Reaching the marginalized

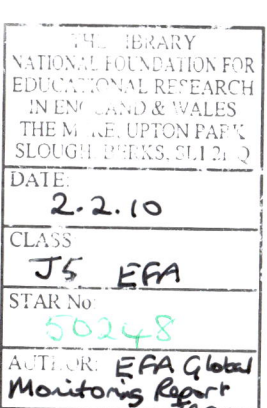

Reaching the marginalized

UNESCO Publishing
United Nations
Educational, Scientific and
Cultural Organization

OXFORD
UNIVERSITY PRESS

This Report is an independent publication commissioned by UNESCO on behalf of the international community. It is the product of a collaborative effort involving members of the Report Team and many other people, agencies, institutions and governments.

The designations employed and the presentation of the material in this publication do not imply the expression of any opinion whatsoever on the part of UNESCO concerning the legal status of any country, territory, city or area, or of its authorities, or concerning the delimitation of its frontiers or boundaries.

The EFA Global Monitoring Report Team is responsible for the choice and the presentation of the facts contained in this book and for the opinions expressed therein, which are not necessarily those of UNESCO and do not commit the Organization. Overall responsibility for the views and opinions expressed in the Report is taken by its Director.

OXFORD
UNIVERSITY PRESS

Great Clarendon Street, Oxford OX2 6DP
Oxford University Press is a department of the University of Oxford.
It furthers the University's objective of excellence in research, scholarship, and education by publishing worldwide in Oxford New York Auckland Cape Town Dar es Salaam Hong Kong (China) Karachi Kuala Lumpur Madrid Melbourne Mexico City Nairobi New Delhi Shanghai Taipei Toronto With offices in Argentina Austria Brazil Chile Czech Republic France Greece Guatemala Hungary Italy Japan Poland Portugal Republic of Korea Singapore Switzerland Thailand Turkey Ukraine Viet Nam
Oxford is a registered trade mark of Oxford University Press in the UK and in certain other countries.

Published jointly by the United Nations Educational, Scientific and Cultural Organization (UNESCO), 7, Place de Fontenoy, 75352 Paris 07 SP, France and Oxford University Press, Great Clarendon Street, Oxford OX2 6DP, United Kingdom.

First published 2010
Published in 2010 by the United Nations Educational, Scientific and Cultural Organization
7, Place de Fontenoy, 75352 Paris 07 SP, France

Graphic design by Sylvaine Baeyens
Layout: Sylvaine Baeyens and Tania Hagemeister

Library of Congress Cataloging in Publication Data
Data available
Typeset by UNESCO
OUP ISBN 9780199584987
UNESCO ISBN 9789231041297

Foreword

This edition of the *EFA Global Monitoring Report 2010, Reaching the marginalized*, comes at a time of great uncertainty. We are still grappling with the far-reaching impact of the global financial and economic crisis not only on the world's banking systems, but on all areas of human development – including education. We are at a crossroads. Either we continue with business as usual and risk undoing the considerable progress made over the past decade, or we use this crisis as an opportunity to create sustainable systems which promote inclusion and put an end to all forms of marginalization.

The gains achieved since the Education for All and Millennium Development Goals were adopted in 2000 are undeniable: great strides have been made towards universal primary education, increased participation in secondary and tertiary education and, in many countries, gender equality. More widely, there have been improvements in overcoming hunger, poverty, and child and maternal mortality.

The global financial crisis could radically change all this. *Reaching the marginalized* demonstrates that declining government revenue and rising unemployment now pose a serious threat to progress in all areas of human development. Government budgets are under even greater pressure and funding for education is especially vulnerable. So are poor households. Rising poverty levels mean that the challenge of meeting basic human needs is a daily struggle. Lessons from the past teach us that children are often the first to suffer – as is their chance to go to school.

In response to this crisis, governments urgently need to create mechanisms to protect the poor and vulnerable. They must also seize the opportunity to build societies that combat inequality, so that all may benefit and prosper. Education is at the front line. Not only do schools teach literacy and lay the groundwork for productive lives, they also play a crucial role in promoting tolerance, peace and understanding between peoples, and in fighting discrimination of all kinds. Schools are the place where indigenous groups can learn to read and write in their mother tongue, where cultural diversity can thrive and where children can try to escape the hardships of conflict and displacement.

This year's *Global Monitoring Report* underscores that there is a long way to travel. There are still at least 72 million children who are missing out on their right to education because of the simple fact of where they are born or who their family is. Millions of youths leave school without the skills they need to succeed in the workforce and one in six adults is denied the right to literacy.

The 2010 Report is a call to action. We must reach the marginalized. Only inclusive education systems have the potential to harness the skills needed to build the knowledge societies of the twenty-first century. The international community has a determining role in supporting countries' efforts to protect and expand their education systems. We must not abandon them at this critical juncture. Promises to help poor countries out of the crisis must now translate into the financial resources that many governments so urgently need.

It is my intention that UNESCO should continue to vigorously advocate for increased investment in education. As the lead agency for Education for All, we have a special responsibility to encourage and support those most at risk from the present crisis. As we stand at the crossroads, with only five years left to meet our collective commitments, let us have the courage and determination to choose the path that lets all children, youths and adults fulfil their right to education.

Irina Bokova

Acknowledgements

This report has been written by the Global Monitoring Report (GMR) team with the support of many people and organizations around the world.

The Global Monitoring Report team would like to thank the members of its International Advisory Board for their valuable guidance.

The EFA Report depends greatly on the work and expertise of the UNESCO Institute for Statistics (UIS). We thank its Director, Hendrik van der Pol, along with Claude Apkabie, Saïd Belkachla, Georges Boade, Michael Bruneforth, Talal El Hourani, Friedrich Huebler, Olivier Labé, Weixin Lu, Adriano Miele, Albert Motivans, Juan Cruz Persua, Pascale Ratovondrahona, Ioulia Sementchouk, Anuja Singh, Saïd Ould Voffal, Peter Wallet and Yanhong Zhang.

The analysis in the EFA Report is informed by commissioned background papers. We thank all authors who prepared material for this year's Report: Abdullahi Haji Abdi, Reda Abou Serie, John Aitcheson, Federico Blanco Allais, Nadir Altinok, Jane Anthony, Laban Ayiro, Gauthier de Beco, Paul Bennell, Herbert Bergmann, Desmond Bermingham, Sonia Bhalotra, Nicholas Biddle, Lyndsay Bird, Michael Bruneforth, Gwang-Chol Chang, Ian Cheffy, Luis Crouch, Santiago Cueto, Mahamadou Diarra, Janice Dolan, Marie Duru-Bellat, Jude Fransman, Franco Gamboa Rocabado, Malini Ghose, George Godia, R. Govinda, Carola Gruen, Gabriela Guerrero, Jialing Han, Ricardo Henriques, George Ingram, Francesca I. Izabel, John Kabutha Mugo, Jean-Francois Kobiané, Ozge Nihan Koseleci, Juan León, Ingrid Lewis, Luis Enrique López, Siobhan Mackay, Cristina Manzanedo, Matthew Martin, Raphaelle Martinez, Geraldo Martins, Juliet McCaffery, Erika Mein, Katharina Michaelowa, Hilaire Mputu, Karen Mundy, Ismael Muñoz, Samir Ranjan Nath, Katy Newell-Jones, Anna Obura, Brendan O'Malley, Zipporah Ongwenyi Nyamauncho, Maciel Pereira, Susan Peters, Marc Pilon, Patrick Quinn, Alan Rogers, Sara Ruto, Alan Sanchez-Jimenez, Elisa Seguin, Nidhi Singal, Devi Sridhar, Pablo Stansbery, Brian Street, Munshi Sulaiman, Tami Tamashiro, Huyen Chi Truong, Yuko Tsujita, Raul Cotera Valdes, Consuelo Vélaz de Medrano, Anna Vignoles, Dan Wagner, Peter Wallet and Kazuhiro Yoshida.

We would also like to thank colleagues who helped us find particular information or identify authors for commissioned background papers, including Izzy Birch, Manuel Contreras, Kate Gooding, Peter Hyll-Larsen, Harounan Kazianga, Louise Meincke, Alemu Melkamnesh, Sophie Qian, Ya Ping Wang and Kai Zhou.

Special mention goes to Kenneth Harttgen, Stephan Klasen and Mark Misselhorn for their work in processing the database on Deprivation and Marginalization in Education, and to Luc-Charles Gacougnolle for his work on the aid to education database.

We are grateful to the Education Policy and Data Center at the Academy for Educational Development for their work on the EFA global costing exercise, and particularly to Babette Wils and her team. The work benefited from extensive support and advice from Gwang-Chol Chang in UNESCO. We are also grateful to Nicola Chanamuto, Caine Rolleston and Jan van Ravens for inputs to specific aspects of the costing work.

We are indebted to several colleagues who reviewed chapters of the report and provided advice and guidance, namely Kwame Akyeampong, Keith Hinchliffe, Jean-Pierre Jarousse and the pôle de Dakar team, Cynthia Lloyd, Paolo de Renzio and Yusuf Sayed, as well as to colleagues who reviewed certain subsections, including Manos Antoninis, Fadila Caillaud, Luis Crouch, Caroline Dyer, David Hulme, Phillippa Lei and Shailen Nandy.

We are indebted to the many colleagues in UNESCO's Education Sector, particularly Steven Obeegadoo and Olav Seim, and to the International Institute for Educational Planning (IIEP), the International Bureau of Education (IBE) and the UNESCO Institute for Lifelong Learning (UIL), who all shared their experience with us. UNESCO's Regional Offices provided advice on country-level activities and commissioned studies. In particular, we would like to express our gratitude to Candy Lugaz and a team from the IIEP Documentation Centre (Corinne Bitoun, Aurore Hagel, Lynne Sergeant, Asunción Valderrama and Aude Zeiler) who, in collaboration with Anton De Grauwe, provided an in-depth review of how marginalization is treated in national education plans. Further thanks are offered to Jean-Mark Bernard, Ulrike Hanemann, Sabine Kube and Clinton Robinson for their advice and guidance on literacy issues; to Kenneth Eklindh and Florence Migeon on inclusion; and to Justine Sass and Yong Feng Liu on HIV and AIDS.

We would like to thank Robert Prouty, Kouassi Soman and Mamadou Thiam of the Fast Track Initiative (FTI) Secretariat; Catherine Dom, Steven Lister and Georgina Rawle of the FTI evaluation team; Julia Benn, Fredrik Ericsson, Valérie Gaveau, Aimée Nichols, Cécile Sangare and Suzanne Steensen of the Development Assistance Committee of the Organisation for Economic Co-operation and Development (OECD-DAC); and Dan Coppard and Asma Zubairi with Development Initiatives for their advice on international cooperation and aid to education.

Special thanks to Alexandre Khan and all those who helped make the public consultation for the 2010 Report a success. Many UNESCO colleagues and partners in non-government organizations went out of their way to help us gather human interest stories, which are a new feature of the Report this year. They are too numerous to mention, but we greatly appreciate their time and effort in making materials available to us and, in some cases, speaking to families and children about their daily difficulties and triumphs in getting to school. Equally, we are extremely grateful to those children and their families who took time to explain to us their views and experiences of education.

We are grateful to the many colleagues within and outside of UNESCO who have helped with the translation and production of the Report.

The clarity of the Report benefited greatly from the editorial expertise of Rebecca Brite, Andrew Johnston and Wenda McNevin, as well as from the support of Isabelle Kite, who assisted in developing this year's bibliography. We also express our appreciation to Jan Worall for preparing the Report's index.

Nino Muñoz Gomez, Sue Williams and the staff of UNESCO's Bureau of Public Information provided timely and energetic assistance in bringing the Report to the attention of global media. A special thanks also to Mariso Sanjines.

The EFA Global Monitoring Report team

Director
Kevin Watkins

Samer Al-Samarrai, Nicole Bella, Marc Philip Boua Liebnitz, Mariela Buonomo, Stuart Cameron, Alison Clayson, Diederick de Jongh, Anna Haas, Julia Heiss, François Leclercq, Anaïs Loizillon, Leila Loupis, Patrick Montjourides, Karen Moore, Claudine Mukizwa, Paula Razquin, Pauline Rose, Sophie Schlondorff, Suhad Varin.

For more information about the Report, please contact:
The Director
EFA Global Monitoring Report team
c/o UNESCO, 7, place de Fontenoy
75352 Paris 07 SP, France
Email: efareport@unesco.org
Tel.: +33 1 45 68 10 36
Fax: +33 1 45 68 56 41
www.efareport.unesco.org

Previous EFA Global Monitoring Reports

2009. Overcoming inequality: why governance matters
2008. Education for All by 2015 – Will we make it?
2007. Strong foundations – Early childhood care and education
2006. Literacy for life
2005. Education for All – The quality imperative
2003/4. Gender and Education for All – The leap to equality
2002. Education for All – Is the world on track?

Any errors or omissions found subsequent to printing will be corrected in the online version at www.efareport.unesco.org

Contents

List of figures, tables and text boxes

Figures

Tables

Text boxes

Highlights of the EFA Report 2010

Ten years have passed since the international community adopted the six Education for All goals in Dakar in 2000. The record since then has been mixed. While much has been achieved over the past decade, many of the world's poorest countries are not on track to meet the 2015 targets. Failure to reach the marginalized has denied many people their right to education. With the effects of the global economic crisis still being felt, there is a real danger that much of the progress of the past ten years will stall or be reversed. Education is at risk, and countries must develop more inclusive approaches, linked to wider strategies for protecting vulnerable populations and overcoming inequality.

Minimizing the impact of the financial crisis on education

The international community needs to identify the threat to education posed by the economic crisis and the rise in global food prices...

- Human development indicators are deteriorating. An estimated 125 million additional people could be pushed into malnutrition in 2009 and 90 million into poverty in 2010.
- With poverty rising, unemployment growing and remittances diminishing, many poor and vulnerable households are having to cut back on education spending or withdraw their children from school.
- National budgets in poor countries are under pressure. Sub-Saharan Africa faces a potential loss of around US$4.6 billion annually in financing for education in 2009 and 2010, equivalent to a 10% reduction in spending per primary-school pupil.

...and develop an effective response:

- Provide up-front, sustained and predictable aid to counteract revenue losses, protect priority social spending and support progress in education.
- Convene a donor pledging conference in 2010 to close the Education for All financing gap.

Reaching the Education for All goals

There has been progress...

- The number of children out of school has dropped by 33 million worldwide since 1999. South and West Asia more than halved the number of children out of school – a reduction of 21 million.
- Some countries have achieved extraordinary advances. Benin started out in 1999 with one of the world's lowest net enrolment ratios but may now be on track for universal primary education by 2015.
- The share of girls out of school has declined from 58% to 54%, and the gender gap in primary education is narrowing in many countries.
- Between 1985–1994 and 2000–2007, the adult literacy rate increased by 10%, to its current level of 84%. The number of adult female literates has increased at a faster pace than that of males.

...but much remains to be done:

- Malnutrition affects around 175 million young children each year and is a health and an education emergency.
- There were 72 million children out of school in 2007. Business as usual would leave 56 million children out of school in 2015.
- Around 54% of children out of school are girls. In sub-Saharan Africa, almost 12 million girls may never enrol. In Yemen, nearly 80% of girls out of school are unlikely ever to enrol, compared with 36% of boys.
- Literacy remains among the most neglected of all education goals, with about 759 million adults lacking literacy skills today. Two-thirds are women.
- Millions of children are leaving school without having acquired basic skills. In some countries in sub-Saharan Africa, young adults with five years of education had a 40% probability of being illiterate. In the Dominican Republic, Ecuador and Guatemala, fewer than half of grade 3 students had more than very basic reading skills.
- Some 1.9 million new teacher posts will be required to meet universal primary education by 2015.

Reaching the marginalized

Governments are failing to address the root causes of marginalization in education. The new Deprivation and Marginalization in Education data set highlights the level of exclusion in eighty countries...

- In twenty-two countries, 30% or more of young adults have fewer than four years of education, and this rises to 50% or more in eleven sub-Saharan African countries.
- In twenty-six countries, 20% or more of young adults have fewer than two years of schooling and, in some countries, including Burkina Faso and Somalia, the share is 50% or more.
- Inequalities often combine to exacerbate the risk of being left behind. In Turkey, 43% of Kurdish-speaking girls from the poorest households have fewer than two years of education, while the national average is 6%; in Nigeria, 97% of poor Hausa-speaking girls have fewer than two years of education.
- Failure to address inequalities, stigmatization and discrimination linked to wealth, gender, ethnicity, language, location and disability is holding back progress towards Education for All.

...and the need to create inclusive education systems:

- Increase access and improve affordability for excluded groups by lowering cost barriers, bringing schools closer to marginalized communities and developing 'second-chance' programmes.
- Improve the learning environment by deploying skilled teachers equitably, targeting financial and learning support to disadvantaged schools, and providing intercultural and bilingual education.
- Expand entitlements and opportunities by enforcing laws against discrimination, providing social protection programmes and redistributing public finance.
- Develop disaggregated data collection systems to identify marginalized groups and monitor their progress.

Meeting the cost of Education for All

The record on aid for education is disappointing...

- Overall aid has been increasing, but commitments are falling short of the US$50 billion increase pledged in 2005. Africa faces the greatest projected shortfall, estimated at US$18 billion.
- Aid to education has been rising, but commitments have recently stagnated. Aid commitments to basic education fell by 22% to US$4.3 billion in 2007.
- Aid to education is not always reaching those who need it most. Some donors continue to give insufficient priority to basic education. Countries affected by conflict are not receiving enough support, undermining prospects for recovery.
- Education lacks a strong multilateral framework for accelerated progress, suffering from a narrow donor base and an absence of funding from private sources.

...donors and recipient governments must both increase resources available to education and improve aid governance:

- Low-income countries could themselves make available an additional US$7 billion a year – or 0.7% of GDP. Even with this effort, large financing gaps will remain. The Report estimates the financing gap to meet the EFA goals in low-income countries at US$16 billion annually.
- Donors should strengthen efforts to implement the Paris agenda on aid effectiveness and review the balance of their support for the different levels of education.
- Donors must also scale up aid to countries affected by conflict, finding innovative ways of providing longer-term, coordinated support.
- The international multilateral framework for cooperation in education needs to be strengthened through fundamental reform of the EFA Fast Track Initiative.
- The United Nations should convene an emergency pledging conference in 2010 to mobilize the additional financing required and to fulfil the Dakar commitment.

Overview

Chapter 1
From financial crisis to human development crisis

© Aubrey Wade/PANOS

The backdrop to the *Education for All Global Monitoring Report 2010* is the most severe global economic downturn since the Great Depression. Education systems in many of the world's poorest countries[1] are experiencing the aftershock of a crisis that originated in the financial systems of the developed world. There is an imminent danger that, after a decade of encouraging advances, progress towards the Education for All goals will stall, or even be thrown into reverse, in the face of rising poverty, slower economic growth and mounting pressure on government budgets. The international community needs to act urgently to avert that danger.

Conditions for a concerted push towards the 2015 targets have deteriorated across the developing world. By 2010, the recession could drive another 90 million people into extreme poverty. Moreover, many of the worst-affected countries are still recovering from high food prices that left an additional 175 million malnourished in 2007 and 2008. Education systems will not be immune to the effects of these deteriorating human conditions. The concern is that the increased vulnerability of poor households and rising child malnutrition will impede efforts to achieve universal primary education and the wider international development targets set for 2015.

© XINHUA/Gamma/Eyedea Presse

Insufficient attention has been paid to the consequences of slower economic growth for the financing of education in the poorest developing countries. While rich countries nurture the 'green shoots' of recovery, developing countries face the prospect of slower growth and diminished revenue collection. In sub-Saharan Africa alone, the potential loss of financing for education as a result of the global recession will average around US$4.6 billion a year in 2009 and 2010 – double the current level of aid to basic education. Spending per primary school pupil could be as much as 10% lower in 2010 than it would have been on pre-crisis economic growth projections.

It is easy to lose sight of what is at stake. Ultimately, the world economy will recover from the recession, but the crisis could create a lost generation of children in the world's poorest countries whose life chances will have been irreparably damaged by a failure to protect their right to education. For those individuals and communities most immediately affected, failure to sustain progress would impose a high price in diminished opportunities to escape poverty and vulnerability. But whole countries also stand to lose out as weaker progress in education leads to slower economic growth, reduced job creation, deteriorating public health and a more marginal place in the increasingly knowledge-based global economy.

National budgets have a vital role to play in preventing the financial crisis from turning into a long-term human development crisis. Rich countries have put in place large-scale fiscal stimulus packages aimed at supporting economic recovery and protecting vital social and economic infrastructure. Education has been seen as a priority area for public spending, notably under the American Recovery and Reinvestment Act. Unlike developed countries, most low-income developing countries lack the capacity to mobilize financing on the scale required to maintain public spending in priority areas. They desperately need an increase in concessional development assistance to provide breathing space to cope with the crisis and maintain spending plans in education and other areas.

The international community has not responded effectively to the challenges facing the poorest countries.

1. Throughout the Report, the word 'countries' should generally be understood as meaning 'countries and territories'.

Rich-country governments and successive summits of the Group of 20 and Group of 8 have moved financial mountains to stabilize financial systems, but have provided an aid molehill for the world's most vulnerable people. Donors have provided some US$2 billion to US$3 billion annually in new and additional finance for low-income countries as a group, principally through the International Monetary Fund, but sub-Saharan Africa alone faces an estimated revenue shortfall, against pre-crisis projections, of US$80 billion per year in 2009 and 2010.

A 'smoke and mirrors' reporting system has led to exaggerated accounts of the international aid directed to low-income countries. Much of the reported support provided to the poorest countries is in fact repackaged or reprogrammed aid. The World Bank has increased assistance principally through early disbursement of existing concessional loans. While such innovative approaches to funding are welcome, the danger is that they will create future financing deficits – and they are no substitute for real resource transfers.

In 2010, the international community will gather at a Millennium Development Goals summit to review progress and assess prospects for achieving the targets set. Those prospects hinge critically on early action to address the threats facing many of the world's poorest countries as a result of the global economic downturn. Education is a priority area. Any slowdown in the rate of progress towards the education goals will have adverse long-term consequences for economic growth, poverty reduction and advances in public health. Early investment is critical.

© Aubrey Wade/PANOS

© Jeroen Oerlemans/PANOS

This Report estimates it will cost US$16 billion a year to achieve universal primary education and wider Education for All goals by 2015. This price tag appears considerable, unless measured against the scale of resources mobilized to rescue ailing financial institutions. It represents about 2% of the amount mobilized to rescue just four major banks in the United Kingdom and the United States. Of course, governments point out that securing the financial assets and balance sheets of banks represents an investment. But the same is true of international aid for education, which is an investment in poverty reduction, shared prosperity and a more equitable pattern of globalization.

The urgent international measures required include:

- increased concessional financial support through bilateral aid and the World Bank's International Development Association (IDA), with a commitment to increase IDA replenishment from US$42 billion to US$60 billion;
- a review of the implications of the global economic downturn for the financing of development targets in advance of the 2010 Millennium Development Goals summit;
- an emergency pledging conference during 2010 to mobilize additional aid for education;
- budget monitoring to pick up early warning signs of fiscal adjustments that threaten education financing, with UNESCO coordinating an international programme to these ends;
- revision of the IMF's loan conditions to ensure consistency with national poverty reduction and Education for All priorities.

Chapter 2
Monitoring progress towards the Education for All goals

The goals adopted in 2000 at the World Education Forum in Dakar remain the benchmark for assessing progress towards Education for All. Much has been achieved: some of the world's poorest countries have registered advances on many fronts, demonstrating that national leadership and good policies make a difference. But the world is unequivocally off track for the Dakar goals and the battle to achieve universal primary education by 2015 is being lost.

Changing this picture will require a far stronger focus on inequality and the most marginalized groups in society. Gender remains a priority area because of the persistence of institutionalized disadvantage for young girls and women. Strategies aimed at equalizing opportunity in education will also have to address disadvantages rooted in poverty and social discrimination. The monitoring evidence points clearly to the need for a greater sense of urgency on the part of governments and donors. With less than five years to the target date, the window of opportunity for putting in place the investment and policies needed to bring the education goals within reach is closing.

Early childhood

Early childhood care and education is the bedrock of Education for All. Good nutrition, effective health care and access to good pre-school facilities can mitigate social disadvantage and lead to improved learning achievement. Yet early childhood provision continues to be marked by neglect.

That neglect starts early. Around a third of all children in developing countries, or 175 million annually, enter primary school having experienced malnutrition that irreparably damages their cognitive development. Unsafe pregnancy and childbirth take a devastating toll. Birth asphyxia leaves around 1 million children a year with learning difficulties and other disabilities. Maternal iodine deficiency poses a risk of mental impairment for around 38 million children a year. These are problems rooted in poverty, gender inequality, and the failure of child and maternal health services to provide affordable access to decent care. Abolishing user fees for these services is an immediate priority. More broadly, it is important that policy-makers develop more integrated approaches to education on the one side, and to child and maternal health care provision on the other.

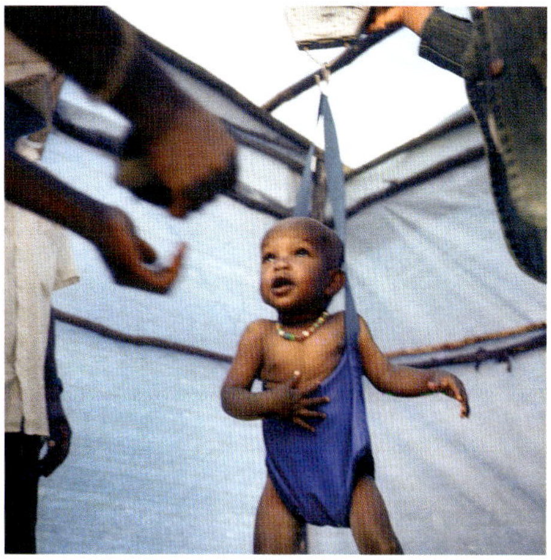

© Alfredo Caliz/PANOS

Participation in early childhood care and education programmes remains uneven. Coverage levels are especially low in South and West Asia, and sub-Saharan Africa. Children from the poorest households potentially have the most to gain from good early childhood care and education. Yet they are the least likely to have access. In Egypt, children from the wealthiest households are twenty-eight times more likely to be in pre-school than children from the poorest households. Such outcomes point to the importance of barriers linked to cost and location. Yet several successful programmes, such as Chile Crece Contigo, demonstrate that targeted investment can break down social disparities.

Universal primary education

Overall progress towards universal primary education in the past decade has been encouraging. In 2007, some 72 million children were out of school – a 28% decline from the start of the decade. Since 1999, enrolment rates in sub-Saharan Africa have been increasing five times as fast as during the 1990s, with countries including Benin, Ethiopia, Mozambique and the United Republic of Tanzania registering rapid advances. In addition, gender disparities in primary school have been narrowing.

© Patrick Le Floch/Explorer/Eyedea Illustration

© Louise Gubb/Corbis

Nevertheless, the world is not on track to meet the universal primary education goal. Current trends will leave some 56 million children out of school in 2015 – and there are worrying indications that the rate of progress towards universal primary education is slowing. Two-thirds of the total decline in out-of-school numbers since the Dakar conference took place from 2002 to 2004. Regional progress has also been uneven. Out-of-school numbers have fallen far more rapidly in South Asia, driven by rapid advances in India, than in sub-Saharan Africa. Most of the countries that are off track for achieving universal primary education by 2015 are low-income countries that, having started from a low base, are either increasing enrolments impressively but too slowly (as in Burkina Faso and the Niger) or stagnating (as in Eritrea and Liberia). Countries affected by conflict figure prominently in this group. More surprisingly, higher-income countries such as the Philippines and Turkey are in danger of failing to achieve the target, largely because of deeply entrenched national inequalities.

Deep-rooted inequalities are a major barrier to universal primary education. Disparities linked to wealth, gender, ethnicity, language and location are holding back progress in many countries. While gender gaps are narrowing, they remain very large in much of South and West Asia and sub-Saharan Africa. In twenty-eight countries, there are still fewer than nine girls in school for every ten boys. Closing the gender divide will require a sustained effort to change attitudes that diminish the value of girls' education, along with practical policies that create incentives for greater equity. Poverty exacerbates the gender divide. In Pakistan there is no discernable gender gap for the wealthiest urban households, but only one-third of girls from the poorest households are in school.

Enrolment is just one measure of overall progress towards universal primary education. While enrolment rates are rising, millions of children enter primary school only to drop out before completing a full primary cycle. Some 28 million pupils in sub-Saharan Africa drop out each year. In South and West Asia, 13% of children entering school drop out in the first grade.

Moreover, current approaches to monitoring and assessment may be putting a positive gloss on underlying problems, for three reasons:

- Data reported by governments may systematically understate real out-of-school numbers for primary school age children. Household survey data indicate that total out-of-school numbers may be as much as one-third higher than those reported by governments.
- Reporting conventions render invisible the 71 million children of lower secondary school age who are out of school.
- Current monitoring tools do not provide an integrated way of measuring the three things that count in progress towards universal primary education: entering school at an appropriate age, progressing smoothly through the system and completing school. Chapter 2 sets out the case for a more comprehensive approach based on the net cohort completion rate.

Adult skills and learning

The global economic crisis has pushed youth and adult skills and learning – goal 3 of the Dakar Framework for Action – to the centre of the Education for All agenda. With youth unemployment rising, governments increasingly see skills development as a vital component of overall strategies to combat marginalization. More broadly, there is recognition that, in an increasingly knowledge-based global economy, the premium on skills as a driver of employment, productivity and economic growth is rising.

Countries vary enormously in the coverage and effectiveness of technical and vocational education. In Germany and Japan, vocational education has played a vital role in smoothing the transition from school to work and in combating youth unemployment. Vocational education in East Asia was an integral part of industrial development strategies that fostered rapid growth, employment creation, and higher levels of skills and wages. It is increasingly recognized that one shot at education is not enough. For youth and young adults who emerge from school lacking basic learning skills, vocational training can help provide a second chance. Experience from Latin America and the United States demonstrates that technical and vocational training can extend opportunities to marginalized young people who dropped out of school, including the chance to re-enter education systems.

While there are many examples of good practice, the overall record of technical and vocational education is open to question. Many national programmes suffer from a combination of underinvestment, poor quality and weak links to employment markets. Governments in the Middle East have invested heavily in vocational education with little to show for it in the way of jobs. In sub-Saharan Africa, vocational education largely bypasses the informal sector (where most marginalized young people work), and is shunned by parents and pupils. Vocational programmes in India reach only about 3% of rural youth and there is little evidence that they enhance employment prospects. The image of technical and vocational provision as a form of second-class education that provides limited benefits for employment remains largely intact.

Changing that image will require far-reaching reforms. Successful vocational education systems typically provide a strong link between the world of school and the world of work, requiring active engagement by the private sector. One of the features of Brazil's model, for example, is that the country's employers' federation is a major provider, with high-quality training geared towards areas characterized by labour market shortages. The curriculum and approaches to teaching also matter. Too often, vocational education focuses on narrow technical abilities rather than broader, more flexible 'learning to learn' skills. Several countries – including Australia and the Republic of Korea – are addressing this problem and the associated poor reputation of traditional programmes, by allowing for greater fluidity between vocational training and academic education.

Adult literacy

Literacy is a vital asset and key component of skills development. Yet adult literacy remains one of the most neglected of the Education for All goals. There are currently some 759 million illiterate youths and adults in the world. Reflecting the legacy of gender disparities in education, two-thirds of this number are women. While gender gaps are narrowing, they remain very large. Except in East Asia – principally China – progress towards the target of halving illiteracy has been painfully slow. On current trends, the world will be less than halfway towards this goal by 2015. India alone will have a shortfall of some 81 million literate people.

There have been some encouraging developments in recent years. Several countries with large numbers of illiterate adults are increasing investment in national literacy programmes. The Literate Brazil Programme, which started in 2003, is an example: it has reached 8 million learners. India is reconfiguring and expanding its national literacy programme to focus more strongly on women, low-caste groups and minorities. Burkina Faso's national education strategy has scaled up investment in literacy from 1% to 7% of the education budget. Governments and donors need to learn from emerging models of good practice and act with greater resolve in prioritizing literacy within wider education strategies.

© REUTERS/Zohra Bensemra

Education quality

The ultimate measure of any education system is not how many children are in school, but what – and how well – they learn. There is growing evidence that the world is moving more quickly to get children into school than to improve the quality of the education offered.

Learning achievement deficits are evident at many levels. International assessment exercises point consistently towards severe global disparities. The 2007 Trends in International Mathematics and Science Study (TIMSS) found that average students in several developing countries, including Ghana, Indonesia and Morocco, performed below the poorest-performing students in countries such as Japan and the Republic of Korea. Inequalities within countries, linked to household disadvantage and the learning environment, are also marked. The problem is not just one of relative achievement. Absolute levels of learning are desperately low in many countries. Evidence from South and West Asia and from sub-Saharan Africa suggests that many children are failing to master basic literacy and numeracy skills, even when they complete a full cycle of primary education.

Low learning achievement stems from many factors. Schools in many developing countries are in a poor state and teachers are in short supply. By 2015, the poorest countries need to recruit some 1.9 million additional primary school teachers, including 1.2 million in sub-Saharan Africa, to create a good learning environment for all children. More equitable teacher deployment is also vital: all too often, the poorest regions and most disadvantaged schools have the fewest and least-qualified teachers. Several countries, including Brazil and Mexico, have introduced programmes targeting schools serving disadvantaged communities. Governments can also raise standards by spotting problems early, using constant monitoring and early-grade reading assessments.

The Education for All financing gap

Achieving the Education for All goals in low-income countries will require a major increase in financing. These countries themselves can do a great deal to mobilize more resources for education. But in the absence of a step increase in aid, efforts to accelerate progress in basic education will be held back by a large financing gap.

This Report provides a detailed assessment of the costs associated with achieving some of the core Education for All goals. Covering forty-six low-income countries, the assessment includes estimates for improved coverage in early childhood programmes, universal primary education and adult literacy. Unlike previous global costing exercises, it includes a provision for reaching the most marginalized. That provision is important because it costs more to extend opportunities to children disadvantaged by poverty, gender, ethnicity, language and remoteness. Among the central findings and recommendations of the Report:

- Low-income developing countries could make available an additional US$7 billion a year – or 0.7% of GDP – by raising more domestic resources and making national budgeting more equitable.

- Even with an increased domestic resource mobilization effort, there will be a global Education for All financing gap of around US$16 billion annually –1.5% of the GDP – for the forty-six low-income countries covered. Sub-Saharan Africa accounts for around two-thirds of the global financing gap, or US$11 billion.

- Current aid to basic education for the forty-six countries – around US$2.7 billion – falls short of what is required to close the gap. Even if donors act on their commitments to increase aid, the financing gap will remain significant at around US$11 billion.

- An emergency pledging conference should be convened in 2010 to mobilize the additional financing required to fulfil the commitment made at Dakar.

© Chretien Eric/Gamma/Eyedea Presse

Chapter 3
Marginalization in education

Governments across the world constantly reaffirm their commitment to equal opportunity in education. Under international human rights conventions they are obligated to act on that commitment. Yet most governments are systematically failing to address extreme and persistent education disadvantages that leave large sections of society marginalized. These disadvantages are rooted in deeply ingrained social, economic and political processes, and unequal power relationships – and they are sustained by political indifference.

Marginalization in education matters at many levels. Having the opportunity for a meaningful education is a basic human right. It is also a condition for advancing social justice. People who are left behind in education face the prospect of diminished life chances in many other areas, including employment, health and participation in the political processes that affect their lives. Moreover, restricted opportunity in education is one of the most powerful mechanisms for transmitting poverty across generations.

Extreme deprivation in education is a particularly striking case of what the economist and philosopher Amartya Sen has described as 'remediable injustices'. The Report looks at the scale of the injustice, examines its underlying causes and identifies policy remedies. The key message to emerge is that failure to place inclusive education at the centre of the Education for All agenda is holding back progress towards the goals adopted at Dakar. Governments have to do far more to extend opportunities to hard-to-reach groups such as ethnic minorities, poor households in slums and remote rural areas, those affected by armed conflict and children with disabilities.

Measuring marginalization: a new data tool

Measuring marginalization in education is inherently difficult. There are no established cross-country benchmarks comparable to those used in assessing extreme income poverty. National data are often not detailed enough to enable marginalized groups to be identified. An underlying problem is that many governments attach little weight to improving data availability relating to some of the most disadvantaged sections of society – child labourers, people living in informal settlements and individuals with disabilities – and to remote regions. This year's Report includes a new tool, the Deprivation and Marginalization in Education (DME) data set, which provides a window on the scale of marginalization within countries and on the social composition of marginalized groups.

Despite the progress of the past decade, absolute deprivation in education remains at extraordinarily high levels. On any global scale, having fewer than four years of education, the minimum required for basic literacy, is an indicator of extreme disadvantage. The DME data set establishes this as a benchmark for 'education poverty', with less than two years in school as an indicator for 'extreme education poverty'. Findings from sixty-three developing countries include the following:

- *Education poverty.* In twenty-two countries, 30% or more of those aged 17 to 22 have fewer than four years of education, and the share rises to 50% or more in eleven countries of sub-Saharan Africa.

- *Extreme education poverty.* In twenty-six countries, 20% or more of those aged 17 to 22 have fewer than two years of schooling and, in some countries, including Burkina Faso and Somalia, the share is 50% or more.

These averages mask extreme inequalities linked to wealth and gender. In the Philippines, education poverty rates among the poor are four times the national average. In some countries, high levels of marginalization among poor females account for a significant share of education poverty. Just under half of poor rural females aged 17 to 22 in Egypt have fewer than four years of education and in Morocco the rate is 88%. Social inequalities also explain some striking cross-country differences. With a per capita income comparable to Viet Nam's, Pakistan has over three times the level of education poverty – a reflection of disparities linked to wealth, gender and region.

The factors leading to marginalization in education do not operate in isolation. Wealth and gender intersect with language, ethnicity, region and rural-urban differences to create mutually reinforcing disadvantages. Detailed DME data for those aged 17 to 22 help identify groups facing particularly extreme restrictions on education opportunity and highlight the scale of national inequalities.

Cross-country analysis reveals complex patterns of marginalization. Some social groups face almost universal disadvantage. Pastoralists in sub-Saharan Africa are an example. In Uganda, which has made strong progress towards universal primary education, Karamajong pastoralists average less than one year in education. Many countries also show large disparities linked to language. In Guatemala, average years in school range from 6.7 for Spanish speakers to 1.8 for speakers of Q'eqchi'.

The DME data set makes it possible to look beyond absolute deprivation to identify some of the key characteristics of those who are being left behind. Using surveys, it identifies people found in the bottom 20% of the national distribution in terms of years in school. The results highlight the powerful influence of social circumstances, over which children have no control, in determining life chances. They also draw attention to unacceptable levels of inequality:

- The wealth divide means that being born into a poor household doubles the risk of being in the bottom 20% in countries ranging from India to the Philippines and Viet Nam.

- Regional divides mean that living in areas such as rural Upper Egypt, northern Cameroon and eastern Turkey increases significantly the risk of falling into the bottom 20%.

- Gender, poverty, language and culture often combine to produce an extremely heightened risk of being left far behind. In Turkey, 43% of Kurdish-speaking girls from the poorest households have fewer than two years of education, while the national average is 6%; in Nigeria, some 97% of poor Hausa-speaking girls have fewer than two years of education.

Time spent in school is just one dimension of marginalization. There are also marked gaps in learning achievement linked to socio-economic status. Children of parents in the wealthiest fourth of the population in Brazil and Mexico score 25% to 30% higher in mathematics test scores, on average, than children of parents in the poorest fourth. Having a home language that is different from the official language of instruction is also associated with lower test scores: in Turkey, Turkish speakers are 30% less likely than non-Turkish speakers to score below a minimum benchmark in mathematics.

© Abbie Trayler-Smith/PANOS

Marginalization in education affects all countries. While absolute average achievement levels are higher in the developed world, extreme relative deprivation is a widespread concern. In the European Union, 15% of young people aged 18 to 24 leave school with only lower secondary school education, and the figure rises to 30% in Spain. Household wealth has a significant bearing on education achievement. In England (United Kingdom), pupils receiving free school meals – an important indicator for social deprivation – score 29% lower, on average, than the national average for mathematics.

Evidence from the United States highlights the powerful influence of wealth and race. African-Americans are twice as likely to be out of school as white Americans, and young adults from poor households are three times as likely to be out of school as those from wealthy homes. International learning assessments illustrate the extent of national disparities. On the TIMSS scale for mathematics, the United States ranks ninth out of forty-eight countries, but schools with high concentrations of poverty score thirteen places lower. The bottom 10% of performers in the United States score 25 places below the national average and below the average for Thailand and Tunisia.

Measuring marginalization is not an end in itself. It should be seen as a means of developing policies and designing targeted interventions that can translate commitment to Education for All into meaningful action. The starting point is for governments to set targets for reducing inequalities and narrowing the gap between marginalized groups and the rest of society. Monitoring progress towards these targets using disaggregated data could help both to provide an evidence base for the development of targeted policies and to increase the visibility of the marginalized.

National equity targets in education should be seen as an integral element of Education for All goals. They could include time-bound commitments to work towards halving gaps in school attendance between, say, the wealthiest and poorest households, the best performing and worst performing regions, boys and girls, and ethnic or linguistic minorities and the rest of the population. Data of the type provided in the DME data set provide a tool for monitoring, auditing and evaluating progress towards equity targets.[2]

Marginalization in education is driven by social inequalities

Marginalization in education is the product of a toxic cocktail of inherited disadvantage, deeply ingrained social processes, unfair economic arrangements and bad policies.

Being born into poverty is one of the strongest factors leading to marginalization in education. Some 1.4 billion of the world's people survive on less than US$1.25 a day. Many are parents struggling to keep their children in school. Household surveys point to parental inability to afford education as a major factor behind non-attendance.

Household poverty goes hand in hand with vulnerability. Even a small economic shock caused by drought, unemployment or sickness, for example, can force parents into coping strategies that damage children's welfare. Girls are often the first to feel the effects. In Pakistan and Uganda, climate-related shocks result in far more girls being taken out of school than boys. Child labour is another corollary of poverty that hurts education. There are an estimated 166 million child labourers in the world. Many of these children are locked in a losing battle to combine work with education. In Mali, around half of all children aged 7 to 14 report that they are working. With labour activities taking up an average of thirty-seven hours a week, most of these children do not attend school.

Language and ethnicity lead to marginalization in education through complex channels. Poverty is an important part of the equation. In Ecuador and Guatemala, malnutrition rates among indigenous children are twice the level for non-indigenous children. Other factors powerfully reinforce the effects of social deprivation. One reason that many linguistic and ethnic minority children perform poorly in school is that they are often taught in a language they struggle to understand. Around 221 million children speak a different language at

2. The DME data set is one of many tools available to support such approaches. It is available online at: http://www.unesco.org/en/efareport/dme.

home from the language of instruction in school, limiting their ability to develop foundations for later learning.

At the same time, language policy in education raises complex issues and potential tensions between group identity on the one hand, and social and economic aspirations on the other. Parents in many countries express a strong preference for their children to learn in the official language, principally because this is seen as a route to enhanced prospects for social mobility.

Stigmatization is a potent source of marginalization that children bring with them to the classroom. From Aboriginals in Australia to the indigenous people of Latin America, failure to provide home language instruction has often been part of a wider process of cultural subordination and social discrimination. Caste systems in South Asia also disadvantage many children. Research from India is instructive. It shows that children from low-caste households score at far lower levels when their caste is publicly announced than when it is unannounced – an outcome that underlines the debilitating effects of stigma on self-confidence.

Livelihoods and location are often strongly linked with social disadvantage in education. One reason pastoralists in South Asia and sub-Saharan Africa register such high levels of deprivation in education is that their livelihoods involve children travelling long distances. Immobile school infrastructure is ill equipped to respond to the needs of highly mobile groups and the schooling provided is often irrelevant to their lives. Slums are also focal points for education deprivation. This is partly because of poverty and partly because many governments fail to provide slum dwellers with the legal rights required to establish an entitlement to education.

Conflict is a potent source of marginalization in education. Worldwide, around 14 million children aged 5 to 17 have been forcibly displaced by conflict, often within countries or across borders, into education systems lacking the most rudimentary education facilities. Less easy to measure than the impact on school attendance are the effects on learning of trauma associated with armed conflict. In 2008 and 2009, Israeli military actions in Gaza led to the deaths of 164 students and 12 teachers, and severely damaged or destroyed 280 schools and kindergartens. In an area where 69% of adolescents were already reported as experiencing post-traumatic stress before the latest episode of violence, many children returned to school carrying with them the effects of anxiety and emotional shock. An investigation into the military actions submitted to the United Nations General Assembly concluded that both Israeli and Palestinian authorities had targeted civilian populations.

© Ami Vitale/PANOS

Some sections of society face problems rooted in public perceptions and official neglect. Children living with disabilities suffer from social attitudes that stigmatize, restrict opportunity and lower self-esteem. These attitudes are frequently reinforced within the classroom, where teachers often lack the training and resources needed to deliver a decent education. Children living with HIV and AIDS, and those who have been orphaned by the disease or are living with affected household members, also face distinctive pressures. Some of these pressures originate in economic hardship and the need to provide care. Others can be traced to practices rooted in social discrimination and to the effects of loss experienced by AIDS orphans. Evidence from many countries suggests that education planners are not responding effectively to these problems.

Reaching and teaching the marginalized

There is no single formula or blueprint for overcoming marginalization in education. Policies need to address underlying causes such as social inequality, gender disparities, ethnic and linguistic disadvantages, and gaps between geographic areas. In each of these areas, equalizing opportunity involves redressing unequal power relationships. The inequalities that the marginalized face start in early childhood and continue through school age years. They are deeply engrained and highly resistant to change. Yet progress is possible with sustained political commitment to social justice, equal opportunity and basic rights.

This Report identifies three broad sets of policies that can make a difference. They can be thought of as three points in an inclusive-education triangle:

Accessibility and affordability. Removing school fees is necessary to make education more affordable for the poorest, but is not sufficient to remove cost barriers. Governments also need to lower indirect costs associated with uniforms, textbooks and informal fees. Financial stipend programmes for identifiably marginalized groups – such as those developed in Bangladesh, Cambodia and Viet Nam – can help provide incentives for education and enhance affordability. Bringing schools closer to marginalized communities is also vital, especially for gender equity – a point demonstrated by the sharp decline in out-of-school numbers in Ethiopia. More flexible approaches to providing education and multigrade teaching in remote areas could bring education within reach of some of the world's most marginalized children. Non-government organizations often play an important role in extending access to hard-to-reach populations, including child labourers, out-of-school adolescents and children with disabilities. In Bangladesh, one non-government organization has developed a system of 'floating schools' in order to reach the Bede (River Gypsy) community, whose livelihood depends on their moving about on boats. The provision of non-government organizations is most successful when it is integrated into national systems, allowing children to continue their studies in formal schooling or to gain meaningful employment.

© Handicap International

The learning environment. Getting marginalized children into school is just a first step. Ensuring that they receive a good education poses significant policy challenges. Targeted financial support and programmes to facilitate improved learning in schools in the most disadvantaged regions can make a difference, as can programmes that draw well-qualified teachers to the schools facing the greatest deprivation. Language policy is another key area. Reforms in Bolivia have emphasized the important role of intercultural and bilingual education in providing ethnic and linguistic minority children with good-quality schooling, and in overcoming social stigmatization. Ensuring that children with disabilities enjoy opportunities for learning in an inclusive environment requires changes in attitude, backed by investment in teacher training and learning equipment. The Convention on the Rights of Persons with Disabilities provides a framework for delivery that should serve as a guide to public policy.

Entitlements and opportunities. Many of the measures needed to overcome marginalization in education operate at the interface between education policy and wider strategies for change.

- *Legal provisions* can play a role in overcoming discrimination and realizing the right to education. Some marginalized groups, such as the Roma in Europe, have successfully challenged the legality of policies that result in institutionalized segregation. Legal provisions are likely to prove most effective when backed by social and political mobilization on the part of marginalized people – New Zealand's Māori language movement and Bolivia's indigenous movements are cases in point.

- *Social protection* is a critical pathway to mitigating the vulnerability that comes with poverty. Conditional cash transfer programmes in Latin America, for example, have a strong track record in improving school attendance and progression. Several countries in sub-Saharan Africa are also investing in social protection programmes. One large-scale example is the Productive Safety Net Programme in Ethiopia, which provides guaranteed employment for communities affected by drought, with positive educational effects. Increased investment in such programmes can enhance equity and accelerate progress towards the Education for All goals. However, equity and cost-effectiveness considerations require detailed attention to the design of interventions, targeting and levels of support.

- *Redistributive public spending* is one of the keys to expanded entitlements and opportunities. Because marginalization in education is associated with poverty,

© Crispin Hughes/PANOS

the regions most affected often have the least capacity to mobilize resources. Most countries have some redistributive element in public finance, but typically it is underdeveloped. The programme of federal government transfers in Brazil is an example of an attempt to narrow large state-level financing gaps in education, with some positive effects.

Overcoming marginalization in education is an imperative for human rights and social justice. It is also the key to accelerated progress towards the Education for All goals set at Dakar. No government seriously committed to the goals can afford to ignore the deep social disparities that are stalling progress in education. Nor can it ignore the wider consequences of marginalization in education for social cohesion and future prosperity. That is why this Report stresses the urgency of all countries developing strategies for more inclusive education linked to wider strategies for overcoming poverty, social discrimination and extreme inequality.

© Franccois Perri

Chapter 4
International aid

The Dakar Framework for Action includes a pledge by donors that 'no countries seriously committed to education for all will be thwarted in their achievement of this goal by a lack of resources'. That pledge has not been honoured. The collective failure of donors to mobilize aid on the scale required is holding back progress in the world's poorest countries. With the global financial crisis adding to pressure on national budgets, it is vital for donors to deliver on the Dakar promise. While primary responsibility for education financing rests with developing country governments, the poorest countries lack the resources to achieve the 2015 goals without a major increase in aid – and an improvement in aid effectiveness.

Aid to education is inevitably influenced by overall development assistance levels. In 2005, donors pledged to increase aid by US$50 billion by 2010, with half the increase going to Africa. After two years of decline, aid flows rose sharply in 2008. However, planned increases fall well short of the levels promised in 2005. Currently programmed aid for Africa points to a potential shortfall against pledges of US$18 billion in aid spending required by 2010.

Donors have a mixed record in delivering on the promises made in 2005. Some countries, including Ireland, the Netherlands, Spain and Sweden, have exceeded their 'fair share' of the commitment. Others have been moving in the wrong direction. Italy has cut its aid-to-GNI ratio (from an already low level) and Japan and the United States fall well short of their 'fair share'. The free riding of bad performers on the commitment of good performers has become a pervasive problem that could worsen as governments respond to fiscal pressures. Some donors – such as the United Kingdom – have undertaken a commitment to maintain, in real terms, planned increases in aid spending. With many low-income countries facing crisis-related budget pressures, this is an approach other donors should consider.

Levels of aid to education remain a source of concern. Overall disbursements of development assistance for basic education have been on a rising trend, reaching US$4.1 billion in 2007. However, commitments stagnated from 2004 and fell by around one-fifth in 2007. One underlying problem is the narrow base of donor support for education: overall flows are dominated by a small group of countries. Another problem is the skewing of aid towards post-primary levels. Three major donors – France, Germany and Japan – commit over half their

© REUTERS/Ahmad Masood

education aid to post-primary levels, with a large share of what is allocated to higher education being spent in domestic institutions. While aid to post-primary education is justified, several donors need to review both their priorities and their aid modalities.

With pressure on aid budgets mounting, it is crucial for donors and recipients to strengthen aid effectiveness. There is evidence of progress – but there is also a great deal of room for improvement. Aid flows are often unpredictable: in 2007, less than half of scheduled aid arrived on time. Use of national public financial management systems is growing, but there is worrying evidence that many donors continue to operate outside these systems, thereby adding to transaction costs.

The education sector has had limited success in tapping into new sources of innovative financing. Several major international companies and philanthropic institutions support initiatives in education, but the overall impact has been diluted by the absence of credible multilateral delivery mechanisms of the type developed in global health initiatives. Advocates for education must seize opportunities to generate new sources of finance. This Report provides an example: it calls for a small (0.4%) 'Better Future' levy on the commercial marketing revenue of the major European football leagues, with the 2010 World Cup providing a launch pad. The initiative could mobilize US$48 million annually and finance quality education for around half a million children a year.

The international donor community has not responded effectively to the problems of low-income countries affected by conflict. These countries account for one-third of out-of-school children, but less than one-fifth of aid to education. Moreover, aid flows are dominated by a small group of conflict-affected states – notably Afghanistan and Pakistan – while a far larger group is neglected.

While conflict and post-conflict environments confront donors with immense challenges, current approaches are leading to lost opportunities for rebuilding education systems. Education receives less than 2% of humanitarian aid, including in countries such as the Democratic Republic of the Congo. And countries such as Burundi and Liberia have received insufficient support for education reconstruction. Overly rigid application of rules on aid governance and reporting has hampered the development of more effective and flexible responses.

The Fast Track Initiative

The Fast Track Initiative (FTI) was hailed at its inception as a 'historic step' towards delivering Education for All, establishing a multilateral framework for strengthening national education plans and galvanizing the financing required to achieve universal primary education, among other goals. While the initiative has registered some important achievements, overall performance has fallen short of expectations – and comprehensive reform is an urgent priority. The international community urgently needs a multilateral architecture fit for the purpose of accelerating progress towards the 2015 targets.

© UNESCO/Samer Al-Samarrai

The reform process starts by setting an appropriate scale of ambition, identifying areas in which a multilateral framework can add value to current efforts and setting out an agenda for governance reform to give developing countries a stronger voice.

Insufficient clarity over the FTI's remit should not be allowed to obscure its weak performance. There is no credible evidence to support the argument that the initiative has spurred an increase in bilateral aid directed through country programmes. The FTI's main financing mechanism, the Catalytic Fund, has made limited financial transfers with high transaction costs. While cumulative donor commitments had reached US$1.2 billion by March 2009, disbursements amounted to just US$491 million. Several countries whose FTI plans were endorsed between 2002 and 2004 have yet to receive their full allocation. Disbursement problems have been compounded by the stringent application of World Bank rules, in some cases forcing governments and bilateral donors to adopt practices that weaken donor coordination and undermine national ownership.

Limited disbursement is not the only FTI weakness. The estimation of financing gaps has been characterized by inconsistency and systematic underestimation, with FTI plans reflecting what donors may be willing to finance rather than what developing countries need to meet the 2015 targets.

Governance is another concern. While the FTI is widely presented as a partnership, it is for practical purposes a 'donor club'. Developing countries are under-represented at all levels and have a weak voice in financing decisions. The FTI also effectively excludes from funding those countries most in need of a multilateral financing mechanism, since most conflict-affected countries have been viewed as not meeting the standards for accessing Catalytic Fund support.

The FTI experience contrasts strongly with multilateral initiatives in health. To take the most notable example, the Global Fund to Fight AIDS, Tuberculosis and Malaria has succeeded in mobilizing and delivering additional resources through a broad donor base. One of the strengths of the Global Fund, in contrast with the FTI, has been the creation of innovative financing windows for philanthropic donations. Governance arrangements differ markedly from those of the FTI. The Global Fund is an independent organization, staffed by a strong secretariat, and developing countries have a strong voice at all levels. It has delivered significant results in terms of impact, including in countries with weak capacity: it had disbursed US$7 billion by 2008 and supplied antiretroviral drugs to 2 million people. Notwithstanding some obvious differences and the problems associated with vertical initiatives geared towards specific diseases, there are important lessons to be drawn for FTI reform.

There are several key ingredients for more effective multilateralism in education. Some of those ingredients can be found in the principles underpinning the FTI, such as the commitment to back national planning and strategies for achieving the Education for All goals with increased aid. However, it is also important to establish a level of ambition commensurate with the challenge ahead. The remit for the FTI should be clearly focused on closing the Education for All financing gap, with a strong commitment to the development of quality education and equity. Provision should be made for attracting support from philanthropic foundations. And developing countries should have a far greater voice in governance. But perhaps the most important ingredient for a more dynamic multilateral architecture, and the ingredient most conspicuous by its absence to date, is high-level political leadership.

The financial crisis: global impact

© XINHUA/Gamma/Eyedea Presse

Chapter 1

Overcoming disadvantage: a boy does homework in Freetown, Sierra Leone

© Aubrey Wade/PANOS

Education at risk: the impact of the financial crisis

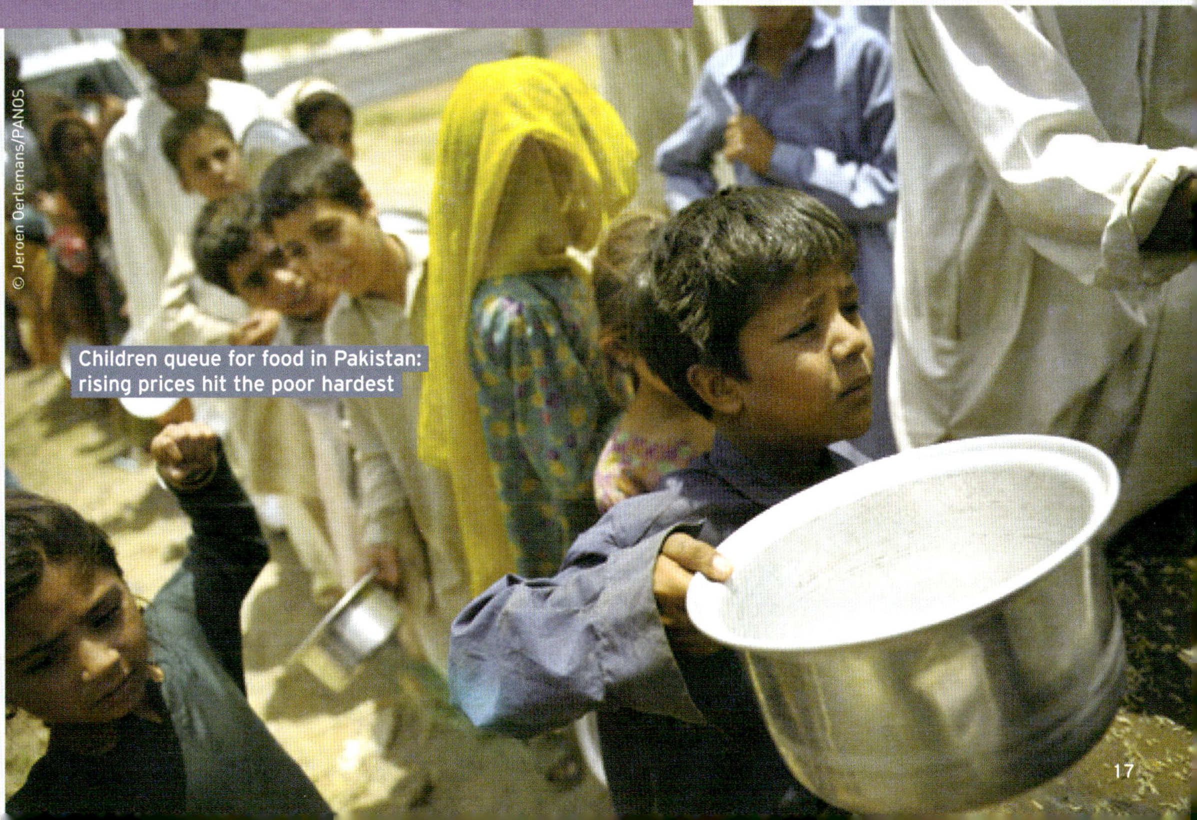

© Jeroen Oerlemans/PANOS

Children queue for food in Pakistan: rising prices hit the poor hardest

The global financial crisis has provided a stark reminder of the realities of global interdependence. With the aftershock now reaching many of the world's poorest countries, poverty levels are rising, malnutrition is worsening and education budgets are coming under pressure. Some of the world's most vulnerable households are feeling the effects of a crisis that originated in the banking systems of the rich world. It is too early to assess exactly what the financial crisis will mean for progress towards the EFA goals. But this year's Report starts by looking at the early warning signs. It then assesses the international response to the crisis and considers what can be done to avoid major setbacks.

Introduction

The backdrop for this edition of the *Education for All Global Monitoring Report* is the deepest economic downturn since the Great Depression. While several financial indicators have improved in recent months, fuelling optimism that the 'green shoots' of recovery are taking root in the developed world, many developing countries stand on the brink of a human development crisis driven by recession and rising poverty.

For the Education for All goals adopted in Dakar at the World Education Forum, 2010 will be a make or break year. The past decade has witnessed remarkable progress on many fronts. The number of children not in school has been falling, gender gaps are narrowing and more children are completing a basic education. Some of the world's poorest countries have demonstrated that universal primary schooling and wider education goals set for 2015 are attainable. With just five years to go to the target date, the challenge is to consolidate these gains and accelerate progress in countries that are off track. The danger is that the aftershock of the financial crisis will slow, stall or even reverse the hard-won gains of the past decade.

Such an outcome would be indefensible. Children living in the urban slums and rural villages of the world's poorest countries played no part in the reckless banking practices and regulatory failures that caused the economic crisis. Yet they stand to suffer for the gambling that took place on Wall Street and other financial centres by losing their chance for an education that could lift them out of poverty. The guiding principle for international action should be a commitment to ensure that the developing world's children do not pay for the excesses of the rich world's bankers.

Policy-makers need to recognize what is at stake. Developments in education – unlike indicators for stock markets, economic growth and the stability of financial systems – take place beyond the glare of media attention and public scrutiny, and are typically reported after the event. Following a decade of broad-based progress, governments might assume that underlying trends will remain positive. But reversals in education can happen, as the experience of the 1990s demonstrated, and they have far-reaching consequences.

Depriving children and youth of opportunities for learning has damaging implications for progress in other areas, including economic growth, poverty reduction, employment creation, health and democracy. If the financial crisis is allowed to create a lost generation in education, this will sound the death knell for the Millennium Development Goals, the international targets set for 2015 – and it will call into question the future of multilateral cooperation on development.

First, avoiding that prospect requires action on two levels. National governments need to strengthen their focus on fairness in public spending to protect poor and vulnerable people from the impact of the economic crisis. Second, the world's richest countries need to support low-income countries by providing concessional financing. Without this lifeline, large-scale and mostly irreversible human development setbacks are inevitable. Education systems will sustain severe damage – and children marginalized by poverty, gender and ethnicity stand to bear the brunt.

The danger is that the aftershock of the financial crisis could reverse the hard-won gains of the past decade

At successive summit meetings, political leaders of the Group of Twenty (G20) and the Group of Eight (G8) have helped stave off a deeper economic crisis by increasing global liquidity, stabilizing financial systems and unlocking credit markets. Unfortunately, little has been done to protect hundreds of millions of the world's most vulnerable people from the impact of a crisis they had no part in creating. The world's richest countries have moved a financial mountain to bail out their banking systems, but have mobilized an aid molehill for the world's poor.

Progress since Dakar has been driven partly by stronger policies in education, but also by accelerated economic growth and poverty reduction. Now, just five years before the 2015 Education for All target date, policy-makers are operating in a far more hostile environment. The financial crisis and steep food price rises have created 'perfect storm' conditions for a major setback. Slower economic growth could trap another 90 million people in poverty in 2010 – and more children face the threat of malnutrition. Meanwhile, national education budgets are coming under intense pressure. In the absence of an effective international response, low-income countries in particular will find it difficult to protect spending on education, let alone to scale up investment.

This chapter has five core messages:

- *The economic slowdown has far-reaching consequences for education financing in the poorest countries.* Slower growth and declining revenue are jeopardizing public spending plans in education. For sub-Saharan Africa, the resources available for education could fall by US$4.6 billion a year on average in 2009 and 2010, or more than twice the current amount of aid to basic education in the region. Spending per primary school pupil could be as much as 10% lower in 2010 because of the effects of the recession. This potentially damaging outcome underlines the importance of real time budget monitoring, with a focus on adjustments to 2009 budgets and spending outcomes, and the formulation of 2010 budgets.

Governments in the world's poorest countries urgently need an increase in development assistance to offset revenue losses

- *Increased international aid would help reduce budget pressures.* Governments in the world's poorest countries urgently need an increase in development assistance to offset revenue losses, sustain high-priority social spending and undertake the countercyclical investment required to create the conditions for recovery. New evidence set out in this chapter shows that low-income countries in sub-Saharan Africa have a limited ability to shield public spending from the effects of the downturn, but a significant capacity to productively absorb increased aid. In addition, a temporary moratorium on official debt payments would reduce pressure on government budgets, potentially releasing resources for spending in areas such as education and health. Such a moratorium would be in the spirit of the fiscal stimulus packages deployed in developed countries, attenuating the impact of the global crisis on economic growth and poverty reduction efforts. The cost of the debt moratorium for forty-nine low-income countries would amount to around US$26 billion for 2009 and 2010 combined.

- *The international response to the financial crisis has failed to address major human development concerns.* Global summits and domestic policies in rich countries have played a crucial role in stabilizing financial systems and establishing the foundations for early recovery. By contrast, the response to the crisis unfolding in the world's poorest countries has been marked by systemic indifference. 'Smoke and mirrors' financial reporting has produced large headline numbers for financial transfers while obscuring the modest level of real resources mobilized. Sub-Saharan Africa stands to lose some US$160 billion in government revenue in 2009–2010 as a result of slower growth and reduced revenue. Best estimates of the international response for low-income countries suggest that additional concessional finance for the period will amount to no more than US$6 billion to US$8 billion.

- *Education for All financing gaps should be closed under a human development recovery plan.* Governments, aid donors and financial institutions urgently need to assess the financing gaps for achieving the Millennium Development Goals. Making available the resources required to close these gaps should be part of the coordinated international response to the global financial crisis. A major new financial costing exercise carried out for this Report (discussed in detail in Chapter 2) puts the Education for All financing gap at around US$16 billion. That headline figure appears large in absolute terms, but has to be placed in context. It represents less than 2% of the financial rescue package put together by governments in just two countries – the United Kingdom and the United States – for four commercial banks and is equal to a small fraction of the wider financial systems bail-out.

- *International action must be taken before the 2010 Millennium Development Goal summit.* The impact of the financial crisis and new evidence on the scale of financing gaps demand an effective international response. With a Millennium Development Goal summit planned for 2010, the United Nations Secretary-General should convene a high-level meeting of donors and governments of low-income countries to reassess the external financing required to achieve the Education for All goals.

This chapter is divided into three parts. Part 1 looks at the mechanisms through which the financial crisis and the food crisis are hurting education systems. Part 2 examines 'fiscal space', the room for manoeuvre that governments have to protect public spending in education and other areas from the effects of the global economic downturn. Part 3 critically reviews the international response to the crisis, highlighting in particular the failure of the current G20 framework.

Double jeopardy: food prices and financial crisis

'We were hearing that there was no work and the factory would be shut down. It all happened quite fast actually. Although there was much talk about the factory shutting down, the authorities did not really tell us anything until almost the last week.'
Anwarul Islam,
a Bangladeshi migrant labourer in Jordan

'Since I lost my job sometimes we eat only once or twice a day. I don't know what to do. We are just camping in front of the factory gates, waiting for the company to pay us.'
Kry Chamnan,
garment worker in Cambodia, February 2009

'My factory retrenched 150 workers including me. I'm in deep trouble thinking about how to live with my two children.'
Lalitha, a 35-year-old worker in Sri Lanka

'You think about your children when you lose your job. That's the first thing that came into my mind – when school starts, how am I going to buy the uniform, the exercise books and all that. The food, you know how expensive that is now...The children depend on me, I'm a single mother.'
Kenia Valle, Managua, Nicaragua

These four voices provide a reminder that, in an increasingly interdependent world, economic shocks travel rapidly across borders (Emmett, 2009). Faced with a daily barrage of reporting on the state of the global economy and recovery prospects for rich countries, it is easy to lose sight of the human costs of the global downturn for those who live away from the media spotlight. The recession, sparked by reckless gambling on Wall Street and the regulatory failures in rich countries, is leaving its mark on people living in slums and remote villages in the world's poorest countries. The effects on education systems are complex and varied, but overwhelmingly destructive.

Economic slowdown threatens education financing

The financial crisis is being transmitted to education systems through various channels. The degree to which countries are integrated into international trade and financial markets, the structure of employment, patterns of import and export, and pre-existing poverty levels all play a part in determining who is affected and for how long (McCord and Vandemoortele, 2009; te Velde et al., 2009). For low-income countries, trade is the primary transmission mechanism from world markets to the national economy, with exporters of minerals and primary commodities hit by a combination of lower prices and falling demand (IMF, 2009*b*, 2009*e*).

Deteriorating prospects for economic growth have far-reaching implications for education financing. Since the onset of the crisis, growth forecasts have been revised downwards on a regular basis. All developing regions are affected. With a pre-crisis growth forecast of over 5%, sub-Saharan Africa now faces the prospect of growing at less than 2%, which is below the rate of population increase. Latin America is projected to face an economic contraction in 2009 (Figure 1.1).

Slower growth and declining export and import activity have adverse consequences for government revenue and hence for public spending (IMF, 2009*b*, 2009*d*). Budgetary pressure is evident in data on fiscal balances. Sub-Saharan Africa is moving from a fiscal surplus in 2008 to a projected 2009 deficit equal to about 6% of gross domestic product (IMF, 2009*e*). The combined effect of slower economic growth and lower levels of revenue collection will translate into losses equivalent to about US$80 billion in 2009 and the same in 2010 (Table 1.1). This is revenue that could have been used for investment in areas ranging from economic infrastructure to health and education.

In an increasingly interdependent world, economic shocks travel rapidly across borders

The importance of economic growth for education financing is not widely recognized. Rising wealth is not automatically associated with improvement in education – and many countries with low average incomes have registered extraordinary progress. But increasing national income does create financing conditions conducive to higher public spending on education. Economic growth expands the resources available to governments through taxation. Moreover, the share of national income collected in government revenue tends to rise as

Figure 1.1: Post-crisis economic growth projections have been revised downwards for all developing regions

Real GDP growth projections since April 2008, selected regions, 2003-2009

Note: Regions shown are those used by UNICEF, which differ to some extent from the Education for All regions.
Source: IMF (2009*f*).

Table 1.1: Potential revenue loss in sub-Saharan Africa, 2008-2010

Constant PPP 2006 $US billions unless specified	2008	2009	2010
Revenues, excluding grants (%GDP) average, April 2009	24.7	20.8	21.6
Pre-crisis government revenue projection[1]	378	402	427
Post-crisis government revenue projection[2]	376	322	347
Potential revenue loss associated with economic crisis	1.4	79.8	80.3
Slower economic growth	1.4	16.4	26.7
Decreased revenue-to-GDP ratio	0.0	63.4	53.6

Notes: These estimates are based on weighted and aggregated single country gross domestic product projections. Countries were weighted using GDP based on the purchasing power parity share of the region. 'Pre-crisis projections' are for April 2008 and 'post-crisis projections' for April 2009. Excludes Somalia and Zimbabwe.

1. Based on April 2008 growth projections and 2008 revenue-to-GDP ratios.
2. Based on April 2009 growth projections and adjusted revenue-to-GDP ratios.

Sources: IMF (2008, 2009*e*, 2009*g*).

poverty falls, and economic growth is an important condition for sustained poverty reduction.

The experience of sub-Saharan Africa is instructive. During the 1990s, economic stagnation and high levels of external debt undermined governments' capacity to finance education, with per capita spending declining in many countries. That picture has changed dramatically, with public spending on primary education rising by 29% over the period from 2000 to 2005 (Figure 1.2). This turnaround was instrumental in reducing the numbers of children out of school and strengthening education infrastructure. Around three-quarters of the increase was directly attributable to economic growth, with the balance accounted for by increased revenue collection and budget redistribution in favour of the education sector.

What does the economic slowdown mean for education financing in sub-Saharan Africa towards 2015? The answer will depend on the duration of the slowdown, the pace of recovery, governments' approach to budget adjustments and the response of international donors. There are many uncertainties in each area. Nevertheless, governments have to draw up public spending plans in an uncertain environment. One way of capturing the potential threat to education financing is to consider a scenario that holds the share of expenditure invested in education constant, with adjustments for reduced economic growth and lower revenue-to-GDP ratios (Figure 1.3).

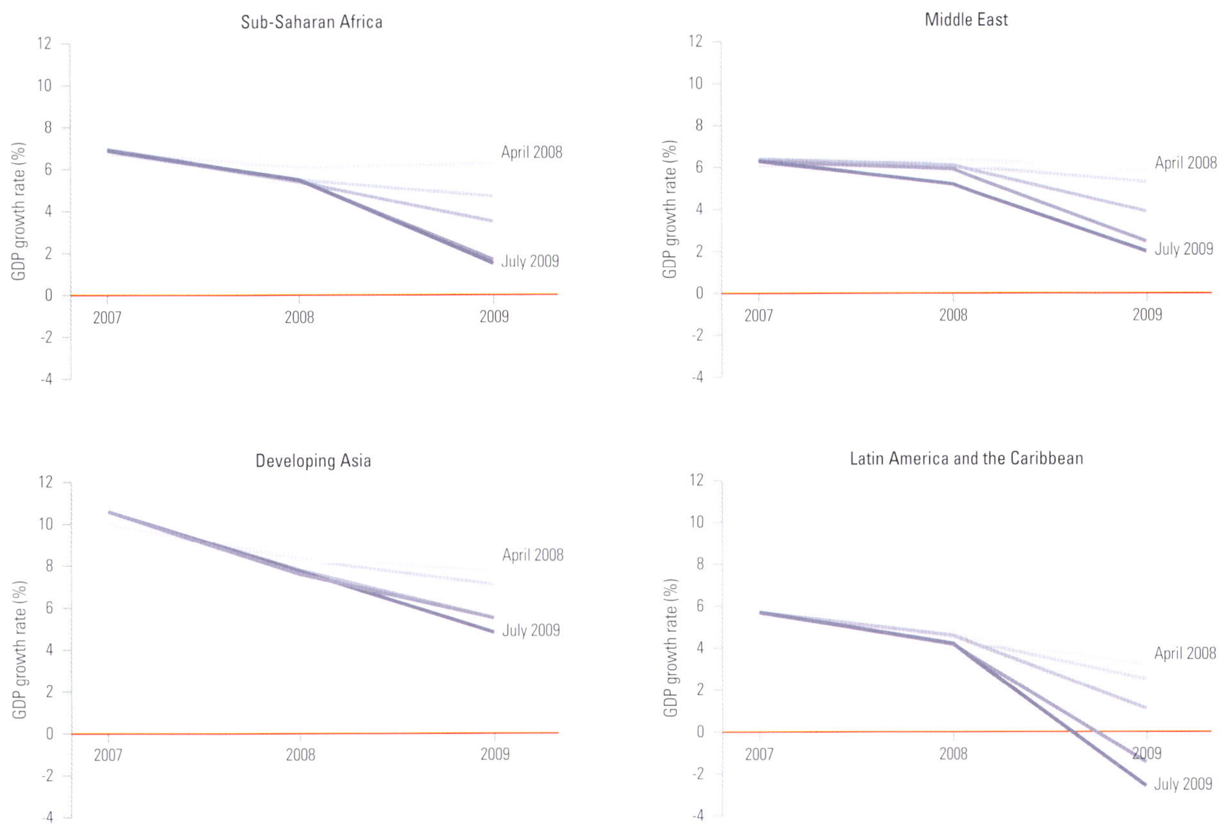

Figure 1.2: Economic growth matters for education financing

Primary education expenditure in sub-Saharan Africa between 2000 and 2005, growth decomposition

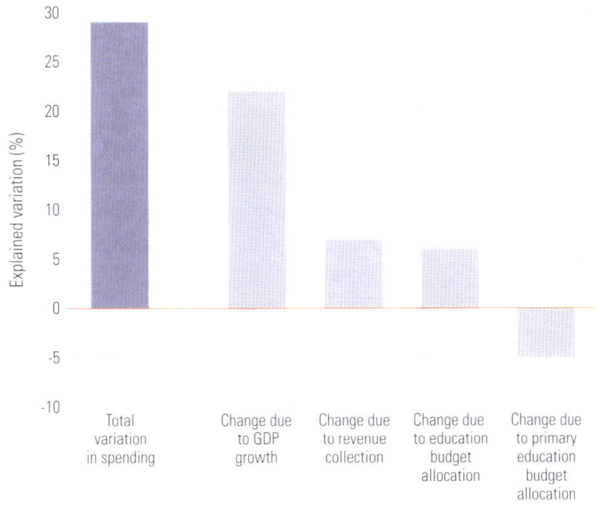

Sources: Pôle de Dakar (2002, 2004, 2005, 2007); UIS database.

Figure 1.3: Education financing in sub-Saharan Africa could suffer from slower economic growth

Estimated forgone income for education due to the crisis in 2009 and 2010

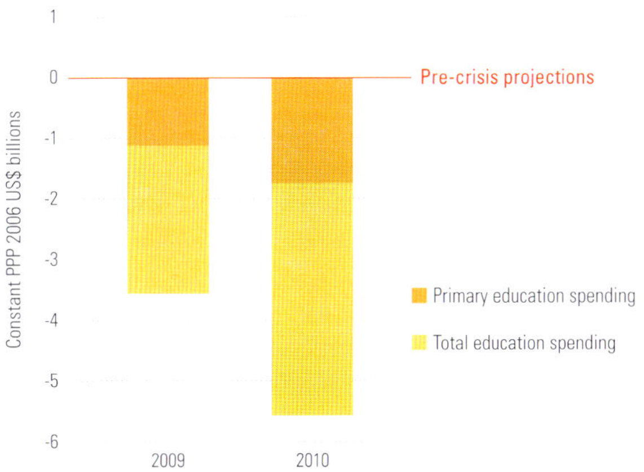

Notes: The shares of GDP devoted to education and primary education have been considered constant and correspond to median shares in 2007 for both data. Forgone income is the difference between education spending estimated with pre-crisis projections and that calculated with the most recent post-crisis projections.

Sources: IMF (2008, 2009*g*); UIS database.

In terms of the potential resources forgone for education spending, such a scenario would result in:

- an average loss over 2009 and 2010 of US$4.6 billion per year, compared with estimated aid disbursements to the region for basic education of US$2 billion;
- a cumulative loss to 2013 of about US$30 billion;
- a loss in 2010 of US$13 per pupil for primary school spending – equivalent to about 10% of current spending per pupil.

These figures provide only an estimate of one possible scenario. They do not chart an inevitable course. Even so, the magnitude of the potential economic growth effect serves to illustrate the budget pressures many countries face. And these new pressures have to be seen against the backdrop of an already large external financing gap – averaging around US$16 billion a year – for the Education for All goals in low-income countries (see Chapter 2).

Rising malnutrition and deteriorating prospects for poverty reduction have far-reaching consequences for education

Wider human impact

The economic downturn in the poorest countries has had direct consequences for vulnerable households. For people surviving below or just above the poverty line, it has meant less secure livelihoods. Income from remittances is falling. Employment prospects are diminishing in many countries. And the downturn has followed hard on the heels of a steep rise in international food prices, with higher levels of poverty superimposed on deteriorating nutrition indicators.

The combination of global food crisis and financial crisis has worsened the environment for achieving the Education for All goals. From 2003 to 2008, corn and wheat prices roughly doubled and rice prices tripled. Domestic price rises have not tracked those of international prices, but food price inflation reached over 17% in sub-Saharan Africa during 2008, rising to 80% in Ethiopia (Lustig, 2009; von Braun, 2008). In other regions, many countries recorded inflation rates in excess of 10%. Because poor households spend a large share of their budgets on food, price rises hit them particularly hard (World Bank, 2008*a*, 2008*e*). Many have had to cope either by diverting spending from other areas or by going hungry. Meanwhile, governments have faced rising food import bills and budget costs for nutrition programmes. Although food prices have started to fall, they remain high by historical standards. At the end of 2008, domestic staple food prices across a large group of developing countries averaged 24% higher than two years earlier (FAO, 2009).

The lethal cocktail of high food prices and economic recession has left a deep imprint on the lives of millions of vulnerable people. According to the Food and Agricultural Organization of the United Nations (FAO), the number of malnourished people in the world increased by 75 million in 2007 and by 100 million in 2008, reaching a global level of just over 1 billion (FAO, 2008). Recent FAO projections for 2009 indicate the financial crisis could push 125 million additional people into malnutrition (Headey et al., 2009). In some regions, drought has exacerbated underlying food security pressure associated with higher prices. For example, in Ethiopia, 12 million people are in immediate need of food and other assistance.

Poverty levels continue to fall, principally as a result of strong economic growth in China and India, but the rate of decline has slowed markedly. According to the World Bank, the downturn will leave an additional 75 million people below the US$1.25 poverty threshold in 2010 and an additional 91 million below the US$2 threshold (Chen and Ravallion, 2009).

Rising malnutrition and deteriorating prospects for poverty reduction have far-reaching consequences for education. Hunger undermines cognitive development, causing irreversible losses in opportunities for learning. There are often long time lags between the advent of malnutrition and data on stunting. But increased malnutrition among pre-school and primary school age children has been reported from several countries, including Guatemala (von Braun, 2008). Rising food prices have also had wider consequences for the place of education spending in household budgets. In Bangladesh, about a third of poor households report cutting spending on education to cope with rising food prices (Raihan, 2009). In Ghana and Zambia, poor households report eating fewer and less nutritious meals, and reducing expenditure on health and education (FAO, 2009). Government budgets have also been affected. In September 2009, Kenya announced plans to delay financing of free education for 8.3 million primary school children and 1.4 million secondary school children, prompting school administrators to press for a temporary restoration of user fees. The government claimed costs associated with emergency feeding programmes forced the delay. More equitable avenues could have been explored, however.

Diminished prospects for reducing poverty will severely damage efforts to accelerate progress towards the Education for All goals. More poverty means parents have less to spend on children's education. Household poverty also pushes children out of school and into employment. Counteracting the impact of rising poverty and deteriorating nutrition will require strengthening of social protection programmes – an issue discussed in Chapter 3.

Sub-Saharan Africa, which has the furthest to travel to achieve universal primary schooling, faces some of the starkest poverty-related threats to education. The region's recent progress has been encouraging, driven by strong economic growth and poverty reduction. For the first time in over a generation, numbers living below the US$1.25-a-day poverty line have fallen: some 4 million people climbed out of poverty between 2000 and 2007. With per capita income set to shrink in 2009, however, poverty levels could rise.

The impact of rising unemployment is already registering on education systems as household budgets come under pressure (World Bank and IMF, 2009). In Zambia, around a quarter of jobs in the copper mining sector have been lost (te Velde et al., 2009). Rising unemployment was also reported in copper mining in the Democratic Republic of the Congo after export prices collapsed. In both countries, there have been reports of unemployed workers having to withdraw children from school (Hossain et al., 2009; *Times of Zambia*, 2009). Women often bear the brunt of deteriorating labour market conditions. One reason is that they are often concentrated in the hardest-hit export industries, such as garments and electronics. Limited employments rights and social insurance further increase their vulnerability (Emmett, 2009; ILO, 2009*b*). Evidence from Cambodia's garment industry points to women being required to work longer hours for less pay, with adverse consequences for education spending.

Household provision for education financing is directly affected by the loss of remittances, a crucial element of financial transfers from richer to poorer countries – the US$308 billion transferred in 2008 far exceeded international development assistance. Flows of remittances are projected to decline by 7% in 2009 (Ratha et al., 2009). Both the decline and its overall effect will be uneven. Flows to Latin America and the Caribbean are falling in a lagged response to the slowdown in the United States, with El Salvador and Mexico recording declines in excess of 10% (Orozco, 2009). Ghana and Kenya report reductions of a similar scale (IMF, 2009*b*). For several countries, the impact will be very marked. In ten sub-Saharan African countries, including Ethiopia, Kenya, Liberia, Senegal, Sierra Leone and Uganda, remittances are equivalent to over 5% of GDP, rising to 20% in Lesotho (Committee of Ten, 2009). Also, with global remittances falling and urban unemployment rising, transfers to rural areas are declining.

Much of the evidence on the impact of these developments on education is anecdotal. Even so, it points in a worrying direction. Remittances are often vital to household spending on education. Evidence from Ghana and Uganda shows that as much as one-quarter of remittance income goes to education, pointing to potentially large losses of household investment (te Velde et al., 2009). In El Salvador and Haiti, where money sent from the United States contributes significantly to financing education, parents report growing difficulties in keeping children in school as remittances decline (Grogg, 2009; Thomson, 2009). It is not just the loss of international remittances that is hurting education. In China, unemployment has forced an estimated 20 million migrants to return to rural areas, and money that was previously being remitted for education has dried up (Mitchell, 2009).

It is critical for rich and poor countries alike to address the human costs of the current downturn

Evidence from previous recessions and other external shocks shows how crucial it is for rich and poor countries alike to address the human costs of the current downturn. The East Asia financial crisis of 1997 resulted in major reversals in child health and education (Ferreira and Schady, 2008; Harper et al., 2009). In Indonesia, infant mortality increased and the proportion of children not enrolled in school doubled in 1998 (Frankenberg et al., 1999; Paxson and Schady, 2005*a*). The number of street children also rose sharply (Harper et al., 2009). Drought and disrupted rainfall have delivered similar setbacks to education in sub-Saharan Africa (Jensen, 2000; World Bank, 2007*c*). Not all the effects on education are straightforward. In some mainly middle-income countries, school enrolment increases during crises, partly because rising unemployment and falling wages lower the economic returns to child labour (Ferreira and Schady, 2008). But the overall impact is universally harmful to progress in education.

The challenge facing policy-makers today is to avoid repeating the experience of past crises. As the effects of the economic downturn are transmitted to more households, those lacking the resources to cope with the shock risk being pushed into a downward spiral. Short-term coping strategies such as cutting spending on health, nutrition and education can have damaging long-term consequences for individuals and societies. Governments and the international community can contain the damage by investing in social protection. But a consistent lesson from previous crises is that early, up-front investment in crisis prevention through social protection is more effective than treatment after the event.

Short-term coping strategies can have damaging long-term consequences for individuals and societies

Budget monitoring matters

Many governments in low-income countries are reassessing public spending plans in the face of mounting fiscal pressure. Their room for manoeuvre depends on a range of factors, including the pre-crisis fiscal balance, recovery prospects, and domestic and international financing options. The impact of budget adjustments on public spending plans for education will vary according to circumstance and policy choice. Options include cutting spending in real terms, scaling down planned increases or maintaining current spending plans through revenue raising and redistribution within the budget. Decisions made over the next year in these areas will have profound consequences for education financing. Public spending cuts, or caps that are set below planned levels, will ultimately translate into fewer classrooms built, fewer teachers recruited and trained, and more children out of school.

Current monitoring exercises do not adequately track budget decision-making processes. International data provide comprehensive cross-country coverage of public spending, but with a significant delay. For example, this year's Report documents expenditure for 2007. While vital for monitoring broad post-Dakar trends, such information reveals nothing about the direction of the public spending plans that will define the future.

This information gap is difficult to defend. Data for the current and previous budget years are available in most countries, as are budget revision and review documents. The problem is that the data are not assembled and made publicly available by international or regional organizations. In the words of an analysis of education budgets in sub-Saharan Africa carried out for this Report: 'It is rather shocking in view of the strong emphasis given to monitoring progress ... that there is not a more current database for analysing education spending' (Martin and Kyrili, 2009, p. 14). The current crisis has added to the urgency of filling this information gap.

One central conclusion is that UNESCO should be far more effective in monitoring current-year public spending on education and reviewing revisions to future spending plans.[1] Through UNESCO regional offices and the UNESCO Institute for Statistics, a regional network of education ministries' planning and budget directors could be established. To further strengthen the monitoring process, national poverty reduction strategy coordinators could be included, along with finance ministry officials overseeing medium-term expenditure strategies.

To assess the threat to Education for All financing, the Global Monitoring Report team commissioned Development Finance International to review the 2009 budgets of all thirty-seven low-income countries in sub-Saharan Africa (Martin and Kyrili, 2009). This should be viewed as both a partial and preliminary exercise. It is partial because detailed and consistent information on education expenditure from the 2009 budget was available for only twelve countries, and it is preliminary because the budget documents consulted reflect pre-crisis conditions. Broad budgetary patterns for the countries covered can be summarized under four headings:

- *Plans to increase expenditure on education in relation to GDP and the overall budget.* Five of the twelve countries are in this category: Burkina Faso, Liberia, Mozambique, Sierra Leone and Zambia. Liberia, Sierra Leone and Zambia envisaged a significant reallocation to education within a growing budget. In Mozambique, education spending was projected to grow significantly as a share of GDP but only marginally as a share of the budget, reflecting a planned rise in non-social sector spending. It should be stressed that governments in several of these countries have raised concerns over their capacity to finance planned education spending. A May 2009 report on Mozambique, for example, projects that revenue will be 1.3% below the level indicated in the approved budget, which could adversely affect spending plans.

- *Plans to maintain education spending at current levels in relation to GDP and total budget*

1. The Education Sector in UNESCO has started to put in place some of the elements of such an approach. In March 2009, it launched a 'Quick Survey' to collect budget information on public expenditure in education. UNESCO professional staff were invited to fill in a questionnaire capturing their assessment of national budget plans. Unfortunately, the methodology was not conducive to accurate reporting of budget information, spending plans or impacts of the financial crisis. UNESCO has acknowledged the need for more rigorous and timely collection of current-year budget data (UNESCO, 2009*b*).

spending. Two countries – Kenya and Uganda – fall into this category. Both have significantly increased financing for education in recent years. Here, too, crisis-related problems could hamper implementation.

- *Plans to increase education spending as a share of GDP but to maintain or cut the share of education in the national budget*. The countries concerned are Lesotho, Rwanda and the United Republic of Tanzania. Lesotho plans to raise the ratio of education spending to GDP while maintaining the budget share. Rwanda's budget envisages a rise in the share of education spending in GDP but a slight fall in the budget percentage because of a shift towards agriculture and infrastructure. The United Republic of Tanzania plans to maintain the GDP share held by education spending but to reduce the budget share, as the country's national poverty reduction strategy entails dramatic increases in expenditure on agriculture, infrastructure and water. All these plans are highly susceptible to economic pressure, which could change patterns of budget allocation to the detriment of basic education. For example, Lesotho's response to the threat of rising unemployment was to shift spending priorities from pre-school and primary education to technical and vocational training.

- *Plans to cut education spending as a share of GDP and total expenditure*. Two countries – Benin and Ghana – fall into this category. In Benin, the planned cut reflects reallocation of budget spending away from education and other social sectors. In Ghana, it is less a direct result of the economic crisis than an effect of a domestic budget crisis inherited from the previous government. In both cases, it is likely that stagnant or declining economic growth will compound the cuts, resulting in significantly fewer resources available for education spending. There is a danger that Benin's strong progress in recent years towards universal primary education, documented in Chapter 2, will be reversed. In Ghana, efforts to address education marginalization in the north could be undermined (see Chapter 3).

This overview contains good news and bad news. The good news is that current evidence indicates that few governments are cutting education spending. The bad news is that the changing picture may look worse than that captured in current budget analyses. Most budgets of low-income African countries reviewed by Development Finance International were approved by parliaments at the end of 2008, before national economies registered any significant impact of the crisis. Mid-term budget reviews may result in marked adjustments in spending. Close monitoring of actual spending on education, and of restrictions on spending, is vital. Formal revisions to 2009 budgets and public spending plans drawn up amid changing fiscal conditions have to be carefully assessed, as do discrepancies between 2009 budget allocations and actual spending. But the full impact of the downturn is likely to be more fully revealed in 2010. There is already evidence of budget revision in some countries. For example, after copper prices collapsed, Zambia's government removed a windfall tax on mining companies that was to have financed an increase in education and other social spending (te Velde et al., 2009).

It is important to base budget monitoring exercises on appropriate benchmarks. Much has been made of the fact that, to date, relatively few low-income countries have cut public spending in general or priority social sector spending in particular. As far as it goes, this is clearly a positive outcome. However, what ultimately matters for progress on the Education for All goals and wider human development measures is whether planned increases in public spending have been compromised. Governments in many low-income countries have drawn up medium-term expenditure plans for education, often as part of wider poverty reduction strategies supported by donors. The plans are linked to activities such as classroom construction, teacher recruitment, purchases of teaching materials and special programmes for marginalized children. These activities are in turn aimed at specific targets for getting children into school and raising the quality of education. To the extent that budget pressures translate into levels of expenditure that are lower than planned, they will compromise any prospect of accelerated progress towards the Dakar goals.

Close monitoring of actual spending on education, and of restrictions on spending, is vital

What happens beyond the education sector is also crucial. Progress in education is inevitably influenced by developments in other key areas, including child and maternal health, and water and sanitation. The national and international response to the economic crisis thus needs to reflect an integrated strategy for protecting human development across a broad front. □

Expanding 'fiscal space': an Education for All priority

Unlike rich countries, most developing countries lack room for manoeuvre in national budgeting

The term 'fiscal space' describes a factor that has profound consequences for governments' capacity to finance vital social and economic programmes. Put most simply, it is about room for manoeuvre in national budgeting. Tax revenue is the primary source of finance for public spending. But governments can also resort to other revenue-raising measures, including domestic or international borrowing, printing money and, in the case of the poorest countries, international aid. The options open to governments vary widely – but they are most limited in the poorest countries.

'Fiscal space' defines the budget parameters within which governments have to operate. The International Monetary Fund (IMF) defines it as 'room in a government's budget that allows it to provide resources for a desired purpose without jeopardizing the sustainability of its financial position or the stability of the economy' (Heller, 2005, p. 32). Less technocratic approaches would incorporate the financing of wider human development goals, including Education for All (Roy et al., 2007). In the context of the global recession, the issue facing governments is that of using national budgets to strengthen demand, stabilize financial systems and maintain vital social investments despite a shrinking revenue base.

Rich countries have responded to the financial crisis by exploiting fiscal space on an epic scale. With their economies contracting, their financial systems requiring support and demands on public spending for social welfare rising, fiscal policy has provided a major stimulus. Overall fiscal deficits are projected to increase by about six percentage points of GDP, with spending financed by a large increase in public debt.[2] Much of this has been used to shore up banking systems.[3] While bank bail-outs are not strictly comparable to aid flows in financial terms, the contrast between what has been mobilized in the two cases is striking. The four largest asset insurance programmes for commercial banks obliged the governments of the United Kingdom and the United States to take on US$786 billion in potential liabilities – over seven times the amount of total international development assistance flows.[4]

Fiscal policy has also played a wider role in advanced economies. Public spending has gone to support demand and unlock credit markets, creating a countercyclical stimulus for recovery. Many governments have used that spending to strengthen the social and education infrastructure. In the United States, the American Recovery and Reinvestment Act (ARRA) passed by Congress in February 2009 delivered a prospective US$789 billion stimulus to the economy. That stimulus also staved off a financing crisis in education that threatened to result in thousands of teachers being laid off and many schools closed (Box 1.1).

Unlike rich countries, most developing countries operate in a highly constrained fiscal environment. Some, including China and India, have been in a position to counteract the impact of the downturn through increased public spending. But the majority of the poorest countries are walking a fiscal tightrope. Overall tax revenue ratios are projected to decline in well over half of all low-income countries and by more than 2% of GDP in one-quarter of them (IMF, 2009*c*). Meanwhile, pressures to increase spending arise from several sources, including the need to finance social protection programmes. The combination of limited fiscal space and revenue decline has the potential to translate into painful public spending adjustments, including in education.

The research for this Report by Development Finance International explored the dimensions of the fiscal space available to thirty-seven low-income countries in sub-Saharan Africa that are facing financing challenges in education (Martin and Kyrili, 2009).[5] This 'fiscal space assessment' starts by defining 'sustainability thresholds', based on comparative international evidence, in three key areas: domestic and international borrowing, revenue mobilization and aid.[6]

2. On average, public debt will climb from around 70% of advanced economy GDP in 2008 to a projected 100% by 2010 (IMF, 2009*g*).

3. Capital injections, debt guarantees and asset guarantees represented 44% of GDP for the United Kingdom and 7% for the United States as of June 2009 (Martin and Kyrili, 2009).

4. The programmes involved Citigroup, Royal Bank of Scotland, Lloyds and Bank of America (Panetta et al., 2009).

5. The countries are those classified by the World Bank as 'IDA-only': eligible only for concessional International Development Association loans. Hence the list includes Cameroon, the Democratic Republic of the Congo and Djibouti, even though the latest World Bank data put them in the lower middle income category.

6. See Martin and Kyrili (2009) for a detailed explanation of the thresholds.

Box 1.1: The Obama rescue plan – protecting education during the economic downturn

Governments across the developed world have used national budgets to counteract the effects of the economic downturn. In the United States, the US$789 billion American Recovery and Reinvestment Act (ARRA) of February 2009 is aimed at providing a platform for early recovery and protecting the social and economic infrastructure, with education a high priority.

ARRA has attempted to turn the threat to education posed by the recession into an opportunity. With public finances damaged by slower economic growth and rising expenditure in other areas, education spending was in jeopardy in many states. Thousands of teachers faced the prospect of being made redundant. Under ARRA, the federal government stepped into the breach left by collapsing state financing (which accounts for around 90% of education spending). Around US$130 billion will be injected into education and related budgets to stabilize finances and extend opportunities for children from disadvantaged backgrounds. The following are among the most important measures:

- States are to benefit from US$39.5 billion designated for public school districts and higher education institutes under the 'state fiscal stabilization' fund.
- School construction and upgrading projects will receive US$22 billion.
- Funding for targeted programmes aimed at special education and children from the most disadvantaged backgrounds will be increased by around US$25.2 billion. ARRA will increase 2009 fiscal year spending on Title I – a set of specialized classroom programmes supporting learning in schools with high concentrations of poor children – to US$20 billion from about US$14.5 billion. Spending on education for children with disabilities will rise to US$17 billion from US$11 billion.
- Head Start and early Head Start pre-school programmes will receive an increase of US$2.1 billion.
- About US$4.3 billion has been allocated to a 'Race to the Top' Fund aimed at recruiting and retaining effective teachers and raising standards in low-performing schools.

ARRA has sparked a wide-ranging debate about the respective roles of federal and state governments in education financing. With the Department of Education's discretionary budget rising from US$60 billion in 2008 to a projected US$146 billion in 2010, the balance between state and federal financing has been dramatically changed. But without the emergency financing, thousands of teachers would have been made redundant, many schools would have closed and education quality would have suffered. As one congressman put it, 'We cannot let education collapse; we have to provide this level of support to schools.'

The world's poorest countries cannot afford to let education collapse either. Yet, unlike rich countries, most lack the budget resources to provide the support their education systems need to avert collapse.

Sources: US Department of Education (2009); National Education Association (2009); Dillon (2009).

- *Sustainable borrowing.* Given the region's long history of unsustainable external debt, borrowing on international markets comes with high risk for most low-income countries in sub-Saharan Africa. The assessment sets a threshold for external debt based on the 'Debt Sustainability Framework' developed by the IMF-World Bank. For domestic debt, it uses the IMF threshold indicator of a nominal debt stock of 15% of GDP as an indicator for sustainability.
- *Sustainable domestic revenue levels.* Raising more revenue is another way for governments to generate resources for public spending. Low-income African countries have made major strides in recent years by increasing taxes and expanding the tax base, but it is widely recognized that there are limits to how much they can increase tax collection. Governments have to avoid creating disincentives for investment and generating deflationary pressure, especially in the current context. In the absence of a viable threshold indicator, the assessment uses an 'acceptable effort' indicator for revenue collection set at 17% of GDP (excluding grants). This is one of the convergence criteria for the CFA franc zone.
- *Sustainable aid levels.* Another way for low-income African countries to expand fiscal space is to obtain more grants. While aid flows to Africa have increased substantially in recent years, they still fall far short of overall pledges made in 2005 and education-specific pledges made in 2000 (see Chapter 4). Studies have indicated that excessive aid dependence can have damaging

In the United States, around US$130 billion will be injected into education and related budgets

consequences for economic growth and governance, but there are no clear parameters for sustainable aid levels. Using evidence from recent studies, the Development Finance Initiative assessment assumes that countries receiving aid levels that exceed 25% of gross national income have no space to increase their aid dependence.

These three pillars of sustainability cannot be viewed in isolation. Even if a country has scope to gain access to more finance through borrowing or aid, it may decide not to exploit this fiscal space because of the risk of macroeconomic instability. The fiscal space assessment therefore includes checks for fiscal balance and inflation.

Increased aid has the most immediate potential for increasing fiscal space

Overall fiscal space is assessed in two steps. First, each country's ability to obtain and use resources through each of the three instruments – debt, domestic revenue and aid – is determined by reference to the thresholds. Countries below all three thresholds are described as having high fiscal space. Countries constrained on one indicator are classed as having moderate space, on two indicators as having low space and on all three as having no space. The second step is to adjust the outcomes to reflect the two check indicators.[7]

Table 1.2 shows the results. After adjustments for fiscal deficits and inflation risk, five countries have no fiscal space. At the other end of the spectrum, four have high space and the option to resort to all three financing instruments. Seventeen countries have 'low space' and eleven 'moderate space', indicating scope to resort to one or two instruments, respectively. Further analysis points to a diverse set of policy options that depend on national circumstances and highlights choices facing governments and the international community over what type of resources should be made available to protect high-priority spending in education and other areas (Figure 1.4).

- *International aid.* Twenty-five countries have the fiscal space to use more development assistance, and eleven have no domestic alternatives. This implies that an increase in grant flows is the primary means open to low-income African countries seeking to avoid cuts and sustain spending plans in high-priority social sectors.

- *Domestic revenue.* Around fifteen countries could raise more revenue on the basis of the 17% of GDP norm, but seeking to raise revenue in the midst of a steep economic downturn is likely to damage recovery prospects.

- *Borrowing.* Between eleven and fourteen countries could borrow more without compromising their overall public debt sustainability. When external and domestic debt are looked at together, however, the scope for expansion is limited.

A vital policy lesson can be drawn from this assessment: increased aid has the most immediate potential for increasing fiscal space. Early action on a sufficient scale could provide the budget resources needed to pre-empt potentially damaging public spending adjustments in education and other areas. It is critical to deliver this aid *before* fiscal pressures convert the financial crisis into an irreversible long-term human development crisis, with attendant consequences for progress in education. □

Table 1.2: Fiscal space in sub-Saharan Africa, selected countries

High (4 countries)	Moderate (11 countries)	Low (17 countries)	None (5 countries)
Mali, Rwanda, Uganda, United Republic of Tanzania	Benin, Burkina Faso, Cameroon, Central African Republic, Chad, Comoros, Lesotho, Madagascar, Mozambique, Niger, Nigeria	Congo, Côte d'Ivoire, Djibouti, Eritrea, Ethiopia, Gambia, Guinea, Guinea-Bissau, Kenya, Malawi, Mauritania, Sao Tome and Principe, Senegal, Sierra Leone, Sudan, Togo, Zimbabwe	Burundi, Democratic Republic of the Congo, Ghana, Liberia, Zambia

Source: Martin and Kyrili (2009).

7. Here the assumption is that a country can use aid but cannot borrow more if its fiscal deficit exceeds 3% of GDP, since this could have damaging inflationary effects. Similarly, if a country has reached the 'acceptable effort' threshold for revenue mobilization, increasing aid grants might push up inflation, whereas if it has scope for revenue-raising, the inflation effects could be neutralized.

Figure 1.4: Many countries lack room for manoeuvre in budget management but could use more aid

Policy options available to increase resources and protect social sector spending, selected sub-Saharan African countries, 2009

Source: Martin and Kyrili (2009).

The international response: missing a human dimension

The threat that the financial crisis poses to internationally agreed human development goals is widely recognized. The G20 communiqué of April 2009 acknowledged the 'human dimensions' of the threat in particularly forthright terms (Group of Twenty, 2009, para. 25):

> *We recognise that the current crisis has a disproportionate impact on the vulnerable in the poorest countries and recognise our collective responsibility to mitigate the social impact of the crisis to minimise long-lasting damage to global potential.*

Subsequent gatherings have reaffirmed the concern. At the G8 summit in July in L'Aquila, Italy, the governments of the world's richest nations declared that they remained focused on the human and social consequences of the crisis. 'We are determined', their communiqué declared, 'to undertake measures to mitigate the impact of the crisis on developing countries, and to continue to support their efforts to achieve the Millennium Development Goals' (Group of Eight, 2009*c*, para. 6). To what extent have political leaders in the countries that caused the crisis acted on their 'collective responsibility' to mitigate its effects?

Much of what has been presented as 'new and additional' finance is in fact repackaged or reprogrammed aid

Financial resources have been made available on a large scale, both domestically and internationally. Advanced economies have spent around US$10 trillion shoring up their financial systems by providing capital, loan guarantees, lending and asset protection. That figure represents around 30% of their combined GDP. Under the G20 recovery plan, the IMF has been used to strengthen global liquidity and bolster fragile financial systems. This national and international response has been vital to staving off a far deeper global crisis and creating the conditions for recovery. After a severe global recession, economic growth has turned positive as wide-ranging public finance interventions have supported demand and reduced financial risk. Yet the report card on support for the poorest countries is deeply unimpressive.

Headline figures on global financing have masked three problems. First, the poorest countries have been largely bypassed (Woods, 2009*b*). As the president of the African Development Bank put it, 'only a small proportion of the resources announced at the G20 summit in London will trickle down to low-income countries' (Kaberuka, 2009). Second, much of the support that does trickle down will arrive too late and on terms that are inappropriate for the financing needs of the poorest countries.

The third concern is that much of what has been presented as 'new and additional' finance is in fact repackaged or reprogrammed aid. This 'smoke and mirrors' financial reporting has obscured the collective failure of developed countries to decisively deliver resources on the required scale. Some new resources have been made available, principally through the IMF. In the case of the World Bank, which G8 and G20 rhetoric places at the centre of the crisis response for the poorest nations, very few additional resources have been mobilized (Woods, 2009*b*). Instead, the institution has been left to reconfigure its resources to mount a response.

Consolidating current financing for low-income countries is problematic because of uncertainties over commitments. On an optimistic assessment, new concessional financing potentially available to low-income countries amounts to between around US$2 billion and US$3 billion annually for the next two to three years.[8] That figure has to be set against the annual revenue loss of US$80 billion for sub-Saharan Africa alone in 2009.

It is easy to lose sight of what is at stake for the international development goals in education. The everyday concerns of parents struggling to keep their children in school in a slum in Lusaka or a poor village in Senegal seem far removed from the international summits on the global financial crisis. Yet the connections are real. As rich countries take the first steps towards economic recovery, the aftershock of the crisis is jeopardizing the efforts of the world's poorest households to secure for their children an education that might lift them out of poverty. Containing the aftershock will require a strengthened focus on financing for human development.

8. In the period to 2010, IMF concessional loans could rise by up to US$8 billion. The estimate for this Report adds US$2 billion for various commitments undertaken through bilateral aid programmes and World Bank trust funds, though this is almost certainly an overestimate.

The crisis response

The framework for the international response to the financial crisis was set at the G20 summit in April 2009, with the ensuing G8 summit supplementing the agreement. The recovery strategy gave the IMF wide-ranging responsibility for strengthening global liquidity by expanding currency reserves to prevent further financial crises and by providing concessional finance for low-income countries. The World Bank was given responsibility for financing measures aimed at strengthening social protection and tackling food supply problems.

The checklist of global financing commitments and provisions for the poorest countries is expansive and superficially impressive. Much of the new financing has come through the IMF:

- *Boosting global liquidity and strengthening financial stability.* Under the G20 plan the IMF has injected US$283 billion into the global economy in Special Drawing Rights (SDRs), currency reserves that can be exchanged for hard currency. New SDR allocations effectively supplement IMF members' existing currency reserves, thereby providing liquidity to the international economic system.[9] The IMF's credit lines for emerging markets have also been reinforced through the creation of a new facility and the strengthening of existing facilities.[10]

- *Scaling up concessional financing.* Measures have been introduced to increase the IMF resources available to low-income countries through the fund's Poverty Reduction and Growth Facility (PRGF). The measures could increase concessional lending by US$17 billion through to 2014, with up to US$8 billion by 2010. Several new financial instruments have been created to provide more concessional support to low-income countries.[11] In addition, the IMF has modified its Exogenous Shocks Facility (ESF), a mechanism aimed at providing support to countries facing exceptional problems as a result of conflict, natural disaster, falling commodity prices or rising food prices (Bredenkamp, 2009*a*, 2009*b*; IMF, 2009*a*, 2009*d*; Woods, 2009*b*).[12]

The G20 meeting signalled a broad agenda for the World Bank. It included what was termed 'a substantial increase in lending of US$100 billion' and increased bilateral contributions for a range of crisis-response facilities aimed at strengthening social protection and wider poverty interventions (Group of Twenty, 2009). These include the new Infrastructure Crisis Facility, Vulnerability Framework and Rapid Social Response Fund. The World Bank was also made institutional lead actor in the response to the global food crisis. At the G8 summit, governments pledged to provide US$20 billion over three years to support countries struggling with higher food import bills (Group of Eight, 2009*b*).

The IMF and World Bank facilities have attracted a great deal of media attention. An impression has been created that rich countries have moved rapidly to extend to the world's poorest countries the same principles applied in their domestic responses to the crisis. That impression owes less to real financial transfers than to some questionable reporting practices.

The initial expansion of post-crisis lending bypassed the poorest countries

Consider first the IMF component of the global recovery package. The initial expansion of post-crisis lending bypassed the poorest countries, principally because it was directed towards financial stabilization in Europe and some emerging markets. Of the eighteen new lending agreements the IMF had approved by late July 2009, 82% were directed to Europe and 1.6% to Africa (Woods, 2009*b*). While low-income countries will have their currency reserves boosted by the new SDR issue, the allocations are linked to the size of national economies (the increased allocation for France exceeds that for all of sub-Saharan Africa). Moreover, an expansion of the national currency reserve does not automatically generate additional resources for high-priority budgets.

What of the increase in concessional lending through the IMF? As of October 2009, this was the only source of new and additional financing linked directly to the global financial crisis. The IMF claims the new arrangements enable it to make up

9. Low-income countries will receive an additional US$17 billion in SDRs (Gottselig, 2009).

10. In April 2009, the IMF announced the creation of a new flexible credit line and increased flexibility for its standard stand-by arrangements.

11. These are the Extended Credit Facility (medium-term support), the Standby Credit Facility (short-term and precautionary support) and the Rapid Credit Facility (emergency support).

12. Much of the additional IMF support to low-income countries in 2009 came through the Exogenous Shocks Facility, whose financing terms are equivalent to those of the PRGF.

Bold language on scaling up social protection has been backed only by a vague pledge of 'voluntary bilateral contributions'

to US$8 billion available in 2009 and 2010, though one-quarter of that figure is accounted for by early disbursement of existing loans. The G20 framework makes about US$6 billion in new concessional lending resources available to the IMF over 2009–2012 (around US$2 billion annually) for all low-income countries. The IMF itself estimates that the increased lending capacity will cover only 2% of low-income countries' external financing needs (IMF, 2009*d*; Woods, 2009*b*). Actual transfers of new financing will be contingent on the rate of disbursement. Given that disbursements through the PRGF are often disrupted because countries cannot comply with loan conditions, there are serious questions over the prospects for timely delivery.

The World Bank's role in the international response to the crisis is characterized by a large gap between words and money. Many commitments in the G20 communiqué, notably those directed to low-income countries, represent not new money but an imaginative 'relaunch' of past pledges.[13] Others effectively exempt the G20 countries from providing new and additional financing, with bold language on scaling up social protection backed only by a vague pledge of 'voluntary bilateral contributions'.

The World Bank has been left to act on the G20 agenda mainly by drawing upon its own resources and facilities. While strong pronouncements have been made declaring that World Bank support to crisis-affected countries is at a 'record high', increased lending has been sustained not by higher donor support, but by a combination of early disbursement of funds – front-loading – and reprogramming.

The Global Food Crisis Response Programme (GFRP) is a case in point. After eighteen months the programme had disbursed US$795 million, or 68% of its original funds – far too slow a pace given the immediacy of the crisis (United Nations Conference on Trade and Development, 2009). Interventions have ranged from support to school feeding programmes in Burundi, Liberia and Senegal to safety-net programmes in Ethiopia, the United Republic of Tanzania and Yemen, and budget support in Bangladesh, Cambodia and Honduras. These programmes provide vital social protection, but the bulk of GFRP finance comes not from increased aid but from existing country allocations, regional International Development Association (IDA) funds and resources transferred from other facilities (Delgado, 2008). The only new source of finance has been a multidonor trust fund that channelled US$200 million to the GFRP. Most of the US$20 billion pledged at the G8 summit for food supplies also involves the diversion of existing aid commitments rather than new money.

Some World Bank programmes appear not to have taken off on any scale. The Rapid Social Response Fund was created to assist poor and vulnerable populations in developing countries, mainly from the World Bank's own resources. As of September 2009, only one programme appears to have been approved – a cash transfer and nutrition intervention for children under 5 in Senegal (World Bank, 2009*i*).

Other programmes have generated large headline numbers under the banner of 'crisis response' with little in the way of new financing. In 2009, the World Bank significantly increased financing provisions for countries affected by the crisis. Commitments under IDA reached US$14 billion in 2009 and a new US$2 billion facility was created to provide early support in key areas of social protection, health and education. Almost half the allocations available had been disbursed by late 2009 (World Bank, 2009*d*). However, most of the new financing came from front-loading of IDA allocations for low-income countries (Figure 1.5). Burkina Faso, Liberia and Senegal, among others, received over 150% of their planned IDA allocations in 2009.

As a crisis response measure, front-loading makes sense. Faced with mounting budget pressure and rising poverty, countries need early aid. For households confronting hunger, health risks and the challenge of keeping children in school, delays in social protection carry a high price. But front-loading does not increase the overall resources available to governments over the full cycle of programme support. Moreover, it comes with its own risks, including the risk of financing deficits in later years.[14]

The upshot is that the World Bank has been involved in an elaborate financial reshuffle. Efforts by the institution itself to address the issue of making new resources available have not been

13. One example is the pledge of US$100 billion in additional multilateral lending, originally made several months before the G20 summit, with India, Indonesia and Ukraine identified as being among the potential beneficiaries.

14. The World Bank is not alone in combating the human development emergency through creative accounting. Plans drawn up by the EU Commission in May 2009 announced an intention to mobilize 8.8 billion euros (approximately US$12 billion at May 2009 exchange rates) in development financing as a crisis response, but almost all the commitments and pledges behind this figure come from pre-existing commitments (Woods, 2009*b*).

Figure 1.5: The World Bank has front-loaded concessional International Development Association loans

Early disbursement as a share of planned allocation under the International Development Association (IDA)

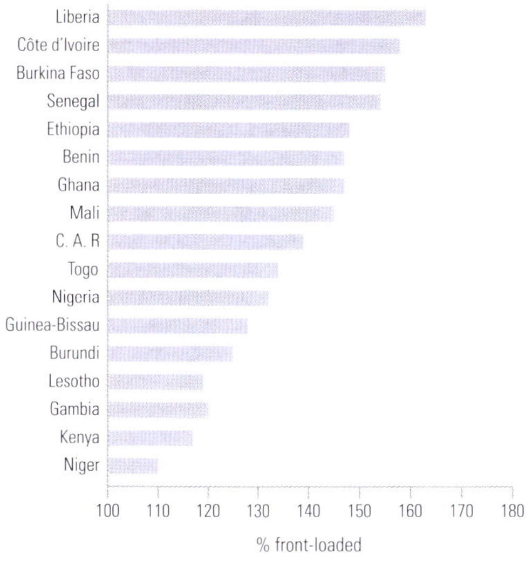

Source: World Bank (2009*b*).

wholly successful. Before the G20 summit, World Bank President Robert Zoellick called on developed countries to put aside the equivalent of 0.7% of their stimulus package for a new Vulnerability Fund (World Bank, 2009*l*). This was an innovative attempt to create a financing base for new and additional aid to countries lacking the fiscal space to respond to the crisis, enabling them to create the conditions for recovery and strengthen social protection. Mr Zoellick noted that the real issue at stake was a choice between an 'age of responsibility or an age of reversal' (Zoellick, 2009). That formulation captures the options rich countries face with respect to the international development goals in education and other areas. Evidence to date suggests that the 'age of reversal' is the default choice.

There are wider problems in the G20 response to the crisis related to the respective roles of the IMF and World Bank. The latter would have been the obvious institution to lead the response to the special challenges facing low-income countries. It has a far stronger capacity than the IMF for rapid assessment of the budgetary implications of the economic downturn on financing for the Millennium Development Goals. It has also played a leading role in supporting and developing social protection programmes. Moreover, the International Development Association, the World Bank's main source of financing for low-income countries, provides loans on more concessional terms than the IMF's Poverty Reduction and Growth Facility.[15] For all of these reasons, the World Bank and the IDA should have been the first line of defence in the response to the crisis.

The IMF's track record in poverty reduction efforts has prompted further questions about its enhanced role. In 2004, the IMF Independent Evaluation Office concluded: 'Success in embedding the PRGF in the overall strategy for growth and poverty reduction has been limited in most cases' (IMF, 2004). Several commentators have identified an inflexible approach to targets, enshrined in loan conditions for inflation, fiscal deficits and public spending, as a source of tension between the IMF approach to macroeconomic stabilization and the financing strategies aimed at achieving the Millennium Development Goals. That tension has been evident in debates over financing for education. For example, the Global Campaign for Education concludes a review of twenty-three IMF programmes by warning of a potential conflict between spending targets set in loan conditions and financing requirements for teacher recruitment (Global Campaign for Education, 2009).

In the wake of the financial crisis, the IMF's senior management has pledged to adopt more flexible approaches to fiscal deficits and inflation (IMF, 2009*d*; Sayeh, 2009). This is vital, because fiscal policy should counteract the crisis, not create deflationary pressures. There is some evidence of greater flexibility being applied at the country level in sub-Saharan Africa. Even before the crisis, inflation targets had been loosened to reflect the impact of higher food prices. In mid-2009, the IMF reported that fiscal targets had been relaxed in eighteen of the twenty-three countries with active programmes (IMF, 2009*d*).[16] However, questions remain over the degree to which the recent declarations reflect a new approach to macroeconomic management. Loan conditions in several countries examined in the United Nations' 2009 *Trade and Development Report* – including Côte d'Ivoire, Ethiopia, Pakistan and Senegal –

The World Bank and the IDA should have been the first line of defence in the response to the crisis

15. PRGF loans are provided at 0.5% interest and are repayable over ten years with a five-year grace period. The PRGF has a grant element of around 30%. IDA provides interest-free credits repayable over thirty-five to forty years with a ten-year grace period. The grant component of IDA is roughly double that of the PRGF.

16. A preliminary review of programmes for thirty-three low-income countries indicates that the deficit is being allowed to widen in around twenty cases (though in some instances just for 2009) and is staying the same or falling in the other countries (Martin and Kyrili, 2009).

include the tightening of fiscal and monetary policy. The authors conclude: 'Policy conditions attached to these IMF loans are fairly similar to those of the past, including a requirement that recipient countries reduce public spending and increase interest rates' (United Nations Conference on Trade and Development, 2009). This would appear to be inconsistent both with the IMF's policy pronouncements and – more importantly – with the need to avoid deflationary measures in the interests of economic recovery and long-term poverty reduction.

Looking ahead

The United Nations Secretary-General has warned in stark terms that the financial crisis has the potential to mutate into a long-term development emergency. 'If we do not act together, if we do not act responsibly, if we do not act now,' he said in May 2009, 'we risk slipping into a cycle of poverty, degradation and despair' (United Nations, 2009*b*). The danger is that as the world economy pulls out of recession, the real victims of the crisis will be forgotten, including millions of children facing the prospect of losing their chance for an education.

The United Nations Secretary-General should convene a high-level meeting on EFA financing

The most immediate priority is for rich countries to respond to the mounting budget pressure facing governments in low-income countries. That means providing more concessional financing before irreparable damage is inflicted on vital social infrastructure. While leaders of the G20 and the G8 have adopted encouraging communiqués, delivery has been woefully inadequate. Behind the global financial pledges, the world's most vulnerable citizens have been left to sink or swim with their own resources. As social and economic pressures mount, there is an imminent threat that progress in education will stall, damaging prospects for economic growth, poverty reduction and health. Political leaders in rich countries need to respond to the human crisis in poor countries with the same level of resolve they have demonstrated in their domestic responses to the crisis.

Action is required at many levels. The following are among the most urgent priorities:

- *Convene a high-level meeting on Education for All financing before the 2010 Millennium Development Goals summit.* Financing gaps for achieving the 2015 Education for All goals have been systematically underestimated. Evidence set out in this Report (see Chapter 2) suggests that the average annual shortfall in financing is around US$16 billion, rather than the US$11 billion previously assumed. With slower economic growth in the poorest countries, prospects for closing this gap are deteriorating. Given the scale of the financing gap and the failure of rich countries to support social and economic recovery in the poorest countries, the United Nations Secretary-General should convene a high-level meeting to elaborate strategies for making more resources available before the Millennium Development Goals summit in September 2010.

- *Scale up aid and provide early support.* If developing countries are to protect and strengthen public financing commitments in the face of an economic downturn, they need a sustained and predictable increase in aid and up-front support to counteract revenue losses from 2008 and 2009. The financial crisis has added to the urgency of rich countries acting on the aid commitments made in 2005 (see Chapter 4). Increased official development assistance should be backed by a temporary debt moratorium for low-income countries for 2009 and 2010, with the savings released for spending in key areas. Such a moratorium would cost around US$26 billion in total (United Nations Conference on Trade and Development, 2009).

- *Make monitoring more effective.* Waiting until the education crisis announces itself in official data is not a sensible course of action. Crisis prevention – which is eminently preferable to response after the event – requires far more effective and current monitoring of government budgets, school attendance and dropout rates. UNESCO should take the lead in this area, working through national education and finance ministries and coordinating a wider donor response. It is particularly important that the implementation of 2009 budgets, real education spending and 2010 budgets are subject to close scrutiny. Beyond outright cuts in public spending, monitoring should focus on disparities between planned spending in education sector strategies and actual spending.

- *Ensure that IMF support is provided on a flexible basis that is consistent with achieving the Education for All goals.* Statements by the IMF leadership pointing to greater flexibility in loan conditions on fiscal deficits, inflation and public spending are welcome, but concerns remain over whether this flexibility will be maintained in 2010 and beyond. In drawing up loan conditions, IMF staff should be required to report explicitly on consistency with the financing requirements for achieving the core Education for All goals by 2015. Special priority should be put on the costs associated with teacher recruitment, training and remuneration.

- *Increase support through the International Development Association.* IDA is the most appropriate multilateral financing vehicle for mitigating the effects of the economic downturn in the poorest countries. While the World Bank has demonstrated a capacity for innovation in front-loading IDA financing, transferring resources from other facilities and redirecting existing country allocations, this approach is neither a sustainable nor a credible response to a systemic crisis in financing for international development goals. Front-loading also raises uncertainty over future financing for education and other high-priority sectors. To guard against this uncertainty and place IDA financing on a more balanced footing, donors should undertake a binding commitment to increase the resources available during the next replenishment. Donors should pledge to increase their support for World Bank concessional loans from US$42 billion in the fifteenth IDA replenishment to US$60 billion in IDA-16, which begins in 2010.

- *Make social protection a high priority.* Protecting education budgets is just one of the requirements for sustained progress towards key Education for All goals. Rising household poverty linked to the economic crisis brings with it the prospect of increased child labour, deteriorating nutrition and reduced capacity for investment in education. Social protection, through cash transfers, nutrition programmes and targeted support in other areas, has been shown in many countries to build the resilience of vulnerable households and strengthen their ability to cope with economic shocks without resorting to damaging measures such as withdrawing children from school. As Chapter 3 shows, government and donor support can make a huge difference in this area. ■

UNESCO should take the lead in the monitoring of government budgets, school attendance and dropout rates

Overcrowded and under-resourced: a classroom in Malawi

© Louise Gubb/Corbis

Chapter 2. Progress

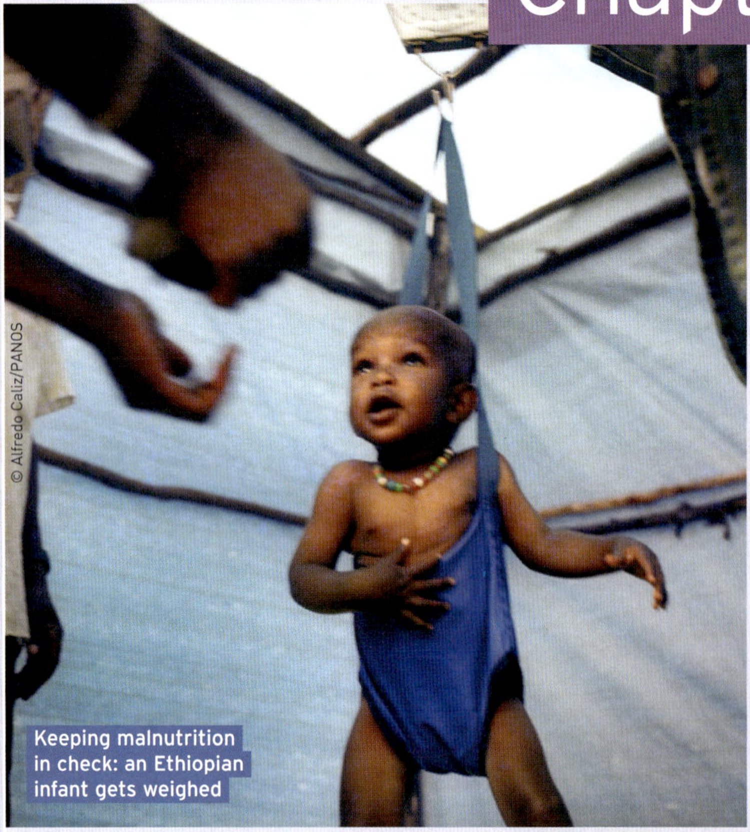

Keeping malnutrition in check: an Ethiopian infant gets weighed

© Alfredo Caliz/PANOS

Continuing education in Lebanon: learning empowers at all ages

© REUTERS/Zohra Bensemra

In the Hindu Kush, Pakistan, a traditional Kalash storyteller captivates his audience

© Chrétien Eric/Gamma/Eyedea Presse

towards the EFA goals

Getting there in rural China: minority children have further to go

© Patrick La Floch/Explorer/Eyedea Illustration

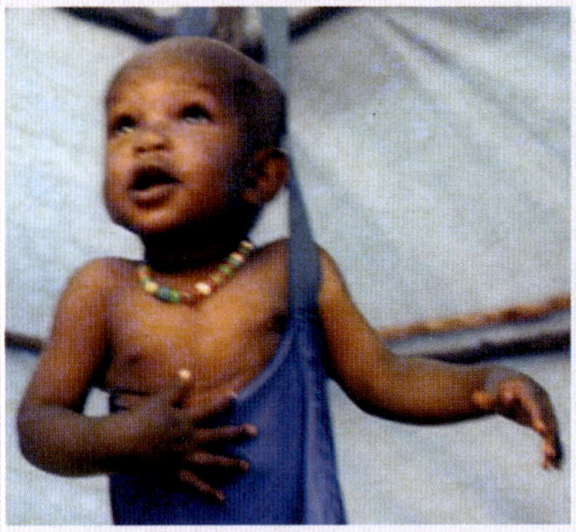

Monitoring national trends is the core task of the *EFA Global Monitoring Report*. This chapter examines progress towards the goals adopted at Dakar. It documents differences across countries and regions, as well as the sometimes dramatic differences that coexist within a single border. It highlights the role of persistent inequalities in holding back advances towards all of the EFA goals and considers the degree to which governments and aid donors are meeting – or falling short – of their promises to invest in basic education. A costing exercise assesses the financing gap for forty-six low-income countries, putting a price tag on the cost of delivering a quality education to every child, youth and adult.

Introduction

The Dakar Framework for Action, adopted by 164 governments in 2000, is one of the most comprehensive, wide-ranging and ambitious of all commitments undertaken by the international community. It pledges to expand learning opportunities for every youth, adult and child – and to achieve specific targets in key areas by 2015.

With just five years to go to the target date, this chapter of the Report monitors progress towards the Education for All goals set under the Dakar Framework. Effective monitoring is vital to achieving international development targets. Apart from keeping the goals themselves in the spotlight, it can highlight examples of success, provide early warning of failure, inform policy and support advocacy. At an international level, measuring progress towards shared goals gives insight into the strengths and weaknesses of national strategies. It demonstrates what can be achieved in practice and shows that all countries, whatever their level of development, can make progress under strong political leadership. Above all, monitoring provides a tool to hold governments accountable for the degree to which they act on the commitments they undertake at international summit meetings.

This chapter starts by highlighting the importance of early childhood care and education in creating the foundations for lifelong learning. It then monitors progress towards universal primary education, an area which raises serious concerns. While the number of children not attending school continues to fall, the most recent school enrolment data suggest that the goal of universal primary education by 2015 will be missed. Moreover, household survey evidence suggests that more children may be out of school than the official data indicate. Progress in school participation continues to outstrip progress in learning achievement, pointing to a widening gap between quantitative and qualitative indicators of progress. The chapter further shows that advances in adult literacy fall far short of the goals. Meanwhile, technical and vocational education programmes have – at best – a mixed record in responding to the learning needs of youth and young adults.

Financing is critical to accelerating progress towards the Education for All goals. Current global estimates of the financing required to meet the 2015 targets are outdated and methodologically flawed, primarily because they do not take into account the cost of reaching disadvantaged groups. This Report provides an updated analysis of the financing needed to reach key targets, adjusted for the incremental cost of extending opportunities to disadvantaged groups. The analysis shows that financing gaps have been underestimated and that developing country governments and aid donors will have to act with urgency to close these gaps.

Progress towards the Dakar goals is far too slow to meet the 2015 targets

Monitoring is about more than technical measurement of progress. This chapter highlights the strong connections between progress towards specific goals and underlying problems of inequality and social marginalization, which Chapter 3 examines further. While national data help illuminate broad trends, they can obscure underlying disparities. Gender disparities are narrowing in many areas, but young girls and women continue to face disadvantages at several levels, from early childhood, through primary and secondary school, and into adulthood. Wider inequalities linked to poverty, language, ethnicity, region and other factors also restrict opportunity on a global scale.

Global monitoring exercises inevitably reveal complex and varied patterns. Two broad messages emerge from the detail of national and regional progress reports on the Education for All goals. The first is good news: there is unequivocal evidence that the world is moving in the right direction, with many of the poorest countries registering impressive advances on many fronts. Their record demonstrates what is achievable – and shows that many of the 2015 goals are still within reach. The second message is cautionary, with a 'bad news' element: on current trends, progress towards the Dakar goals is far too slow to meet the 2015 targets. An underlying problem is the failure of many governments to put higher priority on policies that extend opportunities to the most marginalized sections of society. Failure to change this picture will result in the international community falling far short of the promise made at Dakar in 2000. □

Early childhood care and education

Goal 1: Expanding and improving comprehensive early childhood care and education, especially for the most vulnerable and disadvantaged children.

'Five- and six-year-old children are the inheritors of poverty's curse and not its creators. Unless we act these children will pass it onto the next generation like a family birthmark.'

These remarks by United States President Lyndon B. Johnson (1965) retain a powerful resonance. Early childhood can create the foundations for a life of expanded opportunity – or it can lock children into a future of deprivation and marginalization. There is strong – and growing – evidence that high-quality care in the early years can act as a springboard for success in school. In turn, education provides vulnerable and disadvantaged children with a chance to escape poverty, build a more secure future and realize their potential. The past decade has witnessed rapid and sustained increases in the number of children entering primary school in the world's poorest countries. Yet every year millions of children start school carrying the handicap that comes with the experience of malnutrition, ill health and poverty in their early years.

High-quality care in the early years can act as a springboard for success in school

For many that experience starts, quite literally, in the womb and continues through the early years. Maternal undernutrition and the failure of health systems to provide effective antenatal support, along with safe delivery and post-natal care, contribute to child mortality. They also help transmit educational disadvantage across generations. Malnutrition before children enter school is another formidable barrier to education. Apart from threatening lives, it robs children of the opportunity to develop their potential for learning. That is why the eradication of child malnutrition should be viewed not just as a development imperative in its own right, but as a key element in the Education for All agenda.

With some notable exceptions, governments across the world have failed to accelerate progress in combating child hunger. And with the sharp hike in global food prices during 2007 and 2008, and the economic downturn pushing more children into poverty, a picture that was already bleak has been deteriorating.

Effective early childhood care and education can give children a better chance of escaping what President Johnson called 'poverty's curse'. While much has been achieved, the monitoring evidence set out in this section suggests that far more has to be done. To summarize some of the key messages:

- *Malnutrition needs to be recognized as both a health and an education emergency.* Malnutrition is damaging the bodies and minds of around 178 million young children each year, undermining their potential for learning, reinforcing inequality in education and beyond, and reducing the efficiency of investment in school systems.

- *Improved access to maternal and child health care should be seen as a high priority for education, as well as for public health.* Charging fees for basic services is locking millions of vulnerable women out of health systems and exposing their children to unnecessary risks. As in the education sector, the elimination of user fees should be treated as a high priority.

- *Governments need to tackle inequality in access to early childhood care.* Those in greatest need of early childhood care – and with the most to gain from it – have the least access. In both rich and poor countries, parental income and education heavily influence who attends pre-school programmes, pointing to the need for greater equity in public provision and financing.

This section is divided into two parts. Part 1 reviews progress and the current status of some key indicators of child well-being and nutrition in developing countries, and highlights the strong links between maternal and child health. Part 2 provides a snapshot of access to early childhood programmes across the world, along with evidence that these programmes can play an important role in equalizing opportunity and overcoming marginalization.

Malnutrition and ill health – a 'silent emergency' in education

Retarded growth in the womb, early-childhood stunting and anaemia are not typically viewed as mainstream education issues. The evidence strongly suggests that they should be. Each of these conditions can have profound and irreversible effects on a child's ability to learn, undermining the potential benefits of education.

Neurological science helps explain why education prospects are shaped *in utero* and during the early years of life. The period from about three months before birth is critical to the formation of neural pathways, while the first three years are marked by rapid development of language and memory (Bennett, 2008). Normal brain development during this period creates a foundation for future school achievement and lifelong learning (Harvard University Center on the Developing Child, 2007).

Children who suffer nutritional deprivation *in utero* or during their early years pay a high price later in life. There is a powerful and growing body of evidence that nutritional status during the first two years of life strongly determines later performance in education (Alderman et al., 2001; Glewwe et al., 2001; Grantham-McGregor et al., 2007). Children who experience episodes of early malnutrition tend to score worse on tests of cognitive function, psychomotor development, fine motor skills, activity levels and attention span (Alderman et al., 2006; Behrman, 1996; Maluccio et al., 2009). They also tend to start school later and are at greater risk of dropping out before completing a full primary school cycle. A recent study in Guatemala finds that the impact of being stunted at age 6 is equivalent in its test score effects to losing four grades of schooling (Behrman et al., 2008). The critical but widely ignored insight to emerge from the research evidence is that what children are able to learn in school is heavily influenced by pre-school health and nutrition.

Research carried out for this year's *EFA Global Monitoring Report* adds further weight to evidence of the long-term impact of nutrition on cognitive development (Box 2.1). Drawing on the Young Lives Survey, a unique data set that tracks children in Ethiopia, India, Peru and Viet Nam through their early years, the analysis documents marked nutrition-related disadvantages revealed in test scores at age 4 to 5. By age 7 to 8, the malnutrition penalty is equivalent to the loss of a full term of schooling (Sanchez, 2009).

Child malnutrition – limited progress

Opportunities for education are heavily influenced by the well-being of children before they enter school. It is an unfortunate fact that, at the start of the twenty-first century, the twin scourges of hunger and ill health continue to blight education on a global scale.

Box 2.1: Early malnutrition leads to long-term educational damage

Research carried out for this year's Report strongly reinforces wider evidence on the contribution of malnutrition to educational disadvantage.

Using data from the Young Lives Survey, which tracked children in Ethiopia, India (Andhra Pradesh state), Peru and Viet Nam, the study examines the relationship between early nutrition and cognitive achievements at age 4 to 5, measured on the Peabody Picture Vocabulary Test (PPVT), an international learning achievement scale. It also looks at the relationship between nutrition at age 7 to 8 and outcomes measured in terms of PPVT scores and accumulated years of education at age 11 to 12 (for this cohort, Dercon [2008] presents similar evidence). In both cases, height for age is used as an indicator of nutritional history and status, standardized using the latest World Health Organization (WHO) growth curve references. Although the samples are not nationally representative, they were designed to reflect cultural, ethnic and geographic differences within each country.

The results are striking. After controlling for an extensive set of child, parental and household characteristics, and taking into account the effect of community characteristics, the results point to a strong association between nutritional status measured at 6 to 18 months and cognitive achievement at age 4 to 5. An increase of one standard deviation in early height for age is associated with an improvement of 4% to 12% of the PPVT standard deviation in the Young Lives samples.

Similar findings emerge for the older cohort. In this case, an increase of one standard deviation in nutritional status measured at ages 7 and 8 is associated with a marked increase in school grade attainment that represents 14% to 20% of the grade attainment standard deviation (about 0.2 to 0.4 additional years of schooling). Given the high levels of stunting for both cohorts in all the Young Lives samples, the results underline the significant costs imposed by malnutrition on education.

Source: Sanchez (2009).

One way to gauge how children are faring around the world is to look at child mortality rates. While death rates are falling, the world remains far off track for the Millennium Development Goal of a two-thirds reduction from 1990 levels by 2015. There were 9.3 million child deaths in 2008. On current trends the millennium goal target will be missed by a figure equivalent to more than 4 million additional deaths in 2015. Set against this bad news is the fact that many of the world's poorest countries, including Ethiopia, Malawi, Mozambique and the United Republic of Tanzania, have cut child deaths by 40% or more (UNICEF, 2008*b*).

Child mortality is intimately related to malnutrition. Progress towards the Millennium Development Goal target of halving malnutrition has been painfully slow, with most countries in South Asia and sub-Saharan Africa off track. It is estimated that malnutrition is directly implicated in two of every three deaths of children under age 5. While there have been some advances towards improved child nutrition, and expanded access to Vitamin A supplements and iodized salt, achievements fall far short of the goals that have been set:

Figure 2.1: High levels of child stunting are holding back progress in education

Severe and moderate stunting among children under 5, selected countries, 2000-2007[1]

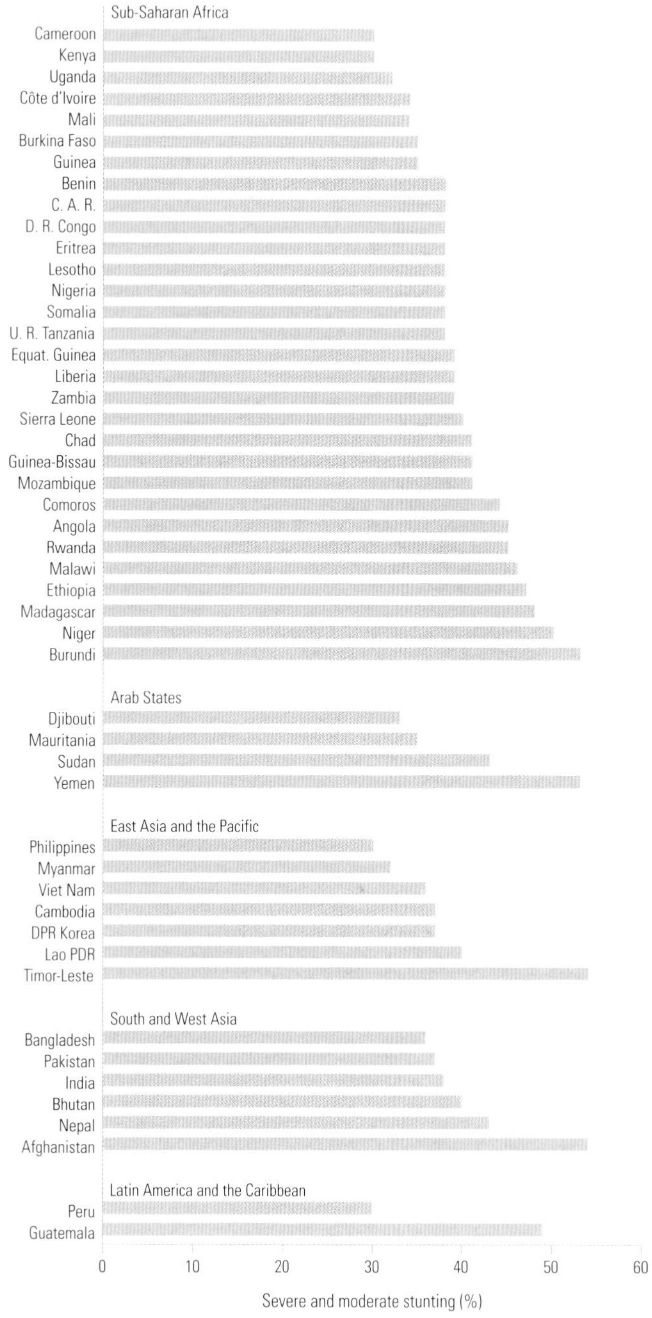

Note: Countries included are those in which the proportion of stunted children is 30% or more.

1. Data are for the most recent year available during the period specified.

Source: Annex, Statistical Table 3A.

- *Childhood stunting.*[1] Around one in three children under age 5 – 178 million in total – suffers severe or moderate stunting. By the time these children enter school, malnutrition will have diminished their potential for learning – a disadvantage they will carry into adulthood. Apart from its damaging consequences for individuals, malnutrition in early childhood inevitably erodes the benefits of investment in education. The highest regional rates of stunting are found in central and eastern Africa and South Asia. Of the forty-nine countries where stunting prevalence rates are in excess of 30%, thirty are in sub-Saharan Africa (Figure 2.1).

- *Low birth weight.* Recent international estimates suggest that about 19 million infants – 14% of all newborns – are delivered with low birth weight (UNICEF, 2008*b*). More than half of these births take place in South Asia: over one in four of the region's children are delivered with low birth weight (Figure 2.2). These children face a heightened risk of early mortality: low birth weight is an underlying factor in 60% to 80% of deaths in the first month. They also face longer-term risks of disadvantage in health and education. Low birth weight is strongly associated with loss of years in school and poorer cognitive skills (Victoria et al., 2008), which undermine the potential benefits of improved access to secondary education. Many of the 8.3 million Indian children born with low birth weight will carry a burden of disadvantage with them into primary school. Moreover, almost half of all children under age 3 in India are underweight for their age, pointing to far deeper nutritional deficits.

- *Micronutrient deficiency.* Early cognitive development can be severely impaired by micronutrient deficiencies. It is estimated that one-third of all pre-school children is affected by iodine deficiency, a condition associated with a loss of ten to fifteen points on IQ tests even in moderate forms. A similar proportion of children is affected by Vitamin A deficiency, a major cause of blindness, ill health and poor concentration (Victoria et al., 2008).

The factors behind malnutrition vary across countries. Poverty, social inequalities and livelihood insecurity all play a role. National wealth is often a

1. Stunting, or low height for age, is caused by long-term insufficiency of nutrient intake and frequent infections. It generally occurs before the age of 2 and the effects are largely irreversible.

poor guide to deprivation. Guatemala is not one of the world's poorest countries, but it has one of the highest levels of child stunting. Almost half of the country's children are malnourished – and in parts of rural Guatemala, where the population is largely Mayan, the figure reaches 80%. Over the past two years, drought and high food prices have made things worse. But the underlying problem is extreme inequality in wealth distribution, allied to the failure of government to mobilize resources for social protection.

Nutritional indicators have been deteriorating in many countries over the past two years. World agricultural prices rose sharply in the two years to 2008, affecting all major traded food staples. While prices have since fallen, they have stabilized at levels far higher than they were before 2007. Effects at the national level have varied considerably, depending on the incidence of poverty and dependence on food imports. However, higher food prices have almost certainly stalled global progress in cutting malnutrition.

Recent estimates from the Food and Agricultural Organization of the United Nations suggest that the number of malnourished people in the world increased from 848 million in 2005 to 963 million in 2008, largely because of rising food prices (FAO, 2008). Another 44 million people may have been pushed into malnutrition during 2008 (Commission on Growth and Development, 2008).

The damage inflicted by higher food prices has been unevenly spread. Outcomes depend on whether households are net sellers or buyers of food, on access to savings or credit and on current nutritional status. For people living below the international poverty threshold of $1.25 a day, many of whom spend 50% to 70% of their income on food, higher food prices pose a stark choice: eat less or decrease spending in other areas (von Braun, 2008; World Bank, 2008*a*). Landless rural households, low-income urban groups and female-headed households have been among the hardest hit. Many have cut already inadequate diets and switched from protein-rich foods to cheaper coarse cereals (Hauenstein Swan et al., 2009; von Braun, 2008). In Bangladesh, where rice and wheat prices almost doubled in 2007, it is estimated that a 50% increase in the price of food staples increases the prevalence of iron deficiency among women and children by 25% (Bouis, 2008).

Figure 2.2: Low birth weight sets the scene for lifelong disadvantage

Average % of infants with low birth weight, selected regions, 2000-2007[1]

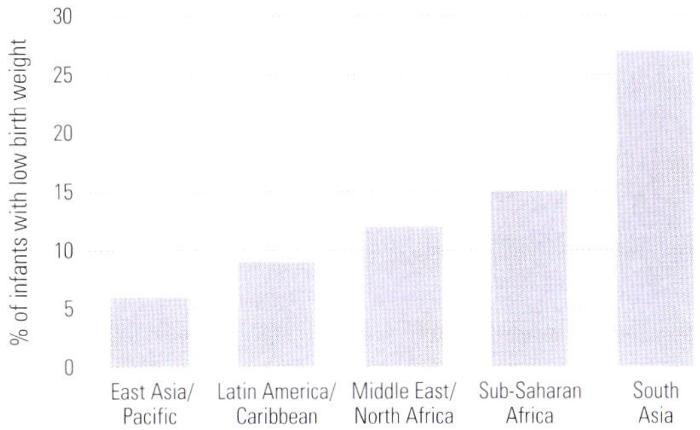

Notes: Regions presented are those used by UNICEF, which differ to some extent from the EFA regions. Low birth weight is defined as less than 2.5 kilograms.
1. Data are for the most recent year available during the period specified.
Source: UNICEF (2008*b*).

Short-term distress in the form of rising malnutrition will have long-term consequences for education. As more children experience episodes of malnutrition in early childhood their prospects for learning will be diminished. At the same time, rising pressure on household budgets will have wider consequences as poor parents are forced to adjust household budgets. There is evidence from Bangladesh, Jamaica and Kenya of households cutting education spending to accommodate higher food prices (Hossain et al., 2009; World Bank, 2008*e*).

Short-term distress in the form of rising malnutrition will have long-term consequences for education

High food prices have not been the only cause of rising malnutrition. In northern Sri Lanka, 300,000 people were displaced by conflict in 2009. It is estimated that about 13% of the displaced were children under 5. A survey covering six of the thirteen camps for displaced people found that one in four children was malnourished and one in three was moderately or severely stunted (Jayatissa, 2009). Failure to adequately protect these children raises wider issues of humanitarian concern. But the consequences for education will also be severe.

Maternal health – critical, but neglected

The health of newborn children – critical for later educational chances – is intimately related to the health of their mothers. Women who are malnourished and suffering from micronutrient deficiency face far higher risks during pregnancy and childbirth, and are more likely to give birth to underweight babies. Restricted growth of the foetus during pregnancy is a major risk factor for maternal health and child survival – and is likely to lead to future educational disadvantage.

More than one in three births in developing countries take place without a skilled birth attendant

Unsafe pregnancy and childbirth exact an immense human toll. An estimated half a million women lose their lives each year from pregnancy and birth-related causes – and for every death another thirty women suffer severe long-term injuries. Almost all these deaths and injuries could be averted through access to antenatal care, skilled attendance during pregnancy and emergency obstetric care. Poor maternal health, inadequate nutrition and limited access to care are also implicated in the deaths of the 4 million newborns who do not survive their first month (Lawn et al., 2006). Two conditions – birth asphyxia and sepsis with pneumonia – cause nearly 60% of these deaths. The real cause, however, is limited access to skilled health professionals at birth and a failure to prioritize maternal and child health in national policy (Thea and Qazi, 2008).

This 'needless human tragedy' (UNICEF, 2008*b*) goes beyond maternal and child mortality and immediate health risks. Undernutrition *in utero*, low birth weight and heightened vulnerability to sickness after birth can cause direct structural damage to the brain that impairs cognitive development and locks children into a future of underachievement. Wider health risks during pregnancy and childbirth also have consequences for education:

- Maternal iodine deficiency in pregnancy causes an estimated 38 million children to be born each year facing risks of mental impairment and congenital abnormalities (UNICEF, 2007*b*).
- Anaemia, which affects around half of all pregnant women, heightens the risks associated with pregnancy and reduces prospects for child survival (UNICEF, 2008*b*).
- Around half of the stunting observed in infants occurs in the uterus and the remainder during the first two years of life (Victoria et al., 2008).
- The absence of skilled health personnel during delivery costs lives and leaves children facing lifetime disadvantages. Asphyxia contributes to around one-quarter of newborn deaths and results in about 1 million children suffering learning difficulties and disabilities such as cerebral palsy (WHO, 2005).

Access to health provision is not the only barrier to improved child and maternal care. Many underlying problems associated with pregnancy and childbirth reflect a failure to protect women's rights. Low status, heavy workloads, a lack of voice in matters of sexual and reproductive health, early marriage and poor access to information all contribute.

Providing quality health care

Inadequate maternal and child health care is holding back advances in education. Progress towards the Millennium Development Goal target of a three-quarters reduction in maternal deaths by 2015 has been close to zero. Meanwhile, limited improvements in survival in the first month of life are preventing progress towards the target on child mortality.

One of the most urgent priorities is providing quality health services. Intrauterine growth restrictions and maternal micronutrient deficiencies can be readily detected through antenatal care and treated at little cost. Access to facilities providing skilled attendance at birth, emergency obstetric care and post-natal care could prevent over 80% of maternal and neonatal deaths, and set children on course for a healthy future (UNICEF, 2008*b*). Yet more than one in three births in developing countries take place without a skilled birth attendant. Skilled attendance rates are lowest in South Asia (41%) and sub-Saharan Africa (45%) (UNICEF, 2008*b*). Not coincidentally, these are the regions with the highest maternal mortality rates.

Poverty undermines maternal health in several ways. It heightens exposure to threats such as malnutrition and infectious disease. It can also reduce access to vital health care, either because care is lacking or because it is unaffordable to the very poor. The poverty risk factor is graphically captured in a UNICEF review of evidence from fifty household surveys that found that neonatal mortality rates among the poorest 20% were typically 20% to 50% higher than for the wealthiest quintile (UNICEF, 2008*b*). These health inequalities fuel education disparities later in life.

The poorest mothers and children are often underserved along the whole continuum of care. In South Asia, being poor reduces by a factor of five the probability of having a skilled health person in attendance during delivery. Even controlling for poverty, indigenous people and ethnic minorities are often severely disadvantaged. In Guatemala, non-indigenous women are more than twice as likely as their indigenous counterparts to give birth in a public health facility with trained personnel. The factors excluding poor and vulnerable households from basic maternal and child health services vary by country but include cost, distance and the poor quality of public care. Whatever the underlying causes of health disadvantage, the consequences include educational disadvantage later in life.

The strength of the links between maternal health and education is often overlooked. Some of those links are very direct. Young women of middle to higher secondary school age, 15 to 19, account for one in seven deaths related to pregnancy and childbirth (WHO and UNICEF, 2003). The younger the age at pregnancy, the greater the health risks for mother and child. Being born to a mother under 18 increases the risk of infant mortality by 60% and the children who survive are more likely to suffer from low birth weight, undernutrition and delayed cognitive development (Lawn et al., 2006; UNICEF, 2008*b*; WHO, 2005).

Empowerment through education is one of the strongest antidotes to maternal risk. Women with higher levels of education are more likely to delay and space out pregnancies, and to seek health care support. In South and West Asia, almost half of women with no education give birth without having received antenatal care, compared with nearly 10% for women with secondary education (Figure 2.3). The 'education advantage' is even more pronounced when it comes to having a skilled birth attendant present during delivery. In Burkina Faso, mothers with primary education are twice as likely to have a skilled attendant present as those with no education, and women with secondary education are almost four times as likely. While the association between education and improved maternal and child indicators is not evidence of causation, the strength of the association points to the importance of the two-way link between investment in health and investment in education.

Figure 2.3: Educated mothers have better access to antenatal care

Children under age 3 born without antenatal care, by maternal education, South and West Asia and sub-Saharan Africa, circa 2005

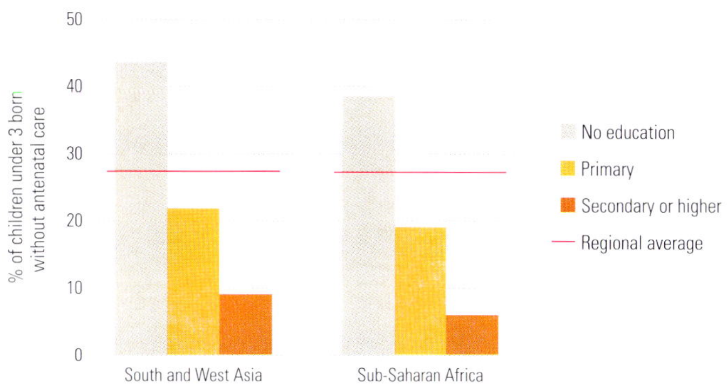

Notes: Figures presented are population weighted averages. The sample of countries used to estimate the South and West Asia average represents more than 90% of the total population of the region and the sample used to estimate the sub-Saharan Africa average more than 80%.
Source: Macro International Inc. (2009).

Rapid progress is possible

Slow progress towards international goals in areas such as maternal health, child nutrition and survival is sometimes viewed as evidence of the cost and complexity of effective measures. That assessment is flawed. Without understating the extent of the challenges, there is compelling evidence that rapid progress is possible.

Cost-effective measures that work include complementary feeding and vitamin supplementation, a continuum of care during pregnancy and childbirth, immunization and wider strategies to tackle killer diseases such as malaria and pneumonia (Black et al., 2008). To make such interventions available, countries need affordable and accessible health systems, allied to wider measures for targeting vulnerable groups and combating malnutrition. Bad news tends to dominate the headlines, but there is positive news too:

- *Scaling up maternal and child health services.* Experience from Bangladesh and Nepal shows that maternal and child survival can be improved in low-income settings by increasing access to skilled attendants, antenatal care and family planning advice (DFID, 2008*b*). In the United Republic of Tanzania, health spending has been increased and focused on diseases that affect the poorest districts. Coverage of key maternal and child health services has expanded, with a marked increase in the recruitment of community-based midwives and health workers. Child nutrition is improving, as reflected in a 40% decline in child mortality between 2000 and 2004 (Masanja et al., 2008).

- *Achieving results through aid.* The GAVI Alliance (formerly Global Alliance for Vaccines and Immunisation), formed in 2000, has supported the immunization of 213 million children, saving an estimated 3.4 million lives. From 2000 to 2006, deaths from measles in Africa fell by 90% (GAVI Alliance, 2009*a*). International partnerships on HIV and AIDS have increased the share of HIV-positive pregnant women receiving antiretroviral therapy from 15% to 33%, helping prevent transmission to children (Global Fund, 2008*a*).

The links between maternal health and education are often overlooked

- *Removing cost barriers to vital maternal and child health services.* Inability to pay is a major factor limiting access to basic maternal and child health services (Gilson and McIntyre, 2005; Pearson, 2004). Recent experience from countries including Ghana, Nepal, Senegal, Uganda and Zambia provides evidence that eliminating charges for basic health services is often followed by a rapid rise in the uptake of services, especially by the poor (Deininger and Mpuga, 2005; Yates, 2009) (Box 2.2).

Box 2.2: Removing cost barriers to maternal and child health services

The removal of cost barriers has played a critical role in opening up opportunities for education. Yet cost barriers to maternal and child health care remain largely intact, with damaging consequences for health *and* education. The inability of poor households to afford health costs often leads to fatal delays in treatment or to their wholesale exclusion from formal health care. Research in countries as diverse as Chad, India and Sudan points to cost as a major factor restricting the use by poor women of maternal and child health services.

As in education, the scale of the barriers that fees create for the very poor is often revealed when fees are removed. When Uganda withdrew health fees in 2001, the number of outpatients visiting hospitals went the same way as school enrolments after fees were withdrawn several years earlier: attendance rates doubled in less than a year, with the poorest groups recording the highest increases. After Burundi removed all health fees for pregnant women and children in 2006, average monthly births in hospitals promptly rose by 61%. In Nepal, the removal of fees, allied to increased investment in the recruitment and training of community health workers, has also increased access to care.

Many governments across Africa and beyond are reconsidering health fees. There is compelling evidence that charging for basic services is ineffective, inefficient – fees generate only 5% to 6% of health sector revenue – and inequitable. In the past two years, Burundi, Ghana, Kenya, Lesotho, Liberia, the Niger, Senegal and Zambia have abolished fees in key areas. Most major development agencies, including the WHO and the World Bank, have also adopted clear positions against fees. Meanwhile, some donors have provided additional aid to countries that have removed fees, including France (for the Niger) and the United Kingdom (for Burundi, Ghana, Nepal and Zambia) .

Eliminating user fees on maternal and child health care should be seen as an urgent priority. However, it is not a stand-alone strategy. Rapid increases in demand for already overstretched services can lead to deterioration in quality and long queues for treatment – outcomes that undermined the benefits of free maternal health care in Ghana. As in the education sector, making access more affordable should be seen as one element in a broader package of policy reforms. Increased investment to strengthen health systems, greater equity in public spending and improved governance are all important. And there is no substitute for recruiting and training more health workers. The shortage of trained health workers is estimated at over 1 million in sub-Saharan Africa alone.

Sources: Yates (2009); Nabyonga et al. (2005); Batungwanayo and Reyntjens (2006); Cohen and Dupas (2007); Gilson and McIntyre (2005); Witter et al. (2009).

- *Putting nutrition at the centre of the poverty reduction agenda.* Over the past two decades Viet Nam has achieved some of the world's most rapid reductions in child malnutrition. Its National Target Programme has focused on the 2,374 communes with the highest rates of poverty and child malnutrition. Supplementary feeding programmes and maternal and child health care have figured prominently. National Institute of Nutrition surveys indicate that stunting rates fell by one-quarter from 1999 to 2005 (Khan et al., 2008). In Brazil, the Zero Hunger programme, a concerted drive to combat malnutrition, contributed to a fall in malnutrition rates in the north-east, the poorest region, from 18% to 16% in the decade to 2005 (Ruel, 2008).

- *Implementing effective social protection.* Programmes that provide parents with income, services and incentives can help combat early childhood deprivation. Large-scale programmes such as Bolsa Familia in Brazil and Oportunidades in Mexico directly link cash transfers to participation in child nutrition programmes – and both have reduced stunting and improved cognitive development (Fiszbein et al., 2009) (Box 2.3).

The artificial separation of health and education in public policy is particularly damaging for early childhood provision. Education planners often measure progress in primary education by numbers entering classrooms, pupil/teacher ratios and the quality of school infrastructure. There is a widespread view that children's nutritional and health status before school age is a health policy matter. This silo mentality produces a distorted picture of policy priorities. Millions of children enter school having suffered irreparable damage to their learning potential as a result of malnutrition and micronutrient deficiencies. Poor maternal health and risks during pregnancy and childbirth are important contributory factors. The upshot of public policy failure in the areas of nutrition and maternal and child health care is not just unnecessary human suffering, but also the erosion of benefits associated with investment in education and progress in getting children into school.

Early childhood education programmes – a mixed record

Learning starts in the home, as children manipulate objects and materials, explore the world around them and develop language. During the crucial formative years, children develop the cognitive and wider skills that will prepare them for school. Pupils from disadvantaged backgrounds often enter school carrying a legacy of disadvantage in many areas, including lower levels of communication, language and literacy skills. The effects of growing up in a disadvantaged home are seldom reversed later in life – in fact, the gaps widen as children progress through their school years (UNESCO, 2005).

Narrowing the opportunity divide

An early start in education is particularly important for children from disadvantaged families. Poverty, low levels of parental education or speaking a minority language at home are among the most powerful transmitters of disadvantage across generations. Good-quality early childhood provision can cut the transmission lines.

By the time children enter school, disparities in language skills linked to income and other factors are often so marked that children can never catch up. Evidence from the United States demonstrates that test scores at the age of 18 are predictable by age 5 (Heckman, 2008). Research in Ecuador indicates that differences in vocabulary test scores between children from different wealth groups are limited at age 3 but that by age 5 the gap is far too wide to be closed in later school years (Paxson and Schady, 2005*b*) (Figure 2.4). In the United Kingdom, longitudinal studies show that test scores at 22 months are a strong predictor for educational qualifications at 22 years (Feinstein, 2003). Moreover, studies have shown that children from low socio-economic backgrounds but with high cognitive ability scores at 22 months are overtaken by children with lower scores from more affluent families between the ages of 5 and 10 years.

Income differences are not the only source of advantage and disadvantage. Parental education, ethnicity and home language all exercise a strong influence on early childhood test scores and subsequent educational achievement (Brooks-Gunn and Markman, 2005; EACEA, 2009; Leseman and van Tuijil, 2005). The issue of language is especially salient. There is strong evidence from the Organisation for Economic Co-operation and Development (OECD) that having a home language that is different from the language used in school significantly decreases achievement for immigrant children in both primary and secondary school (Christensen and Stanat, 2007; Schnepf, 2004). Remedial action often meets with limited success. In Norway, 20% of migrant students placed in special language training groups on entering school never leave them and in Switzerland most migrant children not deemed equipped to enter mainstream classes are still in such groups after two years (Field et al., 2007). Moreover, evidence from several countries shows that catching up through special classes often requires students to miss the normal curriculum (Karsten, 2006).

Box 2.3: Cash transfer in Nicaragua – overcoming cognitive deficits

In many developing countries, serious delays in children's cognitive development damage their prospects in school and their productivity as adults. Understanding the causes of cognitive deficits and developing ways to reduce them are critical policy priorities.

The Atención a Crisis programme in Nicaragua demonstrates the potential benefits of early intervention. Significant cash payments, representing on average about 15% of household income, were made every two months to women in poor rural households. To be eligible, parents had to take children of pre-school age for regular visits to health centres, where they were weighed and received vaccinations and food supplements.

This pilot programme, carried out during 2005 and 2006, included a careful evaluation. Results indicated that the programme improved several dimensions of child development:

- After only nine months in the programme, children aged 3 to 4 years had made up 1.5 months' delayed personal-social and language development on one set of test scores, rising to 2.4 months for children aged 5 to 6 years.
- Participating households were found to have higher values for signs of parental stimulation, including the availability of books, paper and pencils, and the likelihood of parents reading to children.
- Overall food expenditures increased among treated households, especially on nutrient-rich foods.
- Wide-ranging preventive health benefits were identified. Participating children were more likely to have had a growth check-up, received vitamin and iron supplements, and to have been treated with de-worming drugs. The reported health status of mothers had also improved.

Source: Macours et al. (2008).

High-quality early care is particularly important for children from disadvantaged backgrounds

Early childhood education can play an important role in offsetting social, economic and language-based disadvantage. Evidence from around the world indicates that high-quality early care is good for all children, but particularly for those from disadvantaged backgrounds. The following are among the findings to emerge from a range of rigorous evaluations:

- The Head Start Impact Study in the United States randomly evaluated about 5,000 3- and 4-year-olds. It found small to moderate statistically

Figure 2.4: Wealth-based gaps in learning begin early and widen over time

Test scores across ages for the poorest and the fourth deciles in Ecuador, 2003-2004

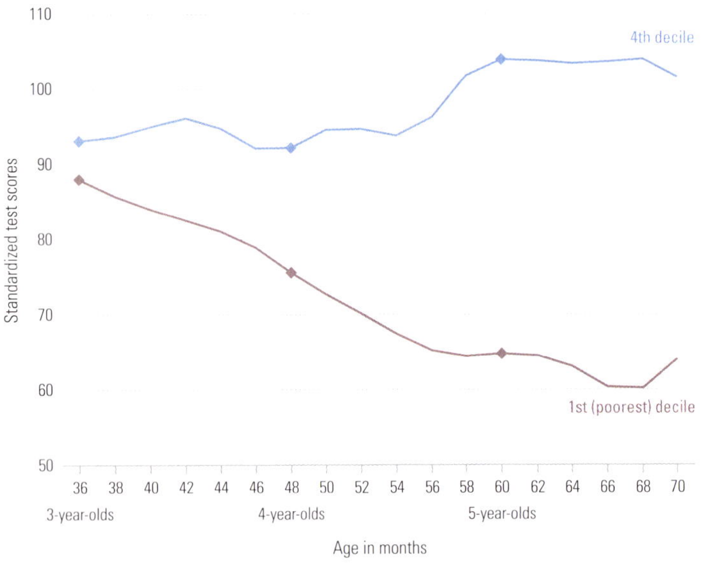

Notes: The test scores used are from the Test de Vocabulario en Imágenes Peabody, the Spanish version of the Peabody Picture Vocabulary Test. The figure presented here, a smoothed version of the original figure (which appears in the source document), has also been reproduced elsewhere (e.g. Fiszbein et al., 2009, and World Bank, 2006*j*).

Source: Paxson and Schady (2005*b*).

significant increases in four key cognitive scores, including pre-reading, pre-writing, literacy skills and vocabulary. While Head Start children scored below average for all children, reflecting racial and social background factors, the programme halved the achievement gap that would have been expected in its absence (US Department of Health and Human Services, 2005).[2]

- Attending the French pre-primary education system (*école maternelle*) increases class retention of low-income and immigrant children in primary school by 9% to 17%, with wider reported benefits for literacy and numeracy (Nusche, 2009).

- Early childhood care can help overcome language-based disadvantage and the problems faced by children of migrants (Cunha et al., 2005). In the Netherlands, children of Turkish and Moroccan immigrants who spent two years in kindergarten halved the average test score gap from the national average (Leseman, 2002).

- In New Zealand, 12-year-olds who had participated in high-quality early education performed better in reading and mathematics, after controlling for household income (UNICEF, 2008*b*).

While these findings relate to developed countries, there is also evidence from developing countries that effective early childhood care and education can both raise learning achievements and narrow disparities. That evidence was extensively reviewed in the *EFA Global Monitoring Report 2007*. While the precise channels of influence are a subject of debate, good-quality early childhood provision clearly has the potential to weaken the influence of parental factors on later education achievement.

Pre-primary education – slow and unequal expansion

'Pre-primary' is an umbrella term covering a wide range of providers and programmes, mostly for children aged 3 and above. Countries differ enormously in the mix of public and private provision, and in financing arrangements and governance. As in other areas of education, data on coverage say little about quality, but high-quality programmes tend to start early, be based in centres, have a critical mass of trained teachers and involve parents (UNICEF, 2008*b*).

Participation in pre-primary education has been steadily increasing. Some 140 million children were enrolled in pre-school programmes worldwide in 2007, up from 113 million in 1999. The gross enrolment ratio (GER) climbed from 33% to 41% over the same period (Table 2.1). Increases have been most pronounced in sub-Saharan Africa, and South and West Asia, albeit from a low base. One in seven children in sub-Saharan Africa is enrolled in an early childhood programme, compared wih one in three for all developing countries.

Looking beyond the regional data reveals a diverse array of country experiences. Among the countries for which data are available, seventeen states in sub-Saharan Africa have coverage rates of less than 10%. In the Arab States, levels of pre-primary coverage are far lower than average income might seem to indicate: out of nineteen countries with data for 2007, fourteen have GERs below 50%. Egypt and Saudi Arabia have lower levels of coverage than some far poorer countries, including Nepal and the United Republic of Tanzania. Indeed, sub-Saharan Africa has increased pre-primary enrolment at three times the rate of the Arab States, with GERs rising by more than 20% since 1999 in several countries, including Burundi, Liberia and Senegal (Annex, Statistical Table 3A). The Arab States region also remains the only one with significant gender disparity at early childhood level: just nine girls are enrolled for every ten boys.

2. In 2005-2006, 24% of children from the poorest 20% of United States households were in centre-based Head Start programmes, compared with 1% of children from the wealthiest 20%. Evaluations of earlier pilot childcare programmes – such as the North Carolina Abecedarian Project and Perry Preschool Program – have also recorded wide-ranging benefits associated with pre-school, extending from primary education to college attendance, employment, wages and crime reduction (Campbell et al., 2008; Karoly et al., 2005; UNESCO, 2008*a*; Schweinhart et al., 2005). Observed effects were strongest for poor children and children whose parents had little education.

Developed countries vary considerably in their blend of crèches, pre-primary schools, centre-based day care and home support. They also differ in the balance between public and private financing and in the age groups that programmes reach. Some countries, notably in the Nordic area, have high rates of coverage for children under 3, though most early childhood programmes in OECD countries cover ages 4 to 6. The duration of pre-primary education varies from one to four years. In Sweden, full-time free early childhood education is available to all children, from age 3, for eleven months of the year; in the United Kingdom, free provision is available part time for 3- and 4-year-olds (EACEA, 2009). Most European Union countries provide two years of free pre-school.[3] By contrast, in the United States, there is no statutory right to pre-school before age 5, though about 60% of children in the pre-school age group were enrolled in 2007.

Differences within countries are often as marked as differences across borders. This is especially true of countries that combine high levels of decentralization with subnational autonomy. The United States provides a striking example. Virtually every 4-year-old in Oklahoma can start school at age 4. In eight other states – including Florida, South Carolina and Texas – more than half of 4-year-olds attend a public pre-school programme. At the other end of the range, twelve states have no regular state pre-school education programme and in eight states less than 20% of children are enrolled (Barnett et al., 2008). There are also marked differences in the quality of provision (Ackerman et al., 2009). Ten benchmarks have been established for assessing quality standards.[4] However, programmes in Florida are required to meet only four benchmarks and Texas sets no limits on class size or staff/child ratios. Spending levels per child also vary markedly: five states spend more than US$8,000 per pupil while another five spend less than US$3,000 (Barnett et al., 2008).

Reaching the vulnerable and disadvantaged

Goal 1 of the Dakar Framework for Action commits governments to expanding early childhood care and education 'especially for the most vulnerable and disadvantaged'. This is for good reason. Children from disadvantaged households have the most to gain from early childhood care – and the most to lose from being excluded. Unfortunately, cross-country evidence strongly suggests that those who need it most receive it least.

Household poverty and low levels of parental education are two of the most pronounced barriers to early childhood programmes. Evidence from a survey of fifty-six developing countries shows that being born into a poor household or having a

Children from disadvantaged households have the most to gain from early childhood care

Table 2.1: Pre-primary enrolment and gross enrolment ratios by region, 1999 and 2007

	Total enrolment			Gross enrolment ratios		
	School year ending in 1999	School year ending in 2007	Change between 1999 and 2007	School year ending in 1999	School year ending in 2007	Change between 1999 and 2007
	(millions)	(millions)	(%)	(%)	(%)	(%)
World	113	139	24	33	41	26
Developing countries	80	106	32	27	36	32
Developed countries	25	26	4	73	80	10
Countries in transition	7	8	7	45	63	39
Sub-Saharan Africa	5	10	82	10	15	53
Arab States	2	3	26	15	19	25
Central Asia	1	1	13	19	28	44
East Asia and the Pacific	37	39	4	40	47	18
East Asia	37	38	4	40	47	19
Pacific	0.4	0.5	12	61	67	11
South and West Asia	21	36	69	21	36	71
Latin America and the Caribbean	16	20	22	56	65	17
Caribbean	0.7	0.8	16	65	74	13
Latin America	16	19	22	55	65	17
North America and Western Europe	19	20	6	75	82	9
Central and Eastern Europe	9	10	5	50	64	30

Source: Annex, Statistical Table 3B.

3. In the European Union, about 87% of 4-year-olds are in school (EACEA, 2009).

4. The standards include teacher and assistant teacher degrees and specialized training, in-service training provision, class size, staff/child ratios, support services, meals and monitoring. Just two states – Alabama and South Carolina – meet all ten benchmarks.

In Chile, a programme aimed at achieving early childhood care for all 4-year-olds has targeted the poorest households

mother with no education carries a large handicap when it comes to early childhood care, regardless of age, gender or place of residence (Figures 2.5 and 2.6). Living in one of Zambia's poorest households cuts the chance of participating in early childhood care by a factor of 12 compared with children in the wealthiest households, and the factor rises to 25 in Uganda and 28 in Egypt (Nonoyama-Tarumi et al., 2008). Such figures demonstrate the degree to which early childhood provision is reinforcing inequalities associated with the home environment.

Why do children from disadvantaged households face the highest barriers to entry? In some cases, it is because facilities are too far from their homes. In others, facilities are accessible but unaffordable – a problem that has held back efforts to expand coverage in Egypt (UNESCO, 2008*a*). However, several countries have succeeded in expanding access. In Chile, a programme aimed at achieving early childhood care for all 4-year-olds has targeted the poorest income groups (Box 2.4).

Figure 2.5: Children from rich families are more likely to participate in early childhood programmes

Likelihood of 3- and 4-year-olds participating in early learning programmes, children from the richest 20% compared with children from the poorest 20%

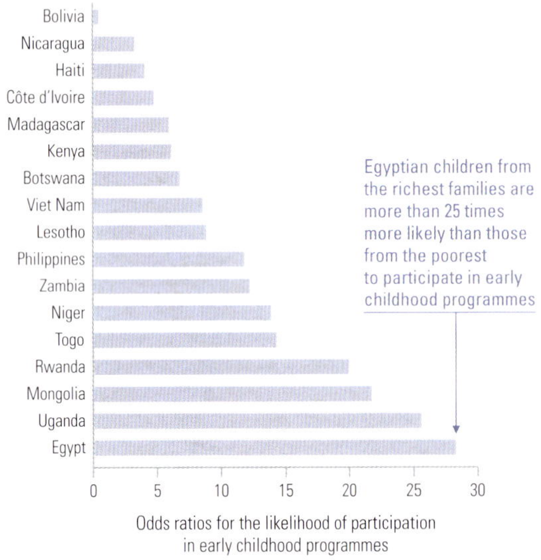

Notes: Using odds ratios (see glossary), this figure compares the likelihood of young children participating in early learning programmes, depending on the wealth status of their families. Specifically, odds ratios provide an estimate of the differences in probability of attending early childhood programmes between one reference group (the poorest 20%) and another (the richest 20%), and they are estimated from a logistic regression with five dependent variables: gender, age, place of residence, mother's level of education and household wealth.
Source: Nonoyama-Tarumi et al. (2008).

Rich countries have also struggled to meet equity goals. There is extensive evidence from the European Union that low-income families and immigrants have less access to good-quality early childhood care (Arnold and Doctoroff, 2003; Nusche, 2009; Sylva et al., 2007).

Evidence from the United States also documents large disparities (Barnett et al., 2008). Families with incomes just above the poverty line face some of the greatest difficulties in gaining access, demonstrating the importance of targeting households at this level. Maternal education also has a marked bearing on United States pre-school participation: attendance rates of 4-year-olds are 55% for children of mothers who have dropped out of secondary school but 87% for children of mothers with a college education (Barnett et al., 2008; Barnett and Yarosz, 2007).

On a more positive note, several governments are scaling up early childhood care as part of wider anti-poverty initiatives. In the United Kingdom, Sure Start, a flagship strategy introduced in 1997 to tackle child poverty, social exclusion and educational disadvantage, now reaches 2.4 million families (Every Child Matters, 2009).

Figure 2.6: Children of educated mothers are more likely to attend pre-school programmes

Likelihood of 3- and 4-year-olds participating in early learning programmes, children of mothers with secondary education or higher compared with children of mothers with no education

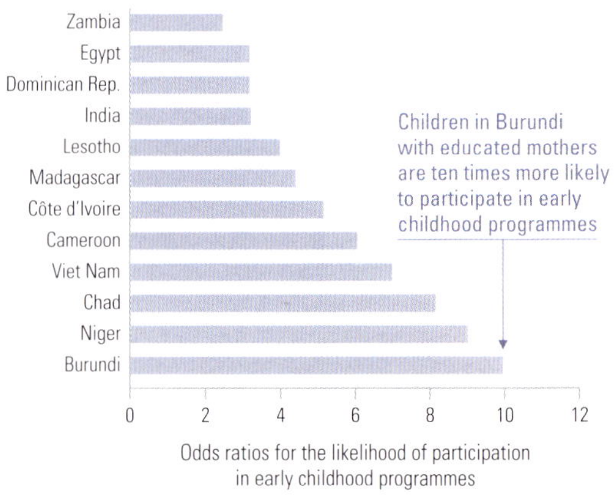

Notes: This figure compares the likelihood of young children participating in early learning programmes, based on the mother's education level. The odds ratios are calculated in the same way as those in Figure 2.5 for different reference groups: one consists of children with a mother with no education and another of children with a mother having secondary education or higher.
Source: Nonoyama-Tarumi et al. (2008).

Box 2.4: Expansion of early childhood education in Chile

Chile has some of the deepest and most persistent education inequalities in Latin America. Recent reforms are attempting to strengthen equity by expanding and improving early childhood care.

After her election in 2006, President Michelle Bachelet initiated a major overhaul of early childhood care, including raising public spending (Larrañaga, 2009; OECD, 2009e). The most ambitious measure involves building 3,000 new childcare facilities and establishing a national child development initiative, Chile Crece Contigo, for all children under 5, as part of the health care system.

Chile Crece Contigo, a result of collaboration by government, child development experts and other interested parties (Frenz, 2007), aims to meet the needs of vulnerable families and children during the critical phases of early childhood development. Families have access to a wide range of social and health services through primary care centres. Their progress is monitored via information technology. Implementation is managed by nine national ministries and coordinated through regional, provincial and local governments.

A concerted effort has been made to reach children from the poorest 40% of households. In that income bracket, young children with mothers at work, in school or seeking employment are eligible for free child care in the *sala cuna* (under 2) or the *jardín infantil* (ages 2 and 3).

Central to the strategy is commitment to quality. Efforts have been made from the outset to measure and assess the development of vocabulary, language and wider skills through Un Buen Comienzo, a programme that runs in sixty schools in thirteen communes of Santiago. Using rigorous evaluation, Un Buen Comienzo seeks to reduce the vocabulary gap between children in low-income families and other children, improve pre-school attendance and reduce later reading difficulties. Teacher development, parental literacy and engagement, and child health are emphasized.

Sources: Frenz (2007); OECD (2009e).

Another striking example comes from New Zealand. Since 2007, all 3- and 4-year-olds in the country have been entitled to twenty hours a week of free early childhood education (Froese, 2008; May, 2008). Efforts are being made to improve the quality of early childhood education available to Māori children. Curricula and teaching materials have been modified through partnerships with Māori groups. Scholarships and incentives have been expanded to attract Māori-language speakers into early childhood teaching. In the five years to 2007, the number of Māori-speaking educators tripled and the share of Māori primary school entrants having been to pre-school rose from 86% to 91% (New Zealand Ministry of Education, 2009).

Conclusion

The Dakar Framework for Action does not set a quantitative goal for early childhood care and education, so what targets – if any – should governments set? And what role should governments play in paying for and providing care?

There are no universal answers to these questions. As the *EFA Global Monitoring Report 2007* documented, many countries have set unrealistic targets. Countries struggling to get children into and through basic education have to weigh arguments for universal early childhood coverage against real resource constraints. At the same time, governments need to recognize the potential efficiency and equity gains from investing in early childhood care. As one Nobel Prize-winning economist has written: 'Early interventions targeted towards disadvantaged children have much higher returns than later interventions. ... At current levels of resources, society over-invests in remedial skill investments at later ages and under-invests in the early years' (Heckman, 2006, p. 1902).

While that reflection is based on evidence from the United States, it is likely to have a wider application. The lesson to be drawn is that public investment should be geared towards narrowing disparities, targeting marginalized groups and providing good-quality services that are accessible to the poor. □

Governments need to recognize the potential efficiency and equity gains from investing in early childhood care

Universal primary education

Goal 2. Ensuring that by 2015 all children, particularly girls, children in difficult circumstances and those belonging to ethnic minorities, have access to and complete, free and compulsory primary education of good quality.

The past decade has seen rapid progress towards universal primary education. Some of the world's poorest countries have dramatically increased enrolment, narrowed gender gaps and extended opportunities for disadvantaged groups. School completion rates are also rising. These achievements provide a marked contrast to the 'lost decade' of the 1990s. But there are limits to the good news. In the midst of an increasingly knowledge-based global economy, millions of children are still out of school and countless millions more start school but drop out before completing primary education. And there is now a real danger that the global economic crisis will stall, and perhaps even reverse, the gains registered over the past decade (see Chapter 1).

Despite encouraging progress, many of the poorest countries are struggling to reach universal primary education

The post-Dakar record has to be assessed against the ambition set out in Goal 2 of the Dakar Framework for Action: universal primary education by 2015. Is the goal still attainable? The answer will depend on decisions taken over the next two years by national governments and aid donors. The window of opportunity for ensuring that all primary school age children currently out of school *complete* a full cycle of primary education is rapidly closing. Getting all children into school by 2015 is still feasible, but the goal will not be achieved with a business-as-usual approach.

The World Education Forum (Dakar, 2000) gave new impetus to education, both nationally and internationally. Yet the hard fact remains that the world will fall short of the targets set and that far more could have been achieved. Many developing countries could have done much more to accelerate progress, notably through policies to overcome inequalities in education. Meanwhile, donors have a mixed record of delivery on their collective commitment to back national programmes with increased financial support – an issue addressed in more detail in Chapter 4.

This section documents progress towards universal primary education. Looking behind the national data, it provides an in-depth look at some of the crucial challenges facing governments in the countdown to 2015. The following are among the key messages to emerge:

- *Out-of-school numbers are dropping for primary school age children, but getting all children into school will require a far stronger focus on the marginalized.* When the Dakar forum was held, over 100 million children of primary school age were out of school. By 2007, the figure had fallen to 72 million. This headline figure bears testimony to national governments' efforts. The bad news is that, on current trends, some 56 million children could still be out of school in 2015. Changing this scenario will require a far stronger commitment by governments to reach girls and other marginalized groups. It will also require a sharper focus on countries affected by conflict or engaged in post-conflict reconstruction.

- *Progress towards universal primary enrolment has been partial and mixed.* Despite encouraging progress, many of the poorest countries are struggling to reach universal enrolment. Less attention has been paid to higher-income countries with significant out-of-school populations, such as the Philippines and Turkey. Such countries will have to target marginalization far more systematically to deliver on the Dakar commitments. New research indicates that official enrolment data may overstate the numbers of children in school at the appropriate age, suggesting that more needs to be done to address the problem of late entry and dropout. Household survey data for a number of countries indicate overestimates of 10% or more in school attendance rates.

- *Gender barriers remain intact.* There has been progress towards greater gender parity in school enrolment. Even so, being born a girl carries with it a significant education disadvantage in many countries. That disadvantage is reflected in the fact that girls still account for 54% of the out-of-school population. Moreover, out-of-school girls are far more likely than boys never to go to school. In twenty-eight countries, there are fewer than nine girls in primary school for every ten boys. Poverty further reinforces gender disparity.

- *Getting children into primary school is just a first step.* Universal primary education involves entering school at an appropriate age, progressing through the system and completing a full cycle. Unfortunately, millions of children enter school late, drop out early and never complete a full cycle. More integrated approaches to monitoring are required to measure the real state of progress towards universal primary education.

- *Out-of-school adolescents are often overlooked.* Monitoring progress towards international development goals in education focuses on the primary school age group. The situation of adolescents has been subject to less scrutiny. There are some 71 million children of lower secondary school age currently out of school. Many have not completed a full primary cycle and face the prospect of social and economic marginalization. Counting adolescents doubles the global headline figure for out-of-school children.

The section is divided into three parts. Part 1 looks at progress towards one of the most important requirements for achieving universal primary education: getting all children into school. It looks beyond the headline numbers to explore the characteristics of the out-of-school population. Removing the barriers that keep children out of school is the first step towards achieving universal primary enrolment – ensuring that the entire primary school age group is in school by 2015. Part 2 looks at enrolment trends. Part 3 examines the problem of retention and progression through primary school, and the transition to secondary education.

Numbers of out-of-school children are declining, but not fast enough

Malina is a 12-year-old living in a rural area of Rattanakiri, a remote hill district in Cambodia. She is a member of a minority ethnic group and has never been to school.

Lucy, 12, lives in the slum of Kibera in the Kenyan capital, Nairobi. When she was 8, she enrolled in primary school, but in the second grade she dropped out. She wants to go back to school but has to take care of her brother, and her mother cannot afford the fees, uniforms and books.

Victor is 14 years old. He lives on the streets of Manila and makes a living by selling newspapers at road junctions. He went to primary school for four years, but left before completing it and has no prospect of returning.

Maria, 15, is in grade 4 of her local primary school in Panama, having started late, repeated two grades and dropped out for a year when she was 12.

Compared with the 1990s, the first decade of the twenty-first century has been one of rapid progress towards universal primary education. Out-of-school numbers are falling and more children are completing primary school. Yet the sheer size of the out-of-school population remains an indictment of national governments and the entire international community. Denying children an opportunity to put even a first step on the education ladder sets them on a course for a lifetime of disadvantage. It violates their basic human right to an education. It also wastes a precious national resource and potential driver of economic growth and poverty reduction.

As the experiences of the children cited above testify, 'out of school' is a simple concept with many meanings. Some children of late primary school age and even secondary school age have never been to school. Others have started school but dropped out. Still others are in a state of flux, moving between in-school and out-of-school status. The out-of-school figures in this section refer only to children of primary school age who are not in school. They represent the tip of the total out-of-school iceberg, since they do not cover adolescents of secondary school age who have not completed primary school. Even within the primary school age group, data for any one year provide only a static snapshot of a dynamic and complicated picture.

There were 72 million children out of school in 2007

The snapshot for 2007, the latest year for which data are available, points to continued progress but still large deficits. There are some remarkable achievements since 1999:

- *Out-of-school numbers are falling.* Worldwide, the number of children of primary school age who are out of school has declined by 33 million since the Dakar pledges were made, from 105 million in 1999 to 72 million in 2007. Seven out of every ten out-of-school children live in South and West Asia, and sub-Saharan Africa (Figure 2.7).

An estimated 56 million children could still be out of school in 2015

- *The gender gap is shrinking.* The share of girls in the out-of-school population declined from 58% to 54%.

- *South and West Asia have achieved rapid progress.* The region more than halved its out-of-school population – a decline of 21 million. The region also cut the share of girls in the out-of-school total, from 63% to 58%.

- *Sub-Saharan Africa has registered strong progress.* During a period in which the size of its school age population increased by 20 million, sub-Saharan Africa reduced its out-of-school population by almost 13 million, or 28%. The strength of the region's progress can be gauged by a comparison with the 1990s. Had the region progressed at the same pace as in the 1990s, 18 million more children would be out of school.

The limits to progress also have to be acknowledged. Not only is the world off track for the Dakar commitments, but there is cause for concern over the pace of change:

- *The 2015 target will be missed.* If the world were to continue the linear trend for 1999–2007, an estimated 56 million children would still be out of school in 2015.[5] Slower economic growth, pressure on education budgets and rising poverty associated with the global economic crisis could significantly inflate this figure (Figure 2.8).

- *Progress has slowed.* The post-1999 overview provides a positive gloss on some disturbing underlying trends. Two-thirds of the total decline in out-of-school numbers took place during the two years to 2004, when the numbers dropped by 22 million. In the three years to 2007, the out-of-school population fell by just 8 million. The slowdown illustrates one of the central challenges now facing governments: the closer countries get to universal primary education, the harder it becomes to reach children still out of school. That is why sustained progress will require a stronger focus on marginalization.

- *South and West Asia dominated the reduction.* Much of the decline took place in India, which reported a fall of almost 15 million in out-of-school numbers in the two years after the 2001 launch of the Sarva Shiksha Abhiyan (universal primary education) programme.[6]

- *The deficit in sub-Saharan Africa remains large.* Fully one-quarter of sub-Saharan Africa's primary school age children were out of school in 2007 – and the region accounted for nearly 45% of the global out-of-school population. Half of the twenty countries with more than 500,000 children out of school were in sub-Saharan Africa (see Figure 2.12 below). Nigeria alone contributed over 10% of the global total. Progress in the region has been uneven. Some countries with large out-of-school populations in 1999 have made major advances; examples include Ethiopia, Kenya, Mozambique, the United Republic of Tanzania and Zambia. Ethiopia and the United Republic of Tanzania each reduced out-of-school numbers by over 3 million between 1999 and 2007. Countries making only limited progress include Liberia, Malawi and Nigeria.

- *Conflict remains a major barrier.* Children living in countries enduring or recovering from conflict are less likely to be in school. Many such countries lack publicly available data and so receive less prominence in international debates than they merit. But a lack of reliable data should not deflect attention from the scale of the

Figure 2.7: Numbers of out-of-school children are declining

Out-of-school children by region, 1999 and 2007

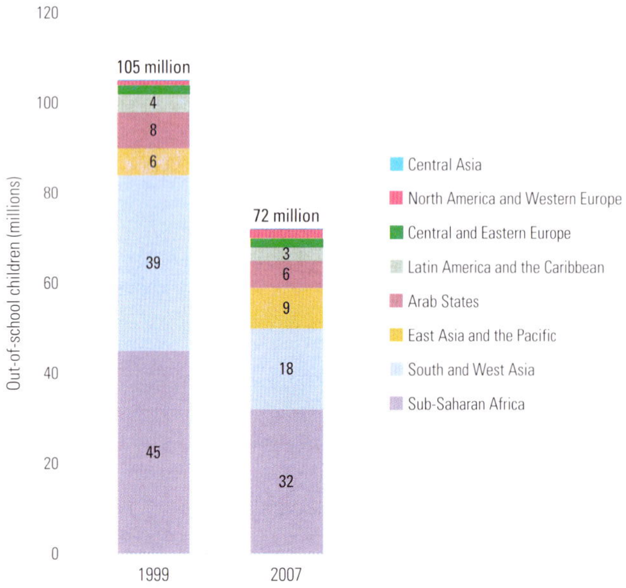

Source: Annex, Statistical Table 5.

5. This figure should not be compared with the partial projection in the *EFA Global Monitoring Report 2009*, which treated a smaller group of countries using a different methodology, and did not include countries such as the Democratic Republic of the Congo and the Sudan.

6. The key aim of the programme is to universalize elementary education by 2010. Commitments include constructing and improving infrastructure in deprived areas, along with measures targeted towards areas with large marginalized populations (scheduled castes, scheduled tribes, Muslims) or low female literacy (Ayyar, 2008; Govinda, 2009); see also Chapter 3.

Figure 2.8: Missing the target – out-of-school trends projected to 2015

Projected numbers of out-of-school children to 2015

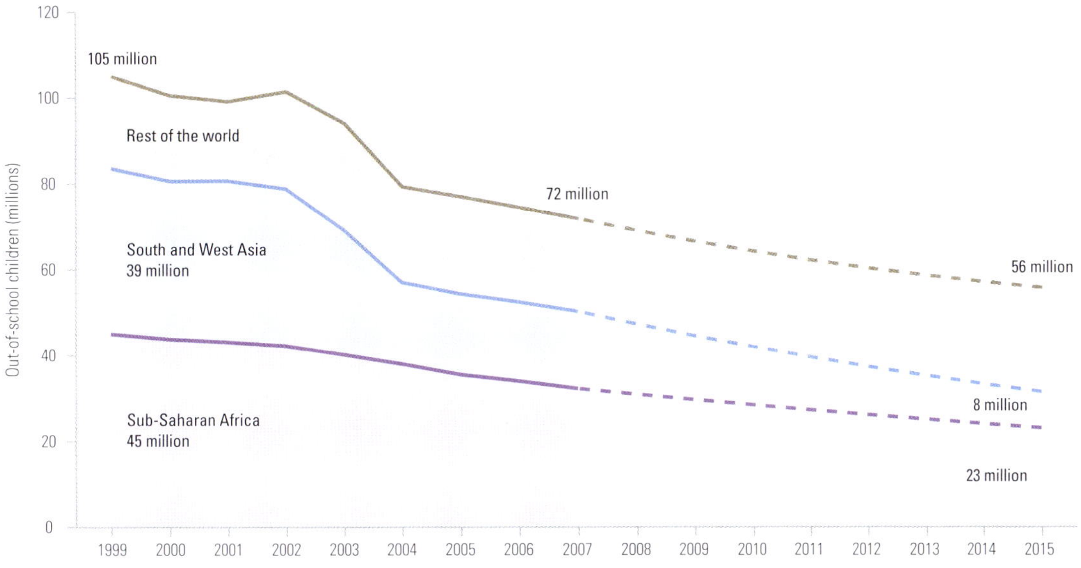

Note: Projections based on regional compound growth rates for 1999–2007.
Source: UIS database (data for 1999–2007).

problem. Best estimates suggest that more than 25 million out-of-school children live in low-income countries affected by conflict – around 35% of the global total.[7] Finding ways to reach children in conflict-affected areas of countries such as Afghanistan, the Central African Republic, the Democratic Republic of the Congo and the Sudan is one of the most urgent of all EFA challenges. Attaching more weight to education in post-conflict recovery is also vital. While Liberia now has peace and stability, 447,000 of its children were out of school in 2008 – an increase of almost 180,000 over 1999.

- *Numbers are probably underestimated.* Estimating the number of children from the relevant age group who are out of primary school is an inexact science. Administrative data that schools report to ministries of education are an important resource and national reporting systems are becoming more effective. However, uncertainties over demographic profiles (and hence the number of children in each age group) can cloud the issue. Household surveys are another source of information, usually obtained through parental reporting on whether their children attend school. There are often significant inconsistencies between these two data sources. For twenty-nine countries in sub-Saharan Africa, and South and West Asia examined in this Report, household surveys show around 50% fewer children in school – 22 million in total – than administrative data indicate. This is equivalent to an increase of 30% in the global out-of-school estimate. Such findings illustrate how different measurement tools can generate different results. They also demonstrate the importance of national governments, international agencies and researchers working together to build a more complete picture of the out-of-school population (Box 2.5).

Who and where are the out-of-school children – and what are their chances of entering school?

Being out of school is not a fixed condition. The category covers children who have dropped out of school temporarily or permanently, those who have never been to school but might start late and those who will never go to school. Data constraints make it difficult to unravel the precise characteristics of the out-of-school population. However, a model developed by the UNESCO Institute for Statistics (UIS) makes it possible to predict, on the basis of past evidence, what share of out-of-school children is likely to enrol in the future (UIS, 2009*a*).

Household survey data suggest an increase of 30% in the global out-of-school estimate

7. The countries included are ones that experienced armed conflicts resulting in at least twenty-five battle-related deaths per year over at least three years between 1999 and 2007 or more than 1,000 battle-related deaths in at least one year during the same period. Of these, only countries categorized as least developed countries by the United Nations or low-income countries by the World Bank in 2007 were included. The proportion of children out of school according to this definition is lower than the frequently quoted figure of more than half. The higher figure is based on calculations using a different methodology, which includes some countries identified as 'fragile' but not in conflict, as well as some middle-income conflict-affected countries (Save the Children, 2009*a*).

Box 2.5: Children count – but counting children in school is difficult

Data on enrolment by age are often treated uncritically as an accurate record of how many primary school age children are actually in primary school. The information passes from schools to education ministries and then to the UNESCO Institute for Statistics (UIS), which compiles the international data used to compare countries, monitor progress and inform international meetings. But is the information accurate?

Research by the UIS compares enrolment figures generated by governments with data reported in Demographic and Health Surveys of households in twenty-nine countries (Figure 2.9). The analysis found that, when compared with household survey data, school registers tend to count more children within the official primary school age range. Correcting that bias would have the effect of reducing the net enrolment ratio – by significant margins in some countries. In the United Republic of Tanzania, the discrepancy was equivalent to twenty-five percentage points. It was over ten percentage points in ten of the twenty-nine countries covered. For nine other countries the bias was in the other direction. The study found that the main factor behind the differences was not the over-reporting of student numbers, but the misreporting of age. Household surveys actually report a greater number of total students attending than administrative data when all students, regardless of their age, are counted.

Age-specific reporting is the main source of discrepancy. Consider the case of Senegal – a country that illustrates the broader pattern (Figure 2.10). For the 5 to 11 age group, administrative data reports an enrolment ratio consistently higher than the attendance rate for the same age group recorded in household survey data. The discrepancy is very large. For age 8, the net enrolment ratio is reported to be 77%, compared with 58% for the net attendance rate. At about age 11, the reporting lines cross: at older ages, household survey data register higher levels of attendance than net enrolment would imply.

The consistent pattern to emerge from the UIS study can be briefly summarized. If the information in household surveys is accurate, net attendance rates covering children in the official primary school age range are lower than reported through net enrolment ratios based on administrative data. This would imply that there are more over-age children in school, and more primary school age children out of school, than indicated by official data.

Simple comparisons between administrative and household survey data do not, however, provide a solid foundation for such conclusions to be drawn. There are many possible factors behind the discrepancies. One is demography. If national population data over- or under-report the size of the primary school age population, net enrolment ratios drawn from administrative data will mirror the inaccuracy.

Uncertainty over the denominator (population size) can be compounded by education reporting systems. Registers may not provide an accurate picture of the age of students, instead treating the class that children are in as a proxy for their age. In some cases institutional incentives may play a role: if the number of students in the appropriate grade for their age determines the allocation of grants or teachers, schools and local governments might have a tendency to inflate the school register.

Household survey exercises have problems as well. Apart from standard sampling errors, the timing of surveys can have a bearing on the results: for example, the data might be affected by the agricultural calendar, drought or major external shocks. The reference period and phrasing of questions can also cause complications. Household surveys examined in the analysis presented here ask whether children attended school at some point during the school year, not whether they are in school for the entire school year. Surveys can also systematically miss parts of the population that are difficult to reach.

All these considerations caution against drawing sweeping policy conclusions. The UIS emphasizes that its technical work comparing household survey and administrative data does not provide a basis for revising estimates of out-of-school children. What is clear is that important issues are at stake – and that more work is needed to clarify the real picture with respect

The model explores the importance of gender, income and location in determining whether or not children are in school. These categories of disadvantage interact with each other and with wider factors – such as language, ethnicity and disability – to create multiple barriers to school entry and survival. Chapter 3 explores the wider factors and their interactions in detail.

Young girls. Disparities between boys and girls are narrowing, but females still accounted for 54% of the global out-of-school population in 2007. Gender parity would cut the number of girls out of school by over 6 million. Gender disadvantage is most pronounced in the Arab States, Central Asia, and South and West Asia. In Pakistan, girls accounted for 60% of out-of-school children in 2006.

Children from poor households. Parental wealth strongly influences prospects of being out of school. Low average income in many of the countries with large out-of-school populations means that poverty extends far beyond the poorest 20%. However, as evidence from household surveys shows, the poorest face distinctive problems. In India, children

Figure 2.9: Different stories – administrative and household measurement of children in school can differ greatly

Differences between net enrolment ratio (administrative data) and net attendance rate (household surveys), selected countries, latest available year

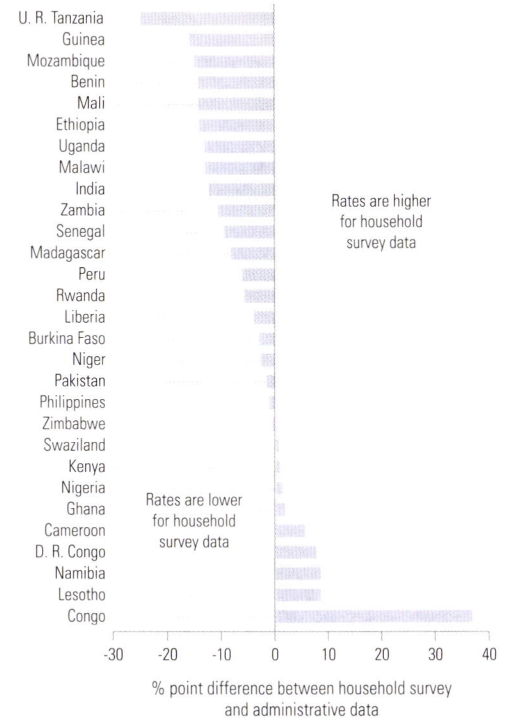

Sources: Bruneforth (2009*a*).

to the core issue in universal primary education: namely, how many children are really out of school. There is strong evidence that administrative data routinely overestimate net enrolment by a considerable margin. In a separate review of the twenty-nine countries covered by the UIS study, this Report estimates that, if the household survey data are accurate:

Figure 2.10: In Senegal, estimates of children in school by age vary with data sources

Age-specific enrolment and attendance rates, Senegal, 2006

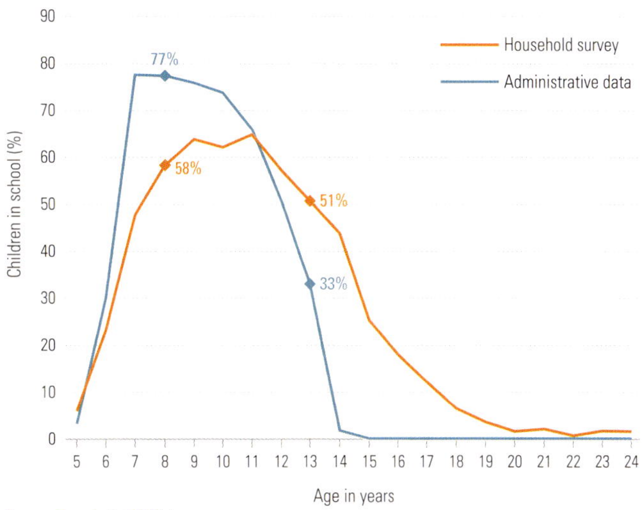

Source: Bruneforth (2009*a*).

- the out-of-school population in these countries would be 66 million, rather than the 44 million reported in administrative data;
- the out-of-school population in India would be 16 million higher, more than twice the administrative data total;
- in sub-Saharan Africa, Ethiopia and the United Republic of Tanzania would each have more than 1.8 million additional children out of school, Mozambique around 600,000 and Uganda over 800,000.

Source: Bruneforth (2009*a*).

from the poorest 20% were over three times more likely to be out of school than children from the richest 20% in 2005 (Bruneforth, 2009*b*).

Rural children. Living in a rural area often puts children at greater risk of being out of school. In Burkina Faso, Cameroon, Ethiopia, Malawi, the Niger, Senegal and Zambia, household survey data suggest that rural children are more than twice as likely not to be in school (Bruneforth, 2009*b*).

Many of those currently not in primary school will probably never enrol. On the basis of past evidence and the UIS model, an estimated 44% of out-of-school children are unlikely to make the transition into school (Figure 2.11). These 31 million children face the most acute disadvantages in education. The problem is most pronounced in sub-Saharan Africa, where 59% of the out-of-school population is unlikely to enrol. In South and West Asia, by contrast, dropout is a more serious problem. More than 60% of the out-of-school population has dropped out, while one-third is unlikely ever to enter. Almost half of the much smaller out-of-school population in the Arab States is unlikely to enter. In East Asia and the Pacific, the problem is

Figure 2.11: Children in sub-Saharan Africa are the least likely to enter school

Distribution of out-of-school children by school exposure, by region, 2007

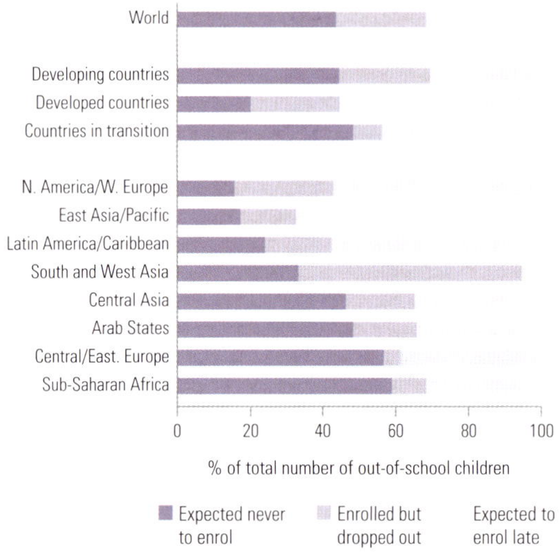

Source: UIS (2009*a*).

In sub-Saharan Africa, almost 12 million girls are expected never to enrol

overwhelmingly one of late entry, though close to one in five out-of-school children is unlikely even to enter school.

Country profiles mirror the regional differences (Figure 2.12). In four of the ten countries in sub-Saharan Africa with large out-of-school populations – Burkina Faso, Mali, the Niger and Senegal – more than 70% of out-of-school children are expected never to enrol.[8] In Pakistan, almost half of the out-of-school population is unlikely to enrol. The pattern is not restricted to low-income countries. One of the most striking results to emerge is the profile of out-of-school children in Turkey, where seven out of ten are unlikely to enter school.

For countries including Bangladesh, India, Indonesia and Nepal, the big challenge is keeping children in school once they enrol. Identifying patterns of exclusion are important for public policy design – the approaches needed to ensure that children not expected to enrol have a chance to enter school are likely to differ from those addressing the constraints facing children at risk of dropout.

How do the three markers for disadvantage – gender, wealth and location – shape prospects that out-of-school children will ever enrol?

Young girls face some of the highest barriers. Not only are they less likely than boys to be in school, but those who are out of school are far more likely than boys never to enter (Figure 2.13). In sub-Saharan Africa, almost 12 million girls are expected never to enrol, compared with 7 million boys. Countries in other regions face similar problems. In Yemen, nearly 80% of out-of-school girls are unlikely ever to enrol, compared with 36% of boys; in Pakistan the figures are 62% for girls and 27% for boys. Gender disadvantages can cut in the other direction: in Bangladesh, Brazil and South Africa, it is more likely that boys will never enrol. However, it is clear that more rapid progress in getting children into school will require measures that target the social, economic and cultural barriers facing young girls.

Prospects for attending school are also heavily conditioned by household location and wealth. Children from rural areas are at a particular disadvantage (Figure 2.14). In Burkina Faso, rural children are almost four times more likely than

Figure 2.12: A child's prospects of entering and staying in school vary by country

Distribution of out-of-school children by school exposure, selected countries, most recent year

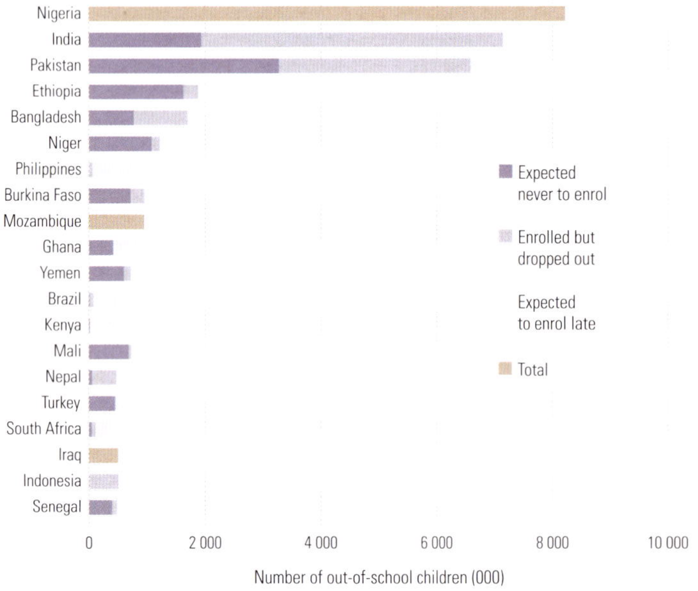

Notes: Countries included had more than 500,000 children out of school in 2007 or the latest year available. For Iraq, Mozambique and Nigeria the breakdown is not available.
Source: Bruneforth (2009*b*).

8. Nigeria could be in a similar situation, but disaggregated data are not available.

Figure 2.13: Left behind: out-of-school girls are less likely ever to get into school

% of out-of-school children who are expected never to enrol, by gender, selected countries, 2007

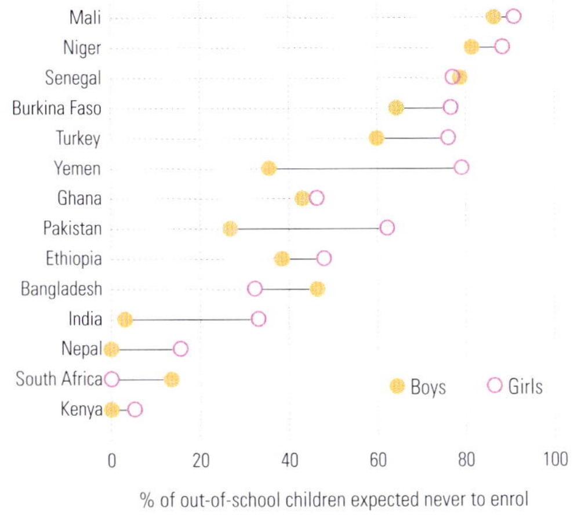

Notes: Countries included had more than 500,000 children out of school in 2007.
Source: Bruneforth (2009*b*).

Figure 2.14: Poor and rural children have much less chance of going to school in Burkina Faso and Ethiopia

School exposure of out-of-school children by location and wealth, Burkina Faso (2003) and Ethiopia (2005)

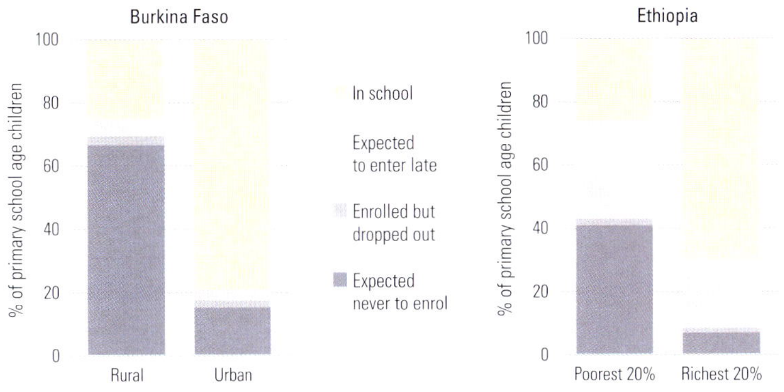

Source: Bruneforth (2009*b*).

urban children to be out of school – and those not in classrooms are over four times less likely ever to go to school. These disparities reflect some of the distinctive problems facing rural communities, including distance to school, poverty and gender disadvantages.

Poverty strongly influences prospects for school entry. Children from the poorest 20% of households dominate the out-of-school populations in many countries and are far less likely than higher-income children ever to enrol. To take one example, around three-quarters of children from the poorest 20% of households in Ethiopia are not in school. Of these, over half are not expected to enter school (Figure 2.14). The heightened risk of never going to school associated with low household wealth underlines the importance of public policies to ensure that poverty does not automatically lead to educational disadvantage.

Enrolment of school age children moving too slowly

Getting children into school is just one of the stepping stones towards universal primary education. As many children will drop out before completing the primary cycle as are currently out of school. The critical challenge is not just getting children into school but ensuring that, once there, they complete a good-quality education.

Universal primary education is easily identified after the event. It exists when almost all primary school age children graduate at roughly the official age. Measuring progress towards this goal is more challenging. No single indicator provides the complete picture, but a combination of measures can help cast light on different parts of a complicated picture. Overall, there is clear evidence that school enrolment and completion are increasing across the world, but a narrow focus on certain indicators may be leading to an underestimation of the distance still to be travelled to achieve universal primary education.

Net enrolment ratios have been rising in the developing world

One commonly used indicator, the net enrolment ratio, measures the proportion of students in the official primary school age group who are enrolled in school. In a system that has achieved universal primary education, the vast majority of children in the official age group will be in primary school.

Universal net enrolment, widely used as a measure of progress towards Goal 2, is a necessary but not sufficient condition for universal primary completion. Countries with a net enrolment ratio close to 100% have most of their primary school age children in the school system, but the measure does not indicate where children are in the cycle. Some children may have dropped out and returned to early grades, while others may be repeating grades having failed school tests.

The critical challenge is to ensure all children complete a good-quality education

Since 1999, South and West Asia and sub-Saharan Africa have increased net enrolment ratios at five times and three times the rate of the 1990s, respectively

For all its limitations, the net enrolment ratio is useful in providing an average picture of progress over time. That picture has been positive since the Dakar forum. Most developing countries that started the current decade a long way from universal primary enrolment have made significant strides (Table 2.2). Since 1999, sub-Saharan Africa and South and West Asia have increased net enrolment ratios at five times and three times the rate of the 1990s, respectively, reaching 73% and 86% in 2007. However, regional aggregates inevitably mask large intraregional differences. Sub-Saharan Africa has a particularly wide range of net enrolment ratios, from 31% in Liberia to 98% in Madagascar and the United Republic of Tanzania. In the Arab States, the spread extends from less than 45% in Djibouti to 75% in Yemen and over 95% in Bahrain and Egypt (Annex, Statistical Table 5).

Progress on enrolment has been uneven

Global progress towards universal net enrolment masks a more complex picture. Countries are moving forwards at different rates, some are not moving – and others are moving backwards.

Figure 2.15 provides a summary progress report. Some countries have achieved extraordinary advances. The United Republic of Tanzania raised its net enrolment ratio from around 50% in 1999 to 98% in 2006. Madagascar, Nicaragua and Zambia have also broken through the 90% threshold towards universal primary enrolment. Benin started out in 1999 with one of the world's lowest net enrolment ratios and could now be on track for universal primary enrolment by 2015. As the education system expands, however, the challenge of extending opportunities to populations that are hard to reach will intensify (Box 2.6). Some of the countries furthest from breaking through the 90% barrier towards universal net enrolment have nonetheless moved a long way, including Burkina Faso, Ethiopia and the Niger.

Past net enrolment trends provide a limited indicator of the potential for countries to achieve universal primary completion. As Figure 2.15 demonstrates, very rapid progress on net enrolment is possible. However, countries with current net enrolment ratios of less than 75% face very steep challenges. Ensuring that all primary school age children progress through the education system is even more challenging, especially when schools are dealing with a large backlog of over-age children.

Several countries in sub-Saharan Africa have tailored their ambitions to current circumstances. Burkina Faso's original goal of attaining universal

Table 2.2: Primary enrolment by region, 1999 and 2007

	Total enrolment		Net enrolment ratios		Gender parity in primary[1]	
	School year ending in		School year ending in		School year ending in	
	1999	2007	1999	2007	1999	2007
	(millions)		(%)		(F/M)	
World	646	694	82	87	0.92	0.96
Developing countries	559	615	80	86	0.91	0.95
Developed countries	70	66	97	96	1.00	1.00
Countries in transition	16	13	88	91	0.99	0.99
Sub-Saharan Africa	82	124	56	73	0.85	0.90
Arab States	35	41	78	84	0.87	0.90
Central Asia	7	6	88	92	0.99	0.98
East Asia and the Pacific	218	191	96	94	0.99	0.99
East Asia	214	188	96	94	0.99	0.99
Pacific	3	3	90	84	0.97	0.97
South and West Asia	155	192	74	86	0.84	0.95
Latin America and the Caribbean	70	68	92	93	0.97	0.97
Caribbean	3	2	75	72	0.98	0.99
Latin America	68	66	93	94	0.97	0.96
North America and Western Europe	53	51	97	95	1.01	1.00
Central and Eastern Europe	26	21	91	92	0.96	0.98

1. Gender parity in primary education is measured by the gender parity index of gross enrolment ratios. See annex for details.
Source: Annex, Statistical Table 5.

Figure 2.15: Most countries improved their primary school enrolment between 1999 and 2007

Change in net enrolment ratios in primary education, 1999-2007

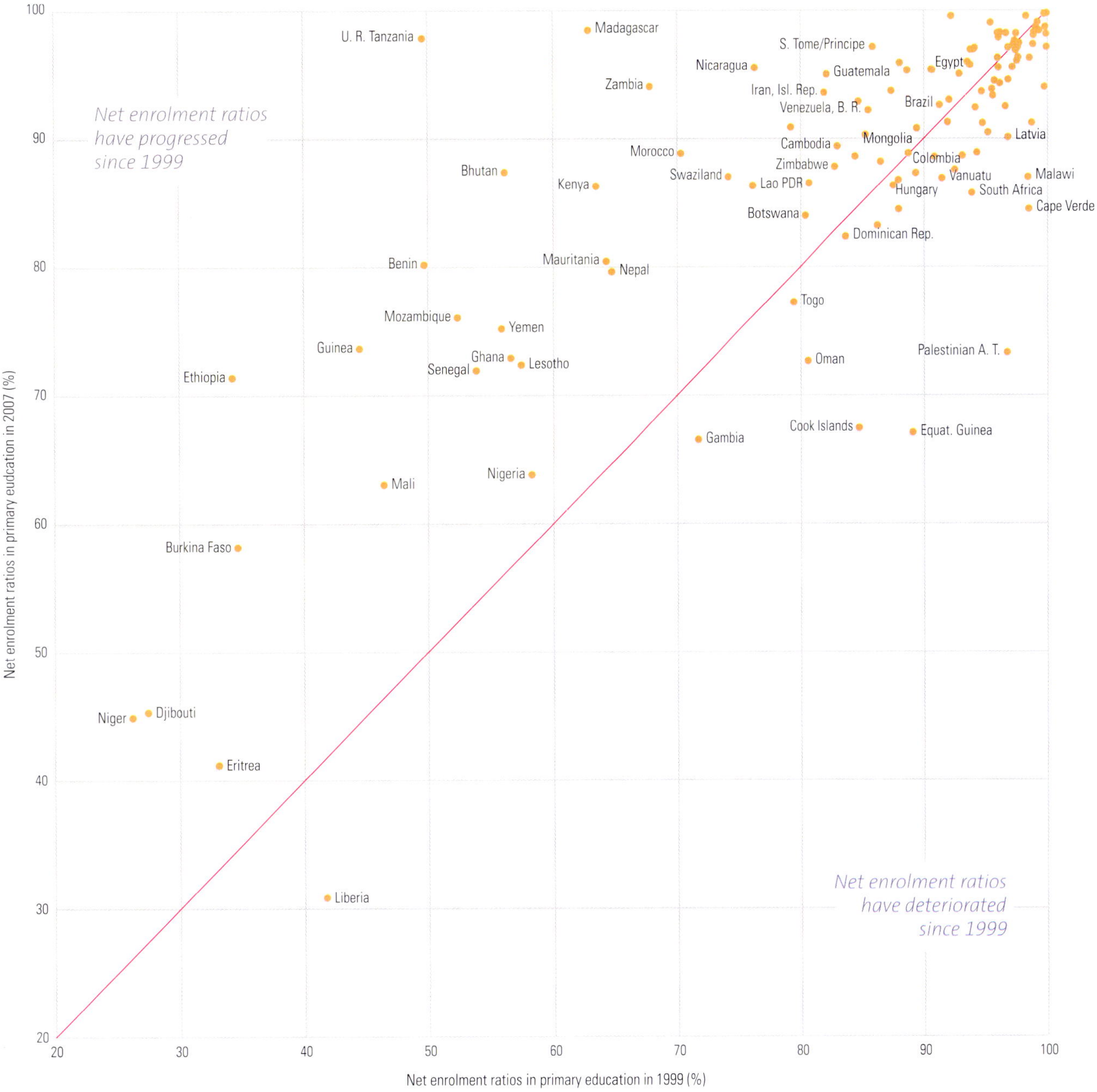

Source: Annex, Statistical Table 5.

primary enrolment by 2015 has been revised downwards in national plans to 70% (Bennell, 2009). Eritrea's current education strategy neatly summarizes the dilemma facing planners: 'achievement of universal primary education by the global target date of 2015 would be extremely difficult. Even if the financial resources were readily available, it would be physically almost impossible to provide the necessary infrastructure and associated inputs (teachers, administrators, etc.) during the next eleven years to cater for all children of primary school age. ... In view of this, it is projected that the net primary school enrolment ratio would reach 82% by 2015 and that UPE would be achieved by 2019' (Eritrea Ministry of National Development, 2005, p. 10).

Box 2.6: Benin — on the right track, but tackling marginalization is a priority

Benin has been among the world's fastest moving countries on primary enrolment, with the net enrolment ratio rising from 50% in 1999 to 80% in 2007. The gender gap also narrowed, from just 67 girls for every 100 boys in school in 1999 to 83 girls in 2006. On current trends, Benin could achieve universal primary enrolment by 2015.

Maintaining the trends will be difficult, however. As in other countries, rapid progress in scaling up enrolment has brought new policy challenges:

- *Raising completion rates.* Achieving Benin's goal of 100% primary school completion by 2015 will require far-reaching measures to ensure that children enrol on time and complete a full primary cycle. Over-age entry remains a significant problem. The gross intake rate into the first grade is 115%, while in 2005 the net intake rate was less than 50%. The disparity points to a concentration of children over 6 years of age in the first grade. Getting children into school on time is important for increasing completion. Fewer than 20% of those who start school complete it at the correct age.
- *Addressing population pressures.* With a population growth rate of 3.2% and almost half of the population under 15 years, Benin's education system will need to expand just to stay in the same position.
- *Reducing regional disparities.* There are marked inequalities across Benin. The gross intake rate for the last grade of primary is only 36% in Alibori Province (one of the poorest regions, with particularly high levels of severe malnutrition for children under 5) compared with a national average of 66%. Reaching vulnerable communities is vital to sustained progress.
- *Tackling poverty.* More than half of Benin's rural population lives in extreme poverty. Children from the wealthiest quintile are at least twice as likely to complete the primary cycle as those in the poorest quintile. This has the effect of skewing education financing towards children from the richest 20% of households, who receive 57% of public expenditure on education compared with just 5% for the poorest.

The government has taken steps in its ten-year education plan (2006-2015) to redress imbalances, including affirmative action for girls and disadvantaged groups and regions – and strong budget commitments. Education spending accounted for 3.9% of GNP and 18% of budget spending in 2006. Just over half of the education budget is directed to primary schooling. To ensure that Benin can go the final step towards universal primary education, international aid donors need to back up this national financing commitment.

Sources: World Bank (2009g); Benin Government (2008).

Twenty-eight countries have still not achieved the 2005 goal of gender parity in primary schooling

Does the scaling down of ambitions mark an unwarranted retreat from the political commitments made at Dakar? Each country has to assess what is achievable in the light of where it currently stands, and the human and financial resources it has available. However, there is strong evidence from several countries that political commitment allied to strong aid partnerships can generate rapid progress.

Gender parity – some progress but a long way to go

The expansion of primary education has gone hand in hand with progress towards greater gender parity, but there are marked differences across and within regions, as witnessed by the gender parity index (GPI).

Twenty-eight countries had GPIs of less than 0.90 in 2007; of these, eighteen are in sub-Saharan Africa. These countries have not yet achieved the goal of gender parity in primary schooling, set for 2005.

There are also marked gender disparities in the Arab States, though the largest gap is found in a South Asian country: Afghanistan, with just 63 girls enrolled in school for every 100 boys. Large gender disparities are inconsistent with sustained rapid progress towards universal primary enrolment.

In countries at low levels of enrolment, such as Burkina Faso, Ethiopia and Yemen, moves towards gender parity from a low starting point have helped generate large increases in primary enrolment. The experience of Yemen demonstrates that rapid progress towards gender parity from a low base is possible and that sustained progress requires a strong political commitment to equity (Box 2.7). Gender parity is usually inversely related to enrolment: the lower the enrolment, the greater the gender disparity (Figure 2.16). An exception is Senegal; while the country still has low net enrolment (72% in 2007), in the space of one primary school generation, the country has moved from a gender parity index of 86 girls per 100 boys

Figure 2.16: The relationship between enrolment and gender parity varies across countries

Net enrolment ratios and gender parity in primary education, 2007

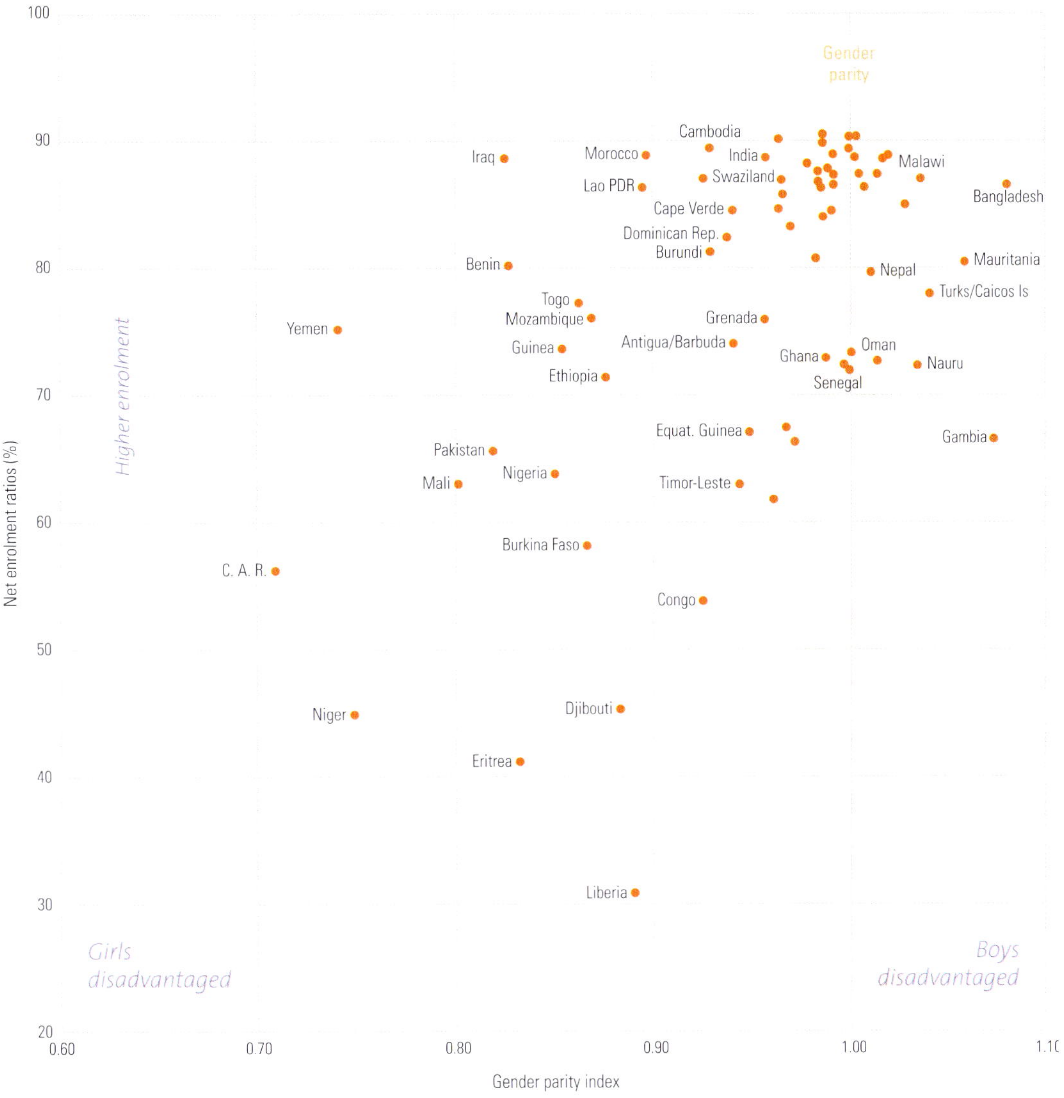

Note: Gender parity in primary education is measured by the gender parity index of gross enrolment ratios. See annex for details.
Source: Annex, Statistical Table 5.

in 1999 to an equal number of girls and boys in 2007. However, not all progress towards gender parity has positive origins. In Equatorial Guinea, Liberia and Togo, greater parity has been driven not by expansion of the education system but by the fact that boys' enrolment has declined (Figure 2.17).

With some of the world's largest gender gaps, several countries in West Africa have adopted policies aimed at strengthening parity as part of the wider strategy for achieving universal primary education. Some of these policies focus on removing one of the greatest obstacles to gender equity: attitudes on girls' and women's place in society. Working through village heads and religious leaders, governments have mounted campaigns to communicate to parents the importance of educating daughters. Other strategies include paying financial incentives, providing water and sanitation in schools (including separate latrines for boys and girls), recruiting female teachers and providing incentives for their deployment to rural areas, and giving teachers gender sensitization training (UNESCO-IIEP, 2009). In remote rural areas, distance to school is often a major security concern for parents of young girls. Governments

Senegal reached gender parity in 2007 in the space of one primary school generation

Figure 2.17: The gender gap is narrowing, but sometimes because enrolment is declining

Changes in net enrolment ratios and gender parity index of gross enrolment ratios in primary education, 1999-2007, selected countries

1999 ○----▶ 2007 The country has improved both participation and gender parity

1999 ○----▶ 2007 The country has improved gender parity but participation has deteriorated

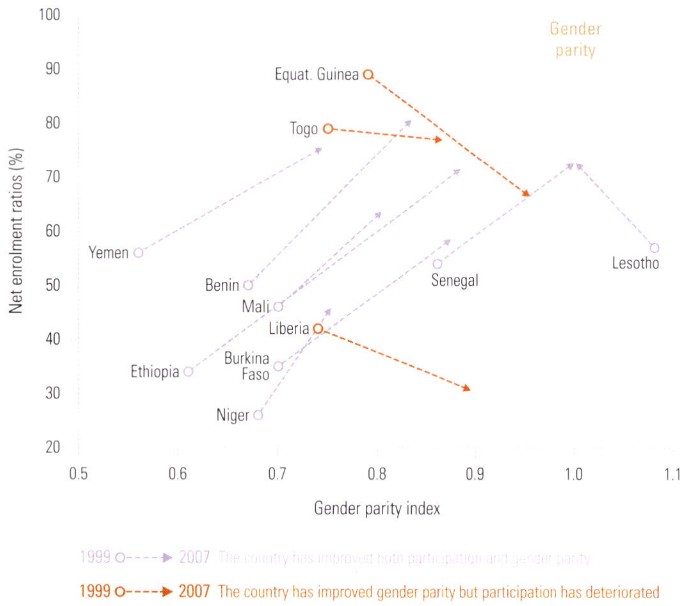

Note: Gender parity in primary education is measured by the gender parity index of gross enrolment ratios. See annex for details.
Source: Annex, Statistical Table 5.

Box 2.7: Yemen – making progress towards

In Yemen, one of the world's poorest countries, enrolment increased from 2.3 million in 1999 to 3.2 million in 2005 and gender disparities shrank. These achievements are all the more remarkable given Yemen's deep poverty, rapid population growth and dispersed rural population.

Girls have benefited from both the overall expansion of education and targeted interventions. Improvement in enrolment in recent years can be traced to policy measures introduced in the late 1990s, including the use of low-cost standardized school designs and consultation with communities on school location. Basic education (grades 1 to 9) has been compulsory and free in principle since the early 1990s, though learners continued to pay for uniforms and textbooks. In 2006/2007 the Ministry of Education made uniforms optional and eliminated textbook fees for girls in grades 1 to 6 and for boys in grades 1 to 3. It has also taken measures to get more female teachers in rural schools.

Further progress will require policy measures that weaken the interaction between gender inequality and poverty. School attendance is lowest, and the gender gap widest, among the poor and in rural areas (Figure 2.18). Of the more than 900,000 primary school age children out of school in 2005, 70% were girls and 88% lived in rural areas. Household survey data show that only 28% of girls and 46% of boys in

have responded by attempting to bring classrooms closer to communities, often by building satellite schools (see Chapter 3).

Getting girls into school demands concerted action to change attitudes and household labour practices

Aid donors can play an important role in supporting efforts to overcome gender disparity. In Chad, a USAID-funded programme is addressing financial and cultural barriers to girls' schooling by providing scholarships and backing community sensitization campaigns. Recognizing that attitudes cannot be changed through top-down directives, the programme supports local agents for change, working through mothers' associations, religious figures, local government and village leaders, and school officials to promote girls' education. The role of imams in asserting the consistency of gender equality in education with the precepts of Islam has been particularly important (Zekas et al., 2009). Initiatives such as these have helped make people more aware that girls have a right to be educated. They also contributed to Chad's progress between 1999 and 2007 in narrowing the gender gap from 58 girls per 100 boys to 70, with greater gender parity helping drive an overall increase in enrolment.

For many countries, sustained progress towards gender parity will require advances on two fronts. Getting girls into school demands concerted action to change attitudes and household labour practices. Keeping them in school once they reach puberty poses another layer of challenges, especially in countries where early marriage is common and where girls' disadvantage interacts with other aspects of marginalization, such as poverty or ethnicity. Countries including Bangladesh and Cambodia have demonstrated that financial incentives can both increase the likelihood of girls entering lower secondary school and raise demand for primary schooling (Filmer and Schady, 2006; Fiszbein et al., 2009). However, public policy interventions are required in many other areas in education and beyond.

In West Africa, some of the world's poorest countries with low enrolment ratios have shown that political leadership and practical measures can override gender discrimination in the household

universal primary education and gender parity

the poorest quintile attended school. Such evidence points to parental attitudes and household labour practices that attach less weight to girls' education than that of boys.

Child labour patterns are also structured by gender disparities. Poverty drives both boys and girls into employment, either because of household cash needs or because parents cannot afford education fees. Children of both sexes also spend time on household chores. Around one-fifth of boys and one-quarter of girls are involved in child labour. However, while 70% of male child labourers attend school, only 52% of females do. The disparity reflects longer work hours among girls, a division of labour that leaves girls with greater responsibility for household labour and a greater weight attached to boys' education.

The complex array of factors keeping children out of school in Yemen points to a need for a twin-track response. Education policies can broaden school infrastructure to reach more children and address gender inequality through financial incentives, recruitment of female teachers and other interventions. At the same time, wider strategies are needed to tackle rural poverty, curtail child labour and challenge attitudes that devalue the education of girls.

Sources: Al-Mekhlafy (2008); Guarcello et al. (2006); Integrated Regional Information Networks (2006, 2007); Kefaya (2007); Ochse (2008).

Figure 2.18: In Yemen, girls' enrolment is lowest in the poorest and rural areas

Primary net attendance rates in Yemen, by gender, wealth and location, 2005

Source: UNESCO-DME (2009).

and beyond. By the same token, failure to narrow gender gaps points to failure in these areas. With a higher income and comparable net enrolment ratio, Pakistan lags far behind Senegal on gender parity. Pakistan's primary net enrolment ratio in 2006 was 73% for boys but only 57% for girls. If Pakistan were to match Senegal's performance, it would have 1.1 million more girls in school. Pakistan's persistent gender disparities, which may be exacerbated by political movements hostile to girls' education, are holding back overall progress in enrolment (Box 2.8). The threat to gender equity is even more marked in neighbouring Afghanistan, where schools and teachers have been targeted with a view to driving girls out of school (see Chapter 3).

Gender disparity is not unidirectional. In a small number of developing countries, girls' enrolment outstrips that of boys. This may happen where demand for boys' labour is higher. To take one example, poor rural families in Lesotho, particularly those in highland areas, often rely on boys to herd cattle, with the result that dropout rates are high after grade 3 (World Bank, 2005*e*). The positive news is that the pace of increase in enrolment has been faster for boys in recent years and gender parity has now been achieved.

Some countries are slipping or stagnating

Positive global trends on net primary enrolment inevitably obscure negative national trends. Several countries with a long way to travel before they achieve universal primary enrolment are not making progress – and some are registering reversals.

Figure 2.15 shows that some countries with low net enrolment ratios and large out-of-school populations – notably Nigeria – are moving in the right direction, but at a snail's pace. More disconcertingly, around twenty-five developing countries with data for both 1999 and 2007 experienced stagnating or declining net enrolment ratios.[9]

Between 1999 and 2007, around twenty-five developing countries have experienced stagnating or declining net enrolment rates

9. This trend is even more apparent in 2006–2007, with forty countries that have yet to achieve universal primary education not moving.

Box 2.8: Pakistan — gender disparities hold back progress

Pakistan is off track for achieving universal primary education by 2015. The country accounts for a significant share of the global out-of-school problem. Failure to tackle gender disadvantages that intersect with poverty and regional differences is at the heart of the problem.

Deep disparities based on location and wealth are a feature of education in Pakistan. In the richest households, over 85% of children go to primary school, with little difference between boys and girls. Attendance rates for children from poor households are far lower, especially for females: only around one-third of poor girls are in school. Similarly, attendance is higher and the gender gap smaller in urban areas than in rural ones, and in the relatively wealthy Punjab province than in Balochistan and Sindh (Figure 2.19).

In Pakistan, only around one-third of poor girls are in school

The North West Frontier Province stands out as having above average attendance for boys but well below average attendance for girls. There is growing concern that this gender gap could be widening further. In the Taliban-occupied parts of the province, 91 girls' schools have been destroyed and 25 damaged, with some boys' schools also suffering.

The factors behind Pakistan's deep gender disparities have been extensively researched. Distance to school matters far more for girls than boys, reflecting security concerns and household labour demands. Girls' enrolment drops off sharply with each 500-metre increase in distance from the closest school admitting girls and this 'distance penalty' accounts for 60% of the gender gap in enrolments. Cost factors can also disadvantage girls because households tend to spend more on boys.

The presence of a government school in the community has a significant positive effect on girls' enrolment. As there has been a marked trend towards sex-segregated primary education, the absence in some areas of all-girl government schools has emerged as a major constraint on girls' schooling. Insufficient recruitment of female teachers is another constraint. Rural parents strongly prefer to have girls educated by women, but the legacy of low investment in girls' education means few local women have appropriate qualifications. It is also difficult to attract qualified female teachers to rural areas from other parts of the country.

Education policy documents increasingly recognize that more weight has to be attached to gender equity, but it is far from clear that the current policy framework provides concrete measures for translating statements into action. Policies indicate community needs as criteria for the location of new government primary schools, for example; however, research suggests that community economic status and the extent of gender disparity have had little influence over the placement of new government schools.

Overall levels of public financing remain low, education is weakly integrated into national poverty reduction strategies and there have been limited attempts to introduce the type of incentives for girls' education that have been successful in Bangladesh, which has moved far ahead of Pakistan in terms of enrolment and gender parity.

Sources: Aly and National Education Policy Review Team (2007); Andrabi et al. (2008); Lloyd et al. (2007); O'Malley (2009); Pakistan Ministry of Education (2003).

Figure 2.19: Pakistan's primary school attendance is marked by gender, regional and wealth inequalities

Primary net attendance rates in Pakistan by gender, wealth, location and region, 2007

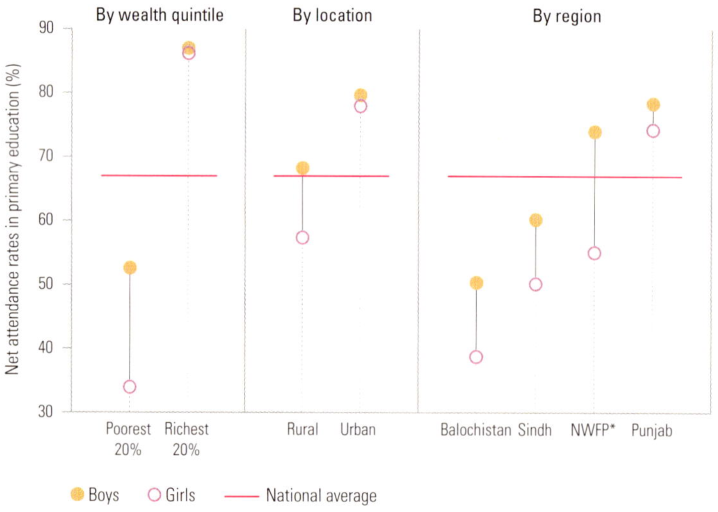

* NWFP: North West Frontier Province.
Source: UNESCO-DME (2009).

Adding in countries that lack enrolment data for both 1999 and 2007 would yield significantly more than twenty-five lagging countries. For example, for the Central African Republic and Pakistan, which had net enrolment ratios below 70% in 2007 and no data for 1999, there is strong evidence that progress has been limited. Other countries have no data available on net enrolment for either 1999 or 2007, including Afghanistan, the Democratic Republic of the Congo, Haiti, Sierra Leone, Somalia and the Sudan. Here, too, there is strong evidence to suggest that progress towards universal net enrolment, if any, has often been very slow, from a low base. Côte d'Ivoire, with a gross enrolment ratio of 72%, and the Sudan at 66% in 2007 are clearly off track.[10] Although Afghanistan's gross enrolment ratio has increased significantly (from 28% in 1999 to 103% in 2007), in part due to the opening up of opportunities for girls' education, there is still a long way to go before all children enter and complete the cycle on time.[11]

Many countries experiencing slow progress or reversals are either in the midst of or recovering from conflict. Developments in Liberia have been particularly disconcerting. After a brutal civil war, the country has now enjoyed several years of peace and has an elected president, Ellen Sirleaf-Johnson, with a strong commitment to education. However, its net enrolment ratio slipped from 42% in 1999 to 31% in 2008. The government plan for education acknowledges that 'realistically, Liberia will likely need more years beyond 2015 to achieve the UPE goals' (Liberia Ministry of Education, 2007*b*). How many more years will depend partly on national efforts and partly on the degree to which aid donors find innovative ways of supporting those efforts (Box 2.9; see also Chapter 4). The large recorded decline in enrolment in the Palestinian Autonomous Territories would also appear to be linked to the combined effects of civil conflict, military incursions, and restrictions on the movement of goods and people.

Eritrea is a further cause for concern. After significant progress increasing enrolment from 1999 to 2006, the country experienced a reversal in 2007.[12] Military tensions appear to be a contributory factor. Since the end of the 1990s, spending on education has more than halved as a share of GNP, from 5.3% in 1999 to 2.4% in 2006. Meanwhile, military spending has been extremely high,[13] crowding out urgently needed spending on education infrastructure.

Box 2.9: Liberia – slipping back in a post-conflict country

Autocratic rule, coups and fourteen years of civil war took a devastating toll on Liberia's education system. Schools were destroyed, public services collapsed, investment fell and parental fears over security led to children being withdrawn from school. The election of President Ellen Sirleaf-Johnson in 2006 created renewed hope, but recovery is proving arduous.

Liberia is one of the world's poorest countries: three-quarters of the population survives on less than US$1.25 a day. Education infrastructure is dilapidated and there are chronic shortages of trained teachers and teaching materials. As well as dealing with children who have enrolled since the end of the conflict, the education system must cope with population growth and the many displaced Liberian families returning from abroad.

Data limitations make it difficult to chart developments, but fragile gains in enrolment at the end of the 1990s are thought to have been reversed during a renewal of violence from 2001 to 2003, with enrolment dropping by about half for girls and one-third for boys because of insecurity and poverty.

In 2007, the Ministry of Education set out a strategy for moving from short-term emergency planning to long-term strategic planning. The strategy envisages strengthening quality and equity, in part by providing a regulatory umbrella that covers the diversity of education providers. In 2008, some 30% of primary enrolment was in private and mission schools, the rest in government and community-funded schools. The equity challenge is particularly daunting, given the large inequalities based on wealth, region and gender.

Liberia's experience raises wider concerns about the failure of aid systems. In countries recovering from conflict, the resources available to government are limited, so aid has a vital role to play. Aid donors were slow to support reconstruction in Liberia, despite the endorsement of the country's economic plan by the Fast Track Initiative. Chapter 4 explores the failure of current aid systems to respond to the needs of countries such as Liberia.

Sources: Center for Global Development (2009); Liberia Ministry of Education (2007*a*); USAID (2007).

Going the final mile – some countries with high net enrolment face problems

Most of the countries facing difficulties in achieving universal net enrolment by 2015 have two characteristics in common. They started with low initial enrolment ratios and they are very poor. There are exceptions to the rule. While enrolment ratios tend to rise with wealth, there are large variations around the average – and some relatively wealthy countries perform worse than might be expected. Moreover, some countries are in grave danger of failing to achieve universal net enrolment by 2015 despite having started at very high levels of school participation.

Figure 2.20 demonstrates that wealth matters for education coverage. It charts the relationship between average income and net enrolment ratios,

10. Because the gross enrolment ratio measures the enrolment of all children irrespective of their age relative to the primary school age group, the net enrolment ratio would be far lower.

11. In 2007, the net intake rate into the primary system in Afghanistan was just 55%.

12. The net enrolment ratio rose from 33% in 1999 to 47% in 2006, but fell back to 41% in 2007.

13. Military expenditure is around one-quarter of GDP, according to the 2007/2008 budget (UNDP, 2007).

Figure 2.20: Most out-of-school children are in poorer countries, but some wealthier countries are underperforming

Primary net enrolment ratios, GNP per capita and out-of-school children headcount in low and middle income countries, 2007

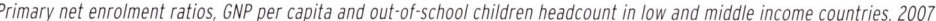

Notes: Bubble size represents the number of out-of-school children. Countries in red have more than 500,000 children out of school.
Source: Annex, Statistical Tables 1 and 5.

The Philippines and Turkey perform less strongly than their national wealth predicts

while at the same time capturing the size of out-of-school populations. There are many reasons for the underlying positive relationship between enrolment and income. As countries grow wealthier, they and their citizens can spend more on education – and as economies grow they tend to generate demand for skilled labour. Of greater interest than the well-established average association is variation around the mean. At the lower end of the enrolment spectrum, countries such as Nigeria and Pakistan are outperformed by poorer countries such as Bangladesh and Ethiopia. At the higher end, countries including the Philippines, South Africa and Turkey perform less strongly than expected.

The Philippines provides a particularly striking example of underperformance.[14] With an average income four times that of the United Republic of Tanzania or Zambia, it has a lower net enrolment ratio. The unfavourable comparisons do not end there. Whereas the United Republic of Tanzania and Zambia have been steadily increasing net enrolment ratios, the Philippines has stagnated. Given the country's starting point in 1999, achieving universal primary education by 2015 should have been a formality. There is now a real danger that, in the absence of decisive political leadership, the country will miss the goal. In 2007, out-of-school numbers for children aged 6 to 11 broke through the 1 million mark and there were over 100,000 more children out of school then than in 1999. Around one-quarter of those entering school drop out before grade 5. Other countries experiencing stagnation or slippage from high levels of net enrolment include Turkey, whose net enrolment ratio has remained unchanged since the beginning of the decade (UIS database).

Why have countries that were so close to universal net enrolment at the end of the 1990s failed to go the extra mile? One factor is the difficulty in extending opportunities to certain regions and parts

14. See Chapter 3 for a fuller analysis of the reasons for the challenges facing the Philippines.

of society. Both the Philippines and Turkey face problems of deeply entrenched marginalization. In the Philippines, marginalization is strongly associated with poverty and location, with the Autonomous Region in Muslim Mindanao and some outlying islands falling far behind. In Turkey, disadvantage is heavily concentrated among young girls in eastern regions who do not have Turkish as their mother tongue (Box 2.10). Chapter 3 explores the problem of reaching marginalized people in more detail, but it is evident in the cases of the Philippines and Turkey that current policies are not breaking down inherited disadvantage. One contributory factor is the low share of national income invested in education. Turkey invested around 4% of GNP in 2004, compared with 6% to 7% in Morocco and Tunisia. The figure was just 2.3% in the Philippines in 2005, compared with an East Asian regional average of 3.6%.[15]

15. The regional figure is the median for those countries with available data.

Box 2.10: Turkey – marginalization keeps universal primary education out of reach

Turkey's advance towards universal primary education has stalled within touching distance of the goal. Much has been achieved over the past decade. But far more has to be done to break down inequalities based on gender, region and wealth.

The country's basic education law requires every child to undergo eight years of schooling and there is a single curriculum for all 6- to 14-year-olds. Primary school enrolment increased rapidly during the second half of the 1990s as a series of programmes expanded school construction, strengthened teacher training, increased textbook supplies and provided transport for children in remote villages.

Since 2000, however, progress has slowed. Enrolment ratios have stagnated at around 90% since 2002 – far below the level predicted on the basis of Turkey's average income. Some 640,000 children of primary school age were out of school in 2007. Around 60% were girls, pointing to deeply entrenched gender inequalities. High levels of exclusion in the early years are holding back progress at higher levels, with adverse consequences for future economic growth, employment and social development. Education quality is another serious source of concern: Turkey figures among the worst performers on the learning achievement tests of the OECD Programme for International Student Assessment (PISA).

Turkey's experience powerfully demonstrates the difficulties governments face as they attempt to reach the most marginalized. One study using Turkey's most recent Demographic and Health Survey highlights deep, overlapping and mutually reinforcing inequalities in opportunity for education, with gender disparities magnifying other gaps:

- *Gender.* Between ages 8 and 12, 7% of girls never make it to school, compared with 2% of boys. By age 15, female enrolment is almost twenty percentage points below male enrolment.
- *Region.* The eastern region lags far behind the rest of the country, mainly because of gender disparity. Enrolment ratios for girls in eastern Turkey, expressed as a share of the level for boys, peak at 85% at age 9 and have dropped below 40% by age 15.
- *Rural location.* Being born in a rural area is disadvantageous for girls across the country. Outside of the eastern region, that disadvantage kicks in from age 13. In the eastern region it starts early: by age 15, fewer than 20% of rural girls are enrolled.
- *Household wealth and other factors.* Children in households that are poor and whose parents have limited formal education are less likely to progress through the school system. Children in the wealthiest 20% of households are five times more likely to reach higher education than their counterparts in the poorest 20%. The strength of the negative correlation between household circumstance and education in Turkey is magnified by gender effects. For example, at age 16 boys of mothers with no education are twice as likely as girls to be in school.

Such findings powerfully illustrate the distance Turkey still has to travel to make the right to education a reality for all of its citizens. As the authors of the research put it, the opportunity profiles that emerge from household surveys show that 'school enrolment in Turkey is evidently not independent from circumstances at birth'.

Patterns of inequality in education raise concerns for the future course of Turkey's social and economic development. High levels of education inequality are holding back efforts to strengthen economic growth, expand employment and create a more equal society. Migration from eastern to western regions, usually from rural to urban settlements, spreads the legacy of education disadvantage across the country. Large numbers of rural migrants to Turkish cities settle in squatter areas called *gecekondular* districts, which are centres of social marginalization and educational disadvantage.

The scale of inequality also highlights the importance of equity in public spending. It is critical to strengthen strategies and incentives for reaching rural girls, especially – though not exclusively – in the eastern region. Addressing the disadvantages faced by children of parents who do not speak Turkish as a home language is another priority area.

Sources: Duman (2008); Ferreira and Gignoux (2008*a*); Otaran et al. (2003).

From enrolment to completion and beyond – a difficult journey that is hard to measure

In half the countries in South and West Asia, and sub-Saharan Africa, almost one child in three drops out

Universal primary education is an apparently simple goal that raises disarmingly complex questions over measurement. Going back to first principles, that goal is about all children entering school at an appropriate age, progressing smoothly through the system and completing a full cycle.

For millions of children entering primary school, the journey through the system is often delayed, hazardous and short-lived. In half the countries in South and West Asia, and sub-Saharan Africa, almost one child in three enrolling in school drops out before completion. Even that figure, stark as it is, understates the problem: many children do not get past the first hurdle. In 2006, 13% of pupils in South and West Asia and 9% in sub-Saharan Africa dropped out before completing the first grade (see annex, Statistical Table 7).[16] Malawi and Uganda have relatively high net enrolment ratios, yet between one-quarter and one-third of pupils drop out during the first grade, in some cases never to return. Repetition of grades is also common. In Burundi, nearly one-third of children in primary school in 2006 were repeating grades.

16. These figures are regional medians for the countries that have the relevant data available.

Charting progress towards universal primary education in school systems marked by high levels of late entry, dropout and grade repetition is a challenging exercise. The tool kits used by governments and the international community comprise a range of instruments for measuring intake, grade progression and completion. Each instrument provides important information. Yet they provide only a partial and in some cases inconsistent insight to where countries are on the road to universal primary education.

Figure 2.21 illustrates the point. It looks at two of the most widely used measures of progress towards universal primary education. The first is the gross intake rate into the last grade of primary school, which expresses the share of children entering the last grade as a proportion of the official age group for that grade. It includes over-age children who started school late or repeated grades. The second measure is the net enrolment ratio, discussed earlier. It provides information on

Figure 2.21: Children's precarious pathway from school entry to completion

Net enrolment ratios and gross intake rates to last grade, selected countries, 2007

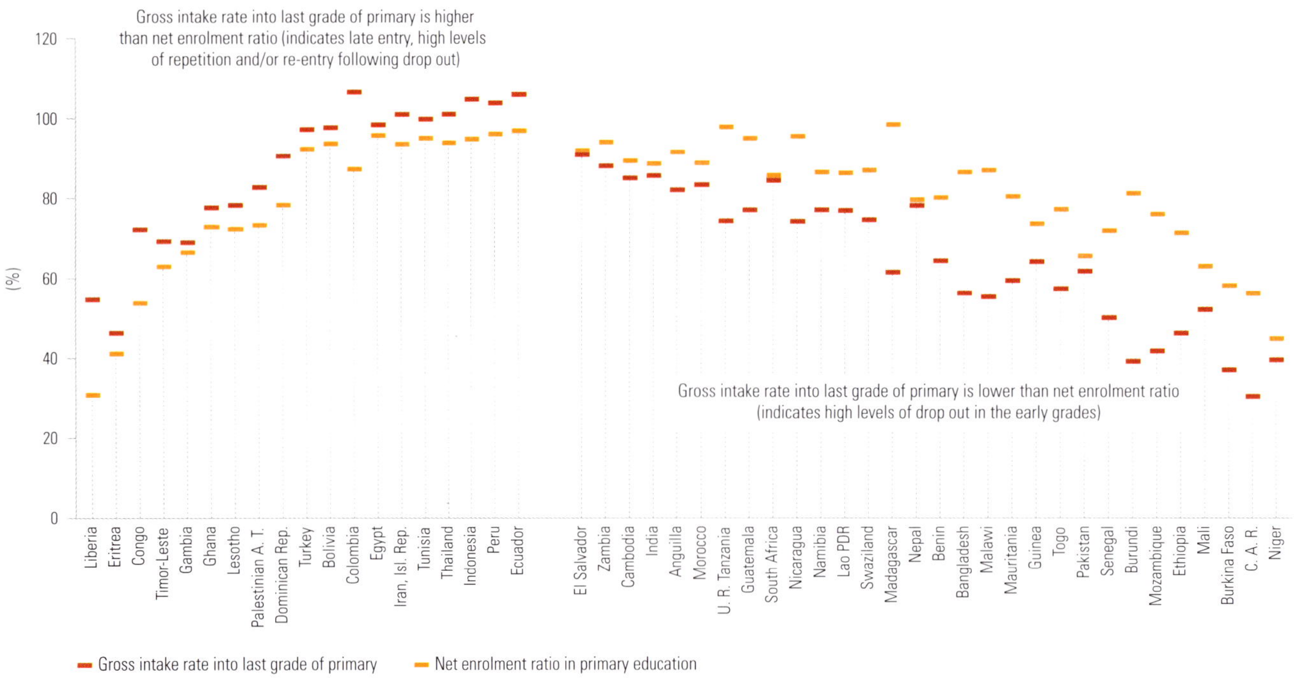

Source: Annex, Statistical Table 5 and UIS database.

the number of primary school age children in the system, but not on where they are in the system, on how many started school over the official age or on the level of grade repetition. Both measures provide important but partial information – and the relationship between the two is highly variable. Countries with gross intake rates that are higher than net enrolment ratios (those on the left of the figure) are characterized by high levels of over-age entry to last grade. Those in the opposite position – Burundi is an example – are characterized by low levels of internal efficiency. But neither measure offers more than a partial insight into how near a country is to achieving universal primary education or how far it may be from that goal.

Cohort tracking can provide a more integrated perspective. Figure 2.22 illustrates one possible

Cohort tracking provides an integrated perspective on progress towards universal primary education

Figure 2.22: Children who start primary school have varying chances to complete the last grade

Net intake rates into first grade of primary through to net cohort completion rates, selected countries, 2006

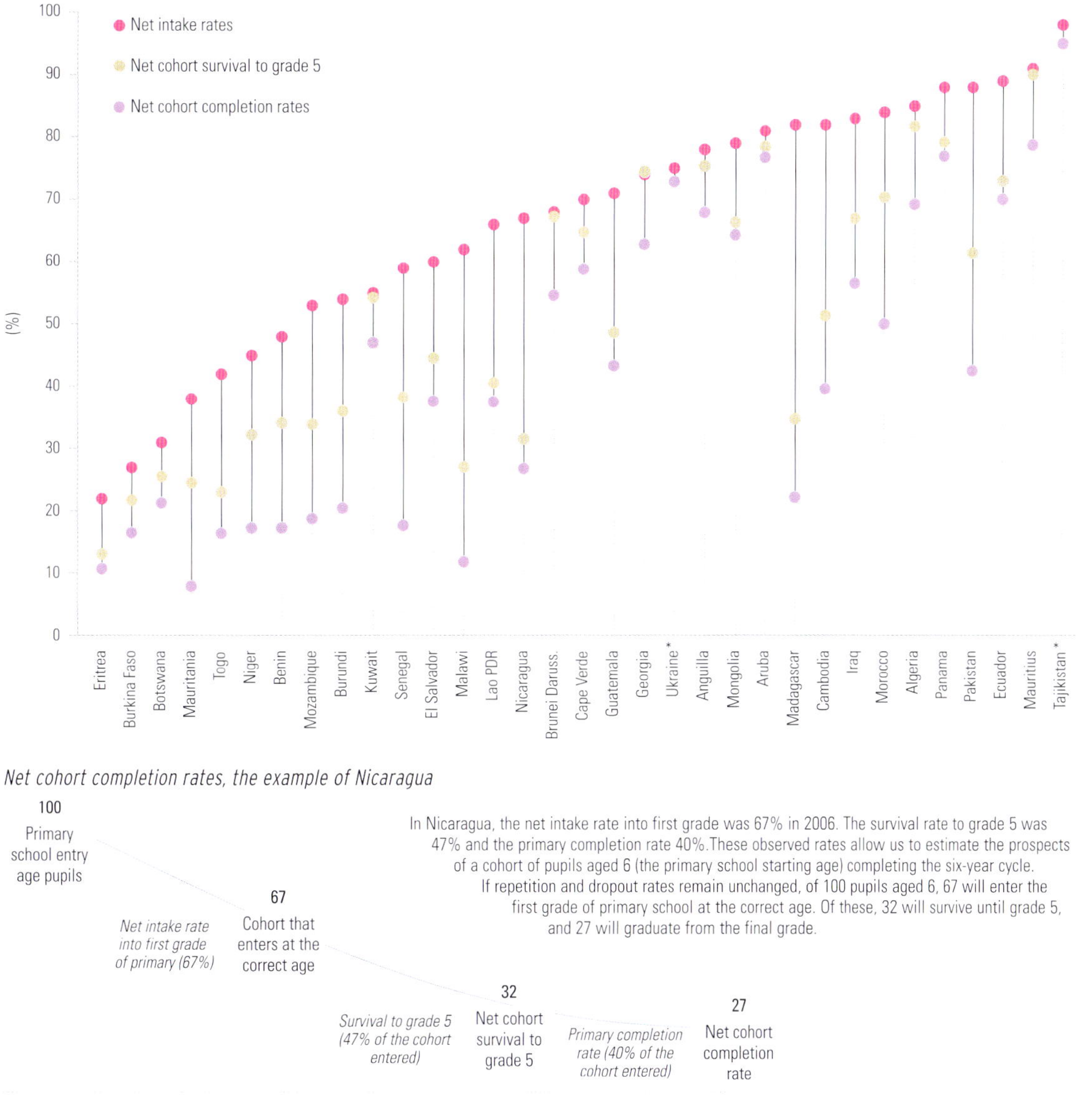

Notes: The lines for each country illustrate the prospects for a cohort of 100 children of primary school entry age completing the cycle if the education system remains in its current state (taking account of current rates of repetition and dropout). Ideally, all children should enter school at the official starting age. The net intake rate is therefore used as the entry point. The net cohort survival rate to grade 5 and the net cohort completion rate are obtained by multiplying the net intake rate by, respectively, the survival rate to grade 5 and the primary cohort completion rate. All countries with available data are included.
* Countries whose primary education cycle is less than five years.
Source: Global Monitoring Report team calculations based on Statistical Tables 4 and 7 (annex).

approach. Starting from the proportion of children entering school at the official age, it uses administrative data to track their progress to grade 5 and, unlike the gross intake rate for the last grade, subsequent completion. For countries seeking to make the transition from school systems characterized by late entry, grade repetition and low completion to a more regular cycle consistent with progress towards universal primary education, the net cohort completion rate is a potentially useful measurement tool.

Nearly 71 million adolescents were out of school in 2007, 54% were girls

One advantage of cohort tracking is that it provides a credible measure of distance from universal primary education. In the case of sub-Saharan Africa, it underlines the daunting scale of the challenge ahead. While intake rates are going up, delayed entry is endemic. Half of all countries in the region had 50% or more children entering school later than the official starting age in 2007. Assuming a five-year school cycle, this implies that governments in the region would have to double the net intake rate by 2010 to make universal primary entry possible by 2015. For some countries, the challenge is to raise the net intake rate while building on a strong but limited completion record. In Burkina Faso, most children entering school at the appropriate age progress through to completion – but the net intake rate in 2006 was just 27%. Conversely, Malawi and Nicaragua have net intake rates over 60% in 2006 where fewer than half the official age entrants make it through to completion.

Out-of-school adolescents

The focus on out-of-school children of primary school age has deflected attention from a far wider problem. Millions in the lower secondary school age group are also out of school, either because they have not completed primary school or could not make the transition to lower secondary school.

Recent data analysis suggests that nearly 71 million adolescents were out of school in 2007 – almost one in five of the total age group (Table 2.3).[17] Viewed through this wider lens, the out-of-school problem is twice as large as it is typically reported to be. The problem is most widespread in sub-Saharan Africa, with 38% of adolescents out of school, and South and West Asia with 28%. As with primary school age children, adolescent girls are more likely than boys to be out of school. Globally, 54% of out-of-school adolescents in 2007 were girls. In the Arab States the figure was 59% (Bruneforth and Wallet, 2009).

Equally disconcerting is the fact that many adolescents in school are still enrolled at the primary level (Figure 2.23). This is the case for 39% of lower secondary school age adolescents in sub-Saharan Africa, for example.

Table 2.3: Number and % of children and adolescents of primary, lower secondary or basic education age not enrolled in primary, secondary or higher education, 2007

	Primary education		Lower secondary education		Basic education (primary and lower secondary combined)	
	Total out-of-school (000)	As % of the primary age group	Total out-of-school (000)	As % of the lower secondary age group	Total out-of-school (000)	As % of the basic education age group
World	71 791	11	70 921	18	142 712	14
Developing countries	68 638	12	68 197	21	136 835	15
Developed countries	2 334	4	1 538	4	3 872	4
Countries in transition	819	6	1 187	6	2 006	6
Sub-Saharan Africa	32 226	26	21 731	38	53 957	30
Arab States	5 752	14	4 009	18	9 761	15
Central Asia	271	5	302	4	573	4
East Asia and the Pacific	9 039	5	10 319	10	19 358	7
South and West Asia	18 031	10	29 905	28	47 937	17
Latin America and the Caribbean	2 989	5	1 885	5	4 873	5
North America and Western Europe	1 931	4	1 319	4	3 250	4
Central and Eastern Europe	1 552	7	1 452	7	3 004	7

Source: Bruneforth and Wallet (2009).

17. For the purposes of this analysis, adolescence is defined in terms of the official lower secondary school age range. Although the range varies by country, it is typically shorter than that for primary school. The lower secondary cycle is usually two to four years, compared with five to seven years of primary schooling in most countries.

The transition from primary school to lower secondary school is hazardous for many children. Problems that may be evident at the primary level are often magnified at the secondary level. Cost, distance to school, labour market demand and – especially for girls – deeply engrained social, cultural and economic barriers figure prominently (Otieno and K'Oliech, 2007). Because secondary schools are often further from home, the importance of distance as a barrier to entry increases. This is especially true for poor households facing labour shortages and for children in rural areas (Mingat and Ndem, 2008). In Mauritania and Senegal, the average journey time to the closest secondary school is eighty minutes in rural areas. The average distance to the closest lower secondary school in Senegal is twenty-five times farther than to the nearest primary school (Glick and Sahn, 2009). Distance can compound the effects of poverty, with poor households often unable to cover the cost either of transport or of boarding school places. Girls face a distinctive set of barriers: longer distances may reinforce security concerns and, in some contexts, early marriage prevents them from progressing beyond primary school.

The transition to lower secondary school is now at the centre of the Education for All agenda in many countries. In sub-Saharan Africa, universal basic education is an increasingly prominent policy goal. For example, Ghana has adopted a basic education cycle embracing six years of primary and three years of lower secondary; in Zambia the cycle is seven years of primary and two years of lower secondary.

There are good reasons for the shift in emphasis towards a longer basic education cycle. As more children get into and progress through primary school, demand for secondary school places is growing. There is also evidence of high social and private returns to education beyond the primary level. Yet governments also face tough choices. In countries that have been unable to deliver affordable, good-quality basic education to large sections of the population, the shift in emphasis raises important questions for equity in public finance. Aid partnerships can help relieve the financing constraints. However, it is important for governments and donors to avoid a premature shift in policy priorities. With millions of children still excluded from primary education and the world off track for the 2015 goals, there is a great deal of unfinished business awaiting urgent attention.

Figure 2.23: Many adolescents are out of school, or still in primary school

Distribution of lower secondary school age children by education level and % out of school

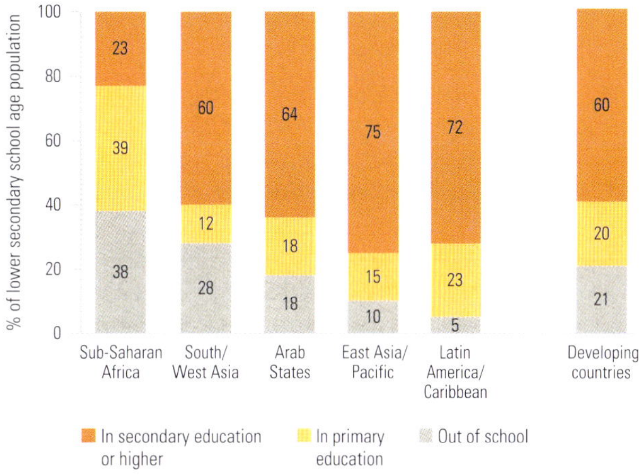

Source: Bruneforth and Wallet (2009).

Conclusion

As in previous years, the progress report on universal primary education is a story of 'glass half empty, glass half full'. Much has been achieved – but the international community has a long way to go if it is to deliver on the promises made in Dakar and in the Millennium Development Goals. The slow-down in getting children into school since 2004 is a particular concern. Another is the evidence of a large mismatch between administrative data on school enrolment and household survey data on school attendance. The out-of-school problem may be far bigger than has previously been assumed, pointing to a need for an urgent policy response at both the national and international levels. □

The transition from primary school to lower secondary school is hazardous for many children

Youth and adult skills – expanding opportunities in the new global economy

Goal 3. Ensuring that the learning needs of all young people and adults are met through equitable access to appropriate learning and life-skills programmes.

The Dakar Framework for Action does not provide targets for youth and adult skills. Rather than agree to quantifiable benchmarks, governments signed up to a third EFA goal that amounts to a vague aspiration. One consequence has been a protracted and unresolved debate over what, if anything, that aspiration means in terms of policy commitments (King and Palmer, 2008). Unlike other parts of the Dakar Framework, goal 3 has been the subject of quiet neglect. It has been conspicuous by its absence not just from the agendas of high-level development summits but also from the campaigns of non-government organizations.

That situation is unfortunate. In the emerging knowledge-based global economy of the twenty-first century, learning and skills play an increasingly important role in shaping prospects for economic growth, shared prosperity and poverty reduction (Sapir, 2005). A country's most important resource is not its raw materials or its geographical location but the skills of its people. Countries that fail to nurture these skills through effective learning face a bleak future, with human capital deficits hindering economic growth, employment creation and social progress (Commission on Growth and Development, 2008; Kok, 2004; OECD, 2004). Within countries, unequal access to opportunities to develop skills will be reflected in deepening social and economic disparities. Youth unemployment, one of the most serious and persistent challenges facing governments across the world, is in part a reflection of a misalignment between skills development and the economy. As one recent report put it: 'Achieving world class skills is *the* key to achieving economic success and social justice in the new global economy' (Leitch Review of Skills, 2006, p. 9).

The global economic crisis has pushed learning and skills up the political agenda

Rich and poor countries alike increasingly recognize that they will pay a high price if they fail to strengthen national skills (DFID, 2007, 2008*a*). The global economic crisis has raised the stakes, pushing learning and skills up the political agenda. While all sections of society have been affected, the economic downturn has left its deepest imprint on vulnerable unskilled workers, especially the young (ILO, 2009*a*; OECD, 2009*d*). Governments across the world are grappling with the twin challenges of providing immediate support to the vulnerable during a period of turbulence while equipping people with the skills they need to re-enter labour markets with higher levels of productivity.

This section looks at some of the lessons to be drawn from current approaches to skills development. Narrowing the wide-angle lens of goal 3, the focus is on skills and learning opportunities for young people provided through technical and vocational education programmes. These programmes can play an important role in strengthening the transition from school to the world of work, in offering second chances and in combating marginalization. In many countries, however, technical and vocational education is in such bad shape that it merits its reputation as a form of second-class schooling. There are no quick fixes for this situation, but four broad messages emerge from this section:

- *Give young people the training they need.* Governments, trade unions and employers need to cooperate to devise effective technical and vocational education that equips young people with the skills they need for success in employment. Too much vocational education delivers skills of limited relevance to economic and social needs, and at high cost, often bypassing the poor and the informal sector. It is often driven by inappropriate curricula and qualifications, with providers insulated from employers' real demands.

- *Skills need a broad base.* Successful transition from school to work requires the development of broad skills, with an emphasis on problem-solving and 'learning to learn', alongside more specialized abilities. Early streaming into specialized vocational education through academic selection should be avoided. Governments also need to address the widespread perception of technical and vocational education as a safety net for failing students or those from poor family backgrounds. Raising the quality and improving the relevance of technical and vocational education is the most effective antidote to that perception.

- *Strengthen basic education.* Effective and equitable skills will not be developed in countries where a majority of the population does not reach secondary school. Strengthening basic education is a key element in providing technical and vocational training.

- *Work towards greater equity.* In many countries, technical and vocational education fails to reach large numbers of marginalized young people, notably young women. Far more could be done to broaden vocational education opportunities, by offering 'second chance' programmes and by better integrating vocational training into national poverty reduction strategies. Designing flexible programmes for young people who have not completed secondary school or gone beyond primary education can help combat youth unemployment.

This section is divided into five parts. Part 1 outlines the diverse ways in which countries approach the task of supplying technical and vocational education and provides a bird's-eye view of global participation in vocational education at the secondary school level. Part 2 looks at one of the most sensitive barometers of the mismatch between training and the economy – youth unemployment. While the global economic crisis is leaving its mark on people across the world, marginalized young people are often bearing the brunt.

Part 3 examines what can happen to technical and vocational programmes when good intentions are undermined by lack of finance, poor design and weak linkage to labour markets. It highlights the particular challenges governments face in the Arab States, India and sub-Saharan Africa. Part 4 explores how vocational education can help young adults avoid marginalization by offering them a second chance to acquire the skills they need. Part 5 considers what kinds of policies lead to effective technical and vocational education programmes that facilitate the transition from school to employment.

Technical and vocational education

The fundamental purpose of technical and vocational education is to equip people with capabilities that can broaden their opportunities in life, and to prepare youth and young adults for the transition from school to work. Skill development in technical and vocational education matters at many levels. For individuals, the skills carried into the labour market have a major influence on job security and wages. For employers, skills and learning play a key role in raising productivity. For society as a whole, raising the overall level of skills, ensuring that young people are not left behind and aligning the supply of skilled labour with the demands of industry are critical to social cohesion. This section focuses principally on the role of vocational education, rather than on training provided by companies, in the generation of skills and capabilities.

Vocational programmes vary across countries

Technical and vocational education programmes emerged in developed countries during the nineteenth century to support industrial development. Their subsequent evolution and their adoption in developing countries reflect complex institutional relationships between education and economic systems.

For individuals, the skills carried into the labour market have a major influence on job security and wages

There are many models of provision. While some countries provide general education in schools, with companies or special training institutes offering vocational options, other countries offer distinctive vocational options in secondary school. Apprenticeship programmes are an important part of technical and vocational education provision, though here, too, arrangements vary. Several broad approaches can be identified:

- *Dual systems.* Some countries combine school-based and work-based training in dual systems, integrating apprenticeships into the formal education structure. OECD countries that typically offer this option include Denmark, Germany, Switzerland and, more recently, Norway (OECD, 2007*a*). The well-known German dual system, which has been widely copied in developing countries, creates opportunities for students to combine school-based classes with in-company training (Barabasch et al., 2009). Four key stakeholders are involved: the federal government, the state government, representatives of employer organizations and trade unions (German Federal Ministry of Education and Research, 2006). Benefits of the German system include firm-based training that equips students with skills suitable for the job market, an assured pool of skilled workers and private sector contributions to financing. Vocational training has played an important role in combating youth unemployment and reducing wage inequalities. On a less positive note, early tracking into vocational education has contributed to deep inequalities in educational achievement, with the school system actively reinforcing social and economic divisions.[18] Germany has some of the largest education disparities between schools and socio-economic groups in the OECD countries, with the children of immigrants far more likely to be tracked into vocational education.[19]

- *School-based systems.* Several countries have traditionally maintained a division of roles between school-based general education and company-based training. In Japan, full-time vocational schooling is followed by full-time employment in enterprises linked to the school (OECD, 2009*c*). As with the German dual system, vocational training in Japan has historically helped facilitate quick settlement of school leavers into secure employment. However, unlike in the German system, with its focus on firm-based training, in Japan students in vocational tracks typically leave full-time education to enter companies that provide training linked to their schools.

- *Mixed models.* Many countries operate hybrid programmes, providing vocational education streams within the school system. This is a characteristic of the French model, though France also operates a small parallel 'dual system' (Grubb, 2006). The United Kingdom operates several 'school and work' programmes involving apprenticeships and general education (UK Learning and Skills Council National Office, 2007). However, the links between employers and educators have traditionally been less institutionalized than in the German or Japanese systems.

In most countries, governments, employers, trade unions, civil society and private agencies are involved in TVET

In most countries, governments hold primary responsibility for setting the overall direction of vocational education policy and for overseeing and regulating standards. A wide range of other interested parties is involved, however, including employers, trade unions, civil society and private agencies. Many countries have created national training authorities to oversee and coordinate activities, with remits that extend from the design of vocational curricula in schools to oversight of training in specialized institutions and in companies. Occupational and standard-setting bodies, along with national qualification frameworks, seek to establish uniform and predictable standards, enabling employers to assess potential employees' skills.

Beyond the school, there is a wide range of training providers. In some cases, government agencies play the lead role in financing and providing training through specialized institutes. Other countries, such as Chile and Mauritius, have split financing from the provision of training and adopted a competitive model for procuring training services.[20] In some countries, the private sector occupies an important position in both financing and providing training. The diversity of governance models is evident in Latin America (CINTERFOR/ILO, 2001; Gallart, 2008). In Colombia and Costa Rica, which have highly effective training models, the public sector plays the dominant role in finance and provision. By contrast, Brazil's Serviço Nacional de Aprendizagem Industrial (SENAI), one of the most successful vocational systems in the developing world, is administered by the Confederação Nacional da Indústria (Box 2.11).

Vocational education is costly

Evidence from developed and developing countries suggests that technical and vocational education is relatively costly to provide. In the fourteen OECD countries for which data are available, expenditure per student is around 15% more than in general education (OECD, 2008*b*). Evidence from sub-Saharan Africa suggests that vocational education is up to fourteen times more expensive than general secondary education (Johanson and Adams, 2004).

Public financing plays the central role in paying for vocational provision through the secondary school system. In dual systems, training costs are typically shared by governments and employers. For example, in Germany, companies cover apprenticeship costs while regional governments pay for the school-based component (Ryan, 2001). Many governments mobilize private finance for national training programmes through payroll taxes levied on companies. Egypt's Training Finance Fund is supported through a 1% levy on payroll taxes (DFID and World Bank, 2005). Twelve countries in sub-Saharan Africa impose a similar levy, albeit on a far narrower tax base (Adams, 2007*b*).

Companies play an important and expanding role

There is strong evidence that investment in training for young people in the workplace is good for the companies involved, for individuals and for national economies. However, governments have to address the fact that workplace training is not always shared fairly. Levels of investment in training tend to rise with the size of the company and the level of

18. 'Tracking' refers to the practice of separating students into different school types, typically academic vs. vocational, at the scondary level.

19. Decisions over the tracking of students are often taken as early as age 10 to 12. The top tier of schooling – *gymnasium* – paves the way to university. Only 18% of immigrant children make it to this top track, compared with 47% of German students. Meanwhile, 40% of immigrant children attend the lowest branch – twice the share for students from German families.

20. The Industrial Vocational Training Board in Mauritius is one example. In Chile, the Servicio Nacional de Capacitación y Empleo (SENCE) has no capacity for delivering training but contracts services from a range of public and private providers.

education of the workforce. While over 80% of companies in Kenya and Zambia with more than 150 employers are active trainers, under 5% of those with fewer than 10 workers fall into this category (Adams, 2007*b*; Tan, 2006). Several countries have adopted innovative approaches aimed at extending company-based opportunities for skills development. Singapore's Skills Development Fund and Malaysia's Human Resources Development Fund are financed by a 1% levy on wages, with the revenue used to subsidize training for workers in smaller companies.[21]

Vocational training through secondary schools

Technical and vocational education is offered through a bewildering array of institutional arrangements, public and private providers, and financing systems, so cross-country comparisons have to be treated with caution. The weakness of many national reporting systems, combined with a lack of consistency, adds a further layer of complication (UNEVOC and UIS, 2006).

Mapping a diverse sector. Detailed mapping of technical and vocational education reveals some broad patterns. The most common format is entry in middle school or upper secondary school, or through college courses combining general and vocational learning. Most courses at this level orient students towards labour markets, though some offer a route into tertiary or general education. Some developed countries, including France and Germany, introduce 'pre-vocational' courses in lower secondary, often targeting them at what are deemed the less academic students. In many developing countries, early tracking is the rule rather than the exception. In the United Republic of Tanzania, two out of three vocational students are tracked after primary school, with the remainder entering specialized technical schools after completing general education (Kahyarara and Teal, 2006).

Participation in technical and vocational education has increased alongside the general expansion of secondary education, but the degree to which secondary education has been 'vocationalized' varies markedly (Lauglo and Maclean, 2005). In 2007, 16% of secondary school students in developed countries were in technical and vocational education, compared with 9% in developing countries.[22] Technical and vocational shares were lowest in secondary enrolment in sub-Saharan Africa (6%), and South and West Asia (2%). (Table 2.4)

Box 2.11: Private vocational training in Brazil: widespread and successful

The best-known graduate of Brazil's Serviço Nacional de Aprendizagem Industrial (SENAI) is President Luiz Inácio Lula da Silva, who trained there as a mechanic.

SENAI operates one of the world's largest integrated vocational systems, administered by the Confederação Nacional da Indústria (National Confederation of Industry). Delivering courses through about 700 training centres in twenty-seven states, it trains 2.8 million professionals a year. Working with government agencies, SENAI has established rigorous, world-class standards for training and certification, enabling graduates to switch between employers and states.

Financed through a payroll tax on industry, the SENAI system is managed by entrepreneurs. Companies play an important role in identifying priority areas for training and in the design of courses. Administration also involves national and regional governments, and trade unions.

Source: SENAI (2009).

Behind these regional averages are very large differences between countries (Annex, Statistical Table 7). In thirteen of the twenty-five countries in sub-Saharan Africa with data, the share of technical and vocational education in secondary enrolment was less than 5%. In Latin America, coverage ranges from less than 5% in Brazil, the Dominican Republic and Nicaragua to over 30% in Argentina and Honduras. Developed countries, too, demonstrate wide variation. Reported enrolment in technical and vocational education at the secondary level ranges from less than 20% in fourteen countries, including France, Spain and the United Kingdom, to over 45% in the Netherlands.

In the United Republic of Tanzania, two out of three vocational students are tracked after primary school

Secondary school enrolment – unequal convergence. One way to assess participation in technical and vocational education is to measure the proportion of secondary school students who are enrolled in such programmes. But to avoid getting a distorted picture, the fact that countries vary widely in levels of secondary school participation must be taken into account. While developing countries have been increasing participation in secondary education and beyond, that process has been highly unequal.

Table 2.5 shows the limits of current progress. Developed countries have achieved near universal secondary education and progression into tertiary education has increased, with the gross enrolment ratio reaching 67% in 2007. Developing regions are catching up at varying speeds and from different

21. Singapore's fund reaches 65% of enterprises with between ten and forty-nine workers. Malaysia's includes a facility for supporting small enterprises in developing training plans and offers incentives for larger firms with excess training capacity to offer places to workers from smaller firms.

22. This uses the conventional benchmark of ICSED 2 and 3 for lower and upper secondary education levels.

Table 2.4: Enrolment in technical and vocational education (TVE) by region, 2007

	Total enrolment in secondary		Total enrolment in TVE			
	Total (000)	Female (%)	Total (000)	Female (%)	% of school age population	% of total enrolment in secondary
World	518 721	47	54 024	46	7	10
Developing countries	409 125	47	37 044	47	6	9
Developed countries	83 335	49	13 553	43	16	16
Countries in transition	26 261	48	3 428	40	12	13
Sub-Saharan Africa	35 580	44	2 221	39	2	6
Arab States	27 453	47	3 157	43	7	11
Central Asia	10 891	48	1 271	46	11	12
East Asia and the Pacific	165 769	48	23 658	49	11	14
East Asia	162 324	48	22 550	49	11	14
Pacific	3 445	48	1 109	44	34	32
South and West Asia	125 705	44	2 412	27	1	2
Latin America and the Caribbean	58 547	51	6 275	54	9	11
Caribbean	1 294	50	51	49	2	4
Latin America	57 253	51	6 225	54	10	11
North America and Western Europe	62 401	49	8 645	43	14	14
Central and Eastern Europe	32 375	48	6 385	39	17	20

Source: Annex, Statistical Table 8.

Table 2.5: Gross enrolment ratios in secondary and tertiary education, 1999 and 2007

	Gross enrolment ratios in secondary (%)				Gross enrolment ratios in tertiary (%)			
	School year ending in				School year ending in			
	1999		2007		1999		2007	
	Total	GPI (F/M)	Total	GPI (F/M)	Total	GPI (F/M)	Total	GPI (F/M)
World	60	0.92	66	0.95	18	0.96	26	1.08
Developing countries	52	0.89	61	0.94	11	0.78	18	0.96
Developed countries	100	1.00	100	1.00	55	1.19	67	1.29
Countries in transition	91	1.01	90	0.98	39	1.21	58	1.29
Sub-Saharan Africa	24	0.82	34	0.79	4	0.67	6	0.66
Arab States	60	0.89	65	0.92	19	0.74	22	1.05
Central Asia	85	0.99	95	0.98	18	0.93	24	1.10
East Asia and the Pacific	65	0.96	78	1.01	14	0.75	26	1.00
East Asia	64	0.96	77	1.01	13	0.73	25	0.99
Pacific	111	0.99	105	0.96	47	1.24	53	1.31
South and West Asia	45	0.75	52	0.85	7	0.64	11	0.77
Latin America and the Caribbean	80	1.07	89	1.08	21	1.12	34	1.19
Caribbean	53	1.03	58	1.03	6	1.30	7	1.36
Latin America	81	1.07	90	1.08	22	1.12	35	1.19
North America and Western Europe	100	0.99	100	1.00	61	1.23	70	1.33
Central and Eastern Europe	87	0.98	88	0.96	38	1.18	62	1.25

Source: Annex, Statistical Tables 8 and 9A.

starting points. Secondary gross enrolment levels ranged from 34% in sub-Saharan Africa to 65% in the Arab States and 90% in Latin America in 2007. Tertiary enrolment was just 6% in sub-Saharan Africa, compared with 22% in the Arab States and 35% in Latin America. These regional averages conceal large intra-regional disparities. While the average secondary participation level was 90% in Latin America and the Caribbean, it was less than 70% for some countries in the region, including El Salvador, Guatemala, Honduras and Nicaragua.

Gender disparities in secondary school have an important bearing on opportunities for technical and vocational education. The two regions with the largest gender disparities are South and West Asia, and sub-Saharan Africa. While the former has achieved a marked improvement in gender parity since 1999, the latter has moved in the opposite direction: the secondary-level GPI for sub-Saharan Africa has slipped from 0.82 to 0.79. This points to the importance of public policy interventions to strengthen opportunities for young girls to make the transition from primary to secondary school. In Latin America and the Caribbean, where more girls than boys attend secondary school, there has been no progress in narrowing the gender gap.

Gender inequalities are often more pronounced in technical and vocational education than in general education. In South and West Asia, and sub-Saharan Africa, girls accounted for 44% of students in secondary school in 2007, but just 27% and 39%, respectively, in technical and vocational education. In nine of the eleven Arab states for which data are available, girls accounted for less than 40% of enrolment. The same is true for twelve of the twenty-five countries in sub-Saharan Africa with reported data. These disparities tell only a small part of a far wider story of gender inequality. In many cases, young girls in technical and vocational streams are being trained for traditional female occupations, often in areas characterized by low pay. Moreover, returns to vocational education are often lowered by gender discrimination in employment and wages.

Prospects for successful vocational education provision are inevitably shaped by the wider learning environment. One of the lessons from successful countries in East Asia and elsewhere is that high levels of literacy, numeracy and broad-based general education are the real foundation for acquiring flexible and transferrable vocational skills. Many countries lack the foundation.

Consider the prospects for 15-year-olds in different parts of the world (Figure 2.24). In OECD countries, 85% of 15- to 19-year-olds are in full-time education and at 15 a student can expect to continue for seven more years (Kuczera et al., 2008; OECD, 2008*b*). This compares with less than one year in South and West Asia. In sub-Saharan Africa, the average 15-year-old does not attend school. In countries including Burkina Faso, Ethiopia and Mozambique, more than 75% of young people who do not go to school report having no education (Garcia and Fares, 2008).

Failures in basic education have important consequences for technical and vocational education. In sub-Saharan Africa, and South and West Asia, technical and vocational education reaches 1% to 2% of the total secondary school age group (Table 2.4). One reason for this is that, in many countries in both regions, only a small share of the secondary school age population reaches the middle grades of secondary school.

One important policy conclusion to be drawn from the data in these regions is that no national policy for developing skills is likely to succeed unless governments dramatically increase the flow of students into secondary school.

In sub-Saharan Africa, the average 15-year-old does not attend school

The foundations for learning are established in primary school and nurtured in the early secondary

Figure 2.24: By age 15, many students in developing countries are nearing the end of their schooling

School life expectancy from primary to tertiary education, by region, 2007

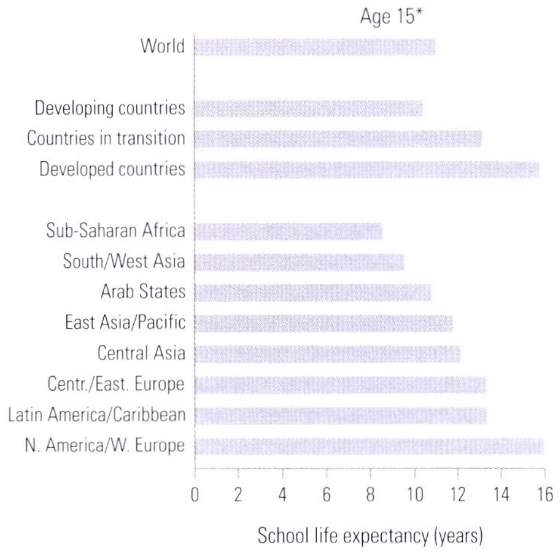

* This is a theoretical threshold that assumes an intake age of 6 in all regions.
Source: Annex, Statistical Table 4.

Youth aged 15 to 24 make up one-quarter of the world's population but almost half of the unemployed

school years. People lacking these foundations are not well placed to develop the type of flexible problem-solving capabilities needed to underpin more specialized learning. For countries where much of the youth population either does not reach secondary school or lacks basic literacy and numeracy, technical and vocational education in secondary school can only have limited success as a national skills development strategy. It may make little sense to rapidly scale up investment in technical and vocational education in countries enrolling only a small proportion of the secondary school age group. Directing resources towards improving access and the quality of education in core subjects is likely to prove far more effective and equitable (Lauglo and Maclean, 2005).

Youth unemployment reveals the skills gap

The broad aim of technical and vocational education is to equip young people and adults with the skills and knowledge they need to cross the bridge from school to work. The economic crisis has made that crossing even more hazardous. Young people who fail to make the transition often face the prospect of long-term unemployment and social marginalization, and run a higher risk of being drawn into illicit activities (Adams, 2008; Brewer, 2004).

While the picture varies by region, governments' records in tackling youth unemployment over the past decade have been disappointing. With global unemployment rising sharply in 2009, the record could deteriorate further as young people are hit hardest by the job crisis.

Pre-crisis trends were not encouraging

Education and demographic trends, coupled with rapid economic growth before the 2008 economic downturn, might have been expected to reduce youth unemployment, with the average number of years spent in school increasing and the youth share in the working age population declining in all regions, with the notable exception of sub-Saharan Africa.

Instead, the International Labour Organization (ILO) reported a 13% rise in youth unemployment, from 63 million in 1996 to 71 million in 2007. Labour market demand is one factor behind this trend. Economic growth has not generated employment on the scale that might have been anticipated. At the same time, rising youth unemployment during a period of sustained economic expansion points to a mismatch between skills acquired in education and labour market demand. The upshot is that young people bear the brunt of unemployment. Before the crisis, the global youth unemployment rate stood at 12%, or around three times the adult unemployment rate (ILO, 2008*a*). In every region, youth unemployment rates are higher than those for older workers. Youth aged 15 to 24 make up one-quarter of the world's population but almost half of the unemployed.

Young people are now in the front line of the global economic downturn. Recent estimates suggest that world unemployment could be 39 million higher by the end of 2009, compared with 2007, and that youth unemployment may rise by between 5 million and 17.7 million. The youth unemployment rate is projected to increase from around 12% in 2008 to between 14% and 15% in 2009 (CINTERFOR/ILO, 2009). Employers are more prone to dismiss young workers – especially unskilled young women – because youth tend to have the least secure employment conditions and are often not covered by labour regulations (CINTERFOR/ILO, 2009).

Youth unemployment patterns vary across the developing regions (Figure 2.25). The ILO reports that the Middle East and North Africa have the highest unemployment rates, with about one-fifth of 15- to 24-year-olds unemployed. In Egypt, youth account for more than 60% of the unemployed. Gender discrimination, both in terms of job segmentation and wages, is deeply entrenched in Arab States' labour markets (Salehi-Isfahani and Dhillon, 2008). In Egypt, fewer than one-quarter of women aged 15 to 29 are economically active – one-third the male rate. The transition from school to work is also more difficult for girls, with fewer than 25% of young women finding work within five years (Assad and Barsoum, 2007). Employer discrimination, early marriage and claims on the labour of women at home all reinforce gender disadvantage in labour markets.

Demography and poverty combine to leave sub-Saharan Africa facing particularly stark challenges in youth employment. The region's share of the world's youth population, currently about 17%, will be some 25% by 2025. Almost two-thirds of the population is under 25. The transition from school to work is enormously difficult for this growing population. Every year between 7 million and 10 million young Africans enter labour markets characterized by high unemployment, low productivity, chronic insecurity and poverty-level incomes (Garcia and Fares, 2008).

Unemployment is just one of the problems young people encounter as they seek to enter the workforce. Many face protracted delays in securing their first jobs. In much of the Middle East and North Africa, the average duration of unemployment for first-time job seekers is measured in years rather than months. In sub-Saharan African countries including Ethiopia, Malawi, Mozambique and Zambia, young people face about five years of reported inactivity before finding work (Garcia and Fares, 2008).

Education is not an automatic panacea for delayed employment. In many Arab states, young people with secondary and tertiary education face longer periods of unemployment than their peers with only basic education. Similarly, in several countries of sub-Saharan Africa, including Burundi, Cameroon, Kenya and Nigeria, youth with secondary and tertiary education have higher rates of unemployment than those with lower levels of attainment (Fares et al., 2005; Garcia and Fares, 2008).

Comparisons across developing regions have to be made with caution. Gender parity in reported youth unemployment in South Asia and sub-Saharan Africa does not imply gender equity in labour markets. In both regions, many young women provide unpaid labour in the household and do not participate in paid employment.[23] Similarly, lower levels of youth unemployment do not necessarily correspond to higher levels of decent employment. Poverty forces millions of people into insecure, low-wage jobs in the informal sector. The ILO estimates that 300 million young people are 'working poor' who live on less than US$2 a day (CINTERFOR/ILO, 2009).

Developed countries also face acute problems

Economic recession in OECD countries is pushing unemployment to record levels. In developed countries as a group, unemployment is projected to peak at 7.3% in 2010, compared with 5.5% in 2007 (OECD, 2009*d*). The scenario could worsen if economic recovery is delayed.

As in developing regions, the economic downturn in rich countries comes against a discouraging backdrop for youth employment (Figure 2.26). Despite strong economic growth from 1997 to 2007, the youth unemployment rate in OECD countries

Figure 2.25: Gender inequalities reinforce high levels of youth unemployment

Youth unemployment rates by region and gender, 2007*

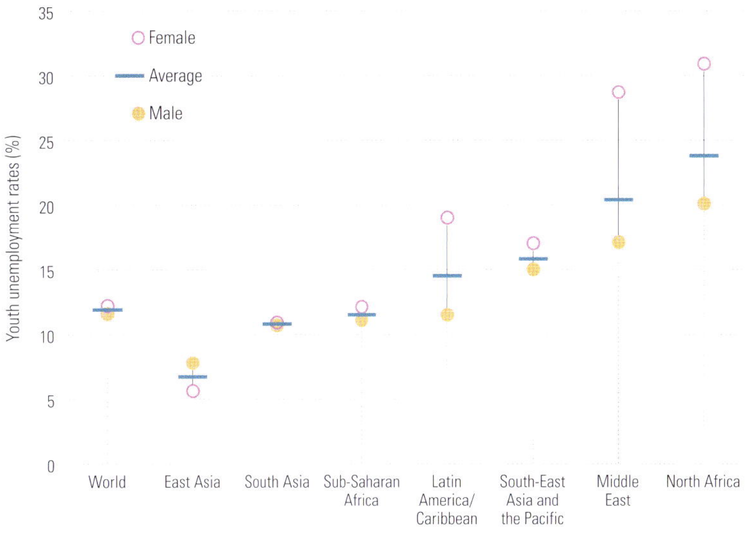

* Regions presented are those used by the ILO, which differ to some extent from the EFA regions.
Sources: ILO (2008*b*); OECD (2009*f*).

Figure 2.26: In most OECD countries, youth face greater risk of unemployment

Youth and adult unemployment rates, selected OECD countries, 2008

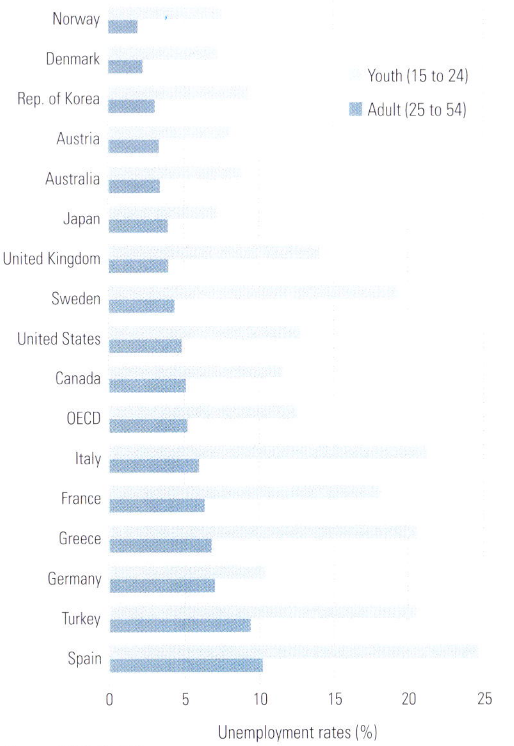

Source: OECD (2009*f*).

In Burundi, Cameroon, Kenya and Nigeria, youth with secondary and tertiary education have higher rates of unemployment than those with lower levels of attainment

23. In South Asia, the ILO reports just 22% of female youth in employment compared with 58% of male youth.

fell only a little, from 15% to 13% (CINTERFOR/ILO, 2008). While some countries, including Australia, Canada, France and Spain, achieved marked reductions, six other countries, including the United Kingdom, experienced increased youth unemployment.

Young people with low skills are especially vulnerable, as was evident even before the deep recession took hold. In the OECD, for example, skilled jobs have been created at five times the rate of unskilled jobs since 2000 (OECD, 2008*b*). The skills gap helps explain the apparent paradox of high growth and stagnant youth unemployment in many countries. In the OECD countries as a group, people with low skills are twice as likely to be unemployed as those with high skills, increasing to four times as likely in the United States. The rising premium on skills has increased the penalties faced by those in the OECD's large pockets of educational deprivation.

Spiralling youth unemployment has added a sense of urgency to national debates over technical and vocational training. While the impact of the economic slowdown is being felt across society, it has fallen most heavily on the young and people with low skills (OECD, 2009*d*). Young people typically find it hard to get established in the labour market because of their lack of experience, which makes them especially vulnerable in a downturn. The young in general and those with low levels of qualification in particular are emerging as prime victims of the slump.

Spiralling youth unemployment has added a sense of urgency to national debates over technical and vocational training

A side effect of the downturn is that it has pushed technical and vocational education and training to the centre of the political agenda. In France, where even before the crisis almost one in five young people was out of work, a quarter of them for more than one year, the government has launched an emergency youth employment programme focused on apprenticeships (CINTERFOR/ILO, 2009). In Japan, though youth unemployment rates are lower than in France, around one-third of workers aged 15 to 24 are in temporary work with insecure contracts (OECD, 2009*c*). Here, too, measures have been introduced to facilitate school-to-work transition through firm-based training. Comparable measures involving incentives for young people to stay in education, training and apprenticeships are being used across the OECD.

Looking beyond the immediate responses, it is important for governments to use the crisis as an opportunity to put in place the long-term investments and policies – in education and beyond – that are needed to combat the marginalization of young people.

Good intentions, poor results: problems in the developing world

Much can be achieved through good-quality vocational education and training. But in many developing countries, vocational programmes have suffered from a combination of underfinancing, poor design and weak links to labour markets. In some regions – notably sub-Saharan Africa and Latin America – deep cuts in spending during the 1980s and 1990s further compromised quality in vocational education (Johanson and Adams, 2004). Public investment has produced disappointing results, calling into question the potential for vocational education to fuel economic growth and reduce poverty.

The poor track record is reflected in student and teacher preferences. In many countries, vocational options are viewed either as a last resort or as a possible route back into general education, rather than as a stepping stone to employment. This is especially true of sub-Saharan Africa, where the reluctance of parents to put their children into vocational streams is supported by evidence confirming that general education generates far higher returns than do vocational alternatives (Kahyarara and Teal, 2006). Thailand adopted the German dual system in 2005; successive governments have attempted to expand vocational education to combat child labour and the marginalization of young people who drop out of school. However, while secondary school enrolment has doubled, vocational enrolment has failed to take off, reflecting concerns of parents and students about the quality of provision and the weakness of links to job markets (World Bank, 2008*g*).

The Middle East: fragmentation and weak links to employment

Faced with the world's highest levels of youth unemployment, governments in the Middle East have identified vocational education as a priority. Two broad models have emerged. At one extreme, students in Egypt are tracked early, but vocational graduates suffer as much unemployment as their secondary school counterparts (Kamel, 2006; Salehi-Isfahani and Dhillon, 2008). In the Islamic Republic of Iran, where tracking into vocational education starts later, it is seen as a sign of failure, prompting many students to drop out. (Box 2.12).

Box 2.12: Training, skills and youth exclusion in the Islamic Republic of Iran

The Islamic Republic of Iran's experience demonstrates the challenges facing policy-makers across the Middle East. Over the past twenty years, the country has made rapid strides in education. Participation at secondary level has increased, average years in education have nearly doubled and gender inequalities have narrowed, especially in urban areas. Vocational education, however, reinforces a mismatch between skills and jobs that perpetuates high youth unemployment.

The education system in the country is heavily oriented towards the university entrance exam, the *concour*, which parents and students see as a route to secure employment, usually in the public sector. Compulsory education ends at around age 15, when students are evaluated and directed on to three separate tracks: the academic curriculum (*Nazari*), technical and vocational education (*Fanni-Herfei*) and basic skills through on-the-job training (*Kardanesh*). The aim of the latter two is explicitly to focus on job skills, but the system fails on several fronts.

Tracking brings high levels of attrition. Of the female students who began their secondary education in 2003/2004, nearly one-third dropped out after tracking (Figure 2.27). Most students pursue the *Nazari* track with a view to passing the *concour*, spurning the vocational tracks because of their low perceived status and quality. But of the nearly 1.5 million who proceed each year to the *concour*, 1.2 million fail and leave school lacking qualifications and job skills.

Iranian policy-makers increasingly recognize the problems with the current system. Of particular concern are the misalignment of education and labour markets, and the poor quality of vocational education, which operates through a network of highly centralized public training centres. Many of these lack equipment and well-trained instructors, and they produce qualifications that employers see as having limited relevance.

The *concour* system creates further problems. Most of the exams are multiple choice, and teaching methods emphasize rote learning. Students other than those entering elite engineering and medical schools often emerge ill prepared to enter productive enterprises.

The mismatch between education and employment is becoming increasingly stark. Steady economic growth has reduced overall unemployment, but youth unemployment remains over 20%. Those who completed upper secondary education have the highest level of unemployment (Figure 2.28). Measured in terms of employment, the benefits of education are dwindling, along with the skills base of the Iranian economy.

Education is only part of the story. Labour market rigidity and discrimination also play a role. Gender barriers to employment appear to be rising, with unemployment rates among women aged 20 to 24 now twice the level for men of that age group.

Whatever the underlying causes, the skills mismatch is a pressing political concern. The rising proportion of young people in the population means the labour force is expanding by almost 4% a year, or nearly 1.2 million people. Many of them will face social exclusion if the Islamic Republic of Iran fails to create enough jobs and give its people the skills they need to fill them.

Sources: Salehi-Isfahani and Egel (2007); Povey (2005).

Figure 2.27: In the Islamic Republic of Iran, vocational tracking comes with high dropout rates

Cohort tracking at lower secondary level, students entered in 2003

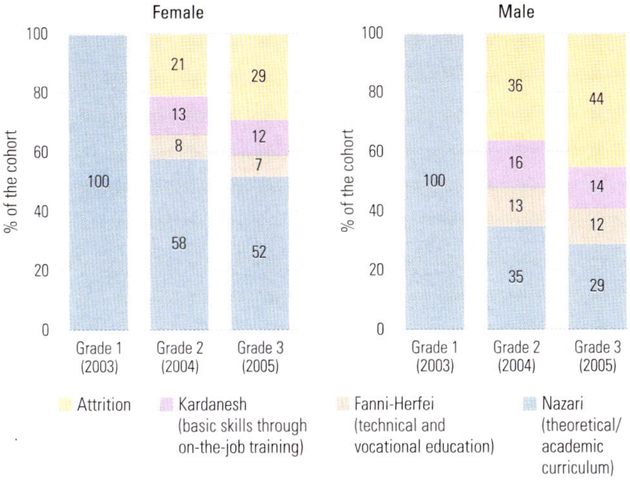

Source: Salehi-Isfahani and Egel (2007).

Figure 2.28: Unemployment increases with level of education, but Iranian women are especially penalized

Unemployment rates by educational attainment and gender, 2005

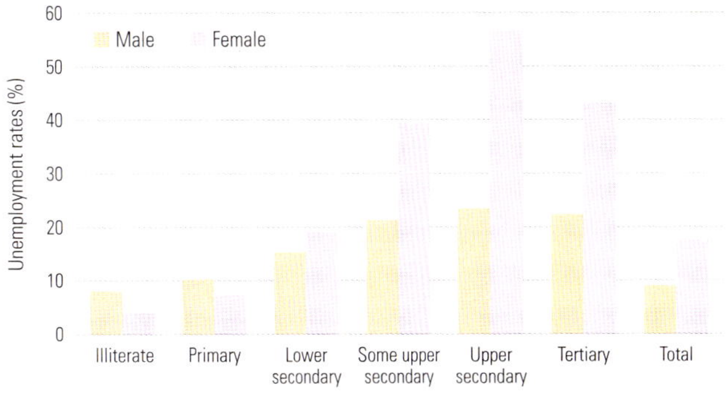

Source: Salehi-Isfahani and Egel (2007).

High youth unemployment in the Middle East is about far more than a failure of vocational education. Slow economic growth, rigid labour markets and gender discrimination have all stymied job creation. In many cases, education systems are part of the employment problem. Courses are geared towards rote learning for university entrance exams that are seen as a route to public sector employment. The upshot is that millions of youth leave school without employable skills and millions more emerge from university lacking the capabilities needed to compete for entry into private sector employment (Salehi-Isfahani and Dhillon, 2008).

Most parents and students in the Middle East see vocational education as unattractive because it receives meagre budget resources, is often delivered by badly trained teachers lacking in motivation, bears little relation to the skills employers seek and produces certificates that are not subject to uniform standards. Part of the problem in many countries is that the private sector has a limited voice in setting priorities and standards (DFID and World Bank, 2005). As a result, the skills delivered through vocational programmes are often of little relevance. In addition, governance typically falls to a range of ministries and government agencies, so it is often fragmented and poorly coordinated. There are some notable exceptions. In Egypt, innovative partnerships are bringing together governments, business and donors.[24] And Morocco has adopted far-reaching governance reforms aimed at improving quality, relevance and equity (Box 2.13).

In the Middle East, millions of youth leave school without employable skills

Box 2.13: Morocco – strengthening vocational governance

In Morocco, vocational education has been overhauled in the past decade. It has its own ministry and a national office for vocational training and work promotion. Syllabuses are adapted to trainees' general education level, with an emphasis on a combination of specific skills and broader capabilities. Vocational schools have achieved good results, with more than half of graduates finding a job within nine months. The proportion of female trainees is rising, reaching 44% in 2006. The vocational system is expanding as the government seeks to foster the skills needed by new sectors such as vehicle manufacture, aeronautics and agro-industry.

Source: African Development Bank/OECD (2008*d*).

24. One prominent example is the Mubarak-Kohl initiative, an arrangement involving the Ministry of Education, the German technical cooperation agency GTZ and business associations. The government provides premises, GTZ supplies technical experts and equipment, and business associations contribute training opportunities and allowances. So far, around 16,000 trainees have been trained in 1,600 companies through 45 technical secondary schools.

In India, limited reach and duplication

Technical and vocational education systems in many countries suffer from inadequate reach as well as limited benefits for participants. In India, only 3% of rural youth and 6% of urban youth have had any kind of vocational training (India Ministry of Health and Family Welfare, 2006; India Planning Commission, 2008). The country's Industrial Training Institutes and various craft centres are not accessible to the vast majority of the poor. India also has some of the world's largest reported gender disparities in technical and vocational education, with girls accounting for just 7% of enrolment at the secondary level and their courses heavily concentrated in traditional areas such as nursing and sewing. In general, the benefits of vocational training are not immediately apparent. Some 60% of graduates from Industrial Training Institutes are still unemployed three years later (World Bank, 2006*g*). Industrial apprentices are more likely to get work, but generally not in the trade for which they trained.

Governance problems have hampered India's efforts to strengthen vocational education. Responsibilities are split among the Ministry of Labour, the Ministry of Human Resource Development, other national bodies and state authorities. Duplication and fragmentation are widespread, there is little control over quality and the certification system is poorly understood by employers. Companies and employer organizations are only marginally involved, though efforts are being made to strengthen their engagement.

Sub-Saharan Africa: failing to reach the marginalized

Governments in sub-Saharan Africa face some of the toughest challenges in reforming technical and vocational education. Finance is part of the problem – institutions across the region suffer from a familiar combination of underinvestment in equipment, low pay for instructors and problems recruiting qualified staff. But not all the difficulties can be traced to financial causes.

Many countries track students into vocational education far too early – often in the face of concerted resistance from parents. Parental concerns are often well grounded. Evaluations point to low rates of absorption of graduates into employment – under half in some countries, including Madagascar, Mali and the United Republic of Tanzania (Johanson and Adams, 2004). The resulting unemployment, even in countries where employers face shortages of skilled secondary school graduates, points to a mismatch between learning and labour market needs.

The high cost of vocational education is another factor. Partly because class sizes are much smaller than in general education and the cost of equipment is higher, vocational education faces far higher per capita costs – about twelve times the average for primary school and four times that for secondary school (Atchoarena and Delluc, 2001).

Problems in vocational education are a legacy of past policy failures and a difficult environment. The quality of provision suffered enormously with deep cuts in spending under structural adjustment programmes in the 1980s and 1990s. Wider problems have also been evident. Vocational systems were designed to meet the needs of formal sector employers, notably in government (Adams, 2008; Africa Commission, 2008). For at least three decades, however, formal sector job creation has stagnated while informal sector employment has grown in importance. In most countries, informal employment and self-employment dominate in both rural and urban areas, typically accounting for over 80% of total employment.[25] Providing training to those employed in the informal sector involves reaching people with lower levels of education. A survey covering Kenya, Senegal, the United Republic of Tanzania, Zambia and Zimbabwe reported that half of informal sector workers had only primary education, if any (Haan, 2006; Liimatainen, 2002).

The need to reduce poverty makes it vital to reach these people, yet most vocational systems fail to deliver. Traditional apprenticeships and on-the-job training are by far the most important routes to skills development for the vast majority of African youth (ILO, 2007; Wachira et al., 2008). On one estimate they account for up to 70% of overall training (Liimatainen, 2002). The strength of traditional apprenticeships is that they provide youth who have low levels of education with practical, employable skills (Monk et al., 2008). On a more negative note, apprenticeships tend to be biased against young women and the very poor. They also perpetuate the use of traditional methods, offering little theoretical knowledge (Adams, 2008).

Vocational education could help redress the equity balance by targeting those who face the most acute disadvantages. Unfortunately, evidence from national evaluations points in the opposite direction. Research in Ghana has highlighted a bias towards regions and social groups that are already better off (Box 2.14). The broader failure to integrate technical and vocational education into strategies for reaching marginalized groups is clear in results from recent evaluations (based on Garcia and Fares, 2008):

- In Burkina Faso, only one-third of interventions involving technical and vocational education were oriented towards disadvantaged groups, mainly through micro-credit programmes.
- In the United Republic of Tanzania, out of twenty-eight programmes reviewed, only three targeted the poorest youth, one targeted youth with no education and three targeted rural areas (where the vast majority of the poor live).
- In a region where 95 million young men and women have no education and are unemployed, have low-paying jobs or have withdrawn from the labour force, second-chance programmes are virtually non-existent. A review covering Burkina Faso, Ethiopia, Uganda and the United Republic of Tanzania concluded that 'most second-chance interventions are small in scale, underevaluated and face severe challenges for sustainability and scalability (Garcia and Fares, 2008, p. xxx).'

Vocational education is failing to target those who face the most acute disadvantages

The problems evident in vocational education in sub-Saharan Africa are widely recognized by governments, regional organizations and aid donors (Africa Commission, 2008; COMEDAF II+, 2007). Across the region, vocational education is undergoing major reform. Several countries have created or strengthened national training authorities, reformed qualification systems and created structures giving the private sector a stronger voice:

- In Cameroon, the four ministries involved in vocational education have developed a sector-wide plan linked to the national poverty reduction strategy (African Development Bank, 2008*a*).
- In Ethiopia, new curricula have been drawn up and qualification systems restructured to bolster the development of skills that labour markets need (African Development Bank, 2008*b*).
- In Rwanda, a strategy adopted in 2007 sets out ambitious goals for changing the image of vocational education. A Workforce Development Agency has been created to oversee coordination and facilitate private sector involvement (African Development Bank/OECD, 2008*f*).

25. Reporting conventions make it difficult to compare across countries (Adams, 2008). The reported share of informal employment in total employment ranges from over 90% in Mali (where agriculture is included) to 22% in the United Republic of Tanzania (where agriculture is excluded).

Box 2.14: Vocational education in Ghana – limited access and poor quality

Since independence half a century ago, political leaders in Ghana have seen technical and vocational education as a means of generating jobs. Yet vocational programmes have suffered from fragmented administration, a proliferation of qualification standards and poor quality.

Public vocational education in Ghana operates through two tracks. The first, extending from lower secondary to post-secondary, is administered by the Ministry of Education and Social Service and operates through Technical Training Institutes. The second track is run by National Vocational Training Institutes attached to the Ministry of Manpower, Youth and Employment. Several other ministries, agencies and private institutions are involved, each offering its own programmes.

The pipeline into vocational education starts in junior secondary school, but parents and students tend to shun vocational streams, with just 5% of students entering public vocational institutions. The share of adults aged 20 to 26 years with formal vocational training stood at just 2% in 2005.

Reviews of Ghana's vocational system have consistently highlighted problems of coherence and coordination. Political oversight has been minimal. Despite what one report describes as a 'dizzying array' of examinations, programmes have failed to provide the skills employers seek. One reason is a multiplicity of certification and testing standards developed without employer advice.

The quality of instruction is far from satisfactory. Ill-trained instructors, low salaries and outdated equipment all contribute. While some public institutions do provide high-quality training, they remain the exception.

There are few evaluations of the benefits of vocational education for Ghana's youth. The available evidence suggests that graduates of the public system, including polytechnics, are prone to high unemployment. This is unsurprising given that teaching is geared towards the demands of the small formal sector, rather than an informal sector that on one estimate delivers 80% to 90% of skills training.

The cost side of the equation is better understood. Vocational programmes account for about 1% of the education budgets. However, recurrent per capita costs in 2006 were five times higher than in primary education and almost three times higher than in senior secondary.

Equity is another major concern. While policy documents emphasize the importance of linking vocational education to the national poverty reduction strategy, marginalized groups are effectively excluded. Participation rises with income levels, with the richest quintile seven times more likely than the poorest to have received vocational education. Regional inequality is marked: the northern region, Ghana's poorest, has one of the lowest levels of vocational enrolment. There is a bias towards males, especially in urban areas. And vocational graduates are twenty times more likely to work in the formal sector than be self-employed as farmers, reflecting a bias against agriculture.

Rather than counteracting the disadvantages associated with limited access to education, apprenticeship programmes have the opposite effect – young people with an incomplete primary education are half as likely to make it into apprenticeship as those with a secondary education.

The government has adopted reforms aimed at establishing a more efficient and equitable system. The Council for Technical and Vocational Education and Training was created in 2006 as an autonomous oversight body, along with the Skills Training and Employment Placement (STEP) programme which targets low-skilled unemployed youth seeking apprenticeships. It is too early to evaluate the latest reforms.

Sources: Adams et al. (2008); African Development Bank/OECD (2008*c*); Akyeampong (2007); Ghana Ministry of Education, Youth and Sports (2004*a*, 2004*b*); Palmer (2007).

In Ghana, vocational programmes have suffered from fragmented administration and poor quality

There are also signs that vocational education is re-emerging as a priority in development assistance. Several countries, notably Germany and Japan, have been giving precedence to support for the sector.

It is too early to evaluate the results of the latest wave of reform. In some cases, old models have proved highly resilient. Mozambique's government set out a bold strategy, the Integrated Professional Reform Programme, aimed at bringing vocational planning under a single umbrella, with a unified qualification and accreditation programme (African Development Bank/OECD, 2008*e*). Two years before the end of its first phase, however, there has been little progress in implementing it.

As in other regions, governments in sub-Saharan Africa have to strike a delicate balance between general and technical and vocational education. The overwhelming priority for the region is to increase enrolment, retention and progression through basic education into secondary school. Vocational education has the potential to play a far greater role, however, not least in providing second-chance opportunities to marginalized youth. Public investment and international aid should be directed towards creating opportunities for the poor, in rural areas and in informal employment, with private spending and investment by companies financing training for higher-income groups.

Offering young people a second chance

Technical and vocational education can extend opportunities for young people still in school. But what of the millions of young adults who have never gone to school or have left education with levels of achievement falling far short of what they need? Can vocational education offer an effective 'second chance' for avoiding a future of marginalization? The economic crisis has given that question renewed relevance because young people suffer most when labour demand is reduced.

Comparing the effectiveness of 'second-chance' programmes and wider targeted interventions for combating marginalization through vocational education is inherently difficult because underlying patterns of marginalization vary. In developed countries, the problem is concentrated at the upper secondary level. Data from the United States indicate that nearly 6.2 million of the country's 16- to 24-year-olds – 16% of the age group – have left secondary school with no diploma.[26] In France, about 18% of young people lack minimum secondary school qualifications (OECD, 2009*b*).

The yardstick for measuring education marginalization in developing countries is different. Millions of young people in Latin America and the Arab States, especially those from the poorest households, have just one or two years of secondary school, or less. In many low-income countries, only a minority of young people have been to secondary school at all – and an incomplete primary education is often the norm.[27]

Evaluations around the world show that 'second-chance' programmes can make a difference. Comprehensive approaches that provide training as part of a wider package are more likely to succeed. In the United States, the Job Corps programme offers 16- to 24-year-olds education and training alongside a wide range of support services (Schochet et al., 2003).[28] Modelled partly on the Job Corps experience, the Jóvenes programmes in several Latin American countries, including Argentina, Chile, Peru and Uruguay, have been particularly successful in reaching the marginalized (Box 2.15).

Skills for the twenty-first century

The Jóvenes programmes are effective because they provide an integrated framework for reaching the marginalized and linking employment with skills training. That key principle also underpins another programme in Latin America and the Caribbean, Entra 21, launched in 2001 by the International Youth Foundation to equip unemployed youth with information technology skills. An evaluation in six countries points to encouraging results for both employment and earnings (Box 2.16).

Remedial education combined with flexible courses targeted at marginal populations provides another way to offer the young a second chance. In Bangladesh, a large-scale programme operated by a non-government organization targets young people who have dropped out of formal education. Classes designed to facilitate early catch-up are followed by vocational programmes developed with companies (World Bank, 2006*j*). In Chile, the Califica programme is aimed at youth and young adults who lack formal secondary education. It includes a secondary education equivalency component that enables people over 18 to study in a certified institution and to gain a certificate that facilitates access to a wide range of vocational courses (Gallart, 2008).

'Second-chance' programmes can help combat youth marginalization

Successful second-chance programmes have to be accessible and affordable to people living in poverty, be flexible enough to fit in with the lives of their target population and be seen to deliver results (Jimenez et al., 2007). One of the most successful models has emerged in Mexico. The Open Secondary School system, aimed at young adults who have dropped out of secondary school, offers second-chance opportunities in thirty-three subjects covered in grades 10 to 12. There are no entrance requirements and no time limit on completion, and students can determine their own schedules. The average period for completion is three to five years, after which

26. It is estimated that secondary school dropouts earn US$485,000 less on average during their lifetime than do secondary school graduates (Center for Labor Market Studies, 2007).

27. These issues are taken up in Chapter 3.

28. The evaluation found that students graduating from Job Corps programmes gained an average increase in income of around 12% (Schochet et al., 2003).

Box 2.15: Linking skills and employment – Jóvenes programmes in Latin America

Experience from Jóvenes programmes in Latin America provides some important insights into the conditions for successful youth training.

Initiated in Chile in 1990, Jóvenes programmes are now well established across the region. They reach out to young people, combining technical training and internship with basic life skills and other support services. More than 60% of participants come from low-income families. The programmes tend to raise the probability of employment and higher wages. In Argentina, Proyecto Joven increased employment and wages by about 10% compared with a control group. Although implementation and management structures vary, evaluations show that successful programmes in Argentina, Chile, Peru and Uruguay share some common elements:

- *Strong targeting.* Programmes are aimed at youth from low-income families and those who have low educational attainment and limited work experience. In some cases, preference is given to household heads with children, in order to combat child poverty.
- *Training is linked with work and wider skills.* Most programmes provide training, work experience, literacy and numeracy courses, and a wide range of auxiliary packages, including job search assistance. The training component is aimed at helping participants attain semi-skilled status in trades for which there is demand. Work experience takes place under the auspices of a company, which assumes a tutoring role but is not obliged to pay trainees or guarantee employment. Training and work experience usually last about six months and include broader life skills such as communication, teamwork and self-esteem.
- *Management and coordination.* The state assumes control of programme design, supervision and full or partial financing, but in most countries, training delivery is decentralized. The private sector provides a link to the job market. In Chile, the programme operates through about 1,000 training providers, ranging from companies to non-government organizations.

Sources: Betcherman et al. (2004, 2007); Gallart (2008); Godfrey (2007).

Box 2.16: Entra 21 – tackling marginalization

Unemployed young people whose education has been disrupted often struggle to break into skilled jobs. The Entra 21 programme is aimed at removing barriers to entry through innovative approaches that give people the skills they need to overcome marginalization.

The programme began in 2001 through collaboration between the International Youth Foundation and the Inter-American Development Bank, in six Latin American countries: Bolivia, the Dominican Republic, El Salvador, Panama, Paraguay and Peru. Courses combine technical training, internship and job placement with life skills and job-seeking skills. Employers help with programme design and job placement. An evaluation of the first phase, which covered 20,000 people, found major benefits:

- Among those who registered for Entra 21, 69% were neither studying nor employed; after completion the figure was 24%.
- The share of graduates from the programme in formal education was 42% – double the share at the time of entry to the course. Another 21% were working and studying.
- While most of the jobs documented were in the formal sector (between 75% and 90%, depending on the country), there were several examples of youth-led microenterprise development in the informal sector, especially in El Salvador and Peru.

The second phase of the programme includes measures aimed at strengthening the focus on marginalized youth. It targets 45,000 young people from low-income households and 5,000 facing increased risk as a result of internal displacement or physical disability.

Source: Lasida and Rodriguez (2006).

students can use their qualifications to re-enter the education system (Flores-Moreno, 2007).

While such examples demonstrate what is possible, second-chance education remains a highly neglected area. Effective government coordination of the wide range of public, private and other non-government actors involved is rare, partly because planning for second-chance programmes is seldom integrated into mainstream education.

There are other ways for governments to enhance skills development and combat youth unemployment. One of the most obvious is to ensure that more young people complete their education and achieve a qualification. In the United States, the American Recovery and Reinvestment Act includes financing provisions: youth who have not finished secondary school can re-enter education through a community college, vocational training or apprenticeship. Several states have introduced programmes led by experienced principals and teachers aimed at facilitating secondary school completion, offering comprehensive after-school and vacation teaching (CNN.com/US, 2009).

Governments can also combine education and employment measures. Providing incentives for companies to offer apprenticeship and vocational programmes to unskilled young people is one option. For example, the OECD has argued that France should gear public assistance and incentives for apprenticeships towards unskilled young people and set a benchmark that increases the share of unskilled youth starting training from 40% to 50% (OECD, 2009*b*). In the United Kingdom, which has some of the deepest skill-based inequalities in the OECD, post-crisis interventions have been generating employment and training for long-term unemployed youth (Box 2.17).

Box 2.17: Skills and employment in the United Kingdom

Even before the global downturn, job prospects for young Britons were deteriorating and school-leavers without qualifications faced severe employment disadvantages. From 2002 to 2007, the youth unemployment rate increased from 11% to 14%. With the recession, it has jumped to 17% – the highest level since 1993. Relatively unskilled youngsters leaving school with poor qualifications are bearing the brunt.

Many of the weaknesses in the United Kingdom's vocational training have deep historical roots. Apprenticeship systems have been based on voluntary provision by employers, with little government involvement. Moreover, vocational qualification systems have suffered from high levels of fragmentation and overspecialization.

Reforms were introduced in 2007 aimed at closing the skills gap. Under new legislation, young people will be required to participate in education and training until they obtain a qualification or turn 18. The qualification system is being overhauled and consolidated around seventeen new diplomas, and is set to become operational in 2015. These will be composite qualifications combining theoretical and practical learning, and including an apprenticeship element. In parallel, long-term job seekers aged 18 to 24 are being offered a range of support and training options.

Responses to the financial crisis have built on this framework. Under the 2009 budget, every 18- to 24-year-old unemployed for a year or more is guaranteed an offer of training or a job, with funding made available through local authorities and voluntary organizations. Questions remain about the degree to which the training offered will equip young people for employment.

Sources: Children England (2009); OECD (2008c); UK Learning and Skills Council (2008).

Programmes that deliver results

How successful are technical and vocational systems in providing young people with skills, meeting company demands and tackling the problems of youth unemployment, low wages and insecurity? There are no easy answers to these questions. Vocational programmes do not operate in isolation. Macroeconomic conditions, labour market regulations and investment patterns have a major bearing on their effectiveness. Vocational education has the potential to make a difference in the lives of young people. Yet that potential is weakened in countries relying on top-down, supply-driven models in which governments determine priorities. Moving towards a demand-driven approach that responds to the needs of individuals, companies and the economy is the overriding priority for reform.

Most rigorous evaluations of technical and vocational education programmes come from developed countries. Reviews that control for selection bias broadly suggest that vocational education improves employment prospects but does not necessarily lead to higher pay (Adams, 2007*a*; Bishop and Mañe, 2005; Ryan, 2001). Evidence from Europe indicates that apprenticeship systems reduce youth unemployment and raise entry into higher-wage occupations (Gangl, 2003; Quintini et al., 2007). Traditional apprenticeship programmes are marked by strong gender bias, however. They achieve far less for women in terms of jobs, careers and wages (Adams, 2007*b*).

Traditional apprenticeships offer far less for women in terms of jobs, careers and wages

As policy-makers seek to address the twin challenges posed by rising unemployment and an increasingly knowledge-based economy, some important lessons may be drawn from the better-performing programmes – along with some cautionary notes.

Reinforce the links between education and labour markets. A major strength of the dual system in Germany is the direct link it establishes between school, work experience and practical education in vocational courses. Companies train students to acquire skills relevant to the needs of the enterprise and, through the involvement of government agencies, the wider economy. Using a very different approach, Japan's system has provided students with a route into company-based training and employment. Contrasts with countries including France and the United Kingdom, where links between education and companies have been far weaker, are striking. In the United States, Career Academies operate through less formal contractual arrangements, but establish strong links between students, companies and educators, combining practical employment opportunities with teaching and job counselling. Rigorous evaluation that controls for selection bias points to strong benefits, including an average earnings increase of about 11% (Kemple and Willner, 2008).

There is a growing sense in which 'what you know' is less important than 'what you are able to learn'

Recognize that past achievements are no guarantee of future success. Rapid economic change is continually shifting the environment for vocational education. Germany's dual system has been coming under pressure as employment growth slows in metalworking, engineering and the automobile sector. The number of new apprenticeship places available is in decline (German Federal Ministry of Education and Research, 2006). In Japan, the 'lost decade' of protracted recession of the 1990s led companies to lower their commitments to training and long-term employment. This is reflected in the large and growing share of young workers in insecure or temporary work (OECD, 2009c). The experience of Germany and Japan serves to highlight the important role of economic growth and employment creation in creating demand among employers for technical and vocational education and training. It also underlines the need for state action to renew vocational programmes in the light of changing circumstances, a task heightened by the current economic downturn.

Rethink the outmoded separation of technical and vocational education from general education. Successful participation in knowledge-based employment markets characterized by rapid change requires problem-solving and creative thinking as well as specific technical skills. There is a growing sense in which 'what you know' is less important than 'what you are able to learn'. Rigid tracking into vocational training, especially at an early age, diminishes the prospect of developing flexible skills and restricts individuals' choices. Vocational students need sufficient academic education to broaden their occupational choices and general students need an opportunity to develop practical skills. Innovative reformers are breaking down barriers between vocational and general education. In the Republic of Korea, academic and vocational students in secondary school share as much as 75% of a joint curriculum, creating opportunities for transition in both directions (Adams, 2007*b*). The share of students enrolled in vocational education at the secondary level has been declining as the emphasis shifts to general education to equip students for post-secondary specialization.[29] Several other countries, including Australia and Switzerland, have actively revised qualification systems to allow for greater mobility between general and vocational education (Hoeckel et al., 2008*a*; Hoeckel et al., 2008*b*).

Develop capability-based qualification systems, involving the private sector. In job markets shaped by rapid technological change, young people need expertise that can be applied to acquiring a wide range of skills. Many countries are introducing or strengthening national qualification frameworks, testing students on the basis of broad abilities and allowing training to be used for transferrable credits into technical and general education (Adams, 2007*b*; Hoeckel et al., 2008*b*; Young, 2005). Involving companies in the development of capability-based training is important because they are well placed to pick up employment market signals. In Australia, programmes developed through industry associations and education authorities have been introduced in the final year of secondary school. At the same time, national skills bodies are bringing together employers, teachers and education ministries to develop and deliver curricula that are relevant to the needs of industry. One of the big challenges is to coordinate the diverse array of partners involved into an administrative framework that avoids fragmentation and duplication.

29. In the Republic of Korea, the share of secondary school enrolment in technical and vocational education dropped steadily from around 45% in the mid-1990s to 29% in 2005.

Integrate vocational programmes into national skills strategies. Some of the most successful models demonstrate that long-term planning of skills development can play a critical role in raising productivity, generating economic growth and creating employment. The Republic of Korea and Singapore both aligned vocational programmes with the needs of high-growth sectors, identifying skills bottlenecks and, as the economy developed, gradually shifting the focus of training from secondary schools to specialized technical institutes and higher education (Law, 2008; Lee, 2008). More recently, Viet Nam has invested heavily in technical and vocational education to improve skills in light manufacturing. There is scope for other developing regions to learn from East Asia, but the conditions for success are difficult to reproduce (Fredriksen and Tan, 2008). They include the integration of vocational education into an active policy for industrial development, rapid economic growth, strong state capacity and – critically – rapid progress in expanding good-quality primary and secondary education. Two distinctive features of the vocational success story in East Asia have been missing from the policy environment of many other developing countries. The first is rapid economic growth, which has created demand for skilled labour and resources for training. Second, provision of technical and vocational education in countries such as the Republic of Korea and Singapore has been integrated into broad-based national strategies for industrial development, employment creation and raising living standards through higher levels of skills and productivity (Lall, 2001) (Box 2.18).

Box 2.18: Singapore's 'jewel in the system'

By helping drive economic growth, overcome shortages of skilled labour and reduce social inequalities, technical and vocational education has played a central role in turning Singapore into a high-income country with one of the world's best-performing education systems. The education minister has described the Institute of Technical Education as 'a shining jewel in our system'.

The Institute of Technical Education was established in the early 1990s in response to growing concerns over the education system's ability to meet the demands of a more productive economy and the needs of the young. It is meant for students who register low scores in general academic education. Courses are designed by government and industry. Companies value its graduates highly: over 90% of students were employed within six months of graduating in 2007. As the economy has evolved, the institute has responded with innovative programmes, including partnering with global industry to set up centres of technology in niche areas such as industrial automation, offering joint certificates with companies such as Microsoft and linking with institutes in Germany to offer diplomas in machine technology.

Perhaps the institute's greatest success has been in combating the stigma associated with vocational education. Successive governments have invested heavily in training teachers, involving the private sector as well, so that the institute's facilities are comparable to those of the country's universities. Qualifications from the institute can be used as a route into tertiary-level technical education through polytechnics, or back into academic education through universities. The emphasis on giving confidence to students and tackling the perception of technical and vocational education as a sign of failure helps explain why Singapore's model has succeeded where others have failed.

Source: Goh and Gopinathan (2008).

Conclusion

In recent decades, the rapid rise of knowledge-based economies, along with persistent youth unemployment and the marginalization of young people lacking skills, has prompted governments to review and revalue technical and vocational education. The economic crisis is another driver of change. Emerging reform models are challenging the image of vocational programmes as second-class education.

Governments face very different types of challenges. The problems with the dual system in Germany are not those of vocational education in Ethiopia. As in other areas of education policy, vocational education is not amenable to quick fixes through the import of successful models from other countries. Policies have to be tailored to reflect governments' abilities to manage them, the realities of labour markets and education systems, and institutional history. What is clear is that no government can afford to ignore the importance of skills and learning in supporting economic growth, combating poverty and overcoming social marginalization. Goal 3 of the Dakar Framework for Action sets out a vision for the learning and skills agenda. Now governments and the international community urgently need to develop meaningful benchmarks for measuring progress and credible policies for achieving greater equity. □

Youth and adult literacy

Literacy remains among the most neglected of all education goals

Goal 4: Achieving a 50 per cent improvement in levels of adult literacy by 2015, especially for women, and equitable access to basic and continuing education for all adults.

Youth and adult illiteracy is the price people and countries are paying for the past failures of education systems. When people emerge from their school years lacking basic reading, writing and numeracy skills, they face a lifetime of disadvantage as illiteracy diminishes their social and economic prospects and damages self-esteem. But the consequences of illiteracy extend beyond the individual. When people lack literacy, society as a whole suffers from lost opportunities for higher productivity, shared prosperity and political participation (Fasih, 2008; Kinsella and He, 2009; UIS, 2008*a*; UNESCO, 2005). Beyond the individual and social costs, illiteracy is a violation of human rights and a global blight on the human condition (Maddox, 2008; Oxenham, 2008). Eradicating it is one of the most urgent development challenges of the twenty-first century.

The international community has failed to rise to the challenge. At the World Education Forum in Dakar in 2000, governments pledged to achieve a 50% improvement in levels of adult literacy by 2015. The pledge was ambitious, but the target was achievable. Unfortunately, the goal will be missed by a large margin. In a world with 759 million illiterate young people and adults, there has been a conspicuous lack of urgency and commitment to literacy on the part of political leaders. The many exceptions to the rule serve to demonstrate that far more could have been achieved – and that far more can be done to get closer to the 2015 target. Among the key messages of this section:

- *Literacy remains among the most neglected of all education goals.* Progress towards the 2015 target of halving illiteracy[30] has been far too slow and uneven. With half the period for achieving the target having elapsed, the regions farthest behind have travelled between a third and half of the distance required. On current trends, there will be 710 million illiterate adults worldwide in 2015. The evidence from monitoring is clear: unless far more is done to accelerate progress, the 2015 targets will not be reached.
- *More rapid progress remains possible.* Several countries have demonstrated through successful policies that more rapid advance towards adult literacy is possible. The National Literacy Mission in India and the Literate Brazil Programme (Programa Brasil Alfabetizado) both reflect a stronger commitment to literacy by political leaders. Several countries have developed highly innovative programmes through partnerships linking communities to governments and non-government groups. Better financing and a renewed effort to reach older adults are critical to accelerated progress.
- *Far more has to be done to overcome the legacy of disadvantage in literacy.* While gender gaps are narrowing, they remain very large – women still account for nearly two-thirds of the world's adult illiterates. Failure to tackle gender disparities and wider inequalities based on wealth, region, ethnicity and language are holding back progress.

This section is divided into two parts. Part 1 provides a global overview of literacy and a post-Dakar progress report. It also looks ahead to 2015, providing a projection of where current trends will leave the world in relation to the goal of achieving a 50% improvement in levels of adult literacy. Part 2 looks at some of the countries that are making progress and identifies approaches that are making a difference.

Progress since the Dakar forum

The precise meaning of 'literacy' continues to be subject to intense academic debate (Benavot, 2008; Fransman, 2005). Unlike the simple dichotomies used in other areas – such as being 'in school' or 'out of school' – there are no clear-cut dividing lines between the literate and non-literate. In any society, there is a continuum of literacy – and people with a fragile hold on literacy in youth can lose that hold in adulthood. However, academic debates over the precise meaning of the word should not detract from common-sense depictions of what the experience of illiteracy means to those affected.

Half a century ago, UNESCO defined a literate person as someone 'who can with understanding both read and write a short simple statement on his or her everyday life' (UNESCO, 1958, p. 3). More recently, the Global Campaign for Education has extended this basic idea: 'Literacy is about the acquisition and use of reading, writing and

30. The target of achieving a 50% improvement in levels of adult literacy is measured by looking at the illiteracy rate, reflecting the original formulation of the goal as expressed in Jomtien in 1990. The adult illiteracy rate is computed by deducting the adult literacy rate from 100.

numeracy skills, and thereby the development of active citizenship, improved health and livelihoods and gender equality' (Global Campaign for Education and ActionAid International, 2005, p. 13). A combination of these two broad definitions captures the reality of illiteracy as a condition that denies people opportunity.

The condition affects much of the world's youth and adult population, especially women in developing countries. While all regions are affected, a relatively small group of countries with large populations dominates the global illiteracy headcount.

The illiteracy scourge continues

An estimated 759 million adults – around 16% of the world's population aged 15 and over – lack the basic reading, writing and numeracy skills needed in everyday life (Table 2.6). More than half live in South and West Asia, and another one-fifth in sub-Saharan Africa. Reflecting the legacy of gender disparity in education, almost two in every three adult illiterates are female (see annex, Statistical Table 2).

Measured in aggregate terms, adult illiterates are heavily concentrated in a small group of large-population countries (Figure 2.29). Just twenty countries account for around 80% of global illiterates, with Bangladesh, China, India and Pakistan making up over half the total. The data in this section highlight the concentration of illiteracy in developing countries. This should not deflect attention from the serious problems in rich countries, where large pockets of illiteracy contribute to wider patterns of social and economic marginalization (Box 2.19).

Aggregate figures mask differences in the incidence of illiteracy. Both South and West Asia, and sub-Saharan Africa have high illiteracy rates, with more than one in three adults affected in both regions (Table 2.6). In sub-Saharan Africa, twelve countries have illiteracy rates in excess of 50%; among these, in Burkina Faso, Guinea, Mali and the Niger, more than 70% of the adult population is illiterate (Figure 2.30). In the Arab States, the proportion is nearly one-third. Gender disparities are a major contributor to the high adult illiteracy rates in all three regions (see annex, Statistical Table 2). For instance:

Table 2.6: Adult (15 and over) illiteracy rates and numbers, by region, 2000-2007[1]

	Illiteracy rates (%)[2]	Illiterates (millions)
World	16	759
Developing countries	20	752
Developed countries	0.7	5
Countries in transition	0.6	1
Sub-Saharan Africa	38	153
Arab States	29	58
Central Asia	1	0.7
East Asia and the Pacific	7	108
East Asia	7	106
Pacific	7	2
South and West Asia	36	391
Latin America and the Caribbean	9	36
Caribbean	25	3
Latin America	9	33
North America and Western Europe	0.6	4
Central and Eastern Europe	2	8

Figure 2.29: Adult illiteracy is heavily concentrated in a small group of large-population countries

Adult (15 and over) illiterates (millions), top ten countries

About 759 million adults lack the basic reading, writing and numeracy skills needed in everyday life

Notes: The population used to generate the number of illiterates is from the United Nations Population Division estimates (2006 revision).
For countries with national observed literacy data, the population used corresponds to the year of the census or survey.
1. Data are for the most recent year available during the period specified. See the web version of the introduction to the statistical tables for a broader explanation of national literacy definitions, assessment methods, and sources and years of data.
2. The illiteracy rate is calculated as 100 minus the literacy rate.
Source: Annex, Statistical Table 2.

The world is far off track for the 2015 target of achieving a 50% improvement in levels of adult literacy

Box 2.19: Rich countries – poor literacy

This section focuses on illiteracy in poor countries, but rich countries also have significant pockets of deprivation. Many adults lack the functional literacy skills they need to apply for jobs, read newspapers or understand documents – on housing, health and the education of children, for example – that affect their lives:

- In France, an estimated 9% of people aged 18 to 65 lack the basic reading, writing, arithmetic and other fundamental skills required for simple everyday situations.
- In the Netherlands, 1.5 million adults (including 1 million native Dutch speakers) are classified as functionally illiterate, implying that they are not equipped to process basic information.
- In the United States, 14% of the population lacks the literacy skills to perform simple, everyday tasks like understanding newspaper articles and instruction manuals. Around 12% lack the literacy skills needed to fill out a job application or understand labels on food and drugs. More than one in five – 22% of the population – has 'below basic' quantitative skills, finding it impossible to balance a chequebook or deduce from an advertisement the amount of interest on a loan.
- In England (United Kingdom), 1.7 million people (5% of those aged 16 to 65) perform below the level expected of 7-year-olds on the national curriculum test, and 5.1 million perform below the level expected of 11-year-olds.

Literacy problems in rich countries are often concentrated in areas of acute social disadvantage, among migrant groups and the poor. Illiteracy is a factor in low pay, insecure employment and social exclusion.

Sources: Burd-Sharps et al. (2008); National Agency to Fight Illiteracy (2007); National Literacy Trust (2009); Reading and Writing Foundation (2009).

- In Afghanistan, 87% of adult women and 57% of men were illiterate in 2000.
- In Chad, Ethiopia and Mali, women are around 1.5 times as likely as men to be illiterate.
- In Algeria and Yemen, the illiteracy rates for females are more than twice those for men.

Contrary to common understanding, the relationship between average income and literacy is highly variable. For example, Egypt's average income is comparable to that of Ecuador, but its literacy rate is 66% while Ecuador's is 84%. Similarly, Algeria has a far higher level of average income than Bolivia but a lower adult literacy rate. In both cases, gender disparities explain much of the discrepancy (see annex, Statistical Table 2).

The contrasting profiles for national literacy point to distinctive policy challenges. As well as making sure that young people emerge from education systems with basic literacy skills, many countries in sub-Saharan Africa, South and West Asia and parts of the Arab world need to extend literacy opportunities to a large share of the adult population. In Brazil and Indonesia, where illiteracy affects 10% or less of the adult population, policy-makers still have to address the task of reaching highly marginalized groups and people, many of them in remote areas.

Measuring literacy is not an exact science. National estimates are typically derived from census and household surveys in which people are asked to report on their own literacy status (Box 2.20). Because the idea of literacy is specific to different cultures and contexts, the word itself can have different meanings to different people (Fransman, 2005; UIS, 2008*a*). National surveys often fail to generate representative data for populations that are hard to reach or people living in informal settlements (Aderinoye and Rogers, 2005). Given that literacy levels are likely to be lower among these groups this can also lead to underestimation of the numbers of illiterates.

The progress report

The world is far off track for the 2015 target of achieving a 50% improvement in levels of adult literacy. In the absence of a concerted international drive to prioritize literacy, there is little prospect of the target being brought within reach. Yet the experience of some countries, and of some programmes within countries, demonstrates that a great deal can be achieved in relatively little time.

Adult literacy rates in the developing world have been rising with every school generation. As more children enter school and leave with basic literacy skills, literacy rates inevitably rise. Literacy programmes have also played a positive role in some countries. From 1985–1994 to 2000–2007,

Figure 2.30: In developing countries, illiteracy can affect up from one to three out of four adults

Adult (15 and over) illiteracy rates in countries with rates of 25% or more in selected regions, 2000-2007[1]

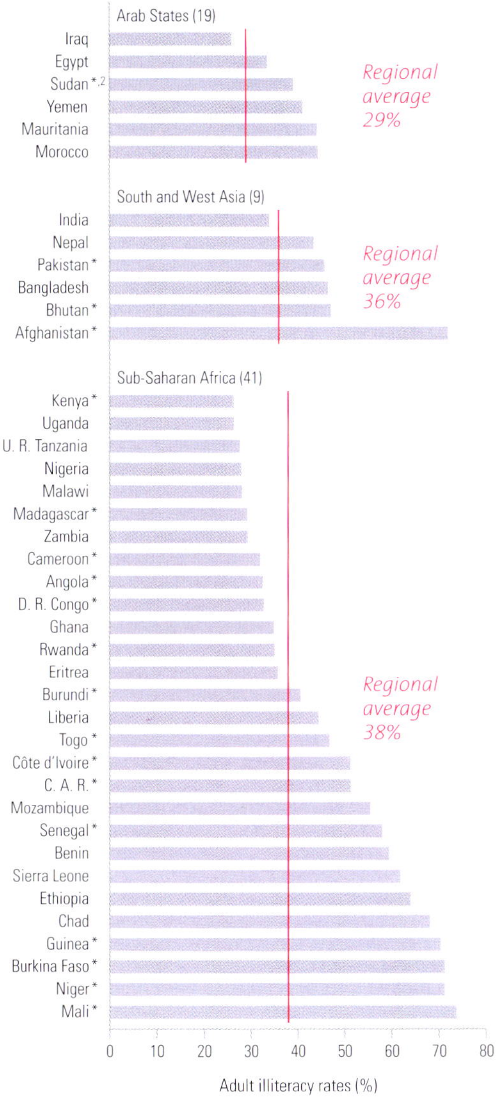

Notes: For countries indicated with *, national observed literacy data are used. For all others, UIS literacy estimates are used. The estimates were generated using the UIS Global Age-specific Literacy Projections model. Figures in parentheses after region names indicate the number of countries with publishable data in the region.

1. Data are for the most recent year available during the period specified. See the web version of the introduction to the statistical tables for a broader explanation of national literacy definitions, assessment methods, and sources and years of data.

2. Data do not include all geographic regions.

Source: Annex, Statistical Table 2.

the number of adult illiterates in the world fell by 13%. Given that population growth pushed the adult population up by around 30% in the same period, the net effect is clearly positive. Adult literacy levels increased more rapidly than in the 1990s (Qiao, 2007), growing by 10% to reach 84% in 2000-2007.

Box 2.20: A new generation of literacy statistics

New approaches to literacy measurement are attempting to address long-standing data problems. One prominent example is the Literacy Assessment and Monitoring Programme (LAMP).

Conventional approaches to literacy measurement are often fundamentally flawed. Asking people to report whether they are literate is of limited use in assessing real capabilities. Similarly, testing literacy by reference to words, objects and experiences that have no relevance in the lives of the people being surveyed can understate achievement levels.

The LAMP approach tests literacy in three domains: continuous texts (prose), non-continuous texts (documents) and numeracy. Results reflect a continuum of achievement, and the tests are designed to be meaningful to respondents. Data generated through the tests are intended for national and cross-national comparisons. Developed by the UIS and administered through ministries of education, LAMP surveys are in the pilot stage in several countries.

Sources: UIS (2009c, 2009d).

The broadly positive global canvas hides some less encouraging developments (Figure 2.31). Almost all the decline in the number of illiterate adults in the developing world took place in just one region, East Asia and the Pacific. In South and West Asia, population growth cancelled out the decline in numbers of illiterate adults. In sub-Saharan Africa, the number of illiterates increased by 19.5 million. The Arab States also experienced an increase. Some countries witnessed large absolute increases in the number of illiterate adults: over 1 million in Burkina Faso, the Philippines, Senegal, the United Republic of Tanzania and Viet Nam, and 4 million in Bangladesh and Ethiopia (see annex, Statistical Table 2).

Adult literacy levels grew by 10% to reach 84% in 2000-2007

The idea that countries are powerless to combat adult illiteracy is refuted by the experience of countries that have achieved rapid progress. The following are examples of positive change between 1985–1994 and 2000–2007:

- Much of the illiteracy reduction in East Asia can be traced to China. The number of adult illiterates there fell by 114 million or 62% between the two periods, with an average increase in the number of adult literates of 4 million between 1990 and 2000 (NCEDR, 2008).

Figure 2.31: The number of adult illiterates is falling despite population growth

Changes in adult (15 and over) illiterates, literacy rates and population, by region, 1985-1994 and 2000-2007[1]

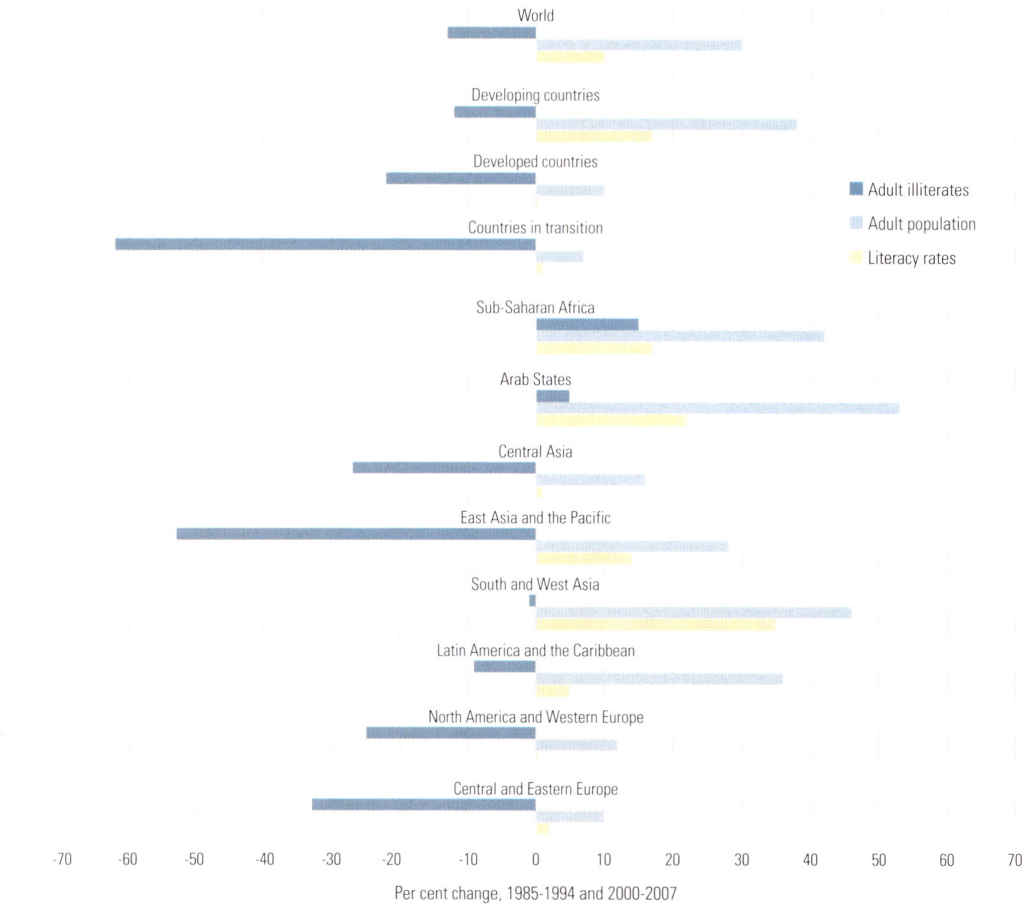

Notes: The population used to generate the number of illiterates is from the United Nations Population Division estimates (2006 revision). For countries with national observed literacy data, the population used corresponds to the year of the census or survey. For countries with UIS estimates, the populations used are for 1994 and 2007.
1. Data are for the most recent year available during each period specified.
Source: Annex, Statistical Table 2.

Burkina Faso and Chad have respectively doubled and almost tripled their literacy rates

- With the world's largest illiterate population, India has been making progress. In 1985–1994 not quite half of adults were literate. The figure is now slightly above two-thirds. Since the adult population increased by 45%, this marks a real advance. It also suggests that the country's Total Literacy Campaign, under the Auspices of the National Literacy Mission, may be having an impact (India Ministry of Human Resource Development and National University of Educational Planning and Administration, 2008).

- Many countries in sub-Saharan Africa have achieved steep rises in adult literacy rates. Burkina Faso and Chad, with some of the world's lowest literacy rates, have respectively doubled and almost tripled their rates.

- Several Arab states have achieved major advances. Egypt's adult literacy rate has increased from 44% to 66%. Yemen has increased the adult literacy rate from 37% to 59%.

Gender parity is improving

Rising literacy has been accompanied by declining gender disparities. Many countries that started with very large gaps between male and female literacy, and from low overall levels, have been on a pathway towards parity.

Gender parity improved in all but eight of the seventy-nine countries with data.[31] In Bangladesh, Burkina Faso, Burundi, Malawi, Nepal and Yemen, female adult literacy rates doubled or

31 The gender parity index (GPI) declined in Ecuador, Ethiopia and Zambia. In Botswana, the GPI improved from 1.09 to 1.00. Gender parity had already been achieved in 1985-1994 in the Maldives, Panama, Seychelles and Uruguay, and was maintained in 2000–2007 (Annex, Statistical Table 2).

tripled, and have increased twice as fast as male rates. Because adult literacy gaps track developments in basic education, this catching up process mirrors a narrowing of the gender gap in basic education. Between the two benchmark periods, the number of adult female literates increased by 14%, compared with 7% for adult males (see annex, Statistical Table 2).

This positive trend has to be placed in context. Women may be catching up, but in many countries they are starting from a long way back. Gender disparities remain very deep – and the share of women in the total number of illiterates has increased slightly. The process of convergence is thus starting from very unequal points (Figure 2.32). In the three regions with the lowest levels of literacy and largest gender disparities – the Arab states, South and West Asia, and sub-Saharan Africa – female adult literacy rates for 2000–2007 were still below the average for male literacy in 1985–1994. On the current trajectory, it will take women in South and West Asia about fifty-six years to catch up.

Gender convergence in adult literacy is proceeding at different rates in different countries. Compare the contrasting experiences of Bangladesh and India. Women aged 25 to 34 in Bangladesh have illiteracy rates 32% higher than men in the same age group. The gap reflects gender disparities that prevailed in the education system when that generation went to school. For 15- to 24-year-olds in Bangladesh today the gender gap has been eliminated. While India has been narrowing the gap, 15- to 24-year-old females are still about twice as likely to be illiterate as males in that group. Among the Arab states, Morocco has been making rapid progress towards improved literacy with every school generation but has been less successful in closing the gender gap, as comparison with China underlines (Figure 2.33).

Improvement in access to education across generations is one of the motors driving increased literacy levels. In almost all countries, literacy rates among younger adults (15 to 24) are higher than the average for all adults (15 and over). In the Arab States, South and West Asia, and sub-Saharan Africa, youth literacy rates in 2000–2007 were 16% to 24% higher than the average for all adults (see annex, Statistical Table 2). Age-group disparities are particularly marked in some countries, including Botswana, Eritrea, the Islamic Republic of Iran, Nigeria and Sri Lanka, where the proportion of illiterates among all adults is double or more the proportion for younger adults.

Figure 2.32: Being so far behind, women have further to travel to reach male literacy rates

Adult (15 and over) literacy rates, by region and gender, 1985-1994 and 2000-2007[1]

1. Data are for the most recent year available during each period specified.
Source: Annex, Statistical Table 2.

Illiteracy mirrors wider disadvantages

National data on literacy can provide insights into the average picture for a country while obscuring disparities within countries, where adult illiteracy may intersect with income, parental education, ethnicity, language and disability. While women are systematically disadvantaged, gender disparities are magnified by wider structures of disadvantage and marginalization.

Low income. Adults from the poorest households are far more likely to be illiterate. In Guatemala, 60% of adults living in extreme poverty and 42% of those living in non-extreme poverty are illiterate, compared with 17% of richer adults (Porta Pallais and Laguna, 2007). Similarly, the literacy rate for the richest Bangladeshi households is 76%, compared with 28% for the poorest (Bangladesh Ministry of Planning and UNESCO Bangladesh, 2008).

Ethnicity, language and group-based disadvantage. Minority language groups and indigenous people often register far lower levels of literacy. In Viet Nam, the literacy rate is 94% among the majority Kinh population, but only 72% for ethnic minorities (Daswani, 2005). In Peru, illiteracy is much more prevalent among

On the current trajectory, it will take women in South and West Asia about fifty-six years to catch up with men

Figure 2.33: Contrasting experiences in reducing illiteracy and the associated gender gap in four countries

Age illiteracy profile in selected countries, by age group and gender, 2007

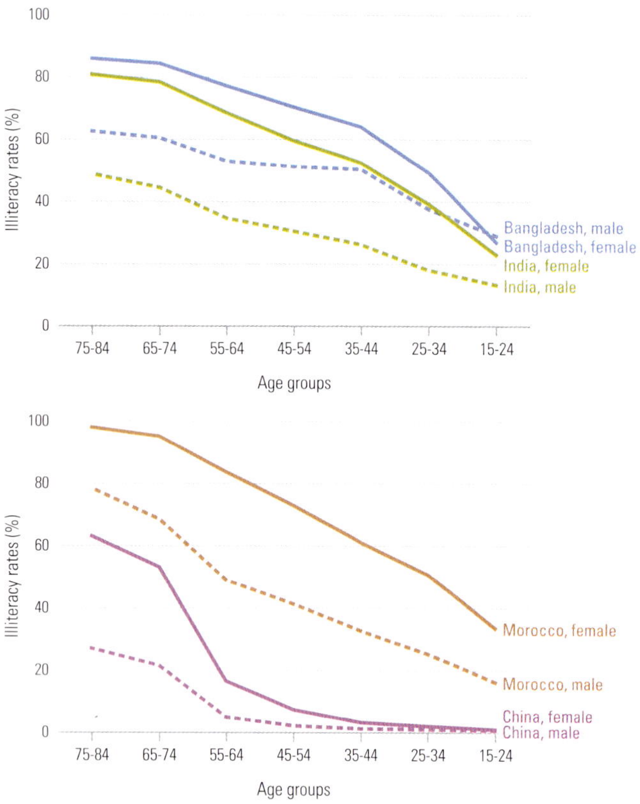

Source: UIS database.

On current trends, 710 million adults will still lack basic literacy skills in 2015.

indigenous-language speakers at 21% of adults compared with 4% for Spanish-speakers (Cueto et al., 2009). In South Asia, literacy gaps between lower and higher castes are pronounced. In Nepal, caste disparities are even larger than wealth and gender disparities (Nepal Ministry of Education and Sports and UNESCO Kathmandu, 2007).

Disparities linked to location. Illiteracy tends to be higher in poorer regions, rural areas and slums. Regional disparities often mirror national poverty maps. For example, in Brazil some of the poorest states in the north-east – Alagoas, Maranhão, Paraíba and Piauí – have illiteracy levels twice as high as in the south-east (The George Washington University, 2006). In India, the regional spectrum extends from almost no illiteracy in the state of Mizoram to 50% illiteracy in Rajasthan (India Ministry of Human Resource Development and National University of Educational Planning and Administration, 2008). Rural areas often lag far behind urban areas (Kinsella and He, 2009).

In Pakistan, urban literacy rates are twice as high as the rural average. Within urban areas illiteracy tends to be concentrated in informal settlements characterized by high levels of poverty (Pakistan Ministry of Education, 2008).

None of these disadvantages exists in isolation. Being female is a near-universal indicator for lower average literacy in many Arab states and most of South and West Asia, and sub-Saharan Africa. But gender disadvantage is compounded by poverty, location and ethnicity (Figure 2.34). The wealth gap in the Philippines is particularly marked: women in the poorest households have literacy rates averaging 65%, compared with over 96% for women in the wealthiest households. In South Africa, white youth and adult women have near-universal literacy levels, compared with just 70% literacy among black women. In Mexico, women who only speak an indigenous language are about fifteen times less likely to be literate than women who only speak Spanish, and women lacking a knowledge of Spanish have literacy levels of just 5%. Literacy rates among Cambodian women living in Ratanakiri, a province dominated by indigenous hill tribes, are just over a third of those among women in the capital, Phnom Penh.

Prospects for achieving the 2015 target

Current trends in adult literacy will leave the world short of the target set for 2015.[32] Progress has been so slow that the target is out of reach. Even in a best-case scenario, not enough children will enter adulthood literate over the next five years to halve the level of illiteracy. Continuing on the current trend will leave a very large gap with the Dakar promise.

Projections provided for the *EFA Global Monitoring Report 2010* give a ballpark estimate of the scale of shortfall: by 2015 the adult illiteracy rate will have fallen between 18% and 25% in the three regions with the lowest rates. In other words, just about half of the journey to the 50% illiteracy reduction target will have been completed.

There is a very real human cost associated with the gap. On the current course, an estimated 710 million adults – 13% of the world's adults – will still lack basic literacy skills in 2015. Regional gaps between target and projected outcome are largest for South and West Asia, sub-Saharan Africa and the Arab States (Figure 2.35). Failure to achieve the Dakar adult literacy goal will translate into very large deficits for many countries. In India the target will be missed on current trends by around 81 million

32. See note for Figure 2.35 for how the literacy target has been measured.

Figure 2.34: Within countries, women's literacy rates are influenced by socio-economic and geographic factors

Female adult (18 and over) literacy rates, by area, ethnicity, income, language, religion or region, selected countries, latest available year

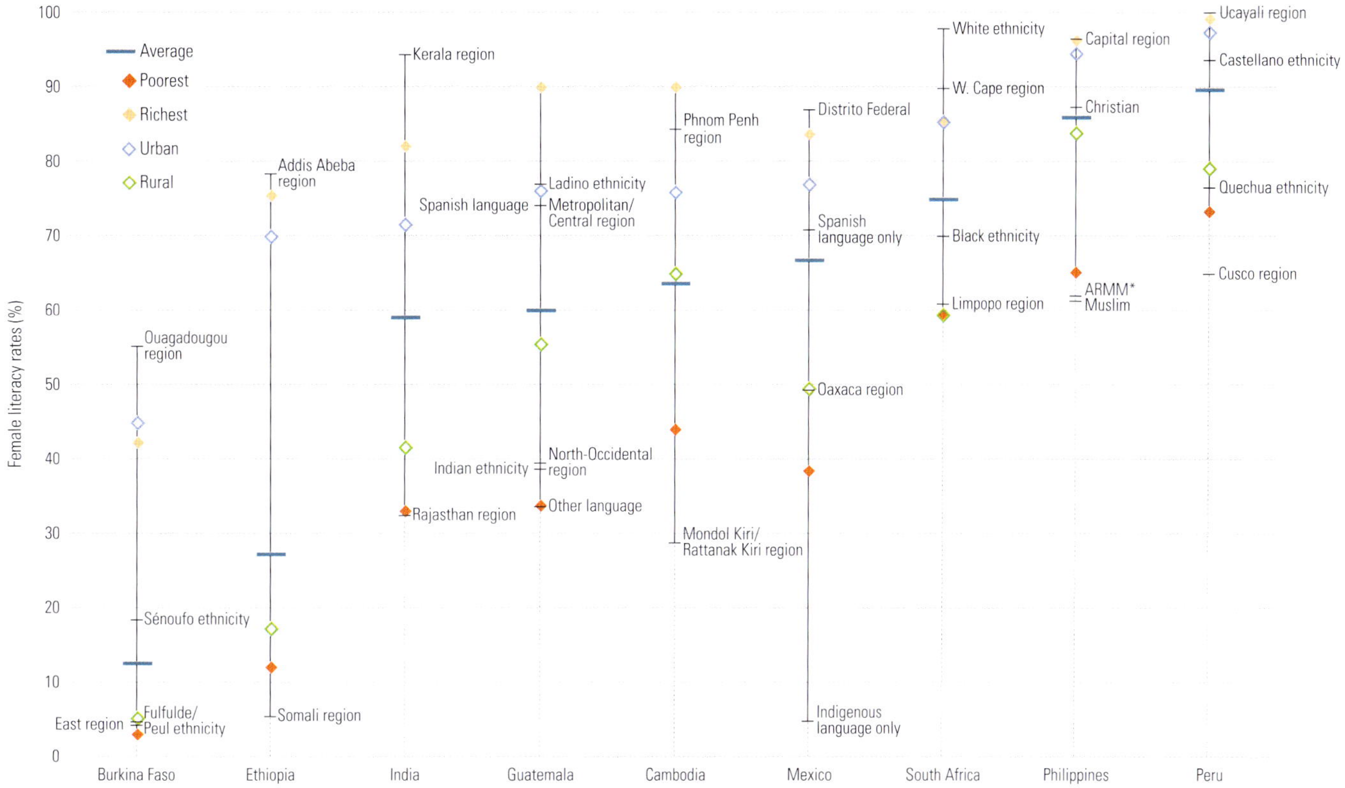

Notes: Data for Burkina Faso (2003), Cambodia (2005), Egypt (2005), Ethiopia (2005), Guatemala (1999), India (2005) and Peru (2004) are from Demographic and Health Surveys. Data for Mexico (2005), the Philippines (2000) and South Africa (2001) are from population censuses. Countries are sorted by average female literacy rate.

* Autonomous Region in Muslim Mindanao.

Source: UNESCO-DME (2009).

people. Bangladesh will have 16 million more illiterates than it would if the 2015 goals were achieved.[33] Among the sub-Saharan African countries, Mozambique will face a deficit of 2.6 million people, based on a target set using 1997 data (UIS, 2009*d*).

Changing the trend – making the literacy decade count

The disappointing progress towards the literacy goal set at Dakar reflects a collective failure of political commitment. While there are many exceptions, governments and aid donors collectively have failed to attach sufficient weight to the eradication of illiteracy. There are encouraging signs, however, that this could be starting to change.

Some are apparent at the international level. In 2003, the United Nations launched a literacy decade, with

33. The Bangladesh and India targets are set using 2001 literacy data from the UIS database.

Figure 2.35: At the present rate, regions furthest behind will miss the literacy target for 2015

Adult (15 and over) illiteracy rates, by region: 2007, projected by 2015 and required by 2015 to achieve the goal

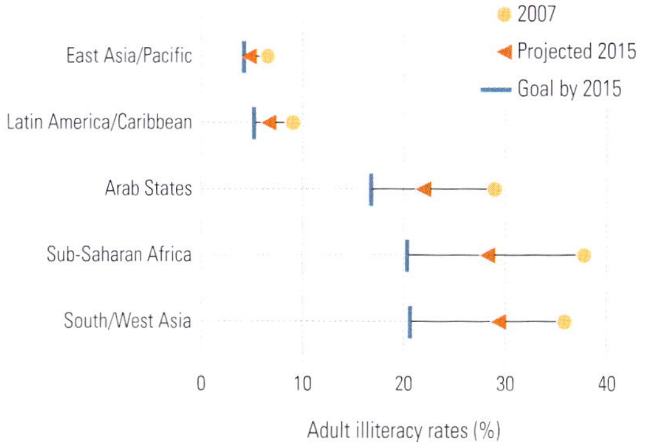

Notes: The goal of achieving a 50% improvement in levels of adult literacy is measured by looking at the 1999 illiteracy rate, reflecting the original formulation of the goal as expressed in Jomtien in 1991. The adult illiteracy rate is computed by deducting the adult literacy rate from 100. Regions are sorted by illiteracy rate goal by 2015.

Sources: Annex, Statistical Table 2; UIS (2009*b*).

governments recognizing that 'literacy is crucial to the acquisition, by every child, youth and adult, of essential life skills that enable them to address the challenges they can face in life, and represents an essential step in basic education' (United Nations, 2002, p. 2). While development decades come and go, usually without meaningful impact, the literacy decade has given rise to intensive regional discussions and raised the profile of the illiteracy problem (Robinson, 2009; UNESCO, 2008*b*). The International Conference on Adult Education scheduled for late 2009 (CONFINTEA VI) provides an opportunity to move from international dialogue to international action.

Large-scale programmes in Brazil, India and the Islamic Republic of Iran are delivering positive results

Literacy continues to receive insufficient attention at many levels. It is not treated as a political priority, it receives insufficient financial commitment and efforts to incorporate strategies for literacy into wider poverty reduction plans remain underdeveloped (Caillods and Hallak, 2004; Giffard-Lindsay, 2008; Lindt, 2008). Even so, some governments have demonstrated through practical action that national programmes deliver results. Others have increased financing commitments for literacy. And a vast array of partnerships and approaches are now promoting literacy at the community level (Oxenham, 2008).

Some governments have openly acknowledged that neglect of literacy was a serious policy failure (Lindt, 2008). One of the most far-reaching efforts to correct that failure is the Literate Brazil Programme (Box 2.21). In the Islamic Republic of Iran, community learning centres initiated by the Literacy Movement Organization, a government agency, have enrolled 3.1 million illiterates from 2000 to 2006 in preliminary basic education courses. Around three-quarters of those enrolled successfully complete their courses (Richmond et al., 2008). In Burkina Faso, the government has adopted the bold target of increasing adult literacy rates from 28% to 40% by 2010. That target has been backed by an increase in the share of the education budget allocated to literacy from 1% to 7% – a move that has facilitated the expansion of permanent literacy training centres and centres for non-formal basic education. Graduation from these centres grew by 24% from 2003 to 2007 (Richmond et al., 2008).

Another example comes from India, where the National Literacy Mission, launched in 1988, has been revitalized. The eleventh five-year plan, which ends in 2012, has quintupled the mission's budget to the equivalent of US$21 billion. Programmes have been redesigned to provide an integrated approach that combines initial literacy training with ongoing post-literacy courses. Decentralization is transferring authority to states and districts, and a much stronger commitment has been made to preparing literacy materials in local languages. In 2009, the Government of India also signaled a stronger focus on gender and equity, first by recasting the National Literacy Mission as the National Female Literacy Mission and then by announcing a strategy for targeting. Commitments have been made to ensure that 85% of targeted beneficiaries will be women and that 50% will come from scheduled castes, tribes and minorities, with a focus on Muslims (India Ministry of Human Resource Development, 2009).

Slow progress in improving literacy is sometimes cited as evidence that little can be done for older generations. There is extensive evidence, however, of problems with past approaches to raising literacy. For two or three decades after 1960, many governments attempted to combat illiteracy through top-down courses that were ill suited to the lives of the intended beneficiaries, badly designed and offered no follow-up. Dropout rates were high and literacy acquisition limited. The needs of indigenous people and minority language groups were often ignored. Literacy programmes have mirrored schools in denying people an opportunity to learn in their local language, diminishing the perceived value of their culture in the process.

Shortcomings persist in national programmes, particularly in targeting. Literacy initiatives often focus on youth and young adults, with insufficient attention paid to older people – especially women – who represent the bulk of the illiterate population. India's and Brazil's programmes principally target people under 30 (India Ministry of Human Resource Development and National University of Educational Planning and Administration, 2008). Reaching older illiterates can be difficult, but far more could be done to extend opportunities through livelihood-based literacy programmes.

Financing is another area of concern. It is encouraging that more governments are adopting bold targets, but those targets are seldom backed by adequate budget support. It is not uncommon for literacy to account for as little as 1% to 2% of total education spending (Lindt, 2008).

Box 2.21: Brazil – 'making people literate'

Around 14 million Brazilian youth, adults and elderly people lack basic reading and writing skills. The Literate Brazil Programme (Programa Brasil Alfabetizado) initiated by President Luiz Inácio Lula da Silva in 2003 is the first concerted national effort to consign illiteracy to the history books.

The programme is coordinated by the Ministry of Education but operates through a highly decentralized structure. It functions in 3,699 municipalities, just over 1,000 of which have been accorded priority status because they have illiteracy rates over 25%. The effort primarily targets disadvantaged groups such as indigenous people, small farmers and farm workers, child labourers (as part of the Programme to Eradicate Child Labour) and people covered under the Bolsa Familia social protection programme.

Literate Brazil is open to anyone over 15 with less than a year of education. Thus far it has provided literacy training to about 8 million learners. Literacy classes typically last six to eight months and are attended by groups of eighteen to twenty-five learners. Federal transfers cover the cost of training and providing grants to literacy facilitators, many of whom are teachers. Literacy textbooks are produced in local languages and reflect local circumstances and needs. Innovative pedagogical approaches have been developed. Teaching is organized around the idea of 'making people literate' through dynamic learning processes that lead to the acquisition of reading, writing and numeracy skills. Students' abilities are assessed and recorded by government agencies, and qualifications are provided that can be used to enter formal education.

Literate Brazil has been about more than providing services. Political leaders have challenged the culture of silence and indifference surrounding illiteracy. A Ministry of Education programme has put the development of textbooks for literacy, a previously neglected subject, on the same footing as books for primary and secondary school. Prizes are awarded for the development of literacy materials and the best entries are integrated into national programmes, with specific prizes for black Brazilians, an educationally disadvantaged group.

Sources: Brazil Ministry of Education (2008); Henriques and Ireland (2007); Ireland (2007, 2008); UIL (2009); UNESCO Brasilia (2009).

Many literacy programmes also continue to suffer from low rates of uptake and completion.

On the other hand, programmes that provide for active learning through a relevant curriculum and offer follow-up have achieved results. Many such programmes are built on partnerships, extending from local communities to non-government actors and government agencies. One prominent example is Reflect. Developed and coordinated by ActionAid, an international charity, it focuses on the learners' own literacy objectives, motivation and skills (Riddell, 2001). It not only promotes the use of real texts from the environment but also encourages participants to generate their own texts. It further aims to transform the broader literacy environment, for example by campaigning for newspapers to use local language or texts more accessible to adult literacy learners (Aderinoye and Rogers, 2005). The programme is currently applied in Bangladesh, Pakistan and many other countries (Duffy et al., 2008).

Bilingual education is critical to the success of literacy programmes aimed at indigenous people and ethnic minorities. Here, too, many governments have openly acknowledged the mistakes of the past. Several governments in Latin America – including those of Chile, Guatemala, Mexico, Paraguay and Peru – and the UN Economic Commission for Latin America and the Caribbean have developed a regional poverty reduction strategy incorporating bilingual literacy training for indigenous groups (Latin American and the Caribbean Demographic Center, 2009; Stockholm Challenge, 2008).

Conclusion

Much has been achieved through the scaling up of literacy initiatives since 2000. However, the monitoring evidence is unambiguous: the 2015 targets will not be reached on the current trajectory. Far more has to be done to accelerate progress. This will require stronger political leadership. Governments across the world continue to attach too little weight to literacy in national planning. This is short-sighted. Illiteracy imposes huge costs on society and the economy – and investments in literacy have the potential to generate large returns in both areas. □

The Literate Brazil Programme has provided literacy training to about 8 million learners

The quality of education

Goal 6: Improving all aspects of the quality of education and ensuring excellence of all so that recognized and measurable learning outcomes are achieved by all, especially in literacy, numeracy and essential life skills.

The core task of any education system is to equip young people with the skills they need to participate in social, economic and political life. Getting children into primary school, through their early grades and into secondary school is not an end in itself but a means of delivering these skills. Success or failure in achieving education for all hinges critically not just on countries delivering more years in school; the ultimate measure lies in what children learn and the quality of their education experience.

Many countries are failing the quality test. Out-of-school children face obvious disadvantages, yet less attention has been paid to the fact that millions of children emerge from primary school each year without having acquired basic literacy and numeracy skills. Unable to formulate or read a simple sentence, these children are ill equipped to make the transition to secondary school – let alone enter employment markets. The problems extend to secondary schools, where many children – sometimes a majority – do not reach even a minimal level of competence.

The core purpose of education is to ensure that children acquire the skills that shape their future life chances

Policy-makers, educators and parents need to focus far more on the core purpose of education: ensuring that children acquire the skills that shape their future life chances. That goal is difficult to achieve – far more difficult, arguably, than getting children into school. Governments need to revise approaches to teaching, learning and curriculum development. With the global financial crisis having tightened already severe budget constraints, cost is often a barrier, but learning achievement can be greatly improved at low cost, in some cases by making better use of resources already being invested in education.

Public concern over the quality of education is evident in many of the world's richest nations, as well as the poorest. This section focuses on the situation in developing countries. There are three key messages:

- *While global gaps in access to school may be narrowing, gaps in school quality remain enormous.* Evidence from learning achievement tests suggests that, in many developing countries, average students are performing close to or below minimum competency levels. Global disparities are reinforced by inequalities within countries. The problem is not just one of relative performance; absolute levels of learning achievement are exceptionally low in many countries.

- *Getting the basics right is important – and many countries are failing to build strong foundations.* Children in the early grades are not mastering the reading skills necessary for further learning. Without these foundations, returns on the huge investment that governments and households make in education will be sub-optimal. Reading skills can be improved relatively easily. Education ministries and teachers need to renew their efforts regarding these basic skills.

- *Children do not start their schooling on an equal footing: more must be done to equalize opportunity.* Circumstances beyond children's control, such as the income and education of their parents, the language they speak and where they live, influence their achievement at school. If the quality goal is to be achieved, ensuring that all learners, regardless of background, achieve basic levels of learning needs to become a central objective. Programmes to improve achievement for the most disadvantaged learners are necessary.

The section is divided into three parts. Part 1 highlights the large disparities in learning achievement among and within countries. Part 2 explores early grade reading – one of the foundations for learning. Part 3 looks at the wider challenge of improving learning in schools and at global trends in teacher recruitment.

The learning gap – from global to local

In an increasingly knowledge-based world, prosperity, employment and poverty reduction – for countries and individuals – depend increasingly on skills and capabilities delivered in the classroom. For large parts of the world's population, however, education systems fall far short of legitimate expectations. Poor quality in education is jeopardizing the future of millions of young people, many of whom face the prospect of lifelong illiteracy.

Cross-country inequalities and achievement deficits

While significant gaps remain, more and more countries are participating in global and regional assessment exercises that make it possible to measure disparities between countries in terms of the skills students attain after a given period of learning.

The fourth cycle of Trends in International Mathematics and Science Study (TIMSS), conducted in 2007 among eighth grade students, shows large gaps in learning achievement between countries (Figure 2.36). One way of looking at these gaps is to consider the range of results. Average test scores for students in the Republic of Korea, the top-performing country, were almost twice as high as for students in Ghana, at the bottom of the league. Viewed from a different vantage point, the average student in El Salvador, Ghana, Indonesia and Morocco figures alongside or below the poorest-performing 10% of students in higher-performing countries.

Few of the poorest developing countries participated in TIMSS 2007. Researchers have attempted to address this limitation by reconfiguring scores from wider test exercises. The results confirm that low-income countries lag far behind others in learning achievement (Altinok, 2008; Hanushek and Woessmann, 2009). One assessment in India, conducted in the states of Orissa and Rajasthan during 2005, used questions from TIMSS to see how students in these states compared with those in countries participating in the original TIMSS survey (Das and Zajonc, 2008). The results showed that ninth grade students in Orissa and Rajasthan ranked alongside students from the poorest-performing TIMSS countries.

Learning assessments allow for more than relative measurement. TIMSS establishes a series of performance thresholds aimed at measuring student capabilities. At the low end (scores of 400 or less), students have only the most basic knowledge of whole numbers, decimals and basic graphs. At the upper end (over 550), students can apply their understanding and knowledge in a variety of complex situations. In eighteen of the countries covered, including Botswana, Egypt and Saudi Arabia, the average student performs below the low threshold (Figure 2.36). This points to

There are large gaps in learning achievement between countries

Figure 2.36: There are large gaps in learning achievement across countries

Distribution of TIMSS mathematics scale score for eighth grade students in 2007

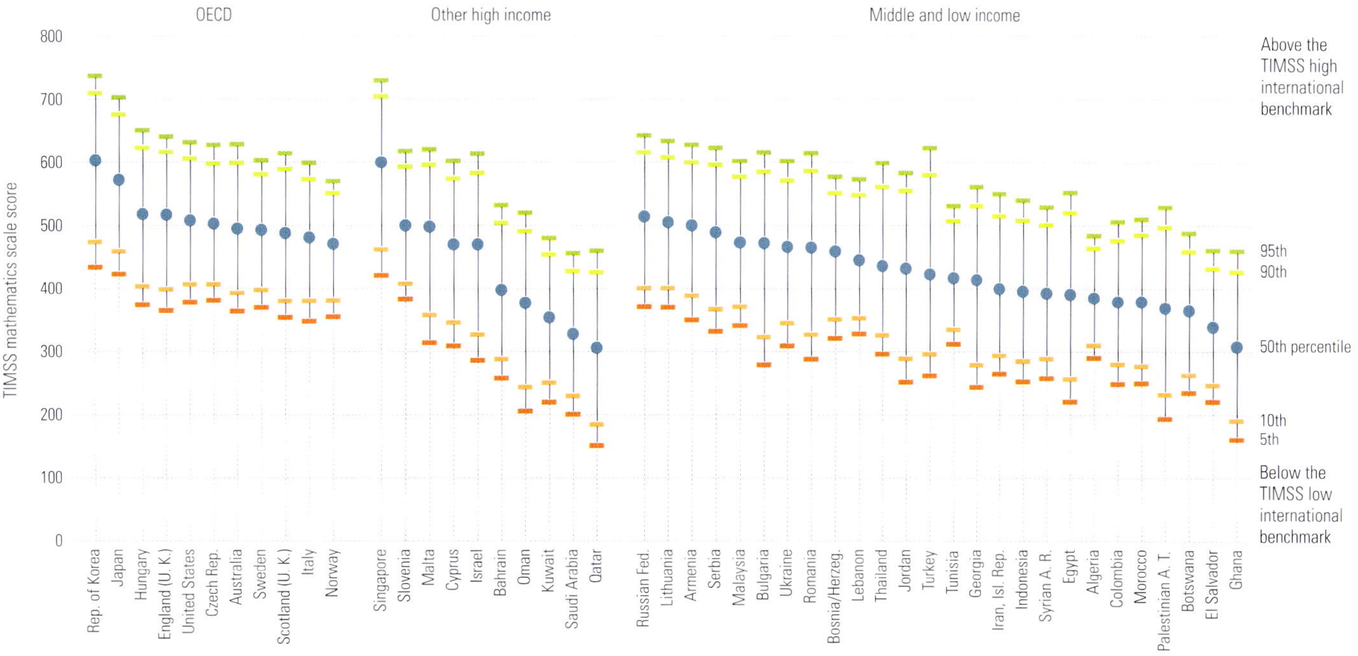

Notes: The markers show the scale score of the indicated percentile. The fiftieth percentile is the median score for the country. This represents the middle of the distribution, with 50% of students scoring above and below the median. Low benchmark – students have some knowledge of whole numbers and decimals, operations and basic graphs. High benchmark – students can organise and draw conclusions from information, make generalizations and solve non-routine problems.

Source: Mullis et al. (2008).

failings in education systems. While average test scores are higher in OECD countries, their education systems still fail a large minority. For example, approximately 10% of students in England (United Kingdom) and the United States, and an even higher share in Italy, score below the low threshold.

Learning achievement does rise with average income, but with large variations and some striking exceptions. Households and governments in wealthier countries can invest more in education and this often leads to higher achievement. For example, average government spending on a secondary school student in Norway was US$13,388 in 2005, compared with US$348 in Ghana (see annex, Statistical Table 11).[34] But the links between income and learning are far from automatic. Among high-income countries, the best performers – the Republic of Korea and Singapore – outperform wealthier countries such as the United States. The most striking exceptions are among Arab states. In Qatar and Saudi Arabia, both high-income countries, three-quarters of students register below the lowest score threshold – a performance comparable with that of Ghana. In the middle-income countries of Algeria, Egypt and Morocco, more than half of students register below the lowest threshold.

Poor quality education in childhood has a major bearing on adult illiteracy

These results point to serious underlying policy problems and help explain the widely observed failure of Arab states to translate investment in education into improved skills, employment creation and economic growth.

International comparison highlights the degree of inequality in learning achievement worldwide, with students from low-income countries faring especially poorly, as Figures 2.37 and 2.38 powerfully demonstrate. At age 10 or 11, in the fourth grade of primary school, fewer than one in five children in Japan or the Netherlands scored below the intermediate benchmark on the relevant TIMSS scale. In Japan, almost all students had at least intermediate levels of proficiency, while in Qatar and Yemen almost no children scored above that level. Meanwhile, fewer than 20% in El Salvador, Morocco and Tunisia scored at the low benchmark (Figure 2.37).

Evidence from international assessments of reading skills is even more disturbing. PISA assesses students with about eight years of education. Students with reading literacy below level 1 are identified as being at risk during the transition to work. They are also unlikely to have achieved sufficient proficiency to be able to benefit from further education and other learning opportunities throughout life (OECD, 2007*b*). In Kyrgyzstan, 70% of students tested in PISA failed to achieve level 1 proficiency in reading (Figure 2.38). In Brazil, Indonesia, Mexico and Thailand, more than 40% of students were at level 1 or below. After eight years of schooling, these children were unable to demonstrate levels of literacy that would typically be achieved by the middle of primary school in OECD countries.

Sub-Saharan Africa is covered poorly by international learning assessments, but there is no shortage of evidence pointing to acute problems. Regional assessments conducted by the Southern and Eastern Africa Consortium for Monitoring Educational Quality (SACMEQ) from 2000 to 2002 for Malawi, Namibia and Zambia found that over 70% of grade 6 students in each country had not achieved basic numeracy. Students in Lesotho and South Africa did not do much better: over half of all students failed to achieve basic levels of numeracy. The evidence from sub-Saharan Africa also demonstrates that income is not the only factor shaping learning achievement. Lesotho and South Africa have much higher per capita incomes and government resources than Kenya, but they registered lower levels of primary school learning achievement.

Poor quality of education in childhood has a major bearing on adult illiteracy. Young adults with no education or just a few years of school inevitably figure prominently in the ranks of adult illiterates. But so do some who have spent several years in school. An analysis of adult literacy in twenty-one countries in sub-Saharan Africa using household survey data found that 22- to 24-year-olds with five years of education had a 40% probability of being illiterate (UNESCO-BREDA, 2007). People with seven years of education had a 20% chance of being illiterate. These figures point not just to an enormous waste of human potential and restricted opportunity, but to a failure of investment in education to deliver results.

In Latin America and the Caribbean, reading proficiency of primary school students also varies widely (Figure 2.39). According to the recent Segundo Estudio Regional Comparativo y Explicativo (SERCE) assessment, less than half of all grade 3 students in the Dominican Republic, Ecuador and Guatemala had more than very basic reading skills (UNESCO-OREALC, 2008).[35] In contrast, over 85%

34. Expressed at purchasing power parity in constant 2006 US dollars.

35. This is based on grade 3 students achieving at or below level 1 performance, as defined by the assessment.

Figure 2.37: There are wide disparities across countries in primary school mathematics performance

% of fourth grade students reaching the TIMSS international benchmarks for mathematics achievement, 2007

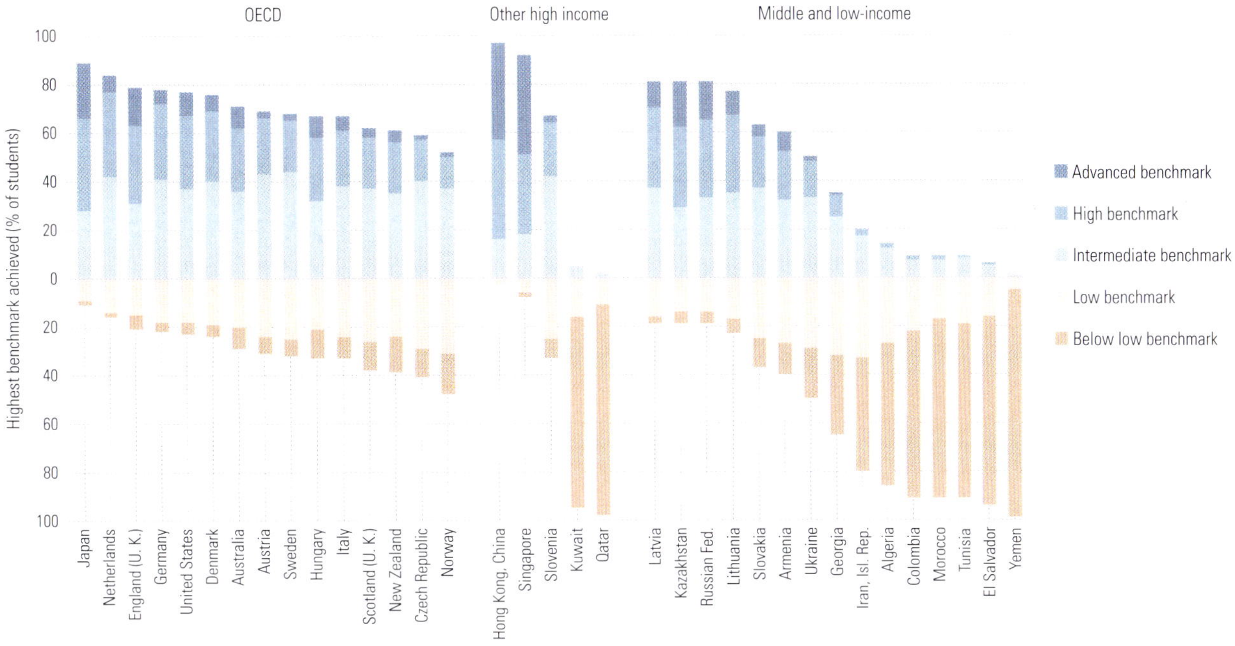

Notes: Low benchmark – students have some basic mathematical knowledge, an understanding of adding and subtracting with whole numbers, and can read information from simple bar graphs and tables. High benchmark – students can apply their mathematical understanding and knowledge in relatively complex situations and explain their meaning.
Source: Mullis et al. (2008).

of students in Costa Rica and Cuba had moved beyond the basics. Primary school students in Cuba performed extremely well. Over 40% of Cuban grade 3 students achieved the highest reading skills assessed, more than double the share in Chile and Mexico. At the other end of the achievement scale, Cuba has the smallest share of students performing below the lowest grade.

Countries in South and West Asia also suffer from significant deficits in levels of learning. In rural Pakistan, a recent survey found that only two-thirds of students in grade 3 could subtract single digit numbers, and only a small proportion could tell the time or carry out simple multiplication and division (Das et al., 2006). In rural India, levels of learning are equally troubling. In 2008, just 28% of grade 3 students could subtract two-digit numbers and only a third could tell the time (Pratham Resource Centre, 2008).

In one important respect international learning assessments understate the problem. This is because they cover only children in school, rather than the entire age group. Factoring in out-of-school children would significantly lower the scores of countries that are far from universal primary enrolment at the level being tested. In Ghana, TIMSS 2007 found that 17% of 16-year-olds scored above the low international benchmark, but only around half of the children of this age were in school. This implies that only 9% of Ghanaian 16-year-olds have mastered the most basic maths skills. In high-income countries such as the Czech Republic and England (United Kingdom), most children at the same stage are still in school and have far higher-level skills in mathematics (Mullis et al., 2008).[36]

Disparities in learning within countries

An equal opportunity to learn is no less a human right than an equal entitlement to be in school, regardless of parental income, gender, language or ethnicity. The Dakar goals in some cases explicitly target greater equity. For example, achieving gender parity in learning achievement is an important part of goal 6 and a key component of achieving gender equality in education by 2015 (goal 5) (Box 2.22). In many countries, however, large disparities in learning achievement point to deep disparities in opportunity. What students achieve is heavily influenced by both the type of school they attend and the characteristics of their family backgrounds.

International learning assessments understate the problem as they only cover children in school

36. For the TIMSS assessment children are assessed in grade 8 of their education careers. In the Czech Republic and England (United Kingdom) the average age of children in grade 8 was 14 compared with 16 in Ghana.

Figure 2.38: Reading ability in secondary school also varies greatly across countries

% of 15-year-old students reaching the PISA standard levels of reading proficiency, 2006

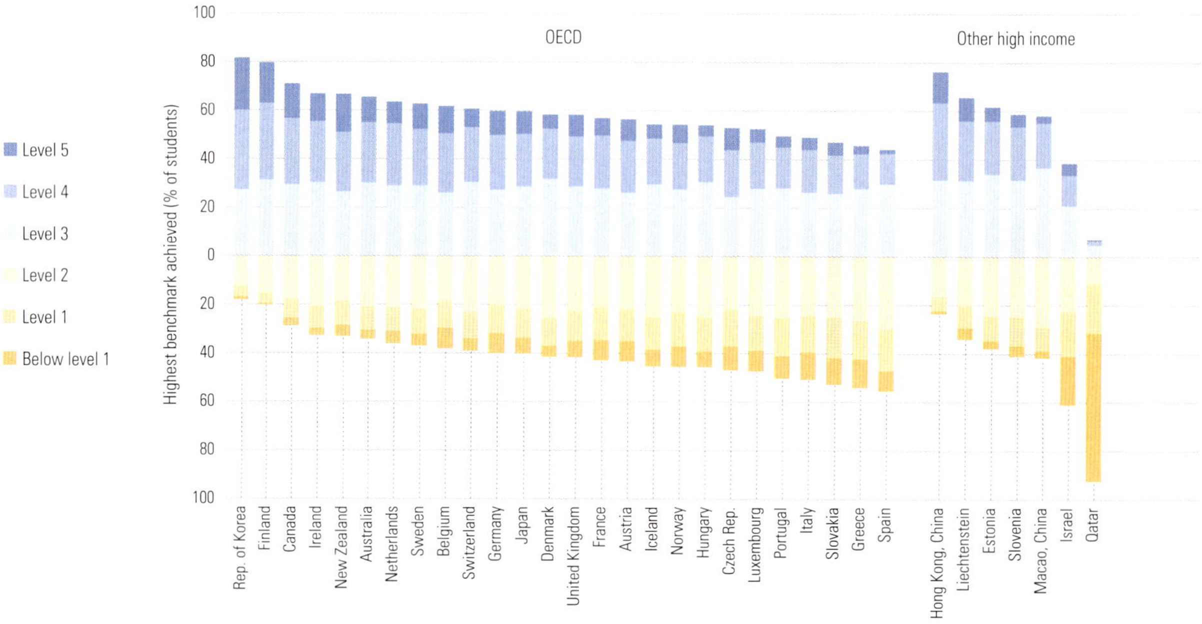

Notes: Below level 1 – students have serious difficulty using reading literacy as an effective tool to advance and extend their knowledge and skills in other areas. Level 5 – students can complete sophisticated reading tasks, such as evaluating critically, building hypotheses, and locating and accommodating concepts contrary to expectations.
Source: OECD (2007*b*).

Figure 2.39: Latin America's reading league has large performance gaps

Levels of reading performance of third grade primary school students in Latin America, 2007

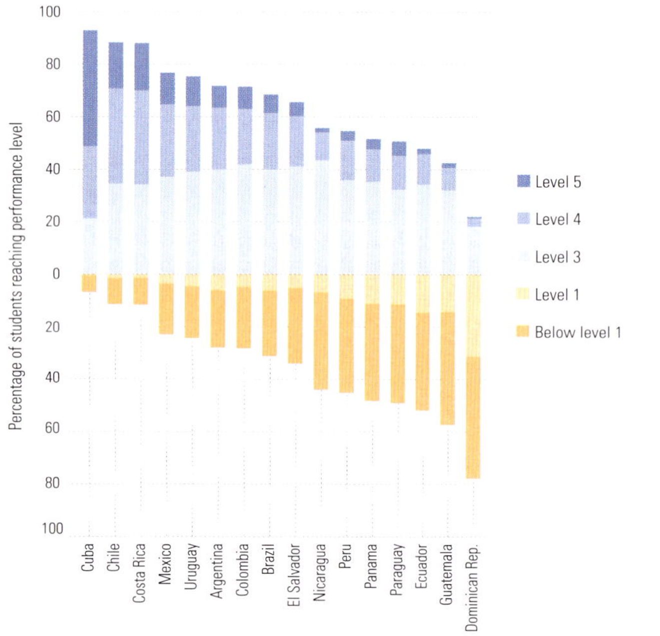

Notes: Level 1 – Students can locate information with a single meaning which is repeated in a prominent part of a text. Level 4 – Students can integrate and generalize information given in a paragraph, read a text and identify new information.
Source: UNESCO-OREALC (2008).

The case for reducing disparities in learning achievement goes beyond education. More equitable education, combined with sustained improvement in overall quality, is likely to be good for economic growth and social cohesion. Achieving greater equity will require a stronger focus on schools that serve the disadvantaged – and on the factors beyond education that diminish learning achievement. Many countries have shown that it is possible to combine equity with high levels of overall achievement.

Measuring equity in learning achievement is inherently difficult. One approach is simply to measure the gap between the best- and worst-performing students. Figure 2.40 applies this measure to grade 4 mathematics results using data from TIMSS. The sizes of the bars show differences in test scores between the best performers (ninety-fifth percentile) and the worst (fifth percentile), expressed as a percentage of the average country score. In OECD countries, disparities in learning are typically smaller than in other countries covered in TIMSS. In Germany, the difference between the best and worst performers is about 42% of the mean score of 525.

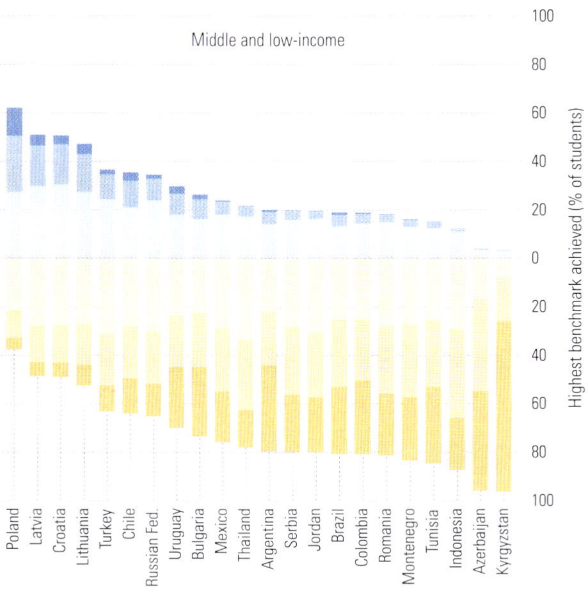

Disparities in learning tend to be much wider in low-income countries, with some of the widest disparities found in Arab states. In Yemen, the difference between the best and worst performers is 368 scale points, or 165% of the mean score of 224. A study of mathematics achievement in the Indian states of Orissa and Rajasthan found that the range in test scores between the best and worst performers was wider than for all TIMSS countries except South Africa (Das and Zajonc, 2008).[37]

Differences between schools play a critical role in the level of equity within education systems, as evidence from the OECD countries shows. Measured on a global scale, these countries have relatively low overall levels of inequality in learning achievement. Where they differ is in the share of inequality that can be traced back to schools. In Nordic countries such as Finland, Iceland and Norway, less than 10% of the variation in science scores is explained by school differences. At the other end of the scale, such differences account for over half the variation in test scores in Germany (Figure 2.41).[38] Such findings demonstrate the degree to which school-based factors can widen – or narrow – learning achievement gaps.

Box 2.22: Gender parity and learning achievement

In many countries, girls are less likely than boys to get into school. Once in school, though, they tend to perform as well as, or better than, their male classmates. While there are important gender-based differences in learning achievement by subject, learning achievement in general is not characterized by deep inequalities.

- *OECD countries.* In PISA 2006, average reading scores for 15-year-old girls were 8% higher than those of boys throughout the OECD. In mathematics, boys held an advantage over girls. The widest gap was found in Austria, where males' test scores were on average 5% higher. Gender differences in science tended to be statistically insignificant.
- *Arab States.* TIMSS 2007 covered thirteen of the twenty Arab States. In most of them, grade 8 girls outperformed boys in mathematics. In Qatar, girls' test scores were 13% higher than boys'. A similar number of countries recorded a female advantage in science, with larger gender gaps in many cases. In Qatar, girls scored on average 25% higher than boys.
- *Central and Eastern Europe.* PISA 2006 covered fifteen of the twenty-one countries in this region. All registered a large female advantage in reading performance. In most, gender gaps in mathematics were statistically insignificant; in the remaining countries boys tended to do slightly better than girls.
- *Latin America and the Caribbean.* Information from sixteen countries in the 2006 SERCE assessment in mathematics shows that boys in the sixth grade performed better than girls. When reading was assessed, girls outperformed boys, but in both subjects the average differences were small.
- *Sub-Saharan Africa.* Among Francophone countries participating in the PASEC assessment, there were no large gender differences in second and fifth grade performance in French or mathematics. For the thirteen countries participating in the 2000-2002 SACMEQ assessments, gender differences in sixth grade English were on the whole either statistically insignificant or small.[1] In mathematics, about half the participating countries showed no statistically significant gender difference. In the rest, males' average scores tended to be higher but the differences were not large.[2]

These findings confirm that gender gaps in overall achievement are modest. Where differences do exist, the data show that, except in the Arab States, girls do better in languages and boys in mathematics and science. Eliminating remaining gaps will be necessary if the goal of education for all is to be achieved. However, it has to be recognized that current data provide an incomplete picture, especially for countries that do not participate in international and regional assessments.

1. Seychelles was the exception, where girls' performance in English compared with that of boys was 0.65 of a standard deviation higher.

2. Seychelles was again the exception, where girls' performance in mathematics compared with that of boys was 0.38 of a standard deviation higher.

Sources: Bonnet (2009); Ma (2007); Mullis et al. (2008); OECD (2007*b*).

37. The study compares test scores of students at the fifth and ninety-fifth percentile of the test score distribution.

38. The overall dispersion of test scores in Germany is 110% of the OECD average, compared with 81% in Finland (OECD, 2007*b*).

Figure 2.40: Learning gaps are higher in poor countries

Learning gaps in TIMSS mathematics scale scores for fourth grade students, 2007

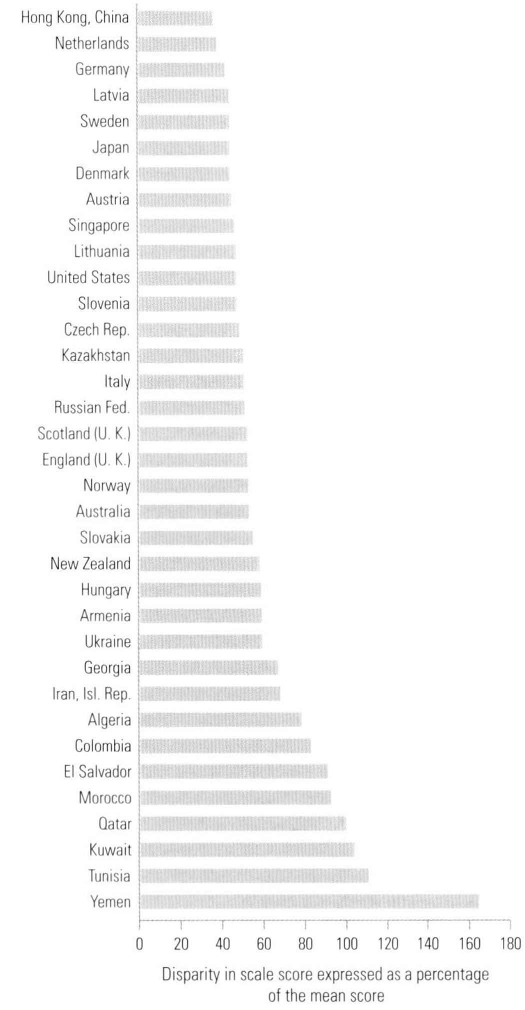

Note: The bars show the difference in test scores between students at the fifth and ninety-fifth percentiles, expressed as a percentage of the country's mean test score.
Source: Mullis et al. (2008).

Figure 2.41: When schools make a difference – inequality in student performance across schools varies widely in rich countries

Variation in PISA science scale scores in OECD countries explained by differences across schools, 2006

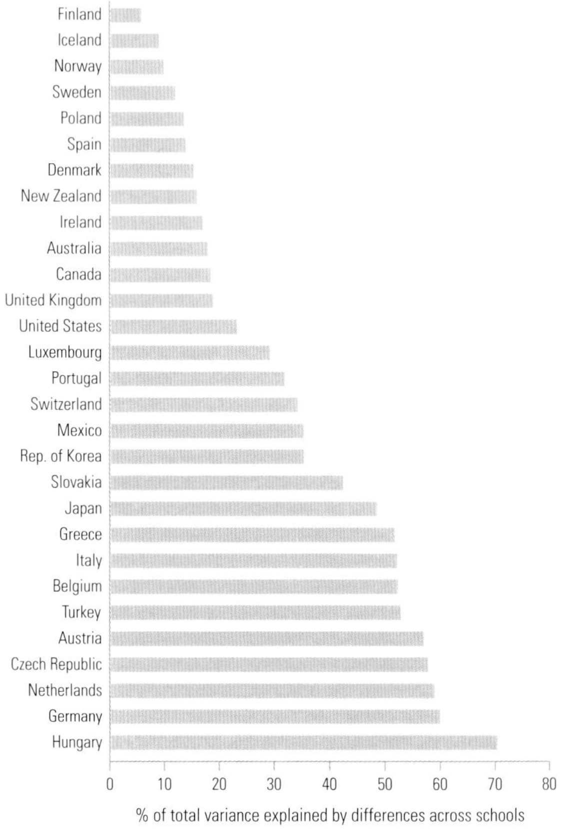

Note: The length of the bars shows the percentage of the total variation in student performance that is accounted for by performance differences between schools.
Source: OECD (2007*b*).

Does greater equity come at the price of reduced average performance? Not in this case: Finland is both more equitable and higher performing than Germany. The greater equity is partly the result of comprehensive education systems that provide similar opportunities for all. In recent years, Poland has achieved substantial reductions in inequality among schools by extending the duration of comprehensive education (Box 2.23). One factor contributing to school-based inequality in many OECD countries is the grouping of students into rigidly separate ability streams, or into academic and vocational tracks or schools (OECD, 2007*b*; Schutz et al., 2008). In Germany, vocational tracks at the secondary level have helped reduce youth unemployment, but early tracking has contributed to high levels of inequality across schools.

In many developing countries, differences in performance across schools are linked to the teaching environment. School systems are often marked by large variations in class size, availability of books and teaching materials, teacher quality and school building standards.[39] In the 2000–2002 SACMEQ assessment, differences among schools accounted for 37% of the variation in student reading performance (Dolata et al., 2004). Research in India and Pakistan has also found that differences in school characteristics help explain inequality in test scores (Das et al., 2006; Das and Zajonc, 2008). In Bolivia and Chile, a study showed that over half the large disparities in learning

39. Performance differences among schools can also arise because households with similar social and economic backgrounds often make the same school choices (e.g. public or private schooling), or because government policy on how students are selected into specific schools has this effect.

between indigenous and non-indigenous students were explained by the poor quality of schools serving indigenous students (McEwan, 2004).

These findings demonstrate that improving school quality and narrowing differences among schools will reduce inequality in student performance. In the mid-1990s, Brazil created the Fundo de Manutenção e Desenvolvimento do Ensino Fundamental e de Valorização do Magistério (FUNDEF), a fund to finance subnational spending on primary and lower secondary education to ensure a more equitable distribution of per-student spending across the country. Preliminary evidence suggests that this redistributive policy has narrowed learning inequalities, though only by a small amount (Gordon and Vegas, 2005). In other countries, per-student funding formulas have been introduced to ensure that resources are more equitably distributed across regions and population groups.

School-based disparities do not operate in isolation. In many cases they interact with and reinforce wider disadvantage. Parental income and education, home language and other factors are all strongly associated with learning achievement levels, as the following cases demonstrate:

- In Pakistan, children from families in the richest third of the population scored on average between 0.25 and 0.5 of a standard deviation higher than children from the poorest households (Das et al., 2006).
- In Peru, in national assessments of mathematics conducted in 2004, sixth grade pupils whose mother tongue was Spanish scored more than one standard deviation higher than children whose mother tongue was an indigenous language (Cueto et al., 2009).
- Fifth grade students from Cameroon's Bamileke language group scored 48% on the PASEC literacy test, compared with 56% for students from the Ewondo language group (Fehrler and Michaelowa, 2009).
- In the 2006 SERCE assessments in Latin America and the Caribbean, students who undertook a significant amount of work, inside and outside the home, had lower levels of mathematics achievement on average. For example, in El Salvador, sixth graders who worked had average scores 6% lower than those of children who did not (Bonnet, 2009).
- A longitudinal study in Ethiopia found that 42% of 12-year-olds who had lost their mothers between ages 8 and 12 were unable to read, while for children with both parents living the figure was 23% (Himaz, 2009). The study attributed the difference to lower school enrolment among orphans, as well as poorer performance in school.

Box 2.23: Improving equity in Poland

In 1999, Poland started providing an additional year of general education before students were split into upper secondary school tracks. By using three rounds of PISA it is possible to assess the reform's impact on equity:

- From 2000 to 2003, average variation in student performance in science fell from 51% of the OECD average to 15%. By 2006, Poland had one of the lowest levels of variation in science performance among participating countries (Figure 2.41). Improvement in equity came about at the same time as general improvement in performance. For example, average reading performance of 15-year-olds increased by twenty-nine score points between 2000 and 2006.
- Most of the improvement occurred among students with poor performance. From 2000 to 2006, the proportion of students failing to score above level 1 in reading competency fell from 23% to 16%.
- Students in the vocational track appear to have benefited most from greater integration of the system.

Source: OECD (2007*b*).

School-based disparities interact with student background and socio-economic status

In countries with more equitable systems, children's backgrounds are less important in determining levels of achievement. In countries where there is a strong relationship between student background and performance, or where large differences in student background exist, reducing differences in school quality is unlikely to be enough to improve equity significantly. Targeted programmes to improve learning among children who are being left behind will also be needed (see Chapter 3). In Mexico, the Consejo Nacional de Fomento Educativo (CONAFE) provides supplemental funds, learning materials – including textbooks in indigenous languages – and teacher support to schools in areas marked by consistent underperformance and disadvantage. Evaluations indicate that these efforts have narrowed the gap in primary school mathematics scores, though they have had little impact on Spanish scores (Vegas and Petrow, 2008).

Teaching reading in the early primary grades is crucial for learning

Children lacking reading and comprehension skills are unable to use textbooks and other written materials and to take advantage of learning opportunities in or out of school. Research shows that children who have difficulties acquiring these skills in their early lives are likely to struggle throughout their school careers (Jukes et al., 2006). Schools in many developing countries are failing to equip young learners with these basic skills. If the EFA quality goal is to be achieved, it is crucial for reading difficulties to be detected early and acted upon quickly.

It is crucial for reading difficulties to be detected early and acted upon quickly

Understanding is central to the achievement of reading skills. Children need to be able to read with sufficient fluency to obtain meaning from what is being read. Reading accurately and quickly has been shown in many cases to be strongly correlated with comprehension (Abadzi, 2006; Fuchs et al., 2001). In a small-scale survey of Peruvian first and second graders, children who could answer a set of three comprehension questions correctly read on average at seventy-seven words per minute, compared with fifteen words per minute for children who only answered one comprehension question correctly (Abadzi et al., 2005).[40] Early grade reading assessments aim to test comprehension by measuring reading fluency (Box 2.24). Estimates vary, but reading fluency in excess of forty words per minute is thought to be required for comprehension (Abadzi, 2006).[41]

Small-scale reading assessments conducted in several low-income countries paint a worrying picture (Table 2.7).[42] While these tests are not nationally representative, they often point to very low levels of fluency in reading. Average performance in many test sites falls far short of automatic reading, implying that large numbers of children are failing to achieve the basic reading skills necessary to facilitate further learning:

- In Gambia, children in grades 1 to 3 were able, on average, to read six words correctly in a minute.
- In Liberia, grade 2 students could read eighteen words per minute. Although fluency increased in grade 3, it was still below the estimated forty words per minute required for comprehension.

Looking beyond the averages reveals the poor outcomes for some children:

- In Ethiopia, a 2008 study of grade 3 students in Woliso district found that 36% could not read a single word in Afan Oromo, the local language (DeStefano and Elaheebocus, 2009).
- In Guatemala, two-thirds of students could read more than forty words correctly per minute but wide disparities across language groups existed. Students whose mother tongue was Mam had average reading speeds below forty words per minute whereas students whose mother tongue was Quiche or Spanish read more than sixty words per minute (Dowd, 2009).

Assessing reading skills early in primary school provides an opportunity to identify children with low learning achievement and take remedial measures that can help prevent dropout and grade repetition. It is far less time-consuming and costly to prevent low achievement at an early age than to act later.

Evidence from several countries demonstrates that policy interventions can make a difference in improving reading skills. Involving schools and communities is a key to success. A programme operated by a non-government organization in Uttar Pradesh, India, has used 'remedial reading camps' run by volunteer trainers to achieve impressive improvements in early reading (Box 2.25). In the Malindi district of Kenya, teachers were trained for five days on a set of carefully designed lessons to teach effective reading skills to grade 2 students (Crouch et al., 2009). Significant improvements resulted: comparing grade 2 results before and after teachers were trained showed that reading speeds had improved by 80%, on average. While it is difficult to attribute all the improvement to the training, the study showed that this relatively small intervention and the information it generated on the poor state of reading skills contributed significantly.[43] Pilot studies in Mali and the Niger in 2007 also demonstrated promising approaches to improving reading skills at relatively low cost (Mitton, 2008).

Whether such pilot programmes can be scaled up to improve reading across national education

40. The positive correlation between comprehension and oral reading fluency has been the subject of much research. For additional examples see Kudo and Bazan (2009) and RTI International (2008).

41. In the United States, children are identified as being at risk of developing learning difficulties if their reading speed is below seventy words per minute in grade 2 and below eighty in grade 3.

42. It is not possible to compare across countries in the table owing to the different languages used and differences in the ages of student populations.

43. The study was set up as a randomized trial but improvement in reading skills was seen in schools where the teachers had received the training as well as in the schools where they did not. The study showed that leakage of teaching techniques and the transfer of teachers between control and treatment schools accounted for similar improvements in both types of schools.

Box 2.24: What are early grade reading assessments and what can they be used for?

Failure to develop reading skills in the early school years can severely compromise later learning, undermining progression through grades and contributing to early dropout. Early grade reading assessments help teachers identify problems and correct them. The components assessed include:

- phonemic awareness – children can focus on, manipulate and break apart the sounds in words;
- ability to use phonics – they can understand and apply knowledge of how letters are linked to sounds to form letter-sound correspondences and spelling patterns;
- fluency – they can read orally with speed, accuracy and proper expression;
- vocabulary – they know an increasing number of words, both orally and in print;
- comprehension – they can actively engage with and derive meaning from texts.

Most of these components are tested by counting the letters and words that children can sound out accurately in one minute. While there are obvious dangers with mechanistic application, the assessments can be used to capture both word recognition and understanding. Similar approaches are used in adult literacy work. Early grade reading assessments are not designed to serve as tests for grading students or ranking schools. They are most useful when integrated into a wider framework for building children's confidence and equipping schools and teachers to respond to their needs.

Sources: Abadzi (2006); Kudo and Bazan (2009); RTI International (2008).

Table 2.7: Results from early grade reading assessments (correct words per minute)

	Year	Grade	Connected text fluency	Sample size
Tests of reading in English				
Gambia	2007	1-3	6	1,200
Malindi, Kenya	2007	2	10	40 schools
Liberia	2008	2	18	429
Liberia	2008	3	28	407
Tests of reading in Spanish				
Nicaragua	2006	3	18	2,206
Junin, Peru	2008	3	57	475
Tests of reading in French				
Senegal	2007	1-3	19	502

Notes: Unless otherwise stated, sample size refers to the number of students tested. The studies recorded in the table also measured other aspects of reading outlined in Box 2.24 and in some cases tested reading in local languages as well.
Sources: Castro and Laguna (2008); Crouch and Korda (2008); Crouch et al (2009); Jammeh (2008); Kudo and Bazan (2009); Sambe and Sprenger-Charolles (2008).

systems is open to question. Many of these programmes succeeded because of intensive efforts to mobilize communities, resources and local professionals. Duplicating these efforts is often difficult for subnational authorities, let alone national ministries. Even so, the success of pilot programmes shows that substantial improvements are possible. Central governments and education authorities can make a difference to early learning through action at many levels, including training teachers more effectively and providing appropriate teaching materials.

Box 2.25: India – remedial reading classes in Uttar Pradesh

A baseline survey conducted in 2005 in Jaunpur district in Uttar Pradesh revealed poor acquisition of basic skills. Among 7- to 14-year-olds, 60% could not read and understand a simple story designed for first grade students. In this context, a randomized evaluation examined the impact on basic education skills of combinations of three interventions:

- encouraging community participation by providing information and facilitating discussion on the status of local schools and outlining to village education committees their roles and responsibilities;
- training community members to assess children's learning and presenting these findings at village meetings;
- training local volunteers in simple techniques for teaching children to read and introducing reading classes after school.

The evaluation found that information-sharing did not improve reading skills but that extra classes after school had a big impact. Overall, the evaluation showed that it was possible to get children who were not fluent readers to read fairly fluently by combining instruction in school with additional reading classes which students attend for two hours a day over a period of three months.

Source: Banerjee et al. (2008).

In India, 'remedial reading camps' have achieved impressive improvements in early reading

Improving learning in schools

In Ethiopia and Guatemala, children were in class and learning for only a third of the time schools were officially open

One of the most important requirements for sustained progress towards better quality in education is an improved learning environment, encompassing the physical school infrastructure, the learning process and the interaction between children and teachers.

Low achievement levels are often associated with a poor school environment. Badly ventilated classrooms, leaking roofs, poor sanitation and lack of materials represent significant barriers to effective learning in many schools. Over half of rural primary students in Peru, the Philippines and Sri Lanka attend schools viewed by the head teacher as needing major rehabilitation (UIS, 2008*b*).[44] A recent survey of primary schools in two Nigerian states found that over 80% of classrooms in Enugu and 50% in Kaduna either did not have a blackboard, or had one that was barely usable (World Bank, 2008*c*). Such conditions are common in many countries.

The fact that the most marginalized children often attend the poorest-quality schools adds to their learning disadvantages. Urban-rural divides figure prominently in school quality disparities. In the Philippines, over 70% of urban grade 4 students attended schools with basic facilities such as blackboards and toilets, but only about 50% of rural students attended schools with these facilities (UIS, 2008*b*). Improving learning in such environments requires redistributing resources towards poorer areas.

Many studies highlight the positive role of appropriate textbooks (Boissiere, 2004; Scheerens, 2004). A detailed evaluation of Ghana's basic education system found that improvements in mathematics and English test scores from 1988 to 2003 had been brought about in part through increased availability of textbooks (White, 2004).

The longer children spend in school over the course of a year, the greater their opportunity to master the curriculum and achieve learning objectives (Boissiere, 2004). The official number of teaching hours varies considerably by country (Benavot, 2004), but time spent on effective learning is what matters for achievement. In effective classrooms, about 80% of class time is spent on learning – a benchmark that many schools in developing countries fail to meet (Abadzi, 2006). Student and teacher absenteeism further reduces learning time. In Nepal, a detailed study of a small number of primary schools showed that, while schools were officially open for 192 days, the average student experienced only 97 days of effective learning (Dowd, 2009). In Ethiopia and Guatemala, children were in class and learning for a third of the time schools were officially open (DeStefano and Elaheebocus, 2009; Dowd, 2009). Better monitoring, improved teacher incentives and targeted support for students struggling to attend regularly can all increase learning time and performance.

Increasing the amount of time children spend learning can be difficult. Chronic overcrowding of classrooms has led many countries to operate double-shift systems in schools. These offer potential efficiency gains in terms of the number of children covered, but the gains sometimes come at a price. In francophone Africa, double-shift teaching has sometimes reduced learning achievement, primarily because children spend less time in school (Michaelowa, 2001). In the longer term, additional classrooms can be built to accommodate a single-shift system. However, policy-makers need to assess whether building classrooms is as cost-effective in improving learning as other investments, such as providing more teaching and learning materials. Creating conditions that enable children to remain in school, ensuring that teachers actually attend and organizing the school day to devote more time to learning are all low-cost options with potentially high returns.

The important role of teachers

Teachers are the single most important education resource in any country. From early childhood through primary and secondary school, the presence of a qualified, well-motivated teacher is vital for effective learning. What students achieve in school is heavily influenced by classroom practices and teachers' skills (Aslam and Kingdon, 2007). In many countries, shortages of trained teachers remain a major barrier to achieving the Education for All goals, especially among marginalized groups.

Pre-primary education. Early childhood teachers and carers play a crucial role in preparing children for school and supporting their social, emotional and cognitive development. The quality of care and teaching depends critically on the pupil/teacher ratio, teacher training and the creation of an active learning environment (Schumacher and Hoffmann, 2008; UNESCO, 2005). Many countries do not meet minimum standards of quality, however. In Bolivia, India, Liberia,[45] Nepal, Uganda and the United

44. This is the percentage of grade 4 pupils in schools where the head stated that the 'school needs complete rebuilding' or 'some classrooms need major repairs'.

45. In Liberia, the pupil/teacher ratio increased from 14 to 142 between 2006 and 2008. This is due to a substantial decrease in volunteer and other untrained teachers previously recruited to meet the teacher demand following the civil crisis (UIS database).

Republic of Tanzania, for example, the pre-primary pupil/teacher ratio was 40:1 or higher in 2007 (see annex, Statistical Table 10A).

Data from within countries highlight particular disadvantages facing the marginalized in this respect. In Kenya, the national ratio of pupils to trained pre-primary teachers is 54:1. In the arid, largely pastoral district of Turkana, one of Kenya's poorest, the ratio is 123:1 (Ruto et al., 2009). In Indonesia, the share of pre-primary teachers with at least a diploma ranges from 60% in Banten, a relatively prosperous area, to only 1% in Maluku, a region with high levels of poverty (Indonesia Ministry of National Education, 2007).

Primary education. Higher enrolment since 1999 has gone hand in hand with an increase in the recruitment of primary teachers. Many countries in sub-Saharan Africa – including Burkina Faso, Burundi, the Niger and Senegal[46] – have more than doubled the teacher workforce in most cases, improving the pupil/teacher ratio (see annex, Statistical Table 10A). As countries seek to accelerate progress towards universal primary education, they will need to sustain a concerted drive to recruit and train teachers.

Despite the progress of the past decade, teacher shortages remain a serious concern. Countries set their own targets for pupil/teacher ratios, making cross-country comparisons difficult (Bennell, 2009). However, the most widely used international ceiling for the pupil/teacher ratio is 40:1 (Takala, 2003; World Bank Independent Evaluation Group, 2006). In 2007, 26 countries out of 171 with data were above this ceiling, all but four of them in sub-Saharan Africa (see annex, Statistical Table 10A). While data coverage is patchy, there are also concerns over the ratio of pupils to *trained* teachers. Countries including Madagascar, Mozambique, Sierra Leone and Togo have ratios of pupils to trained teacher in excess of 80:1 (Figure 2.42). In fifteen of the forty countries with data, the share of trained teachers in the workforce has declined since 1999, in some cases dramatically (see annex, Statistical Table 10A). In Togo, it has fallen from 31% to 15% as recruitment has shifted towards contract teachers.

National average pupil/teacher ratios can conceal large disparities. A recent review of teacher deployment patterns examined differences across regions in ten countries in sub-Saharan Africa (Pôle de Dakar, 2009). In some countries the ratios vary by a factor of three. While low ratios are often

Figure 2.42: Trained teachers are sometimes in short supply

Ratios of pupils to teachers and pupils to trained teachers in primary education, selected countries, 2007

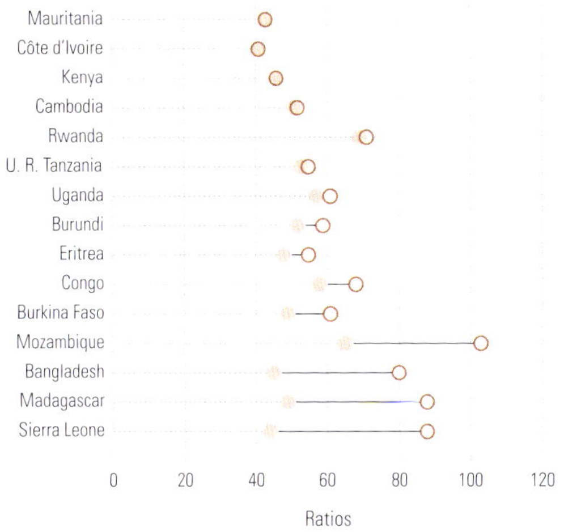

Note: Among countries with available data, only those with pupil/teacher ratios at or above 40:1 are included. Countries sorted by the gap between the pupil/teacher and the pupil/trained teacher ratios.

Sources: Annex, Statistical Table 10A; UIS database.

found in rural areas with highly dispersed populations, high ratios tend to be concentrated in areas marked by poverty and acute disadvantage. In Uganda, northern regions affected by conflict were marked by pupil/teacher ratios in excess of 90:1 – nearly double the national average (Figure 2.43).

Urban-rural differences create another layer of inequality. The pattern of disadvantage is highly variable but overall ratios tend to be higher in urban areas (Zhang et al., 2008). In other countries such as Malawi, though, the average urban pupil/teacher ratio is 46:1, compared with 81:1 in rural areas (Mulkeen, 2009). However, trained teachers are often concentrated in urban areas. Whereas 60% of teachers in the Ugandan capital, Kampala, are trained, the figure falls to 11% in the rural district of Yumbe. In Lesotho, nearly a quarter of teachers in lowland areas are unqualified, compared with about half in the mountainous and less accessible areas (Mulkeen, 2009). These areas also tend to have higher repetition rates and, like other rural areas, poorer test scores (Mulkeen and Chen, 2008).

To some degree, such deployment patterns reflect self-perpetuating processes of selection and inbuilt disadvantage. Trained teachers are more likely to choose to work in urban areas, especially in systems where their remuneration is linked to

In northern Uganda, there were 90 pupils per teacher – nearly double the national average

46. In Senegal, this increase in teachers is due to the creation of more schools, upgrading of schools with incomplete primary education cycles and double-shift teaching (UIS, 2009*b*).

Figure 2.43: National averages can hide large differences in pupil/teacher ratios

Provincial disparities in primary education pupil/teacher ratios, selected sub-Saharan African countries, circa 2005/2006

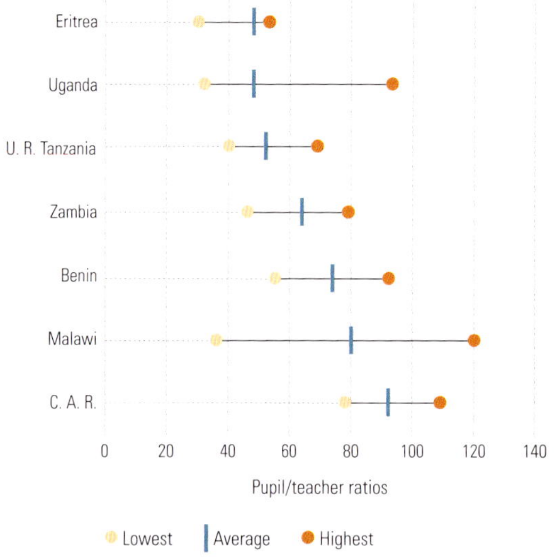

Note: Except where indicated, data do not distinguish between civil servant teachers and community teachers, or between public and private sector teachers. Benin data exclude community teachers. C. A. R. data include community teachers. Countries sorted by average pupil/teacher ratio.
Source: Pôle de Dakar (2009), Table 5.4.

parental contributions. Opportunities for professional development are also more likely to be concentrated in urban areas, enabling urban teachers to gain qualifications more readily than their rural counterparts (Bennell and Akyeampong, 2007). Cities may be seen as preferable to rural areas for other reasons, ranging from the quality of housing, amenities and schools to the proximity of friends and family. Concerns over living in remote and unfamiliar rural communities can also play a role. Such factors play a part in the preference of female teachers for urban areas in many countries. In Uganda and Zambia, the share of female teachers in urban primary schools is about 60%, compared with 15% to 35% in rural areas (Mulkeen, 2009).

Projected primary school teacher requirements to 2015

Future teacher recruitment needs vary enormously by region. They are determined partly by current deficits and partly by a complex mix of demographics, enrolment trends and numbers of children still out of school. The UIS has re-estimated the total number of primary education teachers that will be required to achieve the goal of universal primary education by 2015 (UIS, 2009*e*).[47]

The numbers underline the scale of the challenge facing many countries.

- An additional 1.9 million teachers will have to be recruited to reach universal primary education by 2015.
- Two-thirds of the additional teachers – around 1.2 million – will be needed in sub-Saharan Africa.
- The Arab States account for around 15% of the additional teachers required.

The effort needed to close these gaps varies by country (Figure 2.44). Many governments will have to expand recruitment by 4% to 18% annually. For some countries, this means maintaining the rate of increase registered since 1999. Others will need to step up the pace of recruitment and budget for new posts, including Chad, Côte d'Ivoire, Djibouti, Eritrea, Kenya and Uganda.

In addition to increasing recruitment to achieve universal primary education, governments have to replace teachers expected to retire or leave their posts before 2015.[48] Taking into account the need to replace teachers drives up the regional and global recruitment numbers (UIS, 2009*e*):

- An additional 8.4 million primary teachers will have to be recruited and trained worldwide to replace existing teachers expected to retire or leave their posts before 2015.
- Nearly a quarter of these teachers – around 2.1 million – will be needed in East Asia and the Pacific.
- North America and Western Europe account for 17%, South and West Asia for 19% and sub-Saharan Africa for another 15% of the additional recruitment needed to replace teachers leaving their posts by 2015.

A total of 10.3 million additional teachers will be needed worldwide by 2015, if the 1.9 million new teachers required to achieve universal primary education are added to the 8.4 million needed to replace departing teachers. The number of extra teaching posts that need to be created may seem small compared to the teacher needs resulting from attrition. However, creating new posts requires an increase in the overall budget allocated for teacher salaries. In many countries this requires greater effort than that of filling vacant posts.

An additional 1.9 million teachers will have to be recruited to reach UPE by 2015

47. Estimates of teacher needs are based on assumptions regarding enrolment, repetition and pupil/teacher ratios. For technical details see UIS (2009*e*).

48. These projections are based on a teacher attrition rate of 5% and include additional teachers needed to fill vacancies resulting from increased attrition caused by the expansion of universal primary education and population growth. For results using other attrition assumptions see UIS (2009*e*).

Figure 2.44: The rate at which new teaching posts are created will need to increase if universal primary education is to be achieved by 2015

Annual growth in teacher posts needed to reach universal primary education by 2015, selected countries

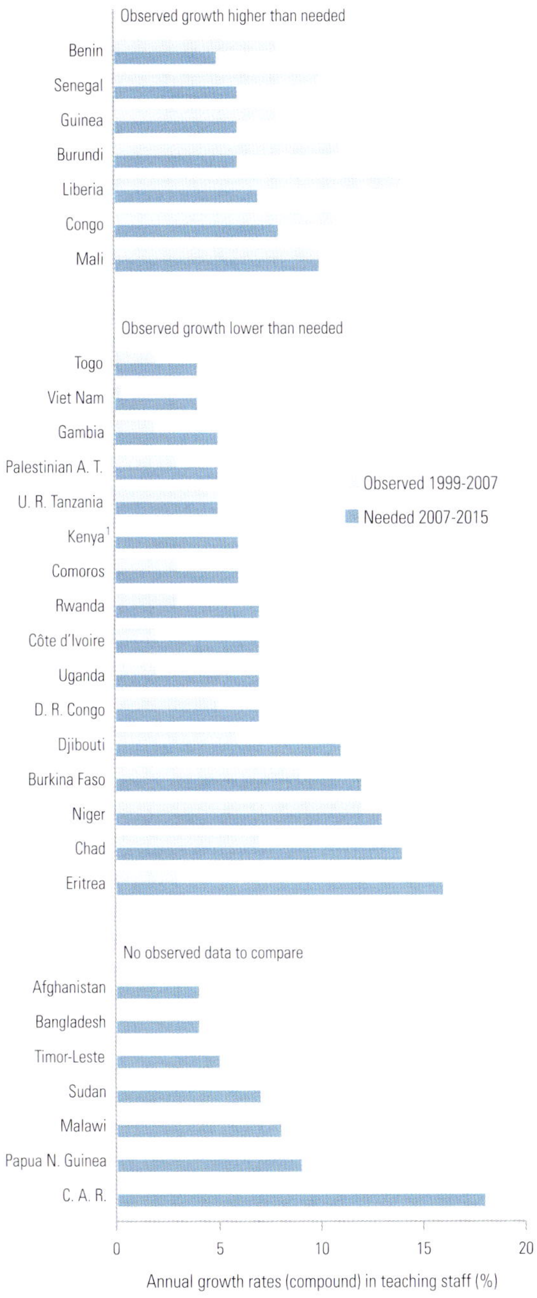

Note: Only countries in which the current number of teachers must expand by at least 30% to reach the projected number needed to achieve universal primary education on time are included.

1. Kenya's observed growth rate between 1999 and 2007 was -0.1% but for expositional purposes this is not shown here.

Source: UIS (2009*e*).

The capacity of countries to finance increased recruitment varies, but for many the prospect of closing the gap will hinge partly on aid donors. A sustained push to recruit teachers will increase the future recurrent costs that governments have to plan for. For low-income countries with a limited revenue base, multiyear aid commitments over five to ten years, backed by predictable delivery, will be vital to the sustainable financing of teacher recruitment. This will require both an increase in aid and a radical change in aid management practices – issues discussed in Chapter 4.

Recruitment is just one part of a far wider set of issues that governments have to address. In many of the world's poorest countries, the problem involves not just low teacher numbers but also poor teacher morale. Attracting and retaining well-qualified candidates is increasingly difficult, as many countries' high attrition rates show. Low pay is endemic, a problem that in many countries not only hinders recruitment of able candidates but forces many teachers to supplement their salaries, thus reducing the time they devote to teaching. In Bangladesh, teachers in state-aided schools are paid less than US$1 a day, and two-thirds report undertaking additional income-earning activities (Financial Management Reform Programme, 2006).

In many of the world's poorest countries, the problem involves low teacher numbers or poor teacher morale

Teacher salaries are a contentious issue in many countries. Governments face an obvious dilemma: how to increase teacher recruitment without creating unsustainable budget pressures. Some countries have attempted to address this dilemma by reducing salary costs, notably by hiring fewer teachers under standard civil service pay terms and hiring more contract teachers at lower levels of remuneration and benefits. Finance ministries and several aid donors have actively encouraged more contract employment. The risk is that this will lead to recruitment of less qualified candidates and to even more pressure on teachers to supplement their incomes through other forms of employment, with attendant implications for morale. There is evidence from West Africa that increased recourse to contract teachers has compromised education quality (UNESCO, 2008*a*). While a balance has to be struck between affordability and good teaching, the limits to cost-cutting also have to be recognized. Governments and donors need to ensure that teacher pay and conditions reflect a commitment to delivering good-quality education through a well-qualified and motivated workforce.

Initial training and professional development are also crucial to morale and effective teaching. Teachers are the product of the education systems they teach in. Where these systems are of low quality it is even more important for teachers to receive effective training and support throughout their careers. Teachers need to understand the content of the curriculum and be able to communicate it to students of varying ability. In many countries, initial training is not good enough to develop these skills. To make matters worse, many teachers do not even receive initial training. In Mozambique, one recent evaluation found that 41% of primary school teachers were untrained (Mulkeen and Chen, 2008). In-service training, which is vital to build on initial skills, is also poorly developed in many low-income countries (Leu, 2004; Lewin and Stuart, 2003).

Conclusion

The ultimate aim of schools is to equip children with the skills and knowledge they need to realize their potential, develop secure livelihoods and participate in society. Evidence presented in this section suggests that many schools are failing to meet even minimum standards for the quality of education. Millions of children, especially those from socially marginalized groups, are completing their primary education without having acquired basic literacy and numeracy skills. At the secondary level, too, many education systems in developing countries are characterized by low levels of learning and high levels of inequality. Equipping schools to provide good quality education will require governments to focus more strongly on recruiting and training teachers, supplying textbooks and developing classroom practices that promote active learning. Support for literacy and reading in early grades has an especially important role to play, as these skills create the foundation for future learning. □

Estimating the cost of achieving Education for All

The Dakar Framework for Action includes strong commitments on education financing. Developing countries pledged to 'enhance significantly investment in basic education' (para. 8[i]), while rich nations promised an increase in aid, mainly in the form of grants and concessional finance, to ensure that 'no countries seriously committed to education for all will be thwarted in their achievement of this goal by a lack of resources' (para. 10).

Ten years later, finance remains a major barrier to Education for All. Developing countries have stepped up their efforts to make domestic resources available, albeit on an uneven basis. Many could do much more to raise their investment in education by strengthening revenue collection and equity in public spending. The international community has also increased aid for basic education, but collectively donors have fallen far short of delivering on their commitments made in Dakar.

This section assesses the scale of the Education for All financing gap. It sets out the results of a costing exercise covering forty-six low-income countries.[49] The exercise looks at the financing requirements for achieving a range of goals in basic education and beyond. Among the key findings:

- *The financing gap is far larger than previously assumed.* Even with an increased domestic resource mobilization effort, low-income countries face a financing gap of about US$16 billion for basic education (literacy, pre-primary and primary education), representing 1.5% of their collective GDP.[50] This is a third higher than the previous estimate. Factoring in lower secondary education would increase the gap to US$25 billion.
- *Low-income countries need to strengthen efficiency and equity in education financing.* There is considerable scope for making more domestic resources available by improving revenue collection, giving education a higher priority and focusing more on basic education. Increased revenue collection and greater equity could enhance domestic financing for basic education by about 0.7% of GDP. This represents US$7 billion, or two-thirds of current levels of spending in the countries included in the study. Several countries have the potential to double the share of GDP allocated to basic education. Exploiting that potential should be part of the Education for All contract between developing countries and donors.
- *Aid donors need to undertake a 'Gleneagles plus' aid commitment.* Aid levels for basic education in the forty-six countries covered need to rise sixfold from their current level, from US$2.7 billion to US$16 billion.[51] Even if donors act on the commitments made at the 2005 Group of Eight summit in Gleneagles, Scotland, and substantially increase aid to the poorest countries, the level will still fall US$11 billion short. An emergency pledging conference should be convened to mobilize the additional financing required.
- *Reaching the marginalized requires additional finance.* Failure to take into account the costs associated with reaching marginalized groups has contributed to systematic underestimation of the financing gap. It costs more to extend education opportunities to the most disadvantaged than it costs to reach better-off households. The new study estimates that additional measures to extend primary school opportunities to social groups facing extreme and persistent deprivation will cost US$3.7 billion annually.

Ten years after Dakar, finance remains a major barrier to Education for All

The revised Education for All financing gap points to challenges for both aid recipients and donors. Developing countries need to increase the level of ambition for public spending in education at a time when slower economic growth is putting budgets under pressure. Most major donors, for their part, are gripped by recession and rising fiscal deficits. Some are cutting aid budgets. Others are reviewing future commitments. As these pressures mount, it is important that governments recognize the crucial role of education investments in creating the foundations for recovery and future poverty reduction efforts.

Part 1 of this section sets out the cost estimates and the assumptions behind them. Part 2 presents the findings on the Education for All financing gap.

49. Full details of the methodology and results of the study are available in (EPDC and UNESCO, 2009).

50. These figures relate to average financing gaps and GDP levels in low-income countries between 2008 and 2015.

51. Chapter 4 reports that annual aid commitments to basic education averaged US$4.9 billion in 2006 and 2007 (see Figure 4.7). The low-income countries included in this costing exercise received 55% of those commitments and US$2.7 billion of total aid to basic education. Chapter 4 shows that low-income countries received 60% of all aid to basic education, but the figure includes some small countries excluded from the costing exercise, as well as India, which the OECD-DAC defined as a low-income country at the time of writing.

Costing the commitment to Education for All goals

Countries need to consider the financing required to reach those who have been left behind

Too often, governments and aid donors have adopted bold goals at international development summits but failed to put in place the financing measures needed to achieve them. How closely are the Education for All goals aligned with current financing?

Several studies have addressed this question. In 2003, the World Bank carried out a detailed analysis of the financing required to achieve universal primary education in low-income countries (Bruns et al., 2003). Basing its estimate on assumptions about economic growth, revenue collection, public spending and aid levels, the study put the annual financing gap at US$3.6 billion (constant 2000 prices). The first *EFA Global Monitoring Report 2002* adjusted this estimate for more moderate economic growth, the impact of HIV and AIDS, and the inclusion of cash-transfer programmes targeted at girls and poor households. These adjustments increased the estimated financing gap for universal primary education to US$5.6 billion (constant 2000 prices). The *EFA Global Monitoring Report 2007* updated this estimate to reflect the fact that aid levels had been lower than expected. Rough estimates were also made of additional financing for early childhood care and education, and literacy.[52] These adjustments produced an annual financing gap estimate in low-income countries of US$11 billion (constant 2003 prices) – a figure that has been widely used as a reference point by the international community.

The costing exercise undertaken for this Report provides a comprehensive review and reassessment of the financing gap (EPDC and UNESCO, 2009). Using the latest available national data, the study updates the global estimate for low-income countries.[53] It covers a wider range of education goals than in the 2003 study, recognizing that Education for All is about more than universal primary education. Another significant departure is the estimation of costs for reaching the most marginalized. Earlier studies assumed the cost of extending education to out-of-school children was the same as the average cost of providing education to those in school, but this assumption is flawed. Many children in the most marginalized groups live in remote areas and suffer chronic poverty and extreme gender disadvantage. Reaching these children requires higher levels of spending, not just on providing schools and teachers but also on supporting demand for education.

There are strong grounds for factoring in these additional costs. Marginalized children have the same right to education as others and that right carries with it a claim on financial resources. Equity in public spending means governments must assess what it takes to deliver equivalent opportunities to children in very different circumstances. The fact that marginalized children have benefited less than others from past public spending reinforces their claim to fairer treatment. Moreover, failure to consider the financing needed to reach those who have been left behind will guarantee that many countries miss the Education for All targets.

Financing gap estimates cannot be considered in isolation. The same level of financing in two different countries can produce widely divergent results. Countries vary not just in their individual cost structures, but also in efficiency and equity in public spending on education. Some countries achieve more for less because they have more efficient procurement systems, school construction programmes and textbook supply arrangements. National differences in teacher remuneration, the biggest single item in most education budgets, can have an enormous bearing on relative cost structures. The level of equity matters because it influences the degree to which increased public spending translates into advances for the most marginalized. For all these reasons, average costs vary widely by country. The marginal costs associated with reaching disadvantaged groups are likely to depend on factors such as the depth of poverty and structures of inequality.

The limitations of global costing exercises have to be recognized. Such exercises can help establish broad orders of magnitude for the financing required to achieve specified goals. But they cannot substitute for detailed estimates drawn up at the national level. Bottom-up estimates provide much clearer insights into the financing needed to achieve policy goals. It is a matter of concern that, almost a decade after the World Education Forum in Dakar, governments and donors continue to address this task in such a fragmented and haphazard fashion – an issue taken up further in Chapter 4. The estimates for the Education for All financing gaps presented in this Report are based on the most recent data available (Box 2.26).

52. The financing gap estimate for the literacy target was half the US$2 billion annual estimate of the cost of literacy programmes in all developing countries – a much larger group than the low-income group used for the other components of the estimate (Van Ravens and Aggio, 2005). It was also assumed that the financing gap for early childhood care and education was similar to that for literacy.

53. The study covers forty-six of the forty-nine countries classified by the World Bank as low income as of April 2009. The study excludes Solomon Islands and Sao Tome and Principe because their populations were below 1 million and the Democratic People's Republic of Korea because of lack of data. It includes the Sudan because southern Sudan has a separate education system and can be considered low income.

Box 2.26: Information used for the global cost estimates

The study has drawn on the most recent cross-country data in preparing the global financing estimates. Variables covered include the size of the school age population, school system structure and capacity, student progression rates (e.g. promotion, repetition and dropout rates) and key costs such as those for teachers, classrooms and textbooks. The three main sources of data are:

- the United Nations World Population Prospects database, for information on school age populations and projections of population growth;
- the UNESCO Institute for Statistics, for information on enrolment, student progression rates, teachers, classrooms and education financing;
- the World Bank and International Monetary Fund, for information on overall government revenue and economic growth projections.

These were supplemented by over thirty other sources, including national education sector reports and plans, and public expenditure reviews. Information was also collected directly from UNESCO offices and other studies commissioned for the costing exercise (Box 2.27). In the few cases where no national data were available, regional aggregates were used. There were often large differences in reported data for a given country, particularly with respect to education costs. Every effort was made to use the best available data. However, in some cases there are large margins of error. Overall, the cost estimates should be treated as indicative of the magnitude of financing gaps in low-income countries.

A detailed outline of the methodology, data and results is available in EPDC and UNESCO (2009).

However, their indicative and provisional nature is readily acknowledged.

Estimating the financing required to meet the Education for All goals poses several problems because the goals set in Dakar do not all include quantitative targets. In addition, quantifying financing gaps means measuring the difference between estimated costs and domestic financing capacity. Determining the latter involves identifying the degree to which low-income countries can make domestic resources available, taking into account economic growth prospects and public spending levels. The following subsections set out the parameters for these areas.

Identifying the targets

In the Dakar Framework for Action, governments made a commitment to achieve universal primary education by 2015. This is a clear, quantifiable and measurable goal, though its precise meaning is open to interpretation. There are also quantifiable targets for adult literacy. Other goals of great importance lack clear targets. Examples include the injunctions to improve education quality and ensure access to appropriate learning programmes for young people and adults. In some cases, goals relating to quality and equity define important principles but do not establish clear benchmarks. Targets chosen for this costing exercise cover four areas (Table 2.8):

- *Early childhood care and education.* It is widely recognized that good early childhood education is important not just in its own right but also as a way to improve participation and learning achievement in primary education. Building on previous work, this exercise adopts a target of providing free pre-primary education to all children living below the poverty line (Van Ravens and Aggio, 2007, 2008). This translates into an average gross enrolment ratio of 52% by 2015 for countries included in the exercise.
- *Universal primary education.* For the purposes of this exercise, it is assumed that all primary school age children enter school on time and progress through school with limited repetition and no dropout, implying a net enrolment ratio of 100% by 2015.[54]
- *Lower secondary education.* The Dakar Framework does not include targets for secondary education, but increasing participation at this level is important. This Report therefore includes a costing exercise that assumes that all children completing primary education by 2015 will make the transition to lower secondary school, implying an average gross enrolment ratio of about 88% by 2015 for countries included in the exercise.
- *Adult literacy.* The Dakar target of halving adult illiteracy will require wide-ranging interventions. Part of the target will be achieved

The costing exercise provides a comprehensive review and reassessment of the EFA financing gap

54. This assumption has the effect of understating costs associated with reaching over-age children currently out of primary school.

Reducing the cost burden on households is a priority for improving access

Table 2.8: Targets for the global costing exercise

Goal	Criteria for achievement by 2015	Average for 46 low-income countries (circa 2007)	Target for 2015
Early childhood care and education	Provision of pre-primary schooling for all children living below the poverty line	Pre-primary gross enrolment ratio = 16%	52%
Universal primary education	Provision of school places of good quality for all children of primary school age	Primary gross enrolment ratio = 95%	108%[1]
		Primary net enrolment ratio = 72%	100%
Expansion of lower secondary schooling	Provision of places in lower secondary school for all children completing primary school	Primary to secondary transition rate = 69%	100%
		Lower secondary gross enrolment ratio = 44%	88%
Adult literacy	Provision of sufficient literacy programme places for illiterate adults to ensure that illiteracy rates are halved from 1999 levels	Adult literacy rate = 59%	80%
Gender parity and equality	Achievement of gender parity in primary enrolment rates and lower secondary transition rates, and male and female literacy rates at or above target levels	—	Full parity
Education quality	Inclusion of a range of quality-enhancing interventions at each education level	—	See Table 2.9

Notes: Targets for early childhood education and adult literacy are country-specific. The targets given in the table are unweighted averages for all countries covered.
1. GER targets are country-specific but imply full enrolment of primary school age children with a maximum of 10% repetition.

Box 2.27: Basic education financing in the Democratic Republic of the Congo and the Sudan

Estimating education costs for countries affected by conflict is problematic. In many such countries, access to the type of data required for a meaningful assessment of need is often lacking.

Innovative work for the global costing exercise set out in this chapter has made it possible to include several conflict-affected countries. UNESCO carried out detailed country-level analysis for the Democratic Republic of the Congo and for the Sudan, where conflict has seriously compromised education planning and data collection. The analysis drew on recent surveys, including a 2006/2007 education census for the Democratic Republic of the Congo (the first in twenty years), as well as detailed evidence on costs from a range of donor, international agency and national ministry sources.

This research draws attention to several important concerns. In both countries, the collapse of public financing for education has shifted the burden to households, which must cover half of overall costs in the Democratic Republic of the Congo and a third in the Sudan. Reducing the burden on households is a priority for improving access.

The case studies also highlight differences within each country. In the Democratic Republic of the Congo, a legacy of weak governance and conflict stretching back over many years has resulted in a highly fragmented education system. Conflict and insecurity in some regions, notably the east, continue to hamper reconstruction prospects. In the Sudan, conflict has led to the development of separate political administrations and parallel education systems in the north and south. Financing for these systems varies. The best estimates indicate that the north devotes 13% of government revenue to education, compared with 6% in southern Sudan, leading to large differences in spending per pupil. Primary school pupil/teacher ratios are 33:1 in the north and 51:1 in the south.

Source: Chang et al. (2009).

through increased participation and improved quality of education at the primary level, with literate school leavers driving down illiteracy rates. The residual element, representing about 42% of the necessary decline, is assumed to occur through adult literacy programmes.

An assumption underpinning the estimates presented in this Report is that education is provided at these levels without fees. This is consistent with the Dakar Framework for Action. However, in many countries, particularly those recently involved in conflict, this would represent a substantial shift in the burden of education costs from households to the state (see Box 2.27).

Setting targets for the cost parameters

The second step in the exercise is to develop targets for key parameters using country-level information on costs. Recurrent costs per capita and capital costs in education vary across and within regions, with significant implications for global cost estimates. Two factors account for most of the variation. First, differences in average efficiency associated with prices for important inputs – such as teacher wages, building materials and textbooks – inevitably influence cost structures. Second, countries have different norms and rules on teacher remuneration, pupil/teacher ratios, school construction and other inputs. Table 2.9 summarizes targets for the core cost parameters used in the estimates.

In setting the parameters, several difficult financing questions were considered. Teacher remuneration is one of the most significant and controversial areas in any costing exercise for education. This is typically the single biggest component in the education budgets of low-income countries, often accounting for three-quarters of total spending. It follows that technical efficiency gains can dramatically reduce costs: adjusting salaries in sub-Saharan Africa to levels found in South and West Asia would cut average costs by 40%. However, the issues at stake go beyond considerations of technical efficiency.

Table 2.9: 2015 targets for main cost parameters

Parameters	Pre-primary	Primary	Lower secondary
Cost drivers			
Teacher salaries			
Sub-Saharan Africa	4.5 times GDP per capita	4.5 times GDP per capita	6 times GDP per capita
Other countries	3 times GDP per capita	3 times GDP per capita	3.5 times GDP per capita
Pupil teacher ratio	20	40	35
Percentage of non-salary costs in recurrent spending	33%	33%	40%
School building and rehabilitation[1]	$ 13,500 per classroom	$ 13,500 per classroom	$ 17,000 per classroom
Share of private enrolment	Maintain current levels	10%	10%
School rehabilitation (% of classroom to be replaced)			
Low income countries	25%	25%	25%
Conflict affected countries	50%	50%	50%
Targeted programmes for the marginalized			
Demand side interventions (e.g. conditional cash transfer programmes, school feeding programmes)	—	5% of GDP per capita per marginalized student	7.5% of GDP per capita per marginalized student
Supply side interventions (e.g. incentives for qualified teachers to work in remote areas, increased resources for schools serving marginalized groups)	—	Additional 33% of per pupil recurrent costs per marginalized student	Additional 33% of per pupil recurrent costs per marginalized student
Effect on per-pupil recurrent costs (constant 2007 US$)			
Estimated current unit costs	106	68	119
Per-pupil costs in 2015 with additional policy measures	102	125	162

Notes: Per-pupil costs for 2015 do not include additional costs of demand-side and supply-side interventions for reaching the marginalized.
1. Includes maintenance, estimated at 2% of construction cost. Classroom construction and rehabilitation include the cost of building school infrastructure (including latrines, offices, water supply, etc.) and providing access for children with disabilities.
Source: EPDC and UNESCO (2009).

Teacher salaries are typically the single biggest component in the education budgets of low-income countries

For example, lowering teacher salaries may cut costs but lead to low morale, making it more difficult to recruit a workforce with sufficient skills and forcing teachers to supplement their pay with other work.

Capital cost estimates raise another set of difficulties. By definition, achieving Education for All requires school infrastructure that is accessible to all children and of sufficient quality to ensure safety and provide an appropriate learning environment. Costs of classroom construction vary enormously. Reasonable-practice standards point to a cost of about US$13,500 per classroom, rising to US$17,000 for lower secondary school.[55] Classrooms obviously need to be built to accommodate children currently out of school. But the dilapidated state of the school infrastructure in many countries means there is also a need for extensive investment in rehabilitation. One recent survey suggests that 30% of classrooms in low-income sub-Saharan Africa need replacing (Theunynck, 2009). Conflict-affected countries face particularly pressing problems. To take one example, half of Liberia's classrooms were destroyed or sustained major damage during the civil war (Liberia Ministry of Education, 2007*b*).

Specific programmes targeting highly marginalized groups are likely to have higher average costs

The parameters set for this Report's costing exercise are derived from international evidence on norms and current practice in key areas. They include the following:

Teacher salaries. Individual countries have to address issues of efficiency, norms and standards for teachers in the light of national circumstances. The costing exercise does not prejudge the appropriate teacher salary level. Instead, it takes the current regional average for primary and lower secondary salaries in sub-Saharan Africa as a long-term target that all countries in the region will converge on.[56] For countries outside sub-Saharan Africa, the benchmark is lower (see Table 2.9).[57]

Rules and norms. While there is some debate about optimal pupil/teacher ratios, here the bar is set at 40:1 for primary school, reflecting the target used in previous costing exercises. Effective teaching also requires access to stationery, textbooks and other learning equipment. Ensuring that one-third of the recurrent budget is directed towards non-salary costs (rising to 40% for lower secondary education) should enable most low-income countries to meet basic needs in this respect.[58]

Wider capital costs. As well as covering the cost of future enrolment, budgets have to absorb the cost of replenishing infrastructure. A conservative estimate is that about a quarter of the classrooms in low-income countries need replacing, rising to half in conflict-affected countries. As with the other targets, it is assumed that all this replacement takes place by 2015.

Cost of adult literacy programmes. In line with previous studies, the unit cost of adult literacy programmes is estimated at 8.9% of GDP per capita for countries in sub-Saharan Africa and 5.3% for all other countries (Van Ravens and Aggio, 2005, 2007).

Reaching the marginalized

Previous global cost estimates for education have assumed that the average cost of reaching out-of-school children is roughly equivalent to a national average benchmark. That assumption is misplaced. Specific programmes targeting highly marginalized groups including child labourers, the extreme poor, ethnic minorities, girls, children with disabilities, and locations such as remote rural areas and slums have to be financed. Moreover, extending education programmes to these groups and areas is likely to raise per capita spending requirements.

Top-down estimates are a particularly blunt tool for assessing the financing required to reach the marginalized. Policy-makers need to consider the interlocking constraints that keep marginalized children out of school or that disrupt their participation and limit their learning achievements (see Chapter 3). Detailed poverty assessments and planning processes that draw on the evidence and perspectives provided by the marginalized themselves are critical to policy design.

With this caveat in mind, international evidence yields some useful insights. Cash transfer programmes that provide social protection can play an important role in insulating vulnerable households from external shocks, enabling them to keep children in school. In some contexts, such programmes have played a particularly crucial role in allowing girls to enter and stay in school. Under the right circumstances, school feeding programmes can also provide strong incentives for children to attend school (as well as crucial health benefits). Effective programmes of this kind typically cost about 5% of GDP per capita (Bundy et al., 2009*a*; Fiszbein et al., 2009*a*)[59].

55. Classroom construction costs include additional infrastructure required for an effective learning environment, such as furniture, latrines and water supply. Unit costs are based on an average of low- and high-cost construction scenarios in Theunynck (2009). Unit costs for lower secondary are assumed to be 25% higher.

56. The regional average also corresponds to average salary targets in national education plans for sub-Saharan Africa (Bennell, 2009*a*).

57. For the low-income countries included in the costing exercise that are not in sub-Saharan Africa, average teacher salaries are 2.5 times GDP per capita in primary school and 3.0 times in secondary.

58. The costs of reaching the marginalized are excluded when non-salary spending as a proportion of total recurrent cost is calculated.

59. The wide range of policy interventions needed to address marginalization are explored in detail in Chapter 3.

International evidence on the incremental costs that might be associated with creating a high-quality learning environment is more fragmented and inconsistent (Chanamuto, 2009). Getting teachers to schools in remote rural areas, slums and other marginalized environments requires incentives, but on what scale? Providing schooling to children whose lives have been blighted by poverty, hunger, stigmatization and low expectations is likely to require supplementary teaching and additional teaching materials, but there is no established benchmark for estimating the additional financing required.

For the purposes of the costing exercise, three criteria are used to introduce equity-based finance:

Assessing the size of the school age population requiring additional support. Drawing on a new statistical source – the Deprivation and Marginalization in Education (DME) data set introduced in Chapter 3 – the Report establishes, for each country, the share of the population aged 17 to 22 with fewer than four years in school. This is used as a proxy indicator for the proportion of the school age population that is marginalized and in need of additional incentives and school resources to participate in basic education. There are obvious limitations to this measure, including the fact that it captures past outcomes rather than the current situation. However, the four-year benchmark is a useful measurement of the scale of marginalization. Chapter 3 explores the use of this measure of marginalization in greater detail.

Providing incentives for marginalized children. The costing exercise includes financial provision for incentives aimed at marginalized groups. It assumes a cost per child of 5% of GDP per capita for primary school students and 7.5% for lower secondary school students.

Creating an incremental financing coefficient. There are no ready-made standards that can be applied on a cross-country basis. For the purposes of the costing exercise, the cost parameter for reaching the marginalized is set at an increment of 33% above average recurrent costs. This is broadly consistent with the sparse evidence available on the cost of financing teacher incentives and other measures to bring good-quality education to marginalized children (Chen and Mulkeen, 2008; Mulkeen, 2009*a*).

The global cost

The aggregate costs that emerge from the analysis are anchored in national data for the forty-six low-income countries covered.[60] For each of the Education for All targets selected, the norms for education inputs are applied to the size of the population that has to be reached in each country. This makes it possible to identify the number of teachers, additional classrooms and teaching materials required. The cost parameters for these inputs are then applied, with adjustments for reaching the marginalized. Table 2.10 shows the resulting cost projections. To summarize:

- Cumulative costs over 2008–2015 for the basic education goals run to US$286 billion, or US$36 billion annually (in constant 2007 US$). Current spending on basic education is about

The financing required to achieve the basic education goals is more than double current levels of spending

Table 2.10: Costs of achieving Education for All in low-income countries

	Pre-primary	Primary	Adult literacy*	Basic education sub-total	Lower secondary	Total
US$ billions (constant 2007 prices)						
Current domestic resources (circa 2007)	0.8	11.1	–	11.9	4.7	16.6
Cumulative cost (2008-2015)	60.4	220.4	5.1	285.9	127.8	413.7
Average annual cost (2008-2015)	7.5	27.5	0.6	35.7	16.0	51.7
Breakdown of costs between 2008-2015 (%)						
Teachers	39	40	–	40	36	39
Classroom construction	41	27	–	30	30	30
Programmes to reach the marginalized	–	14	–	11	12	11
Other	20	20	–	20	22	21

Notes: Breakdown of costs for basic education subtotal relates only to pre-primary and universal primary education. Subtotals are based on non-rounded figures.
* The estimated adult literacy costs for the low-income countries covered are about three times the costs estimated in the original study (see Van Ravens and Aggio, 2005).
Source: EPDC and UNESCO (2009).

60. The base year is 2007 and estimates are based on the 2008–2015 period unless otherwise indicated.

An estimated 6.2 million additional classrooms will be needed in primary and pre-primary education

US$12 billion a year. In other words, the financing required to achieve the basic education goals is three times the current level.

- Some US$3.7 billion, or 14% of annual spending on primary education, is required to finance programmes and interventions aimed at reaching the marginalized at the primary level.
- Additional teacher costs account for 40% of the required spending for basic education, with classroom construction adding just under one-third.
- Factoring in lower secondary education raises the average annual cost by US$16 billion.

Figure 2.45: Spending on teachers has to rise

% increase required from 2007 in spending on primary school teachers to achieve universal primary education by 2015

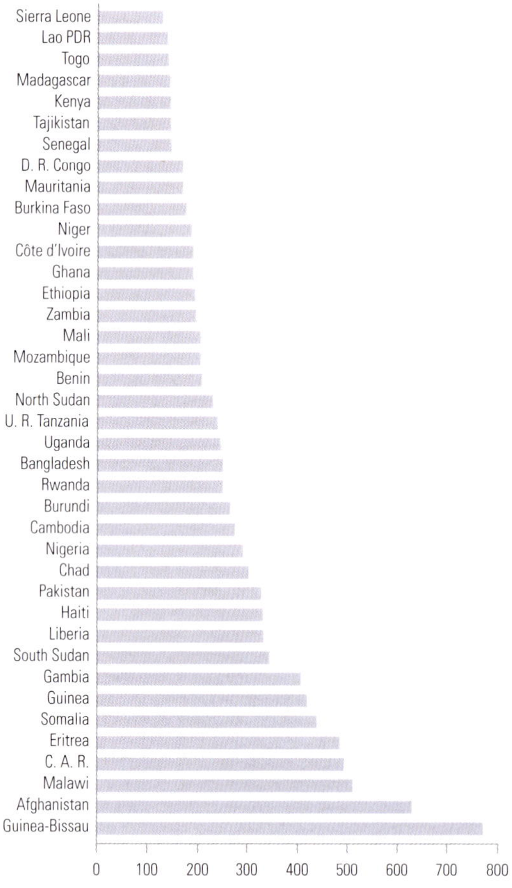

Note: Excludes countries that do not require increases in spending on primary school teachers to achieve universal primary education.
Source: EPDC and UNESCO (2009).

Human resources figure prominently in the cost estimates (Table 2.10). Collectively, the countries covered in the exercise have to recruit 3.2 million more primary and pre-primary teachers to achieve the basic education goals. At the primary level, the global cost of financing recruitment on this scale is some US$9.1 billion annually.[61] Translated into current national budget terms, this implies a significant increase in spending. Ten countries need to more than double spending on primary teacher salaries and thirteen countries more than triple spending, from 2007 levels (Figure 2.45).

Overcoming school infrastructure deficits will require large increases in investment. An estimated 6.2 million additional classrooms will be needed in primary and pre-primary education to accommodate the increase in enrolment required to achieve the targets set.[62] Current rates of construction fall far below the level required in most countries. In Burundi, Rwanda and Uganda, recent rates of classroom construction are less than 15% of the rate required to achieve universal primary education (Figure 2.46). The estimated aggregate costs of expansion are highest in countries with the biggest out-of-school populations. However, a large group of countries will have to increase spending on classroom construction and rehabilitation far above current levels to bring the Education for All targets within reach.

Figure 2.46: Many countries need more classrooms

Current classroom construction as % of required rate of construction necessary to achieve universal primary education by 2015

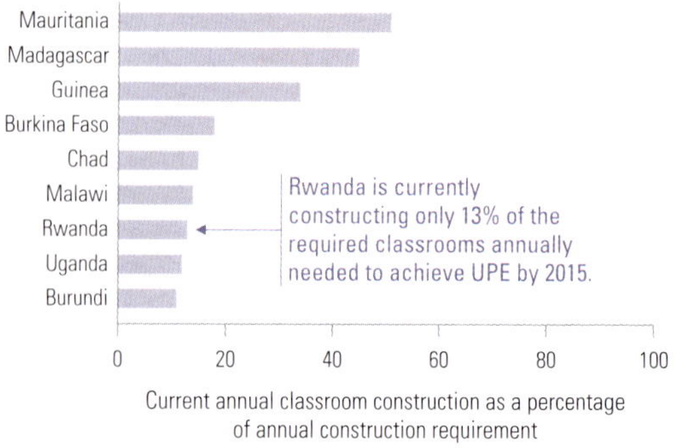

Notes: Estimated classroom needs for universal primary education include replacing old classrooms (the assumption is that classrooms have a forty-year life span) and rebuilding existing stock. The period covered by figures for actual annual growth in classroom stock varies by country. See Table 1.1 in Theunynck (2009) for details.
Sources: EPDC and UNESCO (2009); Theunynck (2009).

61. This figure is reached by multiplying the additional teachers needed from 2008 to 2015 by the target teacher salaries shown in Table 2.9.

62. This includes new classrooms to achieve targeted pupil/classroom ratios and the replacement of old classroom stock.

Estimating the financing gap – and measures to close it

The cost of achieving the internationally agreed Education for All goals has to be assessed against the financing available. National budgets are the primary source of education financing. As the Expanded Commentary on the Dakar Framework for Action recognized, developing countries will have to do far more to make resources available by 'increasing the share of national income and budgets allocated to education and, within that, to basic education' (para. 46). Over and above these broad commitments, action is needed to strengthen the efficiency and equity of education spending, and to curb the diversion of resources associated with corruption.

Most of the countries covered in the costing analysis have the capacity to increase domestic spending on basic education. Increased government revenue, stronger budget commitment and redistribution within the education budget all have a role to play. But even with a stronger domestic effort, many countries will be unable to finance all the investment required. The analysis for this Report estimates the Education for All financing gap as the difference between the total investment requirement indicated by the costing exercise and the domestic financing capacity of governments making a 'best effort' to channel resources to education.

National governments can raise a substantial share of the additional resources needed

Alongside national income, the domestic resource envelope available for public financing of the Education for All goals is ultimately determined by three factors. The first is the *share of national income collected as government revenue.* That share rises on average with the level of per capita income, albeit with large variations by country that reflect policies on taxation, the level of natural resource exports and other national characteristics. The second factor is the *proportion of revenue directed into the overall education budget.* The third is the *share of the education budget allocated to basic education.* The proportion of national income directed towards basic education provides a summary overview of the level of public basic education financing.

Figure 2.47 presents the country-by-country picture. It shows the gap between current levels of spending on basic education and the levels

Figure 2.47: Current national spending falls short of the levels needed to achieve basic education goals

Current and required spending on basic education as a share of GDP

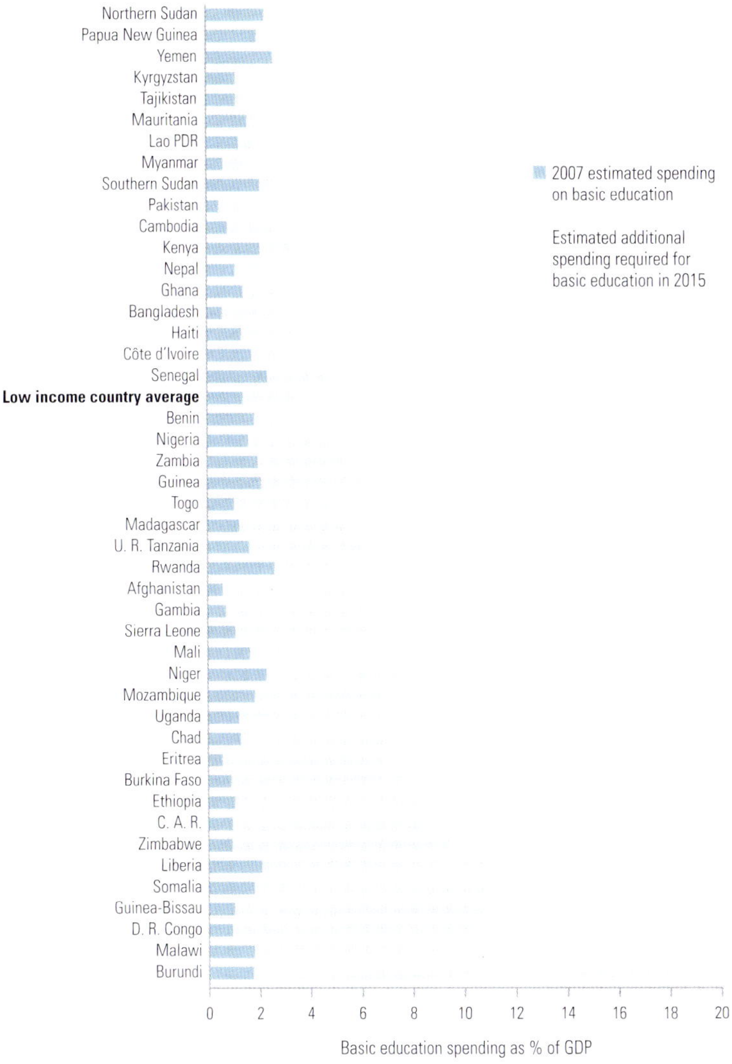

Notes: Spending in 2007 is an estimate of domestic spending on education and excludes grants. Northern and southern Sudan are included separately in the costing study because of their separate education systems (see Box 2.27). Excludes Uzbekistan and Viet Nam which are projected not to require additional spending on basic education.
Source: EPDC and UNESCO (2009).

required to achieve the goals set in this Report's costing exercise. On average, the forty-six countries need to increase public spending on basic education by 2.5% of GDP to meet Education for All goals.[63] However, there are very large variations around this average.

To what extent can low-income countries increase spending on basic education from their own resources? Any attempt to address that question is highly sensitive to assumptions

63. This is an average figure weighted by the size of low-income countries in terms of their GDP.

Many countries can mobilize additional resources for basic education

about economic growth, revenue collection and public spending patterns. For this analysis, a 'best effort' benchmark was established to assess national financing capacity. Factoring in projected economic growth,[64] a significant source of extra revenue, it is possible to estimate the additional resources that can be generated by 2015 if the countries covered (a) increase the average share of government revenue in GDP to at least 17%; (b) raise the share of revenue going to education to at least 20%; and (c) ensure that about 70% of the education budget is devoted to pre-primary, primary and lower secondary.[65] Where countries are already exceeding these thresholds, it is assumed that current values are maintained up to 2015.

Applying these thresholds points to the scope for a far stronger level of national effort. If every country covered in the study reached each threshold, it would expand the financial resource envelope for basic education on average by about 0.9 percentage points of GDP by 2015. Put differently, it would provide slightly more than a third of the additional resources required to achieve the basic education goals by 2015.

The aggregate picture inevitably obscures significant differences between countries (Figure 2.48). Some, such as Benin and Mozambique, are close to the 'best effort' thresholds in all target areas. By contrast, Chad combines high levels of revenue-raising with low levels of financial commitment to education. Nigeria raises 34% of national income in government revenue, but has one of the lowest levels of commitment to primary education among the forty-six countries covered. Pakistan performs poorly on all three counts: government revenue represents a small share of national income, the share of revenue spent on basic education is among the lowest for any of these low-income countries and the share spent on primary education is the very lowest in the group. The country has the potential to more than triple the share of GDP currently allocated to basic education, suggesting that successive governments have failed to address the education

Figure 2.48: Many countries can mobilize additional domestic resources for basic education

Current and additional resources countries devote to basic education as a share of GDP

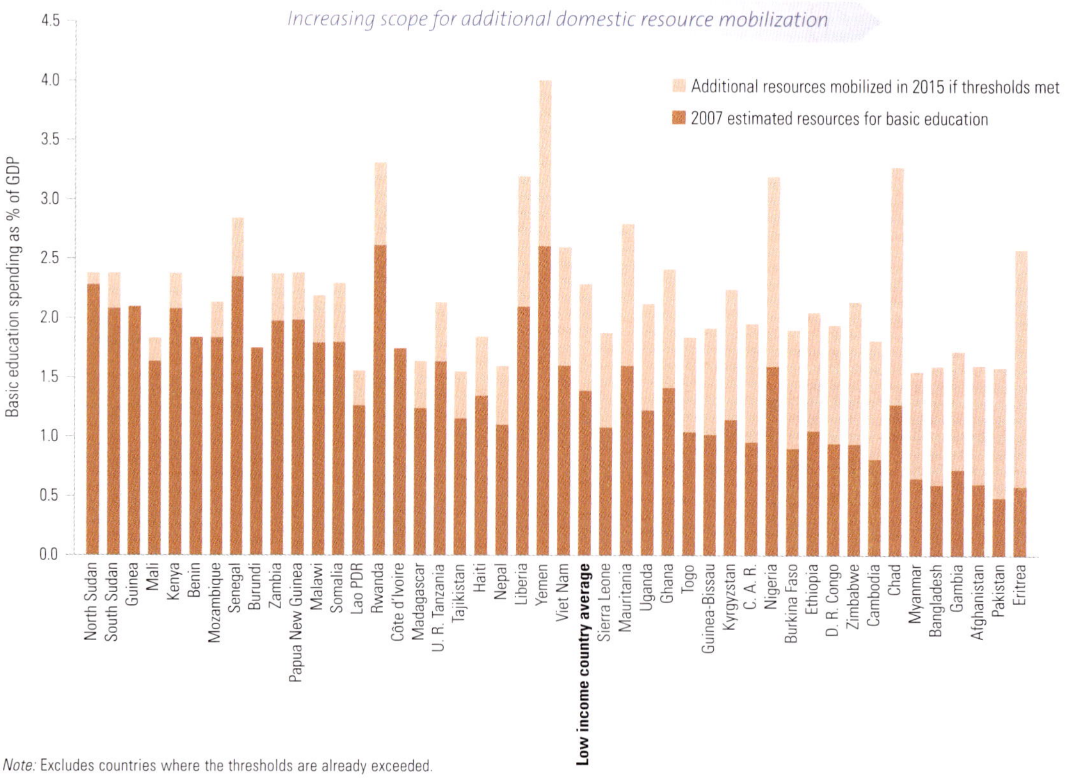

Note: Excludes countries where the thresholds are already exceeded.
Source: EPDC and UNESCO (2009).

64. Resource projections use the latest IMF economic growth forecasts (IMF, 2009f).

65. Targets for the exact share of the budget devoted to Education for All depend on the length of primary and lower secondary cycles. See EPDC and UNESCO (2009) for details. Economic growth projections are taken from the April 2009 IMF forecast (IMF, 2009f).

financing challenge with sufficient urgency. In the cases of Chad and Nigeria, the problem is less one of revenue mobilization than the low priority attached to education in general and basic education in particular.

It should be emphasized that the 'best effort' thresholds used are an imperfect guide to public policy. Revenue-raising capacity partly depends on export structures. Countries with large mineral assets may be better placed than others to increase revenue collection. For countries emerging from conflict, such as Nepal and Sierra Leone, increasing the share of national income collected in revenue may be a slow process involving the restoration of credible public institutions and confidence in government. The estimates here should therefore be treated as an evaluation of what is possible under reasonable conditions, not as a full assessment of what each country can achieve in practice. With the data available, it is difficult to generate precise Education for All financing estimates for countries such as Afghanistan, Liberia and Sierra Leone, but there are strong grounds for recognizing, as most aid donors have done, the urgent need for a large up-front increase in education finance, given the limited capacity of these countries' governments to raise that finance.

Donors need to increase aid to close the remaining gap

Successive issues of the *EFA Global Monitoring Report* have drawn the attention of the donor community to the gap between aid levels and the level of financing required to meet the Dakar targets. The revised global cost estimate suggests the gap is far larger than previously assumed. Any prospect of accelerated progress towards the 2015 targets hinges critically on a scaled-up donor effort. The bottom-line message to emerge from the costing exercise is that two-thirds of the additional resources required will have to be provided through aid.

The residual aid component of the Education for All financing requirement can be extrapolated from the costing exercise. Figure 2.49 summarizes the financing gap that remains once prospects for additional domestic resources have been exhausted. Table 2.11 provides an approximate breakdown of this financing deficit by education

Figure 2.49: Financing gaps are large and unlikely to be eliminated by current donor pledges

Breakdown of annual resource needs to achieve basic education goals

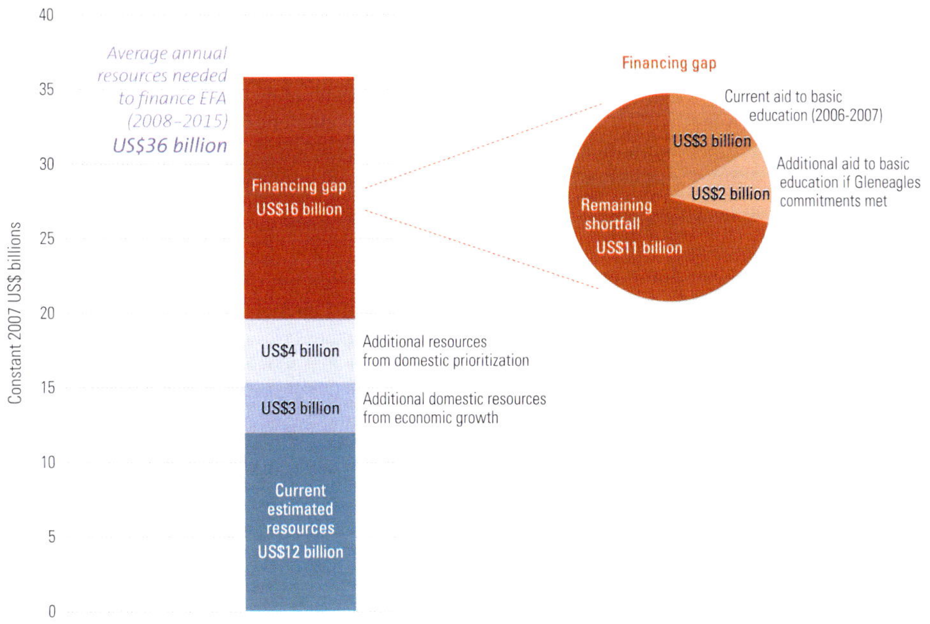

Notes: Breakdown of annual resource needs does not add up to the total due to rounding. The percentage increase in aid between 2005 and 2010 associated with the Gleneagles targets (see Chapter 4) are usual to project 2005 basic education commitments to 2010 for each country covered.

Sources: EPDC and UNESCO (2009); OECD-DAC (2009*d*).

The financing gap for basic education is around US$16 billion annually

Table 2.11: Average annual financing gaps in low-income countries, 2008-2015

Education level	Financing gap (constant 2007 US$ billions)	Sub-Saharan Africa (%)	South Asia (%)	Conflict-affected countries (%)
Pre-primary	5.8	66	23	29
Universal primary education	9.8	68	28	48
Adult literacy	0.6	42	37	51
Basic education financing gap	**16.2**	**66**	**27**	**41**
Lower secondary	8.8	60	35	42
Total financing gap	**25.0**	**64**	**30**	**42**

Note: The financing gap is the difference between the total investment requirement indicated by the costing exercise and levels of domestic financing associated with all countries reaching 'best effort' thresholds by 2015.
Source: EPDC and UNESCO (2009).

sector and region. The deficit that will have to be covered by increased development assistance is projected to widen to 2015 before narrowing as the domestic resource base expands and the need for additional capital spending declines. Results of the analysis include the following:

Sub-Saharan Africa accounts for about two-thirds of the financing gap, or US$10.6 billion

- Estimates of the financing gap for basic education are about 30% higher than the previous global estimates.
- Assuming that all low-income countries reach the 'best effort' thresholds by 2015, the aggregate average annual financing gap in basic education for the low-income countries covered is equivalent to about 1.5% of their collective GDP.[66] The cumulative deficit for basic education, calculated on a country-by-country basis, is around US$16 billion annually from 2008 to 2015.
- Current aid levels cover only a small part of the Education for All financing deficit. For the low-income countries included in this exercise, development assistance for basic education amounts to US$2.7 billion (Figure 2.49).[67] A sixfold increase in aid to basic education will therefore be required if the basic education goals are to be achieved.
- Sub-Saharan Africa accounts for about 66% of the financing gap, or US$10.6 billion.
- Low-income countries affected by conflict account for 41% of the gap, or US$6.7 billion.
- Adding the costs of lower secondary education increases the gap to US$25 billion – a figure that illustrates the enormous increase in resources required if countries are to universalize access. However, without addressing the financing gaps at the basic education level and building strong learning foundations, increased investment in post-primary education is unlikely to be equitable or to lead to the skills improvement that governments and parents demand.

The global costing exercise raises important questions for the international community. With just five years remaining to the target date for the Education for All goals and the wider Millennium Development Goals, the United Nations Secretary-General has called on donors to act on their 2005 commitments, made at Gleneagles to substantially increase aid by 2010. Such a move would clearly help narrow the education financing gap, but it would not fully close it. Holding constant the distribution of aid between low-income and

66. This is calculated by dividing the average financing gap by the average projected GDP of all countries included in the costing exercise from 2008 to 2015.

67. Chapter 4 shows that aid commitments to basic education in 2006 and 2007 averaged US$4.9 billion (see Figure 4.7). The low-income countries included in the costing exercise received 55% of these commitments.

middle-income countries, and between different levels of education, full delivery of the 2005 commitments would leave a deficit of US$11 billion (Figure 2.49). That scenario points to the case for an urgent reassessment of aid commitments and distribution patterns. With an international summit on the Millennium Development Goals planned for 2010, donors should as a matter of urgency convene a pledging conference to close the Education for All financing gap.

Conclusion

The limitations and uncertainties associated with global financial costing models have to be acknowledged. Yet the results of the exercise set out here provide a clear warning sign. In the absence of an urgent, concerted effort to make new and additional resources available for education, there is little prospect of the world's poorest countries getting on track to meet the 2015 targets. If the policy goal is to ensure that all the world's primary school age children are in education systems by 2015, the investment cannot be delayed. The global costing exercise underlines the importance of low-income developing countries and donors doing far more. However, the role of donors is critical because governments in the poorest countries lack the resources to close the Education for All financing gap. ■

Chapter 3

© Ami Vitale/PANOS

Compounded disadvantage: low-caste girls face the greatest obstacles, India

On the move: pastoralist communities require flexible solutions

Reaching the marginalized

Support makes a difference: more girls in Yemen are now going to school

Who are the marginalized? What are the factors contributing to their exclusion and lack of educational opportunity? This chapter looks at the mutually reinforcing interactions between poverty, gender, ethnicity, geographic location, disability, race, language and other factors that create cycles of disadvantage in education. It also shows how integrated anti-marginalization strategies can enable all children – regardless of circumstance – to enjoy their right to education.

Education is the great engine of personal development. It is through education that the daughter of a peasant can become a doctor...that a child of farmworkers can become the president of a great nation. It is what we make out of what we have, not what we are given, that separates one person from another.

– Long Walk to Freedom:
The Autobiography of Nelson Mandela (1994, p. 144)

Introduction

Education has the power to transform lives. It broadens people's freedom of choice and action, empowering them to participate in the social and political lives of their societies and equipping them with the skills they need to develop their livelihoods. For the marginalized, education can be a route to greater social mobility and a way out of poverty. Forged in a society that restricted education on the basis of skin colour and discrimination, Nelson Mandela's words powerfully capture the role of inclusive education in broadening opportunities and building inclusive societies.

This chapter focuses on marginalization in education. Marginalization is the subject of much debate. There is a voluminous literature on how to measure it and how to differentiate the concept from broader ideas about inequality, poverty and social exclusion.[1] Many important issues have been raised. However, debate over definitions can sometimes obscure the political and ethical imperative to combat marginalization. Writing on the idea of justice, Amartya Sen argues that there are limits to the value of perfecting definitions. 'What moves us,' he writes, 'is not the realisation that the world falls short of being completely just (...) but that there are clearly remediable injustices around us which we want to eliminate' (Sen, 2009, p. vii).

The starting point in this Report is that marginalization in education is a form of acute and persistent disadvantage rooted in underlying social inequalities. It represents a stark example of 'clearly remediable injustice'. Removing that injustice should be at the centre of the national and international Education for All agendas.

The focus of this chapter is on schools and basic education. While marginalization typically starts long before children enter school and continues into adult life, schools are in a pivotal position. They can play a vital role in counteracting early childhood disadvantage and help break the transmission of illiteracy across generations. But schools can also reinforce disadvantage and perpetuate marginalization.

The experience of marginalization in education today is seldom a consequence of formal discrimination. Legal restrictions on opportunity, such as those that characterized apartheid South Africa, are rare. Yet informal discrimination is widespread. It is embedded in social, economic and political processes that restrict life chances for some groups and individuals. Marginalization is not random. It is the product of institutionalized disadvantage – and of policies and processes that perpetuate such disadvantage.

Marginalization in education is a form of acute and persistent disadvantage rooted in underlying social inequalities

Half a century ago, governments around the world made a clear statement of intent on education. In the 1960 Convention Against Discrimination in Education, they imposed what amounts to a comprehensive ban not just on discrimination by legal intent, but on processes that have the effect of causing discrimination. As Article 1 of the Convention puts it,

> *the term 'discrimination' includes any distinction, exclusion, limitation or preference which, being based on race, colour, sex, language, religion, political or other opinion, national or social origin, economic condition or birth, has the purpose or effect of nullifying or impairing equality of treatment in education and in particular:*
>
> *(a) Of depriving any person or group of persons of access to education of any type or at any level;*
>
> *(b) Of limiting any person or group of persons to education of an inferior standard[.]* (UNESCO, 1960, Article 1, para. 1).

Underpinning this provision is the simple but compelling idea of equal opportunity. That idea is at the heart of many international human rights provisions, starting with the 1948 Universal Declaration of Human Rights. The 1989 Convention on the Rights of the Child establishes a binding obligation on governments to work towards fulfilling the right to education 'progressively and on the basis of equal opportunity' (United Nations, 1989,

1. See, for example, Kabeer (2005), Sayed et al. (2007), Klasen (2001), Ferreira and Gignoux (2008), World Bank (2005f).

Article 28). The right to equal opportunity for education is also enshrined in most countries' national laws and constitutions. Indeed, few human rights are more widely endorsed – and more widely violated.

Millions of children are denied their human right to education for the simple reason that their parents cannot afford to keep them in school. Social and cultural barriers to education form another formidable obstacle. In many countries, the education of girls is widely perceived as being of less value than that of boys, with traditional practices such as early marriage adding another layer of disadvantage. Members of ethnic minorities often face deeply entrenched obstacles to equal opportunity. Denied an opportunity to learn in their own language and faced with social stigmatization, they are set on an early pathway to disadvantage. Millions of children with disabilities across the world also face far more restricted opportunities than their peers, as do children living in regions affected by conflict.

None of these disadvantages operates in isolation. Poverty, gender, ethnicity and other characteristics interact to create overlapping and self-reinforcing layers of disadvantage that limit opportunity and hamper social mobility.

The interaction between marginalization in education and wider patterns of marginalization operates in both directions. Being educated is a vital human capability that enables people to make choices in areas that matter. The lack of an education restricts choices. It limits the scope people have for influencing decisions that affect their lives. People lacking literacy and numeracy skills face a heightened risk of poverty, insecure employment and ill health. Poverty and ill health, in turn, contribute to marginalization in education. So does the fact that the marginalized have only a weak voice in shaping political decisions affecting their lives.

Extreme and persistent deprivation in education carries a high price for societies as well as for individuals

Reaching marginalized children requires political commitment backed by practical policies. When governments met in 1990 at the World Conference on Education for All in Jomtien, Thailand, they recognized the need to overcome extreme inequalities holding back progress in education. They declared that 'consistent measures must be taken to reduce disparities' and called for active commitment to reach 'underserved groups', including the poor, remote rural populations, ethnic, racial and linguistic minorities, refugees and migrants, and those affected by conflict (UNESCO, 1990, Article 3). The Dakar Framework for Action reaffirmed the commitment to 'explicitly identify, target and respond flexibly to the needs and circumstances of the poorest and the most marginalized' (UNESCO, 2000, IV, para. 52).

While some countries have made impressive efforts to back up such words by extending educational opportunities to their most marginalized populations, action has generally fallen far short of the commitments made at Jomtien and Dakar. Marginalization has remained a peripheral concern. The assumption has been that national progress in education would eventually trickle down to the most disadvantaged. After a decade of steady but uneven national progress, it is time to abandon that assumption. In many countries, large swathes of society are being left behind as a result of inherited disadvantages. Breaking down these disadvantages will require a far stronger focus on the hard to reach.

Tackling marginalization is a matter of urgency on several counts. The targets for 2015 adopted in the Dakar Framework for Action – including universal primary education – will not be achieved unless governments step up their efforts to reach the marginalized. Sustaining progress in basic education and creating the foundations for advances in secondary education will require a renewed drive to extend opportunity to individuals and groups facing the most deeply entrenched disadvantages. Progress in combating marginalization in education would dramatically improve the discouraging scenario that Chapter 2 describes.

The case for action on marginalization goes beyond the 2015 targets. Extreme and persistent deprivation in education carries a high price for societies as well as for individuals. In the increasingly knowledge-based and competitive global economy, depriving people of opportunities for education is a prescription for wastage of skills, talent and opportunities for innovation and economic growth. It is also a recipe for social division. Marginalization in education is an important factor in the widening of social and economic inequalities. Working towards more inclusive education is a condition for the development of more inclusive societies.

The core message of this chapter is that overcoming marginalization must be at the heart of the Education for All agenda. Education should be a driver of equal opportunity and social mobility, not a transmission mechanism for social injustice. The familiar routine of governments endorsing equal opportunity principles, reaffirming human rights commitments and signing up for international summit communiqués on education is not enough. Overcoming marginalization requires practical policies that address the structures of inequality perpetuating marginalization – and it requires political leaders to recognize that marginalization matters. This chapter has four main messages:

■ *Governments across the world are systematically violating the spirit and the letter on United Nations conventions obliging them to work towards equal opportunities for education.* The failure of many governments to act decisively in tackling marginalization in education calls into question their commitment to the human right to education – and it is holding back progress towards the Education for All goals. The scale of the marginalization crisis in education is not widely recognized, partly because the marginalized themselves lack an effective voice.

■ *Disaggregated data can play an important role in identifying social groups and regions characterized by concentrated marginalization.* All too often education policies are developed on the basis of inadequate information about who is being left behind. Data have a vital role to play in providing an evidence base for developing targeted interventions and wider policies. This chapter sets out a new statistical tool – the Deprivation and Marginalization in Education (DME) data set – that looks beyond national averages to provide insight into patterns of marginalization.

■ *Mutually reinforcing layers of disadvantage create extreme and persistent deprivation that restrict opportunity.* Poverty and gender inequalities powerfully magnify disadvantages linked to ethnicity, language, living in rural areas and disability, closing doors to educational opportunities for millions of children. Moreover, stigmatization and social discrimination are potent drivers of marginalization in education.

■ *Good policies backed by a commitment to equity can make a difference.* Education systems can play a central role in overcoming marginalization by giving disadvantaged children access to a good-quality learning environment, including properly financed schools, motivated and well-trained teachers, and instruction in an appropriate language. But strategies in education have to be backed by wider interventions, including investment in social protection, legal provisions to counteract discrimination and wider empowerment measures. The challenge is to ensure that education policies and broader anti-marginalization policies operate within a coherent framework.

The chapter is divided into three parts. Part 1 provides a snapshot of the scale of extreme and persistent deprivation in education. Drawing on the DME data set, it measures marginalization by looking at numbers of years spent in school. Part 1 also explores problems in education quality as captured in measures of learning achievement. Part 2 looks at the social and economic processes behind the data. It explores some key forces behind marginalization, including poverty, gender, ethnicity and location. Part 3 provides an overview of policies and approaches that can break down the structures that perpetuate marginalization in education and beyond. While each country is different and there are no ready-made 'anti-marginalization' blueprints, there are models for good practice. These models can help inform policy choices for governments seeking to act on the obligation to ensure that all of their citizens enjoy a right to education. □

Overcoming marginalization must be at the heart of the Education for All agenda

Measuring marginalization in education

Introduction

In all countries, whatever their level of development, some individuals and groups experience extreme and persistent disadvantage in education that sets them apart from the rest of society. They are less likely to enter school, to start school at the correct age or to complete a full cycle of education, and they are more likely to leave school with lower levels of achievement. As well as being a sign of social deprivation in its own right, disadvantage in education is a cause and an effect of marginalization in other areas and a powerful transmitter of deprivation across generations.

Countries need to invest in more robust and consistent data analysis to identify areas of concentrated disadvantage

Defining *who* is marginalized is problematic because there is seldom an agreed definition of the term within any one country, let alone across countries. Establishing *what* marginalization entails in education presents another set of problems. Most people would accept that it encompasses quantitative deprivation, as measured by years in school or the level of education attained. But it also incorporates a qualitative dimension. The marginalized typically demonstrate lower levels of educational achievement. The Convention on the Rights of the Child calls on governments to provide an education that leads to the 'development of the child's personality, talents and mental and physical abilities to their fullest potential' (United Nations, 1989, Article 29). For many children, though, the experience undermines learning potential, disempowers and stigmatizes them (Klasen, 2001).

This section identifies some of the characteristics that predispose individuals and groups to extreme and persistent disadvantage in education. While all countries endorse the principles of equal opportunity and universal rights, the evidence shows that, when it comes to opportunities for education, some people are more equal than others – the marginalized being the least equal of all. Inequalities linked to parental income, gender, ethnicity, race and other factors continue to restrict life chances and fuel marginalization.

Understanding marginalization is one of the conditions for overcoming it. Too often, governments express commitment to equal opportunity in education but fail to monitor what is happening to the individuals and groups being left behind. One of the central messages of this section is that countries need to invest in more robust and consistent data analysis to identify areas of concentrated disadvantage. The new international data set prepared for this Report provides a tool that governments, non-government organizations and researchers can use to make the marginalized more visible.

Using a quantitative analysis of marginalization in low-income developing countries, this section draws on the DME data set to identify individuals and groups facing heightened risk of marginalization, with respect both to absolute deprivation, defined in terms of years in school, and to disadvantage relative to the rest of society. The section looks also at individual and group-based disadvantage with respect to learning achievement. While the dimensions and characteristics of marginalization differ between developed and developing countries, rich countries are also characterized by extreme and persistent patterns of deprivation.

The Deprivation and Marginalization in Education data set

Measuring marginalization in education is not straightforward. Household surveys and other data provide insights into the relationship between poverty, ethnicity, health, parental literacy and other characteristics on the one side and education on the other. But while these are all characteristics associated with marginalization, they do not operate in isolation. The marginalized in education are often poor and female, and from an ethnic minority living in a remote rural area. Understanding how different layers of disadvantage interact is a first step towards breaking the cycles of disadvantage that push people into marginalization.

Invisibility adds to measurement problems. Concentrated in slums or remote rural regions, the marginalized are often hidden from view and government agencies sometimes have limited access to detailed data for monitoring their condition. All too often the same agencies demonstrate a marked indifference to the social circumstances of the marginalized, reflecting the indifference of political elites.

The new DME data set assembled for this Report is a statistical tool that helps chart the dimensions of marginalization and identifies patterns of individual and group disadvantage. The data are drawn from Demographic and Health Surveys and Multiple Indicator Cluster Surveys covering eighty developing countries, including thirty-eight low-income countries.[2] Data from these sources have been reconstituted to concentrate on key dimensions of education marginalization. The analysis presented in this chapter focuses on three core areas:

- *The bottom line: education poverty.* The marginalized typically fall below a social minimum threshold for years of education. To measure absolute deprivation, this analysis takes four years as the minimum required to gain the most basic literacy and numeracy skills. People aged 17 to 22 who have fewer than four years of education can be thought of as being in 'education poverty'. People with fewer than two years can be thought of as living in 'extreme education poverty'.

- *The bottom 20%.* Time spent in education is one indicator for the distribution of opportunity. Using the DME data set, relative marginalization is measured by organizing individuals aged 17 to 22 according to the number of years they have accumulated in education. The analysis then uses the results to identify the individual and group characteristics of the bottom 20% – the 20% with the fewest years of education.

- *The quality of education.* Acquiring the learning skills that people need to escape marginalization means more than just spending time at school. What children actually learn depends on a wide range of factors, including the quality of education and home circumstances. The analysis looks at marginalization in learning achievement using national and international evidence.

Patterns of marginalization reflect underlying inequalities in opportunity. One advantage of the DME data set is that it provides detailed information on individual and group characteristics of the marginalized, including wealth, gender, location, ethnicity and language. That information provides insight into the weight of 'inherited circumstances'. These represent conditions over which people have little control but which play an important role in shaping their opportunities for education and wider life chances (Bourguignon et al., 2007; Ferreira and Gignoux, 2008; World Bank, 2005*f*).

Measuring marginalization is not a narrowly defined technical matter. It is an integral part of the development of strategies for inclusive education. The DME data set helps increase the visibility of the marginalized and provides a resource that can help inform policy design and public debate. Summary tables are presented at the end of this section and the full data set is available in electronic form.

The scale of marginalization

Falling below the minimum threshold – education poverty

Time spent in education is one of the most important determinants of life chances in all societies. There is no internationally agreed benchmark for education deprivation analogous to the US$2.00 and US$1.25 a day international poverty thresholds. However, people with fewer than four years of schooling are unlikely to have mastered basic literacy or numeracy skills, let alone built a foundation for lifelong learning. Those with fewer than two years are likely to face extreme disadvantages in many areas of their lives. Of course, learning achievement ultimately depends as much on the quality of education as on time spent in school. But the four year and two year thresholds are bottom lines that this analysis treats as indicators for 'education poverty' and 'extreme education poverty', respectively.

Figure 3.1 uses these thresholds to provide a snapshot of education deprivation for sixty-three mostly low-income countries. It covers a reference group of young adults aged 17 to 22. Even taking into account over-age attendance, this is far enough beyond the standard primary school completion age to provide a credible picture of who has completed four years of education.

Three broad themes emerge. The first is the scale of global deprivation and inequality. In rich countries, the vast majority of young adults in this age range will have accumulated ten to fifteen years of education. In twenty-two of the countries covered by the DME data, 30% or more of 17- to 22-year-olds have fewer than four years of education; in eleven of these countries, the figure rises to 50%. Nineteen of the twenty-two countries are in sub-Saharan Africa, with Guatemala, Pakistan and Morocco making up the remainder.

The second theme concerns cross-country differences. On average, as one would expect,

Measuring marginalization is an integral part of the development of strategies for inclusive education

2. Demographic and Health Survey data are collected as part of the MEASURE DHS project implemented by ICF Macro. See http://www.measuredhs.com/. Multiple Indicator Cluster Surveys are collected by UNICEF. See http://www.unicef.org/statistics/index_24302.html.

Figure 3.1: Measuring education poverty across countries

% of national population, the poorest households, and girls in poorest households aged 17 to 22 with fewer than four years and fewer than two years of education, selected countries, most recent year

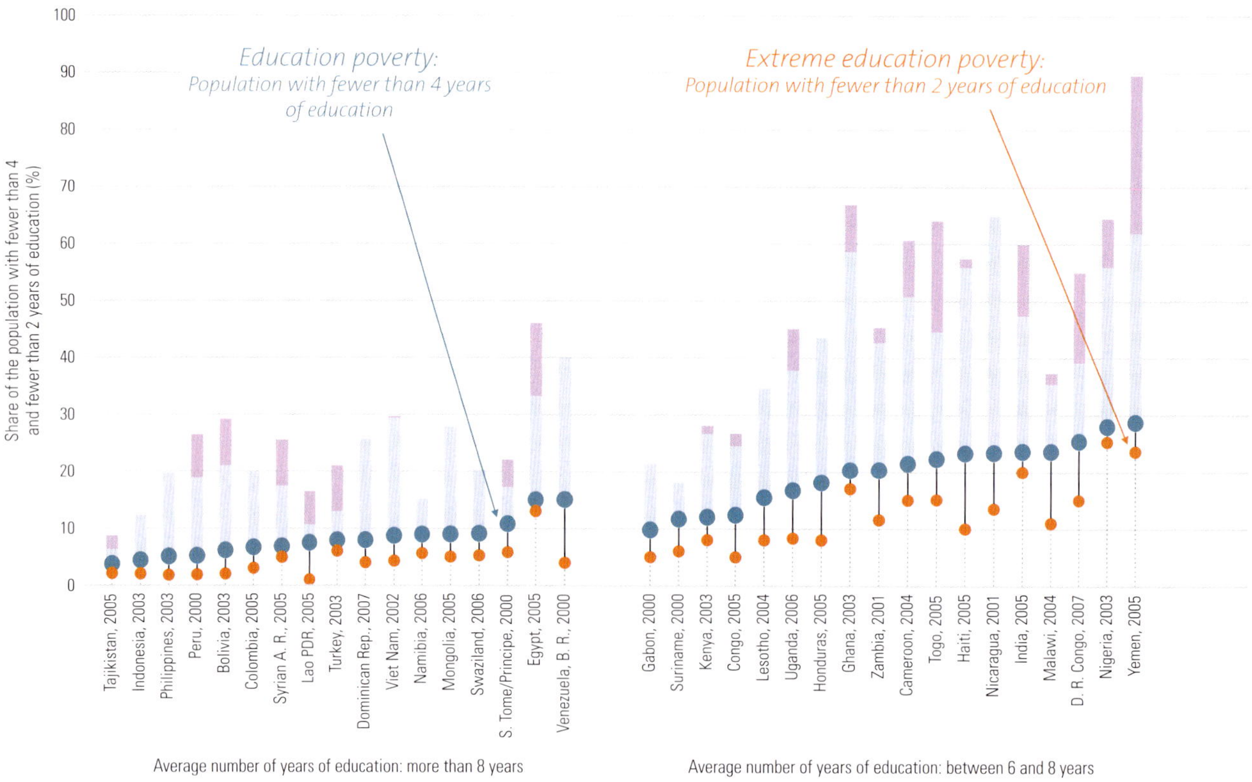

Source: UNESCO-DME (2009).

Wealth-based inequalities are a universal source of disadvantage in education

the share of the population with fewer than four years or fewer than two years of education falls as the national average for years of education rises. Countries averaging more than eight years of education typically have fewer than 10% falling below the four-year threshold. This broad association conceals as much as it reveals, however. For example, Egypt averages more years of education than Kenya but has a larger share of 17- to 22-year-olds with fewer than four years of education. Such comparisons point to deeply entrenched national inequalities that are obscured by national average figures.

Comparisons of the depth of education poverty point in the same direction. In countries with very low average years of education, the majority of people falling below the four-year threshold also have fewer than two years of education. However, Pakistan has a lower share of the population with fewer than four years than Rwanda, but a 50% higher share with fewer than two years. These comparisons illustrate the variation in the degree to which all sections of society share in average progress in education.

The third theme to emerge from Figure 3.1 is the scale of national disparities based on income and gender. Wealth-based inequalities are a universal source of disadvantage in education. Being born into the poorest 20% significantly raises the risk of falling below the four-year threshold. In almost half of the countries including Cambodia, Ghana, Guatemala, India, Nicaragua, Nigeria and Yemen, the incidence of four-year education deprivation among the poor is double the national average. In the Philippines, being poor increases the likelihood of a 17- to 22-year-old having fewer than four years in education by a factor of four compared with the national average.

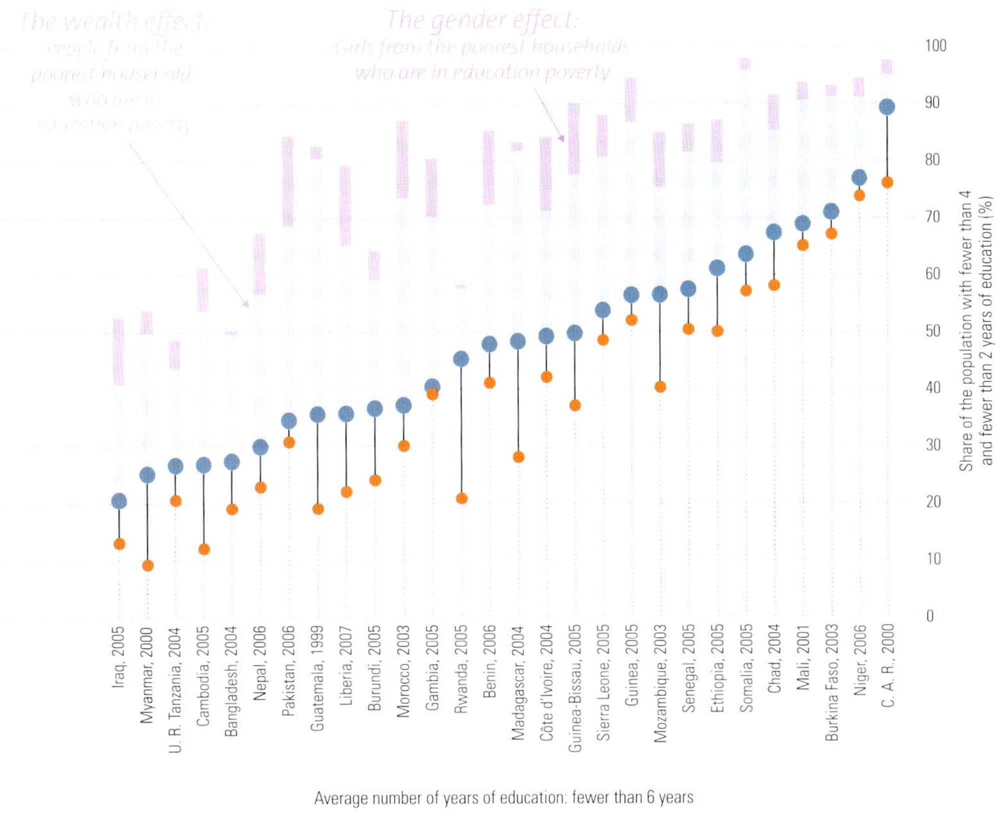

Gender effects magnify poverty effects – and vice versa. Being poor and female carries a double disadvantage in many countries. Figure 3.1 highlights the distance that separates girls in the poorest households, not just from the national average but also from boys in poor households. Gender disparities play an important role in explaining the relatively high level of education poverty in Egypt. Young women in the country are twice as likely as young men to have fewer than four years of education – and four times as likely if they are poor women. The incidence of deprivation among poor women in Egypt is higher than in some other countries, such as Honduras, Uganda and Zambia, at far lower levels of average income. Young women from the poorest households in Morocco are more likely to have fewer than four years in education than their counterparts in Senegal. In Yemen, 90% of poor young women aged 17 to 22 years have fewer than four years in education compared with 30% for poor males.

While data on those aged 17 to 22 provide insight into the legacy of deprivation, current attendance patterns reflect the degree to which disadvantage is transmitted across generations. Figure 3.2 shows income and gender disparities in sub-Saharan Africa, and South and West Asia are narrowing over time but remain very large. The household survey evidence in the DME data set indicates that 38% of children aged 7 to 16 from the poorest households in sub-Saharan Africa and 26% in South and West Asia have never been to school. It also provides worrying evidence of the limited progress achieved in reaching sub-Saharan Africa's poorest 20% of children, especially young girls. The share of young adults aged 17 to 22 from the poorest households who never attended school was higher in South and West Asia than in sub-Saharan Africa. That picture is dramatically reversed for children aged 7-16 years, suggesting that social convergence in school attendance is moving more slowly in sub-Saharan Africa.

Being poor and female carries a double disadvantage in many countries

Figure 3.2: Slow progress for Africa's poorest children

% of the population that has never attended school, by age group, sub-Saharan Africa, and South and West Asia, circa 2005

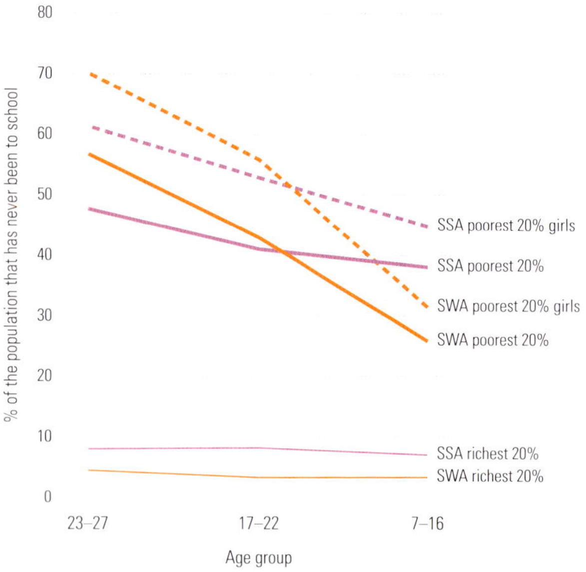

Notes: SSA stands for sub-Saharan Africa, SWA for South and West Asia. Estimates are population weighted averages.
Source: UNESCO-DME (2009).

In Egypt, rich urban girls average ten years in education, declining to under five years for poor rural girls

Inequalities stemming from income and gender help explain the inconsistent relationship between national wealth and acute deprivation in education. Average years of education tend to rise and deprivation to diminish as income rises, but countries vary enormously in the degree to which they convert rising income into declining education deprivation (Figure 3.3). Comparisons across countries at different levels of income reveal some striking results for those aged 17 to 22:

- While it has a per capita income comparable to Viet Nam's, Pakistan has more than three times the share of the age group with fewer than four years of education.

- With double the average income level of Lesotho, Morocco has twice the population share with fewer than four years of education.

- At the same average income level as Egypt, Jordan has an incidence of education poverty seven times lower.

- Average income in Gabon and Turkey is more than double the level in the Dominican Republic, but all three countries have comparable population shares below the four-year threshold.

Such comparisons caution against assuming that economic growth automatically dissolves extreme deprivation in education. Wealth increases the resources available to households and governments for investment in education. Yet the high levels of variation point to the importance of other factors in expanding opportunity for the disadvantaged – notably, the effectiveness of public policies.

Income and gender disparities do not operate in isolation. Education inequalities in both dimensions intersect with inequalities linked to location, ethnicity, language, disability and other factors to limit opportunity and reinforce marginalization.

In many countries, rural households in general and poor rural households in particular lag far behind their urban counterparts. Rural location compounds wealth and gender disadvantages, reflecting the impact of cultural attitudes and the unequal burden of household labour. It also intersects with the wider patterns of group-based deprivation captured in Figure 3.4:

- In Egypt, income differences overlap with rural-urban and gender divides. Rich urban boys and girls both average just over ten years in education. Poor rural males average fewer than eight years, declining to under five years for girls. The rural part of Upper Egypt is an area of particularly deep disadvantage. Over 40% of the population lives in poverty and rural females in the region average just over four years of schooling – a level similar to the national average in Côte d'Ivoire.

- India's wealth divides in education are among the largest in the world – and they are reinforced by regional and gender disparities. While the richest 20% average over eleven years in school, the poorest have an average education expectancy that places them just above the four year 'education poverty line'. Poor rural females are well below that line. Averaging three years in education, they are in a position comparable to the national average for Chad. The average poor rural woman aged 17 to 22 in Bihar averages fewer than two years in education.

- In Nigeria, the average poor rural female is just above the two-year threshold for extreme education deprivation, with less than 40% the national average for years of school and around one-quarter the average for rich urban males. There is a three-year gap between poor rural

Figure 3.3: Education poverty falls with rising income – but the association varies

GNP per capita and % of the population aged 17 to 22 with fewer than four years of education

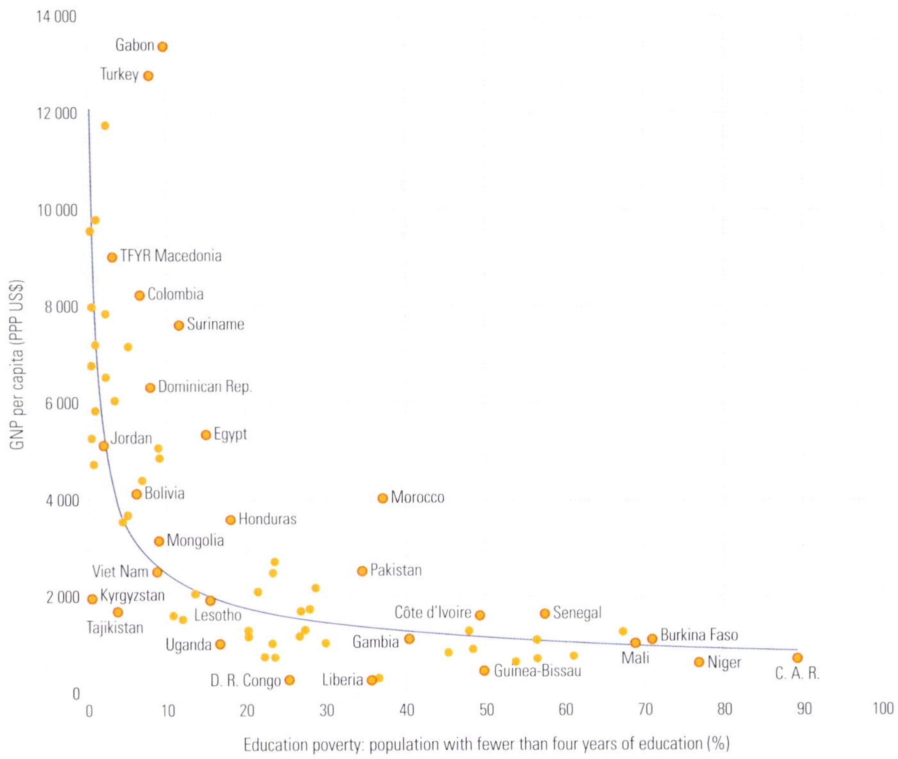

Sources: UNESCO-DME (2009); annex, Statistical Table 1.

females and poor urban males. Poor rural Hausa women are identifiably at the bottom end of the national distribution for opportunities in education, averaging just a few months of schooling. At the other end of the scale, rich boys and girls average around 10 years in education. The Nigerian case powerfully illustrates the mutually reinforcing effects of poverty, rural location and cultural factors in creating extreme disadvantage.

Inequalities associated with specific livelihoods often contribute to national disparities. The experience of pastoralists is a particularly stark example. Living in remote areas, with children heavily involved in tending cattle and livelihoods that involve movement across large distances, pastoralists face major barriers to educational opportunity. Those barriers of time and distance are sometimes reinforced by problems in education policy, including failure to offer relevant curricula, provide appropriate textbooks and respond to the realities of pastoral livelihoods. And they interact with labour practices, cultural traditions and belief systems to perpetuate deep disparities based on gender.

National household survey and census data provide insight into the scale of this disadvantage. In Ethiopia, Kenya and Uganda, for example, pastoralist groups are at the bottom end of the distribution for educational opportunity (Figure 3.5). In Uganda, 85% of Karamojong pastoralists aged 17 to 22 have fewer than two years in school, compared with a national average of over six years. In West Africa, the Peul group, also called the Fula, Fulani and Poular, is among the most educationally disadvantaged in countries including Benin, Chad, Mali and Senegal.

Current school attendance patterns point to a continuation of extreme educational disadvantage across generations, with pastoralist children particularly unlikely to be attending school, as Figure 3.5 shows. In Benin, nearly 90% of Peul children of primary school age do not attend

In Ethiopia, Kenya and Uganda, pastoralist groups are at the bottom end of the distribution for educational opportunity

Figure 3.4: The education inequality tree

Average number of years of education of the population aged 17 to 22 by wealth, gender, location, and other selected drivers of marginalization, latest available year

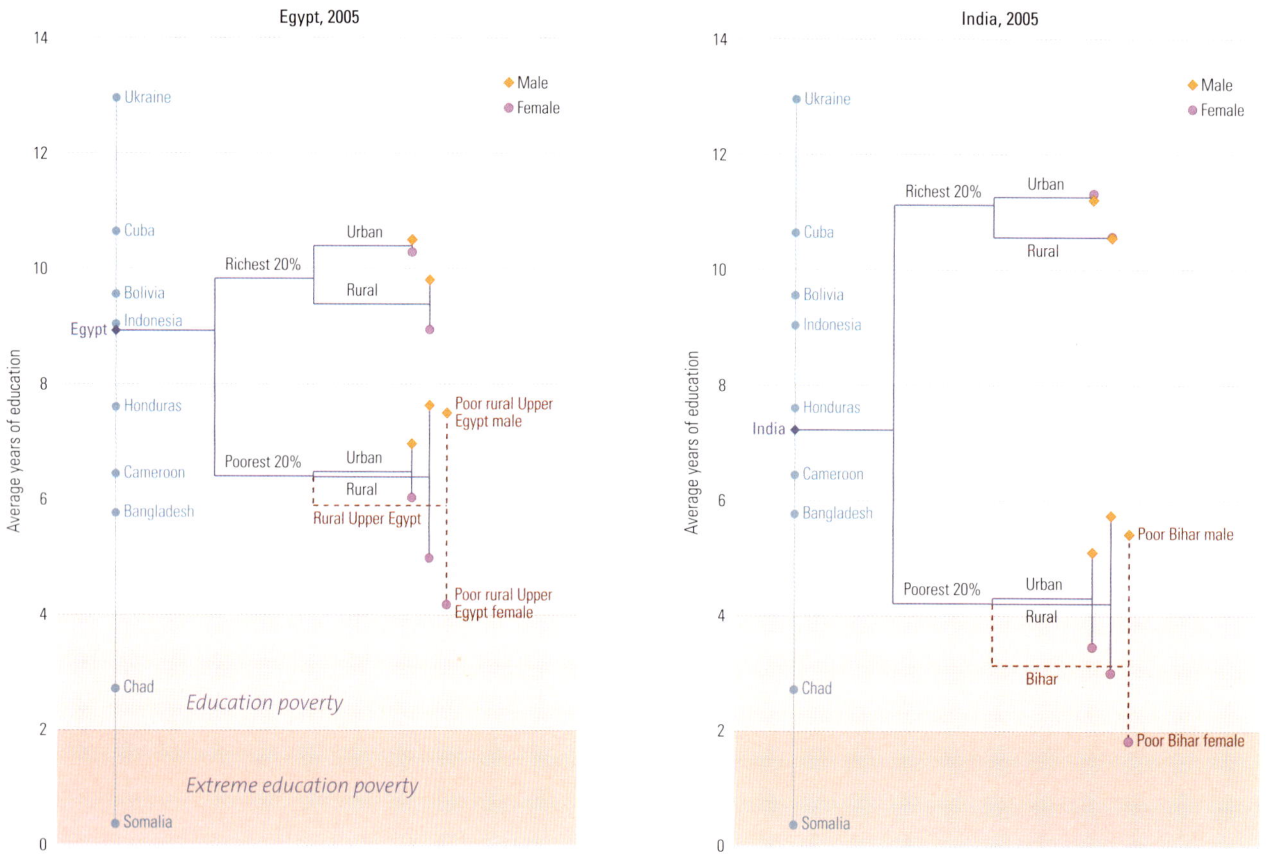

Source: UNESCO-DME (2009).

Figure 3.5: Pastoralists face extreme education deprivation

% of the population aged 17 to 22 with fewer than two years of education and % of primary school age children not attending primary school, by gender and membership of selected pastoralist groups, latest available year

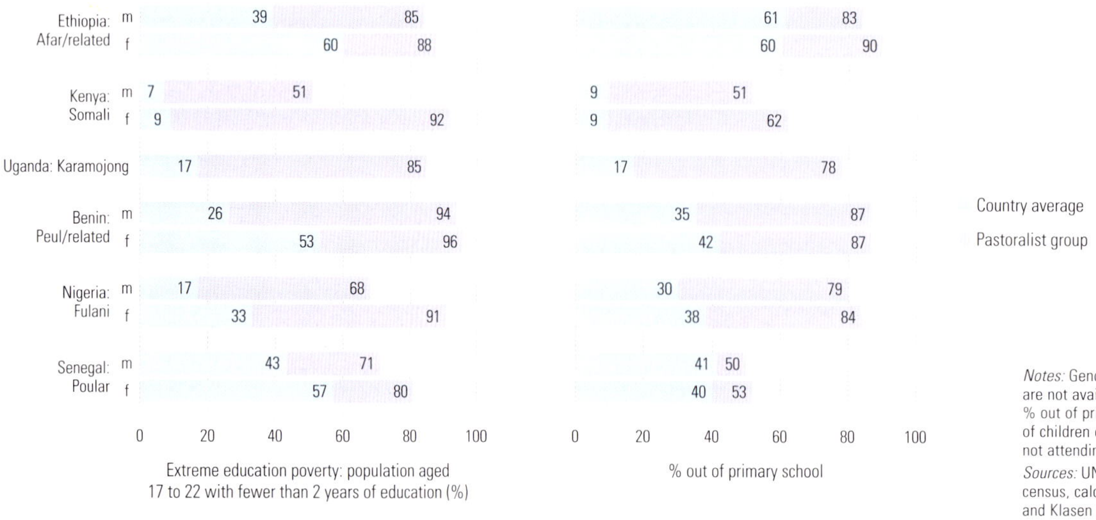

Notes: Gender-disaggregated data are not available for Uganda.
% out of primary school: proportion of children of primary school age not attending primary school.
Sources: UNESCO-DME (2009); census, calculations by Harttgen and Klasen (2009).

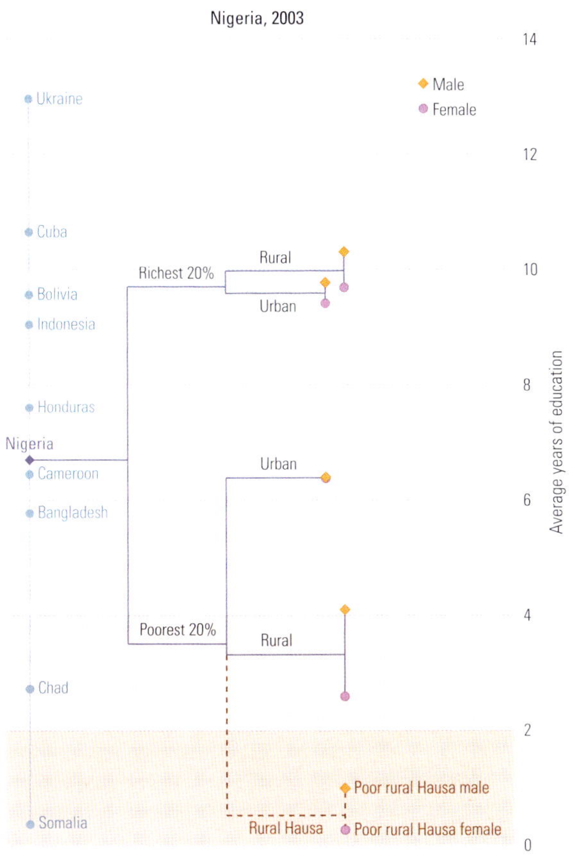

school. Being a Somali in Kenya increases the risk of being out of school by a factor of five or more, depending on gender. Over 60% of Somali girls are not in primary school – some seven times the national average.

Regional disparities figure prominently in the profile of educational disadvantage. Inequalities between regions in the same country are often far larger than inequalities between countries. Figure 3.6, which charts the share of the national population aged 17 to 22 with fewer than four years of school across regions of selected countries, shows that regional differences have a strong influence on educational opportunities. In Nicaragua, the share of the population with fewer than four years of school ranges from less than 7% in Managua to almost 60% in Jinotega.

Marginalized regions are often characterized by high levels of poverty, concentrations of ethnic minority populations and conflict. In Chad's eastern Barh Azoum district, fighting between government and rebel forces has led to large-scale internal displacement. The area is also home to a large population of refugees from the Sudan displaced by Janjaweed militias (Internal Displacement Monitoring Centre, 2009). Over 90% of the district's population aged 17 to 22 has fewer than four years of education and school attendance rates are among the country's lowest. In Uganda, strong national progress towards universal primary education has obscured large pockets of regional marginalization. Education data starkly reveal the devastating impact of conflict and poverty in the north of the country. In the north-eastern districts of Kotido, Moroto and Nakapiripirit, where security concerns and violence linked to cattle raiding have contributed to wider factors holding back progress in education, around 90% of those aged 17 to 22 have fewer than two years of schooling (Box 3.1).

Geographic inequalities are often closely linked to social and economic inequalities, rural-urban differences, ethnicity and language. In Cambodia's most disadvantaged provinces, Mondol Kiri and Rattanak Kiri, large concentrations of hill tribes live in remote areas with high levels of poverty. Fewer than one in three residents aged 17 to 22 have more than four years of education (Figure 3.6). Gender disparities in the area are marked: young women average just 1.8 years of school, compared with 3.2 years for young men. These outcomes reflect the combined effects of poverty, isolation, discrimination and cultural practices, as well as policy failures in education.

In Cambodia's most disadvantaged provinces, young women average just 1.8 years of school, compared with 3.2 years for young men

In the Philippines, there is a close fit between the regional incidence of poverty and the regional incidence of young adults aged 17 to 22 with fewer than four years of education. One of the most educationally disadvantaged areas is the Autonomous Region in Muslim Mindanao, where years of conflict have exacerbated poverty and displaced 750,000 people (Box 3.2).

Another example comes from Mexico, where rapid progress has been made over the past decade, with social protection programmes and targeted transfers eroding regional and income-based inequalities. While regional disparities have fallen over time, they nevertheless remain (Table 3.2):

- The southern 'poverty belt states' of Chiapas, Guerrero, Michoacán, Oaxaca and Veracruz

Figure 3.6: Many countries have large regional disparities in education poverty

% of population aged 17 to 22 with fewer than four years of education, by region, selected countries, latest available year

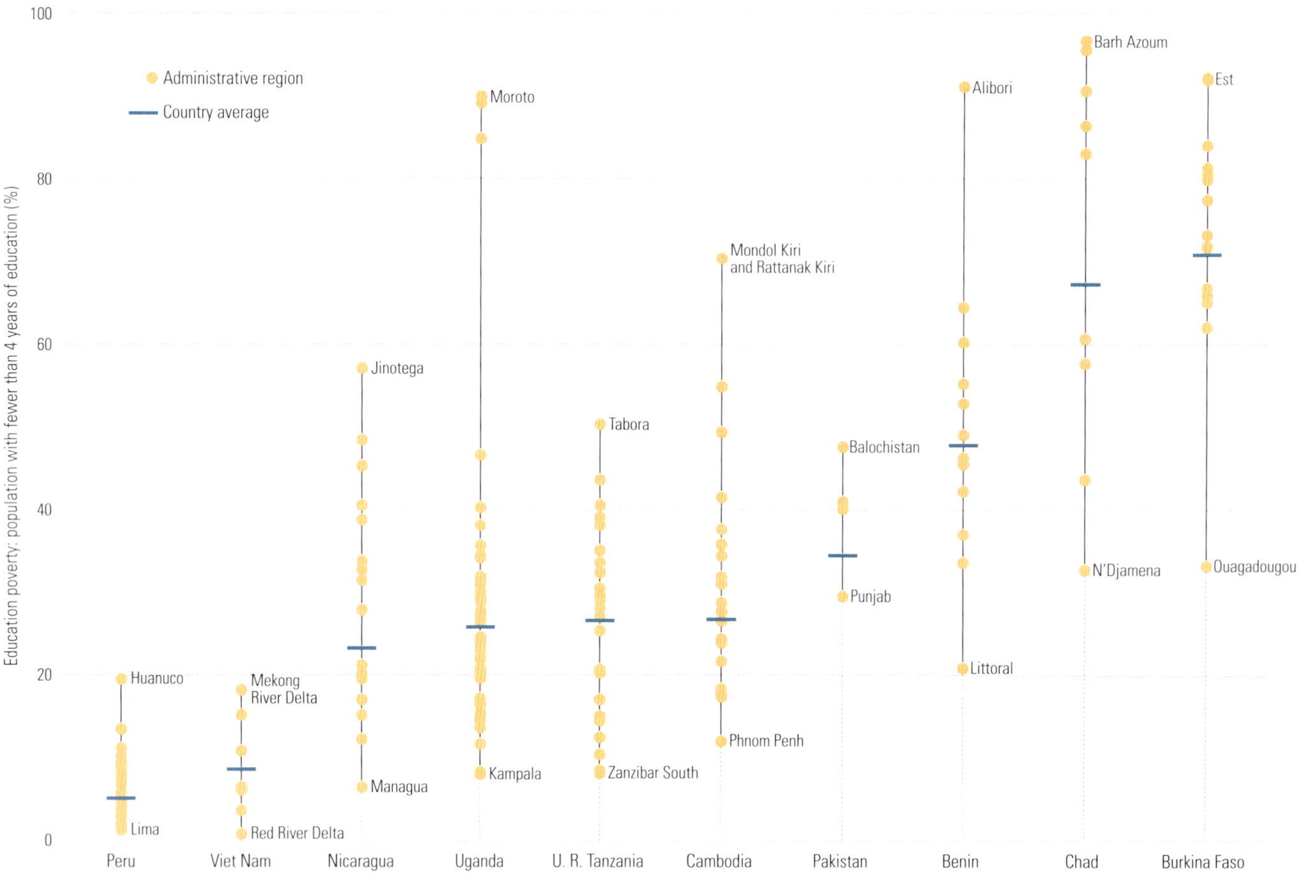

Source: UNESCO-DME (2009).

figure prominently at the bottom end of the educational opportunity scale. Average years of education range from 5.7 for females in Chiapas to over 10 in the Federal District.

- Whereas 11% of those aged 17 to 22 have fewer than four years of education, for Guerrero the figure rises to 19% and for Chiapas 26%.

In Guatemala, the average number of years in school ranges from about 6.7 for Spanish speakers to 1.8 for Q'eqchi' speakers

Indigenous people and ethnic minorities face particularly severe disadvantages in education. Some disadvantages faced by indigenous groups and ethnic minorities are poverty-related. Viet Nam's more than fifty ethnic minority groups account for 13% of the population but 40% of people living below the poverty line (Truong Huyen, 2009). In Bolivia and Guatemala, almost three-quarters of indigenous people are poor, compared with half of the non-indigenous population (Hall and Patrinos, 2006). Higher levels of poverty are associated in turn with discrimination and cultural stigmatization, creating obstacles to education. In Bolivia, Aymara speakers aged 17 to 22 accumulate two years fewer in school than do Spanish speakers and for Quechua speakers the figure is four years. In Guatemala, average years in school range from 6.7 for Spanish speakers to 1.8 for Q'eqchi' speakers.

Poverty and gender discrimination exacerbate education deprivation among indigenous minorities. From Guatemala and Peru to Cambodia and the Lao People's Democratic Republic, indigenous young adults are far more likely than the non-indigenous to experience extreme education deprivation, especially if they are poor and female. An indigenous person aged 17 to 22 in Peru has two years less education than the national average; poor indigenous girls are two years further still down the scale (Figure 3.10).

Box 3.1: Uganda – universal primary education is in sight, but large pockets of marginalization persist

Uganda has made rapid advances in primary education over the past decade. Numbers of out-of-school children have fallen sharply, completion rates are improving and gender disparities are shrinking. Sustaining progress towards universal primary completion will require a renewed effort to reach some of the most marginalized populations. Census and household survey data help identify these populations.

Poverty remains a major barrier. Over 20% of 17- to 22-year-olds in the poorest quintile of the population have fewer than two years of schooling – four times the level for the richest quintile. Increased investment in education and the abolition of school fees have improved access for the poor. Even so, 16% of those aged 7 to 16 from the poorest households are not attending school, pointing to a need for further measures.

Parts of Uganda have been left far behind. Conflict and the activities of the Lord's Resistance Army in the northern districts of Acholi, Apac, Gulu, Kitgum and Lira have had devastating consequences for education. School closures, parental fears over abduction and chronic teacher shortages have held back progress. Insecurity has undermined livelihoods and reinforced poverty, making it difficult for parents to meet indirect education costs. Some 40% of Acholi parents cite cost as the reason for their children dropping out of school, although inability to meet costs and insecurity are mutually reinforcing.

Other northern districts with large pastoralist populations are among the most educationally marginalized in the country. In Kotido, 83% of 17- to 22-year-olds have fewer than two years of education – and only one-fifth of children are currently in primary school (Figure 3.7 and Table 3.1).

Gender disparities are another impediment to progress in the north. Traditional practices often lead to girls as young as 12 being married. Early pregnancy is another problem. One survey found that almost 10% of school dropout in the Acholi subregion was linked to pregnancy or early marriage. Fears over the safety of girls attending schools in conflict-affected areas added to these concerns. And where poverty forces households to choose who goes to school, cultural attitudes lead many to express a preference for boys' education.

Conflict has made it more difficult to attract teachers to the north. For example, in late 2006, 500 teaching positions were advertised in Kitgum, but only 180 viable applications were received. High rates of teacher absenteeism reflect underlying problems. Many schools lack teacher housing, so teachers have to commute long distances, sometimes along insecure routes. Teacher income also tends to be far lower than in more prosperous areas, partly because poverty reduces the supplements households pay.

The fragile peace in the north gives the government and donors an opportunity to support an 'education catch-up'. Seizing the opportunity may require a review of public financing. Mapping of educational disadvantage highlights the special needs of the north, but on a per capita basis the area receives roughly the same in government transfers as the rest of the country. There is a strong case for preferential financing for this disadvantaged area.

Sources: UNICEF (2007*d*); Higgins (2009); Women's Commission for Refugee Women and Children (2005).

Figure 3.7: Education poverty is high in some of Uganda's northern districts

% population aged 17 to 22 with fewer than two years of education

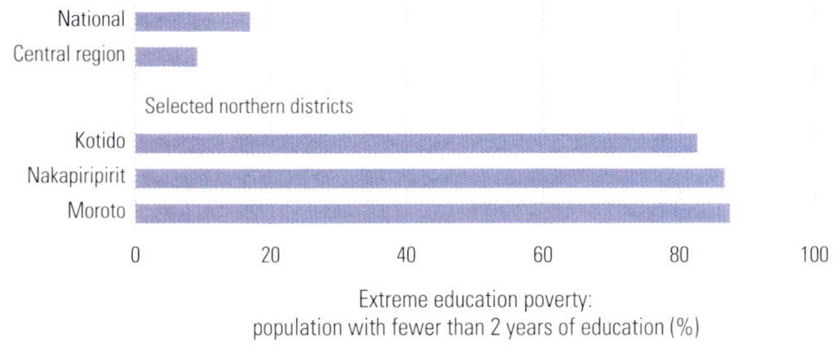

Source: Census, calculations by Harttgen and Klasen (2009).

Table 3.1: Primary net attendance rates in selected regions and districts of Uganda, by gender, 2002

	Primary net attendance rates (%)	
	Male	Female
National	83	83
Central region	89	90
Northern region		
Adjumani	79	76
Apac	79	77
Arua	83	79
Gulu	82	76
Kitgum	84	82
Kotido	22	19
Lira	78	75
Moyo	87	82
Moroto	21	18
Nakapiripirit	17	19
Nobbi	80	72
Pader	82	78
Yumbe	88	81

Box 3.2: The Philippines – leaving the marginalized behind

Education indicators for the Philippines are below what might be expected for a country at its income level. There is a real danger that the country will fail to achieve universal primary education by 2015. Household survey data help identify the large pockets of extreme and persistent deprivation that are holding back progress.

The net enrolment ratio was 92% in 2007, which is comparable with countries at far lower levels of average income, such as Zambia, and below the levels attained by other countries in the region, such as Indonesia. Around 1 million children are out of school – a slight increase over the level in 1999.

Extreme poverty and regional disparities are at the heart of the mismatch between national wealth and education outcome. The gap separating the poorest 20% from the rest of society is far wider than in most countries in the region (Figure 3.8). Those aged 17 to 22 in the poorest quintile average about seven years of education – more than four years fewer than in the wealthiest 20%. Data on school attendance provide evidence that current policies are not reaching the poorest. Around 6% of 7- to 16-year-olds from the poorest households are reported as not attending school or to have ever attended. Extreme economic inequalities fuel education inequalities, notably by pushing many children out of school and into employment.

Regional data reveal deep fault lines in opportunity (Figure 3.9). Nationally, about 6% of those aged 17 to 22 have fewer than four years of education. In the best-performing regions – Ilocos and the National Capital Region – the share falls to 1% to 2%. At the other extreme, in the Autonomous Region in Muslim Mindanao and Zamboanga Peninsula over 10% fall below this threshold.

The disparities are driven by a wide array of factors. The impact of high levels of poverty is exacerbated by conflict in Mindanao, and by the remoteness and wider disadvantage experienced by indigenous people in the Eastern Visayas and Zamboanga.

National authorities face difficult policy choices if the Philippines is to achieve universal primary education by 2015. Far more weight has to be attached to reaching marginalized populations and providing them with good quality education. Social protection and conditional cash transfer programmes, such as those in Brazil and Mexico, could play a vital role in combating child labour and extending educational opportunities to the poor. Another urgent priority is local language teaching in indigenous areas.

Figure 3.8: The Philippines has large wealth gaps in education

Average number of years of education of the population aged 17 to 22, Philippines, 2003

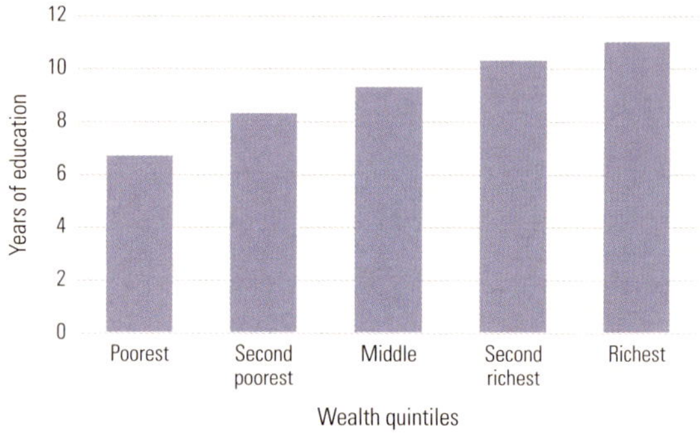

Source: UNESCO-DME (2009).

Large pockets of extreme and persistent deprivation are holding back progress

Table 3.2: Selected education indicators, by region, Mexico, 2005

	Secondary net attendance rates (%)		Years of education*		Fewer than 4 years of education
	Male	Female	Male	Female	(%)*
Disadvantaged southern states					
Chiapas	65	54	6.6	5.7	26
Guerrero	68	64	7.1	7.0	19
Michoacán	59	57	7.1	7.4	14
Oaxaca	69	61	7.1	6.7	16
Veracruz	68	65	7.3	7.1	20
National average	**69**	**66**	**8.2**	**8.2**	**11**
Selected northern and central states					
Baja California	75	74	8.9	9.4	6
Distrito Federal	84	84	10.0	10.1	3
México	74	72	9.0	9.0	6

* Data for population aged 17 to 22.

Source: Census, calculations by Harttgen and Klasen (2009).

The diversity of the challenges sets limits to what the central government can do. Regional and subregional authorities need to develop and implement policies that respond to local needs. However, the central government could do more to create an enabling environment. The education system suffers from chronic shortages of teachers and classrooms, rising class sizes and low levels of learning achievement. Addressing these problems will require an increase in the 2.1% share of national income directed towards education in 2005 – one of the lowest levels in the world.

Figure 3.9: Children in poor, remote, or conflict-affected regions of the Philippines suffer higher levels of education poverty

% of the population aged 17 to 22 with fewer than four years of education and prevalence of poor families by region, Philippines, 2003

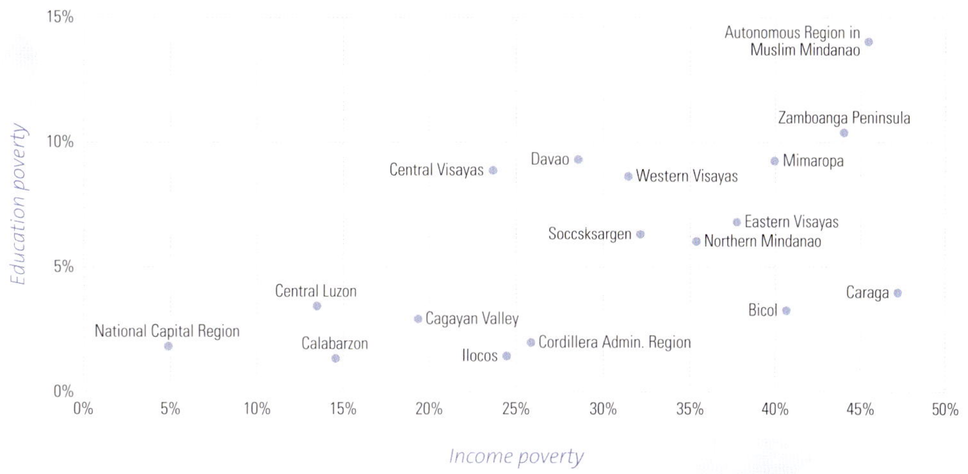

Notes: Education poverty is measured as the proportion of 17- to 22-year-olds with fewer than four years of education. Income poverty rate is the proportion of families whose income puts them below the poverty line for each region.
Sources: UNESCO-DME (2009); Philippines National Statistical Coordination Board (2006).

School attendance patterns revealed in household surveys point to the prospect of marked disparities being transmitted across generations.

Disadvantages associated with language are found across all regions. Having the official language of instruction as a home language significantly lowers the risk of having fewer than four years in education at age 17 to 22. Having Kurdish as a home language in Turkey carries a 30% risk of having fewer than four years of schooling compared with less than 5% for Turkish speakers. While these language effects are strongly associated with regional poverty differences, they are also important in their own right (Figure 3.11).

In countries where the official language is not the most common language spoken at home there are strong links from language to marginalization in education. There are some thirty countries of

Figure 3.10: Wealth and gender widen indigenous education disparities in Latin America

Average number of years of education for indigenous people aged 17 to 22, selected countries, latest available year

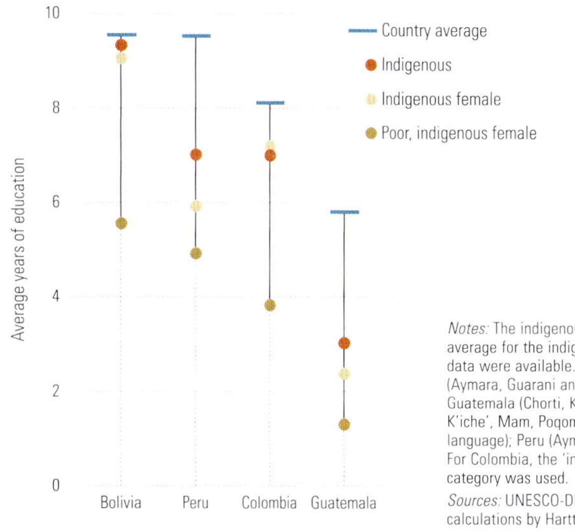

Notes: The indigenous average is the weighted average for the indigenous groups for which data were available. These were: Bolivia (Aymara, Guarani and Quechua ethnicity); Guatemala (Chorti, Kanjobal, Kaqchiquel, K'iche', Mam, Poqomchi', Q'eqchi' and Tzu'Utihil language); Peru (Aymara and Quechua ethnicity). For Colombia, the 'indigenous ethnicity' census category was used.
Sources: UNESCO-DME (2009); census, calculations by Harttgen and Klasen (2009).

Figure 3.11: The language gap in educational opportunity

% of population aged 17 to 22 with fewer than four years of education, by language spoken, selected countries, latest available year

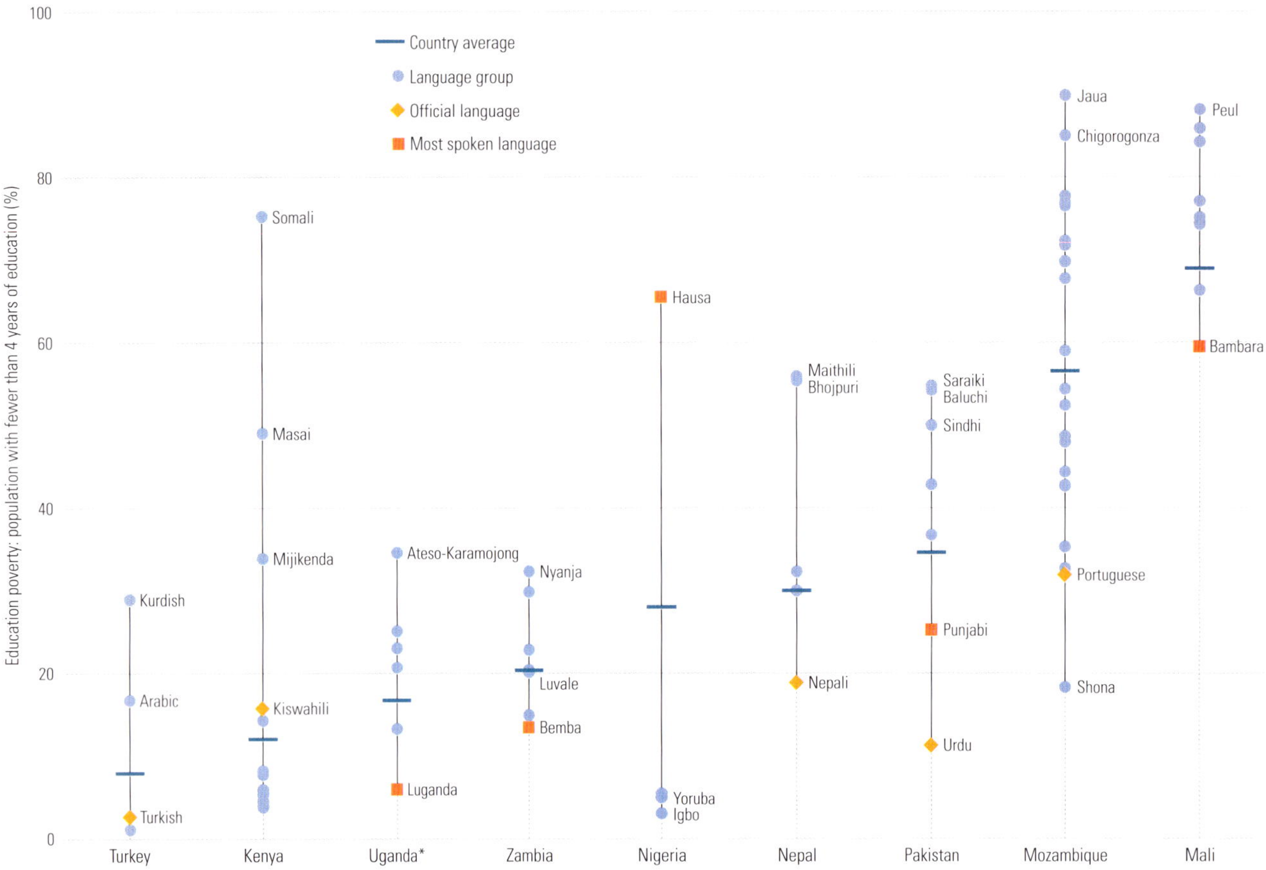

Sources: UNESCO-DME (2009); *Uganda census, calculations by Harttgen and Klasen (2009).

In Nigeria, education poverty levels range from less than 10% for Yoruba speakers to over 60% for Hausa speakers

sub-Saharan Africa where the official language is not the most common home language (Alidou et al., 2006). This means that in many cases children are taught at primary school in a language other than their mother tongue, which contributes to extreme language-based disparities. In Mozambique, speakers of Jaua aged 17 to 22 average one year in education compared with five years for speakers of Portuguese; over 80% have fewer than four years in education. In Nigeria, education poverty levels, defined by the four-year threshold, range from less than 10% for Yoruba speakers to over 60% for Hausa speakers. Across the region, home language has a strong bearing on prospects for getting more than four years of education.

The interaction between language, ethnicity and location is a potent source of marginalization in education. Household survey data can help identify the regions and individuals most severely affected. One striking illustration comes from Turkey. In most regions, 2% to 7% of those aged 17 to 22 have fewer than four years of education, but in the eastern region the figure rises to 21%. Young women speaking a non-Turkish home language – predominantly Kurdish – are among the most educationally marginalized. They average just three years of education – less than the national average for Senegal (Figure 3.12).

The 'bottom 20%': relative deprivation

Marginalization is not just about deprivation in absolute terms. It is also about falling behind the rest of society. The individual and group-based disadvantages discussed above figure prominently in explaining the profile of those left behind in education. This section looks at the characteristics of the 'bottom 20%' in education.

Who are the bottom 20%? Household survey data make it possible to group people aged 17 to 22 on the basis of accumulated years of school. Data analysis can also be used to decompose group membership by identifying social characteristics such as household wealth, gender, ethnicity and location. Unlike the thresholds of deprivation used in the previous section, the 'bottom 20%' provides a relative *national* scale. People at the lowest end of the distribution in, say, the Philippines or Turkey have more years of school than their counterparts in Chad or Mali. What they share is the experience in childhood of restricted opportunity relative to other members in their country.

Household surveys have been widely used to chart overall inequality in education. The new data analysis prepared for this Report makes it possible to look beyond overall inequality to the characteristics of the 'bottom 20%'. The data can be used to assess both the weight of discrete variables such as income, language and gender and – with limitations – the cumulative effects of these variables.

Household wealth. Being born into the poorest 20% of households in a country is strongly associated with heightened risk of being at the bottom end of the distribution for educational opportunity (Figure 3.13). In Colombia, Mongolia, Nicaragua, the Philippines and Viet Nam, the poorest 20% account for twice their population share in the bottom 20% of the education distribution.

Ethnicity and language. In some countries, ethnic and language minority groups account for a large share of the bottom 20% (Figure 3.14). In Nigeria, over half the 'education poor' are Hausa speakers – a group that makes up one-fifth of the population. Reflecting the legacy of disadvantage experienced by indigenous Q'eqchi' speakers in Guatemala, membership of this language group more than doubles the risk of being in the bottom 20% for years in school.

Region and location. Regional differences in years spent in education are often far larger than differences between countries (Figure 3.15). Areas such as northern Kenya, eastern Turkey, rural Upper Egypt and northernmost Cameroon are heavily overrepresented in the lowest 20% of the education distribution for their countries. Single region figures can understate the level of disadvantage. In Cameroon, three regions with just one-quarter of the overall population account

Figure 3.12: Poverty, ethnicity and language fuel education marginalization in Turkey

Average number of years of education of the population aged 17 to 22 by wealth, location, gender and Kurdish language, 2005

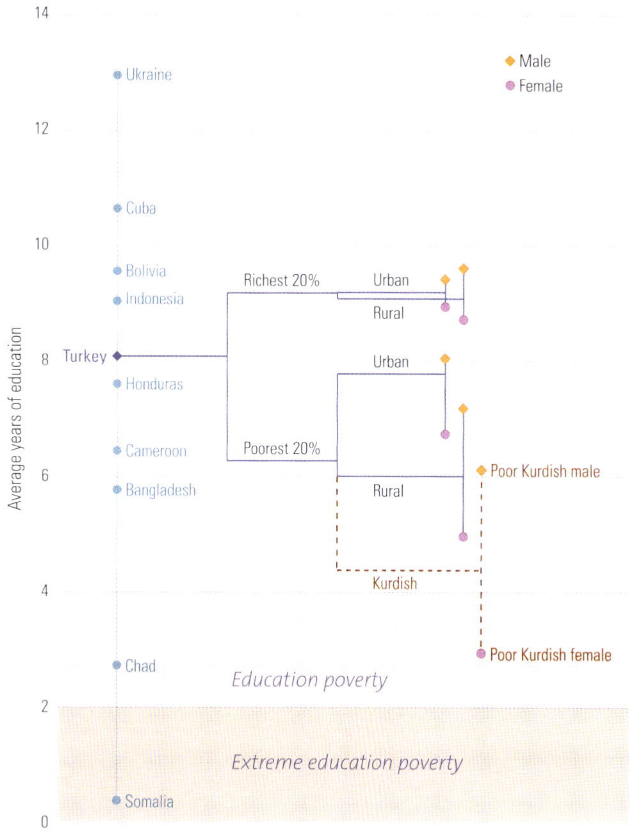

Source: UNESCO-DME (2009).

Figure 3.13: The poorest households are more likely to be left behind in education

Decomposition of the bottom 20% of the education distribution by wealth quintile, selected countries, latest available year

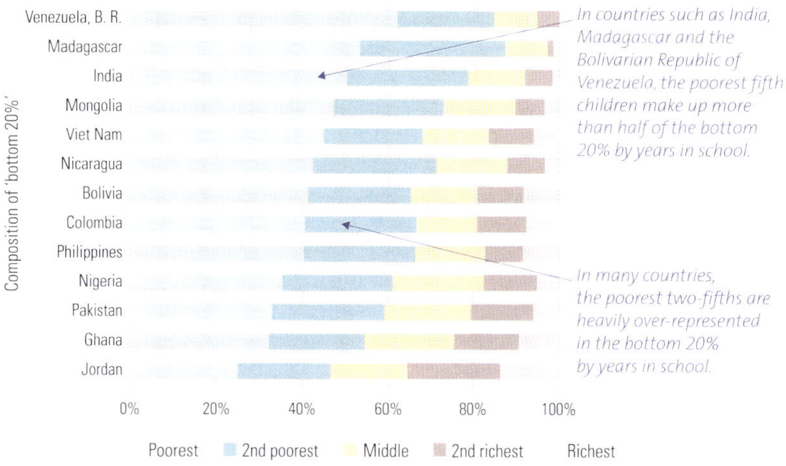

Note: The 'bottom 20%' is the 20% of 17- to 22-year-olds with the fewest years of education.
Source: UNESCO-DME (2009).

Figure 3.14: Language often predicts risk of being in the bottom 20%

% of selected language groups in the bottom 20% of the education distribution, selected countries, latest available year

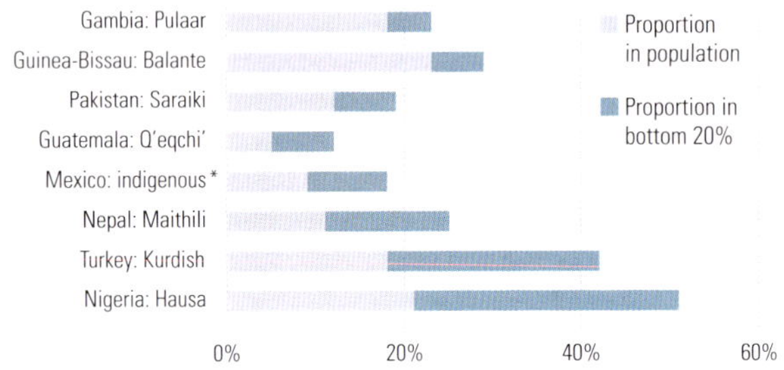

Note: The 'bottom 20%' is the 20% of 17- to 22-year-olds with the fewest years of education.
* The indigenous language category in Mexico consists of those who speak indigenous languages only and do not speak Spanish.
Sources: UNESCO-DME (2009); Mexico census, calculations by Harttgen and Klasen (2009).

for three-quarters of the population in the lowest education quintile. In Nigeria, 86% of the lowest education quintile is in two regions – the north-west and north-east, which account for 43% of the population.

Figure 3.15: Some regions face acute education deprivation

% of selected regions in the bottom 20% of the education distribution, population aged 17 to 22, selected countries, latest available year*

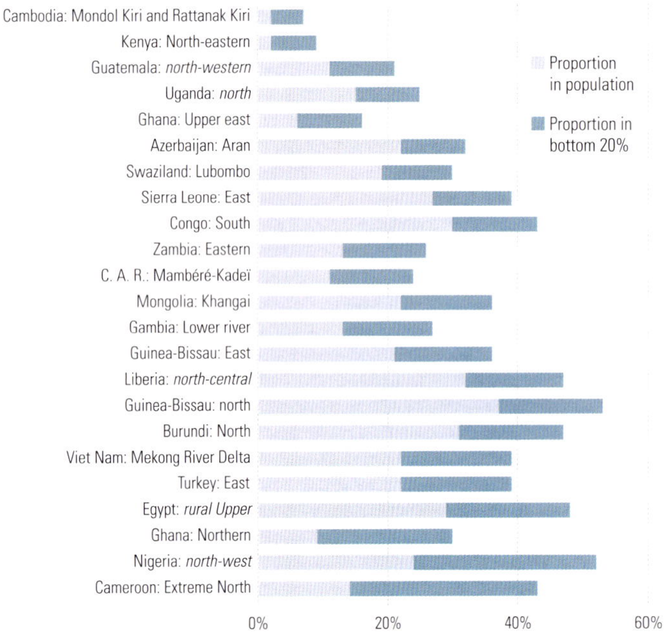

* Regions presented in the graph are the first level of administrative division, except those in italics which are geographical areas.
Sources: UNESCO-DME (2009); census, calculations by Harttgen and Klasen (2009).

The disadvantages that drive people into the bottom 20% in education do not operate in isolation. They intersect and magnify the wider social inequalities that restrict opportunities in education. This is illustrated in Figure 3.16, which uses DME statistics to look at the impact of two or three overlapping dimensions of deprivation. The impact of clustered disadvantage is evident from the combined effects of poverty, gender and other markers for disadvantage. These effects can be captured by reference to the 'extreme education poverty' benchmark of fewer than two years in education and the more recent disadvantages reflected in the school attendance rates for primary school age children:

- Being a rural girl in the Cambodian hill provinces of Mondol Kiri and Rattanak Kiri increases the risk of not being in school by a factor of five. Three-quarters of the group have fewer than two years in school, compared with a national average of 12%.

- In Guatemala, girls from poor households of Indian ethnicity have primary net attendance rates of 60% compared with a national average of 82% and they are over three times more likely to have fewer than two years in school.

- In Turkey, one of the most marginalized groups is Kurdish-speaking girls from the poorest households. Around 43% at ages 17 to 22 have fewer than two years of education, while the national average is 6%.

- In Nigeria, poor Hausa girls face some of the world's most severe education deprivation. Some 97% of 17- to 22-year-olds have fewer than two years of education and just 12% of primary school age Hausa girls attend primary school.

Each of these examples involves a relatively large population group. They represent a statistically significant national policy challenge. But combating marginalization is also about identifying small groups facing intensive deprivation. Figure 3.17 uses the DME data set to illustrate the high levels of marginalization experienced by a number of small population groups. To take one case in point, almost 90% of the Mushahar community in Nepal, a largely landless low-caste group, is in the bottom 20%. The average time spent in school for those aged 17 to 22 in this group is less than three months, and only 29% of girls and 41% of boys attend primary school. Similarly, in Viet Nam

Figure 3.16: Overlapping disadvantages erode education opportunities

Primary net attendance rates and % of the population aged 17 to 22 with fewer than two years of education, selected countries, latest available year

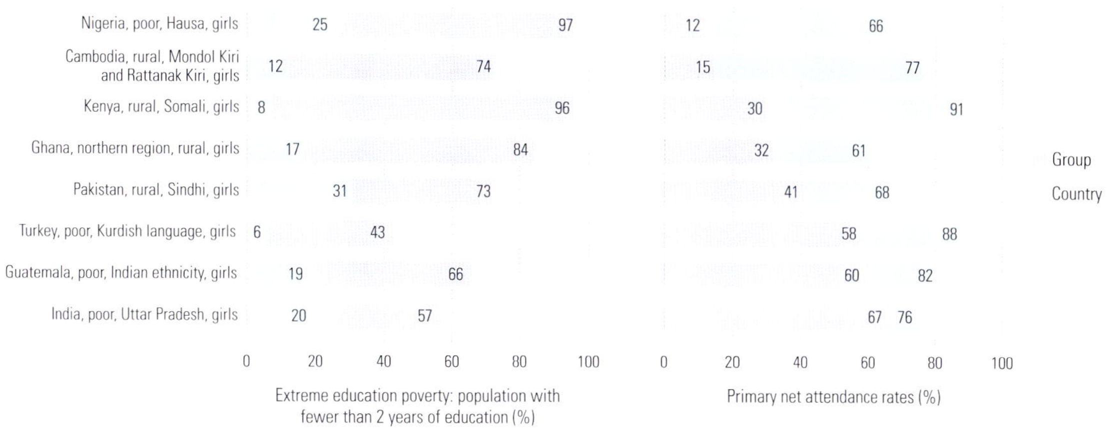

Source: UNESCO-DME (2009).

In Nigeria, 97% of poor Hausa girls have fewer than two years of education

Figure 3.17: Small groups, big disadvantages

Average number of years of education for selected marginalized groups, population aged 17 to 22 selected countries, latest available year

	Mushahar ethnicity	Barh Azoum region	Gourmantché ethnicity	Peul/related ethnicity	Gourmantché ethnicity	Somali ethnicity	Hmong ethnicity	Indigenous language only	North-eastern region
Share of population (%)	1	5	7	4	1	3	1	2	3
Proportion who are in the 'bottom 20%' (%)	89	43	32	43	25	45	88	42	77

Sources: UNESCO-DME (2009); census, calculations by Harttgen and Klasen (2009).

nine out of ten Hmong, members of an ethnic minority group living in northern highland regions, are in the bottom 20% of the national distribution for years in school.

The quality deficit

Marginalized individuals and groups do not just accumulate fewer years of education. When they are in school they often receive a poor-quality education, leading in turn to low levels of learning achievement.

Many of the world's poorest countries have been more successful in expanding access than raising quality. As Chapter 2 shows, average learning achievement is often shockingly low even for children who complete a full primary education cycle. The achievement deficit is widely spread across the population, but is typically concentrated among individuals and groups facing wider disadvantages in access to education.

Household wealth, parental education and home language exercise a pervasive influence on learning achievement

Factors such as household wealth, parental education and home language exercise a pervasive influence on learning achievement. That influence has been extensively documented in developed countries but less widely explored in the world's poorest countries. Research carried out for this Report examined data on learning achievement collected for sub-Saharan Africa, through the PASEC and SACMEQ regional assessment programmes, to identify characteristics associated with students performing at the top, middle and bottom of the test score range. The results are striking. As early as grades 5 and 6, there is a strong association in many countries between wealth and test scores. In Kenya and Zambia, the average household of children scoring in the top 10% has twice as many consumer durables as the average household for children in the lowest 10%. Parental literacy is also strongly associated with test scores (Fehrler and Michaelowa, 2009).

In Latin America, too, assessments reveal the low achievement of students belonging to marginalized populations. The PISA assessment programme uses a composite set of indicators to construct a socio-economic background index for parents of 15-year-olds tested. The results point to a strong association between parental socio-economic status and learning outcomes. In Brazil, Mexico and Uruguay, children of parents in the top quartile achieved a mathematics score 25% to 30% higher than those in the poorest quartile (Vegas and Petrow, 2008). In a national assessment in Uruguay, only 36% of sixth-graders from 'very unfavourable' backgrounds passed the mathematics test and 55% the language test, as opposed to 72% and 87%, respectively, of those from 'favourable' backgrounds (Vegas and Petrow, 2008).

Education outcomes are often substantially worse for indigenous people and ethnic minorities. In Latin America, there is extensive evidence of test score gaps between indigenous and non-indigenous children. In Guatemala, indigenous children in both rural and urban areas scored between 0.8 and 1 standard deviation below non-indigenous children in grades 3 and 6 Spanish tests – a gap of around 17% (McEwan and Trowbridge, 2007). Differences in mathematics tests were smaller but still significant. Recent research from Peru recorded exceptionally large gaps in indigenous and non-indigenous learning achievement (Cueto et al., 2009). At the end of primary school, the gap in mathematics and language scores was above a full standard deviation (1.22 and 1.07, respectively).

Home language often has an important influence on test scores. Research using data from the 2007 TIMSS assessment identifies a strong association between students performing below the lowest international benchmark and the frequency with which the language of the test is spoken at home. In Turkey, grade 8 students who report 'always or almost always' speaking the test language at home are 30% less likely to score below the international mathematics benchmark than those who report speaking it 'sometimes or never' (Altinok, 2009). Evidence from PASEC and SACMEQ also points to a strong link between home language and the language of instruction in influencing test scores (Fehrler and Michaelowa, 2009).

Language, ethnicity and regional factors can combine to produce complex patterns of disadvantage. In Viet Nam, a large-scale survey of grade 5 students in 2001 found strong disparities in achievement among provinces, with school location and students' socio-economic background and ethnicity also having a strong influence (World Bank, 2004). Ethnic minority students who spoke no Vietnamese at home were much less likely to read 'independently' than students whose home language was Vietnamese.

Marginalization in rich countries

Education is an increasingly important engine of social and economic success in rich countries. While education can break the transmission of cycles of disadvantage across generations, it can also reinforce them. Many of those with the lowest education levels come from families characterized by social disadvantage.

Getting a good education can create a virtuous circle of life chances. There is extensive evidence that education improves prospects not just for earnings and employment but also for health, civic engagement and social mobility (Lochner, 2004; Machin et al., 2006). Conversely, low levels of education are associated with entrenched employment disadvantage, restricted social mobility and a wide range of social problems. When individuals and groups emerge from education systems with low levels of achievement, they and their children face a heightened risk of marginalization in many aspects of their lives. Education systems provide a mechanism for offsetting social disadvantage, but when opportunities and outcomes are skewed they can reinforce social divisions.

There are obvious differences in the experience of education marginalization in rich and poor countries. One is in the degree of absolute deprivation. Almost nobody in the rich world enters adulthood with fewer than four years of education, let alone fewer than two years. Relative deprivation is another matter. Many education systems in rich countries have entrenched patterns of marginalization linked to poverty, the social and economic status of parents, ethnicity, race and other factors.

Marginalization in education in France, Germany, the United Kingdom or the United States is clearly not the same as in Cambodia or Mali. Yet there are two parallels. First, the playing field for opportunity is highly uneven: some groups and individuals enter education systems facing a heightened risk of failure. Second, education systems themselves often reinforce and perpetuate wider social disadvantages.

Dropping out of school

Leaving school too early is strongly linked with marginalization. Young people with only a lower secondary education have limited opportunities to realize their potential and develop their learning skills. They face disadvantages in employment and are at greater risk of poverty and social exclusion.

School dropouts represent a significant education underclass in many countries. In the European Union, 15% of people aged 18 to 24 in 2006 left school with only lower secondary education and were not in further education or training. The share affected ranged from just over 10% in some countries, including France and the United Kingdom, to 20% in Italy and 30% in Spain. Cross-country research has identified parental wealth, child poverty, ethnicity and gender as major factors influencing dropout rates (European Commission, 2008).

Evidence from the United States illustrates the pattern of risk factors associated with being out of school. In 2006, about 8% of people aged 16 to 19 were neither enrolled in school nor working. Family poverty contributed strongly to being out of school. Some 17% of youth from poor households were out of school, compared with 5% from non-poor households. Race and ethnicity were also important, with 11% of African-American and Hispanic youth reported as out of school – double the share for white and Asian youth (US Department of Education, 2007).

These data reflect underlying social disadvantages linked to school dropout. One high-profile national report documented a secondary school dropout epidemic in the United States (Bridgeland et al., 2006), with around 1 million school leavers each year lacking a diploma. The epidemic is unequally spread. African-American and Hispanic youth are highly disadvantaged. Whereas the graduation rate for white students is 84%, it falls to 72% for Hispanic and 65% for African-American students (Heckman and LaFontaine, 2007). Parental poverty and low levels of education are other major risk factors. Among student characteristics, low test scores and pregnancy contribute strongly to dropout rates. While the factors behind dropout are varied and complex, the consequences are uniformly severe. Students who drop out typically earn 30% to 35% less than students with a secondary school diploma (Tyler and Lofstrom, 2009).

In the United States, the graduation rate for white students is 84%, but falls to 65% for African-American students

Learning achievement

In a country with equal opportunities for learning, it would be impossible to predict education outcomes on the basis of individual or group characteristics. No country has achieved this state, but countries differ markedly in the degree to which social circumstances shape education opportunity and in the degree to which education systems counteract marginalization.

Students from more advantaged socio-economic backgrounds generally perform better in tests of learning achievement. Analysis of national data from the 2006 PISA science tests given to 15-year-olds shows that, on average, socio-economic background explains 14% of the variation in performance. There is marked variation around the average. Socio-economic characteristics weigh far more heavily in some countries, such as France, Germany, the United Kingdom and the United States, than in others, including Finland, Japan and the Republic of Korea, all of which achieve higher average scores (OECD, 2007*b*).

Socio-economic disadvantage weighs more heavily on test scores in some countries than others

Figure 3.18 illustrates the weight of inherited circumstance in shaping learning achievement. It suggests that high levels of inequality are particularly damaging for children from households at the lower end of the socio-economic distribution. Consider the following comparisons. The share of the national variation in PISA mathematics scores explained by socio-economic status is far greater in Germany than in Finland, with German children in the lowest socio-economic group twice as likely to score at the lowest level in mathematics tests. The contrast between (less equal) France and (more equal) the Republic of Korea is equally striking. Does the higher level of equity achieved in Finland and the Republic of Korea come at the price of lower average performance? On the contrary, both countries have higher mean test scores in PISA than France or Germany.

Figure 3.18: Socio-economic disadvantage in education weighs more heavily in some countries than others

Odds ratio for likelihood of lowest socio-economic status students aged 15 being among the bottom performers and % of mathematics score variance explained by socio-economic status, OECD countries

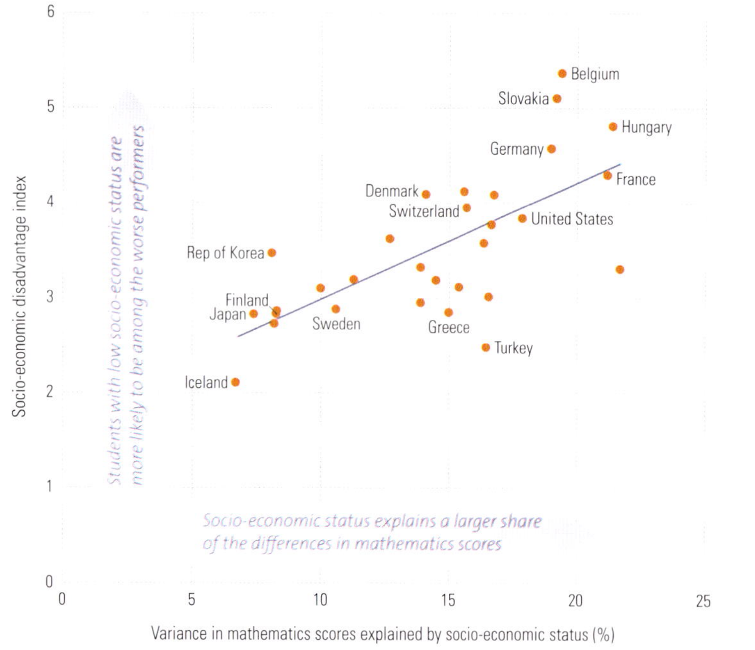

Note: The socio-economic disadvantage index is the relative likelihood of students with the lowest socio-economic status (SES) scoring below or at proficiency level 1 when compared to student with the highest SES.
Sources: OECD (2006*a*, 2007*a*).

Household poverty, a core element in socio-economic disadvantage, is strongly associated with low levels of education achievement. In England, students receiving a free school meal – a sign of household deprivation – have far lower average test scores than other students. The score gap in English is 16% and the gap in mathematics is 29%. The share of this group leaving school with high scores on national tests is one-third the national average (Vignoles, 2009; UK Department for Children, Schools and Families, 2008).

Wealth-based performance differences in France are equally marked. Almost half the children from the poorest households are significantly behind their peers by sixth grade. By age 15, around 15% of the poorest students are at least two years behind the ninth grade performance level – three times the national average. By age 17, almost one in five poor youth have given up their studies (France Council for Employment, 2008).

Poverty effects combine with other factors that contribute to marginalization. In the United States, schools with high concentrations of poverty (with over 75% of students eligible for free or subsidized lunch) had the lowest percentage of white students, the highest percentage of African-American and Hispanic students, and the highest percentage of students who reported always speaking a language other than English at home. They also had the highest percentage of fourth-graders being taught by a teacher with fewer than five years of experience (US Department of Education, 2007). Test score gaps reflect the cumulative disadvantage. On the international TIMSS scale for mathematics in grade 8, the United States ranks ninth out of forty-eight countries. Hispanic students, however, score just above the level of Malaysia. On an international scale, schools with high concentrations of poverty and African-American students score between the average levels of Malaysia and Thailand (Figure 3.19). These very large test score effects point to limited success by the education system in counteracting wide social disadvantages.

Migrant students in many countries face a far higher risk of education marginalization than native students do. Their participation in school is more likely to be disrupted by leaving early – and migrant students often lag in learning achievement. Research based on evidence from PISA surveys shows that, in most OECD countries, first-generation immigrants typically lag an average of about 1.5 years behind their native counterparts (OECD, 2007*b*). In several countries, including Germany, the Netherlands and Switzerland, the proportion of immigrant students failing to reach level 2 in the 2006 PISA assessment was at least three times as high as the proportion of native students (Figure 3.20).

Countries vary also in the degree to which they are narrowing learning achievement gaps. While the gap is narrowing in Sweden and Switzerland, it is widening in Germany and the Netherlands (OECD, 2007*a*). Education policy is just part of the explanation for these trends. Patterns of migrant disadvantage are closely associated in many countries with home language, country of origin, neighbourhood effects and other kinds of social deprivation. But education systems can help narrow or widen the gap.

Early tracking of students into different ability streams and types of school has been found in several cross-country studies to be associated with greater inequality in achievement without any discernible benefits for average performance (Hanushek and Wößmann, 2006). Being labelled as 'low ability' at an early age may lead students to internalize low expectations and lose motivation. Differences in tracking policies may help explain why students of Turkish origin tend to perform better in Switzerland (where tracking is delayed) than in Germany (which tracks students early), two countries where many migrants are channelled into vocational streams (Nusche, 2009; OECD, 2006*b*). They also go some way towards explaining the very large variation in performance between schools in Germany linked to socio-economic status. In Finland, less than 5% of overall performance variation of students can be traced to inequalities between schools, compared with over 70% in Germany – twice the OECD average (OECD, 2006*b*).

Racial and ethnic minority groups experience some of the most severe education disadvantage, which can be traced to deeply engrained and often centuries-old patterns of cultural discrimination and stigmatization. Low educational achievement reflects the durability of these patterns, interacting with social and economic inequalities to perpetuate social exclusion.

Figure 3.19: Same country, different worlds of learning achievement

TIMSS average mathematics scores in the United States and selected countries, grade 8, 2007

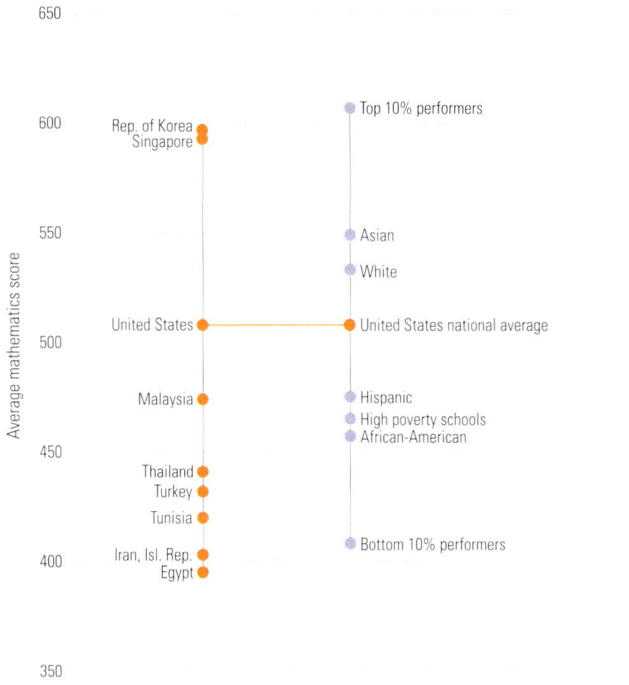

Source: Gonzales et al. (2008).

Figure 3.20: Second-generation immigrants in rich countries perform far below native students in science

% of students aged 15 scoring below proficiency level 2 on PISA mathematics scale, second generation immigrants and native students in Germany, the Netherlands and Switzerland, 2006*

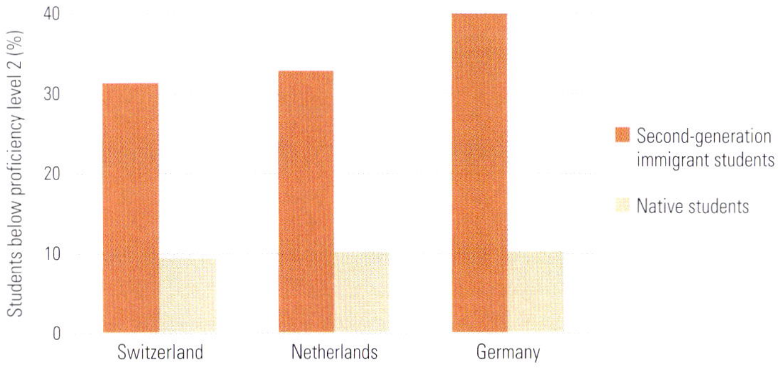

* 'Level 2 on the PISA proficiency scale represents the baseline level of mathematics proficiency at which students begin to demonstrate the kind of skills that enable them to actively use mathematics: for example, they are able to use basic algorithms, formulae and procedures, to make literal interpretations and to apply direct reasoning' (OECD, 2007*a*, p. 107).

Source: OECD (2007*a*).

One particularly stark example of marginalization is the experience of the Roma community.[3] Assessing the full extent of the deprivation faced by Roma children in education is difficult, as data are often partial and unreliable (Box 3.3). The data that are available tell their own story. In most central and eastern European countries no more than 20% to 25% of Roma children attend secondary school and the vast majority of those are enrolled in vocational education. Many drop out of primary school. It is estimated that 15% to 20% of Roma children in Bulgaria and 30% in Romania do not continue beyond fourth grade. The problem is not restricted to central and eastern Europe. It is estimated that half of Italy's Roma children are in primary school but fewer than 2% progress to upper secondary education. While data are scarce, education outcomes for Roma fall well below the levels for the majority population (Open Society Institute, 2007).

In most central and eastern European countries no more than 25% of Roma children attend secondary school

Roma education experiences underline the damage that can be inflicted by bad policies. In many countries, education policies and practices have the effect of creating segregation. Geographic concentration is one factor. In Bulgaria, an estimated 70% of Roma children study in schools where the share of the majority population is less than 50%. Moreover, Roma children are often more likely than their peers to be diagnosed as 'special needs' students and placed in separate schools (Open Society Institute, 2007). In Hungary, one report found that 'about every fifth Roma child is declared to be mildly mentally disabled' (Roma Education Fund, 2007, p. 32). Such practices reflect cultural attitudes and negative stereotyping. One Council of Europe report on Slovakia found that up to half of Roma children in special elementary schools were there as a result of erroneous assessment (European Commission against Racism and Intolerance, 2009).

The legacy of marginalization facing indigenous people in rich countries has received insufficient attention in international education debates. For Native Americans, the Aboriginals of Australia and the Māori of New Zealand, the imprint of discrimination, stigmatization and social breakdown is clearly visible in education data. Only 34% of indigenous Australians aged 15 to 24 are in education, compared with 55% of their non-indigenous peers. Indigenous people also score lower on reading and numeracy tests, especially if they live in remote areas (Figure 3.21). In very remote areas, the share of indigenous Australians falling below the national minimum benchmark for reading is more than double the level for all students. In New Zealand, there is

Box 3.3: Monitoring gaps and marginalization – Roma in Europe

With an estimated population between 8 million and 12 million, Roma are one of Europe's largest minorities. They are also among the most marginalized. Throughout Europe, Roma face institutionalized discrimination, limited opportunities for participation in many aspects of society and poor access to good-quality education.

Lack of data makes it difficult to measure the scale of Roma marginalization. It also limits public debate and the development of effective policy responses. Census data often undercount Roma because the social stigma attached to Roma identity leads many to misreport or refuse to report their identity. Administrative data are also frequently lacking. In some countries, such as Romania and Slovakia, this is because of privacy legislation that restricts reporting on ethnicity.

While data on Roma are scarce overall, the absence of reliable statistics on education is a particular weakness. Problems noted by the European Roma Rights Centre range from under-reported births to unreliable and inconsistent data on school enrolment, dropout and other indicators collected by school authorities. A qualitative study in Bulgaria found that administrative data failed to report a significant number of out-of-school Roma children because households were not registered or school databases were incomplete.

Pressure to improve the scope and reliability of monitoring data on Roma has been building. The Decade of Roma Inclusion 2005-2015, an initiative supported by the World Bank, the United Nations Development Programme, the European Commission, the Council of Europe and the Open Society Institute, has led to a range of initiatives aimed at challenging the use of human rights laws to prohibit data collection and at improving ethnic data disaggregation and clarifying 'Roma identity'.

Sources: Open Society Institute (2007); European Roma Rights Centre (2007); European Commission (2009*a*).

3. Roma – often known as Gypsies – live primarily in central and eastern Europe and are the most populous subgroup of the Romani.

encouraging evidence that Māori children – especially girls – are catching up with non-Māori. Even so, the achievement gaps remain large. Whereas 65% of all students leave school with the National Certificate of Educational Achievement (NCEA) level 2 qualification, the figure drops to 44% for Māori children. Māori learners are three times as likely as non-Māori to leave school with no qualification (New Zealand Ministry of Education, 2009).

Speaking a minority language is also often associated with low levels of education achievement. In many countries, large numbers of children are taught and take tests in languages that they do not speak at home, hindering the early acquisition of reading and writing skills. Their parents may lack literacy skills or familiarity with official languages used in school, so that the home environment reinforces learning opportunity gaps between minority and majority language groups.

International and national learning assessments confirm the importance of home language as a factor in test scores. The TIMSS 2007 assessment found that fourth- and eighth-grade students who reported 'always speaking' at home the language in which the test was conducted score significantly higher. For fourth-grade science students who reported only 'sometimes speaking' the test language at home, the test score was 10% lower. For students who reported 'never speaking' the test language at home, the score was 20% lower (Martin et al., 2008).

Conclusion

Making sure that everyone has a chance to develop their potential through education is an important challenge for all countries. Equal opportunity in education is a basic human right. Moreover, fair and inclusive education is one of the most powerful levers available for making societies more equitable, innovative and democratic. Overcoming the extreme and persistent disadvantages that marginalized groups experience is a vital element in the wider agenda for inclusive education. Extending opportunity to these groups requires more than the general expansion of education and the improvement of average learning achievement levels. It requires policies that target the underlying causes of disadvantage in education and beyond.

Figure 3.21: Indigenous Australians perform consistently below the student average in reading

% of population meeting reading benchmarks at grade 7, indigenous Australians and all students, by location, 2006

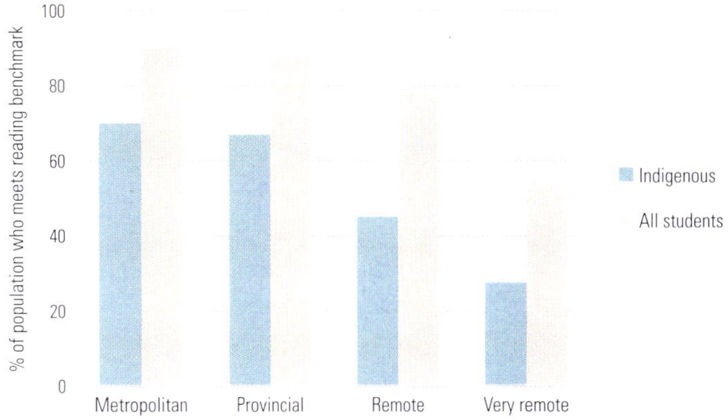

Sources: Australia Department of Education (2008), Table A3.4, p.190; Biddle and Mackay (2009).

Data have an important role to play in the formulation of such policies. Disaggregated household survey data such as those available in the DME data set (Table 3.3) can provide policy-makers with the means to identify social groups and areas characterized by high levels of deprivation. They can also provide insight into the interaction between different patterns of disadvantage, informing approaches to targeting it and the development of strategies aimed at equalizing opportunity. That is why investment in data collection and analysis should be an integral element of any national poverty reduction strategy. □

Investment in disaggregated data collection should be an integral element of any national poverty reduction strategy

Table 3.3: Deprivation and Marginalization in Education, selected data, latest year available[1]

Country	Year of survey	Average number of years of education: Total	Male	Female	Richest 20%	Poorest 20%	Absolute wealth gap	'Bottom 20%' (Share of the poorest wealth quintile in the bottom 20% of the education distribution, by years in school)	Education poverty (Share of the population with fewer than four years of education): Total	Male	Female	Rural girls from the poorest quintile
		(Years)						(%)	(%)			
Albania	2005	9.9	9.9	9.9	11.5	8.7	2.7	32.5	1.0	1.1	0.9	0.9
Armenia	2005	9.2	9.3	9.2	9.8	8.2	1.6	21.5	0.9	1.4	0.6	2.3
Azerbaijan	2006	10.6	10.8	10.5	11.4	9.7	1.7	34.9	2.3	1.3	3.1	6.4
Bangladesh	2004	5.8	5.9	5.7	8.0	3.6	4.4	40.4	27.4	26.4	28.1	50.1
Belize	2005	8.5	8.4	8.6	8.7	7.4	1.3	28.1	3.5	4.7	2.1	2.8
Benin	2006	4.6	6.0	3.4	7.7	2.2	5.6	31.6	47.8	33.4	60.5	85.0
Bolivia	2003	9.6	9.8	9.3	11.2	6.4	4.8	56.6	6.1	4.1	8.1	30.1
Bosnia/Herzeg.	2005	11.2	11.1	11.2	11.7	10.4	1.4	29.4	0.6	0.7	0.4	2.0
Burkina Faso	2003	2.3	2.7	2.0	5.6	0.6	4.9	28.2	70.9	66.5	75.1	93.1
Burundi	2005	4.6	4.8	4.5	6.6	2.6	4.0	32.9	36.6	34.5	38.5	64.6
Cambodia	2005	6.0	6.5	5.5	8.2	3.4	4.8	36.3	26.8	22.5	30.9	62.8
Cameroon	2004	6.4	6.9	6.0	8.8	3.5	5.3	50.8	21.4	16.1	26.2	63.9
C. A. R.	2000	0.9	1.2	0.7	1.7	0.5	1.2	22.0	89.2	86.0	92.3	99.7
Chad	2004	2.7	3.9	1.8	6.7	1.0	5.7	32.9	67.3	53.0	79.0	92.2
Colombia	2005	9.1	8.7	9.5	10.9	6.4	4.5	47.2	6.7	8.4	5.0	18.9
Congo	2005	7.2	7.3	7.1	8.9	5.4	3.5	37.8	12.4	11.1	13.4	27.2
D.R. Congo	2007	6.2	7.0	5.4	9.1	4.4	4.7	29.9	25.4	15.6	34.5	57.0
Côte d'Ivoire	2004	4.3	5.5	3.3	6.3	2.1	4.2	23.8	49.2	36.5	59.5	84.8
Cuba	2005	11.3	11.1	11.6	11.7	10.6	1.1	25.1	1.1	1.4	0.8	0.7
Dominican Rep.	2007	9.2	8.7	9.8	10.8	6.2	4.6	43.0	7.9	10.3	5.5	22.0
Egypt	2005	8.9	9.4	8.5	9.8	6.4	3.4	39.5	15.0	9.7	20.2	47.9
Ethiopia	2005	3.1	3.8	2.5	7.5	1.6	5.9	32.9	61.1	51.8	70.2	87.4
Gabon	2000	7.3	7.6	7.0	8.4	5.0	3.4	41.1	9.8	8.2	11.2	24.2
Gambia	2005	5.4	6.2	4.7	8.1	2.4	5.7	30.0	40.4	31.6	48.0	80.2
Georgia	2005	11.6	11.5	11.8	12.6	10.3	2.2	38.0	0.7	1.0	0.5	0.7
Ghana	2003	7.1	7.5	6.8	9.2	3.3	5.8	52.5	20.3	15.9	23.9	67.2
Guatemala	1999	5.8	6.0	5.7	8.8	1.8	7.0	47.9	35.6	33.1	37.9	86.2
Guinea	2005	3.5	4.9	2.3	5.8	1.0	4.8	31.7	56.4	39.6	71.1	94.5
Guinea-Bissau	2005	3.8	4.7	3.0	6.2	1.7	4.5	36.0	49.7	37.7	59.9	90.3
Haiti	2005	6.4	6.4	6.3	8.5	3.3	5.2	45.4	23.2	23.4	23.1	59.0
Honduras	2005	7.6	7.1	8.1	10.5	4.0	6.5	42.4	18.1	21.4	14.9	42.8
India	2005	7.2	8.1	6.5	11.1	4.2	6.9	50.2	23.6	15.6	30.7	60.1
Indonesia	2003	9.0	9.0	9.1	11.1	6.6	4.5	41.1	4.4	4.3	4.5	12.6
Iraq	2005	5.8	6.2	5.3	7.2	3.9	3.3	39.6	20.6	15.3	26.2	56.9
Jamaica	2005	10.3	10.3	10.4	10.5	10.0	0.5	27.5	0.5	0.3	0.7	0.0
Jordan	2007	11.5	11.3	11.8	12.1	11.4	0.6	21.6	2.0	1.9	2.1	2.5
Kazakhstan	2005	12.3	12.1	12.5	13.2	11.4	1.8	27.0	0.4	0.4	0.3	0.2
Kenya	2003	7.5	7.5	7.5	9.5	5.4	4.1	35.2	12.0	12.3	11.7	27.6
Kyrgyzstan	2005	10.6	10.5	10.7	10.9	10.4	0.5	17.4	0.5	0.7	0.3	1.6
Lao PDR	2000	8.2	8.8	7.7	8.1	5.9	2.3	34.6	13.6	9.6	17.2	42.5
Lesotho	2004	6.8	5.9	7.7	8.8	4.6	4.2	40.4	15.4	25.3	5.5	11.9
Liberia	2007	5.0	5.7	4.5	7.2	2.6	4.6	46.1	35.7	27.6	42.4	79.3

	Education poverty (Share of the population with fewer than four years of education)		Extreme education poverty (Share of the population with fewer than two years of education)			Share of the population aged 7–16 with no education				
Most deprived region[2]	Education poverty	Most deprived region to country average	Total	Male	Female	Total	Male	Female	Rural girls from the poorest quintile	
	(%)	Ratio		(%)				(%)		Country
South	2.0	2.1	0.9	1.1	0.7	0.6	0.7	0.5	0.9	Albania
Aragatsotn	3.2	3.4	0.7	1.0	0.4	3.7	4.0	3.4	5.6	Armenia
Dakhlik Shirvan	5.8	2.5	1.1	0.7	1.4	2.2	1.8	2.7	4.7	Azerbaijan
Sylhet	34.6	1.3	19.5	17.7	20.8	10.6	11.9	9.2	13.5	Bangladesh
Stann Creek	5.5	1.6	2.3	3.5	1.1	0.7	0.7	0.8	0.6	Belize
Alibori	91.2	1.9	40.7	26.1	53.4	28.3	23.3	33.8	54.1	Benin
Potosi	15.2	2.5	1.7	1.0	2.2	1.6	1.5	1.7	4.0	Bolivia
...	...	...	0.3	0.4	0.3	0.8	0.9	0.7	0.5	Bosnia/Herzeg.
Est	92.3	1.3	66.9	61.9	71.6	63.2	59.5	67.0	83.5	Burkina Faso
Nord	52.1	1.4	24.4	22.0	26.6	19.2	17.4	21.0	38.5	Burundi
Mondol Kiri and Rattanak Kiri	70.4	2.6	12.4	8.7	15.9	9.1	9.6	8.7	17.3	Cambodia
Extrême Nord	65.4	3.1	15.0	9.4	20.1	13.0	10.8	15.2	33.2	Cameroon
Vakaga	98.1	1.1	76.5	70.8	82.0	48.2	42.9	53.6	78.3	C. A. R.
Barh Azoum	96.7	1.4	57.6	43.6	69.1	54.2	47.6	60.8	80.3	Chad
Atlantica	8.5	1.3	2.8	3.6	2.1	1.7	2.0	1.3	4.2	Colombia
Nord	18.9	1.5	5.4	4.6	6.0	4.5	4.0	4.9	8.8	Congo
Nord-Kivu	44.5	1.8	15.4	7.5	22.8	18.9	16.2	21.8	35.7	D.R. Congo
Nord	77.0	1.6	41.9	29.7	51.8	33.0	30.0	35.9	52.5	Côte d'Ivoire
Occidente	2.0	1.8	0.6	0.7	0.6	0.3	0.3	0.3	0.1	Cuba
Elías piña	24.7	3.1	4.0	5.2	2.7	1.9	2.4	1.5	3.7	Dominican Rep.
Rural Upper Egypt	28.1	1.9	12.5	6.9	18.2	10.8	8.3	13.5	27.3	Egypt
Somali	86.3	1.4	49.8	39.2	60.4	48.1	46.5	49.9	62.4	Ethiopia
Ngouni and Nyanga	13.3	1.4	5.2	4.5	5.9	2.6	2.6	2.6	3.1	Gabon
Basse	79.4	2.0	38.6	30.3	45.8	29.0	27.8	30.2	48.7	Gambia
Mtskheta-Mtianeti	2.4	3.3	0.6	0.8	0.4	0.5	0.4	0.7	1.1	Georgia
Northern	61.6	3.0	16.6	12.1	20.4	21.0	20.5	21.5	52.5	Ghana
North-west	61.3	1.7	19.1	15.5	22.5	13.0	10.9	15.2	34.2	Guatemala
Kankan	73.7	1.3	52.0	35.4	66.6	44.9	40.8	49.2	68.1	Guinea
Bafatá and Gabu	77.1	1.6	37.3	23.8	48.8	28.0	27.3	28.6	44.2	Guinea-Bissau
Centre	50.8	2.2	10.3	9.4	11.2	11.6	12.5	10.7	26.7	Haiti
Copán	41.5	2.3	7.8	9.4	6.3	5.1	6.1	4.1	9.4	Honduras
Bihar	42.8	1.8	20.3	12.1	27.7	13.2	10.7	15.9	29.1	India
West Kalimantan	12.9	2.9	1.5	1.4	1.7	2.0	2.2	1.9	5.4	Indonesia
North	24.3	1.2	13.1	8.4	18.1	9.9	6.1	13.8	35.1	Iraq
...	...	...	0.4	0.2	0.7	0.3	0.2	0.4	1.3	Jamaica
Central	2.5	1.2	1.6	1.5	1.7	0.8	0.9	0.7	1.2	Jordan
Akmola oblys	1.3	3.3	0.3	0.4	0.3	0.6	0.5	0.6	0.3	Kazakhstan
North eastern	74.7	6.2	7.9	7.0	8.8	6.7	6.3	7.0	17.1	Kenya
Naryn	2.3	5.0	0.3	0.5	0.2	2.1	2.7	1.6	2.3	Kyrgyzstan
South	17.6	1.3	7.8	5.7	9.7	5.4	4.7	6.1	19.9	Lao PDR
Thaba-Tseka	30.6	2.0	8.2	14.7	1.7	5.9	8.5	3.1	5.3	Lesotho
North Western	54.0	1.5	21.9	14.4	28.2	43.9	42.3	45.5	69.2	Liberia

Table 3.3 (continued)

Country	Year of survey	Average number of years of education: Total	Male	Female	Richest 20%	Poorest 20%	Absolute wealth gap	'Bottom 20%' (Share of the poorest wealth quintile in the bottom 20% of the education distribution, by years in school)	Education poverty (Share of the population with fewer than four years of education): Total	Male	Female	Rural girls from the poorest quintile
		(Years)						(%)	(%)			
TFYR Macedonia	2005	10.5	10.1	10.9	11.9	7.3	4.7	22.5	3.2	3.9	2.6	7.0
Madagascar	2004	4.5	4.5	4.5	9.8	1.7	8.1	53.5	48.3	46.9	49.8	83.1
Malawi	2004	6.2	6.5	5.9	8.6	4.8	3.8	29.1	23.6	20.6	26.2	37.4
Mali	2001	2.6	3.3	2.0	5.8	0.7	5.1	26.1	68.8	60.3	76.0	94.0
Mongolia	2005	8.8	8.5	9.1	10.7	6.0	4.7	52.5	9.0	10.6	7.5	22.4
Montenegro	2005	11.2	11.2	11.2	12.2	9.3	2.9	39.6	2.4	1.8	3.0	3.8
Morocco	2004	5.7	6.6	5.0	8.4	2.0	6.4	41.3	37.1	27.0	45.9	87.6
Mozambique	2003	3.2	3.7	2.8	5.0	1.9	3.2	27.8	56.5	49.8	62.7	87.1
Myanmar	2000	5.6	5.7	5.5	7.7	3.6	4.1	32.7	25.1	22.0	27.9	56.1
Namibia	2007	8.4	8.0	8.8	10.5	6.8	3.6	32.2	8.9	12.0	6.2	12.1
Nepal	2006	5.9	7.1	5.0	8.7	3.3	5.4	40.9	29.9	16.8	39.0	67.4
Nicaragua	2001	6.6	6.2	7.0	9.5	2.5	6.9	51.8	23.3	27.5	19.2	60.7
Niger	2006	1.7	2.4	1.2	5.5	0.6	4.9	26.3	76.9	68.4	82.8	94.7
Nigeria	2003	6.7	7.4	6.0	9.7	3.5	6.2	48.5	27.9	19.6	35.4	66.7
Pakistan	2007	5.7	6.5	5.0	9.0	2.4	6.5	34.0	34.5	25.9	42.5	84.9
Peru	2004	10.1	10.2	10.0	11.5	7.4	4.1	53.3	3.5	2.3	5.0	16.9
Philippines	2003	9.4	8.9	10.0	11.0	6.3	4.7	55.4	5.0	6.7	3.2	16.3
Rwanda	2005	3.8	3.8	3.8	5.5	2.9	2.6	28.5	45.3	45.1	45.4	59.1
S. Tome/Principe	2000	8.4	8.9	8.0	11.3	5.9	5.4	30.8	10.8	8.7	12.5	17.8
Senegal	2005	3.2	3.9	2.7	5.1	1.2	4.0	28.6	57.4	50.3	63.3	87.6
Serbia	2005	11.1	10.9	11.3	11.9	8.3	3.6	17.1	1.1	1.3	1.0	3.8
Sierra Leone	2005	3.8	4.8	2.6	6.9	1.4	5.6	32.3	53.7	42.0	67.3	88.9
Somalia	2005	3.1	4.8	2.0	6.6	0.4	6.2	31.5	63.5	44.6	75.7	98.3
Suriname	2000	7.6	7.4	7.9	9.5	6.1	3.4	34.0	11.6	11.7	11.6	13.0
Swaziland	2006	8.0	7.8	8.2	9.4	6.4	3.0	34.7	9.1	10.6	7.7	18.8
Syrian A. R.	2005	8.1	8.1	8.0	9.8	6.2	3.6	37.4	6.8	5.1	8.9	27.0
Tajikistan	2005	9.6	10.3	9.1	10.8	9.2	1.6	24.9	3.7	2.2	5.1	7.7
U. R. Tanzania	2004	5.5	5.6	5.4	7.9	3.9	4.0	37.6	26.7	23.9	29.0	48.8
Togo	2005	6.5	7.2	5.5	8.2	4.1	4.1	34.9	22.3	15.7	30.5	64.4
Trinidad/Tobago	2000	10.4	10.2	10.7	11.9	9.4	2.5	36.9	0.6	0.6	0.7	...
Turkey	2003	8.1	8.8	7.4	9.2	6.3	2.9	28.7	7.9	3.8	12.0	21.4
Uganda	2006	6.5	6.9	6.2	8.5	4.3	4.1	40.6	16.7	12.7	20.1	45.3
Ukraine	2007	13.0	12.8	13.1	13.3	12.4	0.9	21.5	0.3	0.5	0.2	0.0
Venezuela, B. R.	2000	9.1	8.5	9.6	11.8	5.5	6.2	52.6	15.0	20.5	11.0	19.4
Viet Nam	2002	8.3	8.4	8.3	10.4	5.3	5.2	51.0	8.7	8.7	8.7	29.7
Yemen	2005	6.7	8.6	4.9	...	3.2	...	51.6	28.7	10.4	46.2	89.9
Zambia	2001	6.4	6.7	6.1	8.9	4.0	4.9	39.8	20.3	16.0	24.2	46.5
Zimbabwe	2006	8.6	8.7	8.6	9.9	7.0	2.9	45.8	2.8	3.0	2.7	8.0

Notes:

1. Data are for the population aged 17 to 22 unless otherwise stated.
2. Regions presented are the first official administrative division level except those in italics which are geographic areas rather than official administrative divisions.

Source: UNESCO-DME (2009).

	Education poverty (Share of the population with fewer than four years of education)		Extreme education poverty (Share of the population with fewer than two years of education)			Share of the population aged 7–16 with no education				
Most deprived region[2]	Education poverty	Most deprived region to country average	Total	Male	Female	Total	Male	Female	Rural girls from the poorest quintile	
	(%)	Ratio	(%)			(%)				Country
Vardar	7.5	2.3	2.3	2.5	2.1	2.2	1.9	2.5	1.5	TFYR Macedonia
Toliary	68.2	1.4	27.5	26.3	28.8	17.3	18.0	16.6	30.0	Madagascar
Central	26.5	1.1	11.0	8.3	13.4	9.7	10.5	8.9	12.3	Malawi
Mopti	88.6	1.3	65.1	56.7	72.1	52.7	48.4	57.0	75.3	Mali
Eastern	19.0	2.1	4.8	5.9	3.8	2.6	3.3	1.9	5.2	Mongolia
Central	4.0	1.7	2.2	1.6	2.7	1.4	1.5	1.2	0.7	Montenegro
Gharb-Chrarda-Beni Hssen	51.9	1.4	29.9	18.8	39.4	10.5	7.4	13.6	34.9	Morocco
Cabo Delgado	75.1	1.3	40.2	33.4	46.5	26.7	23.3	30.2	44.0	Mozambique
Eastern Shan	74.5	3.0	9.2	7.4	10.8	9.0	9.0	9.0	20.5	Myanmar
Kunene	28.0	3.1	5.6	7.3	4.1	4.4	4.8	4.0	6.5	Namibia
Central (Madhyamanchal)	35.0	1.2	22.8	10.0	31.8	9.3	4.9	13.6	26.2	Nepal
Jinotega	57.1	2.4	13.5	16.1	10.9	11.9	13.6	10.2	32.4	Nicaragua
Tillabéri	86.6	1.1	73.7	64.4	80.3	60.4	53.5	67.5	79.1	Niger
North West	58.0	2.1	25.3	17.0	32.7	25.4	20.9	30.0	54.7	Nigeria
Balochistan	47.6	1.4	30.7	21.6	39.2	23.6	17.1	30.2	63.0	Pakistan
Cajamarca	16.8	4.8	1.2	0.6	2.0	0.7	0.7	0.7	1.8	Peru
Aut. Region in Muslim Mindanao	14.1	2.8	1.8	2.1	1.3	2.4	2.8	1.9	5.9	Philippines
Kibungo	55.4	1.2	20.8	20.1	21.4	10.9	11.6	10.3	13.7	Rwanda
South	24.9	2.3	5.8	4.6	6.9	6.4	6.5	6.4	15.0	S. Tome/Principe
Matam	78.7	1.4	50.4	42.8	56.6	39.0	37.9	40.0	59.1	Senegal
Southeast	2.1	1.8	1.0	1.2	0.8	0.6	0.4	0.8	2.7	Serbia
Northern	66.7	1.2	48.5	37.1	61.8	24.8	22.9	26.7	46.5	Sierra Leone
Central south	72.7	1.1	57.1	39.3	68.6	57.6	48.7	65.2	94.6	Somalia
Sipaliwini	62.1	5.3	6.0	5.2	6.8	3.8	3.8	3.7	2.5	Suriname
Lubombo	16.2	1.8	5.2	5.4	5.1	4.3	4.9	3.6	6.8	Swaziland
Ar-Raqqah	22.4	3.3	4.9	3.4	6.7	2.4	2.1	2.8	7.8	Syrian A. R.
Khatlon	4.9	1.3	2.1	1.7	2.4	5.5	4.6	6.5	8.0	Tajikistan
Tabora	50.3	1.9	20.5	16.8	23.8	19.3	20.0	18.5	28.5	U. R. Tanzania
Savanes	54.5	2.4	15.1	9.8	21.8	15.2	11.9	18.8	34.3	Togo
Tobago	2.1	3.3	0.6	0.6	0.6	0.2	0.2	0.3	...	Trinidad/Tobago
East	21.4	2.7	6.0	2.1	9.9	4.3	2.3	6.3	12.3	Turkey
Northern Region	29.0	1.7	8.3	5.7	10.5	6.3	6.1	6.5	17.1	Uganda
North	0.7	2.2	0.3	0.5	0.1	1.0	1.2	0.7	0.4	Ukraine
...	...	...	4.0	5.7	2.7	4.6	5.5	3.6	12.0	Venezuela, B. R.
Mekong river delta	18.2	2.1	4.3	4.1	4.4	1.7	1.4	2.0	5.7	Viet Nam
Hajjah	54.4	1.9	23.6	6.7	39.8	21.1	14.3	27.9	58.2	Yemen
Eastern	39.5	1.9	11.5	8.9	14.0	23.1	22.9	23.4	39.9	Zambia
...	...	...	1.3	1.3	1.3	1.9	2.1	1.7	2.9	Zimbabwe

Getting left behind

Introduction

Children at risk of marginalization in education are found in all societies. At first glance, the lives of these children may appear poles apart. The daily experiences of slum dwellers in Kenya, ethnic minority children in Viet Nam, a blind girl from a low-income home in Pakistan and a Roma child in Hungary are very different. What they have in common are restricted opportunities to develop their potential, realize their hopes and build a better future through participation in education.

The first part of this chapter identified some of the most marginalized social groups. It documented mutually reinforcing disadvantages linked to poverty, gender and ethnicity. This part looks beyond the data to the processes and power relationships that diminish opportunity. It concentrates mainly on primary school age children in developing countries, while recognizing that early experience tips the balance against many children before they enter school and that educational marginalization continues into adulthood (see Chapter 2).

Stigmatization and discrimination also fuel marginalization in education, locking children into cycles of low expectation and underachievement

Unravelling the threads behind marginalization in education can be difficult. Many factors are involved. Poverty often makes education unaffordable and pushes children out of classrooms and into employment. Gender intersects with low income to create forces of marginalization that are less tangible and less easily measurable than poverty but no less damaging. The low value placed on girls' education can make them the last into school and the first out when poverty strikes. Cultural attitudes and beliefs, stigmatization and discrimination also fuel marginalization, locking children into cycles of low expectation and underachievement. Moreover, many of the processes leading to marginalization in education can be traced to deeply entrenched power relationships that perpetuate poverty and gender disadvantages and group-based inequalities.

The interaction is two-way. Marginalization in education is in part a consequence of marginalization in other areas. But it is also a cause of marginalization. Education systems have the potential to mitigate social disadvantage, yet often they either fail to utilize that potential or they actually magnify underlying problems. As this part of the chapter documents, acts of commission and omission in education policy can place good-quality schooling far beyond the reach of the marginalized, reinforcing wider social divisions in the process.

The interaction between marginalization in education and wider forms of social exclusion does not follow general rules. The national and subnational context matters, as does the specific form of disadvantage that marginalized children experience. Even so, recurrent themes cut across different environments and experiences. This part of the chapter looks at these themes, identifying the global drivers that fuel the local patterns of marginalization explored in the previous part. The first section looks at poverty as a barrier that perpetuates disadvantages in education, partly by pushing children into work. The second examines issues behind group-based marginalization, tracing the routes through which ethnicity, language, stigmatization and poverty often interact to create vicious circles of low expectation and low achievement. The third section considers location-specific factors that intersect with livelihoods, highlighting problems faced by slum dwellers, remote rural communities and conflict-affected regions. The fourth examines disability and the fifth HIV and AIDS – issues that have a marked impact on education.

Poverty and child labour

Household poverty is one of the strongest and most persistent factors contributing to marginalization in education. The transmission mechanisms are well known. Poor households have fewer resources to invest in their children's schooling, health and other assets. Poverty is also a source of vulnerability. When poor people are hit by economic shocks, droughts or health problems, they often lack the resources to cope without cutting spending in key areas, including children's schooling. Education can act as a powerful catalyst in breaking cycles of poverty. But poverty itself is a strong constraint on opportunities for education, fuelling the transmission of disadvantage across generations.

Global poverty trends: a mixed record

The sheer scale of global poverty makes it a formidable barrier to Education for All. In 2005, nearly 1.4 billion people were living on less than US$1.25 a day. More than half the population of sub-Saharan Africa and 40% of people in South Asia fell below this absolute poverty threshold.

Many millions more were living just above the threshold, surviving on less than US$2 a day, rendering them highly vulnerable to acute poverty (Figure 3.22).

Global aggregate figures can obscure the depth of poverty. The average daily consumption level of a poor person in sub-Saharan Africa is just US$0.73 – a figure unchanged in twenty-five years (Chen and Ravallion, 2008). The incidence and depth of poverty are more marked in sub-Saharan Africa than any other region. Depth of poverty matters because it has a bearing on capacity for coping with shocks. For people surviving on US$0.73 a day, even small losses can have catastrophic consequences for nutrition, health and schooling.

The good news is that the number of people worldwide living in extreme poverty has been falling. The decline is driven by strong performance in East Asia; progress in most other regions – notably sub-Saharan Africa – has been far less encouraging. The bad news is that a combination of rising food prices and the global financial crisis has slowed the pace of poverty reduction. For 2009, there may be 55 million to 100 million more people living below the international poverty line than was expected before the crisis. On current economic growth projections, the number of people living in extreme poverty could rise in more than half of all developing countries in 2009 (World Bank, 2009*k*).

Poverty trends in developed countries are also a source of concern. Evidence from the OECD suggests that children are disproportionately disadvantaged by household poverty, with an average of 12% affected.[4] Just as disturbing as this number is the underlying trend. During a decade of sustained economic growth up to the mid-2000s, child poverty rates grew as income inequality rose. Rising unemployment caused by the financial crisis is likely to lead to sharp increases in child poverty during 2009 and 2010 (see Chapter 1). The danger is that rising child poverty will in turn fuel inequalities in education.

Poverty's effects are transmitted to education

Education can help lift people out of poverty by boosting productivity and opening doors to jobs and credit. Conversely, lower educational attainment is strongly associated with higher poverty levels. The evidence thus points to a negative cycle in which poverty begets education disadvantage, which in turn perpetuates poverty. What drives this cycle?

Figure 3.22: Mapping global poverty

Selected poverty indicators by region, 2005

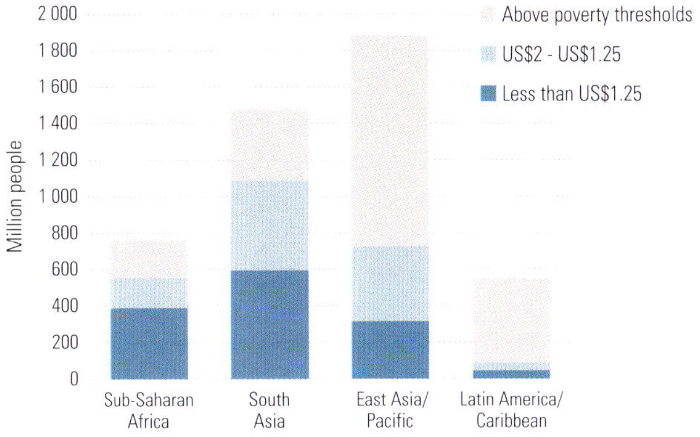

Population living on less than US$1.25 a day

	Sub-Saharan Africa	South Asia	East Asia/ Pacific	Latin America/ Caribbean
Incidence of poverty (%)	51	40	17	8
Average consumption (2005 US$)	0.73	0.93	0.95	0.77

Notes: 'Incidence of poverty' is the proportion of the population whose consumption expenditure is less than US$1.25 a day, at 2005 exchange rates. 'Average consumption' is the average daily consumption expenditure of those below this poverty line.
Source: Chen and Ravallion (2008).

The inability of poor households to support investment in education is one significant factor. In many countries, parents have to pay a high proportion of their income to put their children in school. The costs include official school fees, informal and unofficial charges levied to support teachers' pay and other expenses, and payments for uniforms and textbooks.

For poor people in sub-Saharan Africa, even small losses can have catastrophic consequences for nutrition, health and schooling

For the poorest households, schooling competes with other basic needs, such as health care and food. A study covering four slums in Bangladesh illustrates the extent of the financial burden. For the average household in these slums, expenditure on education amounted to 10% of their income per child in school, rising to 20% for the poorest one-fifth of households. Monthly expenditure per child by the poorest households averaged around US$2 out of an income of less than US$12 per month. Overall, the largest single cost was for supplementary tuition, which many families deem necessary for progress through school (Cameron, 2008).

Eliminating official school fees can help lower financial barriers for the poorest households. From 1999 to 2007, fourteen countries, most of them in sub-Saharan Africa, reported abolishing tuition fees.

4. The OECD defines poverty as living in a household with an equivalized household disposable income of less than half the median for the whole population (OECD, 2009*g*).

This was followed by sharp increases in enrolment in many countries, including Kenya, Uganda and the United Republic of Tanzania (UNESCO, 2007). A study in Burundi in 2006, just after fees were abolished, showed that over 40% of the poorest households reported some of their children would not be in school had fees not been removed. This is consistent with research indicating that, before fees were abolished, a third of children from the poorest households were not in school because their parents could not meet costs (World Bank and Burundi Government, 2008).

Poor people often report inability to afford education for their children, even in countries with nominally free primary schooling. In Cambodia, cost is among the most commonly cited reasons for children being out of school, even though there are no official charges (World Bank, 2006*a*). In Malawi and Uganda, where fees were abolished over a decade ago, many more children from poor households have entered school. Yet in both countries, half the households with children who have dropped out cite lack of money as the main problem (World Bank, 2006*h*, 2007*c*). In a survey covering fifty slums in Delhi, financial constraints were given as the main reason for school age children being out of school or dropping out, even though education is nominally free (Tsujita, 2009).

‘When my child is in school... I have to pay for his uniforms, so money is given out while it is not coming in. [...] School is very costly.’

Parent, Nigeria

Why has fee abolition failed to eliminate cost barriers? In some cases because legislation eliminating fees has been only partly implemented. In the Lao People's Democratic Republic, tuition fees are officially proscribed but about half the schools still levy them (World Bank, 2006*c*). Indonesia's free basic education policy, introduced in 2005, provides incentives for schools to eliminate fees but allows them to opt out (World Bank, 2006*b*). Another problem is that formal fees are just one part of the cost of education. In many cases, parents must also buy uniforms and textbooks. In Sierra Leone, uniforms double the cost associated with school fees (World Bank, 2007*b*). Poor parents in Nigeria no longer face tuition charges, but books and uniforms cost more than fees once did (Lincove, 2009).[5]

Lowering costs is not a stand-alone strategy. Poor parents – like all parents – also consider the quality of the education available. In some countries, the elimination of official fees has led to deterioration in quality, with surges in enrolment increasing class sizes and straining the school infrastructure. To avoid such problems, governments need to assume responsibility for maintaining education resources by raising public spending and sequencing reforms to increase the supply of teachers, classrooms and learning materials (World Bank and UNICEF, 2009).

Social attitudes strongly condition the effects of poverty. The degree to which parents value children's education inevitably influences prospects of participation in school. For Hausa girls in northern Nigeria, the low value many adults ascribe to their education is a powerful source of exclusion (Box 3.4).

Economic shocks can undermine education

While poverty is widely recognized as a barrier to educational opportunity, less attention has been paid to vulnerability. One characteristic of being poor is that precarious livelihoods carry a heightened risk of insecurity. The poorest households often find it impossible to shield their children's schooling from external shocks such as droughts, floods or economic downturns. They often live in hostile environments and have little access to assets such as land, livestock, credit or savings to see them through difficult times. In urban areas, the very poor often work in informal sectors with low wages and limited security.

Cross-country research on past economic crises and climate events shows that the effects of shocks on schooling tend to be more pronounced in low-income countries than in middle-income countries (Ferreira and Schady, 2008). The children of the poorest households are most likely to suffer adverse consequences as regards education, health and nutrition. This risk adds to the threat of poverty persisting across generations.

External shocks can have direct and long-lasting consequences for education. Droughts in sub-Saharan Africa have had significant effects on enrolment and years in school (Alderman et al., 2006; Ferreira and Schady, 2008). In Zambia, over one-third of those aged 7 to 14 belonged to households that experienced some form of economic shock during 2005. Shocks involving loss and destruction of property were particularly damaging for education, raising the probability of children being involved in full-time work by 14% in low-income households (Understanding Children's Work, 2009). In Indonesia, the 1997 financial crisis led to significant declines in enrolment among primary school age children, especially in the poorest households (Thomas et al., 2004).

5. Costs of uniforms and textbooks climb sharply upon the transition from primary to secondary school. One review of textbook provision in sub-Saharan Africa found that in eleven countries textbook costs were entirely financed by parents and that, next to tuition fees, this was the largest item in household spending. (Read et al., 2008).

Box 3.4: Hausa girls in northern Nigeria – losing out in education

Any international ranking of opportunity in education would place Hausa girls in northern Nigeria near the bottom of the scale. In 2003, half of primary school age girls in Kano state were out of school and in Jigawa state the figure was 89%. Being poor and living in a rural area compounds the disadvantage – in this category, over 90% of Hausa women aged 17 to 22 have fewer than two years of education.

Northern states such as Jigawa, Kaduna and Kano are among the poorest in Nigeria. There is evidence that household deprivation hurts girls' education in particular, as poverty intersects with social and cultural practices, beliefs and attitudes.

Some parents attach limited value to girls' education. As one research report put it, 'from birth' a girl 'may be considered as a costly guest in her own home. Her schooling is likely to be considered a waste of time and money, and she is diligently trained to be home as a bearer of many children and a free source of labour' (Rufa'i, 2006, p. 86).

Hausa girls who go to school tend to start late. Around one-quarter of girls aged 6 to 14 in school in Kaduna and Kano were over the usual age for their grade. To compound the problem, marriage at 14 or even younger is common and typically signals the end of education.

Northern Nigeria is predominantly Muslim. Many parents send their daughters to Islamic schools out of distrust for formal public education, concern over the quality of government schools or the distance to them, or fear of sexual harassment in school or on the way there. Yet the quality of Islamic schooling is highly variable – and the education many young girls receive there is both limited and short-lived.

The experience of Hausa girls illustrates some of the wider challenges involved in reaching those on the margins of education. There are public policy measures that can make a difference, such as building classrooms closer to communities, eliminating informal school fees, integrating Islamic schools that meet quality standards into the government system and improving quality through better teacher training. But in northern Nigeria the most tenacious barriers to girls' education are often embedded in parental and community attitudes and gender practices. Removing those obstacles requires more equitable education policies, including wide-ranging incentives for girls' education, backed by social and political dialogue to change attitudes.

Sources: Rufa'i (2006); Akyeampong et al. (2009); UNESCO-DME (2009).

Other effects of such shocks may be less immediate. Malnutrition in young children of poor families, for example, may not just lower school attendance but also impair cognitive development, learning ability and earnings potential. When children are born in a drought year or experience malnutrition early in their lives, the effects can be seen a decade later in their health and nutritional status, and their educational attainment (Alderman et al., 2006; Alderman et al., 2009). In Ethiopia, children born in a year in which drought affected their district are 41% more likely to be stunted at age 5 than children born in a non-drought year (UNDP, 2007). Economic shocks can push households into long-term poverty. One study in Indonesia found that about half of poverty in 2002 could be traced back to the 1997 economic downturn, even though recovery was well under way (Ravallion, 2008). Underlying gender disparities often lead to girls bearing the brunt of economic shocks. In rural Pakistan, for example, unanticipated economic losses reduced the likelihood of girls being in school, but not boys (Lewis and Lockheed, 2007). Similarly, in rural Uganda, crop losses led to sharp declines in girls' enrolment and performance in examinations, while the impact on boys was much smaller (Björkman, 2005).

The current economic downturn, along with increases in food and fuel prices, has increased the vulnerabilities that come with poverty. It is too early to establish the impact on education with any accuracy. One survey in Bangladesh found that the sharp rise in food prices in 2007 and 2008 had forced half the poor households covered to remove children from school as a cost-saving measure (Raihan, 2009). As Chapter 1 indicates, there have also been reports of declines in enrolment and increased absenteeism in other countries. In Kenya and Zambia, for example, crisis-related poverty has left some children hungry and too weak to walk to school. Dropout has increased due to inability to cover the costs of schooling and the need for child labour (Hossain et al., 2009). More broadly, there are grounds for concern that a combination of sluggish economic growth, rising unemployment, falling remittances and slower poverty reduction

In 2007 and 2008 the sharp rise in food prices forced half of poor households surveyed in Bangladesh to remove children from school

will add to the pressures on the poorest households, with potentially damaging consequences for education (see Chapter 1).

Child labour remains a barrier to education

Child labour is a deeply entrenched obstacle to Education for All. Household poverty forces millions of children out of school and into paying jobs or – especially for young girls – domestic chores.

The International Labour Organization put the number of child labourers aged 5 to 14 at 166 million in 2004 (Hagemann et al., 2006). Not all child labourers are kept out of school. Most combine school and work, though often with damaging effects on their education. Some work because their parents cannot afford to send them to school. Others work to help their families make ends meet or to provide labour in the home. Understanding the interplay between educational disadvantage and child labour is critical not only for education, but also for child welfare and wider national poverty reduction efforts.

Evidence from Latin America indicates that combining work with schooling is detrimental to educational achievement

Child labour ranges in scope from young girls collecting water and firewood with their mothers to young boys tending cattle and engaging in paid work, and to more extreme and dangerous forms of work. The worst forms of child labour are a direct source of marginalization in education. Over half the children engaged in labour in 2004 were in hazardous work, involving dangerous conditions, long hours or hazardous machinery (Blanco Allais and Quinn, 2009).[6] Such children can be seen every day scavenging for rubbish in Manila, working on building sites in New Delhi or selling newspapers at traffic junctions in Haiti. They are also forced into more invisible forms of labour, such as involvement in sex work.

The degree to which children combine work and school varies by country. There are no upper limit benchmarks, but children working about thirty hours a week or more are unlikely to attend school (Edmonds, 2007); (Box 3.5). Moreover, it cannot be assumed that ability to combine work and school is conducive to learning. Evidence from eleven Latin American countries indicates that this is detrimental to educational achievement (Gunnarsson et al., 2006). In each country, child labourers achieved significantly lower scores in language and mathematics tests in third and fourth grades, controlling for school and household characteristics. Even modest levels of child labour at early ages had adverse consequences for cognitive abilities, with regular work being most detrimental (Gunnarsson et al., 2006; Sánchez et al., 2009).

Poverty has a very direct bearing on patterns of child labour. Poorer children are more likely than wealthier children to work outside the home and less likely to combine work with school (Blanco Allais and Quinn, 2009). In Zambia, children from households in the lowest income quintile are more likely not only to work, but also to face hazardous work conditions (Understanding Children's Work, 2009).

In urban areas, many child labourers live on streets, either with destitute parents or with other children. These children experience particularly stark forms of marginalization in education. One study covering seven cities in Pakistan found that fewer than 5% of children living on streets had completed primary education (Tufail, 2005). A survey in Bangladesh found that only 8% of street children were in school at the time of the survey and only 14% had completed third grade of primary school (Foundation for Research on Educational Planning and Development, 2003).

Child labour in rural areas is often less visible, but no less widespread or damaging. A 2007 survey of children on cocoa plantations in Côte d'Ivoire and Ghana documented striking examples of children applying toxic pesticides, working in extreme heat and using dangerous implements. In Côte d'Ivoire, many children in cocoa production had been trafficked from Burkina Faso and Mali as bonded labourers (Payson Center for International Development, 2008). Côte d'Ivoire and Ghana have introduced laws aimed at curtailing the practice (World Cocoa Foundation, 2009), but the effectiveness of national action and regional cooperation remain of concern. More broadly, governments are often more adept at adopting statements against child labour than at addressing the underlying causes of the problem.

Child labour often magnifies poverty-related gender disadvantage. A common thread across many countries with large gender disparities in education is the disproportionately large share of the household labour burden that young girls carry. In the Lao People's Democratic Republic, for both urban and rural populations, the average time spent in school falls with poverty and young girls in poor households spend less time in classrooms than young boys. Poor rural girls spend just over two hours a day studying and five hours working, on

6. Hazardous child labour is defined by the International Labour Organization as work in dangerous or unhealthy conditions, or under poor safety and health standards and working arrangements, that could result in a child's death, injury or illness.

average. Young boys spend slightly more time than girls in remunerated employment, while young girls spend more than twice as much time as boys on household activities (King and van de Walle, 2007). The upshot is that young girls from the poorest households are less likely than boys to combine school and work, and more likely to be out of school (Hallman et al., 2007).

Economic shocks can increase the impetus towards child labour. Crop losses, sudden increases in household health costs or parental unemployment can pull children out of school and push them into paying jobs. In the Kagera region of the United Republic of Tanzania, transitory income shocks caused by crop losses were associated with a 30% increase in hours worked by children aged 7 to 15 and a 20% fall in school attendance (Beegle et al., 2006). This example illustrates the interaction between vulnerability and disadvantage in education. Households with a limited coping capacity can be forced to compromise the long-term welfare of children to secure short-term survival.

Child labour confronts policy-makers with wide-ranging challenges. Preventing educational marginalization by saving children from having to work requires not only more effective legislation but also economic incentives aimed at keeping children in school.

Group-based disadvantages

Education for All is a principle rooted in the ideas of human rights and equal citizenship. It does not allow for distinctions based on ethnicity, race, language or culture. Yet these group-based identities are among the deepest fault lines in education. In many countries, children born to parents who are members of an ethnic or linguistic minority, a particular racial group or a low caste enter school with poor prospects of success and emerge with less education and lower achievement than do children without these disadvantages.

The processes that lead to group-based marginalization do not lend themselves to generalization but they include formal and informal discrimination, stigmatization and social exclusion linked to social, economic and political power relationships. Many of these processes have deep historical roots in slavery, dispossession or subjugation. The experiences of the K'iche' in Guatemala, Aboriginals in Australia, low-caste people in India and Kurds in Turkey have evolved from complex histories and are perpetuated through disparate structures. Yet there are some significant common threads, with marginalized groups facing high levels of social discrimination, fewer employment opportunities, more limited rights, and limited prospects for social and economic mobility. All too often their experience in school reinforces and perpetuates their marginalization.

Box 3.5: Mali and Zambia – combining child labour and schooling

Child labour is the rule rather than the exception in Mali and Zambia. Many children in both countries work longer than the average adult in rich countries, with damaging implications for education. However, the consequences vary in scale and severity.

About half of 7- to 14-year-olds in Mali and Zambia were working in 2005, predominantly in rural areas. An alarmingly large proportion of these children – about 80% in both countries – were reported as involved in hazardous work.

Behind these comparable headline figures there were complex variations between school and work. Whereas most working children in Zambia combined the two activities, in Mali about a third of children were reported to be just working and only around 20% combined school and work (Figure 3.23). The average time spent working helps explain the difference. Child labourers in Mali logged an average of thirty-seven hours working each week, compared with twenty-four hours in Zambia.

Figure 3.23: Patterns of school and work vary.

Children aged 7 to 14 by involvement in economic activity and schooling, Mali and Zambia, 2005

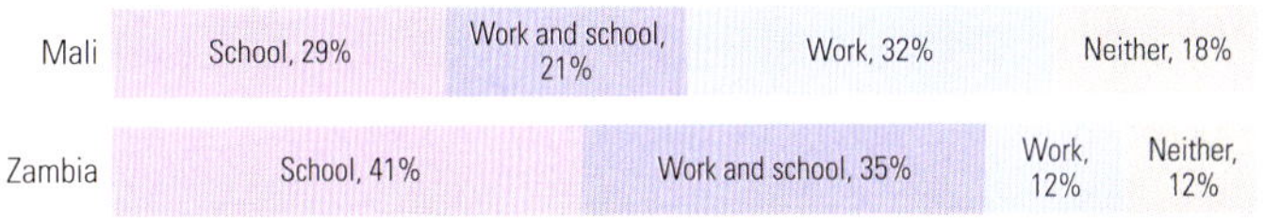

Note: Work does not include household chores.
Sources: Understanding Children's Work (2009), based on Mali National Child Labour Survey, 2005 and Zambia Labour Force Survey, 2005.

These working children have lower levels of school attendance at every age, especially in Mali. School attendance gaps are relatively small in Zambia up to age 13 or 14, again underlining the more marked trade-off between school and work in Mali.

Why does child labour in Zambia seem more compatible with education? Some children in Mali – notably those with inflexible employment conditions such as those working as domestic labourers and in manufacturing that limit the scope for combining school and work – appear to face particularly severe disadvantages. Mali has more and deeper poverty, and greater gender disparities in education. School-related factors, including distance to school, the duration of the school day and flexibility of the school calendar, could also be significant.

Source: Understanding Children's Work (2009).

Social deprivation and educational marginalization

Group-based marginalization has multiple sources. Some, such as race, ethnicity and language, are intimately tied up with the cultural identity of the group in question and with the experience of social discrimination. Other factors are related to poverty, health status and wider social circumstances. The borders between these underlying sources of disadvantage are blurred. For example, ethnicity and language are often two sides of the same coin and ethnic or linguistic minorities may face higher levels of poverty. What is clear from the evidence set out in the first part of this chapter is that group identity is often an aspect of 'multiple exclusion' that has a significant bearing on participation and achievement in education (Lewis and Lockheed, 2007).

'The ridicule we face prevents us from coming to school and sitting with higher-caste children.'

Musahar girl, India

The situation of indigenous groups in Latin America powerfully illustrates the multiple dimensions of deprivation. Indigenous people, especially women and children, have less access to basic health services. They are also more likely to suffer from nutritional problems. In Ecuador and Guatemala, about 60% of indigenous children under 5 are malnourished – roughly twice the national averages (Larrea and Montenegro Torres, 2006; Shapiro, 2006). In Ecuador, non-indigenous women are three times as likely to receive antenatal care and have a skilled attendant present at birth (Larrea and Montenegro Torres, 2006). Being indigenous raises the probability of being in poverty by between 11% and 30%, depending on the country (Hall and Patrinos, 2006).

Poverty magnifies the barriers facing indigenous children, especially girls. In Guatemala, indigenous girls from extremely poor households enrol in school 1.2 years later than indigenous girls from non-poor households, on average, and are far more likely to drop out. Among 7- to 12-year-olds, Mayan boys and girls are twice as likely as non-indigenous children to combine school and work. For non-enrolled indigenous females, lack of money and housework are cited by parents as the main reason for children being out of school (Hallman et al., 2007).

The experience of indigenous people in Latin America also draws attention to the interaction between marginalization in education and employment. Over the past decade, some indigenous people in Latin America have narrowed the gap with the majority population in terms of years in school. But gains in education have enhanced their prospects for employment and higher wages far less than for non-indigenous people, pointing to discrimination in labour markets (Hall and Patrinos, 2006). This helps explain why progress in reducing poverty among indigenous people has been slow despite expanded access to education. The persistence of high levels of household poverty helps explain in turn why child labour, a major cause of school dropout, has tended to fall more slowly among indigenous people than among non-indigenous people.

Australia provides a striking example of extreme marginalization amid high levels of overall development. The country consistently figures in the top five on the United Nations Development Programme's Human Development Index. Yet in 2001, it was estimated that Aboriginals and Torres Strait Islanders in Australia would rank around 103 – below the Philippines and around the level of Viet Nam (Biddle and Mackay, 2009; Cooke et al., 2007). Social disadvantage on this scale inevitably affects what Aboriginal children achieve in school.

The marked racial divisions evident in the United States's education system are also wrapped up in social disparities. Gaps in learning achievement are evident early on. On average, African-American children register lower cognitive development levels by the age of two (Fryer and Levitt, 2006); (Table 3.4). Part of the difference can be traced directly to poverty and to parental education. Other significant factors include the number of books in the home and time spent reading (Ferguson, 2007). These disparities point to the importance of concerted pre-school strategies for overcoming group disadvantage, as discussed in Chapter 2.

Similarly, the restricted opportunities experienced by Roma children in school are intimately linked to poverty, unemployment, poor housing and poor health. A survey has found that one-quarter of the Roma population in southern and eastern Europe lives in dilapidated housing. The poverty rate for Roma in Romania is almost three times the national average (UNICEF, 2007*a*). The invisibility of Roma in national education programmes reinforces their exclusion: in Hungary, most education policies do not mention Roma, the country's most educationally disadvantaged community (Open Society Institute, 2007).

High economic growth and rapid poverty reduction do not automatically dissolve deeply entrenched group-based disadvantages. Since the early 1990s, poverty in Viet Nam has been cut by two-thirds, far surpassing the Millennium Development Goal target. Despite the gains, however, the average poverty rate among the country's 10 million ethnic minority people is 52%, compared with 10% for the majority Kinh (World Bank, 2009*d*). Minorities also have worse health, nutrition and education indicators, and less access to basic services. Partly because of these inequalities, the benefits of rapid economic growth have trickled down more slowly to ethnic minority groups. And the poverty gap has widened over time. At the end of the 1990s, the poverty rate among the non-Kinh population was two and a half times higher than the average for Kinh. By 2006, it was five times higher (Baulch et al., 2009).

The wider social and economic inequalities driving group-based marginalization in Viet Nam have important consequences for education. While education figures for ethnic minority groups are improving, they still lag far behind those of the Kinh population. One-quarter of minority children enter school late, compared with 5% for Kinh children. Around 30% of minority households report at least one child dropping out of primary school, double the Kinh share (World Bank, 2009*d*). Two of the four top reasons for dropping out – inability to afford school fees and need for child labour at home – are directly related to poverty.

Low status and social identity

Low status is intrinsic to marginalization. In parts of South Asia, social practices relating to group status are often based on complex ideas about caste. While caste-based discrimination is frequently outlawed through legislation, underlying practices and attitudes are often difficult to change.

In India, the 1950 Constitution banned 'untouchability' and provided measures to compensate for the extreme social, education and economic disadvantage arising out of that status. Yet, despite progress in many areas including education, deep caste-based disparities remain (Box 3.6). Belonging to a scheduled caste or tribe lowers prospects of school attendance.[7] Being a girl and living in a rural area brings a further layer of disadvantage. In 2004/2005, just 57% of rural girls aged 12 to 14 from scheduled tribes and 66% from scheduled castes were in school, compared with a national average of 80% (Figure 3.24).

Table 3.4: Poverty and early cognitive development by race, United States

	White	African American	National average
Poverty rate (%)	**11**	**25**	**13**
Cognitive development			
2-year-olds: Per cent demonstrating proficiency in listening comprehension	42	30	37
2-year-olds: Per cent demonstrating proficiency in expressive vocabulary	71	56	64
4-year-olds: Per cent proficient at letter recognition	37	28	33
4-year-olds: Average overall mathematics score	24	21	23

Sources:
Poverty rate: Annual Social and Economic Supplement (ASEC) to the 2008 Current Population Survey (CPS), in DeNavas-Walt et al. (2008).
Cognitive development: National Center for Education Statistics (2009). Data for 2-year-olds collected in 2003–04; for 4-year-olds in 2005–06.

Box 3.6: Living with stigma – the 'rat catchers' of Uttar Pradesh and Bihar

'The higher-caste students tell us that we smell bad,' one girl said. Another added, 'The ridicule we face prevents us from coming to school and sitting with higher-caste children.' These girls from the hamlet of Khalispur, near the city of Varanasi, belong to the Musahar or 'rat catcher' community of eastern Uttar Pradesh, India.

Khalispur has a government primary school. Despite an entitlement to receive a stipend, midday meals and uniforms, few Musahar girls attend. The testimony of some of them powerfully demonstrates the force of social attitudes in creating disadvantage: for these girls, school is a place where they experience social exclusion, as stigmatization undermines the self-esteem vital to effective learning. Subtle forms of discrimination reinforce caste hierarchies in the classroom. 'We are forced to sit on the floor,' one girl said. 'The desks and benches in the classroom are meant for the children from the higher castes.'

The Musahar community, which spans eastern Uttar Pradesh and Bihar, has high levels of poverty and low levels of literacy among adults. Apart from catching rats in rice fields, the livelihoods of the Musahar typically revolve around crushing and carrying stones, supplying brick kilns, making leaf plates and performing casual day labour. In contrast to some other low-caste groups, the Musahar have a weak political voice.

According to Musahar elders, government policies have improved but social attitudes have not: 'They do admit our children to school and we now have legal rights, but the behaviour of children from other castes and the teachers is a problem. Our children do not dare attend the school.'

Interviews courtesy of Sudhanshu Joshi, Global March Against Child Labour

7. Scheduled castes are the former untouchables and scheduled tribes are India's indigenous populations. Both are listed in schedules appended to India's constitution as groups deserving affirmative action measures.

Figure 3.24: In India, scheduled castes and tribes remain disadvantaged at all levels in education

Attendance rates by age group in India, by community, rural/urban residence and gender, 2004/2005

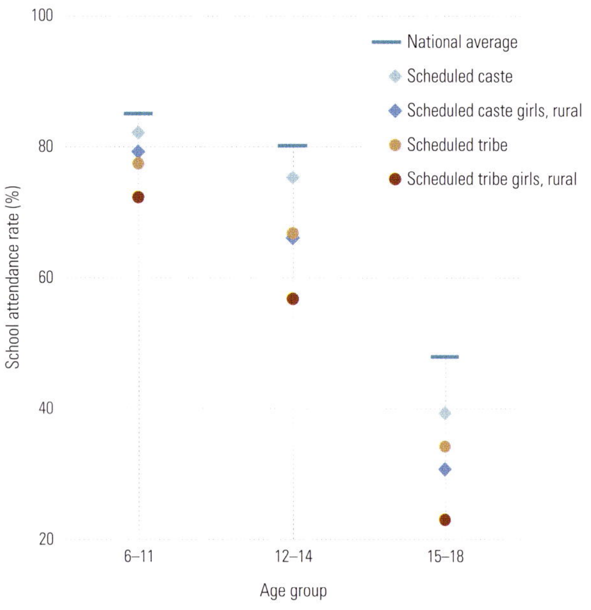

Notes: The attendance rate for an age range is the proportion of children of that age range who report attending school at the time of the survey. The age ranges correspond approximately to primary education, upper primary (or 'middle') education and secondary education, respectively, in the Indian school system.
Source: Bhalotra (2009) based on National Sample Survey data (61st round).

To what extent do these differences stem from distinctive caste and tribe disadvantages rather than wider social and economic factors? That is a key question for policy-makers seeking to equalize opportunity. Research for this Report helps provide a partial answer (Bhalotra, 2009). Using household survey data, and controlling for household and individual characteristics, the study found that about 60% of the attendance gap for scheduled-caste children aged 6 to 14 could be attributed to household characteristics, mainly poverty and lower parental education. For scheduled-tribe children in the same age group, household characteristics weighed less heavily, accounting for about 40% of the attendance gap. One conclusion to be drawn for members of both scheduled groups is that poverty matters a great deal in perpetuating educational disadvantage. However, the non-poverty component is larger for scheduled tribes partly because of the weight of social and cultural discrimination.

Public attitudes have consequences that go beyond school attendance. Institutionalized stigmatization can erode self-confidence and levels of expectation, undermining children's potential for learning.

One particularly striking illustration comes from an experimental investigation into the impact of caste perceptions on test scores (Hoff and Pandey, 2004). Children aged 11 and 12 were chosen at random from a low caste and three high castes, and given a series of puzzles to solve. When caste was not announced to the participants, it had no bearing on the initial score or on the improvement in score registered in subsequent test rounds. But when caste was announced before the test, the scores for low-caste children fell dramatically (Figure 3.25).[8] These findings underline the degree to which social identities that are a product of history, culture and personal experience can create pronounced education disadvantages through their effects on individual expectations.

The critical role of language

Language and ethnicity are deeply intertwined. Having a distinctive language is often a crucial element of personal identity and group attachment. Just as a local language may be a point of association for members of an ethnic group, it can also be an element in their marginalization. People who cannot speak a country's dominant language may have less access to written and spoken sources, restricting their opportunities for employment and social mobility (Smits and Gündüz-Hosgör, 2003; Smits et al., 2008). Parents who do not speak the official language in which their children are being educated may have less opportunity to engage with teachers, education authorities and homework. And their children may not grasp what is being taught if teachers do not speak their home language. The resulting inequalities in opportunity are a major factor

Figure 3.25: Social stigma can undermine test performance

Experimental impact of the announcement of caste on solving puzzles in India

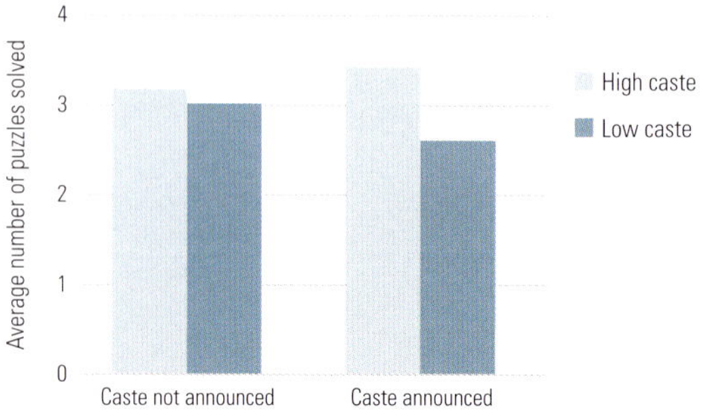

Note: Children aged 11 and 12 were given a packet of fifteen maze puzzles and asked to solve as many as they could in fifteen minutes.
Source: Hoff and Pandey (2004).

8. In three test rounds, scores for low-caste children fell by 14%, 25% and 39%.

in marginalization in countries where ethnicity and language are strongly associated with social deprivation.

The sheer scale of linguistic diversity in the world today and its consequences for achievement in education are not sufficiently recognized. There are nearly 7,000 spoken languages. Every world region is multilingual. Sub-Saharan Africa has 1,200 to 2,000 languages (Alidou et al., 2006). Cameroon alone has more than 200 languages, of which thirty-eight are written. In East Asia, Thailand has over seventy and Indonesia more than 737. Latin America's indigenous peoples speak an estimated 551 languages (Dutcher, 2004).

Education systems seldom reflect linguistic diversity. Many countries stress the importance of children learning in their mother tongue or home language. Nevertheless, about 221 million school age children speak languages that are used at home but not recognized in schools or official settings (Dutcher, 2004).

The degree of alignment between home and school language has a critical bearing on learning opportunities. Children who study in their mother tongue usually learn better and faster than children studying in second languages (UNESCO Bangkok, 2008; Woldemikael, 2003). Pupils who start learning in their home language also perform better in tests taken in the official language of instruction later in their school careers (UNESCO Bangkok, 2008). The benefits extend beyond cognitive skills to enhanced self-confidence, self-esteem and classroom participation (Alidou et al., 2006).

Decades of cognitive research have established the language conditions most conducive to learning (Alidou et al., 2006; Dutcher, 2004; UNESCO Bangkok, 2008). Translating those findings into policies that create an enabling environment for ethnic and linguistic minorities is not straightforward. Linguistic diversity creates challenges within the education system, notably in areas such as teacher recruitment, curriculum development and the provision of teaching materials. Moreover, language policy in education is not just about learning but is intimately wrapped up in power relationships and history.

In many countries, the dominant languages used in education are connected with social, political and cultural subjugation. Colonization has left a deep imprint. For most pupils entering primary school in francophone Africa, French is still their first language of instruction (Alidou et al., 2006). During the 1880s, authorities in New Zealand banned the teaching or use of the Māori language in native schools, arguing that it was an impediment to 'national progress'. One hundred years later, the language was spoken by less than one-quarter of the Māori population and drifting towards extinction (Wurm, 1991). Across much of Latin America, language was key to the exclusion and exploitation of indigenous people by Spanish-mestizo elites (Klein, 2003). Indigenous organizations in the region have seen 'decolonization of the school' as a vital part of wider political emancipation.

Governments have often seen the forging of a common linguistic identity as crucial to the development of a national identity (Daftary and Grin, 2003). The Turkish Constitution of 1923 includes a provision that 'no language other than Turkish shall be taught as mother tongue to Turkish citizens at any institutions of teaching or education' (Kaya, 2009, p. 8). While legislation adopted in 2002 allows greater flexibility, access to minority language primary education remains limited.

About 221 million school age children speak languages at home that are not recognized in schools or official settings

Language policy in education raises complex issues and potential tensions between group identity on the one hand, and social and economic aspirations on the other. Parents in many countries express a strong preference for their children to learn in the official language, principally because this is seen as a route to enhanced prospects for social mobility (Alidou et al., 2006; Cueto et al., 2009; Linehan, 2004). Labour market factors often figure prominently. In response to changing job opportunities and the earnings premium associated with use of English, lower-caste girls and young women in Mumbai are switching from primary and secondary schools teaching in Marathi to those teaching in English (Munshi and Rosenzweig, 2003).

Education systems have to perform a delicate balancing act. First and foremost, they need to create the enabling conditions for effective learning. Ideally, this implies learning the official language as a subject in primary school while receiving instruction in the home language. It also implies a school curriculum that teaches the majority population respect for ethnic minority language and culture. But education systems also have to ensure that children from disadvantaged minority backgrounds learn the skills they need to participate successfully in social and economic life, including language skills.

Breaking long-established institutional patterns is difficult. This is true even in countries with governments that acknowledge the disadvantages ethnic minorities face, as the experience of Viet Nam shows (Box 3.7). In Latin America, most countries have intercultural bilingual education policies, some of them dating from the 1920s. Today, such programmes aim at incorporating indigenous languages into national education systems by giving children a chance to learn in their home language before moving on to Spanish. Despite some significant achievements, however, these programmes face major challenges in several countries:

In parts of Peru, many teachers in bilingual schools can not speak the local indigenous language

- *Limited coverage.* Many indigenous children do not have access to intercultural bilingual education. In Guatemala and Paraguay, legislation provides for bilingual education in just the first three grades of primary school and, in reality, children are often taught only in Spanish. In Guatemala, 74% of children aged 7 to 12 years were reported as receiving classes only in the Spanish language in 2006 (López, 2009). In Peru, only around 10% of indigenous children attend intercultural bilingual schools. Coverage is far lower in urban than in rural areas (Cueto et al., 2009).

- *Poor quality.* Where indigenous language teaching is available, it is often of poor quality, with schooling compounding disadvantages linked to social and economic deprivation. Of about 900 teachers working in indigenous communities in Paraguay, a third have completed only basic education and fewer than two-thirds report speaking the local language (López, 2009). In Peru, which has been implementing the intercultural and bilingual model since 1972, one study in the south of the country found that half of teachers in intercultural and bilingual education schools could not even speak the local indigenous language. Moreover, bilingual materials provided by the Ministry of Education were not being used (Cueto et al., 2009).

- *Limited scope.* Intercultural bilingual education focuses on more effective integration of indigenous children into mainstream education. For many indigenous groups this objective is too limited. In several countries, indigenous political movements have mobilized behind demands for education reforms and for curriculum content that focuses on wider political concerns. In Bolivia, indigenous education councils have been pressing for a new education law that emphasizes multiculturalism, ethnic diversity and the values of indigenous culture. In Guatemala, where indigenous people's rights were brutally suppressed during the civil war, the period since the Peace Accords in 1995 has been marked by the development of a vigorous Mayan political movement focusing on language as one element in a broader campaign against discrimination. In both countries, many indigenous political leaders are looking to strengthen intercultural education to address deeper problems of discrimination and inequality,

Box 3.7: Tackling the ethnic divide in Viet Nam

The government of Viet Nam recognizes that problems facing ethnic minorities are a major barrier to universal primary education. It has established an extensive system of financial transfers targeted at households and communes with large minority populations. A 1999 law allowing minority languages to be used in education recognizes the importance of home language.

Implementing that law has proved difficult, however. Part of the problem is a serious shortage of ethnic minority teachers. While ethnic minority children account for 18% of the primary school age population, ethnic minority teachers make up just 8% of the teaching force. Moreover, few of these teachers are posted to ethnic minority areas. And not all have the training or experience to teach bilingual education. As a result, Kinh remains the dominant language of instruction for most ethnic minority children.

Demographic factors also appear to have an important bearing on the language of instruction. Analysis undertaken for this Report compared home language education in Lao Cai, a mountainous northern province with a large ethnic minority population, with that in Phu Yen, a south-central coastal province in which ethnic minorities account for just 5% of the population. Minority groups in Phu Yen have far less access to home language courses, partly because their children attend overwhelmingly Kinh-dominated schools.

Sources: Truong Huyen (2009); World Bank (2009*d*); UNESCO-DME (2009).

and to help change power relationships in society (López, 2009; Luykx and López, 2007).

Location and livelihoods

Disadvantages linked to poverty, ethnicity and language are often reflected in human geography. Children living in slums, remote rural areas or conflict-affected zones are typically among the poorest and most vulnerable in any society. Potentially, they have the most to gain from education. Yet they live in areas with the most limited access to basic services, including education. Restricted education and livelihood opportunities reinforce the poverty trap. This section looks at institutionalized disadvantages linked to location that perpetuate marginalization in education.

Right to education denied to slum dwellers

Kibera is one of the largest slums in sub-Saharan Africa. Located next to the Royal Nairobi Golf Course and a short distance from leafy suburbs that are home to some of Kenya's wealthiest people, it has an estimated population of 1 million. Most lack access to clean water, sanitation and other public services. It is a short walk from Kibera to some of Kenya's finest primary schools, yet the vast majority of the slum's children are locked out of even the most basic opportunities for education.

Kibera is a microcosm of a wider problem. Half the world's population now lives in cities and urban growth is highest in the developing world (UN-HABITAT, 2008). In the midst of urban prosperity and opportunity, almost every major city has large islands of slums that are centres of social deprivation. On one estimate, one in three urban dwellers in the developing world – 900 million in total – resides in a slum (UN-HABITAT, 2006). In an increasingly urbanized world, slum populations are growing by over 20 million a year as rural poverty and the lure of opportunity create a steady stream of new arrivals.

Not all slum environments are equivalent in the scale of deprivation. One study comparing slums in Nairobi and Dakar, Senegal, found that while the inhabitants of the latter were poorer, they were four times more likely to have access to water and electricity. Just under a third of Nairobi's population lives in slums. Children in these settlements face disadvantages at many levels. Less than 6% of households have piped water in their homes and even fewer have access to sanitation facilities. Poor sanitation and inadequate garbage collection cause major health problems. Children in Nairobi's slums face higher mortality rates than those in rural areas (World Bank, 2009*f*).

Many governments have little idea how many children live in informal settlements and are failing to respond to the major new education policy challenges created by the rapid growth of slums. Because many settlements are 'illegal', they are not recognized in government plans or provided with public water, sanitation, health or education services (UNESCO-IIEP, 2009).

What schooling is available is often supplied by non-government organizations, churches or private entrepreneurs, with little government support or regulation. As evidence from slums in Dhaka, Bangladesh, shows, the poor generally have little if any choice of education provider (Box 3.8). The financing of education in slums such as those in Nairobi is largely private: parents have to pay for poor-quality private schooling, while non-slum children have access to free government education (Oketch et al., 2008). Household poverty, poor child health and nutrition, and extensive child labour combine to create a formidable barrier to education. Even where schools are not far away, security concerns present an additional hurdle to access: 60% of girls interviewed in Kibera expressed fear of being raped. It was not uncommon for boys and girls to have witnessed physical violence. A common response to fear of violence and harassment in slums is to stop going to school (Erulkar and Matheka, 2007; Mudege et al., 2008).

Restricted entitlements are among the most potent elements of educational marginalization in slums. Parents often cannot secure their children's human right to education because they lack official residency status. For purposes of school registration, the authorities do not recognize that these children even exist. One study of 400 slum-dwelling households in Delhi found that only half of primary school age children were in school, compared with a citywide enrolment rate in excess of 90% (Tsujita, 2009). Although government schools were within walking distance, only a third of children in the sample had a birth certificate, which is mandatory for admission to government schools.

In Delhi's slums, only a third of children surveyed had a birth certificate, which is mandatory for admission to government schools

Box 3.8: Slums in Dhaka — marginalization with rapid urban growth

Dhaka, the capital of Bangladesh, is one of the world's fastest-growing cities. An estimated 300,000 to 400,000 new migrants arrive each year and the vast majority head for informal settlements. Around one-third of the city's population – 4 million people – live in slums, many of them in flood zones.

Education figures for Dhaka's slums are among the worst in Bangladesh. One study of four slums found that just 70% of children were enrolled at the primary level, many of them in schools run by non-government organizations.

The study also found high inequality within the slums. The children of better-off families, such as those with small businesses, were far more likely to be not just in school, but in a government or private school. Children from the poorest households were less likely to be in school and almost half those enrolled relied on non-government organizations (Figure 3.26). The parents of these children were predominantly day labourers and rickshaw drivers.

Schools run by non-government organizations play an important function in Dhaka's slums. Unlike private schools, they are usually free and offer flexible hours and classes. Their quality varies, however, and many offer only three or four years of basic education, with limited scope for transition into the formal education system. In some respects non-government education is a symptom of the vacuum created by limited public education. Only a quarter of Dhaka's slums have a government school. Most of these schools are in well-established slum areas, while newer, less formal settlements are left to fend for themselves.

Figure 3.26: Poor slum dwellers in Bangladesh depend on non-government education provision

% of children aged 6 to 11 enrolled, by type of school and wealth, selected slums of Dhaka, 2008

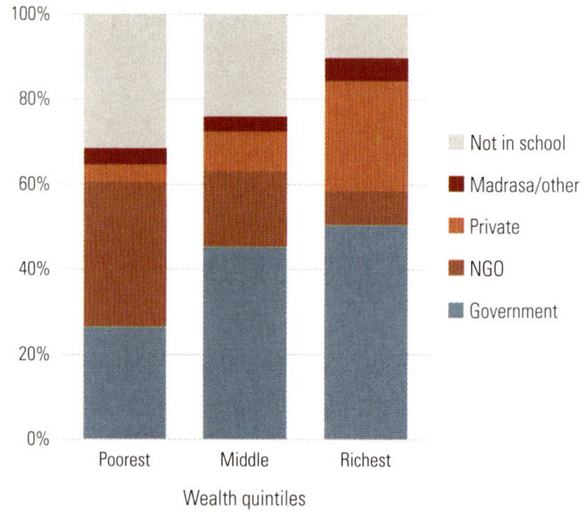

Note: Includes only ages 6 to 11 and enrolment in grades 1 to 5.
Source: Cameron (2009).

As in other slums worldwide, insecure tenure contributes to marginalization in education. Lacking tenancy rights, slum dwellers are in a weak position to demand education and public finance. Moreover, as many city authorities periodically bulldoze informal settlements, some non-government providers are loath to invest in school buildings.

Sources: Cameron (2009); World Bank (2007*a*); Centre for Urban Studies et al. (2006).

'Do we buy food or enrol our child in school?'

Parent, Bangladesh

Residency requirements were another major barrier, as migrants from other states make up a large share of the slum-dwelling population. Rural migrants to urban areas in China face similar problems, with the *hukou* (household registration) system restricting access to basic education (Box 3.9).

Many governments lack credible public policies for providing education and other basic services in fast-growing informal settlements. Authorities often claim that legal entitlement to education and other services in all slums would act as incentives for accelerated rural-urban migration. While this concern is not without foundation, depriving children of their right to an education through government inaction is not an appropriate response.

Remote rural areas are underserved

Rural children face heightened risks of marginalization in education, especially if they are poor and female. Rural-urban divides in education often overlap with wider inequalities. In many countries, rural areas tend to have higher concentrations of poverty and less access to health care. Marginalization in education both mirrors and magnifies these disparities.

Low population density in rural areas often means children have to travel greater distances to school, sometimes across difficult terrain. In addition, rural parents tend to be less educated. These concerns are compounded by government failure to provide schools or attract good teachers to the countryside. Traditional cultural practices and attitudes also play a role.

Box 3.9: China's *hukou* system has restricted education opportunities for migrant children

In China, children's right to education can run up against residency requirements that limit access to schooling.

The full extent of rural-urban migration in China is unknown. One estimate is that 98 million rural migrants live in China's cities, including 14 million children. Attracted by employment and an escape from rural poverty, many migrants live in informal temporary housing in areas with limited public services. Migrant children are among the most educationally marginalized in China, largely because of the registration system called *hukou*.

Under the *hukou* system, city schools can only admit students registered as official inhabitants with a permanent home in the school district. School budgets are based on the number of official students registered by authorities. Individual schools can admit unregistered children, but typically require parents to pay a fee to compensate for the lack of government funds. This arrangement makes education unaffordable for many migrant families.

Education figures for major cities reflect the consequences of the *hukou* system. Only two-thirds of Beijing's 370,000 migrant children were enrolled in public schools. Another quarter were reported as attending unauthorized migrant schools. These schools, a response to exclusion from the public education system, are of questionable quality and some have been forced to close.

Chinese authorities, acknowledging the problems facing rural migrants, have introduced reforms. City authorities have been required to accommodate holders of rural *hukou* with temporary residence and employment permits, reducing the pressure on schools to charge fees. Even so, the children of many migrants, including those working in the informal sector, continue to face restricted opportunities for education.

Sources: Han (2009); Liu, He and Wu (2008); Liang et al. (2008).

Remoteness is one of the strongest factors in marginalization. The poorest households in many rural areas are the furthest from roads, markets, health services and schools. In Nicaragua, the incidence of extreme poverty is 20% higher in the central rural region, where people have to travel twice as far as the national average to reach a school or health clinic (Ahmed et al., 2007).

Distance to school is often a major determinant of participation by ethnic minorities. In India, children from scheduled tribes, many of them living in dispersed communities in remote areas, face some of the longest treks to school in the country (Wu et al., 2007). In the Lao People's Democratic Republic, schools in rural and predominantly non-Lao Tai areas are less likely to offer a full primary education cycle, and the availability of lower secondary schools is far more restricted compared with Lao Tai areas. Only 80% of rural non-Lao Tai children have a primary school in their village and only 4% have a lower secondary school. The shares for the majority Lao Tai children are significantly higher (88% and 17%, respectively). Such differences help explain why only 46% of poor non-Lao Tai girls aged 6 to 12 attend school in rural areas, compared with 70% of poor rural Lao Tai girls (King and van de Walle, 2007).

Lack of nearby facilities has implications for both the time and the energy needed to get to school. Country surveys in West Africa from the 1990s revealed high average walking distances in several countries, including 7.5 km in Chad, 6.6 km in Mali, 5 km in Senegal and 4 km in the Central African Republic. Distances are likely to be higher than these averages in remote areas (Filmer, 2004).

Even relatively short distances to school can significantly reduce demand for education. A 2002–2003 survey of 179 villages in the western Sahelian region of Chad found that for distances over a kilometre, enrolment declined steeply, with fewer than 10% of children typically going to school. Physical barriers such as rivers and forests could considerably increase the time required to reach school (Lehman et al., 2007).

In the western Sahelian region of Chad, enrolment declines steeply when children live over a kilometre from school

Girls' attendance is particularly sensitive to journey times. Household surveys in many countries identify distance as a major factor in parents' decisions to keep daughters out of school (Kane, 2004, and World Bank, 2005*d*, cited in Theunynck, 2009; Glick, 2008; Huisman and Smits, 2009). Explanations vary, but concerns over security and domestic labour needs figure prominently.

Pastoralist lifestyles demand better education responses

Pastoralists in sub-Saharan Africa and South Asia face extreme educational disadvantage (see Figure 3.5 above; Dyer, 2006). By one rough estimate, as many as 8.5 million children from nomadic households do not attend school globally (Carr-Hill, 2009).

Why do pastoralist children face such restricted opportunities for schooling? Livelihood pressures are an important factor. Pastoralists are not always the poorest rural people, especially if their livestock assets are taken into account. But they often rely heavily on boys for tending cattle and girls for domestic chores, restricting children's time available for formal schooling (Ruto et al., 2009) (Box 3.10). Education loses out because labour demands take priority.

'The education system that fits us will be the one that follows us, that follows our animals.'

Village elder, northen Kenya

On the other hand, pastoralists often see education as a route to more diverse and less insecure livelihoods. This finding emerges from research in the Somali region of Ethiopia and among the Turkana of Kenya and the Karamojong of Uganda (Devereux, 2006; Krätli, 2006; Ruto et al., 2009). Paradoxically, environmental degradation, drought and cattle raids may be stimulating interest in the role formal education can play in providing skills needed to cope with contemporary livelihood challenges (Dyer, 2006).

Education systems themselves are often unresponsive to pastoralist demands. Pastoralist livelihoods are inherently mobile, geared towards seasonal calendars for grazing and water availability. Formal education planning, in contrast, is commonly organized around a fixed school infrastructure and a fixed national schedule for the school term and school day. Such planning fails to take into account the realities and demands of pastoral livelihoods. The misalignment between the education supply model and livelihood realities means demands for schooling are often unmet.

School infrastructure is not the only problem. Pastoralists often see curricula as having little relevance to their lives. They are typically absent from the images and stories in primary school textbooks, reinforcing the cultural distance between home and school. If pastoralism is mentioned at all, it may reflect the view of many non-pastoralists that the practice is outdated and ignorant (Krätli, 2006), rather than a specialized and sustainable livelihood.

Early marriage for girls is another barrier to education in some pastoralist communities. So is a deeply engrained belief that female education may be of less value. A proverb of the Gabra community in northern Kenya says: 'God first, then man, then camel, and lastly girl.' This

Box 3.10: Kenya's pastoralists – 'we need schools that follow our herds'

Nasra Hassan, 7, has had a taste of education. She was enrolled in standard one at Basaa Primary School in the Merti Division of Isiolo, a remote district of Northern Kenya. But then the drought hit. The current drought has left an estimated 4 million Kenyans in need of emergency food aid. Pastoralist areas have been among the worst affected. Child malnutrition is rising and households have seen their livestock herds decimated.

The harm to education has been less visible – but no less damaging for long-term efforts to reduce poverty. Nasra's parents no longer have the money they need to pay for her education. And as herders have to travel farther and farther in search of water for their animals, there are fewer people at home to help with household chores, so Nasra is expected to spend more time looking after the smaller animals and collecting water for home use. Instead of studying, she is now busy washing, cooking, and fetching water and firewood. The drought has forced her out of school.

The drought is not the only barrier to education among pastoralist children. Many parents and village elders have ambivalent attitudes to schooling, partly because they are acutely aware of the trade-offs they face. As one parent eloquently put it, 'We have to choose between wealth and knowledge – between having a prosperous herd and having educated children. We need our children to tend the cattle, even though we know they need an education.'

The tension between securing livelihoods and gaining education is a recurrent theme in pastoral areas. Formal education happens in a fixed context – the classroom. By contrast, pastoralist survival often depends on children following herds over large areas.

Resolving the dilemma will require more flexible and more mobile ways to provide education. As one village elder in Isiolo said, 'The education system that fits us will be the one that follows us, that follows our animals.'

Interview courtesy of SOS Sahel

explains a reluctance to sell camels to finance girls' education, unlike for boys (Ruto et al., 2009, p. 11). The social attitudes behind such sentiments are deeply damaging for girls' education.

The diversity of pastoralist experience cautions against generalization. Yet even in countries making strong progress in primary education, pastoralist children are often being left far behind. Kenya is now looking beyond primary schooling to universal secondary education, but that vision contrasts strongly with reality in the country's ten most arid districts. Inhabited predominantly by pastoralist communities, these districts have some of the country's lowest enrolment ratios and largest gender disparities, with net enrolments less than 30% for boys and 20% for girls in the three worst-performing districts located in the North Eastern Province (Figure 3.27).

Figure 3.27: Many of Kenya's arid districts are left behind

Net enrolment ratios in public primary schools for northern arid districts of Kenya, 2007

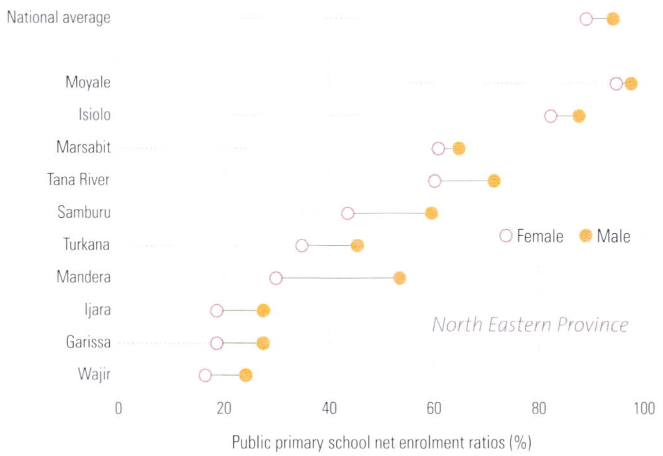

Source: Ruto et al. (2009), based on 2007 data from Ministry of Education Statistics Unit (2009).

Armed conflict fuels educational marginalization

Armed conflict contributes to marginalization in education in many ways. Most obviously, it exposes children to the risk of violence and trauma. In addition to driving people from their homes and creating large refugee populations, conflict can destroy schools and create risks for pupils and teachers. Moreover, conflict can leave a legacy of distrust, instability and weak governance found in many of the world's most fragile states, with governments often unable or unwilling to provide basic services.

While firm evidence of the impact of armed conflict is limited, international data clearly reflect a close association between conflict and marginalization. Over one-third of primary school age children who do not attend school – 25 million in total – live in conflict-affected poor countries (see Chapter 2). Many of these countries have among the world's worst child health and education figures. In Somalia, one in seven children does not survive to age 5 and just 22% of those who do reach primary school age are in school – one of the world's lowest enrolment levels (UNDP, 2009).

Mass displacement caused by conflict locks millions of children into a future of extreme disadvantage in education. Forced to flee their homes, parents often have to resettle in areas ill equipped to provide good basic education. At the end of 2008, there were an estimated 42 million forcibly displaced people worldwide: around 26 million were displaced within their own countries and 16 million had to flee across borders (Internal Displacement Monitoring Centre, 2009; UNHCR, 2009). Children aged 5 to 17 comprise around one-third of the global population of forcibly displaced people (Women's Commission for Refugee Women and Children, 2004). Indigenous peoples and ethnic minorities make up a disproportionate share of displaced populations.

International debates on refugees often focus on issues affecting rich countries. Yet developing countries bear the brunt of cross-border displacement. Countries including Chad, Kenya, Uganda and the United Republic of Tanzania have absorbed millions of people displaced by conflicts in the Democratic Republic of the Congo, Somalia and the Sudan. Pakistan is host to the world's largest refugee population, having absorbed over 2 million people uprooted by violence in Afghanistan (UNHCR, 2009; Winthrop, 2009*a*). Struggling to achieve universal primary education for their own children, these countries are ill equipped to provide education to large, vulnerable, extremely poor refugee populations that often speak different languages. The international aid system offers only limited support. Children end up either studying a curriculum that is alien to them or with no schooling at all. In Pakistan, a refugee census in 2005 estimated that 1 million Afghan refugee children were out of school (Winthrop, 2009*a*).

In Pakistan, a refugee census in 2005 estimated that 1 million Afghan refugee children were out of school

Internal displacement can also create wide-ranging problems for education, overloading the system in areas of resettlement. Pakistan's recent experience

'Students are often absent because they spend hours lining up for rations and water.'

Abdul, Philippines

again illustrates the scale of the problem. With 2.5 million people displaced from the North West Frontier Province in 2008 by fighting between the government and Taliban militants, schools in other parts of the country came under pressure (Winthrop, 2009*b*). In the Philippines, hostilities in 2008 and 2009 between government forces and armed groups led to the displacement of 750,000 people, severely disrupting children's schooling (Amnesty International, 2009) (Box 3.11).

Violent conflict can touch the lives of children in many ways, including enforced recruitment as soldiers. At the end of 2007, child soldiers were directly involved in armed confrontations in seventeen countries, including Afghanistan, Chad, Somalia and the Sudan (Coalition to Stop the Use of Child Soldiers, 2008). In Somalia, the Transitional Federal Government has reportedly recruited over 1,000 children into its armed forces, most of them directly from schools (UN General Assembly Security Council, 2009).

Box 3.11: The human face of conflict in the Philippines

Muhammed's new home is a tent on the grounds of a school, yet he has little time to attend class. For him and many other children in an evacuation camp, helping his parents supplement meagre food rations is now his priority. 'I can only go to classes in the morning because I have to look for vegetables and firewood outside the camp and return before dark,' he said.

Muhammed, 13, is the eldest of five children who are taking refuge with their parents and grandparents in a camp set up in the Datu Gumbay Piang Elementary School in Maguindanao.

Heavy clashes between the military and separatist rebels in the Mindanao region of the Philippines have left hundreds of thousands of civilians stranded in evacuation camps, often set up in schools such as this one. The Datu Gumbay Piang centre has reportedly become home to the highest number of internally displaced persons since the outbreak of the fighting.

For the moment Muhammed and his family consider themselves lucky to have a tent to live in. 'Some of the refugees have no choice but to make their homes inside the classrooms or take shelter under the school buildings when it rains,' said Bernie Abdul, an evacuee working in the school.

Most of the children come to class to escape the dismal living conditions in their tents. But there is no immediate escape from the destruction and violence they have witnessed. 'When the children are in class, they are either lethargic or very nervous because we often hear howitzers being fired not far from us.'

Muhammed is not the only child in the camp who is unable to attend school regularly. Abdul explained: 'Students are often absent because they spend hours lining up for rations and water at the pump or because they're sick. Living in an unhealthy environment without running water and sanitary facilities has affected the children physically and emotionally as well.'

Interviews conducted by Ross Harper Alonso for this Report

Apart from missing out on education, child soldiers often suffer psychological trauma, hampering prospects for a return to education. During the civil war in Sierra Leone that started in 1991, over 15,000 children are estimated to have been forced to serve in military groups. After the end of the conflict in 2002, schooling was seen as a way for the former soldiers to recover some of their lost childhood. However, schools were ill-equipped to provide the psychosocial support necessary to enable them to readjust to normal life (Betancourt et al., 2008).

Other children experience trauma as a result of being part of a civilian population caught in violent conflict. The process of reconstructing education in Gaza will require not only repairing physical infrastructure but also measures to support traumatized children (Box 3.12).

In some cases, education is targeted as a symbol of government authority, with schools subject to armed attack, and pupils and teachers threatened with murder, injury, abduction and rape. In Afghanistan, 670 schools were closed in early 2009 because of security threats, depriving 170,000 children of education. In the three southernmost provinces of Thailand, separatist groups hostile to Buddhist values and Thai-language teaching have attacked schools. In the past five years, 99 teachers have been reported killed and 296 schools have been firebombed (O'Malley, 2009).

Groups within the Taliban in Afghanistan and Pakistan have targeted girls' schools, both to challenge government authority and to assert values hostile to equal opportunity in education. In the Swat district of Pakistan, the Taliban destroyed 108 girls' schools and damaged 64 other schools between 2007 and May 2009. During 2008, local Taliban leaders ordered a ban on women teachers and girls' education. In response, 900 schools closed or stopped admitting girls and fear created by the decree led to the withdrawal of 120,000 girls from school (O'Malley, 2009).

Disability

Disability is one of the least visible but most potent factors in educational marginalization. Beyond the immediate health-related effects, physical and mental impairment carries a stigma that is often a basis for exclusion from society and school. The impact is often worse for poorer households.

Attitudes towards disability have changed over time. Until relatively recently, the 'medical model' was dominant: those with disabilities were seen as having a condition that set them apart from the rest of society. That attitude gave rise to discrimination, isolation and stigmatization. It is now increasingly accepted that, while disabilities involve varying levels and types of impairment, it is social, institutional and attitudinal barriers that limit the full inclusion of people with disabilities. Understanding disability in this way highlights the importance of identifying and removing the barriers. Education has a key role to play in changing attitudes.

Poverty is both a potential cause and a consequence of disability. In several countries, the probability of being in poverty rises in households headed by people with disabilities (McClain-Nhlapo, 2007). In Uganda, evidence from the 1990s found that the probability was as much as 60% higher (Hoogeveen, 2005). Those with disabilities are much less likely to be working. Other family members may also be out of work (or school) to care for them. Inadequate treatment, along with poor families' inability to invest sufficiently in health and nutrition, reinforces the problems people with disabilities face (Bird and Pratt, 2004). These links to poverty, combined with stigma and discrimination, are a significant factor in their educational marginalization.

While globally comparable, reliable data are notoriously difficult to obtain, one widely cited source estimates that 150 million children worldwide live with disabilities (WHO and UNICEF, 2008).[9] Around four in five children with disabilities are in developing countries. In addition, many millions of children live in households with parents or relatives who have disabilities. At all ages, levels of both moderate and severe disability are higher in low- and middle-income countries than in rich countries. They are highest in sub-Saharan Africa (WHO and UNICEF, 2008). The scale of disability and its concentration in the world's poorest countries contributes significantly to marginalization in education.

Box 3.12: Education destruction and reconstruction in Gaza

Conflict in 2008 and 2009 gravely affected the education system in Gaza. The circumstances surrounding the violence are subject to claim and counter-claim. In a report presented to the United Nations General Assembly, Justice Richard Goldstone documented evidence of both sides targeting civilian populations. What is not in question is the scale of the human and physical damage inflicted by Israeli military actions.

Part of the damage can be counted in terms of lives lost and people injured. It is estimated that 164 students and 12 teachers were killed. Many more suffered long-term injuries. Infrastructure was severely affected. While estimates vary, Justice Goldstone reported that some 280 schools and kindergartens were identified as destroyed or badly damaged. Restrictions on transport of building materials have delayed reconstruction.

Less easy to document are the effects of childhood trauma. Violent conflict has left deep scars in Gaza society. Research in Gaza has identified post-traumatic stress disorder as a major problem for young people, with 69% of adolescents affected and 40% reporting moderate or severe depression. Such conditions create severe educational disadvantage.

The scale of violence experienced by civilian populations in 2008 and 2009 has compounded the disadvantage. Many children have returned to school suffering from anxiety, the emotional shock of losing parents or siblings and the memory of acts of extreme violence. The consequences for education are likely to be far reaching and long lasting.

Sources: O'Malley (2009); United Nations (2009*a*); Elbedour et al. (2007).

Systematic under-reporting of disability is a serious problem. To take one example, a 2004 census in Sierra Leone reported only 3,300 cases of mental impairment, while a detailed national survey the year before had estimated the real figure to be ten times higher (World Bank, 2009*c*). One reason for under-reporting is that stigmatization often makes parents and children reluctant to report disability.

Disability is one of the least visible but most potent factors in educational marginalization

Many impairments can be traced back to poverty, poor nutrition and restricted access to basic services (Yeo and Moore, 2003). Asphyxia during birth, often resulting from the absence of a skilled attendant, leaves an estimated 1 million children with impairments such as cerebral palsy and learning difficulties (UNICEF, 2008*b*). Maternal iodine deficiency leads to 18 million babies being born with mental impairments and deficiency in vitamin A leaves about 350,000 children in developing countries blind (Micronutrient Initiative et al., 2009).

Conflict contributes to disability directly through physical threats and indirectly through effects on poverty, nutrition and health care. For every child killed in warfare, it is estimated that three are left

9. In the 1970s, the World Health Organization estimated that 10% of the global population lived with a disability. This rough estimate is still in use today, suggesting that there are about 650 million people with disabilities. It is the basis for the estimate of 150 million of children with disabilities.

with an impairment (UN Enable, 2009 cited in Peters, 2009). Road accidents, a less widely recognized cause of impairment in childhood, are endemic in many of the world's poorest countries. It is conservatively estimated that 10 million children are injured each year on the world's roads and many are left with permanent impairments. Over 80% of road-related injury and death occurs in developing countries (WHO and UNICEF, 2008). The consequences for education of these deaths and injuries have been subject to insufficient scrutiny, notably by national agencies and donors involved in road construction.

In Burkina Faso, just 10% of children with a hearing or speech impairment were in school in 2006

The link between disability and marginalization in education is evident in countries at different ends of the spectrum for primary school enrolment and completion. In Malawi and the United Republic of Tanzania, having disabilities doubles the probability of children never having attended school, and in Burkina Faso it increases the risk of children being out of school by two and a half times (Kobiané and Bougma, 2009; Loeb and Eide, 2004; United Republic of Tanzania Government, 2009). In these countries, inadequate policy attention to disability is clearly holding back national progress towards universal primary education. In some countries that are closer to achieving that goal, people with disabilities represent the majority of those left behind. In Bulgaria and Romania, net enrolment ratios for children aged 7 to 15 were over 90% in 2002 but only 58% for children with disabilities (Mete, 2008).

'Disability' is a generic term covering a multitude of circumstances. Children with, say, severe autism are likely to face very different education-related challenges than children who are partially sighted, or who have lost a limb. Impairments that affect the capacity to communicate and interact in ways common in mainstream schools can impose particularly high practical and social obstacles to participation in education.

A closer look at national data often reveals markedly different consequences for various impairments. In Burkina Faso, children reported as deaf or mute, living with a mental impairment or blind were far less likely to be enrolled in school than those with a physical impairment. In 2006, just 10% of deaf or mute 7- to12-year-olds were in school (Kobiané and Bougma, 2009); (Figure 3.28). The attendance rate for children with a physical impairment was 40%, only slightly below those with no impairment. In Uganda, recent evidence suggests dropout rates are lower among children with visual and physical impairments than among those with mental impairments (Lang and Murangira, 2009).

Children with disabilities face many challenges in education. Three of the most serious involve institutionalized discrimination, stigmatization and neglect, from the classroom to the local community and in the home. Children with disabilities are often isolated within their societies and communities because of a mixture of shame, fear and ignorance about the causes and consequences of their impairment.

One qualitative study of attitudes towards children with autism in Ghana revealed they were widely described as 'useless and not capable of learning, (...) stubborn, lazy, or wilfully disobedient' (Anthony, 2009, pp. 12–13). In a statement with wider application, the Ghanaian Ministry of Education, Sports and Science has powerfully captured the social prejudices that shape the education disadvantages associated with disability: 'The education of children with disabilities is undervalued by families, there is a lack of awareness about the potential of children with disabilities, children with disabilities in mainstream schools receive less attention from teachers and there is an over-emphasis on academic achievement and examination as opposed to all round development of children' (Ghana Ministry of Education, Science and Sports, 2008, pp. 60–61).

Education systems and classroom experience can help counteract the marginalization that children with disabilities face. However, they often have the opposite effect. Insufficient physical access, shortages of trained teachers and limited provision of teaching aids can diminish opportunities. Many schools, particularly in remote rural areas or in slums, are physically inaccessible to some children with disabilities. Children with sensory or mental impairments can find schools noisy, confusing and threatening. The grossly inadequate level of provision for children with disabilities in general schools often drives parents and groups representing people with disabilities to demand separate provision (Lang and Murangira, 2009).

That demand is both understandable and is a symptom of wider problems. Putting children with disabilities in special-needs schools or institutions can reinforce stigmatization. It can also deny them a chance to participate in mainstream education, build relationships and develop in an inclusive environment. Moreover, special schools are often chronically underfunded and lack either skilled teaching staff or the equipment needed to deliver a good education.

Education planners need to recognize that giving children with disabilities a level of access and quality of education equivalent to that enjoyed by other children often entails increased financing. Additional resources are needed to provide teachers with specialized training and children with specially designed learning materials to realize their potential. Families may also require additional financial support. One study in Bangladesh found that the parents of children with disabilities faced costs for aids, appliances and health care that were three times the average household budget for raising children (Chowdhury, 2005, in Marriott and Gooding, 2007). Overcoming a legacy of institutionalized disadvantage can be difficult even in countries with a strong commitment to more inclusive education, such as India (Box 3.13).

Figure 3.28: Burkina Faso's children with disabilities face deep but varied levels of disadvantage

% of children aged 7 to 12 and 13 to 16 attending school, by nature of impairment, Burkina Faso, 2006

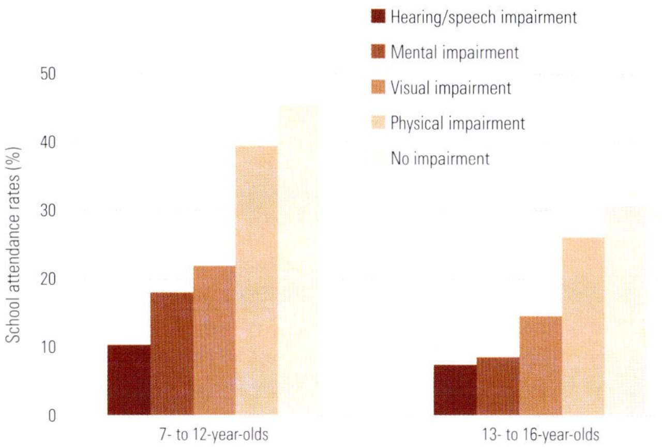

Source: Kobiané and Bougma (2009), based on data from the 2006 Burkina Faso census: Recensement Général de la Population et de l'Habitation.

Box 3.13: Prejudice limits educational opportunities for children with disabilities in India

Education planning documents in India enshrine a strong commitment to inclusive education. The aim is to provide all children with disabilities, irrespective of the type or degree of impairment, with education in an 'appropriate environment', which can include mainstream and special schools as well as alternative schools and home-based learning. Delivering on this commitment requires a concerted political effort backed by reforms in service provision.

Yet disability remains a major brake on progress towards universal primary education in India. While there are inconsistencies in national data, estimates suggest that school participation among children with disabilities never rises above 70%, far below the national average of around 90%. According to a World Bank analysis of India's 2002 National Sample Survey, children with disabilities are five and a half times more likely to be out of school.

Disaggregation of the data highlights important variations. Almost three-quarters of children with severe impairments are out of school, compared with about 35% to 40% among children with mild or moderate impairments. The most likely to be excluded are children with mental illness (two-thirds of whom never enrol in school) or blindness (over half never enrol).

Public attitudes are among the greatest barriers to equal education for people with disabilities in India. Children with mental impairments face some of the most deeply entrenched prejudices. In a public attitude survey covering the states of Uttar Pradesh and Tamil Nadu, almost half of respondents said such children could not attend either regular or special school. Another commonly held view was that those with mental impairments would not find decent employment. People from households with a disabled member shared the general view, reflecting stigmatization in the home.

Institutional constraints reinforce public attitudes. In 2005, just 18% of India's schools were accessible to children with disabilities in terms of facilities such as ramps, appropriately designed classrooms and toilets, and transport.

National education policies reflect growing awareness of the problems associated with disability. Measures introduced so far range from providing aids and appliances in schools to stipends for children with disabilities. Public awareness problems have hampered implementation, however. In a survey in Tamil Nadu and Uttar Pradesh, almost three-quarters of households that included a member with a disability reported being unaware of their eligibility for aids and appliances, and only 2% had directly benefited in 2005. Less than half of these households were aware that stipends were available and only 4% had received them.

Sources: National Sample Survey Organization (2003); Singal (2009); O'Keefe (2007); District Information System for Education (2009).

Giving children with disabilities a level of access and quality of education equivalent to that enjoyed by other children often entails increased financing

Table 3.5: Education indicators by disability status of head of household and wealth, Philippines and Uganda

		7- to 16-year-olds who have never been to school (%)			17- to 22-year-olds with fewer than 4 years of education (%)		
	Year	Average	Disabled*	Disabled* from poorest 20%	Average	Disabled*	Disabled* from poorest 20%
Philippines	2000	3	21	28	6	30	44
Uganda	2002	10	19	23	26	39	49

* 'Disabled' refers to self-reported disability status of the household head.
Source: UNESCO-DME (2009).

Becoming an orphan due to AIDS can inflict severe damage on education prospects

Having disabilities is not the only situation affecting children's educational opportunities. Children whose parents have disabilities often face tensions between schooling and care demands at home. These indirect consequences of adults with disabilities, known as the 'cascade effect', are often very severe.

National census data provide an insight into the scale of the problem. Having a poor parent with a disability increases the likelihood of 7- to 16-year-olds never having been to school by twenty-five percentage points in the Philippines and thirteen points in Uganda – a reminder of how poverty, disability and education interact (Table 3.5).

People affected by HIV and AIDS

HIV and AIDS are principally a global health crisis, but one with profound and wide-ranging consequences for education. As well as threatening lives, keeping children out of school and compromising learning, HIV and AIDS reinforce wider problems arising from poverty and social discrimination, such as economic pressure, orphanhood and stigmatization.

An estimated 33 million people were living with HIV in 2007, two-thirds of them in sub-Saharan Africa. The region is home to 90% of the 2 million children below age 15 living with HIV. Most contracted the virus during pregnancy, birth or breastfeeding – easily preventable forms of HIV transmission (UNAIDS et al., 2008). Without antiretroviral therapy, about 90% of these children die before reaching school age (Pridmore, 2008). Those who live may suffer associated problems, such as respiratory infections, malnutrition and diarrhoeal disease, more often and more severely than do healthy children, affecting their capacity to attend school and learn.[10]

Some of the most devastating effects of HIV and AIDS on education are not reflected in school data, for an obvious reason: many victims do not reach school age. Around 270,000 children under 14 died of AIDS-related illnesses in 2007 (UNAIDS et al., 2008). In many countries HIV and AIDS are reinforcing deep gender disparities in education. In high-prevalence southern African countries, such as Malawi, South Africa and Swaziland, HIV infection rates for girls and young women aged 15 to 24 are 1.8 times to 5.5 times the rates for men (Stirling et al., 2008). These disparities can harm girls' prospects of completing primary school and making the transition to secondary school.

With limited savings and assets, and dependent on physical labour for income, the poorest households are the least equipped to cope with the health costs of HIV and AIDS (UNAIDS et al., 2008). Many must sacrifice spending in other priority areas, including education. Research in Cambodia found that, to pay for health care, two-thirds of families affected by HIV and AIDS reported spending less on children's needs, including nutrition – potentially compromising children's capacity for learning (Alkenbrack et al., 2004). Household members' ill health can also compromise education by increasing demand for child labour (Pridmore, 2008).

Becoming an orphan due to AIDS can inflict severe damage on education prospects. Some 15 million children under 18 have lost one or both parents to AIDS. Evidence from fifty-six countries with recent household survey data indicated that orphans who had lost both parents were 12% less likely to attend school than non-orphans, on average (UNAIDS et al., 2008). Behind this figure are marked variations, some influenced strongly by the gender of the deceased parent. In some sub-Saharan African countries, including Ethiopia, Kenya, Malawi and the United Republic of Tanzania, children whose mothers died were more likely to move to another household and less likely to stay in school (Beegle et al., 2009; Evans and Miguel, 2007; Himaz, 2009; World Bank, 2007c). While the death of a father

10. While access to antiretroviral therapy has risen extremely rapidly over the past few years, increasing the number of HIV-positive children in school and survival rates among their caregivers, in most countries the scale-up rate is insufficient to reach universal access goals by 2010 (UNAIDS, 2009).

in Ethiopia did not significantly affect school enrolment, the death of a mother reduced enrolment among both boys and girls by around 20% and disrupted attendance by enrolled children (Himaz, 2009).

Stigmatization and institutionalized discrimination often reinforce education disadvantages associated with HIV and AIDS. In Thailand, a qualitative study found that those with HIV were denied admission to school, in violation of national laws. Educators expressed concern that other parents would react negatively to the enrolment of HIV-positive students (Save the Children UK, 2006). To some degree, discriminatory school practices hold up a mirror to society. One large household survey in India indicated that 58% of women and 43% of men from households not affected by HIV and AIDS would not send their children to a school with an HIV-positive child (Loudon et al., 2007). The same survey found that stigma was a major reason for dropout. Young children reported losing interest in their studies, becoming depressed and dropping out because of taunts by peers, while adult caregivers reported that stigma and discrimination by teachers were the major educational barrier.

One effect of stigmatization is to force HIV and AIDS underground. In a study examining the educational needs of HIV-positive learners in Namibia and the United Republic of Tanzania, every HIV-positive child interviewed cited experience of the negative consequences of disclosure and emphasized greater safety in silence (UNESCO and EduSector AIDS Response Trust, 2008). Such fears can be well founded. In Brazil and Haiti, teens infected with HIV reported experiencing violence and fighting among their peers in school as a response to their HIV-positive status (Abada-Barrerío and Castro, 2006; Loudon, 2006).

Governments' failure to respond with sufficient urgency to the threat posed by HIV and AIDS in education is often part of the problem. While there has been an increase in the number of orphaned children able to access school thanks to public policy interventions, much needs to be done. A survey of eighteen national education plans in sub-Saharan Africa that have been developed since 2005 found that just ten had specific strategies for children affected by HIV and AIDS, and that only Ethiopia, Kenya, Namibia and Rwanda included detailed integrated strategies (UNESCO-IIEP, 2009). To failures in policy planning can be added a more widespread failure by political leaders to lead public awareness campaigns aimed at challenging misperceptions and overcoming stigmatization. One policy response to stigmatization has been to protect learners by not identifying their HIV status, but this can have unfortunate results. In Namibia, it has led to an absence of information on how many learners are HIV-positive, and hence a lack of special arrangements or allowances for them (UNESCO and EduSector AIDS Response Trust, 2008).

Conclusion

Identifying the underlying causes of marginalization in education is a step towards the development of policies aimed at equalizing opportunity. Children do not choose the circumstances into which they are born. Yet the wealth of their parents, and their own gender, ethnicity or language can greatly influence their achievement in education and beyond.

This chapter has highlighted the interaction of poverty and social attitudes in creating disadvantages that limit opportunities for education, restrict mobility and perpetuate marginalization. What happens in the education systems is critical because schooling can act either as a great leveller or as a driver of disadvantage. But overcoming marginalization in education requires policies that target wider problems rooted in poverty, stigmatization and unequal power relationships.

Teens in Brazil and Haiti reported experiencing violence at school due to their HIV-positive status

There are no policy blueprints. Marginalized people across the world share many experiences in common. By the same token, the circumstances that shape these experiences are highly varied. This is true even within countries. For example, the factors that drive the marginalization in education among pastoralists in northern Kenya are very different than those driving marginalization in Nairobi's slums. Poverty is a near universal source of extreme disadvantage in education, though poverty does not operate in isolation. The poverty-related disadvantages experienced by young girls or ethnic minorities are reinforced by social attitudes that undermine self-confidence and lower the perceived value of education. These differences matter because successful interventions against marginalization have to tackle specific underlying causes that may be missed by blanket interventions.

The ultimate goal for education policy is to create an environment in which effort and talent, rather than pre-determined circumstances, determine learning achievements and life-chances. The next part of this chapter explores routes for attaining this goal. □

Levelling the playing field

Marginalized people are often conspicuous by their absence from national debates on education reform. The implicit assumption of many policy-makers is that, as national education systems become more effective, the benefits will eventually trickle down to the most disadvantaged sections of society. That assumption is flawed. Increasing public spending on education, raising average learning standards and strengthening overall accountability are necessary conditions for overcoming marginalization. But they will not be sufficient to break the cycles of marginalization documented in this Report. Reaching the marginalized will take a concerted effort to tackle the interlocking structures of disadvantage that limit opportunity. The diversity of the processes perpetuating marginalization means there are no simple panaceas or blueprints for reform. To the extent that any general conclusion can be drawn, it is that all governments can, and should, do more to put marginalization at the centre of education reform debates.

Reaching the marginalized will take a concerted effort to tackle the interlocking structures of disadvantage that limit opportunity

How can governments break the cycles of educational disadvantage that trap so many children, restricting their opportunities and fuelling marginalization in other areas? This part of the chapter identifies broad clusters of policies:

- *Make education affordable.* Governments in many countries have withdrawn formal school fees, but this is not enough. Indirect costs and informal charges continue to keep school out of reach for millions of children. Eliminating all school fees is a first step towards improving affordability. Incentives covering other costs linked to school attendance can also play a vital role in enabling marginalized children to participate in school.

- *Ensure that schools are accessible.* Distance to school remains a major barrier to education for all. This is especially true for girls because of the security risks associated with long distance from home. Classroom construction can reduce distance and improve physical accessibility to bring schools closer to marginalized people, provided governments target investment with equity in mind. Ensuring that school construction programmes prioritize remote rural areas and urban slums is key. Some marginalized groups – notably pastoralists – have been bypassed as a result of inflexible models of school provision. More flexible models, including multigrade and mobile schools, can open the doors to education.

- *Develop an inclusive learning environment.* All children deserve a good-quality education but typically those who enter school carrying the weight of disadvantage receive the worst. They are often taught by poorly trained teachers, sometimes in a language they do not understand. They often lack textbooks – and when books are available, they frequently include material that depicts negative stereotypes. Governments can address these problems by creating an environment of non-discrimination and equal opportunity. Providing incentives for skilled teachers to work in areas characterized by high levels of marginalization is a starting point. Supporting intercultural and bilingual education can strengthen achievement among disadvantaged ethnic minorities. Ensuring that teachers and schools are equipped to support children with disabilities is also important for inclusive education. Channelling extra resources and pedagogical support to 'failing' schools can benefit areas of greatest need.

- *Rights and redistribution matter.* Translating the human right to education into concrete entitlements requires action at many levels. National laws can prohibit formal discrimination and create an environment enabling greater equity. Laws are most effective when linked to political mobilization and the development of broad-based alliances to advance Education for All. In addition, governments and donors need to strengthen social protection measures, using cash transfers and risk-management interventions such as employment programmes to build the resilience of vulnerable households. National budgets can play a vital role in equalizing educational opportunities between richer and poorer people and regions. Redistributive public spending can help to narrow gaps. Conversely, failure to prioritize equity in national budgets can reinforce existing disparities.

- *'Joined-up' national strategies.* Marginalization in education is the result of interlocking deprivation. Breaking down disadvantage requires simultaneous public action across a broad front, with education interventions integrated into wider policies for social inclusion, including strategies for tackling social and cultural discrimination, and poor nutrition. In many countries progress towards more inclusive education is being held back by piecemeal, under-resourced and fragmented policy planning.

This part of the chapter starts by setting out the framework for understanding the levels of intervention required to combat marginalization. It identifies three broad layers explored in the subsequent sections: policies for improving access and affordability; the learning environment and factors influencing education quality; and the broader enabling environment for tackling marginalization in education, including poverty reduction measures and legal entitlements. The conclusion highlights the importance of joining up all aspects of these policy approaches into an integrated framework for tackling marginalization.

The analytical framework

Consider the experience of five primary school age children who are all out of school. One is a Hmong girl living in a remote hill region of the Lao People's Democratic Republic. The nearest school is a two-hour walk away and classes are taught in Lao, a language she does not understand. The second child lives a few metres from a public school under a sackcloth tent in Manila. He spends his day collecting and selling rubbish to buy food for himself and his siblings. The third is a young girl in northern Nigeria who has a brother in school but has dropped out herself because she is about to be married. The fourth, a Masai boy from Wajir in northern Kenya, tends cattle during a long trek to grazing land. In a small Brazilian town, the fifth child, who has a severe hearing impairment, does not go to school even though there are several nearby. Local teachers lack training to teach a deaf child and her parents cannot afford a hearing aid.

Each of these children experiences marginalization in education. Yet the underlying causes vary. Distance to school, the language of instruction, child labour and the affordability of education, discrimination and low expectations, and traditional cultural practices and beliefs all play a role. Disentangling the forces behind marginalization is vital, for obvious reasons. Raising teaching standards in schools in Manila will not help children excluded from those schools by poverty and child labour. Increasing the overall education budget in northern Nigeria's Kano state may not deliver the intended results if half the state's children – the female half – face restricted opportunities because of the lower value attached to their schooling by parents or practices such as early marriage. Building a new school in Wajir will not necessarily help educate the children of Masai communities whose livelihoods depend on being mobile.

One way of thinking about marginalization is to identify some of the key ingredients for overcoming it. Figure 3.29 presents these ingredients in a schematic outline.

The inclusive education triangle indentifies three broad strategies for tackling marginalization

- *Accessibility and affordability.* Proximity of schools to communities is an obvious condition for participation in education, especially for young girls, as gender disparities in many countries widen with distance. Schools also need to be affordable. Just as poverty can leave people hungry amid plentiful food, so it can lock poor children out of education even when schools are available. Public policy can ensure that children are not disadvantaged by the location or physical accessibility of classrooms or by cost barriers to education.

- *The learning environment.* Most teachers attempt conscientiously to do a good job, often in difficult circumstances. Yet millions of children face restricted opportunities to learn in an appropriate language and millions more are taught by overstretched, undermotivated,

Figure 3.29: The Inclusive Education Triangle

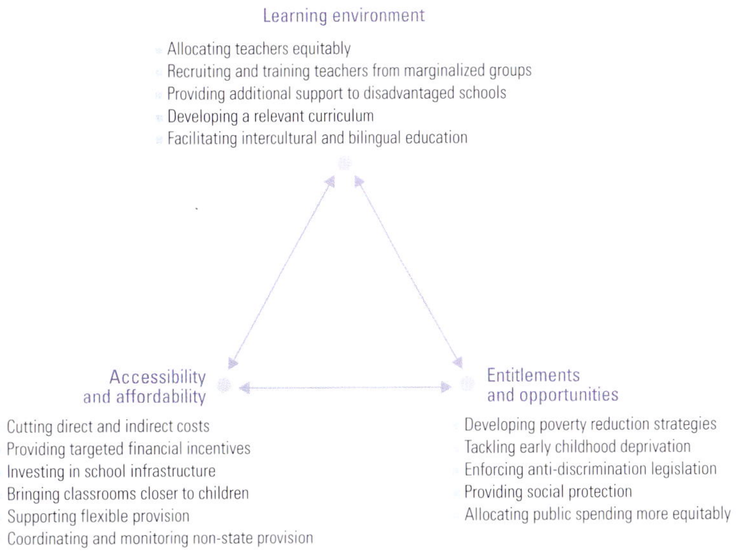

untrained teachers in overcrowded classrooms lacking basic teaching materials. While the problems are often system-wide, it is marginalized children who experience them the most acutely. Strategies to combat marginalization need to ensure that schools serving the poor attract skilled teachers who can teach in an appropriate language with cultural sensitivity, and that sufficient and relevant teaching materials are available.

- *Entitlements and opportunities.* Schools can play an important role in combating marginalization in education and beyond, but there is a limit to what they can do. Mitigating the impact of poverty on education requires measures that increase and stabilize the incomes and food security of poor households. Legal provisions can set standards and equip people with rights that unlock opportunities for education, provided they are enforceable. And public spending can help counteract the disadvantages associated with poverty. In each of these areas, actions by governments can create an enabling environment for greater equity. At the same time, political mobilization by the marginalized, or by civil society more widely, is often a powerful catalyst for change.

Evidence from rich countries shows that much of the attainment gap at the end of secondary school is predictable before age 5

Each point of the triangle needs to be viewed in relation to the others. Making primary education accessible and affordable without tackling problems in education policy is clearly not a prescription for combating marginalization. Conversely, raising the average level of learning for the majority while leaving behind a substantial minority is a route to more marginalization. The wider pattern of entitlements and enabling conditions is vital because it shapes the environment in which the abstract 'human right to education' is translated into meaningful claims and substantive rights. What ultimately matters is the development of an integrated policy response that addresses the multiple and overlapping structures of disadvantage that restrict opportunities for marginalized learners. One powerful example of such a response at a community level comes from Harlem in New York (Box 3.14).

The lesson that emerges from this section is that schools have the potential to make a great deal of difference to the lives of the marginalized. But the processes that drive marginalization start early in life – long before children enter school. As Chapter 2 makes clear, evidence from developing countries shows that malnutrition before age 2 undermines cognitive development and weakens learning achievement. Evidence from rich countries shows that much of the attainment gap at the end of secondary school is predictable before age 5, and that learning achievement is strongly associated with household wealth and parental education (Blanden and Machin, 2008; Feinstein, 2003). Schools can at best mitigate disadvantages accumulated in early childhood. That is why nutrition, maternal and child health, and early childhood care and education are central to an integrated approach for overcoming marginalization.

Box 3.14: 'Tipping points' in Harlem

Numerous initiatives have attempted to close the racial and social divide in American education, but few have achieved a breakthrough in equal opportunity. The Harlem Children's Zone Project is different. Begun in 1997, it traces its roots to 1970s community activism. The failure of social programmes to improve education, tackle unemployment and respond to the breakdown in family and community life that came with crack cocaine use and street trading prompted community leaders to explore new avenues.

In contrast to narrowly based 'school reform' models, the Harlem Children's Zone Project recognizes that poverty, gun crime and drugs are part of a wider culture of low expectations and underachievement. The intent of the project is to create a 'tipping point' by covering at least 65% of children and their parents living in the blocks where the project operates. It sees this as 'a threshold beyond which a shift occurs away from destructive patterns and towards constructive goals' (Harlem Children's Zone, n.d., p. 3).

An ambitious, integrated 'pipeline' model starts before birth with support for maternal health and parenting skills, continues through pre-school to secondary school and college, and encompasses housing, social services and nutrition. The emphasis

Expanding access and improving affordability for excluded groups

Around 72 million children of primary school age are out of school, either because they have never entered the education system or because they have dropped out. Many millions of adolescents enter adulthood without the basic learning skills they need to realize their potential. Changing this picture and accelerating progress towards the goal of universal

is on quality: kindergartens have one teacher for every four children. But scale is also expanding rapidly. From twenty-four blocks in 1997, by 2007 the Harlem Children's Zone Project had expanded to ninety-seven blocks with 7,400 children.

Education is one of the core elements. In 2004, three schools dubbed 'Promise Academies' were opened with funding from government, philanthropists and charities. Many of the children come from highly marginalized backgrounds: 10% live in homeless shelters or foster care. Management of the schools is geared towards the pupils' need for intensive support. The learning environment includes an extended school day, after-school teaching and remedial classes at weekends. Efforts have been made to recruit and retain high-quality teachers. The schools provide meals and medical care (many students come from households without health insurance).

Early results have been very promising. Researchers from Harvard University found that students who enrolled in the sixth grade gained more than a full standard deviation in math, and between one-third and one-half of a standard deviation in English Language Arts (ELA), by eighth grade: 'Taken at face value, these effects are enough to reverse the black-white achievement gap in mathematics (HCZ students outperform the typical white student in New York City and the difference is statistically significant) and reduce it in ELA. Students in the HCZ elementary school gain approximately one and three-quarters of a standard deviation in both math and ELA, closing the racial achievement gap in both subjects' (Dobbie and Fryer, 2009, p. 3).

Can the project's achievements be replicated on a national scale? The Obama administration has outlined plans to reproduce it in twenty cities under a programme of 'Promise Neighborhoods.' Rolling out such an initiative will require more than copying a ready-made blueprint. The high level of community mobilization and the innovation demonstrated by community leaders over many years cannot be readily duplicated. Moreover, expansion to poor neighbourhoods across America will require large-scale public investment during a period of acute budgetary constraints. But the prize of building on the accomplishment of the Harlem Children's Zone Project is potentially enormous. The costs of narrowing the deep divides in American education have to be assessed against the wider social, political and economic costs of allowing marginalization to diminish the potential of the country's children.

Sources: Dobbie and Fryer (2009); Harlem Children's Zone (2007, n.d.); Shulman (2009).

primary education by 2015 requires action at many levels. In most countries in danger of missing that goal, improving opportunities in education means lowering cost barriers and bringing schools closer to marginalized children.

Cutting the costs of entry to school

Many countries have laws or constitutions enshrining the right to free primary education. Yet children often are excluded from education because their parents cannot afford informal school fees. A 2005 survey by the World Bank covering ninety-three countries found that only sixteen charged no fees at all, even though the vast majority made free education nominally available (World Bank and UNICEF, 2009). In reality, free primary schooling remains the exception rather than the rule.

Recent experience powerfully demonstrates the damaging effects of charges on primary education for equity. Countries eliminating user fees for primary education have typically seen large increases in enrolment, especially among disadvantaged groups (Plank, 2007). Even in countries that have moved to eliminate formal charges, however, cost may remain a barrier, with many poor parents continuing to cite inability to afford education as the reason their children do not attend. Why has the move to 'free' education failed to remove this cost barrier for the parents of many marginalized children?

Local school-financing practices have sometimes counteracted national policies. When Ghana introduced a policy eliminating fees in 1996, there was initially only a limited increase in enrolment. The reason: schools faced with a loss of revenue introduced informal fees of their own. In response, the government introduced school grants to make up for the lost fee income – a policy intervention that led to rising enrolment levels (Maikish and Gershberg, 2008). Several other countries, including Ethiopia, Kenya, Mozambique and the United Republic of Tanzania, replaced schools' former user-fee revenue with grants. In addition to reducing pressure on household budgets, school grants give governments a vehicle for targeting disadvantaged groups and regions, for example

'I have spent days without having a full meal but never let Faruk think about leaving school.'

Faruk's mother, Bangladesh

by attaching more weight to rural areas with high concentrations of out-of-school populations (World Bank, 2009*j*).

Like all parents, those of marginalized children care about the quality of education. If fee abolition leads directly to heavily overcrowded classrooms, shortages of teaching materials and unmotivated teachers, parents may question the real value of 'low-cost' education. Evidence from a range of countries that have withdrawn fees shows that sequencing reform is vital (World Bank and UNICEF, 2009). Increasing investment in teacher recruitment and textbook provision in anticipation of rising enrolment is likely to prove more effective than action after the event. Similarly, bringing more marginalized children into school increases the importance of complementary action in other areas, including school-based nutrition programmes (World Bank, 2009*j*).

For poor girls in Cambodia, recieving a secondary school scholarship increased enrolment by 50%

Fee abolition is only a partial response to wider poverty constraints affecting demand for education. Making schools affordable to parents of the most marginalized children is likely to involve removing or cutting costs for uniforms, textbooks and other materials. In western Kenya, one study based on a randomized experiment found that students receiving a free uniform who did not previously own one were 13 percentage points more likely to attend school. For those who already owned a uniform, the estimated impact was small and insignificant (Holla and Kremer, 2009). Such evidence illustrates the need to look at the overall cost barriers confronting poor households, rather than at user fees in isolation. Experience from a broad group of countries points to the positive effects of measures supplementing the abolition of fees:

- In Nepal, the 2004–2009 education strategy included scaling up a stipend programme targeted at low-caste Dalit children. In 2003, about 384,000 out of 527,000 eligible Dalit children received stipends (World Bank, 2006*d*). Scholarships and other incentives have also been made available for girls. Another targeted grant provides a cash transfer to children from households in which no member has completed a primary education. Despite some problems in targeting, the programme appears to have helped girls and children from disadvantaged backgrounds into education (Acharya and Luitel, 2006; Research Centre for Educational Innovation and Development, 2003).

- Viet Nam has introduced a range of financial support mechanisms targeting ethnic minority students. However, school costs are still cited as a cause of children dropping out of school. Under Programme 135, a poverty reduction strategy targeting 2,100 communes with very low human development scores, the government provides children attending semi-boarding schools with a monthly stipend. Those who do not live in communes covered by Programme 135 but are poor or live in a 'commune with extreme difficulties' receive lower stipends. Everywhere, ethnic minority students receive free textbooks and notebooks (Truong Huyen, 2009).

- Several countries have targeted orphans and other vulnerable children. A programme in Mozambique provides around 3,400 orphans and other vulnerable children with vouchers to buy shoes, clothing and stationery. One study points to positive results for enrolment (Ellis et al., 2009).

Stipends at the secondary school level can be effective in counteracting marginalization in primary education. In some countries, there is evidence that parents unable to meet secondary school costs will withdraw their children from primary school before completion. An innovative programme in Cambodia attempted to forestall that decision. In a pilot scholarship programme supported by the Japan Fund for Poverty Reduction, girls who reached the final grade of primary school were eligible for grants of around $45. The cash was provided to families, conditional on their children attending secondary school. It was estimated that the programme increased enrolment among participants by around 30%. An evaluation found that enrolment effects rose with household poverty. For girls from the poorest 20% of households, enrolment increased by 50%, compared with 15% for girls in the wealthiest two quintiles (Filmer and Schady, 2008; Fiszbein et al., 2009).[11] The Bangladesh Female Secondary School Stipend Programme has also introduced wider conditions for transfers. It covers school fees and additional payments for girls who stay in school, remain unmarried to age 18 and pass exams. The stipends are credited not just with increasing secondary school enrolment by around twelve percentage points, but also with creating incentives for households to ensure that girls complete primary education (Khandker et al., 2003). Girls' primary school enrolment now exceeds that of boys.[12]

11. The pilot project, from 2002 to 2005, targeted only girls. A follow-up programme, Cambodian Education Sector Support Project – Scholarships for the Poor, targets both boys and girls with different levels of support. It has also had marked effects on enrolment and attendance (see Annex, p. 294).

12. Another programme in Bangladesh targeting primary school children from poor rural households has been less successful, partly because eligibility criteria have excluded some of the most marginalized children, including many living in slums and informal settlements as well as those attending madrasas and schools run by non-government organizations (Al Samarrai, 2008).

Bringing classrooms closer to marginalized children

Physical access to classrooms remains a major barrier to Education for All. There is no universal benchmark for the appropriate distance to school. One estimate suggests that 2 km, or a thirty-minute walk, should be viewed as an upper limit (Theunynck, 2009). However, much depends on context and circumstance. Where mountains, forests or rivers limit accessibility, even short distances can entail long journey times and high levels of risk.

Increased and more efficient public spending on classroom construction is one way to expand access. Classroom shortages inevitably increase distance to school – and many countries have acute shortages. Low-income countries in sub-Saharan Africa are currently running a deficit of around 1.7 million classrooms. To close that deficit by 2015, the number of classrooms needs to be doubled (EPDC and UNESCO, 2009). Recent estimates for ten sub-Saharan African countries that are off track for the 2015 goals suggest that the number of classrooms is growing at less than half the required rate (Theunynck, 2009).

The location of new schools and classrooms is critical for underserved groups. Too often, classroom construction programmes fail to prioritize areas and groups with greatest need. This is despite the proven benefits of greater equity. In Ethiopia, classroom construction has been a central part of the national strategy to accelerate progress towards universal primary education. Of the 6,000 schools built since 1997, over 85% are in rural areas, significantly reducing average distances to school. The out-of-school population has declined by 3 million and gender disparities have narrowed, underlining the effect of distance on demand for girls' education (UNESCO, 2008*a*).

Combining technology and community participation can help education planners identify underserved groups and areas. Some countries, including Ethiopia, have used geographic information systems to generate information on the spatial distribution of schools, their proximity to pupils' homes and geographic features such as roads, rivers and mountains (Attfield et al., 2002). Communities can supplement this information with local knowledge on the 'cultural distance' that gender, social and ethnic factors can create between schools and marginalized people. Such social mapping is often important. Assessments in India's Rajasthan state in the 1990s found that over 90% of children lived within 1.5 km of a primary school, yet enrolment rates were below 50% because social divisions, including caste, made many parents unwilling to send children to school (Govinda, 1999). This illustrates how social distance can reinforce spatial distance in marginalizing disadvantaged groups.

Children with disabilities – particularly those with visual, physical and severe mental impairments – face obvious disadvantages in negotiating the journey to school and, in many cases, in access to the classroom and other facilities, such as toilets. These disadvantages are reflected in the limited impact of school fee abolition on their enrolment. On one estimate, only one in six Kenyan children with disabilities was attending school after the fee abolition (Mulama, 2004). Difficulties with accessibility cannot readily be separated from wider factors that exclude children with disabilities from school. In many cases, parental concerns over children getting to and into school are compounded by concerns over their experiences in classrooms.

Improving access for children with disabilities requires policy interventions at many levels. Regulations on school design can play an important role in making participation in school possible. Many children with disabilities are effectively excluded from school by the absence of low-cost ramps and appropriate toilet facilities. Getting to school raises wider problems. Public transport systems in many countries are inaccessible to people with disabilities. Sparsely-populated rural areas, where distance to school is the greatest, often have no public transport at all. In urban areas, where the condition of streets often hampers mobility for people with disabilities, the absence of transport effectively prevents many children with disabilities from reaching school. Parental responses to surveys underline the importance of transport. One survey in Bangladesh found that parents of children with disabilities saw the absence of a specialized transport system from home to school in rural areas and the lack of subsidized support for rickshaw transport as major constraints (Ackerman et al., 2005). Education authorities can play a role in addressing access problems through regulations on school design, providing subsidized transport and bringing schools closer to homes.

In sub-Saharan Africa the number of classrooms needs to be doubled by 2015

Some of the most severe classroom shortages are found in areas where conflict has destroyed school infrastructure. After conflict ends, rapid reconstruction and concerted efforts to get children into school are vital. Rwanda's government backed a school rehabilitation programme with a strenuous re-enrolment campaign aimed at overcoming parental security fears and rebuilding trust. Although it took four years for enrolment to return to the levels recorded before the 1994 genocide, by 2005 access was above the level that a simple extrapolation of the trend from 1985 to 1992 would have predicted (Obura and Bird, 2009).

Adapting schools to local contexts

Understanding local context is critical to developing policies for inclusive education. Many marginalized children live in scattered communities in remote areas where low population density can significantly raise the average cost of providing schools and teachers. Household poverty and livelihood systems can also keep children out of school when families rely on children to tend cattle or help with farm work and domestic chores. Other marginalized children live in slums that are not legally recognized and may face problems linked to household vulnerability. Making schools accessible requires innovative policy responses geared towards specific circumstances.

Evidence from some countries suggests multigrade teaching can enhance access without compromising quality

In many countries, low-population density rural areas are marked by highly concentrated patterns of marginalization in education. Individual villages or groups of villages in regions such as the Andean highlands of Peru and Bolivia may have far fewer, and more widely dispersed, primary school age children than other areas. These children are likely to face longer journeys, with harsh terrain compounding the problem of distance. Attending a school in a 'neighbouring' village might involve fording streams and negotiating steep slopes. During the monsoon season in Bangladesh, children living on chars (sand islands in rivers) may have to swim or use banana-leaf rafts to get to school.

Several countries have developed 'satellite school' models aimed at addressing such problems. Schools are organized into clusters, usually consisting of a central, relatively well-resourced school and several smaller satellites. The latter may be one-room schools with one person teaching more than one grade in the same class.

In Bolivia, clusters of schools, known as *núcleos*, have been created to expand the reach of the education system into underserved highland and jungle areas. Each cluster comprises a central school, offering the full cycle of grades up to secondary school, and several satellite schools offering the first three primary grades in multigrade classes. Students and teachers can be redirected to different schools within the cluster to make coverage more even. This system has played a vital role in expanding access to education among indigenous children in highland areas. By providing instruction in Bolivia's three main indigenous languages, as well as Spanish, *núcleos* also promote bilingual and intercultural education (Giordano, 2008). The reform helped increase the public education system's coverage. For instance, in 1992, 82% of urban but only 41% of rural students completed grade 6; by 2001 it was 85% in urban areas and 74% in rural areas (Contreras and Talavera Simoni, 2003).

Satellite systems have to address difficult problems in managing progression through grades. The *núcleo* system in Bolivia aims to ensure that children complete their basic education at the *consolidador*, or central school. Another approach is to create satellite schools that provide a full primary cycle, such as those developed for remote rural communities in Burkina Faso (Theunynck, 2009). The advantage of such a system is that it allows for continuity. But does the provision of multigrade teaching across more grades potentially compromise the quality of provision?

That question is an important one. About one-third of all primary school age children in developing countries are now taught in multigrade settings (Little, 2006*b*). Evidence from some countries suggests multigrade teaching can enhance access without compromising quality. Reviews of the well-established Escuela Nueva, a multigrade system in Colombia, have found higher achievement in Spanish and mathematics than in other primary schools, controlling for other characteristics (Forero-Pineda et al., 2006). Evidence from Burkina Faso, Pakistan and Togo similarly suggests that multigrade classes can perform at least as well as single-grade schools (Little, 2006*b*). Still, not all multigrade schools are successful and much depends upon the effectiveness of institutional support mechanisms (Little, 2006*a*).

The Escuela Nueva system and, to a lesser extent, comparable programmes in Chile and Guatemala have been successful partly because they are linked to wider reforms. Research has highlighted the importance of investment in adequately trained teachers to work in a multigrade setting, the development of curricula and teaching materials that are responsive to student needs and parental concerns, and teaching approaches that encourage students to participate actively in the learning process and to work independently and creatively (McEwan, 2008). Strategies to overcome marginalization need to combine innovative multigrade teaching with support in these key areas.

In pastoral areas, problems posed by low population density are compounded by mobile lifestyles. Improving access to education for pastoralist children requires a break with traditional thinking – and an evidence-based assessment of what works. One such response has been the development of 'mobile schools' that follow the community, with teachers delivering instruction at times when children are not herding. Initiatives in both Ethiopia and Kenya experimented with mobile school programmes, supplemented by boarding schools. While these approaches have created new opportunities, they have often lacked a coherent policy framework or sufficient investment of resources (Rose, 2003; Ruto et al., 2009). Some countries are now starting to take a more integrated approach. In northern Kenya, improved political representation of arid areas has gone hand in hand with the development of broad-based strategies to overcome education marginalization. Much will depend upon the level of support, financial and political, that these strategies attract from the central government and upon the success of wider poverty reduction strategies (Box 3.15).

Improving access to education for pastoralist children requires a break with traditional thinking

Enforced mobility often comes with vulnerabilities that lead to educational marginalization. Refugees, internally displaced people and children migrating to find work in urban areas are all examples. Most children in slums wage a daily battle for survival that involves long hours working for little income.

Box 3.15: Reaching pastoralists in northern Kenya

Marked by unpredictable rainfall and unreliable food supply, along with cattle rustling and banditry, life for pastoralists in the arid lands of northern Kenya is precarious. The region's underdevelopment reinforces the daily challenges: only one district town is connected to the national electricity grid. Against this harsh backdrop, the arid lands were hardest hit by a devastating drought and famine that swept the country in 2009, killing entire herds and sending malnutrition soaring. Turkana children had to hike 30 km for water and some Turkana men abandoned their families, unable to face the shame of being unable to feed their children. Ethnic conflict rose over the last remaining pieces of fertile grazing land.

Education reforms have had a limited impact on the lives of pastoralists. In most of the rest of Kenya, fee abolition led to a surge in enrolment, but it made little difference in pastoral areas. In the North Eastern Province, fewer than 40% of children were enrolled in school in 2007, four years after fees were abolished. Pastoralists' mobile lifestyle and extreme vulnerability mean that reducing the cost of schooling alone was insufficient to enable their children to gain access to education.

To make a difference, an integrated approach to development in the region is needed, along with strategies directly aimed at providing an education relevant to the lives of pastoralists. Such an approach has not been apparent until very recently. Until the late 1990s, the north in general and pastoralists in particular were largely ignored. In education policy, the focus was on persuading pastoralists to abandon their livelihoods and settle in one place where they could more easily be provided with services. This picture has been changing with the emergence of pastoralist civil society organizations and a significant pastoralist group in Parliament – a development that has increased the voice of one of the country's most marginalized groups. The creation of a Ministry of State for the Development of Northern Kenya and other Arid Lands in April 2008 is one of the boldest statements of the government's intention to address challenges in the north more proactively.

As part of its strategy to address the development needs of the region, the new ministry was influential in developing a Nomadic Education Policy, drafted in 2008. Innovations include incorporating traditional knowledge in the curriculum, providing grants to mobile schools, establishing feeder schools within local communities, modifying the formal system to suit the nomadic calendar, recruiting teachers (particularly females) from nomadic areas through affirmative action, and using radio and mobile phones for outreach.

The problem is that the new ministry has a broad mandate with an insufficient budget. For 2009/2010, the ministry was allocated a mere 0.5% of the government budget. Without more serious financial backing, there is a real danger that the ministry's initiatives will fail.

Sources: Gettleman (2009); Ruto et al. (2009); World Bank (2009*f*).

Improving access to education for these children is often difficult, but it is not impossible. The key is to identify the children and ensure that education is provided on a flexible timetable in an accessible environment.

Targeting excluded regions and groups often involves more than the physical presence of a school. Some governments and non-government organizations have used technology in an effort to shrink distances in education. Such technology can complement teacher-student contact by being available at times when children cannot make it to school (whether in the evening or during seasons when they are needed to work) (Cambridge Distance Education Consultancy, 2009). In China, education authorities have developed a range of distance-learning models, using DVDs and satellite broadcasts to provide teaching to schools in remote rural areas. While the benefits of distance learning in primary school can be compromised by the absence of a teacher, in this case the policy was accompanied by investment in training local teachers. Large-scale evaluations in Gansu and Hubei – among the most deprived provinces in western China, with particularly low literacy rates – found improvements linked to distance learning, with most teachers reporting evidence of student stimulation (McQuaide, 2009).

Innovative programmes run by non-government organizations must be integrated into national plans

Providing a second chance to out-of-school children and adolescents

Many marginalized children and youth lack a way back into education. Adolescents who have never attended school or who dropped out early have low levels of literacy and numeracy. Many of the over 71 million adolescents estimated to be out of school are denied a second chance, often because of inflexibility in national education systems. Facilitating re-entry into education is a key strategy for empowering youth and young adults to escape poverty.

Non-government organizations often provide education that is complementary to formal schooling, and can put children and youth on a route back into the formal system. The scale of this provision is not widely recognized. One survey in sub-Saharan Africa recorded 154 programmes in 39 countries reaching 3.5 million children (DeStefano et al., 2006). While the quality of such education is highly variable, the scale of demand demonstrates that complementary education programmes fill an important gap. The more successful programmes combine flexible timing of classes with strong support for learners as well as courses and curricula geared towards relevant skills.

Re-opening the doors to education is a major challenge for education policy. Some programmes focus on building bridges between skills training and employment for marginalized youth and adults. The Jóvenes programmes in Latin America are one example (see Chapter 2). Over-age children and adolescents who have missed out on primary education have different needs. Accelerated learning programmes have been developed in several countries to provide them with opportunities to cover the primary education curriculum over a shorter period. An important requirement for both types of intervention is that they lead to recognized qualifications, allowing graduates to re-enter the formal school system or to gain meaningful employment. This means programmes run by non-government organizations must be acknowledged by governments and integrated into their national plans.

Such programmes have been beneficial in reaching various marginalized groups, from Bangladeshi nomads and street children (Box 3.16) to people in the most educationally disadvantaged region of Ghana (Box 3.17). They also play a vital role in post-conflict settings, where a generation of children may have missed out on education. Sierra Leone's post-conflict reconstruction strategy targeted children aged 10 to 16 through a programme called Complementary Rapid Education for Primary Schools. Although under-resourced, the schools in the programme brought education to thousands of children. These children performed as well as other primary schools in national tests. As a result, many participants transferred to regular primary and secondary schools, and are reported to have continued to do well (Baxter and Bethke, 2008; Johannesen, 2005).

Responding to non-state initiatives

When governments fail to provide marginalized children with an appropriate education, local communities often develop their own schools. How governments respond to such local initiatives can have an important bearing on education opportunities for marginalized groups.

In Zambia, some of the poorest communities set up their own schools after a breakdown in the national education system in the 1990s. In 2006, about one in six basic-level students were attending one of these

Box 3.16: Reaching the most marginalized in Bangladesh through floating schools and programmes for child labourers

Bangladesh has made rapid but uneven progress towards universal primary education. Previously deep gender inequalities have been eliminated in primary education and rural areas have been catching up with urban areas. Enrolment among children living in extreme poverty has been less impressive, however, and the marginalization of this group remains a barrier to universal primary education. Initiatives developed by non-government organizations, which reach over 1 million of the country's most marginalized children, provide powerful evidence that this barrier can be removed.

One example comes from the country's riverbanks. The 800,000 strong Bede, or River Gypsy, community lives on boats in groups of ten to fifteen families. The Bede, among the poorest people in the country, live off trinket selling, fishing, pearl-diving, snake-catching and traditional healing. These activities involve travel over long distances. Because they are not settled, the Bede have traditionally lacked the residency rights necessary to claim school places. Even when they do have formal rights, their mobility makes it difficult for their children to attend school regularly, so teachers are reluctant to enrol them or provide books.

Since 2006, a national non-government organization, the Gram Bangla Unnayan Committee, has provided education through twenty-one 'school boats' that follow the Bede community. Teachers are recruited from the community and given basic training. The boats provide education for two to three years, after which children living with sedentary relatives can gain admission to government primary schools.

Street children are another highly marginalized group. Recognizing the limited success of government efforts to reach these children through formal schooling, non-government organizations opened learning centres as part of the Basic Education for Hard to Reach Urban Working Children programme. In its first phase, the programme trained 346,000 urban working children aged 8 to 14 in basic literacy, numeracy and life skills. They took two-year courses that were equivalent to three years of government primary schooling. Participants were among the most deprived children in the country. One survey revealed that three-quarters of them had never been to school and that 83% of participants' families earned less than US$2 per day.

Accessibility problems were addressed by locating learning centres near children's places of work and shortening the school day to two-and-a-half hours. Few children dropped out of the programme. A remaining challenge is to find a way to enable them to enter the formal system.

Sources: Bangladesh Government (2008); Khan and Chakraborty (2008); Maksud and Rasul (2006); Nath (2009); UNICEF (2008*a*); World Bank (2008*d*).

Box 3.17: Addressing educational deprivation in northern Ghana through complementary education provision

Northern Ghana faces some of the country's most acute educational deprivation. School attendance rates in the region are among the lowest in the country and many children reach adulthood with no more than a few years of education. Parents cite distance to school, cost, seasonal labour demand and, for girls, early marriage as major barriers.

An innovative programme run by non-government organizations is attempting to provide out-of-school children in northern Ghana with a second chance. School for Life offers an intensive nine-month literacy course for children aged 8 to 14, with the aim of preparing them to re-enter primary school. Teaching schedules are designed to accommodate seasonal demands on children's time. Students are given free books and uniforms are not required, reducing the cost of attendance.

The School for Life curriculum is designed to make education meaningful to rural families who feel that formal schools fail to respect the dignity and strengthen the self-esteem of their children. Students are taught in local languages by locally recruited facilitators, many of them volunteers, who receive in-service training.

School for Life has achieved impressive results. Between 1996 and 2007, it reached around 85,000 children in eight districts, with no discernible gender gap. An evaluation in 2007 found that over 90% of students completed the course, 81% met third-grade literacy and numeracy standards and 65% entered the formal education system. Government data indicate that School for Life graduates entering formal school perform above the average in mathematics and English.

Sources: Casely-Hayford et al. (2007); Hartwell (2006); Mfum-Mensah (2009).

8,000 community schools. These schools play a vital role in providing access to education for children in slums and poor rural areas. Government support is erratic: many community schools are staffed by volunteer teachers and lack teaching materials. Yet scaling up government support could be a cost-effective strategy to combat marginalization in education (de Kemp et al., 2008; DeStefano et al., 2006). To be effective, partnerships between governments and non-state providers serving marginalized groups need to be well-defined, with governments taking responsibility for long-term financing, the provision of teaching materials and the monitoring of quality (Akyeampong, 2009).

In some countries, religious schools fill gaps in government education. Some of these schools reach highly marginalized groups and regions. In Kano state, Nigeria, which has some of the worst education indicators in sub-Saharan Africa, around 2.9 million children and youths aged 6 to 21 attend some kind of Islamic school – roughly twice the combined attendance in government and private schools. About half of these schools are community-owned schools, some of which teach the national curriculum and receive state support. Aid donors sometimes express concern over whether Islamic schools foster 'anti-Western' values. Yet these schools reach some of Nigeria's most deprived children and they are often in part a response to poor quality in the state system (Bano, 2008). Here, too, there is potential for the government to work with non-state actors to extend education opportunities in marginalized areas. Integrating these schools into the government system, and providing support by training teachers and supplying textbooks, would help ensure that their students achieved basic literacy and numeracy skills.

Translating the vision of inclusive education into practice requires creating learning environments that give priority to those who are marginalized

Private schools may also fill gaps in education. There may, however, be adverse consequences for equity (UNESCO, 2008*a*). In some cases, it can mean that the poorest slum households pay for education while free government schooling is available to those in less poor urban areas. In Kenya, the government has responded by providing capitation grants from the Free Primary Education budget to private schools willing to comply with ministry guidelines. Many schools do not comply. The government could take more responsibility for regulating these schools, but this is a difficult task, given that they often operate under the government radar. A longer-term solution would be for the government to fulfil its commitment to free primary education for all by extending its provision to slum dwellers (Oketch et al., 2008).

The learning environment

Governments across the world have signed up in large numbers to the principle of inclusive education. At the core of this idea is a compelling vision, set out in the *Salamanca Statement and Framework for Action on Special Needs Education*, of 'the need to work towards "schools for all" – institutions which include everybody, celebrate differences, support learning, and respond to individual needs' (UNESCO and Spain, Ministry of Education and Science, 1994, p. iii). Translating the vision into practice requires creating learning environments that include all children, giving priority to those who are marginalized and excluded.

The learning environment in which children participate is shaped by a vast array of factors. Parental influence, home background, student characteristics, the school and the education system as a whole all play a role. The interaction between these layers and the factors that marginalize children is quite complex. Poverty, gender, ethnicity, minority language and disability do not automatically consign children to a marginalized future, in education or beyond.

Classroom experience, the focus of this section, can help counteract disadvantage but may reinforce it. Schools that give marginalized children access to well-trained and motivated teachers, instruction in a language they are familiar with, a relevant curriculum and adequate teaching materials are powerful vehicles for combating social disadvantage. Many schools lack some or all of these ingredients. All too often, the most marginalized children are taught by the least skilled teachers in the most poorly resourced schools. Tackling this problem requires education systems and political leaders to recognize and respond to the special needs and constraints facing children who have been denied opportunities for education.

Allocating teachers to marginalized areas and schools

Well-trained teachers can help mitigate the disadvantages of marginalized children. Such children stand to gain the most from high-quality teaching, but are the least likely to receive it. The problem is not restricted to developing countries. In France, teachers in lower secondary schools belonging to Zones d'Éducation Prioritaire (ZEPs, or Priority Education Areas) are likely to have less experience than teachers in other schools and teacher turnover is much higher than the national average (Duru-Bellat, 2009). Problems are most acute, however, in poor countries with deprived areas facing acute shortages of skilled teachers.

Recruitment and deployment practices are at the heart of the problem. Many teachers, young women in particular, are understandably reluctant to move to remote areas, especially when they are characterized by high levels of poverty and lack transport, health services and other facilities. Teachers may be similarly reluctant, for career reasons, to serve in what are seen as failing schools. Experienced teachers may use their seniority to get assigned to the smallest classes (often in higher grades), leaving the largest classes, where the marginalized are at particular risk of dropping out, to the least experienced or least qualified teachers.

Changing patterns of recruitment and deployment can help overcome the problems that marginalized children face. As the following examples demonstrate, it is important to encourage people from marginalized communities to become teachers as well as to ensure that the most experienced teachers are allocated to underperforming areas and schools:

- *Recruit teachers from marginalized groups.* Recruiting from marginalized groups can promote positive identities, combat discrimination and ensure that children learn in their own language. But expanding such recruitment is not straightforward. Some countries give ethnic minorities preferential access to teacher training. This approach has achieved some success in Cambodia, which waives the grade 12 entry requirement for candidates from areas where upper secondary education is unavailable. Increasing the pool of teachers from ethnic minorities has been found to have benefits in terms of their understanding of the local culture and motivation to stay in remote areas, as well as ensuring they are able to teach effectively in the vernacular language (Benveniste et al., 2007).

- *Ensure that teachers are deployed to the schools where they are most needed.* Uneven distribution of teachers can result in shortages, particularly of qualified teachers, in the most disadvantaged regions and schools. Even in countries that allocate teachers on the basis of student numbers, teachers can find ways to avoid difficult postings. In Indonesia, which uses a national formula for teacher deployment, there are marked inequities across schools and districts. For instance, 68% of urban primary schools have too many teachers, while 66% of remote primary schools have shortages (World Bank, 2008*f*). Some governments have adopted strategies and rules aimed at achieving more equitable distribution:

  - Better access to and use of data on pupil/teacher ratios in the Philippines has helped reduce disparities in teacher deployment. Using a 'rainbow spectrum' to make disparities visible, districts are colour-coded according to pupil/teacher ratios. Making the information readily available and easily understandable has led to better channelling of new teaching positions to shortage areas and systematic transfer of vacant teaching positions from surplus to shortage areas. As a result, all 7,237 new teaching posts created in 2006 were allocated to red or black zone schools, namely those most in need (World Bank, 2006*e*; UNESCO, 2007).
  - In Eritrea, many teachers start their careers as part of their national service, which facilitates enforcement of deployment rules. Teachers are allocated at the national level to one of the country's six regions, then to schools within the region. They have no choice of location. This has resulted in a more even distribution of teachers. Average pupil/teacher ratios range from 30:1 to 53:1, with the most rural regions having the lowest ratios. However, the least experienced teachers are allocated to the most challenging schools (Mulkeen, 2009).

- *Provide financial incentives.* More equitable rules for teacher deployment may not be enough. Financial and other incentives – such as hardship or travel allowances, subsidized housing, study leave and training opportunities – are often required to encourage teachers to go to demanding schools or to areas with difficult living conditions. Incentives need to be high enough to attract good teachers. Evidence from several countries shows that the incentives offered for teaching in marginalized areas are often too limited to have much effect (Kelleher, 2008; Mulkeen, 2009; Mulkeen and Chen, 2008; UNESCO, 2008*a*). In Bolivia, teachers receive

Some countries, such as Cambodia, give ethnic minorities preferential access to teacher training

Teachers need training to challenge their attitudes to the marginalized and to equip them to effectively teach children from a diversity of backgrounds

extra pay for teaching bilingual students and working in rural areas, but on average the bilingual bonus is 0.3% of annual salary and the rural bonus 1.1% (Vegas and Umansky, 2005). Such low incentives are unlikely to deliver results. Ultimately, inducements for relocation have to be seen by well-trained and experienced teachers as adequate compensation for transfer. The more successful examples include the following:

- In the Gambia, a special allowance was introduced in 2006 to attract and retain teachers in schools more than 3 km from a main road. The allowance represents 30% to 40% of average salary. By 2007, 24% of teachers in several regions had requested transfers to hardship posts, with negligible numbers requesting transfers in the opposite direction (Mulkeen, 2009).
- In Mozambique, bonuses are aimed at attracting the most experienced teachers to remote areas. Schools are placed into four categories, from urban to the most isolated, and teachers are paid a bonus depending on school location and their qualifications. Bonuses effectively double the salary of the most qualified teachers; the least qualified receive no bonus (Mulkeen and Chen, 2008).
- In Uganda, a recent study on teacher attrition found housing to be a key factor in assuring retention, especially in rural areas. The government responded by allocating a grant for the construction of teacher housing in 2005 (Mulkeen and Chen, 2008).
- Several Latin American countries have introduced incentive packages including career development to encourage teachers to work in remote areas. For example, teachers living in isolated areas of Ecuador get not only a bonus but also priority in being granted tenure. The incentives have helped reduce disparities in pupil/teacher ratios, but have also tended to attract the least experienced teachers to remote areas (Mpokosa and Ndaruhutse, 2008).

- *Train teachers to address marginalization.* Beyond recruitment and deployment, teachers need the skills to address marginalization in the classroom. Brazil's FUNDEF programme devoted 60% of its resources to recruiting and training more teachers in poorer states. Qualified teachers helped students to avoid grade repetition and dropout, and possibly also to enter the first grade on time (Vegas, 2007).

Even experienced teachers need training to challenge attitudes to the marginalized and to equip them to teach effectively in classrooms with children from a diversity of backgrounds. This rarely happens, however; when it does, the initiative often comes from non-state groups, reflecting inability or lack of interest on the part of governments. In some cases, partnerships between state and non-state actors have emerged. In the Amazonian region of Peru, the Programa de Formación de Maestros Bilingües de la Amazonía Peruana, a teacher-training programme co-directed by the Ministry of Education and an indigenous organization, led to non-indigenous and indigenous experts cooperating to train bilingual teachers and familiarize them with indigenous culture (López, 2009).

Ability grouping seldom helps the marginalized

Classroom practices often reinforce marginalization. An example is the separation of children into 'ability' groups at an early age. Children from disadvantaged backgrounds may be more likely to be assigned to low ability groups, sometimes because of language problems. Once in a low ability group, disadvantaged learners often fall further behind. Evidence from rich countries strongly suggests that grouping children by ability early in the education cycle reduces equity and can lead to weaker overall results (Duru-Bellat, 2009; Lleras and Rangel, 2009). Research using data from the Early Childhood Longitudinal Study in the United States shows that, among African-American and Hispanic students, reading achievement gains made in the first grade are lower for students who are assigned to low-ability groups than for students with similar characteristics who are taught in non-grouped classes (Lleras and Rangel, 2009). Similarly, research in France shows that studying in a mixed-ability class helps weaker students and that removing streaming has a strong equalizing impact on achievement (Duru-Bellat, 2009).

Tracking, or separating children into different types of school (such as vocational versus general education) according to academic ability at the secondary level, also has adverse consequences. A study based on data from the TIMSS, PIRLS and PISA assessments, covering forty-five mostly OECD countries, finds that the effect of early tracking accounts for one-quarter of the 'equality gap' between the most inequitable and most equitable country, and is also associated with lower mean performance (Hanushek and Wößmann, 2006). In Germany, early tracking seems to be a factor behind the country's large education inequalities and particularly the marginalization of Turkish youth (Crul, 2007). Recognizing the equity implications of tracking, many European countries adopted a unified secondary school system in the 1960s and 1970s. There is evidence that the move weakened the link between family background and educational attainment, with associated benefits for those who would have been sent to the lower tracks (Brunello and Checchi, 2007).

The effects of academic segregation and tracking are widely debated. Evidence from developing countries is both fragmented and limited. However, there are strong equity grounds for planners in rich and poor countries alike to avoid early tracking and to treat academic selection within schools with caution. Both can reinforce exclusion.

Targeting financial and pedagogical support to disadvantaged schools

One way of targeting marginalized children is to target their schools. Targeting criteria can include location, ethnolinguistic composition or the share of poorly performing students, with governments using a range of regulatory instruments and financial mechanisms to raise standards. More intensive support to teachers and school heads, more specialized pedagogical support to students and more per student financing are among the options. One targeted programme in Uruguay is credited with improving learning outcomes in some secondary school grades by up to 30% by combining financial and pedagogical support (Cerdan-Infantes and Vermeersch, 2007; Crouch and Winkler, 2008).[13] In Chile, the 900 Schools Programme provided intensive support to the worst-performing 10% of elementary schools by training teachers, gearing courses to students lagging behind or with behavioural problems and providing textbooks. Evaluations have shown that grade 4 test scores improved significantly for students in the programme, mainly as a result of the introduction of more appropriate pedagogical practices in the classroom and facilitation of a cooperative environment within schools (García-Huidobro, 2006).

Not all school-based targeting has produced such positive results. For almost three decades French governments have given additional support to Zones d'Éducation Prioritaire serving disadvantaged students. In 2008, around 16% of secondary school students were in schools with ZEP status. These schools have more teachers, so class size is lower and students receive additional support. In addition, ZEP teachers receive higher pay. Yet several studies have found only a limited impact on student achievement (Duru-Bellat, 2009). Why have ZEP schools not achieved better results? One reason is that the additional resources are spread too thinly over a large number of schools, so class size is reduced by only two students on average. Schools have also had trouble attracting experienced teachers (Moisan, 2001). High teacher turnover makes it difficult to organize strategies that could improve achievement (Duru-Bellat, 2009). A comparable programme in England (United Kingdom), Excellence in Cities, produced more positive results, yet it too fell short of expectations (Box 3.18).

Experience from programmes targeting disadvantaged schools shows that they can make a difference provided the level of additional financing is sufficient and they are accompanied by incentives to attract and retain qualified teachers.

Learning in an appropriate language and through a relevant curriculum

Inclusive education for ethnic and linguistic minorities requires schools that offer a relevant curriculum in an appropriate language. Sitting in a primary school classroom listening to a teacher providing instruction in a language they do not understand is a short route to marginalization. Bilingual education facilitates learning in a familiar language and equips students with the national language skills they need to make the transition to secondary school and, eventually, to employment and full participation in social and political life (Alidou et al., 2006; Dutcher, 2004; UNESCO Bangkok, 2008).

Evidence from several countries in sub-Saharan Africa demonstrates that bilingual education can improve learning achievement. One example comes from the Écoles Bilingues created in Burkina Faso in the mid-1990s. After five years of instruction in local language and French, 85% of pupils in these schools successfully passed the primary school examination in 2002, compared with a national average of 62% (Alidou et al., 2006). In Zambia, the successful introduction on a pilot basis of local language teaching in the late 1990s was followed in 2002 by reforms that introduced seven local languages into primary school education (Alidou et al., 2006; Linehan, 2004). Ethiopia has gone

Evidence from several countries in sub-Saharan Africa demonstrates that bilingual education can improve learning achievement

13. Learning assessments were used to identify weaker schools. Teachers in selected schools received intensive training together with on-going support throughout the year and were paid an incentive. The school timetable was lengthened from half a day to a full day.

Box 3.18: Achieving 'Excellence in Cities'? A targeted intervention to support deprived urban schools in England (United Kingdom)

England's Excellence in Cities programme was aimed at improving pupil achievement in deprived urban schools. Introduced on a pilot basis in 1999, it was extended nationally until 2006. The programme reached in particular children from non-white backgrounds, those with English as an additional language, those entitled to free school meals and children identified as having special education needs.

Eligible schools received higher than average support per student. In 2005, this amounted to £120 per pupil per year, only 4.4% above the average allocation. Institutional support included four core elements, although specific interventions varied by setting. Local partnerships encouraged schools to work together in developing needs assessments and strategies. Learning Support Units assisted students failing to achieve academically and experiencing behavioural problems. Mentors were provided to children making slow progress in learning. A separate part of the programme sought to identify and support 'gifted and talented' children.

Evaluations revealed some positive outcomes. The greatest impact was on mathematics achievement at age 14. Within the most deprived schools, however, the impact was greatest for children previously achieving medium and higher scores. No impact was found for students using support units and students with a mentor at age 14 made less progress than those without. Pupils designated as 'gifted and talented' registered higher levels of achievement, but there was no evidence of an Excellence in Cities effect.

One possible explanation why this programme failed to achieve stronger outcomes is that insufficient additional finance was provided. Another factor is that schools in deprived urban areas, including those covered by Excellence in Cities, were finding it increasingly difficult to recruit and retain experienced teachers. More fundamentally, it appears that the initiative failed to override the wider structures of disadvantage in the home and beyond that push children towards educational marginalization.

Sources: Vignoles (2009); Kendall et al. (2005).

Schools have a vital role to play in addressing the social attitudes that devalue some cultures

further than many countries, seeking to combine mother tongue instruction with Amharic and English in grades 1 to 8. One recent review of learning assessment data concluded that 'those regions with stronger mother tongue schooling have higher student achievement levels at Grade 8 in all subjects, including English' (Heugh et al., 2006, p. 6). In Mali, bilingual schools have been associated with large declines in dropout and repetition (World Bank, 2005*c*).

Overcoming underlying causes of marginalization associated with language requires more than bilingual provision. Language is wrapped up with cultural identity and schools have a vital role to play in addressing the social attitudes that devalue some cultures. That is why education reform in some Latin American countries has sought to combine intercultural and bilingual education. In Bolivia, reforms that started in the mid-1990s introduced intercultural and bilingual education on a national scale for the three most widely used indigenous languages. Bilingual teaching expanded rapidly, from 75,896 pupils in 1997 to 192,238 in 2002, or 11% of all primary school pupils (Sichra Regalsky, n.d.). Alongside this change, curriculum reforms led to the development of courses and textbooks that attach more weight to the country's multicultural history and the role of indigenous peoples. In other countries, intercultural and bilingual education has suffered from poor design and weak implementation, with intercultural education receiving particularly limited attention. In Peru, which pioneered the approach in the region, it is largely limited to indigenous communities in remote rural areas, and many nominally intercultural and bilingual schools offer no teaching in indigenous languages (Cueto et al., 2009).

Education systems can be instrumental in overcoming marginalization arising from language difficulties. The starting point is to align the rules governing education with broader principles of inclusion. Many countries have not yet done this. In the Lao People's Democratic Republic, the constitution forbids discrimination between ethnic groups and emphasizes the importance of expanding education in ethnic areas. Yet it also establishes Lao as the official language, including of instruction in school – an arrangement that arguably discriminates against children from the 27% of the population that does not have Lao as the mother tongue (Benveniste et al., 2007). Legal recognition of the entitlement to be taught in a familiar language is an important principle still lacking in many countries.

Delivering effective bilingual education requires the development of institutional capacity to train bilingual teachers. This is an area in which national targets are often delinked from public spending allocations and a longer-term strategy for change. One reason Ecuador has been able to deliver strong bilingual teaching is that it has established five specialized teacher-training colleges. Similarly, Bolivia has created three indigenous language universities to support bilingual training (López, 2009).

Children often enter classrooms weighed down by low self-esteem and facing low expectations from teachers. Schools can play an important role in changing this situation. Having teachers from a marginalized community can help widen children's horizons and raise their ambitions. And teachers themselves can be trained to understand the problems faced by ethnic minorities. The Australian Government has set ambitious targets for overcoming disparities between Aboriginal children and the rest of the population. One is to halve the gap in reading, writing and numeracy within a decade. Local initiatives provide pedagogical and curriculum support to address marginalization within the classroom. A pilot programme, Deadly Ways to Learn, has sought to build respect for Aboriginal languages (Box 3.19).

Curriculum reform and intercultural education are not just about reaching the marginalized. They are also about combating marginalization by challenging the stereotypes and the invisibility that sustain it. Textbooks can reinforce gender, racial and ethnic stereotypes that narrow the horizons of many children. Intercultural education has a key role to play in building respect for different cultures, combating prejudice, raising awareness about social inequalities and fostering debate (Luciak, 2006).

Reaching children with disabilities

Rules, attitudes and systems that are unresponsive to the needs of children with disabilities often deny these children an opportunity for education. Excluding children with disabilities restricts their choices, making it more likely that they will live their adult lives in poverty, and has wider costs for society. No country can afford an education system that limits the potential of millions of children to contribute to social, cultural and economic life.

Ecuador has been able to deliver strong bilingual teaching by establishing five specialized teacher-training colleges

Box 3.19: Promoting respect for Aboriginal languages in Australia

Aboriginal children in Australia face language problems at school that had escaped official recognition until recently. The 2006 census indicated that about 11% of the indigenous population aged 5 to 19 speaks an indigenous language at home. The rate rises to 17% in remote Australia and 58% in very remote Australia. The shares are likely to be greater still for Aboriginal English, which many consider a dialect separate from the Standard Australian English taught in primary schools, with a distinctive grammar and vocabulary. While most Aboriginal children enter school speaking English, they often have no idea that their language is different until teachers tell them that it is wrong or inappropriate.

Language problems go beyond the classroom. Aboriginal languages have often been seen as inferior and subjected to ridicule, reflecting wider prejudices about culture, lifestyles and ability to learn. Language problems have often made it difficult for Aboriginal children to understand lessons, absorb information and realize their potential in tests. The result has been a vicious circle of underachievement, with teachers often mistaking a language problem for a learning difficulty.

The Deadly Ways to Learn programme is an attempt to change the ways teachers view Aboriginal languages. It began as a pilot project in fourteen government, private and Catholic schools across rural and urban Western Australia. The name is a play on 'deadly', which Aboriginals use in the same way Standard Australian uses 'great'. The project included the preparation of books such as *Deadly Ways to Teach* and *Talking Deadly* to introduce teachers to the culture, identity and history that inform Aboriginal language. Aboriginal education officers provide support and guidance to teachers in the selected schools. Curriculum and textbook reforms are also involved.

The programme highlights the importance of all students in Australia receiving an education that is sensitive to the history, culture and language of indigenous Australians, and that also takes into account the backgrounds of people from other minority groups. Schools have to become more effective in promoting respect, tolerance and multiculturalism, and in combating the prejudices children bring to school.

Source: Biddle and Mackay (2009).

‘We welcome children with disabilities now because we know that they have the same right to education as the others.’

Teacher, Nicaragua

Governments across the world have recognized that inclusive education for people with disabilities is a human rights imperative. The Convention on the Rights of Persons with Disabilities, which came into force in 2008, has strengthened the entitlements and rights of those with disabilities. It requires governments to ensure that people with disabilities have access to 'an inclusive, quality and free primary education and secondary education on an equal basis with others in the communities in which they live' (United Nations, 2008. Article 24, para. 2b). As of September 2009, seventy countries had ratified the convention.

Putting the principles of inclusive education into practice requires action at many levels, starting with information. Most developing countries have poor data on the number of children with disabilities or the incidence of specific impairments. Government estimates are often inconsistent, reflecting not only problems in monitoring and recording but also, in many cases, the invisibility of people with disabilities and the indifference of political leaders (USAID, 2005). Some countries are working actively to strengthen the monitoring of disability. One example comes from the United Republic of Tanzania, where a 2008 survey provided a detailed profile of the prevalence, distribution and pattern of impairments across the country. It found marked regional disparities and a higher incidence of disability in rural areas (United Republic of Tanzania Government, 2009).

Approaches to reaching people with disabilities vary. Many governments, parents and groups representing them continue to view special schools as the most viable option (Lang and Murangira, 2009). One survey in Uganda found that disability groups and parents favoured this approach partly out of concern about overcrowding and poor resourcing in standard schools (Lang and Murangira, 2009). In some cases, children with severe impairments do need education in specialized institutions. However, special schools can reinforce social exclusion, denying children with disabilities the opportunity to interact with their peers who do not have disabilities, reinforcing stereotypes and segmentation in the process.

Integrating children with disabilities into the standard education system is a preferred policy option because it can break down the segregation that reinforces stereotypes. But integration is not a panacea. Children with severe disabilities may require highly specialized support. Moreover, integrating children with disabilities into poorly resourced, overcrowded schools with restricted access to toilets and other facilities is not a prescription for inclusive education, especially when teachers are not equipped to meet their needs. Placing deaf children in schools where none of the teachers can communicate in sign language will do little to alleviate their disadvantages. And very few schools in the poorest countries, or even in middle-income countries, have access to Braille textbooks or teachers able to teach Braille. It is therefore critical that moves towards integration are part of a broader strategy encompassing teacher training, school financing and other measures.

Several countries are developing education systems that are more responsive to the needs of children with disabilities. The Lao People's Democratic Republic has a network of 539 schools – three for each district in every municipality and province – that teach children with disabilities alongside their peers and provide specialized support. The schools give children with special needs opportunities to learn in an inclusive environment, partly through investment in specialized teacher training. The experience accumulated through the programme is informing wider school reforms (Grimes, 2009). In South Africa, the focus has shifted from special schools to inclusive education in mainstream schools. Authorities have to identify the level of support required by individual learners with disabilities (South Africa Department of Education, 2005; Stofile, 2008). Research in Eastern Cape, one of the poorest provinces, found that inclusive education produced significant gains, ranging from improved physical access to support for specialized teaching practices and increased admission of learners with disabilities (Stofile, 2008).

Non-government organizations have played an important part and in many poor countries are the primary source of education for children with disabilities. Through active engagement with children with disabilities, their parents and education authorities, such groups are producing results that demonstrate what is possible. In 2003, a Bangladeshi non-government organization, BRAC, established a pre-school and primary education programme aimed at increasing participation by children with mild special needs. Training teachers, providing equipment, adapting the curriculum and improving physical access, it had reached about 25,000 children by 2006 (Ryan et al., 2007).

Some non-government organizations and governments, including those of Uganda and the United Republic of Tanzania, have supported 'itinerant teaching' approaches, which enable specialized teachers in central primary schools to reach a larger group of pupils in satellite schools, and support and train teachers (Lynch and McCall, 2007).

Several countries are also attempting to build links between existing special institutions and mainstream schools, with the specialized schools providing learning materials and aids, in-service teacher training and support personnel. In Ethiopia, with the support of the non government organization Handicap International, a school for deaf students operates as both a special school and a resource centre, supporting education for deaf learners in other schools and the development of sign language (Lewis, 2009).

These experiences demonstrate the potential for scaling up local initiatives, but governments need to develop national plans to extend inclusive education for children with disabilities, including detailed targets, strategies for improving access and learning achievement, and comprehensive plans for providing financing and training teachers. The starting point for such a plan is a credible needs assessment based on a national survey of the prevalence of disability.

Entitlements and opportunities

Education systems can do a great deal to address the inequalities that restrict opportunity for children from disadvantaged groups. They can make schools more affordable and accessible, create conditions for effective learning, and act as a vehicle for changing attitudes and beliefs that stigmatize children and corrode self-confidence. But prospects for greater equity in education ultimately depend on what happens to children beyond school, through the social and economic structures that perpetuate marginalization.

This section looks at the interaction between education systems and policies in other sectors. It concentrates on two thematic areas. The first concerns the role of laws, norms and rules in empowering marginalized people. Legal instruments, international as well as national, can enhance equity not just by setting standards for public policy, but also by enabling marginalized people to claim entitlements. Political mobilization by the marginalized and other civil society groups is another way of broadening rights-based claims.

The second area is redistributive finance. Many children are marginalized in education because their families are poor and particularly vulnerable to external shocks, such as drought or economic crisis. The geographic and historical factors underlying regional disparities also limit opportunity. In many cases, the poverty and economic differences that lead to marginalization in education are linked to unequal power relationships and to disparities in financing. Redistributive finance can help redress disadvantages associated with poverty and regional inequality. In particular, social protection can be instrumental in making education more affordable and less susceptible to the economic shocks that pull many poor children out of school.

Enforcing rights and laws

Concerns with equity and fairness inform ethical debates worldwide, crossing political, religious and moral divides. The United Nations Charter encapsulates those concerns in its commitment to universal human rights. Legal institutions and codes enshrine equity in common law traditions (Kritzer, 2002). And political movements for social justice mobilize around agendas emphasizing equal opportunity, non-discrimination and fair distribution of resources. The combined weight of international human rights agreements, laws and political mobilization can act as a powerful catalyst for overcoming marginalization in education.

Political mobilization by the marginalized and other civil society groups is another way of broadening rights-based claims to education

The Universal Declaration of Human Rights remains the foundation for international human rights entitlements. The contemporary human rights regime operating under United Nations auspices comprises a broad array of instruments, many of which set standards for rights in education. These instruments collectively form a comprehensive framework for extending opportunities to children facing exclusion or discrimination in education on the basis of gender, race, ethnicity, language or poverty (see Annex, p. 292).

International conventions and wider human rights instruments set norms, define shared principles and establish an institutional framework for advancing broad-based civil, political, social and economic rights. Principles of international law are often embedded in national legal codes and constitutions. Yet more could be done to use international human rights agreements to empower the marginalized. Ratification of United Nations conventions often fails to lead to action that helps the marginalized. Part of the problem is that the committees overseeing the conventions have for the most part failed either to hold governments to account or to provide transparent and public assessments of national policies. The Committee on the Rights of Persons with Disabilities, the independent body of experts overseeing the new convention, needs to provide a more robust defence of human rights entitlements.

India now legally requires states to provide free education

National legal systems have played a crucial role in addressing equity and marginalization in education. A landmark ruling in the development of civil rights in the United States was the 1954 decision in *Brown* v. *Board of Education*. The Supreme Court determined that laws separating children of different races into different schools violated the equal protection clause of the American constitution. The principles applied in this case were subsequently extended to challenge segregation in other areas. *Brown* thus served as a milestone in the struggle of African-Americans to gain equal civil and political rights.

Recourse to law offers marginalized groups an opportunity to contest discriminatory and inequitable practices. As was the case with *Brown*, legal rulings can have wider importance because of the general principles they establish. To take one example, the European Court of Human Rights has ruled that the Czech Republic's treatment of Roma children is not legal because the policies amount to de facto segregation (Box 3.20). In the United States, education campaigners have mounted legal challenges aimed at securing greater equity in the distribution of public finance, along with wider institutional reforms (Box 3.21).

Both instances illustrate the importance of legal entitlements that can be used to hold governments accountable. Many countries' constitutions include the right to free, non-discriminatory education for all, but constitutional principles are not always enforceable. Article 45 of India's constitution mentions 'free and compulsory education for all children' up to 14 years but this 'directive principle' could not be enforced in court. The Right of Children to Free and Compulsory Education Act adopted in 2009, however, now legally requires states to provide free education to children aged 6 to 14 and reserves 25% of private primary school places for disadvantaged children (*Economic and Political Weekly*, 2009; India Ministry of Law and Justice, 2009).

The entitlement to a formal identity is a critical asset for achieving greater equity in education. The Convention on the Rights of the Child requires all signatories to guarantee the formal identity of children through birth registration. Yet UNICEF

Box 3.20: Roma children's right to education – using the law to challenge the state

The European Court of Human Rights has ruled on several cases in which governments have been accused of violating the education rights of Roma children. Echoing themes raised in *Brown* v. *Board of Education*, the court has applied the principle of non-discrimination to cases of segregation.

Roma children across Europe are often assigned to 'special schools' with little attention to their education needs. Cultural bias and discrimination by teachers and education authorities is widespread. In *D. H. and others* v. *the Czech Republic* the court was asked to pass judgment on a case brought by eighteen Czech nationals of Roma origin living in the Ostrava region of the Czech Republic who had been assigned to schools for children with learning difficulties. Represented by the European Roma Rights Centre, the plaintiffs argued that the assignment was discriminatory and therefore contravened the European Convention on Human Rights. Evidence was presented that 56% of the children enrolled in special schools in Ostrava were Roma, and that half of all Roma children attended such schools compared with less than 2% of non-Roma children.

In 2007 the court ruled that such statistics, although not completely reliable, established a presumption of indirect discrimination. This shifted the burden of proof to the defendant, who failed to show that the difference in treatment had an objective and reasonable justification unrelated to ethnic origin. The court ruled that the assessments through which Roma children were selected for special schools were flawed, notably in failing to consider linguistic and socio-economic conditions.

How successful was the case in addressing Roma marginalization? The trial provided a focal point for Roma and wider human rights groups and the judgment established an important principle, but the European Roma Rights Centre has claimed that the Czech authorities have done little since to address segregation.

Sources: de Beco and Right to Education Project (2009); European Roma Rights Centre (2008).

Box 3.21: Recent legal challenges to educational marginalization in the United States

Education groups in the United States have taken to the courts to address a wide range of concerns. The results have been mixed.

- In *Campaign for Fiscal Equity, Inc.* v. *State of New York*, plaintiffs claimed the state's school finance system underfunded the New York City public schools, thereby denying students their constitutional right to the opportunity for a sound basic education. Evidence was presented that areas with high poverty, learners with disabilities and large numbers of students learning English faced special problems. After ten years of proceedings, the courts finally found in favour of the plaintiffs. In 2007, the New York State Legislature enacted the Education Budget and Reform Act, increasing education funding by an unprecedented amount and establishing transparency and accountability measures for the distribution of funds and school finance reform.
- *Antoine et al.* v. *Winner School District*. This case involved a class action lawsuit brought by the American Civil Liberties Union on behalf of Native American students in South Dakota. Among other issues, the suit charged that the school district disproportionately targeted Native American students for disciplinary action and maintained an educational environment hostile to Native American families. In 2007, a federal court approved a settlement requiring the district to undertake institutional reforms, including hiring a full-time ombudsperson, nominated by the Native American community, to serve as liaison with the community and work with school officials, especially on disciplinary issues. Authorities also agreed to provide training for teachers on 'unconscious racial bias and educational equity', and to include Native American themes in the curriculum.
- Other cases with less positive outcomes include *Horne* v. *Flores*, in which the Supreme Court in June 2009 reversed a federal court decision upholding minimum standards and necessary resources for the education of English-language learners in Arizona primary schools, which have a very large population of Latino students.

Sources: Campaign for Fiscal Equity (2009); Child Rights Information Network (2009); Orfield and Gándara (2009).

estimates that 51 million births per year go unregistered (UNICEF, 2007c). The lack of registration means parents and children may not have the documentation they need to claim a place in school, establish an entitlement to stipends or votes, or seek legal redress. Failure to register births can also mean the most marginalized children are bypassed in national statistics, rendering them invisible to policy-makers.

Several governments have demonstrated that registration gaps can be closed. In 2009, Burkina Faso initiated a one-year programme aimed at registering 5 million people, most of them women and children, by providing free birth certificates (Integrated Regional Information Networks, 2009). Furnishing documentation does not have to be expensive. Senegal's drive to supply modern identity cards to all citizens over 15 is estimated to have cost just US$0.61 per recipient (Levine et al., 2008).

Legal instruments can also make a difference for the millions of young girls every year who face having their education disrupted or terminated by early marriage. By one 2005 estimate, almost half of South Asian females aged 15 to 24 were married before age 18. Poverty, tradition and unequal power relationships between men and women all play a part in early marriage (Levine et al., 2008). These issues have to be addressed on many fronts, but legal prohibition of early marriage, coupled with incentives to keep girls in school and campaigns to change attitudes, can establish norms and a basis for legal recourse.

Wider political mobilization is important

Legal provisions cannot be considered in isolation. *Brown* v. *Board of Education* was the culmination of a decade-long struggle by African-Americans and sympathetic whites against segregation and other discriminatory laws. The legal principles that the Supreme Court laid down were a landmark. But it was the civil rights movement that made the ruling such a powerful force for change. Political mobilization, involving the marginalized and wider social movements, has been essential in reforming laws and rules on education.

Political mobilization against marginalization can become part of a wider movement. One striking example comes from Bolivia, whose education system systematically reinforced subordination of indigenous people. The 1994 Education Reform Law helped establish indigenous people's right to learn in their own language and brought multiculturalism into the curriculum. Education reform in turn played a role in political processes that brought an indigenous political leader to power in 2005. Reforms have seen the strengthening of Indigenous Education Councils, which held their own congress

Legal instruments can make a difference for the millions of young girls every year who have their education disrupted by early marriage

in 2004 and have submitted proposals aimed at broadening and strengthening multiculturalism in Bolivia's schools (Gamboa Rocabado, 2009; Howard, 2009; López, 2009; Luykx and López, 2007).

By helping poor people manage risk, social protection programmes can broaden opportunities in education

The Bolivian experience draws attention to a broader feature of the interaction between politics and law in combating marginalization in education. Political mobilization is important because it gives a voice to social groups facing discrimination and stigmatization. In New Zealand, the *kōhanga reo* language movement provided a social, political and cultural focal point for empowerment of Māori people. Political mobilization has contributed to development of a more multicultural education system, which in turn has extended opportunities for Māori children (Box 3.22). In Bangladesh, a national non-government organization called Nijera Kori ('We do it ourselves') has helped landless labourers, primarily women, strengthen their ability to claim rights and entitlements (Chronic Poverty Research Centre, 2008).

Political mobilization can also pose risks. The marginalized are not a homogenous group, and political parties, social movements and non-government organizations take up their problems unevenly. In India, the rise of political parties representing low-caste groups in northern states has been described as a 'silent revolution' (Jaffrelot, 2003, p. 10). Yet that revolution has done little to address poor schooling for low-caste children, suggesting that political priorities have been in other areas (Mehrotra, 2006). Some highly marginalized groups have a weak voice even within broad-based civil society lobbies seeking improved access to education. The rural poor, ethnic minority women, children with disabilities, slum dwellers and children in conflict zones are groups whose causes have not been widely or effectively taken up.

Social protection: conditional cash transfers and beyond

Household poverty is one of the most potent factors in education marginalization. If a poor family is hit by a disaster such as a drought, a flood, unemployment or a serious illness, it may have no choice but to take children out of school. By helping poor people manage risk without compromising long-term welfare, social protection programmes can also broaden opportunities in education.

Such programmes take many forms. They range from cash transfers to employment-based safety nets and interventions to support nutrition. In addition to reducing destitution, such programmes

Box 3.22: New Zealand's Māori Renaissance

New Zealand's *kōhanga reo* movement has demonstrated what a powerful force indigenous language revitalization can be, not only for education but also for social cohesion.

In the 1970s, the Māori language was on the edge of extinction. A grassroots movement arose to save the language by educating a new generation in total-immersion 'language nests' (from which the movement takes its name). Today it is a national institution widely credited with sparking the language's revival and fuelling a powerful assertion of Māori identity in almost all walks of national life.

The concept is simple. Māori under age 6 get their pre-school education in a community- and family-based environment where only Māori is spoken. They spend their early years surrounded by the culture and values of their people. *Kōhanga reo* are typically found in church halls, schools and *marae*, traditional Māori community centres. Like many social movements, this one started small. It was begun in 1981 by the government's Department of Māori Affairs but grew quickly as a grassroots, mostly volunteer-run movement. Thirteen years later there were 800 *kōhanga reo* catering for 14,000 children.

With their ethos of self-help and commitment to continuity across generations, *kōhanga* reo became a source of inspiration for young Māori parents, many of whom could not speak their ancestral language. The movement nurtured a generation of bilingual Māori speakers, with alumni numbers estimated today at 60,000. In 2008, one-quarter of all Māori children enrolled in early childhood programmes were in *kōhanga reo*.

As graduating Māori speakers turned 5 and started school, they generated demand for Māori immersion schools (*kura kaupapa*). Today, there are sixty-eight *kura kaupapa* with 6,000 students. Year 11 Māori students in immersion schools have recorded significantly better achievement rates than their Māori peers in English-medium schools.

Kōhanga reo have not solved the marginalization in education that many Māori children experience. Māori youth are still twice as likely as their non-Māori counterparts to leave school with no qualification. But the movement has played a crucial role in challenging discrimination and forging a more multicultural national identity.

Sources: Te Kōhanga Reo National Trust (2009); New Zealand Ministry of Education (2008*a*, 2008*b*).

can create incentives supporting children's education, health and nutrition. They can be targeted not just at the very poor, but also at the most marginalized groups or regions.

Cash transfer programmes have grown enormously over the past decade. Many of these programmes are conditional on specific behaviour, such as keeping children in school and attending health clinics. In some countries, including Brazil and Mexico, nationwide social assistance programmes transfer between 1% and 2% of national income to targeted households. In other countries, conditional cash transfer programmes are more localized and often project-based. The degree to which education figures in transfer conditionality and support varies. Some social protection programmes provide direct support for education, including stipends, bursaries, fee waivers and funding for transport and books (Grosh et al., 2008); (see previous section). In other cases, the education benefits associated with social protection are incidental, resulting from employment creation, nutrition programmes or other measures that enable households to get through difficult periods.

Comparisons have to be made with some caution because of data constraints, and differences in evaluation methodology and in the programmes themselves. Even so, evaluations of social protection programmes point to wide-ranging positive effects (see Annex, p. 294).

Evaluations of social protection programmes have documented a range of positive effects, albeit with marked variation across countries and groups. In Mexico, Oportunidades has had a significant impact on children making the transition from primary to secondary school, especially in rural areas (Fiszbein et al., 2009). Nicaragua's Red de Protección Social was targeted at children aged 7 to 13 who had not yet completed grade 4 of primary school. Evaluation results indicated a thirteen percentage point increase in school enrolment, with the extreme poor registering the most marked gains (Villanger, 2008). Employment guarantee programmes have also delivered results, often in contexts marked by deep poverty and acute vulnerability. Ethiopia's Productive Safety Net Programme is an example. Evaluations suggest that around 15% of cash payments have gone to education, while half of beneficiary households report being able to keep children in school longer as a result of the transfers (Slater et al., 2006) (Box 3.23).

Social protection is not a simple antidote to marginalization. Levels of poverty, financing capacity and institutional factors have a bearing on the type of social protection intervention likely to deliver results in various contexts. The cost and effectiveness of any programme will be shaped by factors such as:

- *the scale of transfer;*
- *terms of the transfer;* and
- *targeting of beneficiaries.*

The scale of transfer. Transfer levels vary considerably. One survey found that transfers ranged from around 8% to 23% of the national poverty line in Latin America and from 5% to 30% in sub-Saharan Africa (Yablonski and O'Donnell, 2009). Large-scale conditional cash transfer programmes in Brazil and Mexico have had a marked effect on poverty partly because the money they provide represents a significant increment in the income of the very poor. Ethiopia's Productive Safety Net Programme boosts child education and reduces child labour when the transfers to households are sufficiently large.

Half of beneficiary households in Ethiopia keep children in school longer as a result of the Productive Safety Net Programme

When it comes to supporting poor and vulnerable children, more is clearly better. But policy-makers also have to consider the marginal benefit of increasing transfers and the potential trade-off between reaching more people and providing larger transfers. In the Cambodia Education Sector Support Project scholarship programme, the 25% of students deemed most at risk of dropping out received US$60 and the group next most at risk US$45. Comparing beneficiaries with non-beneficiaries, an evaluation found that while the US$45 transfer significantly increased the probability of a girl being in school, the additional US$15 had a modest additional effect (Filmer and Schady, 2009). In other words, in this case there were diminishing marginal returns to the investment.

Terms of the transfer. Many social protection programmes provide cash transfers to create incentives for behavioural change. To put it crudely, parents get paid for keeping children in school, taking them to health clinics and presenting them for weighing at nutrition centres. The size of transfer influences the strength of the incentive created by this conditionality. Giving transfers to women can result in a higher share of the money being directed towards children – especially girls – than may be the case when men receive the transfers (Kabeer, 2005).

Box 3.23: Ethiopia – Productive Safety Net Programme boosts children's education

Ethiopia's Productive Safety Net Programme is the largest social protection programme in sub-Saharan Africa outside South Africa. Launched in January 2005, the Productive Safety Net Programme now provides regular cash or food transfers to more than 7 million people whose food sources are unreliable. It has produced significant benefits for education.

The programme aims to protect highly vulnerable people against shocks and to build their assets. During periods of stress, one adult per household is guaranteed the option of working in an employment programme that provides payment in cash or in kind as food. In effect, the programme is a social insurance mechanism. It offers people a chance to manage risk without having to sell productive assets, cut spending on nutrition or take children out of school. It has benefits affecting education at various levels:

- *Children's participation in education.* Data for 2006 indicate that about 15% of cash from the programme was used for education purposes. By 2008, spending on education was the most common type of investment of programme resources. Financial support has enabled many families to deal with shocks without taking children out of school. Half of the households interviewed in 2006 reported keeping their children in school longer rather than withdrawing them when cash or food was short; and one-third enrolled more of their children in school. The benefits were strongest in districts where transfers were in cash rather than food.
- *Classroom construction.* The public works component of the programme has included classroom construction and upgrading of schools. In some villages, construction of classrooms has allowed schools to add a grade, enabling pupils to stay on for another year and reducing the attrition associated with transition to more distant schools.
- *Health and nutrition.* Almost a third of recipients spend cash from the programme on health services and the public works component has helped build local clinics. The programme bolsters health and nutrition – receiving a relatively high transfer from the programme reduces the likelihood of low calorific intake by over ten percentage points.

Set against these positive outcomes are some implementation problems. Employment-based support can create incentives for child labour. One study found that about 8% of workers in the programme were under 18. In families facing tight labour constraints, low transfers only partially alleviated resource constraints and in some cases pushed parents into compensating for the transfer of their labour to the programme by increasing demands on young girls. An independent evaluation has concluded that the programme 'could improve child schooling and reduce child labour provided that the transfers are large enough' (Hoddinott et al., 2009, p. 21).

Sources: Devereux et al. (2006); Hoddinott (2008); Hoddinott et al. (2009); Sharp et al. (2006); Slater et al. (2006); Woldehanna (2009).

Well-designed school feeding programmes can provide significant nutritional and educational benefits

Unconditional transfers can also generate strong benefits. In Zambia, a pilot unconditional cash transfer programme supported by German aid involved two districts, Kalomo and Kazungula, marked by large out-of-school populations and high levels of poverty. It resulted in significant declines in absenteeism among children from poor households in Kalomo and an increase in spending on education in both districts (Understanding Children's Work, 2009). Thus, social protection can have an effect even in countries unable to implement and monitor conditional transfers.

School feeding programmes provide another form of social protection. The World Food Programme estimates that 59 million primary students attend school in a state of malnutrition, with 23 million of them in sub-Saharan Africa alone (World Food Programme, 2009). Well-designed school feeding programmes that include micronutrient fortification and deworming provide significant nutritional benefits. They can increase school attendance and educational achievement (Bundy et al., 2009*b*; Kristjansson et al., 2007; Miguel and Kremer, 2004). Many programmes incorporate a strong gender dimension by making special provision for girls' nutrition. One survey in sub-Saharan Africa covering 32 countries and 4,000 primary schools receiving World Food Programme support found that school feeding had marked benefits on school participation (World Food Programme, 2007).

What is less clear is the scale of the benefits and the most effective delivery mechanism. School feeding programmes raise many of the same issues for policy-makers as social protection in other areas. The key to success is equitably and cost-effectively delivering an adequate incentive in terms of the amount of rations provided. There is some evidence that programmes combining take-home rations with on-site meals have the strongest effect on enrolment, though there are large gaps in the evidence available (Bundy et al., 2009*a*).

Contrasting evidence from programmes in Burkina Faso underlines the importance of policy design. In 2005/2006, the World Food Programme assumed responsibility for all school feeding in the country's Sahel region. In some schools it provided lunches to all pupils every school day; in others, girls with 90% attendance received monthly take-home rations of 10 kg of flour. The two models produced different results. While both improved enrolment, take-home rations extended positive nutritional benefits to younger siblings. An evaluation carried out after one year of the programme also found that both approaches increased new enrolment among girls by five to six percentage points, but school lunches did not appear to significantly affect boys' enrolment. Absenteeism declined on average, but increased among girls in households facing severe labour constraints. The reason: siblings took over the off-farm labour of girls eligible for school feeding, who in turn took on more domestic labour. This resulted in higher enrolment but periodic absenteeism as girls were occasionally pulled out of school for chores in the home (Kazianga et al., 2009).

Incorporating school feeding into wider anti-poverty programmes is also important. In Brazil, a school feeding programme covering 37 million children has been a central part of the Zero Hunger strategy. It appears to have delivered strong results, in part because government agencies work through decentralized procurement structures that are well resourced and regulated (Bundy et al., 2009*a*). The Mid-Day Meal Scheme in India, which procures food centrally and distributes it through a network of stores, has achieved wide coverage. But while there is some evidence of nutritional benefits during droughts and improved cognitive skills, the impact on enrolment is less clear cut. Moreover, implementation has been uneven, with wide variations in quality of food provided (Bundy et al., 2009*a*; Singh, 2008).

School feeding programmes have potential to play a greater role in combating marginalization, but problems and limitations have to be recognized. By definition, such programmes do not reach out-of-school children. By targeting schools rather than individuals, they risk providing large transfers to children from high-income homes. In countries lacking cost-effective procurement systems, this can result in a significant diversion of resources away from those in greatest need. More fundamentally, some critics suggest school feeding misses the target, since the primary window of opportunity for addressing malnutrition is during pregnancy and up to age 3 (World Bank, 2006*f*).

Targeting of beneficiaries. Social protection confronts policy-makers with difficult policy choices. Should social transfers be directed to individual households or to districts and regions with high levels of deprivation? Should they have narrow objectives, such as getting children into school, or target specific groups, such as children affected by HIV and AIDS, or have broader objectives and target groups?

Oportunidades shows strong gains in education and decreases in child labour for indigenous children in southern Mexico

There are no simple answers. Much depends on governments' capabilities and the scale and depth of deprivation. In Mexico, Oportunidades has targeted districts and villages with poor human development indicators, as well as individual households. Results include strong gains in education and decreases in child labour for indigenous children in southern Mexico (Lunde et al., 2009). For countries lacking the information or capacity needed to implement finely tuned targeting strategies, self-selection is an option. Ethiopia's Productive Safety Net Programme targets vulnerable regions on the basis of rural poverty and drought indicators but participants choose whether or not to work for the income on offer through employment programmes (Sharp et al., 2006). One potential problem with narrow targeting, in the view of some commentators, is that it can lead to stigmatization. For example, there are concerns that this could happen to people receiving transfers linked to HIV or AIDS status. The Kenyan social transfer programme for orphans and vulnerable children has attempted to address this problem by using wider eligibility indicators linked to poverty, orphanhood and other factors (Lunde et al., 2009).

Child labour is often neglected in poverty reduction strategies (World Bank, 2005*a*). In a survey of forty-four recent national education plans, only eight identified child labourers as a marginalized group and of these just four mentioned specific strategies to reach them (UNESCO-IIEP, 2009). Mali's action plan for accelerating progress towards universal primary education mentions child labourers as a vulnerable group, but contains no specific policies (Understanding Children's Work, 2009).

Social protection provides a mechanism for integrating child labour into wider national poverty reduction efforts. Evidence from Latin America and beyond highlights the potential. Reductions in child work by beneficiaries of conditional cash transfers have been found in Brazil, Cambodia, Ecuador, Mexico and Nicaragua. In Cambodia, the average child receiving a transfer was ten percentage points less likely to work for pay. Reduction of child labour as a result of these programmes is often a by-product of school attendance conditions, or, as in Cambodia, a result of direct transfers for education (Fiszbein et al., 2009).

Without redistributive fiscal transfers, whole regions and historically disadvantaged groups can be left behind

Programmes could go further to target households whose poverty forces them to rely on child labour – but transfers need to be big enough to compensate for the lost income. Targeting the Ultra Poor, a programme launched in 2002 by the Bangladeshi non-government organization BRAC, includes child labour as one indicator of eligibility. In the programme, carefully targeted 'ultra poor' households in rural Bangladesh receive unconditional cash and asset transfers, credit, training and equipment. Income poverty has fallen, nutrition and health have improved, and beneficiaries have increased their access to productive assets. However, the effects on child labour and enrolment have been more muted. As one response, BRAC now includes school enrolment as a monitoring benchmark for graduation from ultra poverty (Sulaiman, 2009). Conditions may also be needed to ensure that children are not kept out of school to take care of livestock assets that the household has been given. At the same time, benefits from the programme need to be sufficient to compensate for lost income from child labour.

Budgeting against marginalization

Government budgets are a major policy tool for combating marginalization in education. Reaching the most marginalized often requires higher spending than for wealthier areas, with a redistribution of public finance helping overcome inherited disadvantage. Yet the marginalized often live in regions with little capacity to mobilize finance. Without redistributive fiscal transfers, whole regions and historically disadvantaged groups can be left behind.

Financial decentralization has often widened opportunity gaps. Devolving responsibility for revenue-raising can bring decision-making on financing closer to the communities affected, but it can also widen financing gaps between richer and poorer regions, and between schools within regions (UNESCO, 2008*a*). In China's highly decentralized financing system, per student expenditure on junior middle schools is eighteen times higher in Beijing and Shanghai than in the poorest provinces (Dollar and Hofman, 2006).

Governments can seek to direct public spending towards marginalized regions and groups through various mechanisms.

Mobilizing resources. Ensuring that excluded groups get a stake in new sources of national wealth is one way to combat marginalization. In practice, this is often a politically fraught exercise because redistribution between subnational bodies involves complex bargaining by central government. The Bolivian Government has introduced several new fiscal transfer mechanisms financed by a Direct Hydrocarbon Tax. Two of these are directly redistributive. The tax finances a cash transfer of around US$50 million to the Juancito Pinto programme. Covering close to 2 million children, it targets districts with high dropout and low attendance. Another social transfer programme provides minimum income support. Together the two programmes represent around 2% of GDP. By far the largest part of the Direct Hydrocarbon Tax revenue takes the form of a block grant to subnational governments. This transfer, estimated in 2009 at US$902 million, or 9% of GDP, is not pro-poor and tends to favour gas-producing departments with relatively low poverty. Thus, the Direct Hydrocarbon Tax has increased overall financing for marginalized children in education, but has done little to narrow financing inequalities. Scaling up the Juancito Pinto programme would strengthen equity by making the tax system more progressive (Gray Molina and Yañez, 2009). Other countries with significant mineral wealth, such as Angola, Nigeria and Peru, could also systematically target transfers to regions of high deprivation in education.

Prioritizing equity. Many countries have adopted rules for the transfer of public finance that attach weight to poverty-related factors, including deficits in education (UNESCO, 2008*a*). One recent example comes from India. Before 2007, equity played only a limited role in determining resource allocation. District population size was the main criterion used in estimating need. A new formula attaches more weight to social indicators, including a district-level Education Development Index. In 2005/2006, the differences in per child allocation between high and low Education Development Index districts were negligible, but in 2008/2009, districts in the lowest quartile on the index received twice as much per child as those in the highest quartile (Jhingran and Sankar, 2009; Figure 3.30). Brazil provides another illustration of equity-based financing, with the education budget weighted to provide additional support to the poorest states and districts (Box 3.24).

Targeting regional development. Education financing can be integrated into financing strategies for regions with high levels of poverty, large ethnic minority populations and geographic disadvantages. The effectiveness of such programmes in narrowing regional disparities depends on the level of redistribution and the overall effect on public spending.

While almost all governments have some redistributive financing mechanisms in place, their effectiveness varies. The United Republic of Tanzania has adopted a needs-based financing formula for education, but it appears to have done little to narrow financing gaps between local government authorities. In fact, recent evidence suggests the gaps may be widening, with damaging consequences for equity in education. For each child aged 7 to 13, the richest thirty local government authorities are allocated twice as much as the poorest thirty. The pupil/teacher ratio is nearly 70:1 in the poorest 20% of authorities and 44:1 in the richest. Such outcomes suggest that underlying inequalities heavily outweigh redistribution. There is a strong relationship between spending per child in each authority and the pass rate at Standard 7 (United Republic of Tanzania Government, 2008; World Bank, 2006*i*).

Budget systems vary in their level of commitment to poverty reduction and the targeting of marginalized areas. Within Kenya's unitary budget system, a broad range of mechanisms is used to support decentralized spending. The Constituency Development Fund allocates 3.5% of government revenue for national poverty reduction efforts but attaches surprisingly little weight (around 25% in the current formula) to poverty levels, as distinct from the overall population in the district. The national budget also identifies 'core poverty programmes' representing around 7% of total planned expenditure. They have played a key role in financing free primary education but have suffered from low levels of disbursement, limited transparency and the inclusion of programmes with weak links to poverty reduction (World Bank, 2009*f*). One result is that areas and groups identified in this Report as centres of marginalization in education – notably the arid and semi-arid north-eastern areas inhabited mainly by pastoralists – receive insufficient support (World Bank, 2009*f*). The Kenyan budget framework thus suffers from both a weak commitment to redistribution and poor delivery.

Figure 3.30: Redistribution of public finance benefits the lowest performing districts in India

Per child allocations to worst and best performance quartiles on Education Development Index, India

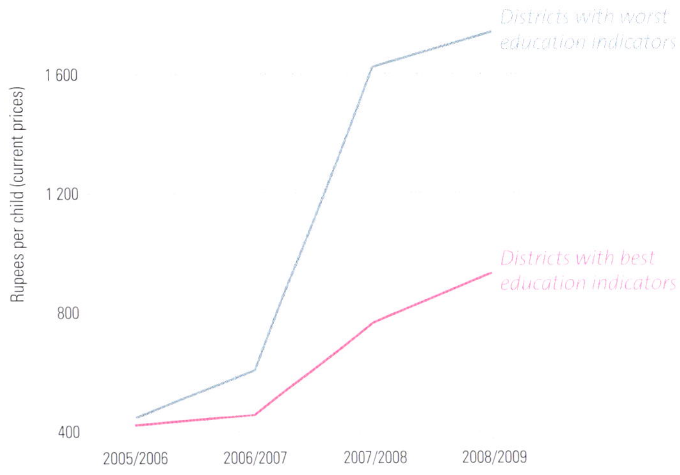

Notes: The allocations shown are those provided under the Sarva Shiksha Abhiyan programme.
The district-level Education Development Index takes into account access (primary school coverage, ratio of upper primary to primary schools); infrastructure (availability of classrooms, toilets and drinking water); pupil/teacher ratio; enrolment of 6- to 14-year-olds; primary and upper primary school completion rates; and equity (girls' enrolment, female literacy).
Source: Jhingran and Sankar (2009).

Overcoming marginalization is likely to require higher levels of per capita spending on the most disadvantaged

Countries with highly devolved financial systems and deep geographical inequalities face distinctive problems. Poor states and regions have the least capacity to raise the revenue they need to deliver good-quality education. Yet they may be home to large populations facing restricted opportunities for education. Overcoming marginalization is likely to require higher levels of per capita spending on the most disadvantaged, while the public financing system is pulling in the other direction. The result is a vicious circle, with poverty and low average income limiting access to education, and deprivation in education reinforcing poverty and regional inequalities.

Breaking the circle requires a strong commitment to redistribution through public finance. That commitment has often been lacking, as witnessed

Box 3.24: Redistributive public financing in Brazil

In Brazil, greater equity in national budgeting has been a central pillar of wider national strategies aimed at breaking the links between poverty, inequality and marginalization in education.

Bolsa Família, one of the developing world's largest social protection programmes, transfers 1% to 2% of Brazil's gross national income to 11 million of its poorest households. The average transfer is around US$35. Most of this is spent on health, education and clothing. The programme has helped improve basic education significantly.

Education budget reforms have attempted to address disparities associated with large inter-state wealth inequalities. Under Brazil's devolved public financing system, the bulk of the revenue directed towards education finance comes from eight taxes. The federal government uses a national formula to determine the share of each tax going to education. Because tax revenue is highly sensitive to wealth, it mirrors inter-state economic inequalities. State and municipal revenues are complemented by transfers from the national budget.

The federal government uses two levers to influence public spending outcomes. The first involves setting regulatory standards to establish national norms for per capita financing. The norms set a minimum threshold for spending at each of twenty-one levels of education, from pre-school to elementary school, secondary school and adult literacy. The norms are weighted for equity. The weighting favours rural over urban schools. It also provides indigenous people and *quilombolas*, a highly marginalized group of black Brazilians, with a level of support 20% above the benchmark.

The second redistributive lever is transfer from the central government. States whose tax revenue leaves them below the stipulated threshold are eligible for complementary federal financing. In 2008, nine states were in this position. These states, located in the poorer north and north-east, are characterized by low average incomes, high levels of poverty and some of the worst education indicators in Brazil.

Table 3.6: Low and high performing Brazilian states on education and poverty indicators, 2007

	Family income per capita (R$)	Late enrolment[1] (%)	Secondary net enrolment (%)
Selected Fundeb recipient states[2]			
Pará	398	27	33
Bahia	377	21	33
Maranhão	314	26	36
Ceará	348	21	42
National average	618	13	48
Best performing states			
Rio Grande do Sul	744	8	52
São Paulo	826	4	67

1. Share of children aged 10 to 14 who are more than two years behind the grade they should be in.
2. Fundeb is the federal complement to state revenue.
Source: Henriques (2009), based on the Brazilian National Household Sample Survey.

Brazil's education budget is weighted to provide additional support to the poorest states and districts

by the deep and persistent regional inequalities documented at the beginning of this chapter. There are exceptions; in recent years, for instance, Brazil has used transfers from the national budget in an effort to redress financing inequalities in education. It has succeeded in narrowing the gap, though large financing disparities remain (Box 3.24).

Conclusion

Most governments claim to have in place a policy framework for combating marginalization in education. Pledges to expand opportunities for education, improve school quality and enhance learning standards for all are a staple part of election campaigns across the world. Unfortunately, the practical policies associated with such pledges are often fragmented and insufficiently coordinated, and they fail to tackle head-on some of the most powerful forces behind marginalization. But accelerated progress towards greater equity is possible.

The building blocks for a concerted drive to combat marginalization are well known. Since the World Education Forum in Dakar in 2000, many developing countries have removed school fees. Primary school enrolment has often increased steeply as a result. Benefits for the marginalized have been most positively pronounced when the withdrawal of fees has been combined with incentives for school attendance by disadvantaged groups – such as young girls and street children – and social protection measures that reduce vulnerability. Some countries have also addressed the problems marginalized learners face in the classroom, deploying qualified teachers to underserved areas, providing additional resources

Targeted regional support has significantly raised education spending in some of the poorest states. Federal transfers have increased per capita spending in Ceará by 21%, rising to 55% in Maranhão. Very large financing gaps remain, however. Per capita spending in better-off states such as Espírito Santo, Acre and Rio Grande do Sul, and in the city of São Paulo, greatly exceeded spending in the eight states receiving complementary support in 2008 (Table 3.6; Figure 3.31). The upshot is that the states lagging furthest behind in education have the most limited resources for catching up with better-performing states.

The problems do not end with inter-state disparities. Some states, including Rio Grande do Sul and Mato Grosso do Sul, may have high average income and per capita education spending but also very large pockets of education marginalization among children of landless agricultural labourers and small farmers. Similarly, children living in the slums of São Paulo and Rio de Janeiro have some of the most restricted opportunities for education in Brazil. Current approaches to public finance do not systematically address these problems.

The experience of Brazil has wider international relevance. Achieving equity is hampered by the sheer scale of inequality, highlighting the limits to the scope of redistribution through the budget and pointing to a need for structural reforms in other areas.

Source: Henriques (2009).

Figure 3.31: Federal government redistribution leaves large gaps in Brazil

State spending per pupil, including the Fundeb transfer from central government, Brazil, 2008

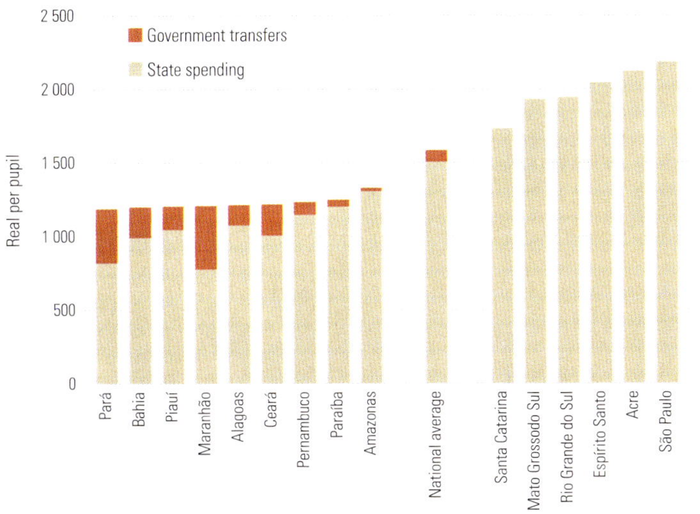

Source: Henriques (2009), based on data from Fundeb.
See http://www.fnde.gov.br/home/index.jsp?arquivo=fundeb.html.

to 'failing' schools, and implementing intercultural and bilingual education programmes. Many governments have also recognized the need to prioritize disadvantaged areas in school construction. While public spending patterns continue to favour wealthier groups and regions in most countries, several countries have acknowledged that levelling the playing field in education requires a commitment to redistributive financing in favour of the marginalized.

Non-government organizations have also demonstrated that progress is possible. They have been instrumental in developing and implementing innovative strategies that reach some of the most marginalized, including street children and pastoralists. These strategies are increasingly being integrated into government systems. One example has been the development of second chance programmes allowing children and youth denied the chance to develop literacy and numeracy skills during their primary school years the opportunity to develop skills for employment, gain qualifications and re-enter the formal education system.

The evidence presented in this chapter demonstrates that 'reaching the marginalized' does not have to be an empty rhetorical pledge. There are strategies that work – but they have to cut across the borders of traditional policy-making. More important, they have to be integrated into a coherent policy framework that simultaneously tackles the multiple underlying causes of marginalization. Setting equity-based targets can help to focus policy and ensure that the marginalized figure more prominently in national planning frameworks and poverty reduction strategies.

'Reaching the marginalized' does not have to be an empty rhetorical pledge

Outdoor learning in Uganda: adapting education to community needs

© Crispin Hughes/PANOS

Chapter 4

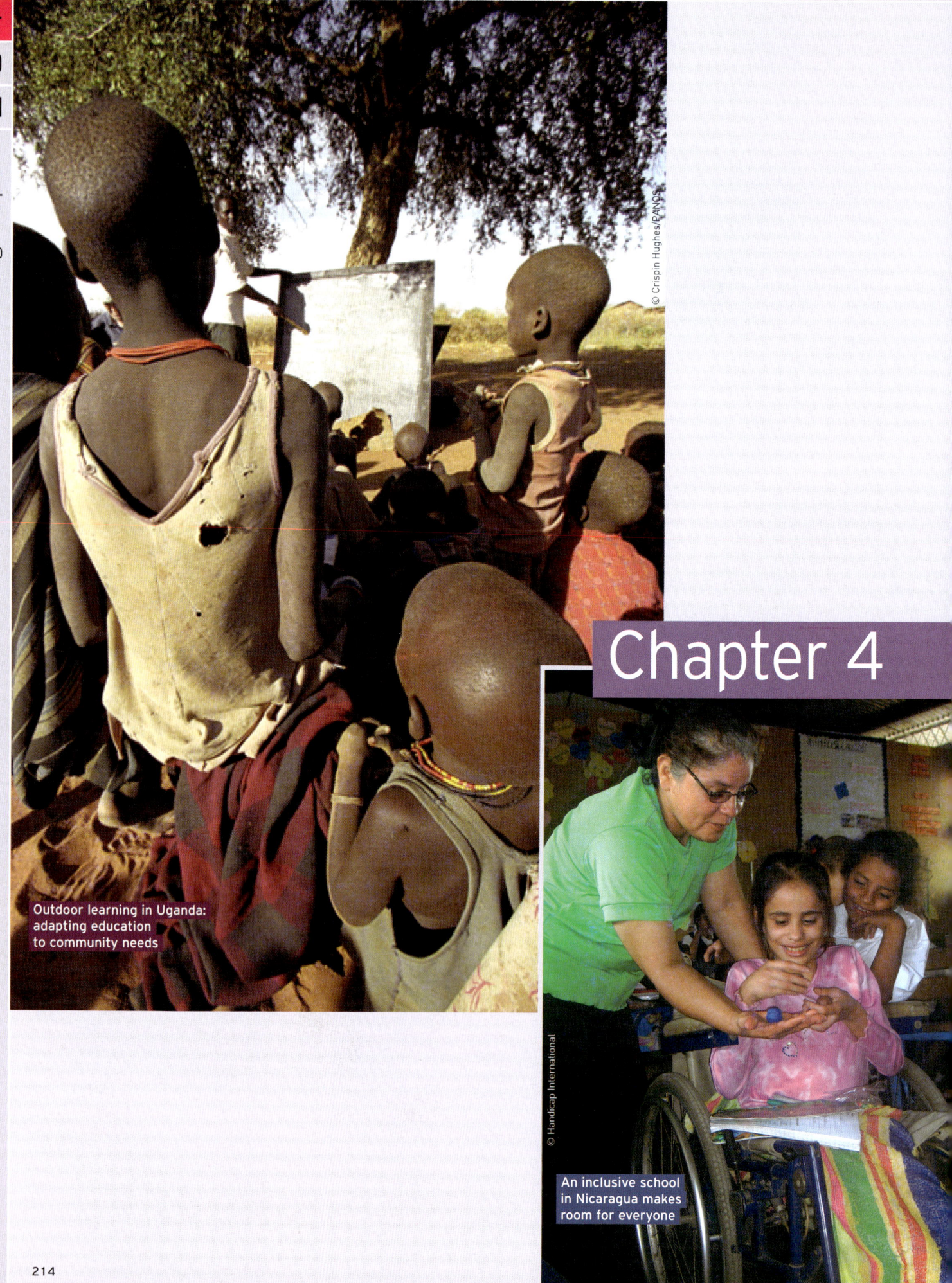

An inclusive school in Nicaragua makes room for everyone

© Handicap International

Conflict and displacement pose particular challenges to education, Afghanistan

© REUTERS/Ahmad Masood

The aid compact: falling short of commitments

Window of opportunity: slum children in and out of school, Bangladesh

© UNESCO/Samer Al-Samarrai

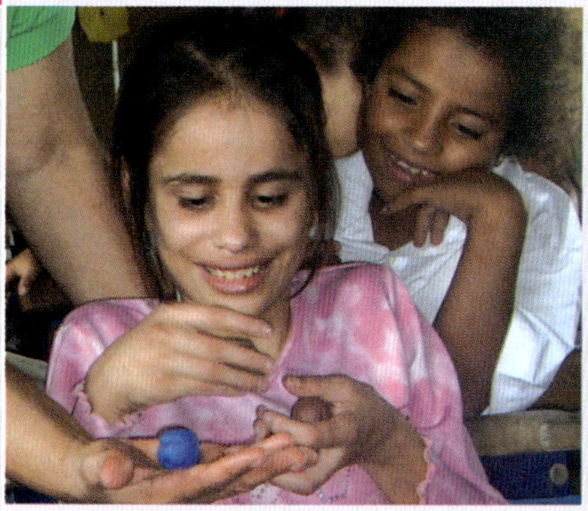

Education budgets in developing countries are under increasing pressure. Concessional aid could help alleviate this pressure. This chapter looks at the donor record on aid delivery and finds a collective failure to act on the pledges made at Dakar. It also assesses ongoing efforts to strengthen aid effectiveness and meet the needs of countries affected by conflict. Finally, it critically reviews the multilateral architecture for aid to education, concluding that far more could be done to scale up financing, give developing countries a greater voice in governance and engage with the private sector. Reform of the Fast Track Initiative is identified as a priority – and lessons are drawn from global initiatives in public health.

Introduction

International aid is a vital part of the Education for All compact. When rich countries signed the Framework for Action in Dakar in 2000, they pledged that no country committed to achieving the EFA goals would be allowed to fail for want of finance. The global economic downturn has reinforced the importance of that commitment. Weaker economic growth and mounting pressure on government budgets threaten not only to slow progress in education, but also to reverse the hard-won gains of the past decade. Countering that threat will require not just increasing aid flows but also improving the quality of aid.

International aid debates often focus on technical issues surrounding aid delivery. The human face of what is at stake is sometimes overlooked. Development assistance can help bring learning opportunities to the marginalized children and young people discussed in previous chapters. The limits to aid for education have to be recognized, but so does the potential for it to help remove the barriers to school created by poverty, gender and other sources of marginalization.

This chapter examines some of the most pressing concerns surrounding aid. The first section looks at how overall trends in development assistance compare with collective commitments made by donors in 2005. While overall aid is rising, several major donors are falling far short of their pledges. In effect, the underperformers are 'free-riding' on the efforts of others. The record on aid for education is disappointing and inconsistent with the Dakar promise. Large financing gaps remain and commitments to basic education are stagnating. The narrow donor base for support to basic education and the skewing of aid towards post-secondary education contribute to the problem. Poor countries affected by conflict, which account for a large share of the world's out-of-school children, are not receiving enough attention, with the result that opportunities to rebuild education systems and societies are being lost.

Improving aid quality is as important as increasing quantity. Development assistance is a scarce resource, and it is vital for donors and aid recipients to work together to maximize the benefits it generates. As the global economic downturn has raised pressure on donor budgets, the need to make aid more efficient has taken on greater significance. The case for scaling up development assistance ultimately rests on demonstrating that more aid can improve access to schools as well as equity and quality in education. Donors and partner countries have agreed to a wide-ranging agenda for strengthening aid effectiveness. The third High-Level Forum on Aid Effectiveness, held in Accra, Ghana, in 2008, gave renewed momentum to that agenda. The record on implementation has been mixed, however, and many donors need to speed up reform.

One of the most important financing initiatives to emerge from the Dakar forum was the EFA Fast Track Initiative (FTI). The second section of this chapter looks at the record of that initiative. The aim of the FTI is to galvanize political and financial support for accelerated progress towards universal primary education and wider goals. Its core principles are as valid today as they were in 2002, when the FTI was created. Unfortunately, very little has been achieved. The initiative has not facilitated mobilization of new financing and its own limited financial contribution has entailed high transaction costs. Protracted delays between aid allocation decisions and disbursement have undermined education planning in many developing countries. Conflict-affected countries have also faced difficulties in receiving support from the FTI. Nevertheless, the world needs a multilateral aid mechanism for education. As the FTI is not currently functional for this purpose, fundamental reforms are needed to fix the financing and governance problems that undermine its ability to deliver aid. □

As the global economic downturn has raised pressure on donor budgets, it is vital for donors and aid recipients to work together to maximize the benefits

Aid for education

Since the Dakar World Education Forum in 2000, the global aid environment has undergone a profound shift. After a steep decline in the 1990s, development assistance budgets have been rising. An important catalyst for change was the Millennium Development Goals (MDGs). Donors and developing country governments see increased aid as vital support for policies aimed at reducing poverty, getting children into school and achieving the wider goals set out in the MDGs.

The evidence does not support intense pessimism on aid effectiveness

Donor commitments – and efforts by campaigners to hold donors to those pledges – reflect a positive view of international aid. Some commentators argue, however, that aid undermines economic growth, distorts national priorities, fuels corruption and delivers little for the poor (Easterly, 2003). As one prominent critic puts it: 'Aid has been, and continues to be, an unmitigated political, economic and humanitarian disaster for most parts of the developing world' (Moyo, 2009, p. xix). Controversies about aid effectiveness go back several decades but recently have taken on a new lease of life, with some commentators calling for development assistance to be curtailed or even eliminated. Yet the evidence does not support this intense pessimism on aid effectiveness.

Consider first the argument that more aid means less economic growth. If it were true, this would clearly be bad not just for poverty reduction, but also for the financing of basic services such as health and education. But there is no robust evidence to support the claim that aid weakens growth prospects. From 2000 to 2008, as aid to sub-Saharan Africa almost doubled, economic growth averaged 5% to 6% a year – double the average of the 1990s. Meanwhile, the incidence of poverty fell from 58% to 51%, with absolute numbers below the poverty line declining for the first time in a generation (Chen and Ravallion, 2008).

Cross-country analysis looking further back suggests aid has a broadly positive impact on growth, though high levels of aid dependence over long periods can have adverse consequences (Clemens et al., 2004). Part of the problem with the argument of aid pessimists is that it fails to differentiate between types of aid. No one would expect aid to basic education or child health to deliver early results for economic productivity. But aid to productive infrastructure has supported growth. One study finds that each US$1 in aid yields US$1.64 in increased income in the recipient country (Radelet et al., 2005).

The association between aid and governance is even more complex. Aid pessimists claim that an assured and abundant supply of development assistance can reduce the incentives for governments to raise domestic revenue, creating a cycle of dependence and weakening accountability to citizens. Another claim is that large inflows of aid can help fuel corruption, especially in countries with weak public financial management systems (Brautigam, 2000). Yet, while there is no shortage of corruption among many governments receiving aid, cross-country studies have generally failed to establish significant, clear or consistent causal links between aid dependence and standards of governance (Coviello and Islam, 2006; Moss et al., 2006). Moreover, aid has played an important role in supporting the development of more accountable institutions in countries including Mozambique, Nepal and the United Republic of Tanzania.

Nevertheless, aid pessimists raise some important issues. Economic growth in many aid-dependent countries has been disappointing. That does not mean aid is the underlying reason, but there are strong grounds for concluding that aid could have achieved far more. Similarly, aid optimists tend to turn a blind eye to corruption. Too much aid that could have been used to build classrooms, train teachers or stock health clinics has been wasted or stolen – sometimes with the collusion of major donors – or otherwise ill-used because of poor governance (Wrong, 2008). There is no doubt that aid is likely to work better in countries that are serious about tackling corruption and strengthening governance.

Developments in education underscore the potential for aid to make a difference. To cite some achievements in countries where aid financing is important:

- Since the overthrow of the Taliban in 2001, Afghanistan has received sizable amounts of aid to restore its education system. With support from many non-government organizations, donors and United Nations agencies, the government has responded to the high demand for education from the Afghan people. Fewer than a million children, most of them boys, were enrolled in primary education at the beginning of the decade. In 2007, over 4.7 million children went to school, more than one-third of them girls.

- Cambodia's Education Sector Support Project, funded by several donors, provides scholarships that help children from poor families make the transition from primary to secondary school. The scholarships have had a marked effect: schools benefiting from the programme have secondary enrolment rates 21% higher than non-participating schools (Fiszbein et al., 2009).

- Over the past decade, Mali has embarked on an ambitious programme to accelerate progress towards universal primary education. Twenty-two donors provide financial and technical assistance. External aid accounted for nearly three-quarters of the programme cost in 2007 – excluding teacher salaries. The primary net enrolment ratio increased from 46% at the end of the 1990s to 63% in 2007. While marked gender disparities remain, the ratio of girls to boys in primary school rose from 70% to 80%. A decade ago, children entered primary schools with very few books, but in 2008 every first grade pupil had two books (Ky, 2009).

- In Mozambique, donors have pooled their support for the national education strategy. Aid has played a key role in financing school construction in rural areas, recruiting and training teachers, and providing textbooks. From 1999 to 2007, the net enrolment ratio in primary education increased from 52% to 76%. The number of children out of school fell by half a million.

- When the Dakar forum was held in 2000, about 3 million children in the United Republic of Tanzania were out of school. The figure is now less than 150,000. The country's education strategy has combined measures aimed at improving access, including the removal of user charges, with increased investment in classroom construction, teacher training and textbooks.

These examples do not represent aid success stories in a narrow sense. They are the result of national policies and national political leadership supported by development assistance. No amount of aid can counteract poor policies and political indifference. But when increased aid is harnessed to strong policies, it is possible to rapidly expand opportunities for basic education. As the case of Afghanistan shows, development assistance can also help rebuild education systems in countries affected by conflict.

This section is divided into four parts. The level of aid to education is a function of two things: overall flows of official development assistance (ODA) and the share of those flows directed into education. Part 1 looks at the first part of that equation, assessing the record of donors in the light of pledges to increase aid by 2010. Part 2 examines the level of aid to education, with a focus on basic education. Part 3 looks at progress towards more effective aid, focusing on aid predictability and donor use of country reporting systems. Part 4 considers the position of countries affected by conflict. The following are among the key messages:

- *Development assistance works.* Aid pessimists argue that development assistance is failing the world's poor. The evidence on education does not support that claim. While much can be done to strengthen aid's effectiveness, it is delivering results.

- *Overall aid levels are rising – but there is a real danger that donors will fall short of their pledges.* Taking into account current spending levels and forward spending plans, projected aid in 2010 may be US$20 billion less than target levels. Budget pressures and political decisions in donor countries may exacerbate the gap. Delivering on commitments made to developing countries in 2005 will require an emergency response on the part of the donor community.

- *Free-riding has emerged as a serious problem.* Donors have adopted bold collective targets, but national targets reveal highly variable levels of ambition, and some countries – including G8 members – are undermining collective commitments by failing to meet their fair share of the burden.

No amount of aid can counteract poor policies and political indifference

- *There are large financing gaps for basic education and aid commitments are stagnating.* With the 2015 deadline for achieving the Dakar targets approaching and many countries off track, it is urgent for donors to close the basic education financing gap. The stagnation in commitments for basic education remains a concern, with several major donors orienting aid towards higher levels of education.

- *Governance problems continue to undermine aid effectiveness.* Aid works best when its provision is predictable and when it operates through viable national reporting and public financial management systems. Under the Paris Declaration on Aid Effectiveness, donors and recipients adopted ambitious targets in these areas. However, progress has been limited. Unpredictable aid and failure to use national systems weaken the ability of developing country governments to undertake long-term financial planning and add to transaction costs.

- *Conflict-affected poor countries receive insufficient support.* Countries enduring or emerging from conflict often have large out-of-school populations, severely damaged education infrastructure, weak governance, and limited financial, technical and human capacity. While there are problems in building aid partnerships in these countries, far more could be done. Opportunities to consolidate peace through the reconstruction of education systems are being lost. Over one-third of out-of-school children are in conflict-affected poor countries. Yet donors commit less than one-fifth of aid to education to these countries.

Donors still have to mobilize an additional US$29 billion – in other words, they are less than halfway to meeting their pledges

Overall aid pledges: the record on delivery

International support for education depends on the size of the global aid envelope and the allocation of resources within that envelope. Here we examine overall aid levels and donors' progress towards the benchmarks set by their own pledges.

Aid flows rose sharply in 2008 after two years of decline, but there is a real danger that commitments made in 2005 to increase overall aid by US$50 billion by 2010 – and to double aid to Africa – will not be honoured. Even before the global economic downturn, spending plans indicated that these targets would be missed by a wide margin. As budgets come under mounting pressure, the deficit could widen, with grave consequences for international development goals in education and beyond.

Aid levels are rising – but too slowly

'Despite the severe impact of the crisis on our economies, we reiterate the importance of fulfilling our commitments to increase aid,' the leaders of the Group of Eight industrialized countries stated at their July 2009 summit in L'Aquila, Italy (Group of Eight, 2009c, p. 35). Their joint communiqué marked the fourth such reaffirmation of a pledge made at the Gleneagles summit and other high-level meetings in 2005. Commitments under that pledge include an increase in overall aid from the US$80 billion spent in 2004 to US$130 billion by 2010, with around half the increase, or US$25 billion, directed towards Africa.[1]

Measuring progress towards these benchmarks is complicated by several factors. High levels of debt relief in 2005 led to a sharp spike in reported aid, followed by a comparative decline in 2006 and 2007. Another difficulty relates to the way aid is measured. The OECD Development Assistance Committee (OECD-DAC) converted donors' initial pledges to targets that expressed aid as a proportion of donor countries' gross national income (GNI). With economic growth projections having fallen, the same aid-to-GNI ratios translate into less real aid. The question is whether the Gleneagles pledge should be adjusted to reflect the new growth projections.

Leaving the aid-to-GNI targets unchanged would contradict the spirit of donors' commitments. For aid recipients, what counts is real financing for schools, teachers, clinics and roads, not the bookkeeping arrangements of the OECD-DAC. This Report, therefore, uses the original pledge of increasing aid by US$50 billion by 2010 as the benchmark for measuring progress.

Overall development assistance rose sharply in 2008 as debt relief reverted to more normal levels. Spending on aid increased by around US$10 billion to US$101 billion in 2008 – a rise of more than 10% from the previous year (Figure 4.1). The share of aid in the GNI of rich countries also increased, to 0.30%.[2]

The positive news on the recovery in aid flows is counterbalanced by the prospect of large shortfalls against the targets set. Two years before the 2010 deadline, donors still have to mobilize an additional US$29 billion. In other words, they are less than halfway to meeting their pledges. Their currently planned increases fall far short of the level required to close the impending 2010 deficit. As Figure 4.1 indicates, the estimated increases leave a global gap between target spending and actual spending of around US$20 billion.

Africa accounts for a large share of the 2010 financing gap. Donors are a long way from the aid spending targets they set for the region at

1. As the 2010 target of increasing aid by US$50 billion is expressed in constant 2004 prices, so are the figures throughout this part.

2. The 2008 aid data were still preliminary at the time of writing.

Gleneagles. The region has accounted for less than one-third of the global increase in aid from 2004 to 2008, whereas the 2010 target share is 50%. The latest OECD-DAC survey of spending plans provides an overview of the regional distribution of future aid flows. Preliminary findings show an increase of only US$2 billion in programmed aid to Africa between 2008 and 2010. This represents one-third of the planned global increase in country programmed aid and a marked slowdown in the rate of increase in planned aid spending for Africa.[3] To achieve the 2010 target, donors need to increase aid spending for Africa by US$18 billion (OECD-DAC, 2009*a* and 2009*d*).

Uncertainty about whether donors will meet their commitments for 2010 is holding back education planning in some of the world's poorest countries. Promises made at summit meetings cannot build schools, pay teachers, buy textbooks or finance incentives for marginalized groups. These activities require real funds. Budget planners need to be confident that donors will deliver on their commitments – and donors' collective performance to date does not breed confidence. As the OECD puts it, 'only a special crisis-related effort can ensure that the 2010 targets for aid are met' (OECD-DAC, 2009*b*, p. 2). Failure to make that effort will undermine education financing in recipient countries and prospects for accelerated progress towards the goals set at Dakar.

Figure 4.1: Africa faces the greatest projected shortfall in total aid

Total ODA, net disbursements for 1999-2008 and simulations for 2009 and 2010

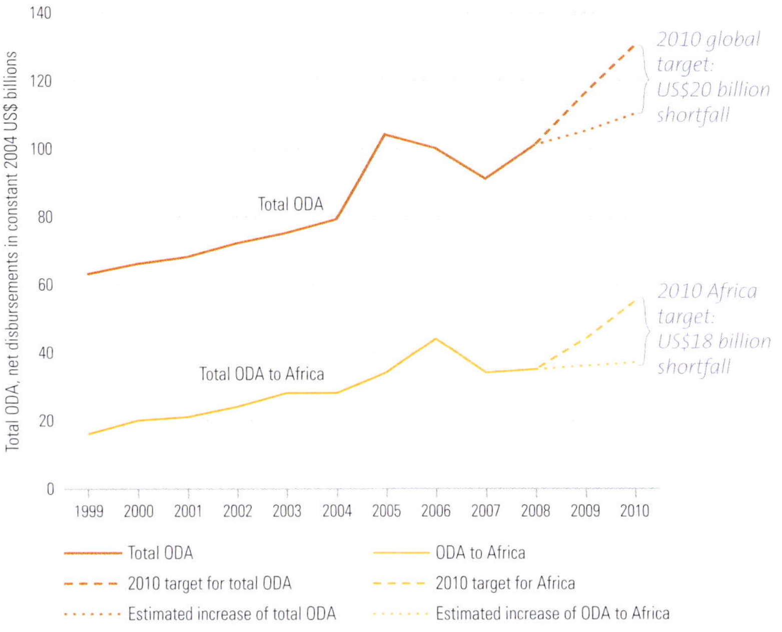

Notes: The simulations are based on the targets of raising total aid to US$130 billion and aid to Africa to US$55 billion by 2010 (at constant 2004 prices). The estimated increases of total aid and of aid to Africa are based on the OECD-DAC Secretariat's 2009 survey of donors' spending plans. It is assumed that aid not classified as country programmable will increase at the same rate as country programmable aid.

Sources: OECD-DAC (2009*a*, 2009*d*).

Donor performance varies

Global monitoring provides an aggregate picture of how well rich countries are meeting their collective commitment to developing countries. But it conceals significant differences between donors, some of whom perform much more strongly than others.

While almost all donors have signed on to collective commitments, there is little uniformity in how they translate these into national targets. European Union members have a shared commitment to reach a collective aid-to-GNI target of 0.56% by 2010 and 0.70% by 2015. Some members have already met the first target and others have set the bar even higher. Japan's national commitment entails an increase of US$10 billion between 2005 and 2009 – nearly double what would have been required to increase aid in line with the Gleneagles goal.[4] Canada's commitment is directed to doubling aid by 2010, but only from the nominal level of aid provided in 2001. The United States has committed to doubling aid to sub-Saharan Africa between 2004 and 2010 but has no global aid target. Further complicating the picture, OECD-DAC members start from very different baselines in terms of their 2004 aid levels.

There are no simple mechanisms for comparing national aid targets, yet it is vital to submit donors' comparative performance to critical scrutiny. One way to place commitments and performance on a common scale is to look at the ratio of aid to gross national income. How do individual donors shape up against each other?

Figure 4.2 provides a partial answer to that question. It captures the wide variation behind the increase in the aggregated OECD-DAC aid-to-GNI ratio, along with the divergence in starting points. By converting the 2010 targets of individual donors into a common unit, it also provides a snapshot of their different levels of ambition.

Five countries surpass the United Nations target of 0.7% and Sweden invests almost 1% of GNI in aid. Three of the four least generous donors – Italy, Japan and the United States – are all G8 countries.

Uncertainty about whether donors will meet their commitments for 2010 is holding back education planning in some of the world's poorest countries

3. Country programmable aid for Africa rose by 7% a year from 2004 to 2007. The planned annual increase for 2008-2010 is 3%.

4. To meet the Gleneagles target, total aid would need to increase by 62.5% from 2004 to 2010. Japan's commitment translates into a 112% increase for the same period.

Figure 4.2: Nearly all donors are falling short of their aid pledges for 2010

OECD-DAC donors' total aid as a share of GNI, 2004-2008 (net disbursements), and targets for 2010

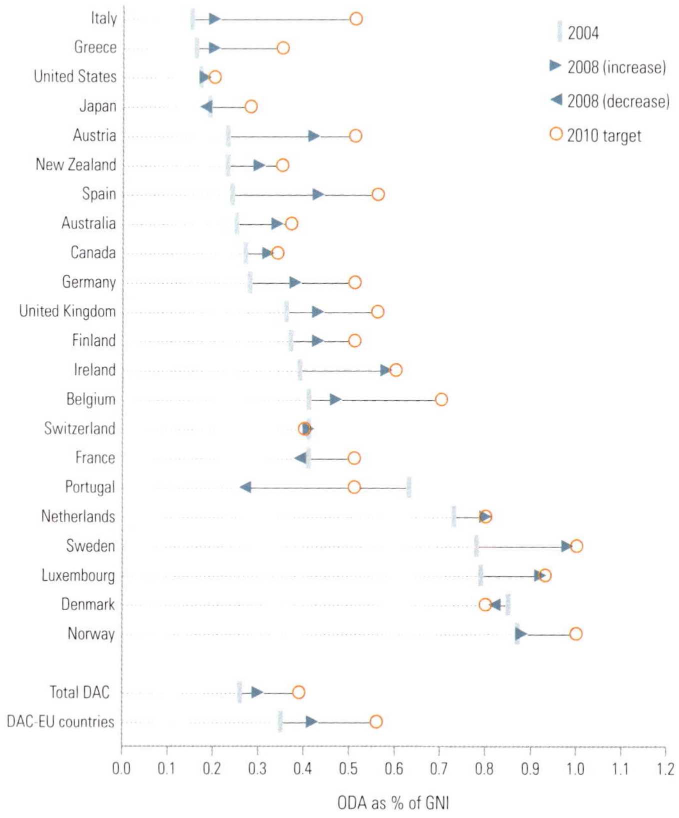

Source: (OECD-DAC, 2009*d*).

Some countries, such as Germany and Spain, have significantly increased aid-to-GNI

While some countries, such as Germany and Spain, have significantly increased aid-to-GNI from the middle of the range, others have registered a marginal increase (Italy), no increase (the United States) or have fallen back (Japan) from a low level.

Some donors have set the bar far higher than others. That is one reason it is problematic to compare donors on the basis of progress towards national targets. Starting from a high level, Norway and Sweden aim to reach an aid-to-GNI level of 1%, while EU members have set a collective target of 0.56%.[5] The financial target for Canadian aid would translate into a 0.34% aid-to-GNI ratio and meeting the Japanese target would produce a ratio of 0.28%.

Another way to measure donors' comparative performance is to look at 'fair shares', allocating each donor responsibility for delivering on a share of the global pledge based on the size of their GNI. Figure 4.3 illustrates this approach with reference to the G8 for the aid target of a US$50 billion increase by 2010. As G8 countries account for two-thirds of global development assistance, the group's collective and individual performance is clearly of great importance in terms of reaching aid targets.

The data show that G8 performance has been variable. Preliminary 2008 data for France, Japan and the United States indicate they have made little progress towards their fair share target while Germany and the United Kingdom are progressing at a rate that would see them surpass that target. Figure 4.4 looks at the broader group of OECD-DAC donors, providing a league table in terms of fair shares. It highlights the strong performance of some countries, including the Netherlands, Spain and Sweden, which have exceeded their share of the overall commitment.

The large prospective 2010 deficit facing sub-Saharan Africa is a source of growing concern. Aid represents a large share of revenue for the region and is a vital source of finance for education. The 2005 Gleneagles commitment was prompted in part by donor recognition that the region was far off track for many of the Millennium Development Goals and that a stronger aid effort could help change this picture. In the event, though, many donors have failed to give higher priority to aid for sub-Saharan Africa (ONE, 2009).

Four years after the 2005 pledges were made, confusion over targets and monitoring criteria continues to hamper effective scrutiny of donor performance. At the 2009 G8 summit in L'Aquila, leaders agreed to explore a 'whole of country' approach to development that takes into account 'a wide range of factors such as government aid and non-aid policies, private sector and civil society efforts' (Group of Eight, 2009*c*, p. 37). It is not clear what this means in practice. An obvious danger is that the conspicuous failure of some donors to deliver on measurable aid pledges will be obscured by a poorly defined reporting system designed to report on indicators that are not comparable – and in some cases not readily measurable.

The financial crisis threatens future aid flows

Prospects for achieving the 2010 aid targets have diminished with the global economic downturn. Donor country governments are grappling with swelling fiscal deficits as they seek to balance a shrinking revenue base with rising expenditure

5. Individual EU country targets differ but represent 0.56% of EU GNI.

for economic recovery and social protection. The impact of the financial crisis will inevitably depend on the severity and duration of the economic slowdown. But there are growing concerns that as aid budgets come under pressure, the pledges made to the poorest countries in 2005 are even less likely to be honoured.

Experience points in a worrying direction. Aid contracted sharply and recovered slowly after the early 1990s' financial crisis. Over the quarter century to 2004, aid tended to decline at times of rising public debt and deteriorating fiscal indicators in rich countries (Roodman, 2008; World Bank and IMF, 2009).

It is encouraging that political leaders have publicly reaffirmed aid targets, notably at the Doha Conference on Financing for Development in late 2008, and the London summit of the G20 and L'Aquila summit of the G8 in 2009. But acting on these reaffirmations in national budget negotiations will require strong political leadership, with governments and development advocates setting out a compelling case in defence of aid.

The record to date has been mixed (Box 4.1). The United Kingdom has committed to maintaining the real financial value of its aid budget, implying a rising share for development assistance in GNI. Public spending reviews in Ireland and Sweden have led to announcements of aid cuts for 2009 and 2010, respectively, albeit in the context of medium-term financing plans that, if implemented, will restore aid levels. There are strong indications that Italy's aid budget may be cut, with no clear framework thus far for recovery and future growth.

Many donor countries have yet to set out clear post-crisis aid spending plans. This has added to the uncertainty over prospects for achieving the 2010 targets. The European Commission has prepared one of the most detailed projections so far, using information from EU members. It indicates that overall EU aid spending in 2010 will represent 0.50% of GNI, against the 0.56% target level (European Commission, 2009*b*).

The varying responses of donors to the economic crisis are conditioned by many factors, including fiscal pressures, the depth of the recession and prospects for recovery. It would be naïve to suppose that aid budgets can be entirely insulated from wider economic developments, but political leadership can make a significant difference.

Figure 4.3: Most G8 countries are falling short of their 'fair share' in aid

G8 donor contributions needed to meet the 2010 aid targets according to the 'fair share' principle and increase in aid achieved from 2004 to 2008

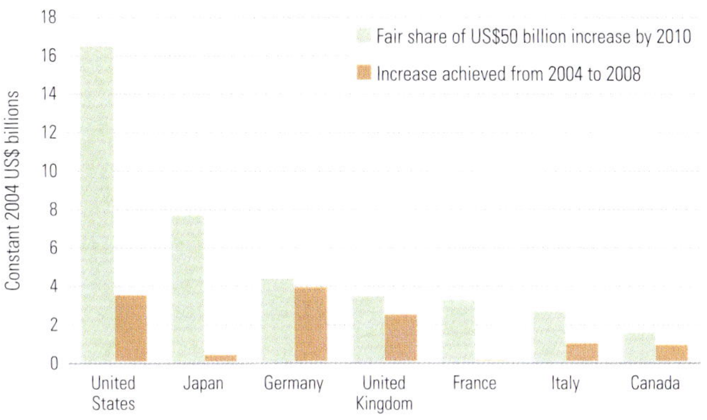

Note: The fair share is based on each DAC donor country's share of total DAC GNI. A donor's fair share of the targeted US$50 billion increase in total net ODA from 2004 to 2010 is measured as its share of the total DAC GNI multiplied by the targeted amount. By convention, the United States share of total DAC GNI is capped at 33%.
Source: OECD-DAC (2009*d*).

Figure 4.4: Most non-G8 donors also have a long way to go

% of 2010 target DAC donors achieved by 2008 according to the 'fair share' principle

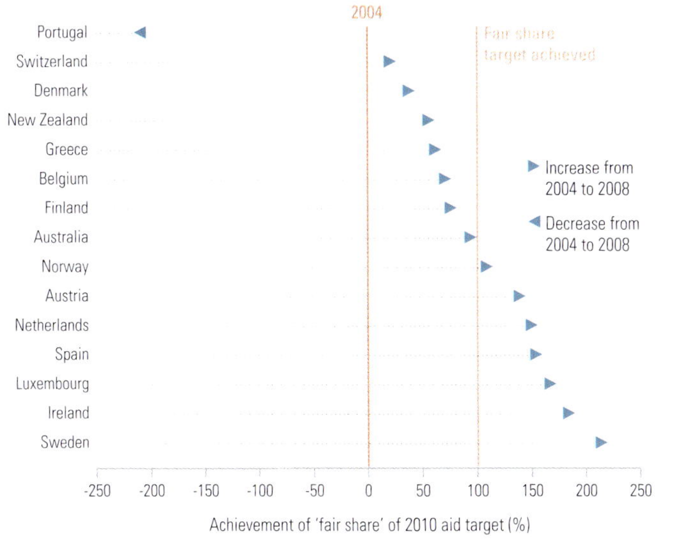

Note: The fair share is based on each DAC donor country's share of total DAC GNI. A donor's fair share of the targeted US$50 billion increase in total net ODA from 2004 to 2010 is measured as its share of the total DAC GNI multiplied by the targeted amount. By convention, the United States share of total DAC GNI is capped at 33%.
Source: OECD-DAC (2009*d*).

Consider the very different positions of Italy and Spain within the European Union. Not only is Italy one of the least generous EU donors, but it has also moved towards shared aid targets more slowly than almost any other member state. Meanwhile, Spanish aid has almost doubled as a share of GNI

Box 4.1: Aid and the financial crisis

People in the world's poorest countries played no part in creating the financial market implosion that caused the global economic downturn, but they stand to be among the biggest losers. International aid has a vital role to play in preventing the short-term global downturn from causing long-term damage to human development.

The impact of the economic crisis on poor countries makes it urgent for donors not only to deliver on past aid commitments but also to respond to the additional needs arising from the crisis. The record to date has been mixed:

- *The United Kingdom: maintaining the real value of commitments.* Given the recession and a lowered forecast for GNI in 2010, the United Kingdom could have made deep cuts in its aid budget and still remained on track for the 0.56% aid-to-GNI ratio. Instead, a public spending review in 2009 announced plans to meet the real spending commitments projected for 2009 and 2010. As a result, the country is expected to reach an aid-to-GNI ratio higher than the 0.56% European target in 2010/2011.
- *Ireland: initial cuts but a commitment to recovery.* The downturn has affected Ireland more than almost any other OECD country. With the national budget absorbing the cost of a large-scale financial rescue package, deep budget cuts have been programmed. Plans announced in 2009 will see the aid budget cut by 22%, reversing a rapid expansion. However, medium-term budget plans reflect a continued commitment to achieving a 0.70% aid-to-GNI ratio by 2012.
- *The United States: announcing real increases.* The new administration has announced an ambitious plan to double national development assistance by 2015, from US$25 billion to US$50 billion, albeit from a very low aid-to-GNI level. The 2010 budget proposal shows a small decline in levels of aid compared with 2009, but it still puts the United States on a path to achieve this goal, though the target date may change depending on the speed of economic recovery.
- *Sweden: making cuts but maintaining a high level of commitment.* The Swedish Government has signalled a major reduction in its 2010 aid budget. The decision is linked to the country's economic recession in 2009 and to its practice of basing development assistance levels on an aid-to-GNI formula. The cut will be about 12%, but the government is committed to continuing to spend 1% of GNI on external aid.
- *Spain: continuing the upward trajectory.* Despite the economic downturn that started in 2008, in early 2009 the Spanish Government adopted a highly ambitious new policy framework setting out multiyear commitments. Public spending targets are on course to achieve the 0.70% aid-to-GNI ratio by 2012, three years ahead of the collective EU schedule.
- *Italy: deep cuts from a low base with little predictability and no recovery plan.* It is difficult to square the actions of the Italian Government with the letter and spirit of the international communiqués it has signed since 2005. The European Commission calls Italy 'the only Member State apparently abandoning its commitments' (European Commission, 2009*b*, p. 27). Grounds for that judgement include

Appreciation of the US dollar against the currencies of other major donors has deflated the value of aid

since 2004 and Spain has overtaken Italy in absolute financial terms. As Figure 4.5 shows, Spain is broadly on course to achieve its national goal of a 0.56% aid-to-GNI level by 2010, while Italy is hopelessly off track in terms of the goals it has endorsed at successive G8 summits, as well as the 2005 EU goal. From a development financing perspective, this shortfall matters. Had Italy's aid level moved towards the 2010 target at the same rate as Spain's, its aid budget would have been around US$3.8 billion larger in 2008 (at constant 2007 prices). In effect, Italy has been free-riding on the strong performance of Spain and the other countries that have pushed the European Union towards its aid targets.

The impact of the economic downturn on aid levels will depend partly on how donors interpret their commitments. With economic growth projections declining, defining commitments in terms of aid-to-GNI ratios has potentially damaging implications for overall aid: a fixed share of declining national income translates into less aid. This is not a technicality: adjusting the 0.56% EU aid-to-GNI commitment to reflect lower projections could result in a loss of nearly US$9 billion from the pre-crisis growth forecast for 2010. If education's share of overall aid remains the same as in 2007, the adjustment could mean a loss of US$890 million in aid to education from European donors in 2010.[6]

Currency movements linked to the financial crisis could also affect development assistance flows. Appreciation of the US dollar against the currencies of other major donors has deflated the value of aid. Preliminary analysis by the World Bank suggests that the losses could be in the order of US$3 billion to US$5 billion annually (World Bank and IMF, 2009).

6. These projections are based on OECD-DAC Secretariat simulations of net ODA disbursements by EU members in 2010. The simulations show the ODA levels resulting from each donor reaching its 2010 aid-to-GNI target. The calculation requires growth projections for each donor country. For the pre-crisis calculation, the same growth projections (from June 2008) were used as in OECD-DAC Secretariat simulations (OECD-DAC, 2008*b*). For the crisis-adjusted amounts, growth projections from the OECD Economic Outlook (24 June 2009) were used.

Figure 4.5: Spain is on track to achieve its national aid target while Italy is off track

Total aid as % of GNI, Spain and Italy, 1999-2008 (net disbursements), and targets for 2010

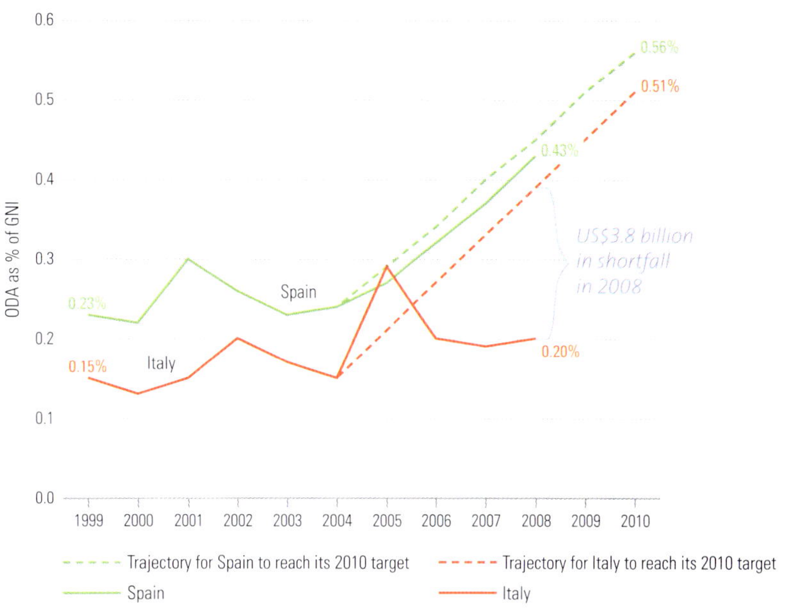

Source: (OECD-DAC, 2009*d*).

plans for significant cuts over 2009-2011 that will lower the aid-to-GNI ratio from 0.20% in 2008 to 0.09% in 2011. Moreover, current public spending plans are uncertain: national authorities have signalled to the OECD that the constraints on Italy's public finance will influence the aid trend (OECD-DAC, 2009c).

- *Canada: modest commitment to continued growth.* Canada has pledged to double development assistance by 2010, but in nominal rather than real terms and from a baseline of 2001 rather than 2004. OECD estimates indicate that meeting this commitment will translate into a 3% increase in aid from 2008 to 2010, lower than for any other G8 country.
- *France and Germany: continued uncertainty.* Both countries have increased aid since 2004, but the European Commission does not consider either one on track for achieving the 2010 targets. As of mid-2009, neither country had prepared multi-annual timetables setting out plans for achieving the targets in the light of weaker economic forecasts.
- *Japan: planned increases from a low base.* In 2008, Japan's aid level rose for the first time since 2005, though the country still has one of the world's lowest aid-to-GNI ratios. While details remain unclear, Japan increased its 2009 development assistance budget by 13%.

Sources: European Commission (2009*b*); Sweden Ministry of Finance (2009); DFID (2009*a*); Ingram (2009); Irish Aid (2009); OECD-DAC (2009*b*); Yoshida (2009); World Bank and IMF (2009).

Conclusion

This is a critical moment for leadership in the donor community. Whatever the immediate budget pressures, there are very good reasons for donors to avoid or minimize aid cuts. Unlike rich countries, many of the world's poorest countries are ill equipped to protect their inhabitants against the economic downturn through fiscal expansion. Cutting aid at a time when poverty levels are rising, budgets are under pressure and financing gaps in education and health are widening would deal a fatal blow to hopes for accelerated progress towards the international development goals. More than that, it would erode the benefits of past aid investments.

The additional financing needed to achieve the 2010 targets needs to be placed in perspective. Expressed in absolute financial terms, the US$20 billion financing gap appears large. Yet it is equivalent to a tiny fraction of the estimated cost of bailing out financial systems in advanced economies – and to 0.05% of DAC donors' collective GNI. Without discounting the very real budget pressures facing donor governments, redeeming the aid pledge is affordable. It might also be viewed as a small price to pay given the expected gains in education, health and poverty reduction.

It would also boost the credibility of international commitments to the Millennium Development Goals. Donors need to go beyond reaffirming their commitments and adopt more credible approaches to monitoring their aid efforts. The long-awaited G8 Preliminary Accountability Report adopted at the L'Aquila summit fundamentally failed the credibility test in important areas (Box 4.2). Looking to the future, the three top priority areas for action are:

- *Clarifying the commitment to real financial targets.* Developing countries widely interpreted donors' 2010 aid targets as constituting a real financial commitment to a US$50 billion increase in overall aid, with US$25 billion directed to Africa. All donors should clarify their commitment to these targets, if necessary by adjusting aid-to-GNI targets for 2010. The United Kingdom decision to maintain real aid commitments for 2010 should serve as a model.

> **Cutting aid at a time when poverty levels are rising, budgets are under pressure and financing gaps in education and health are widening would deal a fatal blow to hopes for accelerated progress**

- *Translating commitments into public spending plans.* Long-term development requires predictable aid flows. Setting clear aid budget plans is therefore a priority. Donors forced to make deep budget adjustments as a result of the crisis should adopt the Irish and Swedish approach of setting a course for recovery.

- *Monitoring donor delivery more closely.* The aid pledge is a collective commitment. Some variation in individual donor performance is inevitable. However, in the case of the 2005 aid pledges it is difficult to escape the conclusion that free-riding has become a problem, with some donors having to compensate for the weak commitment of others. More rigorous monitoring and public reporting is required.

Commitment levels are stagnating and the trend is highly erratic

Box 4.2: The G8's disappointing Accountability Report

The annual G8 summits have produced a steady stream of communiqués making impressive commitments on education. Recognition in recent years of the importance of tracking delivery on these commitments culminated in the G8 Preliminary Accountability Report adopted at the 2009 summit in L'Aquila, Italy. Its contents fell far short of the required reporting standards.

The report claims to account for 'the progress made towards the Education for All goals and the Fast Track Initiative' (p. 16). In fact, it treats G8 commitments to the FTI as the sole measure of performance. In contrast to health, where the G8 has adopted a global financing target aimed at achieving international development goals, there is no global education target. The US$1.2 billion FTI replenishment estimate represents a small fraction of the global basic education financing gap.

To make matters worse, the accounting system for FTI support leaves much to be desired. The United Kingdom is the only G8 member to have been a major source of Fast Track finance. Successive summits have pledged to close the financing gap, with no effect on delivery. The accountability report obscures this failure by including aid for education in countries receiving Fast Track support as aid to the initiative itself.

Further such reports should take a new approach to benchmarking in three areas:

- The G8 should adopt a credible figure for the global financing gap figure for Education for All. This Report estimates that gap at US$16 billion.
- The summit should agree a 'fair share' framework stipulating commitments of individual G8 members to investment in basic education, based on global financing gaps.
- The accountability report should measure real FTI financial commitments and G8 leaders should provide leadership in reforming and revitalizing the initiative.

Source: Group of Eight (2009*a*).

Recent trends in aid to education

As governments look to the 2015 target date for achieving universal primary education and wider goals, prospects for accelerated progress will depend in part on future aid flows. Sustained and predictable increases in those flows can help support more ambitious education strategies, supplementing the resources available to recruit teachers, construct classrooms and reach the marginalized. Aid delivered to education continues to rise, but there is no evidence of a concerted drive to mobilize the additional resources needed to achieve universal primary education and other education goals. Looking ahead, there is a real danger that reduced commitments to basic education will lead to lower levels of disbursements over the next few years.

The share of education in overall aid has not changed

Aid priorities have shifted a great deal in recent years, with the shares of overall aid devoted to various sectors rising, falling or staying the same. Education falls in the third category. The increase in support to education recorded since the Dakar forum in 2000 has been driven principally by the overall increase in aid rather than redistribution from other sectors. In 2006–2007, education accounted for about 12% of all aid commitments to sectors, the same level as in 1999–2000.[7] In contrast, health has been a big winner in aid allocations, with an increased share of sector aid from 11% in 1999–2000 to 17% in 2006–2007. This reflects a surge of bilateral, multilateral and philanthropic aid directed through global funds and national programmes.[8] United Nations agencies, campaigners, governments and the private sector have succeeded in putting health at the centre of the international development agenda.

Education financing has not suffered directly as a result of the rising share of health in aid spending. With overall aid flows increasing, a fixed share still implies an increase in real resources. Moreover, investment in health generates important benefits for education. What matters in the end is whether overall aid flows and aid targets are commensurate with the commitments donors made in 2000 at the

7. Where a two-year period is indicated, figures have been calculated on the basis of two-year averages, in order to smooth out volatility of aid commitments.

8. If education had risen at the same rate as health, direct aid commitments to education would have been US$15.9 billion in 2006-2007. The actual figure was US$10.7 billion.

Dakar forum. Unfortunately, they are not. If donors increased aid in line with their Gleneagles committment and the share directed towards basic education remained constant, there would still be a financing gap of some US$11 billion against the requirements identified in this Report. Donors need to urgently review both the overall level of planned aid and its distribution by sector.

Disbursements are still rising – but are commitments waning?

Effective national planning also requires a clear indication of how much aid can be expected in future years. Recruiting teachers in 2010 has budget implications for salaries in 2012. Similarly, bringing more children into primary school and ensuring that they complete a basic education requires planning classroom construction and purchases of books and other teaching materials. That is why aid commitments, which act as a signal for future disbursements, are important.

Disbursements and commitments are not directly comparable: aid committed by donors this year may be allocated to national programmes over one, two, three or more years. Another complicating factor is that several donors, notably some multilateral institutions, do not report disbursements to the OECD-DAC and so are not included in the analysis of disbursements in this Report.[9]

Disbursed aid has been on a steadily rising trend both for education in general and for basic education (Figure 4.6). Overall aid flows to education reached US$10.8 billion in 2007, more than double the level in 2002.[10] Aid disbursements to basic education grew more slowly – from US$2.1 billion in 2002 to US$4.1 billion in 2007 – indicating a slight distribution shift towards secondary and post-secondary provision: the share of basic education in total education disbursements fell from 41% to 38% over the period.

The picture for aid commitments contrasts strongly with that for disbursements. Overall commitment levels are stagnating and the trend is highly erratic (Figure 4.7). In 2007, reported commitments stood at US$12.1 billion, around the same level as in 2004.

Basic education remains an area of particular concern. While aid commitments rose in the years after Dakar, with an increase of 58% between 1999–2000 and 2003–2004, the period since then has been marked by stagnation punctuated by episodes of steep decline. In real terms, the US$4.3 billion reported in 2007 represented a cut of 22% from 2006 – or about US$1.2 billion in real finance – so that commitments were below the 2003 level. The decline in commitments to basic education was far greater than that for education as a whole.[11]

Several factors contributed to the steep decline in aid commitments for basic education. In 2006, the Netherlands and the United Kingdom made large pledges to the Catalytic Fund of the Fast Track Initiative. The Netherlands also committed resources to UNICEF for education in countries affected by conflict and humanitarian emergencies.[12] As a result, commitments from the Netherlands and the United Kingdom spiked in 2006 and declined the following year. The decline was only partly offset by an increase in commitments from other bilateral donors,

Figure 4.6: Aid disbursements to education have been on a steadily rising trend

Total aid disbursements to education and basic education, 2002-2007

Note: Box 4.3 explains the calculation of total aid to education.
Source: OECD-DAC (2009*d*).

Box 4.3: Assessing the total aid contribution to the education sector

Aid to education comes not only as direct allocations to the education sector but also through general budget support. As in previous *EFA Global Monitoring Reports*, this Report includes part of general budget support as aid to education. It also assumes that half of all aid to education classified as 'level unspecified' is designated for basic education. Thus:

- Total aid to education = direct aid to education + 20% of general budget support.
- Total aid to basic education = direct aid to basic education + 10% of general budget support + 50% of 'level unspecified' aid to education.

9. The African Development Fund, the Asian Development Fund and the International Development Association (IDA) do not report disbursements to the OECD-DAC. Information on IDA disbursements for education for this Report was obtained directly from the World Bank and hence included in the analysis of disbursements.

10. All figures in this subsection are expressed in constant 2007 prices. Data on disbursement are not available before 2002.

11. Commitments for education as a whole fell by 2% from 2006 to 2007.

12. These commitments amounted to US$553 million for the Catalytic Fund and US$231 million for UNICEF.

Figure 4.7: After rising in the early part of the decade, aid commitments to basic education are stagnating

Total aid commitments to education and basic education, 1999-2007

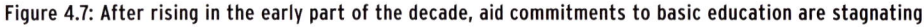

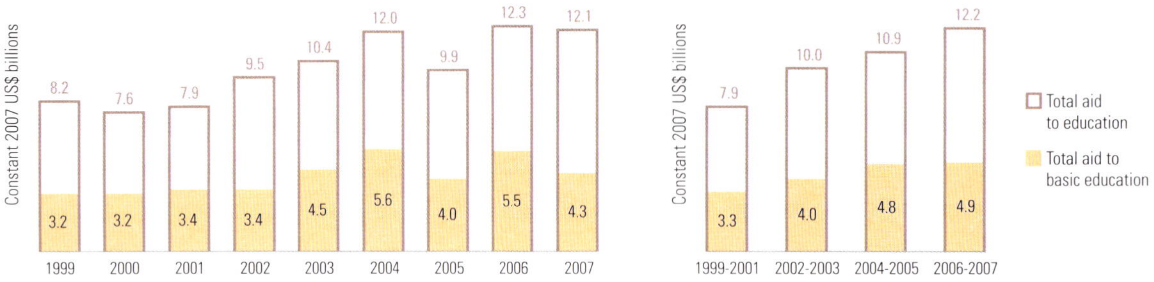

Note: The figure on the right takes two or three year averages in order to smooth out volatility and make the overall trend clearer.
Source: OECD-DAC (2009*d*).

principally the United States, and some multilateral agencies. The net effect was a 31% decline in bilateral aid commitments to basic education from 2006 to 2007, to below US$3 billion. Another important factor behind the decline was the timing of commitments to major aid recipients. Commitments to the twenty largest recipients of aid to basic education, including Ethiopia, Mali and the United Republic of Tanzania, dropped from US$2.8 billion in 2006 to US$2.0 billion in 2007.

A small group of donors dominates aid to education

While fluctuations in commitments are an inevitable part of aid programming, recent trends highlight serious systemic problems. One is that a small group of donors dominates aid to education. In 2006 and 2007, the five largest donors to education – France, Germany, the Netherlands, the United Kingdom and the World Bank's International Development Association (IDA) – accounted for 59% of total commitments to the sector. With a combined commitment of US$3.5 billion, France and Germany account for over one-quarter of overall aid to education. Similarly, the five largest donors in basic education – the European Commission, the IDA, the Netherlands, the United Kingdom and the United States – accounted for 61% of commitments (Figure 4.8). An important consequence of this concentration is that relatively small movements by one or two key donors can have large global consequences, as the combined effect of the Netherlands' and United Kingdom's aid programmes showed in 2006 and 2007.

The record on aid commitments to basic education is a matter of growing concern. Fluctuations on the scale recorded since 2003 raise questions over the predictability of future disbursements. While the data in this section are global, volatile commitment levels have consequences for national budgets and education planning in many aid-dependent countries. Developing a broader base of donor support for education is one key to a less volatile pattern of commitments.

The distribution of aid to low- and middle-income countries has changed little since Dakar (Figure 4.9). In 2006 and 2007, low-income countries received just under half of all aid to education, on average, and almost 60% of aid to basic education. Middle-income countries accounted for nearly two-fifths of overall aid to education. Much of that goes to the post-secondary level, though these countries account for a quarter of aid to basic education.

Primary education needs to be given higher priority

Countries do not expand the choices open to people through primary education alone. Progress towards universal primary education brings increased demand for secondary education – and secondary schools have a vital role to play in training teachers. Investment in post-primary education is also important in developing skills that strengthen prospects for economic growth.

For all these reasons, aid to post-primary education is justified in terms of the Dakar commitments. The challenge for donors – and for aid recipients – is to achieve the right balance of support for the different levels of education. How successfully are they meeting that challenge?

In signing the Dakar Framework for Action, donors pledged to increase the share they devoted to primary education and other forms of basic education.[13]

13. Aid to basic education covers pre-primary, primary, literacy and basic life skills. Comprehensive data on aid to forms of basic education other than primary are not readily available, but previous editions of the *EFA Global Monitoring Report* have shown that the amounts of aid for these purposes are very limited.

Implicitly, this pledge acknowledged that too little aid was being directed to the primary level, especially in countries that were far from achieving universal primary education. Patterns since 2000 do not indicate that any major correction has taken place, however. Around one-quarter of aid is directly committed to basic education, which is slightly below the share reported at the time of the Dakar forum.[14] With the deep cuts in 2007, the share of basic education in all direct education aid commitments fell sharply. Beyond basic education, the post-secondary level dominates, accounting for 38% of total commitments from 1999 to 2007. Sandwiched in between is secondary education, object of around 12% of education aid over the period, though the overall level of support for it is rising – seemingly at the expense of commitments to basic rather than post-secondary education.

This global picture is the result of highly disparate national aid profiles. As Figure 4.10 shows, individual donors vary considerably in their commitments to the different levels of education. Two of the six largest bilateral donors – the Netherlands and the United States – direct over 60% of aid to basic education. Three others – France, Germany and Japan – commit over 55% to post-basic education, underpinning the global distribution of aid beyond the basic level. A closer look at the data reveals a strong bias towards post-secondary, with over 70% of French and German aid directed towards this level. The figure also shows that France and Japan have significantly

14. This refers only to direct aid commitments to basic education, which excludes general budget support and 'level unspecified' aid (see Box 4.3).

Figure 4.8: The lion's share of aid is committed by a small group of donors

Total aid commitments to education and basic education, by donor, 2006-2007 average

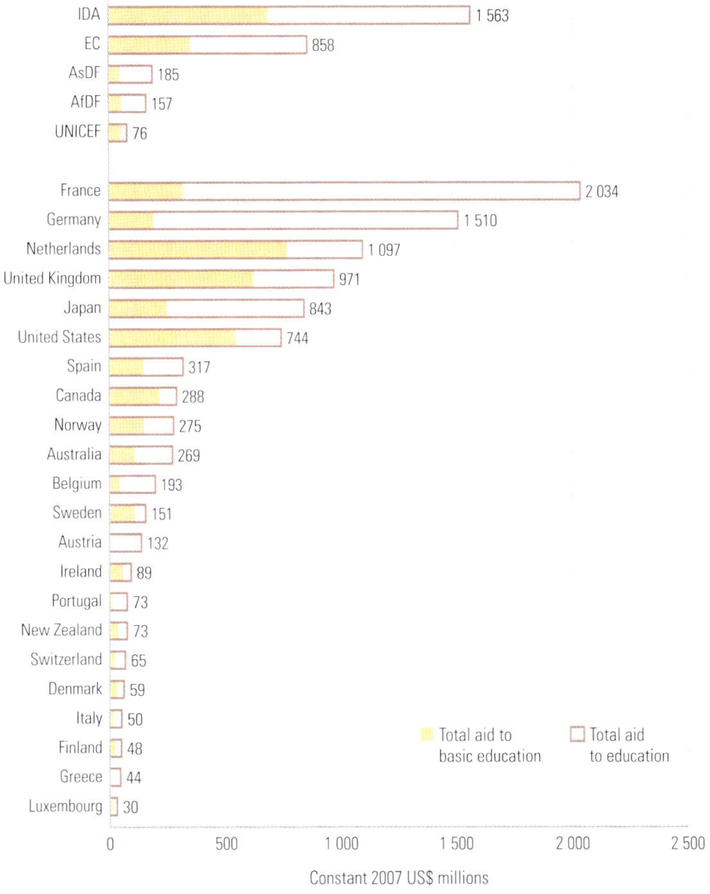

Notes: AfDF = African Development Fund, AsDF = Asian Development Fund, EC = European Commission, IDA = International Development Association.
Source: OECD-DAC (2009*d*).

Figure 4.9: The priority given to low-income countries has not changed since Dakar

Total aid commitments to education and basic education, by country income group, 1999-2007

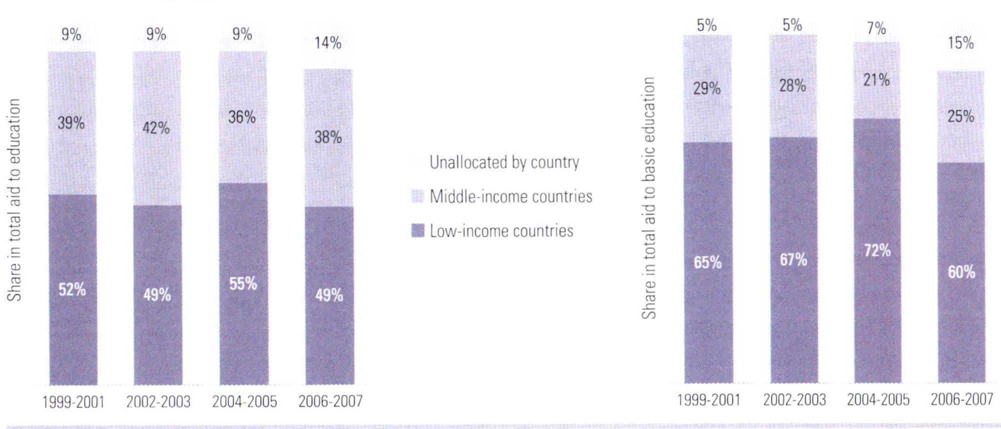

Note: Commitments to the FTI are included in the category 'unallocated by country'. Commitments to the FTI Catalytic Fund have increased in recent years, which explains part of the increase in the share of 'unallocated by country' over 2006–2007. Low-income recipient countries account for a large majority of FTI commitments.
Source: OECD-DAC (2009*d*).

Figure 4.10: Only a few donors give priority to basic education

Direct aid commitments to education by level, 2006-2007 average, and change in the share of post-secondary education between 1999-2000 and 2006-2007

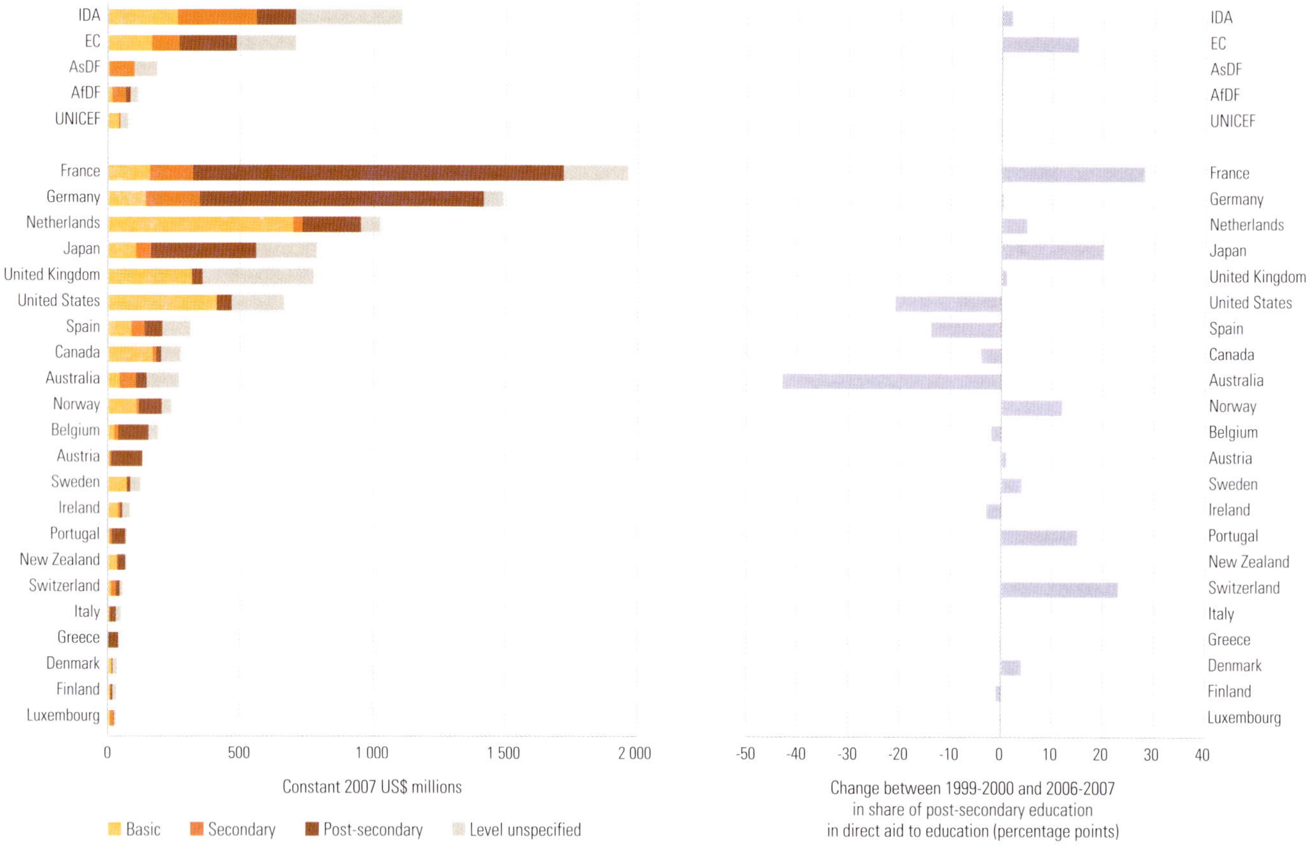

Notes: Direct aid to education falls into four subcategories: basic, secondary, post-secondary and 'level unspecified'. Aid to education not allocated to a particular level of education is recorded as 'level unspecified'. AfDF = African Development Fund, AsDF = Asian Development Fund, EC = European Commission, IDA = International Development Association.
Source: OECD-DAC (2009*d*).

Promotion of higher education often entails high levels of aid spending in the donor country

increased the share of aid commitments directed to post-secondary education. Meanwhile, some other donors have moved in the opposite direction. Spain is one example (Box 4.4).

Promotion of higher education often entails high levels of aid spending in the donor country. The *EFA Global Monitoring Report 2009* critically examined accounting practices associated with the reporting of post-secondary aid levels. In the case of France and Germany, more than four in every five dollars of the aid reported to the OECD-DAC takes the form of 'imputed student costs'. This essentially means that the estimated costs of teaching students from developing countries in French and German tertiary institutions are counted as aid to the students' countries. In Germany, €701 million of the €714 million allocated to higher education in the aid programme is spent in this way, representing around 68% of German aid to education (German Federal Ministry for Economic Cooperation and Development, 2009). While counting domestic spending on higher education as aid is consistent with OECD reporting rules, civil society groups in both countries and some French senators have regularly contested its legitimacy.

Such criticism does not imply that support for higher levels of education is unimportant. As highlighted in Chapter 2, many donors have neglected technical and vocational education and training. An exception is Germany: building on its extensive experience at home, Germany spent €77 million in 2007 supporting vocational education and is one of the largest donors to the subsector in the world. It finances the reform and expansion of vocational education in countries including Egypt, Ethiopia, Mozambique and Uganda. As part of a

Box 4.4: Spain: political will behind increased aid to basic education

The rapid emergence of Spain as a major donor has given important impetus to the wider international aid effort. It has backed its increased aid flows with a stronger commitment to equity, especially in education.

Spanish aid has undergone a remarkable transformation since 2000. The aid-to-GNI ratio has doubled to reach 0.43%. Spain's rapid economic growth means this translates into a large increase in real financial transfers. Moreover, an initially narrow focus (on Latin America) has broadened, and the country has curtailed its tying of aid to Spanish exports and commercial interests. Since the adoption of the Second Master Plan (2005-2008) there has been a much stronger focus on poverty reduction. The plan, which took the Millennium Development Goals as its key reference point, set out a detailed strategy for aligning a wide range of policies and ministries behind Spain's development cooperation goals.

The plan placed Education for All squarely at the centre of the aid agenda. At the time of the World Education Forum, Spain directed most of its aid to education towards the tertiary level. Since Dakar, it has not only increased the level of aid but has shifted it in favour of basic education. Total aid commitments to education grew from an annual average of US$268 million in 1999-2000 to US$316 million in 2006-2007, an 18% expansion. Over the same period, total aid to basic education increased by 79% to US$144 million, or just under half of Spain's total aid to education.

Leadership by the Spanish Government could play an important role in renewing and revitalizing the education aid agenda. In the first half of 2010, Spain assumes the presidency of the European Union. Spain is well placed to call on other EU members to demonstrate a stronger commitment to aid for education, including a commitment to greater equity between sectors.

Sources: Manzanedo and Vélaz de Medrano (2009); OECD-DAC (2009*d*).

Leadership by the Spanish Government could play an important role in renewing and revitalizing the education aid agenda

wider strategy for achieving the Millennium Development Goals, Germany has responded to requests from national governments to scale up support for skills development as a means of raising wages and tackling youth unemployment (German Federal Ministry for Economic Cooperation and Development, 2009). German aid plays an important role in supporting the reform of technical and vocational education, and there is scope for other donors to follow the lead provided. The wider challenge for all donors is to find the right balance. In countries where poverty remains a huge obstacle to achieving universal primary education, the case for investing the bulk of scarce aid resources in higher education that overwhelmingly benefit higher-income students is not credible.

Emerging donors, private giving and innovative finance

OECD-DAC members continue to dominate international development assistance. But important new sources of aid are emerging, some of which could give a significant boost to education.

Overall aid from countries that are not DAC members is on a strong upward trend. While often referred to as 'emerging donors', many members of this diverse group have a long history of providing aid to developing countries. In 2007, aid from non-DAC donors reporting to DAC[15] amounted to US$5.6 billion – four times the level in 1999. The largest emerging donor is Saudi Arabia, which spent US$2.1 billion on aid in 2007. Aid from Brazil has been estimated at US$437 million and that from India at US$1 billion. Official data are not available for China, but estimates point to a total Chinese aid budget of US$1-1.5 billion in 2006 (OECD-DAC, 2009c).

Strong economic growth, the size of the external balances available to major economies such as Brazil, China and India, and growing cooperation in areas such as trade and energy could drive a sustained expansion in aid from non-OECD countries. This makes it all the more important to improve the flow of information and coordination between all donors (Manning, 2006). Achieving that outcome will require a broadening of aid governance structures, which need to be reformed to ensure that the views of emerging donors are taken into account when developing policies and identifying priorities.

Too little is known about the composition of non-DAC donors' aid portfolios to assess their aid to education. China has supported school construction

15. Including the Czech Republic, Hungary, Iceland, Israel, Kuwait, Poland, the Republic of Korea, Saudi Arabia, the Slovak Republic, Turkey and the United Arab Emirates.

programmes in sub-Saharan Africa. It has also increased its support for training in its external aid. By 2007, more than 80,000 people from developing countries had participated in short- and medium-term training courses, in such fields as agriculture, health, management and education, supported by Chinese aid (Brautigam, 2008). The Republic of Korea, which aims to become a member of the DAC in 2010, has a strong focus on infrastructure for social services. Education is one of seven priority sectors in the country's Mid-Term ODA Strategy and accounted for 14% (US$70 million) of its bilateral aid in 2007 (OECD-DAC, 2008*c*). In September 2008, Saudi Arabia joined the launch of Education for All: Class of 2015, a new global initiative. It pledged US$500 million in concessional loan financing for basic education – its first such undertaking and one pointing to a greater share for basic education in its overall lending (Education for All: Class of 2015, 2008).

Data on private aid are not comprehensive, but the available evidence points to strong growth in recent years. In 2007, private aid for international purposes reported to the OECD reached US$18.6 billion, which almost certainly understates the real flow (World Bank and IMF, 2009). International foundations – such as the Bill and Melinda Gates Foundation – and corporations dominate these aid flows, largely directed towards public health. A recent survey showed that 43% of contributions from United States-based foundations were aimed at health in developing countries, with only 6% directed to education (World Bank and IMF, 2009).

In 2007, private aid for international purposes reported to the OECD reached US$18.6 billion, which almost certainly understates the real flow

That picture could be starting to change. Several new education initiatives have emerged recently, many involving innovative private-public partnerships. In 2008, the Open Society Institute contributed US$5 million to the Liberia Primary Education Recovery Program. This is one of the first cases of a private foundation, and multilateral and bilateral donors pooling resources in support of a national education programme – an approach that is well established in the health sector through the Global Fund to Fight AIDS, Tuberculosis and Malaria and the GAVI Alliance (see final section). In 2007, the United Nations refugee agency (UNHCR) launched its 'ninemillion' campaign in cooperation with Nike and Microsoft. It aims to raise US$220 million by 2010 to give 9 million refugee and vulnerable children access to education, sports and technology (UNHCR, 2007). Projects have also been initiated in conjunction with the World Economic Forum, in several cases with a focus on the use of information and communication technology in education. The Jordan Education Initiative, supported by the Jordanian Government, private corporations and non-government organizations, works with teachers and pupils to promote interactive learning in 100 'Discovery Schools' (Light et al., 2008).

There is no shortage of innovative financing models to inform approaches in education. Many lessons can be drawn from experiences in the health sector. The International Finance Facility for Immunisation (IFFIm) has mobilized around US$1.2 billion through government bond issues. The first Advance Market Commitment, a mechanism aimed at creating incentives for the development of new drugs to treat poverty-related diseases, has generated US$1.5 billion (GAVI Alliance, 2009*a*). Climate change is another area increasingly characterized by creative thinking. Education aid agencies and campaigners, however, have been slow to respond to innovative financing models. It is vital to ensure that the interests of the world's 72 million out-of-school children are not crowded out of innovative financing by competing claims in other areas.

Avoiding that outcome will require more effective campaigning and advocacy, backed by more incisive political leadership in the United Nations system. Opportunities for action have to be exploited. One example is the 2010 football World Cup, which is becoming an important focal point for international action and campaigning on Education for All. In 2009, France and the United Kingdom reaffirmed a joint pledge to get an additional 8 million children in school by the start of the World Cup, though details – especially with respect to the French aid budget – remain unclear. The Global Campaign for Education is working with the Fédération Internationale de Football Association (FIFA) and several major European football leagues in the lead-up to the World Cup to raise awareness of the education problems facing sub-Saharan Africa, along with some additional financing (1 Goal, 2009). However, awareness raising and limited voluntary contributions are not enough.

Innovative financing could go on benefiting education well after the 2010 World Cup events are over. An agreement by the major European leagues to place a small (0.4%) EFA levy on future sponsorship and media marketing revenue could generate some US$48 million annually. Channelled through a reformed FTI or another multilateral mechanism, these resources would enable one of the world's most popular sports to make a real difference in the lives of some of the world's poorest children (Box 4.5).

Conclusion

Increases in aid to education since 2000 have been the result of improvements in overall levels of aid, rather than a shift in donor priorities. Aid for basic education has also been rising, but there is a large gap between current levels of provision and the estimated US$16 billion required to achieve the EFA goals. This gap will widen if recent falls in commitments to basic education translate into lower future disbursements. At Dakar, donors pledged to increase the share of aid to education devoted to basic education, but this shift has not taken place. If progress to Education for All is to be accelerated, donors need to make a concerted effort to mobilize the additional resources required.

There is a large gap between current levels of provision and the estimated US$16 billion required to achieve the EFA goals

Box 4.5: Education for All and the football World Cup

In 2010, Africa will host the World Cup for the first time. The event will set a benchmark for global sporting competitions. Apart from being the first such event to be staged in Africa, it will be watched by more people and generate more media and sponsorship revenue than any World Cup in history. With leadership from FIFA, its national members, clubs, footballers and supporters across the world, the World Cup could also set a benchmark for fighting deprivation in education.

Directing to education just a small proportion of the revenue flowing into the industry could make a big difference in the lives of out-of-school children. Consider what might be achieved through a modest levy on media and marketing revenue (Table 4.1).

The 2010 World Cup is setting new records. As of May 2009, it had generated US$3.4 billion in commercial revenue – a 48% increase over the 2006 World Cup. The sale of media rights is the single biggest contributor. Revenue flowing to national members of FIFA in the rich world reflects the growth of the global market for football. The five major rich-country leagues – England, France, Germany, Italy and Spain – account for commercial revenue of US$11.1 billion annually. Their broadcast and sponsorship revenue amounts to US$7.8 billion. To put that figure in context: it is more than double all international aid for basic education in low-income countries.

Table 4.1: Football revenue and school levy

	Annual commercial revenue (US$ million)	Revenue from 0.4% school levy (US$ million)	Estimated number of primary school places provided
Major football leagues			
England	3 511	14	140 430
Germany	2 068	8	82 727
Spain	2 068	8	82 727
Italy	2 044	8	81 749
France	1 422	6	56 897
World Cup	850	3	34 000
Total	**11 963**	**48**	**478 530**

Notes: Based on a recurrent unit cost of US$100 per child in primary school. No account is taken of the capital costs (e.g. classrooms) required to provide primary schooling. The commercial revenue for the World Cup is averaged over four years to provide an annual revenue figure.
Sources: Sportcal (2009); Deloitte LLP (2009).

Placing a modest 'Better Future' levy on football revenue would generate potentially significant amounts. For example, a levy of 0.4% would mobilize around US$48 million annually – less than some European clubs spend on a single footballer yet sufficient to finance a basic education of decent quality for approximately half a million of the world's out-of-school children each year to 2015.

A model that could provide guidance is that of Futbol Club Barcelona, which has created a foundation that receives 0.7% of the club's ordinary income and directs it towards global poverty reduction efforts. To follow this good example, the proposal set out in this box would enable all major football clubs to unite in a global philanthropic effort. Directing the revenue towards a reformed FTI (see 'Reforming the Fast Track Initiative' below) would help maximize the benefits, minimize transaction costs and revitalize multilateral aid for education. Football could do for basic education what the Gates Foundation and other philanthropic interventions have done for the Global Fund in health.

The World Cup is an event that will be remembered for many important goals. But its most lasting legacy could be helping to bring basic education into the lives of some of the world's poorest children and demonstrating to governments that, with good leadership, the goal of universal primary education is still attainable.

Sources: Sportcal (2009); Deloitte LLP (2009).

Ways to make aid more effective

The quality of aid, by its very nature, is more difficult to measure than quantity – but no less important. The 2005 Paris Declaration on Aid Effectiveness marked an attempt by donors and aid recipients to identify institutional arrangements that can strengthen the impact of development assistance. Recognizing the national planning problems caused by uncertainty over the timing of aid flows, donors acknowledged the need for greater predictability in delivery. They also recognized the importance of supporting and working through national public financial management systems. Greater control by recipient countries and improved donor coordination in support of national plans were seen as antidotes to donor-driven aid programmes that bypassed national structures and reinforced aid dependence, often without delivering sustainable results (Deutscher and Fyson, 2008). Specific targets were adopted to change this picture by 2010.

Reporting through national systems, rather than parallel donor systems, can dramatically reduce transaction costs

The Paris agenda has a very direct bearing on aid for education. Perhaps more than in any other sector, planning for education requires predictable medium-term finance. The cost of paying teachers, meeting per pupil costs and financing textbook provision stretches over many years. For governments lacking a sustainable and predictable revenue base, ambitious public investment in education is a high-risk enterprise. Donors' use of public financial management systems in education is also critical. Reporting through national systems, rather than parallel donor systems, can dramatically reduce transaction costs. Similarly, given the significant presence of many donors in aid for education, aid agency coordination in supporting national plans can reduce the burden on already overstretched education planners.

Progress towards the targets set in the Paris agenda has been mixed. Given the 2005 baseline, any overall assessment would be premature. There has been progress in most areas, albeit from a low base. However, its pace will have to pick up over the next three years if the goals are to be attained (Table 4.2). For instance, less than half of development assistance is currently reported in aid recipients' budgets, against a 2010 target of 85%.

The 2008 High-Level Forum on Aid Effectiveness in Accra gave renewed momentum to dialogue between donors and developing countries on aid governance. Donors recognize the need to put in practice the principles underpinning the Paris agenda, but this will require a fundamental shift in the way many donors manage their aid – which will in turn require an even more fundamental shift in how they think about aid partnerships. This section looks at four areas of the broad Paris agenda that have important implications for education:

- the predictability of aid;
- the use of national public financial management systems;
- donor coordination; and
- performance-based aid.

Aid predictability

Predictability is a hallmark of effective aid. If recipients cannot rely on donor commitments, they cannot develop and implement medium-term financing plans for achieving education goals.

There is a great deal of room to improve predictability. In 2007, less than half of aid arrived on schedule. For some countries, the figure was far below that. In Yemen, just one-third of scheduled aid was disbursed. Benin was to receive US$477 million but just US$151 million actually arrived (OECD, 2008*a*). Such shortfalls can have highly damaging effects in education, disrupting school building programmes and limiting the resources available to hire teachers and provide children with textbooks.

Not all the problems associated with unpredictable aid can be traced to donors. If recipient governments cannot account for previously disbursed funds or meet basic reporting conditions, there may be strong grounds for delaying aid. Donor aid management systems are often part of the problem, however, imposing unrealistic conditions or onerous reporting requirements. In most cases, there are problems on both sides of the aid partnership. In the United Republic of Tanzania, disbursements for the Primary Education Development Programme (2001–2006) were consistently below commitments. Delays in approval of work plans, poor quality audit reports and demanding donor reporting requirements all contributed. Using national systems can help strengthen predictability by removing a layer of transactions in reporting. Aid predictability is particularly weak in conflict-affected countries. In 2007, less than half the aid scheduled for disbursement was delivered in the Democratic Republic of the Congo, Nepal and Sierra Leone. In Chad and Liberia, none of the scheduled aid was disbursed that year (OECD, 2008*a*).

Table 4.2: Progress on Paris Declaration targets, 2007

Paris Declaration Principle	Indicator	2005 baseline	2007 results	% of target achieved	2010 targets
Ownership and alignment	Operational development strategies	17%	24%	12%	75% of recipient countries have these strategies
	Reliable public financial management systems	–	36%	–	50% of countries improve quality
	Aid recorded in country budgets	42%	48%	14%	85% of all aid on budget
	Technical assistance coordinated	48%	60%	Achieved	50% coordinated with country programmes
	Donors use country public financial management systems	40%	45%	13%	80% of aid to government using national systems
	Donors use country procurement systems	39%	43%	10%	80% of aid to government using national systems
Aid is predictable and untied	Donors avoid parallel Project Implementation Units	1 817	1 601	18%	611 parallel implementation units
	Aid is disbursed on schedule	41%	46%	17%	71% of funds disbursed in the year scheduled
	Aid is untied	75%	88%	–	Progress over time in percentage of aid untied
Harmonization with partners	Donors use programme-based approaches	43%	47%	17%	66% of aid using these approaches
	Donors coordinate their missions	18%	21%	14%	40% of donor missions coordinated
	Donors coordinate their country studies	42%	44%	9%	66% of country studies undertaken jointly
Managing for results and accountability	Transparent and monitorable performance frameworks	7%	9%	7%	35% of recipient countries with these frameworks
	Mechanisms for mutual accountability	22%	26%	5%	100% of countries have reviews of mutual accountability

Notes: The percentage of target achieved is calculated by dividing the change between 2007 and 2005 by the difference between the target and the baseline figure. The assessment is based on the thirty-three recipient countries included in the first monitoring survey. Targets for the use of country public financial management and procurement systems represent maximums, as targets vary by country depending on system quality in 2005.
Source: OECD-DAC (2008*a*).

While some donors have legislated multiyear aid commitments, most have no binding commitments

One underlying cause of poor predictability is weak donor planning. Recipient countries are encouraged to develop three to five year expenditure frameworks in areas such as health and education, but donors have made little progress providing reliable multiyear aid estimates. While some donors have legislated multiyear aid commitments, most have no binding commitments – and this information is not always shared with recipients (OECD-DAC, 2009*c*). At the 2008 Accra forum on aid effectiveness, donors reaffirmed their commitment to improving medium-term aid predictability and to providing regular, timely information for a three to five year period on the levels of aid developing countries can expect to receive. It is crucial that they act on these pledges.

Use of country public financial management systems

The efficiency, integrity and transparency that governments demonstrate in mobilizing, managing and spending public resources and in reporting to citizens are at the heart of good governance. Aid recipients have made progress in keeping commitments they made in the Paris agenda to strengthen public financial management systems, but donors are not keeping their promise to use those systems as much as possible, thus weakening incentives for reform.

In many developing countries, progress in strengthening public financial management systems has been slow, not least because the institutional arrangements are complex (de Renzio,

2009; de Renzio and Dorotinsky, 2007). However, the latest OECD survey, from 2008, found that one-third of the forty-two low-income countries covered had improved their financial management systems by at least one measure in the Country Policy and Institutional Assessment (CPIA), a World Bank diagnostic tool that ranks performance on an ascending scale from one to five (OECD, 2008*a*).

Donors set an ambitious target of channelling 80% of aid through national systems by 2010, but between 2005 and 2007 the actual amount increased from 40% to just 45%. Moreover, the quality of a country's public financial management system is a weak guide as to whether donors use it, as Figure 4.11 illustrates. Bangladesh scores lower on the CPIA scale than Mozambique, Rwanda or Zambia, yet has a far higher share of aid using national reporting systems.

The quality of a country's public financial management system is a weak guide as to whether donors use it

In any one country, donor perceptions of corruption, organizational incentives, legislation governing aid, the direction of reform and headquarters policies can play a far more important role in shaping policy than a CPIA score. The extent to which individual donors use national financial management systems varies widely (Figure 4.12). More than 60% of aid from France, Japan, the Netherlands, Spain and the United Kingdom goes through national financial management and procurement systems, compared with 35% of aid from the European Commission and only 5% of United States aid. Some countries, such as France and Spain, have been willing to channel aid through weak national systems while supporting efforts to strengthen them.

Channelling aid through national systems gives aid-dependent countries far greater control over budget planning and public spending, and reduces the costly need to create parallel management systems. It makes little sense for the European Commission to require Zambia to meet separate reporting requirements when individual EU members are willing to work through the country's national system. There is much greater scope for donors to work creatively together in supporting and using effective national systems.

Furthermore, scaling up aid to the required level through current financial arrangements is not a viable option. It would entail a proliferation of separate and parallel management structures

Figure 4.11: The extent to which donors use recipients' financial systems is not related to their quality

Donor use and quality of public financial management systems, 2007

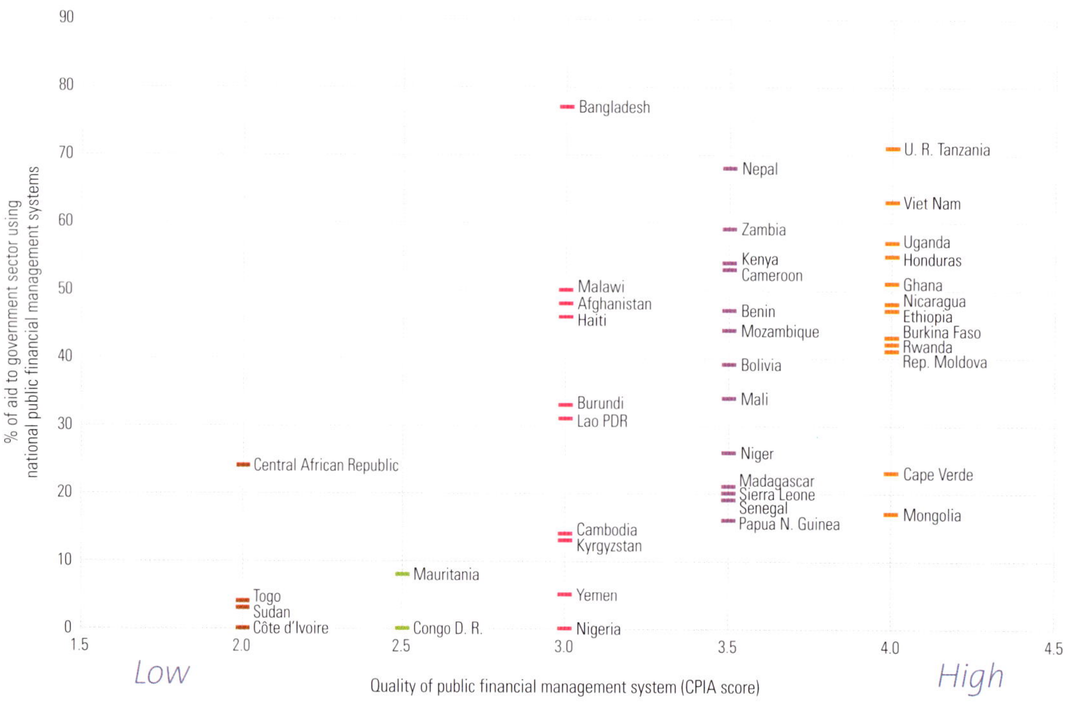

Source: OECD (2009*a*).

that would overload the capacity of developing countries, divert scarce human resources from national planning, weaken budget systems and ultimately diminish the effectiveness of aid.

Aligning aid and coordinating activity

All donors are committed in their policy statements to aligning their activities with the plans of recipient governments. Better alignment also means improved coordination, with donors working collectively to support the goals set out in national plans.

One indicator of progress in this regard is the share of programme-based aid. In 2005–2006, it accounted for some 54% of all aid to basic education, compared with 31% in 1999–2000. In Bangladesh, donors have formed a consortium that works with the government on a unified programme of support for primary education. Mozambique and Zambia have also seen a strong shift towards pooled funding for education, with donors working together through national systems and shared reporting structures. In some cases, donors have cooperated in supporting reforms in planning, reporting and auditing to facilitate a pooled financing arrangement and the scaling up of aid in support of the national education strategy (Box 4.6).

While improved donor coordination is delivering results, it can give rise to new tensions. Negotiations between aid-dependent countries and groups of like-minded donors can reinforce unequal power relationships (Abou Serie et al., 2009). In the United Republic of Tanzania, Education Ministry officials saw dialogue with donors as a source of intrusion, while donors reported concerns over a perceived exclusion from discussions over programme implementation (Box 4.7). Such tensions highlight the complexity of aid partnerships and the importance of setting clear parameters for donor influence.

Managing for results

Under the Paris Declaration on Aid Effectiveness, developing country governments committed to strengthening monitoring of the progress that aid is intended to facilitate and donors pledged to support these efforts and to use national data. 'Managing for results' is the shorthand description of this approach.

There is some evidence that the stronger focus on results is influencing national education programmes supported by aid. In Bangladesh, for example, the national primary education programme

Figure 4.12: The use of recipient financial management systems varies by donor

Selected donors' use of national public financial management systems, 2007

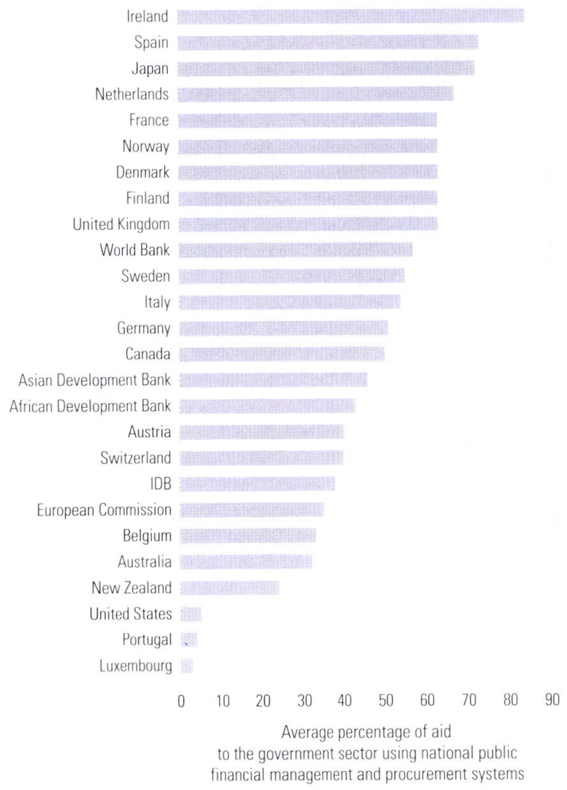

Source: OECD (2009*a*).

Box 4.6: Nicaragua – strengthening management systems through aid alignment

Recent experience from Nicaragua highlights the importance of trust and good communication between government officials and donors in strengthening management systems to increase aid alignment.

With the adoption of the National Education Plan in 2001, Nicaragua set out to harmonize external aid to education. Several instruments were introduced for managing aid, with an emphasis on using national procedures for financial planning, reporting, auditing and procurement. A pooled fund financed by Canada, Denmark and the Netherlands has been a particularly important resource. It provides predictable finance, which can be used flexibly to pay for non-salary activities agreed in the Education Ministry's annual plan.

The introduction of the pooled fund required a strengthening of national management and planning capacities. Close dialogue and frank discussions between senior officials and donors on key management elements were critical to the successful management of the pooled funds. Donors have also agreed to accept a single financial audit for the entire annual budget, replacing multiple donor audits.

Source: Jané (2008).

Box 4.7: Harmonization and alignment in the United Republic of Tanzania education programme

From 2001 to 2006, nine donors pooled funds to support the Primary Education Development Programme in the United Republic of Tanzania, with the World Bank providing additional support. Measures in the programme included the abolition of school fees in 2001, the introduction of capitation grants for primary schools and a major classroom construction programme. Public education spending rose, backed by increased aid commitments. Donors were closely involved with the Ministry of Education in designing and implementing policies, and in financing. While the programme has brought about remarkable improvements in basic education, there have been strains in the aid partnership:

- Pooled fund disbursement was often delayed because of what donors saw as unclear quarterly implementation plans and late, inadequate progress reports from the government.
- Different reporting requirements for the World Bank and for donors working under the pooled fund overstretched government employees responsible for reporting.
- Donors reported concerns over exclusion from discussions at key stages of programme implementation.
- Education Ministry officials felt that policy dialogue with donors was often intrusive, sometimes leading to additional aid conditions, and that donors did not respect the principles of country ownership.
- Civil society representatives reported that they were often crowded out by the large number of donors and a lack of access to information.

In 2007, all donors previously contributing to the pooled fund turned to general budget support. This was partly in response to difficulties managing the pooled fund and partly because the Government of the United Republic of Tanzania said it preferred budget support.

Sources: Williamson et al. (2008); World Bank (2005*b*).

has made result-based management a priority through improved information sharing since 2004. In the past, government departments rarely shared information for sector planning. New systems are breaking down this fragmentation step by step, with an annual report providing an overview of performance measured against key education sector objectives (Bangladesh Government, 2009).

The more extensive use of outcome indicators to measure policy effectiveness is a wholly positive development

At its best, managing for results is about strengthening the capacity of developing country governments to determine what works on the basis of the best available evidence. The more extensive use of outcome indicators to measure policy effectiveness is a wholly positive development. The drive towards results in aid management is not without problems, however.

Some donors see performance-based funding as an obvious corollary of a commitment to management by results. While such funding takes many forms, the broad approach is to create incentives for governments to strengthen policies that are not achieving targets and to reward those that are performing. The United States Millennium Challenge Account, created in 2004, provides funding on the basis of policy reforms and development results. The Global Fund model also uses incentives to improve poorly performing programmes. In Senegal, for example, a grant to combat malaria was stopped due to underperformance and restored only once the national programme had been strengthened. Negative reviews of programmes in the Laos People's Democratic Republic, Lesotho and Nigeria have also led to policy reform (Global Fund, 2009*d*).

Does performance-based funding conflict with the principle of country 'ownership'? All aid is to some degree conditional on recipient governments being seen as viable partners – and on results. Recipients are likely to see performance-based funding as legitimate if they have a role in setting goals and deciding how best to achieve them (Abou Serie et al., 2009). In the case of the Global Fund, the central role of developing country governments and civil society in setting national targets, submitting financing and implementation plans, and jointly reviewing progress creates a basis for country ownership. While there have sometimes been severe tensions over the release of funds, in many cases governments already committed to reform appear to have accepted financing incentives.

Under different conditions it is a small step from performance-based support to old-style conditionality, or worse. Recent proposals in favour of 'cash-on-delivery' aid for education illustrate the problem (Box 4.8).

Box 4.8: Cash-on-delivery aid raises as many problems as it solves

Linking aid to results has an intuitive appeal. If the goal is decent quality education, why not reward governments with a cash payment for every additional child who completes primary education or achieves above a set score on a standardized test? This is the central idea behind cash-on-delivery aid, which aims to provide incentives for recipients to address the institutional and governance problems that can prevent aid from producing results.

The appeal of cash-on-delivery aid is its focus on results. Payments to aid recipients would be made on the basis of verified improvement in outcomes (say, children completing primary education and reaching a specified learning standard) from an established baseline. Recipient governments would be left free to decide on policies and on how to spend the aid they receive. While superficially offering a route to greater ownership, this model poses several problems:

- *Penalizing governments for outcomes they do not control.* School attendance figures and completion rates can be strongly affected by factors such as droughts, floods, unemployment and economic growth. In theory, an external auditor could adjust achieved outcomes (and aid payments) by controlling for exogenous factors, and donors could renegotiate their contract with aid recipients. In practice, unravelling the effects of various influences requires data that are either unavailable or not likely to become available until much later.
- *Shifting the risk.* Development is a risky business. Neither national governments nor aid donors know in advance with any certainty which policy inputs (public investment, targeted incentives, governance reforms and so on) will work. By conditioning aid on broadly shared policy inputs, donors share the risk of failure with the recipient. Basing aid on output transfers risk to the recipient. If a particular input, designed and implemented with a genuine intent to achieve a positive outcome, does not work, the would-be aid recipient loses out while the donor is unaffected. Governments might adopt policies aimed at removing a set of barriers to education of the marginalized, only to find that the policies produce weaker results than expected, incurring cash-on-delivery aid penalties. In effect, this is old-style conditionality on a no-risk basis for donors. Far from encouraging innovation in aid recipient countries, cash-on-delivery could have the opposite effect, creating incentives to avoid risk-taking.
- *Diverting attention from the strengthening of systems.* Cash-on-delivery aid places a premium on achieving short-term targets, such as getting more children through primary school, rather than long-term goals such as strengthening the education system, improving child nutrition and training more teachers. For governments that choose cash-on-delivery aid for quantitative targets, there are also potential tensions with qualitative goals, as has been widely documented in the health sector.
- *Creating incentives for misreporting.* By linking payments to verified results, cash-on-delivery aid has the potential to create perverse incentives, with governments being rewarded for over-reporting – another phenomenon documented in the health sector. Programmes under the auspices of the GAVI Alliance include a payment for every vaccinated child above a baseline. Research indicates that in some countries, including Bangladesh, Indonesia and Mali, official data systematically understate the baseline and overstate subsequent coverage.
- *Bypassing 'underperformers'.* Cash-on-delivery aid effectively penalizes countries that miss their targets. This raises the immediate question of what to do with such countries, many of which are likely to be in the greatest need of support. Should they be disregarded? Or should it be assumed that the prospect of increased aid will create an incentive for policy change?

Accelerated progress towards education for all requires far-reaching changes in monetary and non-monetary incentives, backed by changes in rules for accountability and reporting, aimed at changing institutional behaviour. Under some limited conditions, cash-on-delivery approaches might complement broader performance-based incentives, but they should be developed in the context of national policy, not unequal negotiations between donors and recipients.

Sources: Birdsall et al. (2008); de Renzio and Woods (2007); Lockheed (2008); Lim et al. (2008).

By linking payments to verified results, cash-on-delivery aid has the potential to create perverse incentives

Conclusion

Translating the Paris Declaration principles into practical strategies requires donors and recipients to reconsider the distribution of political power in aid partnerships. Effective aid requires a national policy environment in recipient countries that is conducive to planning. It also requires donors to act on their commitments to deliver more predictable aid. Donors also need to resist the temptation to micromanage aid, either formally (through conditionality) or informally (through control over finance). Delivering development assistance in ways that strengthen national capabilities is not just more effective – it is a route out of aid dependence.

Aid to conflict-affected countries

Low-income countries affected by conflict pose some of the greatest challenges for aid partnerships. People living in these countries need help to rebuild their livelihoods, health and education systems. Yet for donors, working with conflict-affected countries is difficult and often dangerous.

Analysis of the role of aid to education in conflict-affected states is not straightforward. There is no agreed definition or list of such states. Even if a list could be agreed, the status of the countries on it would vary enormously. The situation in the Darfur region of the Sudan is not the same as that of Helmand Province in Afghanistan. Some prefer the broader term 'fragile states' to encompass countries affected by conflict and those facing wider governance challenges, but this does little to add clarity: almost all low-income countries are fragile in some way.

The reconstruction of education systems in countries emerging from conflict can play a vital role in underpinning peace, rebuilding lives and laying the foundations for stability

There is broad agreement, however, that conflict has had devastating consequences for education in many poor countries, affecting millions of children. Whether they are injured or traumatized by bombing in Gaza, living in camps for displaced people in Sri Lanka or recruited as child soldiers in northern Uganda, children are never immune to the impact of conflict. Neither are education systems. Warring factions often destroy schools and target teachers, and education suffers badly when conflict leads to a collapse of governance.

Childhood disrupted as a result of conflict is difficult to mend. Yet education can provide children and youth with protection, a safe space and hope for the future. Similarly, the reconstruction of education systems in countries emerging from conflict can play a vital role in underpinning peace, rebuilding lives and laying the foundations for stability (Aguilar and Retamal, 2009). The experience of Sierra Leone demonstrates what is possible, while the failure to rebuild education in the Democratic Republic of the Congo demonstrates the corrosive effect of slow social reconstruction on peace processes.

Most donors recognize the importance of supporting education in conflict-affected countries. Yet they face difficult policy dilemmas. Donors want aid to be effective, so they focus on conditions such as country ownership, macroeconomic stability and good governance. Few countries emerging from conflict are in a position to meet these conditions. In addition, maintaining access to education during humanitarian emergencies is enormously difficult. Such considerations help explain the highly unequal, volatile and poorly coordinated pattern of aid delivery to conflict-affected countries. Yet adequate education provision in these countries will not be achieved without scaling up aid.

Monitoring aid to conflict-affected countries

How do countries affected by conflict fare in attracting aid, in comparison with other countries? This Report addresses the question by focusing on twenty poor countries meeting established criteria for classification as conflict-affected (Harbom and Wallensteen, 2009; Uppsala Conflict Data Program, 2009).[16]

The diversity of the group underlines the problems in defining conflict-affected countries. Those covered include countries such as Liberia and Rwanda that have embarked on successful post-conflict recovery strategies, countries that have faced localized conflict (Senegal and Uganda) or far broader conflict (Côte d'Ivoire), and those such as Afghanistan where reconstruction is taking place amid continued instability.

The impact of conflict on educational access is clear. Taken collectively, these twenty countries account for about one in three children who are out of school.[17] In many cases, national data make it difficult to establish the full consequences of conflict. For example, there are no reliable estimates of the out-of-school population in Darfur. In other cases, national data can obscure the extent of conflict-related damage to education. While Uganda has made strong national progress towards universal primary education, several northern districts affected by conflict have been left behind.

While aid to conflict-affected poor countries is rising from a low base, it still falls far short of what is needed. For 2006–2007, just under one-fifth of overall aid to education and one-quarter of aid to basic education went to conflict-affected poor countries (Figure 4.13). Data limitations make it difficult to provide an accurate assessment of the levels of aid required for education in these countries. Indicative estimates for this Report put the basic education financing gap in conflict-affected poor countries at approximately US$7 billion or 41% of the total gap for low-income countries (Education Policy and Data Center and UNESCO, 2009). This is substantially more than the US$1.2 billion of aid for basic education committed to these countries in 2006-2007.

16. The countries included are ones that experienced armed conflicts resulting in at least twenty-five battle-related deaths per year over at least three years between 1999 and 2007 or more than 1,000 battle-related deaths in at least one year during the same period. Of these, only countries categorized as least developed countries by the United Nations or low-income countries by the World Bank in 2007 were included.

17. These twenty countries account for 56% of those out of school in low-income countries.

Aid distribution within the group of conflict-affected countries is highly concentrated in Afghanistan, Ethiopia and Pakistan. They accounted for more than half of total aid to basic education in conflict-affected countries in 2006–2007 (Figure 4.14).[18] Comparisons across the group reveal striking disparities in levels of support. Afghanistan received US$19 per primary school age child – eight times as much as the Democratic Republic of the Congo at US$2 (Figure 4.15). Rwanda received US$20 per child and Burundi US$13 (Box 4.9). At US$4 per child, Liberia received less than half the group average in 2006–2007.

Patterns of aid allocation do not correspond to what might be expected on the basis of a global assessment of need. One reason may be that aid priorities have emerged as a key element of a global security agenda. An obvious case in point is Afghanistan, which receives a large amount of aid overall and for education in particular. This is partly because reconstruction of education systems is recognized both as a requirement for human development and greater gender equity, and as a vital element in state-building. However, it is also because of the perceived threat of the country to global security.

Comparisons between Afghanistan and the Democratic Republic of the Congo illustrate the importance of donor priorities. In the Democratic Republic of the Congo, long-running civil conflicts, fuelled in some regions by neighbouring states, have had devastating consequences for education. Household survey data indicate that more than 4 million children are not in school (Democratic Republic of the Congo Ministry of Planning et al., 2008).[19] While the country may be a source of regional instability, donors do not perceive it as a global security threat, unlike Afghanistan. That may explain why it figures among the top ten recipients for only one donor – Belgium, the former colonial power. By contrast, Afghanistan was among the top ten recipients of basic education aid for eight donors in 2007.[20]

18. The twenty countries received 16% of total ODA in 2007, similar to their share of total aid to education. In this group, Afghanistan, Ethiopia and Pakistan are also the biggest recipients of ODA overall (see OECD-DAC, 2009e), suggesting that education is following more general patterns of donor priorities.

19. GMR calculations based on net attendance rate from DRC 2007 DHS and population data from UIS database.

20. Australia, Canada, the European Commission, Germany, the IDA, Japan, Sweden and the United States.

Figure 4.13: Conflict-affected poor countries receive a low share of aid to education

Share of total aid to education and basic education (commitments) allocated to conflict-affected poor countries, 1999-2007

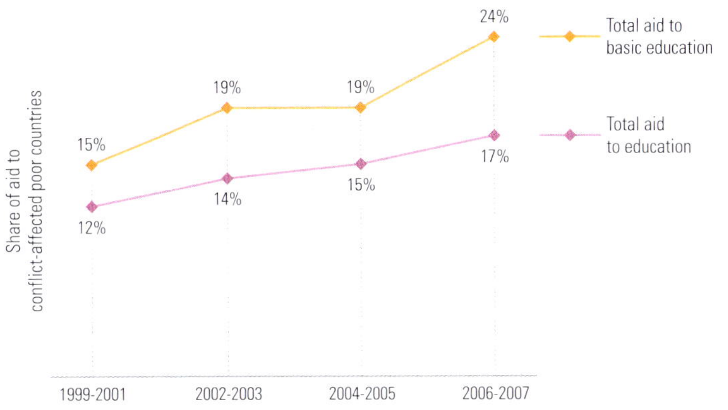

Source: OECD-DAC (2009*d*).

Figure 4.14: Distribution of aid to education among conflict-affected poor countries is uneven

Total aid disbursements to education and basic education in conflict-affected poor countries, 2006-2007 average

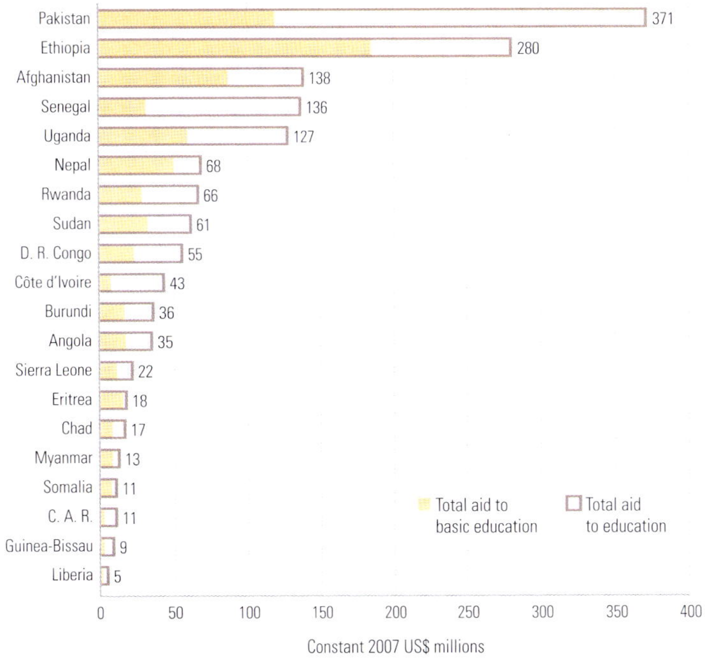

Source: OECD-DAC (2009*d*).

Figure 4.15: Spending per primary school child is low in conflict-affected poor countries

Total aid disbursements to basic education per primary school age child, 2006-2007 average

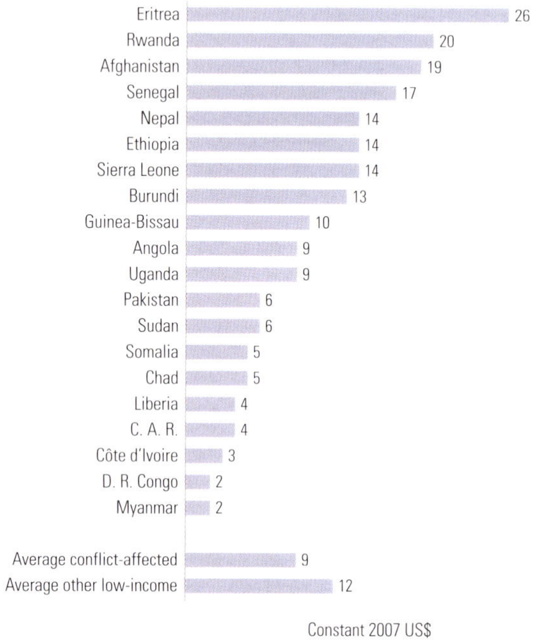

Note: Only low-income countries with a primary school age population above 150,000 are included.
Source: OECD-DAC (2009*d*).

Today, humanitarian aid is dominated by food and emergency nutrition programmes, with long-term aid to agriculture, education and health figuring only marginally

In Afghanistan, aid has played a critical role in expanding education opportunities. Overall, however, the aid allocation patterns raise questions about donor priorities regarding the different recipient countries. In some cases, there are marked disparities in aid levels between conflict-affected countries in the same region, or even neighbouring countries – such as Burundi and Rwanda (Box 4.9).

From humanitarian to development aid – the missing link

'Support for the re-establishment and continuity of education must be a priority strategy for donors and NGOs in conflict and post-conflict situations,' wrote Graça Machel in 1996 (Machel, 1996, p. 47). More than a decade later, most aid for conflict-affected countries continues to be delivered through short-term, uncoordinated projects that fail to lay the foundations on which to rebuild education systems. While donor policy statements increasingly recognize the importance of integrating short-term humanitarian assistance with long-term social and economic reconstruction, progress towards a more 'joined-up' policy framework has been limited.

Humanitarian assistance covers a broad spectrum of activities, but countries affected by violent conflict figure prominently among recipients. Such aid has increased since 1999–2000, though its share in total aid commitments declined from 9% in 1999–2000 to 7% in 2006–2007 (OECD-DAC, 2009*d*). Estimates suggest that education accounted for just 2% of total humanitarian aid – a meagre US$237 million in 2008 (Office for the Coordination of Humanitarian Affairs, 2009).

In many conflict-affected countries, expenditure on security operations and emergency assistance overwhelmingly dominates donor support, with long-term development in general – and education in particular – taking a back seat. In Liberia, for example, the cost of United Nations peacekeeping operations has consistently been more than double total aid flows since 2004. Only 2% of the total aid was allocated to education in 2004–2007. During this post-conflict phase, humanitarian aid continued to play a significant role (OECD-DAC, 2009*d*). But it did not make up the shortfall for education: in humanitarian as in development aid, education accounted for just 2%. This suggests that longer-term, more sustainable approaches to supporting basic service delivery are not yet being addressed (Figure 4.16).

Another example comes from the Democratic Republic of the Congo. In the five years after the signing of the 2003 peace accord, development aid was nominally higher than spending on United Nations peacekeeping. However, this was largely because, under an agreement signed just after the peace accord, creditors wrote off a large share of the country's debt stock, which is counted as aid even though it entails no real financial flows. Humanitarian aid has been a significant proportion of actual assistance from donors, reflecting the difficult environment in which they operate. The 2003 peace accords swiftly broke down, as did subsequent accords. Today, humanitarian aid is dominated by food and emergency nutrition programmes, with long-term aid to agriculture, education and health figuring only marginally. In 2007, US$5 million, or only 1% of humanitarian aid, supported education interventions in the Democratic Republic of the Congo, far short of the US$27 million identified as a minimum requirement for education in the 2007 humanitarian action plan (United Nations, 2007*a*).

The experience of the Democratic Republic of the Congo illustrates both the relative neglect of social

Box 4.9: Non-identical donor responses to education systems in Burundi and Rwanda

Burundi and Rwanda are known in French as *les faux jumeaux* – the non-identical twins. Both have experienced devastating episodes of violent conflict which have left a deep imprint on their education systems. One area where they differ is in the level of support they have received from aid donors in rebuilding those systems.

The three months of genocide in Rwanda in 1994 left 800,000 people dead and 3 million displaced, many of them in neighbouring countries. Some 80% of the country's children experienced death in their immediate family and 90% saw dead bodies. In Burundi, the conflict was more protracted. From 1993 to 2005, out of a population of around 6 million, 300,000 people were killed and 1.6 million fled their homes.

Both countries emerged from conflict with shattered education systems. When a new government assumed office in Rwanda in July 1994, the Education Ministry had no financial resources, no equipment or supplies, and limited manpower. In Burundi, the near-decade of conflict severely weakened education planning and financing. By 2000, just 40% of the school age population were attending primary school, according to household survey data. With large numbers of traumatized children, a bitter legacy of mistrust, shortages of teachers and large financing gaps, both countries urgently needed strong donor support and increased aid.

The donor response has been unequal. Over 2006–2007, Rwanda received US$20 per primary school age child. Burundi received just US$13, even though it is lagging behind Rwanda in progress towards universal primary education, with three times as many children out of school.

Financing disparities of this magnitude are difficult to square with an independent assessment of need, governance or capacity. Other factors have driven aid allocations. The scale of the Rwandan genocide and the failure of the international community to prevent it played a role in eliciting a strong aid response – and rightly so. Public pressure on donors to act was reinforced by graphic media coverage of the genocide. Beyond the humanitarian impulse, many aid donors see Rwanda as a more significant strategic actor than Burundi in the Great Lakes region. The point of the comparison is not to question the level of aid to Rwanda, which has achieved extraordinary progress, but to ask why donors have not supported reconstruction in Burundi more strongly.

Source: Obura and Bird (2009).

reconstruction in humanitarian aid and the complexity of the problems facing donors. Food and nutrition are obvious priorities for emergency support. Yet the failure to put in place a viable strategy and adequate finance for education reconstruction may well have contributed to wider factors that have destabilized successive peace accords.

At one level the aid financing profiles for the Democratic Republic of the Congo and Liberia reflect a compelling set of recovery imperatives. The problem is not that the international community invests too much in security and alleviating hunger. It is that too little is invested in other areas that are no less important to post-conflict reconstruction.

Peace, political stability, access to basic services and economic recovery cannot be viewed in isolation. In a post-conflict environment, failure in any one area can lead to collapse in others. When peace settlements bring an end to violence but fail to restore education systems, the thwarted hopes and ambitions of parents can fuel social tensions and mistrust of government. Distributing food to combat hunger without restoring the economic infrastructure and productive systems that people need for more secure livelihoods can erode prospects for sustainable recovery. The bottom line is that security in the broader sense is about more than the absence of violence and hunger. It is about expanding the real choices open to people and building confidence in the future.

Working effectively in conflict-affected states

There is no ready-made model for working in conflict-affected states. In some cases, peace processes create an opportunity to work with governments committed to reconstruction. In others, donors work amid ongoing conflict, with the risk of being seen as a supporter of one side – a risk that has resulted in a growing number of attacks on aid workers. In still other cases, government unwillingness to participate in peace processes or reconstruction may leave non-government groups as the only potential partners for aid agencies. While the problems are often daunting, there are always opportunities to engage.

The scale of the Rwandan genocide and the failure of the international community to prevent it played a role in eliciting a strong aid response

Figure 4.16: Peacekeeping and reconstruction in the Democratic Republic of the Congo and Liberia*

United Nations peacekeeping expenditure, humanitarian aid and development aid disbursements, Democratic Republic of the Congo and Liberia, 2004-2007

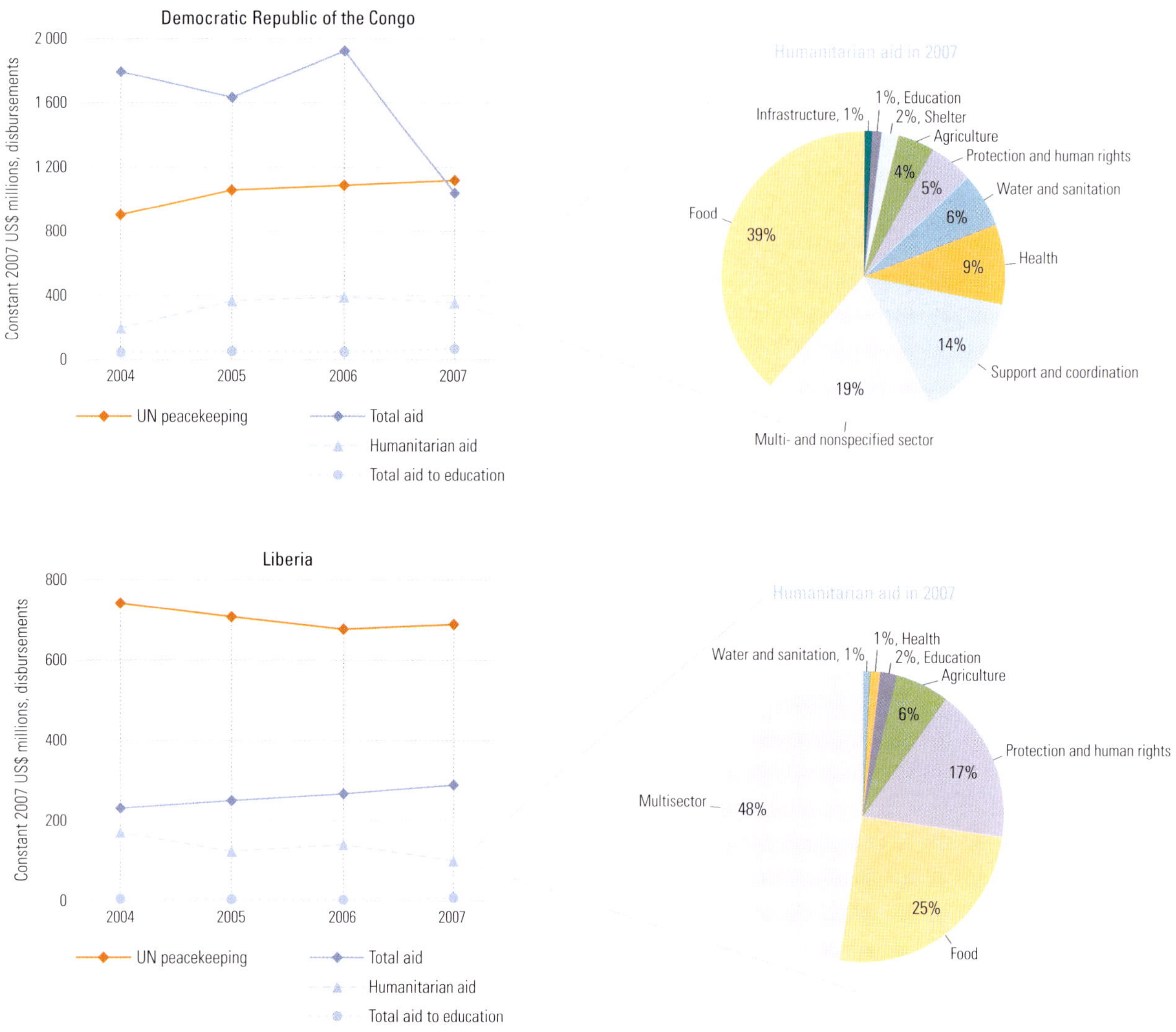

Notes: Data from the United Nations Department of Peacekeeping Operations (UNDPKO) are used as a proxy for peace- and security-related expenditure.
The data indicate the peacekeeping missions under UNDPKO command and the levels of financial support being provided to them by United Nations member states (see OECD-DAC, 2009*e*).
* The sector breakdown in humanitarian aid is taken from the Financial Tracking Service, United Nations Office for the Coordination of Humanitarian Affairs (OCHA). Unlike for the OECD-DAC, reporting to OCHA is voluntary and so likely to be an underestimate. For some countries (notably Liberia in Figure 4.16) multisector aid can be a sizable proportion of humanitarian aid.
In Liberia it was mainly aimed at supporting the return and reintegration of refugees once the political and security situation improved (United Nations, 2007*b*).
Sources: OECD-DAC (2009*d*); Office for the Coordination of Humanitarian Affairs (2009).

The potential for engagement depends partly upon donor governance practices. Stringent rules on reporting may be beyond the capacity of many conflict-affected states. Similarly, the scope for supporting country ownership and using public financial management systems – key elements of the 2005 Paris agenda for aid effectiveness – may be limited. Donors have adopted principles to guide their work in fragile and conflict-affected states,[21] but there is a lack of clarity over the alignment of these principles with those of the Paris agenda – and over how to translate them into action (Oxford Policy Management and IDL Group, 2008).

One principle for international engagement in fragile states emphasizes the importance of acting fast, but also staying involved for long enough to give success a chance (OECD-DAC, 2007). This often does not happen. One reason is that countries emerging from conflict are thought to lack the governance systems to absorb large quantities of aid. That may be true immediately

21. These include 'Principles and Good Practice of Humanitarian Donorship' (2003) and 'Principles for International Engagement in Fragile States and Situations' (2007). The latter include a principle emphasizing the importance of aligning with local priorities in different contexts.

after a conflict, when security and the restoration of basic governance are an immediate priority. But once peace has taken root, there is often a potential for increasing aid (Collier and Hoeffler, 2002).

All too often in the past, donors tended to scale back aid in countries that had emerged from conflict but remained politically unstable two or three years after a peace settlement. The upshot was that aid declined at a time when public concerns were shifting from security to basic services – and when post-conflict governments were building their capacity to use aid more effectively (Weinstein et al., 2004). There are alternatives. Recognizing that uncertainty over future aid flows could compromise efforts to build on the Sierra Leone peace settlement, in 2002 the United Kingdom Department for International Development made a ten-year commitment to support the government. Similar arrangements were later put in place for Afghanistan, Ethiopia and Rwanda (DFID, 2005).

Seizing opportunities for reconstruction requires flexible policies and a strong commitment to working in conflict-affected countries. Some donors are integrating into their policies approaches to providing education in conflict and emergencies (Brannelly et al., 2009). Even so, only ten of the twenty-three OECD-DAC members have policy commitments to providing education in countries affected by conflict and fragility,[22] and only five include education in their emergency policies (Save the Children, 2009*b*).[23]

The risks associated with working in conflict and post-conflict environments can entail high transaction costs for measures such as security assessment, engagement with government and non-government actors, and the design of practical reporting and evaluation systems. Many donors have developed innovative strategies for lowering risks and transaction costs, adapted by context.[24] Investing in pooled funds managed by another donor with a strong track record in the recipient country is one approach (Box 4.10). The Netherlands has committed US$231 million,[25] around 15% of its direct aid to education in 2006, for the period up to 2010 to a joint programme with UNICEF aimed at supporting education in countries in conflict and emergencies. Norway has reduced its bilateral aid for education in Afghanistan and increased support provided through the Afghanistan Reconstruction Trust Fund, a multidonor trust fund managed by the World Bank (Brannelly et al., 2009; Save the Children, 2009*b*). Other innovative approaches to aid delivery in conflict-affected countries include the following:

- In Guatemala, the 1996 peace accords included a commitment to support the development of indigenous education. With the help of funding from Norway directed through Save the Children's Rewrite the Future Campaign, 60,000 children are reported to have benefited from improved education quality, with the recruitment and training of bilingual teachers and curriculum development playing important roles (Save the Children, 2009*b*).

- The development of a basic education programme (focusing on pre-primary, primary and adult education) in Nepal in 2004 shows it is possible for donors and government to work together even amid serious armed conflict. In this case, Denmark, Finland, Norway, the United Kingdom and the World Bank contributed to a pooled fund. There are indications of some gains in educational attainment as a result, despite the conflict (Berry, 2007).

- In Somalia, since the early 1990s the European Commission has supported education through international non-government organizations, focusing on basic education, teacher training and vocational or life-skills training for disadvantaged youth (Brannelly et al., 2009). Support has continued through periods of intense conflict and a non-functioning government.

- Education in northern Uganda has been seriously hindered by violent conflict, with schools and teachers targeted by the Lord's Resistance Army. Aid from the Netherlands has helped finance a bursary programme for former Lord's Resistance Army combatants in the north, along with other programmes helping children and youth catch up on missed schooling (Save the Children, 2009*b*).

Another example comes from Canada, which has dramatically increased its overall aid budget for education and its support for conflict-affected countries. In seeking to align aid financing with a national policy commitment to the reconstruction of education systems, the Canadian International Development Agency (CIDA) has demonstrated a high level of flexibility. In Afghanistan and the Sudan, it has allocated resources to multidonor trust funds and non-government organizations.

Only ten of the twenty-three OECD-DAC members have policy commitments to providing education in countries affected by conflict and fragility

22. Australia, Canada, Denmark, the European Commission, Ireland, the Netherlands, Norway, Spain, the United Kingdom and the United States. The World Bank, which participates in the OECD-DAC as an observer, also has a policy on providing education in conflict-affected countries.

23. Canada, Denmark, Japan, Norway and Sweden.

24. The first principle for International Engagement in Fragile States is to take context as the starting point, recognizing that capacity, political will and legitimacy differ according to whether a country is in a prolonged conflict or recently emerging from conflict, for example.

25. At 2007 prices.

Box 4.10: Multidonor trust funds – a promising approach with mixed results

Multidonor trust funds, which pool the funds of several donors, are usually managed by the World Bank or a United Nations agency. A recent evaluation of such funds identifies them as the best-practice post-crisis funding mechanism. They are among the most important coordination, harmonization and alignment mechanisms open to donors.

In difficult post-conflict environments, multidonor trust funds offer donors several advantages. They spread fiduciary risk and reduce the cost of initiating programmes and providing support. For aid recipients, they can reduce transaction costs and provide early delivery of urgently needed support. Experience in Liberia has shown that funds can be disbursed quickly to support reconstruction of education activities (see Box 4.15). Similarly, the Afghanistan Reconstruction Trust Fund has helped pay the salaries of the expanded teaching force needed for the increased numbers of children entering school since 2002.

Not all multidonor trust funds have been as effective. A World Bank-managed fund in Southern Sudan covers about 12% of donor funding to education. Disbursement has been slow. This is partly because of weak capacity on the part of the new Education Ministry, but it has also been reported that stringent application of World Bank procurement rules has made rapid disbursement difficult.

Multidonor trust funds offer considerable potential for scaling up support to conflict-affected countries. The money currently allocated to such funds is usually a small share of total aid to conflict-affected countries, as some donors continue to provide assistance through separate projects or directly to non-government groups. This dilutes the potential benefits of pooling resources, placing additional transaction costs on recipient governments.

Sources: Scanteam (2007); Brannelly et al. (2009); Greeley (2007); Echessa (2009).

One problem with the global aid architecture is the lack of a single unified multilateral framework for education through which donors can channel resources

In the Palestinian Autonomous Territories, CIDA has a strong focus on providing safe spaces for learning and institutional support for UNRWA, the United Nations agency for Palestinian refugees, rather than providing funding directly to the Palestinian authorities. In Sierra Leone, a country in which Canada has no significant aid programme, support for reintegrating child soldiers has been delivered via non-government organizations (Mundy, 2009).

Aid for conflict-affected countries is not just about development in a narrow sense. In many such countries, donor governments are engaged in wide-ranging military and security operations, diplomatic activity and the rebuilding of basic governance systems. These overlapping roles entail threats and opportunities for effective aid. The threats derive from the risk that aid will be used, or be perceived by the people of recipient countries, as one element in a wider military strategy. Yet the integration of aid into a wider policy framework can create opportunities for more effective delivery.

Some donors are attempting to organize their aid programmes in conflict-affected countries through a 'whole of government' framework linking development, defence and diplomacy (OECD, 2006*c*).[26] For example, in the Democratic Republic of the Congo, the United Kingdom has supported bridge-building programmes aimed at restoring economic infrastructure under a pooled financing arrangement involving the defence ministry's conflict prevention fund (DFID, 2009*b*). Another example, which illustrates the difficult relationship between development and security, comes from Afghanistan, where Canada is developing an education programme in a province marked by severe insecurity (Box 4.11).

Effective multilateral approaches to aid can play a vital role in supporting conflict-affected countries. Such mechanisms enable bilateral donors to pool resources and risk, and to avoid having to create their own delivery systems. One problem with the global aid architecture is the lack of a single unified multilateral framework for education through which donors can channel resources to conflict-affected countries. Hopes that the Fast Track Initiative would fill the gap have not been realized – an issue discussed further in the final section.

26. The 'whole of government' approach is related to one of the principles for international engagement in fragile states, recognizing the link between political security and development objectives.

Box 4.11: Canada's 'whole of government' approach in Afghanistan

The 'whole of government' model that Canada has adopted in Afghanistan is an attempt to unify diplomacy, defence and development within a single policy framework. What does this mean in practice?

Multiple Canadian ministries have joined to create pooled funds, such as the Global Peace and Security Fund, supporting 'whole of government' programmes not only in Afghanistan but also in Haiti, Iraq, the Palestinian Autonomous Territories and the Sudan. The funds are an integrated source of finance covering everything from police training to emergency food aid and education. One aim is to bridge the divide between short-term humanitarian aid and long-term development aid.

Experience in Afghanistan has played an important role in shaping the development of this approach. Education has been a focal point. In 2006 and 2007, Canada provided an average of US$168 million in bilateral aid to Afghanistan. Nearly 13% was allocated to basic education, making Canada one of the country's largest donors to the sector.

Approaches to education have been shaped through a complex interaction between Canadian security commanders and development experts. In 2007, Canadian forces were redeployed to Kandahar Province. Leaders within the forces identified education as a priority concern and called for a strengthened focus on schools, teachers and textbooks. As the Canadian International Development Agency became more involved, clearer guidelines on civil-military interaction in the education sector were negotiated to ensure that Afghanistan's Ministry of Education, rather than Canada, was seen as delivering education services. The Canadian forces support CIDA activities by providing security escorts, assessing and planning infrastructure such as school perimeter walls and providing intelligence about local security.

Critics argue that linking military and human security clashes with poverty-reduction priorities. They raise questions about Canada concentrating resources in Kandahar instead of offering broader national support and about a blurring of civil and military responsibilities. Nevertheless, Canada's experience provides lessons for efforts to support education in conflict-affected contexts where donors might otherwise avoid working for fear of the high risks involved.

Sources: CCIC (2009*a*, 2009*b*); Simpson and Tomlinson (2006); Mundy (2009).

The international development goals for education will not be achieved without scaled up aid efforts in conflict-affected states

Conclusion

The international development goals for education will not be achieved without scaled up aid efforts in conflict-affected states. These states account for a large share of the out-of-school population. The recovery of their education sectors is hampered by inadequate finance, weak technical capacity and chronic shortages of teachers. The difficulties in providing support to the people of these countries are well known. Yet opportunities to rebuild education are being lost as a result of overly rigid aid management practices and the failure to develop an effective multilateral vehicle to support conflict-affected countries. □

Reforming the Fast Track Initiative

When the FTI was launched in 2002, Jim Wolfensohn, then president of the World Bank, hailed it as a 'historic first step towards putting all developing countries on an education fast track that could transform their social and economic prospects' (World Bank, 2002*a*). The FTI was widely seen as a catalyst for accelerated progress towards Education for All. While there have been some real accomplishments, the initiative manifestly has *not* put the poorest developing countries on 'an education fast track'. The overall record is one of sustained underachievement – and reform is an urgent priority.

While there have been some real accomplishments, the initiative manifestly has not put the poorest developing countries on 'an education fast track'

Disappointment in the FTI has been heightened by the gap between its ambitions and its achievements. At its inception, the initiative was seen as embodying a new type of global compact between developing countries and aid donors aimed at achieving international development goals. Developing countries were to put in place credible plans for accelerating progress in education, with donors backing strengthened national efforts through increased, more effective and more predictable aid. Seven years on, the credibility of the initiative is at an all-time low, reflecting its poor record on delivery.

The time is ripe for developing countries, donors and non-government organizations to reassess the FTI. An independent evaluation is scheduled to report on the FTI's effectiveness and formulate proposals for reform.[27] Several donors are pressing for more predictable arrangements for financial replenishment, including an initial US$1.2 billion commitment. Meanwhile, the new United States administration has signalled an intention to create a new global fund for education, though the details remain unclear. This backdrop creates an opportunity for far-reaching reform of the FTI.

Seizing that opportunity is critical for progress towards Education for All. The FTI is not working, but a dynamic multilateral aid initiative could create a powerful new momentum towards reaching the targets set in Dakar in 2000. It could play a vital role in supporting countries that are off track for achieving the EFA goals and in mobilizing resources for marginalized groups. Unlocking the potential will require strong political leadership and greater clarity, notably over the role of the FTI in mobilizing and delivering the additional finance needed to achieve the goals.

This section provides a critical assessment of the Fast Track Initiative. It sets out the problems in governance, finance and country coverage. The scale of these problems rules out business as usual. Bluntly stated, the FTI in its current form is indefensible. Abolishing the current framework and developing a new multilateral blueprint from scratch is not the answer, however. The world needs an ambitious multilateral framework to accelerate progress towards the 2015 goals, and a reformed FTI is the most viable option. The following are among the key messages of this section:

- *The FTI has failed to mobilize and deliver financing on the required scale.* The initiative has delivered too little aid with too many transaction costs. Initially it was envisaged that the FTI would galvanize resources indirectly through an 'endorsement effect', with its stamp of approval unlocking increased donor support. The Catalytic Fund was later introduced to provide direct support. There is no compelling evidence, however, that bilateral aid to FTI-endorsed countries has increased. Meanwhile, the Catalytic Fund has suffered from a weak and erratic donor support base and a large gap between commitments and disbursements.
- *The FTI has left intact a failed approach to the assessment of financing gaps.* Achieving the EFA goals will require a significant increase in aid financing. By this Report's estimate, an additional US$16 billion is required annually to 2015. The FTI has not provided a vehicle for addressing this challenge. National plans still reflect donors' assessments of what they can afford rather than what countries need, and fail to address the additional costs of reaching marginalized groups. Aid financing for education continues to be dominated by short-termism (with typical commitment periods of one to three years), poor predictability and limited support for teacher salaries.
- *The FTI has in some cases weakened efforts to improve aid effectiveness and implement the Paris agenda.* To be eligible for Catalytic Fund support, countries must meet the rules governing the release of funds from the World Bank's International Development Association (IDA). National reporting and procurement

27. The evaluation covers 2002-2008. The report is scheduled for late 2009. Working papers and the preliminary draft report, which were available at the time of writing, were referred to for this section.

systems have often been deemed ineligible, even when bilateral donors use them in harmonized programmes. The result has been long-running tension between FTI practices and the principles underpinning the Paris agenda.

- *The FTI has the rhetoric of an aid partnership with the governance arrangements of a 'donor club'.* Developing countries are under-represented at all levels of the FTI partnership. Governance arrangements are particularly skewed at higher levels, where decisions about funding allocations are made. In addition, FTI decision-making processes are often arbitrary and opaque. New governance rules are needed to increase the voice of developing countries and the transparency of decision-making. The FTI should be reconstituted as an entity operating independently of the World Bank with a larger, more independent secretariat.

- *Conflict-affected countries have not been well served by the FTI.* The initiative is potentially a viable option for supporting countries affected by conflict as it provides a multilateral framework that can help reduce risk and transaction costs. However, the FTI has not responded to the needs of conflict-affected countries. The framework is skewed towards rewarding governments able to meet a 'gold standard' level of planning, effectively excluding many conflict-affected countries. The failure of the donor community to develop a more flexible – and more relevant – model has seriously compromised the education prospects of some of the world's most vulnerable children. Extending the FTI to conflict-affected countries is among the most urgent of all reform priorities.

- *Multilateral initiatives in public health provide lessons for FTI reform.* Global health initiatives have played a vital role in mobilizing development finance. In stark contrast to the FTI, programmes such as the Global Fund to Fight AIDS, Tuberculosis and Malaria and the GAVI Alliance have also provided multilateral frameworks for channelling additional private financing towards shared international development goals and created democratic, transparent and accountable governance structures linking national planning processes to aid disbursements. While multilateral initiatives in health are not without problems and the education sector is different in some key respects, FTI reform should reflect lessons from global health initiatives.

Constructive debate on the FTI has been stymied by a protracted 'blame game'. Donors have criticized one another for perceived failures in financing and delivery and the World Bank for wider governance problems. Unfortunately, the resulting dialogue has diverted attention from deeper structural problems. The FTI cannot be held responsible for donors' failure to act on pledges made at Dakar or for developing countries' failure to prioritize policies for overcoming marginalization. Weak political commitment to international aid for education and to national equity has far deeper roots. Similarly, the highly professional FTI Secretariat in the World Bank cannot be held responsible for governance rules created by the institution's shareholders. While the governance architecture of the FTI is problematic and has weakened its impact, failures of governance are themselves a symptom of weak political leadership.

This section has five parts. Part 1 sets out the background to the FTI, explaining how it operates and documenting delivery to date. Part 2 focuses on financing and the slow pace of disbursement. Part 3 looks at the failure of the FTI to respond to the special needs of countries affected by conflict. Part 4 explores some of the major global initiatives in health, drawing lessons that may be relevant for FTI reform. The section concludes by setting out some of the key conditions for a global initiative in education that can deliver results.

Extending the FTI to conflict-affected countries is among the most urgent of all reform priorities

The Fast Track Initiative framework

Launched in 2002, the Fast Track Initiative was presented as part of a wider global compact for achieving international development goals. At the International Conference on Financing for Development (Monterrey, 2002), developing countries committed to strengthen planning for poverty reduction, while rich countries pledged to mobilize more aid to support 'country-owned' plans.

The FTI became a prototype for the new model, seen as a vehicle for strengthening national planning through development of broad-based education strategies that would be a focal point for donor coordination and resource mobilization. The initiative was geared towards achieving universal primary completion by 2015, rather than the much broader set of EFA objectives set out in the Dakar Framework (Colclough and Fennel, 2004; Rose, 2005; World Bank, 2002*b*). In reality, it has had no significant impact even on this narrow goal.

Tackling gaps in planning and finance

The FTI's core business plan, drawn up in 2002, involved tackling *planning gaps* in three key areas – policy development, data and capacity – and mobilizing additional aid to close *financing gaps* (World Bank, 2002*b*). Four key objectives were established (FTI Secretariat, 2004):

Inconsistency and ambiguity have characterized the Fast Track approach to financing gaps

- increasing aid for basic education by providing sustained, predictable and flexible financial support to countries demonstrating a commitment and capacity to accelerate progress;
- improving aid efficiency and cutting transaction costs by coordinating and harmonizing donor support behind sector-wide education strategies;
- respecting country ownership by aligning aid with national priorities and policies;
- establishing clear benchmarks for the development of credible and sustainable education plans.

The establishment through the FTI of a unified process through which donors could harmonize activities behind country-owned plans linked the initiative to the broad goals set out in the 2005 Paris Declaration on Aid Effectiveness. In practice, however, implementation of FTI planning and financing processes has undermined donor coordination, raised transaction costs and weakened aid effectiveness in some countries.

A restricted approach to financing

The FTI gave donors an opportunity to develop an ambitious new approach to aid financing. With financing gaps identified as major obstacles to universal primary completion by 2015, national planning processes could have been used to develop credible, consistent estimates of the cost of removing those obstacles. Unfortunately, inconsistency and ambiguity have characterized the Fast Track approach to financing gaps.

One problem is the Indicative Framework, a series of benchmarks used to calculate the costs of national plans and associated financing gaps. The indicators included give prominence to overall spending on primary education, average class size, average teacher salaries, spending on inputs other than teacher salaries, and the rate of repetition. Benchmarks for each indicator were established, based on World Bank research that identified countries making good progress towards universal primary completion. The benchmarks were intended to be adapted to country circumstances (Bruns et al., 2003). Some commentators believe the Indicative Framework has created a consistent set of relevant and appropriate benchmarks that have been applied in a fashion consistent with the principles of country ownership (Bermingham, 2009*a*). Others, however, have questioned the weak participation of developing countries and donors in designing the framework, and whether the indicators and benchmarks are appropriate, notably in areas such as teacher remuneration (Carr-Hill, 2009; Rose, 2005).[28] Some have argued that the Indicative Framework could be construed as a new form of policy conditionality (King and Rose, 2005).

National education plans submitted for Fast Track endorsement point to varied approaches towards costing measures to achieve the EFA goals in practice. There is little consistency in approach – and the links to international targets are often unclear. Some national plans are not geared towards achievement of universal primary completion by 2015.[29] Moreover, the vast majority of plans lack credible estimates – in many cases, any estimates – of the cost of reaching marginalized groups (Bennell, 2009).

Factors unrelated to achievement of the 2015 goals appear to have weighed heavily in approaches to estimating financing gaps. The approaches seem to be influenced in part by recipient government expectations of the amount of funding they can hope to receive. Donor considerations of affordability for their own aid budgets also appear to outweigh structured assessment of the financing required to achieve specific targets. This has contributed to what one commentator calls a 'systematic downward bias' in local donor groups' estimation of national financing gaps (Sperling, 2008, p. 4).

Assessments of countries' ability to absorb more aid also play a key role in donor calculations (Dom, 2009; Rawle, 2009). The capacity of aid recipients to use development assistance effectively is an important concern. However, constraints in this area have to be examined in the light of the technical and financing requirements for increasing capacity over time. If inability to absorb aid is a problem, then the solution has to come in part from directing aid towards building absorptive capacity.

The problem in current FTI approaches is that the criteria donors use to assess absorptive capacity

28. The basis for the benchmarks has also been criticized. They are based on averages for each indicator for ten countries identified as good performers in the drive towards universal primary completion. In fact, however, the levels of the indicators diverged considerably across the ten countries.

29. For example, while Mozambique targets universal primary education by 2015, Burkina Faso targets a 70% net enrolment rate, a more realistic target given the country's situation.

lack transparency and consistency. For example, in Cambodia cost estimates for the national education strategy indicate that the country needs an additional US$138 million a year to achieve specified EFA goals agreed with donors. The local donor group decided, for reasons never made public, that only around one-third of that amount could be used effectively. The funding request submitted to the Catalytic Fund was revised downwards to reflect this assessment (FTI Secretariat, 2007*a*). In Cameroon, a proposal to provide funding for the total estimated financing gap of US$47 million was submitted to the Catalytic Fund and the first tranche approved in 2007 (FTI Secretariat, 2007*a*). Leaving aside issues specific to these two cases, the comparison illustrates the *ad hoc* nature of FTI operations and the absence of a strategic planning vision for achieving EFA goals.

Differing views over the role of the FTI in financing have been a source of controversy from the outset. Many developing countries and campaigning organizations argued that a multilateral initiative should play a direct role in financing education plans geared towards international development goals (Rose, 2005; Watkins, 2000). The framework that emerged reflected a less ambitious approach. It saw the FTI as providing an imprimatur for national plans that would unlock additional support from donors operating within developing countries (FTI Secretariat, 2004; Cambridge Education et al., 2009). The emphasis shifted when the multidonor Catalytic Fund was set up as a source of direct finance, initially as a transitional financing mechanism for countries lacking a critical donor base. In 2007 its doors were opened to those with endorsed education plans and a financing gap (FTI Secretariat, 2007*c*).

The creation of the Catalytic Fund added to the confusion over the role of the FTI in financing. Potential aid recipients often saw the new fund as the real core of the initiative. As a recent evaluation of Kenya's recourse to the FTI puts it: 'A striking feature of the Kenya case is that FTI is seen by local stakeholders predominantly as a direct source of funding' (through the FTI Catalytic Fund) (Thomson et al., 2009, p. 83). That perspective is widely shared in developing countries. The role of the Catalytic Fund remains ambiguous, however, with some donors seeing it as a potentially important mechanism for mobilizing and delivering the resources needed to achieve EFA goals and others continuing to view it as a residual financing vehicle.

That ambiguity is apparent in the debate over Catalytic Fund replenishment. The FTI Secretariat estimated that US$1.2 billion is needed over the eighteen months to 2010 to meet expected demand (FTI Task Team on Replenishment of the EFA Fast Track Initiative, 2009). Yet it is not clear whether this estimate reflects an assessment of national financing gaps in relation to universal primary education and other goals, or an assessment of what donors might be willing to allocate. Recent donor discussions on proposals to create a 'needs and performance framework' for allocation of Catalytic Fund resources have added to the confusion. The aim of the framework is to set out a process and criteria for determining how to spread resources among endorsed countries (FTI Secretariat, 2009*b*). In effect, the framework is attempting to establish a basis for rationing without having first established the precise purpose of the Catalytic Fund or its role in global EFA financing.

The Catalytic Fund essentially has become a parallel aid programme supporting a wide range of primarily project-based activities, mainly dealing with school construction, textbook purchasing and distribution, and teacher training. In Madagascar, the fund provided US$21 million from 2005 to 2008 to help finance recruitment and training of community teachers. Support to Rwanda is providing capitation grants to primary schools to help finance the cost of phasing out user fees (World Bank, 2009*h*). These programmes are important, yet most FTI support mirrors activities already backed by in-country donors, including those that finance the Catalytic Fund. Another concern is the lack of provision for ongoing funding to cover, for example, the rising recurrent salary cost of increased teacher recruitment.

The FTI Secretariat estimated that US$1.2 billion is needed over the eighteen months to 2010 to meet expected demand

More fundamentally, the FTI has failed to transform the financing environment for aid to basic education. Accelerated progress towards education for all clearly requires strengthened national planning. But it also requires a commitment by donors to provide predictable, long-term support – over five to ten years – including for teacher salaries. For aid recipients, what matters is timely delivery of donor finance during planning and budget cycles. At present, the FTI neither assures mobilization of additional resources by bilateral donors operating in-country nor offers a reliable source of direct finance through the Catalytic Fund. Practically speaking, it is all but irrelevant to donors' commitment at Dakar to ensure that no country fails to achieve the 2015 goal of universal primary completion for want of additional finance.

Supporting national education planning and building capacity

It is sometimes claimed that the real success of the Fast Track Initiative has been in national planning rather than financing. Such claims are difficult to evaluate. In some cases, FTI processes may have improved the quality of dialogue between donors and governments, and increased donor coordination. But it is not clear from the evidence available that the FTI has strengthened national planning processes overall, either in terms of costing education plans or by giving greater attention to strategies aimed at including marginalized groups, though it may have done so in individual cases (Woods, 2009*a*).[30]

Perhaps the most serious criticism of the EDPF is that it has not helped institutions such as education ministries to plan and monitor progress in education

The Education Programme Development Fund (EPDF), the second multidonor trust fund of the FTI, was established in 2004 to provide technical support and capacity development to help countries meet FTI endorsement standards (FTI Secretariat, 2004). Modelled on a Norwegian trust fund, it has a mixed record. It has successfully supported preparation of technical data and background analysis for some countries (including Sierra Leone, as shown later in this chapter). However, critics question its responsiveness to potential beneficiaries' needs (Box 4.12).

From local to global: governance of the FTI partnership

Governance of the Fast Track Initiative involves a large number of actors and complex processes. National planning, the foundation for entry into the 'FTI partnership', brings together governments and donors. At the global level, the FTI is rooted in wider EFA planning processes through a Board of Directors that includes developing countries and all major donors for education, including bilateral, multilateral and regional agencies, and civil society groups (FTI Secretariat, 2004, 2009*d*; Buse, 2005).

Reform of the governance system has been a perennial item on the FTI agenda. Debate on this point has focused on representation by developing countries and non-government organizations, the

Box 4.12: The Education Programme Development Fund

The EPDF was designed to address the planning constraints facing many developing countries, with a view to improving prospects for FTI endorsement and additional aid. Funding commitments amount to US$114 million for 2005-2010. Norway contributes about 40% of the resources, with the Netherlands and the United Kingdom providing a further 20% between them.

The EPDF is widely acknowledged to have contributed to technical analysis, planning scenarios and regional meetings to promote cross-country learning. There has been criticism of several points, however, including the disparity between allocations and disbursements: at the end of 2008, less than half of the funds allocated since 2004 had been disbursed. Given that the EPDF was created to support capacity-building, the fact that capacity constraints have been cited as a reason for slow disbursement is troubling.

EPDF funds have not targeted countries where capacity is weakest. A 2007 assessment found that only around 40% of EPDF recipient countries were identified as fragile states (according to the OECD-DAC definition) and that these received just 28% of country-specific funding. In some countries, EPDF finance has been directed towards subsectors weakly linked to FTI goals, such as higher education. The fund has largely supported workshops, seminars and traditional types of external technical assistance.

Perhaps the most serious criticism of the EDPF is that it has not helped institutions such as education ministries to plan and monitor progress in education.

Some commentators argue that the EPDF has been weakened through its domination by the World Bank. A 2008 review found that the Bank executed 90% of EPDF activities. This is partly because the management structure delegates proposal development authority to World Bank regional sector managers. The Bank also holds the EPDF Committee chair, adding to potential conflicts of interest.

Several developing country FTI members have indicated that they do not understand the process of securing EDPF funds. This may partly account for the relatively slow pace of disbursement. With the current EPDF commitment period ending in 2010, just two-thirds of funds have been allocated and less than half this amount has been disbursed.

The EPDF remains an underutilized resource. As the single largest source of untied aid available to support capacity development in education, it could be used to address urgent priorities, such as improving the integration into planning processes of policies designed to reach marginalized groups.

Sources: Bermingham (2009*a*); FTI Secretariat (2008*b*, 2009*a*); Bellew and Moock (2008); Riddell (2009).

30. This is one issue assessed by the FTI evaluation. Country studies available at the time of writing had not been able to identify any significant direct FTI influence in national planning. The only other systematic evaluation to date is a World Bank review of twenty-eight education sector plans endorsed by the FTI. While the plans were found to be 'above average', the evaluation concluded that the Indicative Framework benchmarks and assessment guidelines were not used consistently (Woods, 2009a).

role of the secretariat and procedures for endorsing and financing national plans (Visser-Valfrey, 2009). While changes have been made, they have left the underlying institutional structures and power relationships largely intact.

The local education group. The FTI process is open to any developing country with an approved poverty reduction strategy and a 'sound' education plan endorsed by in-country donors. Reflecting the principle of country ownership, the in-country donor group plays a key role, interacting with governments on developing national plans for submission. It also has institutional responsibility for the endorsement of plans and the mobilization of additional financing. By the end of 2008, thirty-six countries had had their education plans endorsed (Figure 4.17). The FTI Secretariat predicts a further twenty-three countries may be added in 2009–2011 (FTI Secretariat, 2009*b*).

Figure 4.17: Between 2002 and 2008, the FTI endorsed thirty-six countries' national plans

Countries with education sector plans endorsed by the FTI, 2002-2008

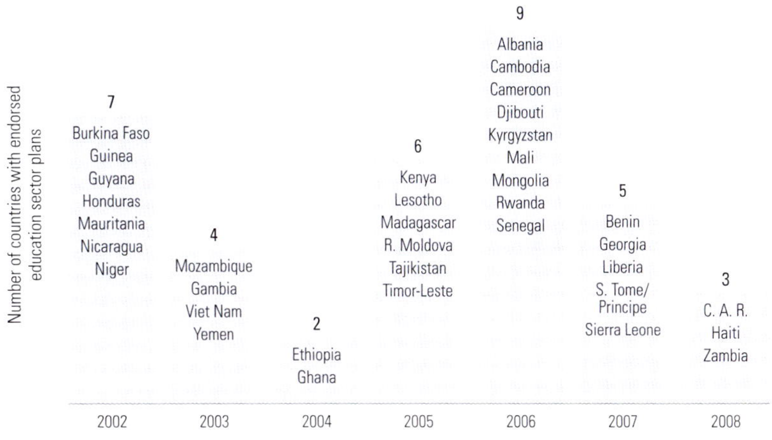

Source: FTI Secretariat (2009*b*).

The World Bank and the FTI Secretariat. The World Bank hosts the FTI Secretariat and serves as trustee and supervising entity for the Catalytic Fund and the Education Programme Development Fund, exercising both fiduciary and decision-making responsibility on the release of finance from the funds. The FTI Secretariat, comprising World Bank staff as well as staff seconded from other FTI partners, provides support to the various FTI activities and committees (World Bank, 2009*a*).

The Board of Directors.[31] This is the governing body of the FTI. It sets policies and strategies, monitors the use of the trust funds and is responsible for mobilizing resources and responding to country concerns. From 2009, the expectation is that the Board of Directors and the FTI partnership overall will be represented by an independent chairperson – a move aimed at bolstering high-level political and intellectual leadership, including in resource mobilization. The chair does not participate in decision-making at any FTI meetings. The board membership is heavily skewed towards donors, with four developing country representatives, two of them from Africa, each serving two years; six bilateral donors, also serving two years each; four multilateral agencies (the World Bank, UNESCO, UNICEF and the European Commission) with one standing representative each; and three civil society organizations (FTI Secretariat, 2009*d*). Not only are developing countries underrepresented, but the rotation of members limits the potential for continuity and sustained dialogue.

The global level. The Partnership Meeting, held every two years, is intended as a high-level forum 'for mutual accountability, enabling a review of progress, challenges and bottlenecks' (FTI Secretariat, 2009*d*, p. 7). The Board of Directors coordinates the meeting with support from the secretariat. Apart from its broad oversight role, the Partnership Meeting provides a platform for 'advocacy in support of continued resource mobilization, improved aid effectiveness, and inclusion of new partners' (FTI Secretariat, 2009*d*, p. 7). As the lead United Nations agency on education, UNESCO provides a link to wider EFA monitoring activities, notably via the High-Level Group created to monitor progress on the Dakar Framework for Action.

The governance structure of any organization has to be assessed in terms of transparency, accountability, effectiveness and perceived legitimacy. FTI governance would score low on each of these. Three distinctive sets of problems have contributed to wider failings:

- *Donor dominance.* The donor community in general and the World Bank in particular dominate FTI processes, from endorsement of national plans to allocations of finance. In effect, donors act as judge, jury and executing agency. There is no independent technical review procedure and no secretariat independent of contributing donors.

- *Poorly 'joined-up' decision-making.* One layer of Fast Track processes takes place at the national

Any organization has to be assessed in terms of transparency, accountability, effectiveness and perceived legitimacy – FTI governance would score low on each of these

31. The Board of Directors was established in July 2009 and has replaced the FTI Steering Committee.

level. Local donor groups, engaged in dialogue with governments over many years, identify FTI priorities in the context of support for sector plans. In many cases, donor groups have developed flexible and innovative strategies for building national capacity and working through national systems. The applications for FTI financing then go through another set of processes at the global level, with World Bank disbursement rules weighing heavily in financing decisions. In many cases, tensions between national donor practices and global FTI rules have stalled delivery.

In many cases, tensions between national donor practices and global FTI rules have stalled delivery

- *Weak global leadership*. The FTI has not galvanized high-level financial and political support, as its narrow donor base and limited success in mobilizing financial resources show. The steering committee has not set a strategic direction and has failed to act decisively in resolving problems over disbursement. A new governance structure has recently been adopted but it is not apparent that it will be able to rectify these problems. Beyond the FTI itself, the High-Level Group has proved ineffective in setting an agenda for change. It was mandated to 'serve as a lever for political commitment and technical and financial resource mobilization', but its annual meetings have become high-level talking shops characterized by long planning cycles, agendas lacking strategic objectives and wide-ranging, unfocused debate. Each meeting has culminated in the adoption of vague communiqués that are long on broad injunctions to governments and largely devoid of practical commitments. The *EFA Global Monitoring Report 2003/4* issued a harsh verdict on the first two meetings: 'Neither the communiqués nor the reports ...', it concluded, 'have had any visible international impact, either in generating political commitment or in mobilizing the resources required to achieve EFA' (UNESCO, 2003, p. 255). That assessment could be extended to all eight High-Level Group meetings.

Delivering finance: too little and too erratic

Confusion has marked the debate over the role of the Fast Track Initiative in mobilizing additional financing. Some observers – including many donors – argue that FTI endorsement has played an important indirect role in generating increased aid through bilateral donors. Others focus on the direct financing provided through the Catalytic Fund.

While indirect financing is difficult to measure, there is little evidence to support a strong 'FTI effect', and the Catalytic Fund has delivered small amounts of finance with high transaction costs.

Financial leverage of FTI endorsement?

Annual reports published by the FTI partnership claim that plan endorsement has helped leverage additional aid (Bermingham, 2009*a*; FTI Secretariat, 2008*a*). That claim is usually supported by reference to studies looking at aid levels before and after FTI endorsement of national plans.

The problem is that these studies lend themselves to selective interpretation. Consider first the widely cited finding that 'the early FTI countries seem to have experienced a greater increase in basic education commitments' (FTI Secretariat, 2008*a*, p. 26). This is based on the observation that countries with plans endorsed in 2002–2004 secured a doubling in aid commitments over 2000–2006, which is greater than the increase for non-endorsed countries. It is not clear why the comparison period begins in 2000 (two years before the creation of the FTI). Moreover, extending the period to 2007 eliminates the positive finding (Rawle, 2009).

The scope for selectivity can be illustrated by reference to another comparison. In the eleven countries endorsed in 2002 and 2003, the annual rate of increase in aid commitments to basic education to 2005 amounted to 4%. This was less than half the increase in commitments recorded for non-FTI low-income countries. Within the FTI group, the increase in commitments was unequally distributed, ranging from annual growth of over 80% in Mauritania and Yemen to 10% in Burkina Faso. Moreover, commitments actually fell in constant 2007 dollar terms in five FTI-endorsed countries. This evidence does not point to a negative FTI effect, but it hardly lends weight to the case for a positive effect.

Preliminary assessment of the FTI mid-term evaluation concludes that aid data 'do not constitute strong evidence that FTI endorsement leads to a surge in aid for basic education' (Cambridge Education et al., 2009, p. 34). Indeed, it was the failure of bilateral donors to scale up support for education sufficiently in countries with endorsed education plans that prompted a broadening of the Catalytic Fund remit in 2007 beyond its initial focus on those lacking a critical base of donors.

The Catalytic Fund: slow disbursement undermines effectiveness

Expansion of the Catalytic Fund's role opened the door for more countries to receive multilateral financing for longer periods (FTI Secretariat, 2007*c*, 2009*b*). It has also served to highlight problems of resource mobilization, disbursement and donor commitments.

Support channelled through the Catalytic Fund has grown steadily. Cumulative cash receipts from donors had reached US$1.2 billion by March 2009. However, overall disbursements amounted to only US$491 million.[32] For 2004–2007, Catalytic Fund receipts averaged around 4% of total aid commitments for basic education (OECD-DAC, 2009*d*). As of the first quarter of 2009, twenty-three developing countries had received Catalytic Fund financing,[33] but distribution was highly uneven, with Kenya, Madagascar and Rwanda accounting for half of all disbursements (FTI Secretariat, 2008*e*, 2009*b*).

The financing base for the Catalytic Fund has remained very narrow. The Fast Track Initiative was created to encourage and coordinate funding from bilateral donors, multilateral agencies and private philanthropy, but bilateral donors dominate Catalytic Fund receipts (Figure 4.18). Fourteen bilateral donors have provided support, with nearly three-quarters of the total over 2004–2008 coming from just three: the Netherlands, Spain and the United Kingdom. In marked contrast to global health financing initiatives, the FTI has not created a window for philanthropic finance.

Support to the Catalytic Fund represents a significant share of some donors' overall aid commitments to education, accounting for an estimated 15% for the Netherlands and 9% for the United Kingdom, from 2004 to 2007. These figures suggest that the performance of the Catalytic Fund influences the programmes of these individual donors.

Poor disbursement rates under the Catalytic Fund have severely compromised the FTI and the wider aid effort. There is inevitably a lag between allocation and disbursement in any aid programme, but in this case the lag has been extremely protracted. Since 2007, some countries have had to wait up to two years after the decision to allocate aid before receiving their first tranche of finance (Figure 4.19). This compares unfavourably with an average gap between allocation and disbursement of nine months before 2007.

Figure 4.18: A small group of countries dominates donor support of the FTI

Total donor allocations to the FTI Catalytic Fund, 2004-2008

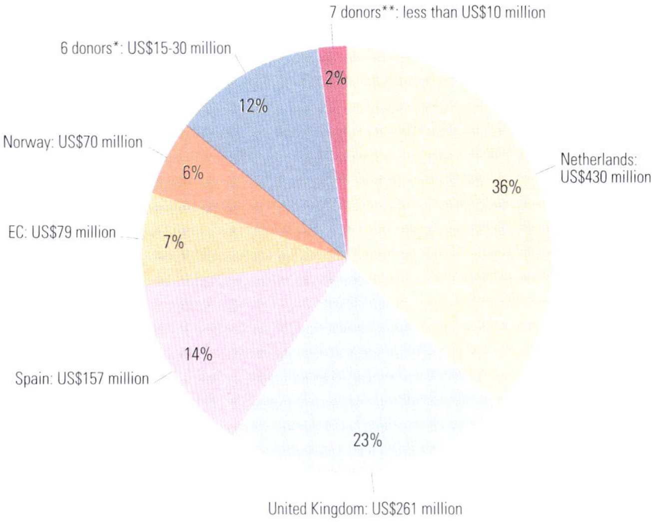

* Canada, Denmark, France, Ireland, Italy and Sweden, each contributing US$15–30 million.
** Australia, Belgium, Germany, Japan, Romania, the Russian Federation and Switzerland, each contributing less than US$10 million.
Source: FTI Secretariat (2009*b*).

While there is some evidence of a slight increase in the rate of disbursement, as of April 2009 only 8% of grants allocated in 2007 had been delivered (Bermingham, 2009*a*).

Delayed disbursement has disrupted planning in many countries. An allocation to Senegal in 2007 was still not disbursed in March 2009. Countries including Cambodia, Mozambique and Sierra Leone have experienced delays of more than a year between allocation and grant agreement. Several countries whose FTI plans were endorsed in 2002–2004 have yet to receive their full allocation. After four years, Nicaragua and Yemen had received less than 60% of their Catalytic Fund allocations (Figure 4.20).

The marked deterioration in disbursement performance can be traced directly to a governance change. Before 2007, Fast Track funds were treated as supplements to IDA projects. In several countries, including Cameroon, Kenya and Rwanda, World Bank staff demonstrated considerable flexibility in adapting project rules to facilitate more rapid disbursement. The experience of Kenya shows what can be achieved through a flexible multilateral financing mechanism, although even in this case support has been short term (Box 4.13).

In marked contrast to global health financing initiatives, the FTI has not created a window for philanthropic finance

32. By August 2009, overall disbursements had increased to US$580 million (FTI Secretariat, 2009*c*).

33. The figure is projected to climb to around thirty countries by the end of 2009.

Figure 4.19: There are long delays between allocation and disbursement from the Catalytic Fund

Number of months between allocation, grant agreement and disbursement from the FTI Catalytic Fund, 2003-2009

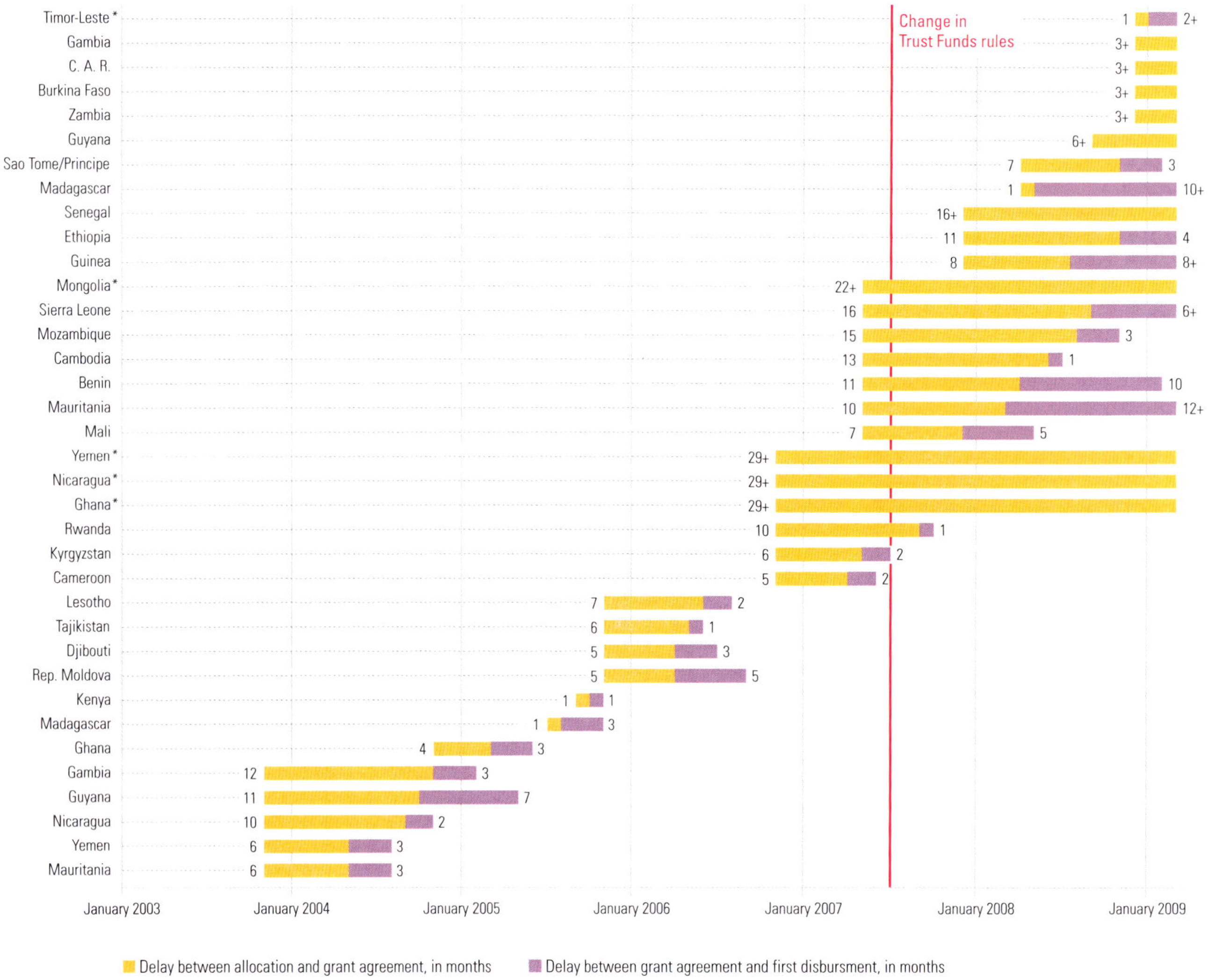

* Third-year grant.

Notes: A plus sign following the number of months means the process is not finished, i.e. the grant agreement has not yet been signed or the first disbursement made.
Some countries appear more than once because they have received more than one allocation since endorsement.

Source: FTI Secretariat (2008*e*, 2009*b*).

Delays in disbursement deter aid recipients from adopting more ambitious reform agendas

Disbursement rates began to slow dramatically with a rule change in 2007. Presented with evidence of a proliferation of trust funds, World Bank directors determined that the institution faced serious financial risk and was failing in its fiduciary responsibilities. A directive required all trust funds – including the FTI Catalytic Fund – to be subject to the same safeguards and management procedures as IDA investment programmes. The change applied retroactively to aid allocated but not yet disbursed (Bermingham, 2009*a*).

Little thought appears to have been given to how the change would affect the FTI. World Bank guidelines on application of the new rules to the Catalytic Fund became available in October 2008 – more than a year after the decision. Several bilateral donors have subsequently been critical of the World Bank for the delays caused in FTI disbursement as a result of the new rules, but this misses an important point: the executive directors who proposed and endorsed the change included representatives of countries contributing to the FTI. Concerned principally with fiduciary responsibility and financial risk, and answerable to finance ministries, they seem not to have considered the impact of the decision on aid to education – an extreme case of failure to 'join up' thinking on development policy.

The oversight proved very costly. Implementation of full IDA financial rules entails thirty-four separate procedures with an average completion time of around eighteen months (Bermingham, 2009*a*). The change was especially problematic for countries without a major World Bank presence, which had to carry out new appraisals before they could receive Catalytic Fund allocations, causing substantial delay and adding to transaction costs. In some cases, the requirement to follow IDA procedures damaged donor efforts to work through national systems – a central objective of the Paris agenda on aid effectiveness (Buse, 2007). The protracted delay in aid delivery to Mozambique illustrates the problem (Box 4.14).

Delays in disbursement deter aid recipients from adopting more ambitious reform agendas. They also weaken donor support of the FTI. In 2008, the Netherlands had to reprogramme US$135 million committed to the FTI because of internal rules linking transfers to disbursement. These resources were effectively lost to the education financing effort.

Efforts have been made to improve Catalytic Fund disbursement. In December 2008, the Catalytic Fund committee agreed for the first time to channel a grant through national budget support, using a World Bank mechanism to deliver US$102 million in FTI funds to Burkina Faso (FTI Secretariat, 2008*d*). This is expected to result in faster disbursement and allow the government to use its own financial management systems, reducing transaction costs.

A second innovation involves delegation of authority from the World Bank to an in-country donor. In Zambia, the local donor group determined that the Netherlands would be better placed to act as the supervising entity for Catalytic Fund aid. The use of an alternative supervising entity shows some flexibility – but does not address the systemic problem. In countries where the World Bank is the FTI supervising body, the theoretical choice for governments is whether to opt for Fast Track support provided on a project basis or to seek direct budget support. Lack of clarity in the criteria for budget support has prompted most countries to choose project support since the rule change.

Figure 4.20: Full disbursement of Catalytic Fund grants can take years

Share of country allocation from the Catalytic Fund disbursed as of the end of 2008

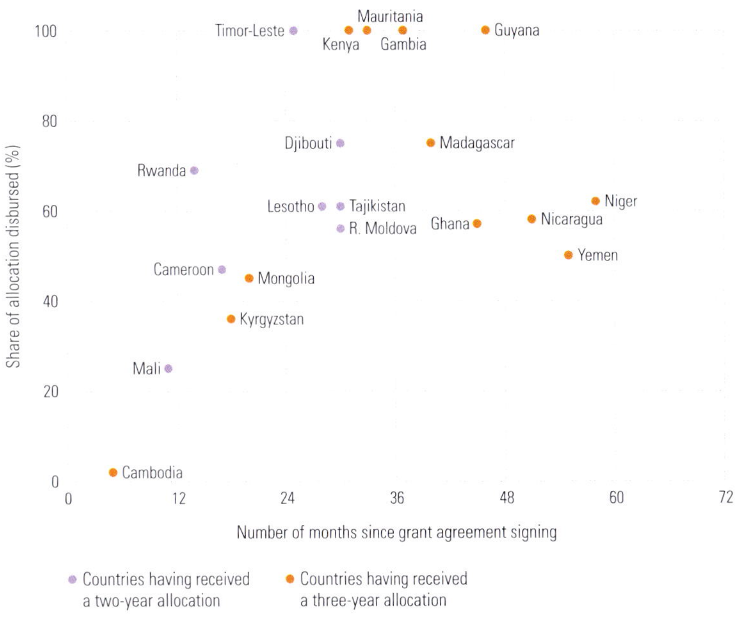

Source: FTI Secretariat (2008*e*).

Box 4.13: Kenya – FTI support for school fee abolition

The experience of Kenya highlights the potential of the FTI to support national reform.

After the abolition of school fees in early 2003, primary school enrolment increased by around a million pupils in the following school year. Per capita grants to schools were designed to replace the lost fee revenue. Even so, classroom overcrowding and textbook shortages threatened to undermine the quality of education. Donors recognized the urgent need for additional resources, while at the same time expressing concern over corruption in procurement.

Under a new donor-supported programme, procurement rules were amended to deliver funds to school committees through the private banking system. These committees of parents and teachers were responsible for purchasing textbooks from an approved list. They also assumed responsibility for verifying and publicizing the receipt of school grants. Despite pervasive corruption in national procurement systems reported at the time, audits found the programme to be effective.

Quick decision-making and rapid disbursement characterized FTI support to Kenya during this critical period. Catalytic Fund grants to Kenya amounted to US$121 million from 2005 to 2008. Administered by the World Bank, these grants were combined with IDA financing and a grant from the United Kingdom Department for International Development to increase support to school committees for the country's 18,000 primary schools. The challenge now is to sustain such support through follow-up Catalytic Fund financing or increased bilateral aid.

Sources: Bermingham (2009*a*); Thomson et al. (2009).

Box 4.14: Mozambique – slow delivery under the Fast Track Initiative

Mozambique's experience graphically illustrates the damaging consequences of the change in Catalytic Fund procedures introduced in 2007. Having built up an impressive track record on reform, the country found its efforts to secure funds, along with donor efforts to align support behind national planning, thwarted by inflexible enforcement of World Bank rules.

Mozambique, one of the first countries to submit an application to the expanded Catalytic Fund, was allocated US$79 million for 2008-2009. The government programmed this into its budget framework for 2008. With support from the local donor group, the government asked for the funds to be channelled through a pooled arrangement developed to support the country's Education Sector Strategic Plan. This well-established sector fund channelled support from six major bilateral donors (Canada, Finland, Germany, Ireland, the Netherlands and the United Kingdom). Donor confidence in improved financial management systems had led to an agreement in which donors committed to using national systems for planning and financial management, including procurement.

Application of the new Catalytic Fund procedures led to problems from the outset. The World Bank did not accept the pooled fund arrangement that complied with IDA rules. It interpreted its fiduciary responsibility as requiring a full financial and management appraisal of systems used by the Ministry of Education and Culture. While the World Bank concluded that the financial management practices in Mozambique were reasonable, and better than average in the education sector, it found that a national law stipulating 'domestic preference' in procurement policy was inconsistent with IDA project rules.

Proposals from the World Bank made the release of finance conditional on either Catalytic Fund support being channelled through a separate project operating outside the pooled funding arrangement, or a change in the rules governing the pooled fund. The government and donors strongly resisted both options. Reversion to project-based aid was seen as a step back from the principles of sector-wide support that the FTI was created to encourage. And there was no support for changing pooled fund rules that had been painstakingly negotiated.

Months of acrimonious discussion followed. Donors asked the Catalytic Fund committee to transfer supervising authority for the Mozambique grant to a member of the local donor group. The committee agreed in principle, but said the decision had to be taken at a local level where negotiations were deadlocked. Under pressure from the World Bank, the Government of Mozambique eventually agreed to a technical annex amending the procurement section of the pooled fund agreement. It registered a strong protest, however, pointing out that the country had been forced to take several steps backwards on donor harmonization and coordination.

As of March 2009, two years after the initial Catalytic Fund allocation, Mozambique had received US$28 million of the US$79 million grant.

Sources: FTI Secretariat (2007*b*); Bermingham (2009*a*); Bartholomew et al. (2009).

Signed pledges from donors amounted to US$389 million in 2008 but fall to US$26 million for 2011

This would appear to be a departure from the principles of the Paris agenda.

Recent innovations underline the fact that reform is possible, but the systemic problems behind the poor disbursement record cannot be resolved case by case. Countries allocated grants in 2007 still have to meet the full rigour of World Bank rules. Several of these countries, including Mauritania and Sierra Leone, were still waiting to receive their first disbursements at the beginning of 2009. Countries with plans endorsed after 2007 also face uncertain prospects.

Long-term predictable financing is still missing

The long-term planning horizons for education require long-term aid financing horizons, with donors making commitments over ten years. The Fast Track Initiative and the Catalytic Fund have failed to address this challenge.

The expanded Catalytic Fund arrangement held out the prospect of more countries getting assistance over longer periods through potentially renewable three year grants. While this time-frame remained too short, it was a step in the right direction. In the event, the fragility of the Catalytic Fund's financing base has compromised even this limited move. Delivering more predictable support requires more predictable donor commitments (FTI Secretariat, 2008*c*). The Catalytic Fund's balance sheet tells its own story. Signed pledges from donors amounted to US$389 million in 2008 but fall to US$26 million for 2011 (FTI Secretariat, 2009*b*).[34] This is not a secure basis for commitments over a typical three to five year medium-term expenditure cycle. As the number of countries with endorsed FTI plans rises, the Catalytic Fund faces the prospect of large financing deficits. Estimates by the FTI Secretariat put the projected deficit by the end of 2009 at US$324 million (FTI Secretariat, 2009*b*).[35] With sixteen countries expected to have education plans endorsed in 2010 or 2011, the deficit is likely to grow.

If the FTI is to emerge as a viable multilateral mechanism, a new financing model is imperative. There is an urgent need for increased predictability and a firmer donor commitment over longer planning cycles of five to ten years. Recognition of the problem has prompted several donors to support calls for a replenishment mechanism that mobilizes around US$3 to 5 billion between 2009 and 2012, with an initial US$1.2 billion for eighteen months from 2009 (FTI Task Team on Replenishment of the EFA - Fast Track Initiative, 2009). Such longer-term arrangements are a characteristic of multilateral initiatives in health, discussed further in the final section. With pledges for 2009 amounting to US$228 million, this implies a rapid scaling up of donor support (FTI Secretariat, 2009*b*). Unfortunately, the FTI's poor disbursement record deters donors from providing the rapid increase this mechanism would require.

Countries affected by conflict

Providing aid for basic education in countries affected by conflict is both an imperative and a challenge. These countries account for a large share of the world's out-of-school population, suffer from acute shortages of teachers and often have severely degraded education infrastructure. Their ability to handle aid is typically weak, with basic finance and public management systems unlikely to meet donor reporting requirements (Berry, 2009). Conflict-affected countries should be at the centre of multilateral financing initiatives in education, enabling donors to pool risks and reduce transaction costs (Dom, 2009). Instead, they are on the periphery.

One of the most serious design flaws in the Fast Track Initiative is that its rules shut out many of the countries and children in the greatest need of support from aid donors. The basic requirements for joining the FTI – a poverty reduction strategy paper and a sound education plan – effectively exclude many countries that are in conflict, undergoing post-conflict reconstruction or suffer from extreme capacity limitations for other reasons.

Reform efforts have been piecemeal and largely unsuccessful. They concentrated initially on development of a 'progressive framework' for plan endorsement. Initially, the broad idea was to attribute 'interim status' to countries moving in the right direction but unable to meet the rigour of full FTI endorsement. Then, with donors unable to agree on how to proceed within the FTI framework, the focus shifted instead to creating a separate Education Transition Fund to provide large-scale support in crisis and post-conflict settings. However, negotiations stalled (see details below). The upshot is that conflict-affected countries still lack access to a multilateral financing mechanism in education.

Difficult journeys through Fast Track Initiative processes

Several conflict-affected countries have travelled through the FTI endorsement process. In 2007, Liberia and Sierra Leone were endorsed, followed a year later by the Central African Republic and Haiti. Southern Sudan is a prospective endorsement candidate in 2009. Unfortunately, plan endorsement has not always led to aid delivery.

In Sierra Leone, the government identified education system reconstruction as a priority after the 2002 peace agreement. Abolition of primary school fees resulted in enrolment doubling between 2001 and 2004, to 1.3 million. Many new entrants faced the prospect of dilapidated schools lacking books and trained teachers (UNICEF, 2009*a*; World Bank, 2007*b*). The FTI Education Programme Development Fund facilitated preparation of a draft education plan, developed with support from UNICEF and the World Bank. Three months after the FTI endorsed the plan, Sierra Leone was approved for US$13.9 million in Catalytic Fund support (FTI Secretariat, 2009*b*). Retroactive application of the IDA rules, however, severely delayed disbursement. As of March 2009, two years after the allocation decision, Sierra Leone was still awaiting its first disbursement.

The process effectively pushed Sierra Leone back into the status of a newly applying country and brought its education sector capacity problems to

Estimates by the FTI Secretariat put the projected deficit by the end of 2009 at US$324 million

34. In March 2009, the FTI balance sheet showed an additional US$14.4 million in unsigned pledges.

35. Taking into account unsigned pledges would reduce this figure to US$197 million.

the fore. The expectation that Sierra Leone could meet the FTI gold standard was flawed from the outset. It was recognized that the government had neither met targets on poverty-related expenditure and domestic resources nor adequately addressed donor concerns about transparency and accountability (UNICEF, 2009*a*). The question was whether the FTI could become more flexible and accept countries like Sierra Leone into the club. The answer in practice was no.

Other conflict-affected countries with similar problems have experienced arbitrary treatment in FTI processes. In Liberia, as in Sierra Leone, the local donor group endorsed a post-conflict reconstruction plan in 2007. With support from some major donors and a government strongly committed to education, the country was well placed to accelerate progress. But the Catalytic Fund committee rejected Liberia's request for financial support for its national education plan, so a pooled fund was set up under UNICEF auspices (Box 4.15).

The experience of the UNICEF-managed pooled fund in Liberia led to the development of a parallel track to provide large-scale support in crisis and post-conflict settings. This involved the proposal to create an Education Transition Fund that would operate under UNICEF auspices. The FTI Secretariat and UNICEF were charged with elaborating rules and procedures for allocation, and several donors – notably the Netherlands and the United Kingdom – signalled a commitment to contribute. But protracted negotiations over the proposed fund between 2008 and 2009 ultimately broke down over concerns about risk and accountability.

In addition, some countries have received mixed messages over where to apply for funding. In December 2008, the Catalytic Fund committee agreed to allocate funds to the Central African Republic. It called the decision 'an exception', on the grounds that 'normally, funding for a country in this status would be through the Education Transition Fund'. It did not explain what it meant by 'in this status' or otherwise identify the grounds for the exception (FTI Secretariat, 2008*d*, p. 2). Nor did it define the conditions under which the allocation is to be disbursed. Moreover, questions remain over the consequences for the Central African Republic of the stalled negotiations on the Education Transition Fund.

For other countries, the FTI's lack of clarity has generated large transaction costs and uncertainties. The local education group in Haiti endorsed the country's education plan in mid-2008, and the government was encouraged to submit a funding request to the Catalytic Fund. By the end of the year, the Haitian Government was being advised to seek financing from the Transition Fund – which did not exist. After a year with an endorsed plan and

The Catalytic Fund committee rejected Liberia's request for financial support for its national education plan

Box 4.15: Liberia — an approved plan with no Catalytic Fund support

Having recently emerged from a brutal conflict, Liberia faces major challenges in education. Just one-third of primary school age children are enrolled, and deep inequality is rife. The FTI could have played an important role by addressing chronic underfinancing in the education sector, but failed to do so.

Liberia's experience underlines the wider limitations of the FTI for conflict-affected countries. Several aid donors worked closely with the government in preparing an education sector strategy, fully recognizing the need to rebuild an effective governance structure. Yet the Catalytic Fund committee rejected Liberia's application, forcing government and donors to develop alternative mechanisms.

Under UNICEF auspices, with initial financial backing from the Netherlands, an Education Pooled Fund was rapidly established to help finance key investments. The fund soon demonstrated more success in disbursing money than the Catalytic Fund. An initial US$7 million grant was used to support the creation of rural teacher-training institutes and the first major postwar procurement of textbooks. Current pledges to the pooled fund amount to US$17 million: US$12 million from the Netherlands and US$5 million from the private philanthropic agency, Open Society Initiative. Nevertheless, a large gap remains, as financing needs over three years are estimated at US$70 million. With no other donors committing to the pooled fund, Liberia's intentions of accelerating progress towards education for all could yet be thwarted.

Sources: UNICEF (2009*b*); Brannelly et al. (2009).

a prepared financing application, Haiti was still unable to submit a request. With some justification, the country's education minister expressed 'disappointment and bitterness' at being locked into such a prolonged process (UNESCO, 2009*a*, p. 4). When it was finally apparent that the Transition Fund would not be established, Haiti was allocated resources through the Catalytic Fund in September 2009.

Efforts to establish an effective multilateral framework for dealing with the problems of conflict-affected states have not been successful. The issues at stake go far beyond the failure of the FTI. In 2006, Haiti had a net enrolment rate of 71%. Almost half the children from the poorest 20% of households are out of school. Chronic underinvestment by government has placed a large financial burden on parents. School fees average US$80 per child, or around one-sixth of average income in 2007. The teacher-training system produces around 500 graduates a year, but some 2,500 are needed (World Bank, 2008*b*). In all these areas, support from the Catalytic Fund could have made a difference.

Lessons from global health funds

The past decade has been marked by the rapid development of global initiatives in health financing.[36] Unlike the FTI, these initiatives have accelerated progress towards international development goals, principally through official development assistance but also by creating multilateral channels for philanthropic financing. The increasing share of health in overall aid can be traced in large measure to the dynamism of such initiatives. About half of all international aid from private sources is now invested in health (Marten and Witte, 2008).

Much of the increase in international aid for health has been directed towards specific diseases or interventions. There are over ninety global health partnerships, and most are in this category (Sridhar and Tamashiro, 2009). Prominent examples include the Global Fund to Fight AIDS, Tuberculosis and Malaria (usually called simply the Global Fund) and the GAVI Alliance[37] (Sridhar and Tamashiro, 2009). Far more than the FTI, these programmes have galvanized political support, keeping health at the centre of the international development agenda.

Do global partnerships in health provide lessons that could help reshape and revitalize the FTI? Caution has to be exercised in drawing direct comparisons. Education is less amenable than health to 'vertical' interventions such as vaccination. Health interventions may also have greater traction in aid debates, especially when the issues at stake involve child survival and keeping people with HIV and AIDS alive.

Yet the differences between health and education can be overstated. Most of the major global partnerships in health have abandoned narrowly defined vertical funding approaches, recognizing that strengthening health systems is vital for effective disease-specific interventions. About a third of the Global Fund's overall support is now geared towards building health systems (Global Fund, 2009*d*).[38]

About half of all international aid from private sources is now invested in health

Many principles and practices developed in governance models for global health partnerships are relevant to the FTI. These partnerships have succeeded in rapidly scaling up aid resources and sustaining high levels of disbursement. They have been far more successful than the FTI in mobilizing new sources of finance that can complement traditional aid, especially from philanthropic foundations.

Governance arrangements have been an important factor in the success of global health funds. These arrangements have avoided the dangers associated with a proliferation of reporting systems and the rules on endorsing plans and delivering finance are more transparent, more effective and more firmly rooted in nationally owned processes than under the FTI. Global health partnerships also provide a far stronger voice to developing countries and civil society. Donor influence is more circumscribed and the World Bank, while an important actor, does not dominate financing decisions. By comparison, the FTI's donor-dominated governance structures appear anachronistic, ineffective and out of touch with political realities when compared with those of the Global Fund and the GAVI Alliance.

The Global Fund

The Global Fund to Fight AIDS, Tuberculosis and Malaria was created to combat diseases claiming over 6 million lives a year. It was first discussed by the G8 in 2000; a year later a United Nations General Assembly Special Session concluded with a commitment to create a new fund and the 2001 G8 summit agreed to mobilize resources (Grubb, 2007). A permanent secretariat was established in January 2002 and the first round of grants for

36. This section draws heavily on Sridhar and Tamashiro (2009).

37. Formerly the Global Alliance for Vaccination and Immunization.

38. The GAVI Alliance has also increased support for health system strengthening, having allocated an additional US$300 million for this purpose in 2008, bringing the total to US$800 million. Current plans aim to ensure that half of all GAVI-eligible countries receive system strengthening support by 2010 (GAVI Alliance 2009a).

thirty-six countries was approved three months later. The fund has supplied anti-retroviral drugs to about 2 million people and tuberculosis treatment to 4.6 million, provided 70 million insecticide-treated bed nets and saved around 3.5 million lives (Global Fund, 2008*a*).

By the end of 2008, it had disbursed US$7 billion (Global Fund, 2009*d*). The current target is to cut the average time between commitment and disbursement from between nine and eleven months – around half the post-2007 FTI disbursement period – to eight months (Sridhar and Tamashiro, 2009). In 2008, 96% of the funding planned in grants was disbursed, and only 16% of active grants had a disbursement rate of less than 75% (Global Fund, 2009*d*). One reason for such rapid disbursement is the development of rules aimed at strengthening and working through national procurement and reporting systems. Another is technical support to countries having trouble meeting disbursement conditions.

Many donors that have given limited backing to the FTI – including France, Germany, Japan and the United States – have actively supported the Global Fund

Effective and accountable governance has been central to sustained delivery. Detailed accounts of the management and administration system are available elsewhere (Global Fund, 2008*d*). For purposes of comparison with the FTI, several distinctive features can be identified:

- *Institutionalized independence.* The Global Fund is legally constituted as a Swiss foundation, rather than a multidonor trust fund, receiving administrative support from the World Health Organization (WHO) and fiduciary support from the World Bank. The Bank's role is limited to disbursing funds on instruction from the Global Fund Secretariat. The secretariat is much larger than the FTI's, with about 470 staff, and it answers to the board as a whole, creating a very different set of institutional incentives than those facing the FTI Secretariat.

- *Broad-based donor support.* To provide sustained and predictable support, the Global Fund works with a system based on replenishments over two year cycles. From 2010, the replenishment arrangement will move to a three year cycle. Total grants for 2008–2010 are expected to reach US$9.5 billion (Global Fund, 2009*a*). Many donors that have given limited backing to the FTI – including France, Germany, Japan and the United States – have actively supported the Global Fund. Notably, United States contributions represented one-quarter of the total (Figure 4.21).

- *Innovative financing.* From 2001 to 2009, contributions from private philanthropy and innovative financing arrangements amounted to US$642 million (Box 4.16). Along with the Bill and Melinda Gates Foundation, thirteen major companies have contributed directly or indirectly.

- *Long-term commitment.* The Global Fund operates on a five year grant cycle (compared with three years for the FTI). As part of the 2007–2010 strategy, a facility was introduced to provide support for high-performing programmes for up to six additional years. The new facility reflects a growing commitment to long-term predictable financing to maintain support following investments in the strengthening of health systems, particularly for recurrent expenditure such as salaries.

- *Broad-based global representation.* The board that oversees the Global Fund sets policy priorities and approves grants. It has twenty-four members, twenty of whom have votes: seven from developing countries, eight from donor countries, three from civil society, one from the private sector and one from the Gates Foundation (Global Health Watch, 2008). This structure gives a far stronger voice to developing countries than that of the FTI.

- *Strong country ownership.* Countries develop plans and submit proposals to the Global Fund through a Country Coordinating Mechanism, a country-level partnership that usually consists of governments and donors, along with representatives of non-government organizations, church groups, the private sector, academics and people affected by the diseases (Global Fund, 2008*b*). The mechanism appoints one or two organizations to act as Principal Recipients, or managers and administrators of Global Fund grants. About two-thirds of Principal Recipients are government agencies, though in some cases responsibility is split. The mechanism facilitates higher levels of engagement between a wider range of actors than is the case with FTI processes.

- *Transparency in decision-making.* Well-defined rules and processes govern endorsement and disbursement. A Technical Review Panel assesses proposals and makes recommendations to the board, setting out its arguments for approval or rejection (Global Fund, 2007). Rejected proposals can be amended and resubmitted, and if it is again rejected, the applicant country can appeal to an independent panel. Another institutional mechanism, the Global Implementation Support Team, has provided funds to build the technical capacity of Country Coordinating Mechanisms.[39] These processes contrast with FTI arrangements in two key respects. First, at the national level the local donor group is just one of several actors deciding whether national plans should be submitted for funding. Second, once plans are submitted, donors have a limited voice in determining whether they are endorsed. In marked contrast, the Catalytic Fund committee can reject applications with no explanation and give applicants no recourse to appeal.

- *Working in fragile states and countries affected by conflict.* From the outset the board of the Global Fund has recognized the need to develop ways of working in conflict-affected countries and fragile states, which receive about a third of total financing (Sridhar and Tamashiro, 2009). While the FTI's Catalytic Fund committee rejected a financing request from Liberia and has failed to disburse funds to Sierra Leone, the Global Fund has delivered about US$54 million to Liberia and US$43 million to Sierra Leone since 2004 (Global Fund, 2009*b*, 2009*e*). Concerns over national capacity and reporting systems in

Figure 4.21: The Global Fund has broad-based donor support

Total donor allocations to the Global Fund to Fight AIDS, Tuberculosis and Malaria, 2001-2009

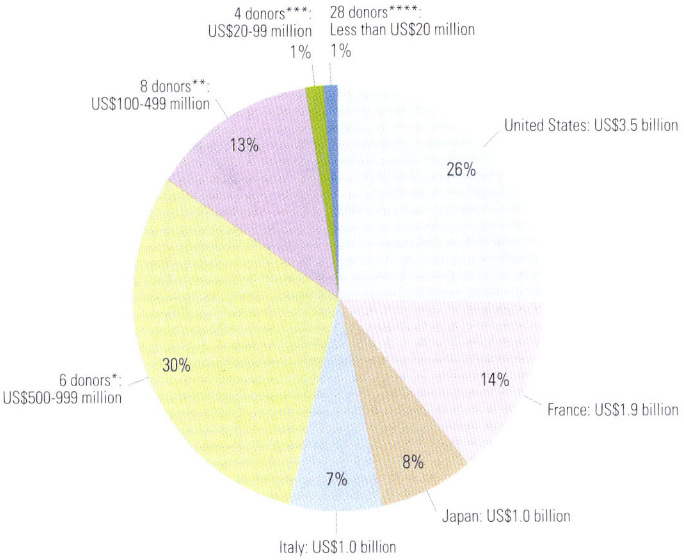

* Canada, the European Commission, the Bill and Melinda Gates Foundation, Germany, the Netherlands and the United Kingdom, each contributing US$500-999 million.

** Australia, Denmark, Ireland, Norway, (RED), the Russian Federation, Spain and Sweden, each contributing US$100-499 million.

*** Belgium, Luxembourg, Switzerland and UNITAID, each contributing US$20-99 million.

**** Brazil, the Chevron Corporation, China, the Communitas Foundation, Debt2Health, Finland, Greece, the Hottokenai campaign, Hungary, Iceland, Idol Gives Back, India, Kuwait, Latvia, Liechtenstein, Mexico, New Zealand, Nigeria, Poland, Portugal, the Republic of Korea, Romania, Saudi Arabia, Singapore, Slovenia, South Africa, Thailand and Uganda, each contributing less than US$20 million.

Allocations are reported up to April 2009.

Source: Global Fund (2009*c*).

Box 4.16: Private sector initiatives

One feature of the Global Fund has been significant contributions from philanthropic organizations, along with a range of innovative financing strategies. Among the most important are:

- *Private foundations.* The Bill and Melinda Gates Foundation has committed over US$11 billion to global health programmes since it was set up in 1994. Since 2001, it has contributed US$550 million to the Global Fund.
- *Debt2Health.* Under a programme begun in 2007, national debt to foreign creditors is converted into a fund to support national health programmes. Germany and Indonesia took the first step, converting US$72 million in debt. Germany has agreed with the Global Fund to make a further US$290 million available by 2010.
- *(Product) RED.* Launched in 2006, (RED) is a brand leased to companies to promote sales in return for the transfer of a small share of the profit to the Global Fund. Partners include American Express, Apple, Dell and Motorola. The initiative has generated more than US$134 million for the Global Fund.
- *UNITAID.* Created in 2006 in a joint initiative by Brazil, Chile, France, Norway and the United Kingdom, this is an international drug purchase facility financed largely by air ticket levies. It has raised more than US$600 million, including around US$39 million directed through the Global Fund.

Sources: Global Fund (2008*a*, 2008*c*, 2009c); UNITAID (2008).

The Bill and Melinda Gates Foundation has committed over US$11 billion to global health programmes

39. Seven agencies – WHO, UNFPA, UNICEF, UNDP, UNAIDS, the Global Fund and the World Bank – formed the Global Implementation Support Team (GIST) in 2005 to address capacity constraints. Based at UNAIDS, it now includes Germany and the United States as well as other organizations. It has developed technical tools and a database to support capacity development.

Developing countries have to be given a stronger voice at all levels

Sierra Leone led to an innovative approach: with the Health Ministry as principle grant recipient, contracts were drawn up with around thirty-nine 'sub-recipients'. Inevitably, there are problems with rapid disbursement in countries where governments lack implementation capacity and cannot meet donor reporting standards. However, reviews have pointed to levels of delivery comparable to those achieved for grants in other countries (Global Fund, 2005; Radelet and Siddiqui, 2007). While the risk of large amounts of vertical funding distorting health systems is even greater in conflict-affected countries (Sridhar, 2009), it is difficult to escape the conclusion that the FTI's record in such countries compares unfavourably with that of the Global Fund.

The GAVI alliance

Launched in 2000 at the World Economic Forum with a start-up grant from the Gates Foundation, the GAVI Alliance is a global health partnership geared towards developing, distributing and evaluating improved vaccines for children in low-income countries.

Like the Global Fund, the GAVI Alliance has scaled up support rapidly in a short time. Donor commitments since 2000 total US$3.8 billion, with annual disbursement projected to reach over US$1 billion in 2009 (GAVI Alliance, 2009*a*). The typical gap between grant application and disbursement is around six months (Sridhar and Tamashiro, 2009).

The WHO estimates that GAVI support for immunization programmes has averted 3.4 million deaths (GAVI Alliance, 2009*a*). Of the seventy-two GAVI-eligible low-income countries, half are in sub-Saharan Africa (Jamison et al., 2006). Special attention has been paid to strengthening health systems in fragile states and countries affected by conflict. Recipient countries include Afghanistan, the Democratic Republic of the Congo and Liberia.

While the GAVI Alliance differs from the Global Fund in scale and mission, there are important governance parallels. GAVI has developed a broad base of financial support, with both bilateral and private donors.[40] Donors and developing country governments are equally represented on the twenty-eight member board, which is supported by a secretariat of about 120 people (Sridhar and Tamashiro, 2009). Grants are made on the basis of a transparent application process. An independent review committee, composed of experts drawn predominantly from developing countries, examines country proposals and makes recommendations to the board. Around 90% of proposals are approved after their first or second submission (Sridhar and Tamashiro, 2009). All this contrasts markedly with the FTI.

As with the Global Fund, innovation is another area of contrast. The GAVI Alliance has developed two mechanisms supported through public-private partnerships. The Advance Market Commitment lets donors commit money to buy vaccines that are not yet available, creating incentives for research into vaccines for diseases such as pneumonia and rotavirus infection (Centers for Disease Control and Prevention, 2008; GAVI Alliance, 2009*b*).[41] The International Finance Facility for Immunisation issues bonds in international capital markets, creating a predictable stream of revenue for the GAVI Alliance, and repays bondholders with funds provided by donors (Lob-Levyt, 2009). The IFFIm has mobilized US$1.2 billion since 2000, with a significant injection of funds during 2007 and 2008 (Sridhar and Tamashiro, 2009).[42] For example, in 2008, La Caixa, one of Spain's leading savings banks, launched a fund-raising campaign among employees and corporate depositors that mobilized US$5 million (GAVI Alliance, 2009*a*).

Some lessons for the Fast Track Initiative

The Global Fund and the GAVI Alliance do not provide blueprints for FTI reform, but they do offer an approach to governance and resource mobilization that could help frame a global education initiative that delivers results.

There are four broad lessons for the FTI. The first is that developing countries have to be given a stronger voice at all levels, from the design of national plans to the framing of finance proposals and decision-making at the global level. The second concerns plan endorsement and the release of finance. FTI arrangements have suffered from opaque rules and arbitrary decision-making. An independent review panel empowered to make recommendations on financing to a more balanced executive board would go some way towards resolving the problem. At the same time, the global health funds have avoided long delays between commitment and disbursement partly because they are not governed by World Bank rules.

The third lesson concerns public-private partnerships. Many private foundations and

40. Between 2000 and 2008, donor governments mobilized US$1.5 billion and private foundations and individuals US$1.1 billion. In 2008, the Gates Foundation provided US$75 million out of US$81.5 million in receipts from individuals and private foundations.

41. Pneumococcal diseases and rotavirus infections (the most common cause of severe diarrhoea) are the two biggest killers of children under age 5.

42. A bond issued by IFFIm and backed by sovereign governments raised US$223 million in 2008 (International Finance Facility for Immunisation, 2008).

companies support education, but they lack a multilateral framework for channelling their support towards meeting shared development goals, adding to transaction costs and reducing aid effectiveness. Unlike the Global Fund and the GAVI Alliance, the FTI has not facilitated private-sector engagement in global initiatives.

The final lesson relates to international advocacy. The FTI partnership has not met one of its central objectives: galvanizing political support for resource mobilization. Although the FTI has become a fixed feature on the agendas of the G8 and the annual IMF and World Bank meetings, little has been achieved. Once again, this is in stark contrast to the Global Fund and, to a lesser extent, the GAVI Alliance. To some degree, it is a chicken-and-egg problem: campaigners have trouble advocating successfully for an initiative that is not delivering.

Although health initiatives can offer lessons for education, they also face real challenges (Sidibe et al., 2006). Donor delivery on pledges made at Global Fund replenishment conferences has been erratic, leading to concern over a potential US$4 billion financing gap for 2008–2010 (Sridhar and Tamashiro, 2009). Moreover, evaluations have highlighted concerns over capacity problems, weak civil society involvement and under-representation of groups advocating for people living with disease (Global Fund, 2008*d*; Lawson, 2004).

In some countries, vertical initiatives in health – notably the Global Fund – have skewed financing towards the diseases donors have targeted, causing distortions in weak and underfunded health systems (Garrett, 2007; Sridhar and Batniji, 2008; Victora et al., 2004). The EU Court of Auditors has expressed concern over parallel distortions in aid priorities, warning that a bias towards specific diseases has diminished aid effectiveness and the strengthening of health systems (Kinst, 2009). The GAVI Alliance has been criticized for skewing health delivery towards immunization rather than wider development of primary health care (Ryman et al., 2008). Its programmes have also been criticized for generating perverse incentives. Recent evaluations have documented evidence of government agencies over-reporting numbers of children vaccinated to secure increased performance-based finance from the GAVI Alliance (Lim et al., 2008; Sternberg, 2008). Any scaled-up global plan for education would have to guard against such outcomes, principally by strengthening national delivery and reporting systems.

Towards a reformed global initiative for education

Not only has the Fast Track Initiative failed to produce results on the ground, it has also failed to act as a focal point for international efforts to mobilize more resources for education. Many commentators argue that it strains credulity to suppose that financial support for the FTI can be scaled up to meet the challenge of accelerating progress towards the 2015 goals.

Against this backdrop it is easy to see why there has been growing interest in alternatives to the FTI. Developments in the United States have attracted particular attention (Bermingham, 2009*b*). During his election campaign, President Barack Obama indicated a broad intent to support a US$2 billion Global Fund for Education (Obama, 2008). Secretary of State Hillary Clinton restated that commitment during her confirmation hearing. Other Obama administration figures have articulated a broad vision for a new global fund that would build on the FTI's strengths while addressing its weaknesses (Sperling, 2008).

The prospect of the Obama administration playing a global leadership role in education is cause for optimism. The danger is that proposals for a new global fund will divert attention and political energy from the more immediate challenge of reforming the FTI (Box 4.17).

A reformed initiative could give renewed impetus to progress towards the Dakar goals

The FTI is at a watershed. Business as usual is no longer an option. However, a reformed initiative could give renewed impetus to progress towards the Dakar goals. It could also help facilitate the development and enhance the effectiveness of any global fund initiative to emerge from the United States, just as the Global Fund and the GAVI Alliance have facilitated American engagement in global health funds. There are seven key ingredients for successful reform:

- *Go back to first principles: identify and close financing gaps.* The FTI's core principle is that there should be a unified process through which (i) low-income countries develop plans for achieving ambitious EFA goals, and (ii) donors back those plans through increased aid and coordinated support. Failure to deliver does not detract from the continued relevance of those objectives. Developing countries need to work out viable cost estimates for universal primary completion and wider education goals, taking

Box 4.17: A new global fund for education?

The 2008 United States election brought to office an administration that has a strong commitment to development and has identified education as a priority area for a scaled-up aid programme. Before Hillary Clinton was appointed secretary of state, she was the principal sponsor in the Senate of a bill aimed at raising United States aid for basic education to US$3 billion from a 2007 level of US$700 million. Part of an increased aid effort could be channelled through a new global fund which under the right conditions could strengthen the multilateral aid architecture for education and enhance the effectiveness of a reformed Fast Track Initiative.

Details of the prospective initiative remain unclear. During his election campaign, President Obama said he would back a proposal to create a US$2 billion Global Education Fund.

Some commentators believe a global education fund should replace the FTI as the focal point for international action. While its positive elements should be retained, this argument runs, the FTI is too discredited to merit strong political support. Critics cite its difficulties securing financial replenishment in support of this conclusion. This assessment is premature and at least partially misplaced.

It is premature because details of the United States proposal remain sketchy. The economic crisis has raised questions over US funding increases for basic education. Moreover, it remains unclear whether the fund would be a bilateral programme (like the Millennium Challenge Account), a United States-led multilateral programme, or a bilateral programme that could be used to finance a global fund (along the lines of the President's Emergency Plan for AIDS Relief, PEPFAR). Details may become clearer with the publication in 2009 of a new USAID education strategy.

Much will depend on governance design. An arrangement like the Millennium Challenge Account could raise problems; only countries meeting stipulated good governance and free market criteria are eligible for grants. Other options could offer greater flexibility. The legislation that authorized PEPFAR in 2003 allows for assistance to be channelled through global funds, provided it does not account for more than one-third of their total finance. In 2007, PEPFAR accounted for 27% of commitments to the Global Fund. However, bilateral PEPFAR support has different reporting requirements than the Global Fund, and much of the support is channelled through United States universities, faith-based organizations and commercial companies.

The new administration has signalled that it wants to strengthen coordination with other donors within a broad commitment to country ownership. However, the nature of United States reporting requirements could make this difficult. Equally difficult may be the use of host-country procurement and reporting systems. Currently only small amounts of United States aid are directed through national budgets, suggesting that much of the potential expenditure could go through American non-government organizations and separate projects.

Such practices cannot serve as the basis for an effective global fund in education. This position, however, does not preclude United States engagement and leadership in reconfiguring the multilateral aid architecture for education. Channelling part of the increase in basic education financing through a reformed FTI could help the United States broaden the geographical coverage of its support without large transaction costs. More active United States involvement in FTI governance would also help strengthen donor coordination.

Experience in the health sector demonstrates what is possible. Through PEPFAR, the United States has been a major contributor to the Global Fund without requiring separate reporting structures. Reforming the FTI along the lines advocated in this chapter would open the door to a similar process of engagement in education.

Sources: PEPFAR (2009); Ingram (2009).

The new administration has signalled that it wants to strengthen coordination with other donors within a broad commitment to country ownership

into account the additional cost of reaching marginalized groups. Donors need to mobilize the additional resources needed – around US$16 billion annually in this Report's estimate – over a five to ten year planning horizon. That is the meaning of the Dakar Framework pledge to ensure that no countries seriously committed to education for all will be thwarted in their achievement of this goal by a lack of resources.

- *Establish the FTI as an independent foundation with a strong independent secretariat and reform governance arrangements to strengthen the voice of developing countries.* Applying lessons from the models developed by global funds for health, the FTI should be legally reconstituted as an independent foundation, staffed by a strengthened independent secretariat and supported by technical review and capacity-building bodies. 'Firewalling' a reformed FTI within the World Bank is a distinctly second-best option because it would leave many governance problems intact, including donor dominance. Developing countries should have representation equal to that of donors at all levels and in all areas, from setting strategic priorities to decision-making over financing.

- *Restructure planning and financing processes.* National plans should be subject to independent review – as happens under the Global Fund – with recommendations acting as a trigger for the board to authorize funding or technical support.

- *Establish a secure and predictable financing base and facilitate partnerships with the private sector to mobilize additional finance.* Donors should make available the US$1.2 billion requested for the eighteen months to 2010, contingent on the development of a reform strategy aimed at transforming the FTI. Subsequent replenishments should reflect financing-gap estimates developed from national planning. A new FTI should support public-private initiatives and invite philanthropic foundations to support EFA goals.

- *Address the needs of conflict-affected countries.* FTI reform provides an opportunity to address needs specific to conflict-affected countries and other fragile states. The principle of a single unified process should apply to all, with assistance geared towards the real circumstances of individual countries. The creation of a US$1 billion Education Reconstruction Fund within a reformed FTI multilateral framework could help facilitate short-term recovery while donors and governments work towards long-term planning goals.

- *Build capacity at the national level.* The FTI needs to be far more responsive to the capacity-building needs of developing countries. A unified process for the Catalytic Fund and the EPDF should go together with an increased institutional and financial commitment to capacity-building.

- *High level political leadership.* Reform blueprints can help define possible routes to the creation of a Fast Track Initiative that is fit for the purpose of driving an ambitious Education for All agenda. But results ultimately depend on political leadership – an ingredient that has been lacking to date. The High-Level Group created to monitor progress on the Dakar Framework for Action has not provided effective leadership, and serious questions remain over its current practices and relevance to the challenges ahead. Successive G8 summits have reported on the FTI in a formulaic fashion, without substantively addressing the initiative's weakness or the underlying reasons for weak donor support. Combined leadership from the United States and the European Union in the context of the 2010 Millennium Development Goal summit and the G20 summit could play a decisive role in charting a new course.

Conclusion

It is widely accepted that the Fast Track Initiative has not delivered on its promise, leaving a large gap in the multilateral aid architecture for education. The danger now is that donors and multilateral agencies will resort to another bout of piecemeal reforms aimed at patching up a mechanism that is not fulfilling its original objectives.

There is an alternative. The FTI could be reconfigured to meet its intended purpose of linking stronger national planning to increased and more predictable aid, with a focus on accelerated progress towards well-defined EFA goals. At present, the initiative is stuck in a vicious circle. Poor delivery has weakened donor commitment, which in turn has made it difficult to strengthen delivery.

Reforms outlined in this section could change that picture. Global health initiatives have demonstrated that multilateral arrangements that deliver results can create a virtuous circle, mobilizing resources and strengthening political commitment nationally and internationally.

FTI reform will require incremental and practical measures, backed by high-level political leadership and a new vision. Immediate reforms are needed to demonstrate that the FTI can deliver and to restore confidence in multilateral approaches to aid for education. The bigger challenge is for champions of education among developing country governments, donors and civil society to work together more effectively in articulating a credible and compelling agenda for change.

Combined leadership from the United States and the European Union could play a decisive role in charting a new course

Whatever it takes: getting to school by boat, Mali

© François Perri

Chapter 5

Rising to the EFA challenge

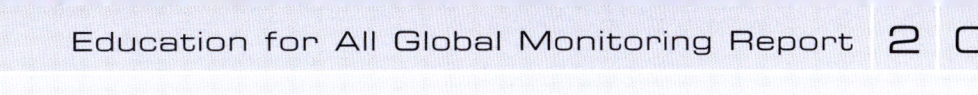

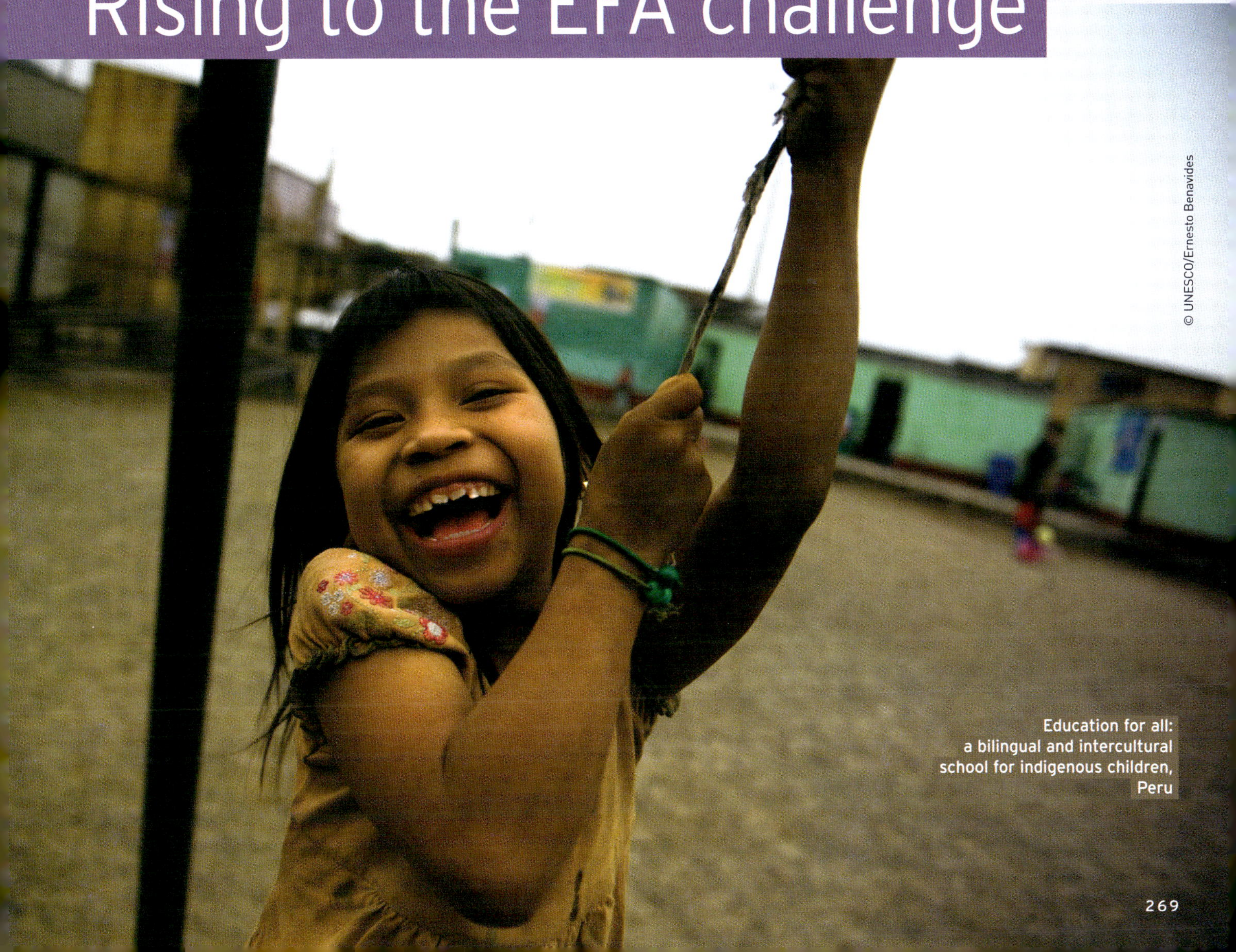

Education for all:
a bilingual and intercultural
school for indigenous children,
Peru

There is no single blueprint for moving towards greater equity in education. When it comes to tackling marginalization, each country faces a different set of challenges – and it has to meet those challenges in the light of the resources available. Just as marginalization is sustained by unequal power relationships, so policies for combating it have to be rooted in political processes and alliances that challenge these relationships. This chapter consolidates some of the broad good practice lessons that emerge from the Report's analysis. It then distills these lessons into a ten-point framework for tackling the challenge posed by marginalization and accelerating progress towards the EFA goals.

Overcoming education marginalization

With five years to go to the 2015 target date for many of the key goals set in the Dakar Framework for Action, progress towards the Education for All goals is at a crossroads. Much has been achieved over the past decade. Yet many of the world's poorest countries are not on track to meet the goals set at Dakar. They could be pushed even further off track. With recovery prospects from the global economic crisis remaining uncertain, there is a real danger that progress in education will stall – and in some countries the hard-won gains made since 2000 could be thrown into reverse.

Such an outcome would be an avoidable tragedy. For many countries, serious question marks now hang over the prospect of achieving the ambition defined in Dakar. What is not in question is the potential for effective national and international policies to sustain and even accelerate progress in the years ahead. The threat posed by the fallout from the financial crisis is real – and an effective response is urgently required. An arguably greater threat is the 'business as usual' mindset of many national governments, international financial institutions and parts of the United Nations system. If the world is to make a big push towards the Dakar goals, all these actors have to demonstrate a higher order of political leadership. The 2010 Millennium Development Goals summit provides an opportunity to set a new course.

This Report has emphasized the critical importance of placing marginalization at the core of the Education for All agenda. Reaching the sections of society and the regions that are being left behind is the right thing to do on ethical grounds – and it is the sensible thing to do for governments committed to the Dakar goals. It is the right thing to do because the Education for All goals are for everyone and they are rooted in a commitment to social justice and human rights. And it is sensible because strengthening commitment to equity and inclusion is the most efficient way to accelerate progress towards the 2015 targets. To put it bluntly, the targets will not be reached in many countries unless governments direct their attention – and resources – towards the most disadvantaged sections of society. Reaching those who are being left behind as a result of disparities linked to poverty, gender, ethnicity, language and other markers of disadvantage should be established as a first order of priority.

Chapter 2 highlighted areas of critical importance for the development of more inclusive education. Among them are:

- a stronger focus on early childhood nutrition, maternal health and more equitable access to pre-school provision of good quality;
- greater clarity on numbers of children out of school, along with the development of monitoring tools enabling more coherent measurement of the key ingredients of universal primary education: timely entry into school, progression through the grades and completion of the cycle;
- a clear commitment to quality and to greater equity in learning achievement;
- development of 'second chance' education options for the millions of adolescents and young adults who have missed out on earlier learning opportunities;
- a strengthening of technical and vocational education to counter youth unemployment and build bridges between school and work;
- renewal of the commitment to combat adult illiteracy through proper resourcing of national programmes;
- a strengthening of the commitment to gender parity and equality in each of the above areas.

Strengthening commitment to equity and inclusion is the most efficient way to accelerate progress towards the 2015 targets

Drawing up global blueprints for accelerated progress towards the Education for All goals is ineffectual. Every country faces different challenges, opportunities and constraints, and has to chart its own course through national political processes. However, there are opportunities for learning across countries. As governments face the run-up to 2015, this Report identifies problems that have to be addressed and it draws on evidence from monitoring and the analysis of country experience to identify some broad policy lessons.

A ten-step plan for overcoming marginalization in education emerges from these lessons.

1 Set equity-based targets for all of the Education for All goals

International development goals such as those adopted at Dakar and the Millennium Development Goals set national targets. Most national education strategies do the same. National average targets are important because they provide valuable benchmarks for measuring progress – but they are not enough. Governments should also set equity-based targets that focus on the marginalized. These targets could be defined in terms of narrowing disparities based on wealth, gender, language and location. National and international reporting on movement towards such targets would help increase the visibility of the marginalized, identify areas of progress and problems, and inform policy choices.

2 Develop data collection systems with a focus on disaggregated statistics to identify marginalized groups and monitor their progress

Monitoring and measurement are critical in combating marginalization. They should be seen as an integral part of strategies aimed at identifying social groups and regions that are being left behind, raising their visibility and identifying what works in terms of policy intervention. Effective monitoring and disaggregated data are also a requirement for assessing progress towards equity-based targets. Too often, national statistical surveys fail to adequately capture the circumstances and conditions of those being left behind, reinforcing their marginalization. Timely data for monitoring equity gaps in learning are even harder to come by.

Governments need to use data to target resources to underperforming schools and areas

The Deprivation and Marginalization in Education data set developed for this Report could be used as part of a larger tool kit to strengthen the focus on equity. To inform policy, governments need to invest more in developing national data systems that allow for a more finely tuned understanding of marginalization and its underlying causes. Governments could also use such data to address the equity gap by targeting resources to underperforming schools and areas. It is also important that data are not seen as a stand-alone policy tool. Qualitative research processes that give a voice to disadvantaged groups are critical to developing policies for more inclusive education. When it comes to understanding marginalization, the marginalized themselves are the real experts.

3 Identify the drivers of marginalization for specific groups

Marginalization in education is the product of inherited disadvantage, deeply ingrained social processes, uneven power relationships, unfair economic arrangements – and bad policies. The overall effect of marginalization is to restrict opportunity as a result of circumstances over which children have no control, such as parental wealth, gender, ethnicity and language. However, the factors underlying this effect are enormously varied. Poverty, stigmatization, social discrimination, restricted legal entitlements and weak political representation all play a role – and they combine in different ways in different contexts. The problems faced by slum dwellers are not the same as those faced by the rural poor. And while poverty is a universal source of marginalization in education, the poverty-related disadvantages experienced by young girls, ethnic minorities or children with disabilities are reinforced by social attitudes that undermine self-confidence and lower the perceived value of education. An understanding of these differences is important because, to be successful, interventions against marginalization have to target specific underlying causes that blanket interventions may miss.

4 Adopt an integrated policy approach that addresses interlocking causes of disadvantage, within education and beyond

There is no substitute for political leadership in combating marginalization in education. Governments need to make achieving greater equity a national policy priority – and they need to communicate the wider social and economic benefits of more inclusive education.

The Inclusive Education Triangle developed for the Report identifies three broad areas of reform:

- Governments need to *improve affordability and accessibility* by removing formal and informal fees and providing targeted support to the marginalized. Bringing schools closer to marginalized communities is also vital, especially for gender parity. More flexible approaches to provision, including mobile schools for pastoralists and multigrade teaching in remote areas, could bring education within reach of some of the world's most marginalized children.

- Broad-based measures are required to *strengthen the learning environment.* Incentives for more equitable teacher deployment and the development of intercultural and bilingual education are high priorities in improving the relevance of education for marginalized groups and helping overcome social stigmatization. Targeting financial and pedagogical support to schools in the most disadvantaged regions or with large numbers of marginalized children can also make a difference.

- *Expanding entitlements and opportunities* for education also involves enforcing laws against discrimination, providing social protection and redistributing public finance. Governments have an obligation to ensure that national legislation is aligned with human rights principles. However, political mobilization on the part of the marginalized and other sections of society is also critical. The experience of the civil rights movement in the United States, which used political mobilization to drive legal reform, retains a powerful relevance.

None of these elements can be viewed in isolation. Just as marginalization is the product of interlocking disadvantages, so strategies for more inclusive education have to incorporate interlocking measures for empowerment. Even the most effective and equitable policies in education will fail to overcome marginalization unless they are part of a wider strategy for combating poverty and extreme inequality. That is why this Report emphasizes the importance of integrated national policies for social inclusion.

5 Increase resource mobilization and strengthen equity in public spending

Many governments have increased financing for education since 2000 and given greater priority to basic education. This is a welcome trend – but more needs to be done. The Report estimates that low-income countries have the potential to increase spending on basic education by around 0.7% of GDP, or some US$7 billion. At the same time, budget pressures resulting from the global economic slowdown have increased the importance of equity in public spending. Too often, budget allocation patterns reinforce inequalities in education and beyond, holding back efforts to combat marginalization.

Redistributive public spending is one of the keys to expanded entitlements and opportunities. Most countries have some redistributive element in public finance, but it is typically underdeveloped. The upshot is that wealthier regions tend to enjoy higher levels of financing. It is important for governments to develop financing formulas that prioritize need, ensuring that the poorest regions and groups are targeted for support. The principle of equity in public spending has to go beyond equalizing per capita expenditure. Providing equal opportunity to children living in remote areas and in households experiencing extreme poverty and social discrimination is likely to require higher levels of financing than in wealthier areas with lower levels of social deprivation. Investment in social programmes geared towards disadvantaged areas and groups is also important in redistributive finance, not least because it has the potential to generate high returns for equity in education. There is extensive evidence that cash transfers, social safety nets and wider interventions can mitigate the vulnerability that can lead parents to withdraw children from school during economic shocks, droughts and other crises. Social protection policies, already highly developed in many middle-income countries, could play a far greater role in tackling marginalization in education in the poorest countries.

It is important for governments to develop financing formulas that ensure that the poorest regions and groups are targeted for support

6 Honour aid donor commitments and convene an Education for All pledging conference

While the performance of individual countries varies, there has been a collective failure on the part of the donor community to back pledges with delivery. Current aid levels fall far short of what is required. Commitments to basic education, already below the level needed to close the Education for All financing gap, fell by around one-fifth in 2007. It is important that 2008 commitments reverse the shortfall and point to a rising trend.

Accelerating progress towards the Education for All goals requires donors to honour the overall aid pledges they made at summits in 2005 and to step up their commitment to education. An immediate priority is the delivery of an additional US$20 billion in global aid by 2010 to fulfil the 2005 promises. Budget pressure resulting from the financial crisis has created a new layer of uncertainty about the future direction of aid financing in many countries. Donors should follow the example set by the United Kingdom in undertaking to maintain real aid increases at the levels set in pre-crisis budgets.

The Education for All financing gap is larger than previously assumed. The global gap is around US$16 billion annually, with sub-Saharan Africa accounting for around two-thirds of the shortfall. For the forty-six countries surveyed for this Report, aid for basic education will have to increase from around US$2.7 billion to around US$16 billion annually.

If the Fast Track Initiative is to have a future, fundamental reform is essential

The global financial crisis has added to the urgency of international action on aid. In many low-income countries, the economic slowdown has created intense fiscal pressure. This pressure could lead to lower public spending on education than was planned in national strategies, or even budget cuts. The result would be to slow, or even reverse, progress in education by undermining investment in teacher recruitment, classroom construction and the development of good learning environments.

With the 2015 target date for achieving the Education for All Goals approaching, it is vital that donors move to close the financing gap. Much of the investment required must be put in place over the next two years if progress is to be accelerated. Given this backdrop, an Education for All pledging conference should be convened by the United Nations Secretary-General in 2010 as part of the wider international strategy for advancing towards the Millennium Development Goals.

7 Improve aid effectiveness, with a strengthened focus on equity and conflict-affected countries

Donors need to strengthen efforts to implement the Paris agenda on aid effectiveness. Despite improvements, aid still often comes with unnecessarily high transaction costs due to poor coordination, failure to use national systems and a preference for working through projects. Such practices not only raise transaction costs but also weaken national capacity and undermine aid effectiveness.

Increased aid needs to be accompanied by a stronger commitment to basic education in low-income countries. While there has been a shift in this direction since Dakar, several donors should review the distribution of their aid budgets across the various levels of education. The financing gaps that remain in basic education call into question the large share of aid directed towards higher education levels by some donors – notably France, Germany and Japan – as well as the practice of counting as aid spending directed at higher education institutions in the donor country.

Poor countries affected by conflict continue to suffer from donor neglect. Support for these countries is uneven and inconsistent – and many countries are bypassed because they are unable to meet inflexible donor reporting requirements. Opportunities for reconstruction are being lost on a large scale, raising the risk of a return to conflict. Working in conflict-affected states confronts governments with wide-ranging governance challenges. Evidence suggests that these challenges can be met through greater flexibility and innovation, and reduced risk aversion. For example, multidonor trust funds have demonstrated that aid can be scaled up even in the most difficult circumstances.

8 Strengthen the multilateral architecture for aid to education

International aid to education continues to suffer from the weakness of the multilateral framework for cooperation. The current architecture is manifestly unfit for the purpose of accelerating progress towards the 2015 goals. It has conspicuously failed either to increase financial resource mobilization on the required scale or to keep education at the centre of the international development agenda. In contrast to the health sector – where global initiatives have succeeded in expanding financing, developing a broad base of donor support and creating multilateral channels for private sector financing – multilateralism in education remains underdeveloped. Political leadership is at the heart of the problem.

The current Fast Track Initiative (FTI) does not provide a credible foundation for the development of an ambitious multilateral framework. While it has registered some important achievements, the FTI has not emerged as the force for change envisaged at its inception. There is little evidence to suggest that it has mobilized significant increases in bilateral aid. The direct financing provided through its two trust funds – the Catalytic Fund and Education Program Development Fund – has been limited. Moreover, the Catalytic Fund has been characterized by slow disbursement and in some cases it has weakened coordinated donor support for nationally owned policies. Countries affected by conflict have received limited support.

If the FTI is to have a future, fundamental reform is essential. Donors should mobilize the US$1.2 billion needed to meet expected Catalytic Fund financing requirements, subject to early implementation of reform measures and commitments to improve disbursement rates. Donors need greater confidence that these resources will be spent effectively and that disbursement rates will improve. As a starting point, the FTI should be reconstituted as an independent organization outside the World Bank. Developing countries should have a greater voice in its governance at all levels. The design of FTI reform should draw on the experiences and lessons of the Global Fund to Fight AIDS, Tuberculosis and Malaria, and similar global initiatives. The limitations of such health funds have to be recognized, notably with respect to distortions associated with vertical financing; nevertheless, these initiatives have mobilized new financing, developed a broad base of donor support, engaged the private sector, created windows for innovative financing and galvanized political support. The ambition for education should be set at a similar level, with a reformed FTI operating under a clear mandate to close the Education for All financing gap.

Effective multilateralism in education will require wider institutional changes. The High-Level Group on Education for All, created to oversee progress, shape the global agenda and galvanize international support, has not functioned effectively. Annual cycles of planning and meetings lack strategic focus and typically culminate in the adoption of vague communiqués, with little or no follow-up. There is a strong case for replacing the current arrangement with a leaner, more results-oriented structure. As an immediate priority, the High-Level Group should provide leadership in developing a more ambitious and effective multilateral architecture in education.

9 Integrate provision by non-government organizations within national education systems

Responsibility for achieving the Education for All goals ultimately rests with governments – and it is governments that have to be held accountable for results. However, non-government organizations have spearheaded efforts to provide education opportunities for marginalized groups. Many such organizations deliver education in slums and remote rural areas. They also work directly with child labourers, pastoralists and children with disabilities in a wide variety of settings. And they have been at the forefront of efforts to provide a second chance to children, youth and adults who were denied an opportunity for education during their primary or early secondary school years. These interventions are most effective when they offer marginalized people a route into meaningful employment or back into formal education – and when they are developed in consultation with the marginalized themselves. Integrating successful interventions by non-government organizations within national education systems can help achieve this level of effectiveness.

10 Expand the entitlements of the marginalized through political and social mobilization

Overcoming marginalization is about more than changing policies. It is also about changing power relationships. Legislative action can be crucial to expanding the entitlements of disadvantaged groups to resources and services, and national laws can establish the principles of non-discrimination and equal opportunity. But legislative action is most effective when accompanied by social and political mobilization. From the civil rights movement in the United States to indigenous peoples' movements in Latin America and the Māori language movement in New Zealand, civil society groups have been instrumental in forging the alliances and framing the demands that have driven change. One of the lessons of history is that marginalization can only be addressed through processes that empower the marginalized and strengthen their voices in political decision-making.

Civil society organizations have an important role to play at the international level by ensuring that these voices are heard in intergovernmental forums. They also have a responsibility for holding aid donors and governments to account for their pledges at Dakar. The Global Campaign for Education, a broad coalition of non-government organizations, teacher unions and other civil society groups, plays a key role in this area. It has raised the profile of education on the international development agenda, built innovative relationships with a broad constituency and developed communications strategies aimed at reaching a wider audience – the '1 Goal' campaign with FIFA to mark the 2010 football World Cup in South Africa is an example. Looking to the future, it is important that the Global Campaign for Education steps up its efforts to hold United Nations agencies and the World Bank accountable for delivering on their Education for All commitments – and for providing higher levels of performance and leadership.

Non-government organizations have been at the forefront of efforts to provide education opportunities for marginalized groups

Persevering against the odds:
a schoolboy braves the floodwaters,
Bangladesh

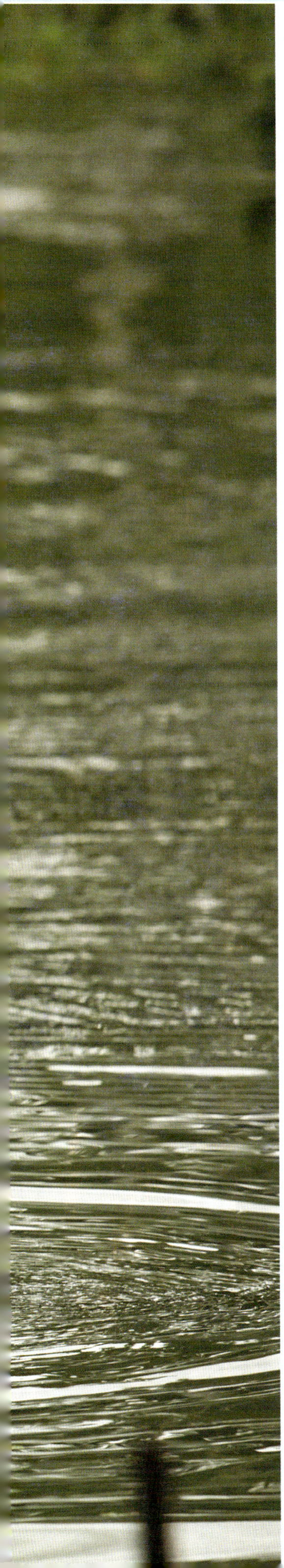

Annex

The Education for All Development Index

While each of the six Education for All goals adopted in 2000 matters in its own right, the commitment undertaken by governments at the World Education Forum in Dakar was to sustain advances on all fronts. The Education for All Development Index (EDI) provides a composite measure of progress, encompassing access, equity and quality. Because of data availability constraints,[1] it includes only the four most easily quantifiable goals, attaching an equal weight to each:

- universal primary education (goal 2), measured by the primary adjusted net enrolment ratio (ANER);[2]
- adult literacy (first part of goal 4), measured by the literacy rate for those aged 15 and above;[3]
- gender parity and equality (goal 5), measured by the gender-specific EFA index (GEI), an average of the gender parity indexes of the primary and secondary gross enrolment ratios and of the adult literacy rate;
- quality of education (goal 6), measured by the survival rate to grade 5.[4]

The EDI value for a given country is the arithmetic mean of the four proxy indicators. It falls between 0 and 1, with 1 representing full EFA achievement.[5]

This section sets out the EDI 2007 situation and rankings, and provides a detailed technical overview of the methodology.

1. Reliable and comparable data relating to goal 1 (early childhood care and education) are not available for most countries, and progress on goal 3 (learning needs of youth and adults) is still not easy to measure or monitor.

2. The primary education adjusted NER measures the proportion of children of primary school age who are enrolled in either primary or secondary education.

3. The literacy data used are based on conventional assessment methods – either self- and third-party declarations or educational attainment proxies – and thus should be interpreted with caution; they are not based on any test and may overestimate actual literacy levels.

4. For countries where primary education lasts fewer than five years, the survival rate to the last grade of primary is used.

5. For further explanation of the EDI rationale and methodology, see the section on choice of indicators, which also includes detailed values and rankings for 2007.

The EDI in 2007

For the school year ending in 2007, the EDI values are calculated for 128 countries.[6] Data limitations continue to prevent a more global assessment. Most of the countries not covered are either affected by conflict[7] or have weak statistical information systems.

Countries' EDI rankings change from year to year, depending on changes in data and on the number of countries covered. For 2007, Norway ranks first and the Niger last, replacing Chad, which is not included this year because of a lack of recent data on the primary adjusted NER.

Table A.1 displays the results of the EDI calculations for 2007 by region. Of the 128 countries included:

- Sixty-two – six more than in 2006 – have either achieved the four most easily quantifiable EFA goals (forty-four countries) or are close to doing so (eighteen countries), with EDI values of 0.950 or above. In addition to high-achieving countries in North America and Europe, the list includes countries from all other EFA regions except sub-Saharan Africa.[8] With a few exceptions,[9] all these countries have achieved balanced progress on the four EFA goals included in the index. The right to education in these countries goes beyond rhetoric; education has been compulsory for decades and is often free.
- Thirty-six countries, mostly in Latin America and the Caribbean (sixteen), sub-Saharan Africa (eight) and the Arab region (six) are in the EDI medium category, with values ranging from 0.80 to 0.94. Most of these countries have a mixed progress report. While school participation is often high (with primary adjusted NER averaging around 93%), indicators for adult literacy and quality are less impressive. Adult literacy is below 80% in some countries in this group, including Algeria,

6. This is one fewer than in 2006.

7. The list of conflict-affected countries includes Afghanistan, Angola, Burundi, the Central African Republic, Chad, the Democratic Republic of the Congo, Côte d'Ivoire, Eritrea, Ethiopia, Guinea-Bissau, Liberia, Myanmar, Nepal, Pakistan, Rwanda, Senegal, Sierra Leone, Somalia, Sudan and Uganda.

8. In the *EFA Global Monitoring Report 2009*, one country in this region, Seychelles, was listed among countries having achieved EFA; it is no longer included because of a lack of recent data on the primary adjusted NER and survival rate to grade 5.

9. The primary adjusted NER remains at 90% or below in the Republic of Moldova and Ukraine, as does the average adult literacy rate in Bahrain and the United Arab Emirates.

Table A.1: Distribution of countries by EDI score and region, 2007

	Far from EFA: EDI below 0.80	Intermediate position: EDI between 0.80 and 0.94	Close to EFA: EDI between 0.95 and 0.96	EFA achieved: EDI between 0.97 and 1.00	Subtotal sample	Total number of countries
Sub-Saharan Africa	17	8			25	45
Arab States	5	6	3		14	20
Central Asia		1	2	5	8	9
East Asia and the Pacific	2	4	2	4	12	33
South and West Asia	5		1		6	9
Latin America and the Caribbean	1	16	5	4	26	41
North America and Western Europe			1	20	21	26
Central and Eastern Europe		1	4	11	16	21
Total	30	36	18	44	128	204

Source: Table A.2.

Belize, Guatemala, Kenya and Zambia, while school retention is particularly poor in Brazil, the Dominican Republic, El Salvador, Guatemala, the Philippines, Sao Tome and Principe, and Suriname.

- Thirty countries, a majority (seventeen) of them in sub-Saharan Africa, have low EDI values, below 0.80. Very low EDI values (below 0.60) are reported in Ethiopia, Mali and the Niger. Countries in other regions listed in this low EDI category include highly populated countries such as Bangladesh, India and Pakistan. With the exception of Madagascar and Nicaragua, which have achieved near universal primary enrolment, countries at low levels of EFA achievement face multiple challenges: school participation is low, quality is poor, adult illiteracy is high and gender disparities are marked.

Change over time in the EDI

For the period from 1999 to 2007, progress on the EDI could be analysed for forty-three countries with data available for both years. As Figure A.1 shows, the EDI increased in a large majority of these countries (thirty out of forty-three), with particularly large gains in some countries, including Ethiopia, Mozambique, Nepal and Zambia (where in each case the EDI went up by more than 12%). With the exceptions of the United Arab Emirates and the Bolivarian Republic of Venezuela, countries moving quickly towards EFA are in the low EDI category.[10]

Expansion of primary school participation is the main reason for the increase in the EDI since 1999: the average increase in the primary adjusted net enrolment ratio was 8.7%. It was followed by the improvements in adult literacy rates (by 3.7%) and education quality as measured by the survival rate to grade 5 (up by 3.4%).

10. The United Arab Emirates moved from the medium EDI category to the high one during the period.

The gender component played a smaller role in the EDI increase (up by 3.0%), except in countries including Nepal and Yemen where the reduction in gender disparities had the greatest impact.

Not all countries have been moving in the right direction. The EDI decreased in thirteen countries, declining by 2% or more from 1999 to 2007 in the Dominican Republic and Fiji, mainly because of a decrease in the rate of survival to grade 5.

The progress report for 2006–2007 provides a similar mix of positive and negative news. Nearly two-thirds of the 120 countries with data available improved or maintained their EDI values (see Table A.5). The EDI increased by 5% or more in Burkina Faso, Namibia, the Niger, and Sao Tome and Principe. On the other hand, the situation worsened in one-third of the remaining countries, particularly Bangladesh, Burundi and Nepal. In Togo, the EDI declined by 8.4%. Analysis of EDI movement can help identify important priority areas and those that have suffered from relative neglect.

Inequalities in overall EFA achievement

Overall progress in the EDI can mask disparities related to wealth, language, rural-urban divides and other factors. These disparities are often comparable to those between nations (UNESCO, 2008). The EFA Inequality Index for Income Groups (EIIIG), developed for the *EFA Global Monitoring Report 2009*, revealed far higher scores for the richest households than for the poorest ones. Similarly, urban areas performed more strongly than rural areas. The disparities are greatest in countries where overall EFA achievement is still low, such as Burkina Faso, Ethiopia, Mali, Mozambique and the Niger. These countries face the double challenge addressed in this year's Report: to develop their education systems while making them more inclusive by reaching and teaching the most marginalized.

Figure A.1: EDI in 2007 and change since 1999 and 2006

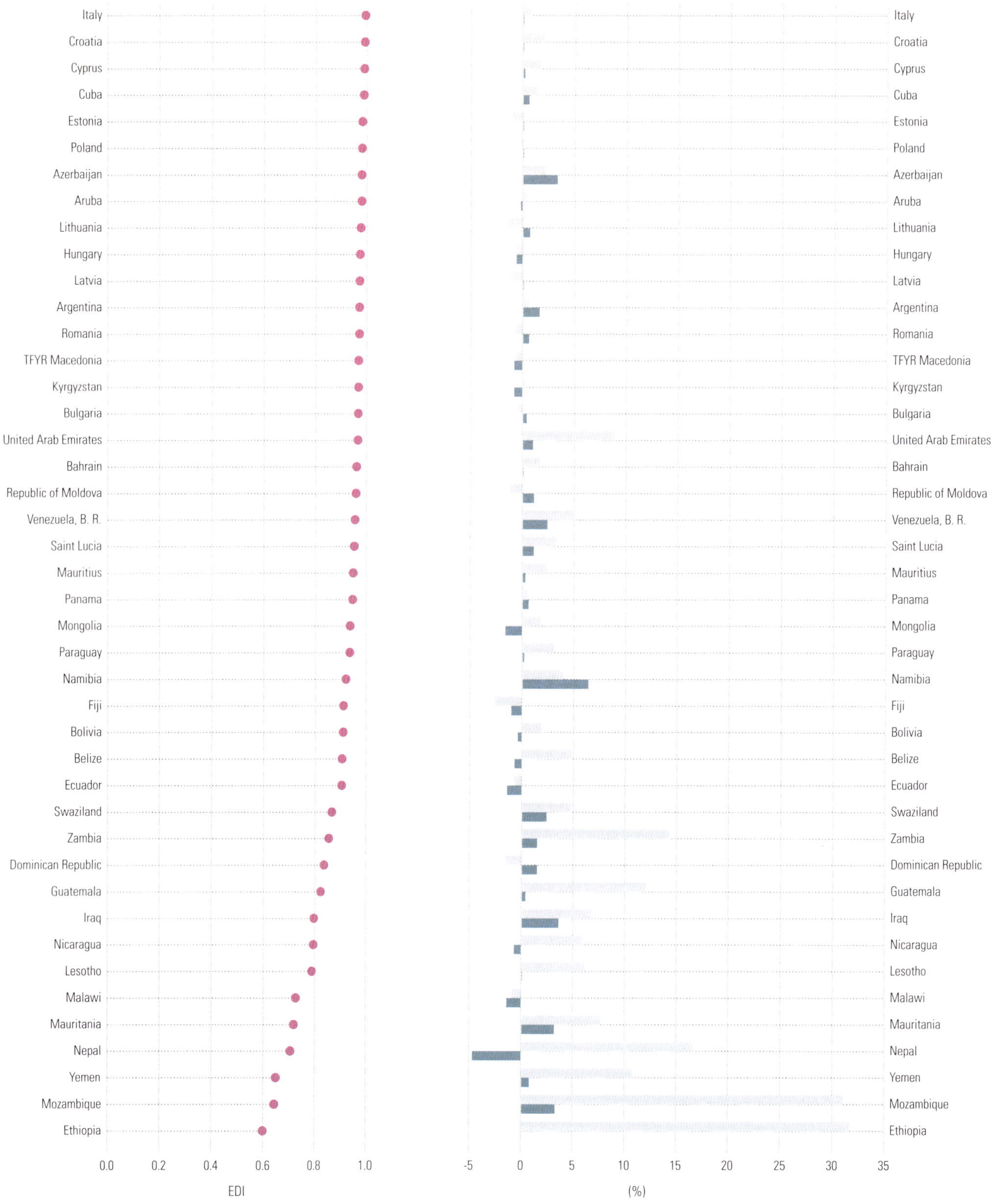

Note: Only countries with EDI values in 1999 and 2007 are included.
Sources: Tables A.4 and A.5.

Choice of indicators as proxy measures of EDI components

Constructing the EDI and selecting the measurement tools involves judgements about the merits of the range of proxy indicators available and their relevance for capturing overall progress. This section explains the choice of indicators and methodology.

Universal primary education

Universal primary education (goal 2) implies both universal access to and universal completion of primary education. However, while both access and participation at this level are relatively easy to measure, there is a lack of consensus on the definition of primary school completion. Therefore, only the universal enrolment aspect of the goal is taken into consideration in the EDI. The indicator selected to measure universal primary enrolment achievement is the primary adjusted net enrolment ratio (ANER), which reflects the percentage of primary school age children who are enrolled in either primary or secondary school. Its value varies from 0 to 100%. An ANER of 100% means all eligible children are enrolled in school in a given school year, even though some of them may not complete it. However, if the ANER is at 100% for many consecutive years, it may imply that all children enrolled do complete at least primary school.

Adult literacy

The adult literacy rate is used as a proxy to measure progress towards the first part of goal 4.[11] This has its limitations. First, the adult literacy indicator, being a statement about the stock of human capital, is slow to change, and thus it could be argued that it is not a good 'leading indicator' of year-by-year progress. Second, the existing data on literacy are not entirely satisfactory. Most of them are based on 'conventional' non-tested methods that usually overestimate the level of literacy among individuals.[12] New methodologies, based on tests and on the definition of literacy as a continuum of skills, are being developed and applied in some countries, including developed countries, to improve the quality of literacy data. Providing a new data series of good quality for most countries will take many years, however. The literacy rates now used are the best currently available internationally.

11. The first part of goal 4 is: 'Achieving a 50 per cent improvement in levels of adult literacy by 2015, especially for women'. To enable progress towards this target to be monitored for all countries, whatever their current adult literacy level, it was decided as of the *EFA Global Monitoring Report 2006* to interpret it in terms of a reduction in the adult illiteracy rate.

12. In most countries, particularly developing countries, current literacy data are derived from methods of self-declaration or third-party reporting (e.g. a household head responding on behalf of other household members) used in censuses or household surveys. In other cases, particularly as regards developed countries, they are based on education attainment proxies as measured in labour force surveys. Neither method is based on any test, and both are subject to bias (overestimation of literacy), which affects the quality and accuracy of literacy data.

Quality of education

There is considerable debate about the concept of quality and how it should be measured. Several proxy indicators are generally used to measure quality of education, among them measures of students' learning outcomes, which are widely used for this purpose, particularly among countries at similar levels of development. However, measures of learning achievement are incomplete, as they are often limited to basic skills (reading, numeracy, science) and do not include values, capacities and other non-cognitive skills that are also important aims of education (UNESCO, 2004, pp. 43–4). They also tell nothing about the cognitive value added by schooling (as opposed to home background) or the distribution of ability among children enrolled in school.[13] Despite these drawbacks, learning outcomes would likely be the most appropriate single proxy for the average quality of education, but as comparable data are not yet available for a large number of countries, it is not yet possible to use them in the EDI.

Among the feasible proxy indicators available for a large number of countries, the survival rate to grade 5 seems to be the best available for the quality of education component of the EDI.[14] Figures A.2, A.3 and A.4 show that there is a clear positive link between such survival rates and learning achievement across various international assessments. The coefficient of correlation (R^2) between survival rates and learning outcomes in reading is 37% (Figure A.2). Education systems capable of retaining a larger proportion of their pupils to grade 5 tend to perform better, on average, in student assessment tests. The survival rate to grade 5 is associated even more strongly with learning outcomes in mathematics (with a coefficient of 52%; Figure A.3) and science (57%; Figure A.4), as shown by the TIMSS 2007 results for fourth-grade students.

Another possible proxy indicator for quality often mentioned is the pupil/teacher ratio. Among countries participating in TIMSS 2007, the association between this indicator and learning outcomes is also strong, but is much lower than for the survival rate to grade 5, with a coefficient of only 19% for both mathematics and science. Many other studies produce ambiguous evidence of the relationship between pupil/teacher ratios and learning outcomes (UNESCO, 2004). In a multivariate context, low pupil/teacher ratios are associated with higher learning outcomes in some studies, but not in many others. In addition, the relationship seems to vary by the level of

13. Strictly speaking, it would be necessary to compare average levels of cognitive achievement for pupils completing a given school grade across countries with similar levels and distributions of income, and with similar NER levels, so as to account for home background and ability cohort effects.

14. See *EFA Global Monitoring Report 2003/4*, Appendix 2, for background.

Figure A.2: Survival rates to grade 5 and learning outcomes in reading at lower secondary level, 2006

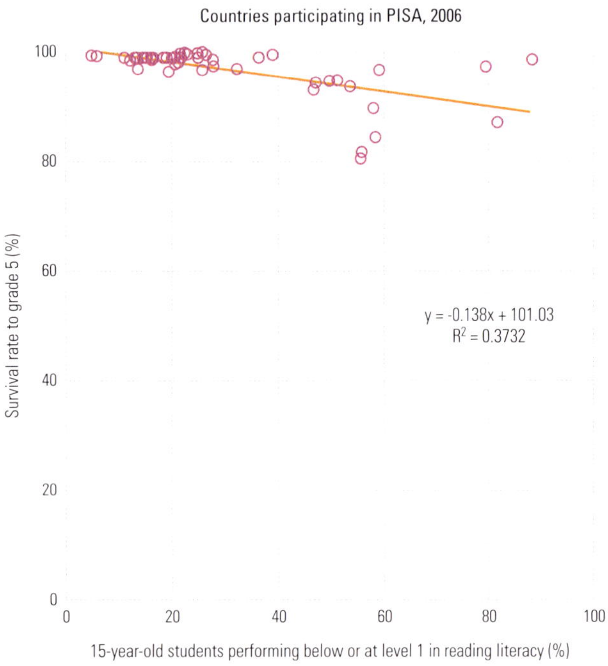

Sources: Annex, Statistical Table 7; OECD (2007).

mean test scores. For low levels of test scores, a decrease in the number of pupils per teacher has a positive impact on learning outcomes, but for higher levels of test scores, additional teachers, which lead to lower ratios, have only limited impact. For all these reasons, the survival rate is used as a safer proxy for learning outcomes and hence for the education quality component of the EDI.[15]

Gender

The fourth EDI component is measured by a composite index, the gender-specific EFA index (GEI). Ideally, the GEI should reflect the whole gender-related Education for All goal, which calls for 'eliminating gender disparities in primary and secondary education by 2005, and achieving gender equality in education by 2015, with a focus on ensuring girls' full and equal access to and achievement in basic education of good quality'. There are thus two subgoals: gender parity (achieving equal participation of girls and boys in primary and secondary education) and gender equality (ensuring that educational equality exists between boys and girls).

15. Another reason is that survival rates, like the other EDI components, but unlike pupil/teacher ratios, range from 0 to 100%. Therefore, the use of the survival rate to grade 5 in the EDI avoids a need to rescale the data.

Figure A.3: Survival rates to grade 5 and learning outcomes in mathematics at primary education level, 2007

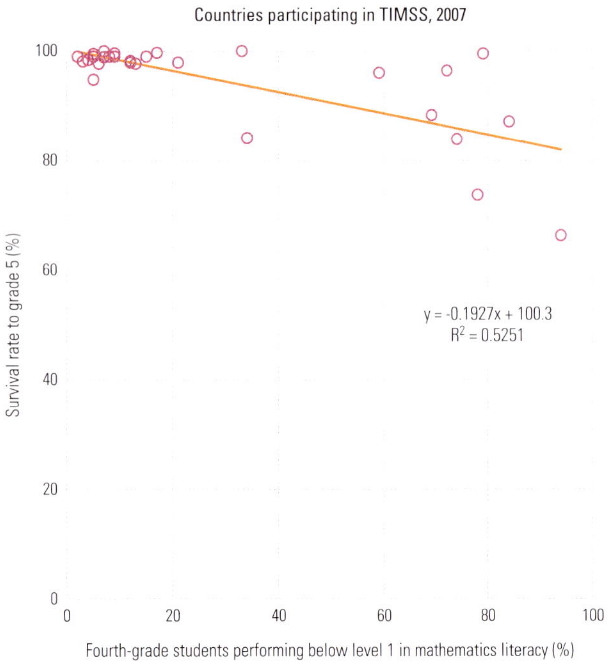

Sources: Annex, Statistical Table 7; Martin et al. (2008).

Figure A.4: Survival rates to grade 5 and learning outcomes in science at primary education level, 2007

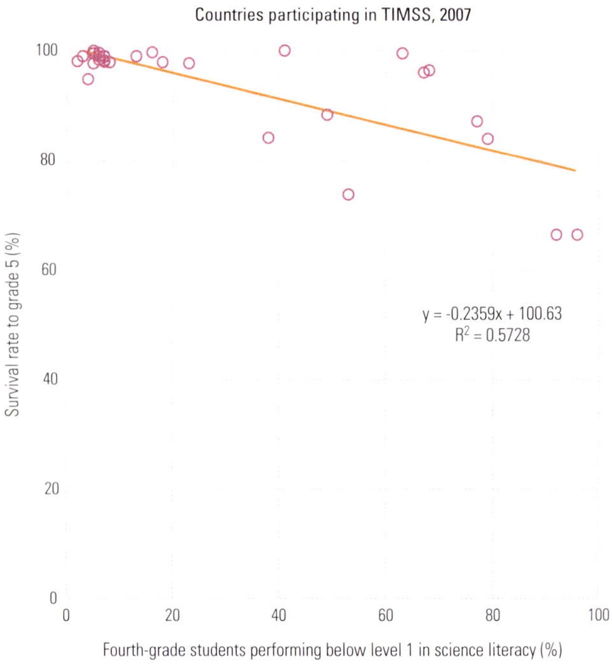

Sources: Annex, Statistical Table 7; Martin et al. (2008).

The first subgoal is measured by the gender parity indexes (GPIs) of the gross enrolment ratios (GERs) at primary and secondary levels. Defining, measuring and monitoring gender equality in education is difficult, as it includes both quantitative and qualitative aspects (see Chapter 2 and UNESCO, 2003). Essentially, measures of outcomes, which are also part of gender equality, are needed for a range of education levels, disaggregated by sex. No such measures are widely available on an internationally comparable basis. As a step in that direction, however, the GEI includes the gender parity measure for adult literacy. Thus, the GEI is calculated as a simple average of three GPIs: for the GER in primary education, for the GER in secondary education and for the adult literacy rate. This means the GEI does not fully reflect the equality aspect of the Education for All gender goal.

The GPI, when expressed as the ratio of female to male enrolment ratios or literacy rates, can exceed unity when more girls/women than boys/men are enrolled or literate. For the purposes of the GEI, the standard F/M formula is inverted to M/F in cases where the GPI is higher than 1. This solves mathematically the problem of including the GEI in the EDI (where all components have a theoretical limit of 1, or 100%) while maintaining the GEI's ability to show gender disparity. Figure A.5 shows how 'transformed' GPIs are arrived at to highlight gender disparities that disadvantage males. Once all three GPI values have been calculated and converted into 'transformed' GPIs (from 0 to 1) where needed, the composite GEI is obtained by calculating a simple average of the three GPIs, with each being weighted equally.

Figure A.6 illustrates the calculation for Spain, using data for the school year ending in 2007. The GPIs in primary education, secondary education and adult literacy were 0.987, 1.063 and 0.986, respectively, resulting in a GEI of 0.971.

GEI = 1/3 (primary GPI)
+ 1/3 (transformed secondary GPI)
+ 1/3 (adult literacy GPI)

GEI = 1/3 (0.987) + 1/3 (0.941) + 1/3 (0.986) = 0.971

Figure A.5: Calculating the 'transformed' GPI

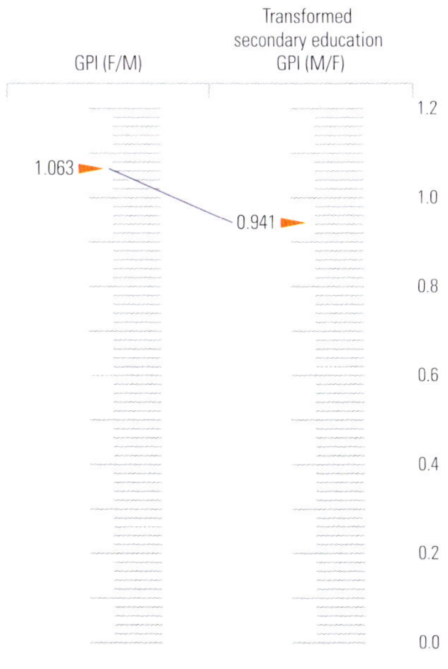

Example used: Spain

Figure A.6: Calculating the GEI

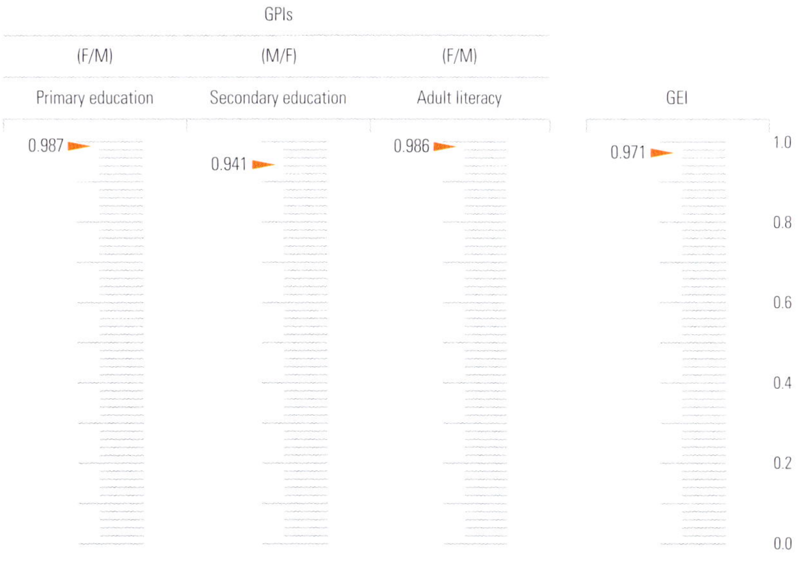

Example used: Spain

Calculating the EDI

The EDI is the arithmetic mean of its four components: primary adjusted NER, adult literacy rate, GEI and survival rate to grade 5. As a simple average, the EDI may mask important variations among its components: for example, results for goals on which a country has made less progress can offset its advances on others. Since all the goals are equally important for Education for All to be achieved as a whole, a synthetic indicator such as the EDI is thus very useful to inform the policy debate on the prominence of all the Education for All goals and to highlight the synergy among them.

Figure A.7 illustrates the calculation of the EDI, again using Spain as an example. The primary adjusted NER, adult literacy rate and GEI are for 2007 while the survival rate to grade 5 is for 2005. Their values were 0.998, 0.979, 0.971 and 0.998, respectively, resulting in an EDI of 0.987.

EDI = 1/4 (primary adjusted NER)
+ 1/4 (adult literacy rate)
+ 1/4 (GEI)
+ 1/4 (survival rate to grade 5)
EDI = 1/4 (0.998) + 1/4 (0.979) + 1/4 (0.971) + 1/4 (0.998)
= 0.987

Figure A.7: Calculating the EDI

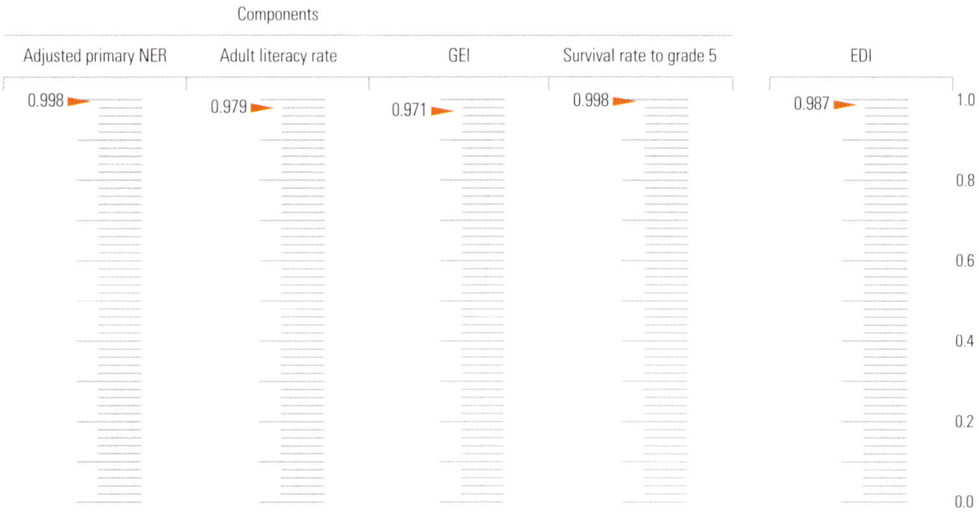

Example used: Spain

Data sources and country coverage

All data used to calculate the EDI for the school year ending in 2007 are from the statistical tables in this annex and the UNESCO Institute for Statistics (UIS) database.

Only the 128 countries with a complete set of the indicators required to calculate the EDI are included in this analysis. Many countries thus are not included in the EDI, among them a number of countries in conflict or post-conflict situations and countries with weak education statistical systems. This fact, coupled with the exclusion of goals 1 and 3, means the EDI does not yet provide a fully comprehensive global overview of Education for All achievement.

Table A.2: The EFA Development Index (EDI) and its components, 2007

Ranking according to level of EDI	Countries/Territories	EDI	Primary adjusted NER[1]	Adult literacy rate	Gender-specific EFA Index (GEI)	Survival rate to grade 5
High EDI						
1	Norway[2]	0.995	0.987	1.000	0.995	0.997
2	Japan[2]	0.994	0.998	0.992	0.997	0.990
3	Germany[2]	0.994	0.998	1.000	0.993	0.984
4	Kazakhstan	0.993	0.990	0.996	0.992	0.995
5	Italy	0.992	0.994	0.989	0.991	0.996
6	New Zealand[2]	0.992	0.993	0.998	0.987	0.990
7	France[2]	0.991	0.992	0.988	0.995	0.990
8	Netherlands	0.990	0.986	0.999	0.986	0.990
9	United Kingdom[2]	0.990	0.984	0.997	0.990	0.990
10	Croatia	0.990	0.989	0.987	0.984	0.998
11	Luxembourg[2]	0.989	0.988	0.990	0.987	0.992
12	Slovenia	0.988	0.972	0.997	0.995	0.990
13	Cyprus	0.988	0.993	0.977	0.983	0.999
14	Cuba	0.987	0.989	0.998	0.992	0.970
15	Finland[2]	0.987	0.965	1.000	0.984	0.999
16	Iceland[2]	0.987	0.975	1.000	0.981	0.991
17	Spain	0.987	0.998	0.979	0.971	0.998
18	Denmark[2]	0.985	0.961	1.000	0.990	0.990
19	Austria[2]	0.985	0.974	1.000	0.985	0.981
20	Sweden[2]	0.984	0.940	1.000	0.996	1.000
21	Republic of Korea[2]	0.984	0.985	0.999	0.972	0.980
22	Georgia[2]	0.983	0.945	0.998	0.989	1.000
23	Belgium[2]	0.983	0.983	0.999	0.988	0.963
24	Greece	0.982	0.998	0.971	0.974	0.985
25	Estonia	0.981	0.968	0.998	0.989	0.969
26	Israel[3]	0.980	0.972	0.971	0.986	0.992
27	Poland[2]	0.980	0.957	0.993	0.993	0.977
28	Ireland[3]	0.980	0.960	0.994	0.976	0.990
29	Aruba	0.979	0.954	0.995	0.981	0.967
30	Azerbaijan	0.979	0.996	0.981	0.971	0.987
31	Switzerland[2]	0.977	0.935	1.000	0.982	0.990
32	Lithuania	0.976	0.936	0.997	0.995	0.977
33	Czech Republic[2]	0.975	0.925	0.999	0.994	0.982
34	Tajikistan	0.975	0.975	0.996	0.934	0.994
35	Hungary[2]	0.973	0.930	0.989	0.991	0.980
36	Slovakia[3]	0.972	0.921	0.996	0.993	0.979
37	Latvia	0.972	0.922	0.998	0.986	0.981
38	Argentina	0.971	0.990	0.976	0.958	0.960
39	Uruguay	0.971	0.976	0.979	0.984	0.944
40	Armenia	0.971	0.939	0.995	0.972	0.977
41	Belarus	0.971	0.902	0.997	0.988	0.995
42	Romania	0.971	0.966	0.976	0.991	0.950
43	Portugal	0.970	0.990	0.949	0.950	0.990
44	Brunei Darussalam	0.970	0.965	0.949	0.972	0.993
45	Uzbekistan	0.969	0.936	0.969	0.978	0.992
46	TFYR Macedonia	0.968	0.942	0.970	0.980	0.982
47	Kyrgyzstan	0.968	0.924	0.993	0.991	0.965
48	Ukraine	0.968	0.899	0.997	0.998	0.979
49	Tonga	0.967	0.985	0.992	0.970	0.921
50	Bulgaria	0.967	0.963	0.983	0.979	0.941
51	Chile	0.966	0.945	0.965	0.975	0.979
52	United Arab Emirates	0.966	0.983	0.900	0.979	1.000
53	Kuwait	0.965	0.941	0.945	0.980	0.995
54	Bahrain	0.961	0.994	0.888	0.972	0.989
55	Mexico	0.959	0.992	0.928	0.971	0.946
56	Republic of Moldova	0.959	0.900	0.992	0.982	0.962
57	Trinidad and Tobago	0.958	0.971	0.987	0.966	0.910
58	Maldives	0.957	0.970	0.970	0.966	0.921
59	Venezuela, B. R.	0.956	0.941	0.952	0.955	0.978
60	Saint Lucia[2]	0.953	0.990	0.913	0.949	0.959
61	Malta	0.953	0.913	0.924	0.984	0.990
62	Macao, China	0.952	0.930	0.935	0.954	0.990

Table A.2 (continued)

Ranking according to level of EDI	Countries/Territories	EDI	Primary adjusted NER[1]	Adult literacy rate	Gender-specific EFA Index (GEI)	Survival rate to grade 5
Medium EDI						
63	Mauritius	0.949	0.954	0.874	0.976	0.990
64	Barbados[2]	0.948	0.970	0.884	0.991	0.946
65	Indonesia	0.947	0.980	0.920	0.962	0.928
66	Panama	0.947	0.990	0.934	0.963	0.900
67	Jordan	0.946	0.929	0.911	0.957	0.988
68	Peru	0.942	0.990	0.896	0.949	0.932
69	Malaysia	0.941	0.975	0.919	0.953	0.917
70	Qatar	0.941	0.983	0.931	0.979	0.871
71	Mongolia	0.937	0.976	0.973	0.958	0.841
72	Paraguay	0.936	0.949	0.946	0.974	0.877
73	Bahamas[2]	0.934	0.912	0.988	0.986	0.850
74	Namibia	0.921	0.881	0.880	0.944	0.978
75	Colombia	0.920	0.909	0.927	0.963	0.883
76	Palestinian A. T.	0.914	0.774	0.938	0.956	0.987
77	Turkey	0.913	0.923	0.887	0.872	0.969
78	Fiji[2]	0.912	0.942	0.929	0.945	0.831
79	Bolivia	0.911	0.950	0.907	0.955	0.833
80	Belize[2]	0.907	0.989	0.796	0.971	0.873
81	Ecuador	0.906	0.993	0.842	0.974	0.817
82	St Vincent/Grenadines[3]	0.904	0.939	0.881	0.917	0.880
83	Sao Tome/Principe	0.899	0.997	0.879	0.933	0.787
84	Lebanon	0.898	0.841	0.896	0.932	0.923
85	Philippines	0.895	0.917	0.934	0.962	0.768
86	Algeria	0.890	0.960	0.754	0.885	0.960
87	Honduras	0.885	0.939	0.836	0.931	0.834
88	Brazil	0.883	0.935	0.900	0.942	0.756
89	Suriname	0.882	0.942	0.904	0.884	0.797
90	Oman	0.879	0.750	0.844	0.938	0.985
91	Cape Verde	0.875	0.852	0.838	0.889	0.922
92	Botswana	0.869	0.841	0.829	0.980	0.825
93	Swaziland	0.867	0.872	0.838	0.938	0.821
94	El Salvador	0.865	0.936	0.820	0.967	0.737
95	Zambia	0.855	0.954	0.706	0.871	0.890
96	Kenya	0.839	0.870	0.736	0.922	0.829
97	Dominican Republic	0.836	0.847	0.891	0.920	0.684
98	Guatemala	0.823	0.968	0.732	0.907	0.683
Low EDI						
99	Iraq	0.796	0.886	0.741	0.750	0.806
100	Bhutan	0.795	0.884	0.528	0.836	0.932
101	Nicaragua	0.794	0.971	0.780	0.954	0.470
102	Ghana	0.791	0.733	0.650	0.896	0.886
103	Lesotho	0.788	0.727	0.822	0.866	0.737
104	Cambodia	0.781	0.894	0.763	0.844	0.622
105	India	0.775	0.943	0.660	0.841	0.658
106	Morocco	0.770	0.893	0.556	0.794	0.839
107	Madagascar	0.762	0.993	0.707	0.924	0.423
108	Uganda	0.761	0.947	0.736	0.873	0.487
109	Lao PDR	0.755	0.863	0.727	0.817	0.615
110	Malawi	0.725	0.876	0.718	0.872	0.434
111	Burundi	0.719	0.813	0.593	0.808	0.662
112	Bangladesh	0.718	0.896	0.535	0.895	0.548
113	Mauritania	0.717	0.810	0.558	0.864	0.637
114	Djibouti[2]	0.709	0.453	0.703	0.783	0.899
115	Nepal	0.704	0.800	0.565	0.835	0.616
116	Gambia[2]	0.678	0.693	0.425	0.865	0.730
117	Pakistan	0.651	0.656	0.542	0.708	0.697
118	Senegal	0.650	0.731	0.419	0.798	0.650
119	Yemen	0.648	0.754	0.589	0.587	0.663
120	Benin	0.647	0.828	0.405	0.640	0.715
121	Mozambique	0.642	0.760	0.444	0.725	0.640
122	Togo	0.629	0.789	0.532	0.650	0.543
123	Guinea	0.622	0.751	0.295	0.615	0.828
124	Eritrea	0.602	0.423	0.642	0.744	0.599
125	Burkina Faso	0.602	0.592	0.287	0.732	0.796
126	Ethiopia	0.598	0.723	0.359	0.667	0.644
127	Mali	0.590	0.630	0.262	0.654	0.812
128	Niger	0.508	0.455	0.287	0.571	0.720

Notes: Data in blue indicate that gender disparities are at the expense of boys or men, particularly at secondary level.

1. Primary adjusted NER includes children of primary school age who are enrolled in either primary or secondary schools.

2. Adult literacy rates are unofficial UIS estimates.

3. The adult literacy rate is a proxy measure based on educational attainment; that is, the proportion of the adult population with at least a complete primary education.

Sources: Annex, Statistical Tables 2, 5, 7 and 8; UIS database.

Table A.3: Countries ranked according to value of EDI and components, 2007

Countries/Territories	EDI	Primary adjusted NER[1]	Adult literacy rate	Gender-specific EFA Index (GEI)	Survival rate to grade 5
High EDI					
Norway[2]	1	25	1	4	8
Japan[2]	2	2	33	2	20
Germany[2]	3	1	1	10	38
Kazakhstan	4	17	25	12	12
Italy	5	8	36	16	9
New Zealand[2]	6	11	16	25	20
France[2]	7	13	37	5	20
Netherlands	8	26	9	30	20
United Kingdom[2]	9	29	18	20	20
Croatia	10	23	39	32	7
Luxembourg[2]	11	24	34	26	16
Slovenia	12	40	22	7	20
Cyprus	13	9	45	36	4
Cuba	14	22	13	13	53
Finland[2]	15	50	1	35	5
Iceland[2]	16	37	1	39	18
Spain	17	3	43	59	6
Denmark[2]	18	52	1	19	20
Austria[2]	19	39	1	31	42
Sweden[2]	20	70	1	3	3
Republic of Korea[2]	21	28	10	57	43
Georgia[2]	22	62	17	21	1
Belgium[2]	23	31	11	23	58
Greece	24	4	50	53	37
Estonia	25	46	14	22	55
Israel[3]	26	41	49	28	17
Poland[2]	27	55	29	9	51
Ireland[3]	28	54	27	48	20
Aruba	29	6	42	60	56
Azerbaijan	30	56	28	40	34
Switzerland[2]	31	77	1	37	20
Lithuania	32	76	21	6	50
Czech Republic[2]	33	82	12	8	39
Tajikistan	34	36	24	87	13
Hungary[2]	35	80	35	14	44
Slovakia[3]	36	86	23	11	46
Latvia	37	85	15	27	41
Argentina	38	16	46	71	60
Uruguay	39	34	44	33	66
Armenia	40	73	26	54	52
Belarus	41	91	19	24	11
Romania	42	48	47	17	63
Portugal	43	15	56	79	31
Brunei Darussalam	44	49	57	56	14
Uzbekistan	45	75	53	47	15
TFYR Macedonia	46	66	52	43	40
Kyrgyzstan	47	83	30	15	57
Ukraine	48	93	20	1	47
Tonga	49	27	32	62	74
Bulgaria	50	51	41	44	67
Chile	51	63	54	50	45
United Arab Emirates	52	32	75	45	1
Kuwait	53	69	59	41	10
Bahrain	54	7	80	55	32
Mexico	55	14	66	58	65
Republic of Moldova	56	92	31	38	59
Trinidad and Tobago	57	43	40	64	76
Maldives	58	44	51	65	73
Venezuela, B. R.	59	68	55	74	49
Saint Lucia[2]	60	18	71	80	62
Malta	61	88	68	34	20
Macao, China	62	79	61	77	20

Table A.3 (continued)

Countries/Territories	EDI	Primary adjusted NER[1]	Adult literacy rate	Gender-specific EFA Index (GEI)	Survival rate to grade 5
Medium EDI					
Mauritius	63	58	86	49	19
Barbados[2]	64	45	82	18	64
Indonesia	65	33	69	69	70
Panama	66	19	63	67	77
Jordan	67	81	72	72	33
Peru	68	20	78	81	69
Malaysia	69	38	70	78	75
Qatar	70	30	64	46	85
Mongolia	71	35	48	70	87
Paraguay	72	60	58	51	83
Bahamas[2]	73	89	38	29	86
Namibia	74	99	84	83	48
Colombia	75	90	67	66	81
Palestinian A. T.	76	113	60	73	35
Turkey	77	84	81	102	54
Fiji[2]	78	65	65	82	91
Bolivia	79	59	73	75	90
Belize[2]	80	21	95	61	84
Ecuador	81	10	88	52	96
St Vincent/Grenadines[3]	82	72	83	94	82
Sao Tome and Principe	83	5	85	88	101
Lebanon	84	106	77	89	71
Philippines	85	87	62	68	102
Algeria	86	53	98	99	61
Honduras	87	71	91	90	89
Brazil	88	78	76	84	103
Suriname	89	67	74	100	99
Oman	90	117	87	85	36
Cape Verde	91	104	90	98	72
Botswana	92	107	92	42	94
Swaziland	93	101	89	86	95
El Salvador	94	74	94	63	105
Zambia	95	57	106	104	79
Kenya	96	102	100	92	92
Dominican Republic	97	105	79	93	110
Guatemala	98	47	102	95	111
Low EDI					
Iraq	99	97	99	117	98
Bhutan	100	98	119	110	68
Nicaragua	101	42	96	76	126
Ghana	102	118	109	96	80
Lesotho	103	120	93	105	104
Cambodia	104	95	97	108	119
India	105	64	108	109	114
Morocco	106	96	115	115	88
Madagascar	107	12	105	91	128
Uganda	108	61	101	101	125
Lao PDR	109	103	103	112	121
Malawi	110	100	104	103	127
Burundi	111	109	111	113	113
Bangladesh	112	94	117	97	123
Mauritania	113	110	114	107	118
Djibouti[2]	114	127	107	116	78
Nepal	115	111	113	111	120
Gambia[2]	116	122	121	106	106
Pakistan	117	123	116	121	109
Senegal	118	119	122	114	115
Yemen	119	115	112	127	112
Benin	120	108	123	125	108
Mozambique	121	114	120	120	117
Togo	122	112	118	124	124
Guinea	123	116	125	126	93
Eritrea	124	128	110	118	122
Burkina Faso	125	125	126	119	100
Ethiopia	126	121	124	122	116
Mali	127	124	128	123	97
Niger	128	126	127	128	107

Notes:

1. Primary adjusted NER includes children of primary school age who are enrolled in either primary or secondary schools.

2. Adult literacy rates are unofficial UIS estimates.

3. The adult literacy rate is a proxy measure based on educational attainment; that is, the proportion of the adult population with at least a complete primary education.

Sources: Annex, Statistical Tables 2, 5, 7 and 8; UIS database.

Table A.4: Change in EDI and its components between 1999 and 2007

Countries/Territories	EFA Development Index 1999	EFA Development Index 2007	Variation 1999–2007 (in relative terms)	Change in EDI components between 1999 and 2007 (% in relative terms): Primary adjusted NER[1]	Adult literacy rate	Gender-specific EFA Index (GEI)	Survival rate to grade 5
Italy	0.984	0.992	0.8	-0.4	0.5	0.1	3.1
Croatia	0.970	0.990	2.1	7.6	0.6	0.3	0.1
Cyprus	0.971	0.988	1.7	1.4	0.9	0.7	4.0
Cuba	0.974	0.987	1.4	-0.3	0.0	2.5	3.5
Estonia	0.991	0.981	-1.0	-3.1	0.0	1.4	-2.2
Poland[2]	0.982	0.980	-0.2	-0.5	0.1	0.6	-0.9
Aruba	0.975	0.979	0.4	1.2	0.9	-0.2	-0.1
Azerbaijan	0.959	0.979	2.1	7.6	0.6	-1.4	2.2
Lithuania	0.991	0.976	-1.4	-4.6	0.0	0.3	-1.6
Hungary[2]	0.982	0.973	-0.8	-4.2	-1.1	0.3	1.2
Latvia	0.983	0.972	-1.1	-6.4	0.0	0.6	1.2
Argentina	0.964	0.971	0.7	-0.3	0.5	-3.1	6.4
Romania	0.978	0.971	-0.7	-3.3	0.3	0.9	-0.7
TFYR Macedonia	0.974	0.968	-0.6	-4.8	0.9	0.9	0.8
Kyrgyzstan	0.965	0.968	0.3	-1.9	0.6	0.6	2.1
Bulgaria	0.971	0.967	-0.4	-2.6	0.1	-0.3	1.3
United Arab Emirates	0.887	0.966	8.8	20.4	7.1	1.1	8.3
Bahrain	0.944	0.961	1.7	0.8	2.6	2.1	1.5
Republic of Moldova	0.971	0.959	-1.2	-6.1	0.8	-0.5	0.9
Venezuela, B. R.	0.910	0.956	5.1	8.2	2.3	2.6	7.7
Saint Lucia[2]	0.922	0.953	3.3	1.8	1.3	3.8	6.5
Mauritius	0.927	0.949	2.4	5.3	3.7	1.4	-0.4
Panama	0.942	0.947	0.5	2.2	1.6	0.1	-2.1
Mongolia	0.920	0.937	1.9	6.8	-0.4	4.6	-3.6
Paraguay	0.909	0.936	3.1	-1.7	2.6	0.7	12.3
Namibia	0.885	0.921	4.0	7.8	3.4	-0.7	6.0
Fiji	0.936	0.912	-2.6	-4.6	0.0	-0.9	-4.9
Bolivia	0.894	0.911	1.9	-1.0	4.6	2.9	1.3
Belize	0.866	0.907	4.8	3.6	3.5	0.9	12.3
Ecuador	0.913	0.906	-0.7	0.3	-7.5	-0.8	6.1
Swaziland	0.829	0.867	4.7	16.6	5.4	-3.5	2.8
Zambia	0.748	0.855	14.3	39.9	3.9	5.4	10.4
Dominican Republic	0.850	0.836	-1.6	-0.5	2.5	-0.7	-8.8
Guatemala	0.734	0.823	12.1	16.0	5.9	6.8	22.0
Iraq	0.744	0.796	6.9	4.8	0.0	2.0	22.9
Nicaragua	0.749	0.794	6.0	21.4	1.7	1.0	-2.9
Lesotho	0.742	0.788	6.2	26.0	0.0	4.6	-0.4
Malawi	0.731	0.725	-0.9	-11.5	10.4	9.6	-11.4
Mauritania	0.666	0.717	7.7	25.9	9.0	4.2	-6.1
Nepal	0.603	0.704	16.7	19.4	16.3	23.5	6.1
Yemen	0.585	0.648	10.8	34.0	27.6	33.3	-24.2
Mozambique	0.490	0.642	31.1	45.1	11.8	18.5	50.1
Ethiopia	0.454	0.598	31.7	107.9	35.1	4.4	14.0

Notes:

1. Primary adjusted NER includes children of primary school age who are enrolled in either primary or secondary schools.
2. Adult literacy rates are unofficial UIS estimates.
3. The adult literacy rate is a proxy measure based on educational attainment; that is, the proportion of the adult population with at least a complete primary education.

Sources: Annex, Statistical Tables 2, 5, 7 and 8; UIS database.

Table A.5: Change in EDI and its components between 2006 and 2007

Countries/Territories	EFA Development Index		Variation 2006–2007 (in relative terms)	Change in EDI components between 2006 and 2007 (% in relative terms)			
	2006	2007		Primary adjusted NER[1]	Adult literacy rate	Gender-specific EFA Index (GEI)	Survival rate to grade 5
High EDI							
Norway[2]	0.994	0.995	0.1	0.7	0.0	-0.1	-0.2
Japan[2]	0.994	0.994	0.0	0.0	0.0	0.0	0.0
Germany[2]	0.994	0.994	-0.1	0.2	0.0	0.1	-0.5
Kazakhstan	0.995	0.993	-0.1	0.0	0.0	-0.1	-0.5
Italy	0.992	0.992	0.0	0.0	0.1	0.0	0.0
New Zealand[2]	0.989	0.992	0.3	-0.2	1.0	0.5	0.0
France[2]	0.991	0.991	0.0	0.0	0.0	0.0	0.0
Netherlands	0.986	0.990	0.4	0.4	1.2	0.1	0.0
United Kingdom[2]	0.993	0.990	-0.3	-1.2	0.0	0.1	0.0
Croatia	0.989	0.990	0.1	0.0	0.1	0.1	0.1
Luxembourg[2]	0.989	0.989	0.0	0.1	0.0	0.4	-0.4
Slovenia	0.988	0.988	0.1	0.4	0.0	-0.2	0.1
Cyprus	0.987	0.988	0.2	-0.2	0.2	-0.1	0.8
Cuba	0.981	0.987	0.6	2.0	0.0	0.6	-0.2
Finland[2]	0.987	0.987	-0.1	-0.5	0.0	-0.2	0.5
Iceland[2]	0.988	0.987	-0.2	-0.2	0.0	-0.5	0.0
Spain	0.985	0.987	0.2	0.1	0.6	0.3	-0.1
Denmark[2]	0.992	0.985	-0.7	-2.6	0.0	-0.1	0.0
Austria[2]	0.987	0.985	-0.2	0.0	0.0	0.0	-0.9
Sweden[2]	0.984	0.984	0.0	-1.0	0.0	-0.1	1.0
Republic of Korea[2]	0.984	0.984	0.0	0.0	0.8	0.5	-1.2
Georgia[2]	0.970	0.983	1.4	4.7	0.0	1.2	0.0
Belgium[2]	0.979	0.983	0.4	0.7	0.9	0.0	-0.2
Greece	0.984	0.982	-0.2	0.1	0.1	-0.8	-0.2
United States	0.972	0.981	1.0	0.5	0.7	0.4	2.2
Estonia	0.980	0.981	0.1	-0.1	0.0	0.4	0.0
Israel[2]	0.980	0.980	0.0	0.2	0.0	0.2	-0.4
Poland[2]	0.981	0.980	0.0	-0.6	1.0	0.3	-0.9
Ireland[3]	0.976	0.980	0.4	1.2	0.0	0.2	0.5
Aruba	0.981	0.979	-0.2	0.1	0.1	-0.9	-0.1
Azerbaijan	0.948	0.979	3.2	11.7	0.0	0.9	1.5
Switzerland[2]	0.976	0.977	0.1	0.0	0.0	0.2	0.0
Lithuania	0.970	0.976	0.7	1.7	0.0	-0.1	1.1
Czech Republic[2]	0.979	0.975	-0.4	0.0	0.0	0.1	-1.6
Tajikistan	0.971	0.975	0.4	0.3	0.0	0.7	0.7
Hungary[2]	0.979	0.973	-0.6	-1.7	-1.1	-0.1	0.1
Slovakia[3]	0.971	0.972	0.2	0.0	0.0	0.2	0.5
Latvia	0.972	0.972	0.0	0.0	0.0	0.0	0.0
Argentina	0.956	0.971	1.6	-0.1	0.1	-0.3	7.0
Uruguay	0.963	0.971	0.8	-2.3	0.1	4.4	1.4
Armenia	0.967	0.971	0.3	3.5	0.0	-0.1	-1.7
Belarus	0.969	0.971	0.2	0.4	0.0	0.1	0.3
Romania	0.965	0.971	0.6	1.1	0.0	0.0	1.4
Portugal	0.969	0.970	0.1	-0.2	0.3	0.4	0.0
Brunei Darussalam	0.972	0.970	-0.2	-0.9	0.3	0.2	-0.4
TFYR Macedonia	0.976	0.968	-0.8	-3.1	0.1	-0.1	0.0
Kyrgyzstan	0.976	0.968	-0.8	-1.1	0.0	0.1	-2.1
Tonga	0.967	0.967	0.0	0.2	0.0	0.0	0.0
Bulgaria	0.963	0.967	0.4	2.6	0.0	-0.1	-0.8
United Arab Emirates	0.956	0.966	1.0	3.3	0.2	-0.5	0.9
Kuwait	0.935	0.965	3.2	6.3	1.3	1.5	3.9
Bahrain	0.959	0.961	0.1	0.0	0.5	0.1	0.0
Mexico	0.956	0.959	0.3	-0.3	1.2	0.3	0.3
Republic of Moldova	0.948	0.959	1.1	5.6	0.1	0.3	-0.8
Trinidad and Tobago	0.941	0.958	1.9	8.6	0.1	-0.8	0.0
Maldives	0.959	0.957	-0.2	-1.0	0.1	0.0	0.0
Venezuela, B. R.	0.934	0.956	2.4	1.0	2.3	0.1	6.3
Saint Lucia[2]	0.942	0.953	1.1	0.2	1.3	3.0	0.0
Malta	0.955	0.953	-0.2	-2.4	1.1	0.3	0.0
Medium EDI							
Macao, China	0.947	0.952	0.6	1.9	0.6	-0.2	0.0
Mauritius	0.946	0.949	0.3	0.4	0.5	0.1	0.2
Barbados[2]	0.943	0.948	0.5	0.8	0.0	1.1	0.0
Indonesia	0.925	0.947	2.4	-0.4	1.0	-0.1	9.9

Table A.5 (continued)

Countries/Territories	EFA Development Index 2006	EFA Development Index 2007	Variation 2006–2007 (in relative terms)	Change in EDI components between 2006 and 2007 (% in relative terms): Primary adjusted NER[1]	Adult literacy rate	Gender-specific EFA Index (GEI)	Survival rate to grade 5
Panama	0.941	0.947	0.6	-0.1	0.2	0.3	2.3
Jordan	0.943	0.946	0.4	-0.8	-1.7	-0.3	4.3
Peru	0.931	0.942	1.2	-0.1	1.0	-0.2	4.1
Malaysia	0.965	0.941	-2.5	-2.4	0.4	0.1	-7.6
Qatar	0.935	0.941	0.7	0.1	3.6	-0.9	0.0
Mongolia	0.952	0.937	-1.6	0.3	0.0	0.5	-7.5
Paraguay	0.935	0.936	0.2	0.0	1.1	-0.3	0.0
Bahamas[2]	0.921	0.934	1.4	3.1	3.1	-0.4	0.0
Namibia	0.865	0.921	6.4	15.3	0.4	-0.7	12.6
Colombia	0.905	0.920	1.7	-1.1	0.4	0.2	8.0
Palestinian A. T.	0.913	0.914	0.1	-3.0	1.6	0.8	0.6
Turkey	0.909	0.913	0.4	1.1	0.6	-0.1	0.0
Fiji[2]	0.921	0.912	-1.0	0.0	0.0	-0.8	-3.3
Bolivia	0.915	0.911	-0.4	-1.3	1.1	0.5	-1.7
Belize[2]	0.913	0.907	-0.7	-0.2	3.5	0.1	-5.3
Ecuador	0.919	0.906	-1.4	-0.1	-8.9	-1.2	5.7
St Vincent/Grenadines[3]	0.901	0.904	0.4	1.5	0.0	0.0	0.0
Sao Tome and Principe	0.857	0.899	4.9	2.1	0.5	-0.2	22.8
Lebanon	0.887	0.898	1.3	1.3	1.5	0.8	1.6
Philippines	0.888	0.895	0.8	-0.3	0.1	0.3	3.9
Algeria	0.888	0.890	0.1	-1.7	1.1	0.6	0.8
Honduras	0.887	0.885	-0.2	-3.2	1.2	1.7	0.0
Brazil	0.901	0.882	-2.1	-2.2	0.0	-0.6	-6.0
Oman	0.885	0.879	-0.6	-1.9	0.8	0.0	-1.5
Cape Verde	0.883	0.875	-0.9	-3.7	1.0	-0.9	0.3
Botswana	0.867	0.869	0.2	0.0	0.9	0.0	0.0
Swaziland	0.847	0.867	2.4	11.0	5.4	-2.9	-2.3
El Salvador	0.867	0.865	-0.2	-2.2	-1.8	1.3	2.2
Zambia	0.842	0.855	1.5	2.0	3.9	1.1	-0.4
Kenya	0.816	0.839	2.8	14.2	0.0	-1.7	0.0
Dominican Republic	0.824	0.836	1.5	6.2	0.4	-0.5	0.0
Guatemala	0.819	0.823	0.4	0.7	1.0	0.7	-0.9
Low EDI							
Iraq	0.768	0.796	3.6	14.4	0.0	0.0	0.0
Bhutan	0.777	0.795	2.4	10.7	-2.8	0.4	0.0
Nicaragua	0.799	0.794	-0.7	6.3	-2.6	0.8	-12.4
Lesotho	0.788	0.788	0.0	0.0	0.0	0.0	0.0
Cambodia	0.778	0.781	0.4	-0.6	0.9	1.4	0.0
India	0.794	0.775	-2.4	-1.9	1.2	0.8	-9.9
Madagascar	0.737	0.762	3.4	3.4	0.0	0.3	18.1
Lao PDR	0.753	0.755	0.3	3.1	0.3	-1.6	-0.9
Malawi	0.735	0.725	-1.4	-4.6	1.3	0.2	-2.0
Burundi	0.757	0.719	-5.0	8.7	0.0	0.0	-24.6
Bangladesh	0.753	0.718	-4.5	-2.8	1.9	-2.1	-15.7
Mauritania	0.695	0.717	3.2	1.4	1.1	0.9	11.0
Djibouti[2]	0.684	0.709	3.8	18.3	0.0	4.3	0.0
Nepal	0.738	0.704	-4.7	-0.2	2.3	2.4	-21.6
Pakistan	0.652	0.651	-0.2	0.0	0.0	-0.8	0.0
Senegal	0.643	0.650	1.0	1.2	-0.2	2.4	0.0
Yemen	0.643	0.648	0.8	0.0	2.7	1.0	0.0
Benin	0.643	0.647	0.7	0.7	2.1	0.5	0.0
Mozambique	0.622	0.642	3.3	0.0	1.4	1.7	11.1
Togo	0.686	0.629	-8.4	-4.6	0.0	1.4	-27.1
Guinea	0.608	0.622	2.4	3.2	0.0	2.6	2.3
Eritrea	0.621	0.602	-3.0	-11.0	11.3	7.1	-18.6
Burkina Faso	0.538	0.602	11.9	23.8	10.6	6.4	9.8
Ethiopia	0.598	0.598	0.0	0.0	0.0	0.0	0.0
Mali	0.570	0.590	3.5	4.2	14.3	3.5	0.0
Niger	0.470	0.508	8.1	3.2	-3.9	-0.8	27.4

Notes:

1. Primary adjusted NER includes children of primary school age who are enrolled in either primary or secondary schools.
2. Adult literacy rates are unofficial UIS estimates.
3. The adult literacy rate is a proxy measure based on educational attainment; that is, the proportion of the adult population with at least a complete primary education.

Sources: Annex, Statistical Tables 2, 5, 7 and 8; UIS database.

Selected international human rights treaties relevant to the EFA goals

Human rights law is a living, breathing process of debate and negotiation between international bodies, states and citizens. The development and adoption of international and regional legal instruments often take years, but this is only the first step in a process that includes ratification by states, absorption into national law and, most crucially, use by individuals and groups to challenge states on violations of rights – including the right to education. This table reviews the status of the main international human rights instruments relevant to education. Not only have important new international instruments emerged in recent years, but states parties continue to sign and ratify even those conventions in existence for decades, reflecting the potential for positive change in national legal contexts.

Instrument	Year	Components relevant to Education for All	Number of signatures[1]	Number of states parties[2]	Recent (2008–2009) signatures (s), ratifications (r) and accessions (a)[3]
International Bill of Human Rights:		• All peoples have the right to freely pursue their economic, social and cultural development. • States to respect and ensure these rights without distinction of any kind, such as race, colour, sex, language, religion, political or other opinion, national or social origin, property, birth or other status. • Right of everyone to education. • Free and compulsory primary education • Secondary and higher education made generally available and accessible to all by every appropriate means; progressive introduction of free education.			
• Universal Declaration of Human Rights	1948				
• International Covenant on Civil and Political Rights (ICCPR)	1966		173	166	Bahamas (s, r), Comoros (s), Cuba (s), Lao People's Democratic Republic (r), Pakistan (s), Papua New Guinea (a), Samoa (a), Vanuatu (r)
– Optional Protocol to the ICCPR[4]	1966		119	115	Brazil (a), Kazakhstan (r), Republic of Moldova (r)
• International Covenant on Economic, Social and Cultural Rights (ICESCR)	1966		167	161	Bahamas (s, r), Comoros (s), Cuba (s), Pakistan (r), Papua New Guinea (a)
– Optional Protocol to the ICESCR[4]	2008		29	0	Signing ceremony held on 24 September 2009; 29 states parties signed within one week.
Discrimination (Employment and Occupation) Convention [No. 111. Adopted by ILO]	1958	• Protection of all persons in vocational training and employment from discrimination (based on distinction, exclusion or preference) made on the basis of race, colour, sex, religion, political opinion, national extraction or social origin.	–	169	Kiribati (r), Lao People's Democratic Republic (r), Samoa (r)
Convention against Discrimination in Education [Adopted by UNESCO]	1960	• Free and compulsory primary education. • Governments shall formulate, develop and apply a national policy tending to promote equality of opportunity and of treatment. • No discrimination in access to or quality of education.	–	96	Latvia (a)
International Convention on the Elimination of All Forms of Racial Discrimination (ICERD)	1965	• Right to education and training with no distinction as to race, colour, or national or ethnic origin. • Adopt measures, particularly in the field of teaching, education, culture and information, to combat prejudices which lead to racial discrimination.	179	173	–
– ICERD Article 14[4]			–	53	Kazakhstan (accepted[5]), San Marino (accepted[5])
Convention on the Elimination of All Forms of Discrimination against Women (CEDAW)	1979	• Eliminate discrimination against women in the field of education. • Ensure equality of access to same curricula, qualified teaching staff, and school facilities and equipment of the same quality. • Elimination of stereotyped concept of the roles of men and women by encouraging coeducation. • Reduction of female dropout rates; organization of programmes for those who left school prematurely.	187	179	Qatar (a)
– Optional Protocol to the CEDAW[4]	1999		114	98	Australia (a), Congo (s), Guinea-Bissau (r), Mauritius (r), Mozambique (a), Rwanda (a), Switzerland (r), Tunisia (a), Turkmenistan (r), Zambia (s)

Instrument	Year	Components relevant to Education for All	Number of signatures[1]	Number of states parties[2]	Recent (2008–2009) signatures (s), ratifications (r) and accessions (a)[3]
Convention concerning Indigenous and Tribal Peoples in Independent Countries (No. 169. Adopted by ILO)	1989	Equal opportunities to obtain education. Education responsive to culture and needs of indigenous peoples. Educational measures to eliminate prejudices.	—	20	Chile (r)
Convention on the Rights of the Child (CRC)	1989	Right to free and compulsory primary schooling without any type of discrimination. Access to higher levels of education. Emphasis on child well-being and development, encouragement of measures to support child care.	195	193	Ratified or acceded to by all states parties, except Somalia and the United States, which have only signed.
Optional Protocol to the CRC on the involvement of children in armed conflict	2000	Limit on voluntary recruitment of children into national armed forces, ban on recruitment of all children into independent armed groups. Condemnation of the targeting of children and schools during armed conflicts.	157	130	Albania (a), Algeria (a), Burundi (r), China (r), Cyprus (s), Iraq (a), Mauritius (r), Netherlands (r), Russian Federation (r), Singapore (r), Solomon Islands (s), South Africa (r), Uzbekistan (a), Zambia (s)
Optional Protocol to the CRC on the sale of children, child prostitution and child pornography	2000	Recognizes the right of the child to be protected from performing any work that is likely to interfere with the child's education.	163	132	Albania (a), Germany (r), Greece (r), Iraq (a), Israel (r), Monaco (r), Solomon Islands (s), United Kingdom (r), Uzbekistan (a), Zambia (s)
International Convention on the Protection of the Rights of All Migrant Workers and Members of their Families	1990	Equality of treatment with nationals of the country concerned as regards access to education. Access to public pre-schools and schools shall not be refused or limited because of the irregularity of stay or employment of either parent, or of the child's stay. Facilitation of teaching of mother tongue and culture for the children of migrant workers.	162	116	Albania (a), Congo (s), Iraq (a), Jamaica (s, r), Niger (a), Nigeria (a), Paraguay (r), Rwanda (a), Uzbekistan (a), Zambia (s)
Convention concerning the Prohibition and Immediate Action for the Elimination of the Worst Forms of Child Labour (No. 182. Adopted by ILO)	1999	Access to free basic education and to vocational training (wherever possible and appropriate) for all children removed from the worst forms of child labour.	—	171	Brunei Darussalam (r), Guinea-Bissau (r), Kiribati (r), Samoa (r), Timor-Leste (r), Uzbekistan (r)
Convention on the Rights of Persons with Disabilities (CRPD)	2006	No exclusion from free and compulsory primary education, or from secondary education, on the basis of disability. Assurance of an inclusive education system at all levels and lifelong learning.	150	70	In 2008, 32 states parties acceded or ratified; an additional 17 signed. In 2009, 24 acceded or ratified (most recently Czech Republic, Dominican Republic, Lao People's Democratic Republic, Malawi, Portugal, Turkey) and 5 signed (Bosnia and Herzegovina, Georgia, Monaco, United States, Uzbekistan).
Optional Protocol to the CRPD[4]	2006		96	45	In 2008, 19 states parties acceded or ratified; an additional 14 signed. In 2009, 18 acceded or ratified (most recently Australia, Dominican Republic, Portugal, United Kingdom) and 5 signed (Bosnia and Herzegovina, Georgia, Solomon Islands, the Former Yugoslav Republic of Macedonia, United Kingdom).

Notes: Information up to date as of 30 September 2009.

1. Indicates the number of states parties that have preliminarily endorsed the convention and intend to examine the treaty domestically and consider ratifying it.
2. Indicates the number of states parties that have agreed to be bound by the convention or protocol through ratification (entering into the convention after signing), accession (signing and ratifying at the same time), or succession (taking on the ratification of an existing or former state party of which the state party was formerly a part).
3. Signatures, ratifications or accessions between January 2008 and April 2009.
4. Optional protocols/articles that allow individuals to seek justice at the international level for violations of the rights established in the main convention, through the establishment of communications, complaint and inquiry procedures.
5. 'Accepted' indicates that the state party recognizes the competence of the Committee on the Elimination of Racial Discrimination as per Article 14.

Sources: ILOLEX (2009); United Nations (2009); UNESCO (2009).

Educational effect of selected social protection programmes

Chapter 3 of this report argues that to mitigate the negative effects of poverty on education, governments and donors need to scale up social protection measures to help poor households manage risk without compromising their children's long-term welfare. The table below reviews evaluations of a range of social protection programmes throughout the developing world, including conditional and unconditional transfers of cash and food. Differences between programmes and in evaluation methodology mean that comparisons have to be made with caution, but overall the evidence points to positive effects on enrolment and attendance, and, in a few cases, on cognitive development and educational achievement.

Country	Programme (year/s)	Targeted beneficiaries of education component	Key instrument of educational component/ scale of transfer	Educational impact[1, 2]
Direct support for education				
Indonesia	**Jaring Pengamanan Sosial (Social Safety Net) scholarship and grant programme** (1998–2005)	Poorest primary and secondary school students, 50% girls	Scholarships of *c.* US$10–30 (1998 exchange rate) depending on school level, sufficient to cover full cost of school fees	↓ of 3 p.p. (mid-school year dropout rate at lower secondary in poorest villages)
Transfers conditional on educational behaviour, or with specific educational goals				
Bangladesh	**Female Secondary School Assistance Programme**, part of Nation Wide Female Stipend Programme (1994–)	Girls aged 11–18 in secondary school (grades 6–10)	• Biannual transfer of stipend, tuition, book allowance and exam fees, totalling between *c.* US$6 and US$24 (2003)/0.6% of per capita expenditure, depending on school level • Conditional on attendance and achievement	↑ enrolment by 12 p.p.
Burkina Faso	**World Food Programme school lunches and take-home rations** (encompassed earlier programmes in 2005–2006)	• School lunches: all children in targeted rural primary schools • Take-home food rations: girls in the last two grades	• Lunch for all children in attendance • Monthly take-home ration of 10 kg cereals for girls in last two grades • Conditional on attendance	• ↑ new enrolments by 5–6 p.p. among younger girls • ↓ absenteeism among girls
Cambodia	**Japan Fund for Poverty Reduction pilot project** (2002–2005)	Girls grades 7–9 (lower secondary school)	• US$45 in three instalments/2–3% of per capita expenditure • Conditional on enrolment, regular attendance and maintaining a passing grade	↑ enrolment by 31.3 p.p.; higher among poorest
	Education Sector Support Project – Scholarships for the Poor Programme (2005–)	Children who have completed grade 6 likely to drop out due to poverty, gender, ethnic minority status, etc.	• US$45 or US$60 in three instalments/2–3% of median household income, depending on estimated 'probability of dropout' • Conditional on enrolment, regular attendance and on-time promotion	• ↑ enrolment by 21.4 p.p. • ↑ attendance by 25 p.p.
Chile	**Chile Solidario** (2002–)	Very poor households	• Decreasing monthly benefits for the first 24 months, from US$21 to US$8 (2006)/ 7% of per capita expenditure • Conditional on attendance	↑ enrolment by 7.5 p.p. among children aged 6-15
Colombia	**Familias en Acción** (2001/2–)	Extremely poor families with children enrolled in school	• About US$8–33 per child per month/17% of per capita expenditure, depending on school level • Conditional on attendance	• Ages 8-13: ↑ enrolment by 2.1 p.p. • Ages 14-17: ↑ enrolment by 5.6 p.p.
Ecuador	**Bono de Desarrollo Humano**[3] (1998– ; relaunched as BDH in 2004)	Families in the poorest two quintiles with children aged 16 or under	• Cash transfer of US$15/month/<10% of per capita monthly income • Conditional on enrolment and attendance	• ↑ enrolment by 10.3 p.p., esp. for poorest quintile, in transition grades • ↑ cognitive development (esp. long-term memory) for poorest decile • No effect on test scores
Honduras	**Programa de Asignación Familiar** (1990– ; relaunched as PRAFII in 2000)	Poor households with children aged 6–12 who have not completed grade 4	• US$60 per household per year/9% of per capita expenditure • Conditional on enrolment and attendance	↑ enrolment by 2.1 p.p.
Jamaica	**Programme of Advancement through Health and Education** (2002–)	Children aged 19 or under (or until they graduate from secondary school)	• About US$7–13 per student per month/ 10% of per capita expenditure; as of 2008, transfer depends on gender (boys receive more) and school level • Conditional on attendance	Over 20-day period, ↑ attendance by 2.5 p.p. (0.5 days)

Country	Programme (year/s)	Targeted beneficiaries of education component	Key instrument of educational component/ scale of transfer	Educational impact[1, 2]
Kenya	**Cash Transfers – Orphans and Vulnerable Children** (2005–)	Ultra-poor households fostering orphan or vulnerable child aged 17 or under not receiving any cash transfer; child cared for by chronically ill adult	• Cash transfers based on the food poverty gap every two months, *c.* US$20/month, for 4 years • Conditional on attendance	Final evaluation not yet available, but improvements in attendance and retention noted. Four-year pilot now being funded to scale up as regular programme
Mexico	**Oportunidades** (1997–)	Extremely poor households with children	• Transfers for stipends and material vary by school level and, from secondary, by gender, *c.* US$35–103 per child per month/20% of per capita expenditure • Plus US$336 in a savings account upon completion of secondary school • Conditional on enrolment, attendance and completion	• Grades 0–5: insignificant impact • Grade 6: ↑ enrolment 8.7 p.p. • Grades 7–9: insignificant impact
Nicaragua	**Atención a Crisis** (2005–2006)	Poor households living in drought-affected region	• US$90 per household per year + US$25 per child per year (for supplies) + US$13 per child per year to school/18% of per capita expenditure • Conditional on enrolment and attendance	• Among children aged 7-15 in grades 1-6: ↑ enrolment by 6.6 p.p. • ↑ cognitive development (esp. language and personal behaviour)
	Red de Protección Social (2000–2005/6)	Extremely poor households with children aged 7–13 in grades 1–4	• US$17 per household every two months + US$20 per child per year (for supplies)/ 27% of per capita expenditure • Conditional on enrolment, attendance and promotion	• ↑ enrolment by 12.8 p.p. (25 p.p. for the poorest) • ↑ proportion advancing 2 grades in 2 years by 7 p.p.
Pakistan	**Punjab Education Sector Reform Programme** (2003–)	Girls aged 10–14	• About US$3 per student per month/ 3% of per capita expenditure • Conditional on enrolment and attendance	↑ enrolment by 11.1 p.p.
Paraguay	**Tekoporã** (2005–)	Households in the poorest districts with low quality of life score and children aged 15 or under	• Cash transfer of c. US$18–36/month • Conditional on school attendance and matriculation	↑ attendance by 5-8 p.p., esp. among boys and older children
Turkey	**Social Risk Mitigation Project** (2002–)	Primary and secondary school students	6% of per capita expenditure	• Primary students: ↓ enrolment by 3 p.p. • Secondary students: no significant increase in enrolment
Other transfers, without specific educational goals or conditions				
Bangladesh	**Challenging the Frontiers of Poverty Reduction – Targeting the Ultra Poor (BRAC)** (2002–)	Ultra-poor households, identified in terms of living in a poor area, labour constraints, lack of assets	• Most generous model provides productive assets (e.g. livestock, sheds worth on average *c.* US$90) and support inputs; weekly stipends (*c.* US$1); income generation training; and other forms of technical, health and social support • Unconditional	• ↑ enrolment by 6.5 p.p. among young boys • No overall effect on enrolment rates • ↑ maximum educational level among 6- to 20-year-olds in household
Ethiopia	**Productive Safety Net Programme** (2005)	Food-insecure, asset-poor households in selected districts	• Cash or food transfers (*c.* US$0.61/day, 2005 prices)/maximum transfer of *c.* US$18 per member per year • Conditional on work on labour-intensive projects designed to build community assets. Labour-constrained households receive unconditional transfers	• ↑ attendance among boys by 19–23 p.p. • ↑ enrolment among *c.* 33% of households • ↑ months in school among *c.* 50% of households • ↑ time studying at home
Integrated programmes				
Burkina Faso	**BRIGHT (Burkinabe Response to Improve Girls' cHances To succeed)** (2005–)	Children, especially girls, in districts where girls' enrolment is lowest	• Daily meals for all; take-home rations (8 kg cereal/month) for girls; school kits and textbooks for all students • Conditional on strong attendance • Other: Construction of rural schools, latrines and teacher housing; mobilization campaign for girls' education; adult literacy training and literacy mentoring for girls; local partner capacity-building	• ↑ enrolment by 20 p.p. • ↑ attendance by 16 p.p. • ↑ math/French test scores of 0.4 s.d. (equivalent of moving from 50th to 80th percentile)

Notes:

1. 'p.p.' = percentage points; 's.d.' = standard deviation.

2. As different methodologies were used to determine the educational impacts of the different programmes, and as target groups and length of intervention vary markedly, these results are not strictly comparable but provide an indication of the range and magnitude of effects.

3. Note that while the Bono de Desarrollo Humano was initially intended to be a cash transfer conditional on education and health behaviour, the education conditions were never monitored or enforced. Nevertheless because of the early information campaign, around one-quarter of households believed sending children to school was a programme requirement (Fiszbein et al., 2009).

Sources: Table adapted from Fiszbein et al. (2009). Additional material from Acharaya and Luitel (2006); Ahmed et al. (2009); Alviar et al. (2009); Barr et al. (2007); Barrientos et al. (2008); Cameron (2009); Devereux et al. (2006); Edmonds and Schady (2008); Filmer and Schady (2009); Grosh et al. (2008); Hoddinott (2008); Hoddinott et al. (2009); Kazianga et al. (2009); Levy et al. (2009); Moore (2008); Sharp et al. (2006); Slater et al. (2006); Soares et al. (2008); Sulaiman (2009); Villanger (2008); WFP (2005); Woldehanna (2009).

Statistical tables[1]

Introduction

The most recent data on pupils, students, teachers and expenditure presented in these statistical tables are for the school year ending in 2007.[2] They are based on survey results reported to and processed by the UNESCO Institute for Statistics (UIS) before the end of May 2009. Data received and processed after this date will be used in the next *EFA Global Monitoring Report*. A small number of countries[3] submitted data for the school year ending in 2008, presented in bold in the statistical tables.

These statistics refer to all formal schools, both public and private, by level of education. They are supplemented by demographic and economic statistics collected or produced by other international organizations, including the United Nations Development Programme (UNDP), the United Nations Children's Fund (UNICEF), the United Nations Population Division (UNPD) and the World Bank.

The statistical tables list a total of 204 countries and territories. Most of them report their data to the UIS using standard questionnaires issued by the Institute. For some countries, however, education data are collected via surveys carried out under the auspices of the World Education Indicators (WEI) or are provided by the Organisation for Economic Co-operation and Development (OECD) and the Statistical Office of the European Communities (Eurostat). These countries are indicated with relevant symbols at the end of the introduction.

Population

The indicators on school access and participation in the statistical tables are based on the 2006 revision of population estimates produced by the UNPD, as the ones from the 2008 revision were not provided in time. Because of possible differences between national population estimates and those of the United Nations, these indicators may differ from those published by individual countries or by other organizations.[4] The UNPD does not provide data by single year of age for countries with a total population of fewer than 80,000. Where no UNPD estimates exist, national population figures, when available, or estimates from the UIS were used to calculate enrolment ratios.

ISCED classification

Education data reported to the UIS are in conformity with the 1997 revision of the International Standard Classification of Education (ISCED). In some cases, data have been adjusted to comply with the ISCED97 classification. Data for the school year ending in 1991 may conform to the previous version of the classification, ISCED76, and therefore may not be comparable in some countries to those for years after 1997.[5] ISCED is used to harmonize data and introduce more international comparability among national education systems. Countries may have their own definitions of education levels that do not correspond to ISCED. Some differences between nationally and internationally reported education statistics may be due, therefore, to the use of these nationally defined education levels rather than the ISCED standard, in addition to the population issue raised above.

Adult participation in basic education

ISCED does not classify education programmes by participants' age. For example, any programme with a content equivalent to primary education, or ISCED 1, may be classed as ISCED 1 even if provided to adults. The guidance the UIS provides for respondents to its regular annual education survey, on the other hand, asks countries to exclude 'data on programmes designed for people beyond regular school age'. As for the guidance for the UIS/OECD/Eurostat (UOE) and WEI questionnaires, until 2005 it stated that 'activities classified as "continuing", "adult" or "non-formal" education should be included' if they 'involve studies with subject content similar to regular educational programmes' or if 'the

1. For more detailed statistics and indicators, please consult the website: www.efareport.unesco.org.

2. This means 2006/2007 for countries with a school year that overlaps two calendar years and 2007 for those with a calendar school year.

3. Bhutan, Burkina Faso, the Central African Republic, Djibouti, the Gambia, Ghana, Kazakhstan, Lebanon, Liberia, Monaco, Nepal, San Marino, Sao Tome and Principe, Thailand and the United Republic of Tanzania.

4. Where obvious inconsistencies exist between enrolment reported by countries and the United Nations population data, the UIS may decide to not calculate or publish the enrolment ratios. This is the case with China, publication of whose net enrolment ratio is suspended pending further review of the population data, and with Myanmar, Singapore and Viet Nam.

5. To improve comparisons over time, the UIS has begun to harmonize time-series data, adjusting data from before 1998 so that they comply with the ISCED97 classification. So far this has been done for gross and net enrolment ratios in primary education and gross enrolment ratios in secondary education.

underlying programmes lead to similar potential qualifications' as the regular programmes. Since 2005, however, the countries involved in the UOE/WEI survey have been requested to report data for such programmes separately so that the UIS can exclude them when calculating internationally comparable indicators. Despite the UIS instructions, data from countries in the annual survey may still include pupils who are substantially above the official age for basic education.

Literacy data

UNESCO has long defined literacy as the ability to read and write, with understanding, a short simple statement related to one's daily life. However, a parallel definition arose with the introduction in 1978 of the notion of functional literacy, which emphasizes the use of literacy skills. That year the UNESCO General Conference approved defining as functionally literate those who can engage in all those activities in which literacy is required for the effective functioning of their group and community and also for enabling them to continue to use reading, writing and calculation for their own and the community's development.

In many cases, the current UIS literacy statistics rely on the first definition and are largely based on data sources that use a 'self-declaration' method: respondents are asked whether they and the members of their household are literate, as opposed to being asked a more comprehensive question or to demonstrate the skill. Some countries assume that persons who complete a certain level of education are literate.[6] As definitions and methodologies used for data collection differ by country, data need to be used with caution.

Literacy data in this report cover adults aged 15 and over as well as youth aged 15 to 24. They refer to two periods, 1985–1994 and 2000–2007. Literacy rates for the first period are mostly national observed information obtained from censuses and household surveys taken during that period. For the second period, most of the literacy data in the table are UIS estimates. They refer to 2007 and are based on the most recent observed national data. These estimates are supplemented with national observed data, indicated with an asterisk (*), for countries for which estimates could not be made or that provided recent data. The reference years and literacy definitions for each country are presented in a longer version of this introduction, posted on the *EFA Global Monitoring Report* website. Both UIS estimates and projections to 2015 presented in the literacy statistical table are produced using the Global Age-specific Literacy Projections Model. For a description of the projection methodology, see p. 261 of the *EFA Global Monitoring Report 2006*, as well as the *Global Age-specific Literacy Projections Model (GALP): Rationale, Methodology and Software*, available at www.uis.unesco.org/TEMPLATE/pdf/Literacy/GALP.pdf.

In many countries, interest in assessing the literacy skills of the population is growing. In response to this interest, the UIS has developed a methodology and data collection instrument called the Literacy Assessment and Monitoring Programme (LAMP). Following the example of the International Adult Literacy Survey (IALS), LAMP is based on the actual, functional assessment of literacy skills. It aims to provide literacy data of higher quality and is based on the concept of a continuum of literacy skills rather than the common literate/illiterate dichotomy.

Estimates and missing data

Both actual and estimated education data are presented throughout the statistical tables. When data are not reported to the UIS using the standard questionnaires, estimates are often necessary. Wherever possible, the UIS encourages countries to make their own estimates, which are presented as national estimates. Where this does not happen, the UIS may make its own estimates if sufficient supplementary information is available. Gaps in the tables may also arise where data submitted by a country are found to be inconsistent. The UIS makes every attempt to resolve such problems with the countries concerned, but reserves the final decision to omit data it regards as problematic.

To fill the gaps in the statistical tables, data for previous school years were included when information for the school year ending in 2007 was not available. Such cases are indicated by a footnote.

Regional averages

Regional figures for literacy rates, gross intake rates, gross and net enrolment ratios, school life expectancy and pupil/teacher ratios are weighted averages, taking into account the relative size of the relevant population of each country in each region. The averages are derived from both published data and broad estimates for countries for which no recent data or reliable publishable data are available.

The figures for the countries with larger populations thus have a proportionately greater influence on the regional

6. For reliability and consistency reasons, the UIS has decided no longer to publish literacy data based on educational attainment proxies. Only data reported by countries based on the 'self-declaration method' and 'household declaration' are included in the statistical tables. However, in the absence of such data, educational attainment proxies are used to compute regional weighted averages and to calculate the EFA Development Index for some countries, particularly developed ones.

aggregates. Where not enough reliable data are available to produce an overall weighted mean, a median figure is calculated for countries with available data only.

Capped figures

There are cases where an indicator theoretically should not exceed 100 (the net enrolment ratio, for example), but data inconsistencies may have resulted nonetheless in the indicator exceeding the theoretical limit. In these cases the indicator is 'capped' at 100 but the gender balance is maintained: the higher value, whether for male or female, is set equal to 100 and the other two values – the lower of male or female plus the figure for both sexes – are then recalculated so that the gender parity index for the capped figures is the same as that for the uncapped figures.

Data processing timetable

The timetable for collection and publication of data used in this report was as follows.

- June 2007 (or December 2007 for some countries with a calendar school year): the final school year in the data collection period ended.
- November 2007 and June 2008: questionnaires were sent to countries whose data are collected directly either by the UIS or through the WEI and UOE questionnaires, with data submission deadlines of 31 March 2008, 1 August 2008 and 30 September 2008, respectively.
- June 2008: after sending reminders by e-mail, fax, phone and/or post, the UIS began to process data and calculate indicators.
- September 2008: estimation was done for missing data.
- October-December 2008: provisional statistical tables were produced and draft indicators sent to member states for their review.
- End February 2009: the first draft of statistical tables was produced for the *EFA Global Monitoring Report*.
- End April 2009: the final statistical tables were sent to the *EFA Global Monitoring Report* team.

Symbols used in the statistical tables (printed and web versions)

*	National estimate
**	UIS estimate
...	Missing data
–	Magnitude nil or negligible
.	Category not applicable
./.	Data included under another category

Footnotes to the tables, along with the glossary following the statistical tables, also provide additional help in interpreting the data and information.

Composition of regions

World classification[7]

- Countries in transition (12):
  Countries of the Commonwealth of Independent States, including 4 in Central and Eastern Europe (Belarus, Republic of Moldova, Russian Federation[w], Ukraine) and the countries of Central Asia minus Mongolia.

- Developed countries (44):
  North America and Western Europe (minus Cyprus[o] and Israel[o]); Central and Eastern Europe (minus Belarus, the Republic of Moldova, the Russian Federation[w], Turkey[o] and Ukraine); Australia[o], Bermuda, Japan[o] and New Zealand[o].

- Developing countries (148):
  Arab States; East Asia and the Pacific (minus Australia[o], Japan[o] and New Zealand[o]); Latin America and the Caribbean (minus Bermuda); South and West Asia; sub-Saharan Africa; Cyprus[o], Israel[o], Mongolia and Turkey[o].

EFA regions[8]

- Arab States (20 countries/territories)
  Algeria, Bahrain, Djibouti, Egypt[w], Iraq, Jordan[w], Kuwait, Lebanon, Libyan Arab Jamahiriya, Mauritania, Morocco, Oman, Palestinian Autonomous Territories, Qatar, Saudi Arabia, Sudan, Syrian Arab Republic, Tunisia[w], United Arab Emirates and Yemen.

- Central and Eastern Europe (21 countries)
  Albania[o], Belarus, Bosnia and Herzegovina[o], Bulgaria[o], Croatia, Czech Republic[o], Estonia[o], Hungary[o], Latvia[o],

7. This is a United Nations Statistical Division world classification, in three main country groupings, as revised in 2004.

8. These are region classifications as defined for the EFA 2000 assessment.

Lithuania[o], Montenegro, Poland[o], Republic of Moldova, Romania[o], Russian Federation[w], Serbia, Slovakia, Slovenia[o], The former Yugoslav Republic of Macedonia[o], Turkey[o] and Ukraine.

- Central Asia (9 countries)
  Armenia, Azerbaijan, Georgia, Kazakhstan, Kyrgyzstan, Mongolia, Tajikistan, Turkmenistan and Uzbekistan.

- East Asia and the Pacific (33 countries/ territories)
  Australia[o], Brunei Darussalam, Cambodia, China[w], Cook Islands, Democratic People's Republic of Korea, Fiji, Indonesia[w], Japan[o], Kiribati, Lao People's Democratic Republic, Macao (China), Malaysia[w], Marshall Islands, Micronesia (Federated States of), Myanmar, Nauru, New Zealand[o], Niue, Palau, Papua New Guinea, Philippines[w], Republic of Korea[o], Samoa, Singapore, Solomon Islands, Thailand[w], Timor-Leste, Tokelau, Tonga, Tuvalu, Vanuatu and Viet Nam.

- East Asia (16 countries/territories)
  Brunei Darussalam, Cambodia, China[w], Democratic People's Republic of Korea, Indonesia[w], Japan[o], Lao People's Democratic Republic, Macao (China), Malaysia[w], Myanmar, Philippines[w], Republic of Korea[o], Singapore, Thailand[w], Timor-Leste and Viet Nam.

- Pacific (17 countries/territories)
  Australia[o], Cook Islands, Fiji, Kiribati, Marshall Islands, Micronesia (Federated States of), Nauru, New Zealand[o], Niue, Palau, Papua New Guinea, Samoa, Solomon Islands, Tokelau, Tonga, Tuvalu and Vanuatu.

- Latin America and the Caribbean (41 countries/territories)
  Anguilla, Antigua and Barbuda, Argentina[w], Aruba, Bahamas, Barbados, Belize, Bermuda, Bolivia, Brazil[w], British Virgin Islands, Cayman Islands, Chile[w], Colombia, Costa Rica, Cuba, Dominica, Dominican Republic, Ecuador, El Salvador, Grenada, Guatemala, Guyana, Haiti, Honduras, Jamaica[w], Mexico[o], Montserrat, Netherlands Antilles, Nicaragua, Panama, Paraguay[w], Peru[w], Saint Kitts and Nevis, Saint Lucia, Saint Vincent and the Grenadines, Suriname, Trinidad and Tobago, Turks and Caicos Islands, Uruguay[w] and the Bolivarian Republic of Venezuela.

- Caribbean (22 countries/territories)
  Anguilla, Antigua and Barbuda, Aruba, Bahamas, Barbados, Belize, Bermuda, British Virgin Islands, Cayman Islands, Dominica, Grenada, Guyana, Haiti, Jamaica[w], Montserrat, Netherlands Antilles, Saint Kitts and Nevis, Saint Lucia, Saint Vincent and the Grenadines, Suriname, Trinidad and Tobago, and Turks and Caicos Islands.

- Latin America (19 countries)
  Argentina[w], Bolivia, Brazil[w], Chile[w], Colombia, Costa Rica, Cuba, Dominican Republic, Ecuador, El Salvador, Guatemala, Honduras, Mexico[o], Nicaragua, Panama, Paraguay[w], Peru[w], Uruguay[w] and the Bolivarian Republic of Venezuela.

- North America and Western Europe (26 countries/territories)
  Andorra, Austria[o], Belgium[o], Canada[o], Cyprus[o], Denmark[o], Finland[o], France[o], Germany[o], Greece[o], Iceland[o], Ireland[o], Israel[o], Italy[o], Luxembourg[o], Malta[o], Monaco, Netherlands[o], Norway[o], Portugal[o], San Marino, Spain[o], Sweden[o], Switzerland[o], United Kingdom[o] and United States[o].

- South and West Asia (9 countries)
  Afghanistan, Bangladesh, Bhutan, India[w], Islamic Republic of Iran, Maldives, Nepal, Pakistan and Sri Lanka[w].

- Sub-Saharan Africa (45 countries)
  Angola, Benin, Botswana, Burkina Faso, Burundi, Cameroon, Cape Verde, Central African Republic, Chad, Comoros, Congo, Côte d'Ivoire, Democratic Republic of the Congo, Equatorial Guinea, Eritrea, Ethiopia, Gabon, Gambia, Ghana, Guinea, Guinea-Bissau, Kenya, Lesotho, Liberia, Madagascar, Malawi, Mali, Mauritius, Mozambique, Namibia, Niger, Nigeria, Rwanda, Sao Tome and Principe, Senegal, Seychelles, Sierra Leone, Somalia, South Africa, Swaziland, Togo, Uganda, United Republic of Tanzania, Zambia and Zimbabwe[w].

  o Countries whose education data are collected through UOE questionnaires

  w WEI project countries

- Least developed countries (50 countries)[9]
  Afghanistan, Angola, Bangladesh, Benin, Bhutan, Burkina Faso, Burundi, Cambodia, Cape Verde, Central African Republic, Chad, Comoros, Democratic Republic of the Congo, Djibouti, Equatorial Guinea, Eritrea, Ethiopia, Gambia, Guinea, Guinea-Bissau, Haiti, Kiribati, Lao People's Democratic Republic, Lesotho, Liberia, Madagascar, Malawi, Maldives, Mali, Mauritania, Mozambique, Myanmar, Nepal, Niger, Rwanda, Samoa, Sao Tome and Principe, Senegal, Sierra Leone, Solomon Islands, Somalia, Sudan, Timor-Leste, Togo, Tuvalu, Uganda, United Republic of Tanzania, Vanuatu, Yemen and Zambia.

9. Fifty countries are currently designated by the United Nations as 'least developed countries' (LDCs). The list of LDCs is reviewed every three years by the Economic and Social Council of the United Nations, in the light of recommendations made by the Committee for Development Policy. The LDC grouping is not presented in the statistical tables.

Table 1
Background statistics

Country or territory	DEMOGRAPHY[1]							HIV AND AIDS[2]		
	Total population (000)	Average annual growth rate (%) total population	Average annual growth rate (%) age 0-4 population	Life expectancy at birth (years)			Total fertility rate (children per woman)	HIV prevalence rate (%) in adults (15-49)	% of women among people (age 15+) living with HIV	Orphans due to AIDS (000)
	2007	2005-2010	2005-2010	2005-2010			2005-2010	2007	2007	2007
				Total	Male	Female		Total		
Arab States										
Algeria	33 858	1.5	1.7	72	71	74	2.4	0.1	29	…
Bahrain	753	1.8	-0.4	76	74	77	2.3	…	…	…
Djibouti	833	1.7	0.3	55	54	56	3.9	3.1	58	5
Egypt	75 498	1.8	0.9	71	69	74	2.9	…	29	…
Iraq	28 993	1.8	0.0	60	58	61	4.3	…	…	…
Jordan	5 924	3.0	1.6	73	71	74	3.1	…	…	…
Kuwait	2 851	2.4	2.3	78	76	80	2.2	…	…	…
Lebanon	4 099	1.1	0.0	72	70	74	2.2	0.1	<33	…
Libyan Arab Jamahiriya	6 160	2.0	1.5	74	72	77	2.7	…	…	…
Mauritania	3 124	2.5	1.2	64	62	66	4.4	0.8	28	3
Morocco	31 224	1.2	1.0	71	69	73	2.4	0.1	28	…
Oman	2 595	2.0	1.2	76	74	77	3.0	…	…	…
Palestinian A. T.	4 017	3.2	1.7	73	72	75	5.1	…	…	…
Qatar	841	2.1	1.6	76	75	76	2.7	…	…	…
Saudi Arabia	24 735	2.2	1.4	73	71	75	3.4	…	…	…
Sudan	38 560	2.2	0.8	59	57	60	4.2	1.4	59	…
Syrian Arab Republic	19 929	2.5	1.6	74	72	76	3.1	…	…	…
Tunisia	10 327	1.1	0.8	74	72	76	1.9	0.1	28	…
United Arab Emirates	4 380	2.8	3.4	79	77	81	2.3	…	…	…
Yemen	22 389	3.0	2.7	63	61	64	5.5	…	…	…
Central and Eastern Europe										
Albania	3 190	0.6	0.0	76	73	80	2.1	…	…	…
Belarus	9 689	-0.6	-0.3	69	63	75	1.2	0.2	30	…
Bosnia and Herzegovina	3 935	0.1	-3.1	75	72	77	1.2	<0.1	…	…
Bulgaria	7 639	-0.7	-0.4	73	69	77	1.3	…	…	…
Croatia	4 555	-0.1	-0.2	76	72	79	1.3	<0.1	…	…
Czech Republic	10 186	0.0	0.4	76	73	80	1.2	…	<33	…
Estonia	1 335	-0.3	1.7	71	66	77	1.5	1.3	24	…
Hungary	10 030	-0.3	-0.7	73	69	77	1.3	0.1	<30	…
Latvia	2 277	-0.5	0.8	73	67	78	1.3	0.8	27	…
Lithuania	3 390	-0.5	-0.2	73	67	78	1.3	0.1	<45	…
Montenegro	598	-0.3	0.5	75	72	77	1.8	…	…	…
Poland	38 082	-0.2	0.2	76	71	80	1.2	0.1	29	…
Republic of Moldova	3 794	-0.9	-0.8	69	65	72	1.4	0.4	30	…
Romania	21 438	-0.4	-0.8	72	69	76	1.3	0.1	50	…
Russian Federation	142 499	-0.5	1.1	65	59	73	1.3	1.1	26	…
Serbia	9 858	0.1	0.8	74	72	76	1.8	0.1	28	…
Slovakia	5 390	0.0	0.6	75	71	79	1.3	<0.1	…	…
Slovenia	2 002	0.0	0.2	78	74	82	1.3	<0.1	…	…
TFYR Macedonia	2 038	0.1	-1.7	74	72	77	1.4	<0.1	…	…
Turkey	74 877	1.3	0.3	72	69	74	2.1	…	…	…
Ukraine	46 205	-0.8	1.0	68	62	74	1.2	1.6	44	…
Central Asia										
Armenia	3 002	-0.2	2.1	72	68	75	1.4	0.1	<42	…
Azerbaijan	8 467	0.8	3.3	67	64	71	1.8	0.2	17	…
Georgia	4 395	-0.8	-1.5	71	67	75	1.4	0.1	<37	…
Kazakhstan	15 422	0.7	4.2	67	62	72	2.3	0.1	28	…
Kyrgyzstan	5 317	1.1	1.9	66	62	70	2.5	0.1	26	…
Mongolia	2 629	1.0	-0.2	67	64	70	1.9	0.1	<20	…
Tajikistan	6 736	1.5	0.1	67	64	69	3.3	0.3	21	…
Turkmenistan	4 965	1.3	0.5	63	59	68	2.5	<0.1	…	…
Uzbekistan	27 372	1.4	0.6	67	64	70	2.5	0.1	29	…
East Asia and the Pacific										
Australia	20 743	1.0	0.5	81	79	84	1.8	0.2	7	…
Brunei Darussalam	390	2.1	0.3	77	75	80	2.3	…	…	…
Cambodia	14 444	1.7	1.2	60	57	62	3.2	0.8	29	…

GNP, AID AND POVERTY							INEQUALITY IN INCOME OR EXPENDITURE[4]				
GNP per capita[3]				Net aid per capita (US$)[4]	Population living on less than US$1 per day[4] (%)	Population living on less than US$2 per day[4] (%)	Share of income or expenditure (%)		Inequality measure		
Current US$		PPP US$					Poorest 20%	Richest 20%	Richest 20% to poorest 20%[6]	Gini index[7]	
1998	2007	1998	2007	2005	1990-2005[5]	1990-2005[5]	1992-2005[5]	1992-2005[5]	1992-2005[5]	1992-2005[5]	Country or territory
											Arab States
1 570	3 620	4 860	7 640	11	…	15	7	43	6	35	Algeria
9 940	…	18 440	…	…	…	…	…	…	…	…	Bahrain
730	1 090	1 590	2 260	99	…	…	…	…	…	…	Djibouti
1 240	1 580	3 370	5 370	13	3	44	9	44	5	34	Egypt
…	…	…	…	…	…	…	…	…	…	…	Iraq
1 590	2 840	2 950	5 150	115	…	7	7	46	7	39	Jordan
17 770	…	36 960	…	…	…	…	…	…	…	…	Kuwait
4 250	5 800	7 350	10 040	68	…	…	…	…	…	…	Lebanon
…	9 010	…	14 710	…	…	…	…	…	…	…	Libyan Arab Jamahiriya
560	840	1 350	2 000	62	26	63	6	46	7	39	Mauritania
1 310	2 290	2 500	4 050	22	…	14	7	47	7	40	Morocco
6 270	…	13 570	…	12	…	…	…	…	…	…	Oman
…	…	…	…	304	…	…	…	…	…	…	Palestinian A. T.
…	…	…	…	…	…	…	…	…	…	…	Qatar
8 030	15 470	17 100	22 950	1	…	…	…	…	…	…	Saudi Arabia
330	950	1 070	1 880	51	…	…	…	…	…	…	Sudan
920	1 780	3 260	4 430	4	…	…	…	…	…	…	Syrian Arab Republic
2 050	3 210	4 110	7 140	38	…	7	6	47	8	40	Tunisia
19 560	…	43 690	…	…	…	…	…	…	…	…	United Arab Emirates
380	870	1 690	2 200	16	16	45	7	41	6	33	Yemen
											Central and Eastern Europe
890	3 300	3 530	7 240	102	…	10	8	40	5	31	Albania
1 550	4 220	4 480	10 750	…	…	…	9	38	5	30	Belarus
1 400	3 790	4 610	8 020	140	…	…	10	36	4	26	Bosnia and Herzegovina
1 270	4 580	5 210	11 100	…	…	6	9	38	4	29	Bulgaria
4 600	10 460	8 620	15 540	28	…	…	8	40	5	29	Croatia
5 580	14 580	13 710	22 690	…	…	…	10	36	4	25	Czech Republic
3 800	12 830	8 310	18 830	…	…	8	7	43	6	36	Estonia
4 320	11 680	9 800	17 470	…	…	…	10	37	4	27	Hungary
2 650	9 920	6 990	15 790	…	…	5	7	45	7	38	Latvia
2 760	9 770	7 710	16 830	…	…	8	7	43	6	36	Lithuania
…	5 270	…	11 780	…	…	…	…	…	…	…	Montenegro
4 310	9 850	9 310	15 500	…	…	…	8	42	6	35	Poland
460	1 210	1 250	2 800	46	…	21	8	41	5	33	Republic of Moldova
1 520	6 390	5 290	12 350	…	…	13	8	39	5	31	Romania
2 140	7 530	5 990	14 330	…	…	12	6	47	8	40	Russian Federation
…	4 540	6 720	9 830	…	…	…	…	…	…	…	Serbia
4 090	11 720	10 250	19 220	…	…	29	9	35	4	26	Slovakia
10 790	21 510	15 620	26 230	…	…	…	9	36	4	28	Slovenia
1 930	3 470	5 220	9 050	113	…	…	6	46	8	39	TFYR Macedonia
4 050	8 030	8 130	12 810	6	3	19	5	50	9	44	Turkey
850	2 560	2 870	6 810	…	…	5	9	38	4	28	Ukraine
											Central Asia
590	2 630	1 820	5 870	64	…	31	9	43	5	34	Armenia
510	2 640	1 810	6 570	27	4	33	7	45	6	37	Azerbaijan
770	2 120	1 960	4 760	69	7	25	6	46	8	40	Georgia
1 390	5 020	3 990	9 600	15	…	16	7	42	6	34	Kazakhstan
350	610	1 140	1 980	52	…	21	9	39	4	30	Kyrgyzstan
460	1 290	1 700	3 170	83	11	45	8	41	5	33	Mongolia
180	460	760	1 710	37	7	43	8	41	5	33	Tajikistan
560	…	…	…	6	…	…	6	48	8	41	Turkmenistan
620	730	1 310	2 430	7	…	…	7	45	6	37	Uzbekistan
											East Asia and the Pacific
21 340	35 760	22 820	33 400	…	…	…	6	41	7	35	Australia
14 480	…	40 160	50 200	…	…	…	…	…	…	…	Brunei Darussalam
290	550	720	1 720	38	34	78	7	50	7	42	Cambodia

Table 1 (continued)

Country or territory	DEMOGRAPHY[1]							HIV AND AIDS[2]		
	Total population (000)	Average annual growth rate (%) total population	Average annual growth rate (%) age 0-4 population	Life expectancy at birth (years)			Total fertility rate (children per woman)	HIV prevalence rate (%) in adults (15-49)	% of women among people (age 15+) living with HIV	Orphans due to AIDS (000)
	2007	2005-2010	2005-2010	2005-2010			2005-2010	2007	2007	2007
				Total	Male	Female		Total		
China	1 328 630	0.6	-0.1	73	71	75	1.7	0.1	29	…
Cook Islands	13	-2.2	…	…	…	…	…	…	…	…
DPR Korea	23 790	0.3	-2.1	67	65	69	1.9	…	…	…
Fiji	839	0.6	-1.1	69	67	71	2.8	0.1	…	…
Indonesia	231 627	1.2	-0.6	71	69	73	2.2	0.2	20	…
Japan	127 967	0.0	-1.4	83	79	86	1.3	…	24	…
Kiribati	95	1.6	…	…	…	…	…	…	…	…
Lao PDR	5 859	1.7	0.8	64	63	66	3.2	0.2	24	…
Macao, China	481	0.7	1.1	81	79	83	0.9	…	…	…
Malaysia	26 572	1.7	-0.1	74	72	77	2.6	0.5	27	…
Marshall Islands	59	2.2	…	…	…	…	…	…	…	…
Micronesia, F. S.	111	0.5	-1.4	69	68	69	3.7	…	…	…
Myanmar	48 798	0.9	-0.3	62	59	65	2.1	0.7	42	…
Nauru	10	0.3	…	…	…	…	…	…	…	…
New Zealand	4 179	0.9	0.3	80	78	82	2.0	0.1	<36	…
Niue	2	-1.8	…	…	…	…	…	…	…	…
Palau	20	0.4	…	…	…	…	…	…	…	…
Papua New Guinea	6 331	2.0	-0.5	57	55	60	3.8	1.5	40	…
Philippines	87 960	1.9	0.4	72	70	74	3.2	…	27	…
Republic of Korea	48 224	0.3	-1.8	79	75	82	1.2	<0.1	28	…
Samoa	187	0.9	-2.5	71	69	75	3.9	…	…	…
Singapore	4 436	1.2	-3.0	80	78	82	1.3	0.2	29	…
Solomon Islands	496	2.3	0.7	64	63	64	3.9	…	…	…
Thailand	63 884	0.7	0.0	71	66	75	1.9	1.4	42	…
Timor-Leste	1 155	3.5	4.6	61	60	62	6.5	…	…	…
Tokelau	1	0.0	…	…	…	…	…	…	…	…
Tonga	100	0.5	0.9	73	72	74	3.8	…	…	…
Tuvalu	11	0.4	…	…	…	…	…	…	…	…
Vanuatu	226	2.4	1.1	70	68	72	3.7	…	…	…
Viet Nam	87 375	1.3	0.0	74	72	76	2.1	0.5	27	…
Latin America and the Caribbean										
Anguilla	13	1.4	…	…	…	…	…	…	…	…
Antigua and Barbuda	85	1.2	…	…	…	…	…	…	…	…
Argentina	39 531	1.0	0.6	75	72	79	2.3	0.5	27	…
Aruba	104	0.0	-1.7	74	71	77	2.0	…	…	…
Bahamas	331	1.2	-0.1	73	71	76	2.0	3.0	26	…
Barbados	294	0.3	-1.2	77	74	80	1.5	1.2	<45	…
Belize	288	2.1	-0.1	76	73	79	2.9	2.1	59	…
Bermuda	65	0.3	…	…	…	…	…	…	…	…
Bolivia	9 525	1.8	0.1	66	63	68	3.5	0.2	28	…
Brazil	191 791	1.3	0.0	72	69	76	2.2	0.6	34	…
British Virgin Islands	23	1.1	…	…	…	…	…	…	…	…
Cayman Islands	47	1.5	…	…	…	…	…	…	…	…
Chile	16 635	1.0	0.2	79	75	82	1.9	0.3	28	…
Colombia	46 156	1.3	-1.0	73	69	77	2.2	0.6	29	…
Costa Rica	4 468	1.5	0.2	79	76	81	2.1	0.4	28	…
Cuba	11 268	0.0	-2.9	78	76	80	1.5	0.1	29	…
Dominica	67	-0.3	…	…	…	…	…	…	…	…
Dominican Republic	9 760	1.5	0.2	72	69	75	2.8	1.1	51	…
Ecuador	13 341	1.1	-0.8	75	72	78	2.6	0.3	28	…
El Salvador	6 857	1.4	-0.3	72	69	75	2.7	0.8	29	…
Grenada	106	0.0	-3.4	69	67	70	2.3	…	…	…
Guatemala	13 354	2.5	1.2	70	67	74	4.2	0.8	98	…
Guyana	738	-0.2	-4.2	67	64	70	2.3	2.5	59	…
Haiti	9 598	1.6	0.5	61	59	63	3.5	2.2	53	…
Honduras	7 106	1.9	0.5	70	67	74	3.3	0.7	28	…
Jamaica	2 714	0.5	-1.2	73	70	75	2.4	1.6	29	…
Mexico	106 535	1.1	-1.0	76	74	79	2.2	0.3	29	…
Montserrat	6	1.2	…	…	…	…	…	…	…	…
Netherlands Antilles	192	1.3	-1.3	75	71	79	1.9	…	…	…
Nicaragua	5 603	1.3	0.3	73	70	76	2.8	0.2	28	…

GNP, AID AND POVERTY							INEQUALITY IN INCOME OR EXPENDITURE[4]				
GNP per capita[3]				Net aid per capita (US$)[4]	Population living on less than US$1 per day[4] (%)	Population living on less than US$2 per day[4] (%)	Share of income or expenditure (%)		Inequality measure		
Current US$		PPP US$					Poorest 20%	Richest 20%	Richest 20% to poorest 20%[6]	Gini index[7]	
1998	2007	1998	2007	2005	1990-2005[5]	1990-2005[5]	1992-2005[5]	1992-2005[5]	1992-2005[5]	1992-2005[5]	**Country or territory**
790	2 370	1 950	5 420	1	10	35	4	52	12	47	China
...	...	...	...	...	...	...	...	...	...	...	Cook Islands
...	...	...	...	...	...	...	...	...	...	...	DPR Korea
2 330	3 750	3 040	4 240	76	...	...	...	...	...	...	Fiji
670	1 650	2 120	3 570	11	8	52	8	43	5	34	Indonesia
32 970	37 790	24 310	34 750	...	...	...	11	36	3	25	Japan
...	1 120	...	2 040	...	...	...	...	...	...	...	Kiribati
310	630	1 100	2 080	50	27	74	8	43	5	35	Lao PDR
15 260	...	20 830	...	...	...	...	...	...	...	...	Macao, China
3 630	6 420	7 520	13 230	1	...	9	4	54	12	49	Malaysia
2 070	3 240	...	...	...	...	...	...	...	...	...	Marshall Islands
2 030	2 280	2 680	3 010	...	...	...	...	...	...	...	Micronesia, F. S.
...	...	420	...	3	...	...	...	...	...	...	Myanmar
...	...	...	...	...	...	...	...	...	...	...	Nauru
15 200	27 080	17 790	25 380	...	...	...	6	44	7	36	New Zealand
...	...	...	...	...	...	...	...	...	...	...	Niue
6 120	8 270	...	...	...	...	...	...	...	...	...	Palau
780	850	1 650	1 870	45	...	...	5	57	13	51	Papua New Guinea
1 080	1 620	2 250	3 710	7	15	43	5	51	9	45	Philippines
9 200	19 730	13 420	24 840	...	...	...	8	38	5	32	Republic of Korea
1 350	2 700	2 610	4 350	238	...	...	...	...	...	...	Samoa
23 490	32 340	28 480	47 950	...	...	...	5	49	10	43	Singapore
900	750	1 590	1 710	415	...	...	...	...	...	...	Solomon Islands
2 120	3 400	4 400	7 880	-3	...	25	6	49	8	42	Thailand
...	1 510	...	3 090	189	...	...	...	...	...	...	Timor-Leste
...	...	...	...	...	...	...	...	...	...	...	Tokelau
1 760	2 480	2 720	3 880	310	...	...	...	...	...	...	Tonga
...	...	...	...	...	...	...	...	...	...	...	Tuvalu
1 360	1 840	3 000	3 410	187	...	...	...	...	...	...	Vanuatu
350	770	1 210	2 530	23	...	...	9	44	5	34	Viet Nam
											Latin America and the Caribbean
...	...	...	...	...	...	...	...	...	...	...	Anguilla
7 810	...	11 410	...	89	...	...	...	...	...	...	Antigua and Barbuda
8 020	6 040	9 140	12 970	3	7	17	3	55	18	51	Argentina
...	...	...	...	...	...	...	...	...	...	...	Aruba
13 220	...	...	...	...	...	...	...	...	...	...	Bahamas
7 680	...	...	...	-8	...	...	...	...	...	...	Barbados
2 710	3 760	3 950	6 080	44	...	...	...	...	...	...	Belize
...	...	...	...	...	...	...	...	...	...	...	Bermuda
1 000	1 260	3 020	4 150	64	23	42	2	63	42	60	Bolivia
4 880	5 860	6 520	9 270	1	8	21	3	61	22	57	Brazil
...	...	...	...	...	...	...	...	...	...	...	British Virgin Islands
...	...	...	...	...	...	...	...	...	...	...	Cayman Islands
5 270	8 190	8 630	12 330	9	...	6	4	60	16	55	Chile
2 550	4 100	5 650	8 260	11	7	18	3	63	25	59	Colombia
3 500	5 520	6 370	10 510	7	3	10	4	54	16	50	Costa Rica
...	...	...	...	8	...	...	...	...	...	...	Cuba
3 300	...	5 580	...	211	...	...	...	...	...	...	Dominica
1 770	3 560	3 530	6 350	9	3	16	4	57	14	52	Dominican Republic
1 810	3 110	4 750	7 110	16	18	41	3	58	17	54	Ecuador
1 870	2 850	4 110	5 640	29	19	41	3	56	21	52	El Salvador
3 040	3 920	4 650	5 480	421	...	...	...	...	...	...	Grenada
1 670	2 450	3 270	4 520	20	14	32	3	60	20	55	Guatemala
880	1 250	1 820	2 580	182	...	...	...	...	...	...	Guyana
400	520	1 020	1 050	60	54	78	2	63	27	59	Haiti
750	1 590	2 380	3 610	95	15	36	3	58	17	54	Honduras
2 660	3 330	4 740	5 300	14	...	14	5	52	10	46	Jamaica
4 020	9 400	7 880	13 910	2	3	12	4	55	13	46	Mexico
...	...	...	...	...	...	...	...	...	...	...	Montserrat
...	...	...	...	...	...	...	...	...	...	...	Netherlands Antilles
670	990	1 590	2 510	135	45	80	6	49	9	43	Nicaragua

Table 1 (continued)

Country or territory	DEMOGRAPHY[1] Total population (000) 2007	Average annual growth rate (%) total population 2005-2010	Average annual growth rate (%) age 0-4 population 2005-2010	Life expectancy at birth (years) 2005-2010 Total	Male	Female	Total fertility rate (children per woman) 2005-2010	HIV AND AIDS[2] HIV prevalence rate (%) in adults (15-49) 2007 Total	% of women among people (age 15+) living with HIV 2007	Orphans due to AIDS (000) 2007
Panama	3 343	1.6	0.1	76	73	78	2.6	1.0	29	...
Paraguay	6 127	1.8	0.3	72	70	74	3.1	0.6	29	...
Peru	27 903	1.2	0.2	71	69	74	2.5	0.5	28	...
Saint Kitts and Nevis	50	1.3	...	...	...	...	...	...	...	...
Saint Lucia	165	1.1	1.1	74	72	76	2.2	...	...	...
St Vincent/Grenadines	120	0.5	-0.1	72	69	74	2.2	...	...	...
Suriname	458	0.6	-1.0	70	67	74	2.4	2.4	28	...
Trinidad and Tobago	1 333	0.4	0.9	70	68	72	1.6	1.5	59	...
Turks and Caicos Islands	26	1.4	...	...	...	...	...	...	...	...
Uruguay	3 340	0.3	-0.8	76	73	80	2.1	0.6	28	...
Venezuela, B. R.	27 657	1.7	0.5	74	71	77	2.5	...	...	...
North America and Western Europe										
Andorra	75	0.4	...	...	...	...	...	...	...	...
Austria	8 361	0.4	-0.3	80	77	83	1.4	0.2	30	...
Belgium	10 457	0.2	-0.5	79	76	82	1.6	0.2	27	...
Canada	32 876	0.9	0.3	81	78	83	1.5	0.4	27	...
Cyprus	855	1.1	1.5	79	76	82	1.6	...	...	...
Denmark	5 442	0.2	-1.1	78	76	81	1.8	0.2	23	...
Finland	5 277	0.3	0.6	79	76	82	1.8	0.1	<42	...
France	61 647	0.5	-0.3	81	77	84	1.9	0.4	27	...
Germany	82 599	-0.1	-1.2	79	77	82	1.4	0.1	29	...
Greece	11 147	0.2	0.2	79	77	82	1.3	0.2	27	...
Iceland	301	0.8	0.6	82	80	83	2.1	0.2	<40	...
Ireland	4 301	1.8	2.2	79	76	81	2.0	0.2	27	...
Israel	6 928	1.7	0.4	81	79	83	2.8	0.1	59	...
Italy	58 877	0.1	-0.1	81	78	83	1.4	0.4	27	...
Luxembourg	467	1.1	0.3	79	76	82	1.7	0.2	...	...
Malta	407	0.4	0.0	79	77	81	1.4	0.1	...	...
Monaco	33	0.3	...	...	...	...	...	...	...	...
Netherlands	16 419	0.2	-2.0	80	78	82	1.7	0.2	27	...
Norway	4 698	0.6	-0.1	80	78	83	1.8	0.1	<33	...
Portugal	10 623	0.4	0.0	78	75	81	1.5	0.5	28	...
San Marino	31	0.8	...	...	...	...	...	...	...	...
Spain	44 279	0.8	1.8	81	78	84	1.4	0.5	20	...
Sweden	9 119	0.4	1.2	81	79	83	1.8	0.1	47	...
Switzerland	7 484	0.4	-0.8	82	79	84	1.4	0.6	37	...
United Kingdom	60 769	0.4	1.0	79	77	82	1.8	0.2	29	...
United States	305 826	1.0	0.8	78	76	81	2.1	0.6	21	...
South and West Asia										
Afghanistan	27 145	3.9	3.6	44	44	44	7.1	...	...	...
Bangladesh	158 665	1.7	-0.3	64	63	65	2.8	...	17	...
Bhutan	658	1.4	-1.6	66	64	67	2.2	0.1	<20	...
India	1 169 016	1.5	-0.1	65	63	66	2.8	0.3	38	...
Iran, Islamic Republic of	71 208	1.4	3.0	71	69	73	2.0	0.2	28	...
Maldives	306	1.8	3.1	68	68	69	2.6	...	...	...
Nepal	28 196	2.0	0.8	64	63	64	3.3	0.5	25	...
Pakistan	163 902	1.8	1.9	65	65	66	3.5	0.1	29	...
Sri Lanka	19 299	0.5	-1.1	72	69	76	1.9	...	38	...
Sub-Saharan Africa										
Angola	17 024	2.8	2.5	43	41	44	6.4	2.1	61	50
Benin	9 033	3.0	2.4	57	56	58	5.4	1.2	63	29
Botswana	1 882	1.2	0.7	51	50	51	2.9	23.9	61	95
Burkina Faso	14 784	2.9	2.4	52	51	54	6.0	1.6	51	100
Burundi	8 508	3.9	5.3	50	48	51	6.8	2.0	59	120
Cameroon	18 549	2.0	0.4	50	50	51	4.3	5.1	60	300
Cape Verde	530	2.2	1.1	72	68	74	3.4	...	...	...
Central African Republic	4 343	1.8	1.0	45	43	46	4.6	6.3	65	72
Chad	10 781	2.9	2.3	51	49	52	6.2	3.5	61	85
Comoros	839	2.5	1.0	65	63	67	4.3	<0.1	<50	<0.1

GNP, AID AND POVERTY							INEQUALITY IN INCOME OR EXPENDITURE[4]				
GNP per capita[3]				Net aid per capita (US$)[4]	Population living on less than US$1 per day[4] (%)	Population living on less than US$2 per day[4] (%)	Share of income or expenditure (%)		Inequality measure		
Current US$		PPP US$					Poorest 20%	Richest 20%	Richest 20% to poorest 20%[6]	Gini index[7]	
1998	2007	1998	2007	2005	1990-2005[5]	1990-2005[5]	1992-2005[5]	1992-2005[5]	1992-2005[5]	1992-2005[5]	Country or territory
3 550	5 500	6 450	10 610	6	7	18	3	60	24	56	Panama
1 650	1 710	3 550	4 520	8	14	30	2	62	26	58	Paraguay
2 240	3 410	4 620	7 200	14	11	31	4	57	15	52	Peru
6 150	9 990	9 320	13 680	73	…	…	…	…	…	…	Saint Kitts and Nevis
3 880	5 520	6 560	9 240	67	…	…	…	…	…	…	Saint Lucia
2 620	4 210	4 360	7 170	41	…	…	…	…	…	…	St Vincent/Grenadines
2 500	4 730	5 370	7 640	98	…	…	…	…	…	…	Suriname
4 440	14 480	9 570	22 420	-2	12	39	6	45	8	39	Trinidad and Tobago
…	…	…	…	…	…	…	…	…	…	…	Turks and Caicos Islands
6 610	6 390	7 860	11 020	4	…	6	5	51	10	45	Uruguay
3 360	7 550	8 450	12 290	2	19	40	3	52	16	48	Venezuela, B. R.
											North America and Western Europe
…	…	…	…	…	…	…	…	…	…	…	Andorra
27 250	41 960	25 860	36 750	…	…	…	9	38	4	29	Austria
25 950	41 110	24 780	35 320	…	…	…	9	41	5	33	Belgium
20 310	39 650	24 630	35 500	…	…	…	7	40	6	33	Canada
14 770	24 940	16 200	24 040	…	…	…	…	…	…	…	Cyprus
32 960	55 440	25 860	36 800	…	…	…	8	36	4	25	Denmark
24 940	44 300	22 140	34 760	…	…	…	10	37	4	27	Finland
25 200	38 810	23 620	33 850	…	…	…	7	40	6	33	France
27 170	38 990	24 000	34 740	…	…	…	9	37	4	28	Germany
13 110	25 740	16 860	27 830	…	…	…	7	42	6	34	Greece
28 400	57 750	27 210	34 070	…	…	…	…	…	…	…	Iceland
20 690	47 610	21 310	37 700	…	…	…	7	42	6	34	Ireland
16 840	22 170	16 920	26 310	…	…	…	6	45	8	39	Israel
21 230	33 490	23 570	30 190	…	…	…	7	42	7	36	Italy
43 620	…	39 620	…	…	…	…	…	…	…	…	Luxembourg
8 790	16 680	14 410	22 460	…	…	…	…	…	…	…	Malta
…	…	…	…	…	…	…	…	…	…	…	Monaco
25 820	45 650	25 230	39 470	…	…	…	8	39	5	31	Netherlands
35 400	77 370	27 110	53 650	…	…	…	10	37	4	26	Norway
11 570	18 950	14 960	21 790	…	…	…	6	46	8	39	Portugal
…	46 770	…	…	…	…	…	…	…	…	…	San Marino
15 220	29 290	18 710	30 750	…	…	…	7	42	6	35	Spain
29 330	47 870	23 920	37 490	…	…	…	9	37	4	25	Sweden
41 620	60 820	31 210	44 410	…	…	…	8	41	6	34	Switzerland
23 030	…	23 190	…	…	…	…	6	44	7	36	United Kingdom
30 620	46 040	31 650	45 840	…	…	…	5	46	8	41	United States
											South and West Asia
…	…	…	…	…	…	…	…	…	…	…	Afghanistan
340	470	740	1 330	9	41	84	9	43	5	33	Bangladesh
600	1 770	1 910	4 980	98	…	…	…	…	…	…	Bhutan
420	950	1 350	2 740	2	34	80	8	45	6	37	India
1 730	3 540	6 320	10 840	2	…	7	5	50	10	43	Iran, Islamic Republic of
1 930	3 190	2 580	4 910	203	…	…	…	…	…	…	Maldives
210	350	730	1 060	16	24	69	6	55	9	47	Nepal
470	860	1 590	2 540	11	17	74	9	40	4	31	Pakistan
820	1 540	2 360	4 200	61	6	42	7	48	7	40	Sri Lanka
											Sub-Saharan Africa
460	2 540	1 800	4 270	28	…	…	…	…	…	…	Angola
340	570	960	1 310	41	31	74	7	45	6	37	Benin
3 350	6 120	7 620	12 880	40	28	56	3	65	20	61	Botswana
240	430	740	1 120	50	27	72	7	47	7	40	Burkina Faso
140	110	300	330	48	55	88	5	48	10	42	Burundi
630	1 050	1 430	2 120	25	17	51	6	51	9	45	Cameroon
1 240	2 430	1 790	2 940	317	…	…	…	…	…	…	Cape Verde
280	370	600	710	24	67	84	2	65	33	61	Central African Republic
220	540	820	1 280	39	…	…	…	…	…	…	Chad
420	680	940	1 150	42	…	…	…	…	…	…	Comoros

Table 1 (continued)

Country or territory	DEMOGRAPHY[1] Total population (000) 2007	Average annual growth rate (%) total population 2005-2010	Average annual growth rate (%) age 0-4 population 2005-2010	Life expectancy at birth (years) 2005-2010 Total	Male	Female	Total fertility rate (children per woman) 2005-2010	HIV AND AIDS[2] HIV prevalence rate (%) in adults (15-49) 2007 Total	% of women among people (age 15+) living with HIV 2007	Orphans due to AIDS (000) 2007
Congo	3 768	2.1	1.2	55	54	57	4.5	3.5	59	69
Côte d'Ivoire	19 262	1.8	0.8	48	48	49	4.5	3.9	60	420
D. R. Congo	62 636	3.2	3.5	46	45	48	6.7	...	...	...
Equatorial Guinea	507	2.4	2.0	52	50	53	5.4	3.4	60	5
Eritrea	4 851	3.2	3.1	58	56	60	5.0	1.3	60	18
Ethiopia	83 099	2.5	1.6	53	52	54	5.3	2.1	60	650
Gabon	1 331	1.5	0.4	57	56	57	3.1	5.9	59	18
Gambia	1 709	2.6	1.3	59	59	60	4.7	0.9	60	3
Ghana	23 478	2.0	0.6	60	60	60	3.8	1.9	60	160
Guinea	9 370	2.2	1.5	56	54	58	5.4	1.6	59	25
Guinea-Bissau	1 695	3.0	3.1	46	45	48	7.1	1.8	58	6
Kenya	37 538	2.7	2.9	54	53	55	5.0	...	...	...
Lesotho	2 008	0.6	-0.4	43	43	42	3.4	23.2	58	110
Liberia	3 750	4.5	4.7	46	45	47	6.8	1.7	59	15
Madagascar	19 683	2.7	1.5	59	58	61	4.8	0.1	26	3
Malawi	13 925	2.6	1.5	48	48	48	5.6	11.9	58	560
Mali	12 337	3.0	3.2	54	52	57	6.5	1.5	60	44
Mauritius	1 262	0.8	-0.5	73	70	76	1.9	1.7	29	<0.5
Mozambique	21 397	1.9	0.6	42	42	42	5.1	12.5	58	400
Namibia	2 074	1.3	0.4	53	52	53	3.2	15.3	61	66
Niger	14 226	3.5	3.1	57	58	56	7.2	0.8	30	25
Nigeria	148 093	2.3	1.2	47	46	47	5.3	3.1	58	1 200
Rwanda	9 725	2.8	4.0	46	45	48	5.9	2.8	60	220
Sao Tome and Principe	158	1.6	0.3	66	64	67	3.9	...	...	...
Senegal	12 379	2.5	1.3	63	61	65	4.7	1.0	59	8
Seychelles	87	0.5	...	...	...	...	...	...	...	...
Sierra Leone	5 866	2.0	1.9	43	41	44	6.5	1.7	59	16
Somalia	8 699	2.9	2.0	48	47	49	6.0	0.5	28	9
South Africa	48 577	0.6	-0.5	49	49	50	2.6	18.1	59	1 400
Swaziland	1 141	0.6	0.2	40	40	39	3.4	26.1	59	56
Togo	6 585	2.6	1.4	58	57	60	4.8	3.3	58	68
Uganda	30 884	3.2	3.1	52	51	52	6.5	5.4	59	1 200
United Republic of Tanzania	40 454	2.5	1.2	53	51	54	5.2	6.2	58	970
Zambia	11 922	1.9	0.9	42	42	42	5.2	15.2	57	600
Zimbabwe	13 349	1.0	0.3	43	44	43	3.2	15.3	57	1 000
	Sum	Weighted average						Sum	Weighted average	
World	6 656 326	1.2	0.5	68.6	66.5	70.8	2.6	0.8	50	15 000
Countries in transition	277 863	-0.1	1.2	66.5	61.0	72.5	1.6	...	...	...
Developed countries	1 020 411	0.4	0.2	79.2	76.2	82.0	1.7	...	...	...
Developing countries	5 358 052	1.4	0.5	66.7	65.1	68.5	2.8	...	...	...
Arab States	321 092	2.0	1.2	68.8	67.0	70.7	3.2	...	...	...
Central and Eastern Europe	403 007	-0.1	0.5	69.9	65.3	74.8	1.5	...	...	...
Central Asia	78 306	1.0	1.5	67.2	63.4	71.0	2.3	...	...	...
East Asia and the Pacific	2 135 015	0.7	-0.2	73.0	71.0	75.1	1.9	...	...	...
East Asia	2 100 437	0.7	-0.2	72.9	70.9	75.1	1.9	0.1	27	...
Pacific	34 578	1.2	0.1	75.7	73.3	78.2	2.3	0.4	30	...
Latin America/Caribbean	567 120	1.2	-0.2	73.4	70.2	76.6	2.2	...	...	...
Caribbean	16 821	1.1	0.0	65.4	63.2	67.6	3.0	1.1	50	...
Latin America	550 299	1.3	-0.2	73.6	70.5	76.8	2.2	0.5	32	...
N. America/W. Europe	749 297	0.6	0.4	79.3	76.6	82.0	1.8	...	...	...
South and West Asia	1 638 396	1.6	0.3	64.7	63.4	66.2	2.9	...	...	...
Sub-Saharan Africa	764 095	2.4	1.8	50.3	49.4	51.2	5.2	5.0	59	11 592

1. The demographic indicators in this table are from the United Nations Population Division estimates, revision 2006 (UNPD, 2007). They are based on the median variant.
2. UNAIDS (2008).
3. World Bank (2009).
4. UNDP (2007).
5. Data are for the most recent year available during the period specified. For more details see UNDP (2007).
6. Data show the ratio of income or expenditure share of the richest group to that of the poorest.
7. A value of 0 represents perfect equality and a value of 100 perfect inequality.

GNP, AID AND POVERTY							INEQUALITY IN INCOME OR EXPENDITURE[4]				
GNP per capita[3]				Net aid per capita (US$)[4]	Population living on less than US$1 per day[4] (%)	Population living on less than US$2 per day[4] (%)	Share of income or expenditure (%)		Inequality measure		
Current US$		PPP US$					Poorest 20%	Richest 20%	Richest 20% to poorest 20%[6]	Gini index[7]	
1998	2007	1998	2007	2005	1990-2005[5]	1990-2005[5]	1992-2005[5]	1992-2005[5]	1992-2005[5]	1992-2005[5]	**Country or territory**
...	...	...	...	362	...	...	...	...	...	...	Congo
730	920	1 510	1 620	7	15	49	5	51	10	45	Côte d'Ivoire
110	140	240	290	32	...	...	...	...	...	...	D. R. Congo
1 120	12 860	5 090	21 220	78	...	...	...	...	...	...	Equatorial Guinea
210	270	720	620	81	...	...	...	...	...	...	Eritrea
130	220	420	780	27	23	78	9	39	4	30	Ethiopia
4 070	7 020	12 210	13 410	39	...	...	...	...	...	...	Gabon
300	320	790	1 140	38	59	83	5	53	11	50	Gambia
370	590	820	1 320	51	45	79	6	47	8	41	Ghana
470	400	810	1 120	19	...	...	7	46	7	39	Guinea
140	200	400	470	50	...	...	5	53	10	47	Guinea-Bissau
440	640	1 110	1 550	22	23	58	6	49	8	43	Kenya
680	1 030	1 340	1 940	38	36	56	2	67	44	63	Lesotho
130	140	250	280	...	...	...	...	...	...	...	Liberia
250	320	690	930	50	61	85	5	54	11	48	Madagascar
200	250	600	760	45	21	63	7	47	7	39	Malawi
280	500	690	1 040	51	36	72	6	47	8	40	Mali
3 760	5 580	6 720	11 410	26	...	...	...	...	...	...	Mauritius
220	330	390	730	65	36	74	5	54	10	47	Mozambique
2 030	3 450	3 350	5 100	61	35	56	1	79	56	74	Namibia
200	280	530	630	37	61	86	3	53	21	51	Niger
270	920	1 120	1 760	49	71	92	5	49	10	44	Nigeria
260	320	550	860	64	60	88	5	53	10	47	Rwanda
...	870	...	1 630	204	...	...	...	...	...	...	Sao Tome and Principe
510	830	1 140	1 650	59	17	56	7	48	7	41	Senegal
7 320	8 960	12 650	15 440	223	...	...	...	...	...	...	Seychelles
160	260	340	660	62	57	75	1	63	58	63	Sierra Leone
...	...	...	...	...	...	...	...	...	...	...	Somalia
3 290	5 720	6 140	9 450	16	11	34	4	62	18	58	South Africa
1 720	2 560	3 410	4 890	41	48	78	4	56	13	50	Swaziland
300	360	680	770	14	...	...	...	...	...	...	Togo
280	370	610	1 040	42	...	...	6	53	9	46	Uganda
230	410	700	1 200	39	58	90	7	42	6	35	United Republic of Tanzania
310	770	810	1 190	81	64	87	4	55	15	51	Zambia
570	...	...	...	28	56	83	5	56	12	50	Zimbabwe

Weighted average							Weighted average				
5 099	7 995	6 280	9 947	16	...	...	...	...	...	...	World
...	...	...	...	...	...	...	...	...	...	...	Countries in transition
...	...	...	...	...	...	...	...	...	...	...	Developed countries
...	...	...	...	17	...	...	...	...	...	...	Developing countries
...	...	...	...	94	...	...	...	...	...	...	Arab States
...	...	...	...	...	...	...	...	...	...	...	Central and Eastern Europe
...	...	...	...	...	...	...	...	...	...	...	Central Asia
826	2 182	2 034	4 969	5	...	...	...	...	...	...	East Asia and the Pacific
...	...	...	...	...	...	...	...	...	...	...	East Asia
...	...	...	...	...	...	...	...	...	...	...	Pacific
3 978	5 801	6 393	9 678	11	...	...	...	...	...	...	Latin America/Caribbean
...	...	...	...	...	...	...	...	...	...	...	Caribbean
...	...	...	...	...	...	...	...	...	...	...	Latin America
...	...	...	...	...	...	...	...	...	...	...	N. America/W. Europe
...	...	...	...	...	...	...	...	...	...	...	South and West Asia
518	951	1 248	1 869	42	...	...	...	...	...	...	Sub-Saharan Africa

Table 2
Adult and youth literacy

Country or territory	ADULT LITERACY RATE (15 and over) (%)									ADULT ILLITERATES (15 and over)					
	1985-1994[1]			2000-2007[1]			Projected 2015			1985-1994[1]		2000-2007[1]		Projected 2015	
	Total	Male	Female	Total	Male	Female	Total	Male	Female	Total (000)	% Female	Total (000)	% Female	Total (000)	% Female
Arab States															
Algeria	50*	63*	36*	75	84	66	81	88	74	6 572	64*	5 974	68	5 392	68
Bahrain	84*	89*	77*	89	90	86	92	93	90	56	56*	63	49	55	49
Djibouti	...	...	...	...	...	...	...	...	...	...	...	...	...	...	...
Egypt	44*	57*	31*	66*	75*	58*	73	80	66	16 428	62*	16 824	63*	16 243	64
Iraq	...	...	...	74*	84*	64*	...	...	...	...	...	3 703	69*	...	...
Jordan	...	...	...	91*	95*	87*	95	98	93	...	...	305	72*	215	73
Kuwait	74*	78*	69*	94*	95*	93*	96	96	95	276	48*	122	46*	114	48
Lebanon	...	...	...	90*	93*	86*	94	96	92	...	...	309	69*	201	70
Libyan Arab Jamahiriya	76	88	63	87	94	78	91	97	84	685	73	569	78	472	81
Mauritania	...	...	...	56	63	48	61	66	55	...	...	832	58	934	57
Morocco	42*	55*	29*	56	69	43	62	74	51	9 602	62*	9 816	66	9 458	67
Oman	...	...	...	84	89	77	89	93	84	...	...	274	61	242	62
Palestinian A. T.	...	...	...	94*	97*	90*	95	98	93	...	...	136	77*	135	76
Qatar	76*	77*	72*	93*	94*	90*	94	95	93	68	30*	47	38*	43	39
Saudi Arabia	71*	80*	57*	85	89	79	89	92	85	2 907	59*	2 473	58	2 176	60
Sudan[2]	...	...	...	61*	71*	52*	...	...	...	...	...	7 449	63*	...	...
Syrian Arab Republic	...	...	...	83	90	76	87	92	82	...	...	2 168	69	2 037	70
Tunisia	...	...	...	78	86	69	83	90	76	...	...	1 733	69	1 464	71
United Arab Emirates	71*	72*	69*	90*	89*	91*	93	93	94	473	31*	328	24*	293	24
Yemen	37*	57*	17*	59	77	40	70	85	55	4 686	66*	5 081	72	4 961	75
Central and Eastern Europe															
Albania	...	...	...	99	99	99	99	99	99	...	...	23	65	19	59
Belarus	98*	99*	97*	100	100	100	100	100	100	166	87*	24	67	16	50
Bosnia and Herzegovina	...	...	...	97*	99*	94*	...	...	...	...	...	105	86*	...	...
Bulgaria	...	...	...	98	99	98	98	98	98	...	...	114	62	118	58
Croatia	97*	99*	95*	99	99	98	99	100	99	120	82*	50	80	31	74
Czech Republic	...	...	...	...	...	...	...	...	...	...	...	...	...	...	...
Estonia	100*	100*	100*	100	100	100	100	100	100	3	79*	2	50	2	47
Hungary	...	...	...	...	...	...	...	...	...	...	...	...	...	...	...
Latvia	99*	100*	99*	100	100	100	100	100	100	11	80*	4	53	4	51
Lithuania	98*	99*	98*	100	100	100	100	100	100	44	76*	9	51	8	52
Montenegro	...	...	...	...	...	...	...	...	...	...	...	...	...	...	...
Poland	...	...	...	...	...	...	...	...	...	...	...	...	...	...	...
Republic of Moldova	96*	99*	94*	99	100	99	100	100	100	114	82*	23	77	12	63
Romania	97*	99*	95*	98	98	97	98	98	97	589	78*	436	66	394	58
Russian Federation	98*	99*	97*	100	100	99	100	100	100	2 290	88*	582	72	398	61
Serbia	...	...	...	...	...	...	...	...	...	...	...	...	...	...	...
Slovakia	...	...	...	...	...	...	...	...	...	...	...	...	...	...	...
Slovenia	100*	100*	99*	100	100	100	100	100	100	7	60*	6	57	5	57
TFYR Macedonia	94*	97*	91*	97	99	95	98	99	97	87	77*	50	77	36	73
Turkey	79*	90*	69*	89*	96*	81*	92	97	86	7 640	75*	6 111	83*	5 234	84
Ukraine	...	...	...	100	100	100	100	100	100	...	...	123	69	83	58
Central Asia															
Armenia	99*	99*	98*	99	100	99	100	100	100	31	77*	12	72	8	63
Azerbaijan	...	...	...	100*	100*	99*	100	100	100	...	...	33	81*	24	76
Georgia	...	...	...	...	...	...	...	...	...	...	...	...	...	...	...
Kazakhstan	98*	99*	96*	100	100	99	100	100	100	278	82*	44	73	34	65
Kyrgyzstan	...	...	...	99	100	99	99	100	99	...	...	26	66	21	55
Mongolia	...	...	...	97	97	98	96	95	98	...	...	52	42	85	32
Tajikistan	98*	99*	97*	100	100	100	100	100	100	68	74*	15	69	11	62
Turkmenistan	...	...	...	100	100	99	100	100	100	...	...	17	70	12	61
Uzbekistan	...	...	...	97*	98*	96*	...	...	...	...	...	481	68*	...	...
East Asia and the Pacific															
Australia	...	...	...	...	...	...	...	...	...	...	...	...	...	...	...
Brunei Darussalam	88*	92*	82*	95	96	93	97	98	96	21	67*	14	65	11	65
Cambodia	...	...	...	76	86	68	81	88	75	...	...	2 195	72	2 146	69
China	78*	87*	68*	93	96	90	96	98	93	184 214	70*	70 583	73	49 848	74

YOUTH LITERACY RATE (15-24) (%)									YOUTH ILLITERATES (15-24)						
1985-1994[1]			2000-2007[1]			Projected 2015			1985-1994[1]		2000-2007[1]		Projected 2015		
Total	Male	Female	Total	Male	Female	Total	Male	Female	Total (000)	% Female	Total (000)	% Female	Total (000)	% Female	Country or territory
															Arab States
74*	86*	62*	92	94	91	95	95	95	1 215	73*	561	61	320	48	Algeria
97*	97*	97*	100	100	100	100	100	100	3	53*	0.3	42	0.1	45	Bahrain
...	...	...	...	...	...	...	...	...	...	...	...	...	...	...	Djibouti
63*	71*	54*	85*	88*	82*	93	94	92	3 473	60*	2 317	59*	1 098	56	Egypt
...	...	...	85*	89*	80*	...	...	...	...	...	764	63*	...	...	Iraq
...	...	...	99*	99*	99*	99	99	100	...	...	12	47*	7	30	Jordan
87*	91*	84*	98*	98*	99*	100	100	100	37	62*	7	44*	0.05	37	Kuwait
...	...	...	99*	98*	99*	99	99	99	...	...	9	36*	7	37	Lebanon
95	99	91	99	100	98	100	100	100	55	89	14	87	0.7	67	Libyan Arab Jamahiriya
...	...	...	66	70	62	71	73	70	...	...	207	54	211	52	Mauritania
58*	71*	46*	75	84	67	83	89	78	2 239	65*	1 605	68	1 017	67	Morocco
...	...	...	98	99	98	99	100	99	...	...	9	63	3	63	Oman
...	...	...	99*	99*	99*	99	99	99	...	...	8	55*	8	54	Palestinian A. T.
90*	89*	91*	99*	99*	99*	100	100	100	6	31*	1	43*	0.4	11	Qatar
88*	94*	81*	97	98	96	99	99	98	369	74*	138	68	75	76	Saudi Arabia
...	...	...	77*	85*	71*	...	...	...	...	...	1 454	64*	...	...	Sudan[2]
...	...	...	94	95	92	96	97	95	...	...	282	63	163	60	Syrian Arab Republic
...	...	...	96	97	94	98	98	97	...	...	91	64	39	57	Tunisia
82*	81*	85*	95*	94*	97*	99	99	99	36	38*	34	24*	5	49	United Arab Emirates
60*	83*	35*	80	93	67	90	97	83	1 122	78*	959	83	587	87	Yemen
															Central and Eastern Europe
...	...	...	99	99	99	99	99	99	...	...	4	44	4	41	Albania
100*	100*	100*	100	100	100	100	100	100	3	43*	3	37	3	33	Belarus
...	...	...	100*	100*	100*	...	...	...	...	...	1	37*	...	...	Bosnia and Herzegovina
...	...	...	97	98	97	96	96	96	...	...	25	49	28	46	Bulgaria
100*	100*	100*	100	100	100	100	100	100	2	53*	2	47	2	44	Croatia
...	...	...	...	...	...	...	...	...	...	...	...	...	...	...	Czech Republic
100*	100*	100*	100	100	100	100	100	100	0.3	35*	0.4	37	0.3	36	Estonia
...	...	...	...	...	...	...	...	...	...	...	...	...	...	...	Hungary
100*	100*	100*	100	100	100	100	100	100	0.8	40*	1.0	41	0.8	42	Latvia
100*	100*	100*	100	100	100	100	100	100	2	44*	1	47	0.8	50	Lithuania
...	...	...	...	...	...	...	...	...	...	...	...	...	...	...	Montenegro
...	...	...	...	...	...	...	...	...	...	...	...	...	...	...	Poland
100*	100*	100*	100	100	100	100	100	100	2	48*	2	48	2	49	Republic of Moldova
99*	99*	99*	97	97	98	96	96	97	35	53*	81	46	86	42	Romania
100*	100*	100*	100	100	100	100	100	100	56	44*	71	40	53	36	Russian Federation
...	...	...	...	...	...	...	...	...	...	...	...	...	...	...	Serbia
...	...	...	...	...	...	...	...	...	...	...	...	...	...	...	Slovakia
100*	100*	100*	100	100	100	100	100	100	0.7	44*	0.4	36	0.3	30	Slovenia
99*	99*	99*	99	99	99	99	99	98	4	62*	4	56	4	52	TFYR Macedonia
93*	97*	88*	96*	99*	94*	97	99	96	867	76*	480	80*	356	77	Turkey
...	...	...	100	100	100	100	100	100	...	...	15	41	12	39	Ukraine
															Central Asia
100*	100*	100*	100	100	100	100	100	100	0.5	49*	1	37	1	33	Armenia
...	...	...	100*	100*	100*	100	100	100	...	...	–	–*	0.6	18	Azerbaijan
...	...	...	...	...	...	...	...	...	...	...	...	...	...	...	Georgia
100*	100*	100*	100	100	100	100	100	100	8	44*	5	38	5	36	Kazakhstan
...	...	...	100	100	100	99	99	100	...	...	5	37	6	31	Kyrgyzstan
...	...	...	95	94	97	91	86	96	...	...	27	30	46	24	Mongolia
100*	100*	100*	100	100	100	100	100	100	3	56*	2	47	2	44	Tajikistan
...	...	...	100	100	100	100	100	100	...	...	2	40	2	33	Turkmenistan
...	...	...	99*	99*	99*	...	...	...	...	...	33	53*	...	...	Uzbekistan
															East Asia and the Pacific
...	...	...	...	...	...	...	...	...	...	...	...	...	...	...	Australia
98*	98*	98*	100	100	100	100	100	100	0.9	49*	0.3	54	0.1	57	Brunei Darussalam
...	...	...	86	90	83	91	93	89	...	...	475	62	313	59	Cambodia
94*	97*	91*	99	99	99	100	100	100	14 352	73*	1 639	58	907	51	China

Table 2 (continued)

Country or territory	ADULT LITERACY RATE (15 and over) (%)									ADULT ILLITERATES (15 and over)					
	1985-1994[1]			2000-2007[1]			Projected 2015			1985-1994[1]		2000-2007[1]		Projected 2015	
	Total	Male	Female	Total	Male	Female	Total	Male	Female	Total (000)	% Female	Total (000)	% Female	Total (000)	% Female
Cook Islands	...	...	...	...	...	...	...	...	...	...	...	...	...	...	...
DPR Korea	...	...	...	...	...	...	...	...	...	...	...	...	...	...	...
Fiji	...	...	...	...	...	...	...	...	...	...	...	...	...	...	...
Indonesia	82*	88*	75*	92*	95*	89*	94	96	91	21 577	68*	13 267	70*	12 237	69
Japan	...	...	...	...	...	...	...	...	...	...	...	...	...	...	...
Kiribati	...	...	...	...	...	...	...	...	...	...	...	...	...	...	...
Lao PDR	...	...	...	73*	82*	63*	80	87	73	...	...	932	68*	898	68
Macao, China	...	...	...	93*	96*	91*	95	97	93	...	...	27	75*	22	73
Malaysia	83*	89*	77*	92	94	90	94	96	93	1 989	66*	1 496	64	1 244	63
Marshall Islands	...	...	...	...	...	...	...	...	...	...	...	...	...	...	...
Micronesia, F. S.	...	...	...	...	...	...	...	...	...	...	...	...	...	...	...
Myanmar	...	...	...	90*	94*	86*	...	...	...	...	...	3 182	70*	...	...
Nauru	...	...	...	...	...	...	...	...	...	...	...	...	...	...	...
New Zealand	...	...	...	...	...	...	...	...	...	...	...	...	...	...	...
Niue	...	...	...	...	...	...	...	...	...	...	...	...	...	...	...
Palau	...	...	...	...	...	...	...	...	...	...	...	...	...	...	...
Papua New Guinea	...	...	...	58	62	53	61	63	60	...	...	1 604	55	1 831	52
Philippines	94*	94*	93*	93	93	94	94	94	95	2 325	53*	3 746	48	4 073	46
Republic of Korea	...	...	...	...	...	...	...	...	...	...	...	...	...	...	...
Samoa	98*	98*	97*	99	99	98	99	99	99	2	60*	1	58	1	54
Singapore	89*	95*	83*	94	97	92	96	98	94	259	78*	203	76	157	74
Solomon Islands	...	...	...	...	...	...	...	...	...	...	...	...	...	...	...
Thailand	...	...	...	94	96	93	96	97	94	...	...	2 946	66	2 387	65
Timor-Leste	...	...	...	...	...	...	...	...	...	...	...	...	...	...	...
Tokelau	...	...	...	...	...	...	...	...	...	...	...	...	...	...	...
Tonga	...	...	...	99	99	99	99	99	99	...	...	0.5	46	0.4	45
Tuvalu	...	...	...	...	...	...	...	...	...	...	...	...	...	...	...
Vanuatu	...	...	...	...	...	...	...	...	...	...	...	...	...	...	...
Viet Nam	88*	93*	83*	90*	94*	87*	...	...	...	4 789	72*	6 033	69*	...	...
Latin America and the Caribbean															
Anguilla	...	...	...	...	...	...	...	...	...	...	...	...	...	...	...
Antigua and Barbuda	...	...	...	99*	98*	99*	...	...	...	...	...	...	...	...	...
Argentina	96*	96*	96*	98	98	98	98	98	98	889	53*	691	51	602	50
Aruba	...	...	...	98	98	98	98	99	98	...	...	2	54	1	54
Bahamas	...	...	...	...	...	...	...	...	...	...	...	...	...	...	...
Barbados	...	...	...	...	...	...	...	...	...	...	...	...	...	...	...
Belize	70*	70*	70*	...	...	...	...	...	...	32	49*	...	...	...	...
Bermuda	...	...	...	...	...	...	...	...	...	...	...	...	...	...	...
Bolivia	80*	88*	72*	91*	96*	86*	93	97	89	825	71*	542	79*	526	79
Brazil	...	...	...	90*	90*	90*	93	92	93	...	...	13 919	50*	11 146	49
British Virgin Islands	...	...	...	...	...	...	...	...	...	...	...	...	...	...	...
Cayman Islands	...	...	...	99*	99*	99*	...	...	...	...	...	...	...	...	...
Chile	94*	95*	94*	97	97	96	97	97	97	547	53*	439	52	367	51
Colombia	81*	81*	81*	93*	92*	93*	95	95	95	4 458	52*	2 401	50*	1 864	49
Costa Rica	...	...	...	96	96	96	97	96	97	...	...	132	47	124	46
Cuba	...	...	...	100	100	100	100	100	100	...	...	19	53	17	54
Dominica	...	...	...	...	...	...	...	...	...	...	...	...	...	...	...
Dominican Republic	...	...	...	89	89	90	92	91	92	...	...	710	49	641	48
Ecuador	88*	90*	86*	84*	87*	82*	91	92	90	731	59*	1 413	59*	970	57
El Salvador	74*	77*	71*	82*	85*	80*	87	89	85	830	58*	816	59*	698	59
Grenada	...	...	...	...	...	...	...	...	...	...	...	...	...	...	...
Guatemala	64*	72*	57*	73	79	68	79	83	74	1 915	61*	2 055	63	2 106	63
Guyana	...	...	...	...	...	...	...	...	...	...	...	...	...	...	...
Haiti	...	...	...	...	...	...	...	...	...	...	...	...	...	...	...
Honduras	...	...	...	84*	84*	83*	89	89	89	...	...	713	52*	607	50
Jamaica	...	...	...	86	81	91	89	85	94	...	...	263	33	218	30
Mexico	88*	90*	85*	93*	94*	91*	95	96	94	6 397	62*	5 368	63*	4 350	62
Montserrat	...	...	...	...	...	...	...	...	...	...	...	...	...	...	...
Netherlands Antilles	95*	95*	95*	96	96	96	97	97	97	7	54*	5	54	5	54
Nicaragua	...	...	...	78*	78*	78*	83	83	84	...	...	746	51*	721	49
Panama	89*	89*	88*	93	94	93	95	95	94	175	52*	155	55	150	55

YOUTH LITERACY RATE (15-24) (%) 1985-1994[1] Total	Male	Female	2000-2007[1] Total	Male	Female	Projected 2015 Total	Male	Female	YOUTH ILLITERATES (15-24) 1985-1994[1] Total (000)	% Female	2000-2007[1] Total (000)	% Female	Projected 2015 Total (000)	% Female	Country or territory
...	...	...	...	...	...	...	...	...	...	...	...	...	...	...	Cook Islands
...	...	...	...	...	...	...	...	...	...	...	...	...	...	...	DPR Korea
...	...	...	...	...	...	...	...	...	...	...	...	...	...	...	Fiji
96*	97*	95*	97*	97*	96*	97	97	98	1 421	65*	1 431	55*	1 099	45	Indonesia
...	...	...	...	...	...	...	...	...	...	...	...	...	...	...	Japan
...	...	...	...	...	...	...	...	...	...	...	...	...	...	...	Kiribati
...	...	...	84*	89*	79*	90	93	87	...	...	195	66*	148	64	Lao PDR
...	...	...	100*	100*	100*	100	100	100	...	...	0.3	43*	0.05	22	Macao, China
96*	96*	95*	98	98	98	99	99	99	155	53*	86	47	51	43	Malaysia
...	...	...	...	...	...	...	...	...	...	...	...	...	...	...	Marshall Islands
...	...	...	...	...	...	...	...	...	...	...	...	...	...	...	Micronesia, F. S.
...	...	...	95*	96*	93*	...	...	...	...	...	495	60*	...	...	Myanmar
...	...	...	...	...	...	...	...	...	...	...	...	...	...	...	Nauru
...	...	...	...	...	...	...	...	...	...	...	...	...	...	...	New Zealand
...	...	...	...	...	...	...	...	...	...	...	...	...	...	...	Niue
...	...	...	...	...	...	...	...	...	...	...	...	...	...	...	Palau
...	...	...	64	63	65	68	63	74	...	...	444	47	490	40	Papua New Guinea
97*	96*	97*	94	94	95	95	94	96	428	45*	975	41	997	38	Philippines
...	...	...	...	...	...	...	...	...	...	...	...	...	...	...	Republic of Korea
99*	99*	99*	99	99	99	100	99	100	0.3	49*	0.2	41	0.2	37	Samoa
99*	99*	99*	100	100	100	100	100	100	6	44*	2	37	1	31	Singapore
...	...	...	...	...	...	...	...	...	...	...	...	...	...	...	Solomon Islands
...	...	...	98	98	98	99	99	99	...	...	181	52	132	49	Thailand
...	...	...	...	...	...	...	...	...	...	...	...	...	...	...	Timor-Leste
...	...	...	...	...	...	...	...	...	...	...	...	...	...	...	Tokelau
...	...	...	100	100	100	100	100	100	...	...	0.1	41	0.1	45	Tonga
...	...	...	...	...	...	...	...	...	...	...	...	...	...	...	Tuvalu
...	...	...	...	...	...	...	...	...	...	...	...	...	...	...	Vanuatu
94*	94*	93*	94*	94*	94*	...	...	...	831	53*	1 105	52*	...	...	Viet Nam
															Latin America and the Caribbean
...	...	...	...	...	...	...	...	...	...	...	...	...	...	...	Anguilla
...	...	...	...	...	...	...	...	...	...	...	...	...	...	...	Antigua and Barbuda
98*	98*	99*	99	99	99	99	99	99	92	43*	59	39	48	37	Argentina
...	...	...	99	99	99	100	99	100	...	...	0.1	43	0.07	40	Aruba
...	...	...	...	...	...	...	...	...	...	...	...	...	...	...	Bahamas
...	...	...	...	...	...	...	...	...	...	...	...	...	...	...	Barbados
76*	76*	77*	...	...	...	...	...	...	9	49*	...	...	...	...	Belize
...	...	...	...	...	...	...	...	...	...	...	...	...	...	...	Bermuda
94*	96*	92*	99*	100*	99*	100	100	100	83	70*	10	77*	10	50	Bolivia
...	...	...	98*	97*	99*	99	98	99	...	...	766	32*	402	31	Brazil
...	...	...	...	...	...	...	...	...	...	...	...	...	...	...	British Virgin Islands
...	...	...	99*	99*	99*	...	...	...	...	...	...	...	...	...	Cayman Islands
98*	98*	99*	99	99	99	99	99	100	38	41*	27	41	17	39	Chile
91*	89*	92*	98*	97*	98*	99	98	99	693	43*	176	38*	126	35	Colombia
...	...	...	98	98	98	98	98	99	...	...	17	38	13	35	Costa Rica
...	...	...	100	100	100	100	100	100	...	...	0.3	53	0.2	64	Cuba
...	...	...	...	...	...	...	...	...	...	...	...	...	...	...	Dominica
...	...	...	96	95	97	97	97	98	...	...	72	37	52	34	Dominican Republic
96*	97*	96*	95*	95*	96*	98	98	99	79	54*	116	47*	42	36	Ecuador
85*	85*	85*	94*	93*	94*	96	95	97	173	51*	82	47*	58	42	El Salvador
...	...	...	...	...	...	...	...	...	...	...	...	...	...	...	Grenada
76*	82*	71*	85	88	83	89	90	88	462	62*	390	60	362	56	Guatemala
...	...	...	...	...	...	...	...	...	...	...	...	...	...	...	Guyana
...	...	...	...	...	...	...	...	...	...	...	...	...	...	...	Haiti
...	...	...	94*	93*	95*	96	95	97	...	...	93	40*	65	35	Honduras
...	...	...	94	91	98	96	94	99	...	...	29	19	20	17	Jamaica
95*	96*	95*	98*	98*	98*	99	99	99	828	56*	354	53*	225	46	Mexico
...	...	...	...	...	...	...	...	...	...	...	...	...	...	...	Montserrat
97*	97*	97*	98	98	98	99	99	99	0.9	44*	0.4	50	0.3	49	Netherlands Antilles
...	...	...	87*	85*	89*	92	90	94	...	...	154	43*	109	38	Nicaragua
95*	95*	95*	96	97	96	97	97	97	25	52*	22	52	21	50	Panama

Table 2 (continued)

Country or territory	ADULT LITERACY RATE (15 and over) (%)									ADULT ILLITERATES (15 and over)					
	1985-1994[1]			2000-2007[1]			Projected 2015			1985-1994[1]		2000-2007[1]		Projected 2015	
	Total	Male	Female	Total	Male	Female	Total	Male	Female	Total (000)	% Female	Total (000)	% Female	Total (000)	% Female
Paraguay	90*	92*	89*	95*	96*	93*	97	97	96	255	59*	216	60*	167	59
Peru	87*	93*	82*	90*	95*	85*	93	97	90	1 848	72*	1 992	75*	1 541	75
Saint Kitts and Nevis	...	...	...	...	...	...	...	...	...	...	...	...	...	...	...
Saint Lucia	...	...	...	...	...	...	...	...	...	...	...	...	...	...	...
Saint Vincent/Grenadines	...	...	...	...	...	...	...	...	...	...	...	...	...	...	...
Suriname	...	...	...	90	93	88	92	94	91	...	...	31	63	27	62
Trinidad and Tobago	97*	98*	96*	99	99	98	99	99	99	26	70*	14	66	10	62
Turks and Caicos Islands	...	...	...	...	...	...	...	...	...	...	...	...	...	...	...
Uruguay	95*	95*	96*	98*	97*	98*	98	98	99	102	46*	55	43*	45	42
Venezuela, B. R.	90*	91*	89*	95*	95*	95*	97	97	97	1 242	54*	931	52*	765	50
North America and Western Europe															
Andorra	...	...	...	...	...	...	...	...	...	...	...	...	...	...	...
Austria	...	...	...	...	...	...	...	...	...	...	...	...	...	...	...
Belgium	...	...	...	...	...	...	...	...	...	...	...	...	...	...	...
Canada	...	...	...	...	...	...	...	...	...	...	...	...	...	...	...
Cyprus	94*	98*	91*	98	99	97	99	99	98	29	81*	16	78	9	75
Denmark	...	...	...	...	...	...	...	...	...	...	...	...	...	...	...
Finland	...	...	...	...	...	...	...	...	...	...	...	...	...	...	...
France	...	...	...	...	...	...	...	...	...	...	...	...	...	...	...
Germany	...	...	...	...	...	...	...	...	...	...	...	...	...	...	...
Greece	93*	96*	89*	97	98	96	98	99	97	615	74*	279	70	200	67
Iceland	...	...	...	...	...	...	...	...	...	...	...	...	...	...	...
Ireland	...	...	...	...	...	...	...	...	...	...	...	...	...	...	...
Israel	...	...	...	...	...	...	...	...	...	...	...	...	...	...	...
Italy	...	...	...	99	99	99	99	99	99	...	...	572	63	386	62
Luxembourg	...	...	...	...	...	...	...	...	...	...	...	...	...	...	...
Malta	88*	88*	88*	92*	91*	94*	95	93	96	31	50*	25	43*	19	37
Monaco	...	...	...	...	...	...	...	...	...	...	...	...	...	...	...
Netherlands	...	...	...	...	...	...	...	...	...	...	...	...	...	...	...
Norway	...	...	...	...	...	...	...	...	...	...	...	...	...	...	...
Portugal	88*	92*	85*	95	97	93	97	98	96	965	67*	459	68	268	68
San Marino	...	...	...	...	...	...	...	...	...	...	...	...	...	...	...
Spain	96*	98*	95*	98*	99*	97*	99	99	98	1 103	73*	782	68*	576	67
Sweden	...	...	...	...	...	...	...	...	...	...	...	...	...	...	...
Switzerland	...	...	...	...	...	...	...	...	...	...	...	...	...	...	...
United Kingdom	...	...	...	...	...	...	...	...	...	...	...	...	...	...	...
United States	...	...	...	...	...	...	...	...	...	...	...	...	...	...	...
South and West Asia															
Afghanistan	...	...	...	28*	43*	13*	...	...	...	...	...	7 822	59*	...	...
Bangladesh	35*	44*	26*	53	59	48	61	64	58	44 458	56*	48 541	55	48 189	53
Bhutan	...	...	...	53*	65*	39*	64	73	54	...	...	201	60*	198	60
India[2]	48*	62*	34*	66	77	54	72	81	62	283 848	61*	269 816	65	261 687	65
Iran, Islamic Republic of	66*	74*	56*	82*	87*	77*	88	92	84	11 124	62*	8 983	64*	7 215	67
Maldives	96*	96*	96*	97	97	97	98	97	98	5	47*	6	48	6	46
Nepal	33*	49*	17*	57	70	44	66	77	56	7 619	63*	7 612	67	7 346	67
Pakistan	...	...	...	54*	68*	40*	62	73	49	...	...	47 060	64*	49 588	64
Sri Lanka[2]	...	...	...	91*	93*	89*	93	94	92	...	...	1 339	61*	1 061	59
Sub-Saharan Africa															
Angola	...	...	...	67*	83*	54*	...	...	...	...	...	2 423	74*	...	...
Benin	27*	40*	17*	41	53	28	47	59	35	2 131	59*	3 022	61	3 476	61
Botswana	69*	65*	71*	83	83	83	87	87	88	247	47*	211	50	176	49
Burkina Faso	14*	20*	8*	29*	37*	22*	36	43	30	4 136	55*	5 684	56*	6 567	56
Burundi	37*	48*	28*	59*	67*	52*	...	...	...	1 945	61*	1 412	62*	...	...
Cameroon	...	...	...	68*	77*	60*	...	...	...	...	...	2 950	64*	...	...
Cape Verde	63*	75*	53*	84	89	79	89	93	86	70	70*	53	69	45	68
Central African Republic	34*	48*	20*	49*	65*	33*	...	...	...	1 085	63*	1 139	67*	...	...
Chad	12*	...	...	32	43	21	39	48	31	3 177	...	3 959	59	4 481	58
Comoros	...	...	...	...	...	...	...	...	...	...	...	...	...	...	...
Congo	...	...	...	...	...	...	...	...	...	...	...	...	...	...	...

YOUTH LITERACY RATE (15-24) (%)									YOUTH ILLITERATES (15-24)						
1985-1994[1]			2000-2007[1]			Projected 2015			1985-1994[1]		2000-2007[1]		Projected 2015		
Total	Male	Female	Total	Male	Female	Total	Male	Female	Total (000)	% Female	Total (000)	% Female	Total (000)	% Female	Country or territory
96*	96*	95*	99*	99*	99*	99	99	99	37	52*	15	50*	13	49	Paraguay
95*	97*	94*	97*	98*	97*	98	98	98	215	67*	143	62*	109	54	Peru
...	...	...	...	...	...	...	...	...	...	...	...	...	...	...	Saint Kitts and Nevis
...	...	...	...	...	...	...	...	...	...	...	...	...	...	...	Saint Lucia
...	...	...	...	...	...	...	...	...	...	...	...	...	...	...	Saint Vincent/Grenadines
...	...	...	95	96	95	96	96	96	...	...	4	55	3	53	Suriname
99*	99*	99*	100	100	100	100	100	100	2	50*	1	49	0.8	48	Trinidad and Tobago
...	...	...	...	...	...	...	...	...	...	...	...	...	...	...	Turks and Caicos Islands
99*	98*	99*	99*	98*	99*	99	99	99	6	37*	6	39*	6	41	Uruguay
95*	95*	96*	98*	98*	99*	99	99	99	176	39*	85	36*	65	41	Venezuela, B. R.
															North America and Western Europe
...	...	...	...	...	...	...	...	...	...	...	...	...	...	...	Andorra
...	...	...	...	...	...	...	...	...	...	...	...	...	...	...	Austria
...	...	...	...	...	...	...	...	...	...	...	...	...	...	...	Belgium
...	...	...	...	...	...	...	...	...	...	...	...	...	...	...	Canada
100*	100*	100*	100	100	100	100	100	100	0.4	44*	0.2	37	0.1	36	Cyprus
...	...	...	...	...	...	...	...	...	...	...	...	...	...	...	Denmark
...	...	...	...	...	...	...	...	...	...	...	...	...	...	...	Finland
...	...	...	...	...	...	...	...	...	...	...	...	...	...	...	France
...	...	...	...	...	...	...	...	...	...	...	...	...	...	...	Germany
99*	99*	99*	99	99	99	99	100	99	16	49*	9	51	6	56	Greece
...	...	...	...	...	...	...	...	...	...	...	...	...	...	...	Iceland
...	...	...	...	...	...	...	...	...	...	...	...	...	...	...	Ireland
...	...	...	...	...	...	...	...	...	...	...	...	...	...	...	Israel
...	...	...	100	100	100	100	100	100	...	...	7	46	4	46	Italy
...	...	...	...	...	...	...	...	...	...	...	...	...	...	...	Luxembourg
98*	97*	99*	98*	97*	99*	99	99	99	1	26*	1	25*	0.5	26	Malta
...	...	...	...	...	...	...	...	...	...	...	...	...	...	...	Monaco
...	...	...	...	...	...	...	...	...	...	...	...	...	...	...	Netherlands
...	...	...	...	...	...	...	...	...	...	...	...	...	...	...	Norway
99*	99*	99*	100	100	100	100	100	100	13	46*	4	44	2	42	Portugal
...	...	...	...	...	...	...	...	...	...	...	...	...	...	...	San Marino
100*	100*	100*	100*	100*	100*	100	100	100	29	47*	21	50*	14	47	Spain
...	...	...	...	...	...	...	...	...	...	...	...	...	...	...	Sweden
...	...	...	...	...	...	...	...	...	...	...	...	...	...	...	Switzerland
...	...	...	...	...	...	...	...	...	...	...	...	...	...	...	United Kingdom
...	...	...	...	...	...	...	...	...	...	...	...	...	...	...	United States
															South and West Asia
...	...	...	34*	51*	18*	...	...	...	...	...	2 576	60*	...	...	Afghanistan
45*	52*	38*	72	71	73	83	80	85	12 833	55*	8 965	47	5 908	41	Bangladesh
...	...	...	74*	80*	68*	88	90	87	...	...	38	58*	17	55	Bhutan
62*	74*	49*	82	87	77	88	90	86	63 893	64*	40 412	61	29 320	58	India[2]
87*	92*	81*	97*	97*	96*	98	98	98	1 399	70*	589	56*	277	49	Iran, Islamic Republic of
98*	98*	98*	98	98	98	98	98	99	1	45*	1	41	1	37	Maldives
50*	68*	33*	79	85	73	88	91	85	1 847	67*	1 189	64	819	60	Nepal
...	...	...	69*	79*	58*	78	83	72	...	...	11 151	65*	8 771	60	Pakistan
...	...	...	97*	97*	98*	99	98	99	...	...	90	40*	43	35	Sri Lanka[2]
															Sub-Saharan Africa
...	...	...	72*	84*	63*	...	...	...	...	...	750	70*	...	...	Angola
40*	55*	27*	52	63	41	60	69	51	612	62*	875	61	895	61	Benin
89*	86*	92*	94	93	95	95	95	96	31	35*	26	40	20	43	Botswana
20*	27*	14*	39*	47*	33*	45	47	43	1 495	54*	1 793	55*	2 068	51	Burkina Faso
54*	59*	48*	73*	77*	70*	...	...	...	495	56*	348	57*	...	...	Burundi
...	...	...	...	...	...	...	...	...	...	...	...	...	...	...	Cameroon
88*	90*	86*	97	97	98	99	98	100	8	58*	3	38	...	...	Cape Verde
48*	63*	35*	59*	70*	47*	...	...	...	270	64*	316	65*	...	...	Central African Republic
17*	...	...	44	53	35	52	55	50	1 042	...	1 170	58	1 280	52	Chad
...	...	...	...	...	...	...	...	...	...	...	...	...	...	...	Comoros
...	...	...	...	...	...	...	...	...	...	...	...	...	...	...	Congo

Table 2 (continued)

Country or territory	ADULT LITERACY RATE (15 and over) (%)									ADULT ILLITERATES (15 and over)					
	1985-1994[1]			2000-2007[1]			Projected 2015			1985-1994[1]		2000-2007[1]		Projected 2015	
	Total	Male	Female	Total	Male	Female	Total	Male	Female	Total (000)	% Female	Total (000)	% Female	Total (000)	% Female
Côte d'Ivoire	34*	44*	23*	49*	61*	39*	...	...	...	4 180	55*	4 831	59*	...	...
D. R. Congo	...	...	...	67*	81*	54*	...	...	...	...	...	9 057	72*	...	...
Equatorial Guinea	...	...	...	87*	93*	80*	...	...	...	...	...	33	76*	...	...
Eritrea	...	...	...	64	76	53	74	83	65	...	...	993	68	934	68
Ethiopia	27*	36*	19*	36*	50*	23*	...	...	...	23 045	57*	27 144	61*	...	...
Gabon	72*	79*	65*	86	90	82	91	94	88	165	64*	120	65	92	66
Gambia	...	...	...	...	...	...	...	...	...	...	...	...	...	...	...
Ghana	...	...	...	65	72	58	71	76	66	...	...	5 077	59	5 152	58
Guinea	...	...	...	29*	43*	18*	...	...	...	...	...	3 404	59*	...	...
Guinea-Bissau	...	...	...	...	...	...	...	...	...	...	...	...	...	...	...
Kenya	...	...	...	74*	78*	70*	...	...	...	...	...	4 579	58*	...	...
Lesotho	...	...	...	82*	74*	90*	...	...	...	...	...	190	32*	...	...
Liberia	41	52	30	56	60	51	64	65	64	652	60	881	55	946	51
Madagascar	...	...	...	71*	77*	65*	...	...	...	...	...	2 613	60*	...	...
Malawi	49*	65*	34*	72	79	65	79	83	74	2 197	68*	2 085	64	2 009	61
Mali	...	...	...	26*	35*	18*	38	46	30	...	...	4 633	58*	5 221	59
Mauritius	80*	85*	75*	87	90	85	90	92	89	150	63*	121	62	103	60
Mozambique	...	...	...	44	57	33	49	58	41	...	...	6 621	64	7 112	60
Namibia	76*	78*	74*	88	89	87	90	90	91	198	56*	156	54	150	49
Niger	...	...	...	29*	43*	15*	36	48	23	...	...	4 897	60*	6 334	60
Nigeria	55*	68*	44*	72	80	64	79	85	74	23 296	64*	23 283	65	21 577	63
Rwanda	58*	...	...	65*	71*	60*	...	...	...	1 468	...	1 491	62*	...	...
Sao Tome and Principe	73*	85*	62*	88	93	83	91	94	88	17	73*	11	73	10	68
Senegal	27*	37*	18*	42*	52*	33*	47	56	40	2 964	56*	4 032	59*	4 769	59
Seychelles	88*	87*	89*	92*	91*	92*	...	...	...	...	...	5	50*	...	...
Sierra Leone	...	...	...	38	50	27	47	58	37	...	...	2 073	61	2 080	61
Somalia	...	...	...	...	...	...	...	...	...	...	...	...	...	...	...
South Africa	...	...	...	88	89	87	91	92	91	...	...	3 977	55	3 107	55
Swaziland	67*	70*	65*	84	84	84	89	88	89	126	59*	113	53	86	51
Togo	...	...	...	53*	69*	38*	...	...	...	...	...	1 404	67*	...	...
Uganda	56*	68*	45*	74	82	66	81	86	75	4 185	64*	4 148	66	4 045	64
United Republic of Tanzania	59*	71*	48*	72	79	66	74	79	70	5 217	65*	6 237	63	7 185	59
Zambia	65*	73*	57*	71	81	61	72	82	63	1 541	62*	1 907	68	2 161	67
Zimbabwe	84*	89*	79*	91	94	88	94	96	93	990	66*	725	67	532	65
	Weighted average									Sum	% F	Sum	% F	Sum	% F
World	76	82	70	84	89	80	87	90	83	869 391	63	758 643	64	709 533	63
Countries in transition	98	99	97	99	100	99	100	100	100	3 778	84	1 433	70	752	59
Developed countries	99	99	99	99	99	99	99	100	99	6 963	67	5 466	63	4 738	60
Developing countries	68	77	59	80	85	74	84	88	79	858 650	63	751 744	64	704 043	63
Arab States	58	70	46	71	80	62	78	86	70	55 364	63	58 360	65	55 780	67
Central and Eastern Europe	96	98	94	98	99	96	98	99	97	11 954	78	8 007	80	6 752	79
Central Asia	98	99	97	99	99	98	99	99	100	1 008	74	734	68	328	50
East Asia and the Pacific	82	89	75	93	96	91	95	97	94	228 906	69	107 875	70	81 923	70
East Asia	82	89	75	93	96	91	95	97	94	227 624	69	106 098	71	80 006	71
Pacific	94	94	93	93	94	92	93	93	93	1 282	56	1 777	55	1 917	52
Latin America/Caribbean	87	88	86	91	92	90	93	94	93	39 602	55	36 084	55	30 126	54
Caribbean	66	65	67	75	73	77	78	76	81	2 897	50	2 770	47	2 718	45
Latin America	87	88	86	91	92	91	94	94	93	36 705	55	33 314	56	27 408	55
N. America/W. Europe	99	99	99	99	100	99	100	100	99	4 695	66	3 540	63	2 821	60
South and West Asia	48	60	34	64	75	53	71	79	62	394 719	61	391 379	63	380 978	63
Sub-Saharan Africa	53	63	45	62	71	54	72	77	66	133 144	61	152 665	62	150 824	60

Source: UNESCO Institute for Statistics database (UIS, 2009).

Note: For countries indicated with (*), national observed literacy data are used. For all others, UIS literacy estimates are used. The estimates were generated using the UIS Global Age-specific Literacy Projections model. Those in the most recent period refer to 2007 and are based on the most recent observed data available for each country.

The population used to generate the number of illiterates is from the United Nations Population Division estimates, revision 2006 (UNPD, 2007). For countries with national observed literacy data, the population corresponding to the year of the census or survey was used. For countries with UIS estimates, populations used are for 1994 and 2007.

YOUTH LITERACY RATE (15-24) (%)									YOUTH ILLITERATES (15-24)						
1985-1994[1]			2000-2007[1]			Projected 2015			1985-1994[1]		2000-2007[1]		Projected 2015		
Total	Male	Female	Total	Male	Female	Total	Male	Female	Total (000)	% Female	Total (000)	% Female	Total (000)	% Female	**Country or territory**
49*	60*	38*	61*	71*	52*	…	…	…	1 054	60*	1 355	62*	…	…	Côte d'Ivoire
…	…	…	70*	78*	63*	…	…	…	…	…	3 029	63*	…	…	D. R. Congo
…	…	…	95*	95*	95*	…	…	…	…	…	4	49*	…	…	Equatorial Guinea
…	…	…	86	90	83	93	94	92	…	…	138	64	82	60	Eritrea
34*	39*	28*	50*	62*	39*	…	…	…	7 404	54*	7 556	62*	…	…	Ethiopia
93*	94*	92*	97	98	96	98	99	97	13	59*	8	66	5	72	Gabon
…	…	…	…	…	…	…	…	…	…	…	…	…	…	…	Gambia
…	…	…	78	80	76	84	84	84	…	…	1 096	53	867	48	Ghana
…	…	…	47*	59*	34*	…	…	…	…	…	904	61*	…	…	Guinea
…	…	…	…	…	…	…	…	…	…	…	…	…	…	…	Guinea-Bissau
…	…	…	80*	80*	81*	…	…	…	…	…	1 352	49*	…	…	Kenya
…	…	…	…	…	…	…	…	…	…	…	…	…	…	…	Lesotho
51	56	47	72	68	76	80	72	87	196	54	211	43	200	31	Liberia
…	…	…	70*	73*	68*	…	…	…	…	…	923	54*	…	…	Madagascar
59*	70*	49*	83	84	82	90	89	91	616	64*	473	52	380	45	Malawi
…	…	…	39*	47*	31*	55	60	50	…	…	1 486	57*	1 460	55	Mali
91*	91*	92*	96	95	97	97	96	98	18	46*	7	37	6	31	Mauritius
…	…	…	53	58	47	57	59	56	…	…	2 000	56	2 225	52	Mozambique
88*	86*	90*	93	91	94	94	91	96	35	40*	35	38	34	32	Namibia
…	…	…	37*	52*	23*	46	56	36	…	…	1 460	64*	1 884	60	Niger
71*	81*	62*	87	89	85	92	92	91	5 091	67*	4 043	57	3 078	51	Nigeria
75*	…	…	78*	79*	77*	…	…	…	305	…	387	54*	…	…	Rwanda
94*	96*	92*	95	95	95	95	93	96	1	65*	2	47	2	35	Sao Tome and Principe
38*	49*	28*	51*	58*	45*	56	60	53	849	58*	1 211	57*	1 311	54	Senegal
99*	98*	99*	99*	99*	99*	…	…	…	…	…	0.1	35*	…	…	Seychelles
…	…	…	54	64	44	67	76	59	…	…	512	61	430	63	Sierra Leone
…	…	…	…	…	…	…	…	…	…	…	…	…	…	…	Somalia
…	…	…	95	95	96	98	97	98	…	…	442	40	218	35	South Africa
84*	83*	84*	94	92	96	96	94	98	24	51*	17	32	10	23	Swaziland
…	…	…	74*	84*	64*	…	…	…	…	…	289	69*	…	…	Togo
70*	77*	63*	86	88	84	91	92	91	1 061	62*	866	57	711	52	Uganda
82*	86*	78*	78	79	76	77	76	77	831	62*	1 848	53	2 306	49	United Republic of Tanzania
66*	67*	66*	75	82	68	74	82	66	543	51*	632	65	790	65	Zambia
95*	97*	94*	91	94	88	99	99	100	102	62*	294	66	25	16	Zimbabwe

Weighted average									Sum	% F	Sum	% F	Sum	% F	
84	88	79	89	91	87	92	93	91	166 321	62	125 401	59	93 365	54	World
100	100	100	100	100	100	100	100	100	123	46	143	43	133	33	Countries in transition
100	100	100	100	100	100	99	99	99	463	50	451	50	791	52	Developed countries
80	85	75	87	90	85	91	92	90	165 735	62	124 807	59	92 442	54	Developing countries
76	84	67	87	91	82	93	95	91	10 921	66	8 494	65	4 681	64	Arab States
98	99	97	99	99	98	99	99	98	1 060	71	749	68	614	64	Central and Eastern Europe
100	100	100	99	99	100	99	99	100	59	47	78	42	108	27	Central Asia
95	97	93	98	98	98	99	99	99	19 892	68	7 226	54	4 706	47	East Asia and the Pacific
95	97	93	98	98	98	99	99	99	19 544	69	6 746	54	4 192	47	East Asia
92	93	92	91	90	91	91	89	92	349	54	480	47	514	40	Pacific
94	93	94	97	97	97	98	98	98	5 640	46	3 029	43	2 049	40	Latin America/Caribbean
78	75	81	87	83	91	91	87	95	580	44	440	35	306	27	Caribbean
94	94	95	97	97	98	98	98	99	5 060	46	2 588	44	1 743	42	Latin America
100	100	100	100	100	100	99	100	99	189	46	163	48	499	52	N. America/W. Europe
61	72	49	80	85	75	87	89	85	92 147	62	65 013	60	46 117	56	South and West Asia
64	70	58	72	77	68	82	83	80	36 413	59	40 649	59	34 590	53	Sub-Saharan Africa

1. Data are for the most recent year available during the period specified.
See the web version of the introduction to the statistical tables for a broader explanation of national literacy definitions, assessment methods, and sources and years of data.
2. Literacy data for the most recent year do not include some geographic regions.

Table 3A
Early childhood care and education (ECCE): care

Country or territory	CHILD SURVIVAL[1]		CHILD WELL-BEING[2]						
				% of children under age 5 suffering from:			% of children who are:		
	Infant mortality rate (‰)	Under-5 mortality rate (‰)	Infants with low birth weight (%)	Underweight moderate and severe	Wasting moderate and severe	Stunting moderate and severe	Exclusively breastfed (<6 months)	Breastfed with complementary food (6-9 months)	Still breastfeeding (20-23 months)
	2005-2010	2005-2010	2000-2007[3]	2000-2007[3]	2000-2007[3]	2000-2007[3]	2000-2007[3]	2000-2007[3]	2000-2007[3]
Arab States									
Algeria	31	33	6	4	3	11	7	39	22
Bahrain	11	14	8	9	5	10	34	65	41
Djibouti	85	126	10	29	21	33	1	23	18
Egypt	29	34	14	6	4	18	38	67	37
Iraq	82	105	15	8	5	21	25	51	36
Jordan	19	22	12	4	2	9	22	66	11
Kuwait	8	10	7	10	11	24	12	26	9
Lebanon	22	26	6	4	5	11	27	35	11
Libyan Arab Jamahiriya	18	20	7	5	3	15	...	...	23
Mauritania	63	92	...	32	13	35	20	78	57
Morocco	31	36	15	10	9	18	31	66	15
Oman	12	14	9	18	7	10	...	91	73
Palestinian A. T.	18	20	7	3	1	10	27	...	...
Qatar	8	10	10	6	2	8	12	48	21
Saudi Arabia	19	22	11	14	11	20	31	60	30
Sudan	65	105	31	41	16	43	16	47	40
Syrian Arab Republic	16	18	9	10	9	22	29	37	16
Tunisia	20	22	7	4	2	12	47	...	22
United Arab Emirates	8	9	15	14	15	17	34	52	29
Yemen	59	79	32	46	12	53	...	...	...
Central and Eastern Europe									
Albania	19	22	7	8	7	22	40	69	22
Belarus	9	12	4	1	1	3	9	38	4
Bosnia and Herzegovina	12	14	5	2	3	7	18	29	10
Bulgaria	12	14	10	...	...	...	...	...	...
Croatia	6	8	5	1	1	1	23	...	...
Czech Republic	4	5	7	...	...	...	...	...	...
Estonia	7	10	4	...	...	...	...	...	...
Hungary	7	8	9	...	...	...	...	...	...
Latvia	10	14	5	...	...	...	...	...	...
Lithuania	9	11	4	...	...	...	...	...	...
Montenegro	22	24	4	3	3	5	19	35	13
Poland	7	8	6	...	...	...	...	...	...
Republic of Moldova	16	19	6	4	4	8	46	18	2
Romania	15	18	8	3	2	10	16	41	...
Russian Federation	17	21	6	3	4	13	...	...	...
Serbia	12	14	5	2	3	6	15	39	8
Slovakia	7	8	7	...	...	...	...	...	...
Slovenia	5	6	6	...	...	...	...	...	...
TFYR Macedonia	15	17	6	2	2	9	37	8	10
Turkey	28	32	16	4	1	12	21	38	24
Ukraine	13	16	4	1	0	3	6	49	11
Central Asia									
Armenia	29	34	8	4	5	13	33	57	15
Azerbaijan	72	86	12	10	5	21	12	44	16
Georgia	39	41	5	2	2	10	11	35	20
Kazakhstan	24	29	6	4	4	13	17	39	16
Kyrgyzstan	53	64	5	3	4	14	32	49	26
Mongolia	40	54	6	6	2	21	57	57	65
Tajikistan	60	78	10	17	7	27	25	15	34
Turkmenistan	75	95	4	11	6	15	11	54	37
Uzbekistan	55	66	5	5	3	15	26	45	38
East Asia and the Pacific									
Australia[6]	4	6	7	...	...	...	...	...	...
Brunei Darussalam	6	7	10	...	...	...	...	...	...
Cambodia	63	89	14	36	7	37	60	82	54

CHILD WELL-BEING[2]					PROVISION FOR UNDER-3s		WOMEN'S EMPLOYMENT AND MATERNITY LEAVE		
% of 1-year-old children immunized against									
Tuberculosis	Diphtheria, Pertussis, Tetanus	Polio	Measles	Hepatitis B	Official programmes targeting children under age 3	Youngest age group targeted in programmes (years)	Female labour force participation rate (age 15 and above)[4] (%)	Duration of paid maternity leave[5] (weeks)	
Corresponding vaccines:									
BCG	DPT3	Polio3	Measles	HepB3					
2007	2007	2007	2007	2007	2005	c. 2005	2003	2007-2009[3]	Country or territory
									Arab States
99	95	95	92	90	...	...	36	14	Algeria
...	97	97	99	97	Yes	0-2	33	6	Bahrain
90	88	88	74	25	...	...	58	14	Djibouti
98	98	98	97	98	Yes	2-3	23	13	Egypt
92	62	66	69	58	...	...	14	9	Iraq
90	98	98	95	98	Yes	0-3	16	10	Jordan
...	99	99	99	99	No	·	43	10	Kuwait
...	74	74	53	74	Yes	0-2	25	7	Lebanon
99	98	98	98	98	...	...	25	7	Libyan Arab Jamahiriya
92	75	75	67	74	...	...	61	14	Mauritania
96	95	95	95	95	No	·	26	14	Morocco
99	99	97	97	99	No	·	20	...	Oman
99	99	99	99	99	Yes	0-4	14	...	Palestinian A. T.
96	94	97	92	94	...	...	40	7	Qatar
96	96	96	96	96	...	...	19	10	Saudi Arabia
83	84	84	79	78	Yes	0-6	31	8	Sudan
99	99	99	98	98	Yes	0-2	20	17	Syrian Arab Republic
99	98	98	98	98	No	·	26	4	Tunisia
98	92	94	92	92	No	·	39	13	United Arab Emirates
64	87	87	74	87	No	·	22	9	Yemen
									Central and Eastern Europe
98	98	99	97	98	No	·	50	52	Albania
98	95	90	99	91	...	...	54	18	Belarus
98	95	95	96	94	Yes	0-3	53	52	Bosnia and Herzegovina
98	95	95	96	95	No	·	47	45	Bulgaria
99	96	96	96	95	...	...	44	58	Croatia
99	99	99	97	99	No	·	51	28	Czech Republic
98	95	95	96	95	Yes	1-6	54	20	Estonia
99	99	99	99	...	Yes	0-2	44	24	Hungary
99	98	98	97	97	No	·	54	16	Latvia
99	95	95	97	96	No	·	51	18	Lithuania
98	92	92	90	90	...	...	...	52	Montenegro
93	99	99	98	98	...	...	47	16	Poland
98	92	94	96	95	...	...	47	18	Republic of Moldova
99	97	96	97	99	No	·	48	18	Romania
96	98	99	99	98	...	...	56	20	Russian Federation
98	94	93	95	99	...	...	...	52	Serbia
98	99	99	99	99	...	...	51	28	Slovakia
...	97	98	96	...	Yes	1-3	54	15	Slovenia
95	95	96	96	96	No	·	42	39	TFYR Macedonia
94	96	96	96	96	Yes	0-2	25	16	Turkey
97	98	99	98	96	Yes	0-3	52	18	Ukraine
									Central Asia
94	88	90	92	85	Yes	2	55	20	Armenia
98	95	97	97	97	Yes	0-2	59	18	Azerbaijan
96	98	88	97	94	Yes	0-2	56	18	Georgia
99	93	94	99	94	Yes	1-6	63	18	Kazakhstan
98	94	94	99	94	Yes	1-3	54	18	Kyrgyzstan
99	95	99	98	98	Yes	2-3	58	17	Mongolia
83	86	85	85	84	No	·	53	20	Tajikistan
99	98	98	99	98	Yes	0-2	59	16	Turkmenistan
99	96	98	99	98	Yes	2-3	58	18	Uzbekistan
									East Asia and the Pacific
...	92	92	94	94	Yes	1-4	57	6	Australia[6]
96	99	99	97	99	...	...	58	...	Brunei Darussalam
90	82	82	79	82	Yes	0-6	75	13	Cambodia

Table 3A (continued)

Country or territory	CHILD SURVIVAL[1]		CHILD WELL-BEING[2]						
				% of children under age 5 suffering from:			% of children who are:		
	Infant mortality rate (‰)	Under-5 mortality rate (‰)	Infants with low birth weight (%)	Underweight moderate and severe	Wasting moderate and severe	Stunting moderate and severe	Exclusively breastfed (<6 months)	Breastfed with complementary food (6-9 months)	Still breastfeeding (20-23 months)
	2005-2010	2005-2010	2000-2007[3]	2000-2007[3]	2000-2007[3]	2000-2007[3]	2000-2007[3]	2000-2007[3]	2000-2007[3]
China	23	29	2	7	...	11	51	32	15
Cook Islands	...	...	3	10	...	...	19	...	...
DPR Korea	48	62	7	23	7	37	65	31	37
Fiji	20	24	10	...	...	...	47	...	...
Indonesia	27	32	9	28	...	...	40	75	59
Japan	3	4	8	...	...	...	...	...	...
Kiribati	...	...	5	13	...	...	80	...	...
Lao People's Democratic Republic	51	67	14	37	7	40	23	10	47
Macao, China	7	8	...	...	...	...	...	...	...
Malaysia	9	11	9	8	...	...	29	...	12
Marshall Islands	...	...	12	...	...	...	63	...	...
Micronesia, Federated States of	34	42	18	15	...	...	60	...	...
Myanmar	66	97	15	32	9	32	15	66	67
Nauru	...	...	...	...	...	...	...	...	...
New Zealand	5	6	6	...	...	...	...	...	...
Niue	...	...	0	...	...	...	...	...	...
Palau	...	...	9	...	...	...	59	...	...
Papua New Guinea[7]	61	84	11	...	...	...	59	74	66
Philippines	23	27	20	28	6	30	34	58	32
Republic of Korea	4	5	4	...	...	...	...	...	...
Samoa	22	27	4	...	...	...	...	...	...
Singapore	3	4	8	3	2	2	...	...	...
Solomon Islands	55	72	13	21	...	...	65	...	...
Thailand	11	15	9	9	4	12	5	43	19
Timor-Leste	67	92	12	49	25	54	31	82	35
Tokelau	...	...	...	...	...	...	...	...	...
Tonga	19	22	3	...	...	...	62	...	...
Tuvalu	...	...	5	...	...	...	...	...	...
Vanuatu	28	34	6	...	...	...	50	...	...
Viet Nam	20	23	7	20	8	36	17	70	23
Latin America and the Caribbean									
Anguilla	...	...	...	...	...	...	...	...	...
Antigua and Barbuda	...	...	5	...	...	...	...	...	...
Argentina	13	16	7	4	1	4	...	...	28
Aruba	17	20	...	...	...	...	...	...	...
Bahamas	14	17	7	...	...	...	...	...	...
Barbados	10	11	14	...	...	...	...	...	...
Belize	16	20	8	6	1	18	10	...	27
Bermuda	...	...	...	...	...	...	...	...	...
Bolivia	46	61	7	8	1	27	54	74	46
Brazil	24	29	8	5	...	...	...	30	17
British Virgin Islands	...	...	...	...	...	...	...	...	...
Cayman Islands	...	...	...	...	...	...	...	...	...
Chile	7	9	6	1	0	1	85	...	...
Colombia	19	26	9	7	1	12	47	65	32
Costa Rica	10	11	7	5	2	6	35	47	12
Cuba	5	7	5	4	2	5	26	47	16
Dominica	...	...	9	...	...	...	...	...	...
Dominican Republic	30	33	11	5	1	7	4	36	15
Ecuador	21	26	16	9	2	23	40	77	23
El Salvador	22	29	7	10	1	19	24	76	43
Grenada	34	41	9	...	...	...	39	...	...
Guatemala	30	39	12	23	2	49	51	67	47
Guyana	43	57	13	12	8	14	11	42	31
Haiti	49	72	25	22	9	24	41	87	35
Honduras	28	42	10	11	1	25	30	69	48
Jamaica	14	17	12	4	4	3	15	36	24
Mexico	17	20	8	5	2	13	38	36	21
Montserrat	...	...	...	...	...	...	...	...	...
Netherlands Antilles	15	17	...	...	...	...	...	...	...
Nicaragua	21	26	12	7	1	17	31	83	43

CHILD WELL-BEING[2]					PROVISION FOR UNDER-3s		WOMEN'S EMPLOYMENT AND MATERNITY LEAVE		
% of 1-year-old children immunized against									
Tuberculosis	Diphtheria, Pertussis, Tetanus	Polio	Measles	Hepatitis B	Official programmes targeting children under age 3	Youngest age group targeted in programmes (years)	Female labour force participation rate (age 15 and above)[4] (%)	Duration of paid maternity leave[5] (weeks)	
Corresponding vaccines: BCG	DPT3	Polio3	Measles	HepB3					
2007	2007	2007	2007	2007	2005	c. 2005	2003	2007-2009[3]	Country or territory
94	93	94	94	92	Yes	0-3	71	13	China
99	99	99	98	99	...	...	...	...	Cook Islands
96	92	99	99	92	Yes	0-3	58	...	DPR Korea
90	83	84	81	84	No	·	39	12	Fiji
91	75	83	80	74	Yes	0-6	49	13	Indonesia
...	98	95	98	...	Yes	0-6	49	14	Japan
90	94	93	93	96	No	·	...	12	Kiribati
56	50	46	40	50	Yes	0-2	79	13	Lao People's Democratic Republic
...	...	...	...	...	No	·	60	...	Macao, China
99	96	96	90	87	Yes	0-3	44	9	Malaysia
92	93	91	94	93	...	...	...	...	Marshall Islands
82	79	79	92	90	...	...	...	...	Micronesia, Federated States of
89	86	84	81	85	...	...	69	12	Myanmar
99	99	99	99	99	...	...	...	...	Nauru
...	88	88	79	88	Yes	0-5	61	14	New Zealand
99	99	99	99	99	...	...	...	...	Niue
...	94	94	91	91	...	...	...	...	Palau
67	60	61	58	59	No	·	71	0	Papua New Guinea[7]
90	87	87	92	88	No	·	49	9	Philippines
96	91	91	92	91	Yes	0-5	50	13	Republic of Korea
91	71	71	63	69	...	...	41	0	Samoa
98	96	96	95	95	Yes	2-6	54	8	Singapore
84	79	77	78	79	No	·	54	12	Solomon Islands
99	98	98	96	96	Yes	0-5	66	13	Thailand
74	70	70	63	...	...	...	56	...	Timor-Leste
...	...	...	...	...	...	...	...	...	Tokelau
99	99	99	99	99	...	...	52	...	Tonga
99	97	97	95	97	...	...	...	...	Tuvalu
82	76	76	65	76	...	...	79	12	Vanuatu
94	92	92	83	67	Yes	0-2	70	17	Viet Nam
									Latin America and the Caribbean
...	...	...	...	...	...	...	...	...	Anguilla
...	99	98	99	97	...	...	...	13	Antigua and Barbuda
99	96	94	99	92	Yes	0-5	50	13	Argentina
...	...	...	...	...	...	...	...	...	Aruba
...	95	95	96	93	...	...	67	13	Bahamas
...	93	93	75	93	Yes	0-2	67	12	Barbados
99	96	97	96	96	...	...	46	14	Belize
...	...	...	...	...	...	...	...	8	Bermuda
93	81	79	81	81	Yes	0-4	67	9	Bolivia
99	98	99	99	95	Yes	0-3	58	17	Brazil
...	...	...	...	...	Yes	0-3	...	13	British Virgin Islands
...	...	...	...	...	...	...	...	...	Cayman Islands
98	94	94	91	94	Yes	0-2	40	18	Chile
93	93	93	95	93	Yes	0-5	63	12	Colombia
91	89	89	90	89	Yes	0-3	43	17	Costa Rica
99	93	99	99	93	Yes	1-6	45	18	Cuba
90	96	93	96	93	...	...	...	12	Dominica
92	79	83	96	70	...	...	56	12	Dominican Republic
99	99	99	99	99	Yes	0-4	52	12	Ecuador
93	96	96	98	96	Yes	0-3	46	12	El Salvador
...	99	99	98	99	Yes	0-2	...	13	Grenada
97	82	82	93	82	Yes	0-6	44	12	Guatemala
97	94	94	96	94	No	·	49	13	Guyana
75	53	52	58	...	Yes	0-3	39	6	Haiti
91	86	86	89	86	Yes	0-3	37	12	Honduras
87	85	85	76	85	No	·	57	8	Jamaica
99	98	98	96	98	Yes	0-3	42	12	Mexico
...	...	...	...	...	...	...	...	...	Montserrat
...	...	...	...	...	...	...	56	...	Netherlands Antilles
99	87	88	99	87	Yes	0-3	37	12	Nicaragua

Table 3A (continued)

Country or territory	CHILD SURVIVAL[1]		CHILD WELL-BEING[2]						
				% of children under age 5 suffering from:			% of children who are:		
	Infant mortality rate (‰)	Under-5 mortality rate (‰)	Infants with low birth weight (%)	Underweight moderate and severe	Wasting moderate and severe	Stunting moderate and severe	Exclusively breastfed (<6 months)	Breastfed with complementary food (6-9 months)	Still breastfeeding (20-23 months)
	2005-2010	2005-2010	2000-2007[3]	2000-2007[3]	2000-2007[3]	2000-2007[3]	2000-2007[3]	2000-2007[3]	2000-2007[3]
Panama	18	24	10	8	1	18	25	38	21
Paraguay	32	38	9	4	1	14	22	60	…
Peru	21	29	10	5	1	30	63	82	47
Saint Kitts and Nevis	…	…	9	…	…	…	56	…	…
Saint Lucia	13	16	11	…	…	…	…	…	…
Saint Vincent and the Grenadines	23	28	8	…	…	…	…	…	…
Suriname	28	35	13	10	5	8	9	25	11
Trinidad and Tobago	12	18	19	6	4	4	13	43	22
Turks and Caicos Islands	…	…	…	…	…	…	…	…	…
Uruguay	13	16	8	5	2	11	54	32	31
Venezuela, Bolivarian Rep. of	17	22	9	5	4	12	7	50	31
North America and Western Europe									
Andorra	…	…	…	…	…	…	…	…	…
Austria	4	5	7	…	…	…	…	…	…
Belgium	4	5	8	…	…	…	…	…	…
Canada	5	6	6	…	…	…	…	…	…
Cyprus	6	7	…	…	…	…	…	…	…
Denmark	4	6	5	…	…	…	…	…	…
Finland	4	5	4	…	…	…	…	…	…
France	4	5	7	…	…	…	…	…	…
Germany	4	5	7	…	…	…	…	…	…
Greece	7	8	8	…	…	…	…	…	…
Iceland	3	4	4	…	…	…	…	…	…
Ireland	5	6	6	…	…	…	…	…	…
Israel	5	6	8	…	…	…	…	…	…
Italy	5	6	6	…	…	…	…	…	…
Luxembourg	5	7	8	…	…	…	…	…	…
Malta	6	8	6	…	…	…	…	…	…
Monaco	…	…	…	…	…	…	…	…	…
Netherlands	5	6	…	…	…	…	…	…	…
Norway[8]	3	4	5	…	…	…	…	…	…
Portugal	5	7	8	…	…	…	…	…	…
San Marino	…	…	…	…	…	…	…	…	…
Spain	4	5	6	…	…	…	…	…	…
Sweden[8]	3	4	4	…	…	…	…	…	…
Switzerland	4	5	6	…	…	…	…	…	…
United Kingdom	5	6	8	…	…	…	…	…	…
United States[7]	6	8	8	2	0	1	…	…	…
South and West Asia									
Afghanistan	157	235	…	39	7	54	…	29	54
Bangladesh	52	69	22	46	16	36	37	52	89
Bhutan	45	65	15	19	3	40	…	…	…
India	55	79	28	46	19	38	46	57	77
Iran, Islamic Republic of	31	35	7	11	5	15	23	68	58
Maldives	34	42	22	30	13	25	10	85	…
Nepal	54	72	21	45	12	43	53	75	95
Pakistan	67	95	19	38	13	37	37	36	55
Sri Lanka	11	13	22	29	14	14	53	…	73
Sub-Saharan Africa									
Angola	132	231	12	31	6	45	11	77	37
Benin	98	146	15	23	7	38	43	72	57
Botswana	46	68	10	13	5	23	34	57	11
Burkina Faso	104	181	16	37	23	35	7	50	85
Burundi	99	169	11	39	7	53	45	88	…
Cameroon	88	144	11	19	6	30	21	64	21
Cape Verde	25	29	13	…	…	…	57	64	13
Central African Republic	97	163	13	29	10	38	23	55	47
Chad	119	189	22	37	14	41	2	77	65
Comoros	48	63	25	25	8	44	21	34	45

CHILD WELL-BEING[2]					PROVISION FOR UNDER-3s		WOMEN'S EMPLOYMENT AND MATERNITY LEAVE		
% of 1-year-old children immunized against									
Tuberculosis	Diphtheria, Pertussis, Tetanus	Polio	Measles	Hepatitis B	Official programmes targeting children under age 3	Youngest age group targeted in programmes (years)	Female labour force participation rate (age 15 and above)[4] (%)	Duration of paid maternity leave[5] (weeks)	Country or territory
Corresponding vaccines:									
BCG	DPT3	Polio3	Measles	HepB3					
2007	2007	2007	2007	2007	2005	c. 2005	2003	2007-2009[3]	
99	88	88	89	88	Yes	2-4	47	14	Panama
68	66	65	80	66	Yes	0-4	70	9	Paraguay
97	80	95	99	80	Yes	0-5	64	13	Peru
97	99	99	99	99	...	...	...	13	Saint Kitts and Nevis
99	99	99	94	99	Yes	0-2	53	13	Saint Lucia
99	99	99	99	99	...	...	54	13	Saint Vincent and the Grenadines
...	84	84	85	84	...	...	39	...	Suriname
...	88	90	91	89	Yes	0-5	57	13	Trinidad and Tobago
...	...	...	...	...	Yes	2	...	...	Turks and Caicos Islands
99	94	94	96	94	Yes	0-3	52	12	Uruguay
83	71	73	55	71	Yes	0-2	51	18	Venezuela, Bolivarian Rep. of
									North America and Western Europe
...	96	96	94	91	Yes	0-3	...	16	Andorra
...	85	85	79	85	Yes	1-3	52	16	Austria
...	99	99	92	94	Yes	1-3	45	15	Belgium
...	94	90	94	14	Yes	0-6	61	15	Canada
...	97	97	87	93	Yes	0-5	53	18	Cyprus
...	75	75	89	...	Yes	0-2	61	18	Denmark
97	99	97	98	...	Yes	0-6	58	18	Finland
84	98	98	87	29	Yes	0-3	50	16	France
...	97	97	94	87	Yes	0-2	51	14	Germany
88	88	87	88	88	Yes	0-3	43	17	Greece
...	97	97	95	...	Yes	0-6	72	13	Iceland
93	92	92	87	...	Yes	0-5	52	26	Ireland
...	96	95	97	99	Yes	0-4	50	12	Israel
...	96	96	87	96	Yes	0-2	38	21	Italy
...	99	99	96	87	No	...	46	16	Luxembourg
...	74	76	79	82	...	...	32	13	Malta
90	99	99	99	99	...	...	...	16	Monaco
...	96	96	96	...	Yes	0-3	56	16	Netherlands
...	93	93	92	...	Yes	0-5	62	48	Norway[8]
98	97	96	95	97	Yes	0-3	56	21	Portugal
...	92	92	92	92	...	...	...	22	San Marino
...	96	96	97	96	Yes	0-3	47	16	Spain
18	99	99	96	4	Yes	1-6	61	84	Sweden[8]
...	93	94	86	...	Yes	0-5	60	14	Switzerland
...	92	92	86	...	Yes	1-3	56	39	United Kingdom
...	96	92	93	92	Yes	0-4	59	0	United States[7]
									South and West Asia
77	83	83	70	83	...	...	29	13	Afghanistan
97	90	96	88	90	No	·	57	12	Bangladesh
94	95	93	95	95	No	·	40	...	Bhutan
85	62	62	67	6	Yes	0-6	35	12	India
99	99	98	97	97	Yes	0-6	31	17	Iran, Islamic Republic of
99	98	98	97	98	Yes	0-3	53	...	Maldives
89	82	82	81	82	No	·	59	7	Nepal
89	83	83	80	83	Yes	0-6	21	12	Pakistan
99	98	98	98	98	...	...	43	12	Sri Lanka
									Sub-Saharan Africa
88	83	83	88	83	...	...	74	13	Angola
88	67	64	61	67	Yes	2-5	58	14	Benin
99	97	97	90	85	Yes	0-4	48	12	Botswana
99	99	99	94	99	...	...	77	14	Burkina Faso
84	74	64	75	74	...	...	90	12	Burundi
81	82	81	74	82	Yes	1-6	53	14	Cameroon
86	81	81	74	79	...	...	45	6	Cape Verde
74	54	47	62	...	Yes	2-5	67	14	Central African Republic
40	20	36	23	...	...	...	71	14	Chad
77	75	75	65	75	...	...	63	14	Comoros

Table 3A (continued)

Country or territory	CHILD SURVIVAL[1]		CHILD WELL-BEING[2]						
				% of children under age 5 suffering from:			% of children who are:		
	Infant mortality rate (‰) 2005-2010	Under-5 mortality rate (‰) 2005-2010	Infants with low birth weight (%) 2000-2007[3]	Underweight moderate and severe 2000-2007[3]	Wasting moderate and severe 2000-2007[3]	Stunting moderate and severe 2000-2007[3]	Exclusively breastfed (<6 months) 2000-2007[3]	Breastfed with complementary food (6-9 months) 2000-2007[3]	Still breastfeeding (20-23 months) 2000-2007[3]
Congo	70	102	13	14	7	26	19	78	21
Côte d'Ivoire	117	183	17	20	7	34	4	54	37
Democratic Rep. of the Congo	114	196	12	31	13	38	36	82	64
Equatorial Guinea	92	155	13	19	7	39	24	...	...
Eritrea	55	77	14	40	13	38	52	43	62
Ethiopia	87	145	20	38	11	47	49	54	...
Gabon	54	86	14	12	3	21	6	62	9
Gambia	74	128	20	20	6	22	41	44	53
Ghana	57	90	9	18	5	22	54	58	56
Guinea	103	156	12	26	9	35	27	41	71
Guinea-Bissau	113	195	24	19	7	41	16	35	61
Kenya	64	104	10	20	6	30	13	84	57
Lesotho[7]	65	98	13	20	4	38	36	79	60
Liberia	133	205	...	26	6	39	35	70	45
Madagascar	66	106	17	42	13	48	67	78	64
Malawi	89	132	14	21	4	46	57	89	72
Mali	129	200	19	32	13	34	38	30	56
Mauritius	14	17	14	15	14	10	21	...	...
Mozambique	96	164	15	24	4	41	30	80	65
Namibia	42	66	14	24	9	24	24	72	28
Niger	111	188	27	44	10	50	9	73	...
Nigeria	109	187	14	29	9	38	17	64	34
Rwanda	112	188	6	23	4	45	88	69	77
Sao Tome and Principe	72	95	8	9	8	23	60	60	18
Senegal	66	115	19	17	8	16	34	61	42
Seychelles	...	...	...	...	...	...	...	...	...
Sierra Leone	160	278	24	30	9	40	8	52	57
Somalia	116	193	...	36	11	38	9	15	35
South Africa	45	66	15	12	3	25	7	46	...
Swaziland[7]	71	114	9	7	2	24	32	77	31
Togo	89	126	12	26	14	24	28	35	44
Uganda	77	127	14	20	5	32	60	80	54
United Republic of Tanzania	73	118	10	22	3	38	41	91	55
Zambia	93	157	12	19	5	39	61	93	42
Zimbabwe	58	94	11	17	6	29	22	79	...
	Weighted average		Weighted average						
World	49	74	14	25	11	28	38	55	50
Countries in transition	31	38	...	...	...	...	...	...	...
Developed countries	6	7	...	...	...	...	...	...	...
Developing countries	54	81	15	26	11	30	39	55	51
Arab States	41	54	12	17	8	26	26	57	36
Central and Eastern Europe	17	21	...	...	...	...	...	...	...
Central Asia	51	62	...	...	...	...	...	...	...
East Asia and the Pacific	24	31	6	14	...	16	43	45	27
East Asia	24	31	...	...	...	...	...	...	...
Pacific	26	36	...	...	...	...	...	...	...
Latin America and the Caribbean	22	27	9	6	2	16	...	...	...
Caribbean	39	56	...	...	...	...	...	...	...
Latin America	21	26	...	...	...	...	...	...	...
N. America/W. Europe	5	7	...	...	...	...	...	...	...
South and West Asia	58	83	...	...	...	...	...	...	...
Sub-Saharan Africa	95	158	15	28	9	38	31	68	51

1. The indicators on child survival in this table are from the United Nations Population Division estimates, revision 2006 (UNPD, 2007). They are based on the median variant.
2. UNICEF (2009).
3. Data are for the most recent year available during the period specified.
4. Employed and unemployed women as a share of the working age population, including women with a job but temporarily not at work (e.g. on maternity leave), home employment for the production of goods and services for own household consumption, and domestic and personal services produced by employing paid domestic staff. Data exclude women occupied solely in domestic duties in their own households (ILO, 2009).

CHILD WELL-BEING[2]					PROVISION FOR UNDER-3s		WOMEN'S EMPLOYMENT AND MATERNITY LEAVE		
% of 1-year-old children immunized against									
Tuberculosis	Diphtheria, Pertussis, Tetanus	Polio	Measles	Hepatitis B	Official programmes targeting children under age 3	Youngest age group targeted in programmes (years)	Female labour force participation rate (age 15 and above)[4] (%)	Duration of paid maternity leave[5] (weeks)	
Corresponding vaccines:									
BCG	DPT3	Polio3	Measles	HepB3					
2007	2007	2007	2007	2007	2005	c. 2005	2003	2007-2009[3]	Country or territory
86	80	80	67	80	...	...	56	15	Congo
94	76	75	67	76	...	...	39	14	Côte d'Ivoire
94	87	87	79	87	...	...	55	14	Democratic Rep. of the Congo
73	33	39	51	...	...	...	45	12	Equatorial Guinea
99	97	96	95	97	Yes	0-6	56	9	Eritrea
72	73	71	65	73	No	.	79	13	Ethiopia
89	38	31	55	38	...	...	62	14	Gabon
95	90	85	85	90	...	...	70	12	Gambia
99	94	94	95	94	Yes	0-2	72	12	Ghana
91	75	62	71	83	Yes	0-3	79	14	Guinea
89	63	64	76	...	...	...	54	9	Guinea-Bissau
92	81	76	80	81	...	...	74	9	Kenya
96	83	80	85	85	No	.	68	0	Lesotho[7]
86	88	84	95	...	Yes	2-6	55	...	Liberia
94	82	81	81	82	Yes	0-3	84	14	Madagascar
95	87	88	83	87	...	...	76	8	Malawi
77	68	62	68	68	Yes	0-3	36	14	Mali
98	97	96	98	97	Yes	0-2	42	12	Mauritius
87	72	70	77	72	...	...	88	9	Mozambique
95	86	81	69	...	Yes	0-1	49	12	Namibia
64	39	55	47	...	Yes	2-6	39	14	Niger
69	54	61	62	41	Yes	0-3	38	12	Nigeria
89	97	98	99	97	...	...	81	8	Rwanda
98	97	98	86	99	...	...	41	9	Sao Tome and Principe
99	94	93	84	94	Yes	0-5	61	14	Senegal
99	99	99	99	99	Yes	0-3	...	12	Seychelles
82	64	64	67	64	No	.	65	...	Sierra Leone
52	39	39	34	...	...	...	54	14	Somalia
99	97	97	83	97	Yes	0-5	47	17	South Africa
99	95	95	91	95	Yes	0-6	62	0	Swaziland[7]
91	88	78	80	...	...	...	52	14	Togo
90	64	59	68	68	...	...	81	12	Uganda
89	83	88	90	83	...	...	87	12	United Republic of Tanzania
92	80	77	85	80	Yes	0-6	60	12	Zambia
76	62	66	66	62	...	...	61	13	Zimbabwe
Weighted average							Median		
89	81	82	82	65	...	...	53	13	World
...	...	...	...	...	...	...	55	18	Countries in transition
...	...	...	...	...	...	...	52	17	Developed countries
89	80	81	81	65	...	...	53	12	Developing countries
92	91	92	89	89	...	...	25	10	Arab States
...	...	...	...	...	...	...	51	20	Central and Eastern Europe
...	...	...	...	...	...	...	58	18	Central Asia
93	89	91	90	87	...	...	58	12	East Asia and the Pacific
...	...	...	...	...	...	...	58	13	East Asia
...	...	...	...	...	...	...	...	...	Pacific
96	92	93	93	89	...	...	52	13	Latin America and the Caribbean
...	...	...	...	...	...	...	54	13	Caribbean
...	...	...	...	...	...	...	50	12	Latin America
...	...	...	...	...	...	...	53	16	N. America/W. Europe
...	...	...	...	...	...	...	40	12	South and West Asia
83	73	74	73	67	...	...	61	12	Sub-Saharan Africa

5. Refers to paid employment-protected leave for employed women around the time of childbirth. The benefit amount varies but is usually a percentage of the average earnings or a function of wage class. A minimum period of employment before childbirth may be required.

6. Maternity leave duration refers to the required unpaid leave for mothers after birth; a birth grant exists in lieu of a maternity benefit.

7. Statutory maternity leave exists but remains unpaid. In some cases, employers may provide a benefit.

8. Maternity leave duration refers to the maximum length of parental leave allocated to the woman.

Sources: For women's maternity leave status, ILO (forthcoming), OECD (2009), United Nations Statistics Division (2009), US Social Security Administration (2008).

Table 3B

Early childhood care and education (ECCE): education

	Country or territory	Age group 2007	ENROLMENT IN PRE-PRIMARY EDUCATION, School year ending in 1999: Total (000)	1999: % F	2007: Total (000)	2007: % F	Enrolment in private institutions as % of total enrolment, School year ending in 1999	2007	GROSS ENROLMENT RATIO (GER) IN PRE-PRIMARY EDUCATION (%), School year ending in 1999: Total	Male	Female	GPI (F/M)
	Arab States											
1	Algeria	5-5	36	49	171	50	.	34	3	3	3	1.01
2	Bahrain	3-5	14	48	19[z]	48[z]	100	100[z]	36	37	36	0.96
3	Djibouti	4-5	0.2	60	**1**	**47**	100	**89**	0.4	0.3	0.5	1.50
4	Egypt	4-5	328	48	580	47	54	30	11	11	10	0.95
5	Iraq	4-5	68	48	*93[y]*	*49[y]*	.	.[y]	5	5	5	0.98
6	Jordan	4-5	74	46	93	47	100	92	29	30	27	0.91
7	Kuwait	4-5	57	49	70	49	24	40[z]	78	78	79	1.02
8	Lebanon	3-5	143	48	**150**	**49**	78	**80**	61	62	60	0.97
9	Libyan Arab Jamahiriya	4-5	10	*48*	22[z]	48[z]	.	17[z]	5	*5*	*5*	*0.97*
10	Mauritania	3-5	…	…	*5[y]*	…	…	*78[y]*	…	…	…	…
11	Morocco	4-5	805	34	706	41	100	96	62	82	43	0.52
12	Oman	4-5	7	45	35	51	100	31	6	6	6	0.88
13	Palestinian Autonomous Territories	4-5	77	48	78	48	100	100	39	40	39	0.96
14	Qatar	3-5	8	48	17	49	100	88	25	25	25	0.98
15	Saudi Arabia	3-5	…	…	179	48*	…	49	…	…	…	…
16	Sudan	4-5	366	…	491	50	*90*	38	19	…	…	…
17	Syrian Arab Republic	3-5	108	46	146	48	67	72	8	9	8	0.90
18	Tunisia	3-5	78	47	…	…	88	…	14	14	13	0.95
19	United Arab Emirates	4-5	64	48	100	48	68	78	64	65	63	0.97
20	Yemen	3-5	12	45	18[y]	45[y]	37	49[y]	0.7	0.7	0.6	0.86
	Central and Eastern Europe											
21	Albania	3-5	82	50	…	…	.	…	40	39	41	1.06
22	Belarus	3-5	263	47*	271	48	–	4	75	77*	73*	0.95*
23	Bosnia and Herzegovina	3-5	…	…	13	47	…	…	…	…	…	…
24	Bulgaria	3-6	219	48	207	48	0.1	0.5	67	67	66	0.99
25	Croatia	3-6	81	48	91	48	5	11	40	40	39	0.98
26	Czech Republic	3-5	312	50	287	48	2	1	90	87	93	1.07
27	Estonia	3-6	55	48	47	49	0.7	3	87	88	87	0.99
28	Hungary	3-6	376	48	328	48	3	5	78	79	77	0.98
29	Latvia	3-6	58	48	65[z]	48[z]	1	3[z]	53	54	51	0.95
30	Lithuania	3-6	94	48	87	48	0.3	0.3	50	50	49	0.97
31	Montenegro	…	…	…	…	…	…	…	…	…	…	…
32	Poland	3-6	958	49	863	49	3	9	50	50	50	1.01
33	Republic of Moldova[1,2]	3-6	103	48	104	48	…	0.1	48	49	48	0.96
34	Romania	3-6	625	49	649	49	0.6	2	62	61	63	1.02
35	Russian Federation	3-6	4 379	…	4 713	53	…	2	68	…	…	…
36	Serbia[1]	3-6	175	46	173	49	…	0.1	*54*	*57*	*51*	*0.90*
37	Slovakia	3-5	169	…	144	48	0.4	3	82	…	…	…
38	Slovenia	3-5	59	46	43	48	1	2	75	78	71	0.91
39	TFYR Macedonia	3-6	33	49	37	49	.	.	27	27	28	1.01
40	Turkey	3-5	261	47	641	48	6	9	6	6	6	0.94
41	Ukraine	3-5	1 103	48	1 081	48	0.0	2	50	50	49	0.98
	Central Asia											
42	Armenia	3-6	57	…	48	51	–	1	26	…	…	…
43	Azerbaijan[1,3]	3-5	88	46	94	47	–	0.2	18	19	17	0.89
44	Georgia	3-5	74	48	78	51	0.1	–	36	36	36	1.00
45	Kazakhstan	3-6	165	48	**355**	**48**	10	**5**	14	15	14	0.96
46	Kyrgyzstan	3-6	48	43	62	50	1	1	10	11	9	0.80
47	Mongolia	3-6	74	54	95	51	4	3	25	23	27	1.21
48	Tajikistan	3-6	56	42	61	46	.	.	8	9	7	0.76
49	Turkmenistan	3-6	…	…	…	…	…	…	…	…	…	…
50	Uzbekistan	3-6	616	47	562	48	…	0.5	24	24	23	0.94
	East Asia and the Pacific											
51	Australia	4-4	…	…	263[z]	48[z]	…	67[z]	…	…	…	…
52	Brunei Darussalam	3-5	11	49	12	49	66	66	50	49	51	1.04
53	Cambodia	3-5	*58*	*50*	111	50	*22*	30	*5*	*5*	*5*	*1.03*
54	China	4-6	24 030	46	22 639	45	…	34	38	38	37	0.97

GROSS ENROLMENT RATIO (GER) IN PRE-PRIMARY EDUCATION (%)				NET ENROLMENT RATIO (NER) IN PRE-PRIMARY EDUCATION (%)				GROSS ENROLMENT RATIO (GER) IN PRE-PRIMARY AND OTHER ECCE PROGRAMMES (%)				NEW ENTRANTS TO THE FIRST GRADE OF PRIMARY EDUCATION WITH ECCE EXPERIENCE (%)			
School year ending in 2007				School year ending in 2007				School year ending in 2007				School year ending in 2007			
Total	Male	Female	GPI (F/M)	Total	Male	Female	GPI (F/M)	Total	Male	Female	GPI (F/M)	Total	Male	Female	
														Arab States	
30	29	30	1.03	26	25	26	1.04	...	...	...	...	30	19	43	1
52[z]	52[z]	51[z]	0.98[z]	51[z]	51[z]	50[z]	0.98[z]	55[z]	56[z]	54[z]	0.97[z]	82[z]	83[z]	81[z]	2
3	**3**	**3**	**0.91**	**2**	**2**	**2**	**0.87**	**3**	**3**	**3**	**0.91**	8	8	8	3
17	18	17	0.94	16	17	16	0.93	17	18	17	0.94	...	...	...	4
6[y]	*6[y]*	*6[y]*	*1.00[y]*	*6[y]*	*6[y]*	*6[y]*	*1.00[y]*	*6[y]*	*6[y]*	*6[y]*	*1.00[y]*	...	...	...	5
32	33	31	0.94	*30[z]*	*31[z]*	*29[z]*	*0.95[z]*	32	33	31	0.94	70	73	68	6
77	78	75	0.97	61	62	60	0.97	77	78	75	0.97	82	81	83	7
67	**68**	**67**	**0.98**	**65**	**66**	**65**	**0.99**	**67**	**68**	**67**	**0.98**	**100**	**100**	**100**	8
9[z]	9[z]	9[z]	0.97[z]	8[z]	8[z]	7[z]	0.96[z]	9[z]	9[z]	9[z]	0.97[z]	...	...	...	9
2[y]	...	...	...	...	...	...	...	...	...	...	...	100	100	100	10
60	69	50	0.72	54	63	45	0.72	60	69	50	0.72	48	48	49	11
31	30	32	1.08	24	23	24	1.08	31	30	32	1.08	...	...	...	12
30	30	30	0.98	19	19	19	1.00	30	30	30	0.98	...	...	...	13
47	47	47	1.01	43	43	44	1.03	...	...	...	...	...	...	...	14
11	11*	10*	0.94*	10*	10*	10*	0.93*	...	...	...	...	...	...	...	15
23	23	24	1.05	...	...	...	...	23	23	24	1.05	62	62	62	16
10	10	10	0.94	10	10	9	0.94	10	10	10	0.94	12[y]	12[y]	12[y]	17
...	...	...	...	...	...	...	...	...	...	...	...	...	...	...	18
85	85	84	0.98	60	61	59	0.98	85	85	84	0.98	82	82	81	19
1[y]	1[y]	1[y]	0.85[y]	...	...	...	...	...	...	...	...	...	...	...	20
														Central and Eastern Europe	
...	...	...	...	...	...	...	...	...	...	...	...	...	...	...	21
103	104	102	0.98	90	91	90	0.99	121	122	120	0.98	...	...	...	22
10	10	9	0.94	...	...	...	...	...	...	...	...	...	...	...	23
81	82	81	0.99	78	78	77	0.99	81	82	81	0.99	...	...	...	24
52	53	51	0.97	52	52	51	0.97	52	53	51	0.97	...	...	...	25
115	117	113	0.97	...	...	...	...	115	117	113	0.97	...	...	...	26
95	95	95	1.00	90	89	90	1.01	...	...	...	...	...	...	...	27
88	88	87	0.99	87	87	87	1.00	88	88	87	0.99	...	...	...	28
89[z]	90[z]	88[z]	0.98[z]	87[z]	87[z]	86[z]	0.99[z]	89[z]	90[z]	88[z]	0.98[z]	...	...	...	29
69	70	69	0.98	69	69	68	0.99	69	70	69	0.98	...	...	...	30
...	...	...	...	...	...	...	...	...	...	...	...	...	...	...	31
60	60	61	1.01	59	58	59	1.01	60	60	61	1.01	...	...	...	32
70	71	69	0.98	68	69	68	0.98	70	71	69	0.98	...	...	...	33
72	72	73	1.01	71	70	72	1.02	72	72	73	1.01	...	...	...	34
88	82	95	1.16	...	...	...	...	88	82	95	1.16	...	...	...	35
59	59	59	1.00	...	...	...	...	...	...	...	...	...	...	...	36
94	96	92	0.97	*86[y]*	*88[y]*	*85[y]*	*0.96[y]*	94	96	92	0.97	...	...	...	37
81	82	79	0.97	79	80	78	0.97	81	82	79	0.97	...	...	...	38
40	39	40	1.02	38	38	39	1.03	40	39	40	1.02	...	...	...	39
16	16	15	0.95	16	16	15	0.95	...	...	...	...	...	...	...	40
94	96	93	0.97	...	...	...	...	94	96	93	0.97	62	...	...	41
														Central Asia	
37	34	42	1.24	...	...	...	...	...	...	...	...	...	...	...	42
30	29	30	1.03	24	24	25	1.05	30	29	30	1.03	7	7	7	43
57	53	62	1.18	41	39	44	1.13	...	...	...	...	...	...	...	44
39	**40**	**39**	**0.97**	**39**	**39**	**38**	**0.98**	...	...	...	...	...	...	...	45
16	15	16	1.04	13	13	13	1.04	16	15	16	1.04	27	28	27	46
54	52	55	1.06	46	45	48	1.06	70	68	72	1.07	49	48	49	47
9	10	9	0.90	7	7	6	0.91	...	...	...	...	1	1	1	48
...	...	...	...	...	...	...	...	...	...	...	...	...	...	...	49
27	27	26	0.94	21[z]	...	...	...	...	...	...	...	...	...	...	50
														East Asia and the Pacific	
104[z]	106[z]	103[z]	0.97[z]	62[y]	62[y]	62[y]	1.00[y]	104[z]	106[z]	103[z]	0.97[z]	...	...	...	51
50	49	51	1.03	44	43	45	1.04	55	54	56	1.04	*99[z]*	*99[z]*	*99[z]*	52
11	11	12	1.06	11	11	12	1.06	11	11	12	1.06	17	16	18	53
42	43	40	0.94	...	...	...	...	42	43	40	0.94	85	...	...	54

Table 3B (continued)

	Country or territory	Age group	ENROLMENT IN PRE-PRIMARY EDUCATION				Enrolment in private institutions as % of total enrolment		GROSS ENROLMENT RATIO (GER) IN PRE-PRIMARY EDUCATION (%)			
			School year ending in				School year ending in		School year ending in			
			1999		2007		1999	2007	1999			
		2007	Total (000)	% F	Total (000)	% F			Total	Male	Female	GPI (F/M)
55	Cook Islands[1]	4-4	0.4	47	0.5	46	25	29	86	87	85	0.98
56	DPR Korea	4-5	...	...	...	...	...	...	...	...	...	...
57	Fiji	3-5	9	49	9[z]	49[z]	...	100[z]	16	16	16	1.02
58	Indonesia	5-6	*1 981*	*49*	3 724	50	*99*	99	*23*	*23*	*23*	*1.01*
59	Japan	3-5	2 962	*49*	3 056	...	65	67	83	*82*	*84*	*1.02*
60	Kiribati	3-5	...	...	...	...	...	...	...	...	...	...
61	Lao People's Democratic Republic	3-5	37	52	55	50	18	28	8	7	8	1.11
62	Macao, China	3-5	17	47	9	49	94	96	87	89	85	0.95
63	Malaysia	4-5	572	50	612[z]	51[z]	49	45[z]	54	53	55	1.04
64	Marshall Islands[1]	4-5	2	50	1	48	19	...	*59*	*57*	*60*	*1.04*
65	Micronesia, Federated States of	3-5	3	...	...	...	...	...	37	...	...	...
66	Myanmar[4]	3-4	41	...	99	50	90	56	...	...	...	...
67	Nauru	3-5	...	...	0.7	59	...	.	...	...	...	...
68	New Zealand	3-4	101	49	104	49	...	98	85	85	85	1.00
69	Niue[1]	4-4	0.6	44	0.03[y]	58[y]	.	...	154	159	147	0.93
70	Palau[1]	3-5	0.7	54	*0.7[y]*	*53[y]*	24	*20[y]*	63	56	69	1.23
71	Papua New Guinea	6-6	...	...	...	...	...	...	...	...	...	...
72	Philippines	5-5	593	50	961	50	47	42	30	30	31	1.05
73	Republic of Korea	5-5	536	47	543	48	75	78	78	82	74	0.89
74	Samoa	3-4	*5*	*53*	5	50	*100*	100	*53*	*48*	*58*	*1.21*
75	Singapore	3-5	...	...	...	...	...	...	...	...	...	...
76	Solomon Islands	3-5	*13*	*48*	...	...	...	...	*35*	*35*	*35*	*1.02*
77	Thailand	3-5	2 745	49	**2 540**	**49**	19	**21**	97	96	97	1.01
78	Timor-Leste	4-5	...	...	7[y]	51[y]	...	...	...	...	...	...
79	Tokelau[1]	3-4	...	...	...	...	...	...	...	...	...	...
80	Tonga	3-4	2	53	*1[y]*	*56[y]*	...	...	30	27	33	1.24
81	Tuvalu[1]	3-5	...	...	0.7[z]	52[z]	...	...	...	...	...	...
82	Vanuatu	3-5	...	...	1[z]	47[z]	...	94[z]	...	...	...	...
83	Viet Nam[4]	3-5	2 179	48	3 113	44	49	57	39	41	38	0.94
	Latin America and the Caribbean											
84	Anguilla[5]	3-4	0.5	52	0.4	47	100	100	...	...	...	...
85	Antigua and Barbuda[1]	3-4	...	...	2	49	...	95	...	...	...	...
86	Argentina	3-5	1 191	50	1 341[z]	49[z]	28	31[z]	57	56	57	1.02
87	Aruba	4-5	3	49	3	50	83	74	99	99	99	1.00
88	Bahamas	3-4	1	51	...	...	...	...	12	11	12	1.09
89	Barbados	3-4	6	49	6	49	...	15	74	75	73	0.98
90	Belize	3-4	4	50	5	51	...	76	27	27	27	1.03
91	Bermuda	4-4	...	...	...	...	...	...	...	...	...	...
92	Bolivia	4-5	208	49	238	49	...	10	45	44	45	1.01
93	Brazil[6]	4-6	5 733	49	6 574	49	28	24	58	58	58	1.00
94	British Virgin Islands[1]	3-4	0.5	53	0.7[z]	52[z]	100	100[z]	62	57	66	1.16
95	Cayman Islands[5]	4-4	0.5	48	0.7[z]	52[z]	88	92[z]	...	...	...	...
96	Chile	3-5	450	49	407	50	45	56	77	77	76	0.99
97	Colombia	3-5	1 034	50	1 081	48	45	41	37	37	38	1.02
98	Costa Rica	4-5	70	49	96	49	10	13	84	84	85	1.01
99	Cuba	3-5	484	50	454	48	.	.	109	107	111	1.04
100	Dominica[1,5]	3-4	3	52	2	50	100	100	80	76	85	1.11
101	Dominican Republic	3-5	195	49	210	49	45	52	32	31	32	1.01
102	Ecuador	5-5	181	50	290	49	39	39	64	63	66	1.04
103	El Salvador	4-6	194	49	230	50	*22*	19	43	42	43	1.01
104	Grenada[1]	3-4	4	50	3	50	...	56	93	93	93	1.01
105	Guatemala	3-6	308	49	457	50	22	20	46	46	45	0.97
106	Guyana	4-5	37	49	28	49	1	2	124	125	124	0.99
107	Haiti	3-5	...	...	...	...	...	...	...	...	...	...
108	Honduras	3-5	...	...	214	50	...	14[z]	...	...	...	...
109	Jamaica	3-5	138	51	142	50	88	91	78	75	81	1.08
110	Mexico	4-5	3 361	50	4 750	49	9	15	74	73	75	1.02
111	Montserrat[1]	3-4	0.1	52	0.1	47	.	–	...	...	...	...
112	Netherlands Antilles	4-5	7	50	...	...	75	...	111	110	112	1.02
113	Nicaragua	3-5	161	50	215	49	17	16	27	27	28	1.04
114	Panama	4-5	49	49	97	49	23	16	39	39	40	1.01

GROSS ENROLMENT RATIO (GER) IN PRE-PRIMARY EDUCATION (%)				NET ENROLMENT RATIO (NER) IN PRE-PRIMARY EDUCATION (%)				GROSS ENROLMENT RATIO (GER) IN PRE-PRIMARY AND OTHER ECCE PROGRAMMES (%)				NEW ENTRANTS TO THE FIRST GRADE OF PRIMARY EDUCATION WITH ECCE EXPERIENCE (%)			
School year ending in 2007				School year ending in 2007				School year ending in 2007				School year ending in 2007			
Total	Male	Female	GPI (F/M)	Total	Male	Female	GPI (F/M)	Total	Male	Female	GPI (F/M)	Total	Male	Female	
94	*97*	*91*	*0.94*	*92*	*94*	*90*	*0.96*	*94*	*97*	*91*	*0.94*	100[y]	100[y]	100[y]	55
...	...	...	...	...	...	...	...	...	...	...	...	...	...	...	56
16[z]	16[z]	16[z]	1.01[z]	15[z]	15[z]	15[z]	1.01[z]	16[z]	16[z]	16[z]	1.01[z]	...	...	...	57
44	43	45	1.04	31	31	32	1.04	44	43	45	1.04	87	87	88	58
86	...	...	...	86	...	...	...	102	...	...	...	...	...	...	59
...	...	...	...	...	...	...	...	...	...	...	...	...	...	...	60
13	13	13	1.04	12	...	...	...	13	13	13	1.04	11	10	11	61
85	85	85	1.00	80	79	81	1.01	85	85	85	1.00	96	96	96	62
57[z]	54[z]	60[z]	1.10[z]	57[z]	54[z]	60[z]	1.10[z]	57[z]	54[z]	60[z]	1.10[z]	76[y]	74[y]	79[y]	63
45	45	45	1.00	...	...	...	...	45	45	45	1.00	...	...	...	64
...	...	...	...	...	...	...	...	...	...	...	...	...	...	...	65
...	...	...	...	...	...	...	...	...	...	...	...	12	...	...	66
89	*71*	*107*	*1.51*	*57*	*58*	*57*	*0.99*	*89*	*71*	*107*	*1.51*	...	...	...	67
93	93	94	1.02	92	91	92.9	1.02	93	93	94	1.02	...	...	...	68
119[y]	108[y]	129[y]	1.19[y]	...	...	...	...	119[y]	108[y]	129[y]	1.19[y]	...	...	...	69
64[y]	*59[y]*	*68[y]*	*1.16[y]*	...	...	...	...	*64[y]*	*59[y]*	*68[y]*	*1.16[y]*	...	...	...	70
...	...	...	...	...	...	...	...	...	...	...	...	...	...	...	71
46	46	47	1.03	37	37	36	0.96	46	46	47	1.03	58[z]	57[z]	60[z]	72
106	104	108	1.04	53	52	54	1.04	106	104	108	1.04	...	...	...	73
48	46	50	1.09	30	29	30	1.05	48	46	50	1.09	...	...	...	74
...	...	...	...	...	...	...	...	...	...	...	...	...	...	...	75
...	...	...	...	...	...	...	...	...	...	...	...	...	...	...	76
95	**94**	**96**	**1.02**	**86**	**85**	**87**	**1.02**	**95**	**94**	**96**	**1.02**	...	...	...	77
10[y]	10[y]	11[y]	1.09[y]	...	...	...	...	10[y]	10[y]	11[y]	1.09[y]	...	...	...	78
...	...	...	...	...	...	...	...	...	...	...	...	...	...	...	79
23[y]	*19[y]*	*26[y]*	*1.37[y]*	...	...	...	...	*23[y]*	*19[y]*	*26[y]*	*1.37[y]*	...	...	...	80
107[z]	98[z]	116[z]	1.18[z]	92[z]	84[z]	100[z]	1.19[z]	...	...	...	...	...	...	...	81
7[z]	7[z]	7[z]	0.95[z]	5[z]	5[z]	5[z]	0.98[z]	7[z]	7[z]	7[z]	0.95[z]	...	...	...	82
...	...	...	...	...	...	...	...	...	...	...	...	...	...	...	83
												Latin America and the Caribbean			
...	...	...	...	...	...	...	...	...	...	...	...	100	100	100	84
72	72	72	1.00	66	66	66	1.00	112	113	111	0.98	...	...	...	85
67[z]	66[z]	67[z]	1.01[z]	66[z]	66[z]	67[z]	1.01[z]	67[z]	66[z]	67[z]	1.01[z]	94[y]	94[y]	94[y]	86
96	95	98	1.03	95	93	96	1.04	96	95	98	1.03	90[y]	90[y]	90[y]	87
...	...	...	...	...	...	...	...	...	...	...	...	52	52	52	88
91	92	90	0.98	82	82	82	1.00	91	92	90	0.98	100	100	100	89
35	33	36	1.07	33	32	34	1.06	35	33	36	1.07	.	.	.	90
...	...	...	...	...	...	...	...	...	...	...	...	...	...	...	91
49	49	49	1.00	40	40	40	1.01	49	49	49	1.00	66[z]	66[z]	66[z]	92
61	61	61	0.99	47	47	47	1.00	...	...	...	...	...	...	...	93
93[z]	88[z]	97[z]	1.11[z]	84[z]	80[z]	88[z]	1.10[z]	166[z]	158[z]	175[z]	1.11[z]	99[z]	...	...	94
...	...	...	...	...	...	...	...	...	...	...	...	90[*,z]	90[*,z]	90[*,z]	95
56	55	57	1.04	53	52	54.1	1.05	56	55	57	1.04	...	...	...	96
41	41	40	0.97	33	33	33	1.01	41	41	40	0.97	...	...	...	97
61	61	61	1.00	...	...	...	...	65	65	64	1.00	76	77	76	98
111	111	112	1.00	100	99	100	1.01	...	...	...	...	100	100	99	99
...	...	...	...	...	...	...	...	...	...	...	...	77	74	81	100
32	32	32	1.01	28	27	28	1.02	32	32	32	1.01	54	54	55	101
100	99	101	1.01	83	83	84	1.01	216	208	223	1.07	64	63	65	102
49	49	50	1.03	42	41	43	1.04	49	49	50	1.03	72	70	74	103
80	80	81	1.01	74	75	74	0.98	80	80	81	1.01	100	100	100	104
29	28	29	1.01	27	27	27	1.01	29	28	29	1.01	...	...	...	105
87	86	87	1.01	75	74	75	1.01	87	86	87	1.01	100	100	100	106
...	...	...	...	...	...	...	...	...	...	...	...	...	...	...	107
38	38	39	1.03	32	31	32	1.04	46	45	47	1.04	...	...	...	108
87	85	88	1.03	82	80	84	1.05	87	85	88	1.03	...	...	...	109
114	114	114	1.01	97	97	98	1.00	114	114	114	1.01	...	...	...	110
91	102	81	0.80	73	83	63	0.76	91	102	81	0.80	100	100	100	111
...	...	...	...	...	...	...	...	...	...	...	...	...	...	...	112
54	53	54	1.02	54	53	54	1.02	...	...	...	...	42	41	42	113
70	71	70	0.99	61	62	61	0.99	70	71	70	0.99	74	73	75	114

Table 3B (continued)

	Country or territory	Age group	ENROLMENT IN PRE-PRIMARY EDUCATION				Enrolment in private institutions as % of total enrolment		GROSS ENROLMENT RATIO (GER) IN PRE-PRIMARY EDUCATION (%)			
			School year ending in				School year ending in		School year ending in			
			1999		2007		1999	2007	1999			
		2007	Total (000)	% F	Total (000)	% F			Total	Male	Female	GPI (F/M)
115	Paraguay	3-5	123	50	148[y]	49[y]	29	28[y]	29	29	30	1.03
116	Peru	3-5	1 017	50	1 204	49	15	24	55	54	56	1.02
117	Saint Kitts and Nevis	3-4	...	...	2	50	...	74	...	...	...	...
118	Saint Lucia	3-4	*4*	*50*	4	50	...	100	*70*	*69*	*71*	*1.03*
119	Saint Vincent and the Grenadines	3-4	...	...	*4[y]*	*49[y]*	...	*100[y]*	...	...	...	...
120	Suriname	4-5	...	...	16	49	...	44	...	...	...	...
121	Trinidad and Tobago	3-4	*23*	*50*	30*	49*	*100*	100[*,y]	*58*	*57*	*58*	*1.01*
122	Turks and Caicos Islands	4-5	0.8	54	1[y]	47[y]	47	65[y]	...	...	...	...
123	Uruguay	3-5	100	49	122	49	...	33	60	59	60	1.02
124	Venezuela, Bolivarian Republic of	3-5	738	50	1 048	49	20	20	45	44	45	1.03
	North America and Western Europe											
125	Andorra[1]	3-5	...	...	3	49	...	2	...	...	...	...
126	Austria	3-5	225	49	219	49	25	27	82	82	82	0.99
127	Belgium	3-5	399	49	412	49	56	53	111	112	110	0.99
128	Canada	4-5	512	49	486[z]	49[z]	8	6[z]	64	64	64	0.99
129	Cyprus[1]	3-5	19	49	20	48	54	50	60	59	60	1.02
130	Denmark	3-6	251	49	252	49	...	...	90	90	90	1.00
131	Finland	3-6	125	49	143	49	10	9	48	49	48	0.99
132	France[7]	3-5	2 393	49	2 594	49	13	13	112	112	112	1.00
133	Germany	3-5	2 333	48	2 420	48	54	63	94	94	93	0.98
134	Greece	4-5	143	49	143	49	3	3	68	67	68	1.01
135	Iceland	3-5	12	48	12	49	*5*	9	88	88	87	0.99
136	Ireland	3-3	...	...	...	...	...	...	...	...	...	...
137	Israel	3-5	355	48	394	48	7	5	105	106	105	0.98
138	Italy	3-5	1 578	48	1 653	48	30	32	95	96	95	0.98
139	Luxembourg	3-5	12	49	15	48	5	7	73	73	73	1.00
140	Malta	3-4	10	48	9[y]	50[y]	37	39[y]	103	103	102	0.99
141	Monaco[5]	3-5	0.9	52	**0.9**	**51**	26	**20**	...	...	...	...
142	Netherlands	4-5	390	49	401	49	69	...	97	98	97	0.99
143	Norway	3-5	139	50	161	...	40	44	75	73	77	1.06
144	Portugal	3-5	220	49	264	49	52	48	69	69	69	0.99
145	San Marino[5]	3-5	...	...	**1**	**46**	...	.	...	...	...	...
146	Spain	3-5	1 131	49	1 560	49	32	36	100	100	100	1.00
147	Sweden	3-6	360	49	333[z]	50[z]	10	12[z]	76	76	76	1.01
148	Switzerland	5-6	158	48	153	48	6	9	89	89	88	0.99
149	United Kingdom[8]	3-4	1 155	49	999	50	6	29	77	77	77	1.00
150	United States	3-5	7 183	48	7 513	48	34	35	58	59	57	0.97
	South and West Asia											
151	Afghanistan	3-6	...	...	...	...	...	...	...	...	...	...
152	Bangladesh	3-5	1 825	50	...	...	...	...	17	17	17	1.04
153	Bhutan	4-5	0.3	48	**0.3**	**51**	100	**100**	0.9	1.0	0.9	0.93
154	India	3-5	13 869	48	29 757[z]	49[z]	...	...	18	18	19	1.02
155	Iran, Islamic Republic of[9]	5-5	220	50	561	51	...	8	13	13	14	1.05
156	Maldives	3-5	12	48	15	50	...	90	54	54	54	1.00
157	Nepal	3-4	...	...	**823**	**46**	...	**63**	...	...	...	...
158	Pakistan	3-4	...	...	4 075[y]	46[y]	...	...	...	...	...	...
159	Sri Lanka	4-4	...	...	...	...	...	...	...	...	...	...
	Sub-Saharan Africa											
160	Angola	3-5	*389*	*40*	...	...	...	...	*28*	*33*	*22*	*0.66*
161	Benin	4-5	18	48	31[z]	50[z]	20	37[y]	4	4	4	0.97
162	Botswana	3-5	...	...	20[y]	50[y]	...	96[y]	...	...	...	...
163	Burkina Faso	4-6	20	50	41	49	34	...	2	2	2	1.04
164	Burundi	4-6	5	50	16	*55*	49	46	0.8	0.8	0.8	1.01
165	Cameroon	4-5	104	48	217	50	57	62	11	11	11	0.95
166	Cape Verde	3-5	...	...	22	50	...	–	...	...	...	...
167	Central African Republic	3-5	...	...	12	52	...	35[y]	...	...	...	...
168	Chad	3-5	...	...	*8[y]*	*33[y]*	...	...	...	...	...	...
169	Comoros	3-5	1	51	*2[y]*	*48[y]*	100	*62[y]*	2	2	2	1.07
170	Congo	3-5	6	61	32	51	85	80	2	2	3	1.59

GROSS ENROLMENT RATIO (GER) IN PRE-PRIMARY EDUCATION (%)				NET ENROLMENT RATIO (NER) IN PRE-PRIMARY EDUCATION (%)				GROSS ENROLMENT RATIO (GER) IN PRE-PRIMARY AND OTHER ECCE PROGRAMMES (%)				NEW ENTRANTS TO THE FIRST GRADE OF PRIMARY EDUCATION WITH ECCE EXPERIENCE (%)			
School year ending in 2007				School year ending in 2007				School year ending in 2007				School year ending in 2007			
Total	Male	Female	GPI (F/M)	Total	Male	Female	GPI (F/M)	Total	Male	Female	GPI (F/M)	Total	Male	Female	
34[y]	34[y]	34[y]	1.01[y]	30[y]	30[y]	31[y]	1.03[y]	34[y]	34[y]	34[y]	1.01[y]	…	…	…	*115*
72	72	73	1.03	69	68	69	1.02	72	72	73	1.03	56	57	56	*116*
120	*114*	*126*	*1.10*	…	…	…	…	*161*	*154*	*168*	*1.09*	99	99	99	*117*
68	67	69	1.02	50	50	51	1.01	…	…	…	…	49	49	50	*118*
88[y]	*89[y]*	*86[y]*	*0.97[y]*	…	…	…	…	*88[y]*	*89[y]*	*86[y]*	*0.97[y]*	*100[y]*	*100[y]*	*100[y]*	*119*
85	83	87	1.04	*83[y]*	*82[y]*	*84[y]*	*1.02[y]*	85	83	87	1.04	100	100	100	*120*
81*	81*	81*	1.00*	65*	65*	65*	1.00*	81*	81*	81*	1.00*	78	78	79	*121*
118[y]	*132[y]*	*106[y]*	*0.80[y]*	*73[y]*	*80[y]*	*68[y]*	*0.85[y]*	*118[y]*	*132[y]*	*106[y]*	*0.80[y]*	100[y]	…	…	*122*
80	80	81	1.01	72	72	72.3	1.01	80	80	81	1.01	96[z]	96[z]	96[z]	*123*
62	62	62	1.00	55	55	55	1.01	84	84	84	1.00	74	74	75	*124*
North America and Western Europe															
101	99	103	1.04	86	84	87	1.04	101	99	103	1.04	100	100	100	*125*
92	92	91	0.99	*87[z]*	*87[z]*	*86[z]*	*0.99[z]*	92	92	91	0.99	…	…	…	*126*
122	122	122	0.99	100	100	100	1.00	122	122	122	0.99	…	…	…	*127*
70[z]	71[z]	70[z]	0.99[z]	…	…	…	…	…	…	…	…	…	…	…	*128*
80	80	79	0.99	70	70	70	0.99	80	80	79	0.99	…	…	…	*129*
96	96	96	1.00	92	91	94	1.03	…	…	…	…	…	…	…	*130*
64	64	64	0.99	63	63	63	1.00	64	64	64	0.99	…	…	…	*131*
113	113	113	1.00	100	100	100	1.00	113	113	113	1.00	…	…	…	*132*
107	108	106	0.99	…	…	…	…	107	108	106	0.99	…	…	…	*133*
69	69	69	1.01	68	68	69	1.02	69	69	69	1.01	…	…	…	*134*
97	97	97	1.00	97	97	97	1.00	97	97	97	1.00	…	…	…	*135*
…	…	…	…	…	…	…	…	…	…	…	…	…	…	…	*136*
98	98	97	0.99	93	92	93	1.01	98	98	97	0.99	…	…	…	*137*
103	104	103	0.99	98	99	98	0.99	103	104	103	0.99	…	…	…	*138*
87	87	87	1.00	85	85	85	1.00	87	87	87	1.00	…	…	…	*139*
97[y]	95[y]	100[y]	1.05[y]	83[y]	82[y]	85[y]	1.04[y]	97[y]	95[y]	100[y]	1.05[y]	…	…	…	*140*
…	…	…	…	…	…	…	…	…	…	…	…	…	…	…	*141*
102	102	102	1.00	100	100	100	1.00	102	102	102	1.00	…	…	…	*142*
92	…	…	…	92	…	…	…	92	…	…	…	…	…	…	*143*
79	79	80	1.01	79	78	79	1.02	79	79	80	1.01	…	…	…	*144*
…	…	…	…	…	…	…	…	…	…	…	…	…	…	…	*145*
122	122	123	1.01	99	99	100	1.01	122	122	123	1.01	…	…	…	*146*
95[z]	93[z]	98[z]	1.05[z]	95[z]	92[z]	98[z]	1.06[z]	95[z]	93[z]	98[z]	1.05[z]	…	…	…	*147*
99	99	99	1.00	73	74	73	0.98	99	99	99	1.00	…	…	…	*148*
73	72	74	1.03	68	67	69	1.03	73	72	74	1.03	…	…	…	*149*
62	63	62	0.98	57	57	57	1.00	62	63	62	0.98	…	…	…	*150*
South and West Asia															
…	…	…	…	…	…	…	…	…	…	…	…	…	…	…	*151*
…	…	…	…	…	…	…	…	…	…	…	…	45[y]	44[y]	46[y]	*152*
1	**1**	**1**	**1.09**	…	…	…	…	**1**	**1**	**1**	**1.09**	…	…	…	*153*
40[z]	39[z]	40[z]	1.04[z]	…	…	…	…	…	…	…	…	…	…	…	*154*
54	51	57	1.11	…	…	…	…	54	51	57	1.11	31[y]	34[y]	29[y]	*155*
85	84	86	1.03	67	67	68	1.01	85	84	86	1.03	88	88	87	*156*
57	**60**	**54**	**0.90**	**35**	**38**	**32**	**0.84**	**57**	**60**	**54**	**0.90**	**35**	**36**	**34**	*157*
52[y]	55[y]	50[y]	0.90[y]	43[y]	45[y]	40[y]	0.89[y]	…	…	…	…	57[y]	52[y]	63[y]	*158*
…	…	…	…	…	…	…	…	…	…	…	…	…	…	…	*159*
Sub-Saharan Africa															
…	…	…	…	…	…	…	…	…	…	…	…	…	…	…	*160*
6[z]	6[z]	6[z]	1.05[z]	*3[y]*	*3[y]*	*3[y]*	*1.03[y]*	…	…	…	…	…	…	…	*161*
15[y]	15[y]	15[y]	1.00[y]	11[y]	11[y]	11[y]	1.01[y]	15[y]	15[y]	15[y]	1.00[y]	…	…	…	*162*
3	3	3	1.01	…	…	…	…	3	3	3	1.01	5	5	5	*163*
2	*2*	*2*	*1.21*	…	…	…	…	2	*2*	*2*	*1.21*	1[z]	1[z]	1[z]	*164*
21	21	21	1.01	14	14	15	1.01	21	21	21	1.01	…	…	…	*165*
53	53	53	1.00	49	49	49	1.01	53	53	53	1.00	85	84	87	*166*
3	3	3	1.07	…	…	…	…	3	3	3	1.07	…	…	…	*167*
1[y]	*1[y]*	*1[y]*	*0.49[y]*	…	…	…	…	…	…	…	…	…	…	…	*168*
3[y]	*3[y]*	*3[y]*	*0.96[y]*	…	…	…	…	…	…	…	…	…	…	…	*169*
10	9	10	1.06	10	9	10	1.06	10	9	10	1.06	12[y]	11[y]	13[y]	*170*

Table 3B (continued)

	Country or territory	Age group	ENROLMENT IN PRE-PRIMARY EDUCATION				Enrolment in private institutions as % of total enrolment		GROSS ENROLMENT RATIO (GER) IN PRE-PRIMARY EDUCATION (%)			
			School year ending in				School year ending in		School year ending in			
			1999		2007		1999	2007	1999			
		2007	Total (000)	% F	Total (000)	% F			Total	Male	Female	GPI (F/M)
171	Côte d'Ivoire	3-5	36	49	52	50	46	46	2	2	2	0.96
172	Democratic Rep. of the Congo	3-5	...	...	172	51	...	69	...	...	...	...
173	Equatorial Guinea	3-6	17	51	40	57	37	49[y]	34	33	34	1.04
174	Eritrea	5-6	12	47	37	49	97	45	5	6	5	0.89
175	Ethiopia	4-6	90	49	219	49	100	95	1	1	1	0.97
176	Gabon	3-5	...	...	...	...	...	...	...	...	...	...
177	Gambia	3-6	29	47	***43***	***50***	...	100	18	19	17	0.91
178	Ghana	3-5	*667*	*49*	**1 258**	**50**	*33*	**19**	*39*	*39*	*39*	*1.02*
179	Guinea	4-6	...	...	86	49	...	86	...	...	...	...
180	Guinea-Bissau	4-6	*4*	*51*	...	...	*62*	...	*3*	*3*	*3*	*1.05*
181	Kenya	3-5	1 188	50	1 691	48	10	35	44	44	43	1.00
182	Lesotho	3-5	*33*	*52*	30[z]	64[z]	*100*	100[z]	*21*	*20*	*22*	*1.08*
183	Liberia	3-5	112	42	**491**	**49**	39	**24**	41	47	35	0.74
184	Madagascar	3-5	*50*	*51*	153	51	*93*	94	*3*	*3*	*3*	*1.02*
185	Malawi	3-5	...	...	...	...	...	...	...	...	...	...
186	Mali	3-6	21	51	55	...	...	...	2	2	2	1.06
187	Mauritius	3-4	42	50	36	50	85	82	96	95	97	1.02
188	Mozambique	3-5	...	...	...	...	...	...	...	...	...	...
189	Namibia	5-6	35	53	33[z]	50[z]	100	...	31	29	33	1.14
190	Niger	4-6	12	50	28	50	33	29	1	1	1	1.04
191	Nigeria	3-5	...	...	2 041[z]	49[z]	...	...	...	...	...	...
192	Rwanda	4-6	...	...	...	...	...	...	...	...	...	...
193	Sao Tome and Principe	3-6	4	52	**6**	**51**	–	**0.5**	25	24	26	1.12
194	Senegal	4-6	24	50	99	52	68	51	3	3	3	1.00
195	Seychelles[1]	4-5	3	49	3	48	5	6	109	107	111	1.04
196	Sierra Leone	3-5	...	...	25	52	...	50	...	...	...	...
197	Somalia	3-5	...	...	...	...	...	...	...	...	...	...
198	South Africa	6-6	207	50	522	50	26	6	21	20	21	1.01
199	Swaziland	3-5	...	...	*15*[y]	*49*[y]	...	.[y]	...	...	...	...
200	Togo	3-5	11	50	23	50	53	55	2	2	2	0.99
201	Uganda	4-5	*66*	*50*	77	51	*100*	100	*4*	*4*	*4*	*1.00*
202	United Republic of Tanzania	5-6	...	...	**896**	**50**	...	**10**	...	...	...	...
203	Zambia	3-6	...	...	...	...	...	...	...	...	...	...
204	Zimbabwe	3-5	*439*	*51*	...	...	...	...	*41*	*40*	*41*	*1.03*

			Sum	% F	Sum	% F	Median		Weighted average			
I	World	...	112 562	48	139 345	48	32	34	33	33	32	0.96
II	Countries in transition	...	7 047	47	7 508	51	0.02	0.8	45	47	44	0.95
III	Developed countries	...	25 376	49	26 308	48	6	9	73	73	73	0.99
IV	Developing countries	...	80 139	47	105 529	48	47	49	27	28	27	0.96
V	Arab States	...	2 441	43	3 079	47	83	72	15	17	13	0.77
VI	Central and Eastern Europe	...	9 455	48	9 924	50	0.7	2	50	50	49	0.97
VII	Central Asia	...	1 273	48	1 433	48	0.1	0.8	19	20	19	0.95
VIII	East Asia and the Pacific	...	37 027	47	38 623	46	49	57	40	40	39	0.98
IX	East Asia	...	36 615	47	38 163	46	57	56	40	40	39	0.98
X	Pacific	...	412	49	460	48	...	...	61	61	61	1.00
XI	Latin America and the Caribbean	...	16 392	49	19 952	49	29	39	56	55	56	1.02
XII	Caribbean	...	672	50	779	51	88	83	65	64	67	1.05
XIII	Latin America	...	15 720	49	19 173	49	23	20	55	55	56	1.01
XIV	North America and Western Europe	...	19 133	48	20 236	48	25	20	75	76	74	0.98
XV	South and West Asia	...	21 425	46	36 225	48	...	...	21	22	20	0.94
XVI	Sub-Saharan Africa	...	5 416	48	9 873	50	53	49	10	10	10	0.94

Source: UNESCO Institute for Statistics database (UIS, 2009).

1. National population data were used to calculate enrolment ratios.
2. Enrolment and population data exclude Transnistria.
3. Enrolment and population data exclude the Nagorno-Karabakh region.
4. Enrolment ratios were not calculated due to inconsistencies in the population data.
5. Enrolment ratios were not calculated due to lack of United Nations population data by age.
6. Enrolment declined from 2005 to 2007 mainly because the data collection reference date was shifted from the last Wednesday of March to the last Wednesday of May to account for duplicates (enrolments), and transfers of students and teachers (from one school to another), common features at the beginning of the year. At this point of the school year, it is believed, the education system becomes stable, so the data collected should represent the current school year.

	GROSS ENROLMENT RATIO (GER) IN PRE-PRIMARY EDUCATION (%) — School year ending in 2007				NET ENROLMENT RATIO (NER) IN PRE-PRIMARY EDUCATION (%) — School year ending in 2007				GROSS ENROLMENT RATIO (GER) IN PRE-PRIMARY AND OTHER ECCE PROGRAMMES (%) — School year ending in 2007				NEW ENTRANTS TO THE FIRST GRADE OF PRIMARY EDUCATION WITH ECCE EXPERIENCE (%) — School year ending in 2007		
	Total	Male	Female	GPI (F/M)	Total	Male	Female	GPI (F/M)	Total	Male	Female	GPI (F/M)	Total	Male	Female
171	3	3	3	1.00	…	…	…	…	3	3	3	1.00	…	…	…
172	3	3	3	1.05	…	…	…	…	3	3	3	1.05	…	…	…
173	66	57	76	1.33	…	…	…	…	…	…	…	…	70[y]	67[y]	72[y]
174	14	14	13	0.96	9	9	9	0.96	14	14	13	0.96	…	…	…
175	3	3	3	0.96	2	2	2	0.96	3	3	3	0.96	…	…	…
176	…	…	…	…	…	…	…	…	…	…	…	…	…	…	…
177	***22***	***22***	***22***	***1.02***	***19***	***19***	***20***	***1.05***	…	…	…	…	…	…	…
178	**68**	**67**	**69**	**1.04**	**47**	**46**	**49**	**1.05**	**78**	**76**	**79**	**1.03**	…	…	…
179	10	10	10	1.01	7	7	7	1.00	10	10	10	1.01	20	20	21
180	…	…	…	…	…	…	…	…	…	…	…	…	…	…	…
181	48	49	47	0.94	26	27	26	0.98	48	49	47	0.94	…	…	…
182	18[z]	13[z]	23[z]	1.79[z]	12[z]	7[z]	16[z]	2.19[z]	…	…	…	…	…	…	…
183	**125**	**127**	**123**	**0.97**	**44**	**44**	**43**	**0.97**	**125**	**127**	**123**	**0.97**	…	…	…
184	8	8	9	1.03	8	8	8	1.03	8	8	9	1.03	…	…	…
185	…	…	…	…	…	…	…	…	…	…	…	…	…	…	…
186	3	…	…	…	…	…	…	…	3	…	…	…	12	12	12
187	99	98	100	1.02	90	89	91	1.02	99	98	100	1.02	100	100	100
188	…	…	…	…	…	…	…	…	…	…	…	…	…	…	…
189	32[z]	32[z]	32[z]	1.00[z]	…	…	…	…	…	…	…	…	…	…	…
190	2	2	2	1.05	2	2	2	1.04	2	2	2	1.05	20	19	21
191	15[z]	15[z]	15[z]	1.00[z]	…	…	…	…	15[z]	15[z]	15[z]	1.00[z]	…	…	…
192	…	…	…	…	…	…	…	…	…	…	…	…	…	…	…
193	**36**	**35**	**37**	**1.06**	**36**	**35**	**37**	**1.06**	…	…	…	…	42	42	43
194	9	9	10	1.12	6	6	7	1.11	…	…	…	…	…	…	…
195	109	110	107	0.97	95	97	92	0.95	109	110	107	0.97	…	…	…
196	5	4	5	1.07	4	4	4	1.07	…	…	…	…	…	…	…
197	…	…	…	…	…	…	…	…	…	…	…	…	…	…	…
198	51	50	51	1.01	11[y]	11[y]	11[y]	1.01[y]	…	…	…	…	…	…	…
199	*17[y]*	*17[y]*	*17[y]*	*0.99[y]*	*11[y]*	*11[y]*	*11[y]*	*0.99[y]*	*17[y]*	*17[y]*	*17[y]*	*0.99[y]*	…	…	…
200	4	4	4	1.01	4	4	4	1.01	4	4	4	1.01	…	…	…
201	4	3	4	1.05	2	2	2	1.04	4	3	4	1.05	…	…	…
202	**35**	**34**	**35**	**1.02**	***35***	***34***	***35***	***1.02***	**35**	**34**	**35**	**1.02**	…	…	…
203	…	…	…	…	…	…	…	…	…	…	…	…	17	16	17
204	…	…	…	…	…	…	…	…	…	…	…	…	…	…	…
	Weighted average				Weighted average				Weighted average				Median		
I	41	41	41	0.99	…	…	…	…	…	…	…	…	…	…	…
II	63	60	66	1.09	…	…	…	…	…	…	…	…	…	…	…
III	80	81	80	0.99	…	…	…	…	…	…	…	…	…	…	…
IV	36	36	35	0.98	…	…	…	…	…	…	…	…	…	…	…
V	19	20	18	0.91	…	…	…	…	…	…	…	…	…	…	…
VI	64	62	66	1.06	…	…	…	…	…	…	…	…	…	…	…
VII	28	28	27	0.98	…	…	…	…	…	…	…	…	…	…	…
VIII	47	48	46	0.96	…	…	…	…	…	…	…	…	…	…	…
IX	47	48	46	0.96	…	…	…	…	…	…	…	…	…	…	…
X	67	68	67	0.98	…	…	…	…	…	…	…	…	…	…	…
XI	65	65	66	1.00	…	…	…	…	…	…	…	…	…	…	…
XII	74	72	76	1.06	…	…	…	…	…	…	…	…	…	…	…
XIII	65	65	65	1.00	…	…	…	…	…	…	…	…	…	…	…
XIV	82	82	81	0.99	…	…	…	…	…	…	…	…	…	…	…
XV	36	36	37	1.02	…	…	…	…	…	…	…	…	…	…	…
XVI	15	15	15	1.00	…	…	…	…	…	…	…	…	…	…	…

7. Data include French overseas departments and territories (DOM-TOM).

8. The decline in enrolment is essentially due to a reclassification of programmes. From 2004, it was decided to include children categorized as being aged '4 rising 5' in primary education enrolment rather than pre-primary enrolment even if they started the school year at the latter level. Such children typically (though not always) start primary school reception classes in the second or third term of the school year.

9. The apparent increase in the gender parity index (GPI) is due to the inclusion in enrolment statistics in recent years of literacy programmes in which 80% of participants are women.

Data in italic are UIS estimates.

Data in bold are for the school year ending in 2008.

(z) Data are for the school year ending in 2006.

(y) Data are for the school year ending in 2005.

(*) National estimate.

Table 4
Access to primary education

Country or territory	Compulsory education (age group)	Legal guarantees of free education[1]	New entrants (000) School year ending in		GROSS INTAKE RATE (GIR) IN PRIMARY EDUCATION (%) School year ending in							
			1999	2007	1999				2007			
					Total	Male	Female	GPI (F/M)	Total	Male	Female	GPI (F/M)
Arab States												
Algeria[2]	6-16	Yes	745	580	101	102	100	0.98	101	102	100	0.98
Bahrain	6-14	Yes	13	15[z]	105	103	107	1.04	125[z]	124[z]	126[z]	1.02[z]
Djibouti	6-15	No	6	**13**	29	33	25	0.74	**63**	**65**	**60**	**0.92**
Egypt[3]	6-14	Yes	*1 451*	1 702	*92*	*94*	*91*	*0.96*	103	105	102	0.97
Iraq	6-11	Yes	*709*	*844*[y]	*102*	*109*	*95*	*0.88*	*108*[y]	*111*[y]	*105*[y]	*0.94*[y]
Jordan[2]	6-16	Yes	126	135	101	100	101	1.00	92	92	93	1.02
Kuwait[2]	6-14	Yes	35	43	97	97	98	1.01	95	97	94	0.98
Lebanon[3]	6-15	Yes	71	**67**	93	97	90	0.92	**89**	**90**	**87**	**0.97**
Libyan Arab Jamahiriya[2]	6-15	Yes	…	…	…	…	…	…	…	…	…	…
Mauritania[3]	6-16	Yes	…	97	…	…	…	…	117	115	120	1.05
Morocco	6-15	Yes	731	680	112	115	108	0.94	114	116	112	0.97
Oman	…	Yes	52	45	87	87	87	1.00	78	77	78	1.01
Palestinian A. T.	6-15	…	95	100	103	103	104	1.01	79	80	79	0.99
Qatar[3]	6-17	Yes	*11*	14	*108*	*109*	*107*	*0.98*	115	115	116	1.01
Saudi Arabia	6-11	Yes	…	538*	…	…	…	…	99*	98*	99*	1.00*
Sudan[3]	6-13	Yes	…	835	…	…	…	…	80	86	74	0.86
Syrian Arab Republic	6-14	Yes	466	565	106	109	103	0.94	121	123	119	0.97
Tunisia	6-16	Yes	204	160	100	100	100	1.00	101	100	101	1.01
United Arab Emirates[2,3]	6-11	Yes	47	61	93	95	92	0.97	107	108	106	0.99
Yemen[3]	6-14	Yes	440	720[y]	76	88	63	0.71	112[y]	122[y]	102[y]	0.83[y]
Central and Eastern Europe												
Albania[3]	6-13	Yes	*67*	…	*96*	*97*	*95*	*0.98*	…	…	…	…
Belarus[3]	6-14	Yes	173	91	131	132	131	0.99	102	103	101	0.99
Bosnia and Herzegovina[3]	…	Yes	…	…	…	…	…	…	…	…	…	…
Bulgaria[2,3]	7-16	Yes	93	69	101	102	100	0.98	109	109	110	1.01
Croatia[3]	7-15	Yes	50	44	94	95	93	0.98	95	95	95	0.99
Czech Republic	6-15	Yes	124	92	100	101	99	0.98	109	110	108	0.98
Estonia	7-15	Yes	18	12	100	101	100	0.99	99	99	98	0.99
Hungary	7-16	Yes	127	95	102	104	101	0.97	97	97	96	0.99
Latvia[3]	7-15	Yes	32	18[z]	98	*99*	*98*	*1.00*	95[z]	95[z]	95[z]	1.00[z]
Lithuania[2]	7-16	Yes	54	34	104	105	104	0.99	99	99	98	0.99
Montenegro	7-14	…	…	…	…	…	…	…	…	…	…	…
Poland[2,4]	7-15	Yes	535	373	101	*101*	*100*	*0.99*	97	…	…	…
Republic of Moldova[3,5,6]	7-15	Yes	62	38	105	*105*	*104*	*1.00*	96	96	96	0.99
Romania[3]	7-14	Yes	269	219	94	95	94	0.99	98	98	98	1.00
Russian Federation[3]	6-15	Yes	1 866	1 244	96	…	…	…	97	…	…	…
Serbia	7-14	Yes	…	…	…	…	…	…	…	…	…	…
Slovakia[2]	6-16	Yes	75	54	102	102	101	0.99	102	103	102	1.00
Slovenia[2]	6-15	Yes	21	18	98	98	97	0.99	100	100	100	1.00
TFYR Macedonia[2,3]	6-15	Yes	32	24	102	102	102	1.00	96	95	96	1.01
Turkey[3]	6-14	Yes	…	*1 335*	…	…	…	…	*97*	*98*	*95*	*0.96*
Ukraine[3]	6-17	Yes	623	390	97	98*	97*	0.99*	100	101*	100*	0.99*
Central Asia												
Armenia[3]	7-15	Yes	…	47	…	…	…	…	131	130	133	1.02
Azerbaijan[3,5,7]	6-16	Yes	175	117	100	99	101	1.02	107	106	107	1.00
Georgia[3]	6-12	Yes	74	51	99	99	100	1.02	106	109	103	0.95
Kazakhstan	7-17	Yes	…	**250**	…	…	…	…	**117**	**117**	**117**	**1.00**
Kyrgyzstan[3]	7-15	Yes	120*	100	100*	99*	100*	1.02*	97	97	97	1.00
Mongolia[3]	7-15	Yes	70	56	109	109	109	1.00	125	124	126	1.02
Tajikistan[3]	7-15	Yes	177	176	99	102	96	0.95	104	106	102	0.96
Turkmenistan[3]	7-15	Yes	…	…	…	…	…	…	…	…	…	…
Uzbekistan[3]	7-17	Yes	677	505	102	…	…	…	93	95	92	0.97
East Asia and the Pacific												
Australia	5-15	Yes	…	*269*[y]	…	…	…	…	*106*[y]	*106*[y]	*105*[y]	*1.00*[y]
Brunei Darussalam	…	Yes	8	7	107	107	106	0.99	98	98	98	1.00
Cambodia[3]	.	Yes	*404*	447	*109*	*112*	*106*	*0.95*	137	141	132	0.94

NET INTAKE RATE (NIR) IN PRIMARY EDUCATION (%)								SCHOOL LIFE EXPECTANCY (expected number of years of formal schooling from primary to tertiary education)						
School year ending in								School year ending in						
1999				2007				1999			2007			
Total	Male	Female	GPI (F/M)	Total	Male	Female	GPI (F/M)	Total	Male	Female	Total	Male	Female	Country or territory
														Arab States
77	79	76	0.97	87	88	85	0.97	…	…	…	12.8[Y]	12.7[Y]	12.9[Y]	Algeria[2]
89	86	91	1.06	99[z]	99[z]	100[z]	1.01[z]	13.3	12.7	13.9	15.1[z]	14.5[z]	16.0[z]	Bahrain
21	24	18	0.75	**41**	**44**	**39**	**0.91**	3.1	3.6	2.6	4.7	5.3	4.1	Djibouti
…	…	…	…	…	…	…	…	12.7	…	…	…	…	…	Egypt[3]
79	83	74	0.90	83[Y]	86[Y]	79[Y]	0.92[Y]	8.2	9.4	7.0	9.7[Y]	11.1[Y]	8.3[Y]	Iraq
67	67	68	1.02	…	…	…	…	…	…	…	13.1	12.9	13.3	Jordan[2]
62	63	61	0.97	56	57	55	0.95	13.6	13.0	14.3	12.5[z]	11.9[z]	13.2[z]	Kuwait[2]
69	70	67	0.95	**62**	**64**	**60**	**0.95**	12.1	12.0	12.2	**13.3**	**12.8**	**13.7**	Lebanon[3]
…	…	…	…	…	…	…	…	…	…	…	…	…	…	Libyan Arab Jamahiriya[2]
…	…	…	…	38	38	38	1.02	7.0	…	…	8.2	…	…	Mauritania[3]
51	53	48	0.92	85	87	84	0.96	8.0	8.9	7.0	10.5	11.1	9.8	Morocco
70	70	71	1.01	53	53	54	1.02	…	…	…	11.5	11.5	11.5	Oman
…	…	…	…	57	58	57	0.98	12.0	12.0	12.1	13.2	12.7	13.7	Palestinian A. T.
…	…	…	…	66	65	67	1.03	12.5	11.7	13.6	13.6	13.3	14.3	Qatar[3]
…	…	…	…	60*	58*	62*	1.06*	…	…	…	13.2[Y]	13.3[Y]	13.0[Y]	Saudi Arabia
…	…	…	…	…	…	…	…	4.6	…	…	…	…	…	Sudan[3]
60	60	59	0.98	58	58	58	1.00	…	…	…	…	…	…	Syrian Arab Republic
…	…	…	…	90	90	90	1.00	12.8	12.9	12.7	14.0	…	…	Tunisia
49	49	49	1.00	42	43	41	0.97	10.8	10.4	11.5	…	…	…	United Arab Emirates[2,3]
25	30	20	0.68	…	…	…	…	7.6	10.2	4.8	8.7[Y]	10.6[Y]	6.6[Y]	Yemen[3]
														Central and Eastern Europe
…	…	…	…	…	…	…	…	10.5	10.5	10.6	…	…	…	Albania[3]
76	77	76	0.99	85	85	84	0.99	13.7	13.4	13.9	14.6	14.2	15.1	Belarus[3]
…	…	…	…	…	…	…	…	…	…	…	12.5	…	…	Bosnia and Herzegovina[3]
…	…	…	…	…	…	…	…	13.0	12.6	13.4	13.7	13.6	13.8	Bulgaria[2,3]
68	69	66	0.97	…	…	…	…	12.0	11.9	12.2	13.7	13.3	14.0	Croatia[3]
…	…	…	…	…	…	…	…	13.3	13.2	13.4	15.2	14.8	15.5	Czech Republic
…	…	…	…	81	83	78	0.95	14.4	13.9	14.9	15.8	14.8	16.8	Estonia
…	…	…	…	65[Y]	67[Y]	63[Y]	0.94[Y]	13.9	13.7	14.2	15.1	14.6	15.7	Hungary
…	…	…	…	…	…	…	…	13.7	13.0	14.4	15.5[z]	14.5[z]	16.6[z]	Latvia[3]
…	…	…	…	…	…	…	…	13.9	13.5	14.4	15.7	14.9	16.6	Lithuania[2]
…	…	…	…	…	…	…	…	…	…	…	…	…	…	Montenegro
…	…	…	…	…	…	…	…	14.6	14.2	14.9	15.2	14.7	15.8	Poland[2,4]
…	…	…	…	76	77	75	0.98	11.4	11.2	11.6	12.1	11.7	12.6	Republic of Moldova[3,5,6]
…	…	…	…	…	…	…	…	11.9	11.7	12.0	14.3	13.9	14.8	Romania[3]
…	…	…	…	…	…	…	…	…	…	…	13.7	13.2	14.3	Russian Federation[3]
…	…	…	…	…	…	…	…	…	…	…	…	…	…	Serbia
…	…	…	…	…	…	…	…	13.2	13.0	13.3	14.9	14.3	15.4	Slovakia[2]
…	…	…	…	…	…	…	…	14.7	14.2	15.1	16.8	16.1	17.6	Slovenia[2]
…	…	…	…	…	…	…	…	11.9	11.9	11.9	12.4	12.3	12.5	TFYR Macedonia[2,3]
…	…	…	…	74[Y]	75[Y]	73[Y]	0.97[Y]	…	…	…	11.6	12.4	10.8	Turkey[3]
69	…	…	…	78	78*	78*	0.99*	12.8	12.6	13.0	14.6	14.2*	14.9*	Ukraine[3]
														Central Asia
…	…	…	…	56	55	57	1.04	11.2	…	…	12.0	11.5	12.5	Armenia[3]
…	…	…	…	79	80	77	0.97	11.0	11.2	10.8	12.8	12.9	12.7	Azerbaijan[3,5,7]
69	68	69	1.02	86	88	85	0.97	11.6	11.6	11.6	12.7	12.6	12.8	Georgia[3]
…	…	…	…	**55**	**57**	**53**	**0.93**	12.1	11.9	12.3	**15.1**	**14.6**	**15.6**	Kazakhstan
58*	59*	58*	0.99*	59	60	58	0.97	11.5	11.3	11.6	12.5	12.1	12.9	Kyrgyzstan[3]
81	81	81	0.99	79	80	78	0.97	8.7	7.8	9.6	13.0	12.2	13.9	Mongolia[3]
93	95	90	0.95	98[z]	100[z]	95[z]	0.95[z]	9.7	10.6	8.9	11.0	12.0	10.0	Tajikistan[3]
…	…	…	…	…	…	…	…	…	…	…	…	…	…	Turkmenistan[3]
…	…	…	…	77[z]	…	…	…	10.6	10.7	10.5	11.6	11.8	11.4	Uzbekistan[3]
														East Asia and the Pacific
…	…	…	…	72[Y]	69[Y]	75[Y]	1.08[Y]	20.2	20.0	20.4	20.7	20.4	20.9	Australia
…	…	…	…	63	64	63	0.99	13.5	13.2	13.9	13.9	13.6	14.2	Brunei Darussalam
64	65	63	0.97	85	86	84	0.98	…	…	…	9.8	10.4	9.2	Cambodia[3]

Table 4 (continued)

Country or territory	Compulsory education (age group)	Legal guarantees of free education[1]	New entrants (000) School year ending in 1999	New entrants (000) School year ending in 2007	GROSS INTAKE RATE (GIR) IN PRIMARY EDUCATION (%) School year ending in 1999 Total	1999 Male	1999 Female	1999 GPI (F/M)	2007 Total	2007 Male	2007 Female	2007 GPI (F/M)
China[3,8]	6-14	Yes	…	17 339	…	…	…	…	93	93	92	0.99
Cook Islands[5]	5-15	…	0.6	0.3	131	…	…	…	*69*	*68*	*70*	*1.04*
DPR Korea	6-16	Yes	…	…	…	…	…	…	…	…	…	…
Fiji	6-15	No	…	*17*	…	…	…	…	*92*	*92*	*92*	*1.00*
Indonesia[3]	7-15	Yes	…	5 279	…	…	…	…	124	127	121	0.96
Japan[4]	6-15	Yes	1 222	1 187	101	102	101	1.00	98	98	99	1.00
Kiribati[5]	6-15	No	3	*3*[y]	109	106	113	1.06	*120*[y]	*119*[y]	*121*[y]	*1.02*[y]
Lao PDR[3]	6-14	Yes	180	192	114	121	108	0.89	131	135	126	0.94
Macao, China	5-14	…	6	4	88	88	89	1.02	96	98	94	0.96
Malaysia	6-11	No	…	513[z]	…	…	…	…	96[z]	96[z]	96[z]	0.99[z]
Marshall Islands[2,5]	6-14	No	1	2	*123*	*122*	*123*	*1.01*	100	105	96	0.91
Micronesia, Federated States of	6-14	No	…	…	…	…	…	…	…	…	…	…
Myanmar[3,9]	5-9	Yes	1 226	1 204	…	…	…	…	…	…	…	…
Nauru	6-16	No	…	0.2*	…	…	…	…	*71*	*65*	*77*	*1.19*
New Zealand[4]	5-16	Yes	…	*58*[y]	…	…	…	…	*104*[y]	*105*[y]	*104*[y]	*1.00*[y]
Niue[5]	5-16	…	0.05	*0.02*[y]	105	79	137	1.73	*81*[y]	*69*[y]	*93*[y]	*1.34*[y]
Palau[2,5]	6-17	Yes	*0.4*	…	*118*	*120*	*115*	*0.96*	…	…	…	…
Papua New Guinea	…	No	…	53[z]	…	…	…	…	…	…	…	…
Philippines[3]	6-12	Yes	2 551	2 657	133	136	129	0.95	130	134	125	0.94
Republic of Korea[2,4]	6-15	Yes	720	609	105	110	100	0.91	114	113	115	1.02
Samoa	5-12	No	5	5	105	106	104	0.98	96	96	95	0.99
Singapore	6-14	No	…	…	…	…	…	…	…	…	…	…
Solomon Islands	…	No	…	…	…	…	…	…	…	…	…	…
Thailand	6-16	Yes	*1 037*	684	*110*	*111*	*107*	*0.96*	77	71	83	1.16
Timor-Leste[3]	6-11	Yes	…	39	…	…	…	…	112	113	111	0.98
Tokelau	.	…	…	…	…	…	…	…	…	…	…	…
Tonga	6-14	No	3	3[z]	104	107	100	0.94	116[z]	118[z]	114[z]	0.97[z]
Tuvalu[5]	7-14	No	*0.2*	*0.3*[z]	*89*	*94*	*83*	*0.89*	*112*[z]	*120*[z]	*104*[z]	*0.86*[z]
Vanuatu	.	No	*6*	…	*109*	*109*	*109*	*1.00*	…	…	…	…
Viet Nam[3,9]	6-14	Yes	2 035	*1 355*[z]	106	110	103	0.93	…	…	…	…
Latin America and the Caribbean												
Anguilla[3,10]	5-17	Yes	0.2	0.2	…	…	…	…	…	…	…	…
Antigua and Barbuda[5]	5-16	Yes	…	2	…	…	…	…	100	103	96	0.93
Argentina[2,3]	5-15	Yes	781	751[z]	112	112	111	0.99	111[z]	111[z]	111[z]	1.00[z]
Aruba	6-16	…	1	1	109	112	106	0.94	98	99	98	0.99
Bahamas	5-16	No	7	6	116	122	111	0.91	112	114	110	0.97
Barbados	5-16	Yes	4	4	99	99	98	0.99	118	119	117	0.98
Belize	5-14	Yes	8	9	128	129	126	0.98	122	120	124	1.04
Bermuda[5]	5-16	…	…	0.8[z]	…	…	…	…	103[z]	…	…	…
Bolivia[3]	6-13	Yes	282	287	124	124	125	1.01	121	121	120	1.00
Brazil[3]	7-14	Yes	…	4 323[y]	…	…	…	…	125[y]	…	…	…
British Virgin Islands[5]	5-16	…	0.4	0.5	106	109	103	0.95	*105*	*105*	*105*	*1.00*
Cayman Islands	5-16	…	0.6	0.7	…	…	…	…	…	…	…	…
Chile[2,3]	6-21	Yes	284	256	95	95	94	0.99	103	103	102	0.98
Colombia[2]	5-15	No	1 267	1 099	137	140	134	0.96	122	123	121	0.98
Costa Rica[3]	6-15	Yes	87	81	104	104	105	1.01	102	101	102	1.01
Cuba	6-14	Yes	164	138	106	109	104	0.95	98	98	98	1.00
Dominica[5,10]	5-16	No	2	1	111	118	104	0.88	…	…	…	…
Dominican Republic[3]	5-14	Yes	267	259	132	137	128	0.94	120	123	116	0.95
Ecuador[3]	5-14	Yes	374	405	134	134	134	1.00	140	141	139	0.99
El Salvador[3]	7-15	Yes	*196*	168	*134*	*138*	*129*	*0.94*	109	111	107	0.97
Grenada[5]	5-16	No	…	2	…	…	…	…	84	87	81	0.93
Guatemala[3]	6-15	Yes	425	468	131	135	127	0.94	123	124	122	0.98
Guyana[3]	6-15	Yes	18	16	126	123	128	1.05	97	98	97	0.99
Haiti	6-11	No	…	…	…	…	…	…	…	…	…	…
Honduras[2,3]	6-13	Yes	…	252[z]	…	…	…	…	137[z]	139[z]	134[z]	0.96[z]
Jamaica	6-12	No	…	*48*	…	…	…	…	*88*	*88*	*88*	*0.99*
Mexico[3]	6-15	Yes	2 509	2 501	111	111	111	1.00	119	120	119	0.99
Montserrat[5]	5-16	…	0.1	0.1	…	…	…	…	99	77	125	1.63
Netherlands Antilles	6-15	…	*4*	…	*112*	*109*	*115*	*1.06*	…	…	…	…
Nicaragua[3]	6-11	Yes	203	223	141	144	137	0.95	166	172	161	0.93

NET INTAKE RATE (NIR) IN PRIMARY EDUCATION (%)								SCHOOL LIFE EXPECTANCY (expected number of years of formal schooling from primary to tertiary education)						
School year ending in								School year ending in						
1999				2007				1999			2007			
Total	Male	Female	GPI (F/M)	Total	Male	Female	GPI (F/M)	Total	Male	Female	Total	Male	Female	Country or territory
…	…	…	…	…	…	…	…	…	…	…	11.4	11.4	11.4	China[3,8]
…	…	…	…	51[Y]	49[Y]	53[Y]	1.08[Y]	10.6	10.5	10.6	9.4	9.3	9.5	Cook Islands[5]
…	…	…	…	…	…	…	…	…	…	…	…	…	…	DPR Korea
…	…	…	…	70[Y]	70[Y]	70[Y]	1.00[Y]	…	…	…	13.0[Y]	12.8[Y]	13.2[Y]	Fiji
…	…	…	…	40	38	41	1.09	…	…	…	12.3	12.5	12.2	Indonesia[3]
…	…	…	…	…	…	…	…	14.4	14.6	14.3	15.0	15.1	14.8	Japan[4]
…	…	…	…	…	…	…	…	11.7	11.2	12.2	12.3[Y]	11.9[Y]	12.7[Y]	Kiribati[5]
52	53	51	0.96	74	73	74	1.00	8.2	9.2	7.2	9.4	10.2	8.5	Lao PDR[3]
63	61	65	1.07	81	82	79	0.97	12.1	12.4	11.9	15.0	15.6	14.6	Macao, China
…	…	…	…	…	…	…	…	11.8	11.7	11.9	12.7[Y]	12.4[Y]	13.1[Y]	Malaysia
…	…	…	…	…	…	…	…	…	…	…	…	…	…	Marshall Islands[2,5]
…	…	…	…	…	…	…	…	…	…	…	…	…	…	Micronesia, Federated States of
…	…	…	…	…	…	…	…	…	…	…	…	…	…	Myanmar[3,9]
…	…	…	…	51	50	52	1.05	…	…	…	8.5[Z]	8.2[Z]	8.8[Z]	Nauru
…	…	…	…	100[Y]	100[Y]	100[Y]	1.00[Y]	17.3	16.7	17.9	19.9	19.1	20.6	New Zealand[4]
…	…	…	…	…	…	…	…	11.9	11.5	12.4	12.3[Y]	12.3[Y]	12.3[Y]	Niue[5]
…	…	…	…	…	…	…	…	…	…	…	…	…	…	Palau[2,5]
…	…	…	…	…	…	…	…	…	…	…	…	…	…	Papua New Guinea
46	47	45	0.95	45[Z]	42[Z]	47[Z]	1.12[Z]	11.6	11.4	11.9	11.8[Z]	11.5[Z]	12.1[Z]	Philippines[3]
96	100	91	0.91	98	…	…	…	15.3	16.3	14.2	16.9	18.0	15.7	Republic of Korea[2,4]
77	77	77	1.00	…	…	…	…	12.3	12.1	12.5	…	…	…	Samoa
…	…	…	…	…	…	…	…	…	…	…	…	…	…	Singapore
…	…	…	…	…	…	…	…	7.3	7.7	6.8	8.5[Y]	8.8[Y]	8.2[Y]	Solomon Islands
…	…	…	…	…	…	…	…	…	…	…	**13.7**	**13.2**	**14.2**	Thailand
…	…	…	…	39	39	40	1.02	…	…	…	…	…	…	Timor-Leste[3]
…	…	…	…	…	…	…	…	…	…	…	…	…	…	Tokelau
48	50	47	0.94	…	…	…	…	13.2	13.0	13.5	…	…	…	Tonga
…	…	…	…	…	…	…	…	…	…	…	…	…	…	Tuvalu[5]
…	…	…	…	…	…	…	…	9.2	…	…	…	…	…	Vanuatu
79	…	…	…	…	…	…	…	10.2	10.7	9.7	…	…	…	Viet Nam[3,9]
														Latin America and the Caribbean
…	…	…	…	…	…	…	…	…	…	…	11.2[Z]	11.0[Z]	11.4[Z]	Anguilla[3,10]
…	…	…	…	…	…	…	…	…	…	…	…	…	…	Antigua and Barbuda[5]
…	…	…	…	99[Z]	100[Z]	97[Z]	0.97[Z]	14.3	13.6	14.9	15.4[Z]	14.4[Z]	16.3[Z]	Argentina[2,3]
90	91	89	0.98	81[Y]	80[Y]	82[Y]	1.02[Y]	13.3	13.1	13.6	13.8	13.5	14.1	Aruba
84	85	82	0.96	71	71	71	1.01	…	…	…	…	…	…	Bahamas
77	77	76	0.99	97	98	96	0.98	13.3	12.7	13.9	15.0	13.9	16.0	Barbados
78	80	76	0.95	68	67	68	1.02	…	…	…	…	…	…	Belize
…	…	…	…	…	…	…	…	…	…	…	13.1[Y]	12.5[Y]	13.7[Y]	Bermuda[5]
69	68	69	1.03	71[Z]	71[Z]	72[Z]	1.01[Z]	13.5	…	…	…	…	…	Bolivia[3]
…	…	…	…	…	…	…	…	14.1	13.9	14.4	13.8	13.5	14.1	Brazil[3]
73	70	76	1.09	70[Y]	66[Y]	74[Y]	1.12[Y]	15.9	15.0	16.8	17.3[Y]	15.5[Y]	19.1[Y]	British Virgin Islands[5]
…	…	…	…	…	…	…	…	…	…	…	…	…	…	Cayman Islands
…	…	…	…	…	…	…	…	12.8	12.9	12.7	14.5	14.6	14.4	Chile[2,3]
60	61	59	0.96	60	60	59	0.99	11.1	10.8	11.4	12.6	12.3	12.9	Colombia[2]
…	…	…	…	64	63	66	1.04	10.3	10.2	10.4	11.7[Y]	11.5[Y]	12.0[Y]	Costa Rica[3]
98	…	…	…	98	98	98	1.00	12.4	12.2	12.6	17.1	15.6	18.8	Cuba
80	83	78	0.94	…	…	…	…	12.3	11.7	13.0	…	…	…	Dominica[5,10]
58	58	58	1.00	72	73	72	0.98	…	…	…	…	…	…	Dominican Republic[3]
84	83	84	1.01	90	90	90	1.01	…	…	…	13.3	13.1	13.5	Ecuador[3]
…	…	…	…	60	59	60	1.02	10.8	11.0	10.7	12.2	12.1	12.4	El Salvador[3]
…	…	…	…	67	70	64	0.92	…	…	…	12.1[Y]	12.0[Y]	12.2[Y]	Grenada[5]
56	58	54	0.92	73	74	72	0.98	…	…	…	10.6	11.0	10.3	Guatemala[3]
91	90	93	1.03	63	63	63	1.00	…	…	…	12.7	12.7	12.6	Guyana[3]
…	…	…	…	…	…	…	…	…	…	…	…	…	…	Haiti
…	…	…	…	70[Z]	69[Z]	72[Z]	1.05[Z]	…	…	…	…	…	…	Honduras[2,3]
…	…	…	…	75[Y]	74[Y]	76[Y]	1.03[Y]	…	…	…	…	…	…	Jamaica
89	89	89	1.01	…	…	…	…	11.8	11.9	11.7	13.6	13.7	13.5	Mexico[3]
…	…	…	…	48	41	56	1.37	…	…	…	15.1	13.8	16.9	Montserrat[5]
77	72	82	1.14	…	…	…	…	14.6	14.3	14.9	…	…	…	Netherlands Antilles
39	40	38	0.95	71	70	72	1.02	…	…	…	…	…	…	Nicaragua[3]

Table 4 (continued)

Country or territory	Compulsory education (age group)	Legal guarantees of free education[1]	New entrants (000) School year ending in 1999	New entrants (000) School year ending in 2007	GROSS INTAKE RATE (GIR) IN PRIMARY EDUCATION (%) School year ending in 1999 Total	1999 Male	1999 Female	1999 GPI (F/M)	2007 Total	2007 Male	2007 Female	2007 GPI (F/M)
Panama[3]	6-14	Yes	69	77	112	113	111	0.99	114	115	113	0.99
Paraguay[3]	6-14	Yes	*179*	158[y]	*131*	*134*	*128*	*0.96*	111[y]	113[y]	110[y]	0.97[y]
Peru[2,3]	6-18	Yes	676	644	110	110	110	1.00	116	114	118	1.04
Saint Kitts and Nevis	5-16	No	...	0.9	...	...	...	...	*86*	*81*	*91*	*1.13*
Saint Lucia	5-15	No	*4*	3	*107*	*109*	*106*	*0.97*	105	106	103	0.97
St Vincent/Grenadines	5-15	No	...	2	...	...	...	...	93	94	92	0.98
Suriname[3]	7-12	Yes	...	10	...	...	...	...	107	108	104	0.96
Trinidad and Tobago[2,3]	6-12	Yes	20	19	94	94	93	0.98	103	106	100	0.95
Turks and Caicos Islands	4-16	...	*0.3*	0.4[y]	...	...	...	...	*83*[y]	*83*[y]	*84*[y]	*1.01*[y]
Uruguay[3]	6-15	Yes	60	53	107	107	107	1.00	104	104	103	0.99
Venezuela, B. R.[2,3]	5-14	Yes	537	589	98	99	97	0.98	105	106	104	0.98
North America and Western Europe												
Andorra[2,5]	6-16	...	...	0.8	...	...	...	...	88	90	85	0.94
Austria[2,4]	6-15	Yes	100	85	106	107	105	0.98	103	105	101	0.97
Belgium[4]	6-18	Yes	...	115	...	...	...	...	100	100	101	1.02
Canada	6-16	Yes	...	351[z]	...	...	...	...	98[z]	98[z]	98[z]	0.99[z]
Cyprus[2,5]	6-15	Yes	...	9	...	...	...	...	107	109	106	0.98
Denmark	7-16	Yes	66	67	100	100	100	1.00	99	98	99	1.01
Finland	7-16	Yes	65	57	100	100	100	1.00	99	99	99	1.00
France[11]	6-16	Yes	736	...	102	*103*	*101*	*0.98*	...	...	...	...
Germany	6-18	Yes	869	794	100	101	100	1.00	102	102	101	0.99
Greece[2]	6-15	Yes	113	107	106	107	105	0.98	103	103	102	1.00
Iceland	6-16	Yes	4	4	99	101	97	0.96	103	102	103	1.01
Ireland	6-15	Yes	51	60	100	101	99	0.98	100	99	101	1.01
Israel[3]	5-15	Yes	...	132	...	...	...	...	101	100	103	1.03
Italy[2]	6-18	Yes	558	567	100	101	99	0.99	107	107	106	0.99
Luxembourg	6-15	Yes	5	6	97	...	...	...	101	103	99	0.96
Malta[2]	5-16	Yes	5	4[y]	102	103	102	0.99	94[y]	93[y]	95[y]	1.02[y]
Monaco[2]	6-16	No	...	...	...	...	...	...	...	...	...	...
Netherlands[2,4]	5-17	Yes	199	204	99	100	99	0.99	103	103	102	0.99
Norway	6-16	Yes	61	60	100	100	99	0.99	101	101	101	0.99
Portugal[2]	6-15	Yes	...	122	...	...	...	...	111	112	110	0.98
San Marino[2,10]	6-16	No	...	**0.3**	...	...	...	...	...	...	...	...
Spain	6-16	Yes	*403*	433	*104*	*104*	*104*	*1.00*	106	106	106	1.00
Sweden	7-16	Yes	127	92	104	105	103	0.98	100	101	100	1.00
Switzerland	7-15	Yes	82	74	93	91	95	1.04	91	89	93	1.05
United Kingdom	5-16	Yes	...	...	...	...	...	...	...	...	...	...
United States	6-17	No	4 322	4 205	104	107	101	0.95	105	102	108	1.05
South and West Asia												
Afghanistan[3]	7-15	Yes	...	811	...	...	...	...	98	116	80	0.69
Bangladesh[3]	6-10	Yes	...	3 986[z]	...	...	...	...	112[z]	110[z]	115[z]	1.04[z]
Bhutan[3]	...	Yes	12	**15**	79	83	75	0.90	**122**	**120**	**123**	**1.03**
India[3]	6-14	Yes	29 639	32 366[z]	120	129	111	0.86	130[z]	133[z]	126[z]	0.95[z]
Iran, Islamic Republic of[3,12]	6-10	Yes	1 563	*1 400*[z]	91	91	91	0.99	*130*[z]	*112*[z]	*150*[z]	*1.35*[z]
Maldives	6-12	No	8	6	102	101	102	1.01	102	102	103	1.00
Nepal[3]	5-10	Yes	879	**904**	132	150	113	0.76	**126**	**125**	**127**	**1.01**
Pakistan	5-9	No	...	4 551	...	...	...	...	118	127	109	0.86
Sri Lanka[2]	5-14	No	...	329[z]	...	...	...	...	112[z]	112[z]	112[z]	1.00[z]
Sub-Saharan Africa												
Angola	6-14	No	...	...	...	...	...	...	...	...	...	...
Benin	6-11	No	...	291[z]	...	...	...	...	115[z]	122[z]	108[z]	0.89[z]
Botswana	6-15	No	50	53[y]	114	115	113	0.99	122[y]	124[y]	120[y]	0.97[y]
Burkina Faso	6-16	No	154	**389**	45	52	37	0.72	**88**	**92**	**85**	**0.92**
Burundi	...	No	*146*	320	*71*	*78*	*64*	*0.83*	140	144	137	0.95
Cameroon	6-11	No	*335*	550	*74*	*82*	*67*	*0.81*	111	118	103	0.88
Cape Verde[2]	6-16	No	*13*	11	*101*	*102*	*100*	*0.98*	83	84	82	0.97
Central African Republic	6-15	No	...	**97**	...	...	...	...	**79**	**90**	**68**	**0.76**
Chad[2,3]	6-14	Yes	175	*316*	72	84	60	0.71	*97*	*111*	*83*	*0.75*
Comoros[2]	6-14	No	13	*16*[y]	70	76	64	0.84	*70*[y]	*74*[y]	*66*[y]	*0.89*[y]

NET INTAKE RATE (NIR) IN PRIMARY EDUCATION (%)								SCHOOL LIFE EXPECTANCY (expected number of years of formal schooling from primary to tertiary education)						
School year ending in								School year ending in						
1999				2007				1999			2007			
Total	Male	Female	GPI (F/M)	Total	Male	Female	GPI (F/M)	Total	Male	Female	Total	Male	Female	Country or territory
84	84	84	1.00	…	…	…	…	12.6	12.1	13.1	13.4[Z]	12.7[Z]	14.1[Z]	Panama[3]
…	…	…	…	69[Y]	68[Y]	70[Y]	1.04[Y]	11.5	11.5	11.5	12.0[Y]	12.0[Y]	12.0[Y]	Paraguay[3]
79	79	79	1.00	81	81	82	1.01	…	…	…	14.0[Z]	13.7[Z]	14.3[Z]	Peru[2,3]
…	…	…	…	60	54	65	1.20	…	…	…	12.3[Y]	12.1[Y]	12.5[Y]	Saint Kitts and Nevis
76	76	75	0.99	75[Z]	73[Z]	77[Z]	1.05[Z]	…	…	…	13.4	12.9	14.0	Saint Lucia
…	…	…	…	62[Y]	66[Y]	58[Y]	0.88[Y]	…	…	…	12.0[Y]	11.8[Y]	12.2[Y]	St Vincent/Grenadines
…	…	…	…	88	88	88	1.00	…	…	…	…	…	…	Suriname[3]
67	66	67	1.02	72	73	72	0.99	11.3	11.1	11.5	11.2[Y]	11.1[Y]	11.4[Y]	Trinidad and Tobago[2,3]
…	…	…	…	54[Y]	57[Y]	51[Y]	0.90[Y]	…	…	…	11.4[Y]	10.9[Y]	11.8[Y]	Turks and Caicos Islands
…	…	…	…	…	…	…	…	13.9	13.0	14.7	15.7	14.9	16.4	Uruguay[3]
60	60	60	1.01	69	69	69	1.01	…	…	…	12.7[Z]	…	…	Venezuela, B. R.[2,3]
														North America and Western Europe
…	…	…	…	41	44	38	0.87	…	…	…	11.1[Z]	10.9[*,Z]	11.4[*,Z]	Andorra[2,5]
…	…	…	…	…	…	…	…	15.2	15.3	15.2	15.2	15.0	15.4	Austria[2,4]
…	…	…	…	…	…	…	…	18.0	17.6	18.5	16.0	15.8	16.3	Belgium[4]
…	…	…	…	…	…	…	…	…	…	…	…	…	…	Canada
…	…	…	…	…	…	…	…	12.5	12.4	12.7	13.8	13.7	13.9	Cyprus[2,5]
…	…	…	…	73[Y]	69[Y]	77[Y]	1.11[Y]	16.1	15.6	16.6	16.9	16.2	17.5	Denmark
…	…	…	…	93[Y]	91[Y]	95[Y]	1.04[Y]	17.2	16.6	18.0	17.1	16.5	17.7	Finland
…	…	…	…	…	…	…	…	15.7	15.5	16.0	16.2	15.9	16.6	France[11]
…	…	…	…	…	…	…	…	…	…	…	…	…	…	Germany
97	97	96	0.99	94[Y]	93[Y]	94[Y]	1.00[Y]	13.8	13.5	14.1	16.5	16.4	16.6	Greece[2]
98	100	96	0.97	96[Y]	98[Y]	95[Y]	0.97[Y]	16.7	16.1	17.3	18.3	17.0	19.7	Iceland
…	…	…	…	…	…	…	…	16.5	16.1	16.9	17.8	17.6	18.1	Ireland
…	…	…	…	…	…	…	…	15.0	14.6	15.4	15.6	15.1	16.0	Israel[3]
…	…	…	…	…	…	…	…	14.7	14.5	15.0	16.5	16.0	16.9	Italy[2]
…	…	…	…	…	…	…	…	13.6	13.5	13.7	13.5[Z]	13.4[Z]	13.6[Z]	Luxembourg
…	…	…	…	…	…	…	…	…	…	…	14.8[Y]	14.8[Y]	14.9[Y]	Malta[2]
…	…	…	…	…	…	…	…	…	…	…	…	…	…	Monaco[2]
…	…	…	…	…	…	…	…	16.4	16.7	16.2	16.6	16.7	16.6	Netherlands[2,4]
…	…	…	…	…	…	…	…	17.2	16.7	17.7	17.5	16.9	18.2	Norway
…	…	…	…	…	…	…	…	15.7	15.3	16.0	15.4	15.1	15.7	Portugal[2]
…	…	…	…	…	…	…	…	…	…	…	…	…	…	San Marino[2,10]
…	…	…	…	…	…	…	…	15.8	15.5	16.2	16.2	15.8	16.7	Spain
…	…	…	…	97	98	97	0.99	18.8	17.2	20.5	15.6	14.9	16.4	Sweden
…	…	…	…	…	…	…	…	14.7	15.1	14.3	14.9	15.1	14.7	Switzerland
…	…	…	…	…	…	…	…	15.9	15.7	16.1	15.9	15.4	16.5	United Kingdom
…	…	…	…	75	72	78	1.07	15.7	…	…	15.8	15.1	16.6	United States
														South and West Asia
…	…	…	…	55	65	45	0.69	…	…	…	…	…	…	Afghanistan[3]
…	…	…	…	86[Z]	86[Z]	86[Z]	1.00[Z]	…	…	…	8.0	7.8	8.1	Bangladesh[3]
20	21	19	0.91	43[Z]	44[Z]	42[Z]	0.95[Z]	7.4	8.1	6.6	10.3[Z]	10.6[Z]	10.0[Z]	Bhutan[3]
…	…	…	…	…	…	…	…	…	…	…	10.0[Z]	10.6[Z]	9.4[Z]	India[3]
44	45	43	0.97	94[Y]	…	…	…	11.6	12.2	10.9	12.8[Y]	12.8[Y]	12.9[Y]	Iran, Islamic Republic of[3,12]
87	86	87	1.01	76	…	…	…	12.0	11.9	12.0	12.3[Z]	12.2[Z]	12.3[Z]	Maldives
…	…	…	…	74	74	74	1.00	…	…	…	9.8	…	…	Nepal[3]
…	…	…	…	92	99	85	0.86	…	…	…	7.1	7.9	6.3	Pakistan
…	…	…	…	…	…	…	…	…	…	…	…	…	…	Sri Lanka[2]
														Sub-Saharan Africa
…	…	…	…	…	…	…	…	…	…	…	…	…	…	Angola
…	…	…	…	48[Y]	51[Y]	45[Y]	0.89[Y]	6.4	7.9	4.8	8.4[Y]	…	…	Benin
23	21	25	1.20	31[Y]	28[Y]	34[Y]	1.22[Y]	11.5	11.4	11.5	11.9[Y]	11.8[Y]	12.0[Y]	Botswana
19	22	16	0.71	**43**	**45**	**40**	**0.91**	3.4	4.0	2.7	**5.7**	**6.2**	**5.1**	Burkina Faso
…	…	…	…	52	53	51	0.97	…	…	…	8.2	8.7	7.7	Burundi
…	…	…	…	…	…	…	…	7.2	…	…	9.0	9.8	8.2	Cameroon
65	64	66	1.03	71	70	71	1.01	…	…	…	11.4	11.1	11.7	Cape Verde[2]
…	…	…	…	…	…	…	…	…	…	…	…	…	…	Central African Republic
22	25	18	0.72	…	…	…	…	…	…	…	5.9[Y]	7.4[Y]	4.3[Y]	Chad[2,3]
16	18	13	0.70	…	…	…	…	6.5	7.1	5.9	…	…	…	Comoros[2]

Table 4 (continued)

Country or territory	Compulsory education (age group)	Legal guarantees of free education[1]	New entrants (000) School year ending in 1999	New entrants (000) School year ending in 2007	GIR 1999 Total	GIR 1999 Male	GIR 1999 Female	GIR 1999 GPI (F/M)	GIR 2007 Total	GIR 2007 Male	GIR 2007 Female	GIR 2007 GPI (F/M)
					GROSS INTAKE RATE (GIR) IN PRIMARY EDUCATION (%) School year ending in							
Congo[3]	6-16	Yes	32	*91*	37	36	37	1.02	*88*	*89*	*86*	*0.97*
Côte d'Ivoire	6-15	No	309	362	64	71	57	0.80	70	76	64	0.84
Democratic Rep. of the Congo[3]	6-15	Yes	767	2 034	50	49	52	1.07	106	114	99	0.87
Equatorial Guinea	7-11	Yes	...	15	...	...	...	...	111	114	109	0.96
Eritrea	7-14	No	57	53	54	60	49	0.81	41	44	38	0.87
Ethiopia	.	No	1 537	3 221	78	92	63	0.69	136	144	128	0.89
Gabon	6-16	Yes	...	...	...	...	...	...	...	...	...	...
Gambia[3]	7-12	Yes	*30*	***42***	*83*	*86*	*79*	*0.92*	***90***	***85***	***94***	***1.10***
Ghana[2,3]	6-15	Yes	469	**659**	85	87	83	0.96	**110**	**109**	**111**	**1.02**
Guinea[2]	7-16	No	119	244	52	58	46	0.80	94	97	90	0.93
Guinea-Bissau[3]	7-12	Yes	*35*	...	*92*	*106*	*79*	*0.74*	...	...	...	...
Kenya	6-13	No	892	*1 113*[y]	102	104	101	0.97	*110*[y]	*112*[y]	*108*[y]	*0.96*[y]
Lesotho	...	No	51	56[z]	99	99	100	1.01	102[z]	105[z]	99[z]	0.94[z]
Liberia[2]	6-16	No	50	**119**	60	73	46	0.63	**100**	**100**	**100**	**1.00**
Madagascar[3]	6-10	Yes	495	970	107	108	106	0.98	169	171	168	0.98
Malawi	6-13	No	616	639	175	174	177	1.02	142	137	147	1.07
Mali[3]	7-15	Yes	*171*	317	*58*	*67*	*50*	*0.75*	85	92	79	0.86
Mauritius[3]	5-16	Yes	22	19	98	96	99	1.04	101	100	102	1.02
Mozambique	6-12	No	536	1 049	104	112	95	0.84	161	166	156	0.94
Namibia[3]	7-16	Yes	54	*56*	98	97	99	1.02	*109*	*108*	*111*	*1.03*
Niger[3]	...	Yes	133	279	43	50	35	0.71	65	72	58	0.81
Nigeria[3]	6-14	Yes	*3 606*	4 127[z]	*99*	*110*	*87*	*0.79*	98[z]	106[z]	90[z]	0.85[z]
Rwanda[3]	7-12	Yes	295	537	127	129	126	0.97	207	209	205	0.98
Sao Tome and Principe[2]	7-13	Yes	4	**5**	106	108	105	0.97	**116**	**115**	**117**	**1.03**
Senegal[3]	7-12	Yes	190	332	66	*68*	*65*	*0.96*	100	98	103	1.05
Seychelles[5]	6-15	Yes	2	1	117	116	118	1.02	127	131	124	0.94
Sierra Leone	6-11	No	...	296	...	...	...	...	180	188	172	0.92
Somalia	...	No	...	...	...	...	...	...	...	...	...	...
South Africa	7-15	No	1 157	*1 092*	115	117	114	0.97	*106*	*110*	*102*	*0.93*
Swaziland	...	Yes	31	31	99	101	97	0.96	110	112	108	0.96
Togo	6-15	No	139	175	91	97	86	0.88	94	97	90	0.94
Uganda	6-12	No	...	1 523	...	...	...	...	149	149	149	1.01
United Republic of Tanzania[3]	7-13	No	714	**1 414**	75	75	74	0.99	**115**	**116**	**114**	**0.98**
Zambia	7-13	No	252	462	84	84	84	1.01	128	126	129	1.02
Zimbabwe	6-12	No	398	...	111	113	109	0.97	...	...	...	...
			Sum		Weighted average							
World	...	...	130 242	137 069	104	109	100	0.92	113	115	110	0.96
Countries in transition	...	...	4 440	3 086	99	100	99	0.99	99	100	98	0.98
Developed countries	...	...	12 380	11 581	102	103	101	0.98	102	101	103	1.02
Developing countries	...	...	113 422	122 401	105	110	100	0.91	114	117	111	0.95
Arab States	...	...	6 297	7 366	90	93	87	0.93	102	104	99	0.94
Central and Eastern Europe	...	...	5 635	4 325	97	99	96	0.97	98	99	97	0.98
Central Asia	...	...	1 785	1 379	101	100	101	1.01	102	103	100	0.98
East Asia and the Pacific	...	...	37 055	32 356	103	103	102	0.99	101	102	101	0.99
East Asia	...	...	36 522	31 949	103	103	102	0.99	102	102	101	0.99
Pacific	...	...	533	408	102	104	101	0.97	76	77	75	0.97
Latin America/Caribbean	...	...	13 176	13 384	119	122	116	0.95	124	126	121	0.96
Caribbean	...	...	565	584	156	153	159	1.04	157	158	156	0.99
Latin America	...	...	12 612	12 800	118	121	115	0.95	122	125	120	0.96
N. America/W. Europe	...	...	9 328	9 010	103	104	101	0.97	103	102	105	1.02
South and West Asia	...	...	40 478	44 207	114	122	104	0.85	125	129	121	0.94
Sub-Saharan Africa	...	...	16 488	25 042	90	96	84	0.87	115	120	110	0.92

Source: UNESCO Institute for Statistics database (UIS, 2009).

1. Tomasevski (2006).

2. Information on compulsory education comes from the Reports under the United Nations Human Rights Treaties.

3. Some primary school fees continue to be charged despite the legal guarantee of free education (Bentaouet-Kattan, 2005; Tomasevski, 2006; World Bank, 2002, 2006).

4. No tuition fees are charged but some direct costs have been reported (Bentaouet-Kattan, 2005; Tomasevski, 2006; World Bank, 2002).

5. National population data were used to calculate enrolment ratios.

6. Enrolment and population data exclude Transnistria.

7. Enrolment and population data exclude the Nagorno-Karabakh region.

NET INTAKE RATE (NIR) IN PRIMARY EDUCATION (%)								SCHOOL LIFE EXPECTANCY (expected number of years of formal schooling from primary to tertiary education)						
School year ending in								School year ending in						
1999				2007				1999			2007			
Total	Male	Female	GPI (F/M)	Total	Male	Female	GPI (F/M)	Total	Male	Female	Total	Male	Female	Country or territory
...	...	...	...	53[z]	54[z]	52[z]	0.96[z]	...	...	...	...	...	...	Congo [3]
26	29	23	0.79	...	...	...	...	*6.1*	*7.4*	*4.8*	...	...	...	Côte d'Ivoire
23	22	24	1.09	42	46	39	0.86	*4.3*	...	...	*7.8*	*9.1*	*6.4*	Democratic Rep. of the Congo [3]
...	...	...	...	37	37	36	0.95	...	...	...	...	...	...	Equatorial Guinea
17	18	16	0.89	*18*	*19*	*17*	*0.92*	*4.1*	*4.6*	*3.5*	...	...	...	Eritrea
20	23	18	0.80	59	61	57	0.94	*3.8*	*4.8*	*2.9*	*7.6*	*8.5*	*6.8*	Ethiopia
...	...	...	...	...	...	...	...	*13.1*	*13.5*	*12.7*	...	...	...	Gabon
...	...	...	...	*51*	*49*	*53*	*1.08*	*7.2*	*8.1*	*6.4*	...	...	...	Gambia [3]
29	*29*	*29*	*1.00*	*35*[z]	*34*[z]	*36*[z]	*1.06*[z]	...	...	...	*9.3*	*9.6*	*9.0*	Ghana [2,3]
20	21	18	0.87	42	43	41	0.95	...	...	...	8.2[z]	9.6[z]	6.8[z]	Guinea [2]
...	...	...	...	...	...	...	...	...	...	...	...	...	...	Guinea-Bissau [3]
30	*29*	*31*	*1.05*	...	...	...	...	...	...	...	*10.5*	*10.8*	*10.1*	Kenya
26	25	27	1.06	*49*[z]	*48*[z]	*49*[z]	*1.01*[z]	9.2	8.7	9.6	10.3[z]	10.1[z]	10.5[z]	Lesotho
...	...	...	...	...	...	...	...	*8.1*	*9.6*	*6.5*	...	...	...	Liberia [2]
...	...	...	...	85	84	85	1.01	...	...	...	*9.4*	*9.6*	*9.2*	Madagascar [3]
...	...	...	...	*70*	*67*	*74*	*1.10*	*10.9*	*11.5*	*10.3*	*9.1*	*9.2*	*9.0*	Malawi
...	...	...	...	27	29	25	0.84	*4.7*	*5.7*	*3.7*	*7.2*	...	...	Mali [3]
72	71	73	1.03	89	88	90	1.02	*12.1*	*12.2*	*12.0*	*13.5*[y]	*13.7*[y]	*13.4*[y]	Mauritius [3]
18	19	17	0.93	*58*	*58*	*57*	*0.99*	*5.4*	...	...	*8.3*[y]	*9.1*[y]	*7.4*[y]	Mozambique
56	54	57	1.06	*62*	*60*	*64*	*1.07*	...	...	...	*10.8*[z]	*10.6*[z]	*10.9*[z]	Namibia [3]
27	32	22	0.68	43	48	38	0.79	...	...	...	*4.0*	*4.7*	*3.3*	Niger [3]
...	...	...	...	...	...	...	...	*7.3*	*8.1*	*6.5*	...	...	...	Nigeria [3]
...	...	...	...	96[z]	97[z]	95[z]	0.99[z]	*6.4*	...	...	*8.6*[y]	*8.5*[y]	*8.6*[y]	Rwanda [3]
...	...	...	...	**46**	**47**	**45**	**0.97**	...	...	...	**10.2**	**10.2**	**10.2**	Sao Tome and Principe [2]
37	*38*	*36*	*0.96*	56	55	57	1.05	*5.2*	...	...	*7.2*	*7.5*	*6.8*	Senegal [3]
75	74	77	1.03	96	97	94	0.97	14.0	13.9	14.2	14.7	14.2	15.4	Seychelles [5]
...	...	...	...	...	...	...	...	...	...	...	...	...	...	Sierra Leone
...	...	...	...	...	...	...	...	...	...	...	...	...	...	Somalia
44	45	43	0.95	*52*[y]	*53*[y]	*50*[y]	*0.95*[y]	*13.5*	*13.3*	*13.6*	*13.1*[z]	*13.0*[z]	*13.2*[z]	South Africa
42	40	43	1.06	52	50	54	1.08	*9.8*	*10.1*	*9.5*	*10.5*[z]	*10.9*[z]	*10.2*[z]	Swaziland
37	40	35	0.87	43	45	42	0.93	...	...	...	*9.0*	...	...	Togo
...	...	...	...	*69*	*67*	*71*	*1.05*	*10.1*	*10.7*	*9.4*	...	...	...	Uganda
14	13	15	1.16	*88*	*87*	*89*	*1.02*	*5.3*	*5.4*	*5.3*	...	...	...	United Republic of Tanzania [3]
37	36	38	1.07	*48*	*46*	*49*	*1.06*	*6.9*	*7.3*	*6.5*	...	...	...	Zambia
...	...	...	...	...	...	...	...	*9.8*	...	...	...	...	...	Zimbabwe
Median								Weighted average						
...	...	...	...	69	68	70	1.04	9.7	10.1	9.2	11.0	11.2	10.7	World
...	...	...	...	77	...	...	...	11.7	11.6	11.8	13.2	12.9	13.4	Countries in transition
...	...	...	...	...	...	...	...	15.5	15.1	15.8	15.8	15.4	16.3	Developed countries
...	...	...	...	64	63	64	1.02	9.0	9.5	8.4	10.4	10.8	10.1	Developing countries
65	65	64	0.99	60	58	60	1.04	9.8	10.5	9.0	10.8	11.3	10.3	Arab States
...	...	...	...	...	...	...	...	12.0	12.1	12.0	13.4	13.3	13.4	Central and Eastern Europe
...	...	...	...	78	...	...	...	10.8	10.9	10.7	12.2	12.2	12.1	Central Asia
...	...	...	...	...	...	...	...	10.5	10.7	10.3	11.8	11.8	11.8	East Asia and the Pacific
...	...	...	...	68	69	68	1.00	10.4	10.6	10.2	11.8	11.8	11.8	East Asia
...	...	...	...	...	...	...	...	14.8	14.8	14.9	14.4	14.3	14.4	Pacific
77	72	82	1.14	71	70	72	1.02	12.5	12.4	12.6	13.4	13.2	13.6	Latin America/Caribbean
...	...	...	...	70	70	71	1.02	10.7	10.8	10.7	10.9	10.8	10.9	Caribbean
69	68	69	1.03	71	71	72	1.02	12.5	12.4	12.6	13.5	13.3	13.7	Latin America
...	...	...	...	...	...	...	...	15.8	15.4	16.2	16.0	15.5	16.5	N. America/W. Europe
...	...	...	...	76	...	...	...	7.9	8.8	6.9	9.6	10.0	9.0	South and West Asia
27	29	26	0.89	51	51	52	1.01	6.6	7.2	5.9	8.6	9.3	7.9	Sub-Saharan Africa

8. Children can enter primary school at age 6 or 7.
9. Enrolment ratios were not calculated due to inconsistencies in the population data.
10. Enrolment ratios were not calculated due to lack of United Nations population data by age.
11. Data include French overseas departments and territories (DOM-TOM).

12. The apparent increase in the gender parity index (GPI) is due to the inclusion in enrolment statistics in recent years of literacy programmes in which 80% of participants are women.

Data in italic are UIS estimates.
Data in bold are for the school year ending in 2008.
(z) Data are for the school year ending in 2006.
(y) Data are for the school year ending in 2005.
(*) National estimate.

Table 5
Participation in primary education

	Country or territory	Age group	School-age population[1] (000)	ENROLMENT IN PRIMARY EDUCATION				Enrolment in private institutions as % of total enrolment		GROSS ENROLMENT RATIO (GER) IN PRIMARY EDUCATION (%)			
				School year ending in				School year ending in		School year ending in			
				1999		2007		1999	2007	1999			
		2007	2006	Total (000)	% F	Total (000)	% F			Total	Male	Female	GPI (F/M)
	Arab States												
1	Algeria	6-11	3 720	4 779	47	4 079	47	.	–	105	110	100	0.91
2	Bahrain	6-11	75	76	49	90[z]	49[z]	19	25[z]	107	106	108	1.01
3	Djibouti	6-11	122	38	41	**56**	**47**	9	**14**	33	39	28	0.71
4	Egypt	6-11	9 544	*8 086*	47	9 988	48	…	8	*102*	*106*	*97*	*0.91*
5	Iraq	6-11	4 612	3 604	44	*4 430[y]*	*44[y]*	.	.[y]	92	101	83	0.82
6	Jordan	6-11	844	706	49	808	49	29	33	98	98	98	1.00
7	Kuwait	6-10	215	140	49	212	49	32	34[z]	100	99	101	1.01
8	Lebanon	6-11	472	395	48	**445**	**48**	66	**70**	105	108	103	0.95
9	Libyan Arab Jamahiriya	6-11	699	822	48	755[z]	48[z]	.	5[z]	120	121	118	0.98
10	Mauritania	6-11	469	346	48	484	50	2	9	89	89	88	0.99
11	Morocco	6-11	3 673	3 462	44	3 939	46	4	8	86	95	77	0.81
12	Oman	6-11	347	316	48	278	49	5	6	91	93	89	0.97
13	Palestinian A. T.	6-9	477	368	49	384	49	9	10	105	105	106	1.01
14	Qatar	6-11	69	61	48	75	49	37	49	102	104	100	0.96
15	Saudi Arabia	6-11	3 234	…	…	3 174	49*	…	8	…	…	…	…
16	Sudan	6-11	5 966	*2 513*	45	3 959	45	*2*	4	*49*	*53*	*45*	*0.85*
17	Syrian Arab Republic	6-9	1 830	2 738	47	2 310	48	4	4	102	107	98	0.92
18	Tunisia	6-11	1 021	1 443	47	1 069	48	0.7	1	113	116	111	0.95
19	United Arab Emirates	6-10	267	270	48	284	49	44	67	90	92	89	0.97
20	Yemen	6-11	3 803	2 303	35	3 220[y]	42[y]	1	2[y]	71	91	51	0.56
	Central and Eastern Europe												
21	Albania	6-9	211	292	48	…	…	.	…	103	104	102	0.98
22	Belarus	6-9	372	632	48	361	48	0.1	0.05	111	111	110	0.99
23	Bosnia and Herzegovina	6-9	196	…	…	192	47	…	…	…	…	…	…
24	Bulgaria	7-10	265	412	48	268	48	0.3	0.5	106	108	105	0.98
25	Croatia	7-10	193	203	49	191	49	0.1	0.2	92	93	92	0.98
26	Czech Republic	6-10	460	655	49	463	48	0.8	1	103	104	103	0.99
27	Estonia	7-12	77	127	48	76	48	1	3	102	103	100	0.97
28	Hungary	7-10	417	503	48	399	48	5	7	102	103	101	0.98
29	Latvia	7-10	79	141	48	79[z]	48[z]	1	1[z]	100	101	99	0.98
30	Lithuania	7-10	151	220	48	144	48	0.4	0.6	102	103	101	0.98
31	Montenegro	7-10	…	…	…	…	…	…	…	…	…	…	…
32	Poland	7-12	2 560	3 434	48	2 485	49	…	2	98	99	97	0.98
33	Republic of Moldova[3,4]	7-10	170*	262	49	161	49	…	0.8	100*	100*	100*	1.00*
34	Romania	7-10	877	1 285	49	918	48	.	0.3	105	106	104	0.98
35	Russian Federation[5]	7-10	5 232	6 743	49	5 010	49	…	0.6	108	109	107	0.98
36	Serbia[3]	7-10	307*	*387*	49	297	49	…	…	*112*	*112*	*111*	*0.99*
37	Slovakia	6-9	226	317	49	231	49	4	5	103	103	102	0.99
38	Slovenia	6-10	92	92	48	95	48	0.1	0.2	100	100	99	0.99
39	TFYR Macedonia	7-10	106	130	48	101	48	.	.	101	102	100	0.98
40	Turkey	6-11	8 399	…	…	*8 065*	*48*	…	*2[z]*	…	…	…	…
41	Ukraine	6-9	1 651	2 200	49	1 648	49*	0.3	0.5	109	110	109	0.99
	Central Asia												
42	Armenia	7-9	116	255	…	128	47	…	2	100	…	…	…
43	Azerbaijan[3,6]	6-9	443*	707	49	513	47	–	0.3	98*	98*	98*	1.00*
44	Georgia	6-11	325	302	49	322	47	0.5	6	98	98	98	1.00
45	Kazakhstan	7-10	900	1 249	49	**956**	**49**	0.5	**0.8**	97	97	98	1.01
46	Kyrgyzstan	7-10	428	470	49	408	49	0.2	1	98	98	97	0.99
47	Mongolia	7-11	240	251	50	239	49	0.5	5	97	96	99	1.04
48	Tajikistan	7-10	682	690	48	680	48	.	.	98	101	96	0.95
49	Turkmenistan	7-9	288	…	…	…	…	…	…	…	…	…	…
50	Uzbekistan	7-10	2 267	2 570	49	2 165	49	…	.	98	99	98	1.00
	East Asia and the Pacific												
51	Australia	5-11	1 840	1 885	49	1 973	49	27	30	100	100	100	1.00
52	Brunei Darussalam	6-11	44	46	47	46	48	36	37	114	115	112	0.97
53	Cambodia	6-11	2 080	2 127	46	2 480	47	2	0.7	97	104	90	0.87
54	China[7]	7-11	95 607	…	…	107 395	47	…	4	…	…	…	…

GROSS ENROLMENT RATIO (GER) IN PRIMARY EDUCATION (%)				NET ENROLMENT RATIO (NER) IN PRIMARY EDUCATION (%)								OUT-OF-SCHOOL CHILDREN (000)[2]				
School year ending in				School year ending in								School year ending in				
2007				1999				2007				1999		2007		
Total	Male	Female	GPI (F/M)	Total	Male	Female	GPI (F/M)	Total	Male	Female	GPI (F/M)	Total	% F	Total	% F	
															Arab States	
110	113	106	0.94	91	93	89	0.96	95	96	95	0.98	357	61	149	59	*1*
120[z]	120[z]	119[z]	1.00[z]	96	95	97	1.03	98[y]	98[y]	98[y]	1.00[y]	1.0	6	0.4[y]	33[y]	*2*
56	**59**	**52**	**0.88**	27	32	23	0.73	**45**	**48**	**43**	**0.89**	83	53	**56**	**52**	*3*
105	107	102	0.95	*94*	*97*	*90*	*0.93*	*96*	*98*	*94*	*0.96*	*285*	*97*	*232*	*96*	*4*
99[y]	*109*[y]	*90*[y]	*0.83*[y]	85	91	78	0.85	*89*[y]	*95*[y]	*82*[y]	*0.86*[y]	605	71	*508*[y]	*78*[y]	*5*
96	95	97	1.02	91	91	91	1.01	89	88	89	1.02	40	46	60	43	*6*
98	100	97	0.98	87	86	87	1.01	88	89	87	0.97	10	46	13	58	*7*
95	**97**	**94**	**0.97**	*86*	*88*	*85*	*0.96*	**83**	**84**	**83**	**0.99**	*44*	*55*	**74**	**50**	*8*
110[z]	113[z]	108[z]	0.95[z]	…	…	…	…	…	…	…	…	…	…	…	…	*9*
103	100	106	1.06	64	65	64	0.99	80	78	83	1.06	139	49	89	42	*10*
107	113	101	0.90	70	76	65	0.85	89	91	86	0.95	1 183	59	395	60	*11*
80	80	81	1.01	81	81	81	1.00	73	72	74	1.02	61	48	87	47	*12*
80	80	80	1.00	97	97	97	1.00	73	73	73	1.00	4	31	108	48	*13*
109	110	109	0.99	92	92	92	1.01	93	93	93	1.00	2	50	1.2	39	*14*
98	100*	96*	0.96*	…	…	…	…	85*	85*	84*	0.99*	…	…	497*	51*	*15*
66	71	61	0.86	…	…	…	…	…	…	…	…	…	…	…	…	*16*
126	129	123	0.96	*92*	*95*	*88*	*0.93*	…	…	…	…	*139*	*84*	…	…	*17*
105	106	103	0.97	93	94	92	0.98	95	95	95	1.01	82	55	35	40	*18*
107	107	106	0.99	79	80	79	0.99	91	91	90	0.99	55	50	5	59	*19*
87[y]	100[y]	74[y]	0.74[y]	56	70	41	0.59	75[y]	85[y]	65[y]	0.76[y]	1 410	65	906[y]	70[y]	*20*
															Central and Eastern Europe	
…	…	…	…	*94*	*95*	*94*	*0.98*	…	…	…	…	*16*	*55*	…	…	*21*
97	98	96	0.99	…	…	…	…	90	…	…	…	…	…	36	…	*22*
98	101	94	0.93	…	…	…	…	…	…	…	…	…	…	…	…	*23*
101	102	100	0.99	97	98	96	0.98	95	95	94	0.99	4	77	10	52	*24*
99	99	99	1.00	85	86	85	0.98	90	91	90	0.99	18	52	2.2	5	*25*
101	101	100	0.99	*97*	*96*	*97*	*1.00*	*93*[y]	*91*[y]	*94*[y]	*1.03*[y]	*21*	*46*	*37*[y]	*41*[y]	*26*
99	100	98	0.99	*96*	*96*	*95*	*0.98*	95	95	94	1.00	*0.1*	*66*	2	44	*27*
96	96	95	0.98	88	88	88	0.99	87	87	86	0.98	15	46	29	48	*28*
95[z]	96[z]	93[z]	0.96[z]	*97*	*98*	*96*	*0.98*	*90*[y]	*89*[y]	*92*[y]	*1.03*[y]	*2*	*56*	*7*[y]	*37*[y]	*29*
95	96	95	0.99	95	96	95	0.99	90	91	90	0.99	4	44	10	48	*30*
…	…	…	…	…	…	…	…	…	…	…	…	…	…	…	…	*31*
97	97	97	1.00	96	96	96	1.00	96	95	96	1.01	133	48	110	45	*32*
94*	95*	94*	0.98*	*93*	…	…	…	88*	88*	87*	0.99*	*11*	…	17*	51*	*33*
105	105	104	0.99	96	96	95	0.99	94	94	94	1.00	2	…	30	46	*34*
96	96	96	1.00	…	…	…	…	…	…	…	…	…	…	…	…	*35*
97*	97*	97*	1.00*	…	…	…	…	95*	95*	95*	1.00*	…	…	9*	47*	*36*
102	103	101	0.99	…	…	…	…	*92*[y]	*92*[y]	*92*[y]	*1.01*[y]	…	…	*19*[y]	*47*[y]	*37*
104	104	103	0.99	96	97	95	0.99	96	96	96	1.00	2	58	3	50	*38*
95	95	95	1.00	93	94	92	0.98	89	89	89	1.00	1.4	95	6	45	*39*
96	*99*	*93*	*0.95*	…	…	…	…	92	94	91	0.97	…	…	643	59	*40*
100	100*	100*	1.00*	…	…	…	…	89	89*	89*	1.00*	…	…	167	49*	*41*
															Central Asia	
110	108	111	1.03	…	…	…	…	85	84	87	1.04	…	…	7	34	*42*
116*	116*	115*	0.99*	89*	88*	89*	1.01*	95*	96*	95*	0.99*	82*	46*	20*	55*	*43*
99	100	98	0.97	…	…	…	…	94	95	92	0.97	…	…	18	60	*44*
109	**108**	**109**	**1.00**	…	…	…	…	**90**	**90**	**90**	**1.00**	…	…	**9**	**25**	*45*
95	96	95	0.99	88*	89*	87*	0.99*	84	85	84	0.99	28*	50*	32	50	*46*
100	99	101	1.02	89	87	90	1.04	89	88	89	1.01	22	38	6	21	*47*
100	102	98	0.96	…	…	…	…	97	99	95	0.96	…	…	17	86	*48*
…	…	…	…	…	…	…	…	…	…	…	…	…	…	…	…	*49*
95	97	94	0.97	…	…	…	…	91	92	90	0.97	…	…	145	59	*50*
															East Asia and the Pacific	
107	107	107	1.00	94	94	94	1.01	97	97	97	1.01	108	46	51	43	*51*
106	106	105	0.99	…	…	…	…	93	93	93	1.00	…	…	2	43	*52*
119	124	115	0.93	*83*	*87*	*79*	*0.91*	89	91	87	0.96	*366*	*61*	220	58	*53*
112	113	112	0.99	…	…	…	…	…	…	…	…	…	…	…	…	*54*

Table 5 (continued)

	Country or territory	Age group	School-age population[1] (000)	ENROLMENT IN PRIMARY EDUCATION, School year ending in 1999		ENROLMENT IN PRIMARY EDUCATION, School year ending in 2007		Enrolment in private institutions as % of total enrolment, School year ending in		GROSS ENROLMENT RATIO (GER) IN PRIMARY EDUCATION (%), School year ending in 1999			
		2007	2006	Total (000)	% F	Total (000)	% F	1999	2007	Total	Male	Female	GPI (F/M)
55	Cook Islands[3]	5-10	*3*	3	46	2	47	15	21	96	99	94	0.95
56	DPR Korea	6-9	1 559	...	...	...	...	...	...	...	...	...	...
57	Fiji	6-11	110	116	48	104	48	...	*99*[y]	109	109	108	0.99
58	Indonesia	7-12	25 412	...	...	29 797	48	...	18	...	...	...	...
59	Japan	6-11	7 209	7 692	49	7 220	49	0.9	1	101	101	101	1.00
60	Kiribati[3]	6-11	...	14	49	16[y]	49[y]	...	...	104	104	105	1.01
61	Lao PDR	6-10	758	828	45	892	46	2	3	111	120	102	0.85
62	Macao, China	6-11	31	47	47	33	47	*95*	96	100	102	97	0.96
63	Malaysia	6-11	3 217	3 040	48	3 133[z]	49[z]	...	0.8[y]	98	99	97	0.98
64	Marshall Islands[3]	6-11	9*	8	48	8	48	25	...	*101*	*102*	*100*	*0.98*
65	Micronesia, F. S.	6-11	17	...	...	19	49	...	*8*	...	...	...	...
66	Myanmar[8]	5-9	...	4 733	49	5 014	...	.	.	...	...	...	...
67	Nauru	6-11	*2*	...	...	1	49	...	.	...	...	...	...
68	New Zealand	5-10	344	361	49	349	49	...	12	100	100	100	1.00
69	Niue[3]	5-10	...	0.3	46	0.2[y]	51[y]	.	...	99	99	98	1.00
70	Palau[3]	6-10	2*	2	47	2	*48*	18	23	114	118	109	0.93
71	Papua New Guinea	7-12	988	...	...	532[z]	44[z]	...	...	...	...	...	...
72	Philippines	6-11	12 017	12 503	49	13 145	48	8	8	113	113	113	1.00
73	Republic of Korea	6-11	3 602	3 946	47	3 838	48	1	1	98	100	96	0.95
74	Samoa	5-10	32	27	48	30	48	16	*17*[y]	99	99	98	0.98
75	Singapore[8]	6-11	...	...	...	301	48	...	5	...	...	...	...
76	Solomon Islands	6-11	77	58	46	75[y]	47[y]	...	...	88	91	86	0.94
77	Thailand	6-11	5 381	6 120	48	**5 565**	**48**	13	**18**	106	107	105	0.99
78	Timor-Leste	6-11	191	...	...	174	47	...	10	...	...	...	...
79	Tokelau	5-10	...	...	...	...	...	...	...	...	...	...	...
80	Tonga	5-10	15	17	46	17[z]	47[z]	7	...	108	110	106	0.96
81	Tuvalu[3]	6-11	...	1	48	1[z]	48[z]	...	...	98	97	99	1.02
82	Vanuatu	6-11	35	34	48	38	48	...	27	111	112	110	0.98
83	Viet Nam[8]	6-10	...	10 250	47	7 041	48	0.3	0.5	108	112	104	0.93
	Latin America and the Caribbean												
84	Anguilla[9]	5-11	...	2	50	2	49	5	8	...	...	...	...
85	Antigua and Barbuda[3]	5-11	11*	...	...	12	49	...	50	...	...	...	...
86	Argentina	6-11	4 092	4 664	49	4 686[z]	49[z]	20	22[z]	113	113	112	0.99
87	Aruba	6-11	9	9	49	10	49	83	78	114	114	114	0.99
88	Bahamas	5-10	36	34	49	37	49	...	29	95	96	94	0.98
89	Barbados	5-10	21	25	49	23	49	...	10	98	99	98	0.98
90	Belize	5-10	42	44	48	52	49	...	95	118	120	116	0.97
91	Bermuda[3]	5-10	...	...	...	5[z]	46[z]	...	35[z]	...	...	...	...
92	Bolivia	6-11	1 397	1 445	49	1 512	49	...	8	113	114	112	0.98
93	Brazil[10]	7-10	13 885	20 939	48	17 996	47	8	11	154	159	150	0.94
94	British Virgin Islands[3]	5-11	*3*	3	49	3	49	13	28	112	113	110	0.97
95	Cayman Islands[9]	5-10	...	3	47	4	48	36	35	...	...	...	...
96	Chile	6-11	1 589	1 805	48	1 679	48	45	55	101	102	99	0.97
97	Colombia	6-10	4 554	5 162	49	5 299	49	20	19	114	114	114	1.00
98	Costa Rica	6-11	487	552	48	536	48	7	8	108	109	107	0.98
99	Cuba	6-11	870	1 074	48	883	48	.	.	111	113	109	0.97
100	Dominica[3,9]	5-11	...	12	48	9	48	24	32	104	107	102	0.95
101	Dominican Republic	6-11	1 268	1 315	49	1 355	48	*14*	19	113	114	111	0.98
102	Ecuador	6-11	1 721	1 899	49	2 039	49	21	28	114	114	114	1.00
103	El Salvador	7-12	912	940	48	1 075	49	*11*	10	112	114	109	0.96
104	Grenada[3]	5-11	17	...	...	14	49	...	77	...	...	...	...
105	Guatemala	7-12	2 159	1 824	46	2 449	48	15	11	101	108	94	0.87
106	Guyana	6-11	97	107	49	109	49	1	2	121	122	120	0.98
107	Haiti	6-11	1 397	...	...	...	...	...	...	...	...	...	...
108	Honduras	6-11	1 096	...	...	1 308	49	...	7[z]	...	...	...	...
109	Jamaica	6-11	339	*316*	49	310	49	*4*	8	*92*	*93*	*92*	*1.00*
110	Mexico	6-11	12 847	14 698	49	14 631	49	7	8	111	112	109	0.98
111	Montserrat[3]	5-11	0.5*	0.4	44	0.5	49	38	31	...	...	...	...
112	Netherlands Antilles	6-11	17	25	48	...	...	74	...	131	135	127	0.95
113	Nicaragua	6-11	823	830	49	953	48	16	15	100	100	101	1.01
114	Panama	6-11	396	393	48	446	48	10	11	108	110	106	0.97
115	Paraguay	6-11	848	*951*	48	934[y]	48[y]	*15*	17[y]	*119*	*121*	*116*	*0.96*

GROSS ENROLMENT RATIO (GER) IN PRIMARY EDUCATION (%)				NET ENROLMENT RATIO (NER) IN PRIMARY EDUCATION (%)								OUT-OF-SCHOOL CHILDREN (000)[2]				
School year ending in				School year ending in								School year ending in				
2007				1999				2007				1999		2007		
Total	Male	Female	GPI (F/M)	Total	Male	Female	GPI (F/M)	Total	Male	Female	GPI (F/M)	Total	% F	Total	% F	
73	*74*	*71*	*0.97*	85	87	83	0.96	*67*	*69*	*66*	*0.96*	0.4	54	*0.9*	*50*	55
...	...	...	...	...	...	...	...	...	...	...	...	...	...	...	...	56
94	96	93	0.97	99	98	99	1.01	91[z]	91[z]	91[z]	1.00[z]	1.4	30	6[z]	47[z]	57
117	120	115	0.96	...	...	...	...	95	97	93	0.96	...	...	507	...	58
100	100	100	1.00	100	...	...	...	100	...	...	...	3	...	16	...	59
113[y]	112[y]	114[y]	1.01[y]	*97*	*96*	*98*	*1.01*	...	...	...	...	*0.1*	...	...	...	60
118	124	111	0.90	76	79	73	0.92	86	88	84	0.95	178	56	104	57	61
108	112	103	0.92	85	84	85	1.01	93	94	91	0.97	7	47	2	59	62
98[z]	98[z]	98[z]	0.99[z]	98	99	97	0.98	97[z]	98[z]	97[z]	1.00[z]	70	70	82[z]	52[z]	63
93	94	92	0.97	...	...	...	...	66	67	66	0.99	...	...	3	49	64
110	109	110	1.01	...	...	...	...	...	...	...	...	...	...	...	...	65
...	...	...	...	...	...	...	...	...	...	...	...	...	...	...	...	66
79	*78*	*80*	*1.03*	...	...	...	...	*72*	*72*	*73*	*1.01*	...	...	*0.4*	*47.0*	67
102	101	102	1.01	99	99	99	1.00	99	99	99	1.01	2.0	45	2.5	24	68
105[y]	107[y]	102[y]	0.95[y]	99	99	98	1.00	...	...	...	...	0.0	50	...	...	69
99	*98*	*100*	*1.02*	*97*	*99*	*94*	*0.94*	...	...	...	...	*0.1*	*91*	...	...	70
55[z]	60[z]	50[z]	0.84[z]	...	...	...	...	...	...	...	...	...	...	...	...	71
109	110	109	0.98	92	92	92	1.00	91	90	92	1.02	895	48	1 003	43	72
107	107	106	0.98	97	99	94	0.95	98[z]	...	...	...	129	84	57[z]	...	73
95	96	95	1.00	92	92	91	0.99	...	...	...	...	1.6	50	...	...	74
...	...	...	...	...	...	...	...	...	...	...	...	...	...	...	...	75
101[y]	102[y]	98[y]	0.96[y]	...	...	...	...	62[y]	62[y]	61[y]	0.99[y]	...	...	29[y]	48[y]	76
104	**104**	**104**	**1.00**	...	...	...	...	**95**	**95**	**96**	**1.01**	...	...	**264**	**43**	77
91	93	88	0.94	...	...	...	...	63	64	62	0.96	...	...	71	50	78
...	...	...	...	...	...	...	...	...	...	...	...	...	...	...	...	79
113[z]	116[z]	110[z]	0.95[z]	88	90	86	0.96	96[y]	97[y]	94[y]	0.97[y]	2	56	0.2[y]	...	80
106[z]	106[z]	105[z]	0.99[z]	...	...	...	...	...	...	...	...	...	...	...	...	81
108	110	106	0.97	91	92	91	0.99	87	88	86	0.99	2.5	51	4	51	82
...	...	...	...	95	...	...	...	...	...	...	...	447	...	...	...	83
Latin America and the Caribbean																
...	...	...	...	...	...	...	...	...	...	...	...	...	...	...	...	84
102	106	99	0.94	...	...	...	...	74	75	73	0.98	...	...	3	52	85
114[z]	115[z]	113[z]	0.98[z]	99	99	99	0.99	98[z]	...	...	...	26	82	39[z]	...	86
114	115	112	0.97	98	97	100	1.03	100	100	100	1.00	0.1	...	0.04	46	87
103	103	103	1.00	89	90	89	0.99	91	89	92	1.03	4	50	3	41	88
105	105	105	1.00	*94*	*94*	*94*	*0.99*	97	96	97	1.01	*2*	*51*	0.7	41	89
123	124	122	0.99	*94*	*94*	*94*	*0.99*	97	96	98	1.01	*2*	*49*	0.5	...	90
100[z]	108[z]	92[z]	0.85[z]	...	...	...	...	*92*[z]	...	...	...	...	...	*0.3*[z]	...	91
108	108	108	1.00	95	95	95	1.00	94	93	94	1.01	52	51	70	45	92
130	134	125	0.93	91	...	...	...	93	93	93	1.00	1 033	...	901	49	93
108	*110*	*105*	*0.96*	*96*	*95*	*97*	*1.02*	*93*	*93*	*94*	*1.01*	*0.04*	*42*	*0.1*	*27*	94
...	...	...	...	...	...	...	...	...	...	...	...	...	...	...	...	95
106	108	103	0.95	...	...	...	...	94	95	94	0.99	...	...	87	53	96
116	117	116	0.99	89	*89*	*90*	*1.01*	87	87	87	1.00	369	*46*	413	47	97
110	111	110	0.99	...	...	...	...	...	...	...	...	...	...	...	...	98
102	103	100	0.98	97	97	98	1.01	98	98	98	1.00	9	...	10	58	99
...	...	...	...	*94*	*95*	*93*	*0.98*	...	...	...	...	*0.4*	*61*	...	...	100
107	110	103	0.94	84	83	84	1.01	82	82	83	1.01	174	47	194	47	101
118	119	118	1.00	97	97	98	1.01	97	96	97	1.01	17	16	12	...	102
118	118	118	1.00	...	...	...	...	92	92	92	1.01	...	...	58	46	103
81	83	79	0.96	...	...	...	...	76	77	75	0.97	...	...	4	51	104
113	117	110	0.94	82	86	78	0.91	95	97	93	0.96	299	61	69	76	105
112	113	111	0.98	...	...	...	...	...	...	...	...	...	...	...	...	106
...	...	...	...	...	...	...	...	...	...	...	...	...	...	...	...	107
119	120	119	1.00	...	...	...	...	93	93	94	1.01	...	...	66	43	108
91	91	92	1.01	*88*	*87*	*88*	*1.00*	86	86	87	1.02	*38*	*49*	45	45	109
114	115	112	0.97	97	97	97	1.00	98	...	...	...	55	17	109	...	110
107	101	113	1.12	...	...	...	...	92	89	96	1.08	...	...	0.02	...	111
...	...	...	...	...	...	...	...	...	...	...	...	...	...	...	...	112
116	117	115	0.98	76	76	77	1.01	96	95	96	1.01	165	47	24	39	113
113	114	111	0.97	96	96	96	0.99	98	99	98	0.99	11	53	4	62	114
111[y]	113[y]	110[y]	0.97[y]	96	96	96	1.00	94[y]	94[y]	95[y]	1.01[y]	28	46	43[y]	46[y]	115

Table 5 (continued)

	Country or territory	Age group 2007	School-age population[1] (000) 2006	ENROLMENT IN PRIMARY EDUCATION, School year ending in 1999: Total (000)	1999: % F	2007: Total (000)	2007: % F	Enrolment in private institutions as % of total enrolment, School year ending in 1999	2007	GROSS ENROLMENT RATIO (GER) IN PRIMARY EDUCATION (%), School year ending in 1999: Total	Male	Female	GPI (F/M)
116	Peru	6-11	3 411	4 350	49	3 994	49	13	19	122	123	121	0.99
117	Saint Kitts and Nevis	5-11	*7*	…	…	6	49	…	22	…	…	…	…
118	Saint Lucia	5-11	20	26	49	22	49	*2*	3	109	110	108	0.98
119	Saint Vincent/Grenadines	5-11	16	…	…	16	48	…	4	…	…	…	…
120	Suriname	6-11	55	…	…	65	48	…	46	…	…	…	…
121	Trinidad and Tobago	5-11	130	172	49	130	49	*72*	73	96	96	95	1.00
122	Turks and Caicos Islands	6-11	…	2	49	2[y]	51[y]	18	30[y]	…	…	…	…
123	Uruguay	6-11	315	366	49	359	48	…	14	111	112	111	0.99
124	Venezuela, B. R.	6-11	3 320	3 261	49	3 521	48	15	15	100	101	99	0.98
	North America and Western Europe												
125	Andorra[3]	6-11	5*	…	…	4	47	…	2	…	…	…	…
126	Austria	6-9	344	389	48	347	48	4	5	103	103	102	0.99
127	Belgium	6-11	713	763	49	732	49	55	54	105	105	105	0.99
128	Canada	6-11	2 295	2 429	49	2 305[z]	49[z]	6	6[z]	99	99	99	1.00
129	Cyprus[3]	6-11	56*	64	48	58	49	4	6	97	98	97	1.00
130	Denmark	7-12	420	372	49	416	49	11	12	101	102	101	1.00
131	Finland	7-12	374	383	49	365	49	1	1	99	99	99	1.00
132	France[11]	6-10	3 723	3 944	49	4 106	48	15	15	107	107	106	0.99
133	Germany	6-9	3 177	3 767	49	3 311	49	2	3	106	106	105	0.99
134	Greece	6-11	631	646	48	639	49	7	7	94	94	95	1.00
135	Iceland	6-12	31	30	48	30	49	1	2	99	100	98	0.98
136	Ireland	4-11	456	457	49	476	49	0.9	0.9	104	104	103	0.99
137	Israel	6-11	746	722	49	826	49	…	.	112	112	111	0.99
138	Italy	6-10	2 695	2 876	48	2 820	48	7	7	103	103	102	0.99
139	Luxembourg	6-11	35	31	49	36	49	7	8	101	100	102	1.02
140	Malta	5-10	28	35	49	30[y]	48[y]	36	38[y]	107	106	107	1.01
141	Monaco[9]	6-10	…	2	50	**2**	**47**	31	**25**	…	…	…	…
142	Netherlands	6-11	1 200	1 268	48	1 281	48	68	…	108	109	107	0.98
143	Norway	6-12	436	412	49	431	49	1	2	101	101	101	1.00
144	Portugal	6-11	655	815	48	754	47	9	11	123	126	121	0.96
145	San Marino[9]	6-10	…	…	…	**2**	**48**	…	.	…	…	…	…
146	Spain	6-11	2 418	2 580	48	2 556	48	33	33	106	106	105	0.99
147	Sweden	7-12	636	763	49	601	49	3	8	110	108	111	1.03
148	Switzerland	7-12	525	530	49	511	49	3	4	102	102	102	1.00
149	United Kingdom	5-10	4 243	4 661	49	4 409	49	5	5	101	101	101	1.00
150	United States	6-11	24 730	24 938	49	24 492	49	12	10	101	100	102	1.03
	South and West Asia												
151	Afghanistan	7-12	4 600	957	7	4 718	37	…	…	28	51	4	0.08
152	Bangladesh	6-10	17 842	…	…	16 313	51	…	42	…	…	…	…
153	Bhutan	6-12	98	81	46	**106**	**50**	2	**3**	75	81	69	0.85
154	India	6-10	124 425	110 986	43	139 170[z]	47[z]	…	…	93	100	85	0.84
155	Iran, Islamic Republic of[12]	6-10	5 917	8 667	47	7 152	55	…	5	96	99	94	0.95
156	Maldives	6-12	45	74	49	50	48	3	1	134	134	135	1.01
157	Nepal	5-9	3 574	3 588	42	**4 419**	**49**	…	**10**	114	128	98	0.77
158	Pakistan	5-9	19 534	…	…	17 979	44	…	34[z]	…	…	…	…
159	Sri Lanka	5-9	1 484	…	…	1 612[z]	49[z]	…	–[z]	…	…	…	…
	Sub-Saharan Africa												
160	Angola	6-9	1 968	…	…	…	…	…	9	…	…	…	…
161	Benin	6-11	1 452	872	39	1 357[z]	44[z]	7	13[z]	74	89	59	0.67
162	Botswana	6-12	303	322	50	327[y]	49[y]	5	…	104	104	104	1.00
163	Burkina Faso	7-12	2 391	816	40	**1 742**	**46**	11	**13**	43	51	36	0.70
164	Burundi	7-12	1 303	*702*	44	1 491	48	*0.8*	1	*60*	*67*	*54*	*0.80*
165	Cameroon	6-11	2 846	2 134	45	3 120	46	28	22	84	92	75	0.82
166	Cape Verde	6-11	78	92	49	79	48	–	0.4	119	122	116	0.96
167	Central African Republic	6-11	700	…	…	**522**	**42**	…	**13**	…	…	…	…
168	Chad	6-11	1 790	840	37	1 324	41	25	34[z]	63	79	46	0.58
169	Comoros	6-11	132	83	45	*107[y]*	*46[y]*	12	*10[y]*	76	82	69	0.85
170	Congo	6-11	587	276	49	622	48	10	35	56	58	55	0.95
171	Côte d'Ivoire	6-11	3 022	1 911	43	2 180	44	12	12	69	79	59	0.74

GROSS ENROLMENT RATIO (GER) IN PRIMARY EDUCATION (%)				NET ENROLMENT RATIO (NER) IN PRIMARY EDUCATION (%)								OUT-OF-SCHOOL CHILDREN (000)[2]				
School year ending in				School year ending in								School year ending in				
2007				1999				2007				1999		2007		
Total	Male	Female	GPI (F/M)	Total	Male	Female	GPI (F/M)	Total	Male	Female	GPI (F/M)	Total	% F	Total	% F	
117	117	118	1.01	*98*	*98*	*97*	*1.00*	96	95	97	1.02	*6*	...	35	...	116
94	*93*	*94*	*1.01*	...	...	...	...	*87*	*86*	*88*	*1.02*	...	...	*0.6*	*42*	117
109	111	108	0.97	*96*	*97*	*96*	*0.99*	98	98	97	0.99	*0.7*	*52*	0.2	62	118
102	105	100	0.94	...	...	...	...	91	94	88	0.94	...	...	1.0	65	119
119	120	118	0.98	...	...	...	...	94	93	95	1.02	...	...	3	41	120
100	101	99	0.97	87	87	88	1.01	94	94	93	0.99	16	46	4	58	121
90[Y]	*88*[Y]	*92*[Y]	*1.04*[Y]	...	...	...	...	*78*[Y]	*75*[Y]	*81*[Y]	*1.07*[Y]	...	...	*0.5*[Y]	*42*[Y]	122
114	116	113	0.97	...	...	...	...	97	97	97	1.00	...	...	7.4	47	123
106	107	105	0.97	86	85	86	1.01	92	92	92	1.00	424	47	195	46	124
North America and Western Europe																
88	89	87	0.98	...	...	...	...	81	81	80	0.99	...	...	0.9	49	125
101	101	100	0.99	*97*	*97*	*98*	*1.01*	*97*[Z]	*97*[Z]	*98*[Z]	*1.01*[Z]	*10*	*38*	*9*[Z]	*38*[Z]	126
103	103	103	1.00	99	99	99	1.00	98	98	98	1.01	6	43	12	42	127
99[Z]	99[Z]	99[Z]	0.99[Z]	99	99	99	1.00	...	...	...	...	30	42	...	...	128
102	103	102	0.99	95	95	95	1.00	99	99	99	1.00	1.3	49	0.4	56	129
99	99	99	1.00	97	97	97	1.00	96	95	96	1.01	8	42	17	39	130
98	98	97	1.00	99	99	98	1.00	96	96	96	1.00	5	57	13	46	131
110	111	110	0.99	99	99	99	1.00	99	98	99	1.00	9	34	29	32	132
104	104	104	1.00	*100*	...	...	...	*98*	*98*	*98*	*1.00*	*3*	...	*7*	...	133
101	101	101	1.00	92	92	93	1.01	100	100	100	1.00	31	44	1.4	49	134
97	97	98	1.00	99	100	98	0.98	97	97	97	1.00	0.3	...	0.8	46	135
104	105	104	1.00	94	93	94	1.01	96	96	96	1.01	28	45	18	43	136
111	110	112	1.01	98	98	98	1.00	97	97	98	1.01	15	51	21	39	137
105	105	104	0.99	99	99	99	0.99	99	99	98	0.99	7	...	17	73	138
102	102	103	1.00	97	96	98	1.03	97	97	98	1.01	0.6	16	0.4	19	139
100[Y]	101[Y]	99[Y]	0.98[Y]	95	94	96	1.02	91[Y]	92[Y]	91[Y]	0.99[Y]	2	41	2.6[Y]	51[Y]	140
...	...	...	...	...	...	...	...	...	...	...	...	...	...	...	...	141
107	108	106	0.98	99	100	99	0.99	98	99	98	0.99	6.4	99	17	70	142
99	99	99	1.00	100	100	100	1.00	99	99	99	1.00	0.6	60	6	49	143
115	118	112	0.95	...	...	...	...	99	99	98	0.99	...	...	6	70	144
...	...	...	...	...	...	...	...	...	...	...	...	...	...	...	...	145
106	106	105	0.99	100	100	100	1.00	100	100	100	1.00	6	69	5.5	80	146
94	95	94	1.00	100	...	...	...	94	94	94	1.00	2	...	38	50	147
97	98	97	0.99	94	94	94	1.00	89	89	89	0.99	10	37	34	48	148
104	104	104	1.01	100	100	100	1.00	97	97	98	1.01	2	25	68	37	149
99	99	99	1.00	94	94	94	1.00	92	92	93	1.01	1 215	49	1 564	43	150
South and West Asia																
103	125	78	0.63	...	...	...	...	...	...	...	...	...	...	...	...	151
91	88	95	1.08	...	...	...	...	*87*[Z]	*83*[Z]	*90*[Z]	*1.08*[Z]	...	...	*1 837*[Z]	*33*[Z]	152
111	**111**	**111**	**1.00**	56	60	53	0.89	**87**	**86**	**88**	**1.02**	47	53	**11**	**45**	153
112[Z]	114[Z]	109[Z]	0.96[Z]	...	...	...	...	89[Z]	90[Z]	87[Z]	0.96[Z]	...	...	7 142[Z]	65[Z]	154
121	106	137	1.29	*82*	*83*	*81*	*0.97*	*94*[Z]	...	...	...	*1 616*	*52*	*391*[Z]	...	155
111	112	109	0.97	98	97	98	1.01	96	96	97	1.01	1.1	41	1.4	39.1	156
124	**123**	**125**	**1.01**	65*	72*	57*	0.79*	**80**	**81**	**78**	**0.96**	1 043*	61*	**714**	**53**	157
92	101	83	0.82	...	...	...	...	*66*[Z]	*73*[Z]	*57*[Z]	*0.78*[Z]	...	...	*6 821*[Z]	*60*[Z]	158
108[Z]	108[Z]	108[Z]	1.00[Z]	...	...	...	...	...	...	...	...	...	...	...	...	159
Sub-Saharan Africa																
...	...	...	...	...	...	...	...	...	...	...	...	...	...	...	...	160
96[Z]	105[Z]	87[Z]	0.83[Z]	50*	59*	40*	0.68*	80[Z]	87[Z]	73[Z]	0.84[Z]	586*	59*	244[Z]	71[Z]	161
107[Y]	107[Y]	106[Y]	0.99[Y]	80	79	82	1.04	84[Y]	83[Y]	85[Y]	1.03[Y]	55	44	49[Y]	45[Y]	162
71	**76**	**66**	**0.87**	35	41	28	0.70	**58**	**62**	**54**	**0.86**	1 231	54	**1 002**	**54**	163
114	119	110	0.93	...	...	...	...	81	82	80	0.98	...	...	244	53	164
110	118	101	0.86	...	...	...	...	...	...	...	...	...	...	...	...	165
101	105	98	0.94	*99*	*99*	*98*	*0.98*	85	85	84	0.98	*0.8*	*90*	12	52	166
74	**86**	**61**	**0.71**	...	...	...	...	**56**	**65**	**48**	**0.74**	...	...	**310**	**60**	167
74	87	61	0.70	51	63	39	0.62	...	...	...	...	654	62	...	...	168
85[Y]	*91*[Y]	*80*[Y]	*0.88*[Y]	49	54	45	0.85	...	...	...	...	53	54	...	...	169
106	110	102	0.93	...	...	...	...	*54*	*56*	*52*	*0.92*	...	...	*244*	*52*	170
72	81	64	0.79	52	60	45	0.75	...	...	...	...	1 290	58	...	...	171

Table 5 (continued)

	Country or territory	Age group 2007	School-age population[1] (000) 2006	ENROLMENT IN PRIMARY EDUCATION, School year ending in 1999: Total (000)	1999: % F	2007: Total (000)	2007: % F	Enrolment in private institutions as % of total enrolment, School year ending in 1999	2007	GROSS ENROLMENT RATIO (GER) IN PRIMARY EDUCATION (%), School year ending in 1999: Total	Male	Female	GPI (F/M)
172	Democratic Rep. of the Congo	6-11	10 383	4 022	47	8 840	45	19	11	48	51	46	0.90
173	Equatorial Guinea	7-11	65	75	44	81	49	33	30[y]	142	159	125	0.79
174	Eritrea	7-11	604	262	45	332	45	11	9	52	57	47	0.82
175	Ethiopia	7-12	13 415	5 168	38	12 175	47	...	...	48	59	36	0.61
176	Gabon	6-11	183	265	50	...	...	17	...	148	148	148	1.00
177	Gambia	7-12	253	170	46	**217**	**51**	14	**18**	87	94	81	0.86
178	Ghana	6-11	3 446	2 377	47	**3 616**	**49**	13	**17**	75	78	72	0.92
179	Guinea	7-12	1 451	727	38	1 318	45	15	27	57	70	45	0.64
180	Guinea-Bissau	7-12	274	*145*	40	...	...	*19*	...	*70*	*84*	*56*	*0.67*
181	Kenya	6-11	5 937	4 782	49	6 688	49	...	10	93	94	91	0.97
182	Lesotho	6-12	373	365	52	425[z]	50[z]	...	0.4[z]	102	98	106	1.08
183	Liberia	6-11	614	396	42	**539**	**47**	38	**30**	85	98	73	0.74
184	Madagascar	6-10	2 714	2 012	49	3 837	49	22	19	93	95	92	0.97
185	Malawi	6-11	2 526	2 582	49	2 943	50	...	1[z]	137	140	134	0.96
186	Mali	7-12	2 065	959	41	1 717	44	22	38	59	70	49	0.70
187	Mauritius	5-10	118	133	49	119	49	24	26	105	105	106	1.00
188	Mozambique	6-12	4 111	2 302	43	4 564	46	...	2	70	80	59	0.74
189	Namibia	7-13	375	383	50	410	50	4	4	107	107	108	1.01
190	Niger	7-12	2 316	530	39	1 235	41	4	4	31	37	25	0.68
191	Nigeria[13]	6-11	24 111	17 907	44	22 862[z]	45[z]	*4*	5[z]	88	98	78	0.79
192	Rwanda	7-12	1 459	1 289	50	2 150	51	...	2	92	93	91	0.98
193	Sao Tome and Principe	7-12	25	24	49	**33**	**49**	–	–	108	109	106	0.97
194	Senegal	7-12	1 882	1 034	46	1 572	50	12	12	64	*69*	*59*	*0.86*
195	Seychelles[3]	6-11	7*	10	49	9	49	5	6	116*	117*	116*	0.99*
196	Sierra Leone	6-11	899	...	...	1 322	48	...	3	...	...	...	...
197	Somalia	6-12	1 581	148	35	...	...	...	...	12	16	9	0.54
198	South Africa	7-13	7 134	7 935	49	7 312	49	2	2	116	117	114	0.97
199	Swaziland	6-12	205	213	49	233	48	–	.[y]	100	102	97	0.95
200	Togo	6-11	1 052	954	43	1 022	46	36	42	112	127	96	0.75
201	Uganda	6-12	6 489	6 288	47	7 538	50	...	10	125	130	119	0.92
202	United Republic of Tanzania	7-13	7 436	4 190	50	**8 624**	**50**	0.2	1	67	67	67	1.00
203	Zambia	7-13	2 346	1 556	48	2 790	49	...	3	80	84	77	0.92
204	Zimbabwe	6-12	2 396	2 460	49	2 446[z]	50[z]	88	...	100	101	98	0.97

			Sum	Sum	% F	Sum	% F	Median		Weighted average			
I	World	...	653 493	646 227	47	693 877	47	7	8	99	103	95	0.92
II	Countries in transition	...	12 875	16 443	49	12 628	49	0.2	0.7	104	105	104	0.99
III	Developed countries	...	65 378	70 414	49	66 334	49	4	5	102	102	102	1.00
IV	Developing countries	...	575 240	559 370	46	614 914	47	11	10	98	103	93	0.91
V	Arab States	...	41 457	35 402	46	40 506	47	4	8	90	96	84	0.87
VI	Central and Eastern Europe	...	22 041	26 063	48	21 421	48	0.3	0.6	102	104	100	0.96
VII	Central Asia	...	5 690	6 857	49	5 687	48	0.3	1.0	98	99	98	0.99
VIII	East Asia and the Pacific	...	173 175	217 665	48	190 901	47	8	9	112	113	112	0.99
IX	East Asia	...	169 703	214 493	48	187 736	47	2	4	113	113	112	0.99
X	Pacific	...	3 471	3 172	48	3 165	48	...	21	95	97	94	0.97
XI	Latin America/Caribbean	...	58 223	70 049	48	68 037	48	15	19	121	123	119	0.97
XII	Caribbean	...	2 232	2 500	49	2 400	49	21	30	112	113	111	0.98
XIII	Latin America	...	55 991	67 549	48	65 637	48	15	14	121	123	119	0.97
XIV	N. America/W. Europe	...	50 571	52 882	49	51 500	49	7	6	103	102	103	1.01
XV	South and West Asia	...	177 522	155 083	44	191 678	47	...	5	89	96	81	0.84
XVI	Sub-Saharan Africa	...	124 815	82 226	46	124 146	47	12	10	78	85	72	0.85

Source: UNESCO Institute for Statistics database (UIS, 2009).

1. Data are for 2006 except for countries with a calendar school year, in which case data are for 2007.
2. Data reflect the actual number of children not enrolled at all, derived from the age-specific enrolment ratios of primary school age children, which measures the proportion of those who are enrolled either in primary or in secondary schools (ANER).
3. National population data were used to calculate enrolment ratios.
4. Enrolment and population data exclude Transnistria.
5. In the Russian Federation two education structures existed in the past, both starting at age 7. The most common or widespread one lasted three years and was used to calculate indicators; the second one, in which about one-third of primary pupils were enrolled, had four grades. Since 2004, the four-grade structure has been extended all over the country.
6. Enrolment and population data exclude the Nagorno-Karabakh region.
7. Children enter primary school at age 6 or 7. Since 7 is the most common entrance age, enrolment ratios were calculated using the 7-11 age group for population.
8. Enrolment ratios were not calculated due to inconsistencies in the population data.
9. Enrolment ratios were not calculated due to lack of United Nations population data by age.

GROSS ENROLMENT RATIO (GER) IN PRIMARY EDUCATION (%)				NET ENROLMENT RATIO (NER) IN PRIMARY EDUCATION (%)								OUT-OF-SCHOOL CHILDREN (000)[2]				
School year ending in				School year ending in								School year ending in				
2007				1999				2007				1999		2007		
Total	Male	Female	GPI (F/M)	Total	Male	Female	GPI (F/M)	Total	Male	Female	GPI (F/M)	Total	% F	Total	% F	
85	94	76	0.81	33	34	32	0.95	...	...	...	...	5 570	51	...	...	*172*
124	128	121	0.95	89	...	...	...	67	68	66	0.97	...	...	20	52	*173*
55	60	50	0.83	33	36	31	0.86	41	44	38	0.88	335	52	349	52	*174*
91	97	85	0.88	34	41	28	0.69	71	74	68	0.92	7 069	55	3 721	55	*175*
...	...	...	...	...	...	...	...	...	...	...	...	...	...	...	...	*176*
83	**80**	**86**	**1.07**	72	76	67	0.89	**67**	**64**	**69**	**1.09**	53	58	**80**	**45**	*177*
104	**104**	**103**	**0.99**	*57*	*58*	*55*	*0.96*	**73**	**73**	**73**	**1.01**	*1 349*	*50*	**930**	**48**	*178*
91	98	84	0.85	45	52	36	0.69	74	79	69	0.87	698	56	362	60	*179*
...	...	...	...	*45*	*53*	*37*	*0.71*	...	...	...	...	*114*	*57*	...	...	*180*
113	113	112	0.99	63	63	64	1.01	86	86	86	1.00	1 859	49	769	50	*181*
114[z]	115[z]	114[z]	1.00[z]	57	54	61	1.12	72[z]	71[z]	74[z]	1.04[z]	152	46	101[z]	47[z]	*182*
83	**88**	**79**	**0.89**	42	47	36	0.77	**31**	**32**	**30**	**0.93**	268	55	**447**	**51**	*183*
141	144	139	0.97	63	63	63	1.01	98	98	99	1.01	796	50	20	16	*184*
116	114	119	1.04	98	99	97	0.98	87	84	90	1.07	20	...	314	37	*185*
83	92	74	0.80	*46*	*55*	*38*	*0.70*	63	70	56	0.80	*862*	*58*	763	59	*186*
101	101	101	1.00	91	90	91	1.01	95	95	96	1.01	12	47	5	42	*187*
111	119	103	0.87	52	58	46	0.79	76[z]	79[z]	73[z]	0.93[z]	1 574	56	954[z]	56[z]	*188*
109	110	109	0.99	81	78	83	1.07	87	84	89	1.06	65	42	45	38	*189*
53	61	46	0.75	26	31	21	0.68	45	51	38	0.75	1 255	52	1 262	55	*190*
97[z]	104[z]	89[z]	0.85[z]	*58*	*64*	*52*	*0.82*	*64[z]*	*68[z]*	*60[z]*	*0.88[z]*	*8 218*	*57*	*8 221[z]*	*55[z]*	*191*
147	146	149	1.02	...	...	...	...	94	92	95	1.03	...	...	88	40	*192*
130	**131**	**129**	**0.98**	86	86	85	0.99	**97**	**98**	**97**	**0.99**	2.7	50	**0.1**	...	*193*
84	84	84	1.00	54	*57*	*50*	*0.88*	72	72	72	1.00	740	*54*	506	50	*194*
125*	126*	125*	0.99*	...	...	...	...	...	...	...	...	...	...	...	...	*195*
147	155	139	0.90	...	...	...	...	...	...	...	...	...	...	...	...	*196*
...	...	...	...	...	...	...	...	...	...	...	...	...	...	...	...	*197*
103	104	101	0.97	94	93	94	1.01	*86*	*86*	*86*	*1.00*	97	2	*642*	*44*	*198*
113	118	109	0.93	74	73	75	1.02	87	86	88	1.02	54	48	26	47	*199*
97	104	90	0.86	79	89	70	0.79	77	82	72	0.88	148	81	222	63	*200*
116	116	117	1.01	...	...	...	...	95	93	96	1.03	...	...	341	36	*201*
112	**112**	**113**	**1.00**	50	49	50	1.04	98[z]	98[z]	97[z]	0.99[z]	3 148	49	143[z]	65[z]	*202*
119	121	117	0.97	68	69	67	0.96	94	94	94	1.01	616	52	108	44	*203*
101[z]	102[z]	101[z]	0.99[z]	83	83	83	1.01	88[z]	87[z]	88[z]	1.01[z]	406	49	281[z]	47[z]	*204*
Weighted average				Weighted average								Sum	% F	Sum	% F	
106	109	104	0.96	82	85	79	0.93	87	88	86	0.97	105 035	58	71 791	54	*I*
98	99	98	0.99	88	89	88	0.99	91	91	90	0.99	1 471	51	819	50	*II*
101	102	101	1.00	97	97	97	1.00	96	95	96	1.01	1 791	50	2 334	44	*III*
107	110	104	0.95	80	83	77	0.92	86	87	84	0.97	101 773	58	68 638	55	*IV*
98	103	93	0.90	78	82	74	0.90	84	88	81	0.92	7 980	59	5 752	61	*V*
97	98	96	0.98	91	93	90	0.97	92	92	91	0.99	2 036	59	1 552	52	*VI*
100	101	99	0.98	88	88	88	0.99	92	93	91	0.98	464	50	271	58	*VII*
110	111	109	0.99	96	96	96	1.00	94	94	93	1.00	5 992	52	9 039	48	*VIII*
111	111	110	0.99	96	96	96	1.00	94	94	94	1.00	5 674	52	8 484	48	*IX*
91	93	90	0.97	90	91	89	0.98	84	85	83	0.97	318	54	555	52	*X*
117	119	115	0.97	92	93	91	0.98	93	94	93	1.00	3 538	54	2 989	50	*XI*
107	108	107	0.99	75	76	74	0.97	72	73	70	0.97	493	50	621	51	*XII*
117	119	115	0.96	93	94	92	0.98	94	94	94	1.00	3 045	55	2 367	49	*XIII*
102	102	102	1.00	97	97	97	1.00	95	95	95	1.01	1 420	50	1 931	44	*XIV*
108	110	105	0.95	74	80	67	0.84	86	87	84	0.96	38 594	63	18 031	58	*XV*
99	104	94	0.90	56	60	53	0.89	73	76	71	0.93	45 012	54	32 226	54	*XVI*

10. Enrolment declined from 2005 to 2007 mainly because the data collection reference date was shifted from the last Wednesday of March to the last Wednesday of May to account for duplicates (enrolments), and transfers of students and teachers (from one school to another), common features at the beginning of the year. At this point of the school year, it is believed, the education system becomes stable, so the data collected should represent the current school year.

11. Data include French overseas departments and territories (DOM-TOM).

12. The apparent increase in the gender parity index (GPI) is due to the inclusion in enrolment statistics in recent years of literacy programmes in which 80% of participants are women.

13. Due to the continuing discrepancy in enrolment by single age, the net enrolment ratio in primary education is estimated using the age distribution of the 2004 DHS data.

Data in italic are UIS estimates.

Data in bold are for the school year ending in 2008.

(z) Data are for the school year ending in 2006.

(y) Data are for the school year ending in 2005.

(*) National estimate.

Table 6

Internal efficiency: repetition in primary education

	Country or territory	Duration[1] of primary education	REPETITION RATES BY GRADE IN PRIMARY EDUCATION (%)											
			School year ending in 2006											
			Grade 1			Grade 2			Grade 3			Grade 4		
		2007	Total	Male	Female	Total	Male	Female	Total	Male	Female	Total	Male	Female
	Arab States													
1	Algeria	6	12.0	13.8	9.9	10.6	12.8	8.2	9.5	12.1	6.8	8.3	10.6	5.7
2	Bahrain	6	3.0^{x}	2.4^{x}	3.5^{x}	3.2^{x}	3.7^{x}	2.6^{x}	3.4^{x}	4.0^{x}	2.8^{x}	2.5^{x}	3.2^{x}	1.8^{x}
3	Djibouti	6	**3.6**	**3.4**	**3.7**	**8.0**	**7.8**	**8.1**	**6.5**	**5.9**	**7.3**	…	…	…
4	Egypt	6	–	–	–	*1.8*	…	…	*2.5*	…	…	*4.1*	…	…
5	Iraq	6	*9.2^{x}*	*10.3^{x}*	*7.9^{x}*	*7.7^{x}*	*8.7^{x}*	*6.5^{x}*	*6.4^{x}*	*7.4^{x}*	*5.2^{x}*	*7.2^{x}*	*8.5^{x}*	*5.5^{x}*
6	Jordan	6	0.6	…	…	0.5	…	…	0.6	…	…	1.3	…	…
7	Kuwait	5	0.7	0.8	0.5	0.3	0.3	0.2	1.5	1.7	1.3	1.3	1.6	1.1
8	Lebanon	6	**5.2**	**6.2**	**4.1**	**5.9**	**7.1**	**4.5**	**5.7**	**6.9**	**4.4**	**15.4**	**17.6**	**12.9**
9	Libyan Arab Jamahiriya	6	…	…	…	…	…	…	…	…	…	…	…	…
10	Mauritania	6	0.4	0.4	0.3	0.8	0.8	0.7	1.0	1.0	1.0	5.8	5.9	5.6
11	Morocco	6	15.6	16.8	14.3	13.3	14.8	11.6	13.3	15.4	10.8	11.1	13.3	8.4
12	Oman	6	–	–	–	–	–	–	–	–	–	–	–	–
13	Palestinian A. T.	4	0.0	0.0	0.0	0.0	0.0	0.0	0.0	0.0	0.0	2.1	2.2	1.9
14	Qatar	6	1.0	1.2	0.8	…	…	…	…	…	…	…	…	…
15	Saudi Arabia	6	…	…	…	…	…	…	…	…	…	…	…	…
16	Sudan	6	2.7	2.8	2.6	2.6	2.7	2.4	3.2	3.3	3.0	2.8	2.9	2.7
17	Syrian Arab Republic	4	11.8	12.8	10.6	7.9	9.1	6.6	4.7	5.6	3.7	2.9	3.6	2.2
18	Tunisia	6	1.3	1.5	1.1	9.6	10.9	8.1	2.2	2.7	1.8	12.5	15.0	9.6
19	United Arab Emirates	5	2.7	2.8	2.6	1.6	1.6	1.6	1.7	1.8	1.6	2.2	2.4	2.0
20	Yemen	6	4.4^{x}	4.3^{x}	4.6^{x}	4.4^{x}	4.4^{x}	4.3^{x}	5.1^{x}	5.4^{x}	4.7^{x}	6.2^{x}	6.9^{x}	5.3^{x}
	Central and Eastern Europe													
21	Albania	4	…	…	…	…	…	…	…	…	…	…	…	…
22	Belarus	4	0.2	0.1	0.2	0.0	0.0	0.0	0.0	0.0	0.0	0.0	0.0	0.0
23	Bosnia and Herzegovina	4	…	…	…	…	…	…	…	…	…	…	…	…
24	Bulgaria	4	0.5	0.7	0.3	2.6	3.0	2.1	2.1	2.5	1.6	3.1	3.5	2.7
25	Croatia	4	0.6	0.6	0.5	0.3	0.3	0.2	0.2	0.2	0.1	0.1	0.2	0.1
26	Czech Republic	5	1.0	1.2	0.9	0.5	0.6	0.4	0.5	0.6	0.4	0.5	0.6	0.5
27	Estonia	6	–	–	–	…	…	…	…	…	…	…	…	…
28	Hungary	4	3.8	4.4	3.2	1.4	1.6	1.1	1.1	1.3	0.9	*1.2*	*1.4*	*0.9*
29	Latvia	4	4.8^{y}	6.4^{y}	3.0^{y}	2.0^{y}	2.7^{y}	1.3^{y}	1.8^{y}	2.4^{y}	1.1^{y}	2.2^{y}	3.0^{y}	1.4^{y}
30	Lithuania	4	1.3	1.5	1.1	0.5	0.6	0.3	0.4	0.4	0.4	0.3	0.4	0.3
31	Montenegro	4	…	…	…	…	…	…	…	…	…	…	…	…
32	Poland	6	0.8	…	…	0.4	…	…	0.4	…	…	0.9	…	…
33	Republic of Moldova	4	0.4	0.5	0.3	0.1	0.1	0.1	0.0	0.1	0.0	0.1	0.1	0.0
34	Romania	4	0.9	0.9	0.8	1.7	2.0	1.3	1.2	1.5	0.8	1.3	1.6	1.0
35	Russian Federation	4	0.8	…	…	0.5	…	…	0.3	…	…	…	…	…
36	Serbia	4	…	…	…	…	…	…	…	…	…	…	…	…
37	Slovakia	4	5.3	5.6	4.9	2.1	2.3	1.9	1.5	1.8	1.3	1.8	1.9	1.6
38	Slovenia	5	0.5	0.5	0.4	…	…	…	…	…	…	…	…	…
39	TFYR Macedonia	4	0.3^{x}	0.3^{x}	0.2^{x}	0.2^{x}	0.2^{x}	0.2^{x}	0.1^{x}	0.1^{x}	0.1^{x}	0.2^{x}	0.2^{x}	0.1^{x}
40	Turkey	6	*3.9*	*4.2*	*3.5*	*1.8*	*1.8*	*1.8*	*1.8*	*1.6*	*2.0*	*2.2*	*1.8*	*2.6*
41	Ukraine	4	0.3	0.3*	0.3*	0.1	0.1*	0.1*	0.0	0.0*	0.0*	0.0	0.0*	0.0*
	Central Asia													
42	Armenia	3	–	–	–	0.3	0.3	0.3	0.3	0.3	0.2	…	…	…
43	Azerbaijan	4	0.4	0.4	0.4	0.3	0.3	0.2	0.2	0.2	0.2	0.3	0.3	0.2
44	Georgia	6	0.5	*0.7*	*0.3*	0.3	…	…	0.3	…	…	0.3	…	…
45	Kazakhstan	4	**0.1**	**0.1**	**0.1**	**0.1**	**0.1**	**0.1**	**0.1**	**0.1**	**0.0**	**0.0**	**0.1**	**0.0**
46	Kyrgyzstan	4	0.1	0.1	0.1	0.1	0.1	0.1	0.1	0.1	0.0	0.1	0.1	0.1
47	Mongolia	5	1.2	1.3	1.1	1.2	1.3	1.1	0.1	0.1	0.1	0.1	0.1	0.1
48	Tajikistan	4	0.1	0.1	–	0.3	…	…	0.2	…	…	0.2	…	…
49	Turkmenistan	3	…	…	…	…	…	…	…	…	…	…	…	…
50	Uzbekistan	4	0.0	0.0	0.0	0.0	0.0	0.0	0.0	0.0	0.0	0.0	0.0	0.0
	East Asia and the Pacific													
51	Australia	7	…	…	…	…	…	…	…	…	…	…	…	…
52	Brunei Darussalam	6	0.7	0.9	0.5	0.9	1.4	0.4	0.8	1.0	0.5	1.8	2.5	0.9
53	Cambodia	6	20.6	21.7	19.4	13.5	14.7	12.2	11.2	12.5	9.6	7.8	9.0	6.5
54	China	5	1.2	1.3	1.1	…	…	…	…	…	…	…	…	…
55	Cook Islands	6	…	…	…	…	…	…	…	…	…	…	…	…

REPETITION RATES BY GRADE IN PRIMARY EDUCATION (%)									REPEATERS, ALL GRADES (%)						
School year ending in 2006									School year ending in						
Grade 5			Grade 6			Grade 7			1999			2007			
Total	Male	Female	Total	Male	Female	Total	Male	Female	Total	Male	Female	Total	Male	Female	
														Arab States	
11.0	14.1	7.5	13.1	15.4	10.4	.	.	.	11.9	14.6	8.7	11.1	13.6	8.2	*1*
2.8[x]	3.5[x]	2.1[x]	1.9[x]	3.1[x]	0.8[x]	.	.	.	3.8	4.6	3.1	2.7[z]	3.0[z]	2.3[z]	*2*
…	…	…	.	.	.	.	.	.	16.6	*16.9*	*16.1*	**10.6**	**10.6**	**10.5**	*3*
3.9	…	…	*6.8*	…	…	.	.	.	*6.0*	*7.1*	*4.6*	3.1	3.9	2.2	*4*
13.1[x]	*15.2*[x]	*10.2*[x]	*4.2*[x]	*4.4*[x]	*3.8*[x]	.	.	.	10.0	10.7	9.2	*8.0*[y]	*9.1*[y]	*6.5*[y]	*5*
1.6	…	…	1.8	…	…	.	.	.	0.7	0.7	0.7	1.1	1.1	1.1	*6*
1.0	1.3	0.6	…	…	…	.	.	.	3.3	3.4	3.1	0.9	1.1	0.7	*7*
9.8	**11.1**	**8.4**	**9.0**	**10.3**	**7.7**	.	.	.	9.1	10.5	7.7	**8.7**	**10.2**	**7.2**	*8*
…	…	…	…	…	…	.	.	.	…	…	…	…	…	…	*9*
8.4	8.4	8.4	13.7	13.4	14.0	.	.	.	…	…	…	3.4	3.4	3.4	*10*
8.7	10.9	6.2	8.1	10.1	5.7	.	.	.	12.4	14.1	10.2	11.9	13.7	9.7	*11*
4.0	3.0	5.0	2.6	2.4	2.9	.	.	.	8.0	9.5	6.4	1.3	1.0	1.5	*12*
…	…	…	…	…	…	.	.	.	2.1	2.2	2.0	0.5	0.6	0.5	*13*
…	…	…	…	…	…	.	.	.	*2.7*	*3.5*	*1.9*	0.9	0.9	0.8	*14*
…	…	…	…	…	…	.	.	.	…	…	…	3.2*	3.4*	2.9*	*15*
2.8	2.9	2.6	3.4	3.6	3.1	.	.	.	*11.3*	*10.9*	*11.8*	2.8	2.9	2.7	*16*
…	…	…	…	…	…	.	.	.	6.5	7.2	5.6	7.0	8.0	5.9	*17*
2.6	3.3	1.9	11.2	13.7	8.3	.	.	.	18.3	20.0	16.4	7.4	9.0	5.7	*18*
1.5	2.0	1.0	…	…	…	.	.	.	3.5	4.4	2.5	1.9	2.0	1.7	*19*
5.8[x]	6.5[x]	4.7[x]	5.0[x]	5.6[x]	3.9[x]	.	.	.	10.6	11.7*	8.7*	4.9[y]	5.3[y]	4.3[y]	*20*
												Central and Eastern Europe			
.	.	.	.	.	.	.	.	.	*3.9*	*4.6*	*3.2*	…	…	…	*21*
.	.	.	.	.	.	.	.	.	0.5	0.5	0.5	0.1	0.1	0.1	*22*
.	.	.	.	.	.	.	.	.	…	…	…	0.5	0.8	0.2	*23*
.	.	.	.	.	.	.	.	.	3.2	3.7	2.7	2.1	2.5	1.8	*24*
.	.	.	.	.	.	.	.	.	0.4	0.5	0.3	0.3	0.3	0.2	*25*
0.5	0.6	0.3	.	.	.	.	.	.	1.2	1.5	1.0	0.6	0.7	0.5	*26*
…	…	…	–	–	–	.	.	.	2.5	3.5	1.4	–	–	–	*27*
.	.	.	.	.	.	.	.	.	2.2	2.1	2.2	1.9	2.3	1.6	*28*
.	.	.	.	.	.	.	.	.	2.1	*2.7*	*1.3*	2.8[z]	3.8[z]	1.8[z]	*29*
.	.	.	.	.	.	.	.	.	0.9	1.3	0.5	0.6	0.8	0.5	*30*
…	…	…	…	…	…	.	.	.	…	…	…	…	…	…	*31*
1.0	…	…	0.6	…	…	.	.	.	1.2	…	…	0.7	1.1	0.3	*32*
.	.	.	.	.	.	.	.	.	0.9	*0.9*	*0.9*	0.1	0.2	0.1	*33*
.	.	.	.	.	.	.	.	.	3.4	4.1	2.6	1.3	1.5	1.0	*34*
.	.	.	.	.	.	.	.	.	1.4	…	…	0.5	…	…	*35*
.	.	.	.	.	.	.	.	.	…	…	…	…	…	…	*36*
.	.	.	.	.	.	.	.	.	2.3	2.6	2.0	2.7	2.9	2.5	*37*
.	.	.	.	.	.	.	.	.	1.0	1.3	0.7	0.5	0.6	0.4	*38*
.	.	.	.	.	.	.	.	.	0.0	0.1	0.0	0.1	0.1	0.1	*39*
…	…	…	…	…	…	.	.	.	…	…	…	*2.7*	*2.5*	*2.8*	*40*
…	…	…	.	.	.	.	.	.	0.8	0.8*	0.8*	0.1	0.1*	0.1*	*41*
													Central Asia		
.	.	.	.	.	.	.	.	.	…	…	…	0.2	0.2	0.2	*42*
.	.	.	.	.	.	.	.	.	0.4	0.4	0.4	0.3	0.3	0.2	*43*
0.4	…	…	0.4	*0.6*	*0.3*	.	.	.	0.3	*0.5*	*0.2*	0.4	…	…	*44*
.	.	.	.	.	.	.	.	.	0.3	…	…	**0.1**	**0.1**	**0.1**	*45*
.	.	.	.	.	.	.	.	.	0.3	0.4	0.2	0.1	0.1	0.1	*46*
0.1	0.1	0.1	.	.	.	.	.	.	0.9	1.0	0.8	0.5	0.5	0.5	*47*
.	.	.	.	.	.	.	.	.	0.5	*0.5*	*0.6*	0.2	…	…	*48*
.	.	.	.	.	.	.	.	.	…	…	…	…	…	…	*49*
.	.	.	.	.	.	.	.	.	0.1	…	…	0.0	0.0	0.0	*50*
												East Asia and the Pacific			
…	…	…	…	…	…	.	.	.	…	…	…	…	…	…	*51*
1.2	1.8	0.7	6.9	9.0	4.5	.	.	.	.	.	.	2.1	2.8	1.3	*52*
5.2	6.0	4.2	2.8	3.3	2.2	.	.	.	*24.6*	*25.4*	*23.5*	11.6	12.8	10.4	*53*
…	…	…	.	.	.	.	.	.	…	…	…	0.2	0.3	0.2	*54*
…	…	…	…	…	…	.	.	.	2.6	…	…	1.7	…	…	*55*

Table 6 (continued)

	Country or territory	Duration[1] of primary education 2007	REPETITION RATES BY GRADE IN PRIMARY EDUCATION (%) School year ending in 2006 — Grade 1 Total	Grade 1 Male	Grade 1 Female	Grade 2 Total	Grade 2 Male	Grade 2 Female	Grade 3 Total	Grade 3 Male	Grade 3 Female	Grade 4 Total	Grade 4 Male	Grade 4 Female
56	DPR Korea	4	...	...	...	...	...	...	...	...	...	...	...	...
57	Fiji	6	*4.0*	*4.8*	*3.2*	*2.0*	...	...	*1.3*	...	...	*1.2*	...	...
58	Indonesia	6	6.8	7.8	5.7	4.1	4.9	3.2	3.7	4.5	2.8	2.7	3.3	2.1
59	Japan	6	–	–	–	...	...	...	...	...	...	...	...	...
60	Kiribati	6	.[x]	.[x]	.[x]	.[x]	.[x]	.[x]	...	...	...	...	...	...
61	Lao PDR	5	30.6	31.3	29.8	17.1	18.3	15.7	11.4	12.8	9.8	7.2	8.5	5.7
62	Macao, China	6	2.1	...	...	2.8	...	...	...	...	...	...	...	...
63	Malaysia	6	.[y]	.[y]	.[y]	.[y]	.[y]	.[y]	.[y]	.[y]	.[y]	.[y]	.[y]	.[y]
64	Marshall Islands	6	...	...	...	...	...	...	...	...	...	...	...	...
65	Micronesia, F. S.	6	...	...	...	...	...	...	...	...	...	...	...	...
66	Myanmar	5	0.9	1.1	0.7	0.6	...	...	0.5	...	...	0.5	...	...
67	Nauru	6	–	–	–	...	...	...	...	...	...	...	...	...
68	New Zealand	6	...	...	...	...	...	...	...	...	...	...	...	...
69	Niue	6	...	...	...	...	...	...	...	...	...	...	...	...
70	Palau	5	...	...	...	...	...	...	...	...	...	...	...	...
71	Papua New Guinea	6	–[y]	–[y]	–[y]	...	...	...	...	...	...	...	...	...
72	Philippines	6	5.3	6.2	4.2	2.6	3.5	1.8	1.8	2.5	1.2	1.4	1.8	0.8
73	Republic of Korea	6	0.0	0.0	0.0	0.0	0.0	0.0	0.0	0.0	0.0	0.0	0.0	0.0
74	Samoa	6	...	...	...	...	...	...	...	...	...	...	...	...
75	Singapore	6	...	...	...	...	...	...	...	...	...	...	...	...
76	Solomon Islands	6	...	...	...	...	...	...	...	...	...	...	...	...
77	Thailand	6	...	...	...	...	...	...	...	...	...	...	...	...
78	Timor-Leste	6	...	...	...	...	...	...	...	...	...	...	...	...
79	Tokelau	6	...	...	...	...	...	...	...	...	...	...	...	...
80	Tonga	6	.[y]	.[y]	.[y]	.[y]	.[y]	.[y]	.[y]	.[y]	.[y]	.[y]	.[y]	.[y]
81	Tuvalu	6	.[y]	.[y]	.[y]	.[y]	.[y]	.[y]	.[y]	.[y]	.[y]	.[y]	.[y]	.[y]
82	Vanuatu	6	...	...	...	...	...	...	...	...	...	...	...	...
83	Viet Nam	5	*2.9*[y]	...	...	*0.9*[y]	...	...	*0.7*[y]	...	...	*0.6*[y]	...	...
	Latin America and the Caribbean													
84	Anguilla	7	–	–	–	–	–	–	–	–	–	–	–	–
85	Antigua and Barbuda	7	...	...	...	...	...	...	...	...	...	...	...	...
86	Argentina	6	10.1[y]	11.5[y]	8.5[y]	7.0[y]	8.2[y]	5.8[y]	6.2[y]	7.3[y]	5.0[y]	6.1[y]	7.3[y]	4.9[y]
87	Aruba	6	13.4	15.3	11.6	10.6	11.6	9.6	9.1	10.5	7.5	8.9	9.4	8.3
88	Bahamas	6	–	–	–	–	–	–	–	–	–	–	–	–
89	Barbados	6	.	.	.	.	.	.	.	.	.	.	.	.
90	Belize	6	13.8	14.9	12.6	9.6	11.0	8.2	8.5	10.2	6.6	9.3	11.3	7.3
91	Bermuda	6	.[y]	...	...	.[y]	...	...	.[y]	...	...	.[y]	...	...
92	Bolivia	6	2.6	2.7	2.4	2.3	2.5	2.1	2.7	2.9	2.5	2.1	2.3	1.9
93	Brazil	4	24.4[x]	...	...	19.2[x]	...	...	14.2[x]	...	...	14.3[x]	...	...
94	British Virgin Islands	7	7.1	11.6	2.3	...	...	...	...	...	...	...	...	...
95	Cayman Islands	6	–	–	–	–	–	–	–	–	–	–	–	–
96	Chile	6	2.7	3.2	2.2	2.5	2.9	2.0	2.2	2.8	1.7	1.8	2.2	1.3
97	Colombia	5	5.7	6.3	5.1	4.1	4.5	3.7	3.3	3.7	2.9	2.8	3.2	2.4
98	Costa Rica	6	13.9	15.6	12.0	8.1	9.3	6.7	7.2	8.4	5.9	9.3	10.9	7.5
99	Cuba	6	–	–	–	1.7	2.4	0.9	–	–	–	0.8	1.1	0.4
100	Dominica	7	9.9	13.8	5.5	4.5	6.1	3.1	5.7	8.0	3.2	3.1	3.8	2.3
101	Dominican Republic	6	6.4	...	...	...	...	...	...	...	...	...	...	...
102	Ecuador	6	2.9	3.2	2.6	2.0	2.2	1.7	1.2	1.4	1.0	0.9	1.1	0.8
103	El Salvador	6	13.3	14.7	11.8	6.6	7.5	5.6	5.2	6.2	4.2	5.4	6.5	4.2
104	Grenada	7	*1.7*[y]	*2.6*[y]	*0.8*[y]	*3.0*[y]	*3.3*[y]	*2.6*[y]	*2.9*[y]	*3.7*[y]	*2.0*[y]	...	...	...
105	Guatemala	6	24.3	25.8	22.8	14.1	15.2	12.9	10.5	11.5	9.4	7.0	7.9	5.9
106	Guyana	6	...	...	...	...	...	...	...	...	...	...	...	...
107	Haiti	6	...	...	...	...	...	...	...	...	...	...	...	...
108	Honduras	6	16.4[y]	17.6[y]	15.1[y]	9.5[y]	10.8[y]	8.2[y]	6.4[y]	7.2[y]	5.5[y]	4.1[y]	4.6[y]	3.5[y]
109	Jamaica	6	*3.9*[x]	*5.1*[x]	*2.6*[x]	...	...	...	...	...	...	...	...	...
110	Mexico	6	6.1	7.2	5.0	6.1	7.2	4.8	4.2	5.1	3.2	3.4	4.2	2.5
111	Montserrat	7	11.8	11.1	12.5	–	–	–	3.0	2.3	4.3	1.3	2.4	–
112	Netherlands Antilles	6	...	...	...	...	...	...	...	...	...	...	...	...
113	Nicaragua	6	13.8	15.0	12.4	11.1	12.8	9.3	7.0	8.0	6.0	7.3	8.6	6.0
114	Panama	6	9.0	10.1	7.7	8.4	9.8	6.9	6.2	7.4	4.9	4.2	5.2	3.1
115	Paraguay	6	10.2[x]	11.5[x]	8.7[x]	6.9[x]	8.3[x]	5.5[x]	5.1[x]	6.1[x]	4.0[x]	3.4[x]	4.2[x]	2.5[x]
116	Peru	6	3.8	4.0	3.6	12.9	13.4	12.5	10.9	11.2	10.6	7.7	8.0	7.4
117	Saint Kitts and Nevis	7	.[x]	.[x]	.[x]	.[x]	.[x]	.[x]	...	...	...	...	...	...

REPETITION RATES BY GRADE IN PRIMARY EDUCATION (%)									REPEATERS, ALL GRADES (%)						
School year ending in 2006									School year ending in						
Grade 5			Grade 6			Grade 7			1999			2007			
Total	Male	Female	Total	Male	Female	Total	Male	Female	Total	Male	Female	Total	Male	Female	
...	...	...	...	...	...	.	.	.	...	...	...	...	...	...	*56*
1.0	...	...	*3.1*	...	...	.	.	.	...	...	...	*2.2*	*2.7*	*1.7*	*57*
1.9	...	...	0.3	...	...	.	.	.	...	...	...	3.3	4.0	2.7	*58*
...	...	...	...	...	...	.	.	.	...	...	...	...	...	...	*59*
...	...	...	...	...	...	.	.	.	.	.	.	.[y]	.[y]	.[y]	*60*
4.0	4.8	3.0	.	.	.	.	.	.	20.9	22.4	19.1	16.9	18.0	15.7	*61*
...	...	...	...	...	...	.	.	.	6.3	7.3	5.1	5.8	7.4	4.0	*62*
.[y]	.[y]	.[y]	.[y]	.[y]	.[y]	.	.	.	.	.	.	.[z]	.[z]	.[z]	*63*
...	...	...	...	...	...	.	.	.	.	.	.	.	.	.	*64*
...	...	...	...	...	...	.	.	.	...	...	...	...	...	...	*65*
0.3	...	...	.	.	.	.	.	.	1.7	*1.7*	*1.7*	0.6	...	...	*66*
...	...	...	...	...	...	.	.	.	...	...	...	...	...	...	*67*
...	...	...	...	...	...	.	.	.	...	...	...	...	...	...	*68*
...	...	...	...	...	...	.	.	.	.	.	.	.[y]	.[y]	.[y]	*69*
...	...	...	.	.	.	.	.	.	–	–	–	...	...	...	*70*
...	...	...	...	...	...	.	.	.	...	...	...	...	...	...	*71*
1.1	1.6	0.7	0.6	0.8	0.3	.	.	.	1.9	2.4	1.4	2.3	3.0	1.6	*72*
0.0	0.0	0.0	0.0	0.0	0.0	.	.	.	–	–	–	0.0	0.0	0.0	*73*
...	...	...	...	...	...	.	.	.	1.0	1.1	0.9	1.2	1.5	0.9	*74*
...	...	...	...	...	...	.	.	.	...	...	...	0.3*	0.4*	0.3*	*75*
...	...	...	...	...	...	.	.	.	...	...	...	...	...	...	*76*
...	...	...	...	...	...	.	.	.	3.5	3.4	3.5	9.2	11.8	6.5	*77*
...	...	...	...	...	...	.	.	.	...	...	...	14.5	15.3	13.5	*78*
...	...	...	...	...	...	.	.	.	...	...	...	...	...	...	*79*
.[y]	.[y]	.[y]	20.2[y]	22.7[y]	17.3[y]	.	.	.	8.8	8.5	9.2	5.2[z]	5.9[z]	4.4[z]	*80*
.[y]	.[y]	.[y]	.[y]	.[y]	.[y]	.	.	.	.	.	.	.[z]	.[z]	.[z]	*81*
...	...	...	...	...	...	.	.	.	*10.6*	*11.1*	*9.9*	...	...	...	*82*
0.1[y]	...	...	...	...	...	.	.	.	3.8	4.2	3.2	*1.0*[z]	...	...	*83*
Latin America and the Caribbean															
–	–	–	...	...	...	...	...	...	0.3	0.4	0.3	–	–	–	*84*
...	...	...	...	...	...	...	...	...	...	...	...	2.1	2.4	1.7	*85*
5.6[y]	6.9[y]	4.4[y]	4.7[y]	5.7[y]	3.7[y]	.	.	.	5.9	6.9	4.9	6.6[z]	7.7[z]	5.3[z]	*86*
7.2	8.4	6.0	3.5	3.9	3.1	.	.	.	7.7	9.5	5.9	8.4	9.3	7.5	*87*
–	–	–	...	...	...	.	.	.	.	.	.	–	–	–	*88*
.	.	.	.	.	.	.	.	.	.	.	.	.	.	.	*89*
7.3	8.7	5.9	7.1	8.1	6.1	.	.	.	9.7	10.8	8.4	9.4	10.9	7.9	*90*
.[y]	...	...	.[y]	...	...	.	.	.	...	...	...	.[z]	.[z]	.[z]	*91*
2.2	2.5	2.0	3.0	3.5	2.5	.	.	.	2.4	2.6	2.3	2.5	2.7	2.2	*92*
...	...	...	...	...	...	.	.	.	24.0	24.0	24.0	18.7[y]	...	...	*93*
...	...	...	...	...	...	...	...	...	*3.8*	*4.1*	*3.6*	4.5	6.2	2.7	*94*
–	–	–	...	...	...	.	.	.	*0.2*	*0.2*	*0.1*	–	–	–	*95*
...	...	...	...	...	...	.	.	.	2.4	2.9	1.9	2.4	2.9	1.8	*96*
2.4	2.8	2.0	.	.	.	.	.	.	5.2	5.8	4.6	3.7	4.2	3.2	*97*
5.9	6.9	4.8	0.8	0.9	0.6	.	.	.	9.2	10.4	7.9	7.6	8.8	6.3	*98*
0.3	0.5	0.2	0.2	0.2	0.1	.	.	.	1.9	2.6	1.1	0.5	0.7	0.3	*99*
2.3	3.2	1.4	2.7	3.7	1.5	2.6	3.5	1.6	3.6	3.8	3.5	4.5	6.2	2.7	*100*
...	...	...	...	...	...	.	.	.	4.1	4.5	3.7	5.6	6.9	4.1	*101*
0.6	0.8	0.5	0.3	0.4	0.3	.	.	.	2.7	3.0	2.4	1.4	1.6	1.2	*102*
4.5	5.5	3.4	4.3	5.3	3.3	.	.	.	*7.1*	*7.7*	*6.4*	6.6	7.9	5.4	*103*
...	...	...	...	...	...	...	...	...	...	...	...	2.4	3.0	1.7	*104*
4.7	5.4	3.9	1.4	1.7	1.2	.	.	.	14.9	15.8	13.8	12.2	13.2	11.2	*105*
...	...	...	...	...	...	.	.	.	3.1	3.6	2.5	1.4	1.7	1.2	*106*
...	...	...	...	...	...	.	.	.	...	...	...	...	...	...	*107*
2.6[y]	3.1[y]	2.1[y]	0.7[y]	0.9[y]	0.6[y]	.	.	.	...	...	...	6.8	6.8	6.8	*108*
...	...	...	...	...	...	.	.	.	...	...	...	3.0	3.5	2.5	*109*
2.4	3.2	1.7	0.5	0.6	0.4	.	.	.	6.6	7.6	5.5	3.8	4.7	2.9	*110*
...	...	...	...	...	...	...	...	...	0.8	1.4	–	3.2	3.6	2.9	*111*
...	...	...	...	...	...	.	.	.	*12.0*	*14.5*	*9.3*	...	...	...	*112*
4.0	4.8	3.2	2.2	2.6	1.8	.	.	.	4.7	5.3	4.1	9.0	10.2	7.6	*113*
2.9	3.7	2.1	1.2	1.6	0.8	.	.	.	6.4	7.4	5.2	5.5	6.5	4.4	*114*
2.0[x]	2.5[x]	1.4[x]	1.0[x]	1.3[x]	0.7[x]	.	.	.	7.8	8.8	6.7	5.1[y]	6.1[y]	4.1[y]	*115*
6.5	6.9	6.1	3.5	3.7	3.4	.	.	.	10.2	10.5	9.9	7.8	8.1	7.5	*116*
...	...	...	...	...	...	...	...	...	...	...	...	1.8	2.6	1.0	*117*

Table 6 (continued)

	Country or territory	Duration[1] of primary education	REPETITION RATES BY GRADE IN PRIMARY EDUCATION (%)											
			School year ending in 2006											
			Grade 1			Grade 2			Grade 3			Grade 4		
		2007	Total	Male	Female	Total	Male	Female	Total	Male	Female	Total	Male	Female
118	Saint Lucia	7	6.3	7.9	4.7	2.2	3.0	1.4	1.5	2.2	0.8	1.2	1.5	0.9
119	Saint Vincent/Grenadines	7	5.3[x]	6.5[x]	3.9[x]	...	...	...	...	...	...	...	...	...
120	Suriname	6	18.4	21.1	15.2	14.3	17.3	10.9	15.1	17.4	12.5	13.8	16.2	11.2
121	Trinidad and Tobago	7	10.8[*,x]	12.8[*,x]	8.6[*,x]	3.5[*,x]	2.7[*,x]	4.3[*,x]	4.1[*,x]	5.1[*,x]	3.0[*,x]	4.1[*,x]	4.9[*,x]	3.2[*,x]
122	Turks and Caicos Islands	6	...	...	...	...	...	...	...	...	...	...	...	...
123	Uruguay	6	14.2	16.7	11.5	9.1	10.3	7.8	6.9	8.1	5.5	5.3	6.4	4.2
124	Venezuela, B. R.	6	8.1	9.6	6.5	6.4	7.8	4.9	6.2	7.8	4.6	4.5	5.7	3.2
	North America and Western Europe													
125	Andorra	6	2.0	1.6	2.3	6.3	6.3	6.2	1.3	1.7	0.9	3.1	3.9	2.2
126	Austria	4	–	–	–	–	–	–	–	–	–	–	–	–
127	Belgium	6	6.5	6.8	6.2	4.4	4.4	4.5	2.8	2.9	2.8	2.5	2.7	2.3
128	Canada	6	...	...	...	...	...	...	...	...	...	...	...	...
129	Cyprus	6	1.2	1.5	0.8	0.1	0.0	0.1	0.0	–	0.1	0.0	0.0	0.0
130	Denmark	6	–	–	–	–	–	–	–	–	–	...	...	...
131	Finland	6	0.9	1.2	0.7	0.9	1.2	0.7	0.3	0.4	0.2	0.2	0.3	0.1
132	France	5	...	...	...	...	...	...	...	...	...	...	...	...
133	Germany	4	1.2	1.2	1.1	1.4	1.4	1.4	1.3	1.4	1.2	0.7	0.8	0.6
134	Greece	6	1.4	1.6	1.2	0.7	0.8	0.6	0.6	0.6	0.5	0.4	0.5	0.4
135	Iceland	7	–	–	–	–	–	–	–	–	–	–	–	–
136	Ireland	8	1.9	2.1	1.7	1.2	1.4	1.0	0.7	0.8	0.6	...	...	...
137	Israel	6	1.7	...	...	0.9	...	...	1.0	...	...	1.2	...	...
138	Italy	5	0.5	0.6	0.3	0.2	0.3	0.2	0.2	0.2	0.1	0.1	0.2	0.1
139	Luxembourg	6	4.8	5.3	4.2	5.3	5.9	4.6	5.6	6.9	4.3	3.1	3.5	2.7
140	Malta	6	0.8[x]	0.8[x]	0.8[x]	0.8[x]	0.9[x]	0.7[x]	...	...	...	...	...	...
141	Monaco	5	...	...	...	...	...	...	...	...	...	...	...	...
142	Netherlands	6	.	.	.	.	.	.	.	.	.	.	.	.
143	Norway	7	.	.	.	.	.	.	.	.	.	.	.	.
144	Portugal	6	–	–	–	...	...	...	...	...	...	...	...	...
145	San Marino	5	–	–	–	–	–	–	–	–	–	–	–	–
146	Spain	6	–	–	–	...	...	...	...	...	...	...	...	...
147	Sweden	6	–	–	–	–	–	–	–	–	–	–	–	–
148	Switzerland	6	...	...	...	...	...	...	...	...	...	...	...	...
149	United Kingdom	6	...	...	...	...	...	...	...	...	...	...	...	...
150	United States	6	–	–	–	–	–	–	–	–	–	–	–	–
	South and West Asia													
151	Afghanistan	6	*8.8*[x]	*8.1*[x]	*10.5*[x]	...	...	...	...	...	...	...	...	...
152	Bangladesh	5	11.5[y]	11.9[y]	11.2[y]	10.6[y]	10.8[y]	10.3[y]	13.6[y]	13.6[y]	13.5[y]	12.7[y]	12.6[y]	12.8[y]
153	Bhutan	7	8.1[y]	8.6[y]	7.5[y]	7.8[y]	8.9[y]	6.6[y]	7.9[y]	8.7[y]	7.1[y]	5.9[y]	6.5[y]	5.4[y]
154	India	5	3.7[y]	3.7[y]	3.7[y]	2.7[y]	2.7[y]	2.7[y]	3.8[y]	3.8[y]	3.9[y]	4.1[y]	4.2[y]	4.0[y]
155	Iran, Islamic Republic of	5	*4.0*[y]	*4.9*[y]	*3.2*[y]	...	...	...	...	...	...	...	...	...
156	Maldives	7	0.5[y]	...	...	0.4[y]	...	...	...	...	...	...	...	...
157	Nepal	5	**30.0**	**30.1**	**29.8**	**12.9**	**12.6**	**13.3**	**9.8**	**9.6**	**10.0**	**9.5**	**9.5**	**9.4**
158	Pakistan	5	6.5	6.6	6.3	...	...	...	...	...	...	...	...	...
159	Sri Lanka	5	*0.5*[y]	*0.6*[y]	*0.5*[y]	*0.9*[y]	*1.0*[y]	*0.8*[y]	*0.9*[y]	*1.0*[y]	*0.8*[y]	*1.1*[y]	*1.2*[y]	*0.9*[y]
	Sub-Saharan Africa													
160	Angola	4	...	...	...	...	...	...	...	...	...	...	...	...
161	Benin	6	1.4[y]	1.6[y]	1.1[y]	9.3[y]	9.4[y]	9.2[y]	11.2[y]	11.1[y]	11.3[y]	11.5[y]	11.0[y]	12.2[y]
162	Botswana	7	.[x]	.[x]	.[x]	.[x]	.[x]	.[x]	.[x]	.[x]	.[x]	.[x]	.[x]	.[x]
163	Burkina Faso	6	**5.0**	**5.1**	**4.7**	**8.9**	**9.2**	**8.6**	**10.4**	**10.7**	**10.1**	**13.4**	**13.5**	**13.3**
164	Burundi	6	34.4	33.6	35.1	34.2	34.2	34.2	32.3	31.7	32.9	30.9	29.9	32.0
165	Cameroon	6	26.4	26.9	25.8	17.9	18.2	17.7	23.2	...	...	15.8	...	...
166	Cape Verde	6	1.5	...	...	22.5	...	...	13.2	...	...	14.2	...	...
167	Central African Republic	6	**28.5**	**27.3**	**30.2**	**23.2**	**22.7**	**23.8**	**31.1**	**30.8**	**31.6**	**27.1**	**26.4**	**28.1**
168	Chad	6	*22.8*	*22.1*	*23.8*	...	...	...	...	...	...	...	...	...
169	Comoros	6	*33.3*[x]	*35.0*[x]	*31.2*[x]	*28.9*[x]	*27.5*[x]	*30.4*[x]	*28.5*[x]	*30.4*[x]	*26.2*[x]	*24.1*[x]	*26.0*[x]	*21.9*[x]
170	Congo	6	27.7[x]	...	...	...	...	...	...	...	...	...	...	...
171	Côte d'Ivoire	6	20.3	21.3	19.2	18.0	19.3	16.6	21.6	22.1	21.0	20.7	20.7	20.8
172	Democratic Rep. of the Congo	6	...	...	...	...	...	...	...	...	...	...	...	...
173	Equatorial Guinea	5	...	...	...	...	...	...	...	...	...	...	...	...
174	Eritrea	5	13.0	13.0	12.9	15.6	16.0	15.3	13.6	13.8	13.3	13.8	13.8	13.8
175	Ethiopia	6	7.1	7.4	6.8	5.2	5.6	4.8	5.8	6.4	5.1	7.6	8.2	6.8

REPETITION RATES BY GRADE IN PRIMARY EDUCATION (%)									REPEATERS, ALL GRADES (%)						
School year ending in 2006									School year ending in						
Grade 5			Grade 6			Grade 7			1999			2007			
Total	Male	Female	Total	Male	Female	Total	Male	Female	Total	Male	Female	Total	Male	Female	
0.9	1.2	0.7	…	…	…	…	…	…	*2.4*	*2.8*	*2.0*	2.7	3.3	2.0	118
…	…	…	…	…	…	16.0[x]	21.9[x]	11.2[x]	…	…	…	4.1[y]	5.0[y]	3.0[y]	119
13.9	15.9	11.9	16.8	16.8	16.7	…	…	…	…	…	…	15.7	17.8	13.5	120
4.2[*,x]	5.0[*,x]	3.3[*,x]	5.2[*,x]	6.5[*,x]	4.0[*,x]	3.2[*,x]	2.9[*,x]	3.4[*,x]	4.7	4.9	4.4	2.9	3.5	2.3	121
…	…	…	…	…	…	.	.	.	…	…	…	2.9[y]	3.2[y]	2.6[y]	122
4.1	5.2	2.9	1.9	2.4	1.5	.	.	.	7.9	9.3	6.5	7.0	8.2	5.6	123
2.9	3.8	2.1	1.1	1.5	0.8	.	.	.	*7.0*	*8.5*	*5.5*	4.9	6.1	3.7	124
North America and Western Europe															
1.1	1.3	0.9	…	…	…	.	.	.	…	…	…	2.9	3.3	2.5	125
…	…	…	…	…	…	.	.	.	1.5	1.8	1.3	…	…	…	126
2.5	2.8	2.2	1.0	1.1	0.9	.	.	.	…	…	…	3.2	3.3	3.1	127
…	…	…	…	…	…	.	.	.	…	…	…	–[z]	–[z]	–[z]	128
0.0	0.0	–	0.0	0.1	0.0	.	.	.	0.4	0.5	0.3	0.2	0.3	0.2	129
…	…	…	…	…	…	.	.	.	–	–	–	–	–	–	130
0.1	0.2	0.1	0.2	0.2	0.1	.	.	.	0.4	0.6	0.3	0.4	0.6	0.3	131
…	…	…	…	…	…	.	.	.	4.2	*4.2*	*4.2*	…	…	…	132
…	…	…	…	…	…	.	.	.	1.7	1.9	1.5	1.2	1.2	1.1	133
0.4	0.5	0.4	0.5	0.6	0.4	.	.	.	–	–	–	0.7	0.8	0.6	134
–	–	–	–	–	–	–	…	…	–	–	–	–	–	–	135
…	…	…	…	…	…	–	…	…	1.8	2.1	1.6	0.7	0.8	0.6	136
1.2	…	…	1.0	…	…	.	.	.	…	…	…	1.4	1.9	0.9	137
0.3	0.3	0.2	…	…	…	.	.	.	0.4	0.5	0.3	0.2	0.3	0.2	138
3.8	4.5	3.1	1.1	1.4	0.7	.	.	.	…	…	…	4.0	4.6	3.3	139
…	…	…	…	…	…	.	.	.	2.1	2.4	1.8	2.6[y]	2.9[y]	2.2[y]	140
…	…	…	…	…	…	.	.	.	–	–	–	…	…	…	141
.	.	.	.	.	.	.	.	.	.	.	.	.	.	.	142
.	.	.	.	.	.	.	.	.	.	.	.	.	.	.	143
…	…	…	…	…	…	.	.	.	…	…	…	*10.2*[y]	…	…	144
–	–	–	…	…	…	.	.	.	…	…	…	–	–	–	145
…	…	…	…	…	…	.	.	.	…	…	…	2.8[z]	3.2[z]	2.4[z]	146
–	–	–	–	–	–	.	.	.	–	–	–	–	–	–	147
…	…	…	…	…	…	.	.	.	1.8	1.9	1.6	1.5	1.6	1.3	148
…	…	…	…	…	…	.	.	.	–	–	–	–	–	–	149
–	–	–	–	–	–	.	.	.	–	–	–	–	–	–	150
South and West Asia															
…	…	…	…	…	…	.	.	.	…	…	…	–	–	–	151
5.2[y]	5.5[y]	5.0[y]	…	…	…	.	.	.	…	…	…	10.9[z]	11.2[z]	10.7[z]	152
9.1[y]	10.4[y]	7.7[y]	5.8[y]	6.1[y]	5.5[y]	3.5[y]	3.7[y]	3.4[y]	12.1	12.5	11.7	**6.4**	**7.2**	**5.5**	153
4.0[y]	4.1[y]	3.8[y]	.	.	.	.	.	.	4.0	4.0	4.1	3.4[z]	3.4[z]	3.4[z]	154
…	…	…	.	.	.	.	.	.	…	…	…	*2.0*	*2.8*	*1.4*	155
…	…	…	…	…	…	.	.	.	…	…	…	4.7[z]	5.5[z]	3.7[z]	156
7.5	**7.4**	**7.5**	.	.	.	.	.	.	22.9	22.2	23.8	**16.8**	**16.8**	**16.7**	157
4.0	4.5	3.3	.	.	.	.	.	.	…	…	…	5.3	5.5	4.9	158
1.3[y]	*1.5*[y]	*1.1*[y]	.	.	.	.	.	.	…	…	…	0.9[z]	1.1[z]	0.8[z]	159
Sub-Saharan Africa															
…	…	…	…	…	…	.	.	.	…	…	…	…	…	…	160
12.2[y]	11.5[y]	13.2[y]	4.4[y]	4.6[y]	4.1[y]	.	.	.	…	…	…	7.8[z]	7.9[z]	7.8[z]	161
.[x]	.[x]	.[x]	.[x]	.[x]	.[x]	.[x]	.[x]	.[x]	3.3	3.9	2.7	.[y]	.[y]	.[y]	162
13.6	**12.9**	**14.5**	**28.8**	**26.8**	**31.4**	.	.	.	17.7	17.5	18.0	**10.5**	**10.6**	**10.5**	163
42.2	40.4	44.2	49.1	46.4	52.3	.	.	.	*20.3*	*20.3*	*20.4*	32.0	31.5	32.4	164
18.3	…	…	20.3	…	…	.	.	.	*26.7*	*26.8*	*26.5*	20.1	20.0	20.1	165
9.2	…	…	10.2	…	…	.	.	.	*11.6*	*12.8*	*10.3*	12.9	15.3	10.3	166
26.2	**25.4**	**27.3**	**30.8**	**31.2**	**30.2**	.	.	.	…	…	…	**26.3**	**26.0**	**26.8**	167
…	…	…	*23.0*	*22.5*	*23.9*	.	.	.	25.9	25.7	26.3	*21.8*	*21.1*	*22.8*	168
22.7[x]	*23.6*[x]	*21.7*[x]	*26.2*[x]	*27.9*[x]	*24.3*[x]	.	.	.	26.0	26.4	25.5	*27.1*[y]	*28.2*[y]	*25.9*[y]	169
…	…	…	…	…	…	.	.	.	39.1	40.0	38.2	*21.2*	*21.5*	*20.9*	170
23.0	22.7	23.3	31.7	32.4	30.7	.	.	.	23.7	*22.8*	*24.9*	21.6	22.3	20.7	171
…	…	…	…	…	…	.	.	.	15.5	18.8	11.9	15.9	15.6	16.4	172
…	…	…	.	.	.	.	.	.	11.8	9.3	14.9	24.3	25.1	23.4	173
9.5	9.7	9.1	…	…	…	.	.	.	19.4	18.2	20.8	14.6	14.9	14.2	174
9.0	9.6	8.3	7.1	8.1	5.7	.	.	.	10.6	9.8	11.9	6.0	6.6	5.4	175

Table 6 (continued)

	Country or territory	Duration[1] of primary education 2007	REPETITION RATES BY GRADE IN PRIMARY EDUCATION (%) School year ending in 2006 Grade 1 Total	Grade 1 Male	Grade 1 Female	Grade 2 Total	Grade 2 Male	Grade 2 Female	Grade 3 Total	Grade 3 Male	Grade 3 Female	Grade 4 Total	Grade 4 Male	Grade 4 Female
176	Gabon	6	…	…	…	…	…	…	…	…	…	…	…	…
177	Gambia	6	**9.2**	**9.0**	**9.3**	**5.7**	**5.8**	**5.7**	**4.5**	**4.6**	**4.4**	**4.1**	**4.4**	**3.8**
178	Ghana	6	**8.1**	**8.2**	**8.0**	**7.5**	**8.5**	**6.5**	**7.9**	…	…	**5.4**	…	…
179	Guinea	6	3.9	3.8	4.1	12.1	11.7	12.6	5.0	4.6	5.5	12.6	12.0	13.4
180	Guinea-Bissau	6	…	…	…	…	…	…	…	…	…	…	…	…
181	Kenya	6	*6.2*[x]	*6.4*[x]	*5.9*[x]	*5.8*[x]	*6.0*[x]	*5.6*[x]	*6.1*[x]	*6.4*[x]	*5.8*[x]	*6.2*[x]	*6.5*[x]	*5.9*[x]
182	Lesotho	7	28.1[y]	31.5[y]	24.1[y]	24.5[y]	28.2[y]	20.1[y]	21.0[y]	25.0[y]	16.6[y]	21.1[y]	24.9[y]	17.1[y]
183	Liberia	6	…	…	…	…	…	…	…	…	…	…	…	…
184	Madagascar	5	13.0	13.4	12.6	27.1	28.2	26.0	26.7	27.6	25.8	9.2	9.3	9.0
185	Malawi	6	23.4	23.7	23.2	21.9	22.4	21.4	22.9	23.6	22.3	17.7	18.4	17.1
186	Mali	6	9.9	9.8	10.1	…	…	…	…	…	…	…	…	…
187	Mauritius	6	.	.	.	.	.	.	.	.	.	.	.	.
188	Mozambique	7	3.6	3.7	3.4	9.0	9.1	8.8	4.3	4.4	4.1	4.5	4.7	4.3
189	Namibia	7	*20.0*	*22.1*	*17.7*	*13.6*	*16.6*	*10.6*	*13.0*	*15.4*	*10.5*	*13.9*	*16.6*	*11.2*
190	Niger	6	0.1	0.1	0.1	2.9	2.8	2.9	3.5	3.3	3.8	4.9	4.5	5.5
191	Nigeria	6	…	…	…	…	…	…	…	…	…	…	…	…
192	Rwanda	6	19.9	20.8	19.1	…	…	…	…	…	…	…	…	…
193	Sao Tome and Principe	6	**25.4**	**27.5**	**23.2**	**24.0**	**26.4**	**21.6**	**21.5**	**23.3**	**19.6**	**18.2**	**19.6**	**16.8**
194	Senegal	6	4.9	5.0	4.8	…	…	…	…	…	…	…	…	…
195	Seychelles	6	.	.	.	.	.	.	.	.	.	.	.	.
196	Sierra Leone	6	…	…	…	…	…	…	…	…	…	…	…	…
197	Somalia	7	…	…	…	…	…	…	…	…	…	…	…	…
198	South Africa	7	*6.7*	*6.7*	*6.6*	…	…	…	…	…	…	…	…	…
199	Swaziland	7	21.7	24.4	18.6	18.7	21.9	15.1	21.2	24.7	17.2	17.9	20.6	14.9
200	Togo	6	23.8	24.0	23.7	22.2	22.0	22.4	24.5	24.2	24.9	22.0	21.3	22.9
201	Uganda	7	12.3[x]	11.1[x]	13.6[x]	*12.2*[x]	*12.5*[x]	*11.9*[x]	*14.3*[x]	*15.2*[x]	*13.4*[x]	*13.2*[x]	*13.2*[x]	*13.2*[x]
202	United Republic of Tanzania	7	*8.5*	*8.6*	*8.4*	*4.9*	*5.1*	*4.7*	*4.2*	*4.2*	*4.2*	*8.7*	*8.7*	*8.8*
203	Zambia	7	5.6	5.6	5.7	5.5	5.6	5.4	5.8	6.0	5.5	6.4	6.7	6.0
204	Zimbabwe	7	…	…	…	…	…	…	…	…	…	…	…	…
I	World[2]	…	2.9	…	…	2.5	2.8	2.2	2.5	…	…	2.8	3.2	2.4
II	Countries in transition	…	0.2	0.2	0.2	0.2	…	…	0.1	0.1	0.1	0.1	0.1	0.0
III	Developed countries	…	0.5	0.6	0.4	0.5	0.6	0.4	0.4	0.4	0.4	0.3	0.3	0.2
IV	Developing countries	…	5.5	5.9	5.0	5.6	5.7	5.6	5.0	5.4	4.7	4.7	4.6	4.9
V	Arab States	…	2.7	2.8	2.6	3.2	3.7	2.6	3.2	3.3	3.0	3.5	…	…
VI	Central and Eastern Europe	…	0.8	…	…	0.5	0.6	0.4	0.4	…	…	0.7	…	…
VII	Central Asia	…	0.1	0.1	0.1	0.3	…	…	0.2	0.2	0.1	0.1	0.1	0.1
VIII	East Asia and the Pacific	…	0.8	1.0	0.6	…	…	…	…	…	…	…	…	…
IX	East Asia	…	1.7	…	…	1.8	2.4	1.1	0.8	1.0	0.5	1.4	1.8	0.8
X	Pacific	…	…	…	…	…	…	…	…	…	…	…	…	…
XI	Latin America/Caribbean	…	6.7	…	…	5.3	6.6	4.0	5.1	6.1	4.0	3.7	4.4	3.0
XII	Caribbean	…	5.3	6.5	3.9	1.1	1.5	0.7	2.9	3.7	2.0	1.3	2.0	0.5
XIII	Latin America	…	9.0	10.1	7.7	7.0	8.2	5.6	6.2	7.3	5.0	4.3	5.4	3.2
XIV	N. America/W. Europe	…	0.5	0.6	0.3	0.5	0.5	0.4	0.2	0.2	0.1	0.1	0.2	0.1
XV	South and West Asia	…	6.5	6.6	6.3	5.2	5.8	4.6	7.9	8.7	7.1	5.9	6.5	5.4
XVI	Sub-Saharan Africa	…	9.9	9.8	10.1	12.2	12.5	11.9	13.0	15.4	10.5	13.2	13.2	13.2

Source: UNESCO Institute for Statistics database (UIS, 2009).
1. Duration in this table is defined according to ISCED97 and may differ from that reported nationally.
2. All values shown are medians.

Data in italic are UIS estimates.
Data in bold are for the school year ending in 2007 for repetition rates by grade, and the school year ending in 2008 for percentage of repeaters (all grades).

(z) Data are for the school year ending in 2006.
(y) Data are for the school year ending in 2005.
(x) Data are for the school year ending in 2004.
(*) National estimate.

REPETITION RATES BY GRADE IN PRIMARY EDUCATION (%)									REPEATERS, ALL GRADES (%)						
School year ending in 2006									School year ending in						
Grade 5			Grade 6			Grade 7			1999			2007			
Total	Male	Female	Total	Male	Female	Total	Male	Female	Total	Male	Female	Total	Male	Female	
...	...	...	...	...	...	.	.	.	...	...	...	...	...	...	176
3.2	**3.2**	**3.1**	**2.4**	**2.4**	**2.4**	.	.	.	*8.5*	*8.6*	*8.5*	**5.2**	**5.3**	**5.1**	177
5.7	...	...	**6.7**	...	...	.	.	.	4.2	4.3	4.1	**6.5**	**7.0**	**6.0**	178
5.1	4.7	5.6	19.5	18.1	21.5	.	.	.	26.2	25.5	27.4	9.1	8.7	9.5	179
...	...	...	...	...	...	.	.	.	*24.0*	*23.6*	*24.5*	...	...	...	180
5.9[x]	...	...	*5.5*[x]	...	...	.	.	.	...	...	...	*5.8*[y]	*6.0*[y]	*5.6*[y]	181
17.6[y]	20.4[y]	14.9[y]	13.4[y]	15.1[y]	12.1[y]	16.0[y]	14.5[y]	17.1[y]	20.3	22.9	17.9	20.9[z]	24.3[z]	17.6[z]	182
...	...	...	...	...	...	.	.	.	...	...	...	**6.7**	**7.4**	**5.9**	183
19.3	19.2	19.4	.	.	.	.	.	.	*28.3*	*27.7*	*28.9*	19.1	19.8	18.4	184
16.8	17.2	16.3	13.4	13.7	13.1	.	.	.	14.4	14.4	14.4	20.7	21.1	20.3	185
...	...	...	*25.4*	*24.4*	*26.9*	.	.	.	17.4	17.2	17.7	*17.0*	*16.7*	*17.3*	186
.	.	.	17.8	20.5	14.9	.	.	.	3.8	4.1	3.5	3.7	4.4	3.0	187
13.2	13.4	12.9	2.0	2.2	1.8	10.6	10.7	10.4	23.8	23.2	24.7	5.9	6.1	5.7	188
23.0	*26.4*	*19.5*	*15.4*	*17.3*	*13.6*	*16.9*	*17.5*	*16.3*	12.3	13.9	10.7	*16.4*	*18.7*	*14.2*	189
6.2	5.7	6.9	23.4	22.5	24.9	.	.	.	12.2	12.4	11.8	4.9	4.8	5.1	190
...	...	...	...	...	...	.	.	.	*3.1*	*3.0*	*3.1*	*2.9*[z]	*2.8*[z]	*3.0*[z]	191
...	...	...	...	...	...	.	.	.	29.1	29.2	29.0	*14.6*	*14.6*	*14.6*	192
27.6	**29.0**	**26.2**	**36.3**	**36.7**	**35.9**	.	.	.	30.7	32.6	28.7	**24.2**	**25.6**	**22.8**	193
...	...	...	*24.0*	*23.8*	*24.1*	.	.	.	14.4	14.5	14.2	*10.6*	*10.8*	*10.5*	194
.	.	.	.	.	.	.	.	.	.	.	.	.	.	.	195
...	...	...	...	...	...	.	.	.	...	...	...	9.9	9.7	10.2	196
...	...	...	...	...	...	.	.	.	...	...	...	...	...	...	197
...	...	...	...	...	...	*5.2*	*5.2*	*5.3*	10.4	11.6	9.2	*8.0*	*8.4*	*7.5*	198
18.6	20.5	16.5	18.0	19.5	16.4	6.8	7.3	6.4	17.1	19.5	14.5	18.0	20.5	15.3	199
23.3	22.9	23.9	21.8	21.4	22.2	.	.	.	31.2	30.9	31.6	23.7	23.5	24.0	200
13.8[x]	*13.7*[x]	*13.9*[x]	*13.2*[x]	*11.9*[x]	*14.5*[x]	*10.2*[x]	*10.8*[x]	*9.5*[x]	...	...	...	*13.1*[y]	*13.0*[y]	*13.3*[y]	201
0.1	*0.1*	*0.1*	*0.0*	*0.0*	*0.0*	*0.0*	*0.0*	*0.0*	3.2	3.1	3.2	4.2	4.3	4.2	202
6.4	6.7	6.2	7.2	7.5	6.9	12.4	13.9	10.7	*6.1*	*6.4*	*5.8*	6.5	6.8	6.2	203
...	...	...	...	...	...	...	...	...	.	.	.	...	...	...	204
2.1	2.5	1.7	0.9	1.1	0.6	.	.	.	3.6	4.1	3.0	2.9	3.4	2.5	I
.	.	.	.	.	.	.	.	.	0.5	0.5	0.5	0.2	0.2	0.1	II
.	.	.	.	.	.	.	.	.	1.0	1.3	0.6	0.6	0.8	0.4	III
4.0	4.5	3.3	3.3	...	...	.	.	.	6.8	8.1	5.5	5.0	6.1	3.9	IV
3.9	...	...	5.0	5.6	3.9	.	.	.	8.0	9.5	6.4	3.2	3.4	2.9	V
.	.	.	.	.	.	.	.	.	1.2	1.5	1.0	0.6	0.8	0.4	VI
.	.	.	.	.	.	.	.	.	0.3	0.5	0.2	0.2	...	...	VII
...	...	...	...	...	...	.	.	.	1.7	1.7	1.7	1.5	...	...	VIII
1.1	1.6	0.7	0.0	0.0	0.0	.	.	.	2.7	2.9	2.5	2.2	2.9	1.5	IX
...	...	...	...	...	...	.	.	.	.	.	.	...	...	...	X
2.6	3.1	2.1	1.7	2.0	1.3	.	.	.	4.7	5.3	4.4	3.8	4.4	2.8	XI
0.9	1.2	0.7	...	...	...	.	.	.	3.1	3.6	2.5	2.8	3.3	2.1	XII
2.9	3.7	2.1	1.2	1.5	0.8	.	.	.	6.5	7.5	5.3	5.6	6.9	4.1	XIII
0.1	0.2	0.1	...	...	...	.	.	.	0.2	0.2	0.1	0.4	0.6	0.3	XIV
4.6	5.0	4.4	.	.	.	.	.	.	...	...	...	4.7	5.5	3.7	XV
13.2	13.4	12.9	14.4	15.5	13.3	.	.	.	16.3	19.1	13.2	13.0	14.1	11.8	XVI

Table 7
Internal efficiency: primary education dropout and completion

Country or territory	Duration[1] of primary education 2007	DROPOUT RATES BY GRADE IN PRIMARY EDUCATION (%) School year ending in 2006 Grade 1 Total	Grade 1 Male	Grade 1 Female	Grade 2 Total	Grade 2 Male	Grade 2 Female	Grade 3 Total	Grade 3 Male	Grade 3 Female	Grade 4 Total	Grade 4 Male	Grade 4 Female	Grade 5 Total	Grade 5 Male	Grade 5 Female
Arab States																
Algeria	6	0.7	1.2	0.3	0.8	1.0	0.5	0.7	0.9	0.5	1.5	1.8	1.1	3.7	4.6	2.7
Bahrain	6	–[x]	–[x]	–[x]	–[x]	–[x]	–[x]	0.0[x]	–[x]	0.4[x]	0.2[x]	–[x]	0.5[x]	0.1[x]	–[x]	0.2[x]
Djibouti	6	2.2	5.1	–	2.7	3.7	1.5	–	…	…	…	…	…	…	…	…
Egypt	6	*1.9*	*2.4*	*1.3*	–	…	…	*0.3*	…	…	*3.0*	…	…	–	…	…
Iraq	6	*11.1*[x]	*9.1*[x]	*13.4*[x]	*1.4*[x]	–[x]	*3.7*[x]	*1.1*[x]	–[x]	*2.9*[x]	*5.2*[x]	*3.2*[x]	*7.8*[x]	*11.2*[x]	*8.8*[x]	*14.6*[x]
Jordan	6	–	…	…	2.1	…	…	–	…	…	0.0	…	…	–	…	…
Kuwait	5	0.4	0.8	–	–	–	–	–	–	–	–	–	–	…	…	…
Lebanon	6	**2.0**	**2.4**	**1.5**	**0.6**	**0.7**	**0.5**	**1.0**	**1.3**	**0.7**	**3.4**	**4.4**	**2.4**	**3.1**	**4.3**	**1.8**
Libyan Arab Jamahiriya	6	…	…	…	…	…	…	…	…	…	…	…	…	…	…	…
Mauritania	6	9.1	10.4	7.7	7.0	7.4	6.7	10.6	10.6	10.6	14.6	14.5	14.6	13.3	12.2	14.4
Morocco	6	4.6	4.5	4.6	2.0	1.7	2.3	3.4	3.0	3.8	4.9	4.6	5.2	6.9	6.2	7.8
Oman	6	1.3	1.9	0.7	0.4	0.6	0.1	0.0	–	0.2	–	–	–	0.9	0.8	0.9
Palestinian A. T.	4	0.8	0.9	0.7	0.6	0.5	0.7	–	–	–	…	…	…	.	.	.
Qatar	6	4.9[y]	5.5[y]	4.3[y]	5.5[y]	6.1[y]	5.0[y]	3.2[y]	0.6[y]	5.9[y]	–[y]	–[y]	–[y]	–[y]	–[y]	–[y]
Saudi Arabia	6	…	…	…	…	…	…	…	…	…	…	…	…	…	…	…
Sudan	6	7.6	7.6	7.7	8.2	7.4	9.0	7.2	6.3	8.3	9.5	9.6	9.4	11.5	10.8	12.4
Syrian Arab Republic	4	2.2	2.4	2.0	1.2	1.3	1.0	1.1	1.1	1.1	…	…	…	.	.	.
Tunisia	6	0.4	0.3	0.5	0.6	0.7	0.6	0.5	0.3	0.7	1.8	1.9	1.6	2.2	2.3	2.0
United Arab Emirates	5	–	–	–	1.2	1.1	1.4	–	–	–	–	–	–	…	…	…
Yemen	6	13.5[x]	15.1[x]	11.5[x]	8.9[x]	8.5[x]	9.4[x]	6.7[x]	5.4[x]	8.5[x]	7.9[x]	6.7[x]	9.9[x]	9.6[x]	8.4[x]	11.7[x]
Central and Eastern Europe																
Albania	4	…	…	…	…	…	…	…	…	…	…	…	…	.	.	.
Belarus	4	0.1	0.4	–	0.2	0.3	0.2	0.1	–	0.4	…	…	…	.	.	.
Bosnia and Herzegovina	4	…	…	…	…	…	…	…	…	…	…	…	…	.	.	.
Bulgaria	4	2.3	2.3	2.4	2.1	2.4	1.8	1.5	1.4	1.6	…	…	…	.	.	.
Croatia	4	0.0	0.4	–	–	–	–	–	–	–	…	…	…	.	.	.
Czech Republic	5	1.0	1.3	0.8	0.3	0.4	0.3	0.3	0.3	0.2	0.2	0.1	0.2	…	…	…
Estonia	6	1.0[y]	1.1[y]	0.8[y]	0.7[y]	0.8[y]	0.5[y]	0.6[y]	0.6[y]	0.5[y]	0.9[y]	0.6[y]	1.3[y]	0.6[y]	1.1[y]	0.1[y]
Hungary	4	1.5	1.8	1.3	0.4	0.4	0.4	0.1	0.1	0.1	…	…	…	.	.	.
Latvia	4	1.4[y]	1.6[y]	1.2[y]	0.3[y]	–[y]	0.8[y]	0.1[y]	0.4[y]	–[y]	…	…	…	.	.	.
Lithuania	4	0.7	0.8	0.7	0.7	0.7	0.6	0.8	0.9	0.7	…	…	…	.	.	.
Montenegro	4	…	…	…	…	…	…	…	…	…	…	…	…	.	.	.
Poland	6	0.8	…	…	0.4	…	…	0.5	…	…	0.5	…	…	0.4	…	…
Republic of Moldova	4	1.2	1.1	1.3	1.4	1.4	1.3	1.2	1.4	1.1	…	…	…	.	.	.
Romania	4	2.3	2.5	2.1	1.4	1.6	1.1	1.4	1.4	1.3	…	…	…	.	.	.
Russian Federation	4	2.9	…	…	1.1	…	…	1.2	…	…	…	…	…	.	.	.
Serbia	4	…	…	…	…	…	…	…	…	…	…	…	…	.	.	.
Slovakia	4	1.2	1.2	1.3	0.5	0.5	0.4	0.3	0.5	0.2	…	…	…	.	.	.
Slovenia	5	…	…	…	…	…	…	…	…	…	…	…	…	…	…	…
TFYR Macedonia	4	1.0[x]	1.5[x]	0.5[x]	0.1[x]	0.0[x]	0.3[x]	0.6[x]	0.8[x]	0.5[x]	…	…	…	.	.	.
Turkey	6	0.1[x]	0.5[x]	–[x]	0.8[x]	0.7[x]	0.9[x]	1.0[x]	0.9[x]	1.2[x]	1.1[x]	0.6[x]	1.6[x]	2.9[x]	1.9[x]	3.9[x]
Ukraine	4	1.0	1.2*	0.8*	0.7	0.9*	0.5*	0.5	0.7*	0.3*	…	…	…	.	.	.
Central Asia																
Armenia	3	1.8	1.1	2.6	0.5	0.9	0.1	…	…	…	.	.	.	.	.	.
Azerbaijan	4	0.2	0.6	–	0.4	0.8	0.1	0.4	0.7	–	…	…	…	.	.	.
Georgia	6	0.3	…	…	–	–	–	–	–	–	–	–	–	–	–	–
Kazakhstan	4	**0.0**	**0.1**	–	**0.4**	**0.7**	**0.1**	**0.1**	**0.1**	**0.0**	…	…	…	.	.	.
Kyrgyzstan	4	1.2	1.3	1.0	1.3	1.6	1.0	1.1	1.0	1.1	…	…	…	.	.	.
Mongolia	5	…	…	…	…	…	…	…	…	…	…	…	…	…	…	…
Tajikistan	4	–	–	–	0.4	…	…	0.6	…	…	…	…	…	.	.	.
Turkmenistan	3	…	…	…	…	…	…	…	…	…	.	.	.	.	.	.
Uzbekistan	4	–	–	–	0.5	0.3	0.6	0.4	0.2	0.5	…	…	…	.	.	.
East Asia and the Pacific																
Australia	7	…	…	…	…	…	…	…	…	…	…	…	…	…	…	…
Brunei Darussalam	6	0.3	–	1.0	0.1	0.3	–	–	–	–	–	–	–	2.2	2.6	1.8
Cambodia	6	9.4	9.1	9.8	9.3	9.7	8.8	9.5	10.0	8.9	10.6	11.1	10.1	11.7	11.7	11.8

PRIMARY EDUCATION COMPLETION															
SURVIVAL RATE TO GRADE 5 (%)						SURVIVAL RATE TO LAST GRADE (%)						PRIMARY COHORT COMPLETION RATE (%)			
School year ending in						School year ending in						School year ending in			
1999			2006			1999			2006			2006			
Total	Male	Female	Total	Male	Female	Total	Male	Female	Total	Male	Female	Total	Male	Female	Country or territory
															Arab States
95	94	96	96	95	97	91	90	93	92	89	95	81.2	76.5	86.5	Algeria
97	*97*	*98*	99[x]	100[x]	98[x]	*92*	*91*	*93*	99[x]	100[x]	97[x]	…	…	…	Bahrain
77	71	85	…	…	…	…	…	…	…	…	…	…	…	…	Djibouti
99	*99*	*99*	*97*	…	…	*99*	*99*	*99*	*97*	…	…	…	…	…	Egypt
66	*67*	*63*	*81[x]*	*87[x]*	*73[x]*	*49*	*51*	*47*	*70[x]*	*78[x]*	*61[x]*	*68.1[x]*	*75.1[x]*	*60.4[x]*	Iraq
98	98	97	…	…	…	97	97	97	99	…	…	…	…	…	Jordan
…	…	…	100	100	99	94	93	95	100	100	99	86.3[y]	82.7[y]	90.3[y]	Kuwait
91	88	95	**92**	**90**	**95**	91	88	95	**89**	**86**	**93**	…	…	…	Lebanon
…	…	…	…	…	…	…	…	…	…	…	…	…	…	…	Libyan Arab Jamahiriya
68	*70*	*66*	64	63	65	*61*	…	…	54	54	55	20.5[x]	20.8[x]	20.1[x]	Mauritania
82	82	82	84	85	83	75	75	76	78	79	76	59.6[y]	63.2[y]	55.8[y]	Morocco
94	94	94	98	98	99	92	92	92	98	97	98	…	…	…	Oman
.	.	.	.	.	.	99	100	99	99	99	99	…	…	…	Palestinian A. T.
…	…	…	…	…	…	…	…	…	89[y]	89[y]	89[y]	…	…	…	Qatar
…	…	…	…	…	…	…	…	…	…	…	…	…	…	…	Saudi Arabia
84	*81*	*88*	70	72	69	*77*	*74*	*81*	62	64	60	…	…	…	Sudan
.	.	.	.	.	.	87	87	87	95	95	96	…	…	…	Syrian Arab Republic
92	91	93	96	96	96	87	86	88	94	94	94	…	…	…	Tunisia
92	93	92	100	100	100	90	90	89	100	100	100	98.4	98.8	100.0	United Arab Emirates
87	…	…	66[x]	67[x]	65[x]	*80*	…	…	59[x]	61[x]	57[x]	…	…	…	Yemen
															Central and Eastern Europe
.	.	.	.	.	.	*92*	*90*	*95*	…	…	…	…	…	…	Albania
.	.	.	.	.	.	99	99	99	100	99	100	98.0	96.4	99.6	Belarus
.	.	.	.	.	.	…	…	…	…	…	…	…	…	…	Bosnia and Herzegovina
.	.	.	.	.	.	93	93	93	94	94	94	…	…	…	Bulgaria
.	.	.	.	.	.	100	99	100	100	100	100	…	…	…	Croatia
98	98	99	98	98	99	98	98	99	98	98	99	…	…	…	Czech Republic
99	99	99	97[y]	97[y]	97[y]	99	98	99	96[y]	96[y]	97[y]	…	…	…	Estonia
.	.	.	.	.	.	97	96	98	98	98	98	…	…	…	Hungary
.	.	.	.	.	.	97	97	97	98[y]	98[y]	98[y]	…	…	…	Latvia
.	.	.	.	.	.	99	99	100	98	98	98	…	…	…	Lithuania
.	.	.	.	.	.	…	…	…	…	…	…	…	…	…	Montenegro
99	…	…	98	…	…	98	…	…	97	…	…	…	…	…	Poland
.	.	.	.	.	.	95	…	…	96	96	96	…	…	…	Republic of Moldova
.	.	.	.	.	.	96	95	96	95	95	95	…	…	…	Romania
.	.	.	.	.	.	95	…	…	95	…	…	…	…	…	Russian Federation
.	.	.	.	.	.	…	…	…	…	…	…	…	…	…	Serbia
.	.	.	.	.	.	97	96	98	98	98	98	…	…	…	Slovakia
…	…	…	…	…	…	…	…	…	…	…	…	…	…	…	Slovenia
.	.	.	…	…	…	97	96	99	98[x]	98[x]	99[x]	…	…	…	TFYR Macedonia
…	…	…	97[x]	97[x]	97[x]	…	…	…	94[x]	95[x]	93[x]	…	…	…	Turkey
.	.	.	.	.	.	97	96*	97*	98	97*	99*	96.6[y]	…	…	Ukraine
															Central Asia
.	.	.	.	.	.	…	…	…	98	98	97	…	…	…	Armenia
.	.	.	.	.	.	97	96	98	99	98	100	97.7	95.6	100.0	Azerbaijan
…	…	…	100	…	…	99	99	100	100	…	…	84.5[y]	…	…	Georgia
.	.	.	.	.	.	…	…	…	**100**	**99**	**100**	99.1[y]	98.6[y]	99.6[y]	Kazakhstan
.	.	.	.	.	.	95*	95*	94*	96	96	97	94.6[y]	92.5[y]	96.8[y]	Kyrgyzstan
…	…	…	84	86	83	87	85	90	84	86	83	81.6	82.2	81.0	Mongolia
.	.	.	.	.	.	97	*100*	*94*	99	…	…	97.3[x]	*95.7[x]*	*99.0[x]*	Tajikistan
.	.	.	.	.	.	…	…	…	…	…	…	…	…	…	Turkmenistan
.	.	.	.	.	.	100	*100*	*99*	99	99	99	…	…	…	Uzbekistan
															East Asia and the Pacific
…	…	…	…	…	…	…	…	…	…	…	…	…	…	…	Australia
…	…	…	99	99	100	…	…	…	98	97	99	80.7	75.6	86.1	Brunei Darussalam
56	*58*	*54*	62	61	64	*49*	*52*	*45*	54	53	56	48.0	47.6	48.5	Cambodia

Table 7 (continued)

Country or territory	Duration[1] of primary education 2007	DROPOUT RATES BY GRADE IN PRIMARY EDUCATION (%) School year ending in 2006 — Grade 1			Grade 2			Grade 3			Grade 4			Grade 5		
		Total	Male	Female	Total	Male	Female	Total	Male	Female	Total	Male	Female	Total	Male	Female
China	5	–	–	–	…	…	…	…	…	…	…	…	…	…	…	…
Cook Islands	6	…	…	…	…	…	…	…	…	…	…	…	…	…	…	…
DPR Korea	4	…	…	…	…	…	…	…	…	…	…	…	…	.	.	.
Fiji	6	*6.0*	*6.2*	*5.7*	–	…	…	*8.0*	…	…	*4.3*	…	…	*9.0*	…	…
Indonesia	6	3.6	3.7	3.4	3.1	3.4	2.8	0.5	0.7	0.2	–	–	–	–	…	…
Japan	6	…	…	…	…	…	…	…	…	…	…	…	…	…	…	…
Kiribati	6	…	…	…	…	…	…	…	…	…	…	…	…	…	…	…
Lao PDR	5	13.8	13.8	13.8	6.8	6.8	6.8	7.9	7.9	8.0	7.4	6.5	8.5	…	…	…
Macao, China	6	–	…	…	–	…	…	…	…	…	…	…	…	…	…	…
Malaysia	6	2.2^{y}	2.4^{y}	2.0^{y}	2.1^{y}	2.0^{y}	2.2^{y}	2.0^{y}	2.0^{y}	2.0^{y}	2.2^{y}	2.2^{y}	2.1^{y}	2.6^{y}	2.7^{y}	2.5^{y}
Marshall Islands	6	…	…	…	…	…	…	…	…	…	…	…	…	…	…	…
Micronesia, F. S.	6	…	…	…	…	…	…	…	…	…	…	…	…	…	…	…
Myanmar	5	10.4	…	…	5.5	…	…	6.3	…	…	8.0	…	…	…	…	…
Nauru	6	…	…	…	…	…	…	…	…	…	…	…	…	…	…	…
New Zealand	6	…	…	…	…	…	…	…	…	…	…	…	…	…	…	…
Niue	6	…	…	…	…	…	…	…	…	…	…	…	…	…	…	…
Palau	5	…	…	…	…	…	…	…	…	…	…	…	…	…	…	…
Papua New Guinea	6	…	…	…	…	…	…	…	…	…	…	…	…	…	…	…
Philippines	6	12.6	14.2	10.8	4.4	5.4	3.4	3.6	4.6	2.5	3.6	4.6	2.5	4.6	5.7	3.6
Republic of Korea	6	0.2	0.2	0.1	0.5	0.4	0.6	0.6	0.5	0.7	0.7	0.7	0.7	0.7	0.6	0.7
Samoa	6	…	…	…	…	…	…	…	…	…	…	…	…	…	…	…
Singapore	6	…	…	…	…	…	…	…	…	…	…	…	…	…	…	…
Solomon Islands	6	…	…	…	…	…	…	…	…	…	…	…	…	…	…	…
Thailand	6	…	…	…	…	…	…	…	…	…	…	…	…	…	…	…
Timor-Leste	6	…	…	…	…	…	…	…	…	…	…	…	…	…	…	…
Tokelau	6	…	…	…	…	…	…	…	…	…	…	…	…	…	…	…
Tonga	6	4.2^{y}	4.3^{y}	4.0^{y}	1.6^{y}	0.2^{y}	3.1^{y}	2.8^{y}	3.8^{y}	1.5^{y}	–^{y}	–^{y}	–^{y}	1.3^{y}	2.3^{y}	0.2^{y}
Tuvalu	6	…	…	…	…	…	…	…	…	…	…	…	…	…	…	…
Vanuatu	6	…	…	…	…	…	…	…	…	…	…	…	…	…	…	…
Viet Nam	5	*2.1*^{y}	…	…	*1.6*^{y}	…	…	*2.0*^{y}	…	…	*2.3*^{y}	…	…	…	…	…
Latin America and the Caribbean																
Anguilla	7	1.0^{x}	3.2^{x}	–^{x}	–^{x}	–^{x}	–^{x}	0.9^{x}	–^{x}	1.9^{x}	1.0^{x}	0.9^{x}	1.3^{x}	–^{x}	…	…
Antigua and Barbuda	7	…	…	…	…	…	…	…	…	…	…	…	…	…	…	…
Argentina	6	2.1^{y}	2.2^{y}	2.0^{y}	0.5^{y}	0.7^{y}	0.3^{y}	0.2^{y}	0.3^{y}	0.1^{y}	0.9^{y}	1.1^{y}	0.7^{y}	1.5^{y}	2.1^{y}	0.8^{y}
Aruba	6	2.4	2.5	2.3	1.0	1.1	1.0	–	–	–	0.8	0.5	1.1	1.0	1.5	0.5
Bahamas	6	8.7^{y}	10.6^{y}	6.7^{y}	3.0^{y}	5.3^{y}	0.7^{y}	2.0^{y}	0.7^{y}	3.2^{y}	2.0^{y}	2.3^{y}	1.7^{y}	4.3^{y}	4.2^{y}	4.3^{y}
Barbados	6	3.2^{y}	1.6^{y}	4.8^{y}	0.5^{y}	1.6^{y}	–^{y}	0.8^{y}	–^{y}	1.6^{y}	1.0^{y}	2.6^{y}	–^{y}	–^{y}	…	…
Belize	6	8.1	7.7	8.5	0.8	1.0	0.5	2.0	2.4	1.5	0.7	0.6	0.8	3.6	5.4	1.6
Bermuda	6	1.6^{y}	…	…	1.4^{y}	…	…	9.8^{y}	…	…	–^{y}	–^{y}	–^{y}	3.7^{y}	…	…
Bolivia	6	8.3	8.5	8.0	2.3	2.1	2.4	4.3	4.2	4.5	2.4	2.3	2.6	3.6	3.0	4.3
Brazil	4	13.8^{x}	…	…	2.4^{x}	…	…	3.8^{x}	…	…	…	…	…	.	.	.
British Virgin Islands	7	–	–	–	…	…	…	…	…	…	…	…	…	.	.	.
Cayman Islands	6	5.6^{x}	4.9^{x}	6.3^{x}	5.7^{x}	1.9^{x}	9.9^{x}	6.6^{x}	7.8^{x}	5.4^{x}	6.4^{x}	9.8^{x}	2.0^{x}	–^{x}	…	…
Chile	6	1.7	1.9	1.4	0.5	0.6	0.4	–	–	–	0.8	0.6	0.9	…	…	…
Colombia	5	7.1	7.6	6.5	1.0	3.0	–	4.8	5.4	4.2	–	–	–	…	…	…
Costa Rica	6	3.3	3.7	2.9	2.3	2.6	2.1	2.0	1.9	2.1	4.0	4.7	3.2	4.1	4.4	3.8
Cuba	6	1.3	1.8	0.9	1.4	1.4	1.4	0.4	0.1	0.6	–	–	–	–	–	–
Dominica	7	4.6	1.6	8.0	2.1	4.0	0.3	3.0	2.7	3.4	0.5	0.3	0.7	2.8	2.6	3.0
Dominican Republic	6	8.0^{y}	8.0^{y}	8.0^{y}	7.1^{y}	7.5^{y}	6.7^{y}	8.9^{y}	10.2^{y}	7.4^{y}	9.0^{y}	9.7^{y}	8.2^{y}	10.1^{y}	11.3^{y}	8.9^{y}
Ecuador	6	11.6	12.0	11.1	2.0	2.5	1.4	2.6	2.9	2.4	2.7	3.1	2.4	1.4	1.4	1.3
El Salvador	6	9.6	10.2	8.9	5.3	5.8	4.8	5.2	5.4	5.0	6.7	7.1	6.2	6.2	6.4	6.0
Grenada	7	…	…	…	…	…	…	…	…	…	…	…	…	…	…	…
Guatemala	6	9.5	9.6	9.5	5.8	5.5	6.2	7.2	6.5	7.9	8.1	7.6	8.7	8.2	8.2	8.2
Guyana	6	…	…	…	…	…	…	…	…	…	…	…	…	…	…	…
Haiti	6	…	…	…	…	…	…	…	…	…	…	…	…	…	…	…
Honduras	6	6.9^{y}	8.0^{y}	5.7^{y}	2.7^{y}	3.5^{y}	1.9^{y}	2.8^{y}	3.4^{y}	2.3^{y}	3.2^{y}	3.5^{y}	2.9^{y}	2.9^{y}	3.7^{y}	2.1^{y}
Jamaica	6	…	…	…	…	…	…	…	…	…	…	…	…	…	…	…
Mexico	6	1.8	2.0	1.6	0.8	0.9	0.7	1.5	1.7	1.3	1.0	1.3	0.7	2.3	2.6	2.0
Montserrat	7	2.4	2.2	2.5	–	–	–	4.5	7.0	–	2.7	2.4	2.9	…	…	…
Netherlands Antilles	6	…	…	…	…	…	…	…	…	…	…	…	…	…	…	…
Nicaragua	6	26.2	27.2	25.1	9.7	10.9	8.5	11.1	12.5	9.6	12.8	14.2	11.3	6.5	7.4	5.5

PRIMARY EDUCATION COMPLETION															
SURVIVAL RATE TO GRADE 5 (%)						SURVIVAL RATE TO LAST GRADE (%)						PRIMARY COHORT COMPLETION RATE (%)			
School year ending in						School year ending in						School year ending in			
1999			2006			1999			2006			2006			
Total	Male	Female	Total	Male	Female	Total	Male	Female	Total	Male	Female	Total	Male	Female	Country or territory
...	...	...	...	...	...	...	...	...	...	...	...	...	...	...	China
...	...	...	...	...	...	...	...	...	...	...	...	...	...	...	Cook Islands
.	.	.	.	.	.	...	...	...	...	...	...	...	...	...	DPR Korea
87	89	86	*83*	...	...	82	82	82	*76*	...	...	...	...	...	Fiji
...	...	...	...	...	...	...	...	...	95	...	...	...	...	...	Indonesia
...	...	...	...	...	...	...	...	...	...	...	...	...	...	...	Japan
...	...	...	...	...	...	...	...	...	...	...	...	...	...	...	Kiribati
54	55	54	61	62	61	54	55	54	61	62	61	56.8	56.5	57.2	Lao PDR
...	...	...	...	...	...	...	...	...	...	...	...	...	...	...	Macao, China
...	...	...	92[y]	92[y]	92[y]	...	...	...	89[y]	89[y]	90[y]	...	...	...	Malaysia
...	...	...	...	...	...	...	...	...	...	...	...	...	...	...	Marshall Islands
...	...	...	...	...	...	...	...	...	...	...	...	...	...	...	Micronesia, F. S.
...	...	...	73	...	...	...	...	...	73	...	...	72.6	...	...	Myanmar
...	...	...	...	...	...	...	...	...	...	...	...	...	...	...	Nauru
...	...	...	...	...	...	...	...	...	...	...	...	...	...	...	New Zealand
...	...	...	...	...	...	...	...	...	...	...	...	...	...	...	Niue
...	...	...	...	...	...	...	...	...	...	...	...	...	...	...	Palau
...	...	...	...	...	...	...	...	...	...	...	...	...	...	...	Papua New Guinea
...	...	...	77	73	81	...	...	...	73	69	78	...	...	...	Philippines
100	100	100	98	98	98	99	100	99	97	97	97	...	...	...	Republic of Korea
94	91*	96*	...	...	...	92	91*	94*	...	...	...	...	...	...	Samoa
...	...	...	...	...	...	...	...	...	...	...	...	...	...	...	Singapore
...	...	...	...	...	...	...	...	...	...	...	...	...	...	...	Solomon Islands
...	...	...	...	...	...	...	...	...	...	...	...	...	...	...	Thailand
...	...	...	...	...	...	...	...	...	...	...	...	...	...	...	Timor-Leste
...	...	...	...	...	...	...	...	...	...	...	...	...	...	...	Tokelau
...	...	...	92[y]	92[y]	92[y]	...	...	...	91[y]	90[y]	92[y]	...	...	...	Tonga
...	...	...	...	...	...	...	...	...	...	...	...	...	...	...	Tuvalu
72	72	72	...	...	...	69	67	71	...	...	...	...	...	...	Vanuatu
83	80	86	*92*[y]	...	...	83	80	86	*92*[y]	...	...	...	...	...	Viet Nam
															Latin America and the Caribbean
...	...	...	97[x]	94[x]	100[x]	...	...	...	93[x]	...	...	87.5[x]	...	...	Anguilla
...	...	...	...	...	...	...	...	...	...	...	...	...	...	...	Antigua and Barbuda
90	88	92	96[y]	95[y]	97[y]	89	86	91	95[y]	93[y]	96[y]	...	...	...	Argentina
97	97	96	97	96	97	97	99	95	96	94	97	94.6[x]	92.5[x]	96.7[x]	Aruba
...	...	...	85[y]	82[y]	88[y]	...	...	...	81[y]	79[y]	84[y]	...	...	...	Bahamas
93	95	92	...	...	...	94	95	93	97[y]	...	...	...	...	...	Barbados
78	76	79	87	87	88	77	77	76	84	82	86	...	...	...	Belize
...	...	...	90[y]	...	...	...	...	...	86[y]	...	...	...	...	...	Bermuda
82	83	81	83	83	83	80	82	77	80	81	80	...	...	...	Bolivia
.	.	.	.	.	.	...	...	...	76[x]	...	...	...	...	...	Brazil
.	.	.	.	.	.	...	...	...	...	...	...	...	...	...	British Virgin Islands
74	...	...	...	...	...	...	...	...	78[x]	...	...	...	...	...	Cayman Islands
100	100	100	98	98	98	100	99	100	...	...	...	...	...	...	Chile
67	64	69	88	85	92	67	64	69	88	85	92	74.6[x]	72.7[x]	76.7[x]	Colombia
91	90	93	88	86	89	88	86	89	84	82	86	75.3*	73.4*	77.2*	Costa Rica
94	94	94	97	97	97	93	92	93	97	97	97	...	...	...	Cuba
91	...	...	89	91	87	...	...	...	87	87	87	...	...	...	Dominica
75	71	79	68[y]	66[y]	71[y]	71	66	75	61[y]	58[y]	65[y]	...	...	...	Dominican Republic
77	77	77	82	80	83	75	74	75	81	79	82	78.5	77.1	80.0	Ecuador
65	*64*	*66*	74	72	76	*62*	*63*	*62*	69	67	71	62.2	57.1	67.7	El Salvador
...	...	...	...	...	...	...	...	...	...	...	...	...	...	...	Grenada
56	55	58	68	69	67	52	50	54	62	63	62	60.9[x]	62.7[x]	58.9[x]	Guatemala
95	...	...	...	...	...	93	...	...	...	...	...	...	...	...	Guyana
...	...	...	...	...	...	...	...	...	...	...	...	...	...	...	Haiti
...	...	...	83[y]	80[y]	87[y]	...	...	...	81[y]	77[y]	85[y]	...	...	...	Honduras
...	...	...	...	...	...	...	...	...	...	...	...	...	...	...	Jamaica
89	88	90	95	94	95	87	86	88	92	91	94	...	...	...	Mexico
...	...	...	90	86	97	...	...	...	...	...	...	...	...	...	Montserrat
84	*80*	*88*	...	...	...	*84*	*78*	*91*	...	...	...	...	...	...	Netherlands Antilles
48	44	53	47	43	51	46	42	50	44	40	48	40.0	35.9	44.6	Nicaragua

Table 7 (continued)

Country or territory	Duration[1] of primary education	DROPOUT RATES BY GRADE IN PRIMARY EDUCATION (%)														
		School year ending in 2006														
		Grade 1			Grade 2			Grade 3			Grade 4			Grade 5		
	2007	Total	Male	Female	Total	Male	Female	Total	Male	Female	Total	Male	Female	Total	Male	Female
Panama	6	4.3	4.6	4.0	1.6	1.5	1.6	1.4	1.6	1.3	2.3	2.3	2.4	1.9	2.1	1.7
Paraguay	6	4.9[x]	5.2[x]	4.5[x]	1.7[x]	2.1[x]	1.2[x]	2.0[x]	2.4[x]	1.5[x]	3.4[x]	4.0[x]	2.8[x]	4.2[x]	4.7[x]	3.6[x]
Peru	6	2.1	2.4	1.8	1.9	1.9	1.9	1.1	1.0	1.2	1.3	1.2	1.4	3.5	3.2	3.7
Saint Kitts and Nevis	7	…	…	…	…	…	…	…	…	…	…	…	…	…	…	…
Saint Lucia	7	1.5[x]	1.8[x]	1.1[x]	1.1[x]	–[x]	2.3[x]	0.2[x]	0.1[x]	0.3[x]	1.2[x]	1.8[x]	0.6[x]	2.0[x]	3.3[x]	0.7[x]
Saint Vincent/Grenadines	7	…	…	…	…	…	…	…	…	…	…	…	…	…	…	…
Suriname	6	4.1	4.1	4.1	3.6	4.3	2.8	3.2	4.1	2.3	7.6	6.7	8.5	13.0	15.9	9.9
Trinidad and Tobago	7	–[*,x]	–[*,x]	–[*,x]	3.8[*,x]	5.1[*,x]	2.4[*,x]	3.9[*,x]	4.7[*,x]	3.1[*,x]	1.6[*,x]	1.4[*,x]	1.9[*,x]	4.1[*,x]	4.3[*,x]	3.8[*,x]
Turks and Caicos Islands	6	…	…	…	…	…	…	…	…	…	…	…	…	…	…	…
Uruguay	6	2.9	3.6	2.2	0.1	0.2	–	0.9	1.2	0.6	1.2	1.5	0.8	0.8	0.8	0.7
Venezuela, B. R.	6	–	–	–	–	–	–	–	–	–	0.6	1.2	–	0.5	1.0	–
North America and Western Europe																
Andorra	6	0.1	–	0.2	0.1	–	1.4	–	–	–	–	–	–	…	…	…
Austria	4	2.2	3.2	1.0	0.1	0.2	–	–	–	–	…	…	…	.	.	.
Belgium	6	1.6	2.0	1.1	1.0	1.1	0.8	0.5	0.6	0.5	0.6	0.7	0.5	2.9	3.3	2.5
Canada	6	…	…	…	…	…	…	…	…	…	…	…	…	…	…	…
Cyprus	6	0.4	0.6	0.2	–	–	–	–	–	–	–	–	–	–	–	–
Denmark	6	1.0[x]	0.8[x]	1.3[x]	4.8[x]	4.8[x]	4.9[x]	1.6[x]	1.6[x]	1.6[x]	–[x]	–[x]	–[x]	1.4[x]	1.5[x]	1.3[x]
Finland	6	–	–	–	–	–	–	–	–	–	–	–	–	–	–	–
France	5	…	…	…	…	…	…	…	…	…	…	…	…	…	…	…
Germany	4	–	–	–	1.4	1.6	1.1	0.9	0.9	0.9	…	…	…	.	.	.
Greece	6	1.4	1.7	1.0	–	–	–	0.1	0.3	0.0	0.1	0.2	–	0.2	0.2	0.2
Iceland	7	0.8	2.9	–	–	–	–	–	–	–	–	…	…	–	…	…
Ireland	8	–	–	–	–	–	–	–	–	–	…	…	…	…	…	…
Israel	6	–	…	…	–	…	…	–	…	…	–	…	…	0.1	…	…
Italy	5	–	–	–	–	–	–	–	–	–	–	–	–	…	…	…
Luxembourg	6	–	–	–	–	–	–	–	–	–	0.7	1.1	0.2	11.3	12.6	9.9
Malta	6	…	…	…	…	…	…	…	…	…	…	…	…	…	…	…
Monaco	5	…	…	…	…	…	…	…	…	…	…	…	…	…	…	…
Netherlands	6	…	…	…	…	…	…	…	…	…	…	…	…	…	…	…
Norway	7	–	–	–	–	–	–	–	–	–	–	–	–	–	–	–
Portugal	6	…	…	…	…	…	…	…	…	…	…	…	…	…	…	…
San Marino	5	…	…	…	…	…	…	…	…	…	…	…	…	…	…	…
Spain	6	–[y]	–[y]	–[y]	–[y]	–[y]	–[y]	–[y]	–[y]	–[y]	–[y]	–[y]	–[y]	–[y]	–[y]	–[y]
Sweden	6	0.5	0.6	0.3	–	–	–	–	–	–	–	–	–	–	–	–
Switzerland	6	…	…	…	…	…	…	…	…	…	…	…	…	…	…	…
United Kingdom	6	…	…	…	…	…	…	…	…	…	…	…	…	…	…	…
United States	6	1.6	4.5	–	–	–	–	–	…	…	–	…	…	–	…	…
South and West Asia																
Afghanistan	6	…	…	…	…	…	…	…	…	…	…	…	…	…	…	…
Bangladesh	5	13.2[y]	14.1[y]	12.4[y]	9.1[y]	10.1[y]	8.0[y]	11.2[y]	12.8[y]	9.6[y]	15.4[y]	15.6[y]	15.2[y]	…	…	…
Bhutan	7	–[y]	–[y]	–[y]	1.8[y]	1.8[y]	1.8[y]	3.1[y]	3.9[y]	2.2[y]	1.5[y]	2.4[y]	0.7[y]	4.4[y]	5.1[y]	3.8[y]
India	5	15.4[y]	16.2[y]	14.4[y]	9.7[y]	9.5[y]	10.0[y]	9.3[y]	9.0[y]	9.7[y]	3.5[y]	2.6[y]	4.7[y]	…	…	…
Iran, Islamic Republic of	5	…	…	…	…	…	…	…	…	…	…	…	…	…	…	…
Maldives	7	…	…	…	…	…	…	…	…	…	…	…	…	…	…	…
Nepal	5	**13.2**	**13.5**	**12.8**	**9.7**	**10.0**	**9.3**	**7.1**	**7.6**	**6.5**	**6.6**	**7.6**	**5.4**	…	…	…
Pakistan	5	15.3[x]	15.4[x]	15.1[x]	4.7[x]	6.1[x]	2.5[x]	3.8[x]	4.7[x]	2.5[x]	9.2[x]	9.1[x]	9.4[x]	…	…	…
Sri Lanka	5	1.2[y]	1.2[y]	1.3[y]	1.4[y]	1.4[y]	1.3[y]	1.9[y]	2.0[y]	1.9[y]	2.2[y]	2.3[y]	2.0[y]	…	…	…
Sub-Saharan Africa																
Angola	4	…	…	…	…	…	…	…	…	…	…	…	…	.	.	.
Benin	6	10.0[y]	10.3[y]	9.7[y]	6.6[y]	6.9[y]	6.4[y]	5.0[y]	4.7[y]	5.5[y]	7.9[y]	7.3[y]	8.7[y]	7.6[y]	5.9[y]	10.1[y]
Botswana	7	8.8[x]	9.2[x]	8.3[x]	2.6[x]	2.9[x]	2.4[x]	–[x]	–[x]	–[x]	8.5[x]	10.4[x]	6.4[x]	3.5[x]	3.8[x]	3.1[x]
Burkina Faso	6	**6.7**	**6.7**	**6.8**	**2.2**	**1.9**	**2.6**	**7.2**	**8.1**	**6.1**	**3.9**	**4.9**	**2.7**	**11.5**	**11.7**	**11.3**
Burundi	6	14.6	14.4	14.9	1.7	2.0	1.3	3.6	4.2	3.0	2.5	3.6	1.2	3.7	5.3	1.9
Cameroon	6	0.9	2.6	–	3.0	–	6.7	–	…	…	10.7	…	…	24.4	…	…
Cape Verde	6	–	…	…	2.7	…	…	1.7	…	…	3.6	…	…	3.6	…	…
Central African Republic	6	**8.3**	**9.1**	**7.3**	–	–	–	**11.6**	**11.6**	**11.6**	**12.9**	**11.9**	**14.4**	**10.5**	**9.3**	**12.3**
Chad	6	19.3[y]	18.0[y]	21.1[y]	14.2[y]	13.7[y]	14.9[y]	15.4[y]	14.5[y]	16.6[y]	17.9[y]	16.6[y]	20.0[y]	16.1[y]	13.8[y]	19.9[y]
Comoros	6	1.4[x]	1.7[x]	1.2[x]	2.2[x]	2.3[x]	2.2[x]	3.2[x]	4.1[x]	2.3[x]	7.0[x]	6.1[x]	8.2[x]	7.4[x]	8.8[x]	5.9[x]

PRIMARY EDUCATION COMPLETION

SURVIVAL RATE TO GRADE 5 (%)						SURVIVAL RATE TO LAST GRADE (%)						PRIMARY COHORT COMPLETION RATE (%)			
School year ending in						School year ending in						School year ending in			
1999			2006			1999			2006			2006			
Total	Male	Female	Total	Male	Female	Total	Male	Female	Total	Male	Female	Total	Male	Female	Country or territory
92	92	92	90	90	90	90	90	91	88	88	89	87.6	87.3	87.8	Panama
78	*76*	*80*	88[x]	86[x]	90[x]	*73*	*71*	*76*	84[x]	82[x]	86[x]	…	…	…	Paraguay
87	88	87	93	93	93	83	84	82	90	90	90	…	…	…	Peru
…	…	…	…	…	…	…	…	…	…	…	…	…	…	…	Saint Kitts and Nevis
90	…	…	…	…	…	…	…	…	96[x]	95[x]	97[x]	…	…	…	Saint Lucia
…	…	…	…	…	…	…	…	…	…	…	…	…	…	…	Saint Vincent/Grenadines
…	…	…	80	78	81	…	…	…	68	63	72	…	…	…	Suriname
…	…	…	91[*,x]	90[*,x]	92[*,x]	…	…	…	84[*,x]	80[*,x]	87[*,x]	…	…	…	Trinidad and Tobago
…	…	…	…	…	…	…	…	…	…	…	…	…	…	…	Turks and Caicos Islands
…	…	…	94	93	96	…	…	…	94	92	95	…	…	…	Uruguay
91	88	94	98	96	100	88	84	92	97	95	100	95.1	92.2	98.3	Venezuela, B. R.
															North America and Western Europe
…	…	…	98	100	96	…	…	…	…	…	…	…	…	…	Andorra
.	.	.	.	.	.	…	…	…	98	97	99	…	…	…	Austria
…	…	…	96	95	97	…	…	…	93	92	95	…	…	…	Belgium
…	…	…	…	…	…	…	…	…	…	…	…	…	…	…	Canada
96	95	97	100	100	100	96	95	97	100	100	100	…	…	…	Cyprus
100	100	100	93[x]	93[x]	93[x]	100	100	100	92[x]	92[x]	92[x]	…	…	…	Denmark
100	100	100	100	100	100	100	100	100	100	100	100	…	…	…	Finland
98	*98*	*97*	…	…	…	98	*98*	*97*	…	…	…	…	…	…	France
.	.	.	.	.	.	99	99	100	98	98	99	…	…	…	Germany
…	…	…	98	99	98	…	…	…	98	98	98	…	…	…	Greece
100	100	100	94	…	…	100	…	…	93	…	…	…	…	…	Iceland
95	94	97	…	…	…	…	…	…	…	…	…	…	…	…	Ireland
…	…	…	…	…	…	…	…	…	99	…	…	…	…	…	Israel
97	…	…	100	99	100	97	…	…	100	99	100	…	…	…	Italy
96	*93*	*100*	99	98	100	*89*	*84*	*94*	90	88	92	…	…	…	Luxembourg
99	100	99	…	…	…	99	…	…	…	…	…	…	…	…	Malta
…	…	…	…	…	…	…	…	…	…	…	…	…	…	…	Monaco
100	100	100	…	…	…	100	100	100	…	…	…	…	…	…	Netherlands
100	100	100	100	100	99	100	100	100	99	100	99	…	…	…	Norway
…	…	…	…	…	…	…	…	…	…	…	…	…	…	…	Portugal
…	…	…	…	…	…	…	…	…	…	…	…	…	…	…	San Marino
…	…	…	100[y]	100[y]	100[y]	…	…	…	100[y]	100[y]	100[y]	…	…	…	Spain
99	99	99	100	100	100	100	100	99	100	100	100	…	…	…	Sweden
…	…	…	…	…	…	…	…	…	…	…	…	…	…	…	Switzerland
…	…	…	…	…	…	…	…	…	…	…	…	…	…	…	United Kingdom
94	…	…	…	…	…	92	…	…	95	…	…	…	…	…	United States
															South and West Asia
…	…	…	…	…	…	…	…	…	…	…	…	…	…	…	Afghanistan
…	…	…	55[y]	52[y]	58[y]	…	…	…	55[y]	52[y]	58[y]	…	…	…	Bangladesh
90	89	92	93[y]	91[y]	95[y]	81	78	86	84[y]	81[y]	88[y]	…	…	…	Bhutan
62	63	60	66[y]	66[y]	65[y]	62	63	60	66[y]	66[y]	65[y]	…	…	…	India
…	…	…	…	…	…	…	…	…	…	…	…	…	…	…	Iran, Islamic Republic of
…	…	…	…	…	…	…	…	…	…	…	…	…	…	…	Maldives
58	56	61	**62**	**60**	**64**	58	56	61	**62**	**60**	**64**	*57.0*[x]	*50.9*[x]	*65.2*[x]	Nepal
…	…	…	70[x]	68[x]	72[x]	…	…	…	70[x]	68[x]	72[x]	48.3[x]	46.7[x]	50.5[x]	Pakistan
…	…	…	*93*[y]	*93*[y]	*94*[y]	…	…	…	*93*[y]	*93*[y]	*94*[y]	…	…	…	Sri Lanka
															Sub-Saharan Africa
.	.	.	.	.	.	…	…	…	…	…	…	…	…	…	Angola
…	…	…	72[y]	72[y]	71[y]	…	…	…	65[y]	67[y]	63[y]	36.3[x]	37.9[x]	34.2[x]	Benin
87	84	89	83[x]	80[x]	85[x]	82	79	86	75[x]	71[x]	78[x]	69.1[x]	…	…	Botswana
68	67	70	**80**	**78**	**81**	61	59	63	**69**	**68**	**71**	60.6	60.0	61.4	Burkina Faso
…	…	…	66	65	68	…	…	…	58	56	61	37.8	44.9	27.3	Burundi
81	…	…	84	…	…	*78*	…	…	59	…	…	45.2	…	…	Cameroon
…	…	…	92	…	…	…	…	…	88	…	…	83.8	…	…	Cape Verde
…	…	…	**59**	**61**	**57**	…	…	…	**50**	**53**	**47**	…	…	…	Central African Republic
55	58	50	38[y]	41[y]	34[y]	47	50	41	30[y]	33[y]	25[y]	…	…	…	Chad
…	…	…	*80*[x]	*79*[x]	*81*[x]	…	…	…	*72*[x]	*69*[x]	*74*[x]	…	…	…	Comoros

Table 7 (continued)

Country or territory	Duration[1] of primary education 2007	DROPOUT RATES BY GRADE IN PRIMARY EDUCATION (%) School year ending in 2006 Grade 1 Total	Grade 1 Male	Grade 1 Female	Grade 2 Total	Grade 2 Male	Grade 2 Female	Grade 3 Total	Grade 3 Male	Grade 3 Female	Grade 4 Total	Grade 4 Male	Grade 4 Female	Grade 5 Total	Grade 5 Male	Grade 5 Female
Congo	6	...	...	...	...	...	...	...	...	...	...	...	...	...	...	...
Côte d'Ivoire	6	3.0	2.9	3.1	4.3	3.1	5.8	4.6	2.9	6.7	6.7	5.2	8.5	2.5	–	6.5
D. R. Congo	6	...	...	...	...	...	...	...	...	...	...	...	...	...	...	...
Equatorial Guinea	5	...	...	...	...	...	...	...	...	...	...	...	...	...	...	...
Eritrea	5	9.9	10.8	8.8	9.0	9.3	8.7	9.2	9.1	9.3	13.1	13.1	13.2	...	...	...
Ethiopia	6	15.7	15.8	15.6	12.9	13.2	12.5	8.5	8.7	8.3	1.4	1.8	0.9	9.2	9.7	8.7
Gabon	6	...	...	...	...	...	...	...	...	...	...	...	...	...	...	...
Gambia	6	***12.6***	***11.7***	***13.5***	***4.6***	***6.4***	***2.8***	***3.9***	***5.6***	***2.3***	***6.8***	***7.2***	***6.4***	***12.0***	***11.7***	***12.2***
Ghana	6	**9.2**	**9.6**	**8.7**	**0.6**	**0.2**	**1.0**	–	...	...	**2.7**	...	...	**5.5**	...	...
Guinea	6	0.4	–	2.1	2.9	1.4	4.7	7.2	6.7	7.7	6.1	5.7	6.5	6.4	5.5	7.7
Guinea-Bissau	6	...	...	...	...	...	...	...	...	...	...	...	...	...	...	...
Kenya	6	*9.1*[x]	*9.9*[x]	*8.3*[x]	*5.9*[x]	*6.6*[x]	*5.1*[x]	–[x]	–[x]	–[x]	*4.0*[x]	*4.2*[x]	*3.8*[x]	–[x]	...	...
Lesotho	7	9.3[y]	9.8[y]	8.8[y]	2.0[y]	2.9[y]	0.9[y]	3.7[y]	4.8[y]	2.5[y]	6.3[y]	7.8[y]	4.7[y]	7.1[y]	9.7[y]	4.6[y]
Liberia	6	...	...	...	...	...	...	...	...	...	...	...	...	...	...	...
Madagascar	5	21.8	22.0	21.5	13.0	13.3	12.7	12.0	12.1	11.9	15.9	15.9	16.0	...	...	...
Malawi	6	24.7	24.2	25.1	6.5	5.9	7.0	14.7	14.4	15.0	11.0	10.6	11.4	14.6	14.0	15.2
Mali	6	2.9[y]	2.9[y]	3.0[y]	3.5[y]	2.9[y]	4.1[y]	5.1[y]	4.7[y]	5.6[y]	5.3[y]	5.0[y]	5.6[y]	7.1[y]	6.3[y]	8.2[y]
Mauritius	6	–	–	–	0.4	0.2	0.6	0.4	0.3	0.6	0.3	0.2	0.4	1.2	1.2	1.1
Mozambique	7	10.8	10.0	11.8	9.6	8.6	10.9	9.6	8.7	10.6	9.9	8.1	11.9	19.6	18.8	20.7
Namibia	7	*2.7*	*3.5*	*1.8*	–	–	–	–	–	–	–	–	–	*6.5*	*5.7*	*7.2*
Niger	6	10.4	9.5	11.6	6.4	5.6	7.6	7.7	7.2	8.5	6.2	5.9	6.5	2.7	2.6	3.0
Nigeria	6	...	...	...	...	...	...	...	...	...	...	...	...	...	...	...
Rwanda	6	...	...	...	...	...	...	...	...	...	...	...	...	...	...	...
Sao Tome and Principe	6	**5.8**	**4.8**	**6.8**	**2.5**	**1.8**	**3.2**	**3.6**	**2.7**	**4.5**	**5.7**	**4.5**	**7.0**	**3.8**	**3.8**	**3.8**
Senegal	6	17.4[y]	17.6[y]	17.2[y]	6.6[y]	6.2[y]	7.0[y]	8.7[y]	8.9[y]	8.6[y]	4.3[y]	4.4[y]	4.1[y]	15.6[y]	15.2[y]	16.2[y]
Seychelles	6	...	...	...	...	...	...	...	...	...	...	...	...	...	...	...
Sierra Leone	6	...	...	...	...	...	...	...	...	...	...	...	...	...	...	...
Somalia	7	...	...	...	...	...	...	...	...	...	...	...	...	...	...	...
South Africa	7	...	...	...	...	...	...	...	...	...	...	...	...	...	...	...
Swaziland	7	4.7	4.5	4.8	–	–	–	7.6	12.1	2.5	3.8	4.0	3.5	4.0	5.7	2.3
Togo	6	13.1	12.6	13.7	7.0	6.3	7.7	11.1	9.9	12.5	11.6	10.0	13.4	13.4	11.1	16.3
Uganda	7	*31.6*[x]	*32.8*[x]	*30.5*[x]	*3.9*[x]	*4.7*[x]	*3.0*[x]	*7.1*[x]	*4.5*[x]	*9.6*[x]	*11.4*[x]	*11.7*[x]	*11.1*[x]	*15.2*[x]	*14.4*[x]	*16.0*[x]
United Republic of Tanzania	7	*1.2*	*2.3*	*0.1*	*2.1*	*2.5*	*1.7*	*1.1*	*2.4*	–	*7.9*	*7.2*	*8.5*	*1.3*	*1.3*	*1.2*
Zambia	7	5.1	3.8	6.4	0.3	–	1.2	2.9	1.6	4.1	2.4	0.5	4.4	7.9	6.4	9.4
Zimbabwe	7	...	...	...	...	...	...	...	...	...	...	...	...	...	...	...
World[2]	...	2.2	2.7	1.5	1.4	1.5	1.2	1.2	...	...	2.4	1.4	3.4	1.4	1.5	1.3
Countries in transition	...	0.6	...	...	0.5	0.6	0.3	0.5	0.7	0.3	...	...	...	.	.	.
Developed countries	...	0.9	2.0	0.4	0.2	0.2	0.2	0.1	0.4	–	...	...	...	.	.	.
Developing countries	...	4.4	4.5	4.3	2.1	3.2	1.0	2.9	1.6	4.1	3.4	4.0	2.8	3.6	...	...
Arab States	...	1.9	2.4	1.4	1.2	1.2	1.2	0.6	0.6	0.6	1.8	1.9	1.6	2.2	2.3	2.0
Central and Eastern Europe	...	1.0	1.4	0.7	0.6	0.7	0.5	0.6	...	...	...	...	...	.	.	.
Central Asia	...	0.2	0.6	0.0	0.4	0.8	0.1	0.4	0.5	0.3	...	...	...	.	.	.
East Asia and the Pacific	...	...	...	...	...	...	...	...	...	...	...	...	...	...	...	...
East Asia	...	2.2	2.4	2.0	2.6	2.7	2.5	2.0	2.0	2.0	2.3	...	...	...	...	...
Pacific	...	...	...	...	...	...	...	...	...	...	...	...	...	...	...	...
Latin America/Caribbean	...	3.7	3.9	3.5	1.7	2.1	1.2	2.0	1.9	2.1	1.5	1.3	1.7	2.8	2.6	3.0
Caribbean	...	2.4	2.5	2.3	1.2	...	...	2.5	1.7	3.3	1.1	1.3	0.9	2.4	2.9	1.8
Latin America	...	4.9	5.2	4.5	1.9	1.9	1.9	2.0	1.9	2.1	2.4	2.3	2.5	2.9	3.7	2.1
N. America/W. Europe	...	0.1	–	0.2	–	–	–	–	–	–	–	–	–	–	...	...
South and West Asia	...	13.2	13.8	12.6	6.9	8.1	5.3	5.5	6.2	4.5	5.1	5.1	5.0	...	...	...
Sub-Saharan Africa	...	9.1	9.9	8.3	3.0	–	6.7	5.0	4.7	5.5	6.3	7.8	4.7	7.1	8.0	6.4

Source: UNESCO Institute for Statistics database (UIS, 2009).

1. Duration in this table is defined according to ISCED97 and may differ from that reported nationally.

2. All regional values shown are medians.

Data in italic are UIS estimates.

Data in bold are for the school year ending in 2007.

(y) Data are for the school year ending in 2005.

(x) Data are for the school year ending in 2004.

(*) National estimate.

PRIMARY EDUCATION COMPLETION															
SURVIVAL RATE TO GRADE 5 (%)						SURVIVAL RATE TO LAST GRADE (%)						PRIMARY COHORT COMPLETION RATE (%)			
School year ending in						School year ending in						School year ending in			
1999			2006			1999			2006			2006			
Total	Male	Female	Total	Male	Female	Total	Male	Female	Total	Male	Female	Total	Male	Female	Country or territory
...	...	...	...	...	...	...	...	...	...	...	...	...	...	...	Congo
69	73	65	78	83	73	62	67	56	75	83	66	...	...	...	Côte d'Ivoire
...	...	...	...	...	...	...	...	...	...	...	...	...	...	...	D. R. Congo
...	...	...	...	...	...	...	...	...	...	...	...	...	...	...	Equatorial Guinea
95	97	93	60	59	61	95	97	93	60	59	61	49.5	48.3	51.0	Eritrea
56	55	59	64	64	65	51	49	54	58	57	59	...	...	...	Ethiopia
...	...	...	...	...	...	...	...	...	...	...	...	...	...	...	Gabon
92	*93*	*92*	***73***	***71***	***75***	*86*	*88*	*83*	***64***	***62***	***66***	...	...	...	Gambia
...	...	...	**89**	...	...	...	...	...	**83**	...	...	...	...	...	Ghana
...	...	...	83	87	79	...	...	...	77	82	72	...	...	...	Guinea
...	...	...	...	...	...	...	...	...	...	...	...	...	...	...	Guinea-Bissau
...	...	...	*83*[x]	*81*[x]	*85*[x]	...	...	...	*84*[x]	...	...	...	...	...	Kenya
74	67	80	74[y]	68[y]	80[y]	58	50	66	62[y]	53[y]	71[y]	...	...	...	Lesotho
...	...	...	...	...	...	...	...	...	...	...	...	...	...	...	Liberia
51	51	52	42	42	43	51	51	52	42	42	43	27.0[y]	...	...	Madagascar
49	55	43	43	44	43	37	39	34	36	37	35	17.9	22.3	13.8	Malawi
78	*79*	*77*	81[y]	83[y]	79[y]	*66*	*67*	*63*	73[y]	75[y]	70[y]	...	...	...	Mali
99	100	99	99	99	99	99	100	99	98	98	98	86.5	81.8	91.3	Mauritius
43	47	37	64	68	60	28	31	25	45	48	41	35.6	38.3	32.6	Mozambique
92	92	93	*98*	*97*	*99*	82	79	84	*88*	*87*	*87*	...	...	...	Namibia
...	...	...	72	74	69	...	...	...	70	72	67	38.7[x]	40.1[x]	36.5[x]	Niger
...	...	...	...	...	...	...	...	...	...	...	...	...	...	...	Nigeria
45	...	...	...	...	...	30	...	...	...	...	...	...	...	...	Rwanda
...	...	...	**79**	**82**	**75**	...	...	...	**74**	**77**	**71**	...	...	...	Sao Tome and Principe
...	...	...	65[y]	65[y]	65[y]	...	...	...	53[y]	54[y]	53[y]	30.1[y]	24.3[y]	36.9[y]	Senegal
99	98	100	...	...	...	99	99	100	...	...	...	...	...	...	Seychelles
...	...	...	...	...	...	...	...	...	...	...	...	...	...	...	Sierra Leone
...	...	...	...	...	...	...	...	...	...	...	...	...	...	...	Somalia
65	65	64	...	...	...	57	59	56	...	...	...	...	...	...	South Africa
80	72	88	82	76	88	64	62	66	74	71	76	...	...	...	Swaziland
52	54	49	54	58	50	44	47	40	45	49	39	38.6	44.3	32.4	Togo
...	...	...	*49*[x]	*49*[x]	*49*[x]	...	...	...	*25*[x]	*26*[x]	*25*[x]	...	...	...	Uganda
...	...	...	*87*	*85*	*89*	...	...	...	*83*	*81*	*85*	...	...	...	United Republic of Tanzania
81	83	78	89	94	84	66	70	62	75	83	67	...	...	...	Zambia
...	...	...	...	...	...	...	...	...	...	...	...	...	...	...	Zimbabwe
...	...	...	...	...	...	90	90	91	89	87	91	...	...	...	World[2]
.	.	.	.	.	.	97	96	98	98	97	99	...	...	...	Countries in transition
...	...	...	...	...	...	98	...	...	98	98	98	...	...	...	Developed countries
81	...	...	83	...	...	...	...	...	81	78	83	...	...	...	Developing countries
...	...	...	...	...	...	90	89	92	94	94	94	...	...	...	Arab States
.	.	.	.	.	.	97	96	98	98	97	98	...	...	...	Central and Eastern Europe
.	.	.	.	.	.	97	98	96	99	99	99	96	94	98	Central Asia
...	...	...	...	...	...	...	...	...	...	...	...	...	...	...	East Asia and the Pacific
...	...	...	...	...	...	...	...	...	89	89	90	...	...	...	East Asia
...	...	...	...	...	...	...	...	...	...	...	...	...	...	...	Pacific
86	...	...	88	85	92	84	78	91	84	82	86	...	...	...	Latin America/Caribbean
...	...	...	...	...	...	...	...	...	86	...	...	...	...	...	Caribbean
82	83	81	88	86	90	81	83	80	84	82	86	...	...	...	Latin America
98	98	97	...	...	...	99	99	100	99	100	99	...	...	...	N. America/W. Europe
...	...	...	68	67	69	...	...	...	68	67	69	...	...	...	South and West Asia
...	...	...	76	75	76	...	...	...	69	68	71	...	...	...	Sub-Saharan Africa

Table 8
Participation in secondary education[1]

	Country or territory	TRANSITION FROM PRIMARY TO SECONDARY GENERAL EDUCATION (%) School year ending in 2006			ENROLMENT IN SECONDARY EDUCATION								
					Age group	School-age population[2] (000)	Total enrolment School year ending in 1999		Total enrolment School year ending in 2007		Enrolment in private institutions as % of total enrolment School year ending in 2007	Enrolment in technical and vocational education School year ending in 2007	
		Total	Male	Female	2007	2006	Total (000)	% F	Total (000)	% F		Total (000)	% F
	Arab States												
1	Algeria	81	78	84	12-18	5 113	...	...	*3 756*[y]	*51*[y]	.[y]	*464*[y]	*39*[y]
2	Bahrain	96[y]	95[y]	98[y]	12-17	73	59	51	74[z]	50[z]	17[z]	15[z]	39[z]
3	Djibouti	88	90	85	12-18	137	16	42	**41**	**41**	**12**	**2**	**39**
4	Egypt	...	...	...	12-17	9 414	*7 671*	*47*	...	...	...	...	...
5	Iraq	*70*[x]	*73*[x]	*66*[x]	12-17	4 039	1 105	38	*1 751*[y]	*39*[y]	.[y]	*140*[y]	*32*[y]
6	Jordan	98	98	97	12-17	751	579	49	671	50	17	...	...
7	Kuwait	100	100	100	11-17	272	*235*	*49*	247	49	29[z]	5	11
8	Lebanon	**86**	**83**	**89**	12-17	454	372	52	**370**	**52**	**56**	**57**	**40**
9	Libyan Arab Jamahiriya	...	...	...	12-18	769	...	...	733[z]	53[z]	2[z]	...	...
10	Mauritania	52	57	47	12-17	406	*63*	*42*	*102*	*46*	17[*,z]	...	...
11	Morocco	80	80	79	12-17	3 892	1 470	43	2 173	*46*	5[z]	122	...
12	Oman	97	97	97	12-17	341	229	49	306	48	1	.	.
13	Palestinian A. T.	97	97	98	10-17	759	444	50	702	50	5	6	34
14	Qatar	99	97	100	12-17	59	44	50	61	50	34	0.8	–
15	Saudi Arabia	...	...	...	12-17	3 009	...	...	2 826	...	11	80	...
16	Sudan	88	88	88	12-16	4 386	*965*	...	1 463	47	10	31	21
17	Syrian Arab Republic	95	95	96	10-17	3 537	1 030	47	2 549	48	4	104	40
18	Tunisia	88[y]	86[y]	90[y]	12-18	1 440	1 059	49	1 268	...	5	120	...
19	United Arab Emirates	98	98	99	11-17	337	202	50	*311*	*49*	*49*	...	...
20	Yemen	83[x]	83[x]	82[x]	12-17	3 368	1 042	26	1 455[y]	32[y]	2[y]	10[y]	6[y]
	Central and Eastern Europe												
21	Albania	...	...	...	10-17	492	364	48	...	...	...	...	...
22	Belarus	100	100	100	10-16	863	978	50	823	49	0.1	5	31
23	Bosnia and Herzegovina	...	...	...	10-17	403	...	...	345	50	...	...	...
24	Bulgaria	95	94	95	11-17	599	700	48	633	48	1.0	191	38
25	Croatia	100	99	100	11-18	429	416	49	393	50	1	150	47
26	Czech Republic	99	99	99	11-18	979	928	50	937	49	8	360	46
27	Estonia	98[y]	...	...	13-18	114	116	50	114	49	2	19	34
28	Hungary	*98*	*100*	*95*	11-18	981	1 007	49	937	49	11	128	39
29	Latvia	97[y]	97[y]	97[y]	11-18	247	255	50	258[z]	49[z]	1[z]	38[z]	39[z]
30	Lithuania	99	99	99	11-18	403	407	49	394	49	0.6	38	35
31	Montenegro	...	...	...	11-18	...	...	...	...	...	...	...	...
32	Poland	*92*[y]	...	...	13-18	3 211	3 984	49	3 206	48	3	784	36
33	Republic of Moldova[3,4]	99	99	99	11-17	415*	415	50	368	50	1	37	43
34	Romania	98	99	98	11-18	2 234	2 218	49	1 954	49	1	669	43
35	Russian Federation	...	...	...	11-17	12 808	...	...	10 798	48	0.6	1 842	37
36	Serbia[3]	...	...	...	11-18	700*	*737*	*49*	616	49	0.2	220	47
37	Slovakia	98	97	98	10-18	658	674	50	617	49	8	215	46
38	Slovenia	...	...	...	11-18	176	220	49	165	49	1	57	42
39	TFYR Macedonia	100[x]	100[x]	99[x]	11-18	247	219	48	208	48	0.6	58	42
40	Turkey	92[x]	93[x]	90[x]	12-16	6 896	...	...	*5 527*	*44*	*2*[z]	1 172	38
41	Ukraine	100	100*	100*	10-16	3 936	5 214	50*	3 709	49*	0.4	297	35*
	Central Asia												
42	Armenia	99	99	100	10-16	378	347	...	337	50	1	2	33
43	Azerbaijan[3,5]	100	99	100	10-16	1 160*	929	49	1 030	48	0.5	*3*	*28*
44	Georgia	98	...	...	12-16	356	442	49	321	*49*	4.8	7	...
45	Kazakhstan	**100**	**100**	**100**	11-17	2 020	1 966	49	**1 778**	**48**	**0.8**	**107**	**30**
46	Kyrgyzstan	99	99	99	11-17	826	633	50	714	49	1	29	33
47	Mongolia	96	95	97	12-17	358	205	55	328	52	6	25	46
48	Tajikistan	98	...	...	11-17	1 211	769	46	1 012	45	.	23	25
49	Turkmenistan	...	...	...	10-15	672	...	...	...	...	...	.	...
50	Uzbekistan	100	100	100	11-17	4 490	3 411	49	4 598	49	.	1 075	49
	East Asia and the Pacific												
51	Australia[6]	...	...	...	12-17	1 690	2 491	49	2 511	48[z]	28	1 009	44
52	Brunei Darussalam	93	92	95	12-18	47	34	51	46	49	13	3	37
53	Cambodia	79	81	78	12-17	2 168	*318*	*34*	875	44	2	19	47

GROSS ENROLMENT RATIO (GER) IN SECONDARY EDUCATION (%)																NET ENROLMENT RATIO (NER) IN SECONDARY EDUCATION (%)				
Lower secondary				Upper secondary				Total secondary								Total secondary				
School year ending in 2007				School year ending in 2007				School year ending in 1999				2007				School year ending in 2007				
Total	Male	Female	GPI (F/M)	Total	Male	Female	GPI (F/M)	Total	Male	Female	GPI (F/M)	Total	Male	Female	GPI (F/M)	Total	Male	Female	GPI (F/M)	
																				Arab States
108[y]	*111[y]*	*105[y]*	*0.95[y]*	*58[y]*	*50[y]*	*67[y]*	*1.36[y]*	…	…	…	…	*83[y]*	*80[y]*	*86[y]*	*1.08[y]*	…	…	…	…	*1*
104[z]	104[z]	104[z]	1.00[z]	100[z]	96[z]	104[z]	1.08[z]	95	91	98	1.08	102[z]	100[z]	104[z]	1.04[z]	93[z]	91[z]	96[z]	1.05[z]	*2*
37	**43**	**31**	**0.72**	**19**	**23**	**15**	**0.63**	14	16	12	0.72	**29**	**35**	**24**	**0.70**	***24***	***28***	***20***	***0.72***	*3*
…	…	…	…	…	…	…	…	*82*	*86*	*79*	*0.92*	…	…	…	…	…	…	…	…	*4*
58[y]	*70[y]*	*45[y]*	*0.64[y]*	*32[y]*	*38[y]*	*26[y]*	*0.70[y]*	34	41	26	0.63	*45[y]*	*54[y]*	*36[y]*	*0.66[y]*	*38[y]*	*45[y]*	*32[y]*	*0.70[y]*	*5*
96	95	96	1.02	76	74	78	1.06	89	88	90	1.02	89	88	91	1.03	*87*	*86*	*87*	*1.01*	*6*
96	97	96	0.98	83	80	86	1.07	*98*	*98*	99	*1.02*	91	90	92	1.02	*80*	*80*	*80*	*1.01*	*7*
85	**82**	**89**	**1.09**	**75**	**70**	**80**	**1.13**	74	70	77	1.09	**80**	**76**	**84**	**1.10**	**73**	**70**	**77**	**1.10**	*8*
116[z]	117[z]	115[z]	0.99[z]	77[z]	65[z]	91[z]	1.41[z]	…	…	…	…	94[z]	86[z]	101[z]	1.17[z]	…	…	…	…	*9*
26	*28*	*24*	*0.85*	*24*	*25*	*23*	*0.93*	*19*	*21*	*16*	*0.77*	*25*	*27*	*24*	*0.89*	*17*	*18*	*16*	*0.88*	*10*
74	*81*	*68*	*0.84*	38	*40*	*36*	*0.90*	37	41	32	0.79	56	*60*	*51*	*0.86*	…	…	…	…	*11*
94	96	92	0.96	86	87	84	0.97	75	75	75	1.00	90	91	88	0.96	79	78	79	1.01	*12*
98	96	99	1.04	75	69	82	1.18	80	79	82	1.04	92	90	95	1.06	89	86	91	1.06	*13*
106	106	105	0.98	101	102	100	0.98	87	83	92	1.11	103	105	102	0.98	93	94	92	0.98	*14*
96	…	…	…	92	…	…	…	…	…	…	…	94	…	…	…	73*	*70*	*76*	*1.08*	*15*
45	48	43	0.89	25	25	25	0.98	*26*	…	…	…	33	35	32	0.93	…	…	…	…	*16*
95	97	93	0.96	34	34	35	1.02	40	42	38	0.91	72	73	71	0.97	66	67	65	0.97	*17*
113	113	113	1.00	71	…	…	…	72	72	73	1.02	88	…	…	…	…	…	…	…	*18*
101	102	100	0.98	*81*	*77*	*86*	*1.11*	76	74	78	1.06	*92*	*91*	*94*	*1.03*	*83*	*81*	*84*	*1.03*	*19*
51[y]	67[y]	34[y]	0.52[y]	40[y]	54[y]	25[y]	0.46[y]	41	58	22	0.37	46[y]	61[y]	30[y]	0.49[y]	*37[y]*	*48[y]*	*26[y]*	*0.53[y]*	*20*
																				Central and Eastern Europe
…	…	…	…	…	…	…	…	71	72	70	0.98	…	…	…	…	…	…	…	…	*21*
107	109	105	0.97	72	66	79	1.21	85	83	87	1.05	95	94	96	1.02	87	…	…	…	*22*
95	93	97	1.04	77	76	78	1.02	…	…	…	…	85	84	87	1.03	…	…	…	…	*23*
88	91	86	0.94	125	127	123	0.97	91	92	90	0.98	106	108	103	0.96	88	89	87	0.99	*24*
99	97	100	1.03	85	84	87	1.04	84	84	85	1.02	92	90	93	1.03	*87[z]*	*86[z]*	*88[z]*	*1.02[z]*	*25*
99	99	98	1.00	93	92	94	1.03	83	81	84	1.04	96	95	96	1.01	…	…	…	…	*26*
106	109	102	0.94	95	91	100	1.10	93	91	95	1.04	100	99	101	1.02	90	89	91	1.03	*27*
97	97	96	0.99	94	94	95	1.01	94	93	94	1.02	96	96	95	1.00	89	89	90	1.00	*28*
103[z]	104[z]	101[z]	0.97[z]	93[z]	91[z]	96[z]	1.06[z]	88	87	90	1.04	99[z]	98[z]	99[z]	1.00[z]	…	…	…	…	*29*
99	100	98	0.98	94	91	97	1.06	95	95	96	1.01	98	98	98	1.00	91	90	92	1.02	*30*
…	…	…	…	…	…	…	…	…	…	…	…	…	…	…	…	…	…	…	…	*31*
101	101	100	0.98	99	99	99	1.00	99	100	99	0.99	100	100	99	0.99	94	93	95	1.02	*32*
91	91	90	0.99	84	79	90	1.13	83	84	82	0.98	89	87	90	1.03	81	79	82	1.03	*33*
99	100	99	0.99	79	79	79	1.00	79	79	80	1.01	87	88	87	0.99	73	74	72	0.97	*34*
82	82	83	1.01	88	91	85	0.93	…	…	…	…	84	85	83	0.98	…	…	…	…	*35*
97	97	96	0.99	80	77	82	1.07	*93*	*93*	*94*	*1.01*	88	87	89	1.03	…	…	…	…	*36*
95	96	94	0.98	92	91	94	1.03	85	84	86	1.02	94	93	94	1.01	…	…	…	…	*37*
88	88	88	1.00	98	99	98	0.99	100	98	101	1.03	94	94	93	0.99	89	88	89	1.01	*38*
93	93	93	1.00	76	78	74	0.95	82	83	81	0.97	84	85	83	0.97	81[y]	82[y]	80[y]	0.98[y]	*39*
89	*96*	*82*	*0.86*	74	82	66	0.80	…	…	…	…	*80*	*88*	*72*	*0.82*	*69*	*75*	*64*	*0.86*	*40*
95	95*	95*	1.00*	93	93*	92*	0.99*	98	97*	100*	1.03*	94	94*	94*	1.00*	84	84*	85*	1.01*	*41*
																				Central Asia
92	91	93	1.03	83	78	88	1.12	91	…	…	…	89	87	91	1.05	85	83	88	1.06	*42*
97	99	95	0.97	71	73	68	0.94	78	79	78	0.99	89	91	87	0.96	83	84	82	0.97	*43*
90	91	90	0.99	90	*90*	*90*	*1.00*	79	80	78	0.98	90	*90*	*90*	*1.00*	82	*82*	*82*	*1.01*	*44*
105	**104**	**105**	**1.00**	**66**	**69**	**63**	**0.92**	92	92	92	1.00	**92**	**93**	**91**	**0.98**	**86**	**86**	**85**	**0.99**	*45*
92	91	93	1.02	73	73	73	1.00	83	83	84	1.02	86	86	87	1.01	81	80	81	1.02	*46*
95	91	98	1.07	86	79	94	1.18	58	51	65	1.27	92	87	97	1.11	81	77	85	1.11	*47*
95	100	90	0.91	55	68	41	0.61	74	80	68	0.86	84	91	76	0.84	81	87	75	0.86	*48*
…	…	…	…	…	…	…	…	…	…	…	…	…	…	…	…	…	…	…	…	*49*
97	98	96	0.98	115	116	114	0.98	86	87	86	0.98	102	103	101	0.98	92	93	90	0.97	*50*
																				East Asia and the Pacific
114	114	114	1.00	217	226	207	0.91	157	158	157	1.00	149	152	145	0.96	88	87	89	1.02	*51*
115	117	113	0.97	84	79	88	1.11	85	81	89	1.09	97	96	99	1.04	89	87	91	1.05	*52*
56	60	52	0.87	23	27	19	0.70	*17*	*22*	*12*	*0.53*	40	44	36	0.82	*34*	*36*	*32*	*0.88*	*53*

Table 8 (continued)

	Country or territory	TRANSITION FROM PRIMARY TO SECONDARY GENERAL EDUCATION (%) School year ending in 2006			ENROLMENT IN SECONDARY EDUCATION								
					Age group	School-age population[2] (000)	Total enrolment School year ending in 1999		Total enrolment School year ending in 2007		Enrolment in private institutions as % of total enrolment, School year ending in 2007	Enrolment in technical and vocational education, School year ending in 2007	
		Total	Male	Female	2007	2006	Total (000)	% F	Total (000)	% F		Total (000)	% F
54	China	…	…	…	12-17	131 690	77 436	…	101 831	48	8	17 229	50
55	Cook Islands[3]	…	…	…	11-17	*3*	2	50	2	50	15	.	.
56	DPR Korea	…	…	…	10-15	2 472	…	…	…	…	…	…	…
57	Fiji	*99[y]*	*99[y]*	*100[y]*	12-18	120	98	51	99	51	*92[y]*	3	34
58	Indonesia	99	99	98	13-18	25 472	…	…	18 717	49	49	2 402	41
59	Japan	…	…	…	12-17	7 362	8 959	49	7 427	49	19	922	43
60	Kiribati[3]	…	…	…	12-17	…	9	53	11[y]	52[y]	…	–[y]	–[y]
61	Lao PDR	78	79	76	11-16	922	240	40	404	43	2	4	35
62	Macao, China	96	93	98	12-17	46	32	51	45	49	95	1	44
63	Malaysia	*99[y]*	*100[y]*	*98[y]*	12-18	3 661	2 177	51	2 489[y]	51[y]	3[y]	146[y]	43[y]
64	Marshall Islands[3]	…	…	…	12-17	8*	6	50	5	49	…	0.2	50
65	Micronesia, F. S.	…	…	…	12-17	16	…	…	*15*	…	…	…	…
66	Myanmar[7]	73	75	70	10-15	…	2 059	50	2 686	50	.	–	–
67	Nauru	…	…	…	12-17	*1*	…	…	0.7	51	.	.	.
68	New Zealand	…	…	…	11-17	435	437	50	527	49	20	…	…
69	Niue[3]	…	…	…	11-16	…	0.3	54	0.2[y]	48[y]	…	.[y]	.[y]
70	Palau[3]	…	…	…	11-17	3*	2	49	2	*50*	28	…	.
71	Papua New Guinea	…	…	…	13-18	831	…	…	…	…	…	…	…
72	Philippines	98	98	97	12-15	7 646	5 117	51	6 366	51	20	.	.
73	Republic of Korea	99	99	98	12-17	3 985	4 177	48	3 917	47	32	494	46
74	Samoa	…	…	…	11-17	32	22	50	*24[y]*	*51[y]*	*32[y]*	.[y]	.[y]
75	Singapore[7]	…	…	…	12-15	…	…	…	232	48	6	28	36
76	Solomon Islands	…	…	…	12-18	78	17	41	22[y]	43[y]	…	.[y]	.[y]
77	Thailand	87	85	89	12-17	5 736	…	…	**4 729**	**51**	18	**777**	**44**
78	Timor-Leste	…	…	…	12-17	154	…	…	75[y]	49[y]	…	3[y]	40[y]
79	Tokelau	…	…	…	11-15	…	…	…	…	…	…	…	…
80	Tonga	62[y]	62[y]	62[y]	11-16	15	15	50	14[z]	48[z]	…	…	…
81	Tuvalu	…	…	…	12-17	…	…	…	…	…	…	…	…
82	Vanuatu	64	63	65	12-18	37	9	45	…	…	…	…	…
83	Viet Nam[7]	*93[y]*	…	…	11-17	…	7 401	47	9 845	50	11	516	56
	Latin America and the Caribbean												
84	Anguilla[8]	98[x]	100[x]	96[x]	12-16	…	1	53	1	52	.	…	…
85	Antigua and Barbuda	…	…	…	12-16	7*	…	…	8	51	19	…	…
86	Argentina	94[y]	93[y]	95[y]	12-17	4 153	3 344	50	3 481[z]	52[z]	28[z]	1 231[z]	54[z]
87	Aruba	97	95	100	12-16	7	6	51	8	51	92	2	39
88	Bahamas	99	…	…	11-16	36	27	49	34	50	32	.	.
89	Barbados	98	…	…	11-15	20	22	51	21	50	5	.	.
90	Belize	88	87	90	11-16	39	22	51	30	51	74	1	50
91	Bermuda[3]	95[y]	…	…	11-17	…	…	…	5[z]	51[z]	42[z]	.[z]	.[z]
92	Bolivia	90	90	90	12-17	1 285	830	48	1 052	48	13	.	.
93	Brazil[9]	82[x]	…	…	11-17	23 396	24 983	52	23 424	52	11	997	58
94	British Virgin Islands[3]	95	100	91	12-16	*2*	2	47	2	54	12	0.4	50
95	Cayman Islands[8]	92	…	…	11-16	…	2	48	3	49	29	.	.
96	Chile	97[x]	96[x]	98[x]	12-17	1 779	1 305	50	1 612	50	55	389	47
97	Colombia	99	99	100	11-16	5 472	3 589	52	4 657	52	23	266	54
98	Costa Rica	97	…	…	12-16	432	235	51	378	50	10	57	51
99	Cuba	98	98	98	12-17	970	740	50	899	49	.	253	42
100	Dominica[3,8]	98	…	…	12-16	…	7	57	7	50	26	0.3	73
101	Dominican Republic	96	93	98	12-17	1 163	611	55	920	54	23[z]	35	60
102	Ecuador	79	81	77	12-17	1 640	904	50	1 142	49	32	261	51
103	El Salvador	91	90	91	13-18	832	406	49	536	50	19	104	53
104	Grenada[3]	…	…	…	12-16	13	…	…	13	49	60	1	35
105	Guatemala	92	94	90	13-17	1 554	435	45	864	48	74	247	51
106	Guyana	…	…	…	12-16	68	66	50	73	49	2	7	31
107	Haiti	…	…	…	12-18	1 518	…	…	…	…	…	…	…
108	Honduras	71[y]	68[y]	74[y]	12-16	866	…	…	554	55	…	171	56
109	Jamaica	*99[x]*	*100[x]*	*97[x]*	12-16	286	*231*	*50*	257	50	6[y]	8	63
110	Mexico	94	95	94	12-17	12 533	8 722	50	11 122	51	15	1 676	56
111	Montserrat[3]	…	…	…	12-16	0.3*	0.3	47	0.3	46	.	.	.
112	Netherlands Antilles	…	…	…	12-17	17	15	54	…	…	…	…	…
113	Nicaragua	…	…	…	12-16	683	*321*	*54*	471	52	24	19	55

GROSS ENROLMENT RATIO (GER) IN SECONDARY EDUCATION (%)																NET ENROLMENT RATIO (NER) IN SECONDARY EDUCATION (%)				
Lower secondary				Upper secondary				Total secondary								Total secondary				
School year ending in 2007				School year ending in 2007				School year ending in 1999				School year ending in 2007				School year ending in 2007				
Total	Male	Female	GPI (F/M)	Total	Male	Female	GPI (F/M)	Total	Male	Female	GPI (F/M)	Total	Male	Female	GPI (F/M)	Total	Male	Female	GPI (F/M)	
96	96	96	1.00	60	60	61	1.03	62	…	…	…	77	77	78	1.01	…	…	…	…	*54*
…	…	…	…	…	…	…	…	60	58	63	1.08	*73*	*70*	*76*	*1.08*	*70*	*68*	*73*	*1.07*	*55*
…	…	…	…	…	…	…	…	…	…	…	…	…	…	…	…	…	…	…	…	*56*
97	94	100	1.06	62	55	69	1.25	80	76	84	1.11	82	78	87	1.12	79[Z]	76[Z]	83[Z]	1.10[Z]	*57*
90	90	91	1.02	57	57	56	0.98	…	…	…	…	73	73	74	1.01	68	67	68	1.01	*58*
101	101	101	1.00	101	101	101	1.00	102	101	102	1.01	101	101	101	1.00	98	98	98	1.00	*59*
112[Y]	*109[Y]*	*115[Y]*	*1.06[Y]*	*65[Y]*	*57[Y]*	*74[Y]*	*1.30[Y]*	84	77	91	1.18	88[Y]	82[Y]	94[Y]	1.14[Y]	*68[Y]*	*65[Y]*	*72[Y]*	*1.11[Y]*	*60*
53	58	47	0.81	34	39	30	0.76	33	39	27	0.69	44	49	39	0.79	*36*	*38*	*33*	*0.87*	*61*
116	119	114	0.95	85	82	88	1.06	76	73	79	1.08	99	99	99	1.00	78	76	79	1.04	*62*
90[Y]	89[Y]	91[Y]	1.02[Y]	53[Y]	48[Y]	58[Y]	1.22[Y]	65	63	68	1.07	69[Y]	66[Y]	72[Y]	1.10[Y]	69[Y]	66[Y]	72[Y]	1.10[Y]	*63*
82	82	83	1.01	59	59	60	1.02	*72*	*70*	*74*	*1.06*	66	66	67	1.02	45	43	47	1.08	*64*
100	100	99	0.99	…	…	…	…	…	…	…	…	*91*	…	…	…	…	…	…	…	*65*
…	…	…	…	…	…	…	…	…	…	…	…	…	…	…	…	…	…	…	…	*66*
47	*43*	*51*	*1.17*	*45*	*40*	*50*	*1.25*	…	…	…	…	*46*	*42*	*50*	*1.19*	…	…	…	…	*67*
104	104	104	1.00	143	139	148	1.07	113	110	115	1.05	121	119	123	1.03	…	…	…	…	*68*
…	…	…	…	…	…	…	…	98	93	103	1.10	99[Y]	96[Y]	102[Y]	1.07[Y]	…	…	…	…	*69*
98	…	…	…	96	97	96	0.99	101	98	105	1.07	97	*98*	*96*	*0.97*	…	…	…	…	*70*
…	…	…	…	…	…	…	…	…	…	…	…	…	…	…	…	…	…	…	…	*71*
87	84	90	1.07	73	66	79	1.21	76	72	79	1.09	83	79	87	1.10	61	56	67	1.20	*72*
101	106	97	0.91	95	97	93	0.96	98	97	98	1.01	98	102	95	0.93	97	100	94	0.94	*73*
100[Y]	*100[Y]*	*100[Y]*	*1.00[Y]*	*72[Y]*	*66[Y]*	*79[Y]*	*1.20[Y]*	79	76	84	1.10	*81[Y]*	*76[Y]*	*86[Y]*	*1.13[Y]*	…	…	…	…	*74*
…	…	…	…	…	…	…	…	…	…	…	…	…	…	…	…	…	…	…	…	*75*
46[Y]	49[Y]	44[Y]	0.89[Y]	17[Y]	19[Y]	14[Y]	0.74[Y]	25	28	21	0.76	30[Y]	32[Y]	27[Y]	0.84[Y]	…	…	…	…	*76*
101	**99**	**102**	**1.03**	**67**	**61**	**74**	**1.21**	…	…	…	…	**83**	**79**	**88**	**1.10**	**81**	**77**	**85**	**1.11**	*77*
68[Y]	67[Y]	69[Y]	1.02[Y]	37[Y]	38[Y]	37[Y]	0.96[Y]	…	…	…	…	53[Y]	53[Y]	53[Y]	1.00[Y]	…	…	…	…	*78*
…	…	…	…	…	…	…	…	…	…	…	…	…	…	…	…	…	…	…	…	*79*
99[Z]	100[Z]	99[Z]	1.00[Z]	81[Z]	75[Z]	88[Z]	1.17[Z]	102	97	108	1.11	94[Z]	92[Z]	96[Z]	1.04[Z]	*60[Z]*	*54[Z]*	*67[Z]*	*1.25[Z]*	*80*
…	…	…	…	…	…	…	…	…	…	…	…	…	…	…	…	…	…	…	…	*81*
…	…	…	…	…	…	…	…	30	32	28	0.87	…	…	…	…	…	…	…	…	*82*
…	…	…	…	…	…	…	…	62	65	58	0.90	…	…	…	…	…	…	…	…	*83*
Latin America and the Caribbean																				
…	…	…	…	…	…	…	…	…	…	…	…	…	…	…	…	*81[Y]*	*83[Y]*	*79[Y]*	*0.96[Y]*	*84*
…	…	…	…	…	…	…	…	…	…	…	…	105*	107*	103*	0.96*	…	…	…	…	*85*
102[Z]	99[Z]	104[Z]	1.06[Z]	66[Z]	59[Z]	74[Z]	1.24[Z]	84	82	86	1.05	84[Z]	79[Z]	89[Z]	1.12[Z]	78[Z]	74[Z]	83[Z]	1.11[Z]	*86*
114	117	110	0.94	99	92	107	1.16	99	96	103	1.07	105	102	108	1.06	82	80	85	1.06	*87*
98	96	100	1.04	89	88	91	1.03	79	79	78	0.99	94	92	96	1.03	86	84	89	1.05	*88*
99	100	97	0.97	110	104	116	1.11	100	98	103	1.05	103	102	105	1.03	90	88	93	1.05	*89*
88	86	90	1.04	59	54	64	1.19	64	62	67	1.08	79	76	81	1.07	67	64	70	1.09	*90*
91[Z]	93[Z]	89[Z]	0.96[Z]	79[Z]	74[Z]	85[Z]	1.15[Z]	…	…	…	…	84[Z]	82[Z]	87[Z]	1.06[Z]	…	…	…	…	*91*
93	95	91	0.97	76	77	75	0.97	78	80	75	0.93	82	83	81	0.97	70	70	70	0.99	*92*
108	106	109	1.04	90	81	100	1.23	99	94	104	1.11	100	95	105	1.11	77	73	81	1.11	*93*
112	*106*	*117*	*1.10*	*84*	*77*	*90*	*1.17*	99	103	94	0.91	*101*	*95*	*106*	*1.11*	*84*	*79*	*89*	*1.12*	*94*
…	…	…	…	…	…	…	…	…	…	…	…	…	…	…	…	…	…	…	…	*95*
99	100	99	0.98	86	84	88	1.05	79	78	81	1.04	91	89	92	1.03	85	84	87	1.03	*96*
94	90	97	1.08	68	62	74	1.18	70	67	74	1.11	85	81	90	1.11	67	64	71	1.11	*97*
105	104	105	1.01	63	58	67	1.15	57	55	60	1.09	87	85	90	1.05	…	…	…	…	*98*
93	95	92	0.97	92	91	93	1.03	77	75	80	1.07	93	93	93	1.00	86	85	87	1.02	*99*
…	…	…	…	…	…	…	…	90	77	104	1.35	…	…	…	…	…	…	…	…	*100*
83	79	87	1.10	77	68	86	1.26	57	51	63	1.24	79	72	86	1.20	61	55	68	1.22	*101*
79	80	77	0.97	60	58	62	1.07	57	56	57	1.03	70	69	70	1.01	59	59	60	1.02	*102*
80	80	80	1.00	48	45	50	1.11	52	52	51	0.98	64	63	66	1.04	54	53	56	1.05	*103*
98	101	95	0.94	99	96	102	1.06	…	…	…	…	99	99	98	0.99	*79[Y]*	*78[Y]*	*80[Y]*	*1.02[Y]*	*104*
61	64	57	0.88	48	47	48	1.01	33	36	30	0.84	56	58	53	0.92	*38[Z]*	*40[Z]*	*37[Z]*	*0.92[Z]*	*105*
129	136	122	0.90	69	67	70	1.03	82	82	83	1.02	107	111	103	0.93	…	…	…	…	*106*
…	…	…	…	…	…	…	…	…	…	…	…	…	…	…	…	…	…	…	…	*107*
66	61	72	1.17	60	50	70	1.40	…	…	…	…	64	57	71	1.25	…	…	…	…	*108*
95	95	96	1.01	82	76	87	1.14	*88*	*87*	*88*	*1.02*	90	87	92	1.05	76	74	79	1.06	*109*
114	112	117	1.05	62	61	62	1.01	70	69	70	1.01	89	88	90	1.03	72	72	72	1.00	*110*
101	96	109	1.14	103	111	96	0.86	…	…	…	…	102	101	103	1.02	96	95	96	1.01	*111*
…	…	…	…	…	…	…	…	92	85	99	1.16	…	…	…	…	…	…	…	…	*112*
78	75	80	1.06	55	48	62	1.30	*52*	*47*	*56*	*1.19*	69	65	73	1.13	*46*	*42*	*49*	*1.15*	*113*

Table 8 (continued)

	Country or territory	TRANSITION FROM PRIMARY TO SECONDARY GENERAL EDUCATION (%)			ENROLMENT IN SECONDARY EDUCATION								
		School year ending in 2006			Age group	School-age population[2] (000)	Total enrolment School year ending in 1999		Total enrolment School year ending in 2007		Enrolment in private institutions as % of total enrolment School year ending in 2007	Enrolment in technical and vocational education School year ending in 2007	
		Total	Male	Female	2007	2006	Total (000)	% F	Total (000)	% F		Total (000)	% F
114	Panama	99	100	98	12-17	371	230	51	261	51	16	43	48
115	Paraguay	89x	89x	89x	12-17	810	425	50	529y	50y	21y	47y	47y
116	Peru	98	99	96	12-16	2 919	2 278	48	2 861	50	26	257	61
117	Saint Kitts and Nevis	…	…	…	12-16	*4*	…	…	5	50	4	.	.
118	Saint Lucia	97	…	…	12-16	16	12	56	15	52	4	0.3	29
119	Saint Vincent/Grenadines	84x	79x	88x	12-16	12	…	…	10y	55y	25y	0.4y	34y
120	Suriname	46	41	50	12-18	59	…	…	47	57	18	23	51
121	Trinidad and Tobago	93*,x	94*,x	92*,x	12-16	115	117	52	*98*	*51*	24*,y	…	…
122	Turks and Caicos Islands	88x	84x	92x	12-16	…	1	51	*2y*	*48y*	*16y*	*0.1y*	*48y*
123	Uruguay	77	71	83	12-17	320	284	53	295	49	13	44	43
124	Venezuela, B. R.	98	98	98	12-16	2 740	1 439	54	2 175	52	26	117	50
	North America and Western Europe												
125	Andorra[3]	…	…	…	12-17	5*	…	…	4	49	3	0.2	50
126	Austria	99	100	99	10-17	765	748	48	778	48	10	301	44
127	Belgium	99	100	99	12-17	750	1 033	51	822z	48z	68	343	44
128	Canada	…	…	…	12-17	2 593	…	…	2 632z	48z	6z	.z	.z
129	Cyprus[3]	99	98	100	12-17	66*	63	49	65	49	14	4	15
130	Denmark	97	97	96y	13-18	399	422	50	475	49	13	126	44
131	Finland	100	100	*100y*	13-18	389	480	51	433	50	7	126	46
132	France[10]	…	…	…	11-17	5 237	5 955	49	5 940	49	26	1 180	42
133	Germany	99	99	98	10-18	8 004	8 185	48	7 982	48	8	1 727	42
134	Greece	97	…	…y	12-17	670	771	49	682	47	5	109	35
135	Iceland	100	100	100	13-19	31	32	50	34	50	7	7	43
136	Ireland	99x	…	…	12-16	279	346	50	316	51	0.7	51	54
137	Israel	71	71	71	12-17	673	569	49	616	49	.	123	43
138	Italy	100	100	99	11-18	4 502	4 450	49	4 553	48	5	1 687	39
139	Luxembourg	…	…	…	12-18	39	33	50	38	50	18	12	48
140	Malta	94x	93x	94x	11-17	38	…	…	38y	49y	28y	4y	33y
141	Monaco[8]	…	…	…	11-17	…	3	51	**3**	**48**	**22**	**0.4**	**41**
142	Netherlands	…	…	…	12-17	1 208	1 365	48	1 444	48	…	671	46
143	Norway	100	100	99	13-18	372	378	49	420	48	7y	135	42
144	Portugal	…	…	…	12-17	673	848	51	680	51	16	125	42
145	San Marino[8]	…	…	…	11-18	…	…	…	**2**	**49**	.	**0.5**	**30**
146	Spain	…	…	…	12-17	2 570	3 299	50	3 080	50	28	492	50
147	Sweden	…	…	…	13-18	734	946	55	760	49	12	223	44
148	Switzerland	100	99	100	13-19	639	544	47	592	47	7	191	40
149	United Kingdom	…	…	…	11-17	5 445	5 192	49	5 306	49	26	1 008	50
150	United States	…	…	…	12-17	26 248	22 445	…	24 731	49	9	.	.
	South and West Asia												
151	Afghanistan	…	…	…	13-18	3 753	…	…	1 036	26	…	7	11
152	Bangladesh	97y	95y	100y	11-17	24 101	9 912	49	10 445	50	96	254	30
153	Bhutan	93y	92y	94y	13-18	93	20	44	**52**	**48**	**9**	–	–
154	India	84y	86y	82y	11-17	169 164	67 090	39	91 529z	43z	…	750z	7z
155	Iran, Islamic Republic of	*83*	*89*	*77*	11-17	11 457	9 727	47	9 942y	47y	*8y*	876y	38y
156	Maldives	81	76	85	13-17	39	15	51	*33z*	*50z*	*12z*	…	…
157	Nepal	**81**	**81**	**81**	10-16	4 688	1 265	40	**2 305**	**47**	**14**	**15**	…
158	Pakistan	76	75	76	10-16	28 103	…	…	9 145	42	31	331	35
159	Sri Lanka	*97y*	*96y*	*97y*	10-17	2 556	…	…	…	…	…	…	…
	Sub-Saharan Africa												
160	Angola	…	…	…	10-16	2 974	300	43	…	…	…	…	…
161	Benin	71y	72y	70y	12-18	1 415	213	31	*435y*	*35y*	*25y*	*58y*	*43y*
162	Botswana	97x	97x	98x	13-17	220	158	51	169y	51y	…	11y	38y
163	Burkina Faso	**52**	**54**	**50**	13-19	2 272	173	38	**424**	**42**	**43**	**26**	**49**
164	Burundi	31	37	24	13-19	1 377	…	…	210	42	7	13	44
165	Cameroon	36*	35*	37*	12-18	2 985	*626*	*45*	751*	44*	28*	124*	39*
166	Cape Verde	83	80	87	12-17	77	…	…	61	54	12	2	43
167	Central African Republic	*47y*	*44y*	*51y*	12-18	706	…	…	…	…	…	…	…
168	Chad	*64*	*64*	*65*	12-18	1 670	123	21	314	31	23z	4	46
169	Comoros	*63x*	*70x*	*55x*	12-18	127	29	44	*43y*	*43y*	*41y*	*0.2y*	*7y*

GROSS ENROLMENT RATIO (GER) IN SECONDARY EDUCATION (%)																NET ENROLMENT RATIO (NER) IN SECONDARY EDUCATION (%)				
Lower secondary				Upper secondary				Total secondary								Total secondary				
School year ending in 2007				School year ending in 2007				School year ending in 1999				2007				School year ending in 2007				
Total	Male	Female	GPI (F/M)	Total	Male	Female	GPI (F/M)	Total	Male	Female	GPI (F/M)	Total	Male	Female	GPI (F/M)	Total	Male	Female	GPI (F/M)	
85	84	86	1.02	55	51	59	1.17	67	65	69	1.07	70	68	73	1.08	*64[z]*	*61[z]*	*67[z]*	*1.11[z]*	114
79[y]	79[y]	80[y]	1.01[y]	53[y]	52[y]	55[y]	1.05[y]	58	57	59	1.04	66[y]	66[y]	67[y]	1.03[y]	57[y]	56[y]	59[y]	1.06[y]	115
114	111	117	1.06	74	74	74	1.00	84	87	81	0.94	98	96	100	1.04	76	76	77	1.01	116
118	*123*	*113*	*0.92*	*86*	*90*	*82*	*0.91*	…	…	…	…	*105*	*110*	*100*	*0.91*	*84*	*89*	*80*	*0.91*	117
104	102	107	1.04	77	67	88	1.32	71	62	79	1.29	93	88	99	1.13	*82*	*76*	*88*	*1.17*	118
90[y]	83[y]	96[y]	1.16[y]	54[y]	44[y]	64[y]	1.46[y]	…	…	…	…	75[y]	67[y]	83[y]	1.24[y]	*64[y]*	*57[y]*	*71[y]*	*1.23[y]*	119
96	89	104	1.18	58	38	78	2.04	…	…	…	…	80	67	93	1.39	*68[y]*	*57[y]*	*79[y]*	*1.38[y]*	120
88	86	90	1.05	*84*	*80*	*88*	*1.10*	77	74	81	1.10	*86*	*83*	*89*	*1.07*	*73*	*71*	*76*	*1.07*	121
86[y]	*89[y]*	*84[y]*	*0.95[y]*	*85[y]*	*89[y]*	*82[y]*	*0.92[y]*	…	…	…	…	*86[y]*	*89[y]*	*83[y]*	*0.94[y]*	*70[y]*	*72[y]*	*69[y]*	*0.96[y]*	122
101	97	105	1.08	83	88	78	0.89	92	84	99	1.17	92	93	91	0.99	68	64	71	1.11	123
89	86	93	1.08	65	59	71	1.20	56	51	62	1.22	79	75	84	1.12	68	64	73	1.14	124
North America and Western Europe																				
89	88	90	1.02	69	62	77	1.25	…	…	…	…	82	79	86	1.08	72	70	74	1.07	125
102	102	102	0.99	101	104	98	0.94	99	101	97	0.96	102	103	100	0.96	…	…	…	…	126
112	115	108	0.95	109	111	108	0.98	143	138	148	1.07	110	112	108	0.97	*87[z]*	*89[z]*	*85[z]*	*0.96[z]*	127
97[z]	98[z]	96[z]	0.99[z]	104[z]	105[z]	103[z]	0.97[z]	…	…	…	…	102[z]	103[z]	100[z]	0.98[z]	…	…	…	…	128
96	96	96	1.00	99	98	101	1.04	93	92	95	1.03	98	97	99	1.02	95	94	96	1.02	129
117	115	118	1.03	122	120	124	1.03	125	121	128	1.06	119	117	121	1.03	90	88	91	1.03	130
102	102	102	1.00	121	116	126	1.09	121	116	126	1.09	111	109	114	1.05	97	97	97	1.01	131
111	111	111	0.99	117	116	118	1.02	111	111	111	1.00	113	113	114	1.01	98	97	99	1.02	132
100	100	100	1.00	100	102	97	0.95	98	99	97	0.98	100	101	99	0.98	…	…	…	…	133
104	108	100	0.92	99	101	98	0.97	90	89	92	1.04	102	105	99	0.95	91	91	91	0.99	134
101	101	100	0.99	118	113	124	1.10	110	107	113	1.06	111	108	114	1.06	91	89	92	1.03	135
105	104	107	1.03	125	118	132	1.12	107	104	111	1.06	113	110	117	1.07	88	86	90	1.05	136
75	74	75	1.01	109	109	109	1.00	90	90	90	1.00	92	91	92	1.00	88	87	88	1.01	137
103	105	101	0.97	100	100	100	1.00	92	92	91	0.99	101	102	100	0.99	94	93	94	1.01	138
108	108	109	1.01	88	86	91	1.06	98	96	99	1.04	97	96	99	1.04	85	83	86	1.04	139
104[y]	103[y]	105[y]	1.03[y]	89[y]	92[y]	87[y]	0.94[y]	…	…	…	…	99[y]	99[y]	100[y]	1.00[y]	*87[y]*	*84[y]*	*90[y]*	*1.07[y]*	140
…	…	…	…	…	…	…	…	…	…	…	…	…	…	…	…	…	…	…	…	141
128	131	125	0.95	111	111	112	1.01	124	126	121	0.96	120	121	118	0.98	89	*88*	*90*	*1.02*	142
97	97	97	0.99	129	131	128	0.98	120	118	121	1.02	113	114	112	0.99	97	97	97	1.01	143
117	117	117	1.00	86	79	93	1.18	106	102	110	1.08	101	98	105	1.07	88	84	92	1.09	144
…	…	…	…	…	…	…	…	…	…	…	…	…	…	…	…	…	…	…	…	145
117	117	117	1.00	125	115	136	1.18	108	105	112	1.07	120	116	124	1.06	95	93	96	1.03	146
103	104	103	0.99	104	104	104	0.99	157	137	177	1.29	104	104	103	0.99	100	100	100	1.00	147
107	106	109	1.03	81	86	76	0.89	94	98	90	0.92	93	95	90	0.96	82	84	80	0.96	148
98	97	98	1.01	97	96	99	1.03	101	101	101	1.00	97	96	99	1.02	91	90	93	1.04	149
100	100	100	1.00	89	88	89	1.01	95	…	…	…	94	94	95	1.01	88	87	89	1.02	150
South and West Asia																				
38	53	21	0.40	16	24	8	0.34	…	…	…	…	28	39	15	0.38	*26*	*37*	*14*	*0.38*	151
60	56	64	1.13	30	31	30	0.97	45	45	45	1.01	43	42	45	1.06	41	39	42	1.07	152
69	**70**	**67**	**0.96**	**32**	**36**	**29**	**0.82**	37	41	33	0.81	**56**	**58**	**54**	**0.93**	**45**	**45**	**45**	**1.00**	153
71[z]	75[z]	66[z]	0.89[z]	42[z]	47[z]	36[z]	0.77[z]	44	52	36	0.71	55[z]	59[z]	49[z]	0.83[z]	…	…	…	…	154
86[y]	90[y]	82[y]	0.91[y]	77[y]	79[y]	76[y]	0.96[y]	78	81	75	0.93	81[y]	83[y]	78[y]	0.94[y]	77[y]	79[y]	75[y]	0.94[y]	155
124[z]	117[z]	132[z]	1.13[z]	…	…	…	…	43	42	44	1.07	*83[z]*	*80[z]*	*86[z]*	*1.07[z]*	*69*	*67*	*71*	*1.06*	156
68	**70**	**66**	**0.94**	**32**	**34**	**31**	**0.91**	34	40	28	0.70	**48**	**50**	**47**	**0.93**	*42*	*44*	*40*	*0.92*	157
45	52	39	0.75	23	26	20	0.77	…	…	…	…	33	37	28	0.76	32	37	28	0.76	158
…	…	…	…	…	…	…	…	…	…	…	…	…	…	…	…	…	…	…	…	159
Sub-Saharan Africa																				
…	…	…	…	…	…	…	…	13	15	11	0.76	…	…	…	…	…	…	…	…	160
41[y]	*51[y]*	*30[y]*	*0.58[y]*	*20[y]*	*27[y]*	*14[y]*	*0.52[y]*	19	26	12	0.47	*32[y]*	*41[y]*	*23[y]*	*0.57[y]*	…	…	…	…	161
89[y]	86[y]	92[y]	1.07[y]	58[y]	58[y]	58[y]	1.00[y]	74	72	76	1.07	76[y]	75[y]	78[y]	1.05[y]	*56[y]*	*52[y]*	*60[y]*	*1.14[y]*	162
24	**28**	**21**	**0.77**	**8**	**10**	**6**	**0.61**	10	12	7	0.62	**18**	**21**	**15**	**0.74**	**14**	**16**	**12**	**0.74**	163
20	23	17	0.75	8	10	6	0.63	…	…	…	…	15	18	13	0.72	…	…	…	…	164
32*	35*	28*	0.80*	16*	18*	14*	0.78*	*25*	*27*	*23*	*0.83*	25*	28*	22*	0.79*	…	…	…	…	165
99	93	105	1.13	60	53	67	1.28	…	…	…	…	79	73	86	1.18	61	57	65	1.14	166
…	…	…	…	…	…	…	…	…	…	…	…	…	…	…	…	…	…	…	…	167
23	33	14	0.41	12	15	9	0.56	10	16	4	0.26	19	26	12	0.45	…	…	…	…	168
41[y]	*47[y]*	*35[y]*	*0.75[y]*	*27[y]*	*30[y]*	*24[y]*	*0.78[y]*	25	28	22	0.81	*35[y]*	*40[y]*	*30[y]*	*0.76[y]*	…	…	…	…	169

Table 8 (continued)

	Country or territory	TRANSITION FROM PRIMARY TO SECONDARY GENERAL EDUCATION (%) School year ending in 2006 Total	Male	Female	ENROLMENT IN SECONDARY EDUCATION Age group 2007	School-age population[2] (000) 2006	Total enrolment School year ending in 1999 Total (000)	1999 % F	2007 Total (000)	2007 % F	Enrolment in private institutions as % of total enrolment School year ending in 2007	Enrolment in technical and vocational education School year ending in 2007 Total (000)	% F
170	Congo	*63*[x]	*65*[x]	*62*[x]	12-18	584	...	...	...	...	...	...	...
171	Côte d'Ivoire	48	49	48	12-18	3 210	*592*	*35*	...	...	...	...	...
172	D. R. Congo	...	...	...	12-17	8 441	1 235	34	2 815	35	...	562	...
173	Equatorial Guinea	...	...	...	12-18	76	20	27	...	...	...	...	...
174	Eritrea	77	78	76	12-18	747	115	41	218	41	5	1	46
175	Ethiopia	89	90	87	13-18	11 258	1 060	40	3 430	40	...	191	44
176	Gabon	...	...	...	12-18	211	87	46	...	...	...	...	...
177	Gambia	***80***	***81***	***79***	13-18	208	47	40	**105**	**48**	**25**	–	–
178	Ghana	**93**	**90**	**96**	12-17	3 210	1 024	44	**1 729**	**46**	**16**[z]	**67**	**46**
179	Guinea	65	69	59	13-19	1 410	*168*	*26*	*531*	*35*	16[z]	*5*	*14*
180	Guinea-Bissau	...	...	...	13-17	184	...	...	...	...	...	...	...
181	Kenya	...	...	...	12-17	5 170	1 822	49	2 729	46	11	25	62
182	Lesotho	68[y]	68[y]	68[y]	13-17	255	74	57	94[z]	56[z]	3[z]	2[z]	53[z]
183	Liberia	...	...	...	12-17	499	114	39	...	...	...	...	...
184	Madagascar	61	61	60	11-17	3 170	...	...	*836*	*49*	*41*	*30*	*35*
185	Malawi	74	76	71	12-17	2 030	556	41	574	45	10[z]	.	.
186	Mali	64	...	...	13-18	1 688	218	34	534	39	28	55	51
187	Mauritius	71	65	77	11-17	147	104	49	*128*[y]	*49*[y]	...	*18*[y]	*31*[y]
188	Mozambique	58	56	61	13-17	2 426	103	39	445	42	13	28	31
189	Namibia	*77*	*75*	*80*	14-18	268	116	53	158	54	5	.	.
190	Niger	40	42	37	13-19	2 017	105	38	214	38	15	3	17
191	Nigeria	49[y]	49[y]	49[y]	12-17	20 683	3 845	47	6 436[z]	44[z]	12[z]	166[z]	35[z]
192	Rwanda	...	...	...	13-18	1 474	105	51	267	48	41	...	...
193	Sao Tome and Principe	**48**	**44**	**52**	13-17	18	...	...	**9**	**51**	–	**0.1**	**43**
194	Senegal	*60*	*62*	*57*	13-19	1 922	237	39	*505*	*43*	23[y]	...	...
195	Seychelles[3]	...	...	...	12-16	7*	8	50	8	50	6	.	.
196	Sierra Leone	...	...	...	12-17	757	...	...	240	41	7	12	60
197	Somalia	...	...	...	13-17	901	...	...	...	...	...	...	...
198	South Africa	*94*	*93*	*94*	14-18	4 924	4 239	53	*4 780*	*51*	3[y]	...	...
199	Swaziland	89[y]	90[y]	87[y]	13-17	153	62	50	83	47	.	.	.
200	Togo	53	56	49	12-18	1 039	232	29	409	*35*	31[z]	32	*38*
201	Uganda	*58*	*59*	*57*	13-18	4 442	*318*	*40*	*1 001*	*45*	...	...	...
202	United Republic of Tanzania	***65***	***71***	***59***	14-19	5 335	*271*	*45*	...	...	...	...	...
203	Zambia	58	54	64	14-18	1 408	237	*43*	607	47	...	51	39
204	Zimbabwe	...	...	...	13-18	2 081	835	47	831[z]	48[z]	...	.[z]	.[z]
		Median				Sum	Sum	% F	Sum	% F	Median	Sum	% F
I	World	93	93	94	...	782 790	436 797	47	518 721	47	11	54 024	46
II	Countries in transition	99	99	100	...	29 135	31 719	49	26 261	48	0.7	3 428	40
III	Developed countries	99	...	...	...	82 951	84 564	49	83 335	49	7	13 553	43
IV	Developing countries	88	89	86	...	670 705	320 514	46	409 125	47	15	37 044	47
V	Arab States	88	86	90	...	42 556	22 682	46	27 453	47	10	3 157	43
VI	Central and Eastern Europe	98	99	98	...	36 792	39 582	49	32 375	48	1	6 385	39
VII	Central Asia	99	99	100	...	11 470	9 356	49	10 891	48	1	1 271	46
VIII	East Asia and the Pacific	...	...	...	...	213 360	133 579	47	165 769	48	19	23 658	49
IX	East Asia	93	92	95	...	210 090	130 307	47	162 324	48	12	22 550	49
X	Pacific	...	...	...	...	3 270	3 272	49	3 445	48	...	1 109	44
XI	Latin America/Caribbean	95	...	...	...	66 153	52 575	51	58 547	51	20	6 275	54
XII	Caribbean	95	100	91	...	2 233	1 151	50	1 294	50	19	51	49
XIII	Latin America	94	94	94	...	63 919	51 424	51	57 253	51	22	6 225	54
XIV	N. America/W. Europe	99	99	99	...	62 328	60 661	49	62 401	49	9	8 645	43
XV	South and West Asia	84	87	84	...	243 954	97 783	41	125 705	44	13	2 412	27
XVI	Sub-Saharan Africa	64	64	65	...	106 177	20 578	45	35 580	44	14	2 221	39

Source: UNESCO Institute for Statistics database (UIS, 2009).

1. Refers to lower and upper secondary education (ISCED levels 2 and 3).
2. Data are for 2006 except for countries with a calendar school year, in which case data are for 2007.
3. National population data were used to calculate enrolment ratios.
4. Enrolment and population data exclude Transnistria.
5. Enrolment and population data exclude the Nagorno-Karabakh region.
6. Enrolment data for upper secondary education include adult education (students over age 25), particularly in pre-vocational/vocational programmes, in which males are in the majority. This explains the high level of GER and the relatively low GPI.
7. Enrolment ratios were not calculated due to inconsistencies in the population data.
8. Enrolment ratios were not calculated due to lack of United Nations population data by age.

GROSS ENROLMENT RATIO (GER) IN SECONDARY EDUCATION (%)																NET ENROLMENT RATIO (NER) IN SECONDARY EDUCATION (%)				
Lower secondary				Upper secondary				Total secondary								Total secondary				
School year ending in 2007				School year ending in 2007				School year ending in 1999				2007				School year ending in 2007				
Total	Male	Female	GPI (F/M)	Total	Male	Female	GPI (F/M)	Total	Male	Female	GPI (F/M)	Total	Male	Female	GPI (F/M)	Total	Male	Female	GPI (F/M)	
…	…	…	…	…	…	…	…	…	…	…	…	…	…	…	…	…	…	…	…	170
…	…	…	…	…	…	…	…	*22*	*28*	*15*	*0.54*	…	…	…	…	…	…	…	…	171
46	58	33	0.58	27	36	17	0.49	18	24	12	0.52	33	44	23	0.53	…	…	…	…	172
…	…	…	…	…	…	…	…	33	48	18	0.37	…	…	…	…	…	…	…	…	173
43	50	36	0.73	18	22	15	0.67	21	25	17	0.69	29	34	24	0.70	25	29	21	0.72	174
39	47	32	0.67	11	13	8	0.64	12	15	10	0.68	30	36	24	0.67	*24*[z]	*29*[z]	*19*[z]	*0.64*[z]	175
…	…	…	…	…	…	…	…	49	53	46	0.86	…	…	…	…	…	…	…	…	176
60	**60**	**59**	**0.98**	**36**	**38**	**35**	**0.91**	30	36	24	0.67	**49**	**50**	**47**	**0.96**	**40**	**40**	**40**	**1.00**	177
74	**77**	**71**	**0.92**	**32**	**35**	**29**	**0.82**	37	41	33	0.80	**53**	**56**	**50**	**0.89**	*45*	*47*	*43*	*0.91*	178
47	58	35	0.61	*24*	*33*	*15*	*0.45*	*14*	*20*	*7*	*0.37*	*38*	*48*	*27*	*0.57*	30	37	22	0.60	179
…	…	…	…	…	…	…	…	…	…	…	…	…	…	…	…	…	…	…	…	180
87	93	82	0.88	35	38	33	0.86	38	39	37	0.96	53	56	49	0.88	*45*	*47*	*43*	*0.91*	181
45[z]	40[z]	51[z]	1.29[z]	24[z]	22[z]	27[z]	1.22[z]	31	26	35	1.35	37[z]	33[z]	41[z]	1.27[z]	*24*[z]	*19*[z]	*29*[z]	*1.55*[z]	182
…	…	…	…	…	…	…	…	29	35	23	0.65	…	…	…	…	…	…	…	…	183
36	*37*	*35*	*0.96*	*12*	*12*	*11*	*0.91*	…	…	…	…	*26*	*27*	*26*	*0.95*	*21*	*21*	*21*	*1.01*	184
39	42	36	0.87	16	18	14	0.74	36	42	30	0.70	28	31	26	0.83	24	25	23	0.91	185
44	53	34	0.64	18	22	14	0.65	16	22	11	0.52	32	39	25	0.64	…	…	…	…	186
99[y]	98[y]	100[y]	1.02[y]	*80*[y]	*81*[y]	*78*[y]	*0.96*[y]	76	76	75	0.98	*88*[y]	*89*[y]	*88*[y]	*0.99*[y]	*82*[y]	*81*[y]	*82*[y]	*1.02*[y]	187
26	29	22	0.74	7	8	5	0.66	5	6	4	0.62	18	21	15	0.73	3	3	2	0.83	188
76	70	82	1.17	32	30	35	1.16	58	55	61	1.11	59	54	64	1.17	*50*	*44*	*55*	*1.23*	189
15	18	12	0.64	4	5	2	0.50	7	9	5	0.60	11	13	8	0.61	9	11	7	0.62	190
35[z]	39[z]	32[z]	0.82[z]	28[z]	31[z]	25[z]	0.79[z]	23	24	22	0.89	32[z]	35[z]	28[z]	0.81[z]	*27*[z]	*30*[z]	*24*[z]	*0.82*[z]	191
24	25	23	0.92	13	14	12	0.85	9	10	9	0.99	18	19	17	0.89	…	…	…	…	192
64	**61**	**67**	**1.11**	**18**	**19**	**17**	**0.88**	…	…	…	…	**46**	**45**	**48**	**1.07**	38	36	40	1.11	193
35	38	31	0.80	*14*	*17*	*11*	*0.65*	15	19	12	0.64	*26*	*30*	*23*	*0.76*	*22*	*25*	*19*	*0.78*	194
116	111	121	1.09	106	96	116	1.21	113	111	115	1.04	112	105	119	1.13	94	…	…	…	195
46	54	37	0.69	17	20	14	0.69	…	…	…	…	32	37	26	0.69	23	27	19	0.71	196
…	…	…	…	…	…	…	…	…	…	…	…	…	…	…	…	…	…	…	…	197
95	95	94	0.99	*99*	*94*	*103*	*1.09*	89	83	94	1.13	*97*	*95*	*99*	*1.05*	*73*	*71*	*76*	*1.06*	198
66	70	61	0.87	38	39	37	0.94	45	45	45	1.00	54	58	51	0.89	29	32	27	0.85	199
49	*62*	*35*	*0.57*	*26*	*36*	*15*	*0.42*	28	40	16	0.40	39	*52*	*27*	*0.53*	…	…	…	…	200
27	*29*	*25*	*0.87*	12	15	10	0.67	*10*	*12*	*8*	*0.66*	*23*	*25*	*20*	*0.83*	*19*	*20*	*18*	*0.90*	201
…	…	…	…	…	…	…	…	*6*	*7*	*5*	*0.82*	…	…	…	…	…	…	…	…	202
58	60	55	0.91	33	35	30	0.86	20	*23*	*18*	*0.77*	43	46	41	0.89	41	44	38	0.87	203
58[z]	59[z]	58[z]	0.99[z]	31[z]	33[z]	28[z]	0.87[z]	43	46	40	0.88	40[z]	41[z]	38[z]	0.93[z]	37[z]	38[z]	36[z]	0.96[z]	204
Weighted average																Weighted average				
78	80	76	0.95	54	56	53	0.95	60	62	57	0.92	66	68	65	0.95	59	60	58	0.96	I
91	91	91	0.99	89	91	86	0.95	91	90	91	1.01	90	91	89	0.98	84	84	83	0.98	II
102	103	102	1.00	99	98	99	1.01	100	100	100	1.00	100	100	100	1.00	90	90	91	1.01	III
75	77	72	0.94	48	50	46	0.94	52	55	49	0.89	61	63	59	0.94	54	55	52	0.95	IV
76	80	72	0.89	52	53	51	0.97	60	63	57	0.89	65	67	62	0.92	57	59	56	0.95	V
90	91	89	0.98	85	88	83	0.94	87	88	87	0.98	88	90	86	0.96	80	82	79	0.97	VI
97	98	97	0.98	89	91	87	0.96	85	86	84	0.99	95	96	94	0.98	88	89	86	0.97	VII
93	93	93	1.00	63	62	64	1.03	65	66	63	0.96	78	77	78	1.01	71	71	72	1.02	VIII
93	93	93	1.00	62	61	63	1.03	64	65	63	0.96	77	77	78	1.01	71	71	72	1.02	IX
88	89	87	0.97	136	140	132	0.94	111	111	111	0.99	105	107	103	0.96	70	71	70	0.99	X
101	99	103	1.04	74	69	78	1.14	80	77	82	1.07	89	85	92	1.08	71	68	73	1.07	XI
73	72	73	1.02	44	43	45	1.06	53	53	54	1.03	58	57	59	1.03	41	39	42	1.08	XII
102	100	104	1.04	75	70	80	1.14	81	78	83	1.07	90	86	93	1.08	72	69	74	1.07	XIII
103	103	102	1.00	98	97	98	1.01	100	101	100	0.99	100	100	100	1.00	90	90	91	1.02	XIV
67	71	63	0.89	39	43	35	0.81	45	51	38	0.75	52	55	47	0.85	46	49	42	0.86	XV
40	44	35	0.79	26	29	23	0.78	24	26	21	0.82	34	37	30	0.79	27	29	24	0.82	XVI

9. Enrolment declined from 2005 to 2007 mainly because the data collection reference date was shifted from the last Wednesday of March to the last Wednesday of May to account for duplicates (enrolments) and transfers of students and teachers (from one school to another), common features at the beginning of the year. At this point of the school year, it is believed, the education system becomes stable, so the data collected should represent the current school year.

10. Data include French overseas departments and territories (DOM-TOM).

Data in italic are UIS estimates.

Data in bold are for the school year ending in 2007 for transition rates, and the school year ending in 2008 for enrolment and enrolment ratios.

(z) Data are for the school year ending in 2006.
(y) Data are for the school year ending in 2005.
(x) Data are for the school year ending in 2004.
(*) National estimate.

Table 9A
Participation in tertiary education

Country or territory	ENROLMENT IN TERTIARY EDUCATION											
	Total students enrolled				Gross enrolment ratio (GER) (%)							
	School year ending in				School year ending in							
	1999		2007		1999				2007			
	Total (000)	% F	Total (000)	% F	Total	Male	Female	GPI (F/M)	Total	Male	Female	GPI (F/M)
Arab States												
Algeria	*456*	...	902	57	*14*	...	...	...	24	20	28	1.40
Bahrain	11	*60*	18[z]	68[z]	22	*16*	*28*	*1.76*	32[z]	19[z]	47[z]	2.46[z]
Djibouti	0.2	51	2.2	40	0.3	0.3	0.3	1.05	3	3	2	0.69
Egypt	*2 447*	...	*2 594*[y]	...	*37*	...	...	...	*35*[y]	...	...	...
Iraq	272	34	*425*[y]	*36*[y]	11	15	8	0.54	*16*[y]	*20*[y]	*12*[y]	*0.59*[y]
Jordan	...	...	232	51	...	...	...	...	40	38	42	1.10
Kuwait	*32*	*68*	38[z]	65[z]	*23*	*14*	*33*	*2.40*	18[z]	11[z]	26[z]	2.32[z]
Lebanon	113	50	**197**	**55**	33	33	33	1.00	**54**	**48**	**60**	**1.24**
Libyan Arab Jamahiriya	308	*49*	...	...	50	*51*	*50*	*0.98*	...	...	...	...
Mauritania	13	...	12	...	5	...	...	...	4	...	...	...
Morocco	273	42	369	48	9	11	8	0.71	11	12	11	0.89
Oman	...	...	69	53	...	...	...	...	25	23	28	1.18
Palestinian Autonomous Territories	66	46	169	54	25	26	23	0.89	46	42	51	1.22
Qatar	*9*	*72*	9	64	*23*	*11*	*41*	*3.82*	16	9	27	2.87
Saudi Arabia	350	57	636[z]	58[z]	20	16	24	1.50	30[z]	25[z]	36[z]	1.46[z]
Sudan	201	47	...	...	6	6	6	0.92	...	...	...	...
Syrian Arab Republic	...	...	...	...	...	...	...	...	...	...	...	...
Tunisia	*157*	*48*	326	59	*17*	*17*	*17*	*0.97*	31	25	37	1.51
United Arab Emirates	*40*	*67*	**77**	**60**	*18*	*10*	*29*	*2.97*	**23**	**15**	**35**	**2.32**
Yemen	164	21	*209*[z]	*26*[z]	10	16	4	0.28	*9*[z]	*14*[z]	*5*[z]	*0.37*[z]
Central and Eastern Europe												
Albania	39	60	...	...	15	12	17	1.43	...	...	...	...
Belarus	387	56	557	57	51	44	58	1.30	69	57	80	1.41
Bosnia and Herzegovina	...	...	99	...	...	...	...	...	37	...	...	...
Bulgaria	270	59	259	54	45	36	55	1.54	50	45	55	1.22
Croatia	96	53	140	54	31	28	33	1.16	46	41	51	1.23
Czech Republic	231	50	363	55	26	26	27	1.03	55	49	61	1.26
Estonia	49	58	69	61	50	42	59	1.40	65	50	81	1.63
Hungary	279	54	432	58	33	30	37	1.24	69	56	82	1.46
Latvia	82	62	131[z]	63[z]	50	38	63	1.65	74[z]	53[z]	95[z]	1.80[z]
Lithuania	107	60	200	60	44	35	53	1.53	76	59	93	1.57
Montenegro	...	...	...	...	...	...	...	...	...	...	...	...
Poland	1 399	57	2 147	57	45	38	52	1.38	67	56	78	1.40
Republic of Moldova[1,2]	104	56	148*	57*	33	29	37	1.29	41	35	48	1.39
Romania	408	51	928	56	22	21	23	1.09	58	50	67	1.33
Russian Federation	...	...	9 370	57	...	...	...	...	75	64	86	1.35
Serbia	...	...	...	...	...	...	...	...	51	41	61	...
Slovakia	123	52	218	59	26	25	28	1.11	51	41	61	1.49
Slovenia	79	56	116	58	53	45	61	1.36	86	70	102	1.45
TFYR Macedonia	35	55	58	55	22	19	24	1.28	36	31	40	1.27
Turkey	1 465	40	2 454	43	22	25	17	0.68	36	41	31	0.76
Ukraine	1 737	53	2 819	54	47	44	50	1.15	76	68	85	1.24
Central Asia												
Armenia	61	54	107	55	24	22	25	1.11	34	31	37	1.20
Azerbaijan[1,3]	108	39	135	46	16	19	12	0.62	15	16	14	0.88
Georgia	130	52	141	52	36	35	37	1.07	37	35	39	1.12
Kazakhstan	324	53	**720**	**58**	24	23	26	1.15	**47**	**39**	**56**	**1.44**
Kyrgyzstan	131	51	239	56	29	28	30	1.04	43	37	48	1.30
Mongolia	65	65	142	61	26	18	34	1.88	48	37	58	1.56
Tajikistan	76	25	147	27	14	20	7	0.35	20	29	11	0.38
Turkmenistan	...	...	...	...	...	...	...	...	...	...	...	...
Uzbekistan	296	45	289	41	13	14	12	0.82	10	11	8	0.71
East Asia and the Pacific												
Australia	846	54	1 084	55	65	59	72	1.22	75	66	85	1.29
Brunei Darussalam	3.7	66	5	65	12	8	16	1.98	15	11	20	1.88
Cambodia	...	...	92	35	...	...	...	...	5	7	4	0.56

DISTRIBUTION OF STUDENTS BY ISCED LEVEL (%)						FOREIGN STUDENTS				
Total students			Percentage of females at each level							
School year ending in 2007			School year ending in 2007			School year ending in				
						1999		2007		
Level 5A	Level 5B	Level 6	Level 5A	Level 5B	Level 6	Total (000)	% F	Total (000)	% F	Country or territory
										Arab States
86	10	5	59	47	46	...	...	6	...	Algeria
92[z]	8[z]	0[z]	70[z]	51[z]	–[z]	...	...	0.7[z]	49[z]	Bahrain
...	...	.	...	...	.	–	–	–[z]	–[z]	Djibouti
...	...	...	...	...	...	...	...	...	...	Egypt
78[y]	*17*[y]	*5*[y]	*39*[y]	*22*[y]	*35*[y]	...	...	...	...	Iraq
88	11	1	51	59	30	...	...	22[z]	28[z]	Jordan
97[z]	.[z]	3[z]	66[z]	.[z]	51[z]	...	...	...	...	Kuwait
84	**15**	**1**	**55**	**55**	**39**	16	...	23	54	Lebanon
...	...	...	...	...	...	...	...	...	...	Libyan Arab Jamahiriya
...	...	...	...	...	...	...	...	...	...	Mauritania
69	24	8	49	48	36	4	16	7	26	Morocco
87	12	1	52	65	26	...	...	0.2	36	Oman
90	10	.	55	47	.	3	29	–	–	Palestinian Autonomous Territories
76	24	.	74	33	.	...	...	2	51	Qatar
83[z]	15[z]	2[z]	65[z]	23[z]	41[z]	6	25	14[z]	33[z]	Saudi Arabia
...	...	...	...	...	...	...	...	...	...	Sudan
...	...	...	...	...	...	...	...	...	...	Syrian Arab Republic
60	31	9	...	...	...	3[j]	...	...	...	Tunisia
72	**28**	.	**61**	**57**	.	...	...	...	...	United Arab Emirates
...	...	...	...	...	...	...	...	...	...	Yemen
										Central and Eastern Europe
...	...	...	...	...	...	0.8	27	...	...	Albania
72	27	1	59	54	55	3	...	4	...	Belarus
96	4	–	...	...	...	...	...	...	...	Bosnia and Herzegovina
88	10	2	54	52	50	8	42	9	42	Bulgaria
69	30	1	56	49	45	0.5[j]	...	3	52	Croatia
85	9	7	54	70	39	5	*41*	24	51	Czech Republic
62	34	3	61	61	55	0.8	58	1.0	53	Estonia
92	6	2	58	68	49	9[j]	54	15	47	Hungary
85[z]	14[z]	1[z]	64[z]	60[z]	60[z]	2[j]	...	2[y]	...	Latvia
70	28	1	60	60	58	0.5	22	1.9	48	Lithuania
...	...	...	...	...	...	...	...	...	...	Montenegro
97	1	1	57	80	50	6[j]	48	13	50	Poland
87*	11*	1*	58	56*	50	2	...	1.9	25	Republic of Moldova [1,2]
96	1	3	56	56	46	13	40	9	46	Romania
78	20	2	58	53	43	...	...	90[y]	...	Russian Federation
...	...	...	...	...	...	...	...	...	...	Serbia
94	1	5	60	69	45	...	...	1.9	49	Slovakia
57	42	1	62	53	48	0.7	40	1.2	57	Slovenia
96	4	0	54	63	50	0.3	43	0.9	40	TFYR Macedonia
69	29	1	43	41	41	18[v]	28	19	33	Turkey
82	17	1	55	52	55	18	...	30	...	Ukraine
										Central Asia
99	.	1	55	.	37	...	...	4	42	Armenia
99	.	1	46	.	28	2	35	4	20	Azerbaijan [1,3]
100	.	0	52	.	63	0.3	...	0.4	...	Georgia
100	.	**0**	**58**	.	**64**	8	...	**11**	...	Kazakhstan
99	.	1	56	.	60	...	...	27	63	Kyrgyzstan
96	3	1	60	70	58	0.3	50	1	48	Mongolia
99	.	1	27	.	30	5	...	3	46	Tajikistan
...	...	...	...	...	...	...	...	...	...	Turkmenistan
99	.	1	41	.	45	...	...	0.2	...	Uzbekistan
										East Asia and the Pacific
81	16	4	56	53	51	117	49	212	46	Australia
65	35	0	67	60	30	0.1	53	0.1	55	Brunei Darussalam
100	.	–	35	.	–	0.0	25	0.1[z]	10[z]	Cambodia

Education for All Global Monitoring Report 2010

Table 9A (continued)

Country or territory	ENROLMENT IN TERTIARY EDUCATION											
	Total students enrolled				Gross enrolment ratio (GER) (%)							
	School year ending in				School year ending in							
	1999		2007		1999				2007			
	Total (000)	% F	Total (000)	% F	Total	Male	Female	GPI (F/M)	Total	Male	Female	GPI (F/M)
China	6 366	…	25 346	48	6	…	…	…	23	23	23	1.01
Cook Islands	.	.	.	.	.	.	.	.	.	.	.	.
DPR Korea	…	…	…	…	…	…	…	…	…	…	…	…
Fiji	…	…	*13*[y]	*53*[y]	…	…	…	…	*15*[y]	*14*[y]	*17*[y]	*1.20*[y]
Indonesia	…	…	3 755	50	…	…	…	…	17	17	17	1.00
Japan	3 941	45	4 033	46	45	49	41	0.85	58	62	54	0.88
Kiribati	.	.	.[z]	.[z]	.	.	.	.	.[z]	.[z]	.[z]	.[z]
Lao People's Democratic Republic	12	32	75	42	2	3	2	0.49	12	13	10	0.72
Macao, China	7	46	24	49	28	32	24	0.76	57	59	55	0.92
Malaysia	473	50	749[z]	54[z]	23	23	23	1.02	30[z]	27[z]	33[z]	1.22[z]
Marshall Islands	…	…	…	…	…	…	…	…	…	…	…	…
Micronesia, Federated States of	2	…	…	…	14	…	…	…	…	…	…	…
Myanmar[4]	…	…	508	58	…	…	…	…	…	…	…	…
Nauru	.	.	.[z]	.[z]	.	.	.	.	.[z]	.[z]	.[z]	.[z]
New Zealand	167	59	243	59	64	52	77	1.46	80	64	96	1.49
Niue	.	.	.[z]	.[z]	.	.	.	.	.[z]	.[z]	.[z]	.[z]
Palau	…	…	…	…	…	…	…	…	…	…	…	…
Papua New Guinea	*9.9*	*35*	…	…	*2*	*3*	*1*	*0.55*	…	…	…	…
Philippines	2 209	55	2 484[z]	54[z]	29	25	32	1.26	28[z]	25[z]	32[z]	1.24[z]
Republic of Korea	2 838	35	3 209	38	73	92	52	0.57	95	113	75	0.67
Samoa	2	47	…	…	11	11	12	1.04	…	…	…	…
Singapore[4]	…	…	184	49	…	…	…	…	…	…	…	…
Solomon Islands	.	.	.[z]	.[z]	.	.	.	.	.[z]	.[z]	.[z]	.[z]
Thailand	1 814	53	**2 422**	**54**	33	31	36	1.16	**48**	**44**	**53**	**1.21**
Timor-Leste	…	…	…	…	…	…	…	…	…	…	…	…
Tokelau	.	.	.[z]	.[z]	.	.	.	.	.[z]	.[z]	.[z]	.[z]
Tonga	0.4	55	…	…	3	3	4	1.29	…	…	…	…
Tuvalu	.	.	.	.	.	.	.	.	.	.	.	.
Vanuatu	*0.6*	…	…	…	*4*	…	…	…	…	…	…	…
Viet Nam[4]	810	43	1 588	49	11	12	9	0.76	…	…	…	…
Latin America and the Caribbean												
Anguilla[5]	.	.	0.05	83	.	.	.	.	…	…	…	…
Antigua and Barbuda	.	.	…	…	.	.	.	.	…	…	…	…
Argentina	1 601	62	2 202[z]	60[z]	49	37	60	1.63	67[z]	53[z]	81[z]	1.52[z]
Aruba	1.4	54	2.2	58	27	25	29	1.19	33	27	39	1.45
Bahamas	…	…	…	…	…	…	…	…	…	…	…	…
Barbados	7	69	11	68	33	20	45	2.28	53	34	73	2.18
Belize	…	…	…	…	…	…	…	…	…	…	…	…
Bermuda	…	…	0.9	71	…	…	…	…	…	…	…	…
Bolivia	253	…	…	…	33	…	…	…	…	…	…	…
Brazil	2 457	56	5 273	56	14	13	16	1.26	30	26	34	1.29
British Virgin Islands[1]	0.9	70	*1.2*[y]	*69*[y]	60	36	86	2.40	*75*[y]	*46*[y]	*106*[y]	*2.28*[y]
Cayman Islands[5]	*0.4*	*74*	0.6[z]	72[z]	…	…	…	…	…	…	…	…
Chile	451	47	753	49	38	39	36	0.91	52	52	52	1.01
Colombia	878	52	1 373	51	22	21	23	1.11	32	30	33	1.09
Costa Rica	59	53	*111*[y]	*54*[y]	16	15	17	1.17	*25*[y]	*23*[y]	*28*[y]	*1.26*[y]
Cuba	153	53	865	64	21	19	22	1.19	109	77	143	1.85
Dominica	.	.	.[y]	.[y]	.	.	.	.	.[y]	.[y]	.[y]	.[y]
Dominican Republic	…	…	…	…	…	…	…	…	…	…	…	…
Ecuador	…	…	444	54	…	…	…	…	35	32	39	1.22
El Salvador	118	55	132	55	18	16	20	1.24	22	20	24	1.22
Grenada	.	.	.[y]	.[y]	.	.	.	.	.[y]	.[y]	.[y]	.[y]
Guatemala	…	…	234	51	…	…	…	…	18	18	18	1.00
Guyana	…	…	8	68	…	…	…	…	12	8	17	2.09
Haiti	…	…	…	…	…	…	…	…	…	…	…	…
Honduras	*85*	*56*	…	…	*14*	*13*	*16*	*1.24*	…	…	…	…
Jamaica	…	…	…	…	…	…	…	…	17	15	20	1.37
Mexico	1 838	48	2 529	50	18	19	17	0.91	27	28	26	0.93
Montserrat	.	.	.	.	…	…	…	…	.	.	.	.
Netherlands Antilles	2	53	…	…	19	18	20	1.11	…	…	…	…
Nicaragua	…	…	…	…	…	…	…	…	…	…	…	…

DISTRIBUTION OF STUDENTS BY ISCED LEVEL (%)						FOREIGN STUDENTS				
Total students			Percentage of females at each level							
School year ending in			School year ending in			School year ending in				
2007			2007			1999		2007		
Level 5A	Level 5B	Level 6	Level 5A	Level 5B	Level 6	Total (000)	% F	Total (000)	% F	**Country or territory**
…	45	…	…	50	…	…	…	42	45	China
.	.	.	.	.	.	.	.	.	.	Cook Islands
…	…	…	…	…	…	…	…	…	…	DPR Korea
86[y]	*12*[y]	*1*[y]	*52*[y]	*63*[y]	*43*[y]	…	…	…	…	Fiji
79	20	0	48	56	39	0.3	…	3	…	Indonesia
75	23	2	41	61	30	57	43	126	49	Japan
.[z]	.[z]	.[z]	.[z]	.[z]	.[z]	.	.	.	.	Kiribati
47	53	.	41	42	.	0.1	14	0.3	…	Lao People's Democratic Republic
85	13	2	48	61	24	…	…	12	38	Macao, China
52[z]	46[z]	2[z]	59[z]	50[z]	48[z]	4	…	24[z]	…	Malaysia
…	…	…	…	…	…	…	…	…	…	Marshall Islands
…	…	…	…	…	…	…	…	…	…	Micronesia, Federated States of
99	0	1	58	74	84	…	…	0.1	…	Myanmar[4]
.[z]	.[z]	.[z]	.[z]	.[z]	.[z]	.	.	.	.	Nauru
71	27	2	59	58	51	7	51	33	49	New Zealand
.[z]	.[z]	.[z]	.[z]	.[z]	.[z]	.	.	.	.	Niue
…	…	…	…	…	…	…	…	…	…	Palau
…	…	…	…	…	…	*0.3*	*32*	…	…	Papua New Guinea
89[z]	10[z]	0[z]	55[z]	53[z]	61[z]	4	…	5[z]	…	Philippines
63	36	1	37	39	34	3	40	32	47	Republic of Korea
…	…	…	…	…	…	0.1	39	…	…	Samoa
55	42	3	50	47	36	…	…	…	…	Singapore[4]
.[z]	.[z]	.[z]	.[z]	.[z]	.[z]	.	.	…	…	Solomon Islands
84	***16***	***1***	***55***	***47***	***49***	2[i]	55	**11**	**45**	Thailand
…	…	…	…	…	…	…	…	…	…	Timor-Leste
.[z]	.[z]	.[z]	.[z]	.[z]	.[z]	.	.	.[y]	.[y]	Tokelau
…	…	…	…	…	…	…	…	…	…	Tonga
.	.	.	.	.	.	.	.	.	.	Tuvalu
…	…	…	…	…	…	…	…	…	…	Vanuatu
65	32	3	60	29	41	0.5	15	3	…	Viet Nam[4]
										Latin America and the Caribbean
81	19	.	82	90	.	.	.	–	–	Anguilla[5]
…	…	…	…	…	…	.	.	…	…	Antigua and Barbuda
74[z]	25[z]	0[z]	57[z]	69[z]	57[z]	…	…	…	…	Argentina
32	68	.	71	53	.	…	…	0.2[z]	59[z]	Aruba
…	…	…	…	…	…	…	…	…	…	Bahamas
51	49	1	68	68	55	…	…	0.9	…	Barbados
…	…	…	…	…	…	…	…	…	…	Belize
.	100	.	.	71	.	…	…	…	…	Bermuda
…	…	…	…	…	…	…	…	…	…	Bolivia
91	8	1	57	41	51	…	…	…	…	Brazil
67[y]	*33*[y]	.[y]	*75*[y]	*56*[y]	.[y]	.	.	…	…	British Virgin Islands[1]
11[z]	89[z]	.[z]	90[z]	69[z]	.[z]	…	…	0.2[z]	71[z]	Cayman Islands[5]
59	40	0	53	44	43	2	…	8	…	Chile
82	18	0	52	47	38	…	…	…	…	Colombia
…	…	…	…	…	…	…	…	…	…	Costa Rica
100	.	0	64	.	48	…	.	27	…	Cuba
.[y]	.[y]	.[y]	.[y]	.[y]	.[y]	.	…	.	…	Dominica
…	…	…	…	…	…	…	…	…	…	Dominican Republic
…	…	…	…	…	…	…	…	…	…	Ecuador
86	14	0	55	54	14	…	…	0.8	46	El Salvador
.[y]	.[y]	.[y]	.[y]	.[y]	.[y]	…	…	.	.	Grenada
…	…	.	…	…	.	…	…	…	…	Guatemala
73	27	.	64	80	.	…	…	0.0	…	Guyana
…	…	…	…	…	…	…	…	…	…	Haiti
…	…	…	…	…	…	…	…	…	…	Honduras
…	…	…	…	…	…	0.6	…	…	…	Jamaica
96	3	1	51	43	42	2	…	…	…	Mexico
.	.	.	.	.	.	.	.	.	…	Montserrat
…	…	…	…	…	…	…	…	…	…	Netherlands Antilles
…	…	…	…	…	…	…	…	…	…	Nicaragua

Table 9A (continued)

Country or territory	ENROLMENT IN TERTIARY EDUCATION: Total students enrolled, School year ending in 1999: Total (000)	1999: % F	2007: Total (000)	2007: % F	Gross enrolment ratio (GER) (%), School year ending in 1999: Total	1999: Male	1999: Female	1999: GPI (F/M)	2007: Total	2007: Male	2007: Female	2007: GPI (F/M)
Panama	109	61	131[z]	61[z]	41	31	50	1.59	45[z]	35[z]	56[z]	1.61[z]
Paraguay	66	57	*156[y]*	*52[y]*	13	11	15	1.38	*26[y]*	*24[y]*	*27[y]*	*1.13[y]*
Peru	...	...	*952[z]*	*51[z]*	...	...	...	...	*35[z]*	*34[z]*	*36[z]*	*1.06[z]*
Saint Kitts and Nevis	.	.	.	.	.	.	.	.	.	.	.	.
Saint Lucia	...	...	1.4	71	...	...	...	...	9	5	12	2.41
Saint Vincent and the Grenadines	.	.	.	.	.	.	.	.	.	.	.	.
Suriname	...	...	...	...	...	...	...	...	...	...	...	...
Trinidad and Tobago	8	57	*17[y]*	*56[y]*	6	5	7	1.38	*11[y]*	*10[y]*	*13[y]*	*1.28[y]*
Turks and Caicos Islands	.	.	.	.	.	.	.	.	.	.	.	.
Uruguay	*91*	*63*	159	63	*34*	*25*	*44*	*1.76*	64	47	82	1.75
Venezuela, Bolivarian Republic of	...	...	1 381[*,z]	...	...	...	...	...	52[*,z]	...	...	...
North America and Western Europe												
Andorra[1]	...	...	0.4[z]	53[z]	...	...	...	...	10[z]	9[z]	11[z]	1.25[z]
Austria	253	50	261	54	54	52	55	1.05	51	46	56	1.20
Belgium	352	53	394	55	57	53	61	1.15	62	55	70	1.26
Canada	1 221	56	...	...	60	52	69	1.34	...	...	...	...
Cyprus[1]	11	56	22	50	21	19	23	1.25	36	36	36	0.99
Denmark	190	56	232	58	56	48	64	1.33	80	67	94	1.41
Finland	263	54	309	54	82	74	91	1.23	94	84	104	1.23
France[6]	2 012	54	2 180	55	52	47	58	1.24	56	49	62	1.27
Germany	...	...	...	...	...	...	...	...	...	...	...	...
Greece	388	50	603	50	47	45	49	1.11	91	86	95	1.10
Iceland	8	62	16	64	40	30	50	1.69	73	52	96	1.86
Ireland	151	54	190	55	46	42	50	1.20	61	54	68	1.27
Israel	247	58	327	56	48	40	57	1.44	60	52	69	1.32
Italy	1 797	55	2 034	57	47	41	53	1.28	68	57	80	1.40
Luxembourg	2.7	52	3[z]	52[z]	11	10	11	1.10	10[z]	10[z]	11[z]	1.12[z]
Malta	6	51	9[y]	56[y]	20	18	21	1.13	32[y]	27[y]	36[y]	1.35[y]
Monaco	.	...	.[z]	.[z]	.	.	.	.	.[z]	.[z]	.[z]	.[z]
Netherlands	470	49	590	51	49	49	50	1.01	60	58	63	1.09
Norway	187	57	215	60	66	55	77	1.40	76	60	94	1.57
Portugal	357	56	367	54	45	39	51	1.30	56	51	62	1.22
San Marino[5]	...	.	**0.9**	**57**	...	...	...	...	...	...	...	...
Spain	1 787	53	1 777	54	57	52	62	1.18	69	62	76	1.24
Sweden	335	58	414	60	64	53	75	1.41	75	59	92	1.57
Switzerland	156	42	213	48	36	41	30	0.73	47	49	45	0.93
United Kingdom	2 081	53	2 363	57	60	55	64	1.16	59	49	69	1.40
United States	13 769	*56*	17 759	57	73	*63*	*83*	*1.31*	82	68	96	1.41
South and West Asia												
Afghanistan	...	...	...	...	...	...	...	...	...	...	...	...
Bangladesh	709	32	1 145	35	5	7	4	0.51	7	9	5	0.57
Bhutan	*1.5*	*36*	4	31	*3*	*3*	*2*	*0.58*	5	7	3	0.51
India	...	...	12 853[z]	40[z]	...	...	...	...	12[z]	14[z]	10[z]	0.72[z]
Iran, Islamic Republic of	1 308	43	2 829	52	19	21	17	0.80	31	29	34	1.15
Maldives	.	...	–[z]	–[z]	.	.	.	.	–[z]	–[z]	–[z]	–[z]
Nepal	...	...	321	...	...	...	...	...	11	...	...	...
Pakistan	...	...	955[*]	45[*]	...	...	...	...	5[*]	6[*]	5[*]	0.85[*]
Sri Lanka	...	...	...	...	...	...	...	...	...	...	...	...
Sub-Saharan Africa												
Angola	8	39	49[z]	...	0.6	0.7	0.5	0.63	3[z]	...	...	...
Benin	19	*20*	43[z]	...	3	*5*	*1*	*0.25*	5[z]	...	...	...
Botswana	5.5	44	11[y]	50[y]	3	3	3	0.79	5[y]	5[y]	5[y]	1.00[y]
Burkina Faso	10	23	**42**	**33**	0.9	1.4	0.4	0.30	**3**	**4**	**2**	**0.50**
Burundi	5	30	16	32	1.0	1.4	0.6	0.41	2	3	1	0.46
Cameroon	67	...	132	44	5	...	...	...	7	8	6	0.79
Cape Verde	1	...	5	55	2	...	...	...	9	8	10	1.21
Central African Republic	6	16	4[z]	22[z]	2	3	1	0.18	1.1[z]	1.7[z]	0.5[z]	0.28[z]
Chad	...	...	*10[y]*	*13[y]*	...	...	...	...	*1.2[y]*	*2.0[y]*	*0.3[y]*	*0.14[y]*
Comoros	0.6	43	...	...	1	1	0.9	0.75	...	...	...	...

DISTRIBUTION OF STUDENTS BY ISCED LEVEL (%)						FOREIGN STUDENTS				
Total students			Percentage of females at each level			School year ending in				
School year ending in 2007			School year ending in 2007			1999		2007		
Level 5A	Level 5B	Level 6	Level 5A	Level 5B	Level 6	Total (000)	% F	Total (000)	% F	**Country or territory**
91[z]	9[z]	0[z]	61[z]	58[z]	63[z]	...	...	...	...	Panama
90[y]	*10*[y]	...	51[y]	66[y]	...	...	...	...	...	Paraguay
60[z]	*40*[z]	...	47[z]	57[z]	...	...	...	...	...	Peru
.	.	.	.	.	.	.	.	.	.	Saint Kitts and Nevis
93	7	.	73	36	.	...	...	0.1	...	Saint Lucia
.	.	.	.	.	.	.	.	.	.	Saint Vincent and the Grenadines
...	...	...	...	...	...	...	...	...	...	Suriname
...	*34*[y]	...	...	*48*[y]	...	1	46	...	...	Trinidad and Tobago
.	.	.	.	.	.	.	.	.	.	Turks and Caicos Islands
91	9	0	63	61	42	0.9	...	...	...	Uruguay
64[*,z]	36[*,z]	...	...	...	...	...	...	...	...	Venezuela, Bolivarian Republic of
										North America and Western Europe
40[z]	60[z]	.[z]	59[z]	49[z]	.[z]	...	...	...	...	Andorra[1]
84	9	7	53	66	46	30	49	44	54	Austria
47	51	2	52	58	43	36	48	25	61	Belgium
...	...	...	...	...	...	40	...	76[y]	45[y]	Canada
22	76	2	71	44	48	2	39	6	23	Cyprus[1]
85	13	2	59	47	46	12	61	13	59	Denmark
93	0	7	54	10	52	5	41	10	44	Finland
72	25	3	56	56	46	131[±]	...	247	50	France[6]
...	...	...	48	61	...	178	46	535	20	Germany
61	35	4	54	45	42	...	...	21	...	Greece
97	2	1	65	39	57	0.2	72	0.8	61	Iceland
68	29	3	58	50	47	7[eo]	51	17	60	Ireland
79	18	3	56	55	53	...	...	...	...	Israel
98	1	2	57	57	52	23	50	57	59	Italy
68[z]	...	...	...	...	...	0.7[j]	...	1[z]	...	Luxembourg
85[y]	14[y]	1[y]	56[y]	57[y]	30[y]	0.3[j]	53	0.6[y]	57[y]	Malta
.[z]	.[z]	.[z]	.[z]	.[z]	.[z]	.	.	...	...	Monaco
99	.	1	52	.	42	14	46	27	57	Netherlands
97	1	3	61	61	47	9	53	16	58	Norway
94	1	5	54	62	56	...	...	18	48	Portugal
27	**73**	.	**56**	**58**	.	...	...	...	...	San Marino[5]
83	13	4	55	52	52	33	51	21	...	Spain
90	5	5	61	52	50	24	45	22	47	Sweden
74	18	8	49	43	41	25	44	38	50	Switzerland
74	22	4	55	66	45	233	47	351	48	United Kingdom
77	21	2	57	60	52	452	42	596	...	United States
										South and West Asia
...	...	...	...	...	...	...	...	...	...	Afghanistan
90	9	1	36	25	25	...	...	0.7	...	Bangladesh
...	...	...	...	...	...	...	...	–	–	Bhutan
100[z]	–[z]	0[z]	40[z]	–[z]	40[z]	...	...	...	...	India
73	26	1	56	42	33	...	...	2	41	Iran, Islamic Republic of
–[z]	–[z]	–[z]	–[z]	–[z]	–[z]	.	.	...	...	Maldives
79	20	0	...	...	...	...	...	...	...	Nepal
94*	5*	1*	45*	45*	27*	...	...	...	...	Pakistan
...	...	...	...	...	...	...	...	...	...	Sri Lanka
										Sub-Saharan Africa
100[z]	–[z]	–[z]	...	.[z]	.[z]	...	...	...	...	Angola
...	...	...	...	...	...	...	...	...	...	Benin
94[y]	6[y]	–[y]	52[y]	16[y]	–[y]	...	...	0.7[y]	...	Botswana
...	...	...	...	...	...	...	...	0.9[y]	38[y]	Burkina Faso
5	95	1	27	32	–	0.1	...	...	...	Burundi
81	17	2	43	49	33	...	...	1	...	Cameroon
98	.	2	55	.	41	...	...	...	...	Cape Verde
77[z]	23[z]	.[z]	20[z]	30[z]	.[z]	...	...	0.5[z]	9[z]	Central African Republic
...	...	...	...	...	...	...	...	...	...	Chad
...	...	...	...	...	...	.	.	...	...	Comoros

Table 9A (continued)

Country or territory	ENROLMENT IN TERTIARY EDUCATION											
	Total students enrolled				Gross enrolment ratio (GER) (%)							
	School year ending in				School year ending in							
	1999		2007		1999				2007			
	Total (000)	% F	Total (000)	% F	Total	Male	Female	GPI (F/M)	Total	Male	Female	GPI (F/M)
Congo	10.7	21	...	...	4	6	1	0.26	...	...	...	...
Côte d'Ivoire	97	26	157	33	6	9	3	0.36	8	11	5	0.50
Democratic Rep. of the Congo	*60*	...	238	26*	*1*	...	...	...	4	6*	2*	0.35*
Equatorial Guinea	...	...	...	...	...	...	...	...	...	...	...	...
Eritrea	4.0	14	...	...	1.0	1.7	0.3	0.16	...	...	...	...
Ethiopia	52	19	210	25	0.9	1.4	0.3	0.23	3	4	1	0.34
Gabon	7	36	...	...	7.1	9.3	5.0	0.54	...	...	...	...
Gambia	1.2	23	...	...	1.0	1.6	0.5	0.30	...	...	...	...
Ghana	...	...	140	34	...	...	...	...	6	8	4	0.54
Guinea	...	...	43^z	21^z	...	...	...	...	5^z	8^z	2^z	0.28^z
Guinea-Bissau	*0.5*	*16*	...	...	*0.4*	*0.7*	*0.1*	*0.18*	...	...	...	...
Kenya	...	...	140	36	...	...	...	...	3	4	3	0.57
Lesotho	4	64	9^z	55^z	2	2	3	1.65	4^z	3^z	4^z	1.19^z
Liberia	21	19	...	...	8	13	3	0.24	...	...	...	...
Madagascar	31	*46*	58	47	2	*2*	*2*	*0.84*	3	3	3	0.89
Malawi	3	28	6	34	0.3	0.4	0.2	0.37	0.5	0.7	0.3	0.51
Mali	19	32	51	...	2	3	1	0.45	4	...	...	...
Mauritius	8	46	**14**	**53**	7	7	6	0.88	**14**	**13**	**15**	**1.17**
Mozambique	10	...	28^y	33^y	0.6	...	...	...	1^y	2^y	1^y	0.49^y
Namibia	...	...	13^z	47^z	...	...	...	...	6^z	7^z	6^z	0.88^z
Niger	...	...	11	29	...	...	...	...	1	2	0.5	0.33
Nigeria	699	43	$1\,392^y$	41^y	6	7	5	0.76	10^y	12^y	8^y	0.69^y
Rwanda	6	...	*26^y*	*39^y*	1	...	...	...	*3^y*	*3^y*	*2^y*	*0.62^y*
Sao Tome and Principe	.	.	.	.	.	.	.	.	.	.	.	.
Senegal	29	...	**91**	**35**	3	...	...	...	**8**	**10**	**5**	**0.55**
Seychelles	.	.	.	.	.	.	.	.	.	.	.	.
Sierra Leone	...	...	...	...	...	...	...	...	...	...	...	...
Somalia	...	...	...	...	...	...	...	...	...	...	...	...
South Africa	633	54	741^z	55^z	14	13	15	1.16	15^z	14^z	17^z	1.24^z
Swaziland	5	48	6^z	50^z	5	5	4	0.86	4^z	4^z	4^z	0.98^z
Togo	...	...	33	...	...	...	...	...	5	...	...	...
Uganda	41	*35*	...	...	2	*2*	*1*	*0.53*	...	...	...	...
United Republic of Tanzania	19	21	55	32	0.6	1.0	0.3	0.27	1	2	1	0.48
Zambia	*23*	*32*	...	...	*2*	*3*	*1*	*0.46*	...	...	...	...
Zimbabwe	*43*	...	...	...	*3*	...	...	...	...	...	...	...
	Sum	% F	Sum	% F	Weighted average				Weighted average			
World	92 533	48	150 498	51	18	18	17	0.96	26	25	27	1.08
Countries in transition	8 673	54	14 747	56	39	35	42	1.21	58	51	66	1.29
Developed countries	36 358	53	44 420	55	55	51	60	1.19	67	59	76	1.29
Developing countries	47 502	43	91 331	48	11	12	10	0.78	18	19	18	0.96
Arab States	5 165	42	7 146	50	19	22	16	0.74	22	22	23	1.05
Central and Eastern Europe	12 421	53	20 750	55	38	35	41	1.18	62	55	69	1.25
Central Asia	1 212	48	1 994	52	18	19	18	0.93	24	23	25	1.10
East Asia and the Pacific	22 947	41	46 294	48	14	16	12	0.75	26	26	26	1.00
East Asia	21 907	41	44 936	48	13	16	11	0.73	25	25	25	0.99
Pacific	1 039	55	1 357	55	47	42	52	1.24	53	46	61	1.31
Latin America and the Caribbean	10 664	53	17 757	54	21	20	23	1.12	34	31	37	1.19
Caribbean	81	57	111	58	6	5	6	1.30	7	6	8	1.36
Latin America	10 583	53	17 646	54	22	21	23	1.12	35	32	38	1.19
North America and Western Europe	28 230	54	34 008	56	61	55	68	1.23	70	60	80	1.33
South and West Asia	9 758	37	18 409	42	7	9	6	0.64	11	13	10	0.77
Sub-Saharan Africa	2 136	40	4 140	40	4	4	3	0.67	6	7	4	0.66

Source: UNESCO Institute for Statistics database (UIS, 2009).

1. National population data were used to calculate enrolment ratios.
2. Enrolment and population data exclude Transnistria.
3. Enrolment and population data exclude the Nagorno-Karabakh region.
4. Enrolment ratios were not calculated due to inconsistencies in the population data.
5. Enrolment ratios were not calculated due to lack of United Nations population data by age.
6. Data include French overseas departments and territories (DOM-TOM).

Country or territory	DISTRIBUTION OF STUDENTS BY ISCED LEVEL (%): Total students, School year ending in 2007: Level 5A	Level 5B	Level 6	Percentage of females at each level, School year ending in 2007: Level 5A	Level 5B	Level 6	FOREIGN STUDENTS, School year ending in 1999: Total (000)	% F	2007: Total (000)	% F
Congo	...	...	...	...	...	...	...	...	...	...
Côte d'Ivoire	54	39	7	30	39	26	...	...	...	...
Democratic Rep. of the Congo	...	...	...	...	...	...	...	...	...	...
Equatorial Guinea	...	...	...	...	...	...	...	...	...	...
Eritrea	...	...	...	...	...	...	0.1	16	...	...
Ethiopia	100	.	0	25	.	2	...	...	...	...
Gabon	...	...	...	...	...	...	0.4	...	...	...
Gambia	...	...	...	...	...	...	...	...	...	...
Ghana	73	26	0	35	33	26	...	...	2	52
Guinea	...	...	.^{z}	...	...	.^{z}	...	...	0.9^{z}	26^{z}
Guinea-Bissau	...	...	...	...	...	...	...	...	...	...
Kenya	83	15	2	36	38	43	...	...	...	...
Lesotho	79^{z}	21^{z}	.^{z}	51^{z}	70^{z}	.^{z}	1	46	0.1^{z}	...
Liberia	...	...	...	...	...	...	...	...	...	...
Madagascar	72	25	4	48	45	41	1	...	1.1	22
Malawi	100	.	.	34	.	.	...	...	...	...
Mali	86	4	11	...	...	...	1	...	...	...
Mauritius	**73**	**26**	**2**	**54**	**53**	**39**	...	...	...	...
Mozambique	100^{y}	.^{y}	.^{y}	33^{y}	.^{y}	.^{y}	...	...	...	...
Namibia	61^{z}	39^{z}	0^{z}	43^{z}	52^{z}	45^{z}	...	...	0.2^{z}	...
Niger	71	29	–	21	47	–	...	...	0.2	34
Nigeria	52^{y}	47^{y}	1^{y}	36^{y}	46^{y}	24^{y}	...	...	...	...
Rwanda	*65*^{y}	*35*^{y}	.^{y}	*41*^{y}	*35*^{y}	.^{y}	0.1	...	...	...
Sao Tome and Principe	.	.	.	.	.	.	.	.	.	.
Senegal	...	...	...	...	...	...	1	...	...	...
Seychelles	.	.	.	.	.	.	.	.	.^{z}	.^{z}
Sierra Leone	...	...	...	...	...	...	...	...	...	...
Somalia	...	...	...	...	...	...	...	...	...	...
South Africa	62^{z}	36^{z}	1^{z}	55^{z}	56^{z}	42^{z}	...	...	*61*	...
Swaziland	99^{z}	.^{z}	1^{z}	50^{z}	.^{z}	50^{z}	0.1	...	0.1^{z}	...
Togo	88	12	–	...	...	–	0.5	33	0.5	32
Uganda	...	...	...	...	...	...	...	...	...	...
United Republic of Tanzania	...	...	...	...	...	...	...	...	...	...
Zambia	...	...	...	...	...	...	...	...	...	...
Zimbabwe	...	...	...	...	...	...	...	...	...	...

	Median			Median			Sum	% F	Sum	% F
World	79	18	3	54	47	39	...	...	...	...
Countries in transition	99	.	1	55	26	46	...	...	...	...
Developed countries	82	14	4	56	57	47	...	...	...	...
Developing countries	74	25	0.5	50	43	26	...	...	...	...
Arab States	84	15	1	57	47	30	...	...	...	...
Central and Eastern Europe	85	11	4	58	56	50	...	...	...	...
Central Asia	99	.	1	53	.	51	...	...	...	...
East Asia and the Pacific	65	35	0.4	48	47	30	...	...	...	...
East Asia	75	23	2	50	50	36	...	...	...	...
Pacific	.	.	.	.	.	.	...	...	...	...
Latin America and the Caribbean	65.4	34.5	...	55	53	.	...	...	...	...
Caribbean	.	.	.	.	.	.	...	...	...	...
Latin America	88	12	...	55	54	43	...	...	...	...
North America and Western Europe	78	19	3	56	54	46	...	...	...	...
South and West Asia	85	15	0.4	40	25	27	...	...	...	...
Sub-Saharan Africa	77	23	.	...	33	.	...	...	...	...

(eo) Full-time only.
(j) Data refer to ISCED levels 5A and 6 only.
(v) Data do not include ISCED level 6.
(±) Partial data.
Data in italic are UIS estimates.
Data in bold are for the school year ending in 2008.
(z) Data are for the school year ending in 2006.
(y) Data are for the school year ending in 2005.
(*) National estimate.

Table 9B. **Tertiary education: distribution of students by field of study and female share in each field, school year ending in 2007**

Country or territory	Total enrolment		PERCENTAGE DISTRIBUTION BY FIELD OF STUDY								
	Total (000)	% F	Education	Humanities and arts	Social sciences, business and law	Science	Engineering, manufacturing and construction	Agriculture	Health and welfare	Services	Not known or unspecified
Arab States											
Algeria	902	57	1.7	18.6	38.7	7.7	9.2	2.0	6.1	0.9	15.2
Bahrain	18[z]	68[z]	2.1[z]	8.8[z]	51.8[z]	9.2[z]	8.6[z]	.[z]	7.0[z]	3.0[z]	9.6[z]
Djibouti	2.2	40	.[z]	23.3[z]	43.9[z]	22.6[z]	5.9[z]	.[z]	.[z]	4.3[z]	–[z]
Egypt	*2 594*[y]	…	…	…	…	…	…	…	…	…	…
Iraq	*425*[y]	*36*[y]	…	…	…	…	…	…	…	…	…
Jordan	232	51	13.7	15.4	25.2	14.9	13.2	1.6	14.2	0.4	1.4
Kuwait	38[z]	65[z]	…	…	…	…	…	…	…	…	…
Lebanon	**197**	**55**	**3.6**	**16.2**	**45.4**	**12.4**	**11.2**	**0.4**	**9.3**	**0.9**	**0.5**
Libyan Arab Jamahiriya	…	…	…	…	…	…	…	…	…	…	…
Mauritania	12	…	3.6[y]	13.0[y]	19.8[y]	6.2[y]	–[y]	–[y]	–[y]	–[y]	57.4[y]
Morocco	369	48	1.3	14.5	48.2	22.2	6.7	0.7	5.0	1.4	–
Oman	69	53	25.4	6.3	21.9	13.6	7.4	2.0	7.0	–	16.3
Palestinian A. T.	169	54	34.5	10.7	31.7	9.6	6.6	0.6	6.1	0.2	0.0
Qatar	9	64	5.3	24.0	32.2	12.2	17.6	.	7.3	0.9	0.6
Saudi Arabia	636[z]	58[z]	4.3[z]	39.5[z]	16.6[z]	20.6[z]	5.3[z]	0.9[z]	6.7[z]	–[z]	6.1[z]
Sudan	…	…	…	…	…	…	…	…	…	…	…
Syrian Arab Republic	…	…	…	…	…	…	…	…	…	…	…
Tunisia	326	59	1.0[z]	20.0[z]	17.5[z]	14.8[z]	10.7[z]	2.7[z]	7.7[z]	12.9[z]	12.6[z]
United Arab Emirates	**77**	**60**	**4.5**	**9.1**	**38.8**	**10.4**	**10.6**	**0.1**	**5.8**	**0.9**	**19.9**
Yemen	*209*[z]	*26*[z]	…	…	…	…	…	…	…	…	…
Central and Eastern Europe											
Albania	…	…	…	…	…	…	…	…	…	…	…
Belarus	557	57	12.2	5.6	38.4	2.3	25.7	8.0	4.1	3.6	–
Bosnia and Herzegovina	99	…	…	…	…	…	…	…	…	…	…
Bulgaria	259	54	6.4	7.9	44.0	5.1	19.7	2.5	6.2	8.0	0.2
Croatia	140	54	4.1	9.7	41.7	7.7	15.7	3.8	7.0	10.2	–
Czech Republic	363	55	12.7	8.7	28.6	8.7	14.2	3.7	11.9	4.1	7.4
Estonia	69	61	6.9	11.4	39.8	9.9	13.1	2.4	8.3	8.1	–
Hungary	432	58	11.8	8.6	40.6	6.9	11.5	2.7	8.8	9.1	–
Latvia	131[z]	63[z]	12.2[z]	7.0[z]	54.2[z]	5.2[z]	10.0[z]	1.2[z]	5.2[z]	4.9[z]	0.1[z]
Lithuania	200	60	12.2	7.1	42.8	5.9	18.2	2.2	8.4	3.1	–
Montenegro	…	…	…	…	…	…	…	…	…	…	…
Poland	2 147	57	13.6	10.2	40.3	9.5	12.6	2.2	6.1	5.6	–
Republic of Moldova[1]	148*	57*	…	…	…	…	…	…	…	…	…
Romania	928	56	2.5	9.9	51.0	6.2	17.2	2.7	5.6	4.3	0.6
Russian Federation	9 370	57	…	…	…	…	…	…	…	…	…
Serbia	…	…	…	…	…	…	…	…	…	…	…
Slovakia	218	59	15.5	6.2	29.4	8.9	15.7	2.6	16.2	5.5	–
Slovenia	116	58	8.4	7.8	41.7	5.6	16.7	3.2	7.2	9.5	–
TFYR Macedonia	58	55	13.3[y]	10.9[y]	32.8[y]	7.4[y]	18.1[y]	4.0[y]	9.0[y]	4.5[y]	–[y]
Turkey	2 454	43	11.5	6.2	48.7	7.5	13.1	3.7	5.6	3.8	–
Ukraine	2 819	54	9.0	5.1	42.5	4.1	22.0	4.5	5.1	6.1	1.7
Central Asia											
Armenia	107	55	14.7	4.4	28.4	0.2	6.5	4.7	15.6	2.9	22.5
Azerbaijan[2]	135	46	…	…	…	…	…	…	…	…	…
Georgia	141	52	3.4	38.2	30.0	5.1	8.9	2.8	9.1	2.5	0.0
Kazakhstan	**720**	**58**	…	…	…	…	…	…	…	…	…
Kyrgyzstan	239	56	25.4	10.4	36.1	5.7	11.3	1.3	3.1	6.7	–
Mongolia	142	61	10.6	9.6	39.7	6.7	15.9	2.9	8.1	5.6	0.8
Tajikistan	147	27	7.9	27.8	33.6	14.6	8.5	2.1	3.4	1.7	0.3
Turkmenistan	…	…	…	…	…	…	…	…	…	…	…
Uzbekistan	289	41	34.3	11.6	20.3	6.2	14.5	4.0	6.7	2.3	–
East Asia and the Pacific											
Australia	1 084	55	8.8	11.6	38.5	9.7	10.3	1.3	16.1	3.5	0.1
Brunei Darussalam	5	65	51.7	9.4	12.5	7.5	7.3	–	7.2	–	4.3
Cambodia	92	35	19.8	0.7	51.4	11.0	3.5	3.2	6.4	–	4.0
China	25 346	48	…	…	…	…	…	…	…	…	…

PERCENTAGE FEMALE IN EACH FIELD									
Education	Humanities and arts	Social sciences, business and law	Science	Engineering, manufacturing and construction	Agriculture	Health and welfare	Services	Not known or unspecified	Country or territory
									Arab States
69	75	59	61	31	47	60	29	45	Algeria
51^{z}	83^{z}	70^{z}	75^{z}	21^{z}	$.^{z}$	85^{z}	69^{z}	72^{z}	Bahrain
$.^{z}$	48^{z}	47^{z}	22^{z}	21^{z}	$.^{z}$	$.^{z}$	49^{z}	$-^{z}$	Djibouti
...	...	...	...	...	...	...	...	...	Egypt
...	...	...	...	...	...	...	...	...	Iraq
84	63	39	51	29	54	48	53	60	Jordan
...	...	...	...	...	...	...	...	...	Kuwait
94	**67**	**52**	**53**	**24**	**54**	**68**	**53**	**60**	Lebanon
...	...	...	...	...	...	...	...	...	Libyan Arab Jamahiriya
17^{y}	24^{y}	26^{y}	21^{y}	$-^{y}$	$-^{y}$	$-^{y}$	$-^{y}$	25^{y}	Mauritania
38	52	50	41	29	38	67	48	–	Morocco
63	69	43	56	23	74	66	–	48	Oman
70	66	40	46	30	18	57	31	40	Palestinian A. T.
85	85	65	68	25	.	76	.	40	Qatar
73^{z}	73^{z}	53^{z}	59^{z}	2^{z}	23^{z}	44^{z}	$-^{z}$	24^{z}	Saudi Arabia
...	...	...	...	...	...	...	...	...	Sudan
...	...	...	...	...	...	...	...	...	Syrian Arab Republic
...	...	...	...	...	...	...	...	...	Tunisia
92	**76**	**55**	**55**	**29**	**74**	**80**	**30**	**70**	United Arab Emirates
...	...	...	...	...	...	...	...	...	Yemen
									Central and Eastern Europe
...	...	...	...	...	...	...	...	...	Albania
...	...	...	...	...	...	...	...	...	Belarus
...	...	...	...	...	...	...	...	...	Bosnia and Herzegovina
69	65	61	47	31	41	67	46	49	Bulgaria
91	70	64	42	26	46	73	25	–	Croatia
76	66	62	33	25	57	75	42	33	Czech Republic
92	74	66	38	26	52	90	52	–	Estonia
74	66	65	28	19	45	76	60	–	Hungary
85^{z}	77^{z}	67^{z}	30^{z}	21^{z}	49^{z}	86^{z}	52^{z}	86^{z}	Latvia
78	73	69	32	24	49	84	44	–	Lithuania
...	...	...	...	...	...	...	...	...	Montenegro
73	71	62	36	27	53	74	49	–	Poland
...	...	...	...	...	...	...	...	...	Republic of Moldova [1]
88	67	62	57	30	38	68	39	38	Romania
...	...	...	...	...	...	...	...	...	Russian Federation
...	...	...	...	...	...	...	...	...	Serbia
76	61	64	37	29	43	82	44	–	Slovakia
81	73	67	34	25	57	79	49	–	Slovenia
74^{y}	68^{y}	60^{y}	55^{y}	32^{y}	34^{y}	74^{y}	38^{y}	$-^{y}$	TFYR Macedonia
53	49	44	39	19	47	61	31	–	Turkey
...	...	...	...	...	...	...	...	...	Ukraine
									Central Asia
94	57	47	26	23	25	72	26	46	Armenia
...	...	...	...	...	...	...	...	...	Azerbaijan [2]
94	57	43	57	35	30	75	10	94	Georgia
...	...	...	...	...	...	...	...	...	Kazakhstan
82	58	54	49	33	22	50	21	–	Kyrgyzstan
76	72	64	43	38	60	80	41	59	Mongolia
...	...	...	...	...	...	...	...	...	Tajikistan
...	...	...	...	...	...	...	...	...	Turkmenistan
57	66	22	57	11	14	45	29	–	Uzbekistan
									East Asia and the Pacific
74	62	54	36	21	52	76	54	63	Australia
69	57	62	57	36	–	73	–	73	Brunei Darussalam
35	27	43	12	5	25	39	–	28	Cambodia
...	...	...	...	...	...	...	...	...	China

Table 9B (continued)

Country or territory	Total enrolment		PERCENTAGE DISTRIBUTION BY FIELD OF STUDY								
	Total (000)	% F	Education	Humanities and arts	Social sciences, business and law	Science	Engineering, manufacturing and construction	Agriculture	Health and welfare	Services	Not known or unspecified
Cook Islands	.	.	.	.	.	.	.	.	.	.	.
DPR Korea	…	…	…	…	…	…	…	…	…	…	…
Fiji	*13*^{y}	*53*^{y}	…	…	…	…	…	…	…	…	…
Indonesia	3 755	50	15.0	0.5	50.7	8.1	16.4	4.9	3.9	–	0.4
Japan	4 033	46	7.3	15.7	29.1	2.9	15.8	2.2	12.5	5.7	8.8
Kiribati	.^{z}	.^{z}	.	.	.	.	.	.	.	.	.
Lao PDR	75	42	21.9	20.1	38.8	2.8	6.3	5.7	1.9	2.5	–
Macao, China	24	49	4.1	7.2	66.3	3.7	2.0	–	5.3	11.5	–
Malaysia	749^{z}	54^{z}	9.4^{z}	9.2^{z}	26.9^{z}	19.3^{z}	22.9^{z}	2.8^{z}	6.4^{z}	3.0^{z}	0.1^{z}
Marshall Islands	…	…	…	…	…	…	…	…	…	…	…
Micronesia, Federated States of	…	…	…	…	…	…	…	…	…	…	…
Myanmar	508	58	1.5	48.2	28.5	21.7	–	–	–	–	–
Nauru	.^{z}	.^{z}	.	.	.	.	.	.	.	.	.
New Zealand	243	59	10.2^{z}	17.5^{z}	34.8^{z}	13.9^{z}	6.6^{z}	1.0^{z}	12.6^{z}	2.7^{z}	0.7^{z}
Niue	.^{z}	.^{z}	.	.	.	.	.	.	.	.	.
Palau	…	…	…	…	…	…	…	…	…	…	…
Papua New Guinea	…	…	…	…	…	…	…	…	…	…	…
Philippines	2 484^{z}	54^{z}	…	…	…	…	…	…	…	…	…
Republic of Korea	3 209	38	6.3	18.2	21.9	8.8	27.8	1.2	9.3	6.4	–
Samoa	…	…	…	…	…	…	…	…	…	…	…
Singapore	184	49	3.2	9.0	34.1	16.9	30.7	–	5.6	0.6	–
Solomon Islands	.^{z}	.^{z}	.	.	.	.	.	.	.	.	.
Thailand	***2 422***	***54***	…	…	…	…	…	…	…	…	100.0
Timor-Leste	…	…	…	…	…	…	…	…	…	…	…
Tokelau	.^{z}	.^{z}	.	.	.	.	.	.	.	.	.
Tonga	…	…	…	…	…	…	…	…	…	…	…
Tuvalu	.	.	.	.	.	.	.	.	.	.	.
Vanuatu	…	…	…	…	…	…	…	…	…	…	…
Viet Nam	1 588	49	25.6	3.6	34.1	–	23.5	6.5	3.0	–	3.7
Latin America and the Caribbean											
Anguilla	0.05	83	29.6	–	70.4	–	–	–	–	–	–
Antigua and Barbuda	…	…	…	…	…	…	…	…	…	…	…
Argentina	2 202^{z}	60^{z}	10.2^{z}	12.4^{z}	39.6^{z}	9.5^{z}	8.1^{z}	3.5^{z}	12.8^{z}	3.0^{z}	0.9^{z}
Aruba	2.2	58	14.5	–	49.2	–	18.7	–	17.6	–	–
Bahamas	…	…	…	…	…	…	…	…	…	…	…
Barbados	11	68	…	…	…	…	…	…	…	…	…
Belize	…	…	…	…	…	…	…	…	…	…	…
Bermuda	0.9	71	4.1	9.3	33.0	12.5	6.0	–	7.7	3.3	24.3
Bolivia	…	…	…	…	…	…	…	…	…	…	…
Brazil	5 273	56	19.4	3.2	40.5	7.7	7.8	2.1	14.5	1.9	2.9
British Virgin Islands	*1.2*^{y}	*69*^{y}	…	…	…	…	…	…	…	…	…
Cayman Islands	0.6^{z}	72^{z}	.^{z}	.^{z}	81.0^{z}	16.4^{z}	.^{z}	.^{z}	.^{z}	.^{z}	2.6^{z}
Chile	753	49	13.8	6.4	27.0	7.2	17.8	3.4	15.6	8.3	0.5
Colombia	1 373	51	10.4	4.3	43.8	2.2	28.0	2.1	9.2	–	–
Costa Rica	*111*^{y}	*54*^{y}	…	…	…	…	…	…	…	…	…
Cuba	865	64	26.5	1.3	34.3	2.3	1.7	1.5	23.2	8.2	1.1
Dominica	.^{y}	.^{y}	.	.	.	.	.	.	.	.	.
Dominican Republic	…	…	…	…	…	…	…	…	…	…	…
Ecuador	444	54	14.2	0.7	49.1	6.6	11.7	3.1	10.6	0.6	3.4
El Salvador	132	55	9.2	4.7	45.4	11.2	11.9	1.2	16.4	0.0	–
Grenada	.^{y}	.^{y}	.	.	.	.	.	.	.	.	.
Guatemala	234	51	13.1^{*,z}	0.7^{*,z}	46.0^{*,z}	2.3^{*,z}	18.6^{*,z}	2.9^{*,z}	7.0^{*,z}	–^{*,z}	9.4^{*,z}
Guyana	8	68	30.3	3.1	38.2	8.2	4.9	3.7	9.5	0.7	1.4
Haiti	…	…	…	…	…	…	…	…	…	…	…
Honduras	…	…	…	…	…	…	…	…	…	…	…
Jamaica	…	…	…	…	…	…	…	…	…	…	…
Mexico	2 529	50	10.2	4.6	39.8	12.2	18.8	2.4	8.9	3.0	0.2
Montserrat	.	.	.	.	.	.	.	.	.	.	.
Netherlands Antilles	…	…	…	…	…	…	…	…	…	…	…
Nicaragua	…	…	…	…	…	…	…	…	…	…	…
Panama	131^{z}	61^{z}	14.9^{z}	9.8^{z}	39.6^{z}	8.0^{z}	11.2^{z}	1.1^{z}	8.0^{z}	6.9^{z}	0.5^{z}
Paraguay	*156*^{y}	*52*^{y}	…	…	…	…	…	…	…	…	…

PERCENTAGE FEMALE IN EACH FIELD									
Education	Humanities and arts	Social sciences, business and law	Science	Engineering, manufacturing and construction	Agriculture	Health and welfare	Services	Not known or unspecified	**Country or territory**
.	.	.	.	.	.	.	.	.	Cook Islands
...	...	...	...	...	...	...	...	...	DPR Korea
...	...	...	...	...	...	...	...	...	Fiji
50	50	50	50	49	50	50	–	39	Indonesia
69	67	35	25	12	38	59	80	50	Japan
.	.	.	.	.	.	.	.	.	Kiribati
49	50	41	34	12	24	58	26	–	Lao PDR
63	75	43	14	14	–	74	65	–	Macao, China
55^{z}	58^{z}	63^{z}	55^{z}	37^{z}	79^{z}	61^{z}	64^{z}	$–^{z}$	Malaysia
...	...	...	...	...	...	...	...	...	Marshall Islands
...	...	...	...	...	...	...	...	...	Micronesia, Federated States of
73	57	56	60	–	–	–	–	–	Myanmar
.	.	.	.	.	.	.	.	.	Nauru
82^{z}	64^{z}	56^{z}	43^{z}	25^{z}	58^{z}	80^{z}	48^{z}	63^{z}	New Zealand
.	.	.	.	.	.	.	.	.	Niue
...	...	...	...	...	...	...	...	...	Palau
...	...	...	...	...	...	...	...	...	Papua New Guinea
...	...	...	...	...	...	...	...	...	Philippines
70	57	36	29	16	32	62	31	–	Republic of Korea
...	...	...	...	...	...	...	...	...	Samoa
70	66	58	46	28	–	71	51	–	Singapore
.	.	.	.	.	.	.	.	.	Solomon Islands
...	...	...	...	...	...	...	...	54	Thailand
...	...	...	...	...	...	...	...	...	Timor-Leste
.	.	.	.	.	.	.	.	.	Tokelau
...	...	...	...	...	...	...	...	...	Tonga
.	.	.	.	.	.	.	.	.	Tuvalu
...	...	...	...	...	...	...	...	...	Vanuatu
60	70	59	–	23	40	46	–	47	Viet Nam
									Latin America and the Caribbean
94	–	79	–	–	–	–	–	–	Anguilla
...	...	...	...	...	...	...	...	...	Antigua and Barbuda
81^{z}	66^{z}	59^{z}	49^{z}	32^{z}	43^{z}	70^{z}	56^{z}	58^{z}	Argentina
79	–	61	–	11	–	86	–	–	Aruba
...	...	...	...	...	...	...	...	...	Bahamas
...	...	...	...	...	...	...	...	...	Barbados
...	...	...	...	...	...	...	...	...	Belize
89	72	78	59	4	–	93	62	75	Bermuda
...	...	...	...	...	...	...	...	...	Bolivia
73	57	52	32	26	40	73	64	50	Brazil
...	...	...	...	...	...	...	...	...	British Virgin Islands
$.^{z}$	$.^{z}$	74^{z}	60^{z}	$.^{z}$	$.^{z}$	$.^{z}$	$.^{z}$	80^{z}	Cayman Islands
71	52	54	23	19	44	72	47	49	Chile
65	48	58	51	32	39	69	–	–	Colombia
...	...	...	...	...	...	...	...	...	Costa Rica
70	57	63	46	24	31	73	41	44	Cuba
.	.	.	.	.	.	.	.	.	Dominica
...	...	...	...	...	...	...	...	...	Dominican Republic
71	47	60	36	18	32	66	41	63	Ecuador
74	55	57	36	24	37	73	31	–	El Salvador
.	.	.	.	.	.	.	.	.	Grenada
$56^{*,z}$	$68^{*,z}$	$51^{*,z}$	$61^{*,z}$	$25^{*,z}$	$17^{*,z}$	$59^{*,z}$	$–^{z}$	$43^{*,z}$	Guatemala
85	83	62	60	18	32	80	67	82	Guyana
...	...	...	...	...	...	...	...	...	Haiti
...	...	...	...	...	...	...	...	...	Honduras
...	...	...	...	...	...	...	...	...	Jamaica
71	56	57	39	25	37	64	59	50	Mexico
.	.	.	.	.	.	.	.	.	Montserrat
...	...	...	...	...	...	...	...	...	Netherlands Antilles
...	...	...	...	...	...	...	...	...	Nicaragua
77^{z}	60^{z}	65^{z}	46^{z}	31^{z}	24^{z}	76^{z}	58^{z}	58^{z}	Panama
...	...	...	...	...	...	...	...	...	Paraguay

Table 9B (continued)

Country or territory	Total enrolment		PERCENTAGE DISTRIBUTION BY FIELD OF STUDY								
	Total (000)	% F	Education	Humanities and arts	Social sciences, business and law	Science	Engineering, manufacturing and construction	Agriculture	Health and welfare	Services	Not known or unspecified
Peru	*952[z]*	*51[z]*	...	...	...	...	...	...	...	...	...
Saint Kitts and Nevis	.	.	.	.	.	.	.	.	.	.	.
Saint Lucia	1.4	71	5.1	0.2	15.9	7.0	0.2	.	.	.	71.6
Saint Vincent/Grenadines	.	.	.	.	.	.	.	.	.	.	.
Suriname	...	...	...	...	...	...	...	...	...	...	...
Trinidad and Tobago	*17[y]*	*56[y]*	...	...	...	...	...	...	...	...	...
Turks and Caicos Islands	.	.	.	.	.	.	.	.	.	.	.
Uruguay	159	63	16.0	4.7	40.2	11.7	9.6	3.2	13.3	1.2	–
Venezuela, B. R.	1 381*[,z]	...	...	...	...	...	...	...	...	...	...
North America and Western Europe											
Andorra	0.4[z]	53[z]	–[z]	6.7[z]	55.1[z]	24.7[z]	–[z]	–[z]	13.5[z]	–[z]	–[z]
Austria	261	54	12.4	15.4	36.5	12.0	12.7	1.1	7.9	1.8	0.2
Belgium	394	55	12.3	10.9	29.5	6.5	9.5	2.5	19.4	1.9	7.5
Canada	...	...	...	...	...	...	...	...	...	...	...
Cyprus	22	50	9.7	9.5	49.9	11.9	6.8	0.1	6.1	6.1	–
Denmark	232	58	11.3	15.3	29.0	8.7	10.1	1.5	22.0	2.2	–
Finland	309	54	5.2	14.6	22.7	11.2	25.4	2.2	13.7	4.9	–
France[3]	2 180	55	2.8	16.0	35.6	12.4	12.8	1.1	15.1	3.4	0.8
Germany	...	...	...	...	...	...	...	...	...	...	...
Greece	603	50	5.7	13.5	31.8	13.6	17.0	5.8	9.6	3.1	–
Iceland	16	64	16.5	14.6	38.5	7.9	7.7	0.6	12.7	1.5	–
Ireland	190	55	5.6	14.7	22.0	11.0	10.3	1.2	13.1	4.9	17.2
Israel	327	56	14.9	10.6	38.5	9.1	17.8	0.5	7.5	.	1.2
Italy	2 034	57	7.3	15.3	35.6	7.9	15.6	2.3	12.9	2.7	0.4
Luxembourg	3[z]	52[z]	22.7[z]	8.2[z]	45.2[z]	8.4[z]	15.0[z]	.[z]	0.4[z]	–[z]	–[z]
Malta	9[y]	56[y]	15.7[y]	13.5[y]	41.6[y]	5.9[y]	7.8[y]	0.8[y]	14.5[y]	0.2[y]	–[y]
Monaco	.[z]	.[z]	.	.	.	.	.	.	.	.	.
Netherlands	590	51	14.5	8.4	37.0	6.4	8.0	1.1	16.6	6.1	1.8
Norway	215	60	14.1	11.6	32.3	8.8	7.0	0.8	19.8	4.0	1.7
Portugal	367	54	5.8	8.5	32.0	7.3	22.3	1.9	16.5	5.7	–
San Marino	**0.9**	**57**	...	...	...	...	...	...	...	...	...
Spain	1 777	54	9.2	10.3	31.6	10.5	17.6	2.0	11.7	5.6	1.4
Sweden	414	60	15.0	12.5	26.3	9.4	16.1	0.9	17.7	2.0	0.2
Switzerland	213	48	10.3	12.7	37.0	10.5	13.2	1.1	11.0	3.5	0.6
United Kingdom	2 363	57	9.2	17.1	26.9	13.4	8.4	0.9	16.0	3.1	5.0
United States	17 759	57	9.4	10.6	27.3	8.9	6.7	0.6	13.9	5.1	17.6
South and West Asia											
Afghanistan	...	...	...	...	...	...	...	...	...	...	...
Bangladesh	1 145	35	2.3	25.0	44.6	10.5	3.3	1.1	2.2	0.2	10.8
Bhutan	4	31	36.1	12.2	11.7	2.3	8.5	2.8	0.5	...	26.0
India	12 853[z]	40[z]	1.3[y]	36.0[y]	13.5[y]	14.3[y]	5.9[y]	–[y]	2.2[y]	–[y]	26.8[y]
Iran, Islamic Republic of	2 829	52	5.4	12.1	30.2	12.0	28.5	4.5	4.8	2.4	–
Maldives	–[z]	–[z]	...	...	...	...	...	...	...	...	...
Nepal	321	...	...	...	...	...	...	...	...	...	...
Pakistan	955*	45*	4.6*	11.5*	18.3*	4.6*	5.6*	1.5*	7.5*	.*	46.3*
Sri Lanka	...	...	...	...	...	...	...	...	...	...	...
Sub-Saharan Africa											
Angola	49[z]	...	...	...	...	...	...	...	...	...	...
Benin	43[z]	...	...	...	...	...	...	...	...	...	...
Botswana	11[y]	50[y]	...	...	...	...	...	...	...	...	...
Burkina Faso	**42**	**33**	**5.1**	**15.2**	**54.7**	**16.1**	**1.2**	**0.6**	**6.5**	**0.5**	–
Burundi	16	32	...	...	...	...	...	...	...	...	...
Cameroon	132	44	6.9	6.9	61.3	18.7	2.7	0.5	1.8	0.6	0.6
Cape Verde	5	55	...	...	...	...	...	...	...	...	...
Central African Republic	4[z]	22[z]	...	...	...	...	...	...	...	...	...
Chad	*10[y]*	*13[y]*	...	...	...	...	...	...	...	...	...
Comoros	...	...	...	...	...	...	...	...	...	...	...
Congo	...	...	...	...	...	...	...	...	...	...	...
Côte d'Ivoire	157	33	1.5	13.1	48.1	14.7	9.2	0.4	6.3	4.3	2.4
Democratic Rep. of the Congo	238	26*	...	...	...	...	...	...	...	...	...

PERCENTAGE FEMALE IN EACH FIELD									
Education	Humanities and arts	Social sciences, business and law	Science	Engineering, manufacturing and construction	Agriculture	Health and welfare	Services	Not known or unspecified	Country or territory
...	...	...	...	...	...	...	...	...	Peru
.	.	.	.	.	.	.	.	.	Saint Kitts and Nevis
71	100	76	38	33	.	.	.	73	Saint Lucia
.	.	.	.	.	.	.	.	.	Saint Vincent/Grenadines
...	...	...	...	...	...	...	...	...	Suriname
...	...	...	...	...	...	...	...	...	Trinidad and Tobago
.	.	.	.	.	.	.	.	.	Turks and Caicos Islands
78	63	64	49	39	45	77	31	–	Uruguay
...	...	...	...	...	...	...	...	...	Venezuela, B. R.
									North America and Western Europe
–[z]	78[z]	63[z]	11[z]	–[z]	–[z]	78[z]	–[z]	–[z]	Andorra
75	67	55	34	23	64	67	46	51	Austria
72	56	54	30	20	52	74	50	51	Belgium
...	...	...	...	...	...	...	...	...	Canada
86	74	45	35	19	9	62	48	–	Cyprus
71	62	51	35	33	54	80	22	–	Denmark
80	71	62	40	19	52	84	71	–	Finland
74	68	61	36	24	38	71	42	50	France[3]
...	...	...	...	...	...	...	...	...	Germany
62	69	55	37	26	45	66	49	–	Greece
83	66	60	38	32	46	85	78	–	Iceland
77	63	56	43	17	46	79	47	56	Ireland
83	62	56	40	28	56	77	.	66	Israel
86	72	57	50	29	46	65	48	58	Italy
...	...	...	...	...	...	...	...	...	Luxembourg
72[y]	57[y]	56[y]	35[y]	28[y]	31[y]	67[y]	33[y]	–[y]	Malta
.	.	.	.	.	.	.	.	.	Monaco
74	54	47	16	15	51	74	49	43	Netherlands
74	62	57	35	25	58	80	47	62	Norway
82	59	58	48	25	56	77	48	–	Portugal
...	...	...	...	...	...	...	...	...	San Marino
78	60	59	34	28	46	74	56	49	Spain
76	63	61	43	28	59	80	61	74	Sweden
71	59	47	29	15	49	70	50	54	Switzerland
75	62	55	37	20	60	77	78	61	United Kingdom
79	58	56	39	16	50	80	53	56	United States
									South and West Asia
...	...	...	...	...	...	...	...	...	Afghanistan
40	43	35	28	19	25	42	19	27	Bangladesh
36	36	34	16	22	31	35	...	23	Bhutan
44[y]	44[y]	36[y]	40[y]	24[y]	–[y]	35[y]	–[y]	38[y]	India
72	68	57	67	28	45	74	52	–	Iran, Islamic Republic of
...	...	...	...	...	...	...	...	...	Maldives
...	...	...	...	...	...	...	...	...	Nepal
65*	43*	22*	21*	15*	16*	47*	.	58*	Pakistan
...	...	...	...	...	...	...	...	...	Sri Lanka
									Sub-Saharan Africa
...	...	...	...	...	...	...	...	...	Angola
...	...	...	...	...	...	...	...	...	Benin
...	...	...	...	...	...	...	...	...[y]	Botswana
19	**36**	**39**	**15**	**7**	**28**	**31**	**40**	–	Burkina Faso
...	...	...	...	...	...	...	...	...	Burundi
...	...	...	...	...	...	...	...	...	Cameroon
...	...	...	...	...	...	...	...	...	Cape Verde
...	...	...	...	...	...	...	...	...	Central African Republic
...	...	...	...	...	...	...	...	...	Chad
...	...	...	...	...	...	...	...	...	Comoros
...	...	...	...	...	...	...	...	...	Congo
44	32	41	18	13	19	40	26	55	Côte d'Ivoire
...	...	...	...	...	...	...	...	...	Democratic Rep. of the Congo

Table 9B (continued)

Country or territory	Total enrolment: Total (000)	Total enrolment: % F	Education	Humanities and arts	Social sciences, business and law	Science	Engineering, manufacturing and construction	Agriculture	Health and welfare	Services	Not known or unspecified
			PERCENTAGE DISTRIBUTION BY FIELD OF STUDY								
Equatorial Guinea	...	...	...	...	...	...	...	...	...	...	...
Eritrea	...	...	...	...	...	...	...	...	...	...	...
Ethiopia	210	25	26.8	2.9	36.9	7.0	8.0	8.5	9.1	–	0.8
Gabon	...	...	...	...	...	...	...	...	...	...	...
Gambia	...	...	...	...	...	...	...	...	...	...	...
Ghana	140	34	...	...	...	...	...	...	...	...	...
Guinea	43[z]	21[z]	4.3[z]	11.1[z]	32.0[z]	19.4[z]	3.9[z]	10.9[z]	7.8[z]	1.1[z]	9.5[z]
Guinea-Bissau	...	...	...	...	...	...	...	...	...	...	...
Kenya	140	36	...	...	...	...	...	...	...	...	...
Lesotho	9[z]	55[z]	32.4[y]	8.2[y]	33.3[y]	23.2[y]	0.7[y]	1.1[y]	1.1[y]	–[y]	–[y]
Liberia	...	...	...	...	...	...	...	...	...	...	...
Madagascar	58	47	2.4	10.8	57.9	11.5	7.2	2.3	7.0	0.3	0.7
Malawi	6	34	...	...	...	...	...	...	...	...	...
Mali	51	...	...	...	...	...	...	...	...	...	...
Mauritius	**14**	**53**	**14.6**	**5.7**	**45.4**	**11.4**	**19.9**	**2.8**	**0.0**	**0.2**	–
Mozambique	28[y]	33[y]	7.6[y]	11.1[y]	43.9[y]	13.9[y]	9.9[y]	5.2[y]	5.2[y]	2.7[y]	0.5[y]
Namibia	13[z]	47[z]	...	...	...	...	...	...	...	...	...
Niger	11	29	2.0	27.5	34.9	6.2	–	3.0	19.5	–	6.9
Nigeria	1 392[y]	41[y]	...	...	...	...	...	...	...	...	...
Rwanda	*26*[y]	*39*[y]	...	...	...	...	...	...	...	...	...
Sao Tome and Principe	.	.	.	.	.	.	.	.	.	.	.
Senegal	**91**	**35**	...	...	...	...	...	...	...	...	...
Seychelles	.	.	.	.	.	.	.	.	.	.	.
Sierra Leone	...	...	...	...	...	...	...	...	...	...	...
Somalia	...	...	...	...	...	...	...	...	...	...	...
South Africa	741[z]	55[z]	13.3[z]	4.9[z]	52.9[z]	10.4[z]	9.5[z]	1.8[z]	5.9[z]	1.2[z]	0.0[z]
Swaziland	6[z]	50[z]	10.7[z]	21.1[z]	45.5[z]	5.7[z]	3.1[z]	6.1[z]	7.0[z]	0.8[z]	.[z]
Togo	33	...	...	...	...	...	...	...	...	...	...
Uganda	...	...	...	...	...	...	...	...	...	...	...
United Republic of Tanzania	55	32	*12.9*[y]	*7.1*[y]	*20.2*[y]	*15.2*[y]	*9.0*[y]	*4.7*[y]	*6.6*[y]	*1.7*[y]	*22.4*[y]
Zambia	...	...	...	...	...	...	...	...	...	...	...
Zimbabwe	...	...	...	...	...	...	...	...	...	...	...

	Sum	% F	Median								
World	150 498	51	8.9	8.3	40.5	6.9	16.1	2.9	10.6	4.8	0.9
Countries in transition	14 747	56	11.8	4.8	35.4	2.1	14.3	4.6	10.4	4.5	12.1
Developed countries	44 420	55	9.8	14.1	31.1	11.4	6.7	0.8	13.3	3.9	9.1
Developing countries	91 331	48	5.4	18.0	31.2	12.1	23.0	2.3	6.0	1.6	0.3
Arab States	7 146	50	3.6	13.0	19.8	6.2	–	–	–	–	57.4
Central and Eastern Europe	20 750	55	11.8	8.6	40.6	6.9	11.5	2.7	8.8	9.1	–
Central Asia	1 994	52	12.7	7.0	34.0	3.4	11.2	3.8	11.9	4.3	11.7
East Asia and the Pacific	46 294	48	5.2	12.7	44.1	6.2	14.9	0.6	7.3	8.9	–
East Asia	44 936	48	9.4	9.2	26.9	19.3	22.9	2.8	6.4	3.0	0.1
The Pacific	1 357	55	.	.	.	.	.	.	.	.	.
Latin America and the Caribbean	17 757	54	10.2	4.6	39.8	12.2	18.8	2.4	8.9	3.0	0.2
Caribbean	111	58	.	.	.	.	.	.	.	.	.
Latin America	17 646	54	13.8	6.4	27.0	7.2	17.8	3.4	15.6	8.3	0.5
N. America/W. Europe	34 008	56	9.7	9.5	49.9	11.9	6.8	0.1	6.1	6.1	–
South and West Asia	18 409	42	4.6	11.5	18.3	4.6	5.6	1.5	7.5	.	46.3
Sub-Saharan Africa	4 140	40	...	...	...	...	...	...	...	...	...

Source: UNESCO Institute for Statistics database (UIS, 2009).
1. Enrolment data exclude Transnistria.
2. Enrolment data exclude the Nagorno-Karabakh region.
3. Data include French overseas departments and territories (DOM-TOM).

Data in italic are UIS estimates.
Data in bold are for the school year ending in 2008.

(z) Data are for the school year ending in 2006.
(y) Data are for the school year ending in 2005.
(*) National estimate.

PERCENTAGE FEMALE IN EACH FIELD									
Education	Humanities and arts	Social sciences, business and law	Science	Engineering, manufacturing and construction	Agriculture	Health and welfare	Services	Not known or unspecified	**Country or territory**
...	...	...	...	...	...	...	...	...	Equatorial Guinea
...	...	...	...	...	...	...	...	...	Eritrea
24	32	31	23	15	15	26	–	26	Ethiopia
...	...	...	...	...	...	...	...	...	Gabon
...	...	...	...	...	...	...	...	...	Gambia
...	...	...	...	...	...	...	...	...	Ghana
30[z]	20[z]	24[z]	16[z]	12[z]	17[z]	33[z]	15[z]	20[z]	Guinea
...	...	...	...	...	...	...	...	...	Guinea-Bissau
...	...	...	...	...	...	...	...	...	Kenya
58[y]	67[y]	56[y]	54[y]	37[y]	61[y]	53[y]	–[y]	–[y]	Lesotho
...	...	...	...	...	...	...	...	...	Liberia
45	60	50	33	21	41	51	50	52	Madagascar
...	...	...	...	...	...	...	...	...	Malawi
...	...	...	...	...	...	...	...	...	Mali
66	**75**	**60**	**46**	**26**	**63**	**50**	–	–	Mauritius
33[y]	36[y]	41[y]	21[y]	10[y]	27[y]	54[y]	21[y]	23[y]	Mozambique
...	...	...	...	...	...	...	...	...	Namibia
15	24	31	7	–	15	37	–	41	Niger
...	...	...	...	...	...	...	...	...	Nigeria
...	...	...	...	...	...	...	...	...	Rwanda
.	.	.	.	.	.	.	.	.	Sao Tome and Principe
...	...	...	...	...	...	...	...	...	Senegal
.	.	.	.	.	.	.	.	.	Seychelles
...	...	...	...	...	...	...	...	...	Sierra Leone
...	...	...	...	...	...	...	...	...	Somalia
72[z]	61[z]	57[z]	44[z]	26[z]	43[z]	67[z]	66[z]	50[z]	South Africa
53[z]	63[z]	49[z]	36[z]	9[z]	18[z]	65[z]	62[z]	.[z]	Swaziland
...	...	...	...	...	...	...	...	...	Togo
...	...	...	...	...	...	...	...	...	Uganda
38[y]	56[y]	41[y]	24[y]	10[y]	26[y]	29[y]	16[y]	32[y]	United Republic of Tanzania
...	...	...	...	...	...	...	...	...	Zambia
...	...	...	...	...	...	...	...	...	Zimbabwe
Median									
71	52	61	41	21	31	69	41	54	World
...	...	...	...	...	...	...	...	...	Countries in transition
75	62	58	40	24	59	79	70	68	Developed countries
56	63	57	58	31	48	60	32	22	Developing countries
69	70	50	54	30	33	59	30	43	Arab States
76	68	64	37	26	47	75	44	–	Central and Eastern Europe
82	58	47	49	33	25	72	26	46	Central Asia
53	53	42	19	12	–	48	–	–	East Asia and the Pacific
63	57	50	34	16	25	59	26	14	East Asia
.	.	.	.	.	.	.	.	.	The Pacific
71	52	54	23	19	44	72	47	49	Latin America and the Caribbean
.	.	.	.	.	.	.	.	.	Caribbean
71	56	57	39	25	37	64	59	50	Latin America
75	64	55	36	22	62	72	62	56	N. America/W. Europe
44	43	35	28	22	25	42	...	27	South and West Asia
...	...	...	...	...	...	...	...	...	Sub-Saharan Africa

Table 10A

Teaching staff in pre-primary and primary education

Country or territory	PRE-PRIMARY EDUCATION											
	Teaching staff				Trained teachers (%)[1]						Pupil/teacher ratio[2]	
	School year ending in				School year ending in						School year ending in	
	1999		2007		1999			2007			1999	2007
	Total (000)	% F	Total (000)	% F	Total	Male	Female	Total	Male	Female		
Arab States												
Algeria	1	93	7	67	...	...	...	...	...	...	28	25
Bahrain	0.7	100	1[z]	100[z]	18	–	18	58[z]	100[z]	58[z]	21	16[z]
Djibouti	0.01	100	***0.1***	***87***	...	...	...	47	56	43	29	***17***
Egypt	*14*	*99*	23	99	...	...	...	...	...	...	*24*	25
Iraq	5	100	*6*[y]	*100*[y]	...	...	...	...	...	...	15	*16*[y]
Jordan	3	100	5	100	...	...	...	...	...	...	22	19
Kuwait	4	100	6	100	100	100	100	100	100	100	15	12
Lebanon	11	95	**9**	**99**	...	...	...	**9**	**5**	**10**	13	**16**
Libyan Arab Jamahiriya	1	100	2[z]	96[z]	...	...	...	...	...	...	8	9[z]
Mauritania	...	...	*0.3*[y]	*100*[y]	...	...	...	...	...	...	...	*19*[y]
Morocco	40	40	40	61	...	...	...	100	100	100	20	17
Oman	0.4	100	2	100	93	–	93	100	100	100	20	19
Palestinian Autonomous Territories	3	100	3	100	...	...	...	100	100	100	29	24
Qatar	*0.4*	*96*	0.9[z]	99[z]	...	...	...	36[z]	67[z]	35[z]	*21*	18[z]
Saudi Arabia	...	...	16*	100*	...	...	...	...	...	...	...	11*
Sudan	*12*	*84*	28	100	...	...	...	60[z]	60[z]	60[z]	*30*	17
Syrian Arab Republic	5	96	6	98	87	84	87	19	25	18	24	24
Tunisia	4	95	...	...	...	...	...	...	...	...	20	...
United Arab Emirates	3	100	5	100	59	71	59	100	100	100	19	21
Yemen	0.8	93	1[y]	97[y]	...	...	...	...	...	...	17	15[y]
Central and Eastern Europe												
Albania	4	100	...	...	...	...	...	...	...	...	20	...
Belarus	53	...	44	99	...	...	...	63	63	63	5	6
Bosnia and Herzegovina	...	...	1	94	...	...	...	...	...	...	...	13
Bulgaria	19	*100*	18	100	...	...	...	...	...	...	11	11
Croatia	6	100	6	99	76	86	76	...	...	...	13	14
Czech Republic	17	*100*	21	100	...	...	...	...	...	...	18	14
Estonia	7	100	6[z]	100[z]	...	...	...	...	...	...	8	8[z]
Hungary	32	100	31	100	...	...	...	...	...	...	12	11
Latvia	7	99	6[z]	100[z]	...	...	...	...	...	...	9	10[z]
Lithuania	13	99	12	100	...	...	...	...	...	...	7	7
Montenegro	...	...	...	...	...	...	...	...	...	...	...	...
Poland	*77*	...	49	98	...	...	...	...	...	...	*12*	18
Republic of Moldova	13	100	11	100	*92*	–	*92*	90	...	...	8	10
Romania	37	100	37	100	...	...	...	...	...	...	17	18
Russian Federation	642	100*	628[z]	100[*,z]	...	...	...	...	...	...	7	7[z]
Serbia	8	*98*	10	98	...	...	...	...	...	...	21	17
Slovakia	16	100	11	100	...	...	...	...	...	...	10	13
Slovenia	3	*99*	*2*[z]	*100*[z]	...	...	...	...	...	...	18	*18*[z]
TFYR Macedonia	3	99	3	98	...	...	...	...	...	...	10	11
Turkey	17	*99*	25	95	...	...	...	...	...	...	15	26
Ukraine	143	100	127	99	...	...	...	...	...	...	8	9
Central Asia												
Armenia	8	...	5	100	...	...	...	...	...	...	7	9
Azerbaijan	12	100	11	100	78	–	78	90	100	90	7	9
Georgia	6	100	7	100	...	...	...	...	...	...	13	11
Kazakhstan	19	...	**34**	**99**	...	...	...	...	...	...	9	**10**
Kyrgyzstan	3	100	2	99	32	–	32	42	44	42	18	25
Mongolia	3	100	3	100	99	75	99	92	86	92	25	29
Tajikistan	5	100	5	100	...	...	...	82	.	82	11	13
Turkmenistan	...	...	...	...	...	...	...	...	...	...	...	...
Uzbekistan	66	96	61	95	...	...	...	100	100	100	9	9
East Asia and the Pacific												
Australia	...	...	...	...	...	...	...	...	...	...	...	...
Brunei Darussalam	0.6*	83*	0.6	97	...	...	...	66	89	66	20*	21
Cambodia	*2*	*99*	4	97	...	...	...	88[z]	...	...	*27*	25
China	875	94	1 009	98	...	...	...	...	...	...	27	22

PRIMARY EDUCATION

Teaching staff: 1999 Total (000)	Teaching staff: 1999 % F	Teaching staff: 2007 Total (000)	Teaching staff: 2007 % F	Trained teachers (%)[1]: 1999 Total	Trained teachers (%)[1]: 1999 Male	Trained teachers (%)[1]: 1999 Female	Trained teachers (%)[1]: 2007 Total	Trained teachers (%)[1]: 2007 Male	Trained teachers (%)[1]: 2007 Female	Pupil/teacher ratio[2]: 1999	Pupil/teacher ratio[2]: 2007	Country or territory
												Arab States
170	46	170	53	94	92	96	99	…	…	28	24	Algeria
…	…	…	…	…	…	…	…	…	…	…	…	Bahrain
1	28	**2**	**26**	…	…	…	**80**	**81**	**78**	40	**34**	Djibouti
346	*52*	*369*	*56*	…	…	…	…	…	…	*23*	*27*	Egypt
141	72	*216y*	*72y*	…	…	…	…	…	…	25	*21y*	Iraq
…	…	…	…	…	…	…	…	…	…	…	…	Jordan
10	73	22	88	100	100	100	100	100	100	13	10	Kuwait
28	82	**32**	**86**	15	…	…	**13**	**15**	**13**	14	**14**	Lebanon
…	…	…	…	…	…	…	…	…	…	…	…	Libyan Arab Jamahiriya
7	26	11	35	…	…	…	100	100	100	47	43	Mauritania
123	39	144	47	…	…	…	100	100	100	28	27	Morocco
12	52	*21*	*63*	100	100	99	*100z*	*100z*	*100z*	25	*13*	Oman
10	54	13	67	100	100	100	100	100	100	38	30	Palestinian Autonomous Territories
5	75	7z	85z	…	…	…	69z	…	…	13	11z	Qatar
…	…	283*	52*	…	…	…	91*	97*	87*	…	11*	Saudi Arabia
…	…	108	64	…	…	…	59z	73z	52z	…	37	Sudan
110	*65*	…	…	81	…	…	…	…	…	25	…	Syrian Arab Republic
60	50	59	53	…	…	…	…	…	…	24	18	Tunisia
17	73	17	85	…	…	…	100	100	100	16	17	United Arab Emirates
103	*20*	…	…	…	…	…	…	…	…	*22*	…	Yemen
												Central and Eastern Europe
13	*75*	…	…	…	…	…	…	…	…	*23*	…	Albania
32	99	23	99	…	…	…	100	100	100	20	16	Belarus
…	…	…	…	…	…	…	…	…	…	…	…	Bosnia and Herzegovina
23	*91*	17	93	…	…	…	…	…	…	18	16	Bulgaria
11	89	11	91	100	100	100	…	…	…	19	17	Croatia
36	85	25	94	…	…	…	…	…	…	18	19	Czech Republic
8	*86*	6	94	…	…	…	…	…	…	16	13	Estonia
47	85	40	96	…	…	…	…	…	…	11	10	Hungary
9	97	7z	97z	…	…	…	…	…	…	15	12z	Latvia
13	98	11	97	…	…	…	…	…	…	17	13	Lithuania
…	…	…	…	…	…	…	…	…	…	…	…	Montenegro
…	…	234	84	…	…	…	…	…	…	…	11	Poland
12	96	10	97	…	…	…	…	…	…	21	16	Republic of Moldova
69	86	55	87	…	…	…	…	…	…	19	17	Romania
367	98	301z	98z	…	…	…	…	…	…	18	17z	Russian Federation
23	…	*22*	…	…	…	…	…	…	…	*17*	*13*	Serbia
17	93	15	85	…	…	…	…	…	…	19	15	Slovakia
6	96	6	98	…	…	…	…	…	…	14	16	Slovenia
6	66	6	72	…	…	…	…	…	…	22	18	TFYR Macedonia
…	…	…	…	…	…	…	…	…	…	…	…	Turkey
107	98	101	99*	100	…	…	100	…	…	20	16	Ukraine
												Central Asia
…	…	7	100	…	…	…	77y	22y	78y	…	19	Armenia
37	83	44	87	100	100	100	100	100	100	19	12	Azerbaijan
17	92	…	…	…	…	…	…	…	…	17	…	Georgia
…	…	**57**	**98**	…	…	…	…	…	…	…	**17**	Kazakhstan
19	95	17	97	48	49	48	62	62	62	24	24	Kyrgyzstan
8	93	8	95	…	…	…	99	100	99	32	32	Mongolia
31	56	31	64	…	…	…	87	…	…	22	22	Tajikistan
…	…	…	…	…	…	…	…	…	…	…	…	Turkmenistan
123	84	119	85	…	…	…	100	100	100	21	18	Uzbekistan
												East Asia and the Pacific
105	…	…	…	…	…	…	…	…	…	*18*	…	Australia
3*	66*	4	74	…	…	…	83	90	80	14*	13	Brunei Darussalam
45	*37*	49	43	…	…	…	98	…	…	*48*	51	Cambodia
…	…	6 074	56	…	…	…	…	…	…	…	18	China

Table 10A (continued)

Country or territory	PRE-PRIMARY EDUCATION													
	Teaching staff				Trained teachers (%)[1]						Pupil/teacher ratio[2]	
	School year ending in				School year ending in						School year ending in	
	1999		2007		1999			2007			1999	2007
	Total (000)	% F	Total (000)	% F	Total	Male	Female	Total	Male	Female		
Cook Islands	0.03	100	0.03	100	...	...	...	41	.	41	14	15
DPR Korea	...	...	...	...	...	...	...	...	...	...	...	...
Fiji	...	...	0.5[z]	...	...	...	...	...	...	...	...	19[z]
Indonesia	*118*	*98*	280	96	...	...	...	...	...	...	*17*	13
Japan	96	...	108	...	...	...	...	...	...	...	31	28
Kiribati	...	...	...	...	...	...	...	...	...	...	...	...
Lao People's Democratic Republic	2	100	3	99	86	100	86	81	67	81	18	17
Macao, China	0.5	100	0.5	100	93	–	93	98	100	98	31	19
Malaysia	21	100	30[y]	96[y]	...	...	...	...	...	...	27	23[y]
Marshall Islands	0.1	...	...	...	...	...	...	...	...	...	11	...
Micronesia, Federated States of	...	...	...	...	...	...	...	...	...	...	...	...
Myanmar	2	...	5	99	...	...	...	54	...	...	22	19
Nauru	...	...	0.04	97	...	...	...	82	–	84	...	17
New Zealand	7	98	8	99	...	...	...	...	...	...	15	14
Niue	0.01	100	...	...	...	...	...	...	...	...	11	...
Palau	...	...	...	...	...	...	...	...	...	...	...	...
Papua New Guinea	...	...	...	...	...	...	...	...	...	...	...	...
Philippines	18	*92*	28[z]	97[z]	*100*	...	...	...	...	...	33	33[z]
Republic of Korea	22	100	29	99	...	...	...	...	...	...	24	19
Samoa	...	...	...	...	...	...	...	...	...	...	...	...
Singapore	...	...	...	...	...	...	...	...	...	...	...	...
Solomon Islands	...	...	...	...	...	...	...	...	...	...	...	...
Thailand	111	79	**104**	**78**	...	...	...	...	...	...	25	**24**
Timor-Leste	...	...	0.2[y]	97[y]	...	...	...	...	...	...	...	29[y]
Tokelau	...	...	...	...	...	...	...	...	...	...	...	...
Tonga	0.1	100	...	...	...	...	...	...	...	...	18	...
Tuvalu	...	...	...	...	...	...	...	...	...	...	...	...
Vanuatu	...	...	0.1[z]	91[z]	...	...	...	...	...	...	...	12[z]
Viet Nam	94	100	164	99	44	–	44	89	...	...	23	19
Latin America and the Caribbean												
Anguilla	0.03	100	0.04	100	38	–	38	45	.	45	18	11
Antigua and Barbuda	...	...	0.2	100	...	...	...	29	.	29	...	13
Argentina	50	96	72[z]	96[z]	...	...	...	...	...	...	24	19[z]
Aruba	0.1	100	0.1	99	100	–	100	100	100	100	26	21
Bahamas	0.2	97	...	...	53	*50*	*53*	...	...	...	9	...
Barbados	*0.3*	*93*	0.3	97	...	...	...	50	10	51	*18*	19
Belize	0.2	98	0.3	99	...	...	...	9	–	9	19	17
Bermuda	...	...	...	...	...	...	...	...	...	...	...	...
Bolivia	5	93	*6*[y]	*92*[y]	...	...	...	...	...	...	42	*41*[y]
Brazil[3]	304	98	330	97	...	...	...	...	...	...	19	20
British Virgin Islands	*0.03*	*100*	0.05[z]	100[z]	*29*	–	*29*	...	...	...	*13*	15[z]
Cayman Islands	0.1	96	0.05[z]	100[z]	92	50	94	100[z]	.[z]	100[z]	9	13[z]
Chile	...	...	22	98	...	...	...	...	...	...	...	19
Colombia	59	94	50	96	...	...	...	...	...	...	18	22
Costa Rica	4	97	7	94	92	...	...	81	60	82	19	13
Cuba	26	98	28	100	98	–	100	100	.	100	19	16
Dominica	0.1	100	0.1	100	75	–	75	...	...	...	18	14
Dominican Republic	8	95	10*	94*	54	59	53	77*	73*	77*	24	22*
Ecuador	10	90	17	87	...	...	...	75	62	76	18	17
El Salvador	...	...	7	91	...	...	...	90	55	93	...	31
Grenada	0.2	96	0.2	100	...	...	...	42	.	42	18	14
Guatemala	12	...	19	91	...	...	...	...	...	...	26	24
Guyana	2	99	2	99	38	41	38	53	36	53	18	15
Haiti	...	...	...	...	...	...	...	...	...	...	...	...
Honduras	...	...	8[z]	...	...	...	...	...	...	...	...	26[z]
Jamaica	5	...	6	98	...	...	...	...	...	...	25	24
Mexico	150	94	167	96	...	...	...	...	...	...	22	28
Montserrat	0.01	100	0.01	100	100	–	100	100	.	100	12	11
Netherlands Antilles	0.3	99	...	...	100	100	100	...	...	...	21	...
Nicaragua	6	97	10	94	32	19	33	39	43	39	26	22
Panama	3	98	5	94	36	35	36	41	8	43	19	18

PRIMARY EDUCATION

Teaching staff				Trained teachers (%)[1]						Pupil/teacher ratio[2]		
School year ending in				School year ending in						School year ending in		
1999		2007		1999			2007			1999	2007	
Total (000)	% F	Total (000)	% F	Total	Male	Female	Total	Male	Female			Country or territory
0.1	86	0.1	77	…	…	…	79	79	79	18	16	Cook Islands
…	…	…	…	…	…	…	…	…	…	…	…	DPR Korea
…	…	4[y]	57[y]	…	…	…	…	…	…	…	28[y]	Fiji
…	…	1 584	58	…	…	…	…	…	…	…	19	Indonesia
367	…	391	…	…	…	…	…	…	…	21	18	Japan
0.6	62	1[y]	75[y]	…	…	…	…	…	…	25	25[y]	Kiribati
27	43	30	47	76	69	85	90	87	93	31	30	Lao People's Democratic Republic
2	87	2	88	81	62	84	89	76	91	31	20	Macao, China
143	66	195[z]	68[z]	…	…	…	…	…	…	21	16[z]	Malaysia
0.6	…	…	…	…	…	…	…	…	…	15	…	Marshall Islands
…	…	1	…	…	…	…	…	…	…	…	17	Micronesia, Federated States of
155	73	172	83	60	60	60	99	…	…	31	29	Myanmar
…	…	0	90	…	…	…	74	50	77	…	20	Nauru
20	82	22	83	…	…	…	…	…	…	18	16	New Zealand
0.02	100	0[y]	100[y]	…	…	…	…	…	…	16	12[y]	Niue
0.1	82	0[y]	…	…	…	…	…	…	…	15	13[y]	Palau
…	…	15[z]	43[z]	…	…	…	…	…	…	…	36[z]	Papua New Guinea
360	87	390	87	100	…	…	…	…	…	35	34	Philippines
122	67	150	77	…	…	…	…	…	…	32	26	Republic of Korea
1	71	1	78	…	…	…	98	…	…	24	24	Samoa
…	…	15	81	…	…	…	96	94	97	…	20	Singapore
3	41	…	…	…	…	…	…	…	…	19	…	Solomon Islands
298	63	**348**	**60**	…	…	…	…	…	…	21	**16**	Thailand
…	…	6	32	…	…	…	…	…	…	…	31	Timor-Leste
…	…	…	…	…	…	…	…	…	…	…	…	Tokelau
0.8	67	0.8[z]	…	…	…	…	…	…	…	21	22[z]	Tonga
0.07	…	…	…	…	…	…	…	…	…	19	…	Tuvalu
1	49	…	…	…	…	…	…	…	…	24	…	Vanuatu
337	78	345	78	78	75	78	98	94	99	30	20	Viet Nam
												Latin America and the Caribbean
0.07	87	0.1	95	76	78	76	54	20	55	22	16	Anguilla
…	…	0.5	92	…	…	…	67	71	67	…	22	Antigua and Barbuda
221	88	287[z]	88[z]	…	…	…	…	…	…	21	16[z]	Argentina
0.5	78	0.6	83	100	100	100	100	100	100	19	17	Aruba
2	63	3	85	58	57	59	85	69	88	14	14	Bahamas
1	76	2	78	…	…	…	70	73	70	18	15	Barbados
2	64	2	72	…	…	…	45	58	41	24	23	Belize
…	…	0.6[z]	89[z]	…	…	…	100[z]	100[z]	100[z]	…	8[z]	Bermuda
58	61	…	…	…	…	…	…	…	…	25	…	Bolivia
807	93	754	91	…	…	…	…	…	…	26	24	Brazil[3]
0.2	86	0.2	90	72	55	75	72	57	73	18	14	British Virgin Islands
0.2	89	0.3	90	98	96	98	96	94	96	15	11	Cayman Islands
56	77	67	78	…	…	…	…	…	…	32	25	Chile
215	77	188	76	…	…	…	…	…	…	24	28	Colombia
20	80	28	80	93	…	…	89	90	89	27	19	Costa Rica
91	79	92	76	100	100	100	100	100	100	12	10	Cuba
0.6	75	0.5	84	64	46	70	61	42	65	20	17	Dominica
…	…	57*	76*	…	…	…	88*	81*	90*	…	24*	Dominican Republic
71	68	90	70	…	…	…	72	71	72	27	23	Ecuador
…	…	27	68	…	…	…	93	92	94	…	40	El Salvador
…	…	0.9	77	…	…	…	69	70	69	…	16	Grenada
48	…	80	65	…	…	…	…	…	…	38	30	Guatemala
4	86	4	88	52	52	52	57	54	58	27	26	Guyana
…	…	…	…	…	…	…	…	…	…	…	…	Haiti
…	…	46[z]	…	…	…	…	…	…	…	…	28[z]	Honduras
…	…	12[y]	89[y]	…	…	…	…	…	…	…	28[y]	Jamaica
540	62	523	67	…	…	…	…	…	…	27	28	Mexico
0.02	84	0.03	100	100	100	100	77	.	77	21	16	Montserrat
1	86	…	…	100	100	100	…	…	…	20	…	Netherlands Antilles
24	83	31	76	79	63	82	72	61	76	34	31	Nicaragua
15	75	18	76	79	86	77	91	93	90	26	25	Panama

Table 10A (continued)

Country or territory	PRE-PRIMARY EDUCATION											
	Teaching staff				Trained teachers (%)[1]						Pupil/teacher ratio[2]	
	School year ending in				School year ending in						School year ending in	
	1999		2007		1999			2007			1999	2007
	Total (000)	% F	Total (000)	% F	Total	Male	Female	Total	Male	Female		
Paraguay	…	…	…	…	…	…	…	…	…	…	…	…
Peru	…	…	58	96	…	…	…	…	…	…	…	21
Saint Kitts and Nevis	…	…	0.4	100	…	…	…	*46*[y]	.[y]	*46*[y]	…	7
Saint Lucia	*0.3*	*100*	0.4	100	…	…	…	*56*[y]	.[y]	*56*[y]	*13*	11
Saint Vincent and the Grenadines	…	…	*0.3*[y]	*100*[y]	…	…	…	*59*[y]	.[y]	*59*[y]	…	*11*[y]
Suriname	…	…	0.8	100	…	…	…	…	…	…	…	20
Trinidad and Tobago	*2*	*100*	2*	…	*20*	–	*20*	…	…	…	*13*	14*
Turks and Caicos Islands	*0.1*	*92*	*0.1*[y]	*95*[y]	*61*	*40*	*63*	*76*[y]	*25*[y]	*78*[y]	*13*	*12*[y]
Uruguay	3	*98*	5	…	…	…	…	…	…	…	31	23
Venezuela, Bolivarian Republic of	…	…	63[y]	94[y]	…	…	…	86[y]	70[y]	87[y]	…	15[y]
North America and Western Europe												
Andorra	…	…	0.2	95	…	…	…	100	100	100	…	13
Austria	14	99	16	99	…	…	…	…	…	…	16	14
Belgium	…	…	30	98	…	…	…	…	…	…	…	14
Canada	30	*68*	…	…	…	…	…	…	…	…	17	…
Cyprus	1	99	1	99	…	…	…	…	…	…	19	17
Denmark	45	92	…	…	…	…	…	…	…	…	6	…
Finland	10	96	13	97	…	…	…	…	…	…	12	11
France	128	78	141	82	…	…	…	…	…	…	19	18
Germany	…	…	207	98	…	…	…	…	…	…	…	12
Greece	9	*100*	12	99	…	…	…	…	…	…	16	12
Iceland	*2*	*98*	2	97	…	…	…	…	…	…	*5*	6
Ireland	…	…	…	…	…	…	…	…	…	…	…	…
Israel	…	…	…	…	…	…	…	…	…	…	…	…
Italy	119	99	142	99	…	…	…	…	…	…	13	12
Luxembourg	…	…	1	98	…	…	…	…	…	…	…	12
Malta	0.9	99	0.9[y]	99[y]	…	…	…	…	…	…	12	10[y]
Monaco	*0.1*	*100*	…	…	…	…	…	…	…	…	*18*	…
Netherlands	…	…	…	…	…	…	…	…	…	…	…	…
Norway	…	…	…	…	…	…	…	…	…	…	…	…
Portugal	…	…	17	97	…	…	…	…	…	…	…	16
San Marino	…	…	**0.1**	**97**	…	…	…	…	…	…	…	**8**
Spain	68	93	120	88	…	…	…	…	…	…	17	13
Sweden	…	…	34[z]	96[z]	…	…	…	…	…	…	…	10[z]
Switzerland	…	…	…	…	…	…	…	…	…	…	…	…
United Kingdom	…	…	44[z]	97[z]	…	…	…	…	…	…	…	22[z]
United States	327	95	468	91	…	…	…	…	…	…	22	16
South and West Asia												
Afghanistan	…	…	…	…	…	…	…	…	…	…	…	…
Bangladesh	68	33	33[y]	89[y]	…	…	…	…	…	…	27	…
Bhutan	0.01	31	*0.02*[z]	…	100	100	100	…	…	…	22	*23*[z]
India	…	…	738[z]	100[z]	…	…	…	…	…	…	…	40[z]
Iran, Islamic Republic of	9	98	19[y]	89[y]	…	…	…	…	…	…	23	27[y]
Maldives	0.4	90	0.6	97	47	46	47	45[z]	46[z]	45[z]	31	24
Nepal	…	…	**20**	**93**	…	…	…	**73**	**75**	**72**	…	**41**
Pakistan	…	…	…	…	…	…	…	…	…	…	…	…
Sri Lanka	…	…	…	…	…	…	…	…	…	…	…	…
Sub-Saharan Africa												
Angola	…	…	…	…	…	…	…	…	…	…	…	…
Benin	0.6	61	0.6[z]	78[z]	100	100	100	…	…	…	28	49[z]
Botswana	…	…	0.9[y]	55[y]	…	…	…	50[y]	…	…	…	22[y]
Burkina Faso	…	…	2	*71*	…	…	…	38[z]	96[z]	14[z]	…	24
Burundi	*0.2*	*99*	0.4*	87*	…	…	…	…	…	…	*28*	37*
Cameroon	4	97	12	97	…	…	…	43	38	43	23	18
Cape Verde	…	…	1.0	100	…	…	…	18	.	18	…	22
Central African Republic	…	…	0.4	92	…	…	…	…	…	…	…	34
Chad	…	…	*0.2*[y]	…	…	…	…	…	…	…	…	*38*[y]
Comoros	*0.05*	*94*	…	…	…	…	…	…	…	…	*26*	…
Congo	0.6	100	2	94	…	…	…	53[y]	–[y]	62[y]	10	20

PRIMARY EDUCATION

Teaching staff: 1999 Total (000)	Teaching staff: 1999 % F	Teaching staff: 2007 Total (000)	Teaching staff: 2007 % F	Trained teachers (%)[1]: 1999 Total	1999 Male	1999 Female	Trained teachers (%)[1]: 2007 Total	2007 Male	2007 Female	Pupil/teacher ratio[2]: 1999	Pupil/teacher ratio[2]: 2007	Country or territory
...	...	...	...	...	...	...	...	...	...	...	...	Paraguay
...	...	180	65	...	...	...	...	...	...	...	22	Peru
...	...	0.4	87	...	...	...	62	...	...	...	17	Saint Kitts and Nevis
1	*84*	1.0	87	...	...	...	82	80	83	22	23	Saint Lucia
...	...	0.9	77	...	...	...	78	69	80	...	17	Saint Vincent and the Grenadines
...	...	5	92	...	...	...	...	...	...	...	13	Suriname
8	76	8	77	71	74	71	89	95	87	21	16	Trinidad and Tobago
0.1	*92*	*0.1*[Y]	*89*[Y]	*81*	*63*	*82*	*82*[Y]	*81*[Y]	*83*[Y]	*18*	*15*[Y]	Turks and Caicos Islands
18	*92*	23	...	...	...	...	...	...	...	20	16	Uruguay
...	...	184[Y]	81[Y]	...	...	...	84[Y]	70[Y]	87[Y]	...	19[Y]	Venezuela, Bolivarian Republic of
												North America and Western Europe
...	...	0.4	77	...	...	...	100	100	100	...	10	Andorra
29	89	29	89	...	...	...	...	...	...	13	12	Austria
...	...	65	80	...	...	...	...	...	...	...	11	Belgium
141	*68*	...	...	...	...	...	...	...	...	17	...	Canada
4	67	4	82	...	...	...	...	...	...	18	16	Cyprus
37	63	...	...	...	...	...	...	...	...	10	...	Denmark
22	71	24	77	...	...	...	...	...	...	17	15	Finland
209	78	217	82	...	...	...	...	...	...	19	19	France
221	82	243	84	...	...	...	...	...	...	17	14	Germany
48	*57*	62	65	...	...	...	...	...	...	14	10	Greece
3	*76*	*3*[Z]	*80*[Z]	...	...	...	...	...	...	*11*	*10*[Z]	Iceland
21	85	30	84	...	...	...	...	...	...	22	16	Ireland
54	...	62	86	...	...	...	...	...	...	13	13	Israel
254	95	273	95	...	...	...	...	...	...	11	10	Italy
...	...	3	72	...	...	...	...	...	...	...	11	Luxembourg
2	87	3[Y]	86[Y]	...	...	...	...	...	...	20	12[Y]	Malta
0.1	*87*	...	...	...	...	...	...	...	...	*16*	...	Monaco
...	...	...	...	...	...	...	...	...	...	...	...	Netherlands
...	...	...	...	...	...	...	...	...	...	...	...	Norway
...	...	64	82	...	...	...	...	...	...	...	12	Portugal
...	...	**0.2**	**91**	...	...	...	...	...	...	...	**6**	San Marino
172	68	199	72	...	...	...	...	...	...	15	13	Spain
62	80	61	81	...	...	...	...	...	...	12	10	Sweden
...	...	...	...	...	...	...	...	...	...	...	...	Switzerland
244	76	250[Z]	81[Z]	...	...	...	...	...	...	19	18[Z]	United Kingdom
1 618	86	1 775	89	...	...	...	...	...	...	15	14	United States
												South and West Asia
...	...	110	28	...	...	...	...	...	...	...	43	Afghanistan
...	...	364	40	...	...	...	56	55	57	...	45	Bangladesh
2	32	**4**	...	100	100	100	**91**	...	...	42	**30**	Bhutan
3 135*	33*	...	...	...	...	...	...	...	...	35*	...	India
327	53	373	58	...	...	...	100[Y]	100[Y]	100[Y]	27	19	Iran, Islamic Republic of
3	60	3	71	67	70	65	66	68	65	24	15	Maldives
92	23	**117**	**35**	46	50	35	**66**	**67**	**66**	39	**38**	Nepal
...	...	450	46	...	...	...	85[Z]	92[Z]	75[Z]	...	40	Pakistan
...	...	69[Z]	84[Z]	...	...	...	...	...	...	...	23[Z]	Sri Lanka
												Sub-Saharan Africa
...	...	95	40	...	...	...	...	...	...	...	41	Angola
16	23	31[Z]	17[Z]	58	52	77	72[Z]	71[Z]	76[Z]	53	44[Z]	Benin
12	81	13[Y]	78[Y]	90	81	92	87[Y]	89[Y]	86[Y]	27	24[Y]	Botswana
17	25	**36**	**33**	...	...	...	**88**	**86**	**91**	49	**49**	Burkina Faso
12	*54*	29	53	...	...	...	87	81	94	*57*	52	Burundi
41	36	70	43	...	...	...	62[*,Z]	58[*,Z]	67[*,Z]	52	44	Cameroon
3	*62*	3	67	...	...	...	83	79	85	*29*	25	Cape Verde
...	...	**6**	**13**	...	...	...	...	...	...	...	**90**	Central African Republic
12	9	22	13	...	...	...	35[Z]	30[Z]	71[Z]	68	60	Chad
2	26	*3*[Y]	*33*[Y]	...	...	...	...	...	...	35	*35*[Y]	Comoros
5	42	11	44	...	...	...	87	82	92	61	58	Congo

Table 10A (continued)

	PRE-PRIMARY EDUCATION											
	Teaching staff				Trained teachers (%)[1]						Pupil/teacher ratio[2]	
	School year ending in				School year ending in						School year ending in	
	1999		2007		1999			2007			1999	2007
Country or territory	Total (000)	% F	Total (000)	% F	Total	Male	Female	Total	Male	Female		
Côte d'Ivoire	2	96	3	97	...	...	...	100	100	100	23	17
Democratic Rep. of the Congo	...	...	7	95	...	...	...	93	92	93	...	26
Equatorial Guinea	0.4	36	2	87	...	...	...	...	...	...	43	24
Eritrea	0.3	97	1	97	65	22	66	66	70	65	36	35
Ethiopia	2	93	8	62	63	37	65	66	12	100	36	27
Gabon	...	...	...	...	...	...	...	...	...	...	...	...
Gambia	...	...	...	...	...	...	...	...	...	...	...	...
Ghana	*26*	*91*	**36**	**84**	*24*	*14*	*25*	**25**	**22**	**26**	*25*	**35**
Guinea	...	...	3	50	...	...	...	34[z]	31[z]	38[z]	...	33
Guinea-Bissau	*0.2*	*73*	...	...	...	...	...	...	...	...	*21*	...
Kenya	44	55	76	87	...	...	...	71	55	73	27	22
Lesotho	...	...	2[z]	99[z]	...	...	...	–[y]	–[y]	–[y]	...	19[z]
Liberia	6	19	**3**	**52**	...	...	...	**100**	**100**	**100**	18	**142**
Madagascar	...	...	5	97	...	...	...	17	18	17	...	31
Malawi	...	...	...	...	...	...	...	...	...	...	...	...
Mali	...	...	2	93	...	...	...	...	...	...	...	36
Mauritius	3	100	3	100	100	–	100	100	.	96	16	15
Mozambique	...	...	...	...	...	...	...	...	...	...	...	...
Namibia	1	88	...	...	77	12	86	...	...	...	27	...
Niger	0.6	98	1	88	96	91	96	96	95	96	21	23
Nigeria	...	...	...	...	...	...	...	...	...	...	...	...
Rwanda	...	...	...	...	...	...	...	...	...	...	...	...
Sao Tome and Principe	0.1	95	*0.2*[z]	...	...	...	...	...	...	...	28	*23*[z]
Senegal	1	78	6	68	...	...	...	...	...	...	19	17
Seychelles	0.2	100	0.2	100	86	–	86	...	...	...	16	15
Sierra Leone	...	...	1	79	...	...	...	52	53	52	...	20
Somalia	...	...	...	...	...	...	...	...	...	...	...	...
South Africa	...	...	...	...	...	...	...	...	...	...	...	...
Swaziland	...	...	*0.5*[y]	*75*[y]	...	...	...	...	...	...	...	*32*[y]
Togo	0.6	97	0.9	92	...	...	...	29	24	30	20	25
Uganda	*3*	*70*	2[z]	70[z]	...	...	...	...	...	...	*25*	42[z]
United Republic of Tanzania	...	...	18	56	...	...	...	14	8	19	...	43
Zambia	...	...	...	...	...	...	...	...	...	...	...	...
Zimbabwe	...	...	...	...	...	...	...	...	...	...	...	...
	Sum	**% F**	**Sum**	**% F**	**Median**						**Weighted average**	
World	5 432	91	6 823	94	...	...	...	...	...	...	21	20
Countries in transition	977	100	967	99	...	...	...	...	...	...	7	8
Developed countries	1 448	94	1 747	93	...	...	...	...	...	...	18	15
Developing countries	3 006	87	4 109	93	...	...	...	...	...	...	27	26
Arab States	117	77	169	89	...	...	...	60	60	60	21	18
Central and Eastern Europe	1 122	100	1 078	100	...	...	...	...	...	...	8	9
Central Asia	129	97	135	97	...	...	...	90	100	90	10	11
East Asia and the Pacific	1 430	94	1 821	96	...	...	...	...	...	...	26	21
East Asia	1 404	94	1 794	97	...	...	...	...	...	...	26	21
Pacific	26	94	27	92	...	...	...	...	...	...	16	17
Latin America and the Caribbean	748	96	928	96	...	...	...	59	.	59	22	22
Caribbean	22	97	25	99	61	40	63	53	36	53	31	32
Latin America	726	96	903	96	...	...	...	...	...	...	22	21
North America and Western Europe	1 100	92	1 424	92	...	...	...	...	...	...	17	14
South and West Asia	601	69	916	93	...	...	...	...	...	...	36	40
Sub-Saharan Africa	185	67	352	68	...	...	...	...	...	...	29	28

Source: UNESCO Institute for Statistics database (UIS, 2009).

1. Data on trained teachers (defined according to national standards) are not collected for countries whose education statistics are gathered through the OECD, Eurostat or the World Education Indicators questionnaires.

2. Based on headcounts of pupils and teachers.

3. The number of teachers declined from 2005 to 2007 mainly because the data collection reference date was shifted from the last Wednesday of March to the last Wednesday of May to account for duplicates (enrolments) and transfers of students and teachers (from one school to another), common features at the beginning of the year. At this point of the school year, it is believed, the education system becomes stable, so the data collected should represent the current school year.

PRIMARY EDUCATION

Country or territory	Teaching staff, 1999: Total (000)	Teaching staff, 1999: % F	Teaching staff, 2007: Total (000)	Teaching staff, 2007: % F	Trained teachers (%)[1], 1999: Total	Trained teachers (%)[1], 1999: Male	Trained teachers (%)[1], 1999: Female	Trained teachers (%)[1], 2007: Total	Trained teachers (%)[1], 2007: Male	Trained teachers (%)[1], 2007: Female	Pupil/teacher ratio[2], 1999	Pupil/teacher ratio[2], 2007
Côte d'Ivoire	45	20	53	24	...	...	...	100	100	100	43	41
Democratic Rep. of the Congo	155	21	231	26	...	...	...	96	97	95	26	38
Equatorial Guinea	1	28	3	34	...	...	...	31	32	29	57	28
Eritrea	6	35	7	48	73	75	69	87	92	82	47	48
Ethiopia	112	28	...	...	...	...	...	...	...	...	46	...
Gabon	6	42	...	...	...	...	...	...	...	...	44	...
Gambia	5	29	5	33	72	*72*	*72*	...	...	...	37	41
Ghana	80	32	**112**	**33**	72	64	89	**49**	**40**	**68**	30	**32**
Guinea	16	25	29	26	...	...	...	68[z]	65[z]	74[z]	47	45
Guinea-Bissau	*3*	*20*	...	...	...	...	...	...	...	...	*44*	...
Kenya	148	42	*147*	*44*	...	...	...	*99*	*98*	*100*	32	*46*
Lesotho	8	80	11[z]	78[z]	78	68	81	66[z]	49[z]	71[z]	44	40[z]
Liberia	10	19	**23**	**12**	...	...	...	**40**	**39**	**47**	39	**24**
Madagascar	43	58	79	61	...	...	...	55	51	58	47	49
Malawi	...	...	44	38	...	...	...	...	...	...	...	67
Mali	15*	23*	33	27	...	...	...	...	...	...	62*	52
Mauritius	5	54	6	65	100	100	100	100	100	100	26	22
Mozambique	37	25	70	34	...	...	...	63	59	71	61	65
Namibia	12	67	14	*65*	29	27	30	95	...	...	32	30
Niger	13	31	31	43	98	98	98	98	98	99	41	40
Nigeria	432	48	566[z]	50[z]	...	...	...	51[z]	41[z]	62[z]	41	40[z]
Rwanda	24	55	31	53	49	52	46	98	98	98	54	69
Sao Tome and Principe	0.7	...	*1*[z]	*55*[z]	...	...	...	...	...	...	36	*31*[z]
Senegal	21	*23*	46	28	...	...	...	...	...	...	49	34
Seychelles	0.7	85	0.7	85	82	76	83	...	...	...	15	12
Sierra Leone	...	...	30	26	...	...	...	49	45	63	...	44
Somalia	5	35	...	...	...	...	...	...	...	...	28	...
South Africa	227	78	236	77	63	66	62	...	...	...	35	31
Swaziland	6	75	7	70	91	89	92	94	93	94	33	32
Togo	23	13	26	12	31	29	46	15	14	22	41	39
Uganda	110	33	132	39	...	...	...	93	93	94	57	57
United Republic of Tanzania	104	45	**164**	***49***	...	...	...	**99**	...	...	40	**53**
Zambia	33	49	57	48	94	93	95	...	...	...	47	49
Zimbabwe	60	47	64[z]	...	...	...	...	...	...	...	41	38[z]

	Sum	% F	Sum	% F	Median						Weighted average	
World	25 773	58	27 846	62	...	...	...	...	...	...	25	25
Countries in transition	842	93	736	93	...	...	...	94	...	...	20	17
Developed countries	4 485	81	4 662	83	...	...	...	...	...	...	16	14
Developing countries	20 445	52	22 448	56	...	...	...	85	69	88	27	27
Arab States	1 554	52	1 959	59	...	...	...	100	...	...	23	21
Central and Eastern Europe	1 384	82	1 214	80	...	...	...	...	...	...	19	18
Central Asia	331	84	318	86	...	...	...	93	...	...	21	18
East Asia and the Pacific	10 092	55	9 961	60	...	...	...	...	...	...	22	19
East Asia	9 936	55	9 791	59	...	...	...	...	...	...	22	19
Pacific	156	71	170	75	...	...	...	...	...	...	20	19
Latin America and the Caribbean	2 684	76	2 905	78	...	...	...	80	74	81	26	23
Caribbean	104	50	112	58	76	78	76	75	.	75	24	21
Latin America	2 580	77	2 792	78	...	...	...	...	...	...	26	24
North America and Western Europe	3 443	81	3 718	85	...	...	...	...	...	...	15	14
South and West Asia	4 297	35	4 950	45	...	...	...	76	80	70	36	39
Sub-Saharan Africa	1 988	43	2 822	44	...	...	...	87	82	92	41	44

Data in italic are UIS estimates.
Data in bold are for the school year ending in 2008.
(z) Data are for the school year ending in 2006.
(y) Data are for the school year ending in 2005.
(*) National estimate.

Table 10B

Teaching staff in secondary and tertiary education

		SECONDARY EDUCATION											
		Teaching staff											
		Lower secondary				Upper secondary				Total secondary			
		School year ending in				School year ending in				School year ending in			
		1999		2007		1999		2007		1999		2007	
	Country or territory	Total (000)	% F	Total (000)	% F	Total (000)	% F	Total (000)	% F	Total (000)	% F	Total (000)	% F
	Arab States												
1	Algeria	...	...	...	...	...	...	...	...	...	...	...	...
2	Bahrain	...	...	...	...	...	...	...	...	...	...	...	...
3	Djibouti	0.5	24	...	...	0.2	17	...	...	0.7	22	**1**	**23**
4	Egypt	*207*	*44*	*220*	*46*	*247*	*38*	*270*	*39*	*454*	*41*	*491*	*42*
5	Iraq	*34*	*77*	*61*[y]	*59*[y]	*23*	*57*	*32*[y]	*56*[y]	*56*	*69*	*93*[y]	*58*[y]
6	Jordan	...	...	...	...	10	48	18	52	...	...	...	...
7	Kuwait	*11*	*58*	14	55	*11*	*53*	12	...	*22*	*56*	26	*53*
8	Lebanon	*27*	*57*	**19**	**62**	*15*	*42*	**22**	**48**	*42*	*51*	**41**	**55**
9	Libyan Arab Jamahiriya	...	...	...	...	...	...	74[z]	71[z]	...	...	...	...
10	Mauritania	1	11	*2*	*11*	1	10	*2*	*10*	2	10	*4*	*10*
11	Morocco	*53*	*35*	...	...	*35*	*29*	...	...	*88*	*33*	...	...
12	Oman	7	48	...	...	5	51	...	...	13	50	*21*	*56*
13	Palestinian A. T.	14	49	22	50	3	38	6	45	*18*	*48*	28	49
14	Qatar	*2*	*56*	3[z]	56[z]	*2*	*57*	3[z]	56[z]	*4*	*57*	6[z]	56[z]
15	Saudi Arabia	...	...	133*[,y]	...	...	...	101*[,y]	53*[,y]	...	...	234*[,y]	*53*[y]
16	Sudan	...	...	38	60	18	47	41	44	...	...	79	52
17	Syrian Arab Republic	...	...	...	...	...	...	39	47	54	...	...	...
18	Tunisia	*27*	*46*	...	...	*30*	*35*	...	...	*56*	*40*	80	...
19	United Arab Emirates	8	54	13	57	8	55	*11*	*53*	16	55	*24*	*55*
20	Yemen	*29*	*20*	...	...	19	18	...	...	*48*	*19*	...	...
	Central and Eastern Europe												
21	Albania	*16*	*51*	...	...	6	54	...	...	*22*	*52*	...	...
22	Belarus	...	...	...	...	...	...	...	...	107	77	102	80
23	Bosnia and Herzegovina	...	...	...	...	...	...	11	54	...	...	...	...
24	Bulgaria	27	*76*	23	80	29	*70*	32	76	56	*73*	55	78
25	Croatia	16	67	18	72	18	62	24	65	33	64	42	68
26	Czech Republic[3]	...	...	43[z]	74[z]	...	...	48[z]	57[z]	...	...	92[z]	65[z]
27	Estonia	5	*85*	5	80	6	*78*	6	75	11	*81*	11	77
28	Hungary	47	86	49[z]	78[z]	53	59	*41*[z]	*64*[z]	100	71	*90*[z]	*72*[z]
29	Latvia	16	83	15[z]	85[z]	9	76	10[z]	85[z]	25	80	25[z]	85[z]
30	Lithuania	*24*	*81*	39	82	*12*	*76*	...	...	*36*	*79*	42	81
31	Montenegro	...	...	...	...	...	...	...	...	...	...	...	...
32	Poland	...	...	*128*[z]	*73*[z]	...	...	*134*[z]	*65*[z]	...	...	*261*[z]	*69*[z]
33	Republic of Moldova	25	74	22	77	8	68	8	73	33	72	30	76
34	Romania	104	67	86	68	73	60	68	65	177	64	154	67
35	Russian Federation	...	...	...	...	...	...	...	...	...	...	1 284[z]	80[z]
36	Serbia	*24*	...	*25*	...	24	58	27	63	*48*	...	*52*	...
37	Slovakia	29	77	25	78	*25*	*66*	23	70	*54*	*72*	48	74
38	Slovenia	7	77	8	79	9	62	8	65	17	69	16	72
39	TFYR Macedonia	8	46	9	52	5	53	6	56	13	49	15	54
40	Turkey	...	...	...	...	...	...	168[z]	42[z]	...	...	...	...
41	Ukraine	...	...	...	...	...	...	...	...	400	76	351	79*
	Central Asia												
42	Armenia	...	...	...	...	...	...	...	...	...	...	43	84
43	Azerbaijan	...	...	...	...	...	...	...	...	118	63	132	66
44	Georgia	...	...	...	...	...	...	...	...	59	77	...	...
45	Kazakhstan	...	...	...	...	...	...	...	...	...	...	**178**	**86**
46	Kyrgyzstan	...	...	...	...	...	...	...	...	48	68	53	74
47	Mongolia	8	69	10	75	3	67	6	72	11	69	17	74
48	Tajikistan	...	...	...	...	...	...	...	...	47	43	61	49
49	Turkmenistan	...	...	...	...	...	...	...	...	...	...	...	...
50	Uzbekistan	...	...	...	...	...	...	...	...	307	57	352	63
	East Asia and the Pacific												
51	Australia	...	...	...	...	...	...	...	...	...	...	...	...
52	Brunei Darussalam	2*	48*	...	...	1*	47*	...	...	3	48	4	60
53	Cambodia	*14*	*28*	21	34	*4*	*24*	10	27	*18*	*27*	30	32

SECONDARY EDUCATION									TERTIARY EDUCATION				
Trained teachers (%)[1]			Pupil/teacher ratio[2]						Teaching staff				
Total secondary			Lower secondary		Upper secondary		Total secondary						
School year ending in			School year ending in		School year ending in		School year ending in		School year ending in				
2007			1999	2007	1999	2007	1999	2007	1999		2007		
Total	Male	Female							Total (000)	% F	Total (000)	% F	
												Arab States	
...	...	...	...	...	...	...	...	...	...	...	32	*35*	*1*
...	...	...	...	...	...	...	...	...	...	...	*0.8*[y]	*41*[y]	*2*
...	...	...	26	...	16	...	23	**34**	0.02	30	0.1	17	*3*
...	...	...	*22*	...	*13*	...	*17*	...	...	...	...	...	*4*
...	...	...	*22*	*19*[y]	*16*	*19*[y]	*20*	*19*[y]	12	31	*19*[y]	*35*[y]	*5*
...	...	...	...	...	17	10	...	...	...	...	9	23	*6*
100[y]	100[y]	100[y]	*12*	11	*9*	8	*11*	9	*2*	...	*2*[z]	*27*[z]	*7*
13	**14**	**13**	*9*	**10**	***8***	**8**	***9***	**9**	9	28	**23**	**39**	*8*
...	...	...	...	...	...	5[z]	...	...	12	*13*	...	...	*9*
100[*,z]	100[*,z]	100[*,z]	*28*	*29*	*24*	*24*	*26*	*27*	...	...	0.4[z]	4[z]	*10*
...	...	...	*19*	...	*14*	...	*17*	...	16	23	18	19	*11*
100[z]	*100*[z]	*100*[z]	19	...	16	...	18	*15*	...	...	3	29	*12*
100	100	100	26	26	19	21	*24*	25	3	13	6	17	*13*
68[z]	72[z]	65[z]	*13*	10[z]	*8*	9[z]	*10*	9[z]	*0.7*	*32*	1	37	*14*
...	...	...	...	10[*,y]	...	12[*,y]	...	11[*,y]	20	36	28[z]	33[z]	*15*
80[z]	...	...	...	22	*22*	16	...	18	4	23	...	...	*16*
...	...	...	...	...	...	12	19	...	...	...	...	...	*17*
...	...	...	*23*	...	*15*	...	*19*	16	6	41	18	41	*18*
46[y]	47[y]	46[y]	14	15	10	*11*	12	*13*	...	...	**5**	**31**	*19*
...	...	...	*22*	...	21	...	*22*	...	5	1	*6*[y]	*16*[y]	*20*
												Central and Eastern Europe	
...	...	...	*16*	...	17	...	*16*	...	2	36	...	...	*21*
...	...	...	...	...	...	...	9	8	30	51	42	56	*22*
...	...	...	...	...	...	14	...	...	...	...	...	...	*23*
...	...	...	13	12	12	11	13	12	24	*41*	21	45	*24*
...	...	...	14	11	11	8	12	9	...	...	13	41	*25*
...	...	...	...	11[z]	...	10[z]	...	11[z]	19	*38*	23[z]	38[z]	*26*
...	...	...	11	10	10	10	10	10	6	49	*6*[z]	*48*[z]	*27*
...	...	...	11	10[z]	9	*12*[z]	10	*11*[z]	21	38	23	37	*28*
...	...	...	10	10[z]	10	11[z]	10	10[z]	6	52	6[z]	57[z]	*29*
...	...	...	*11*	8	*11*	...	*11*	9	15	50	16	55	*30*
...	...	...	...	...	...	...	...	...	...	...	...	...	*31*
...	...	...	...	*13*[z]	...	*13*[z]	...	*13*[z]	*76*	...	99	42	*32*
...	...	...	13	11	12	14	13	12	7	50	9*	58*	*33*
...	...	...	12	11	13	15	13	13	26	37	31	44	*34*
...	...	...	...	...	...	...	...	9[z]	...	...	656	57	*35*
...	...	...	*17*	*13*	14	11	*15*	*12*	...	...	...	...	*36*
...	...	...	13	13	*12*	13	*13*	13	*11*	*38*	14	43	*37*
...	...	...	14	9	13	11	13	10	2	21	6	35	*38*
...	...	...	16	13	16	15	16	14	3	42	3	45	*39*
...	...	...	...	...	...	17[z]	...	...	60	35	89	39	*40*
...	...	...	...	...	...	...	13	11	133	...	197	...	*41*
												Central Asia	
...	...	...	...	...	...	...	...	8	9	42	13	47	*42*
...	...	...	...	...	...	...	8	8	13	36	16	40	*43*
...	...	...	...	...	...	...	8	...	26	47	16	52	*44*
...	...	...	...	...	...	...	...	**10**	27	58	**41**	**63**	*45*
79	78	80	...	...	...	...	13	14	8	32	13	56	*46*
99	98	99	19	21	17	18	19	20	6	*47*	9	56	*47*
...	...	...	...	...	...	...	16	17	6	29	8	32	*48*
...	...	...	...	...	...	...	...	...	...	...	...	...	*49*
100	100	100	...	...	...	...	11	13	17	36	23	36	*50*
												East Asia and the Pacific	
...	...	...	...	...	...	...	...	...	...	...	...	...	*51*
82	80	83	12*	...	10*	...	11	11	0.5	32	0.6	43	*52*
99	...	...	*16*	31	*21*	25	*18*	29	1	19	3[z]	11[z]	*53*

Table 10B (continued)

	Country or territory	SECONDARY EDUCATION – Teaching staff – Lower secondary – School year ending in 1999 – Total (000)	% F	Lower secondary 2007 – Total (000)	% F	Upper secondary – School year ending in 1999 – Total (000)	% F	Upper secondary 2007 – Total (000)	% F	Total secondary – School year ending in 1999 – Total (000)	% F	Total secondary 2007 – Total (000)	% F
54	China	3 213	41	3 637	47	...	...	2 584	43	...	...	6 221	45
55	Cook Islands	...	...	...	...	...	...	...	...	...	...	0.1	78
56	DPR Korea	...	...	...	...	...	...	...	...	...	...	...	...
57	Fiji	...	...	...	...	...	...	...	...	...	...	4	50
58	Indonesia	...	...	842	48	...	...	593	50	...	...	1 435	49
59	Japan	268	...	260	...	362	...	347	...	630	...	608	...
60	Kiribati	0.2	59	0.3[y]	52[y]	0.3	38	0.3[y]	42[y]	0.5	46	0.7[y]	47[y]
61	Lao PDR	9	40	...	...	3	40	...	...	12	40	17	43
62	Macao, China	0.9	59	1	65	0.5	49	1	53	1	56	2	59
63	Malaysia	76	65	...	...	...	...	...	...	...	...	147[y]	63[y]
64	Marshall Islands	0.1	...	...	...	0.2	...	...	...	0.3	...	...	...
65	Micronesia, Federated States of	...	...	...	...	...	...	...	...	...	...	...	...
66	Myanmar	54	77	59	84	14	73	23	80	68	76	82	83
67	Nauru	...	...	...	...	...	...	...	...	...	...	0.03	79
68	New Zealand	13	63	17	66	15	54	19	58	28	58	36	62
69	Niue	0.02	43	...	...	0.0	50	...	...	0.03	44	0.03[y]	68[y]
70	Palau	0.1	54	...	...	0.1	49	...	...	0.2	51	...	...
71	Papua New Guinea	...	...	...	...	...	...	...	...	...	...	...	...
72	Philippines	100	76	127	76	50	76	54	77	150	76	181	76
73	Republic of Korea	87	56	101	66	101	28	116	41	189	41	217	53
74	Samoa	0.3	76	...	...	0.8	49	...	...	1.1	57	...	...
75	Singapore	...	...	7	65	...	...	7	66	...	...	14	66
76	Solomon Islands	...	...	...	...	...	...	...	...	1	33	...	...
77	Thailand	...	...	**137**	**56**	...	...	**86**	**54**	...	...	**223**	**55**
78	Timor-Leste	...	...	1.3	24	...	...	1.3	22	...	...	2.6	23
79	Tokelau	...	...	...	...	...	...	...	...	...	...	...	...
80	Tonga	0.7	49	...	...	0.3	48	...	...	1	48	...	...
81	Tuvalu	...	...	...	...	...	...	...	...	...	...	...	...
82	Vanuatu	...	...	...	...	...	...	...	...	0.4	47	...	...
83	Viet Nam	194	70	311	67	64	51	141	56	258	65	451	64
	Latin America and the Caribbean												
84	Anguilla	...	...	...	...	...	...	...	...	0.1	63	0.1	69
85	Antigua and Barbuda	...	...	...	...	...	...	0.5	69	...	...	...	...
86	Argentina	171	73	127[z]	74[z]	...	...	146[z]	65[z]	...	...	273[z]	69[z]
87	Aruba	0.2	49	...	...	0.2	49	...	...	0.4	49	0.5	57
88	Bahamas	0.6	73	1.5	70	0.6	75	1.3	69	1.2	74	2.8	70
89	Barbados	0.7	58	...	...	0.5	58	...	...	1	58	1[z]	59[z]
90	Belize	0.7	63	1	61	0.2	60	0.5	59	0.9	62	2	61
91	Bermuda	...	...	0.4[z]	68[z]	...	...	0.4[z]	67[z]	...	...	0.7[z]	67[z]
92	Bolivia	14	59	...	...	25	48	22[z]	48[z]	39	52	...	...
93	Brazil[4]	703	84	733	74	401	70	530	63	1 104	79	1 263	69
94	British Virgin Islands	0.2	64	0.1	83	0.05	57	0.1	61	0.2	63	0.2	74
95	Cayman Islands	0.1	52	0.1[z]	61[z]	0.1	41	0.2[z]	56[z]	0.2	46	0.3[z]	58[z]
96	Chile	16	78	24	78	29	54	44	55	45	62	68	63
97	Colombia	138	50	...	...	48	50	...	...	187	50	164	52
98	Costa Rica	9	51	15*	57*	4	54	6*	59*	13	52	21*	58*
99	Cuba	40	68	46	64	25	49	48	48	65	60	93	56
100	Dominica	0.3	68	0.3	67	0.1	67	0.2	64	0.4	68	0.5	65
101	Dominican Republic	...	...	13*	71*	14	47	18*	52*	...	...	32*	60*
102	Ecuador	31	49	45	50	23	50	33	50	54	50	78	50
103	El Salvador	...	...	12	50	...	...	8	44	...	...	20	48
104	Grenada	...	...	0.6[y]	60[y]	...	...	0.3[y]	57[y]	...	...	0.9[y]	59[y]
105	Guatemala	20	...	34	44	13	...	19	42	33	...	54	44
106	Guyana	3	63	...	...	0.9	63	...	...	4	63	5	57
107	Haiti	...	...	...	...	...	...	...	...	...	...	...	...
108	Honduras	...	...	...	...	...	...	...	...	...	...	...	...
109	Jamaica	...	...	...	...	...	...	...	...	...	...	13	69
110	Mexico	321	46	373	50	198	40	248	44	519	44	621	47
111	Montserrat	0.02	63	...	...	0.01	60	...	...	0.03	62	0.03	66
112	Netherlands Antilles	0.7	46	...	...	0.4	66	...	...	1	53	...	...
113	Nicaragua	7*	56*	10	60	3*	56*	5	56	10*	56*	15	59

SECONDARY EDUCATION									TERTIARY EDUCATION				
Trained teachers (%)[1]			Pupil/teacher ratio[2]						Teaching staff				
Total secondary			Lower secondary		Upper secondary		Total secondary						
School year ending in 2007			School year ending in		School year ending in		School year ending in		School year ending in				
			1999	2007	1999	2007	1999	2007	1999		2007		
Total	Male	Female							Total (000)	% F	Total (000)	% F	
...	...	...	17	16	...	16	...	16	504	...	1 326	43	*54*
79	76	80	...	...	...	...	...	15	.	.	.	.	*55*
...	...	...	...	...	...	...	...	...	...	...	...	...	*56*
96	96	96	...	...	...	...	...	23	...	...	...	...	*57*
...	...	...	...	14	...	12	...	13	...	...	266	41	*58*
...	...	...	16	14	13	11	14	12	465	...	516	...	*59*
...	...	...	21	*21*[y]	19	*13*[y]	20	17[y]	.	.	.[z]	.[z]	*60*
93	92	95	20	...	22	...	20	24	1	31	3	33	*61*
69	57	78	24	21	21	20	23	21	0.7	...	2	31	*62*
...	...	...	18	...	...	...	...	17[y]	...	...	40[z]	48[z]	*63*
...	...	...	28	...	18	...	22	...	...	...	...	...	*64*
...	...	...	...	...	...	...	...	...	0.1	...	...	...	*65*
97	99	97	28	34	38	28	30	33	*9*	*76*	11	82	*66*
36	43	35	...	...	...	...	...	21	.	.	.[z]	.[z]	*67*
...	...	...	18	15	13	15	15	15	11	43	14	50	*68*
...	...	...	6	...	21	...	11	8[y]	.	.	.[z]	.[z]	*69*
...	...	...	14	...	12	...	13	...	...	...	...	...	*70*
...	...	...	...	...	...	...	...	...	*1*	*20*	...	...	*71*
...	...	...	41	39	21	25	34	35	94	...	*113*[y]	*56*[y]	*72*
...	...	...	22	20	22	16	22	18	137	26	202	32	*73*
...	...	...	*26*	...	17	...	*20*	...	0.2	41	...	...	*74*
95	94	95	...	17	...	17	...	17	...	...	14	35	*75*
...	...	...	...	...	...	...	13	...	.	.	.[z]	.[z]	*76*
...	...	...	...	**20**	...	**23**	...	**21**	50	53	***75***	***68***	*77*
...	...	...	...	...	...	...	...	...	...	...	...	...	*78*
...	...	...	...	...	...	...	...	...	.	.	.[z]	.[z]	*79*
...	...	...	*15*	...	*13*	...	*15*	...	0.07	21	...	...	*80*
...	...	...	...	...	...	...	...	...	.	.	.	.	*81*
...	...	...	...	...	...	...	23	...	...	...	...	...	*82*
98[z]	...	...	29	20	29	26	29	22	28	37	54	44	*83*
Latin America and the Caribbean													
60	57	62	...	...	...	...	*15*	10	.	.	0.01	43	*84*
...	...	...	...	...	...	...	...	...	.	.	...	...	*85*
...	...	...	12	17[z]	...	9[z]	...	13[z]	102	54	142[z]	53[z]	*86*
93[z]	95[z]	92[z]	*16*	...	*16*	...	16	14	0.2	43	0.2	50	*87*
86	80	88	*23*	13	*23*	12	*23*	12	...	...	...	...	*88*
57[z]	57[z]	57[z]	*18*	...	*18*	...	*18*	15[z]	*0.6*	*41*	0.8	49	*89*
37	34	39	*24*	18	*23*	14	*24*	17	...	...	0.1[y]	*49*[y]	*90*
100[z]	100[z]	100[z]	...	6[z]	...	6[z]	...	6[z]	...	...	0.09	55	*91*
...	...	...	*24*	...	20	29[z]	*21*	...	13	...	...	...	*92*
...	...	...	23	20	21	17	23	19	174	41	368	44	*93*
...	...	...	6	10	10	6	7	9	0.08	49	*0.1*[y]	*55*[y]	*94*
100[z]	99[z]	100[z]	11	11[z]	7	7[z]	9	9[z]	0.02	42	0.05[z]	24[z]	*95*
...	...	...	32	24	27	23	29	24	...	...	55	39	*96*
...	...	...	*19*	...	*20*	...	*19*	28	86	34	*88*	*35*	*97*
85*	87*	85*	*18*	18*	*18*	17*	*18*	18*	...	...	...	...	*98*
100	100	100	12	10	10	10	11	10	24	48	136	56	*99*
41	40	41	*21*	21	*15*	10	*19*	16	.	.	.[y]	.[y]	*100*
85*	73*	93*	...	25*	28	32*	...	29*	...	...	...	...	*101*
71	64	77	*17*	15	*17*	15	*17*	15	...	...	23	28	*102*
88	87	89	...	28	...	25	...	27	7	32	8	33	*103*
35[y]	39[y]	33[y]	...	*14*[y]	...	18*,[y]	...	15*,[y]	.	.	.[y]	.[y]	*104*
...	...	...	15	17	11	14	13	16	...	...	4[z]	31[z]	*105*
55[y]	*46*[y]	*60*[y]	*19*	...	*19*	...	*19*	14	...	...	0.6	50	*106*
...	...	...	...	...	...	...	...	...	...	...	...	...	*107*
...	...	...	...	...	...	...	...	...	...	...	...	...	*108*
...	...	...	...	...	...	...	...	20	...	...	...	...	*109*
...	...	...	18	20	14	15	17	18	192	...	275	...	*110*
59	50	63	*11*	...	*10*	...	10	12	.	.	.	.	*111*
...	...	...	12	...	21	...	15	...	*0.2*	*42*	...	...	*112*
60	57	62	31*	32	*31*	29	*31*	31	...	...	...	...	*113*

Table 10B (continued)

	Country or territory	SECONDARY EDUCATION — Teaching staff — Lower secondary — School year ending in 1999 — Total (000)	% F	Lower secondary 2007 — Total (000)	% F	Upper secondary — School year ending in 1999 — Total (000)	% F	Upper secondary 2007 — Total (000)	% F	Total secondary — School year ending in 1999 — Total (000)	% F	Total secondary 2007 — Total (000)	% F
114	Panama	8	55	10	62	6	55	7	54	14	55	17	58
115	Paraguay	…	…	…	…	…	…	…	…	…	…	…	…
116	Peru	…	…	…	…	…	…	…	…	…	…	159	…
117	Saint Kitts and Nevis	…	…	0.3	64	…	…	0.2	64	…	…	0.4	64
118	Saint Lucia	*0.4*	*65*	…	…	*0.3*	*62*	…	…	0.7	*64*	0.9	66
119	Saint Vincent/Grenadines	…	…	*0.4[y]*	*58[y]*	…	…	*0.2[y]*	*57[y]*	…	…	*0.5[y]*	*58[y]*
120	Suriname	…	…	2	63	…	…	1	55	…	…	3	60
121	Trinidad and Tobago	*3*	*61*	4*	…	*2*	*55*	*3*	…	*6*	*59*	*7*	…
122	Turks and Caicos Islands	*0.08*	*61*	*0.1[y]*	*61[y]*	*0.05*	*63*	*0.07[y]*	*64[y]*	*0.1*	*62*	*0.2[y]*	*62[y]*
123	Uruguay	14	75	14	…	5	65	7	…	19	72	21	…
124	Venezuela, B. R.	…	…	116[y]	65[y]	…	…	72[y]	60[y]	…	…	188[y]	63[y]
	North America and Western Europe												
125	Andorra	…	…	0.4[y]	61[y]	…	…	0.1[y]	51[y]	…	…	0.5[y]	59[y]
126	Austria	43	64	42	69	30	49	29	52	73	57	72	62
127	Belgium	…	…	43[z]	60[z]	…	…	…	…	…	…	*82[z]*	*57[z]*
128	Canada	71	*68*	…	…	68	*68*	…	…	139	*68*	…	…
129	Cyprus	*2*	*54*	3	68	*2*	*49*	3	56	*5*	*51*	6	62
130	Denmark	20	63	…	…	24	30	…	…	44	45	…	…
131	Finland	20	71	21[y]	72[y]	…	…	*14[y]*	*59[y]*	…	…	*35[y]*	*67[y]*
132	France	255	…	243	64	240	…	248	54	495	57	491	59
133	Germany	365	57	409	61	168	39	184	48	533	51	593	57
134	Greece	37	*64*	42	67	38	*49*	44	48	75	*56*	87	58
135	Iceland	*1.1*	*78*	*1[z]*	*80[z]*	1.4	44	2[z]	53[z]	*2.5*	*58*	*3[z]*	*65[z]*
136	Ireland	…	…	…	…	…	…	…	…	…	…	30[z]	62[z]
137	Israel	19	…	19	78	36	…	33	67	55	…	52	71
138	Italy	177	73	191	76	245	59	260	61	422	65	451	67
139	Luxembourg	…	…	…	…	…	…	…	…	…	…	4	47
140	Malta	3.4	50	3[y]	60[y]	0.2	31	…	…	3.6	48	4[y]	57[y]
141	Monaco	*0.2*	*69*	…	…	*0.2*	*54*	…	…	*0.4*	*61*	**0.5**	**68**
142	Netherlands	…	…	…	…	…	…	…	…	…	…	108	46
143	Norway	…	…	…	…	26	44	…	…	…	…	…	…
144	Portugal	…	…	51	70	…	…	42	67	…	…	93	69
145	San Marino	…	…	**0.2**	**76**	…	…	…	…	…	…	…	…
146	Spain	…	…	165	59	…	…	120	54	…	…	285	57
147	Sweden	28	…	39	67	35	50	40	51	63	…	79	59
148	Switzerland	…	…	…	…	…	…	…	…	…	…	…	…
149	United Kingdom	142	55	147[z]	61[z]	212	56	221[*,z]	61[*,z]	355	56	368[*,z]	61[*,z]
150	United States	764	60	922	68	740	51	776	56	1 504	56	1 698	62
	South and West Asia												
151	Afghanistan	…	…	24	28	…	…	9	27	…	…	33	28
152	Bangladesh	136	13	220	20	129	13	193	20	265	13	414	20
153	Bhutan	0.4	32	**1.4**	**38**	0.2	32	**0.8**	**25**	0.6	32	**2.2**	**33**
154	India	…	…	…	…	…	…	…	…	*1 995*	*34*	…	…
155	Iran, Islamic Republic of	…	…	236[y]	49[y]	…	…	294[y]	47[y]	…	…	530[y]	48[y]
156	Maldives	0.8	25	3	39	0.1	27	…	…	0.9	25	…	…
157	Nepal	22	12	**28**	**19**	18	7	**28**	**11**	40	9	**56**	**15**
158	Pakistan	…	…	…	…	…	…	…	…	…	…	…	…
159	Sri Lanka	…	…	69[z]	69[z]	…	…	…	…	…	…	…	…
	Sub-Saharan Africa												
160	Angola	…	…	…	…	…	…	…	…	*16*	*33*	…	…
161	Benin	*6*	*12*	…	…	*3*	*14*	…	…	*9*	*12*	…	…
162	Botswana	…	…	…	…	…	…	…	…	9	45	*12[y]*	*54[y]*
163	Burkina Faso	*5*	…	…	…	*1*	…	…	…	*6*	…	**14**	**17**
164	Burundi	…	…	…	…	…	…	…	…	…	…	8	24
165	Cameroon	*13*	*28*	…	…	*13*	*28*	…	…	*26*	*28*	*43[z]*	*26[z]*
166	Cape Verde	…	…	2	41	…	…	1	38	…	…	3	39
167	Central African Republic	…	…	…	…	…	…	…	…	…	…	…	…
168	Chad	2.3	5	…	…	1.3	6	…	…	3.6	5	*10*	…
169	Comoros	…	…	*2[y]*	*16[y]*	…	…	*1[y]*	*9[y]*	…	…	*3[y]*	*13[y]*

SECONDARY EDUCATION									TERTIARY EDUCATION				
Trained teachers (%)[1]			Pupil/teacher ratio[2]						Teaching staff				
Total secondary			Lower secondary		Upper secondary		Total secondary						
School year ending in 2007			School year ending in		School year ending in		School year ending in		School year ending in				
			1999	2007	1999	2007	1999	2007	1999		2007		
Total	Male	Female							Total (000)	% F	Total (000)	% F	
91	89	92	17	16	15	14	16	15	8	…	12^{z}	46^{z}	*114*
…	…	…	…	…	…	…	…	…	…	…	…	…	*115*
…	…	…	…	…	…	…	…	18	…	…	…	…	*116*
40	…	…	…	10	…	10	…	10	.	.	$.^{y}$	$.^{y}$	*117*
57^{z}	53^{z}	59^{z}	*19*	…	*16*	…	18	17	…	…	0.3	54	*118*
55^{y}	*58*^{y}	*53*^{y}	…	*18*^{y}	…	*18*^{y}	…	*18*^{y}	.	.	$.^{y}$	$.^{y}$	*119*
…	…	…	…	15	…	12	…	14	…	…	…	…	*120*
…	…	…	*22*	14*	*19*	*14*	*21*	*14*	0.5	31	*2*^{y}	*33*^{y}	*121*
100^{y}	*100*^{y}	*100*^{y}	*9*	*9*^{y}	*9*	*9*^{y}	*9*	*9*^{y}	.	.	$.^{y}$	$.^{y}$	*122*
…	…	…	12	11	23	19	15	14	11	…	16	…	*123*
83^{y}	76^{y}	86^{y}	…	12^{y}	…	9^{y}	…	11^{y}	…	…	$109^{*,z}$	…	*124*
									North America and Western Europe				
…	…	…	…	7^{y}	…	14^{y}	…	8^{y}	…	…	0.08^{z}	40^{z}	*125*
…	…	…	9	9	12	13	10	11	26	…	29	32	*126*
…	…	…	…	7^{z}	…	…	…	*10*^{z}	…	…	26	42	*127*
…	…	…	17	…	…	…	…	…	129	*41*	…	…	*128*
…	…	…	*14*	11	*12*	10	*13*	11	1	34	2	40	*129*
…	…	…	10	…	9	…	10	…	…	…	…	…	*130*
…	…	…	10	10^{y}	…	*17*^{y}	…	*12*^{y}	*18*	*46*	*19*^{z}	*46*^{z}	*131*
…	…	…	13	13	11	11	12	12	102	40	…	…	*132*
…	…	…	15	12	16	16	15	13	272	30	295	36	*133*
…	…	…	10	8	10	8	10	8	17	*31*	29	35	*134*
…	…	…	*11*	*10*^{z}	14	12^{z}	*13*	*11*^{z}	1	43	2	45	*135*
…	…	…	…	…	…	…	…	11^{z}	10	33	12	39	*136*
…	…	…	12	13	9	11	10	12	…	…	…	…	*137*
…	…	…	10	9	11	11	11	10	73	28	104	35	*138*
…	…	…	…	…	…	…	…	10	…	…	…	…	*139*
…	…	…	…	8^{y}	…	…	…	10^{y}	0.7	25	*0.7*^{y}	*23*^{y}	*140*
…	…	…	*10*	…	*7*	…	*8*	**6**	.	.	$.^{z}$	$.^{z}$	*141*
…	…	…	…	…	…	…	…	13	…	…	45	37	*142*
…	…	…	…	…	8	…	…	…	14	36	19	41	*143*
…	…	…	…	8	…	7	…	7	…	…	36	43	*144*
…	…	…	…	**6**	…	…	…	…	…	…	…	…	*145*
…	…	…	…	12	…	9	…	11	108	35	144	39	*146*
…	…	…	12	10	17	10	15	10	29	…	36	43	*147*
…	…	…	…	…	…	…	…	…	8	16	33^{z}	31^{z}	*148*
…	…	…	16	16^{z}	14	$14^{*,z}$	15	$15^{*,z}$	92	32	126^{z}	41^{z}	*149*
…	…	…	16	14	14	15	15	15	992	*41*	1 310	45	*150*
									South and West Asia				
…	…	…	…	32	…	31	…	32	…	…	…	…	*151*
39	39	41	43	29	32	21	37	25	45	14	64	18	*152*
83	…	…	35	**31**	27	**12**	32	**24**	…	…	0.4^{z}	…	*153*
…	…	…	…	…	…	…	*34*	…	…	…	…	…	*154*
100^{y}	100^{y}	100^{y}	…	19^{y}	…	19^{y}	…	19^{y}	65	17	133	24	*155*
…	…	…	18	11	9	…	17	…	.	.	$-^{z}$	$-^{z}$	*156*
…	…	…	38	**52**	24	**30**	32	**41**	…	…	10	…	*157*
…	…	…	…	…	…	…	…	…	…	…	52*	37*	*158*
…	…	…	…	19^{z}	…	…	…	…	…	…	…	…	*159*
									Sub-Saharan Africa				
…	…	…	…	…	…	…	*18*	…	0.8	20	1^{z}	…	*160*
…	…	…	*27*	…	*15*	…	*24*	…	*0.7*	*9*	…	…	*161*
…	…	…	…	…	…	…	18	*14*^{y}	*0.5*	*28*	0.5^{y}	37^{y}	*162*
27	**26**	**32**	*29*	…	*23*	…	*28*	**30**	0.8	…	**2**	**8**	*163*
…	…	…	…	…	…	…	…	28	0.4	…	1	…	*164*
…	…	…	*26*	…	*21*	…	*24*	*16*^{z}	3	…	3	…	*165*
75	75	77	…	20	…	18	…	19	…	…	0.6	39	*166*
…	…	…	…	…	…	…	…	…	0.3	5	…	…	*167*
…	…	…	41	…	23	…	34	*33*	…	…	*1*^{y}	*3*^{y}	*168*
…	…	…	…	*16*^{y}	…	*11*^{y}	…	*14*^{y}	0.1	10	…	…	*169*

Table 10B (continued)

	Country or territory	SECONDARY EDUCATION — Teaching staff											
		Lower secondary				Upper secondary				Total secondary			
		School year ending in				School year ending in				School year ending in			
		1999		2007		1999		2007		1999		2007	
		Total (000)	% F	Total (000)	% F	Total (000)	% F	Total (000)	% F	Total (000)	% F	Total (000)	% F
170	Congo	...	...	7[y]	14[y]	...	...	3[y]	14[y]	...	...	10[y]	14[y]
171	Côte d'Ivoire	13	...	...	...	7	13	...	...	20	...	...	...
172	Democratic Rep. of the Congo	...	...	...	...	...	...	...	...	89	10	180	10
173	Equatorial Guinea	0.7	5	...	...	0.1	7	...	...	0.9	5	...	...
174	Eritrea	1	12	2	12	1	11	2	11	2	12	4	12
175	Ethiopia	...	...	...	...	...	...	...	...	...	...	...	...
176	Gabon	2.3	17	...	...	0.7	15	...	...	3.1	16	...	...
177	Gambia	1.7	16	3	18	0.6	12	1	11	2.3	15	4	16
178	Ghana	40	24	**74**	**23**	12	16	**25**	**20**	52	22	**99**	**22**
179	Guinea	4	11	9	7	...	...	5	5	...	...	14	6
180	Guinea-Bissau	...	...	...	...	...	...	...	...	...	...	...	...
181	Kenya	...	...	49	44	...	...	54	36	...	...	102	40
182	Lesotho	2	51	...	...	1.0	53	...	...	3	51	4[z]	55[z]
183	Liberia	4	16	...	...	3	16	...	...	7	16	...	...
184	Madagascar	...	...	25	...	...	...	9	...	...	...	34	...
185	Malawi	...	...	...	...	...	...	10	19	...	...	...	...
186	Mali	5*	17*	11	14	3	10	4	...	8*	14*	15	...
187	Mauritius	...	...	...	...	...	...	...	...	5	47	8	56
188	Mozambique	...	...	10	16	...	...	2	18	...	...	12	16
189	Namibia	4	45	...	...	1	49	...	...	5	46	6	50
190	Niger	2	23	6	18	2	12	2	13	4	18	8	17
191	Nigeria	...	...	113[z]	40[z]	...	...	89[z]	36[z]	129	36	202[z]	38[z]
192	Rwanda	...	...	...	...	...	...	...	...	...	...	12	53
193	Sao Tome and Principe	...	...	...	...	...	...	...	...	...	...	0.4[z]	13[z]
194	Senegal	6	14	15	15	3	13	5	16	9	14	20	15
195	Seychelles	0.4	54	...	...	0.2	55	...	...	0.6	54	0.6	55
196	Sierra Leone	...	...	...	...	...	...	...	...	...	...	10	16
197	Somalia	...	...	...	...	...	...	...	...	...	...	...	...
198	South Africa	...	...	...	...	...	...	...	...	145	50	165	53
199	Swaziland	...	...	...	...	...	...	...	...	...	...	4	48
200	Togo	4	11	...	...	2	16	...	...	7	13	12	7
201	Uganda	...	...	...	...	...	...	...	...	...	...	54	22
202	United Republic of Tanzania	...	...	...	...	...	...	...	...	...	...	...	...
203	Zambia	4	28	...	...	6	27	...	...	10	27	14	39
204	Zimbabwe	...	...	...	...	...	...	...	...	31	37	...	...

		Sum	% F	Sum	% F	Sum	% F	Sum	% F	Sum	% F	Sum	% F
I	World	...	...	...	...	...	...	...	...	24 138	52	29 346	52
II	Countries in transition	...	...	...	...	...	...	...	...	2 767	74	2 581	76
III	Developed countries	...	...	...	...	...	...	...	...	6 286	55	6 557	59
IV	Developing countries	...	...	...	...	...	...	...	...	15 085	47	20 209	47
V	Arab States	...	...	...	...	...	...	...	...	1 387	46	1 913	51
VI	Central and Eastern Europe	...	...	...	...	...	...	...	...	3 158	72	2 869	74
VII	Central Asia	...	...	...	...	...	...	...	...	855	65	914	69
VIII	East Asia and the Pacific	...	...	...	...	...	...	...	...	7 699	46	10 005	48
IX	East Asia	...	...	...	...	...	...	...	...	7 472	46	9 758	47
X	Pacific	...	...	...	...	...	...	...	...	226	57	247	56
XI	Latin America and the Caribbean	1 683	67	...	...	1 063	58	...	...	2 746	64	3 283	60
XII	Caribbean	33	46	...	...	20	40	...	...	53	44	69	40
XIII	Latin America	1 650	68	...	...	1 043	59	...	...	2 693	64	3 215	60
XIV	N. America/W. Europe	...	...	...	...	...	...	...	...	4 487	56	4 842	61
XV	South and West Asia	...	...	...	...	...	...	...	...	2 956	35	4 117	36
XVI	Sub-Saharan Africa	...	...	...	...	...	...	...	...	851	31	1 403	30

Source: UNESCO Institute for Statistics database (UIS, 2009).

1. Data on trained teachers (defined according to national standards) are not collected for countries whose education statistics are gathered through the OECD, Eurostat or the World Education Indicators questionnaires.

2. Based on headcounts of pupils and teachers.

3. Teaching staff in upper secondary includes full- and part-time teachers.

4. The number of teachers declined from 2005 to 2007 mainly because the data collection reference date was shifted from the last Wednesday of March to the last Wednesday of May to account for duplicates (enrolments) and transfers of students and teachers (from one school to another), common features at the beginning of the school year. At this point of the school year, it is believed, the education system becomes stable, so the data collected should represent the current school year.

SECONDARY EDUCATION									TERTIARY EDUCATION				
Trained teachers (%)[1]			Pupil/teacher ratio[2]						Teaching staff				
Total secondary			Lower secondary		Upper secondary		Total secondary						
School year ending in 2007			School year ending in		School year ending in		School year ending in		School year ending in				
			1999	2007	1999	2007	1999	2007	1999		2007		
Total	Male	Female							Total (000)	% F	Total (000)	% F	
...	...	...	...	*30*[y]	...	...	...	...	*0.4*	*5*	...	...	170
...	...	...	*34*	...	*21*	...	*29*	...	...	...	...	...	171
...	...	...	...	...	...	...	14	16	4	6	17	...	172
...	...	...	25	...	15	...	23	...	...	...	...	...	173
57	57	60	55	57	45	40	51	49	0.2	13	...	...	174
...	...	...	...	...	...	...	...	...	2	6	8	9	175
...	...	...	*28*	...	*28*	...	*28*	...	0.6	17	...	...	176
...	...	...	20	22	21	24	20	23	0.1	15	...	...	177
69	**65**	**82**	20	**17**	19	**20**	20	**17**	*2*	*13*	4	11	178
...	...	...	31	44	...	*28*	...	*38*	...	...	1[z]	3[z]	179
...	...	...	...	...	...	...	...	...	*0.03*	*18*	...	...	180
95	*95*	*97*	...	*31*	...	23	...	*27*	...	...	...	...	181
87[z]	78[z]	95[z]	*24*	...	*17*	...	22	25[z]	0.4	*45*	0.6[z]	47[z]	182
...	...	...	17	...	18	...	17	...	0.6	15	...	...	183
...	...	...	...	*28*	...	*16*	...	*24*	1	31	3	30	184
...	...	...	...	...	...	15	...	...	0.5	25	0.9	*34*	185
...	...	...	31*	36	24	34	28*	36	1.0	...	1.0	...	186
...	...	...	...	...	...	...	20	...	*0.6*	*26*	...	...	187
62	60	74	...	40	...	25	...	37	...	...	3[y]	21[y]	188
97[y]	...	...	25	...	21	...	24	25	...	...	0.8[z]	42[z]	189
21[z]	21[z]	20[z]	34	31	12	16	24	27	...	...	1[z]	*6*[z]	190
70[z]	66[z]	77[z]	...	33[z]	...	30[z]	30	32[z]	52	31	...	...	191
53	94	17	...	...	...	...	...	22	0.4	10	*2*[y]	*12*[y]	192
...	...	...	...	...	...	...	...	*22*[z]	.	.	.	.	193
...	...	...	*29*	26	*19*	*24*	*25*	*25*	...	...	...	...	194
...	...	...	*14*	...	*14*	...	14	13	.	.	.	.	195
82	81	89	...	...	...	...	...	24	...	...	...	...	196
...	...	...	...	...	...	...	...	...	...	...	...	...	197
...	...	...	...	...	...	...	29	*29*	...	...	44[z]	51[z]	198
99	...	...	...	...	...	...	...	19	0.2	32	0.5[z]	40[z]	199
50[z]	...	...	44	...	20	...	35	*36*	0.4	10	0.5	*11*	200
...	...	...	...	...	...	...	...	*18*	2	17	...	...	201
...	...	...	...	...	...	...	...	...	2	14	3	18	202
...	...	...	*29*	...	*19*	...	*23*	43	...	...	...	...	203
...	...	...	...	...	...	...	27	...	...	...	...	...	204
Median			Weighted average						Sum	% F	Sum	% F	
...	...	...	...	...	...	...	18	18	6 434	39	9 475	42	I
...	...	...	...	...	...	...	11	10	756	54	1 039	55	II
...	...	...	...	...	...	...	13	13	2 784	34	3 447	38	III
...	...	...	...	...	...	...	21	20	2 893	39	4 989	41	IV
...	...	...	...	...	...	...	16	14	205	33	296	34	V
...	...	...	...	...	...	...	13	11	941	50	1 273	52	VI
...	...	...	...	...	...	...	11	12	115	44	144	50	VII
...	...	...	...	...	...	...	17	17	1 619	33	2 715	38	VIII
...	...	...	...	...	...	...	17	17	1 543	33	2 641	38	IX
...	...	...	...	...	...	...	14	14	75	44	75	43	X
71	64	77	20	...	17	...	19	18	832	45	1 439	46	XI
57	57	57	22	...	22	...	22	19	6	47	10	52	XII
...	...	...	20	...	17	...	19	18	826	45	1 429	46	XIII
...	...	...	...	...	...	...	14	13	2 043	38	2 618	41	XIV
...	...	...	...	...	...	...	33	31	563	32	815	35	XV
...	...	...	...	...	...	...	24	25	116	29	174	26	XVI

Data in italic are UIS estimates.
Data in bold are for the school year ending in 2008.
(z) Data are for the school year ending in 2006.
(y) Data are for the school year ending in 2005.
(*) National estimate.

Table 11

Commitment to education: public spending

Country or territory	Total public expenditure on education as % of GNP		Total public expenditure on education as % of total government expenditure		Public current expenditure on education as % of total public expenditure on education		Public current expenditure on primary education as % of public current expenditure on education		Public current expenditure on primary education per pupil (unit cost) at PPP in constant 2006 US$		Public current expenditure on primary education as % of GNP	
	1999	2007	1999	2007	1999	2007	1999	2007	1999	2007	1999	2007
Arab States												
Algeria	...	...	...	...	...	...	...	...	...	...	...	...
Bahrain	...	...	...	...	...	...	...	...	...	...	...	...
Djibouti	7.5	7.8	...	22.8	...	...	...	...	...	...	...	...
Egypt	...	3.7	...	12.6	...	...	...	...	...	...	...	...
Iraq	...	...	...	...	...	...	...	...	...	...	...	...
Jordan	5.0	...	20.6	...	...	...	...	...	455	538[z]	1.9	1.6[z]
Kuwait	...	*3.3*[z]	...	*12.9*[z]	...	*92.3*[z]	...	*21.3*[z]	...	...	...	0.6[z]
Lebanon	2.0	2.7	10.4	9.6	...	92.1	...	*33.3*[y]	...	*714*[y]	...	*0.8*[y]
Libyan Arab Jamahiriya	...	...	...	...	68.4	...	...	...	...	...	...	...
Mauritania	*2.8*	2.8[z]	...	10.1[z]	...	99.3[z]	...	*62.0*[y]	...	*169*[y]	...	*1.4*[y]
Morocco	5.5	5.6[z]	25.7	26.1[z]	90.8	93.3[z]	39.1	45.5[y]	471	554	2.0	1.8
Oman	4.2	4.2[z]	21.3	31.1[z]	...	92.2[z]	...	50.1[y]	...	...	1.4	1.6[y]
Palestinian A. T.	...	...	...	...	...	...	...	...	...	...	...	...
Qatar	...	...	...	19.6[y]	...	*88.4*[x]	...	...	...	...	...	...
Saudi Arabia	7.0	6.7[x]	26.0	27.6[x]	...	...	...	...	...	...	...	...
Sudan	...	...	...	...	...	...	...	...	...	...	...	...
Syrian Arab Republic	...	...	...	...	...	...	...	...	370	694[z]	1.7	2.0[z]
Tunisia	7.2	7.5[z]	...	20.5[z]	...	89.0[z]	...	*35.1*[y]	...	*1 243*[y]	...	*2.3*[y]
United Arab Emirates	...	1.6[*,x]	...	*28.3*[y]	...	...	...	...	...	...	0.7	0.3[z]
Yemen	...	...	...	...	...	...	...	...	...	...	...	...
Central and Eastern Europe												
Albania	...	...	...	...	...	...	...	...	...	...	...	...
Belarus	6.0	5.3	...	9.3	...	93.7	...	...	...	...	...	...
Bosnia and Herzegovina	...	...	...	...	...	...	...	...	...	...	...	...
Bulgaria	...	4.3[z]	...	11.6[z]	...	93.1[z]	...	19.9[z]	...	2 272[z]	...	0.8[z]
Croatia	...	4.6[x]	...	...	...	95.0[x]	...	*18.0*[x]	...	...	...	*0.8*[x]
Czech Republic	4.1	4.8[z]	9.7	10.5[z]	*90.9*	89.2[z]	*17.8*	13.3[z]	*1 674*	2 597[z]	*0.7*	0.6[z]
Estonia	7.0	5.1[y]	15.4	14.6[y]	...	90.9[y]	...	25.3[y]	...	3 029[y]	...	1.2[y]
Hungary	5.0	5.8[z]	12.8	10.4[z]	*91.4*	92.8[z]	*19.5*	20.0[z]	*2 238*	4 434[z]	*0.9*	1.1[z]
Latvia	5.8	5.2[z]	...	13.4[z]	...	...	...	...	...	...	...	...
Lithuania	...	5.0[z]	...	14.4[z]	...	92.2[z]	...	14.7[z]	...	2 349[z]	...	0.7[z]
Montenegro	...	...	...	...	...	...	...	...	...	...	...	...
Poland	4.7	5.6[y]	11.4	12.7[x]	*93.0*	95.2[y]	...	30.5[y]	...	3 065[y]	...	1.6[y]
Republic of Moldova	4.6	7.3	16.4	19.8	...	90.5	...	17.1	...	755	...	1.1
Romania	*3.6*	3.6[y]	...	14.3[y]	...	94.5[y]	...	*14.1*[y]	...	*1 003*[y]	...	*0.5*[y]
Russian Federation	...	4.0[z]	...	12.9[x]	...	...	...	...	...	...	...	...
Serbia	...	...	...	...	...	...	...	...	...	...	...	...
Slovakia	4.2	3.9[z]	13.8	10.2[z]	*95.8*	93.8[z]	*14.5*	17.9[z]	*1 264*	2 601[z]	*0.6*	0.7[z]
Slovenia	...	5.9[z]	...	12.9[z]	...	91.6[z]	...	*19.7*[y]	...	*5 426*[y]	...	*1.1*[y]
TFYR Macedonia	*4.2*	...	...	...	...	...	...	...	...	...	...	...
Turkey	4.0	4.1[x]	...	...	...	90.5[x]	...	*40.0*[x]	...	*1 039*[x]	...	*1.5*[x]
Ukraine	3.7	5.4	13.6	20.2	...	92.9[z]	...	...	...	...	...	...
Central Asia												
Armenia	2.2	2.6[z]	...	15.0[z]	...	...	...	...	...	...	...	...
Azerbaijan	4.3	2.9	24.4	12.6	99.2	96.6	...	*16.6*[z]	...	*315*[z]	...	*0.4*[z]
Georgia	2.0	2.6	10.3	7.8	...	97.3[x]	...	...	...	...	...	...
Kazakhstan	4.0	3.2	14.4	...	...	...	...	...	...	...	...	...
Kyrgyzstan	4.3	5.4	21.4	19.2	86.3	91.8[z]	...	...	...	...	...	...
Mongolia	6.0	5.2	...	...	...	88.6	...	27.1	...	420	...	1.3
Tajikistan	2.1	3.5	11.8	18.2	90.0	88.1[y]	...	*27.1*[y]	...	*121*[y]	...	*0.9*[y]
Turkmenistan	...	...	...	...	...	...	...	...	...	...	...	...
Uzbekistan	...	...	...	...	...	...	...	...	...	...	...	...
East Asia and the Pacific												
Australia	5.2	5.4[z]	...	...	*96.1*	95.4[z]	*32.9*	33.0[z]	*4 808*	5 417[z]	*1.7*	1.7[z]
Brunei Darussalam	4.9	...	*9.3*	...	96.6	...	...	...	...	...	...	...
Cambodia	1.0	1.7	8.7	12.4	...	97.7	...	...	...	...	...	...
China	1.9	...	13.0	...	*93.2*	...	*34.3*	...	...	...	*0.6*	...

Public current expenditure on primary education per pupil as % of GNP per capita		Public current expenditure on secondary education as % of public current expenditure on education		Public current expenditure on secondary education per pupil (unit cost) at PPP in constant 2006 US$		Public current expenditure on secondary education as % of GNP		Public current expenditure on secondary education per pupil as % of GNP per capita		Primary teachers' compensation as % of public current expenditure on primary education, in public institutions		
1999	2007	1999	2007	1999	2007	1999	2007	1999	2007	1999	2006	**Country or territory**
												Arab States
...	...	...	...	...	...	...	...	...	...	...	...	Algeria
...	...	...	...	...	...	...	...	...	...	...	...	Bahrain
...	...	...	...	...	...	...	...	...	...	...	...	Djibouti
...	...	...	...	...	...	...	...	...	...	...	...	Egypt
...	...	...	...	...	...	...	...	...	...	...	...	Iraq
12.6	11.1[z]	...	...	527	701[z]	1.8	1.7[z]	14.6	14.5[z]	77.8	88.0[z]	Jordan
...	8.0[z]	...	37.8[z]	...	...	...	1.1[z]	...	12.3[z]	...	76.9[z]	Kuwait
...	7.3[y]	...	29.8[y]	...	798[y]	...	0.7[y]	...	8.2[y]	69.1	83.6[y]	Lebanon
...	...	...	...	...	...	...	...	...	...	...	...	Libyan Arab Jamahiriya
...	9.3[y]	...	32.6[y]	...	424[y]	...	0.7[y]	...	23.3[y]	...	...	Mauritania
15.9	14.2	43.5	38.2[y]	1 237	1 454	2.2	2.6	41.7	37.4	...	...	Morocco
10.5	13.8[y]	...	41.5[y]	...	...	2.0	1.4[y]	20.3	11.6[y]	74.9	90.7[x]	Oman
...	...	...	...	...	...	...	...	...	...	...	...	Palestinian A. T.
...	...	...	...	...	...	...	...	...	...	...	...	Qatar
...	...	...	...	...	...	...	...	...	...	...	...	Saudi Arabia
...	...	...	...	...	...	...	...	...	...	...	...	Sudan
10.0	16.9[z]	...	...	639	...	1.1	...	17.3	...	...	...	Syrian Arab Republic
...	19.8[y]	...	42.6[y]	...	1 441[y]	...	2.8[y]	...	23.0[y]	...	...	Tunisia
7.8	4.2[z]	...	...	...	...	0.7	0.4[z]	10.2	5.8[z]	...	70.2[z]	United Arab Emirates
...	...	...	...	...	...	...	...	...	...	...	...	Yemen
												Central and Eastern Europe
...	...	...	...	...	...	...	...	...	...	...	...	Albania
...	...	...	...	...	...	...	...	...	...	...	...	Belarus
...	...	...	...	...	...	...	...	...	...	...	...	Bosnia and Herzegovina
...	22.5[z]	...	44.9[z]	...	2 116[z]	...	1.8[z]	...	21.0[z]	...	52.7[z]	Bulgaria
...	...	...	50.6[x]	...	...	...	2.2[x]	...	...	...	...	Croatia
10.3	12.5[z]	49.8	48.3[z]	3 299	4 623[z]	1.8	2.1[z]	20.4	22.2[z]	45.0	47.7[z]	Czech Republic
...	18.4[y]	...	42.9[y]	...	3 530[y]	...	2.0[y]	...	21.4[y]	...	...	Estonia
18.0	26.3[z]	40.6	41.1[z]	2 329	3 984[z]	1.8	2.2[z]	18.7	23.6[z]	...	...	Hungary
...	...	...	...	...	...	...	...	...	...	...	...	Latvia
...	15.4[z]	...	50.7[z]	...	2 977[z]	...	2.4[z]	...	19.5[z]	...	...	Lithuania
...	...	...	...	...	...	...	...	...	...	...	...	Montenegro
...	22.7[y]	...	36.4[y]	...	2 894[y]	...	1.9[y]	...	21.4[y]	...	...	Poland
...	26.5	...	48.4	...	936	...	3.2	...	32.8	...	...	Republic of Moldova
...	10.7[y]	...	45.5[y]	...	1 501[y]	...	1.5[y]	...	16.0[y]	...	...	Romania
...	...	...	...	...	...	...	...	...	...	...	...	Russian Federation
...	...	...	...	...	...	...	...	...	...	...	...	Serbia
10.0	15.1[z]	55.7	50.0[y]	2 280	2 371[y]	2.2	1.9[y]	18.0	15.2[y]	62.1	51.9[z]	Slovakia
...	23.1[y]	...	49.3[y]	...	6 995[y]	...	2.7[y]	...	29.7[y]	...	41.0[y]	Slovenia
...	...	...	...	...	...	...	...	...	...	...	...	TFYR Macedonia
...	13.3[x]	...	33.6[x]	...	1 288[x]	...	1.2[x]	...	16.5[x]	...	...	Turkey
...	...	...	...	...	...	...	...	...	...	...	...	Ukraine
												Central Asia
...	...	...	...	...	...	...	...	...	...	...	...	Armenia
...	5.9[z]	...	49.7[z]	...	484[z]	...	1.1[z]	...	9.0[z]	...	...	Azerbaijan
...	...	...	...	...	...	...	...	...	...	...	...	Georgia
...	...	...	...	...	...	...	...	...	...	...	...	Kazakhstan
...	...	...	...	...	...	...	...	...	...	47.5	...	Kyrgyzstan
...	13.7	...	35.2	...	397	...	1.6	...	12.9	...	48.1	Mongolia
...	8.2[y]	...	49.9[y]	...	157[y]	...	1.6[y]	...	10.6[y]	...	...	Tajikistan
...	...	...	...	...	...	...	...	...	...	...	...	Turkmenistan
...	...	...	...	...	...	...	...	...	...	...	...	Uzbekistan
												East Asia and the Pacific
16.6	17.7[z]	39.5	38.8[z]	4 373	4 869[z]	2.0	2.0[z]	15.1	15.9[z]	59.6	63.7[z]	Australia
...	...	...	...	...	...	...	...	...	...	...	...	Brunei Darussalam
...	...	...	...	...	...	...	...	...	...	...	...	Cambodia
...	...	38.4	...	283	...	0.7	...	11.2	...	...	...	China

Table 11 (continued)

Country or territory	Total public expenditure on education as % of GNP		Total public expenditure on education as % of total government expenditure		Public current expenditure on education as % of total public expenditure on education		Public current expenditure on primary education as % of public current expenditure on education		Public current expenditure on primary education per pupil (unit cost) at PPP in constant 2006 US$		Public current expenditure on primary education as % of GNP	
	1999	2007	1999	2007	1999	2007	1999	2007	1999	2007	1999	2007
Cook Islands	0.4	…	*13.1*	…	98.6	…	53.0	…	…	…	0.2	…
DPR Korea	…	…	…	…	…	…	…	…	…	…	…	…
Fiji	5.4	6.2[x]	18.3	…	…	97.4[x]	…	40.1[x]	…	771[x]	…	2.4[x]
Indonesia	…	*3.6*	…	*17.5*	…	…	…	…	…	…	…	…
Japan	3.5	3.4[z]	9.3	9.5[z]	…	…	…	…	…	…	…	…
Kiribati	7.9	…	…	…	…	…	…	…	…	…	…	…
Lao PDR	1.0	3.6	…	15.8	…	37.4	…	45.9[y]	…	53[y]	…	0.5[y]
Macao, China	3.6	…	13.5	14.9[z]	…	88.7[x]	…	…	…	…	…	…
Malaysia	6.1	4.7[z]	25.2	25.2[x]	…	88.2[x]	…	29.0[x]	…	1 411[x]	…	1.6[x]
Marshall Islands	13.3	*9.5*[x]	…	…	…	…	…	…	…	…	…	…
Micronesia, Federated States of	6.5	…	…	…	…	…	…	…	…	…	…	…
Myanmar	0.6	…	8.1	…	63.8	…	…	…	…	…	…	…
Nauru	…	…	…	…	…	…	…	…	…	…	…	…
New Zealand	7.2	6.3	…	19.7[z]	*95.1*	99.8	*26.7*	23.9	*4 005*	3 798	*1.8*	1.5
Niue	…	…	…	…	99.7	…	31.9	…	…	…	…	…
Palau	…	…	…	…	…	…	…	…	…	…	…	…
Papua New Guinea	…	…	…	…	…	…	…	…	…	…	…	…
Philippines	…	2.3[y]	…	15.2[y]	…	93.5[y]	…	53.6[y]	…	252[y]	…	1.2[y]
Republic of Korea	3.8	4.4[y]	13.1	15.3[y]	*80.3*	86.9[y]	*43.5*	35.1[y]	*2 602*	3 547[y]	*1.3*	1.4[y]
Samoa	4.5	…	13.3	…	98.9	…	*32.4*	…	*270*	…	*1.4*	…
Singapore	…	**3.0**	…	**15.3**	…	**90.3**	…	**20.5**	…	…	…	**0.6**
Solomon Islands	*3.3*	…	…	…	…	…	…	…	…	…	…	…
Thailand	5.1	4.0	28.1	20.9	…	…	…	…	…	…	…	…
Timor-Leste	…	…	…	…	…	…	…	…	…	…	…	1.0
Tokelau	…	…	…	…	…	…	…	…	…	…	…	…
Tonga	*6.7*	4.9[x]	…	…	…	…	…	…	…	…	…	…
Tuvalu	…	…	…	…	…	…	…	…	…	…	…	…
Vanuatu	6.7	…	17.4	…	83.7	…	38.9	…	416	…	2.2	…
Viet Nam	…	…	…	…	…	…	…	…	…	…	…	…
Latin America and the Caribbean												
Anguilla	…	4.0[y]	…	14.0[y]	…	89.9[y]	…	30.5[y]	…	…	…	1.1[y]
Antigua and Barbuda	3.4	…	…	…	100.0	…	…	…	…	1 110	…	0.9
Argentina	4.6	4.6[z]	13.3	14.0[z]	94.0	97.9[z]	36.7	34.9[z]	1 322	1 544[z]	1.6	1.6[z]
Aruba	…	5.1[y]	13.8	15.4[y]	89.5	83.8[y]	29.9	30.2[y]	…	…	…	1.3[y]
Bahamas	…	…	…	…	…	…	…	…	…	…	…	…
Barbados	5.3	6.7	15.4	16.4[y]	91.6	96.0	*21.5*	*28.3*[y]	…	…	*1.0*	*2.0*[y]
Belize	*5.7*	5.8[x]	*17.1*	…	…	87.6[x]	…	47.2[x]	…	767[x]	…	2.4[x]
Bermuda	…	1.2[z]	…	…	…	96.9[y]	…	*40.7*[y]	…	…	…	*0.8*[y]
Bolivia	5.8	…	15.8	…	84.3	…	*41.0*	…	*404*	…	*2.0*	…
Brazil	4.0	5.2[z]	10.5	16.2[z]	*95.1*	94.2[z]	*33.3*	31.7[z]	*804*	1 257[y]	*1.3*	1.6[z]
British Virgin Islands	…	3.4	…	14.6	…	93.0	…	26.8	…	…	…	0.8
Cayman Islands	…	2.9[z]	…	…	…	…	…	…	…	…	…	…
Chile	4.0	3.8	15.6	18.2	87.6	93.7	44.5	35.1	1 323	1 496	1.5	1.2
Colombia	4.5	5.1	16.9	12.6	…	88.2	…	41.0	…	1 044	…	1.9
Costa Rica	5.5	4.9	…	20.6[z]	99.6	79.4[x]	47.2	56.0[x]	1 340	1 480[x]	2.6	2.3[x]
Cuba	7.7	13.6	13.7	20.6	…	96.9	…	30.6	…	…	…	4.0
Dominica	*5.5*	5.5	…	…	…	…	…	…	…	1 082	…	1.8
Dominican Republic	…	2.6	…	11.0	…	…	…	…	…	549	…	1.2
Ecuador	2.0	…	9.7	…	92.7*	…	…	…	…	…	…	…
El Salvador	*2.4*	3.1*	*17.1*	13.1*	…	89.9*	…	46.3*	…	51	…	1.3
Grenada	…	…	…	…	…	…	…	…	…	…	…	…
Guatemala	…	3.1	…	…	…	93.6	…	61.3	…	431	…	1.8
Guyana	*9.3*	6.5	*18.4*	12.5	…	90.6	…	33.1	…	372	…	2.0
Haiti	…	…	…	…	…	…	…	…	…	…	…	…
Honduras	…	…	…	…	…	…	…	…	…	…	…	…
Jamaica	…	7.0	…	8.8[y]	…	91.8	…	36.7	…	1 155	…	2.4
Mexico	4.5	5.6[z]	22.6	25.6[x]	95.0	96.8[z]	40.8	39.1[z]	1 210	1 798[z]	1.8	2.1[z]
Montserrat	…	…	*10.7*	…	47.3	65.0[x]	…	…	…	…	…	…
Netherlands Antilles	…	…	14.0	…	93.8	…	…	…	…	…	…	…
Nicaragua	4.0	…	17.8	…	…	…	…	…	…	217[z]	…	1.6[z]
Panama	5.1	*4.1*[x]	…	*8.9*[x]	…	…	…	…	1 073	899	1.9	1.2
Paraguay	5.1	4.1[x]	8.8	10.0[x]	87.9	95.5[x]	…	46.0[x]	…	425[x]	…	1.8[x]

Public current expenditure on primary education per pupil as % of GNP per capita		Public current expenditure on secondary education as % of public current expenditure on education		Public current expenditure on secondary education per pupil (unit cost) at PPP in constant 2006 US$		Public current expenditure on secondary education as % of GNP		Public current expenditure on secondary education per pupil as % of GNP per capita		Primary teachers' compensation as % of public current expenditure on primary education, in public institutions		
1999	2007	1999	2007	1999	2007	1999	2007	1999	2007	1999	2006	**Country or territory**
1.6*	...	40.0	...	...	...	0.2	...	1.9*	...	...	...	Cook Islands
...	...	...	...	...	...	...	...	...	...	...	...	DPR Korea
...	17.5[x]	...	33.5[x]	...	716[x]	...	2.0[x]	...	16.3[x]	...	...	Fiji
...	...	...	...	...	...	...	...	...	...	...	...	Indonesia
...	...	...	...	...	...	...	...	...	...	...	...	Japan
...	...	...	...	...	...	...	...	...	...	...	...	Kiribati
...	3.1[y]	...	30.2[y]	...	79[y]	...	0.3[y]	...	4.7[y]	...	...	Lao PDR
...	...	...	...	...	...	...	...	...	...	...	...	Macao, China
...	12.7[x]	...	34.4[x]	...	2 049[x]	...	1.9[x]	...	18.5[x]	69.6	63.7[x]	Malaysia
...	...	...	...	...	...	...	...	...	...	...	...	Marshall Islands
...	...	...	...	...	...	...	...	...	...	...	...	Micronesia, Federated States of
...	...	...	...	...	...	...	...	...	...	...	...	Myanmar
...	...	...	...	...	...	...	...	...	...	...	...	Nauru
19.3	17.9	*39.8*	40.2	*4 989*	4 282	*2.7*	2.5	*24.0*	20.1	...	...	New Zealand
...	...	59.3	...	...	...	...	...	...	...	...	...	Niue
...	...	...	...	...	...	...	...	...	...	...	...	Palau
...	...	...	...	...	...	...	...	...	...	...	...	Papua New Guinea
...	7.6[y]	...	27.0[y]	...	262[y]	...	0.6[y]	...	7.9[y]	...	94.5[x]	Philippines
15.7	16.2[y]	*38.3*	41.1[y]	*2 161*	4 422[y]	*1.2*	1.6[y]	*13.1*	20.2[y]	77.6	65.0[y]	Republic of Korea
9.1	...	*26.9*	...	*286*	...	*1.2*	...	*9.6*	...	...	...	Samoa
...	**8.5**	...	**25.0**	...	...	...	**0.7**	...	**13.4**	...	...	Singapore
...	...	...	...	...	...	...	...	...	...	...	...	Solomon Islands
...	...	...	...	...	...	...	...	...	...	...	...	Thailand
...	5.9	...	...	...	...	...	0.7	...	...	...	...	Timor-Leste
...	...	...	...	...	...	...	...	...	...	...	...	Tokelau
...	...	...	...	...	...	...	...	...	...	...	...	Tonga
...	...	...	...	...	...	...	...	...	...	...	...	Tuvalu
11.8	...	51.9	...	2 119	...	2.9	...	60.2	...	94.3	...	Vanuatu
...	...	...	...	...	...	...	...	...	...	...	...	Viet Nam
												Latin America and the Caribbean
...	9.3[y]	...	49.7[y]	...	...	...	1.8[y]	...	21.4[y]	...	**100.0**	Anguilla
...	6.5	...	...	...	...	...	...	...	...	66.4	47.4	Antigua and Barbuda
12.5	13.2[z]	35.4	39.9[z]	1 777	2 381[z]	1.5	1.8[z]	16.9	20.4[z]	...	67.7[z]	Argentina
...	13.0[y]	32.3	32.0[y]	...	...	...	1.4[y]	...	19.8[y]	...	...	Aruba
...	...	...	...	...	...	...	...	...	...	...	...	Bahamas
11.9	*25.8*[y]	31.3	33.2	...	...	1.5	2.1	19.8	30.1	...	72.4	Barbados
...	13.4[x]	...	43.6[x]	...	1 112[x]	...	2.2[x]	...	19.5[x]	...	86.4[x]	Belize
...	*10.9*[y]	...	*52.3*[y]	...	...	...	*1.0*[y]	...	*14.0*[y]	...	...	Bermuda
11.3	...	*22.2*	...	*381*	...	*1.1*	...	*10.7*	...	...	...	Bolivia
10.4	15.0[y]	*36.1*	44.3[z]	*729*	1 093[y]	*1.4*	2.2[z]	*9.4*	13.0[y]	...	72.9[z]	Brazil
...	7.6[z]	...	36.9	...	...	...	1.2	...	15.4[z]	...	70.0	British Virgin Islands
...	...	...	...	...	...	...	...	...	...	...	88.7[z]	Cayman Islands
13.0	12.2	36.5	38.0	1 499	1 689	1.3	1.3	14.8	13.8	...	84.1	Chile
...	16.1	...	28.9	...	838	...	1.3	...	12.9	91.0*	74.1	Colombia
18.0	17.3[x]	29.1	34.3[x]	1 940	1 489[x]	1.6	1.4[x]	26.0	17.4[x]	...	69.6	Costa Rica
...	51.4	...	35.5	...	...	...	4.7	...	58.7	...	69.1[y]	Cuba
...	15.4	...	...	...	1 032	...	1.5	...	14.7	...	...	Dominica
...	8.9	...	...	...	241	...	0.4	...	3.9	...	63.6	Dominican Republic
...	...	...	...	...	...	...	...	...	...	...	...	Ecuador
...	8.3	...	24.4*	...	55	...	0.7	...	8.8	...	67.5	El Salvador
...	...	...	...	...	...	...	...	...	...	...	...	Grenada
...	9.8	...	12.9	...	257	...	0.4	...	5.8	...	*87.6*[y]	Guatemala
...	13.3	...	28.8	...	486	...	1.7	...	17.3	...	85.3	Guyana
...	...	...	...	...	...	...	...	...	...	...	...	Haiti
...	...	...	...	...	...	...	...	...	...	...	...	Honduras
...	20.4	...	33.4	...	1 269	...	2.2	...	22.4	...	86.2	Jamaica
11.6	15.0[z]	...	29.9[z]	...	1 843[z]	...	1.6[z]	...	15.4[z]	86.3	86.0[z]	Mexico
...	...	...	...	...	...	...	...	...	...	...	...	Montserrat
...	...	...	...	...	...	...	...	...	...	...	...	Netherlands Antilles
...	9.1[z]	...	...	...	96[z]	...	0.3[z]	...	4.0[z]	...	88.4[z]	Nicaragua
13.7	8.7	...	...	1 530	1 179	1.5	0.9	19.5	11.4	...	98.9[y]	Panama
...	11.1[x]	29.7	30.1[x]	668	491[x]	1.3	1.2[x]	16.5	12.8[x]	...	82.2[x]	Paraguay

Table 11 (continued)

Country or territory	Total public expenditure on education as % of GNP		Total public expenditure on education as % of total government expenditure		Public current expenditure on education as % of total public expenditure on education		Public current expenditure on primary education as % of public current expenditure on education		Public current expenditure on primary education per pupil (unit cost) at PPP in constant 2006 US$		Public current expenditure on primary education as % of GNP	
	1999	2007	1999	2007	1999	2007	1999	2007	1999	2007	1999	2007
Peru	3.4	2.7	21.1	16.4	87.9	92.2	40.4	40.8	393	495	1.2	1.0
Saint Kitts and Nevis	*5.6*	10.9[Y]	*13.3*	…	…	37.4[Y]	…	…	…	…	…	…
Saint Lucia	8.8	6.9[Z]	21.3	19.1[Z]	78.5	73.7[Z]	*52.7*	38.9[Z]	*1 783*	1 217[Z]	*3.6*	2.0[Z]
Saint Vincent/Grenadines	*7.2*	7.5	…	16.1[Y]	…	67.7[Y]	…	50.0[Y]	…	1 293	…	2.5
Suriname	…	…	…	…	…	…	…	…	…	…	…	…
Trinidad and Tobago	3.9	…	*16.4*	…	96.0	…	39.8	…	1 312	…	1.5	…
Turks and Caicos Islands	…	…	17.4	11.8[Y]	72.8	88.4[Y]	29.7	*20.0[Y]*	…	…	…	…
Uruguay	2.8	3.0[Z]	…	11.6[Z]	92.3	…	32.4	…	686	…	0.8	…
Venezuela, B. R.	…	3.7	…	…	…	97.3	…	32.5	…	1 071	…	1.2
North America and Western Europe												
Andorra	…	2.6	…	…	…	93.6[Z]	…	24.7[Z]	…	…	…	0.6
Austria	6.4	5.5[Y]	12.4	10.9[Y]	*94.1*	96.3[Y]	*19.0*	19.1[Y]	*7 362*	7 881[Y]	*1.1*	1.0[Y]
Belgium	…	6.0[Z]	…	12.4[Z]	…	97.5[Z]	…	23.3[Z]	…	6 612[Z]	…	1.4[Z]
Canada	5.9	5.0[Y]	…	…	*98.4*	95.0[Y]	…	…	…	…	…	…
Cyprus	5.3	7.3[Z]	…	9.5[Z]	86.2	89.5[Z]	33.9	26.7[Z]	3 627	5 614[Z]	1.6	1.7[Z]
Denmark	8.2	8.2[Y]	14.9	15.5[Y]	…	95.4[Y]	…	22.5[Y]	*7 318*	7 913[Y]	*1.6*	1.8[Y]
Finland	6.2	6.1[Z]	12.5	12.6[Z]	*93.7*	92.9[Z]	*21.1*	20.2[Z]	*4 330*	5 345[Z]	*1.2*	1.1[Z]
France	5.7	5.6[Z]	11.5	10.6[Z]	*91.4*	91.2[Z]	*20.2*	20.6[Z]	*4 621*	5 167[Z]	*1.1*	1.0[Z]
Germany	4.5	4.4[Z]	9.5	9.7[Z]	…	98.1[Z]	…	15.0[Z]	…	5 137[Z]	…	0.6[Z]
Greece	2.8	3.5[Y]	7.0	9.2[Y]	*78.0*	78.2[Y]	*25.2*	*26.2[Y]*	*2 308*	*3 641[Y]*	*0.5*	*0.7[Y]*
Iceland	…	8.5[Z]	…	18.1[Z]	…	89.8[Z]	…	33.7[Z]	…	8 360[Z]	…	2.6[Z]
Ireland	4.9	5.7[Z]	13.2	14.4[Z]	*91.2*	91.5[Z]	*32.2*	33.0[Z]	*3 183*	5 591[Z]	*1.4*	1.7[Z]
Israel	7.5	6.3[Z]	13.9	…	*93.7*	95.8[Z]	*34.1*	36.3[Z]	*4 150*	4 659[Z]	*2.4*	2.2[Z]
Italy	4.7	4.8[Z]	9.6	9.7[Z]	94.0	95.0[Z]	*26.1*	25.1[Z]	*6 244*	6 919[Z]	*1.2*	1.1[Z]
Luxembourg	*3.7*	…	*8.5*	…	…	…	…	…	…	*11 519[Y]*	…	*1.5[Y]*
Malta	*4.9*	4.9[X]	…	10.5[X]	…	94.6[X]	…	21.8[X]	…	2 655[X]	…	1.0[X]
Monaco	…	…	5.1	…	91.9	91.2[X]	17.7	16.8[X]	…	…	…	…
Netherlands	4.6	5.4[Z]	10.4	12.0[Z]	*96.2*	100.0[Z]	*25.5*	25.2[Z]	*4 671*	6 487[Z]	*1.1*	1.4[Z]
Norway	7.2	6.6[Z]	15.6	16.2[Z]	89.6	91.9[Z]	*24.7*	24.6[Z]	*7 800*	8 382[Z]	*1.6*	1.5[Z]
Portugal	*5.4*	5.5[Z]	*12.8*	11.3[Z]	*92.6*	97.2[Z]	*31.0*	30.7[Z]	*3 760*	4 611[Z]	*1.5*	1.6[Z]
San Marino	…	…	…	…	…	…	…	…	…	…	…	…
Spain	4.4	4.4[Z]	11.3	11.1[Z]	*91.1*	89.6[Z]	*28.1*	26.7[Z]	*4 370*	5 299[Z]	*1.1*	1.0[Z]
Sweden	7.5	7.0[Z]	13.6	12.6[Z]	…	95.1[Z]	…	24.3[Z]	…	8 001[Z]	…	1.6[Z]
Switzerland	5.0	5.1[Z]	15.2	16.3[Z]	90.2	92.2[Z]	31.6	28.6[Z]	7 153	8 027[Z]	1.4	1.4[Z]
United Kingdom	4.6	5.4[Y]	11.4	12.5[Y]	…	92.7[Y]	…	25.9[Y]	…	5 326[Y]	…	1.3[Y]
United States	5.0	5.7[Z]	…	14.8[Z]	…	…	…	…	…	…	…	…
South and West Asia												
Afghanistan	…	…	…	…	…	…	…	…	…	…	…	…
Bangladesh	2.3	2.4	15.3	15.8	63.7	85.8	38.9	43.4	…	99	0.6	0.9
Bhutan	…	5.8	…	17.2[Y]	…	64.1	…	26.9	…	249	…	1.0
India	4.5	3.2[Y]	12.7	…	*98.0*	99.3[Y]	*29.9*	35.8[Y]	*192*	179[Y]	*1.3*	1.2[Y]
Iran, Islamic Republic of	4.5	5.6	18.7	19.5	90.9	87.5	…	29.5	…	1 235	…	1.4
Maldives	…	8.3[Z]	…	11.0[Z]	…	*80.6[Y]*	…	*54.1[Y]*	…	*714[Y]*	…	*3.5[Y]*
Nepal	*2.9*	**3.8**	*12.5*	…	*73.6*	**90.5**	*52.7*	**62.9**	*61*	…	*1.1*	**2.2**
Pakistan	2.6	2.8	…	11.2	88.9	73.9	…	…	…	…	…	…
Sri Lanka	…	…	…	…	…	…	…	…	…	…	…	…
Sub-Saharan Africa												
Angola	*3.4*	3.0[Z]	*6.4*	…	*88.7*	75.3[Z]	…	27.6[Z]	…	109[Z]	…	0.6[Z]
Benin	3.0	3.9[Z]	15.6	18.0[Z]	88.0	90.4[Z]	…	54.4[Z]	…	156[Z]	…	1.9[Z]
Botswana	…	8.8	…	21.0	…	*75.1*	…	*19.3*	…	1 228[Y]	…	1.3
Burkina Faso	…	4.5[Z]	…	15.4[Z]	…	94.7[Z]	…	65.7[Z]	…	314[Z]	…	2.8[Z]
Burundi	3.5	5.2[Y]	…	17.7[Y]	93.9	97.6[Y]	38.9	52.1[Y]	*42*	65[Y]	1.3	2.7[Y]
Cameroon	*2.1*	3.9	*9.8*	17.0	…	67.4	…	37.6	123	121	1.0	1.0
Cape Verde	…	5.9	…	16.4	…	85.0	…	47.4	…	459	…	2.4
Central African Republic	…	1.3[Z]	…	…	…	98.3[Z]	…	52.4[Z]	…	50[Z]	…	0.7[Z]
Chad	*1.7*	2.3[Y]	…	10.1[Y]	…	50.3[Y]	…	47.8[Y]	…	56[Y]	…	0.6[Y]
Comoros	…	…	…	…	…	…	…	…	…	…	…	…
Congo	6.0	2.5[Y]	22.0	8.1[Y]	92.9	91.0[Y]	35.9	27.3[Y]	469	94[Y]	2.0	0.6[Y]
Côte d'Ivoire	5.6	…	…	…	74.0	…	43.4	…	285	…	1.8	*0.1[Y]*
Democratic Rep. of the Congo	…	…	…	…	…	…	…	…	…	…	…	…

Public current expenditure on primary education per pupil as % of GNP per capita		Public current expenditure on secondary education as % of public current expenditure on education		Public current expenditure on secondary education per pupil (unit cost) at PPP in constant 2006 US$		Public current expenditure on secondary education as % of GNP		Public current expenditure on secondary education per pupil as % of GNP per capita		Primary teachers' compensation as % of public current expenditure on primary education, in public institutions		
1999	2007	1999	2007	1999	2007	1999	2007	1999	2007	1999	2006	**Country or territory**
7.1	7.0	28.4	37.1	528	628	0.9	0.9	9.5	8.9	87.8	63.8	Peru
…	…	…	…	…	…	…	…	…	…	…	67.7^{Y}	Saint Kitts and Nevis
21.8	13.6^{Z}	*32.6*	30.2^{Z}	2 385	1 581^{Z}	*2.2*	1.5^{Z}	*29.1*	17.6^{Z}	87.6	79.1^{Z}	Saint Lucia
…	18.5	…	29.8^{Y}	…	1 223^{Y}	…	1.8	…	19.8^{Y}	…	84.9^{Y}	Saint Vincent/Grenadines
…	…	…	…	…	…	…	…	…	…	…	…	Suriname
11.3	…	31.1	…	1 507	…	1.2	…	12.9	…	77.5	…	Trinidad and Tobago
…	…	39.6	29.8^{Y}	…	…	…	…	…	…	*63.5*	…	Turks and Caicos Islands
7.6	…	36.9	…	1 008	…	1.0	…	11.1	…	71.3	51.8^{X}	Uruguay
…	9.2	…	16.7	…	891	…	0.6	…	7.7	…	…	Venezuela, B. R.
												North America and Western Europe
…	12.1*	…	22.3^{Z}	…	…	…	0.6	…	13.6*	…	49.2	Andorra
23.4	23.0^{Y}	*45.1*	46.7^{Y}	*9 076*	8 931^{Y}	*2.7*	2.5^{Y}	*28.9*	26.0^{Y}	71.5	55.2^{Y}	Austria
…	19.7^{Z}	…	43.2^{Y}	…	10 609^{Y}	…	2.5^{Y}	…	32.4^{Y}	…	65.6^{Z}	Belgium
…	…	…	…	…	…	…	…	…	…	…	…	Canada
16.6	22.5^{Z}	52.5	44.3^{Z}	5 725	8 599^{Z}	2.4	2.9^{Z}	26.2	34.4^{Z}	…	74.8^{Z}	Cyprus
23.5	23.0^{Y}	…	36.3^{Y}	*11 535*	11 389^{Y}	*2.9*	2.8^{Y}	*37.0*	33.1^{Y}	48.9	51.2^{Y}	Denmark
16.4	16.2^{Z}	*39.3*	41.3^{Z}	*6 434*	9 373^{Z}	*2.3*	2.3^{Z}	*24.4*	28.4^{Z}	59.0	57.9^{Z}	Finland
15.6	16.0^{Z}	*49.8*	46.6^{Z}	*7 555*	7 774^{Z}	*2.6*	2.4^{Z}	*25.5*	24.1^{Z}	…	52.8^{Z}	France
…	16.0^{Z}	…	48.0^{Z}	…	6 591^{Z}	…	2.1^{Z}	…	20.5^{Z}	…	…	Germany
9.2	*12.3*^{Y}	*37.5*	37.0^{Y}	*2 873*	4 679^{Y}	*0.8*	1.0^{Y}	*11.5*	15.8^{Y}	…	*91.3*^{Y}	Greece
…	25.5^{Z}	…	33.6^{Z}	…	7 474^{Z}	…	2.5^{Z}	…	*27.8*^{Z}	…	…	Iceland
11.9	15.9^{Z}	*36.8*	35.4^{Z}	*4 791*	8 831^{Z}	*1.6*	1.8^{Z}	*17.9*	25.1^{Z}	83.3	75.4^{Z}	Ireland
20.4	19.2^{Z}	*30.2*	29.0^{Z}	*4 654*	4 861^{Z}	*2.1*	1.7^{Z}	*22.8*	20.0^{Z}	…	…	Israel
22.9	24.1^{Z}	*46.5*	46.7^{Z}	*7 189*	7 930^{Z}	*2.1*	2.1^{Z}	*26.4*	27.6^{Z}	…	67.8^{Z}	Italy
…	*19.0*^{Y}	…	…	…	13 774^{Z}	…	1.8^{Z}	…	22.2^{Z}	…	*74.2*^{Y}	Luxembourg
…	13.1^{X}	…	41.6^{X}	…	3 772^{X}	…	1.9^{X}	…	18.6^{X}	…	58.0^{X}	Malta
…	…	50.9	46.2^{X}	…	…	…	…	…	…	…	…	Monaco
14.0	17.3^{Z}	*39.5*	39.7^{Z}	*6 712*	9 284^{Z}	*1.7*	2.1^{Z}	*20.1*	24.8^{Z}	…	…	Netherlands
17.2	16.2^{Z}	*31.9*	35.3^{Y}	*10 973*	13 338^{Y}	*2.0*	2.3^{Y}	*24.2*	26.2^{Y}	…	78.4^{Z}	Norway
19.3	23.0^{Z}	*44.0*	40.7^{Z}	*5 127*	6 925^{Z}	*2.2*	2.2^{Z}	*26.3*	34.6^{Z}	…	85.5^{Z}	Portugal
…	…	…	…	…	…	…	…	…	…	…	…	San Marino
17.5	18.4^{Z}	*47.5*	40.1^{Z}	*5 776*	6 437^{Z}	*1.9*	1.6^{Z}	*23.1*	22.4^{Z}	78.3	71.8^{Z}	Spain
…	23.4^{Z}	…	37.9^{Z}	…	10 427^{Z}	…	2.5^{Z}	…	30.5^{Z}	49.8	53.6^{Z}	Sweden
19.2	19.6^{Z}	40.5	37.9^{Z}	8 898	9 400^{Z}	1.8	1.8^{Z}	23.9	22.9^{Z}	72.4	70.9^{Z}	Switzerland
…	16.8^{Y}	…	34.9^{Y}	…	5 802^{Y}	…	1.8^{Y}	…	18.3^{Y}	52.4	52.8^{Y}	United Kingdom
…	…	…	…	…	…	…	…	…	…	55.9	54.7^{Z}	United States
												South and West Asia
…	…	…	…	…	…	…	…	…	…	…	…	Afghanistan
…	8.5	*42.0*	43.5	*81*	159	*0.6*	0.9	*9.2*	13.6	…	…	Bangladesh
…	6.3	…	53.9	…	1 134	…	2.0	…	28.8	…	…	Bhutan
11.7	9.0^{Y}	*37.6*	42.9^{Y}	*400*	333^{Y}	*1.7*	1.4^{Y}	*24.3*	16.7^{Y}	78.6	80.1^{Y}	India
…	14.1	…	47.2	…	868^{Y}	…	2.3	…	10.7^{Y}	…	…	Iran, Islamic Republic of
…	*17.9*^{Y}	…	…	…	…	…	…	…	…	…	…	Maldives
7.3	**13.8**	*28.9*	**24.2**	*94*	…	*0.6*	**0.8**	*11.3*	**10.2**	…	**71.8**	Nepal
…	…	…	…	…	…	…	…	…	…	…	…	Pakistan
…	…	…	…	…	…	…	…	…	…	…	…	Sri Lanka
												Sub-Saharan Africa
…	2.8^{Z}	…	42.7^{Z}	…	1 239^{Z}	…	1.0^{Z}	…	31.8^{Z}	…	…	Angola
…	12.4^{Z}	…	25.2^{Z}	…	*297*^{X}	…	0.9^{Z}	…	*23.9*^{X}	…	84.6^{Z}	Benin
…	11.6^{Y}	…	*48.3*	…	*3 958*^{Y}	…	3.2	…	*37.5*^{Y}	…	…	Botswana
…	29.1^{Z}	…	12.2^{Z}	…	253^{Z}	…	0.5^{Z}	…	23.4^{Z}	…	…	Burkina Faso
11.8	20.1^{Y}	36.5	33.0^{Y}	…	*248*^{Y}	1.2	1.7^{Y}	…	*77.2*^{Y}	…	…	Burundi
7.2	5.9	…	57.0	267	761*	0.6	1.5	*15.7*	36.9*	…	…	Cameroon
…	16.0	…	31.6	…	396	…	1.6	…	13.9	…	86.0^{Z}	Cape Verde
…	7.0^{Z}	…	23.7^{Z}	…	…	…	0.3^{Z}	…	…	…	…	Central African Republic
…	4.5^{Y}	…	29.3^{Y}	…	*184*^{Y}	…	0.3^{Y}	…	*14.7*^{Y}	…	…	Chad
…	…	…	…	…	…	…	…	…	…	…	…	Comoros
22.6	3.7^{Y}	23.8	41.2^{Y}	…	…	1.3	0.9^{Y}	…	…	…	…	Congo
15.8	…	36.4	…	*772*	…	1.5	0.5^{Y}	*42.8*	…	…	…	Côte d'Ivoire
…	…	…	…	…	…	…	…	…	…	…	…	Democratic Rep. of the Congo

Table 11 (continued)

Country or territory	Total public expenditure on education as % of GNP 1999	2007	Total public expenditure on education as % of total government expenditure 1999	2007	Public current expenditure on education as % of total public expenditure on education 1999	2007	Public current expenditure on primary education as % of public current expenditure on education 1999	2007	Public current expenditure on primary education per pupil (unit cost) at PPP in constant 2006 US$ 1999	2007	Public current expenditure on primary education as % of GNP 1999	2007
Equatorial Guinea	...	...	...	...	...	...	...	...	...	...	...	...
Eritrea	5.3	2.4[z]	...	...	*69.5*	80.4[z]	...	39.2[z]	...	50[z]	...	0.8[z]
Ethiopia	*3.5*	5.5	...	23.3	...	67.5	...	50.9	...	73	...	1.9
Gabon	*3.5*	...	...	...	*87.3*	...	...	...	...	...	...	...
Gambia	3.1	*2.1*[x]	14.2	...	86.8	...	...	...	...	...	...	...
Ghana	*4.2*	5.5[y]	...	...	...	85.6[y]	...	34.4[y]	...	147[y]	...	1.6[y]
Guinea	*2.1*	1.7[y]	...	...	...	...	...	...	...	...	...	...
Guinea-Bissau	5.6	...	11.9	...	40.8	...	...	...	...	...	...	...
Kenya	5.4	7.0[z]	...	17.9[y]	95.5	94.1[z]	...	54.7[z]	...	258[z]	...	3.6[z]
Lesotho	10.2	11.0[z]	25.5	29.8[y]	74.1	91.4[z]	42.8	38.2[z]	250	301[z]	3.2	3.8[z]
Liberia	...	...	...	...	...	...	...	...	...	...	...	...
Madagascar	*2.5*	3.4	...	16.4	...	90.0	...	51.6	...	73	...	1.6
Malawi	4.7	...	24.6	...	81.8	...	...	...	...	...	...	...
Mali	*3.0*	4.9[z]	...	16.8[z]	*89.6*	73.4[z]	*48.9*	60.2[z]	*117*	159[z]	*1.3*	2.2[z]
Mauritius	4.2	3.9[z]	17.7	12.7[z]	91.1	87.5[z]	31.9	27.9[z]	864	991[z]	1.2	1.0[z]
Mozambique	*2.2*	5.8[z]	...	21.0[z]	...	73.2[z]	...	56.2[z]	...	79[z]	...	2.4[z]
Namibia	7.9	...	...	...	93.9	...	59.4	...	865	668[y]	4.4	3.1[y]
Niger	...	3.3[z]	...	17.6[z]	...	80.7[z]	...	64.0[z]	...	130[z]	...	1.7[z]
Nigeria	...	...	...	...	...	...	...	...	...	...	...	...
Rwanda	...	4.9	...	19.0	...	94.5	...	45.3	...	80	...	2.1
Sao Tome and Principe	...	...	...	...	...	...	...	...	...	...	...	...
Senegal	*3.2*	4.9[z]	...	26.3[z]	...	91.5[z]	...	46.1[y]	...	257[y]	...	2.0[y]
Seychelles	5.5	6.6[z]	...	12.6[z]	...	88.2[z]	...	*30.6*[x]	...	*2 089*[x]	...	*1.6*[x]
Sierra Leone	...	*3.9*[y]	...	...	...	*99.4*[y]	...	...	...	...	...	...
Somalia	...	...	...	...	...	...	...	...	...	...	...	...
South Africa	6.2	5.5	22.2	17.4	98.1	96.1	45.2	41.3	1 097*	1 225	2.7	2.2
Swaziland	5.7	7.9[z]	...	24.4[z]	100.0	100.0[x]	33.2	*37.7*[x]	448	*459*[x]	1.9	*2.4*[x]
Togo	4.3	3.8	26.2	**15.8**	96.7	**95.9**	36.8	**38.1**	69	76	1.5	1.5
Uganda	...	*5.3*[x]	...	*18.3*[x]	...	*75.0*[x]	...	*61.9*[x]	...	*66*[x]	...	**2.1**
United Republic of Tanzania	*2.2*	...	...	...	...	...	...	...	...	...	...	...
Zambia	2.0	1.7	...	14.8[x]	...	76.0	...	59.4[y]	...	63[y]	...	1.3[y]
Zimbabwe	...	...	...	...	...	...	...	...	...	...	...	...
World[1]	4.6	4.9	...	15.0	...	91.8	...	33.1	...	1 003	...	1.4
Countries in transition	3.9	3.5	14.4	16.6	...	92.3	...	...	...	...	...	...
Developed countries	5.0	5.3	11.5	12.4	...	93.7	...	23.9	...	5 312	...	1.1
Developing countries	4.5	4.5	...	...	...	90.0	...	...	...	...	...	1.6
Arab States	...	4.0	...	20.5	...	...	...	...	...	...	...	...
Central and Eastern Europe	4.4	5.1	...	12.9	...	92.9	...	18.8	...	2 597	...	0.9
Central Asia	4.0	3.2	14.4	15.0	...	91.8	...	...	...	...	...	...
East Asia and the Pacific	4.9	...	...	...	...	...	...	...	...	...	...	...
East Asia	3.6	3.6	13.0	15.3	...	...	...	...	...	...	...	...
Pacific	6.5	...	...	...	...	...	...	...	...	...	...	...
Latin America and the Caribbean	4.9	4.8	15.7	14.3	...	91.8	...	...	...	1 071	...	1.6
Caribbean	...	5.8	...	...	...	88.4	...	33.1	...	...	...	1.9
Latin America	4.5	4.1	15.7	14.0	92.5	94.0	...	40.0	...	972	...	1.6
N. America/W. Europe	5.0	5.5	11.9	12.2	91.9	93.6	25.8	24.9	4 496	5 614	1.3	1.4
South and West Asia	2.9	3.8	...	15.8	88.9	85.8	...	39.6	...	249	...	1.3
Sub-Saharan Africa	3.5	4.5	...	17.5	...	88.2	...	46.8	...	130	...	1.8

Source: UNESCO Institute for Statistics database (UIS, 2009).
1. All regional values shown are medians.
Data in italic are UIS estimates.
Data in bold are for 2008.

(z) Data are for 2006.
(y) Data are for 2005.
(x) Data are for 2004.
(*) National estimate.

Public current expenditure on primary education per pupil as % of GNP per capita		Public current expenditure on secondary education as % of public current expenditure on education		Public current expenditure on secondary education per pupil (unit cost) at PPP in constant 2006 US$		Public current expenditure on secondary education as % of GNP		Public current expenditure on secondary education per pupil as % of GNP per capita		Primary teachers' compensation as % of public current expenditure on primary education, in public institutions		
1999	2007	1999	2007	1999	2007	1999	2007	1999	2007	1999	2006	**Country or territory**
...	...	...	...	...	...	...	...	...	...	...	...	Equatorial Guinea
...	9.7[Z]	...	12.8[Z]	...	26[Z]	...	0.2[Z]	...	5.1[Z]	...	...	Eritrea
...	12.0	...	7.9	...	40	...	0.3	...	6.6	...	...	Ethiopia
...	...	...	...	...	...	...	...	...	...	...	...	Gabon
...	...	...	...	...	...	...	...	...	...	...	74.8[X]	Gambia
...	12.5[Y]	...	37.4[Y]	...	*348*[Y]	...	1.8[Y]	...	*29.6*[Y]	...	...	Ghana
...	...	...	...	...	...	...	...	...	...	...	...	Guinea
...	...	...	...	...	...	...	...	...	...	...	...	Guinea-Bissau
...	21.2[Z]	...	22.8[Z]	...	*266*[Z]	...	1.5[Z]	...	*21.9*[Z]	...	...	Kenya
16.0	18.0[Z]	24.4	18.5[Z]	730	654[Z]	1.9	1.9[Z]	46.8	39.0[Z]	84.5	...	Lesotho
...	...	...	...	...	...	...	...	...	...	...	...	Liberia
...	8.1	...	16.7	...	*109*	...	0.5	...	*12.1*	...	62.7	Madagascar
...	...	...	...	...	...	...	...	...	...	...	...	Malawi
13.5	16.0[Z]	*33.7*	27.4[Z]	*355*	246[Z]	*0.9*	1.0[Z]	*41.0*	24.7[Z]	...	...	Mali
11.0	9.6[Z]	36.7	42.6[Z]	1 275	*1 462*[Z]	1.4	1.5[Z]	16.2	*14.1*[Z]	...	...	Mauritius
...	12.0[Z]	...	28.5[Z]	...	458[Z]	...	1.2[Z]	...	69.0[Z]	...	92.5[X]	Mozambique
20.6	15.1[Y]	27.7	...	1 413	...	2.1	...	33.6	...	...	...	Namibia
...	20.7[Z]	...	25.3[Z]	...	267[Z]	...	0.7[Z]	...	42.4[Z]	...	...	Niger
...	...	...	...	...	...	...	...	...	...	...	...	Nigeria
...	9.5	...	19.8	...	282	...	0.9	...	33.4	...	...	Rwanda
...	...	...	...	...	...	...	...	...	...	...	...	Sao Tome and Principe
...	16.4[Y]	...	25.5[Y]	...	506[Y]	...	1.1[Y]	...	32.3[Y]	...	...	Senegal
...	*15.1*[X]	...	*30.0*[X]	...	*2 463*[X]	...	*1.6*[X]	...	*17.8*[X]	...	68.2[Z]	Seychelles
...	...	...	...	...	...	...	...	...	...	...	...	Sierra Leone
...	...	...	...	...	...	...	...	...	...	...	...	Somalia
14.3*	14.3	33.7	32.8	1 543*	*1 476*	2.0	1.7	20.2*	*17.2*	...	82.4	South Africa
8.9	*12.7*[X]	26.9	*28.0*[X]	1 266	*1 141*[X]	1.5	*1.8*[X]	25.1	*31.6*[X]	...	...	Swaziland
8.4	9.9	33.6	**33.7**	259	151	1.4	1.2	31.4	19.5	79.4	96.6	Togo
...	**8.7**	...	*19.9*[X]	...	*227*[X]	...	**0.8**	...	***24.3***	...	...	Uganda
...	...	...	...	...	...	...	...	...	...	...	...	United Republic of Tanzania
...	5.7[Y]	...	14.6[Y]	...	*98*[Y]	...	0.3[Y]	...	*8.7*[Y]	...	92.8[X]	Zambia
...	...	...	...	...	...	...	...	...	...	...	...	Zimbabwe
...	13.7	...	36.3	...	...	...	1.6	...	19.5	...	...	World[1]
...	...	...	...	...	...	...	...	...	...	...	...	Countries in transition
...	17.8	...	41.3	...	6 758	...	2.1	...	22.3	...	57.9	Developed countries
...	12.5	...	...	...	...	...	1.3	...	17.3	...	...	Developing countries
...	...	...	...	...	...	...	...	...	...	...	...	Arab States
...	18.4	...	46.9	...	2 894	...	2.0	...	21.4	...	...	Central and Eastern Europe
...	...	...	...	...	...	...	...	...	...	...	...	Central Asia
...	...	...	...	...	...	...	...	...	...	...	...	East Asia and the Pacific
...	...	...	...	...	...	...	...	...	...	...	...	East Asia
...	...	...	...	...	...	...	...	...	...	...	...	Pacific
...	13.0	...	33.2	...	...	...	1.4	...	15.0	...	76.6	Latin America and the Caribbean
...	13.3	...	33.2	...	...	...	1.7	...	19.5	...	84.9	Caribbean
...	11.1	...	32.2	...	865	...	1.2	...	12.8	...	72.9	Latin America
17.3	18.7	42.2	39.9	6 573	8 599	2.1	2.1	24.3	24.5	...	65.6	N. America/W. Europe
...	11.4	...	43.5	...	...	...	1.4	...	13.6	...	...	South and West Asia
...	12.0	...	27.7	...	290	...	1.0	...	24.1	...	...	Sub-Saharan Africa

Table 12

Trends in basic or proxy indicators to measure EFA goals 1, 2, 3, 4 and 5

		GOAL 1			GOAL 2						GOAL 3			
		Early childhood care and education			Universal primary education						Learning needs of all youth and adults			
		GROSS ENROLMENT RATIO (GER) IN PRE-PRIMARY EDUCATION			NET ENROLMENT RATIO (NER) IN PRIMARY EDUCATION						YOUTH LITERACY RATE (15-24)			
		School year ending in			School year ending in									
		1991	1999	2007	1991		1999		2007		1985-1994[1]		2000-2007[1]	
	Country or territory	Total (%)	Total (%)	Total (%)	Total (%)	GPI (F/M)	Total (%)	GPI (F/M)	Total (%)	GPI (F/M)	Total (%)	GPI (F/M)	Total (%)	GPI (F/M)
	Arab States													
1	Algeria	…	3	30	89	0.88	91	0.96	95	0.98	74	0.72*	92	0.96
2	Bahrain	27	36	52[z]	99	1.00	96	1.03	98[y]	1.00[y]	97	0.99*	100	1.00
3	Djibouti	1	0.4	**3**	29	*0.72*	27	0.73	**45**	**0.89**	…	…	…	…
4	Egypt	6	11	17	*86*	*0.84*	*94*	*0.93*	*96*	*0.96*	63	0.76*	85	0.93*
5	Iraq	8	5	*6*[y]	*94*	*0.88*	85	0.85	*89*[y]	*0.86*[y]	…	…	85	0.91*
6	Jordan	21	29	32	…	…	91	1.01	89	1.02	…	…	99	1.00*
7	Kuwait	33	78	77	*49*	*0.93*	87	1.01	88	0.97	87	0.93*	98	1.00*
8	Lebanon	…	61	**67**	*66*	*0.97*	*86*	*0.96*	**83**	**0.99**	…	…	99	1.01*
9	Libyan Arab Jamahiriya	…	5	9[z]	…	…	…	…	…	…	95	0.92	99	0.98
10	Mauritania	…	…	*2*[y]	*36*	*0.78*	64	0.99	80	1.06	…	…	66	0.89
11	Morocco	58	62	60	56	0.70	70	0.85	89	0.95	58	0.64*	75	0.79
12	Oman	3	6	31	69	0.95	81	1.00	73	1.02	…	…	98	0.99
13	Palestinian A. T.	21	39	30	…	…	97	1.00	73	1.00	…	…	99	1.00*
14	Qatar	28	25	47	89	0.98	92	1.01	93	1.00	90	1.03*	99	1.00*
15	Saudi Arabia	7	…	11	59	0.80	…	…	85*	0.99*	88	0.86*	97	0.98
16	Sudan[2]	18	19	23	…	…	…	…	…	…	…	…	77	0.84*
17	Syrian Arab Republic	6	8	10	91	0.91	*92*	*0.93*	…	…	…	…	94	0.96
18	Tunisia	*8*	14	…	93	0.93	93	0.98	95	1.01	…	…	96	0.97
19	United Arab Emirates	56	64	85	99	0.98	79	0.99	91	0.99	82	1.04*	95	1.04*
20	Yemen	1	0.7	1[y]	…	…	56	0.59	75[y]	0.76[y]	60	0.43*	80	0.71
	Central and Eastern Europe													
21	Albania	59	40	…	…	…	*94*	*0.98*	…	…	…	…	99	1.00
22	Belarus	84	75	103	*85*	*0.96*	…	…	90	…	100	1.00*	100	1.00
23	Bosnia and Herzegovina	…	…	10	79	1.00	…	…	…	…	…	…	100	1.00*
24	Bulgaria	91	67	81	…	…	97	0.98	95	0.99	…	…	97	1.00
25	Croatia	28	40	52	…	…	85	0.98	90	0.99	100	1.00*	100	1.00
26	Czech Republic	95	90	115	*87*	*1.00*	*97*	*1.00*	*93*[y]	*1.03*[y]	…	…	…	…
27	Estonia	76	87	95	*100*	*0.99*	*96*	*0.98*	95	1.00	100	1.00*	100	1.00
28	Hungary	113	78	88	…	…	88	0.99	87	0.98	…	…	…	…
29	Latvia	47	53	89[z]	*94*	*0.99*	*97*	*0.98*	*90*[y]	*1.03*[y]	100	1.00*	100	1.00
30	Lithuania	58	50	69	…	…	95	0.99	90	0.99	100	1.00*	100	1.00
31	Montenegro	…	…	…	…	…	…	…	…	…	…	…	…	…
32	Poland	47	50	60	…	…	96	1.00	96	1.01	…	…	…	…
33	Republic of Moldova[3,4]	70	48	70	*86*	*1.01*	*93*	…	88	0.99	100	1.00*	100	1.00
34	Romania	76	62	72	*81*	*1.00*	96	0.99	94	1.00	99	1.00*	97	1.00
35	Russian Federation[5]	74	68	88	*98*	*1.00*	…	…	…	…	100	1.00*	100	1.00
36	Serbia[3]	…	*54*	59	…	…	…	…	95	1.00	…	…	…	…
37	Slovakia	86	82	94	…	…	…	…	*92*[y]	*1.01*[y]	…	…	…	…
38	Slovenia	66	75	81	*96*	*1.01*	96	0.99	96	1.00	100	1.00*	100	1.00
39	TFYR Macedonia	…	27	40	…	…	93	0.98	89	1.00	99	0.99*	99	1.00
40	Turkey	4	6	16	89	*0.92*	…	…	92	0.97	93	0.92*	96	0.96*
41	Ukraine	86	50	94	*81*	*1.00*	…	…	89	1.00*	…	…	100	1.00
	Central Asia													
42	Armenia	37	26	37	…	…	…	…	85	1.04	100	1.00*	100	1.00
43	Azerbaijan[3,6]	19	18	30	89	0.99	89	1.01	95	0.99	…	…	100	1.00*
44	Georgia	59	36	57	*97*	*1.00*	…	…	94	0.97	…	…	…	…
45	Kazakhstan	73	14	**39**	*88*	*0.99*	…	…	**90**	**1.00**	100	1.00*	100	1.00
46	Kyrgyzstan	34	10	16	*92*	*1.00*	88*	0.99*	84	0.99	…	…	100	1.00
47	Mongolia	39	25	54	*90*	*1.02*	89	1.04	89	1.01	…	…	95	1.04
48	Tajikistan	16	8	9	*77*	*0.98*	…	…	97	0.96	100	1.00*	100	1.00
49	Turkmenistan	…	…	…	…	…	…	…	…	…	…	…	100	1.00
50	Uzbekistan	73	24	27	*78*	*0.99*	…	…	91	0.97	…	…	99	1.00*
	East Asia and the Pacific													
51	Australia	71	…	104[z]	99	1.00	94	1.01	97	1.01	…	…	…	…
52	Brunei Darussalam	48	50	50	92	0.98	…	…	93	1.00	98	1.00*	100	1.00
53	Cambodia	4	*5*	11	*72*	*0.84*	*83*	*0.91*	89	0.96	…	…	86	0.92
54	China[7]	22	38	42	98	0.96	…	…	…	…	94	0.94*	99	1.00

GOAL 4				GOAL 5																
Improving levels of adult literacy				Gender parity in primary education						Gender parity in secondary education										
ADULT LITERACY RATE (15 and over)				GROSS ENROLMENT RATIO (GER)						GROSS ENROLMENT RATIO (GER)										
				School year ending in						School year ending in										
1985-1994[1]		2000-2007[1]		1991		1999		2007		1991		1999		2007						
Total (%)	GPI (F/M)	Total (%)	GPI (F/M)	Total (%)	GPI (F/M)	Total (%)	GPI (F/M)	Total (%)	GPI (F/M)	Total (%)	GPI (F/M)	Total (%)	GPI (F/M)	Total (%)	GPI (F/M)					
Arab States																				
50	0.57*	75	0.79	96	0.85	105	0.91	110	0.94	60	0.80	…	…	*83[y]*	*1.08[y]*	1				
84	0.87*	89	0.96	110	1.00	107	1.01	120[z]	1.00[z]	100	1.04	94.5	1.08	102[z]	1.04[z]	2				
…	…	…	…	34	0.72	33	0.71	**56**	**0.88**	11	*0.66*	14.0	0.72	**29**	**0.70**	3				
44	0.55*	66	0.77*	94	0.83	*102*	*0.91*	105	0.95	71	0.79	*82.5*	*0.92*	…	…	4				
…	…	74	0.76*	108	0.83	92	0.82	*99[y]*	*0.83[y]*	*44*	*0.63*	33.6	0.63	*45[y]*	*0.66[y]*	5				
…	…	91	0.91*	107	0.99	98	1.00	96	1.02	82	1.04	88.8	1.02	89	1.03	6				
74	0.88*	94	0.98*	60	0.95	100	1.01	98	0.98	*43*	*0.98*	*98.4*	*1.02*	91	1.02	7				
…	…	90	0.92*	*97*	*0.97*	105	0.95	**95**	**0.97**	…	…	73.5	1.09	**80**	**1.10**	8				
76	0.71	87	0.83	…	…	120	0.98	110[z]	0.95[z]	…	…	…	…	94[z]	1.17[z]	9				
…	…	56	0.76	52	0.77	89	0.99	103	1.06	14	0.49	*19.0*	*0.77*	*25*	*0.89*	10				
42	0.52*	56	0.63	64	0.69	86	0.81	107	0.90	36	0.72	36.7	0.79	56	*0.86*	11				
…	…	84	0.87	85	0.92	91	0.97	80	1.01	45	0.81	75.2	1.00	90	0.96	12				
…	…	94	0.93*	…	…	105	1.01	80	1.00	…	…	80.3	1.04	92	1.06	13				
76	0.94*	93	0.96*	101	0.93	102	0.96	109	0.99	84	1.06	87.5	1.11	103	0.98	14				
71	0.72*	85	0.89	73	0.85	…	…	98	0.96*	44	0.80	…	…	94	…	15				
…	…	61	0.73*	49	0.77	*49*	*0.85*	66	0.86	21	0.79	*26.0*	…	33	0.93	16				
…	…	83	0.85	101	0.90	102	0.92	126	0.96	48	0.73	40.3	0.91	72	0.97	17				
…	…	78	0.80	113	0.90	113	0.95	105	0.97	45	0.79	72.4	1.02	88	…	18				
71	0.95*	90	1.02*	114	0.97	90	0.97	107	0.99	68	1.16	76.1	1.06	*92*	*1.03*	19				
37	0.30*	59	0.53	…	…	71	0.56	87[y]	0.74[y]	…	…	40.6	0.37	46[y]	0.49[y]	20				
Central and Eastern Europe																				
…	…	99	0.99	102	1.01	103	0.98	…	…	88	0.93	71.4	0.98	…	…	21				
98	0.97*	100	1.00	95	*0.96*	111	0.99	97	0.99	93	…	85.0	1.05	95	1.02	22				
…	…	97	0.95*	…	…	…	…	98	0.93	…	…	…	…	85	1.03	23				
…	…	98	0.99	94	0.98	106	0.98	101	0.99	86	1.00	90.9	0.98	106	0.96	24				
97	0.96*	99	0.99	…	…	92	0.98	99	1.00	…	…	84.5	1.02	92	1.03	25				
…	…	…	…	97	1.00	103	0.99	101	0.99	91	0.97	82.7	1.04	96	1.01	26				
100	1.00*	100	1.00	112	0.97	102	0.97	99	0.99	100	*1.09*	92.9	1.04	100	1.02	27				
…	…	…	…	95	0.99	102	0.98	96	0.98	86	1.00	93.7	1.02	96	1.00	28				
99	0.99*	100	1.00	98	1.00	100	0.98	95[z]	0.96[z]	92	1.02	88.1	1.04	99[z]	1.00[z]	29				
98	0.99*	100	1.00	92	*0.95*	102	0.98	95	0.99	92	…	95.3	1.01	98	1.00	30				
…	…	…	…	…	…	…	…	…	…	…	…	…	…	…	…	31				
…	…	…	…	98	0.98	98	0.98	97	1.00	87	1.02	99.5	0.99	100	0.99	32				
96	0.96*	99	0.99	90	1.02	100	1.00	94	0.98	78	1.10	82.9	0.98	89	1.03	33				
97	0.96*	98	0.99	91	1.00	105	0.98	105	0.99	92	0.99	79.2	1.01	87	0.99	34				
98	0.97*	100	1.00	108	1.00	108	0.98	96	1.00	93	*1.06*	…	…	84	0.98	35				
…	…	…	…	…	…	*112*	*0.99*	97	1.00	…	…	*93.1*	*1.01*	88	1.03	36				
…	…	…	…	…	…	103	0.99	102	0.99	…	…	85.3	1.02	94	1.01	37				
100	1.00*	100	1.00	100	…	100	0.99	104	0.99	89	…	99.7	1.03	94	0.99	38				
94	0.94*	97	0.97	…	…	101	0.98	95	1.00	…	…	82.3	0.97	84	0.97	39				
79	0.76*	89	0.84*	99	0.92	…	…	*96*	*0.95*	48	0.63	…	…	*80*	*0.82*	40				
…	…	100	1.00	89	1.00	109	0.99	100	1.00*	94	…	98.2	1.03*	94	1.00*	41				
Central Asia																				
99	0.99*	99	1.00	…	…	100	…	110	1.03	…	…	91.2	…	89	1.05	42				
…	…	100	0.99*	*111*	*0.99*	98	1.00	116	0.99	88	1.01	78.5	0.99	89	0.96	43				
…	…	…	…	97	1.00	98	1.00	99	0.97	95	0.97	79.1	0.98	90	*1.00*	44				
98	0.97*	100	1.00	89	*0.99*	97	1.01	**109**	**1.00**	100	*1.03*	92.0	1.00	**92**	**0.98**	45				
…	…	99	1.00	…	…	98	0.99	95	0.99	100	1.02	83.4	1.02	86	1.01	46				
…	…	97	1.01	97	1.02	97	1.04	100	1.02	82	1.14	58.3	1.27	92	1.11	47				
98	0.98*	100	1.00	91	0.98	98	0.95	100	0.96	102	…	74.1	0.86	84	0.84	48				
…	…	100	1.00	…	…	…	…	…	…	…	…	…	…	…	…	49				
…	…	97	0.98*	81	0.98	98	1.00	95	0.97	99	*0.91*	86.5	0.98	102	0.98	50				
East Asia and the Pacific																				
…	…	…	…	108	0.99	100	1.00	107	1.00	83	1.03	157.5	1.00	149	0.96	51				
88	0.89*	95	0.97	114	0.94	114	0.97	106	0.99	77	1.09	85.0	1.09	97	1.04	52				
…	…	76	0.79	90	*0.81*	97	0.87	119	0.93	25	*0.43*	*17.1*	*0.53*	40	0.82	53				
78	0.78*	93	0.93	126	0.93	…	…	112	0.99	40	0.75	61.9	…	77	1.01	54				

Table 12 (continued)

	Country or territory	GOAL 1 Early childhood care and education GROSS ENROLMENT RATIO (GER) IN PRE-PRIMARY EDUCATION			GOAL 2 Universal primary education NET ENROLMENT RATIO (NER) IN PRIMARY EDUCATION						GOAL 3 Learning needs of all youth and adults YOUTH LITERACY RATE (15-24)			
		School year ending in			School year ending in									
		1991	1999	2007	1991		1999		2007		1985-1994[1]		2000-2007[1]	
		Total (%)	Total (%)	Total (%)	Total (%)	GPI (F/M)	Total (%)	GPI (F/M)	Total (%)	GPI (F/M)	Total (%)	GPI (F/M)	Total (%)	GPI (F/M)
55	Cook Islands[3]	…	86	*94*	…	…	85	0.96	*67*	*0.96*	…	…	…	…
56	DPR Korea	…	…	…	…	…	…	…	…	…	…	…	…	…
57	Fiji	14	16	16[z]	…	…	99	1.01	91[z]	1.00[z]	…	…	…	…
58	Indonesia	18	*23*	44	96	0.96	…	…	95	0.96	96	0.98*	97	0.99*
59	Japan	48	83	86	100	1.00	100	…	100	…	…	…	…	…
60	Kiribati[3]	…	…	…	…	…	*97*	*1.01*	…	…	…	…	…	…
61	Lao PDR	7	8	13	*62*	*0.86*	76	0.92	86	0.95	…	…	84	0.88*
62	Macao, China	89	87	85	*81*	*0.98*	85	1.01	93	0.97	…	…	100	1.00*
63	Malaysia	37	54	57[z]	93	0.99	98	0.98	97[z]	1.00[z]	96	0.99*	98	1.00
64	Marshall Islands[3]	…	*59*	45	…	…	…	…	66	0.99	…	…	…	…
65	Micronesia, F. S.	…	37	…	98	1.04	…	…	…	…	…	…	…	…
66	Myanmar[8]	…	…	…	*99*	…	…	…	…	…	…	…	95	0.98*
67	Nauru	…	…	*89*	…	…	…	…	*72*	*1.01*	…	…	…	…
68	New Zealand	76	85	93	98	1.00	99	1.00	99	1.01	…	…	…	…
69	Niue[3]	…	154	119[y]	…	…	99	1.00	…	…	…	…	…	…
70	Palau[3]	…	63	*64*[y]	…	…	*97*	*0.94*	…	…	…	…	…	…
71	Papua New Guinea	0	…	…	66	0.86	…	…	…	…	…	…	64	1.04
72	Philippines	12	30	46	*96*	*0.99*	92	1.00	91	1.02	97	1.01*	94	1.02
73	Republic of Korea	55	78	106	100	1.01	97	0.95	98[z]	…	…	…	…	…
74	Samoa	…	*53*	48	…	…	92	0.99	…	…	99	1.00*	99	1.00
75	Singapore[8]	…	…	…	…	…	…	…	…	…	99	1.00*	100	1.00
76	Solomon Islands	36	*35*	…	84	0.86	…	…	62[y]	0.99[y]	…	…	…	…
77	Thailand	49	97	**95**	*88*	*0.99*	…	…	**95**	**1.01**	…	…	98	1.00
78	Timor-Leste	…	…	10[y]	…	…	…	…	63	0.96	…	…	…	…
79	Tokelau	…	…	…	…	…	…	…	…	…	…	…	…	…
80	Tonga	…	30	*23*[y]	97	0.97	88	0.96	96[y]	0.97[y]	…	…	100	1.00
81	Tuvalu[3]	…	…	107[z]	…	…	…	…	…	…	…	…	…	…
82	Vanuatu	…	…	7[z]	71	1.01	91	0.99	87	0.99	…	…	…	…
83	Viet Nam[8]	28	39	…	*90*	*0.92*	95	…	…	…	94	0.99*	94	0.99*
	Latin America and the Caribbean													
84	Anguilla[9]	…	…	…	…	…	…	…	…	…	…	…	…	…
85	Antigua and Barbuda[3]	…	…	72	…	…	…	…	74	0.98	…	…	…	…
86	Argentina	50	57	67[z]	94	1.00*	99	0.99	98[z]	…	98	1.00*	99	1.00
87	Aruba	…	99	96	…	…	98	1.03	100	1.00	…	…	99	1.00
88	Bahamas	…	12	…	*90*	*1.03*	89	0.99	91	1.03	…	…	…	…
89	Barbados	…	74	91	*79*	*0.98*	*94*	*0.99*	97	1.01	…	…	…	…
90	Belize	23	27	35	…	…	*94*	*0.99*	97	1.01	76	1.01*	…	…
91	Bermuda[3]	…	…	…	…	…	…	…	*92*[z]	…	…	…	…	…
92	Bolivia	32	45	49	…	…	95	1.00	94	1.01	94	0.95*	99	0.99*
93	Brazil[10]	48	58	61	…	…	91	…	93	1.00	…	…	98	1.02*
94	British Virgin Islands[3]	…	62	93[z]	…	…	*96*	*1.02*	*93*	*1.01*	…	…	…	…
95	Cayman Islands[9]	…	…	…	…	…	…	…	…	…	…	…	99	0.99*
96	Chile	72	77	56	89	0.98	…	…	94	0.99	98	1.01*	99	1.00
97	Colombia	13	37	41	68	1.15	89	*1.01*	87	1.00	91	1.03*	98	1.01*
98	Costa Rica	65	84	61	87	1.01	…	…	…	…	…	…	98	1.01
99	Cuba	102	109	111	94	1.00	97	1.01	98	1.00	…	…	100	1.00
100	Dominica[3,9]	…	80	…	…	…	*94*	*0.98*	77[z]	1.06[z]	…	…	…	…
101	Dominican Republic	…	32	32	…	…	84	1.01	82	1.01	…	…	96	1.02
102	Ecuador	42	64	100	*98*	*1.01*	97	1.01	97	1.01	96	0.99*	95	1.00*
103	El Salvador	21	43	49	…	…	…	…	92	1.01	85	1.00*	94	1.01*
104	Grenada[3]	…	93	80	100	1.00	…	…	76	0.97	…	…	…	…
105	Guatemala	25	46	29	64	0.91*	82	0.91	95	0.96	76	0.87*	85	0.94
106	Guyana	74	124	87	89	1.00	…	…	…	…	…	…	…	…
107	Haiti	33	…	…	21	1.05	…	…	…	…	…	…	…	…
108	Honduras	13	…	38	*88*	*1.01*	…	…	93	1.01	…	…	94	1.03*
109	Jamaica	78	78	87	96	1.00	*88*	*1.00*	86	1.02	…	…	94	1.08
110	Mexico	63	74	114	98	*0.97*	97	1.00	98	…	95	0.99*	98	1.00*
111	Montserrat[3]	…	…	91	…	…	…	…	92	1.08	…	…	…	…
112	Netherlands Antilles	…	111	…	…	…	…	…	…	…	97	1.01*	98	1.00
113	Nicaragua	13	27	54	70	1.03	76	1.01	96	1.01	…	…	87	1.04*
114	Panama	57	39	70	92	1.00	96	0.99	98	0.99	95	0.99*	96	1.00
115	Paraguay	31	29	34[y]	94	0.99	96	1.00	94[y]	1.01[y]	96	0.99*	99	1.00*

GOAL 4				GOAL 5												
Improving levels of adult literacy				Gender parity in primary education						Gender parity in secondary education						
ADULT LITERACY RATE (15 and over)				GROSS ENROLMENT RATIO (GER)						GROSS ENROLMENT RATIO (GER)						
				School year ending in						School year ending in						
1985-1994[1]		2000-2007[1]		1991		1999		2007		1991		1999		2007		
Total (%)	GPI (F/M)	Total (%)	GPI (F/M)	Total (%)	GPI (F/M)	Total (%)	GPI (F/M)	Total (%)	GPI (F/M)	Total (%)	GPI (F/M)	Total (%)	GPI (F/M)	Total (%)	GPI (F/M)	
…	…	…	…	…	…	96	0.95	*73*	*0.97*	…	…	60.3	1.08	*73*	*1.08*	55
…	…	…	…	…	…	…	…	…	…	…	…	…	…	…	…	56
…	…	…	…	133	1.00	109	0.99	94	0.97	56	0.95	80.1	1.11	82	1.12	57
82	0.86*	92	0.93*	114	0.98	…	…	117	0.96	45	0.83	…	…	73	1.01	58
…	…	…	…	100	1.00	101	1.00	100	1.00	97	1.02	101.8	1.01	101	1.00	59
…	…	…	…	…	…	104	1.01	113[Y]	1.01[Y]	…	…	84.2	1.18	88[Y]	1.14[Y]	60
…	…	73	0.77*	103	0.79	111	0.85	118	0.90	23*	0.62*	33.0	0.69	44	0.79	61
…	…	93	0.94*	99	0.96	100	0.96	108	0.92	65*	1.11*	75.7	1.08	99	1.00	62
83	0.87*	92	0.95	93	0.99	98	0.98	98[Z]	0.99[Z]	57	1.05	65.5	1.07	69[Y]	1.10[Y]	63
…	…	…	…	…	…	*101*	*0.98*	93	0.97	…	…	*72.2*	*1.06*	66	1.02	64
…	…	…	…	…	…	…	…	110	1.01	…	…	…	…	*91*	…	65
…	…	90	0.92*	114	0.97	…	…	…	…	23	0.99	…	…	…	…	66
…	…	…	…	…	…	…	…	*79*	*1.03*	…	…	…	…	*46*	*1.19*	67
…	…	…	…	102	0.99	100	1.00	102	1.01	90	1.02	112.7	1.05	121	1.03	68
…	…	…	…	…	…	99	1.00	105[Y]	0.95[Y]	…	…	98.2	1.10	99[Y]	1.07[Y]	69
…	…	…	…	…	…	114	0.93	99	*1.02*	…	…	101.2	1.07	97	*0.97*	70
…	…	58	0.86	65	0.85	…	…	55[Z]	0.84[Z]	12	0.62	…	…	…	…	71
94	0.99*	93	1.01	109	0.99	113	1.00	109	0.98	71	*1.04*	75.7	1.09	83	1.10	72
…	…	…	…	105	1.01	98	0.95	107	0.98	90	0.97	97.6	1.01	98	0.93	73
98	0.99*	99	0.99	124	1.02	99	0.98	95	1.00	33	1.96	79.5	1.10	*81*[Y]	*1.13*[Y]	74
89	0.87*	94	0.94	…	…	…	…	…	…	…	…	…	…	…	…	75
…	…	…	…	88	0.87	88	0.94	101[Y]	0.96[Y]	15	0.61	25.1	0.76	30[Y]	0.84[Y]	76
…	…	94	0.97	113	0.98	106	0.99	**104**	**1.00**	33	0.96	…	…	**83**	**1.10**	77
…	…	…	…	…	…	…	…	91	0.94	…	…	…	…	53[Y]	1.00[Y]	78
…	…	…	…	…	…	…	…	…	…	…	…	…	…	…	…	79
…	…	99	1.00	112	0.98	108	0.96	113[Z]	0.95[Z]	98	1.04	102.1	1.11	94[Z]	1.04[Z]	80
…	…	…	…	…	…	98	1.02	106[Z]	0.99[Z]	…	…	…	…	…	…	81
…	…	…	…	95	0.96	111	0.98	108	0.97	18	0.80	30.2	0.87	…	…	82
88	0.89*	90	0.93*	107	*0.93*	108	0.93	…	…	*32*	…	61.5	0.90	…	…	83
Latin America and the Caribbean																
…	…	…	…	…	…	…	…	…	…	…	…	…	…	…	…	84
…	…	99	1.01*	…	…	…	…	102	0.94	…	…	…	…	105	0.96	85
96	1.00	98	1.00	108	…	113	0.99	114[Z]	0.98[Z]	72	…	84.3	1.05	84[Z]	1.12[Z]	86
…	…	98	1.00	…	…	114	0.99	114	0.97	…	…	99.3	1.07	105	1.06	87
…	…	…	…	96	*1.03*	95	0.98	103	1.00	…	…	78.6	0.99	94	1.03	88
…	…	…	…	*92*	*1.00*	98	0.98	105	1.00	…	…	100.3	1.05	103	1.03	89
70	1.00*	…	…	113	0.96	118	0.97	123	0.99	66	1.09	64.3	1.08	79	1.07	90
…	…	…	…	…	…	…	…	100[Z]	0.85[Z]	…	…	…	…	84[Z]	1.06[Z]	91
80	0.82*	91	0.90*	…	…	113	0.98	108	1.00	…	…	77.5	0.93	82	0.97	92
…	…	90	1.01*	131	…	154	0.94	130	0.93	58	…	99.1	1.11	100	1.11	93
…	…	…	…	…	…	112	0.97	*108*	*0.96*	…	…	98.8	0.91	*101*	*1.11*	94
…	…	99	1.00*	…	…	…	…	…	…	…	…	…	…	…	…	95
94	0.99*	97	1.00	101	0.98	101	0.97	106	0.95	73	1.07	79.5	1.04	91	1.03	96
81	1.00*	93	1.00*	103	1.02	114	1.00	116	0.99	50	1.19	70.3	1.11	85	1.11	97
…	…	96	1.00	103	0.99	108	0.98	110	0.99	45	1.06	57.1	1.09	87	1.05	98
…	…	100	1.00	100	0.97	111	0.97	102	0.98	94	1.15	77.3	1.07	93	1.00	99
…	…	…	…	…	…	104	0.95	…	…	…	…	90.0	1.35	…	…	100
…	…	89	1.01	…	…	113	0.98	107	0.94	…	…	57.1	1.24	79	1.20	101
88	0.95*	84	0.94*	116	*0.99*	114	1.00	118	1.00	55*	…	56.5	1.03	70	1.01	102
74	0.92*	82	0.94*	97	0.99	112	0.96	118	1.00	36	1.13	51.5	0.98	64	1.04	103
…	…	…	…	117	*0.85*	…	…	81	0.96	100	1.16	…	…	99	0.99	104
64	0.80*	73	0.86	81	0.87	101	0.87	113	0.94	23	…	33.4	0.84	56	0.92	105
…	…	…	…	94	0.99	121	0.98	112	0.98	79	1.06	82.5	1.02	107	0.93	106
…	…	…	…	46	0.95	…	…	…	…	21*	0.94*	…	…	…	…	107
…	…	84	1.00*	107	1.04	…	…	119	1.00	33	1.23	…	…	64	1.25	108
…	…	86	1.13	*101*	*0.99*	*92*	*1.00*	91	1.01	65	*1.06*	*87.7*	*1.02*	90	1.05	109
88	0.94*	93	0.97*	112	0.97	111	0.98	114	0.97	53	0.99	69.7	1.01	89	1.03	110
…	…	…	…	…	…	…	…	107	1.12	…	…	…	…	102	1.02	111
95	1.00*	96	1.00	…	…	131	0.95	…	…	93	1.19	92.0	1.16	…	…	112
…	…	78	1.00*	91	1.06	100	1.01	116	0.98	42	*1.20*	*51.7*	*1.19*	69	1.13	113
89	0.99*	93	0.99	105	…	108	0.97	113	0.97	62	…	66.8	1.07	70	1.08	114
90	0.96*	95	0.98*	106	0.97	*119*	*0.96*	111[Y]	0.97[Y]	31	1.05	57.8	1.04	66[Y]	1.03[Y]	115

Table 12 (continued)

	Country or territory	GOAL 1: Early childhood care and education — GROSS ENROLMENT RATIO (GER) IN PRE-PRIMARY EDUCATION — School year ending in 1991 Total (%)	1999 Total (%)	2007 Total (%)	GOAL 2: Universal primary education — NET ENROLMENT RATIO (NER) IN PRIMARY EDUCATION — School year ending in 1991 Total (%)	1991 GPI (F/M)	1999 Total (%)	1999 GPI (F/M)	2007 Total (%)	2007 GPI (F/M)	GOAL 3: Learning needs of all youth and adults — YOUTH LITERACY RATE (15-24) — 1985-1994[1] Total (%)	1985-1994[1] GPI (F/M)	2000-2007[1] Total (%)	2000-2007[1] GPI (F/M)
116	Peru	30	55	72	88	0.99	98	1.00	96	1.02	95	0.97*	97	0.99*
117	Saint Kitts and Nevis	…	…	120	99*	0.99*	…	…	87	1.02	…	…	…	…
118	Saint Lucia	51	70	68	95	0.97	96	0.99	98	0.99	…	…	…	…
119	Saint Vincent/Grenadines	45	…	88[y]	91	0.99	…	…	91	0.94	…	…	…	…
120	Suriname	79	…	85	81	1.06	…	…	94	1.02	…	…	95	0.99
121	Trinidad and Tobago	8	58	81*	89	1.00	87	1.01	94	0.99	99	1.00*	100	1.00
122	Turks and Caicos Islands	…	…	118[y]	…	…	…	…	78[y]	1.07[y]	…	…	…	…
123	Uruguay	43	60	80	91	1.01	…	…	97	1.00	99	1.01*	99	1.01*
124	Venezuela, B. R.	40	45	62	…	…	86	1.01	92	1.00	95	1.02*	98	1.01*
	North America and Western Europe													
125	Andorra[3]	…	…	101	…	…	…	…	81	0.99	…	…	…	…
126	Austria	69	82	92	88	1.02	97	1.01	97[z]	1.01[z]	…	…	…	…
127	Belgium	105	111	122	96	1.02	99	1.00	98	1.01	…	…	…	…
128	Canada	61	64	70[z]	98	1.00	99	1.00	…	…	…	…	…	…
129	Cyprus[3]	48	60	80	87	1.00	95	1.00	99	1.00	100	1.00*	100	1.00
130	Denmark	99	90	96	98	1.00	97	1.00	96	1.01	…	…	…	…
131	Finland	34	48	64	98	1.00	99	1.00	96	1.00	…	…	…	…
132	France[11]	83	112	113	100	1.00	99	1.00	99	1.00	…	…	…	…
133	Germany	…	94	107	84	1.03	100	…	98	1.00	…	…	…	…
134	Greece	57	68	69	95	0.99	92	1.01	100	1.00	99	1.00*	99	1.00
135	Iceland	…	88	97	100	0.99	99	0.98	97	1.00	…	…	…	…
136	Ireland	101	…	…	90	1.02	94	1.01	96	1.01	…	…	…	…
137	Israel	85	105	98	…	…	98	1.00	97	1.01	…	…	…	…
138	Italy	94	95	103	100	1.00	99	0.99	99	0.99	…	…	100	1.00
139	Luxembourg	92	73	87	…	…	97	1.03	97	1.01	…	…	…	…
140	Malta	103	103	97[y]	97	0.99	95	1.02	91[y]	0.99[y]	98	1.02*	98	1.02*
141	Monaco[9]	…	…	…	…	…	…	…	…	…	…	…	…	…
142	Netherlands	99	97	102	95	1.04	99	0.99	98	0.99	…	…	…	…
143	Norway	88	75	92	100	1.00	100	1.00	99	1.00	…	…	…	…
144	Portugal	51	69	79	98	1.00	…	…	99	0.99	99	1.00*	100	1.00
145	San Marino[9]	…	…	…	…	…	…	…	…	…	…	…	…	…
146	Spain	58	100	122	100	1.00	100	1.00	100	1.00	100	1.00*	100	1.00*
147	Sweden	65	76	95[z]	100	1.00	100	…	94	1.00	…	…	…	…
148	Switzerland	60	89	99	84	1.02	94	1.00	89	0.99	…	…	…	…
149	United Kingdom	52	77	73	98	1.00	100	1.00	97	1.01	…	…	…	…
150	United States	63	58	62	97	1.00	94	1.00	92	1.01	…	…	…	…
	South and West Asia													
151	Afghanistan	…	…	…	25	0.55	…	…	…	…	…	…	34	0.36*
152	Bangladesh	…	17	…	76	0.87	…	…	87[z]	1.08[z]	45	0.73*	72	1.03
153	Bhutan	…	1	**1**	55	…	56	0.89	**87**	**1.02**	…	…	74	0.85*
154	India[2]	3	18	40[z]	…	…	…	…	89[z]	0.96[z]	62	0.67*	82	0.89
155	Iran, Islamic Republic of[12]	12	13	54	92	0.92	82	0.97	94[z]	…	87	0.88*	97	0.99*
156	Maldives	…	54	85	87	1.00	98	1.01	96	1.01	98	1.00*	98	1.01
157	Nepal	…	…	**57**	63	0.50	65*	0.79*	**80**	**0.96**	50	0.48*	79	0.86
158	Pakistan	…	…	52[y]	33	…	…	…	66[z]	0.78[z]	…	…	69	0.74*
159	Sri Lanka[2]	…	…	…	84	0.95	…	…	…	…	…	…	97	1.01*
	Sub-Saharan Africa													
160	Angola	47	28	…	50	0.95	…	…	…	…	…	…	72	0.75*
161	Benin	2	4	6[z]	41	0.54	50*	0.68*	80[z]	0.84[z]	40	0.48*	52	0.65
162	Botswana	…	…	15[y]	88	1.08	80	1.04	84[y]	1.03[y]	89	1.07*	94	1.03
163	Burkina Faso	1	2	3	27	0.65	35	0.70	**58**	**0.86**	20	0.53*	39	0.71*
164	Burundi	…	0.8	2	53	0.85	…	…	81	0.98	54	0.81*	73	0.92*
165	Cameroon	12	11	21	69	0.88	…	…	…	…	…	…	…	…
166	Cape Verde	…	…	53	91	0.95	99	0.98	85	0.98	88	0.96*	97	1.01
167	Central African Republic	6	…	3	52	0.66	…	…	**56**	**0.74**	48	0.56*	59	0.67*
168	Chad	…	…	1[y]	34	0.45	51	0.62	…	…	17	…	44	0.66
169	Comoros	…	2	3[y]	57	0.73	49	0.85	…	…	…	…	…	…
170	Congo	3	2	10	82	0.94	…	…	54	0.92	…	…	…	…
171	Côte d'Ivoire	1	2	3	45	0.71	52	0.75	…	…	49	0.63*	61	0.74*
172	Democratic Rep. of the Congo	…	…	3	54	0.78	33	0.95	…	…	…	…	70	0.81*

GOAL 4 Improving levels of adult literacy ADULT LITERACY RATE (15 and over)				GOAL 5 Gender parity in primary education GROSS ENROLMENT RATIO (GER)						Gender parity in secondary education GROSS ENROLMENT RATIO (GER)						
1985-1994[1]		2000-2007[1]		School year ending in 1991		1999		2007		School year ending in 1991		1999		2007		
Total (%)	GPI (F/M)	Total (%)	GPI (F/M)	Total (%)	GPI (F/M)	Total (%)	GPI (F/M)	Total (%)	GPI (F/M)	Total (%)	GPI (F/M)	Total (%)	GPI (F/M)	Total (%)	GPI (F/M)	
87	0.88*	90	0.89*	118	0.97	122	0.99	117	1.01	67	0.94	84.0	0.94	98	1.04	*116*
...	...	...	...	*119*	*1.02*	...	...	*94*	*1.01*	*85*	*1.11*	...	...	*105*	*0.91*	*117*
...	...	...	...	139	*0.94*	109	0.98	109	0.97	53	1.45	70.5	1.29	93	1.13	*118*
...	...	...	...	112	0.98	...	...	102	0.94	58	1.24	...	...	75[y]	1.24[y]	*119*
...	...	90	0.95	104	1.03	...	...	119	0.98	58	1.16	...	...	80	1.39	*120*
97	0.98*	99	0.99	94	1.00	96	1.00	100	0.97	82	1.04	77.5	1.10	*86*	*1.07*	*121*
...	...	...	...	...	...	...	...	*90[y]*	*1.04[y]*	...	...	...	...	*86[y]*	*0.94[y]*	*122*
95	1.01*	98	1.01*	108	0.99	111	0.99	114	0.97	84	...	91.6	1.17	92	0.99	*123*
90	0.98*	95	1.00*	109	0.99	100	0.98	106	0.97	53	1.24	56.2	1.22	79	1.12	*124*
North America and Western Europe																
...	...	...	...	...	...	...	...	88	0.98	...	...	...	...	82	1.08	*125*
...	...	...	...	101	1.00	103	0.99	101	0.99	102	0.93	98.8	0.96	102	0.96	*126*
...	...	...	...	100	1.01	105	0.99	103	1.00	101	1.01	142.8	1.07	110	0.97	*127*
...	...	...	...	104	0.98	99	1.00	99[z]	0.99[z]	101	1.00	...	...	102[z]	0.98[z]	*128*
94	0.93*	98	0.98	90	1.00	97	1.00	102	0.99	72	1.02	93.2	1.03	98	1.02	*129*
...	...	...	...	98	1.00	101	1.00	99	1.00	109	1.01	124.6	1.06	119	1.03	*130*
...	...	...	...	99	0.99	99	1.00	98	1.00	116	1.19	120.8	1.09	111	1.05	*131*
...	...	...	...	108	0.99	107	0.99	110	0.99	98	1.05	110.7	1.00	113	1.01	*132*
...	...	...	...	101	*1.01*	106	0.99	104	1.00	98	*0.97*	98.0	0.98	100	0.98	*133*
93	0.93*	97	0.98	98	0.99	94	1.00	101	1.00	94	0.98	90.4	1.04	102	0.95	*134*
...	...	...	...	101	*0.99*	99	0.98	97	1.00	100	0.96	109.6	1.06	111	1.06	*135*
...	...	...	...	102	1.00	104	0.99	104	1.00	100	1.09	107.4	1.06	113	1.07	*136*
...	...	...	...	97	1.04	112	0.99	111	1.01	92	1.06	90.2	1.00	92	1.00	*137*
...	...	99	1.00	104	1.00	103	0.99	105	0.99	83	1.00	91.7	0.99	101	0.99	*138*
...	...	...	...	91	1.08	101	1.02	102	1.00	*75*	...	97.5	1.04	97	1.04	*139*
88	1.01*	92	1.03*	108	0.96	107	1.01	100[y]	0.98[y]	83	0.94	...	...	99[y]	1.00[y]	*140*
...	...	...	...	...	...	...	...	...	...	...	...	...	...	...	...	*141*
...	...	...	...	102	1.03	108	0.98	107	0.98	120	0.92	123.6	0.96	120	0.98	*142*
...	...	...	...	100	1.00	101	1.00	99	1.00	103	1.03	119.8	1.02	113	0.99	*143*
88	0.92*	95	0.97	119	0.95	123	0.96	115	0.95	66	1.16	106.1	1.08	101	1.07	*144*
...	...	...	...	...	...	...	...	...	...	...	...	...	...	...	...	*145*
96	0.97*	98	0.99*	106	0.99	106	0.99	106	0.99	105	1.07	108.3	1.07	120	1.06	*146*
...	...	...	...	100	1.00	110	1.03	94	1.00	90	1.05	156.6	1.29	104	0.99	*147*
...	...	...	...	90	1.01	102	1.00	97	0.99	99	0.95	93.7	0.92	93	0.96	*148*
...	...	...	...	105	1.01	101	1.00	104	1.01	*87*	*1.04*	101.0	1.00	97	1.02	*149*
...	...	...	...	103	0.98	101	1.03	99	1.00	92	1.01	95.1	...	94	1.01	*150*
South and West Asia																
...	...	28	0.29*	29	0.55	28	0.08	103	0.63	16	0.51	...	...	28	0.38	*151*
35	0.58*	53	0.82	...	...	...	...	91	1.08	...	...	45.1	1.01	43	1.06	*152*
...	...	53	0.59*	...	...	75	0.85	**111**	**1.00**	...	...	37.4	0.81	**56**	**0.93**	*153*
48	0.55*	66	0.71	94	0.77	93	0.84	112[z]	0.96[z]	*42*	*0.60*	44.4	0.71	55[z]	0.83[z]	*154*
66	0.76*	82	0.89*	109	0.90	96	0.95	121	1.29	57	0.75	77.8	0.93	81[y]	0.94[y]	*155*
96	1.00*	97	1.00	...	...	134	1.01	111	0.97	...	...	42.9	1.07	*83[z]*	*1.07[z]*	*156*
33	0.35*	57	0.62	110	0.63	114	0.77	**124**	**1.01**	34	0.46	34.0	0.70	**48**	**0.93**	*157*
...	...	54	0.59*	...	...	...	...	92	0.82	25	0.48	...	...	33	0.76	*158*
...	...	91	0.96*	115	0.96	...	...	108[z]	1.00[z]	71	1.09	...	...	...	...	*159*
Sub-Saharan Africa																
...	...	67	0.65*	80	0.92*	...	...	...	...	11	...	12.8	0.76	...	...	*160*
27	0.42*	41	0.53	54	0.51	74	0.67	96[z]	0.83[z]	*10*	*0.42*	19.1	0.47	*32[y]*	*0.57[y]*	*161*
69	1.09*	83	1.00	107	1.07	104	1.00	107[y]	0.99[y]	48	1.18	74.0	1.07	76[y]	1.05[y]	*162*
14	0.42*	29	0.59*	33	0.64	43	0.70	**71**	**0.87**	7	*0.54*	9.7	0.62	**18**	**0.74**	*163*
37	0.57*	59	0.78*	71	0.84	*60*	*0.80*	114	0.93	5	0.58	...	...	15	0.72	*164*
...	...	68	0.78*	94	0.86	84	0.82	110	0.86	26	0.71	*25.0*	*0.83*	25*	0.79*	*165*
63	0.71*	84	0.88	111	*0.94*	119	0.96	101	0.94	21*	...	...	...	79	1.18	*166*
34	0.42*	49	0.52*	63	0.64	...	...	**74**	**0.71**	11	0.40	...	...	...	...	*167*
12	...	32	0.48	51	0.45	63	0.58	74	0.70	*7*	*0.20*	9.8	0.26	19	0.45	*168*
...	...	...	...	75	0.73	76	0.85	*85[y]*	*0.88[y]*	18*	0.65*	25.0	0.81	*35[y]*	*0.76[y]*	*169*
...	...	...	...	121	0.90	56	0.95	106	0.93	46	*0.72*	...	...	...	...	*170*
34	0.53*	49	0.63*	64	0.71	69	0.74	72	0.79	*21*	*0.48*	*21.6*	*0.54*	...	...	*171*
...	...	67	0.67*	70	0.75	48	0.90	85	0.81	...	...	18.1	0.52	33	0.53	*172*

Table 12 (continued)

	Country or territory	GOAL 1: Early childhood care and education — GROSS ENROLMENT RATIO (GER) IN PRE-PRIMARY EDUCATION, School year ending in 1991: Total (%)	1999: Total (%)	2007: Total (%)	GOAL 2: Universal primary education — NET ENROLMENT RATIO (NER) IN PRIMARY EDUCATION, School year ending in 1991: Total (%)	1991: GPI (F/M)	1999: Total (%)	1999: GPI (F/M)	2007: Total (%)	2007: GPI (F/M)	GOAL 3: Learning needs of all youth and adults — YOUTH LITERACY RATE (15-24), 1985-1994[1]: Total (%)	1985-1994[1]: GPI (F/M)	2000-2007[1]: Total (%)	2000-2007[1]: GPI (F/M)
173	Equatorial Guinea	…	34	66	*96*	*0.97*	89	…	67	0.97	…	…	95	1.00*
174	Eritrea	…	5	14	*15*	*1.00*	33	0.86	41	0.88	…	…	86	0.92
175	Ethiopia	1	1	3	*22*	*0.75*	34	0.69	71	0.92	34	0.71*	50	0.62*
176	Gabon	…	…	…	*94*	*1.00*	…	…	…	…	93	0.98*	97	0.98
177	Gambia	…	18	***22***	*46*	*0.72*	72	0.89	**67**	**1.09**	…	…	…	…
178	Ghana	…	*39*	**68**	*54*	*0.89*	*57*	*0.96*	**73**	**1.01**	…	…	78	0.95
179	Guinea	…	…	10	*27*	*0.52*	45	0.69	74	0.87	…	…	47	0.57*
180	Guinea-Bissau	…	*3*	…	*38*	*0.56*	*45*	*0.71*	…	…	…	…	…	…
181	Kenya	35	44	48	…	…	63	1.01	86	1.00	…	…	80	1.01*
182	Lesotho	…	*21*	18[z]	72	1.24	57	1.12	72[z]	1.04[z]	…	…	…	…
183	Liberia	…	41	**125**	…	…	42	0.77	**31**	**0.93**	51	0.84	72	1.12
184	Madagascar	…	*3*	8	*64*	*1.00*	63	1.01	98	1.01	…	…	70	0.94*
185	Malawi	…	…	…	49	0.93	98	0.98	87	1.07	59	0.70*	83	0.98
186	Mali	…	2	3	*25*	*0.60*	*46*	*0.70*	63	0.80	…	…	39	0.65*
187	Mauritius	…	96	99	91	1.00	91	1.01	95	1.01	91	1.01*	96	1.02
188	Mozambique	…	…	…	42	0.79	52	0.79	76[z]	0.93[z]	…	…	53	0.81
189	Namibia	13	31	32[z]	86	1.08	81	1.07	87	1.06	88	1.06*	93	1.04
190	Niger	1	1	2	24	0.61	26	0.68	45	0.75	…	…	37	0.44*
191	Nigeria[13]	…	…	15[z]	*55*	*0.77*	*58*	*0.82*	*64*[z]	*0.88*[z]	71	0.77*	87	0.96
192	Rwanda	…	…	…	67	0.94	…	…	94	1.03	75	…	78	0.98*
193	Sao Tome and Principe	…	25	**36**	96	0.94	86	0.99	**97**	**0.99**	94	0.96*	95	1.01
194	Senegal	2	3	9	*45*	*0.75*	54	*0.88*	72	1.00	38	0.57*	51	0.77*
195	Seychelles[3]	…	109	109	…	…	…	…	…	…	99	1.01*	99	1.01*
196	Sierra Leone	…	…	5	*43*	*0.73*	…	…	…	…	…	…	54	0.68
197	Somalia	…	…	…	…	…	…	…	…	…	…	…	…	…
198	South Africa	*21*	21	51	90	1.03	94	1.01	*86*	*1.00*	…	…	95	1.02
199	Swaziland	…	…	*17*[y]	*75*	*1.05*	74	1.02	87	1.02	84	1.01*	94	1.05
200	Togo	3	2	4	64	0.71	79	0.79	77	0.88	…	…	74	0.76*
201	Uganda	…	*4*	4	51	0.83	…	…	95	1.03	70	0.82*	86	0.95
202	United Republic of Tanzania	…	…	**35**	51	1.02	50	1.04	98[z]	0.99[z]	82	0.90*	78	0.97
203	Zambia	…	…	…	78	0.96	68	0.96	94	1.01	66	0.97*	75	0.82
204	Zimbabwe	…	*41*	…	84	1.00	83	1.01	88[z]	1.01[z]	95	0.98*	91	0.94
		Weighted average			Weighted average						Weighted average			
I	World	…	33	41	81	0.88	82	0.93	87	0.97	84	0.90	89.3	0.95
II	Countries in transition	…	45	63	89	0.99	88	0.99	91	0.99	100	1.00	99.7	1.00
III	Developed countries	…	73	80	96	1.00	97	1.00	96	1.01	100	1.00	99.7	1.00
IV	Developing countries	…	27	36	78	0.85	80	0.92	86	0.97	80	0.88	87.5	0.94
V	Arab States	…	15	19	75	0.81	78	0.90	84	0.92	76	0.80	86.6	0.91
VI	Central and Eastern Europe	…	50	64	90	0.98	91	0.97	92	0.99	98	0.98	98.8	0.99
VII	Central Asia	…	19	28	84	0.99	88	0.99	92	0.98	100	1.00	99.5	1.00
VIII	East Asia and the Pacific	…	40	47	97	0.97	96	1.00	94	1.00	95	0.96	98.0	1.00
IX	East Asia	…	40	47	97	0.97	96	1.00	94	1.00	95	0.96	98.1	1.00
X	Pacific	…	61	67	91	0.97	90	0.98	84	0.97	92	0.99	90.6	1.01
XI	Latin America/Caribbean	…	56	65	87	0.99	92	0.98	93	1.00	94	1.01	97.1	1.01
XII	Caribbean	…	65	74	51	1.02	75	0.97	72	0.97	78	1.07	86.9	1.09
XIII	Latin America	…	55	65	88	0.99	93	0.98	94	1.00	94	1.01	97.4	1.01
XIV	N. America/W. Europe	…	75	82	96	1.00	97	1.00	95	1.01	100	1.00	99.8	1.00
XV	South and West Asia	…	21	36	70	0.67	74	0.84	86	0.96	61	0.69	80.0	0.89
XVI	Sub-Saharan Africa	…	10	15	53	0.86	56	0.89	73	0.93	64	0.83	72.4	0.88

Source: UNESCO Institute for Statistics database (UIS, 2009).

1. Data are for the most recent year available during the period specified. See the web version of the introduction to the statistical tables for a broader explanation of national literacy definitions, assessment methods, and sources and years of data. For countries indicated with (*), national observed literacy data are used. For all others, UIS literacy estimates are used. The estimates were generated using the UIS Global Age-specific Literacy Projections model. Those in the most recent period refer to 2007 and are based on the most recent observed data available for each country.

2. Literacy data for the most recent year do not include some geographic regions.

3. National population data were used to calculate enrolment ratios.

4. Enrolment and population data used to calculate enrolment rates exclude Transnistria.

5. In the Russian Federation two education structures existed in the past, both starting at age 7. The most common or widespread one lasted three years and was used to calculate indicators; the second one, in which about one-third of primary pupils were enrolled, had four grades. Since 2004, the four-grade structure has been extended all over the country.

6. Enrolment and population data exclude the Nagorno-Karabakh region.

7. Children enter primary school at age 6 or 7. Since 7 is the most common entrance age, enrolment ratios were calculated using the 7-11 age group for both enrolment and population.

GOAL 4: Improving levels of adult literacy — ADULT LITERACY RATE (15 and over)				GOAL 5: Gender parity in primary education — GROSS ENROLMENT RATIO (GER) — School year ending in						GOAL 5: Gender parity in secondary education — GROSS ENROLMENT RATIO (GER) — School year ending in						
1985-1994[1]		2000-2007[1]		1991		1999		2007		1991		1999		2007		
Total (%)	GPI (F/M)	Total (%)	GPI (F/M)	Total (%)	GPI (F/M)	Total (%)	GPI (F/M)	Total (%)	GPI (F/M)	Total (%)	GPI (F/M)	Total (%)	GPI (F/M)	Total (%)	GPI (F/M)	
...	...	87	0.86*	*173*	*0.96*	142	0.79	124	0.95	...	...	33.0	0.37	...	...	*173*
...	...	64	0.70	20	0.95	52	0.82	55	0.83	...	...	21.3	0.69	29	0.70	*174*
27	0.51*	36	0.46	30	0.66	48	0.61	91	0.88	13	0.75	12.2	0.68	30	0.67	*175*
72	0.82*	86	0.91	*155*	*0.98*	148	1.00	...	...	...	...	49.4	0.86	...	...	*176*
...	...	...	...	59	*0.70*	87	0.86	**83**	**1.07**	17	0.50	29.9	0.67	**49**	**0.96**	*177*
...	...	65	0.81	74	0.85	75	0.92	**104**	**0.99**	*34*	*0.65*	37.3	0.80	**53**	**0.89**	*178*
...	...	29	0.43*	37	0.48	57	0.64	91	0.85	10	0.34	*14.1*	*0.37*	*38*	*0.57*	*179*
...	...	...	...	*50*	*0.55*	*70*	*0.67*	...	...	...	...	...	...	...	...	*180*
...	...	74	0.90*	98	0.97	93	0.97	113	0.99	*46*	*0.85*	38.2	0.96	53	0.88	*181*
...	...	82	1.23*	109	1.22	102	1.08	114[z]	1.00[z]	24	1.42	30.6	1.35	37[z]	1.27[z]	*182*
41	0.57	56	0.84	...	...	85	0.74	**83**	**0.89**	...	...	29.3	0.65	...	...	*183*
...	...	71	0.85*	93	0.98	93	0.97	141	0.97	*17*	*0.97*	...	...	*26*	*0.95*	*184*
49	0.51*	72	0.82	66	0.84	137	0.96	116	1.04	8	*0.46*	36.1	0.70	28	0.83	*185*
...	...	26	0.52*	30	0.59	59	0.70	83	0.80	8	0.50	16.3	0.52	32	0.64	*186*
80	0.88*	87	0.94	109	1.00	105	1.00	101	1.00	*55*	*1.04*	75.5	0.98	*88*[y]	*0.99*[y]	*187*
...	...	44	0.58	60	0.74	70	0.74	111	0.87	7	0.57	5.2	0.62	18	0.73	*188*
76	0.95*	88	0.99	128	1.03	107	1.01	109	0.99	45	1.22	57.6	1.11	59	1.17	*189*
...	...	29	0.35*	28	0.61	31	0.68	53	0.75	7	0.37	6.9	0.60	11	0.61	*190*
55	0.65*	72	0.80	83	0.79	88	0.79	97[z]	0.85[z]	24	0.72	23.1	0.89	32[z]	0.81[z]	*191*
58	...	65	0.84*	71	0.93	92	0.98	147	1.02	9	0.73	9.5	0.99	18	0.89	*192*
73	0.73*	88	0.88	...	...	108	0.97	**130**	**0.98**	...	...	...	...	**46**	**1.07**	*193*
27	0.48*	42	0.63*	55	0.73	64	*0.86*	84	1.00	*15*	*0.53*	15.4	0.64	*26*	*0.76*	*194*
88	1.02*	92	1.01*	...	...	116	0.99	125	0.99	...	...	112.6	1.04	112	1.13	*195*
...	...	38	0.54	*53*	*0.70*	...	...	147	0.90	17	0.57	...	...	32	0.69	*196*
...	...	...	...	...	...	12	0.54	...	...	...	...	...	...	...	...	*197*
...	...	88	0.98	109	0.99	116	0.97	103	0.97	69	1.18	88.5	1.13	*97*	*1.05*	*198*
67	0.94*	84	1.00	94	0.99	100	0.95	113	0.93	*42*	*0.96*	45.3	1.00	54	0.89	*199*
...	...	53	0.56*	94	0.65	112	0.75	97	0.86	20	0.34	28.0	0.40	39	*0.53*	*200*
56	0.66*	74	0.80	*70*	*0.84*	125	0.92	116	1.01	*11*	*0.59*	*9.6*	*0.66*	*23*	*0.83*	*201*
59	0.67*	72	0.83	70	0.98	67	1.00	**112**	**1.00**	5	0.77	*6.1*	*0.82*	...	...	*202*
65	0.79*	71	0.75	95	...	80	0.92	119	0.97	*23*	...	20.3	*0.77*	43	0.89	*203*
84	0.88*	91	0.94	106	0.97	100	0.97	101[z]	0.99[z]	49	0.79	42.9	0.88	40[z]	0.93[z]	*204*
Weighted average				**Weighted average**												
76	0.85	84	0.90	99	0.89	99	0.92	106	0.96	50	0.83	60	0.92	66	0.95	*I*
98	0.98	99	1.00	97	0.99	104	0.99	98	0.99	95	1.03	91	1.01	90	0.98	*II*
99	0.99	99	1.00	103	0.99	102	1.00	101	1.00	93	1.01	100	1.00	100	1.00	*III*
68	0.77	80	0.86	99	0.87	98	0.91	107	0.95	41	0.75	52	0.89	61	0.94	*IV*
58	0.66	71	0.77	87	0.79	90	0.87	98	0.90	49	0.76	60	0.89	65	0.92	*V*
96	0.96	98	0.97	100	0.97	102	0.96	97	0.98	82	0.98	87	0.98	88	0.96	*VI*
98	0.98	99	0.99	90	0.99	98	0.99	100	0.98	98	0.99	85	0.99	95	0.98	*VII*
82	0.84	93	0.94	118	0.95	112	0.99	110	0.99	45	0.83	65	0.96	78	1.01	*VIII*
82	0.84	93	0.94	118	0.95	113	0.99	111	0.99	45	0.83	64	0.96	77	1.01	*IX*
94	0.99	93	0.99	98	0.97	95	0.97	91	0.97	66	1.00	111	0.99	105	0.96	*X*
87	0.98	91	0.99	113	0.99	121	0.97	117	0.97	56	1.01	80	1.07	89	1.08	*XI*
66	1.02	75	1.05	70	0.98	112	0.98	107	0.99	44	1.03	53	1.03	58	1.03	*XII*
87	0.97	91	0.98	114	0.99	121	0.97	117	0.96	57	1.01	81	1.07	90	1.08	*XIII*
99	1.00	99	1.00	104	0.99	103	1.01	102	1.00	94	1.02	100	0.99	100	1.00	*XIV*
48	0.57	64	0.72	89	0.77	89	0.84	108	0.95	39	0.60	45	0.75	52	0.85	*XV*
53	0.71	62	0.76	73	0.84	78	0.85	99	0.90	22	0.76	24	0.82	34	0.79	*XVI*

8. Enrolment ratios were not calculated due to inconsistencies in the population data.
9. Enrolment ratios were not calculated due to lack of United Nations population data by age.
10. Enrolment ratios declined from 2005 to 2007 mainly because the data collection reference date was shifted from the last Wednesday of March to the last Wednesday of May to account for duplicates (enrolments), and transfers of students and teachers (from one school to another), common features at the beginning of the year. At this point of the school year, it is believed, the education system becomes stable, so the data collected should represent the current school year.
11. Data include French overseas departments and territories (DOM-TOM).
12. The apparent increase in the gender parity index (GPI) of pre-primary and primary education GER is due to the inclusion in enrolment statistics in recent years of literacy programmes in which 80% of participants are women.
13. Due to the continuing discrepancy in enrolment by single age, the net enrolment ratio in primary education is estimated using the age distribution of the 2004 DHS data.

Data in italic are UIS estimates.

Data in bold are for the school year ending in 2008.

(z) Data are for the school year ending in 2006.

(y) Data are for the school year ending in 2005.

(*) National estimate.

Table 13

Trends in basic or proxy indicators to measure EFA goal 6

Country or territory	GOAL 6 — Educational quality: SURVIVAL RATE TO GRADE 5 — School year ending in 1991: Total (%)	1991: GPI (F/M)	1999: Total (%)	1999: GPI (F/M)	2006: Total (%)	2006: GPI (F/M)	PUPIL/TEACHER RATIO IN PRIMARY EDUCATION[1] — School year ending in 1991	1999	2007	% FEMALE TEACHERS IN PRIMARY EDUCATION — School year ending in 1991	1999	2007
Arab States												
Algeria	95	0.99	95	1.02	96	1.03	28	28	24	39	46	53
Bahrain	89	1.01	*97*	*1.01*	99[x]	0.98[x]	19*	…	…	54*	…	…
Djibouti	87	1.81	77	1.19	…	…	43	40	**34**	37	28	**26**
Egypt	…	…	*99*	*1.01*	*97*	…	*24*	*23*	*27*	*52*	*52*	*56*
Iraq	…	…	*66*	*0.94*	*81*[x]	*0.84*[x]	25	25	*21*[y]	70	72	*72*[y]
Jordan	…	…	98	0.99	…	…	…	…	…	…	…	…
Kuwait	…	…	…	…	100	0.99	18	13	10	61	73	88
Lebanon	…	…	91	1.07	**92**	1.05	…	14	**14**	…	82	**86**
Libyan Arab Jamahiriya	…	…	…	…	…	…	…	…	…	…	…	…
Mauritania	75	0.99	*68*	*0.94*	64	1.04	45	47	43	18	26	35
Morocco	75	1.02	82	1.00	84	0.98	27	28	27	37	39	47
Oman	97	0.99	94	1.00	98	1.01	28	25	*13*	47	52	*63*
Palestinian A. T.	…	…	…	.	.	.	…	38	30	…	54	67
Qatar	64	1.02	…	…	…	…	11	13	11[z]	72	75	85[z]
Saudi Arabia	83	1.03	…	…	…	…	16	…	11*	48	…	52*
Sudan	94	1.09	*84*	*1.10*	70	0.96	34	…	37	51	…	64
Syrian Arab Republic	96	0.98	92	.	…	…	25	25	…	64	*65*	…
Tunisia	86	0.83	92	1.02	96	1.00	28	24	18	45	50	53
United Arab Emirates	80	0.99	92	0.99	100	1.00	18	16	17	64	73	85
Yemen	…	…	*87*	…	66[x]	0.96[x]	…	*22*	…	…	*20*	…
Central and Eastern Europe												
Albania	…	…	…	.	.	.	…	*23*	…	…	*75*	…
Belarus	…	…	…	.	.	.	…	20	16	…	99	99
Bosnia and Herzegovina	…	…	…	.	.	.	…	…	…	…	…	…
Bulgaria	…	…	…	.	.	.	…	18	16	…	*91*	93
Croatia	…	…	…	.	.	.	…	19	17	…	89	91
Czech Republic	…	…	98	1.01	98	1.01	23	18	19	…	85	94
Estonia	…	…	99	1.01	97[y]	1.00[y]	…	16	13	…	*86*	94
Hungary	…	…	…	.	.	.	…	11	10	…	85	96
Latvia	…	…	…	.	.	.	15	15	12[z]	…	97	97[z]
Lithuania	…	…	…	.	.	.	18	17	13	94	98	97
Montenegro	…	…	…	.	.	.	…	…	…	…	…	…
Poland	98	1.08	99	…	98	…	…	…	11	…	…	84
Republic of Moldova	…	…	…	.	.	.	23	21	16	97	96	97
Romania	…	…	…	.	.	.	22	19	17	84	86	87
Russian Federation	…	…	…	.	.	.	22	18	17[z]	99	98	98[z]
Serbia	…	…	…	.	.	.	…	*17*	*13*	…	…	…
Slovakia	…	…	…	.	.	.	…	19	15	…	93	85
Slovenia	…	…	…	…	…	…	…	14	16	…	96	98
TFYR Macedonia	…	…	…	…	…	…	…	22	18	…	66	72
Turkey	98	0.99	…	…	97[x]	0.99[x]	30	…	…	43	…	…
Ukraine	…	…	…	.	.	.	*22*	20	16	*98*	98	99*
Central Asia												
Armenia	…	…	…	.	.	.	…	…	19	…	…	100
Azerbaijan	…	…	…	.	.	.	…	19	12	…	83	87
Georgia	…	…	…	…	100	…	17	17	…	92	92	…
Kazakhstan	…	…	…	.	.	.	21	…	**17**	96	…	**98**
Kyrgyzstan	…	…	…	.	.	.	…	24	24	81	95	97
Mongolia	…	…	…	…	84	0.97	28	32	32	90	93	95
Tajikistan	…	…	…	.	.	.	21	22	22	49	56	64
Turkmenistan	…	…	…	.	.	.	…	…	…	…	…	…
Uzbekistan	…	…	…	.	.	.	24	21	18	79	84	85
East Asia and the Pacific												
Australia	99	1.01	…	…	…	…	*17*	*18*	…	*72*	…	…
Brunei Darussalam	…	…	…	…	99	1.01	15	14*	13	57	66*	74
Cambodia	…	…	*56*	*0.93*	62	1.04	33	*48*	51	31	*37*	43

GOAL 6

Educational quality

TRAINED PRIMARY-SCHOOL TEACHERS[2] as % of total		PUBLIC CURRENT EXPENDITURE ON PRIMARY EDUCATION as % of GNP			PUBLIC CURRENT EXPENDITURE ON PRIMARY EDUCATION PER PUPIL (unit cost) at PPP in constant 2006 US$			
School year ending in		School year ending in			School year ending in			
1999	2007	1991	1999	2007	1991	1999	2007	**Country or territory**
								Arab States
94	99	4.5	…	…	1 639	…	…	Algeria
…	…	…	…	…	…	…	…	Bahrain
…	**80**	1.8	…	…	895	…	…	Djibouti
…	…	…	…	…	…	…	…	Egypt
…	…	…	…	…	…	…	…	Iraq
…	…	…	1.9	1.6[z]	…	455	538[z]	Jordan
100	100	1.5	…	0.6[z]	…	…	…	Kuwait
15	**13**	…	…	*0.8*[y]	…	…	*714*[y]	Lebanon
…	…	…	…	…	…	…	…	Libyan Arab Jamahiriya
…	100	…	…	*1.4*[y]	…	…	*169*[y]	Mauritania
…	100	1.6	2.0	1.8	460	471	554	Morocco
100	*100*[z]	1.5	1.4	1.6[y]	…	…	…	Oman
100	100	…	…	…	…	…	…	Palestinian A. T.
…	69[z]	…	…	…	…	…	…	Qatar
…	91*	…	…	…	…	…	…	Saudi Arabia
…	59[z]	…	…	…	…	…	…	Sudan
81	…	…	1.7	2.0[z]	…	370	694[z]	Syrian Arab Republic
…	…	…	…	*2.3*[y]	…	…	*1 243*[y]	Tunisia
…	100	…	0.7	0.3[z]	…	…	…	United Arab Emirates
…	…	…	…	…	…	…	…	Yemen
								Central and Eastern Europe
…	…	…	…	…	…	…	…	Albania
…	100	1.8	…	…	…	…	…	Belarus
…	…	…	…	…	…	…	…	Bosnia and Herzegovina
…	…	…	…	0.8[z]	…	…	2 272[z]	Bulgaria
100	…	…	…	*0.8*[x]	…	…	…	Croatia
…	…	…	*0.7*	0.6[z]	…	*1 674*	2 597[z]	Czech Republic
…	…	…	…	1.2[y]	…	…	3 029[y]	Estonia
…	…	…	*0.9*	1.1[z]	…	*2 238*	4 434[z]	Hungary
…	…	…	…	…	…	…	…	Latvia
…	…	…	…	0.7[z]	…	…	2 349[z]	Lithuania
…	…	…	…	…	…	…	…	Montenegro
…	…	…	…	1.6[y]	…	…	3 065[y]	Poland
…	…	…	…	1.1	…	…	755	Republic of Moldova
…	…	…	…	*0.5*[y]	…	…	*1 003*[y]	Romania
…	…	…	…	…	…	…	…	Russian Federation
…	…	…	…	…	…	…	…	Serbia
…	…	…	*0.6*	0.7[z]	…	*1 264*	2 601[z]	Slovakia
…	…	1.0	…	*1.1*[y]	2 636	…	*5 426*[y]	Slovenia
…	…	…	…	…	…	…	…	TFYR Macedonia
…	…	1.3	…	*1.5*[x]	580	…	*1 039*[x]	Turkey
100	100	…	…	…	…	…	…	Ukraine
								Central Asia
…	77[y]	…	…	…	…	…	…	Armenia
100	100	…	…	*0.4*[z]	…	…	*315*[z]	Azerbaijan
…	…	…	…	…	…	…	…	Georgia
…	…	…	…	…	…	…	…	Kazakhstan
48	62	…	…	…	…	…	…	Kyrgyzstan
…	99	…	…	1.3	…	…	420	Mongolia
…	87	…	…	*0.9*[y]	…	…	*121*[y]	Tajikistan
…	…	…	…	…	…	…	…	Turkmenistan
…	100	…	…	…	…	…	…	Uzbekistan
								East Asia and the Pacific
…	…	…	*1.7*	1.7[z]	…	*4 808*	5 417[z]	Australia
…	83	…	…	…	2 645	…	…	Brunei Darussalam
…	98	…	…	…	…	…	…	Cambodia

Table 13 (continued)

Country or territory	GOAL 6 — Educational quality: SURVIVAL RATE TO GRADE 5 (School year ending in) 1991 Total (%)	1991 GPI (F/M)	1999 Total (%)	1999 GPI (F/M)	2006 Total (%)	2006 GPI (F/M)	PUPIL/TEACHER RATIO IN PRIMARY EDUCATION[1] (School year ending in) 1991	1999	2007	% FEMALE TEACHERS IN PRIMARY EDUCATION (School year ending in) 1991	1999	2007
China	86	1.36	…	…	…	…	22	…	18	43	…	56
Cook Islands	…	…	…	…	…	…	…	18	16	…	86	77
DPR Korea	…	…	…	.	.	.	…	…	…	…	…	…
Fiji	87	0.97	87	0.96	*83*	…	31	…	*28*^{y}	57	…	*57*^{y}
Indonesia	84	2.27	…	…	…	…	23	…	19	51	…	58
Japan	100	1.00	…	…	…	…	21	21	18	58	…	…
Kiribati	92	…	…	…	…	…	29	25	25^{y}	58	62	75^{y}
Lao PDR	…	…	54	0.98	61	0.99	27	31	30	38	43	47
Macao, China	…	…	…	…	…	…	…	31	20	…	87	88
Malaysia	97	1.00	…	…	92^{y}	1.00^{y}	20	21	16^{z}	57	66	68^{z}
Marshall Islands	…	…	…	…	…	…	…	15	…	…	…	…
Micronesia, F. S.	…	…	…	…	…	…	…	…	*17*	…	…	…
Myanmar	…	…	…	…	73	…	48	31	29	62	73	83
Nauru	…	…	…	…	…	…	…	…	20	…	…	90
New Zealand	…	…	…	…	…	…	17	18	16	80	82	83
Niue	…	…	…	…	…	…	20	16	*12*^{y}	…	100	*100*^{y}
Palau	…	…	…	…	…	…	…	15	*13*^{y}	…	82	…
Papua New Guinea	69	0.97	…	…	…	…	31	…	*36*^{z}	34	…	*43*^{z}
Philippines	…	…	…	…	77	1.12	33	35	34	…	87	87
Republic of Korea	99	1.00	100	1.00	98	1.00	36	32	26	50	67	77
Samoa	…	…	94	1.05*	…	…	26	*24*	24	72	*71*	78
Singapore	…	…	…	…	…	…	26	…	20	…	…	81
Solomon Islands	88	1.28	…	…	…	…	21	19	…	…	41	…
Thailand	…	…	…	…	…	…	22	21	**16**	…	63	**60**
Timor-Leste	…	…	…	…	…	…	…	…	31	…	…	32
Tokelau	…	…	…	…	…	…	…	…	…	…	…	…
Tonga	…	…	…	…	92^{y}	1.00^{y}	23	21	22^{z}	67	67	…
Tuvalu	…	…	…	…	…	…	…	19	…	…	…	…
Vanuatu	…	…	72	0.99	…	…	29	24	…	40	49	…
Viet Nam	…	…	83	1.08	*92*^{y}	…	35	30	20	…	78	78
Latin America and the Caribbean												
Anguilla	…	…	…	…	97^{x}	1.06^{x}	…	22	16	…	87	95
Antigua and Barbuda	…	…	…	…	…	…	…	…	22	…	…	92
Argentina	…	…	90	1.04	96^{y}	1.01^{y}	…	21	16^{z}	…	88	88^{z}
Aruba	…	…	97	0.99	97	1.02	…	19	17	…	78	83
Bahamas	84	…	…	…	85^{y}	1.07^{y}	…	14	14	…	63	85
Barbados	…	…	93	0.97	…	…	*18*	*18*	15	*72*	*76*	78
Belize	67	0.96	78	1.04	87	1.01	…	*24*	23	…	*64*	72
Bermuda	…	…	…	…	90^{y}	…	…	…	8^{z}	…	…	89^{z}
Bolivia	…	…	82	0.97	83	1.00	…	*25*	…	…	*61*	…
Brazil	…	…	…	.	.	.	…	26	24	…	93	91
British Virgin Islands	…	…	…	.	.	.	19	18	14	…	86	90
Cayman Islands	…	…	*74*	…	…	…	…	15	11	…	89	90
Chile	92	0.97	100	1.00	98	1.00	25	32	25	73	77	78
Colombia	76	…	67	1.08	88	1.09	30	24	28	…	77	76
Costa Rica	84	1.02	91	1.03	88	1.04	32	27	19	80	80	80
Cuba	92	…	94	1.00	97	1.01	13	12	10	79	79	76
Dominica	75	…	*91*	…	89	0.96	29	20	17	81	75	84
Dominican Republic	…	…	75	1.11	68^{y}	1.09^{y}	…	…	24*	…	…	76*
Ecuador	…	…	77	1.01	82	1.03	30	27	23	…	68	70
El Salvador	58	1.08	*65*	*1.02*	74	1.05	…	…	40	…	…	68
Grenada	…	…	…	…	…	…	…	…	16	…	…	77
Guatemala	…	…	56	1.06	68	0.98	34	38	30	…	…	65
Guyana	…	…	95	…	…	…	30	27	26	76	86	88
Haiti	…	…	…	…	…	…	23	…	…	45	…	…
Honduras	…	…	…	…	83^{y}	1.08^{y}	38	…	28^{z}	74	…	…
Jamaica	…	…	…	…	…	…	*34*	…	*28*^{y}	…	…	*89*^{y}
Mexico	80	2.06	89	1.02	95	1.02	31	27	28	…	62	67
Montserrat	…	…	…	…	90	1.12	…	21	16	…	84	100
Netherlands Antilles	…	…	*84*	*1.10*	…	…	…	20	…	…	86	…
Nicaragua	44	3.33	48	1.19	47	1.18	36	34	31	86	83	76

GOAL 6

Educational quality

TRAINED PRIMARY-SCHOOL TEACHERS[2] as % of total		PUBLIC CURRENT EXPENDITURE ON PRIMARY EDUCATION as % of GNP			PUBLIC CURRENT EXPENDITURE ON PRIMARY EDUCATION PER PUPIL (unit cost) at PPP in constant 2006 US$			
School year ending in		School year ending in			School year ending in			
1999	2007	1991	1999	2007	1991	1999	2007	Country or territory
…	…	…	*0.6*	…	…	…	…	China
…	79	…	0.2	…	…	…	…	Cook Islands
…	…	…	…	…	…	…	…	DPR Korea
…	…	…	…	2.4[x]	…	…	771[x]	Fiji
…	…	…	…	…	…	…	…	Indonesia
…	…	…	…	…	…	…	…	Japan
…	…	…	…	…	…	…	…	Kiribati
76	90	…	…	0.5[y]	…	…	53[y]	Lao PDR
81	89	…	…	…	…	…	…	Macao, China
…	…	1.5	…	1.6[x]	756	…	1 411[x]	Malaysia
…	…	…	…	…	…	…	…	Marshall Islands
…	…	…	…	…	…	…	…	Micronesia, F. S.
60	99	…	…	…	…	…	…	Myanmar
…	74	…	…	…	…	…	…	Nauru
…	…	1.7	*1.8*	1.5	3 300	*4 005*	3 798	New Zealand
…	…	…	…	…	…	…	…	Niue
…	…	…	…	…	…	…	…	Palau
…	…	…	…	…	…	…	…	Papua New Guinea
100	…	…	…	1.2[y]	…	…	252[y]	Philippines
…	…	1.3	*1.3*	1.4[y]	1 369	*2 602*	3 547[y]	Republic of Korea
…	98	…	*1.4*	…	…	*270*	…	Samoa
…	96	…	…	**0.6**	…	…	…	Singapore
…	…	2.2	…	…	256	…	…	Solomon Islands
…	…	1.5	…	…	524	…	…	Thailand
…	…	…	…	1.0	…	…	…	Timor-Leste
…	…	…	…	…	…	…	…	Tokelau
…	…	…	…	…	…	…	…	Tonga
…	…	…	…	…	…	…	…	Tuvalu
…	…	…	2.2	…	…	416	…	Vanuatu
78	98	…	…	…	…	…	…	Viet Nam
								Latin America and the Caribbean
76	54	…	…	1.1[y]	…	…	…	Anguilla
…	67	…	…	0.9	…	…	1 110	Antigua and Barbuda
…	…	…	1.6	1.6[z]	…	1 322	1 544[z]	Argentina
100	100	…	…	1.3[y]	…	…	…	Aruba
58	85	…	…	…	…	…	…	Bahamas
…	70	…	*1.0*	*2.0[y]*	…	…	…	Barbados
…	45	…	…	2.4[x]	…	…	767[x]	Belize
…	100[z]	1.1	…	*0.8[y]*	…	…	…	Bermuda
…	…	…	*2.0*	…	…	*404*	…	Bolivia
…	…	…	*1.3*	1.6[z]	…	*804*	1 257[y]	Brazil
72	72	…	…	0.8	…	…	…	British Virgin Islands
98	96	…	…	…	…	…	…	Cayman Islands
…	…	…	1.5	1.2	…	1 323	1 496	Chile
…	…	…	…	1.9	…	…	1 044	Colombia
93	89	1.2	2.6	2.3[x]	503	1 340	1 480[x]	Costa Rica
100	100	…	…	4.0	…	…	…	Cuba
64	61	…	…	1.8	…	…	1 082	Dominica
…	88*	…	…	1.2	…	…	549	Dominican Republic
…	72	…	…	…	…	…	…	Ecuador
…	93	…	…	1.3	…	…	51	El Salvador
…	69	…	…	…	…	…	…	Grenada
…	…	…	…	1.8	…	…	431	Guatemala
52	57	…	…	2.0	…	…	372	Guyana
…	…	0.7	…	…	141	…	…	Haiti
…	…	…	…	…	…	…	…	Honduras
…	…	1.5	…	2.4	618	…	1 155	Jamaica
…	…	0.8	1.8	2.1[z]	468	1 210	1 798[z]	Mexico
100	77	…	…	…	…	…	…	Montserrat
100	…	…	…	…	…	…	…	Netherlands Antilles
79	72	…	…	1.6[z]	…	…	217[z]	Nicaragua

Table 13 (continued)

Country or territory	GOAL 6 – Educational quality: SURVIVAL RATE TO GRADE 5 (School year ending in) 1991 Total (%)	1991 GPI (F/M)	1999 Total (%)	1999 GPI (F/M)	2006 Total (%)	2006 GPI (F/M)	PUPIL/TEACHER RATIO IN PRIMARY EDUCATION[1] (School year ending in) 1991	1999	2007	% FEMALE TEACHERS IN PRIMARY EDUCATION (School year ending in) 1991	1999	2007
Panama	…	…	92	1.01	90	1.01	…	26	25	…	75	76
Paraguay	74	1.02	*78*	*1.05*	88[x]	1.05[x]	25	…	…	…	…	…
Peru	…	…	87	0.98	93	1.00	29	…	22	…	…	65
Saint Kitts and Nevis	…	…	…	…	…	…	*22*	…	17	*74*	…	87
Saint Lucia	96	…	*90*	…	…	…	*29*	22	23	*83*	*84*	87
Saint Vincent/Grenadines	…	…	…	…	…	…	20	…	17	67	…	77
Suriname	…	…	…	…	80	1.04	22	…	13	84	…	92
Trinidad and Tobago	…	…	…	…	91[*,x]	1.03[*,x]	26	21	16	70	76	77
Turks and Caicos Islands	…	…	…	…	…	…	…	*18*	*15*[y]	…	*92*	*89*[y]
Uruguay	97	1.03	…	…	94	1.04	22	20	16	…	*92*	…
Venezuela, B. R.	86	1.09	91	1.08	98	1.04	…	…	19[y]	…	…	81[y]
North America and Western Europe												
Andorra	…	…	…	…	98	0.96	…	…	10	…	…	77
Austria	…	…	…	.	.	.	11	13	12	82	89	89
Belgium	91	1.02	…	…	96	1.02	…	…	11	…	…	80
Canada	97	1.04	…	…	…	…	15	17	…	69	*68*	…
Cyprus	100	1.00	96	1.03	100	1.00	21	18	16	60	67	82
Denmark	94	1.00	100	1.00	93[x]	1.00[x]	…	10	…	…	63	…
Finland	100	1.00	100	1.00	100	1.00	…	17	15	…	71	77
France	96	1.37	98	*0.99*	…	…	…	19	19	…	78	82
Germany	…	…	…	.	.	.	…	17	14	…	82	84
Greece	100	1.00	…	…	98	1.00	19	14	10	52	*57*	65
Iceland	…	…	100	1.00	94	…	…	*11*	*10*[z]	…	*76*	*80*[z]
Ireland	100	1.01	95	1.03	…	…	27	22	16	77	85	84
Israel	…	…	…	…	…	…	…	13	13	…	…	86
Italy	…	…	97	…	100	1.01	12	11	10	91	95	95
Luxembourg	…	…	*96*	*1.08*	99	1.02	13	…	11	51	…	72
Malta	99	1.01	99	0.99	…	…	21	20	12[y]	79	87	86[y]
Monaco	83	0.81	…	…	…	…	…	*16*	…	…	*87*	…
Netherlands	…	…	100	1.00	…	…	17	…	…	53	…	…
Norway	100	1.01	100	1.00	100	0.99	…	…	…	…	…	…
Portugal	…	…	…	…	…	…	14	…	12	81	…	82
San Marino	88	…	…	…	…	…	6	…	**6**	89	…	**91**
Spain	…	…	…	…	100[y]	1.00[y]	22	15	13	73	68	72
Sweden	100	1.00	99	1.00	100	1.00	*10*	12	10	*77*	80	81
Switzerland	…	…	…	…	…	…	…	…	…	…	…	…
United Kingdom	…	…	…	…	…	…	20	19	18[z]	78	76	81[z]
United States	…	…	94	…	…	…	…	15	14	…	86	89
South and West Asia												
Afghanistan	…	…	…	…	…	…	…	…	43	…	…	28
Bangladesh	…	…	…	…	55[y]	1.10[y]	…	…	45	…	…	40
Bhutan	…	…	90	1.04	93[y]	1.04[y]	…	42	**30**	…	32	…
India	…	…	62	0.95	66[y]	0.99[y]	*47*	35[*]	…	*28*	33[*]	…
Iran, Islamic Republic of	90	0.98	…	…	…	…	31	27	19	53	53	58
Maldives	…	…	…	…	…	…	…	24	15	…	60	71
Nepal	51	0.99	58	1.10	**62**	1.07	39	39	**38**	14	23	**35**
Pakistan	…	…	…	…	70[x]	1.07[x]	…	…	40	*27*	…	46
Sri Lanka	92	1.01	…	…	*93*[y]	*1.00*[y]	*31*	…	23[z]	…	…	84[z]
Sub-Saharan Africa												
Angola	…	…	…	.	.	.	32	…	41	…	…	40
Benin	55	1.02	…	…	72[y]	0.98[y]	36	53	44[z]	25	23	17[z]
Botswana	84	1.06	87	1.06	83[x]	1.05[x]	30	27	24[y]	78	81	78[y]
Burkina Faso	70	0.96	68	1.05	**80**	1.04	57	49	**49**	27	25	**33**
Burundi	62	0.89	…	…	66	1.04	67	*57*	52	46	*54*	53
Cameroon	…	…	*81*	…	84	…	51	52	44	30	36	43
Cape Verde	…	…	…	…	92	…	…	*29*	25	…	*62*	67
Central African Republic	23	0.90	…	…	**59**	0.94	77	…	**90**	25	…	**13**
Chad	*51*	*0.74*	55	0.86	38[y]	0.83[y]	66	68	60	6	9	13
Comoros	…	…	…	…	*80*[x]	*1.02*[x]	37	35	*35*[y]	…	26	*33*[y]

GOAL 6								
	Educational quality								
TRAINED PRIMARY-SCHOOL TEACHERS[2] as % of total		PUBLIC CURRENT EXPENDITURE ON PRIMARY EDUCATION as % of GNP			PUBLIC CURRENT EXPENDITURE ON PRIMARY EDUCATION PER PUPIL (unit cost) at PPP in constant 2006 US$				
School year ending in		School year ending in			School year ending in				
1999	2007	1991	1999	2007	1991	1999	2007	Country or territory	
79	91	1.7	1.9	1.2	762	1 073	899	Panama	
…	…	…	…	1.8ˣ	…	…	425ˣ	Paraguay	
…	…	…	1.2	1.0	…	393	495	Peru	
…	62	1.1	…	…	…	…	…	Saint Kitts and Nevis	
…	82	2.5	*3.6*	2.0ᶻ	701	*1 783*	1 217ᶻ	Saint Lucia	
…	78	3.0	…	2.5	641	…	1 293	Saint Vincent/Grenadines	
…	…	…	…	…	…	…	…	Suriname	
71	89	…	1.5	…	…	1 312	…	Trinidad and Tobago	
81	*82ʸ*	…	…	…	…	…	…	Turks and Caicos Islands	
…	…	0.9	0.8	…	581	686	…	Uruguay	
…	84ʸ	…	…	1.2	…	…	1 071	Venezuela, B. R.	
								North America and Western Europe	
…	100	…	…	0.6	…	…	…	Andorra	
…	…	0.9	*1.1*	1.0ʸ	4 981	*7 362*	7 881ʸ	Austria	
…	…	1.1	…	1.4ᶻ	4 116	…	6 612ᶻ	Belgium	
…	…	…	…	…	…	…	…	Canada	
…	…	1.2	1.6	1.7ᶻ	2 086	3 627	5 614ᶻ	Cyprus	
…	…	…	*1.6*	1.8ʸ	…	*7 318*	7 913ʸ	Denmark	
…	…	1.7	1.2	1.1ᶻ	4 786	*4 330*	5 345ᶻ	Finland	
…	…	0.9	*1.1*	1.0ᶻ	3 038	*4 621*	5 167ᶻ	France	
…	…	…	…	0.6ᶻ	…	…	5 137ᶻ	Germany	
…	…	0.5	*0.5*	*0.7ʸ*	1 282	*2 308*	*3 641ʸ*	Greece	
…	…	…	…	2.6ᶻ	…	…	8 360ᶻ	Iceland	
…	…	1.5	*1.4*	1.7ᶻ	2 129	*3 183*	5 591ᶻ	Ireland	
…	…	…	*2.4*	2.2ᶻ	…	*4 150*	4 659ᶻ	Israel	
…	…	0.8	*1.2*	1.1ᶻ	3 663	*6 244*	6 919ᶻ	Italy	
…	…	…	…	*1.5ʸ*	…	…	*11 519ʸ*	Luxembourg	
…	…	0.9	…	1.0ˣ	1 383	…	2 655ˣ	Malta	
…	…	…	…	…	…	…	…	Monaco	
…	…	0.9	*1.1*	1.4ᶻ	3 391	*4 671*	6 487ᶻ	Netherlands	
…	…	2.4	*1.6*	1.5ᶻ	11 509	*7 800*	8 382ᶻ	Norway	
…	…	1.7	*1.5*	1.6ᶻ	2 698	*3 760*	4 611ᶻ	Portugal	
…	…	…	…	…	…	…	…	San Marino	
…	…	0.8	*1.1*	1.0ᶻ	2 394	*4 370*	5 299ᶻ	Spain	
…	…	3.1	…	1.6ᶻ	10 928	…	8 001ᶻ	Sweden	
…	…	2.1	1.4	1.4ᶻ	12 204	7 153	8 027ᶻ	Switzerland	
…	…	1.2	…	1.3ʸ	3 309	…	5 326ʸ	United Kingdom	
…	…	…	…	…	…	…	…	United States	
								South and West Asia	
…	…	…	…	…	…	…	…	Afghanistan	
…	56	…	0.6	0.9	…	…	99	Bangladesh	
100	**91**	…	…	1.0	…	…	249	Bhutan	
…	…	…	*1.3*	1.2ʸ	…	*192*	179ʸ	India	
…	100ʸ	…	…	1.4	…	…	1 235	Iran, Islamic Republic of	
67	66	…	…	*3.5ʸ*	…	…	*714ʸ*	Maldives	
46	**66**	…	*1.1*	**2.2**	…	*61*	…	Nepal	
…	85ᶻ	…	…	…	…	…	…	Pakistan	
…	…	…	…	…	…	…	…	Sri Lanka	
								Sub-Saharan Africa	
…	…	…	…	0.6ᶻ	…	…	109ᶻ	Angola	
58	72ᶻ	…	…	1.9ᶻ	…	…	156ᶻ	Benin	
90	87ʸ	…	…	1.3	…	…	1 228ʸ	Botswana	
…	**88**	…	…	2.8ᶻ	…	…	314ᶻ	Burkina Faso	
…	87	1.5	1.3	2.7ʸ	69	*42*	65ʸ	Burundi	
…	62 *,ᶻ	…	1.0	1.0	…	123	121	Cameroon	
…	83	…	…	2.4	…	…	459	Cape Verde	
…	…	1.2	…	0.7ᶻ	95	…	50ᶻ	Central African Republic	
…	35ᶻ	0.7	…	0.6ʸ	85	…	56ʸ	Chad	
…	…	…	…	…	…	…	…	Comoros

Table 13 (continued)

	GOAL 6 Educational quality														
	SURVIVAL RATE TO GRADE 5						PUPIL/TEACHER RATIO IN PRIMARY EDUCATION[1]			% FEMALE TEACHERS IN PRIMARY EDUCATION		
	School year ending in						School year ending in			School year ending in		
	1991		1999		2006		1991	1999	2007	1991	1999	2007
Country or territory	Total (%)	GPI (F/M)	Total (%)	GPI (F/M)	Total (%)	GPI (F/M)						
Congo	60	1.16	…	…	…	…	65	61	58	32	42	44
Côte d'Ivoire	73	0.93	69	0.89	78	0.88	*37*	43	41	*18*	20	24
Democratic Rep. of the Congo	55	0.86	…	…	…	…	*40*	26	38	*24*	21	26
Equatorial Guinea	…	…	…	…	…	…	…	57	28	…	28	34
Eritrea	…	…	95	0.95	60	1.03	38	47	48	45	35	48
Ethiopia	18	1.47	56	1.06	64	1.03	36	46	…	24	28	…
Gabon	…	…	…	…	…	…	…	44	…	…	42	…
Gambia	…	…	*92*	*0.99*	***73***	*1.07*	31	37	41	*31*	29	33
Ghana	80	0.98	…	…	**89**	…	29	30	**32**	36	32	**33**
Guinea	59	0.76	…	…	83	0.91	40	47	45	22	25	26
Guinea-Bissau	…	…	…	…	…	…	…	*44*	…	…	*20*	…
Kenya	77	1.04	…	…	*83*[x]	*1.05*[x]	…	32	*46*	…	42	*44*
Lesotho	66	1.26	74	1.20	74[y]	1.18[y]	54	44	40[z]	80	80	78[z]
Liberia	…	…	…	…	…	…	…	39	**24**	…	19	**12**
Madagascar	21	0.96	51	1.02	42	1.04	40	47	49	…	58	61
Malawi	64	0.80	49	0.77	43	0.96	61	…	67	31	…	38
Mali	*70*	*0.95*	*78*	*0.97*	81[y]	0.96[y]	*47*	62*	52	*25*	23*	27
Mauritius	97	1.01	99	0.99	99	1.00	21	26	22	45	54	65
Mozambique	34	0.87	43	0.79	64	0.89	55	61	65	23	25	34
Namibia	62	1.08	92	1.02	*98*	*1.02*	…	32	30	…	67	*65*
Niger	62	1.06	…	…	72	0.93	42	41	40	33	31	43
Nigeria	89	…	…	…	…	…	39	41	40[z]	43	48	50[z]
Rwanda	60	0.97	45	…	…	…	57	54	69	46	55	53
Sao Tome and Principe	…	…	…	…	**79**	0.92	…	36	*31*[z]	…	…	*55*[z]
Senegal	85	…	…	…	65[y]	1.00[y]	53	49	34	*27*	*23*	28
Seychelles	93	1.03	99	1.02	…	…	…	15	12	…	85	85
Sierra Leone	…	…	…	…	…	…	*35*	…	44	…	…	26
Somalia	…	…	…	…	…	…	…	28	…	…	35	…
South Africa	…	…	65	0.99	…	…	27	35	31	58	78	77
Swaziland	77	1.09	80	1.22	82	1.15	32	33	32	78	75	70
Togo	48	0.80	52	0.90	54	0.87	58	41	39	19	13	12
Uganda	36	…	…	…	*49*[x]	*0.99*[x]	*33*	57	57	…	33	39
United Republic of Tanzania	*81*	*1.02*	…	…	*87*	*1.05*	36	40	**53**	40	45	***49***
Zambia	…	…	81	0.94	89	0.89	…	47	49	…	49	48
Zimbabwe	76	1.12	…	…	…	…	39	41	38[z]	40	47	…

	Median						Weighted average			Weighted average		
World	…	…	…	…	…	…	26	25	25	56	58	62
Countries in transition	…	…	.	.	.	.	22	20	17	93	93	93
Developed countries	…	…	…	…	…	…	17	16	14	78	81	83
Developing countries	…	…	81	…	83	…	29	27	27	48	52	56
Arab States	87	1.00	…	…	…	…	25	23	21	52	52	59
Central and Eastern Europe	…	…	.	.	.	.	22	19	18	82	82	80
Central Asia	…	…	.	.	.	.	21	21	18	85	84	86
East Asia and the Pacific	…	…	…	…	…	…	23	22	19	48	55	60
East Asia	…	…	…	…	…	…	23	22	19	48	55	59
Pacific	…	…	…	…	…	…	19	20	19	67	71	75
Latin America/Caribbean	…	…	86	…	88	1.09	25	26	23	75	76	78
Caribbean	…	…	…	…	…	…	25	24	21	65	50	58
Latin America	80	…	82	0.97	88	1.05	25	26	24	76	77	78
N. America/W. Europe	…	…	98	0.99	…	…	16	15	14	80	81	85
South and West Asia	…	…	…	…	68	1.03	45	36	39	31	35	45
Sub-Saharan Africa	63	0.93	…	…	76	1.01	37	41	44	…	43	44

Source: UNESCO Institute for Statistics database (UIS, 2009).

1. Based on headcounts of pupils and teachers.

2. Data on trained teachers (defined according to national standards) are not collected for countries whose education statistics are gathered through the OECD, Eurostat or the World Education Indicators questionnaires.

Data in italic are UIS estimates.

Data in bold are for the school year ending in 2007 for survival rates to grade 5, and the school year ending in 2008 for the remaining indicators.

GOAL 6

Educational quality

TRAINED PRIMARY-SCHOOL TEACHERS[2] as % of total		PUBLIC CURRENT EXPENDITURE ON PRIMARY EDUCATION as % of GNP			PUBLIC CURRENT EXPENDITURE ON PRIMARY EDUCATION PER PUPIL (unit cost) at PPP in constant 2006 US$			
School year ending in		School year ending in			School year ending in			
1999	2007	1991	1999	2007	1991	1999	2007	**Country or territory**
…	87	…	2.0	0.6[y]	…	469	94[y]	Congo
…	100	…	1.8	*0.1*[y]	…	285	…	Côte d'Ivoire
…	96	…	…	…	…	…	…	Democratic Rep. of the Congo
…	31	…	…	…	…	…	…	Equatorial Guinea
73	87	…	…	0.8[z]	…	…	50[z]	Eritrea
…	…	1.1	…	1.9	99	…	73	Ethiopia
…	…	…	…	…	…	…	…	Gabon
72	…	1.3	…	…	157	…	…	Gambia
72	**49**	…	…	1.6[y]	…	…	147[y]	Ghana
…	68[z]	…	…	…	…	…	…	Guinea
…	…	…	…	…	…	…	…	Guinea-Bissau
…	*99*	…	…	3.6[z]	…	…	258[z]	Kenya
78	66[z]	…	3.2	3.8[z]	…	250	301[z]	Lesotho
…	**40**	…	…	…	…	…	…	Liberia
…	55	…	…	1.6	…	…	73	Madagascar
…	…	1.1	…	…	43	…	…	Malawi
…	…	…	*1.3*	2.2[z]	…	*117*	159[z]	Mali
100	100	1.3	1.2	1.0[z]	563	864	991[z]	Mauritius
…	63	…	…	2.4[z]	…	…	79[z]	Mozambique
29	95	…	4.4	3.1[y]	…	865	668[y]	Namibia
98	98	…	…	1.7[z]	…	…	130[z]	Niger
…	51[z]	…	…	…	…	…	…	Nigeria
49	98	…	…	2.1	…	…	80	Rwanda
…	…	…	…	…	…	…	…	Sao Tome and Principe
…	…	1.7	…	2.0[y]	272	…	257[y]	Senegal
82	…	…	…	*1.6*[x]	…	…	*2 089*[x]	Seychelles
…	49	…	…	…	…	…	…	Sierra Leone
…	…	…	…	…	…	…	…	Somalia
63	…	…	2.7	2.2	1 442	1 097*	1 225	South Africa
91	94	1.4	1.9	*2.4*[x]	312	448	*459*[x]	Swaziland
31	15	…	1.5	1.5	…	69	76	Togo
…	93	…	…	**2.1**	…	…	*66*[x]	Uganda
…	**99**	…	…	…	…	…	…	United Republic of Tanzania
94	…	…	…	1.3[y]	…	…	63[y]	Zambia
…	…	4.3	…	…	…	…	…	Zimbabwe
Median		**Median**			**Median**			
…	…	…	…	1.4	…	…	1 003	World
…	94	…	…	…	…	…	…	Countries in transition
…	…	…	…	1.1	…	…	5 312	Developed countries
…	85	…	…	1.6	…	…	…	Developing countries
…	100	…	…	…	…	…	…	Arab States
…	…	…	…	0.9	…	…	2 597	Central and Eastern Europe
…	93	…	…	…	…	…	…	Central Asia
…	…	…	…	…	…	…	…	East Asia and the Pacific
…	…	…	…	…	…	…	…	East Asia
…	…	…	…	…	…	…	…	Pacific
…	80	…	…	1.6	…	…	1 071	Latin America/Caribbean
76	75	…	…	1.9	…	…	…	Caribbean
…	…	…	…	1.6	…	…	972	Latin America
…	…	1.2	1.3	1.4	3 350	4 496	5 614	N. America/W. Europe
…	76	…	…	1.3	…	…	249	South and West Asia
…	87	…	…	1.8	…	…	130	Sub-Saharan Africa

(z) Data are for the school year ending in 2006.
(y) Data are for the school year ending in 2005.
(*) National estimate.

Aid to disadvantaged families can help get working children back into school, the Philippines

Aid tables

Introduction

Most of the data on aid used in this Report are derived from the OECD's International Development Statistics (IDS) database, which records information provided annually by all member countries of the OECD Development Assistance Committee (DAC). The IDS comprises the DAC database, which provides aggregate data, and the Creditor Reporting System, which provides project- and activity-level data. The IDS is available online at www.oecd.org/dac/stats/idsonline. It is updated frequently. The data presented in this Report were downloaded between February and June 2009.

The focus of this section of the annex, on aid data, is official development assistance. This term and others used in describing aid data are explained below to help in understanding the tables in this section and the data presented in Chapter 4. Private funds are not included.

Aid recipients and donors

Official development assistance (ODA) is public funds provided to developing countries to promote their economic and social development. It is concessional: that is, it takes the form either of a grant or of a loan carrying a lower rate of interest than is available in the market and, usually, a longer than normal repayment period. ODA may be provided directly by a government (bilateral ODA) or through an international agency (multilateral ODA). ODA can include technical cooperation (see below).

Developing countries are those in Part I of the DAC List of Aid Recipients, which essentially comprises all low- and middle-income countries. Twelve central and eastern European countries, including new independent states of the former Soviet Union, plus a set of more advanced developing countries are in Part II of the list, and aid to them is referred to as official aid (OA). The data presented in this Report do not include OA unless indicated.

Bilateral donors are countries that provide development assistance directly to recipient countries. The majority (Australia, Austria, Belgium, Canada, Denmark, Finland, France, Germany, Greece, Ireland, Italy, Japan, Luxembourg, the Netherlands, New Zealand, Norway, Portugal, Spain, Sweden, Switzerland, the United Kingdom and the United States) are members of the DAC, a forum of major bilateral donors established to promote aid volume and effectiveness. Non-DAC bilateral donors include the Republic of Korea and some Arab states. Bilateral donors also contribute substantially to the financing of multilateral donors through contributions recorded as multilateral ODA. The financial flows from multilateral donors to recipient countries are also recorded as ODA receipts.

Multilateral donors are international institutions with government membership that conduct all or a significant part of their activities in favour of developing countries. They include multilateral development banks (e.g. the World Bank and the Inter-American Development Bank), United Nations agencies (e.g. UNDP and UNICEF) and regional groupings (e.g. the European Commission and Arab agencies). The development banks also make non-concessional loans to several middle- and higher-income countries, and these are not counted as part of ODA.

Types of aid

Direct aid to education: term used in this Report for the aid to education in the DAC database that is reported as direct allocations to the education sector. Direct aid to education falls into four subcategories: basic, secondary, post-secondary and 'level unspecified' aid to education.

Total aid to education: term used in this Report to refer to direct aid to education plus part of general budget support (aid provided to governments without being earmarked for specific projects or sectors), some of which benefits the education sector. A review of World Bank Poverty Reduction Support Credits found that between 15% and 25% of budget support aid typically benefits the education sector (FTI Secretariat, 2006). Total aid to education is calculated by adding 20% of all general budget support to direct aid to education. Similarly, total aid to basic education is calculated by adding 10% of all general budget support to direct aid to basic education. In addition, it is assumed that half of 'level unspecified' aid for education benefits basic education. Hence:

- Total aid to education = direct aid to education + 20% of general budget support.
- Total aid to basic education = direct aid to basic education + 10% of general budget support + 50% of 'level unspecified' aid to education.

Unallocated aid: some contributions are not susceptible to allocation by sector and are reported as non-sector allocable aid. Examples are aid for general development purposes (direct budget support), balance-of-payments support, action relating to debt (including debt relief) and emergency assistance.

Basic education: the definition of basic education varies by agency. The DAC defines it as covering primary education, basic life skills for youth and adults, and early childhood education.

Education, level unspecified: the aid to education reported in the DAC database includes basic, secondary and post-secondary education, and 'education, level unspecified'. This subcategory covers aid related to any activity that cannot be attributed solely to the development of a single level of education.

Technical cooperation (sometimes referred to as technical assistance): according to the DAC Directives, technical cooperation is the provision of know-how in the form of personnel, training, research and associated costs. It includes (a) grants to nationals of aid recipient countries receiving education or training at home or abroad; and (b) payments to consultants, advisers and similar personnel as well as teachers and administrators serving in recipient countries (including the cost of associated equipment). Where such assistance is related specifically to a capital project, it is included with project and programme expenditure, and is not separately reported as technical cooperation. The aid activities reported in this category vary by donor, as interpretations of the definition are broad.

Debt relief: this includes debt forgiveness, i.e. the extinction of a loan by agreement between the creditor (donor) and the debtor (aid recipient), and other action on debt, including debt swaps, buy-backs and refinancing. In the DAC database, debt forgiveness is reported as a grant. It raises gross ODA but not necessarily net ODA (see below).

Commitments and disbursements: a commitment is a firm obligation by a donor, expressed in writing and backed by the necessary funds, to provide specified assistance to a country or multilateral organization. The amount specified is recorded as a commitment. Disbursement is the release of funds to, or purchase of goods or services for, a recipient; in other words, the amount spent. Disbursements record the actual international transfer of financial resources or of goods or services valued by the donor. As the aid committed in a given year can be disbursed later, sometimes over several years, the annual aid figures based on commitments differ from those based on disbursements.

Gross and net disbursements: gross disbursements are the total aid extended. Net disbursements are the total aid extended minus amounts of loan principal repaid by recipients or cancelled through debt forgiveness.

Current and constant prices: aid figures in the DAC database are expressed in US$. When other currencies are converted into dollars at the exchange rates prevailing at the time, the resulting amounts are at current prices and exchange rates. When comparing aid figures between different years, adjustment is required to compensate for inflation and changes in exchange rates. Such adjustments result in aid being expressed in constant dollars, i.e. in dollars fixed at the value they held in a given reference year, including their external value in terms of other currencies. Thus, amounts of aid for any year and in any currency expressed in 2007 constant dollars reflect the value of that aid in terms of the purchasing power of dollars in 2007. In this Report, most aid data are presented in 2007 constant dollars. The indices used for adjusting currencies and years (called deflators) are derived from Table 36 of the statistical annex of the 2009 DAC Annual Report (OECD-DAC, 2009*e*). In previous editions of the *EFA Global Monitoring Report*, amounts of aid were based on the constant prices of different years (the 2007 Report used 2003 constant prices), so amounts for a given country for a given year in these editions differ from the amounts presented in this Report for the same year. For more detailed and precise definitions of terms used in the DAC database, see the DAC Directives, available at www.oecd.org/dac/stats/dac/directives.

Source: OECD-DAC (2009*d*).

Table 1: Bilateral and multilateral ODA

	Total ODA			Net disbursements as % of GNI				Sector-allocable ODA			Debt relief and other actions relating to debt		
	Constant 2007 US$ millions							Constant 2007 US$ millions			Constant 2007 US$ millions		
	1999–2000 annual average	2006	2007	1999–2000 annual average	2006	2007	2008*	1999–2000 annual average	2006	2007	1999–2000 annual average	2006	2007
Australia	1 825	2 608	1 710	0.27	0.30	0.32	0.34	1 357	1 437	1 455	12	319	12
Austria	782	1 207	1 382	0.24	0.47	0.50	0.42	233	296	360	244	800	904
Belgium	783	1 725	1 587	0.33	0.50	0.43	0.47	505	951	1 076	71	448	190
Canada	2 164	2 917	3 715	0.27	0.29	0.29	0.32	953	1 592	2 121	61	268	29
Denmark	1 412	1 520	1 481	1.04	0.80	0.81	0.82	1 081	827	946	15	285	0
Finland	353	680	650	0.32	0.40	0.39	0.43	204	435	387	26	2	1
France	6 721	11 112	8 464	0.34	0.47	0.38	0.39	2 505	4 698	5 132	1 552	4 335	1 707
Germany	5 424	10 528	9 644	0.27	0.36	0.37	0.38	4 144	6 303	5 977	364	3 369	2 994
Greece	154	212	249	0.18	0.17	0.16	0.20	0	167	205	0	0	0
Ireland	267	699	824	0.30	0.54	0.55	0.58	74	460	528	7	0	0
Italy	1 129	2 797	1 465	0.14	0.20	0.19	0.20	510	810	630	277	1 809	586
Japan	11 777	13 297	12 912	0.28	0.25	0.17	0.18	6 703	7 959	8 823	887	3 746	1 578
Luxembourg	166	227	253	0.69	0.90	0.91	0.92	0	143	175	0	0	0
Netherlands	3 959	11 365	4 800	0.82	0.81	0.81	0.80	1 507	4 917	2 856	272	1 634	392
New Zealand	174	351	289	0.26	0.27	0.27	0.30	0	240	172	0	0	0
Norway	1 926	2 946	2 883	0.82	0.89	0.95	0.88	1 223	1 894	1 985	33	251	39
Portugal	529	244	277	0.26	0.21	0.22	0.27	249	179	308	215	0	1
Spain	1 637	2 743	3 641	0.23	0.32	0.37	0.43	1 259	1 850	2 730	119	592	301
Sweden	2 021	3 484	2 292	0.75	1.02	0.93	0.98	804	2 160	1 307	0	329	76
Switzerland	1 058	1 322	1 531	0.35	0.39	0.37	0.41	639	720	800	0	103	66
United Kingdom	3 884	10 375	7 379	0.28	0.51	0.36	0.43	4 032	5 424	4 591	181	3 966	29
United States	12 215	24 947	24 725	0.10	0.18	0.16	0.18	7 542	17 302	18 621	123	1 731	104
Total DAC	**60 360**	**107 308**	**92 153**	**0.22**	**0.31**	**0.28**	**0.30**	**35 526**	**60 764**	**61 183**	**4 458**	**23 986**	**9 010**
African Development Fund	962	1 811	1 976	...	...	...	...	785	1 489	1 823	...	...	...
Asian Development Fund	1 493	1 274	1 857	...	...	...	...	1 424	1 274	1 857	...	...	...
European Commission	10 009	13 728	13 209	...	...	...	...	6 366	10 242	9 690	...	...	...
International Development Association	7 969	9 450	12 827	...	...	...	...	6 468	7 754	9 893	...	...	...
Inter-American Development Bank Special Fund	410	392	413	...	...	...	...	410	392	413	...	...	...
UNICEF	239	840	750	...	...	...	...	210	576	750	...	...	...
Total multilaterals**	**21 911**	**30 753**	**34 857**	...	...	...	...	**16 437**	**24 927**	**28 217**	...	...	...
Total	**82 271**	**138 062**	**127 010**	...	...	...	...	**51 963**	**85 691**	**89 399**	...	...	...

Notes:

* Preliminary data.

** The total includes ODA from other multilaterals not listed above.

(...) indicates that data are not available.

All data represent commitments unless otherwise specified.

Source: OECD-DAC (2009*d*).

Table 2: Bilateral and multilateral aid to education

	Total aid to education			Total aid to basic education			Direct aid to education			Direct aid to basic education			Direct aid to secondary education		
	Constant 2007 US$ millions			Constant 2007 US$ millions			Constant 2007 US$ millions			Constant 2007 US$ millions			Constant 2007 US$ millions		
	1999–2000 annual average	2006	2007	1999–2000 annual average	2006	2007	1999–2000 annual average	2006	2007	1999–2000 annual average	2006	2007	1999–2000 annual average	2006	2007
Australia	291	178	360	89	85	127	291	178	359	80	38	49	26	4	118
Austria	97	117	147	6	6	7	97	117	147	4	4	5	3	6	9
Belgium	103	182	203	18	46	42	101	179	203	5	33	15	12	12	18
Canada	114	313	262	57	245	179	112	309	240	33	222	113	20	24	5
Denmark	81	48	69	49	30	38	73	18	53	40	14	13	22	0	5
Finland	29	50	45	13	21	26	28	37	29	3	5	10	2	4	1
France	1 831	2 074	1 994	426	342	293	1 766	1 996	1 929	106	117	199	331	80	245
Germany	940	1 541	1 479	135	172	208	937	1 518	1 464	110	120	165	110	237	172
Greece	0	27	61	0	3	2	0	26	61	0	0	0	0	0	0
Ireland	20	76	102	10	50	61	20	71	96	4	41	34	1	9	5
Italy	61	51	49	17	15	13	58	47	49	2	3	3	13	5	4
Japan	502	894	792	210	239	257	302	874	703	42	99	112	33	60	51
Luxembourg	0	33	27	0	12	11	0	33	27	0	6	7	0	15	13
Netherlands	309	1 501	693	200	1 249	293	267	1 433	618	145	1 197	199	11	44	26
New Zealand	0	71	74	0	23	51	0	69	70	0	20	45	0	4	2
Norway	170	296	254	105	150	137	165	261	222	89	113	102	10	9	9
Portugal	42	74	72	11	10	10	40	73	71	5	7	5	5	10	9
Spain	268	262	371	81	99	190	268	260	365	25	48	128	36	48	52
Sweden	78	237	64	51	172	35	51	200	48	27	120	19	1	2	0
Switzerland	47	72	58	20	29	14	47	64	50	15	18	3	21	19	18
United Kingdom	512	1 314	629	376	936	311	372	1 017	534	274	590	41	18	1	0
United States	375	567	920	206	414	682	353	489	841	186	283	538	46	0	5
Total DAC	5 872	9 980	8 723	2 079	4 350	2 990	5 348	9 270	8 178	1 193	3 100	1 805	721	593	765
African Development Fund	89	224	90	56	76	30	81	159	67	22	32	0	0	72	31
Asian Development Fund	149	206	165	11	28	69	149	206	165	0	0	9	124	149	36
European Commission	808	761	956	516	337	366	581	658	761	384	220	110	69	117	91
International Development Association	946	1 113	2 013	487	647	732	730	782	1 430	170	234	290	63	52	546
Inter-American Development Bank Special Fund	6	0	10	3	0	10	6	0	10	0	0	10	0	0	0
UNICEF	34	44	107	34	42	68	34	44	107	34	41	39	0	0	10
Total multilaterals*	2 041	2 350	3 342	1 110	1 132	1 276	1 590	1 852	2 542	611	527	458	257	391	715
Total	7 912	12 330	12 065	3 189	5 482	4 266	6 938	11 121	10 720	1 804	3 627	2 263	978	984	1 480

Notes:

* The total also includes ODA for education from UNDP.

(…) indicates that data are not available.

All data represent commitments unless otherwise specified.

Source: OECD-DAC (2009*d*).

Direct aid to post-secondary education Constant 2007 US$ millions			Education, level unspecified Constant 2007 US$ millions			Share of education in total ODA (%)			Share of education in total sector-allocable ODA (%)			Share of basic education in total aid to education (%)			
1999–2000 annual average	2006	2007	1999–2000 annual average	2006	2007	1999–2000 annual average	2006	2007	1999–2000 annual average	2006	2007	1999–2000 annual average	2006	2007	
168	42	36	18	93	157	16	7	21	21	12	25	30	48	35	Australia
86	103	129	4	4	3	12	10	11	42	39	41	6	5	5	Austria
61	110	116	22	24	55	13	11	13	20	19	19	17	25	21	Belgium
12	21	12	48	42	111	5	11	7	12	20	12	50	78	68	Canada
0	2	1	12	1	35	6	3	5	7	6	7	61	62	55	Denmark
5	10	1	19	18	17	8	7	7	14	12	12	44	41	59	Finland
754	1 427	1 361	574	371	124	27	19	24	73	44	39	23	17	15	France
670	1 079	1 055	47	81	73	17	15	15	23	24	25	14	11	14	Germany
0	20	57	0	6	4	0	13	24	...	16	30	...	12	4	Greece
2	7	8	12	14	48	7	11	12	27	17	19	51	66	60	Ireland
15	20	21	28	18	21	5	2	3	12	6	8	28	29	27	Italy
91	456	338	136	258	201	4	7	6	7	11	9	42	27	33	Japan
0	0	1	0	12	7	0	15	11	...	23	16	...	36	39	Luxembourg
42	157	280	69	35	113	8	13	14	21	31	24	65	83	42	Netherlands
0	40	15	0	4	7	0	20	26	...	30	43	...	33	69	New Zealand
40	98	74	28	41	37	9	10	9	14	16	13	62	51	54	Norway
21	50	47	10	7	10	8	30	26	17	41	23	26	14	15	Portugal
94	64	67	112	100	118	16	10	10	21	14	14	30	38	51	Spain
3	11	13	19	67	15	4	7	3	10	11	5	65	73	55	Sweden
1	13	15	11	13	14	4	5	4	7	10	7	43	41	24	Switzerland
16	31	48	64	395	445	13	13	9	13	24	14	74	71	49	United Kingdom
104	22	87	17	184	212	3	2	4	5	3	5	55	73	74	United States
2 185	**3 786**	**3 783**	**1 250**	**1 790**	**1 826**	**10**	**9**	**9**	**17**	**16**	**14**	**35**	**44**	**34**	**Total DAC**
0	32	0	59	24	36	9	12	5	11	15	5	62	34	33	African Development Fund
4	0	0	21	57	119	10	16	9	10	16	9	7	14	42	Asian Development Fund
91	190	242	37	131	319	8	6	7	13	7	10	64	44	38	European Commission
79	0	292	418	495	302	12	12	16	15	14	20	51	58	36	International Development Association
0	0	0	6	0	0	2	0	2	2	0	2	50	...	100	Inter-American Development Bank Special Fund
0	0	0	0	3	58	14	5	14	16	8	14	100	97	63	UNICEF
175	**222**	**534**	**547**	**711**	**835**	**9**	**8**	**10**	**12**	**9**	**12**	**54**	**48**	**38**	**Total multilaterals***
2 360	4 008	4 317	1 796	2 501	2 661	10	9	9	15	14	13	40	44	35	Total

Table 3: ODA recipients

	Total ODA			Per capita ODA			Sector-allocable ODA			Debt relief and other actions relating to debt		
	Constant 2007 US$ millions			Constant 2007 US$			Constant 2007 US$ millions			Constant 2007 US$ millions		
	1999–2000 annual average	2006	2007	1999–2000 annual average	2006	2007	1999–2000 annual average	2006	2007	1999–2000 annual average	2006	2007
Arab States	**6 710**	**18 501**	**19 287**	**25**	**60**	**62**	**5 236**	**11 712**	**11 156**	**548**	**3 857**	**4 805**
Unallocated within the region	*309*	*506*	*413*	...	...	...	*217*	*430*	*207*	*1*	*0*	*0*
Algeria	214	537	442	7	16	13	185	483	408	0	27	10
Bahrain	0	0	0	1	0	0	0	0	0	0	0	0
Djibouti	94	90	131	131	110	157	71	74	88	2	8	0
Egypt	1 827	1 685	1 645	28	23	22	1 489	1 324	1 204	336	148	145
Iraq	136	8 233	9 102	6	289	314	19	4 460	4 186	0	3 634	4 553
Jordan	633	572	653	133	100	110	464	373	444	89	19	72
Lebanon	142	739	788	38	182	192	123	277	522	0	0	14
Libyan Arab Jamahiriya	2	39	17	0	6	3	2	38	16	0	0	0
Mauritania	272	333	180	108	109	58	181	300	142	23	3	7
Morocco	867	1 345	1 256	30	44	40	770	1 316	1 227	73	2	2
Oman	7	7	3	3	3	1	6	7	3	0	0	0
Palestinian A. T.	620	1 161	1 435	200	298	357	535	833	966	0	0	0
Saudi Arabia	3	12	14	0	0	1	3	11	12	0	0	0
Sudan	341	2 218	1 802	10	59	47	73	904	562	5	3	0
Syrian Arab Republic	127	163	231	8	8	12	123	154	211	0	0	0
Tunisia	587	525	836	62	51	81	570	440	690	0	2	2
Yemen	528	336	339	29	15	15	404	290	268	20	10	1
Central and Eastern Europe	**6 525**	**6 725**	**4 874**	**45**	**46**	**33**	**3 607**	**5 245**	**4 525**	**327**	**854**	**4**
Unallocated within the region	*2 974*	*3 165*	*1 811*	...	...	...	*1 388*	*1 819*	*1 620*	*0*	*854*	*0*
Albania	677	477	299	220	150	94	452	473	283	2	0	0
Belarus	0	69	76	0	7	8	0	63	73	0	0	0
Bosnia and Herzegovina	1 350	541	473	361	138	120	699	527	460	325	0	0
Croatia	105	258	259	23	57	57	87	254	255	0	0	0
Republic of Moldova	176	202	273	42	53	72	126	169	189	0	0	4
TFYR Macedonia	419	225	182	209	110	89	240	222	170	0	0	0
Turkey	825	1 241	942	12	17	13	616	1 177	924	0	0	0
Ukraine	0	547	559	0	12	12	0	543	551	0	0	0
Central Asia	**1 936**	**2 801**	**2 238**	**26**	**36**	**29**	**1 517**	**2 473**	**1 977**	**2**	**43**	**58**
Unallocated within the region	*0*	*191*	*232*	...	...	...	*0*	*179*	*224*	*0*	*0*	*0*
Armenia	286	507	354	93	169	118	239	449	291	0	4	0
Azerbaijan	294	286	198	36	34	23	244	279	187	0	0	0
Georgia	343	725	329	72	163	75	254	608	218	0	6	57
Kazakhstan	196	138	257	13	9	17	192	124	255	2	0	0
Kyrgyzstan	292	262	210	59	50	40	186	229	196	0	17	1
Mongolia	183	269	220	74	103	84	153	244	210	0	17	0
Tajikistan	170	269	267	28	41	40	94	213	227	0	0	0
Turkmenistan	26	19	25	6	4	5	22	18	25	0	0	0
Uzbekistan	146	135	146	6	5	5	134	131	143	0	0	0
East Asia and the Pacific	**12 917**	**12 554**	**12 859**	**7**	**6**	**7**	**10 647**	**11 126**	**11 266**	**161**	**200**	**91**
Unallocated within the region	*118*	*371*	*446*	...	...	...	*104*	*313*	*352*	*0*	*0*	*24*
Cambodia	548	630	556	43	44	38	423	595	472	0	0	1
China	2 498	2 716	2 618	2	2	2	2 351	2 624	2 593	0	0	0
Cook Islands	3	42	10	199	3 090	748	3	7	8	0	27	0
DPR Korea	217	56	111	10	2	5	8	16	62	0	0	0
Fiji	25	66	40	31	79	47	23	62	38	0	0	0
Indonesia	2 077	3 265	2 919	10	14	13	1 065	2 616	2 219	110	99	62
Kiribati	25	17	30	303	185	317	25	17	29	0	0	0
Lao PDR	221	267	281	43	46	48	193	244	248	3	0	0

Table 3 (continued)

	Total ODA			Per capita ODA			Sector-allocable ODA			Debt relief and other actions relating to debt		
	Constant 2007 US$ millions			Constant 2007 US$			Constant 2007 US$ millions			Constant 2007 US$ millions		
	1999–2000 annual average	2006	2007	1999–2000 annual average	2006	2007	1999–2000 annual average	2006	2007	1999–2000 annual average	2006	2007
Malaysia	942	117	70	41	4	3	941	113	67	0	0	0
Marshall Islands	63	57	54	1 203	989	905	27	54	52	0	0	0
Micronesia, F. S.	112	115	109	1 049	1 039	978	39	113	107	0	0	0
Myanmar	65	168	214	1	3	4	38	129	121	12	4	1
Nauru	0	22	24	16	2 165	2 330	0	21	22	0	0	0
Niue	1	9	23	624	5 610	14 660	1	9	7	0	0	0
Palau	33	34	31	1 725	1 658	1 510	20	23	30	0	0	0
Papua New Guinea	590	351	372	111	57	59	547	340	365	0	0	0
Philippines	1 396	489	728	19	6	8	1 313	429	692	0	0	1
Republic of Korea	33	0	0	1	0	0	31	0	0	0	0	0
Samoa	35	49	78	199	264	415	35	46	76	0	0	0
Solomon Islands	132	228	266	322	472	536	93	226	258	0	0	0
Thailand	1 253	370	219	21	6	3	1 120	318	159	0	0	2
Timor-Leste	360	226	307	442	202	266	242	192	288	0	0	0
Tokelau	0	13	11	101	9 423	7 902	0	5	4	0	0	0
Tonga	17	30	40	171	301	400	17	28	37	0	0	0
Tuvalu	8	6	19	788	586	1 821	8	6	16	0	0	0
Vanuatu	39	120	66	208	541	293	36	116	58	1	0	0
Viet Nam	2 106	2 721	3 218	27	32	37	1 944	2 463	2 886	35	69	0
Latin America and the Caribbean	**8 480**	**9 381**	**7 888**	**17**	**17**	**14**	**6 647**	**7 959**	**6 599**	**595**	**507**	**358**
Unallocated within the region	*411*	*571*	*599*	...	...	...	*300*	*524*	*503*	*0*	*0*	*0*
Anguilla	7	12	6	601	935	446	6	12	6	0	0	0
Antigua and Barbuda	8	0	1	99	4	15	7	0	1	0	0	0
Argentina	68	90	153	2	2	4	67	86	144	0	0	3
Aruba	0	0	0	2	0	0	0	0	0	0	0	0
Barbados	2	7	20	8	25	67	2	7	20	0	0	0
Belize	43	18	20	178	65	69	41	18	19	0	0	0
Bolivia	1 082	757	812	131	81	85	756	619	757	257	72	0
Brazil	271	324	330	2	2	2	259	308	310	0	0	0
Chile	76	51	141	5	3	8	71	47	135	1	0	0
Colombia	985	1 651	781	24	36	17	949	1 520	704	3	0	0
Costa Rica	63	203	60	16	46	13	51	199	55	10	0	0
Cuba	83	59	76	7	5	7	56	52	71	0	0	0
Dominica	21	9	30	310	132	442	16	7	15	0	1	0
Dominican Republic	347	283	186	40	29	19	320	191	152	1	16	5
Ecuador	207	255	289	17	19	22	158	225	277	0	6	1
El Salvador	231	195	599	38	29	87	182	177	576	2	1	2
Grenada	14	11	17	139	108	159	10	11	3	0	0	0
Guatemala	405	621	464	36	48	35	331	330	240	0	202	180
Guyana	191	65	271	259	88	367	145	53	245	24	2	0
Haiti	279	629	671	33	67	70	193	543	446	5	1	59
Honduras	1 053	521	444	172	75	63	700	301	367	97	162	49
Jamaica	137	86	123	53	32	45	87	72	100	5	8	1
Mexico	195	480	236	2	5	2	185	475	225	0	0	0
Montserrat	49	27	19	9 083	4 630	3 163	34	27	19	0	0	0
Nicaragua	844	1 102	378	166	199	67	588	955	307	68	15	3
Panama	39	62	216	13	19	65	39	56	214	0	0	0
Paraguay	54	328	82	10	55	13	50	291	76	0	0	0
Peru	1 034	745	474	41	27	17	807	683	392	122	3	13
Saint Kitts and Nevis	5	4	18	119	82	359	5	4	4	0	0	0
Saint Lucia	31	12	20	203	74	122	21	11	20	0	0	0
Saint Vincent/Grenadines	15	12	71	127	99	588	11	12	29	0	0	41
Suriname	40	62	148	91	136	324	39	39	47	0	18	0
Trinidad and Tobago	10	44	17	8	33	13	8	43	16	0	0	0
Turks and Caicos Islands	5	15	6	292	594	227	5	0	0	0	0	0
Uruguay	21	27	61	6	8	18	20	25	55	0	0	0
Venezuela, B. R.	156	40	51	6	1	2	124	38	48	0	0	0

Table 3 (continued)

	Total ODA			Per capita ODA			Sector-allocable ODA			Debt relief and other actions relating to debt		
	Constant 2007 US$ millions			Constant 2007 US$			Constant 2007 US$ millions			Constant 2007 US$ millions		
	1999–2000 annual average	2006	2007	1999–2000 annual average	2006	2007	1999–2000 annual average	2006	2007	1999–2000 annual average	2006	2007
North America and Western Europe	**29**	**31**	**585**	**4**	**0**	**0**	**29**	**31**	**585**	**0**	**0**	**0**
Unallocated within the region	*27*	*31*	*585*	...	...	...	*27*	*31*	*585*	*0*	*0*	*0*
Malta	2	0	0	4	0	0	2	0	0	0	0	0
South and West Asia	**7 401**	**15 046**	**17 457**	**5**	**9**	**11**	**5 943**	**12 408**	**14 550**	**595**	**356**	**88**
Unallocated within the region	*0*	*50*	*101*	...	...	...	*0*	*40*	*55*	*0*	*0*	*0*
Afghanistan	206	3 563	4 387	10	137	162	60	3 026	3 553	0	0	58
Bangladesh	2 261	2 597	2 455	16	17	15	1 847	2 101	1 965	154	245	11
Bhutan	82	79	130	148	121	198	80	61	97	0	0	0
India	2 588	4 839	5 824	2	4	5	2 280	4 761	5 529	1	0	0
Iran, Islamic Republic of	146	130	107	2	2	2	119	77	84	0	0	
Maldives	36	58	31	133	194	100	35	21	29	0	0	0
Nepal	537	530	776	22	19	28	509	451	689	17	31	16
Pakistan	915	2 369	2 825	6	15	17	434	1 289	1 873	423	6	0
Sri Lanka	630	831	822	34	43	43	578	582	675	0	73	4
Sub-Saharan Africa	**21 666**	**45 977**	**37 297**	**34**	**62**	**49**	**13 854**	**21 637**	**26 857**	**2 170**	**16 338**	**3 544**
Unallocated within the region	*813*	*1 910*	*2 645*	...	...	...	*689*	*1 532*	*2 182*	*1*	*1*	*0*
Angola	398	282	354	29	17	21	217	239	335	1	0	0
Benin	482	867	465	68	99	52	342	741	324	36	15	2
Botswana	51	84	255	30	45	135	44	77	253	3	5	1
Burkina Faso	656	792	700	56	55	47	475	567	479	44	21	3
Burundi	206	639	444	31	78	52	110	402	257	9	15	1
Cameroon	632	2 357	2 075	40	130	112	340	623	577	170	1 519	1 485
Cape Verde	164	158	340	368	304	641	117	125	158	1	1	1
Central African Republic	146	281	230	38	66	53	83	153	127	23	13	6
Chad	392	294	418	47	28	39	321	130	174	14	8	7
Comoros	27	39	48	40	48	58	15	32	45	3	2	1
Congo	139	455	159	44	123	42	32	112	133	86	301	9
Côte d'Ivoire	742	457	413	44	24	21	294	200	373	276	65	5
D. R. Congo	203	2 201	1 546	4	36	25	117	843	1 087	18	905	124
Equatorial Guinea	32	44	38	75	89	74	27	40	37	3	2	0
Eritrea	300	123	166	83	26	34	169	75	120	0	0	0
Ethiopia	995	2 442	3 315	15	30	40	462	2 034	2 949	3	37	3
Gabon	99	168	142	84	128	107	67	165	139	31	0	0
Gambia	69	75	55	51	45	32	56	69	52	1	0	0
Ghana	1 127	1 516	1 675	57	66	71	779	938	1 412	8	31	10
Guinea	289	242	326	36	26	35	240	199	290	30	17	2
Guinea-Bissau	114	90	136	85	55	80	53	70	101	12	8	0
Kenya	1 041	1 707	2 387	34	47	64	775	1 322	2 204	19	69	5
Lesotho	104	126	186	56	63	93	100	121	161	0	0	0
Liberia	48	381	927	16	106	247	24	212	344	0	0	15
Madagascar	678	675	665	43	35	34	338	477	418	95	31	90
Malawi	775	770	595	68	57	43	505	523	457	31	67	37
Mali	672	838	1 352	68	70	110	502	655	1 073	41	32	124
Mauritius	44	86	171	37	69	136	44	85	41	0	0	0
Mozambique	1 905	1 492	2 276	106	71	106	1 126	1 082	1 479	303	86	9
Namibia	137	219	301	73	107	145	129	213	298	0	0	0
Niger	326	600	365	30	44	26	190	400	234	38	15	2
Nigeria	658	13 358	2 419	5	92	16	646	1 291	1 711	0	12 059	669
Rwanda	569	855	721	72	90	74	254	465	586	22	109	0
Sao Tome and Principe	50	29	43	362	189	272	44	25	29	3	2	7
Senegal	997	1 079	606	98	89	49	650	832	549	224	188	3
Seychelles	5	15	3	64	173	40	5	12	3	0	2	0
Sierra Leone	349	263	464	78	46	79	121	142	221	0	35	194

Table 3 (continued)

	Total ODA			Per capita ODA			Sector-allocable ODA			Debt relief and other actions relating to debt		
	Constant 2007 US$ millions			Constant 2007 US$			Constant 2007 US$ millions			Constant 2007 US$ millions		
	1999–2000 annual average	2006	2007	1999–2000 annual average	2006	2007	1999–2000 annual average	2006	2007	1999–2000 annual average	2006	2007
Somalia	142	478	439	21	57	50	51	110	141	4	1	0
South Africa	595	957	1 037	13	20	21	567	944	1 029	0	0	0
Swaziland	30	47	59	29	41	52	24	45	44	0	0	0
Togo	113	70	198	21	11	30	73	55	184	20	7	8
Uganda	1 280	1 338	1 873	53	45	61	846	882	1 453	110	11	6
U. R. Tanzania	1 494	2 941	2 788	45	75	69	924	1 136	1 682	196	8	648
Zambia	1 319	1 752	1 028	128	150	86	640	942	693	290	648	65
Zimbabwe	255	382	448	20	29	34	226	299	223	0	0	2
Unallocated by country	*10 821*	*26 659*	*22 324*	…	…	…	*4 484*	*13 101*	*11 885*	*63*	*1 855*	*92*
Total	76 486	137 675	124 809	15	25	23	51 963	85 691	89 399	4 460	24 010	9 041
Upper middle income countries	3 693	4 974	5 372	10	13	13	3 267	4 315	4 797	45	36	61
Low middle income countries	25 867	34 289	33 062	11	14	13	19 449	25 936	24 531	1 449	5 360	5 159
High income countries	123	0	0	3	0	0	114	0	0	0	0	0
Unallocated by income	12 779	31 357	27 469	…	…	…	5 927	16 848	15 968	65	1 856	117
Least developed countries	21 204	34 245	35 486	32	44	44	13 621	22 997	25 485	1 815	2 591	1 512
Low income countries	34 025	67 054	58 906	15	27	23	23 207	38 591	44 103	2 902	16 758	3 704
Middle income countries	29 559	39 263	38 435	11	14	13	22 715	30 251	29 329	1 493	5 395	5 220
Total	76 486	137 675	124 809	15	25	23	51 963	85 691	89 399	4 460	24 010	9 041
Arab States	6 710	18 501	19 287	25	60	62	5 236	11 712	11 156	548	3 857	4 805
Central and Eastern Europe	6 525	6 725	4 874	45	46	33	3 607	5 245	4 525	327	854	4
Central Asia	1 936	2 801	2 238	26	36	29	1 517	2 473	1 977	2	43	58
East Asia and the Pacific	12 917	12 554	12 859	7	6	7	10 647	11 126	11 266	161	200	91
Latin America and the Caribbean	8 480	9 381	7 888	17	17	14	6 647	7 959	6 599	595	507	358
North America and Western Europe	29	31	585	4	0	0	29	31	585	0	0	0
South and West Asia	7 401	15 046	17 457	5	9	11	5 943	12 408	14 550	595	356	88
Sub-Saharan Africa	21 666	45 977	37 297	34	62	49	13 854	21 637	26 857	2 170	16 338	3 544
Unallocated by region	*10 821*	*26 659*	*22 324*	…	…	…	*4 484*	*13 101*	*11 885*	*63*	*1 855*	*92*
Total	76 486	137 675	124 809	15	25	23	51 963	85 691	89 399	4 460	24 010	9 041

Notes:
(…) indicates that data are not available.
All data represent commitments unless otherwise specified.
Totals may not match those presented in Table 1 due to the use of different databases.
Source: OECD-DAC (2009*d*).

Table 4: Recipients of aid to education

	Total aid to education			Total aid to basic education			Total aid to basic education per primary school-age child			Direct aid to education			Direct aid to basic education		
	Constant 2007 US$ millions			Constant 2007 US$ millions			Constant 2007 US$			Constant 2007 US$ millions			Constant 2007 US$ millions		
	1999–2000 annual average	2006	2007	1999–2000 annual average	2006	2007	1999–2000 annual average	2006	2007	1999–2000 annual average	2006	2007	1999–2000 annual average	2006	2007
Arab States	**1 223**	**1 828**	**1 726**	**359**	**577**	**525**	**9**	**14**	**13**	**1 194**	**1 774**	**1 614**	**162**	**323**	**281**
Unallocated within the region	*28*	*76*	*71*	*7*	*9*	*0*	...	...	...	*28*	*76*	*71*	*4*	*3*	*0*
Algeria	139	221	174	42	21	1	9	6	0	139	221	174	0	0	0
Bahrain	1	0	0	0	0	0	0	0	0	1	0	0	0	0	0
Djibouti	54	39	33	16	10	18	134	84	146	51	39	27	1	7	15
Egypt	161	164	341	43	125	183	5	13	19	161	164	286	39	124	71
Iraq	9	64	129	1	27	60	0	6	13	9	64	129	0	2	2
Jordan	29	113	122	3	77	73	4	92	86	25	78	99	0	59	42
Lebanon	48	73	92	10	6	15	26	12	32	48	73	89	1	5	12
Libyan Arab Jamahiriya	2	7	5	0	0	0	0	1	1	2	7	5	0	0	0
Mauritania	46	100	22	13	44	8	33	96	18	37	99	22	1	11	8
Morocco	296	354	332	72	40	42	18	11	11	296	354	332	12	15	36
Oman	1	1	1	0	0	0	0	1	1	1	1	1	0	0	0
Palestinian A. T.	62	104	45	31	58	18	87	125	37	60	103	34	19	31	10
Saudi Arabia	2	7	9	0	2	2	0	1	1	2	7	9	0	2	2
Sudan	23	188	75	6	95	52	1	16	9	14	187	72	1	12	41
Syrian Arab Republic	44	73	70	5	2	7	2	1	4	44	73	70	0	1	6
Tunisia	200	185	125	51	10	2	40	9	2	199	170	125	33	2	1
Yemen	78	59	78	59	50	43	18	13	11	77	59	68	49	48	33
Central and Eastern Europe	**456**	**472**	**526**	**146**	**50**	**70**	**12**	**4**	**6**	**414**	**455**	**508**	**97**	**25**	**31**
Unallocated within the region	*70*	*100*	*157*	*11*	*19*	*37*	...	...	...	*67*	*86*	*157*	*1*	*4*	*15*
Albania	36	48	48	12	11	5	45	53	26	28	48	46	2	8	2
Belarus	0	26	18	0	0	0	0	0	0	0	26	18	0	0	0
Bosnia and Herzegovina	41	35	35	12	2	3	70	10	17	31	35	35	2	1	1
Croatia	22	21	16	1	0	1	2	1	7	22	21	16	0	0	1
Republic of Moldova	11	28	29	4	8	8	15	44	42	4	26	15	0	7	1
TFYR Macedonia	28	21	22	12	6	11	97	55	107	14	21	20	4	5	10
Turkey	247	119	144	94	3	3	11	0	0	247	119	144	87	1	1
Ukraine	0	74	56	0	1	1	0	0	0	0	74	56	0	0	0
Central Asia	**114**	**219**	**199**	**28**	**68**	**36**	**4**	**12**	**6**	**92**	**196**	**183**	**9**	**36**	**20**
Unallocated within the region	*0*	*0*	*16*	*0*	*0*	*0*	...	...	...	*0*	*0*	*16*	*0*	*0*	*0*
Armenia	12	42	44	2	6	7	8	52	57	10	36	35	0	0	1
Azerbaijan	8	7	5	3	0	0	3	0	0	7	7	5	0	0	0
Georgia	23	50	30	5	13	5	17	38	14	14	35	25	0	4	1
Kazakhstan	17	12	19	2	1	2	2	1	2	17	12	19	2	0	1
Kyrgyzstan	11	22	10	4	12	3	9	27	7	4	22	10	0	7	1
Mongolia	16	46	30	6	20	11	23	81	46	14	46	30	4	12	10
Tajikistan	9	10	8	4	3	6	5	5	8	8	8	6	1	2	4
Turkmenistan	4	1	4	0	0	2	1	1	8	4	1	4	0	0	1
Uzbekistan	15	28	32	2	12	1	1	5	0	15	28	32	1	11	0
East Asia and the Pacific	**1 326**	**2 076**	**2 118**	**402**	**687**	**556**	**2**	**4**	**3**	**1 129**	**2 018**	**1 960**	**180**	**454**	**192**
Unallocated within the region	*17*	*10*	*124*	*6*	*3*	*5*	...	...	...	*15*	*10*	*124*	*4*	*1*	*5*
Cambodia	44	68	31	17	52	12	8	25	6	37	68	20	8	50	5
China	188	894	697	30	139	39	0	1	0	188	894	697	19	72	4
Cook Islands	0	4	3	0	2	1	0	675	...	0	4	3	0	1	1
DPR Korea	1	2	2	0	0	1	0	0	1	1	2	2	0	0	1
Fiji	7	10	5	1	4	2	10	35	19	7	10	5	1	0	0
Indonesia	293	463	519	133	306	237	5	12	9	175	443	440	62	237	72
Kiribati	8	3	2	3	1	1	251	76	...	8	3	2	0	0	0
Lao PDR	35	21	26	6	5	14	7	6	18	32	19	22	2	1	10

Direct aid to secondary education			Direct aid to post-secondary education			Aid to education, level unspecified			Share of education in total ODA			Share of education in total sector-allocable ODA			Share of basic education in total aid to education		
Constant 2007 US$ millions			Constant 2007 US$ millions			Constant 2007 US$ millions			(%)			(%)			(%)		
1999–2000 annual average	2006	2007	1999–2000 annual average	2006	2007	1999–2000 annual average	2006	2007	1999–2000 annual average	2006	2007	1999–2000 annual average	2006	2007	1999–2000 annual average	2006	2007
233	**133**	**83**	**434**	**864**	**873**	**364**	**454**	**376**	**18**	**10**	**9**	**23**	**16**	**15**	**29**	**32**	**30**
2	*5*	*5*	*15*	*57*	*66*	*6*	*11*	*1*	*9*	*15*	*17*	*13*	*18*	*34*	*26*	*12*	*1*
6	8	3	49	170	169	84	42	2	65	41	39	75	46	43	31	10	1
0	0	0	0	0	0	0	0	0	...	...	...	...	...	...	...	...	...
14	0	0	10	25	12	25	7	0	58	43	25	77	52	38	29	26	54
51	13	3	64	25	44	7	2	168	9	10	21	11	12	28	27	77	54
0	2	2	8	11	11	1	50	115	7	1	1	49	1	3	8	42	46
4	1	2	20	17	17	1	1	39	5	20	19	6	30	28	9	68	59
11	12	9	19	55	66	16	1	2	34	10	12	39	26	18	20	8	16
0	0	0	1	7	4	0	0	0	96	18	30	103	19	32	11	5	7
5	11	1	15	13	12	14	65	0	17	30	12	26	34	16	28	44	37
68	23	24	95	265	261	120	51	11	34	26	26	38	27	27	24	11	13
0	0	0	1	0	0	0	0	0	11	12	32	11	13	35	13	23	34
11	4	5	8	16	15	23	52	5	10	9	3	12	12	5	50	56	39
0	3	2	1	2	4	1	1	0	69	65	62	69	71	70	13	30	28
1	1	2	11	9	9	1	165	19	7	8	4	32	21	13	27	51	70
1	1	1	34	68	61	9	3	2	34	45	30	35	47	33	10	3	10
57	50	9	75	117	114	34	1	1	34	35	15	35	42	18	25	5	2
1	0	15	7	8	9	20	3	10	15	18	23	19	20	29	76	84	56
54	**39**	**38**	**206**	**357**	**379**	**56**	**33**	**60**	**7**	**7**	**11**	**13**	**9**	**12**	**32**	**11**	**13**
2	*13*	*12*	*47*	*53*	*86*	*17*	*16*	*44*	*2*	*3*	*9*	*5*	*5*	*10*	*15*	*19*	*24*
3	14	6	10	19	34	13	8	5	5	10	16	8	10	17	35	24	11
0	0	0	0	25	17	0	0	0	...	37	23	...	41	24	...	1	0
0	3	1	18	29	29	10	3	4	3	6	7	6	7	8	30	6	9
0	0	1	21	20	13	1	0	0	21	8	6	25	8	6	2	1	9
0	7	1	3	12	12	1	0	1	6	14	11	9	17	15	37	29	29
2	1	0	6	14	9	2	2	1	7	10	12	12	10	13	43	28	52
46	1	15	101	114	124	13	3	3	30	10	15	40	10	16	38	2	2
0	0	0	0	72	55	0	1	1	...	13	10	...	14	10	...	1	1
25	**28**	**54**	**43**	**91**	**94**	**15**	**42**	**14**	**6**	**8**	**9**	**8**	**9**	**10**	**24**	**31**	**18**
0	*0*	*1*	*0*	*0*	*15*	*0*	*0*	*0*	...	*0*	*7*	...	*0*	*7*	...	*0*	*0*
0	10	22	8	19	11	2	6	0	4	8	13	5	9	15	15	15	15
0	0	0	3	7	5	4	0	0	3	2	3	3	3	3	33	2	2
0	3	1	13	25	22	1	2	2	7	7	9	9	8	14	22	26	15
10	2	8	5	9	9	1	2	2	9	9	7	9	10	8	11	8	9
1	0	1	2	5	5	0	11	3	4	9	5	6	10	5	38	53	28
1	1	1	7	17	16	2	17	3	9	17	14	10	19	14	36	44	37
3	4	0	0	1	1	3	1	1	5	4	3	10	5	4	41	33	69
3	0	0	0	1	1	0	0	2	14	8	17	17	8	17	10	15	51
7	7	20	4	7	10	3	3	1	10	21	22	11	22	22	16	43	3
190	**68**	**206**	**512**	**1 088**	**992**	**247**	**407**	**569**	**10**	**17**	**16**	**12**	**19**	**19**	**30**	**33**	**26**
1	*0*	*118*	*9*	*6*	*1*	*2*	*4*	*1*	*14*	*3*	*28*	*16*	*3*	*35*	*35*	*28*	*4*
4	1	2	15	12	10	10	5	3	8	11	6	10	11	7	38	77	39
10	11	10	136	676	614	22	135	69	8	33	27	8	34	27	16	16	6
0	1	1	0	1	0	0	1	2	3	10	33	3	57	38	0	47	42
0	0	0	1	1	1	0	0	0	1	3	2	16	11	3	4	11	42
0	0	0	6	3	1	0	7	4	30	16	12	32	17	12	15	38	44
19	21	8	70	68	109	24	116	251	14	14	18	28	18	23	46	66	46
0	0	0	1	1	0	7	1	1	31	15	6	31	15	6	43	41	41
4	8	2	22	4	7	4	6	3	16	8	9	18	8	11	16	24	52

Table 4 (continued)

	Total aid to education Constant 2007 US$ millions			Total aid to basic education Constant 2007 US$ millions			Total aid to basic education per primary school-age child Constant 2007 US$			Direct aid to education Constant 2007 US$ millions			Direct aid to basic education Constant 2007 US$ millions		
	1999–2000 annual average	2006	2007	1999–2000 annual average	2006	2007	1999–2000 annual average	2006	2007	1999–2000 annual average	2006	2007	1999–2000 annual average	2006	2007
Malaysia	84	86	20	1	2	1	0	0	0	84	86	20	0	0	0
Marshall Islands	4	13	14	2	7	7	233	767	792	0	13	14	0	0	0
Micronesia, F. S.	9	28	29	4	14	14	222	829	856	1	28	29	0	0	0
Myanmar	3	21	33	2	17	28	0	4	7	3	21	33	1	17	28
Nauru	0	2	1	0	1	1	0	642	469	0	2	1	0	0	0
Niue	0	0	4	0	0	2	0	211	...	0	0	1	0	0	0
Palau	2	3	1	1	2	1	386	998	335	0	1	1	0	0	0
Papua New Guinea	116	38	40	72	24	21	90	24	21	110	38	40	66	16	3
Philippines	170	46	125	59	23	64	5	2	5	168	46	125	5	15	15
Republic of Korea	32	0	0	4	0	0	1	0	0	32	0	0	0	0	0
Samoa	9	24	4	4	7	2	142	211	56	9	24	4	2	0	0
Solomon Islands	15	5	44	4	2	30	63	20	384	8	5	44	0	1	28
Thailand	51	36	34	13	2	2	2	0	0	28	36	34	0	0	0
Timor-Leste	9	31	46	3	19	26	19	100	136	9	30	46	2	13	13
Tokelau	0	2	2	0	1	1	...	3 267	...	0	0	0	0	0	0
Tonga	2	18	3	0	12	1	21	807	96	2	18	3	0	10	0
Tuvalu	1	0	3	0	0	0	312	33	...	1	0	3	0	0	0
Vanuatu	14	13	9	1	6	4	20	164	110	14	13	8	0	3	1
Viet Nam	211	237	295	36	38	40	4	5	5	194	205	237	6	13	4
Latin America and the Caribbean	**605**	**832**	**794**	**270**	**284**	**289**	**5**	**5**	**5**	**577**	**782**	**743**	**184**	**154**	**177**
Unallocated within the region	*30*	*13*	*39*	*11*	*3*	*2*	...	...	...	*28*	*12*	*39*	*2*	*0*	*1*
Anguilla	3	0	0	0	0	0	...	0	...	3	0	0	0	0	0
Antigua and Barbuda	2	0	0	1	0	0	...	0	9	2	0	0	0	0	0
Argentina	18	20	39	3	3	3	1	1	1	18	20	39	0	2	2
Aruba	0	0	0	0	0	0	0	0	0	0	0	0	0	0	0
Barbados	0	0	0	0	0	0	1	0	0	0	0	0	0	0	0
Belize	1	1	1	1	0	0	23	7	10	1	1	1	1	0	0
Bolivia	45	47	60	33	19	17	26	14	12	43	45	60	29	13	13
Brazil	52	70	73	12	14	11	1	1	1	52	70	73	6	9	3
Chile	22	19	27	3	3	3	2	2	2	22	19	27	1	2	3
Colombia	39	51	49	14	9	8	3	2	2	39	51	49	4	7	7
Costa Rica	4	6	6	0	1	1	1	2	3	4	6	6	0	1	1
Cuba	9	5	7	1	1	1	1	1	1	9	5	7	0	0	1
Dominica	1	0	3	1	0	2	46	2	...	0	0	0	0	0	0
Dominican Republic	24	98	13	8	45	7	7	36	5	24	88	13	7	6	5
Ecuador	11	40	57	2	13	37	1	8	22	11	40	57	1	3	34
El Salvador	16	21	37	8	9	19	9	10	21	15	21	37	5	2	6
Grenada	0	0	4	0	0	3	4	1	176	0	0	2	0	0	2
Guatemala	34	26	24	22	11	13	12	5	6	34	26	24	19	8	10
Guyana	7	4	8	1	2	4	9	19	46	6	2	3	0	0	2
Haiti	35	58	81	20	13	47	15	9	34	31	55	68	12	6	28
Honduras	25	24	43	14	19	27	14	17	25	22	24	43	5	16	15
Jamaica	24	6	11	20	5	9	58	14	26	18	6	7	16	4	7
Mexico	24	52	46	4	5	5	0	0	0	24	52	46	1	4	4
Montserrat	2	0	0	1	0	0	3 891	0	0	0	0	0	0	0	0
Nicaragua	84	116	45	68	81	21	82	97	25	82	97	45	59	57	12
Panama	15	3	3	1	1	1	3	2	2	15	3	3	1	0	0
Paraguay	5	16	10	3	7	5	3	9	6	5	9	10	2	3	5
Peru	31	74	44	10	15	17	3	4	5	31	71	44	7	8	12
Saint Kitts and Nevis	0	0	7	0	0	3	0	0	490	0	0	4	0	0	0
Saint Lucia	3	1	3	2	1	0	66	28	17	1	1	3	0	1	0
Saint Vincent/Grenadines	1	0	17	1	0	8	35	6	538	1	0	17	0	0	0
Suriname	1	2	21	0	0	10	1	0	181	1	2	1	0	0	0
Trinidad and Tobago	1	39	1	0	0	0	0	0	0	1	39	1	0	0	0
Turks and Caicos Islands	2	3	1	2	1	1	...	...	...	2	0	0	2	0	0
Uruguay	6	4	5	1	1	1	3	3	4	6	4	5	0	1	1
Venezuela, B. R.	25	12	10	2	1	1	1	0	0	25	12	10	1	1	1

Direct aid to secondary education			Direct aid to post-secondary education			Aid to education, level unspecified			Share of education in total ODA			Share of education in total sector-allocable ODA			Share of basic education in total aid to education		
Constant 2007 US$ millions			Constant 2007 US$ millions			Constant 2007 US$ millions			(%)			(%)			(%)		
1999–2000 annual average	2006	2007	1999–2000 annual average	2006	2007	1999–2000 annual average	2006	2007	1999–2000 annual average	2006	2007	1999–2000 annual average	2006	2007	1999–2000 annual average	2006	2007
2	1	1	81	81	17	2	3	2	9	73	29	9	76	30	1	2	7
0	0	0	0	0	0	0	12	13	7	23	26	16	24	27	44	50	50
0	0	0	1	0	0	0	27	28	8	24	26	22	25	27	44	50	50
0	0	0	1	4	4	1	0	2	5	13	16	9	17	28	58	81	85
0	0	0	0	0	0	0	2	1	52	9	6	52	10	7	0	50	49
0	0	0	0	0	0	0	0	0	32	4	17	35	4	54	0	10	52
0	0	0	0	0	0	0	0	0	5	8	2	8	13	2	39	57	74
10	2	1	27	4	1	6	16	35	20	11	11	21	11	11	62	61	51
31	5	3	26	9	10	105	17	97	12	9	17	13	11	18	35	51	51
0	0	0	23	0	0	9	0	0	97	...	...	105	...	...	14	...	...
1	2	1	1	9	0	5	12	3	25	48	5	25	51	5	46	28	44
2	0	12	5	3	1	1	0	3	11	2	17	16	2	17	28	30	67
6	1	1	20	32	30	2	3	3	4	10	15	5	11	21	25	5	5
0	1	2	6	5	5	1	11	26	3	14	15	4	16	16	29	61	57
0	0	0	0	0	0	0	0	0	93	13	15	93	32	45	0	43	50
0	2	0	2	2	0	0	3	3	14	59	8	14	63	9	15	68	42
0	0	0	0	0	3	1	0	0	16	1	17	16	2	20	34	50	6
6	0	0	6	4	2	1	6	5	35	11	14	38	11	16	5	44	42
93	12	45	52	161	175	43	18	14	10	9	9	11	10	10	17	16	13
64	**107**	**113**	**185**	**312**	**281**	**144**	**209**	**172**	**7**	**9**	**10**	**9**	**10**	**12**	**45**	**34**	**36**
1	*2*	*2*	*8*	*6*	*35*	*16*	*5*	*1*	*7*	*2*	*7*	*10*	*2*	*8*	*37*	*20*	*4*
3	0	0	0	0	0	1	0	0	52	0	0	54	0	0	12	...	...
0	0	0	0	0	0	2	0	0	25	4	18	25	4	18	50	0	44
3	1	18	10	14	16	5	2	2	27	23	26	27	24	27	15	16	9
0	0	0	0	0	0	0	0	0	0	...	...	0	...	...	...	...	...
0	0	0	0	0	0	0	0	0	4	2	0	4	2	0	23	0	0
0	0	0	0	0	0	0	0	1	3	3	4	3	3	4	77	54	53
1	14	32	7	8	8	5	10	8	4	6	7	6	8	8	73	40	28
5	5	8	28	45	46	13	11	15	19	22	22	20	23	23	24	20	15
3	1	1	14	14	22	4	1	2	29	38	19	31	41	20	13	15	13
2	6	7	14	33	33	18	4	2	4	3	6	4	3	7	35	18	17
1	1	1	3	4	4	0	1	1	6	3	11	8	3	12	11	20	23
3	0	0	5	4	6	2	0	1	11	8	9	17	10	10	11	13	12
0	0	0	0	0	0	0	0	0	5	4	11	7	5	22	48	7	45
12	4	3	3	10	3	1	69	3	7	35	7	7	51	9	34	46	51
2	6	6	6	11	11	3	20	5	5	16	20	7	18	20	19	33	66
2	2	2	3	3	3	5	14	26	7	11	6	9	12	6	50	44	52
0	0	0	0	0	0	0	0	0	1	1	26	1	1	...	47	29	68
2	3	3	7	10	6	5	5	5	8	4	5	10	8	10	64	41	53
6	0	0	0	0	0	0	1	0	4	6	3	5	7	3	10	45	59
2	9	1	4	29	14	13	12	25	12	9	12	18	11	18	59	22	58
1	1	1	2	1	2	14	6	25	2	5	10	4	8	12	55	79	64
0	0	0	1	0	0	0	1	0	18	7	9	28	8	11	81	80	77
1	4	4	16	42	36	5	1	2	12	11	19	13	11	20	17	9	10
0	0	0	0	0	0	0	0	0	4	0	0	6	0	0	54	0	...
3	8	13	4	2	4	16	30	17	10	10	12	14	12	15	81	70	46
2	1	1	13	1	1	0	1	1	40	5	2	40	6	2	7	22	21
0	2	1	1	2	2	2	3	2	9	5	12	10	5	13	56	47	55
6	33	4	12	18	18	6	11	10	3	10	9	4	11	11	33	21	39
0	0	0	0	0	0	0	0	4	0	1	36	0	1	...	5	0	49
0	0	2	0	0	0	0	0	0	9	10	13	13	11	13	58	47	14
0	0	0	0	0	0	1	0	17	9	3	24	12	3	57	50	28	50
0	0	0	1	2	1	0	0	0	3	4	14	3	6	44	6	1	48
0	0	0	1	39	1	0	0	0	10	89	5	11	90	5	9	0	0
0	0	0	0	0	0	0	0	0	35	20	19	35	...	...	100	50	50
1	1	1	3	2	2	2	1	1	29	15	7	30	16	8	16	27	26
1	2	1	20	8	8	3	1	0	16	29	20	20	30	21	8	11	9

Table 4 (continued)

	Total aid to education			Total aid to basic education			Total aid to basic education per primary school-age child			Direct aid to education			Direct aid to basic education		
	Constant 2007 US$ millions			Constant 2007 US$ millions			Constant 2007 US$			Constant 2007 US$ millions			Constant 2007 US$ millions		
	1999–2000 annual average	2006	2007	1999–2000 annual average	2006	2007	1999–2000 annual average	2006	2007	1999–2000 annual average	2006	2007	1999–2000 annual average	2006	2007
North America and Western Europe	**3**	**0**	**352**	**0**	**0**	**140**	**2**	**0**	**0**	**3**	**0**	**352**	**0**	**0**	**92**
Unallocated within the region	*2*	*0*	*352*	*0*	*0*	*140*	...	...	...	*2*	*0*	*352*	*0*	*0*	*92*
Malta	1	0	0	0	0	0	2	0	0	1	0	0	0	0	0
South and West Asia	**948**	**1 074**	**1 604**	**501**	**521**	**672**	**3**	**3**	**4**	**931**	**915**	**1 295**	**382**	**357**	**381**
Unallocated within the region	*0*	*0*	*0*	*0*	*0*	*0*	...	...	...	*0*	*0*	*0*	*0*	*0*	*0*
Afghanistan	8	159	277	2	117	168	1	26	37	8	155	208	1	91	87
Bangladesh	149	258	250	91	82	118	5	5	7	149	228	195	86	65	69
Bhutan	6	10	15	1	3	5	11	34	52	6	6	9	0	0	0
India	522	177	423	331	84	49	3	1	0	505	177	380	229	56	20
Iran, Islamic Republic of	88	55	56	5	1	1	1	0	0	88	55	56	0	1	0
Maldives	18	5	8	0	2	1	6	43	14	18	5	8	0	1	0
Nepal	66	60	175	55	29	96	17	8	27	66	60	175	54	11	92
Pakistan	31	296	316	11	198	197	1	10	10	31	176	180	6	129	111
Sri Lanka	60	52	83	5	5	36	3	4	24	60	52	83	4	3	2
Sub-Saharan Africa	**2 686**	**4 182**	**3 630**	**1 352**	**2 248**	**1 698**	**13**	**18**	**14**	**2 056**	**3 343**	**2 990**	**727**	**1 287**	**897**
Unallocated within the region	*47*	*50*	*94*	*25*	*9*	*40*	...	...	...	*46*	*50*	*94*	*19*	*0*	*36*
Angola	25	42	28	9	24	10	6	12	5	25	42	28	4	21	3
Benin	49	89	76	23	49	32	19	34	22	32	68	51	9	36	14
Botswana	15	2	3	1	1	1	2	2	3	15	2	3	0	0	0
Burkina Faso	81	213	112	42	151	69	22	65	29	60	182	78	28	125	46
Burundi	7	49	55	2	28	32	2	22	24	5	29	41	0	14	18
Cameroon	125	169	120	33	34	9	13	12	3	106	128	120	6	12	7
Cape Verde	30	36	40	8	3	4	102	33	57	24	33	34	2	1	1
Central African Republic	32	27	14	8	11	4	13	15	6	25	7	8	3	1	1
Chad	35	7	12	13	2	5	9	1	3	26	7	12	6	2	3
Comoros	8	12	11	4	1	1	34	10	4	7	12	11	0	0	1
Congo	18	24	33	8	1	1	16	1	1	18	24	33	0	1	1
Côte d'Ivoire	156	39	65	57	9	9	20	3	3	129	39	65	25	8	5
D. R. Congo	16	35	261	8	15	196	1	1	19	16	34	261	4	12	155
Equatorial Guinea	11	9	11	5	4	4	95	61	65	11	9	11	3	0	0
Eritrea	39	2	2	31	0	0	61	1	0	39	2	2	29	0	0
Ethiopia	59	445	186	28	339	89	3	26	7	58	443	186	20	260	15
Gabon	58	38	35	17	4	0	96	23	0	58	38	35	12	0	0
Gambia	13	10	6	11	6	5	56	24	18	12	10	6	10	5	4
Ghana	138	371	188	100	188	125	31	55	36	103	268	145	82	25	74
Guinea	47	36	24	21	9	1	17	7	1	47	36	24	17	9	1
Guinea-Bissau	16	7	12	6	2	4	28	6	13	9	7	7	2	1	1
Kenya	73	235	69	45	130	47	9	23	8	39	235	69	26	62	43
Lesotho	18	2	18	2	2	11	6	6	29	18	2	18	2	2	4
Liberia	2	19	108	1	10	59	3	16	97	2	19	21	1	1	15
Madagascar	85	96	82	30	47	30	14	18	11	48	74	63	1	34	17
Malawi	160	61	67	110	23	48	57	9	19	121	41	56	79	11	36
Mali	106	339	136	54	281	77	33	140	38	85	318	112	23	242	52
Mauritius	28	21	47	4	1	15	29	12	126	28	21	21	0	1	2
Mozambique	176	210	384	95	128	213	28	32	52	127	154	246	37	82	80
Namibia	28	8	14	19	4	9	50	11	23	28	8	14	16	4	7
Niger	37	52	46	16	26	25	9	12	11	21	39	34	4	10	17
Nigeria	83	86	489	47	18	164	2	1	7	83	86	489	26	11	48
Rwanda	89	134	98	43	65	70	30	45	48	47	84	78	5	13	53
Sao Tome and Principe	6	14	6	1	4	0	60	165	12	6	14	6	1	0	0
Senegal	169	341	153	91	141	49	56	76	26	153	334	149	47	41	29
Seychelles	1	0	1	1	0	0	73	18	24	1	0	1	0	0	0

Direct aid to secondary education Constant 2007 US$ millions			Direct aid to post-secondary education Constant 2007 US$ millions			Aid to education, level unspecified Constant 2007 US$ millions			Share of education in total ODA (%)			Share of education in total sector-allocable ODA (%)			Share of basic education in total aid to education (%)		
1999–2000 annual average	2006	2007	1999–2000 annual average	2006	2007	1999–2000 annual average	2006	2007	1999–2000 annual average	2006	2007	1999–2000 annual average	2006	2007	1999–2000 annual average	2006	2007
0	**0**	**164**	**3**	**0**	**0**	**0**	**0**	**96**	**11**	**0**	**60**	**11**	**0**	**60**	**6**	**0**	**40**
0	*0*	*164*	*2*	*0*	*0*	*0*	*0*	*96*	*7*	*0*	*60*	*7*	*0*	*60*	*6*	*0*	*40*
0	0	0	1	0	0	0	0	0	43	...	...	44	...	...	7	...	...
131	**213**	**388**	**197**	**175**	**253**	**222**	**171**	**271**	**13**	**7**	**9**	**16**	**9**	**11**	**53**	**49**	**42**
0	*0*	*0*	*0*	*0*	*0*	*0*	*0*	*0*	...	*0*	*0*	...	*0*	*0*	...	...	...
1	9	3	5	8	24	1	47	93	4	4	6	14	5	8	22	73	61
44	148	65	9	11	18	10	3	43	7	10	10	8	12	13	61	32	47
2	0	4	2	3	2	2	3	3	7	12	12	7	16	16	20	36	33
14	5	289	75	59	56	187	57	16	20	4	7	23	4	8	63	48	12
0	1	0	78	53	55	9	0	1	60	43	53	74	72	67	6	2	1
12	1	6	5	1	1	0	3	1	50	9	26	52	26	27	2	37	8
4	1	17	6	13	57	1	36	8	12	11	22	13	13	25	83	48	55
1	9	1	14	20	32	10	18	37	3	13	11	7	23	17	35	67	62
53	36	4	2	8	8	1	5	69	10	6	10	10	9	12	8	10	44
251	**253**	**338**	**458**	**721**	**793**	**620**	**1 081**	**962**	**12**	**9**	**10**	**19**	**19**	**14**	**50**	**54**	**47**
5	*0*	*10*	*11*	*32*	*38*	*11*	*19*	*9*	*6*	*3*	*4*	*7*	*3*	*4*	*54*	*19*	*43*
1	4	3	8	11	8	11	6	15	6	15	8	11	18	9	38	57	35
6	1	1	6	27	24	11	4	12	10	10	16	14	12	24	47	55	43
2	1	1	13	0	1	0	1	2	31	2	1	35	3	1	3	28	30
11	22	3	13	15	18	7	19	11	12	27	16	17	38	23	52	71	61
0	0	5	3	7	4	2	8	15	3	8	12	6	12	21	32	57	58
4	3	3	62	111	107	33	3	3	20	7	6	37	27	21	26	20	7
3	2	4	13	29	28	6	0	1	18	23	12	26	29	25	26	7	11
11	0	1	9	6	6	2	0	0	22	9	6	39	17	11	24	40	31
2	0	2	15	5	5	3	0	2	9	3	3	11	6	7	36	26	39
1	0	0	0	10	10	6	1	0	30	30	22	54	37	23	46	11	5
0	1	10	2	22	22	15	0	0	13	5	21	57	21	25	44	3	2
25	1	22	42	30	30	37	0	8	21	9	16	53	20	18	37	22	13
1	2	5	4	15	18	8	5	84	8	2	17	14	4	24	47	42	75
2	1	0	2	1	2	4	7	8	33	21	29	39	23	29	47	42	40
3	1	0	3	1	1	4	0	0	13	2	1	23	3	1	80	18	12
5	4	5	19	21	18	14	157	148	6	18	6	13	22	6	46	76	48
20	1	8	16	28	28	11	8	0	59	23	25	86	23	26	30	11	0
0	2	0	0	1	0	1	2	2	19	13	11	23	14	11	84	60	81
12	4	4	8	16	7	1	224	59	12	24	11	18	40	13	72	51	67
10	1	0	12	26	22	7	1	1	16	15	7	20	18	8	45	26	6
1	1	2	5	4	4	1	0	0	14	8	9	30	10	12	38	24	30
3	22	6	6	14	13	4	137	7	7	14	3	9	18	3	62	55	68
15	0	1	1	0	0	1	0	13	18	2	10	18	2	11	12	93	59
0	0	2	0	0	1	1	17	2	4	5	12	9	9	31	67	51	55
9	4	5	17	32	34	20	5	7	13	14	12	25	20	20	35	49	37
17	25	1	1	1	7	24	4	12	21	8	11	32	12	15	69	38	71
12	2	12	8	17	21	42	56	27	16	40	10	21	52	13	51	83	57
0	2	2	20	17	17	7	0	0	63	24	27	63	24	...	13	7	32
9	24	12	15	11	25	66	37	129	9	14	17	16	19	26	54	61	56
3	2	2	3	1	2	6	0	3	21	3	5	22	4	5	67	54	62
6	1	4	3	9	8	8	19	4	11	9	13	20	13	20	42	50	55
4	50	106	11	11	104	41	15	231	13	1	20	13	7	29	57	21	33
4	1	3	5	16	7	33	54	15	16	16	14	35	29	17	48	48	72
2	1	1	3	5	5	1	8	0	13	47	15	15	55	23	21	29	5
10	21	8	24	78	75	71	194	37	17	32	25	26	41	28	54	41	32
0	0	0	0	0	1	1	0	0	26	3	20	26	4	22	47	29	24

Table 4 (continued)

	Total aid to education			Total aid to basic education			Total aid to basic education per primary school-age child			Direct aid to education			Direct aid to basic education		
	Constant 2007 US$ millions			Constant 2007 US$ millions			Constant 2007 US$			Constant 2007 US$ millions			Constant 2007 US$ millions		
	1999–2000 annual average	2006	2007	1999–2000 annual average	2006	2007	1999–2000 annual average	2006	2007	1999–2000 annual average	2006	2007	1999–2000 annual average	2006	2007
Sierra Leone	27	15	17	13	9	7	20	11	8	2	8	14	1	5	4
Somalia	6	17	9	3	15	8	2	10	5	6	17	9	1	14	7
South Africa	95	88	37	44	35	20	6	5	3	95	88	37	38	22	14
Swaziland	2	0	5	0	0	4	1	1	21	2	0	5	0	0	4
Togo	16	21	20	7	4	1	8	4	1	13	21	20	2	3	1
Uganda	172	172	92	103	98	45	20	16	7	116	136	56	54	66	13
U. R. Tanzania	95	431	219	49	237	85	8	33	11	37	88	142	18	62	43
Zambia	158	100	119	106	77	65	54	34	28	85	78	71	62	64	21
Zimbabwe	27	7	5	9	2	1	4	1	1	26	7	5	2	2	1
Unallocated by country	*550*	*1 648*	*1 117*	*131*	*1 047*	*280*	...	...	...	*542*	*1 637*	*1 077*	*64*	*990*	*190*
Total	7 912	12 330	12 065	3 189	5 482	4 266	5	9	7	6 938	11 121	10 720	1 804	3 627	2 263
Upper middle income countries	738	633	872	195	76	213	4	2	4	731	628	833	147	46	127
Low middle income countries	2 412	3 810	3 851	731	1 105	1 074	3	5	5	2 184	3 674	3 624	329	681	442
High income countries	43	0	0	5	0	0	1	0	0	43	0	0	0	0	0
Unallocated by income	688	1 825	1 543	183	1 076	343	...	...	...	675	1 815	1 502	93	995	233
Least developed countries	2 384	4 130	3 597	1 238	2 362	1 923	12	20	16	1 834	3 391	2 856	695	1 476	1 114
Low income countries	4 031	6 062	5 799	2 076	3 224	2 635	7	10	8	3 304	5 004	4 761	1 235	1 905	1 460
Middle income countries	3 150	4 443	4 724	926	1 181	1 287	3	5	5	2 915	4 303	4 457	476	728	570
Total	7 912	12 330	12 065	3 189	5 482	4 266	5	9	7	6 938	11 121	10 720	1 804	3 627	2 263
Arab States	1 223	1 828	1 726	359	577	525	9	14	13	1 194	1 774	1 614	162	323	281
Central and Eastern Europe	456	472	526	146	50	70	12	4	6	414	455	508	97	25	31
Central Asia	114	219	199	28	68	36	4	12	6	92	196	183	9	36	20
East Asia and the Pacific	1 326	2 076	2 118	402	687	556	2	4	3	1 129	2 018	1 960	180	454	192
Latin America and the Caribbean	605	832	794	270	284	289	5	5	5	577	782	743	184	154	177
North America and Western Europe	3	0	352	0	0	140	2	0	0	3	0	352	0	0	92
South and West Asia	948	1 074	1 604	501	521	672	3	3	4	931	915	1 295	382	357	381
Sub-Saharan Africa	2 686	4 182	3 630	1 352	2 248	1 698	13	18	14	2 056	3 343	2 990	727	1 287	897
Unallocated by region	*550*	*1 648*	*1 117*	*131*	*1 047*	*280*	...	...	...	*542*	*1 637*	*1 077*	*64*	*990*	*190*
Total	7 912	12 330	12 065	3 189	5 482	4 266	5	9	7	6 938	11 121	10 720	1 804	3 627	2 263

Notes:
(...) indicates that data are not available.
All data represent commitments unless otherwise specified.
Source: OECD-DAC (2009*d*).

Direct aid to secondary education			Direct aid to post-secondary education			Aid to education, level unspecified			Share of education in total ODA			Share of education in total sector-allocable ODA			Share of basic education in total aid to education		
Constant 2007 US$ millions			Constant 2007 US$ millions			Constant 2007 US$ millions			(%)			(%)			(%)		
1999–2000 annual average	2006	2007	1999–2000 annual average	2006	2007	1999–2000 annual average	2006	2007	1999–2000 annual average	2006	2007	1999–2000 annual average	2006	2007	1999–2000 annual average	2006	2007
0	0	6	1	1	1	0	2	3	8	6	4	22	10	8	49	65	43
0	1	0	0	0	0	5	2	2	4	4	2	11	16	7	51	89	84
12	13	3	32	27	8	12	25	13	16	9	4	17	9	4	46	40	54
1	0	0	0	0	0	0	0	0	6	1	8	7	1	11	7	47	94
0	1	2	4	16	17	7	1	1	15	30	10	23	39	11	42	17	6
3	24	7	18	17	7	41	29	29	13	13	5	20	20	6	60	57	49
7	3	60	9	16	31	3	7	7	6	15	8	10	38	13	51	55	39
4	2	6	4	8	3	15	3	41	12	6	12	25	11	17	67	77	55
4	0	0	6	5	3	15	1	1	10	2	1	12	2	2	35	30	29
31	*144*	*97*	*321*	*400*	*651*	*126*	*104*	*139*	*5*	*6*	*5*	*12*	*13*	*9*	*24*	*64*	*25*
978	**984**	**1 480**	**2 360**	**4 008**	**4 317**	**1 796**	**2 501**	**2 661**	**10**	**9**	**10**	**15**	**14**	**13**	**40**	**44**	**35**
109	47	198	386	480	375	90	55	133	20	13	16	23	15	18	26	12	24
385	302	234	894	1 979	1 912	576	711	1 035	9	11	12	12	15	16	30	29	28
1	0	0	33	0	0	10	0	0	35	...	...	38	...	...	11	...	...
41	153	233	375	514	856	165	153	180	5	6	6	12	11	10	27	59	22
257	**345**	**292**	**346**	**538**	**574**	**538**	**1 033**	**876**	**11**	**12**	**10**	**18**	**18**	**14**	**52**	**57**	**53**
443	**482**	**814**	**671**	**1 036**	**1 174**	**956**	**1 582**	**1 313**	**12**	**9**	**10**	**17**	**16**	**13**	**51**	**53**	**45**
494	**350**	**432**	**1 280**	**2 459**	**2 287**	**666**	**766**	**1 168**	**11**	**11**	**12**	**14**	**15**	**16**	**29**	**27**	**27**
978	**984**	**1 480**	**2 360**	**4 008**	**4 317**	**1 796**	**2 501**	**2 661**	**10**	**9**	**10**	**15**	**14**	**13**	**40**	**44**	**35**
233	133	83	434	864	873	364	454	376	18	10	9	23	16	15	29	32	30
54	39	38	206	357	379	56	33	60	7	7	11	13	9	12	32	11	13
25	28	54	43	91	94	15	42	14	6	8	9	8	9	10	24	31	18
190	68	206	512	1 088	992	247	407	569	10	17	16	12	19	19	30	33	26
64	107	113	185	312	281	144	209	172	7	9	10	9	10	12	45	34	36
0	0	164	3	0	0	0	0	96	11	0	60	11	0	60	6	0	40
131	213	388	197	175	253	222	171	271	13	7	9	16	9	11	53	49	42
251	253	338	458	721	793	620	1 081	962	12	9	10	19	19	14	50	54	47
31	*144*	*97*	*321*	*400*	*651*	*126*	*104*	*139*	*5*	*6*	*5*	*12*	*13*	*9*	*24*	*64*	*25*
978	**984**	**1 480**	**2 360**	**4 008**	**4 317**	**1 796**	**2 501**	**2 661**	**10**	**9**	**10**	**15**	**14**	**13**	**40**	**44**	**35**

Glossary

Achievement. Performance on standardized tests or examinations that measure knowledge or competence in a specific subject area. The term is sometimes used as an indication of education quality within an education system or when comparing a group of schools.

Adult education. Educational activities, offered through formal, non-formal or informal frameworks, targeted at adults and aimed at advancing, or substituting for, initial education and training.

Adult literacy rate. Number of literate persons aged 15 and above, expressed as a percentage of the total population in that age group.

Age-specific enrolment ratio (ASER). Enrolment of a given age or age group, regardless of the level of education in which pupils or students are enrolled, expressed as a percentage of the population of the same age or age group.

Basic education. The whole range of educational activities taking place in various settings (formal, non-formal and informal) that aim to meet basic learning needs; in the Dakar Framework the term is synonymous with the broad EFA agenda. Similarly, the OECD-DAC and standard aid classifications use a definition that includes early childhood education, primary education, and basic life skills for youths and adults, including literacy. According to the International Standard Classification of Education, basic education comprises primary education (first stage of basic education) and lower secondary education (second stage).

Basic learning needs. As defined in the World Declaration on Education for All (Jomtien, Thailand, 1990): essential learning tools (literacy, oral expression, numeracy, problem-solving) and basic learning content (knowledge, skills, values, attitudes) required by human beings to survive, develop their full capacities, live and work in dignity, participate fully in development, improve the quality of their lives, make informed decisions and continue learning.

Child- or under-5 mortality rate. Probability of dying between birth and the fifth birthday, expressed per 1,000 live births.

Constant prices. Prices of a particular item adjusted to remove the overall effect of general price changes (inflation) since a given baseline year.

Continuing or further education. A general term referring to a wide range of educational activities designed to meet the learning needs of adults. See also Adult education.

Disability. As used in this Report, the term describes an interaction of three factors: (i) physical or mental impairments; (ii) the resulting limitations on activities that such impairments entail; and (iii) restrictions on participation resulting from discrimination, stigmatization and social attitudes that exclude people from opportunities to participate in society.

Dropout rate by grade. Percentage of pupils or students who drop out of a given grade in a given school year.

Early childhood care and education (ECCE). Programmes that, in addition to providing children with care, offer a structured and purposeful set of learning activities either in a formal institution (pre-primary or ISCED 0) or as part of a non-formal child development programme. ECCE programmes are normally designed for children from age 3 and include organized learning activities that constitute, on average, the equivalent of at least 2 hours per day and 100 days per year.

Education attainment rate. The percentage of a population belonging to a particular age group that has attained or completed a specified education level (typically primary, secondary or tertiary) or grade in school.

EFA Development Index (EDI). Composite index aimed at measuring overall progress towards EFA. At present, the EDI incorporates four of the most easily quantifiable EFA goals – universal primary education as measured by the primary adjusted net enrolment ratio, adult literacy as measured by the adult literacy rate, gender parity as measured by the gender-specific EFA index and quality of education as measured by the survival rate to grade 5. Its value is the arithmetic mean of the observed values of these four indicators.

EFA Inequality Index for Income Groups (EIIIG). A composite index measuring inequality in overall EFA achievement across different population groups. The EIIIG measures the (unequal) distribution of overall EFA achievement within countries according to household wealth and other socio-demographic markers, using a set of indicators from household surveys that differs from those in the EDI.

Enrolment. Number of pupils or students enrolled at a given level of education, regardless of age. See also Gross enrolment ratio and Net enrolment ratio.

Equivalency education. Programmes primarily organized for children and youth who did not have access to, or who dropped out of, formal primary/basic education. Typically, these programmes aim at providing equivalency to formal primary/basic education.

Gender parity index (GPI). Ratio of female to male values (or male to female, in certain cases) of a given indicator. A GPI of 1 indicates parity between sexes; a GPI above or below 1 indicates a disparity in favour of one sex over the other.

Gender-specific EFA index (GEI). A composite index measuring gender parity in total participation in primary and secondary education, and in adult literacy. The GEI is calculated as the arithmetic mean of the gender parity indices of the primary and secondary gross enrolment ratios and of the adult literacy rate.

Gross enrolment ratio (GER). Total enrolment in a specific level of education, regardless of age, expressed as a percentage of the population in the official age group corresponding to this level of education. For the tertiary level, the population used is that of the five-year age group following on from the secondary school leaving age. The GER can exceed 100% due to early or late entry and/or grade repetition.

Gross intake rate (GIR). Total number of new entrants to a given grade of primary education, regardless of age, expressed as a percentage of the population at the official school entrance age for that grade.

Gross domestic product (GDP). The value of all final goods and services produced in a country in one year (see also Gross national product). GDP can be measured by aggregating an economy's (a) income (wages, interest, profits, rents) or (b) expenditure (consumption, investment, government purchases), plus net exports (exports minus imports).

Gross domestic product per capita. GDP divided by the total population at mid-year.

Gross national product (GNP). The value of all final goods and services produced in a country in one year (gross domestic product) plus income that residents have received from abroad, minus income claimed by nonresidents.

Gross national product per capita. GNP divided by the total population at mid-year.

HIV prevalence rate. Estimated number of people of a given age group living with HIV/AIDS at the end of a given year, expressed as a percentage of the total population of the corresponding age group.

Illiterate. See Literate.

Infant mortality rate. Probability of dying between birth and the first birthday, expressed as deaths per 1,000 live births.

International Standard Classification of Education (ISCED). Classification system designed to serve as an instrument for assembling, compiling and presenting comparable indicators and statistics of education both within countries and internationally. The system, introduced in 1976, was revised in 1997 (ISCED97).

Labour force participation rate. The share of employed plus unemployed people in comparison with the working age population.

Life expectancy at birth. Approximate number of years a newborn infant would live if prevailing patterns of age-specific mortality rates in the year of birth were to stay the same throughout the child's life.

Literacy. According to UNESCO's 1958 definition, the term refers to the ability of an individual to read and write with understanding a simple short statement related to his/her everyday life. The concept of literacy has since evolved to embrace multiple skill domains, each conceived on a scale of different mastery levels and serving different purposes.

Literate/illiterate. The term refers to a person who can/cannot read and write with understanding a simple statement related to his/her everyday life.

Net attendance rate (NAR). Number of pupils in the official age group for a given level of education who attend school in that level, expressed as a percentage of the population in that age group.

Net enrolment ratio (NER). Enrolment of the official age group for a given level of education, expressed as a percentage of the population in that age group.

Net intake rate (NIR). New entrants to the first grade of primary education who are of the official primary school entrance age, expressed as a percentage of the population of that age.

New entrants. Pupils entering a given level of education for the first time; the difference between enrolment and repeaters in the first grade of the level.

New entrants to the first grade of primary education with ECCE experience (%). Number of new entrants to the first grade of primary school who have attended the equivalent of at least 200 hours of organized ECCE programmes, expressed as a percentage of the total number of new entrants to the first grade.

Non-formal education. Learning activities typically organized outside the formal education system. The term is generally contrasted with formal and informal education. In different contexts, non-formal education covers educational activities aimed at imparting adult literacy, basic education for out-of-school children and youth, life skills, work skills and general culture.

Odds ratio. A number comparing the probability of one group achieving a particular outcome, compared with another group. For instance, if a group has an odds ratio of 2 for being able to read and write, people in that group are twice as likely to be literate as the comparison group. Odds ratios are used to interpret the results of statistical techniques such as logistic regression.

Out-of-school children. Children in the official primary school age range who are not enrolled in either primary or secondary school.

Post-secondary non-tertiary education (ISCED level 4). Programmes that lie between the upper secondary and tertiary levels from an international point of view, even though they might clearly be considered upper secondary or tertiary programmes in a national context. They are often not significantly more advanced than programmes at ISCED level 3 (upper secondary) but they serve to broaden the knowledge of students who have completed a programme at that level. The students are usually older than those at ISCED level 3. ISCED 4 programmes typically last between six months and two years.

Pre-primary education (ISCED level 0). Programmes at the initial stage of organized instruction, primarily designed to introduce very young children, aged at least 3 years, to a school-type environment and provide a bridge between home and school. Variously referred to as infant education, nursery education, pre-school education, kindergarten or early childhood education, such programmes are the more formal component of ECCE. Upon completion of these programmes, children continue their education at ISCED 1 (primary education).

Primary adjusted net attendance rate (ANAR). Number of pupils of the official primary school age group who attend school in either primary or secondary education, expressed as a percentage of the population in that age group.

Primary adjusted net enrolment ratio (ANER). Enrolment of children of the official primary school age group in either primary or secondary schools, expressed as a percentage of the population in that age group.

Primary cohort completion rate. Proxy measure of primary school completion. It focuses on children who have access to school, measuring how many successfully complete it. The primary cohort completion rate is the product of the survival rate to the last grade and the percentage of those in the last grade who successfully graduate.

Primary education (ISCED level 1). Programmes normally designed on a unit or project basis to give pupils a sound basic education in reading, writing and mathematics, and an elementary understanding of subjects such as history, geography, natural sciences, social sciences, art and music.

Private enrolment/institutions. Number of pupils/students enrolled in private institutions, that is, in institutions that are not operated by public authorities but are controlled and managed, whether for profit or not, by private bodies such as nongovernment organizations, religious bodies, special interest groups, foundations or business enterprises.

Public enrolment/institutions. Number of students enrolled in public institutions, that is, institutions controlled and managed by public authorities or agencies (national/federal, state/provincial or local), whatever the origins of their financial resources.

Public expenditure on education. Total current and capital expenditure on education by local, regional and national governments, including municipalities. Household contributions are excluded. The term covers public expenditure for both public and private institutions.

Pupil/teacher ratio (PTR). Average number of pupils per teacher at a specific level of education.

Pupil/trained-teacher ratio. Average number of pupils per trained teacher at a specific level of education.

Purchasing power parity (PPP). An exchange rate adjustment that accounts for price differences between countries, allowing international comparisons of real output and incomes.

Repeaters. Number of pupils enrolled in the same grade or level as the previous year, expressed as a percentage of the total enrolment in that grade or level.

Repetition rate by grade. Number of repeaters in a given grade in a given school year, expressed as a percentage of enrolment in that grade the previous school year.

School age population. Population of the age group officially corresponding to a given level of education, whether enrolled in school or not.

School life expectancy (SLE). Number of years a child of school entrance age is expected to spend in school or university, including years spent on repetition. It is the sum of the age-specific enrolment ratios for primary, secondary, post-secondary non-tertiary and tertiary education. A school life expectancy can be calculated for each level of education, including pre-primary education.

Secondary education (ISCED levels 2 and 3). Programme made up of two stages: lower and upper secondary. Lower secondary education (ISCED 2) is generally designed to continue the basic programmes of the primary level but the teaching is typically more subject-focused, requiring more specialized teachers for each subject area. The end of this level often coincides with the end of compulsory education. In upper secondary education (ISCED 3), the final stage of secondary education in most countries, instruction is often organized even more along subject lines and teachers typically need a higher or more subject-specific qualification than at ISCED level 2.

Stunting rate. Proportion of children in a given age group whose height for their age is between two and three standard deviations (moderate stunting) or three or more standard deviations (severe stunting) below the reference median established by the National Center for Health Statistics and the World Health Organization. Low height for age is a basic indicator of malnutrition.

Survival rate by grade. Percentage of a cohort of students who are enrolled in the first grade of an education cycle in a given school year and are expected to reach a specified grade, regardless of repetition.

Teacher compensation. A base teaching salary plus bonuses. Base salary refers to the minimum scheduled gross annual salary for a full-time teacher with the minimum training necessary to be qualified at the beginning of his or her teaching career.

Teachers/teaching staff. Number of persons employed full time or part time in an official capacity to guide and direct the learning experience of pupils and students, irrespective of their qualifications or the delivery mechanism (i.e. face to face and/or at a distance).

Technical and vocational education and training (TVET). Programmes designed mainly to prepare students for direct entry into a particular occupation or trade (or class of occupations or trades).

Tertiary or higher education (ISCED levels 5 and 6). Programmes with an educational content more advanced than what is offered at ISCED levels 3 and 4. The first stage of tertiary education, ISCED level 5, includes level 5A, composed of largely theoretically based programmes intended to provide sufficient qualifications for gaining entry to advanced research programmes and professions with high skill requirements; and level 5B, where programmes are generally more practical, technical and/or occupationally specific. The second stage of tertiary education, ISCED level 6, comprises programmes devoted to advanced study and original research, and leading to the award of an advanced research qualification.

Total fertility rate. Average number of children that would be born to a woman if she were to live to the end of her childbearing years (15 to 49) and bear children at each age in accordance with prevailing age-specific fertility rates.

Transition rate to secondary education. New entrants to the first grade of secondary education in a given year, expressed as a percentage of the number of pupils enrolled in the final grade of primary education in the previous year. The indicator measures transition to secondary general education only.

Youth literacy rate. Number of literate persons aged 15 to 24, expressed as a percentage of the total population in that age group.

Education for All Global Monitoring Report 2010

Bibliography*

1 Goal. 2009. *Join 1 Goal Everywhere: Education for All.* http://www.join1goal.org/en/about-us (Accessed 31 August 2009.)

Abada-Barrerío, C. E. and Castro, A. 2006. Experiences of stigma and access to HAART in children and adolescents living with HIV/AIDS in Brazil. *Social Science & Medicine*, Vol. 62, No. 5, pp. 1219–28.

Abadzi, H. 2006. *Efficient Learning for the Poor: Insights from the Frontier of Cognitive Neuroscience.* Washington, DC, World Bank. (Directions in Development.)

Abadzi, H., Crouch, L. A., Echegaray, M., Pasco, C. and Sampe, J. 2005. Monitoring basic skills acquisition through rapid learning assessments: a case study of Peru. *Prospects*, Vol. 35, No. 2, pp. 137–56.

Abou Serie, R., Ayiro, L., Crouch, L., Godia, G. and Martins, G. 2009. Absorptive capacity: from donor perspectives to recipients' professional views. Background paper for *EFA Global Monitoring Report 2010.*

Acharya, S. and Luitel, B. C. 2006. *The Functioning and Effectiveness of Scholarship and Incentive Schemes in Nepal.* Kathmandu, UNESCO. (UNESCO Kathmandu Series of Monographs and Working Papers, 9.)

Ackerman, D., Barnett, W. S., Hawkinson, L. E., Brown, K. and McConigle, E. A. 2009. *Providing Preschool Education for All 4 Year Olds: Lessons From Six State Journeys.* New Brunswick, NJ., National Institute for Early Education Research. (Preschool Policy Brief.)

Ackerman, P., Thormann, M. S. and Huq, S. 2005. *Assessment of Educational Needs of Disabled Children in Bangladesh.* Washington, DC, US Agency for International Development.

Adams, A. V. 2007*a*. Helping youth make the transition from school to work. *Development OUTREACH*, Vol. 9, No. 2, pp. 22–25.

——. 2007*b*. *The Role of Youth Skills Development in the Transition to Work: A Global Review.* Washington, DC, World Bank. (HDNCY No. 5.)

——. 2008. *Skills Development in the Informal Sector of Sub-Saharan Africa.* Washington, DC, World Bank.

Adams, A. V., Coulombe, H., Wodon, Q. and Razmara, S. 2008. *Education, Skills and Labor Market Outcomes in Ghana*, Washington, DC, World Bank. (Mimeo.)

Aderinoye, R. and Rogers, A. 2005. Urban literacies: the intervention of the Literacy Shop Approach in Bodija Market, Ibadan, Nigeria. Rogers, A. (ed.), *Urban Literacy: Communication, Identity and Learning in Development Contexts.* Hamburg, Germany, UNESCO Institute for Education, pp. 253–77.

Africa Commission. 2008. *Africa Commission Thematic Conference on the African Youth and Employment, Accra 5 September 2008.* Accra, Africa Commission. (Background paper.)

African Development Bank/OECD. 2008*a*. *African Economic Outlook – Cameroon.* Paris, African Development Bank/Organisation for Economic Co-operation and Development. (African Economic Outlook report.)

——. 2008*b*. *African Economic Outlook – Ethiopia.* Paris, African Development Bank/Organisation for Economic Co-operation and Development. (African Economic Outlook report.)

——. 2008*c*. *African Economic Outlook – Ghana.* Paris, African Development Bank/Organisation for Economic Co-operation and Development. http://www.africaneconomicoutlook.org/en/countries/west-africa/ghana/ (Accessed 29 September 2009.)

——. 2008*d*. *African Economic Outlook – Morocco.* Paris, African Development Bank/Organisation for Economic Co-operation and Development. (African Economic Outlook report.)

——. 2008*e*. *African Economic Outlook – Mozambique.* Paris, African Development Bank/Organisation for Economic Co-operation and Development. (African Economic Outlook report.)

——. 2008*f*. *African Economic Outlook – Rwanda.* Paris, African Development Bank/Organisation for Economic Co-operation and Development. (African Economic Outlook report.)

Aguilar, P. and Retamal, G. 2009. Protective environments and quality education in humanitarian contexts. *International Education of Educational Development*, Vol. 29, No. 1, pp. 3–16.

Ahmed, A. U., Hill, R. V., Smith, L. C., Wiesmann, D. M. and Frankenberger, T. 2007. *The World's Most Deprived: Characteristics and Causes of Extreme Poverty and Hunger.* Washington, DC, International Food Policy Research Institute. (2020 Discussion Paper.)

* All background papers for *EFA Global Monitoring Report 2010* are available at www.efareport.unesco.org

Akyeampong, K. 2007. *50 Years of Educational Progress and Challenge in Ghana.* Brighton, UK, University of Sussex, Centre for International Education.

——. 2009. Revisiting free compulsory basic education (FCUBE) in Ghana. *Comparative Education,* Vol. 45, No. 2, pp. 175–95.

Akyeampong, K., Sabates, R., Hunt, F. and Anthony, J. 2009. *Review of Research on Basic Education Provision in Nigeria (ESSPIN).* Brighton, UK, University of Sussex, Centre for International Education. (Unpublished.)

Al-Mekhlafy, T. A. 2008. Strategies for gender equality in basic and secondary education: a comprehensive and integrated approach in the Republic of Yemen. Tembon, M. and Fort, L. (eds), *Girls' Education in the 21st Century: Gender Equality, Empowerment and Economic Growth.* Washington, DC, World Bank, pp. 269–78.

Al Samarrai, S. 2008. Governance and education inequality in Bangladesh. Background paper for *EFA Global Monitoring Report 2009.*

Alderman, H., Behrman, J., Lavy, V. and Menon, R. 2001. Child health and school enrollment: a longitudinal analysis. *The Journal of Human Resources,* Vol. 36, No. 1, pp. 185–205.

Alderman, H., Hoddinott, J. and Kinsey, B. 2006. Long term consequences of early childhood malnutrition. *Oxford Economic Papers,* Vol. 58, No. 3, pp. 450–74.

Alderman, H., Hoogeveen, H. and Rossi, M. 2009. Preschool nutrition and subsequent schooling attainment: longitudinal evidence from Tanzania. *Economic Development and Cultural Change,* Vol. 57, No. 2, pp. 239–60.

Alidou, H., Boly, A., Brock-Utne, B., Diallo, Y. S., Heugh, K. and Wolff, H. E. 2006. *Optimizing Learning and Education in Africa – the Language Factor: A Stock-taking Research on Mother Tongue and Bilingual Education in Sub-Saharan Africa.* ADEA 2006 Biennial Meeting, Libreville, Gabon, 27–31 March.

Alkenbrack, S., Chettra, T. and Forsythe, S. 2004. *The Social and Economic Impact of HIV/AIDS on Families with Adolescents and Children in Cambodia.* Phnom Penh, Government of Cambodia, Child Welfare Department, Technical Directorate of the Ministry of Social Affairs, Veterans and Youth Rehabilitation/the POLICY Project Cambodia.

Altinok, N. 2008. An international perspective on trends in the quality of learning achievement (1965–2007). Background paper for *EFA Global Monitoring Report 2009.*

——. 2009. An empirical approach to marginalization in education based on the TIMSS 2007 study. Background paper for *EFA Global Monitoring Report 2010.*

Alviar, C., Ayala, F. and Handa, S. Forthcoming. Testing combined targeting systems for cash transfer programmes: the case of the CT-OVC programme in Kenya. Lawson, D., Hulme, D., Matin, I. and Moore, K. (eds), *What Works for the Poorest? Poverty Reduction Programmes for the World's Ultra-Poor.* Rugby, UK, Practical Action.

Aly, J. H. and National Education Policy Review Team. 2007. *Education in Pakistan: A White Paper. Document to Debate and Finalize the National Education Policy.* Islamabad.

Amnesty International. 2009. *Shattered Lives: Beyond the 2008–2009 Mindnanao Armed Conflict.* London, Amnesty International.

Andrabi, T., Das, J., Khwaja, A. I., Vishwanath, T., Zajonc, T. and the LEAPS Team. 2008. *Pakistan Learning and Educational Achievements in Punjab Schools (LEAPS): Insights to Inform the Education Policy Debate.* Washington, DC, World Bank.

Anthony, J. 2009. Access to education for students with autism in Ghana: Implications for EFA. Background paper for *EFA Global Monitoring Report 2010.*

Arnold, D. H. and Doctoroff, G. L. 2003. The early education of socioeconomically disadvantaged children. *Annual Review of Psychology,* Vol. 54, pp. 517–45.

Aslam, M. and Kingdon, G. 2007. *What Can Teachers Do to Raise Pupil Achievement?* Oxford, UK, University of Oxford, Department of Economics. (Centre for the Study of African Economies, CSAE WPS/2007-14.)

Assad, R. and Barsoum, G. 2007. *Youth Exclusion in Egypt: In Search of a "Second Chance".* Washington, DC/ Dubai, United Arab Emirates, Wolfensohn Center for Development, Brookings Institution/Dubai School of Government (Middle East Youth Initiative Working Papers, 2.)

Atchoarena, D. and Delluc, A. M. 2001. *Revisiting technical and vocational education in sub-Saharan Africa: provision, patterns and policy issues.* Paris, UNESCO International Institute for Educational Planning.

Attfield, I., Tamiru, M., Parolin, B. and Grauwe, A. D. 2002. *Improving micro-level planning through a Geographical Information System: Studies on Ethiopia and Palestine.* Paris, UNESCO International Institute for Educational Planning.

Australia Department of Education. 2008. *National Report to Parliament on Indigenous Education and Training, 2006.* Canberra, Department of Education, Employment and Workplace Relations.

Ayyar, R. V. V. 2008. Country-agency relationship in development cooperation: an Indian experience. Background paper for *EFA Global Monitoring Report 2009.*

Banerjee, A., Banerji, R., Duflo, E., Glennerster, R. and Khemani, S. 2008. *Pitfalls of participatory programmes: evidence from a randomised evaluation in education in India.* Washington, DC, World Bank, Development Research Group, Human Development and Public Services Team. (Impact Evaluation Series, 21. Policy Research Working Papers, 4584.)

Bangladesh Government. 2008. *Final Mid-term Evaluation Report of the Basic Education for Hard to Reach Urban Children's Project (2nd phase).* Dhaka, Government of the People's Republic of Bangladesh.

——. 2009. *Bangladesh Primary Education Annual Sector Performance Report 2009.* Dhaka, Government of the People's Republic of Bangladesh.

Bangladesh Ministry of Planning and UNESCO Bangladesh. 2008. *Literacy Assessment Survey 2008.* Dhaka, Ministry of Planning, Planning Division, Bangladesh Bureau of Statistics/UNESCO Bangladesh.

Bano, M. 2008. *Islamiyya, Quranic and Tsangaya Education (IQTE) Integration Strategy.* Kano/London, Kano State Government/CUBE, UK Department for International Developent.

Barabasch, A., Hang, S. and Lawson, R. 2009. Planned policy transfer: the impact of the German model on Chinese vocational education. *Compare: A Journal of Comparative and International Education,* Vol. 39, No. 1, pp. 5–20.

Barnett, W. S., Epstein, D. J., Friedman, A. A., Boyd, J. S. and Hustedt, J. T. 2008. *The State of Preschool 2008: State Preschool Yearbook.* New Brunswick, NJ, National Institute for Early Education Research.

Barnett, W. S. and Yarosz, D. J. 2007. Who goes to preschool and why does it matter? *Preschool Policy Matters,* Issue 15, November.

Bartholomew, A., Takala, T. and Ahmed, Z. 2009. *Mid-Term Evaluation of the EFA Fast Track Initiative. Country Case Study: Mozambique.* Cambridge/Oxford, UK, Cambridge Education/Mokoro Ltd/Oxford Policy Management. (Draft.)

Batungwanayo, C. and Reyntjens, L. 2006. *L'Impact du Décret Présidentiel pour la Gratuité des Soins sur la Qualité des Services de Santé au Burundi* [Impact of the presidential decree of free treatment on quality of health care services in Burundi]. Bujumbura, Burundi Ministry of Public Health, Direction Générale de la Santé Publique.

Baulch, B., Nguyen, T. M. H., Nguyen, T. T. P. and Pham, T. H. 2009. *Ethnic Minority Poverty in Vietnam.* Background paper for *Country Social Analysis: Ethnicity and Development in Vietnam.* Washington, DC, World Bank. (Discussion draft.)

Baxter, P. and Bethke, L. 2008. *Filling the Gap: What is the Role of Alternative Education Programmes?* Reading, UK/Paris, CfBT Education Trust/UNESCO International Institute for Educational Planning.

Beegle, K., De Weerdt, J. and Dercon, S. 2009. The intergenerational impact of the African orphans crisis: a cohort study from an HIV/AIDS affected area. *International Journal of Epidemiology,* Vol. 38, No. 2, pp. 561–8.

Beegle, K., Dehejia, R. H. and Gatti, R. 2006. Child labor and agricultural shocks. *Journal of Development Economics,* Vol. 81, No. 1, pp. 80–96.

Behrman, J. R. 1996. Impact of health and nutrition on education. *The World Bank Research Observer,* Vol. 11, No. 1, pp. 23–37.

Behrman, J. R., Hoddinot, J., Maluccio, J. A., Soler-Hampejsek, E., Behrman, E. R., Martorell, R., Ramirez-Zea, M. and Stein, A. D. 2008. *What Determines Adult Cognitive Skills: Impacts of Pre-schooling, Schooling and Post-schooling Experiences in Guatemala.* Washington, DC, International Food Policy Research Institute. (IFPRI Discussion Papers, 00826.)

Belfield, C. R. 2007. Introduction to the special issue 'The Economics of Early Childhood Education'. *Economics of Education Review,* Vol. 26, No. 1, pp. 1–2.

Bellew, R. and Moock, P. 2008. *Fast Track Initiative Education Program Development Fund (EPDF): Review of Activities and Allocations 2005–2007.* Washington, DC, Fast Track Initiative Secretariat.

Benavot, A. 2004. A global study of intended instructional time and official school curricula, 1980–2000. Background paper for *EFA Global Monitoring Report 2005.*

——. 2008. Meeting the lifelong learning needs of youth and adults. Duke, C. and Hinzen, H. (eds), *Knowing More, Doing Better: Challenges for CONFINTEA VI from Monitoring EFA in Non-Formal Youth and Adult Education.* Bonn, Germany, dvv International, pp. 8–14. (International Perspectives in Adult Education.)

Benin Government. 2008. *Benin: Poverty Reduction Strategy Paper – Growth Strategy for Poverty Reduction.* Washington, DC, IMF/Republic of Benin. (Country Reports, 08/125.)

Bennell, P. 2009. A review of EFA expenditure projections made by national education plans in sub-Saharan Africa. Background paper for *EFA Global Monitoring Report 2010*

Bennell, P. and Akyeampong, K. 2007. *Teacher Motivation in sub-Saharan Africa and South Asia.* London, UK Department for International Development, Central Research Department. (Educational Papers; Researching the Issues, 71.)

Bennett, J. 2008. *Early Childhood Services in the OECD Countries: Review of the Literature and Current Policy in the Early Childhood Field.* Florence, Italy, UNICEF Innocenti Research Centre. (Innocenti Working Paper.)

Benveniste, L., Marshall, J. and Santibañez, L. 2007. *Teaching in Lao PDR.* Washington, DC/Vientiane, World Bank/ Lao People's Democratic Republic Ministry of Education.

Bermingham, D. 2009*a*. Scaling up aid for education: lessons from the Education for All Fast Track Initiative (FTI). Background paper for *EFA Global Monitoring Report 2010.*

____. 2009*b*. *We Don't Need No Education? Why the United States Should Take the Lead on Global Education.* Washington, DC, Center for Global Development. (CGD Notes.)

Berry, C. 2009. A framework for assessing the effectiveness of the delivery of education aid in fragile states. *Journal of Education for International Development (JEID),* Vol. 4, No. 1.

Betancourt, T. S., Simmons, S., Borisova, I., Brewer, S. E., Iweala, U. and de la Soudière, M. 2008. High hopes, grim realities: reintegration and the education of former child soldiers in Sierra Leone. *Comparative Education Review,* Vol. 52, No. 4, pp. 565–87.

Betcherman, G., Godfrey, M., Puerto, S., Rother, F. and Stavreska, A. 2007. *A Review of Interventions to Support Young Workers: Findings of the Youth Employment Inventory.* Washington, DC, World Bank. (Discussion paper, 0715.)

Betcherman, G., Olivas, K. and Dar, A. 2004. *Impacts of Active Labor Market Programs: New Evidence from Evaluations with Particular Attention to Developing and Transition Countries.* Washington, DC, World Bank, Human Development Network. (Social Protection Discussion Paper Series; Discussion paper, 0402.)

Bhalotra, S. 2009. Educational deficits and social identity in India. Background paper for *EFA Global Monitoring Report 2010.*

Biddle, N. and Mackay, S. 2009. Understanding the educational marginalisation of indigenous Australians: extent, processes and policy responses. Background paper for *EFA Global Monitoring Report 2010.*

Bird, K. and Pratt, N. 2004. *Fracture Points in Social Policies for Chronic Poverty Reduction.* Manchester, Chronic Poverty Research Centre. (CPRC Working Paper.)

Birdsall, N., Savedoff, W. and Vyborny, K. 2008. *Cash on delivery aid for education: a hands-off approach.* Washington, DC, Center for Global Development.

Bishop, J. H. and Mañe, F. 2005. Economic Return to Vocational Courses in U.S. High Schools. Lauglo, J. and Maclean, R. (eds), *Vocationalisation of Secondary Education Revisited* (Technical and Vocational Education and Training: Issues, Concerns and Prospects, Vol. 1.) Dordrecht, The Netherlands, Springer, pp. 329–62.

Björkman, M. 2005. *Income Shocks and Gender Gaps in Education: Evidence from Uganda.* Stockholm, Institute for International Economic Studies, Stockholm University.

Black, R. E., Allen, L. H., Bhutta, Z. A., Caulfield, L. E., de Onis, M., Ezzati, M., Mathers, C. and Rivera, J. 2008. Maternal and child undernutrition: global and regional exposures and health consequences. *The Lancet (Maternal and Child Undernutrition 1),* Vol. 371, No. 9608, pp. 243–60.

Blanco Allais, F. and Quinn, P. 2009. Marginalisation and child labour. Background paper for *EFA Global Monitoring Report 2010.*

Blanden, J. and Machin, S. 2008. Up and down the generational income ladder in Britain: past changes and future prospects. *National Institute Economic Review,* Vol. 205, No. 1, pp. 101–16.

Boissiere, M. 2004. *Determinants of Primary Education Outcomes in Developing Countries.* Washington, DC, World Bank, Operations Evaluation Department. (Background paper for evaluation of World Bank support to primary education.)

Bonnet, G. 2009. Marginalization in Latin America and the Caribbean. Background paper for *EFA Global Monitoring Report 2010.*

Bouis, H. 2008. *Rising Food Prices Will Result in Severe Declines in Mineral and Vitamin Intakes of the Poor.* Washington, DC, HarvestPlus, International Food Policy Research Institute.

Bourguignon, F., Ferreira, F. and Walton, M. 2007. Equity, efficiency and inequality traps: a research agenda. *Journal of Economic Inequality,* Vol. 5, No. 2, pp. 235–56.

Brannelly, L., Ndaruhutse, S. and Rigaud, C. 2009. *Donors' Engagement in Education in Fragile and Conflict-Affected States.* Reading, UK/Paris, CfBT Education Trust/UNESCO International Institute for Educational Planning. (Policy brief.)

Brautigam, D. A. 2000. *Aid Dependence and Governance.* Stockholm, Expert Group on Development Issues, Swedish Ministry for Foreign Affairs.

____. 2008. *China's African Aid: Transatlantic Challenges.* Washington, DC, German Marshall Fund of the United States, Program on Aid Effectiveness.

Brazil Ministry of Education. 2008. *National Report from Brazil.* National report for CONFINTEA VI, Belém, Brazil, 1–4 December. Brasília/Hamburg, Germany, Brazil Ministry of Education/UNESCO Institute for Lifelong Learning.

Bredenkamp, H. 2009*a*. *Helping low-income countries confront the worst economic crisis in 60 years.* Washington, DC, International Monetary Fund. http://blog-imfdirect.imf.org/2009/08/31/twin-crises/ (Accessed 29 September 2009.)

____. 2009*b*. *Low-income countries: different strokes for different folks.* Washington, DC, International Monetary Fund. http://blog-imfdirect.imf.org/2009/09/02/differe3nt-nee/ (Accessed 29 September 2009.)

Brewer, L. 2004. *Youth at Risk: The Role of Skills Development in Facilitating the Transition to Work.* Geneva, Switzerland, ILO, InFocus Programme on Skills, Knowledge and Employability. (Skills Working Papers.)

Bridgeland, J., Dilulio, J. J., Jr. and Morison, K. B. 2006. *The Silent Epidemic. Perspectives of High School Dropouts.* Washington, DC, Civic Enterprises, LLC/Peter D. Hart Research Associates for the Bill & Melinda Gates Foundation.

Brooks-Gunn, J. and Markman, L. B. 2005. The contribution of parenting to ethnic and racial gaps in school readiness. *The Future of Children*, Spring, School Readiness: Closing Racial and Ethnic Gaps, Vol. 15, No. 1, pp. 139–68.

Bruneforth, M. 2009*a*. *Differences in the Age Distribution of Primary Pupils Between Administrative and Household Data and the Impact on Monitoring of Enrolment Rates.* Montreal, Qué, UNESCO Institute for Statistics.

____. 2009*b*. Social background and a typology of out-of-school children in 27 countries. Background paper for *EFA Global Monitoring Report 2010.*

Bruneforth, M. and Wallet, P. 2009. Developing indicators to monitor out-of-school adolescents. Background paper for *EFA Global Monitoring Report 2010.*

Brunello, G. and Checchi, D. 2007. Does school tracking affect equality of opportunity? New international evidence. *Economic Policy*, Vol. 22, No. 52, pp. 781-861.

Bruns, B., Mingat, A. and Rakotomalala, R. 2003. *Achieving Universal Primary Education by 2015: A Chance for Every Child.* Washington, DC, World Bank.

Bundy, D. A., Burbano, C., Grosh, M., Gelli, A., Jukes, M. and Drake, L. 2009*a*. *Rethinking School Feeding: Social Safety Nets, Child Development, and the Education Sector.* Washington, DC/Rome, World Bank/World Food Programme.

Bundy, D. A., Kremer, M., Bleakley, H., Jukes, M. C. H. and Miguel, E. 2009*b*. Deworming and development: asking the right questions, asking the questions right. *PLoS Neglected Tropical Diseases*, Vol. 3, No. 1, e362.

Burd-Sharps, S., Lewis , K. and Borges Martins, E. 2008. *The Measure of America: American Human Development Report, 2008–2009.* Brooklyn, NY, Social Science Research Council, American Human Development Project. (A Columbia/SSRC Book.)

Buse, K. 2005. *Education for All – Fast Track Initiative: Review of the Governance and Management Structures.* Washington, DC/London, World Bank/UK Overseas Development Institute.

____. 2007. *Education for All – Fast Track Initiative: An Embodiment of the Paris Declaration on Aid Effectiveness?* Washington, DC/London, World Bank/UK Overseas Development Institute.

Caillods, F. and Hallak, J. 2004. *Education and PRSPs: A Review of Experiences.* Paris, UNESCO International Institute for Educational Planning.

Cambridge Distance Education Consultancy. 2009. *Open and Distance Learning for Basic Education: Its Potential for Hard to Reach Children and Children in Conflict and Disaster Areas*, Cambridge, UK/ Kathmandu, CDED/UNICEF Regional Office for South Asia. (Report prepared by CDEC for UNICEF-ROSA.)

Cambridge Education, Mokoro and OPM. 2009. *Mid-Term Evaluation of the EFA Fast Track Initiative. Preliminary Report.* Cambridge/Oxford, UK, Cambridge Education/Mokoro Ltd/Oxford Policy Management. (Draft.)

Cameron, S. 2008. *Education decisions in slums of Dhaka, Bangladesh.* British Association of International and Comparative Education, Glasgow, UK.

____. 2009. *Education Decisions in Slums of Dhaka.* Falmer, Consortium for Research on Educational Access, Transitions and Equity (CREATE). (Pathways to Access.)

Campaign for Fiscal Equity. 2009. *A Sound Basic Education for All Children.* http://www.cfequity.org (Accessed 24 September 2009.)

Campbella, F. A., Wasika, B. H., Pungelloa, E., Burchinala, M., Barbarina, O., Kainza, K., Sparlinga, J. J. and Rameyb, C. T. 2008. Young adult outcomes of the Abecedarian and CARE early childhood educational interventions. *Early Childhood Research Quarterly*, Vol. 23, No. 4, pp. 452–66.

Carr-Hill, R. 2009. *Mid-Term Evaluation of the EFA Fast Track Initiative: Issues in Data and Monitoring and Evaluation.* Oxford/Cambridge, UK, Mokoro Ltd/Cambridge Education/Oxford Policy Management. (Working Paper 3.)

Casely-Hayford, L., Ghartey, A. B. and SfL Internal Impact Assessment Team. 2007. *The Leap to Literacy and Life Change in Northern Ghana: An impact assessment of School for Life (SfL).* Tamale, Ghana, School for Life.

Castro, V. and Laguna, J. R. 2008. *Review of Results from Pilots in Spanish: Nicaragua*. Paper presented at the Early Grade Reading Assessment (EGRA) Second 2nd Workshop, Washington, DC, 12–14 March.

CCIC. 2009*a*. *Aid in the Crosshairs: Civil-military Relations in Afghanistan*. Ottawa, Canadian Council for International Co-operation. (CCIC Briefing Note.)

___. 2009*b*. *Backgrounder on the Kandahar Provincial Reconstruction Team*. Ottawa, Canadian Council for International Co-operation.

Center for Global Development. *Liberia's Recovery From Devastation*. http://www.cgdev.org/section/initiatives/_active/liberia/recovery (Accessed 13 July 2009.)

Center for Labor Market Studies. 2007. *Left Behind in America: The Nation's Dropout Crisis*. Boston, Mass., Northeastern University, Center for Labor Market Studies.

Centers for Disease Control and Prevention. 2008. Progress toward introduction of *Haemophilus influenzae* type b vaccine in low-income countries – worldwide, 2004-2007. *Morbidity and Mortality Weekly Report*, Vol. 57, No. 06, pp. 148–51.

Centre for Urban Studies, National Institute of Population Research and Training and MEASURE Evaluation. 2006. *Slums of Urban Bangladesh: Mapping and Census*. Dhaka/Chapel Hill, NC, CUS/NIPORT/MEASURE Evaluation.

Cerdan-Infantes, P. and Vermeersch, C. 2007. *More Time Is Better: An Evaluation of the Full-Time School Program in Uruguay*. Washington, DC, World Bank. (Impact Evaluation Series, 13. Policy Research Working Papers, 4167.)

Chanamuto, N. 2009. Annotated bibliography on the costs of reaching and teaching the marginalised. Background paper for *EFA Global Monitoring Report 2010*.

Chang, G.-C., Martinez, R. and Mputu, H. 2009. Estimating the costs of education development: case study for Democratic Republic of Congo, Nigeria and Sudan. Background paper for *EFA Global Monitoring Report 2010*.

Chen, S. and Ravallion, M. 2008. *The Developing World is Poorer Than We Thought, but No Less Successful in the Fight Against Poverty*. Washington, DC, World Bank. (Policy Research Working Papers, 4703)

___. 2009. *The Impact of the Global Financial Crisis on the World's Poorest*. VoxEU.org. http://www.voxeu.org/index.php?q=node/3520 (Accessed 5 November 2009.)

Child Rights Information Network. 2009. *Discrimination/indigenous rights: Antoine et al v. Winner School District (USA)*. http://www.crin.org/Law/instrument.asp?InstID=1227 (Accessed September 24 2009.)

Children England. 2009. *Children England HM Treasury Budget 2009*. London, Children England. (Briefing of key announcements.)

Chowdhury, J. 2005. *Disability and Chronic Poverty: An Empirical Study on Bangladesh*. Oxford, UK, Oxford University. (MPhil Thesis.)

Christensen, G. and Stanat, P. 2007. *Language Policies and Practices for Helping Immigrants and Second-Generation Students Succeed*. Washington, DC, Migration Policy Institute/Bertelsmann Stiftung. (Transatlantic Taskforce on Immigration and Integration.)

Chronic Poverty Research Centre. 2008. *The Chronic Poverty Report 2008–09: Escaping Poverty Traps*. Manchester, UK, CPRC.

CINTERFOR/ILO. 2001. *Modernization in vocational education and training in Latin America and the Caribbean*. Montevideo, International Labour Organization, CINTERFOR (Inter-American Research and Documentation Centre on Vocational Training).

___. 2008. *Global Employment Trends for Youth: October 2008*. Geneva, Switzerland, International Labour Office.

___. 2009. *Global Employment Trends: Update, May 2009*. Geneva, Switzerland, International Labour Office.

Clemens, M., Radelet, S. and Bhavnani, R. 2004. *Counting Chickens When They Hatch: the Short Term Effect of Aid on Growth*. Washington, DC, Center for Global Development. (Working Paper.)

CNN. 2009. *'High school dropout crisis' continues in US, study says*. CNN, Atlanta, Ga. http://edition.cnn.com/2009/US/05/05/dropout.rate.study/ (Accessed 29 September 2009.)

Coalition to Stop the Use of Child Soldiers. 2008. *Child Soldiers: Global Report 2008*. London, Coalition to Stop the Use of Child Soldiers.

Cohen, J. and Dupas, P. 2007. *Free distribution or cost-sharing: evidence from a randomized malaria prevention experiment*. Cambridge, Mass., Poverty Action Lab. http://www.povertyactionlab.org/papers/Dupas%20Free_Distribution_vs_Cost-Sharing_10.15.07.pdf (Accessed 29 September 2009.)

Colclough, C. and Fennel, S. 2004. *The Fast Track Initiative: Towards a New Strategy for Meeting the Education MDGs*. London, UK Department for International Development. (Policy paper.)

Collier, P. and Hoeffler, A. 2002. *Aid, Policy and Growth in Post-Conflict Societies*. Washington, DC, World Bank. (Policy Research Working Papers, 2927.)

COMEDAF II+. 2007. *Strategy to Revitalize Technical and Vocational Education and Training (TVET) in Africa*. Meeting of the Bureau of the Conference of Ministers of Education of the African Union, 29–31 May, Addis Ababa, January.

Commission on Growth and Development. 2008. *The Growth Report: Strategies for Sustained Growth and Inclusive Development*. Washington, DC, World Bank, Commission on Growth and Development.

Committee of Ten. 2009. *Impact of the Crisis on African Economies: Sustaining Growth and Poverty Reduction – African Perspectives and Recommendations to the G20*. Tunis-Belvedère, Tunisia, African Development Bank.

Contreras, M. E. and Talavera Simoni, M. L. 2003. *The Bolivian Education Reform 1992-2002: Case Studies in Large-Scale Education Reform*. Washington, DC, World Bank.

Cooke, M., Mitrou, F., Lawrence, D., Guimond, E. and Beavon, D. 2007. Indigenous well-being in four countries: an application of the UNDP's human development index to indigenous peoples in Australia, Canada, New Zealand, and the United States. *BMC International Health and Human Rights*, Vol. 7, No. 9.

Coviello, D. and Islam, R. 2006. *Does aid help improve economic institutions?* Washington, DC, World Bank. (Policy Research Working Papers, 3990.)

Crouch, L. and Winkler, D. 2008. Governance, management and financing of education for all: basic frameworks and case studies. Background paper for *EFA Global Monitoring Report 2009*.

Crouch, L. A. and Korda, M. 2008. *EGRA Liberia: Baseline Assessment of Reading Levels and Associated Factors*. Washington, DC, USAID/World Bank.

Crouch, L. A., Korda, M. and Mumo, D. 2009. *Improvements in Reading Skills in Kenya: An Experiment in the Malindi District*. Washington, DC, USAID. (EdData II.)

Crul, M. 2007.. *Pathways to Success for the Children of Immigrants*. Washington, DC, Migration Policy Institute/Bertelsmann Stiftung. (Transatlantic Taskforce on Immigration and Integration.)

Cueto, S., Guerrero, G., León, J., Seguin, E. and Muñoz, I. 2009. Explaining and overcoming marginalization in education: a focus on ethnic/language minorities in Peru. Background paper for *EFA Global Monitoring Report 2010*.

Cunha, F., Heckman, J. J., Lochner, L. and Masterov, D. V. 2005. *Interpreting the Evidence on Life Cycle Skill Formation*. Cambridge, Mass., National Bureau of Economic Research. (Working Paper/Chapter for Handbook of the Economics of Education.)

Daftary, F. and Grin, F. 2003. *Nation-Building, Ethnicity and Language Politics in Transition Countries*. Budapest, Local Government and Public Service Reform Initiative, Open Society Institute.

Das, J., Pandey, P. and Zajonc, T. 2006. *Learning levels and gaps in Pakistan*. Washington, DC, World Bank. (Policy Research Working Papers, 4067.)

Das, J. and Zajonc, T. 2008. *India Shining and Bharat Drowning: Comparing Two Indian States to the Worldwide Distribution in Mathematics Achievement*. Washington. DC, World Bank. (Policy Research Working Papers, 4644.)

Daswani, C. J. 2005. Urban people and urban literacies: some Indian experiences. Rogers, A. (ed.), *Urban Literacy: Communication, Identity and Learning in Development Contexts*. Hamburg, Germany, UNESCO Institute for Education, pp. 15–22.

de Beco, G. and Right to Education Project. 2009. The right to education: human rights indicators and the right to education of Roma children in Slovakia. Background paper for *EFA Global Monitoring Report 2010*.

de Kemp, A., Elbers, C., Gunning, J. W., van den Berg, E. and de Hoop, K. 2008. *Primary education in Zambia*. The Hague, OBT.

de Renzio, P. 2009. *Taking Stock: What Do PEFA Assessments Tell Us about PFM Systems across Countries?* London, UK Overseas Development Institute. (Working Paper, 302.)

de Renzio, P. and Dorotinsky, B. 2007. *Tracking progress in the quality of PFM systems in HIPCs: an update on past assessments using PEFA data*. Washington, DC., Public Expenditure and Financial Accountability (PEFA) Program.

de Renzio, P. and Woods, N. 2007. *The Trouble with Cash on Delivery Aid: A Note on its Potential Effects on Recipient Country Institutions*. Washington, DC, Center for Global Development. (Note prepared for CGD initiative on 'Cash on Delivery Aid'.)

Deininger, K. and Mpuga, P. 2005. Economic and welfare impact of the abolition of health user fees: evidence from Uganda. *Journal of African Economies*, Vol. 14, No. 1, pp. 55–99.

Delgado, C. 2008. *The Global Food Crisis Response Program (GFRP) at the World Bank*. Paper presented at the Food and Energy Price Increases and Policy Options Workshop, Washington, DC, World Bank, 9–10 July.

Deloitte LLP. 2009. *Deloitte Annual Review of Football Finance*. London, Deloitte LLP.

Democratic Republic of the Congo Ministry of Planning, Democratic Republic of Congo Ministry of Health and Macro International Inc. 2008. *Enquête Démographique et de Santé 2007* [2007 Demographic and Health Survey]. Kinshasa/Calverton, Md., Democratic Republic of the Congo Ministry of Planning and Ministry of Health/ Macro International Inc.

DeNavas-Walt, C., Proctor, B. D. and Smith, J. C. 2008. *Income, Poverty, and Health Insurance Coverage in the United States: 2007.* Washington, DC, US Census Bureau. (Current Population Reports.)

DeStefano, J. and Elaheebocus, N. 2009. *School Effectiveness in Woliso, Ethiopia: Measuring Opportunity to Learn and Early Grade Reading Fluency.* Washington, DC, USAID/Save the Children USA.

DeStefano, J., Schuh Moore, A.-M., Balwanz, D. and Hartwell, A. 2006. *Meeting EFA: Reaching the Underserved through Complementary Models of Effective Schooling.* Washington, DC, USAID/Academy for Educational Development. (EQUIP2 Working Paper.)

Deutscher, E. and Fyson, S. 2008. Improving the effectiveness of aid. *Finance and Development,* Vol. 45, No. 3, pp. 15–9.

Devereux, S. 2006. *Vulnerable Livelihoods in Somali Region, Ethiopia.* Falmer, UK, Institute of Development Studies. (Research Report, 57.)

Devereux, S., Sabates-Wheeler, R., Tefera, M. and Taye, H. 2006. *Ethiopia's Productive Safety Net Programme (PSNP): Trends in PSNP Transfers Within Targeted Households – Final Report.* Falmer, UK/Addis Ababa, Institute of Development Studies/Indak International PLC.

DFID. 2005. *Why We Need to Work More Effectively in Fragile States.* London, UK Department for International Development.

——. 2007. *Technical and vocational skills development.* London, UK Department for International Development. (Briefing; a DFID Practice Paper.)

——. 2008*a*. *Jobs, Labour Markets and Shared Growth: The Role of Skills.* London, UK Department for International Development. (Briefing; a DFID Practice Paper, TD/TNC 95.324.)

——. 2008*b*. *Maternal Health Strategy – Reducing Maternal Deaths: Evidence and Action.* London, UK Department for International Development. (Progress report.)

——. 2009*a*. *Budget 2009 – Keeping our Promises to the World's Poorest People.* London, UK Department for International Development. http://www.dfid.gov.uk/Media-Room/News-Stories/2009/Budget-2009--keeping-our-promises-to-the-worlds-poorest-people/ (Accessed 29 September 2009.)

——. 2009*b*. *Eliminating World Poverty: Building our Common Future.* London, UK Department for International Development.

DFID and World Bank. 2005. *Integrating TVET into the Knowledge Economy: Reform and Challenges in the Middle East and North Africa.* London/Washington, DC, UK Department for International Development/European Training Foundation/World Bank. (Research report.)

Dillon, S. 2009. Stimulus plan would provide flood of aid to education. *The New York Times,* 27 January.

District Information System for Education. 2009. *Elementary Education in India: Progress towards UEE – DISE 2007–08.* New Delhi, National University of Educational Planning and Administration/India Ministry of Human Resource Development, Department of School Education and Literacy.

Dobbie, W. and Fryer, R. G., Jr. 2009. *Are High-Quality Schools Enough to Close the Achievement Gap? Evidence from a Bold Social Experiment in Harlem.* Cambridge, Mass., Harvard University.

Dolata, S., Ikeda, M. and Murimba, S. 2004. Different pathways to EFA for different school systems. *IIEP Newsletter,* Vol. 22, No. 1, pp. 8–9.

Dollar, D. and Hofman, B. 2006. *Intergovernmental Fiscal Reforms, Expenditure Assignment, and Governance.* Paper presented at the Roundtable Conference on Public Finance for a Harmonious Society, Session on Expenditure Assignments within a Framework of Decentralization. Beijing, June 28–27, World Bank.

Dom, C. 2009. *Mid-Term Evaluation of the EFA Fast Track Initiative. FTI and Fragile States and Fragile Partnerships: Background Literature Review.* Cambridge/Oxford, UK, Cambridge Education/Mokoro Ltd/Oxford Policy Management. (Working Paper 6.)

Dowd, A. J. 2009. *A Day in School: Are Students Getting an Opportunity to Learn?* Paper presented at the Comparative and International Education Society Conference, Charleston, SC, 24 March.

Duffy, M., Fransman, J. and Pearce, E. 2008. *Review of 16 Reflect Evaluations.* London, ActionAid UK.

Duman, A. 2008. Education and income inequality in Turkey: does schooling matter? *Financial Theory and Practice,* Vol. 32, No. 3, pp. 369–87.

Duru-Bellat, M. 2009. Accès à l'éducation: quelles inégalités dans la France d'aujourd'hui? [Access to education: what are the inequalities in France today?] Background paper for *EFA Global Monitoring Report 2010.*

Dutcher, N. 2004. *Expanding Educational Opportunity in Linguistically Diverse Societies.* Washington, DC, Center for Applied Linguistics.

Dyer, C. 2006. *The Education of Nomadic Peoples: Current Issues, Future Prospects.* Oxford, UK, Berghahn.

EACEA. 2009. *Tackling Social and Cultural Inequalities through Early Childhood Education and Care in Europe.* Brussels, Education, Audiovisual and Culture Executive Agency. (Eurydice study.)

Easterly, W. 2003. Can foreign aid buy growth? *Journal of Economic Perspectives,* Vol. 17, No. 3, pp. 23–48.

Echessa, E. 2009. *Effective Education Financing in Fragile Contexts – Challenges and Opportunities: Southern Sudan Case,* Inter-agency Network for Education in Emergencies.

Economic and Political Weekly. 2009. Editorial: half measure on the right to education. *Economic and Political Weekly,* Vol. 44, No. 33, p. 6.

Edmonds, E. V. 2007. *Child Labor.* Bonn, Germany, Institute for the Study of Labor (IZA). (IZA Discussion Papers, 2606.)

Education for All: Class of 2015. 2008. *Education for All: Class of 2015. Launch Event Communiqué.* 25 September. Johannesburg, Global Campaign for Education, Class of 2015.

EPDC (Education Policy and Data Center) and UNESCO. 2009. Estimating the costs of achieving Education for All in low income countries. Background paper for *EFA Global Monitoring Report 2010.*

Elbedour, S., Onwuegbuzie, A. J., Ghannam, J., Whitcome, J. A. and Hein, F. A. 2007. Post-traumatic stress disorder, depression, and anxiety among Gaza Strip adolescents in the wake of the second Uprising (Intifada). *Child Abuse & Neglect,* Vol. 31, No. 7, pp. 719–29.

Ellis, F., Devereux, S. and White, P. 2009. *Social Protection in Africa.* Cheltenham UK/Northampton, Mass., Edward Elgar Publishing Ltd.

Emmett, B. 2009. *Paying the Price for the Economic Crisis.* Oxford, UK, Oxfam International. (Oxfam International Discussion Paper.)

Eritrea Ministry of National Development. 2005. *Millennium Development Goals Report.* Asmara, Eritrea Ministry of National Development.

Erulkar, A. S. and Matheka, J. K. 2007. *Adolescence in the Kibera Slums of Nairobi, Kenya.* Nairobi, Population Council.

European Commission. 2008. Child Poverty and Well-being in the EU: Current Status and Way Forward. European Commission, Directorate-General for Employment, Social Affairs and Equal Opportunities, Unit E2.

——. 2009*a. EU Action against Discrimination: Activity Report 2007–08.* Luxembourg, European Commission, Directorate-General for Employment, Social Affairs and Equal Opportunities, Unit G4.

——. 2009*b. Supporting Developing Countries in Copying with the Crisis: Where Does the EU Go From Doha? What Prospects for Meeting the EU Targets of 2010 and 2015?* Annual Progress Report 2009 on Financing for Development. Brussels, European Commission. (Commission Staff Working Paper.)

European Commission against Racism and Intolerance. 2009. *ECRI Report on Slovakia (Fourth Monitoring Cycle).* Strasbourg, France, Council of Europe, Directorate General of Human Rights and Legal Affairs, ECRI Secretariat. (CRI(2009)20.)

European Roma Rights Centre. 2007. *The Impact of Legislation and Policies on School Segregation of Romani Children: a Study of Anti-Discrimination Law and Government Measures to Eliminate Segregation in Education in Bulgaria, Czech Republic, Hungary, Romania and Slovakia.* Budapest, European Roma Rights Centre.

——. 2008. *Rights Groups Press Czech Government on Roma Education.* Budapest, European Roma Rights Centre. http://www.errc.org/cikk.php?cikk=2982&archiv=12009. (Accessed 29 September 2009.)

Evans, D. and Miguel, E. 2007. Orphans and schooling in Africa: a longitudinal analysis. *Demography,* Vol. 44, No. 1, pp. 35–57.

Every Child Matters. 2009. *Sure Start Children's Centres.* London, Every Child Matters, UK Department for Children, Schools and Families. http://www.surestart.gov.uk/surestartservices/settings/surestartchildrenscentres (Accessed 29 September 2009.)

FAO. 2008. *The State of Food Insecurity in the World 2008 – High Food Prices and Food Security: Threats and Opportunities.* Rome, Food and Agriculture Organization of the United Nations.

——. 2009. *The State of Food Insecurity in the World – Economic Crises: Impacts and Lessons Learned.* Rome, Food and Agriculture Organization of the United Nations.

Fares, J., Guarcello, L., Manacorda, M., Rosati, F. C., Lyon, S. and Valdivia, C. 2005. *School to Work Transition in Sub-Saharan Africa: An Overview.* Rome, ILO/UNICEF/World Bank, Understanding Children's Work Project, University of Rome Tor Vergata, Faculty of Economics. (Working paper.)

Fasih, T. 2008. *Linking Education Policy to Labor Market Outcomes*. Washington, DC, World Bank. (Directions in Development. Human Development.)

Fehrler, S. and Michaelowa, K. 2009. Education marginalization in sub-Saharan Africa. Background paper for *EFA Global Monitoring Report 2010*.

Feinstein, L. 2003. Inequality in the early cognitive development of British children in the 1970 cohort. *Economica*, Vol. 70, No. 277, pp. 73–97.

Ferguson, R. F. 2007. Toward excellence with equity: the role of parenting and transformative school reform. Belfield, C. R. and Levin, H. M. (eds), *The Price We Pay: Economic and Social Consequences of Inadequate Education*. Washington, DC, Brookings Institution Press, pp. 225–54.

Ferreira, F. H. G. and Gignoux, J. 2008. *The Measurement of Inequality of Opportunity: Theory and an Application to Latin America*. Washington, DC, World Bank, Development Research Group, Poverty Team. (Policy Research Working Papers, 4659.)

Ferreira, F. H. G. and Schady, N. 2008. *Aggregate Economic Shocks, Child Schooling and Child Health*. Washington, DC, World Bank Development Research Group, Poverty, Human Development and Public Services Teams. (Policy Research Working Papers, 4701.)

Field, S., Kuczera, M. and Pont, B. 2007. *No More Failures: Ten Steps to Equity in Education*. Paris, Organisation for Economic Co-operation and Development, Education and Training Policy Division. (Comparative Report.)

Filmer, D. 2004. *If You Build It, Will They Come? School Availability and School Enrollment in 21 Poor Countries*. Washington, DC, World Bank.

Filmer, D. and Schady, N. 2006. *Getting girls into school: Evidence from a scholarship program in Cambodia*. Washington, DC, World Bank. (Policy Research Working Papers, 3910.)

——. 2008. Getting girls into school: evidence from a scholarship program in Cambodia. *Economic Development and Cultural Change*, Vol. 56, No. 3, pp. 581–617.

——. 2009. *Are There Diminishing Returns to Transfer Size in Conditional Cash Transfers?* Washington, DC, World Bank, Development Research Group, Human Development and Public Services Team. (Impact Evaluation Series, 35. Policy Research Working Papers, 4999.)

Financial Management Reform Programme. 2006. *Primary education in Bangladesh: Assessing service delivery*. Dhaka/Oxford, UK FMRP/Oxford Policy Management. (Social Sector Performance Surveys.)

Fiszbein, A., Schady, N., with Ferreira, F. H. G., Grosh, M., Kelleher, N., Olinto, P. and Skoufias, E. 2009. *Conditional Cash Transfers: Reducing Present and Future Poverty*. Washington, DC, World Bank.

Flores-Moreno, C. 2007. Mexico. Non-formal education. Background paper for *EFA Global Monitoring Report 2008*.

Forero-Pineda, C., Escobar-Rodríguez, D. and Molina, D. 2006. *Escuela Nueva*'s impact on the peaceful social interaction of children in Colombia. Little, A. W. (ed.), *Education for All and Multigrade Teaching: Challenges and Opportunities*. Dordrecht, The Netherlands, Springer.

Foundation for Research on Educational Planning and Development. 2003. *A Baseline Survey of Street Children in Bangladesh*. Dhaka, FREPD. (Report submitted to the Bangladesh Bureau of Statistics.)

France Council for Employment, Income and Social Cohesion. 2008. *A National Responsibility: the School-to-Work Transition of Young People Without Diplomas*. Paris, CERC. (Report No. 9.)

Frankenberg, E., Thomas, D. and Beegle, K. 1999. *The Real Costs of Indonesia's Economic Crisis: Preliminary Finding from the Indonesia Family Life Surveys*. Santa Monica, Calif., RAND Corporation, Labor and Population Program. (Working Paper, 99–04.)

Fransman, J. 2005. Understanding literacy: a concept paper. Background paper for *EFA Global Monitoring Report 2006*.

Fredriksen, B. and Tan, J. P. 2008. *An African Exploration of the East Asian Experience*. Washington, DC, World Bank.

Frenz, P. 2007. *Innovative Practices for Intersectoral Action on Health: A Case Study of Four Programmes for Social Equity*. Santiago, Chile Ministry of Health, Division of Health Planning, Social Determinants of Health Initiative/World Health Organization, Commission on Social Determinants of Health. (Country Case Studies on Intersectoral Action for Health.)

Froese, N. 2008. *Early Effects of Free Early Childhood Education*. Wellington, New Zealand Ministry of Education. (Research report.)

Fryer, R. G. and Levitt, S. D. 2006. The black-white test score gap through third grade. *American Law and Economics Review*, Vol. 8, No. 2, pp. 249–81.

FTI Secretariat. 2004. *Accelerating Progress Towards Quality Universal Primary Education: Framework*. Washington, DC, Fast Track Initiative Secretariat.

——. 2007*a*. *Catalytic Fund Beneficiary Countries Implementation Progress Report. An Update*. Washington, DC, Fast Track Initiative Secretariat. (Prepared in collaboration with country teams for the Catalytic Fund Committee meeting, Dakar, 10 December.)

——. 2007*b*. *Catalytic Fund Committee Meeting*, Dakar, 10 December. Washington, DC, Fast Track Initiative Secretariat. (Minutes.)

——. 2007*c*. *Expanded Catalytic Fund: Concept Note*. Washington, DC, Fast Track Initiative Secretariat.

——. 2008*a*. *Annual Report 2008 – The Road to 2015: Reaching the Education Goals*. Washington, DC, Fast Track Initiative Secretariat.

——. 2008*b*. *Education Program Development Fund (EPDF): Summary Progress Report*. Washington, DC, Fast Track Initiative Secretariat. (Prepared for the EPDF Committee meeting, Oslo, 14–15 December.)

——. 2008*c*. *EFA-FTI Trust Funds – Replenishment Strategy. Draft Update on Progress and Issues*. Washington, DC, Fast Track Initiative Secretariat. (Report prepared for the Catalytic Fund Committee meeting, Oslo, 13–14 December.)

——. 2008*d*. *FTI Catalytic Fund Committee Meeting*. Oslo, 13–14 December. Washington, DC, Fast Track Initiative Secretariat. (Minutes.)

——. 2008*e*. *FTI Catalytic Fund: Annual Status Report*. Washington, DC, Fast Track Initiative Secretariat. (Prepared for the Catalytic Fund Committee Meeting, Oslo, 13–14 December.)

——. 2009*a*. *Education Program Development Fund (EPDF): Interim Progress Report*. Washington, DC, Fast Track Initiative Secretariat. (Prepared for the EPDF Committee meeting, Copenhagen, 22 April.)

——. 2009*b*. *FTI Catalytic Fund: Interim Status Report*. Washington, DC, Fast Track Initiative Secretariat. (Prepared for the Catalytic Fund Committee meeting, Copenhagen, 22 April.)

——. 2009*c*. *FTI Catalytic Fund: Quarterly Financial Update*. Washington, DC, Fast Track Initiative Secretariat. (Prepared for the FTI Board of Directors meeting, Paris, 10 September.)

——. 2009*d*. *Governance of the Partnership*. Washington, DC, Fast Track Initiative Secretariat.

FTI Task Team on Replenishment of the EFA-Fast Track Initiative. 2009. *Report to Steering Committee: Setting out a Proposal on Replenishment*. Washington, DC, Fast Track Initiative Task Team on Replenishment. (Prepared for Steering Committee meeting, Copenhagen, 19 April.)

Fuchs, L., Fuchs, D., Hosp, M. K. and Jenkins, J. 2001. Oral reading fluency as an indicator of reading competence: a theoretical, empirical, and historical analysis. *Scientific Studies of Reading*, Vol. 5, No. 3, pp. 239–56.

Gallart, M. A. 2008. *Skills, Productivity and Employment Growth. The Case of Latin America*. Montevideo, International Labour Organization, CINTERFOR (Inter-American Research and Documentation Centre on Vocational Training), Skills and Employment Department.

Gamboa Rocabado, F. 2009. De las críticas contra el sistema al ejercicio del poder: los movimientos sociales indígenas y las políticas de reforma educativa en Bolivia [From criticism of the system to the exercise of power: indigenous social movements and education reform policies in Bolivia]. Background paper for *EFA Global Monitoring Report 2010*.

Gangl, M. 2003. Returns to education in context: individual education and transition outcomes in European labour markets. Müller, W. and Gangl, M. (eds), *Transitions from Education to Work in Europe: The Integration of Youth into EU Labour Markets*. New York, Oxford University Press, pp. 156–86.

García-Huidobro, J. E. 2006. *900 Schools and Critical Schools Programs (Chile): Two Experiences of Positive Discrimination*. Paper presented at Latin American Lessons in Promoting Education for All, Cartagena de Indias, Colombia, World Bank, 9–11 October.

Garcia, M. and Fares, J. 2008. *Youth in Africa's Labor Market*. Washington, DC, World Bank. (Directions in Development Series: Human Development.)

Garrett, L. 2007. The challenge of global health. *Foreign Affairs*, No. 86, pp. 14–38.

GAVI Alliance. 2009*a*. *GAVI Alliance Progress Report 2008*. Geneva, Switzerland, GAVI Alliance.

——. 2009*b*. *GAVI partners fulfil promise to fight pneumococcal disease*. Geneva, Switzerland, GAVI Alliance. http://www.gavialliance.org/media_centre/press_releases/2009_06_12_AMC_lecce_kick_off.php (Accessed 29 August 2009.)

German Federal Ministry for Economic Cooperation and Development. 2009. *Briefing Note: Education in Development Cooperation*. Bonn, Germany, BMZ.

German Federal Ministry of Education and Research. 2006. *Report on Vocational Education and Training for the Year 2006*. Bonn, Germany, BMBF.

Gettleman, J. 2009. Drought sows misery and conflict across Kenya. *International Herald Tribune*, 8 September.

Ghana Ministry of Education, Science and Sports. 2008. *Preliminary Education Sector Performance Report.* Accra, Ghana, Ministry of Education, Science and Sports.

Ghana Ministry of Education Youth and Sports. 2004*a*. *TVET Policy for Ghana*, Ghana Ministry of Education, Youth & Sports. (Executive summary.)

___. 2004*b*. *White Paper on the Report of Education Reform Review Committee.* Accra, Ghana Ministry of Education, Youth and Sports.

Giffard-Lindsay, K. 2008. Poverty Reduction Strategies and governance, with equity, for education – four case studies: Cambodia, Ethiopia, Ghana, and Nepal. Background paper for *EFA Global Monitoring Report 2009.*

Gilson, L. and McIntyre, D. 2005. Removing user fees for primary care in Africa: the need for careful action. *BMJ*, No. 331, pp. 762–5.

Giordano, E. A. 2008. *School Clusters and Teacher Resource Centres.* Paris, UNESCO International Institute for Educational Planning. (Fundamentals of Educational Planning, 86.)

Glewwe, P., Jacoby, H. G. and King, E. M. 2001. Early childhood nutrition and academic achievement: a longitudinal analysis. *Journal of Public Economics*, Vol. 81, No. 3, pp. 345–68.

Glick, P. 2008. What policies will reduce gender schooling gaps in developing countries: evidence and interpretation. *World Development*, Vol. 36, No. 9, pp. 1623–46.

Glick, P. and Sahn, D. E. 2009. Cognitive skills among children in Senegal: disentangling the roles of schooling and family background. *Economics of Education Review*, Vol. 28, No. 2, pp. 178–88.

Global Campaign for Education. 2009. *Education on the Brink: Will the IMF's New Lease on Life Ease or Block Progress towards Education Goals?* Johannesburg, Global Campaign for Education.

Global Campaign for Education and ActionAid International. 2005. Global benchmarks for adult literacy. Background paper for *EFA Global Monitoring Report 2006.*

Global Fund. 2005. *Global Fund Investments in Fragile States: Early Results.* Geneva, Switzerland, Global Fund to Fight AIDS, Tuberculosis and Malaria.

___. 2007. *Guidelines for proposals. Round 7.* Geneva, Switzerland, Global Fund to Fight AIDS, Tuberculosis and Malaria.

___. 2008*a*. *Annual Report. A New Era for the Global Fund.* Geneva, Switzerland, Global Fund to Fight AIDS, Tuberculosis and Malaria.

___. 2008*b*. *Country Coordinating Mechanisms. Governance and Civil Society Participation.* Geneva, Switzerland, Global Fund to Fight AIDS, Tuberculosis and Malaria. (Implementer Series.)

___. 2008*c*. *Innovative Financing of the Global Fund: DEBT2HEALTH.* Geneva, Switzerland, Global Fund to Fight AIDS, Tuberculosis and Malaria.

___. 2008*d*. *Lessons Learned in the Field: Health Financing and Governance. A Report on the Country Coordinating Mechanism Model.* Geneva, Switzerland, Global Fund to Fight AIDS, Tuberculosis and Malaria.

___. 2009*a*. *Donors Assess Global Fund Resource Needs.* Geneva, Switzerland, Global Fund. (Press release.)

___. 2009*b*. *Liberia and the Global Fund: Portfolio of Grants.* http://www.theglobalfund.org/programs/portfolio/?countryID=LBR&lang=en (Accessed 5 November 2009.)

___. 2009*c*. *Pledges and Contributions.* Geneva, Switzerland, Global Fund to Fight AIDS, Tuberculosis and Malaria. http://www.theglobalfund.org/en/pledges/?lang=en (Accessed June 30 2009.)

___. 2009*d*. *Scaling up for Impact. Results Report.* Geneva, Switzerland, Global Fund to Fight AIDS, Tuberculosis and Malaria.

___. 2009*e*. *Sierra Leone and the Global Fund: Portfolio of Grants.* http://www.theglobalfund.org/programs/portfolio/?countryID=SLE&lang=en (Accessed 5 November 2009.)

Global Health Watch. 2008. The Global Fund to Fight AIDS, Tuberculosis and Malaria. *Global Health Watch 2: An Alternative World Health Report.* London/New York, Zed Books, pp. 260–76.

Godfrey, M. 2007. *Youth Employment Policy in Developing and Transition Countries: Prevention as well as Cure* Washington, DC, World Bank, Human Development Network, Social Protection Unit. (Social Protection Discussion Series, 0320.)

Goh, C. B. and Gopinathan, S. 2008. Education in Singapore: Developments since 1965. Tan, J.-P. and Fredriksen, B. (eds), *An African Exploration of the East Asian Education Experience.* Washington, DC, World Bank, pp. 80–108.

Gonzales, P., Williams, T., Jocelyn, L., Roey, S., Kastberg, D. and Brenwald, S. 2008. *Highlights From TIMSS 2007: Mathematics and Science Achievement of US Fourth and Eighth-grade Students in an International Context.* Washington, DC, US Department of Education, National Center for Education Statistics, Institute of Education Sciences.

Gordon, N. and Vegas, E. 2005. Educational finance equalisation, spending, teacher quality, and student outcomes: the case of Brazil's FUNDEF. Vegas, E. (ed.), *Incentives to Improve Teaching: Lessons from Latin America.* Washington, DC, World Bank, pp. 151–86.

Gottselig, G. 2009. Combating the global crisis: IMF injecting $283 billion in SDRs into global economy, boosting reserves. *IMF Survey Magazine,* 28 August.

Govinda, R. 1999. *Reaching the Unreached through Participatory Planning: School Mapping in Lok Jumbish, India.* Paris, UNESCO International Institute for Educational Planning. (School Mapping and Local-level Planning.)

——. 2009. India's policies towards children marginalized from education. *EFA Global Monitoring Report 2010.*

Grantham-McGregor, S., Cheung, Y. B., Cueto, S., Glewwe, P., Richter, L., Strupp, B. and International Child Development Steering Group. 2007. Developmental potential in the first 5 years for children in developing countries. *The Lancet,* Vol. 369, No. 9555, pp. 60–70.

Gray Molina, G. and Yañez, E. 2009. *The Dynamics of Inequality in the Best and Worst of Times, Bolivia 1997-2007.* Paper prepared for project on Markets, the State and the Dynamics of Inequality. New York, UNDP Regional Bureau for Latin America and the Caribbean. (Working Paper ID-16-2009.)

Greeley, M. 2007. *Financing Primary Education in Afghanistan.* Brighton, UK, University of Sussex, International Development Studies Institute. (Prepared for Save the Children Alliance.)

Grimes, P. 2009. *A Quality Education for All: A History of the Lao PDR Inclusive Education Project 1993–2009.* Oslo/Vientiane, Save the Children Norway.

Grogg, P. 2009. Latin America: remittance drop will hurt poor. *Inter Press Service.* http://ipsnews.net/news.asp?idnews=47032 (Accessed 5 November 2009.)

Grosh, M., del Ninno, C., Tesliuc, E. and Ouerghi, A. 2008. *For Protection and Promotion: the Design and Implementation of Effective Safety Nets.* Washington, DC, World Bank.

Group of Eight. 2009*a*. *G8 Preliminary Accountability Report. L'Aquila G8 Summit (2009).* G8 Summit 2009: From La Maddalena to L'Aquila. L'Aquila, Italy, Group of Eight, 8–10 July.

——. 2009*b*. *L'Aquila Joint Statement on Global Food Security. L'Aquila Food Security Initiative (AFSI).* G8 Summit 2009: From La Maddalena to L'Aquila. L'Aquila, Italy, Group of Eight, 8–10 July.

——. 2009*c*. *Responsible Leadership for a Sustainable Future.* G8 Summit 2009: From La Maddalena to L'Aquila. L'Aquila, Italy, Group of Eight, 8–10 July..

Group of Twenty. 2009. *The Global Plan for Recovery and Reform.* London, Group of Twenty, 2 April.

Grubb, I. 2007. *Investing in our Future. The Global Fund to Fight AIDS, Tuberculosis and Malaria.* Financing and Action for Global Health Conference 2007, London, ACGH, 13 September.

Grubb, W. N. 2006. Vocational Education and Training: Issues for a Thematic Review. *OECD Meeting of Experts,* 9–10 November.

Guarcello, L., Lyon, S. and Rosati, F. C. 2006. *Promoting School Enrolment, Attendance and Retention among Disadvantaged Children in Yemen: The Potential of Conditional Cash Transfers.* Rome, ILO/UNICEF/World Bank, Understanding Children's Work Project/University of Rome Tor Vergata, Faculty of Economics..

Gunnarsson, V., Orazem, P. F. and Sánchez, M. A. 2006. Child labor and school achievement in Latin America. *The World Bank Economic Review,* Vol. 20, No. 1, pp. 31–54.

Haan, H. C. 2001. *Training for Work in the Informal Sector: Fresh Evidence from Eastern and Southern Africa.* Turin, Italy, International Labour Organization, International Training Center.

Hagemann, F., Diallo, Y., Etienne, A. and Mehran, F. 2006. *Global Child Labour Trends 2000 to 2004.* Geneva, Switzerland, International Labour Organization, International Programme on the Elimination of Child Labour, Statistical Information and Monitoring Programme on Child Labour.

Hall, G. and Patrinos, H. A. (eds). 2006. *Indigenous Peoples, Poverty and Human Development in Latin America.* New York, Palgrave Macmillan.

Hallman, K., Peracca, S., with, Catino, J. and Ruiz, M. J. 2007. Indigenous girls in Guatemala: Poverty and location. Lewis, M. and Lockheed, M. (eds), *Exclusion, Gender and Schooling: Case Studies from the Developing World.* Washington, DC, Center for Global Development, pp. 145–75.

Han, J. 2009. Education of migrant children in China. Background paper for *EFA Global Monitoring Report 2010.*

Hanushek, E. and Woessmann, L. 2009. *Do better schools lead to more growth? Cognitive skills, economic outcomes, and causation.* Cambridge, Mass., National Bureau of Economic Research. (Working Papers, 14633.)

Hanushek, E. A. and Wößmann, L. 2006. Does educational tracking affect performance and inequality? Differences-in-differences evidence across countries. *The Economic Journal,* Vol. 116, No. 510, pp. C63–76.

Harbom, L. and Wallensteen, P. 2009. Armed Conflict, 1946–2008. *Journal of Peace Research*, Vol. 46, No. 4, pp. 577–87.

Harlem Children's Zone. 2007. *Harlem Children's Zone 2006–2007. Biennial Report*. New York, Harlem Children's Zone.

——. n.d. *The Harlem Children's Zone Project Model: Executive Summary*. New York, Harlem Children's Zone.

Harper, C., Jones, N., McKay, A. and Espey, J. 2009. *Children in Times of Economic Crisis: Past Lessons, Future Policies*. London, UK Overseas Development Institute. (ODI Background Note.)

Harttgen, K. and Klasen, S. 2009. Educational marginalization across developed and developing countries. Background paper for *EFA Global Monitoring Report 2010*.

Hartwell, A. 2006. *Meeting EFA: Ghana School for Life*. Washington, DC, USAID/Academy for Educational Development. (EQUIP2 Working Paper.)

Harvard University Center on the Developing Child. 2007. *A Science-Based Framework for Early Childhood Policy: Using Evidence to Improve Outcomes in Learning, Behavior and Health for Vulnerable Children*. Cambridge, Mass., Harvard University, Center on the Developing Child, National Scientific Council on the Developing Child, National Forum on Early Childhood Program Evaluation.

Hauenstein Swan, S., Hadley, S. and Cichon, B. 2009. *Feeding Hunger and Insecurity: Field analysis of volatile global food commodity prices, food security and child malnutrition*. Paris/ACF International Network. (A Hunger Watch Publication.)

Headey, D., Malaiyandi, S. and Fan, S. 2009. *Navigating the Perfect Storm: Reflections on the Food, Energy, and Financial Crises*. Washington, DC, International Food Policy Research Institute. (IFPRI Discussion Paper.)

Heckman, J. J. 2008. *Schools, Skills and Synapses*. Bonn, Germany, Institute for the Sudy of Labor (IZA). (IZA Discussion Papers, 3515.)

Heckman, J. J. and LaFontaine, P. A. 2007. *The American High School Graduation Rate: Trends and Levels*. Cambridge, Mass., National Bureau of Economic Research. (NBER Working Papers, 13670.)

Heller, P. 2005. Back to basics – fiscal space: what it is and how to get it. *Finance and Development*, Vol. 42, No. 2, pp. 32–3.

Henriques, R. 2009. Educational marginalization in Brazil. Background paper for *EFA Global Monitoring Report 2010*.

Henriques, R. and Ireland, T. D. 2007. Brazil's national programme for adult and youth education. Singh, M. and Castro Mussot Meyer-Bisch, L. M. (eds), *Literacy, Knowledge and Development: South-South Policy Dialogue on Quality Education for Adults and Young People*. Hamburg, Germany/Mexico City, UNESCO Institute for Lifelong Learning/Mexican National Institute for Adult Education, pp. 61–90.

Heugh, K., Bogale, B., Benson, C. and Yohannes, M. A. G. 2006. *Final Report: Study on Medium of Instruction in Primary Schools in Ethiopia*. Addis Ababa, Ethiopia Ministry of Education.

Higgins, K. 2009. *Regional Inequality and Primary Education in Northern Uganda*. London, UK Overseas Development Institute. (Policy Brief 2, prepared for *World Development Report 2009*.)

Himaz, R. 2009. *The Impact of Parental Death on Schooling and Subjective Well-being: Evidence from Ethiopia using Longitudinal Data*. Oxford, UK, UK Department of International Development, Young Lives. (Working Paper, 44.)

Hoddinott, J. 2008. *Ethiopia's Productive Safety Net Programme (PSNP): 2008 Assessment Report – Executive Summary*. Washington, DC, World Bank/International Food Policy Research Institute.

Hoddinott, J., Gilligan, D. O. and Taffesse, A. S. 2009. *The Impact of Ethiopia's Productive Safety Net Program on Schooling and Child Labor*. Washington, DC, World Bank/International Food Policy Research Institute.

Hoeckel, K., Field, S. and Grubb, W. N. 2008*a*. *Learning for Jobs: OECD Reviews of Vocational Education and Training. Switzerland*. Paris, Organisation for Economic Co-operation and Development.

Hoeckel, K., Field, S., Justesen, T. R. and Kim, M. 2008*b*. *Learning for Jobs: OECD Reviews of Vocational Education and Training. Australia*. Paris, Organisation for Economic Co-operation and Development.

Hoff, K. and Pandey, P. 2004. *Belief Systems and Durable Inequalities: An Experimental Investigation of Indian Caste*. World Bank. (Policy Research Working Papers, 3351.)

Holla, A. and Kremer, M. 2009. *Pricing and Access: Lessons from Randomized Evaluations in Education and Health*. Washington, DC, Center for Global Development. (Working Paper.)

Hoogeveen, J. G. 2005. Measuring welfare for small but vulnerable groups. Poverty and disability in Uganda. *Journal of African Economies*, Vol. 14, No. 4, pp. 603–31.

Hossain, N., Eyben, R., Rashid, M., Fillaili, R., Moncrieffe, J., Nyonyinto Lubaale, G. and Mulumbi, M. 2009. *Accounts of Crisis: Poor People's Experiences of the Food, Fuel and Financial Crises in Five Countries – Report on a Pilot Study in Bangladesh, Indonesia, Jamaica, Kenya and Zambia*. Brighton, UK, UK Department for International Development.

Howard, R. 2009. Education reform, indigenous politics, and decolonisation in the Bolivia of Evo Morales. *International Journal of Educational Development*, Vol. In Press. (Corrected proof.)

Huisman, J. and Smits, J. 2009. Effects of household- and district-level factors on primary school enrollment in 30 developing countries. *World Development*, Vol. 37, No. 1, pp. 179–93.

ICF Macro. 2009. *MEASURE DHS online tools: STATcompiler*. Calverton, Md., ICF Macro. http://www.statcompiler.com (Accessed 20 August 2009.)

ILO. 2007. *Apprenticeship in the Informal Economy in Africa*. Geneva, Switzerland, International Labour Organization. (Employment Sector report. Workshop Report, Geneva, 3–4 May.)

——. 2008*a*. *Conclusions on Skills for Improved Productivity, Employment Growth and Development*. Geneva, Switzerland, International Labour Organization.

——. 2008*b*. *Global Employment Trends for Youth. October 2008*. Geneva, Switzerland, International Labour Organization.

——. 2009*a*. *The Financial and Economic Crisis: A Decent Work Response*. Geneva, Switzerland, ILO Governing Body, Committee on Employment and Social Policy. (GB.304/ESP/2.)

——. 2009*b*. *Global Employment Trends for Women, March 2009*. Geneva, International Labour Organization.

IMF. 2004. *Evaluation of the IMF's Role in Poverty Reduction Strategy Papers and the Poverty Reduction and Growth Facility*. Washington, DC, International Monetary Fund, Independent Evaluation Office.

——. 2008. *World Economic Outlook. April 2008. Housing and the Business Cycle*. Washington, DC, International Monetary Fund. (World Economic and Financial Surveys.)

——. 2009*a*. *IMF Announces Unprecedented Increase in Financial Support to Low-Income Countries*. Washington, DC, International Monetary Fund, Press Release No. 09/268, 29 July. http://www.imf.org/external/np/sec/pr/2009/pr09268.htm (Accessed 29 September 2009.)

——. 2009*b*. *Impact of the Global Financial Crisis on Sub-Saharan Africa*. Washington, DC, International Monetary Fund, African Department.

——. 2009*c*. *The Implications of the Global Financial Crisis for Low-Income Countries*. Washington, DC, International Monetary Fund.

——. 2009*d*. *The International Community's Response to the Economic and Financial Crisis and its Impact on Development: IMF Contribution to the United Nations Conference, New York, June 24-26, 2009*. Washington, DC, International Monetary Fund.

——. 2009*e*. *Regional Economic Outlook. April 2009. Sub-Saharan Africa*. Washington, DC, International Monetary Fund. (World Economic and Financial Surveys.)

——. 2009*f*. *World Economic Outlook Database*, International Monetary Fund. http://www.imf.org/external/ns/cs.aspx?id=28 (Accessed 29 September 2009.)

——. 2009*g*. *World Economic Outlook. April 2009. Crisis and Recovery*. Washington, DC, International Monetary Fund. (World Economic and Financial Surveys.)

India Ministry of Health and Family Welfare. 2006. *2005–2006 National Family Health Survey (NFHS-3)*. Mumbai, India, Ministry of Health and Family Welfare. (National fact sheet, provisional data.)

India Ministry of Human Resource Development. 2009. *Saakshar Bharat*. New Delhi, Ministry of Human Resource Development, Department of School Education & Literacy.

India Ministry of Human Resource Development and National University of Educational Planning and Administration. 2008. *Education for All Mid-Decade Assessment: Reaching the Unreached. India*. New Delhi, Ministry of Human Resource Development, Department of School Education & Literacy/NUEPA.

India Ministry of Law and Justice. 2009. *The Right of Children to Free and Compulsory Education Act, 2009*. New Delhi, Ministry of Law and Justice.

India Planning Commission. 2008. *The Eleventh Five Year Plan (2007–2012)*. New Delhi, Oxford University Press.

Indonesia Ministry of National Education. 2007. *EFA Mid Decade Assessment: Indonesia*. Jakarta, Ministry of National Education, EFA Secretariat.

Ingram, G. M. 2009. US assistance for basic education. Background paper for *EFA Global Monitoring Report 2010*.

Integrated Regional Information Networks. 2006. *YEMEN: Hear Our Voices: "I hate my classmates calling me a servant"*. UN Office for the Coordination of Humanitarian Affairs, IRIN. http://www.irinnews.org/Report.aspx?ReportId=62346 (Accessed 29 September 2009.)

——. 2007. *YEMEN: Rapid population growth threatening development*. UN Office for the Coordination of Humanitarian Affairs, IRIN. http://www.irinnews.org/Report.aspx?ReportId=76011 (Accessed 29 September 2009.)

___. 2009. *BURKINA FASO: Millions to Receive Birth Certificates*, UN Office for the Coordination of Humanitarian Affairs, IRIN. http://www.irinnews.org/Report.aspx?ReportId=842242009 (Accessed 29 September 2009.)

Internal Displacement Monitoring Centre. 2009. *Internal Displacement Global Overview of Trends and Developments in 2008*. Geneva, Switzerland, IDMC/Norwegian Refugee Council.

International Finance Facility for Immunisation. 2008. *Bringing Together Capital Market Investors and Children in the World's Poorest Countries. Both Benefit*. London, IFFIm.

Ireland, T. D. 2007. Partnerships for lifelong learning policies: a Brazilian experience. *Convergence*, Vol. 40, No. 3/4, p. 43.

___. 2008. The provision of basic non-formal basic education for youths and adults in Brazil: country profile. Duke, C. and Hinzen, H. (eds), *Knowing More, Doing Better: Challenges for CONFINTEA VI from Monitoring EFA in Non-Formal Youth and Adult Education*. Bonn, Germany, dvv International, pp. 62–72. (International Perspectives in Adult Education.)

Irish Aid. 2009. *Statement on Overseas Development Assistance by the Minister for Foreign Affairs, Micheál Martin, T.D., and the Minister of State for Overseas Development, Peter Power, T.D.* Dublin, Irish Aid.

Jaffrelot, C. 2003. *India's Silent Revolution: The Rise of the Low Castes in North Indian Politics*. Delhi, Permanent Black.

Jamison, D. T., Feachem, R. G., Makgoba, M. W., Bos, E. R., Baingana, F. K., Hofman, K. J. and Khama O. Rogo (eds). 2006. *Disease and Mortality in Sub-Saharan Africa*. Washington, DC, World Bank.

Jammeh, J. 2008. *Review of Results from Pilots in English: The Gambia*. Paper presented at the Early Grade Reading Assessment (EGRA) Second Workshop, Washington, DC, 12–14 March 2008.

Jané, E. 2008. Assessment of the sector-wide approach in the education sector in Nicaragua. Background paper for *EFA Global Monitoring Report 2010*.

Jayatissa, R. 2009. *Rapid Assessment of Nutritional Status Among Post conflict Displaced Children in Vavuniya*. Colombo, Medical Research Institute, Nutrition Department.

Jensen, R. 2000. Agricultural volatility and investments in children. *The American Economic Review*, Vol. 90, No. 2, pp. 399–404.

Jhingran, D. and Sankar, D. 2009. *Addressing Educational Disparity Using District Level Education Development Indices for Equitable Resource Allocations in India*. Washington, DC, World Bank, South Asia Region, Human Development Department. (WPS4955.)

Jimenez, E. Y., Kiso, N. and Ridao-Cano, C. 2007. Never Too Late to Learn? Investing in Educational Second Chances for Youth. *Journal of International Cooperation in Education*, Vol. 10, No. 1, pp. 89–100.

Johannesen, E. M. 2005. *Evaluation Report: the Complementary Rapid Education for Primary Schools (CREPS) and the Distance Education Programme (DEP) in Sierra Leone*. Oslo, Norwegian Refugee Council/EDUCARE.

Johanson, R. K. and Adams, A. A. 2004. *Skills Development in Sub-Saharan Africa*. Washington, DC, World Bank. (World Bank Regional and Sectoral Studies.)

Johnson, L. B. 1965. *Remarks on Project Head Start. May 18, 1965*. http://www.presidency.ucsb.edu/ws/index.php?pid=26973 (Accessed 29 September 2009.)

Jukes, M., Vagh, S. B. and Kim, Y. S. 2006. *Development of Assessments of Reading Ability and Classroom Behavior*. Washington, DC, World Bank.

Kabeer, N. 2005. Social Exclusion: Concepts, Findings and Implications for the MDGs. Background paper for *Reducing Poverty by Tackling Social Exclusion*, UK Department for International Development policy paper.

Kaberuka, D. 2009. Making Africa's voice heard. *The Banker*, 7 July.

Kahyarara, G. and Teal, F.. 2006. *To Train or to Educate? Evidence from Tanzania*. Oxford, UK, Global Poverty Research Group/Economic & Social Research Council. (GPRG-WPS-051.)

Kamel, M. 2006. *Situation Analysis of Youth Employment in Egypt*. Cairo, Egypt Ministry of International Cooperation, Centre for Project Evaluation and Macroeconomic Analysis.

Kane, E. 2004. *Girls' Education in Africa: What Do We Know about Strategies that Work?* Washington, DC, World Bank. (Africa Region Human Development Working Paper, 73.)

Karoly, L. A., Kilburn, M. R. and Cannon, J. 2005. *Early Childhood Interventions. Proven Results, Future Promise*. Santa Monica, Calif., RAND Corporation. (Monographs.)

Karsten, S. 2006. Policies for disadvantaged children under scrutiny: the Dutch policy compared with policies in France, England, Flanders and the USA. *Comparative Education*, Vol. 42, No. 2, pp. 261–82.

Kaya, N. 2009. *Forgotten or Assimilated? Minorities in the Education System of Turkey*. London, Minority Rights Group International.

Kefaya, N. A. 2007. *Yemen. Country Case Study*. Paris, UNESCO. Background paper for *EFA Global Monitoring Report 2008*.

Kelleher, F. (ed.). 2008. *Primary School Teacher Deployment. A Comparative Study.* London, Commonwealth Secretariat.

Kemple, J. J. and Willner, C. J. 2008. *Career Academies. Long-Term Impacts on Labor Market Outcomes, Educational Attainment, and Transitions to Adulthood.* New York, MDRC.

Kendall, L., O'Donnell, L., Golden, S., Ridley, K., Machin, S., Rutt, S., McNally, S., Schagen, I., Meghir, C., Stoney, S., Morris, M., West, A. and Noden, P. 2005. *Excellence in Cities; The National Evaluation of a Policy to Raise Standards in Urban Schools 2000–2003.* London, Department for Children, Schools and Families. (Research Report.)

Khan, M. S. H. and Chakraborty, N. 2008. *Rapid assessment of the BEHTRUWC project on completion of 1st learning cycle.* Dhaka, Associates for Community and Population Research.

Khan, N. C., Hop, L. T., Tuyen, L. D., Khoi, H. H., Son, T. H., Duong, P. H. and Vietnam Huynh Nam Phuong National Institute of Nutrition. 2008. A national Plan of Action to accelerate stunting reduction in Vietnam. *SCN News – Accelerating the Reduction of Maternal and Child Undernutrition*, No. 36, pp. 30–8.

Khandker, S. R., Pitt, M. M. and Fuwa, N. 2003. *Subsidy to Promote Girls' Secondary Education: The Female Stipend Program in Bangladesh.* Washington, DC, World Bank.

King, E. M. and van de Walle, D. 2007. Girls in Lao PDR: Ethnic affiliation, poverty, and location. Lewis, M. and Lockheed, M. (eds), *Exclusion, Gender and Education: Case Studies from the Developing World.* Washington, DC, Center for Global Development, pp. 31-70.

King, K. and Palmer, R. 2008. *Skills for Work, Growth and Poverty Reduction. Challenges and Opportunities in the Global Analysis and Monitoring of Skills.* London, British Council/UK National Commission for UNESCO. (Briefing note for UK Institute of Education Seminar, 31 October.)

King, K. and Rose, P. 2005. International development targets and education: towards a new international compact or a new conditionality? *Journal of International Development*, Vol. 17, No. 1, pp. 97–100.

Kinsella, K. and He, W. 2009. *An Ageing World: 2008.* Washington, DC, US Department of Health and Human Services, National Institutes of Health, National Institute on Aging/US Department of Commerce, Economics and Statistics Administration, US Census Bureau. (International Population Reports, P95/09-1.)

Kinst, J. 2009. *Introduction to the Special Report 10/2008: "EC Development Assistance to Health Services in sub-Saharan Africa".* Brussels, Europa, press releases RAPID. http://europa.eu/rapid/pressReleasesAction.do?reference=ECA/09/5&format=HTML&aged=0&language=EN&guiLanguage=en (Accessed 31 August 2009.)

Klasen, S. 2001. Social exclusion, children, and education: implications of a rights-based approach. *European Societies*, Vol. 3, No. 4, pp. 413–45.

Klein, H. 2003. *A concise history of Bolivia.* Cambridge University Press.

Kobiané, J.-F. and Bougma, M. 2009. *Burkina Faso. RGPH 2006. Rapport d'Analyse du Thème IV. Instruction, Alphabétisation et Scolarisation* [Analytical Report on Theme IV: Teaching, Literacy Training and Schooling]. Ouagadougou, Institut National de la Statistique et de la Démographie.

Kok, W. 2004. *Facing the Challenge. The Lisbon Strategy for Growth and Employment.* Luxembourg, European Commission.

Krätli, S. 2006. Cultural roots of poverty? Education and pastoral livelihood in Turkana and Karamoja. Dyer, C. (ed.), *The Education of Nomadic Peoples: Current Issues, Future Prospects.* New York, Berghahn Books, pp. 120–40.

Kristjansson, B., Robinson, V., Petticrew, M., MacDonald, B., Krasevec, J., Janzen, L., Greenhalgh, T., Wells, G. A., MacGowan, J., Farmer, A. P., Shea, B. J., Mayhew, A. and Tugwell, P. 2007. *School Feeding for Improving the Physical and Psychosocial Health of Disadvantaged Elementary School Children (Campbell Review).* Copenhagen, SFI Campbell. (Campbell Systematic Reviews.)

Kritzer, H. 2002. *Legal systems of the world: a political, social and cultural encyclopaedia.* Santa Barbara, Calif., ABC-CLIO.

Kuczera, M. S., Field, N. H. and Wolter, S. 2008. *Learning for Jobs: OECD Reviews of Vocational Education and Training. Sweden.* Paris, Organisation for Economic Co-operation and Development.

Kudo, I. and Bazan, J. 2009. *Measuring Beginner Reading Skills. An Empirical Evaluation of Alternative Instruments and their Potential Use for Policymaking and Accountability in Peru.* Washington, DC, World Bank. (Policy Research Working Papers, 4812.)

Ky, A. 2009. *Rapport d'Evaluation à Mi-Parcours de la Seconde Phase du Programme d'Invesstissement dans le Secteur de l'Education (PISE II) et de l'Initiative Fast Track* [Mid-Term Evaluation Report on the Second Phase of the Investment Programme for the Education Sector (PISE II) and the Fast Track Initiative].

Lall, S. 2001. *Competiveness, Technology and Skills.* Cheltenham, UK/Northampton, Mass., Edward Elgar Publishing Ltd.

Lang, R. and Murangira, A. 2009. *Disability Scoping Study: Final Report.* Kampala, DFID Uganda.

Larrañaga, O. 2009. *Inequality, Poverty and Social Policy: Recent Trends in Chile.* Paris, Organisation for Economic Co-operation and Development. (OECD Social, Employment and Migration Working Papers, 85.)

Larrea, C. and Montenegro Torres, F. 2006. Ecuador. Hall, G. and Patrinos, H. A. (eds), *Indigenous Peoples, Poverty and Human Development in Latin America.* New York, Palgrave Macmillan, pp. 67–105.

Lasida, J. and Rodriguez, E. 2006. *Entering the World of Work: Results from Six Entra 21 Youth Employment Projects.* Baltimore, Md, International Youth Foundation. (Learning Series, 2.)

Latin American and the Caribbean Demographic Center. 2009. *Bi-Literacy Regional Programs: Long-Term Objective.* Santiago, Economic Commission for Latin America and the Caribbean, Latin American and the Caribbean Demographic Center, Population Division. http://www.eclac.cl/cgi-bin/getprod.asp?xml=/bialfa/noticias /paginas/7/11507/P11507.xml&xsl=/bialfa/tpl/p18f.xsl&base=/bialfa/tpl-i/top-bottom.xsl (Accessed 10 February 2009.)

Lauglo, J. and Maclean, R. 2005. *Vocationalisation of Secondary Education Revisited.* (Technical and Vocational Education and Training: Issues, Concerns and Prospects, Vol. 1.) Dordrecht, The Netherlands, Springer.

Law, S. S. 2008. Vocational technical education and economic development – the Singapore Experience. *Towards a Better Future: Education and Training for Economic Development in Singapore Since 1965.* Washington, DC, World Bank.

Lawn, J. E., Zupan, J., Begkoyian, G. and Knippenberg, R. 2006. Newborn survival. Jamison, D. T., Breman, J. G., Measham, A. R., Alleyne, G., Claeson, M., Evans, D. B., Jha, P., Mills, A. and Musgrove, P. (eds), *Disease Control Priorities in Developing Countries.* New York, Oxford University Press, pp. 531–49.

Lawson, P. 2004. *The Top 10 Problems Faced by CCMs.* Paper presented at the Global Fund: How CCMs can be More Effective, Satellite Meeting, Bangkok AIDS 2004, 14 July.

Lee, C. J. 2008. Education in the Republic of Korea: approaches, achievements, and current challenges. Tan, J.-P. and Fredriksen, B. (eds), *An African Exploration of the East Asian Education Experience.* Washington, DC, World Bank, pp. 155–217.

Lehman, D. C., Buys, P., Atchina, G. F. and Laroche, L. 2007. *Shortening the Distance to Education for All in the African Sahel.* Washington, DC, World Bank.

Leitch Review of Skills. 2006. *Prosperity for All in the Global Economy – World Class Skills. Final Report.* Norwich, UK, UK Treasury.

Leseman, P. P. M. 2002. *Early Childhood Education and Care for Children from Low-income or Minority Backgrounds.* OECD Oslo Workshop, Paris, Organisation for Economic Co-operation and Development, 6–7June 2002.

Leseman, P. P. M. and van Tuijil, C. 2005. Cultural diversity in early literacy: findings in Dutch studies. Neuman, S. B. and Dickinson, D. K. (eds), *Handbook of Early Literacy Research*, Vol. 2. New York, The Guilford Press, pp. 211–28.

Leu, E. 2004. *The Patterns and Purposes of School-based and Cluster Teacher Professional Development Programs.* Washington, DC, USAID, EQUIP1. (Study of School-based Teacher Inservice Programs and Clustering of Schools, Working Paper 2.)

Levine, R., Lloyd, C., Greene, M. and Grown, C. 2008. *Girls Count: A Global Investment & Action Agenda.* Washington, DC, Center for Global Development.

Lewin, K. M. and Stuart, J. S. 2003. *Researching Teacher Education: New Perspectives on Practice, Performance and Policy. Multi-Site Teacher Education Research Project (MUSTER). Synthesis Report.* London, UK Department for International Development. (Researching the Issues, 49a.)

Lewis, I. 2009. Education for Disabled People in Ethiopia and Rwanda. Background paper for *EFA Global Monitoring Report 2010.*

Lewis, M. and Lockheed, M. (eds). 2007. *Exclusion, Gender and Schooling: Case Studies from the Developing World.* Washington, DC, Center for Global Development.

Liang, Z., Guo, L. and Duan, C. C. 2008. Migration and the well-being of children in China. *Yale China Health Journal*, No. 5, pp. 25–46.

Liberia Ministry of Education. 2007*a*. *Appraisal and Endorsement of the Liberian Primary Education Recovery Program, Prepared for Fast Track Initiative.* Monrovia, Ministry of Education.

——. 2007*b*. *Liberian Primary Education Recovery Program, Prepared for Fast Track Initiative.* Monrovia, Ministry of Education.

Light, D., Method, F., Rockman, C., Cressman, G. M. and Daly, J. 2008. *Evaluation of the Jordan Education Initiative. Synthesis Report. Overview and Recommendations to the Jordan Education Initiative.* Washington, DC, Education Development Center.

Liimatainen, M.-R. 2002. *Training and Skills Acquisition in the Informal Sector: A Literature Review.* Geneva, Switzerland, International Labour Organization. (Informal Economy Series. Working paper.)

Lim, S. S., Stein, D. B., Charrow, A. and Murray, C. J. L. 2008. Tracking progress towards universal childhood immunisation and the impact of global initiatives: a systematic analysis of three-dose diphtheria, tetanus, and pertussis immunisation coverage. *The Lancet*, Vol. 372, No. 9655, pp. 2031–46.

Lincove, J. A. 2009. Determinants of schooling for boys and girls in Nigeria under a policy of free primary education. *Economics of Education Review*, Vol. 28, No. 4, pp. 474–84.

Lindt, A. 2008. *Literacy for All: Making a Difference*. Paris, UNESCO International Institute for Educational Planning. (Fundamentals of Educational Planning, 89.)

Linehan, S. 2004. Language of instruction and the quality of basic education in Zambia. Background paper for *EFA Global Monitoring Report 2005*.

Little, A. W. 2006*a*. Education for all: multigrade realities and histories. Little, A. W. (ed.), *Education for All and Multigrade Teaching: Challenges and Opportunities*. Dordrecht, The Netherlands, Springer, pp. 1–46.

——. 2006*b*. Multigrade lessons for EFA: a synthesis. Little, A. W. (ed.), *Education for All and Multigrade Teaching: Challenges and Opportunities*. Dordrecht, The Netherlands, Springer, pp. 300–48.

Liu, Y., He, S. and Wu, F. 2008. Urban pauperization under China's social exclusion: a case study of Nanjing. *Journal of Urban Affairs*, Vol. 30, No. 1, pp. 21–36.

Lleras, C. and Rangel, C. 2009. Ability grouping practices in elementary school and African/Hispanic achievement. *American Journal of Education*, Vol. 115, No. 2, pp. 279–304.

Lloyd, C. B., Mete, C. and Grant, M. 2007. Rural girls in Pakistan: constraints of policy and culture. Lewis, M. A. and Lockheed, M. E. (eds), *Exclusion, Gender and Education: Case Studies from the Developing World*. Washington, DC, Center for Global Development, pp. 99–118.

Lob-Levyt, J. 2009. Vaccine coverage and the GAVI Alliance Immunization Services Support initiative. *The Lancet*, Vol. 373, No. 9685, pp. 260–3.

Lochner, L. 2004. Education, work and crime: a human capital approach. *International Economic Review*, Vol. 45, No. 3, pp. 811–43.

Lockheed, M. 2008. *Measuring progress with tests of learning: Pros and cons for 'cash on delivery aid' in education*. Washington, DC, Center for Global Development. (Working Paper, 147.)

Loeb, M. E. and Eide, A. H. 2004. *Living Conditions among People with Activity Limitations in Malawi. A National Representative Study*. Oslo, SINTEF Health Research.

López, L. E. 2009. Reaching the unreached: indigenous intercultural bilingual education in Latin America. Background paper for *EFA Global Monitoring Report 2010*.

Loudon, M. 2006. *A Study of Integrated Interventions for Children Made Vulnerable by HIV/AIDS in Haiti – A Case Study of La Maison l'Arc-en-Ciel*. Panama, Joint United Nations Programme on HIV/AIDS/UNICEF.

Loudon, M., Bhaskar, M., Bhutia, Y., Deshpande, A., Ganesh, V., Mohanraj, R., Prakasam, C. P., Royal, K. N. and Saoor, S. B. 2007. *Barriers to Service for Children with HIV-positive Parents in Five high HIV Prevalence States of India*. New Delhi, UNICEF India/India Ministry of Women and Child Development/National HIV/AIDS Control Organization.

Luciak, M. 2006. Minority schooling and intercultural education: a comparison of recent developments in the old and new EU member states. *Intercultural Education*, Vol. 17, No. 1, pp. 73–80.

Lunde, T., Moreno, V. G. and Ramirez, A. 2009. *Moving Out of Poverty – Understanding Growth and Freedom from the Bottom Up:Mexico Country Study*. Washington, DC, World Bank.

Lustig, N. 2009. *Coping with Rising Food Prices: Policy Dilemmas in the Developing World*. New Orleans, La., Tulane University, Department of Economics. (Working Papers, 0907.)

Luykx, A. and López, L. E. 2007. Schooling in Bolivia. Beech, J. and Gvirtz, S. (eds), *Going to School in Latin America*. Westport, Conn., Greenwood Press, pp. 35–54. (The Global School Room.)

Lynch, P. and McCall, S. 2007. The itinerant teacher's role in the educational inclusion of children with low vision in local schools in Africa. *The Educator*, Vol. 20, No. 1, pp. 49–53.

Ma, X. 2007. Gender differences in learning outcomes. Background paper for *EFA Global Monitoring Report 2008*.

Machel, G. 1996. *Impact of Armed Conflict on Children*. New York, UNICEF.

Machin, S., Telhaj, S., and Wilson, J. 2006. The mobility of English school children. *Fiscal Studies*, Vol. 27, No. 3, pp. 253–80.

Macours, K., Schady, N. and Vakis, R. 2008. *Cash Transfers, Behavioral Changes, and Cognitive Development in Early Childhood: Evidence from a Randomized Experiment*. Washington, DC, World Bank, Development Research Group. (Impact Evaluation Series, 25. Policy Research Working Papers, 4759.)

Maddox, B. 2008. What good is literacy? Insights and implications of the capabilities approach. *Journal of Human Development*, Vol. 9, No. 2, pp. 185–206.

Maikish, A. and Gershberg, A. 2008. Targeting education funding to the poor: universal primary education, education decentralization and local level outcomes in Ghana. Background paper for *EFA Global Monitoring Report 2009*.

Maksud, A. K. M. and Rasul, I. 2006. *The Nomadic Bede Community and their Mobile School Program*. Paper presented at What Works for the Poorest: Knowledge, Policies and Practices, Dhaka, Bangladesh, 3–5 December 2006.

Maluccio, J. A., Hoddinot, J. F., Behrman, J., Martorell, R., Quisumbing, A. R. and Stein, A. D. 2009. The impact of nutrition during early childhood on education among Guatemalan adults. *The Economic Journal*, Vol. 119, No. 537, pp. 734–63.

Mandela, N. 1994. *Long Walk to Freedom: the Autobiography of Nelson Mandela*. Boston, New York, Toronto, London, Little, Brown and Company.

Manning, R. 2006. Will 'emerging donors' change the face of international co-operation? *Development Policy Review*, Vol. 24, No. 4, pp. 371–85.

Manzanedo, C. and Vélaz de Medrano, C. 2009. Spain's aid to education. Background paper for *EFA Global Monitoring Report 2010*.

Marriott, A. and Gooding, K. 2007. *Social Assistance and Disability in Developing Countries*. Haywards Heath, UK, Sightsavers International.

Marten, R. and Witte, J. M. 2008. *Transforming Development? The Role of Philanthropic Foundations in International Development Cooperation*. Berlin, Global Public Policy institute (GPPi). (GPPi Research Series.)

Martin, M. and Kyrili, K. 2009. The impact of the financial crisis on fiscal space for education expenditure in Africa. Background paper for *EFA Global Monitoring Report 2010*.

Martin, M. O., Mullis, I. V. S., Foy, P., with Olson, J. F., Erberber, E., Preuschoff, C. and Galia, J. 2008. *TIMSS 2007 International Science Report: Findings from IEA's Trends in International Mathematics and Science Study at the Fourth and Eighth Grades*. Chestnut Hill, Mass., Boston College, Lynch School of Education, TIMSS & PIRLS International Study Center.

Masanja, H., de Savigny, D., Smithson, P., Schellenberg, J., John, T., Mbuya, C., Upunda, G., Boerma, T., Victora, C., Smith, T. and Mshinda, H. 2008. Child survival gains in Tanzania: analysis of data from demographic and health surveys. *The Lancet*, Vol. 371, No. 9620, pp. 1276–83.

May, H. 2008. Towards the right of New Zealand children for free early childhood education. *International Journal of Child Care and Education Policy*, Vol. 2, No. 1, pp. 77–91.

McClain-Nhlapo, C. 2007. *Including People with Disabilities in Actions to Reduce Poverty and Hunger*. Washington, DC, International Food Policy Research Institute. (2020 Focus Brief on the World's Poor and Hungry People.)

McColl, K. 2008. Europe told to deliver more aid for health. *The Lancet*, Vol. 371, No. 9630, pp. 2072–3.

McCord, A. and Vandemoortele, M. 2009. *The Global Financial Crisis: Poverty and Social Protection. Evidence from 10 Country Case Studies*. London, UK Overseas Development Institute. (ODI Briefing Paper, 51.)

McEwan, P. 2004. The indigenous test score gap in Bolivia and Chile. *Economic Development and Cultural Change*, Vol. 53, No. 1, pp. 435–52.

___. 2008. Evaluating multigrade school reform in Latin America. *Comparative Education*, Vol. 44, No. 4, pp. 465–83.

McEwan, P. J. and Trowbridge, M. 2007. The achievement of indigenous students in Guatemalan primary schools. *International Journal of Educational Development*, Vol. 27, No. 1, pp. 61–76.

McQuaide, S. 2009. Making education equitable in rural China through distance learning. *International Review of Research in Open and Distance Learning*, Vol. 10, No. 1.

Mehrotra, S. 2006. Well-being and caste in Uttar Pradesh: why UP is not like Tamil Nadu. *Economic and Political Weekly*, Vol. 41, No. 40, pp. 4261–71.

Mete, C. 2008. Introduction. Mete, C. (ed.), *Economic Implications of Chronic Illness and Disability in Eastern Europe and the Former Soviet Union*. Washington, DC, World Bank.

Mfum-Mensah, O. 2009. An exploratory study of the curriculum development process of a complementary education program for marginalized communities in Northern Ghana. *Curriculum Inquiry*, Vol. 39, No. 2, pp. 343–67.

Michaelowa, K. 2001. Primary education quality in francophone Sub-Saharan Africa: Determinants of learning achievement and efficiency considerations. *World Development*, Vol. 29, No. 10, pp. 1699–716.

Micronutrient Initiative, Flour Fortification Initiative, Gain, USAID, World Bank and UNICEF. 2009. *Investing in the Future: A United Call to Action on Vitamin and Mineral Deficiencies: Global Report 2009*. Ottawa, Micronutrient Initiative.

Miguel, E. and Kremer, M. 2004. Worms: identifying impacts on education and health in the presence of treatment externalities. *Econometrica*, Vol. 72, pp. 159–217

Mingat, A. and Ndem, F. 2008. *La dimension rurale des scolarisations dans les pays d'Afrique au Sud du Sahara: situation actuelle et defis pour le developpement de la couverture scolaire au niveau du premier cycle secondaire* [The rural dimension of schooling in sub-Saharan African countries: current situation and challenges for the expansion of lower secondary enrolment]. Dijon, Université de Bourgogne, IREDU-CNRS. (Working Paper.)

Misselhorn, M., Harttgen, K. and Klasen, S. 2009. Comparing marginalization across countries. Background paper for *EFA Global Monitoring Report 2010*.

Mitchell, T. 2009. China schools offer parents incentive to stay put. *The Financial Times*, 3 September.

Mitton, G. 2008. *Success in Early Reading: Pilot Project in Mali and Niger: Implementation Report*. Washington, DC/Woking, UK, USAID/Plan International. (Implementation report, GAD MLI0080 & NER064.)

Moisan, C. 2001. Les ZEP: bientôt vingt ans [Priority education zones (ZEPs): twenty years on]. *Education et formations*, No. 61, pp. 13–22.

Monk, C., Sandefur, J. and Teal, F. 2008. *Does Doing an Apprenticeship Pay Off? Evidence from Ghana*. Oxford, UK, University of Oxford, Department of Economics, Centre for the Study of African Economies.

Moss, T., Pettersson, G. and van de Walle, N. 2006. *An Aid-Institutions Paradox? A Review Essay on Aid Dependency and State Building in Sub-Saharan Africa*. Washington, DC, Center for Global Development. (Working Papers, 74.)

Moyo, D. 2009. *Dead Aid: Why Aid Is Not Working and How There Is Another Way for Africa*. London, Penguin Books Ltd.

Mpokosa, C. and Ndaruhutse, S. 2008. *Managing Teachers: The Centrality of Teacher Management to Quality Education. Lessons from Developing Countries*. London, London/Reading, UK, VSO International /CfBT Education Trust.

Mudege, N. N., Zulu, E. M. and Izugbara, C. 2008. How insecurity impacts on school attendance and school dropout among urban slum children in Nairobi. *International Journal of Conflict and Violence*, Vol. 2, No. 1, pp. 98–112.

Mulama, J. 2004. *Education – Kenya: 'Schooling for All' an Empty Slogan for Disabled Children*. http://ipsnews.net/news.asp?idnews=24246 (Accessed September 17 2009.)

Mulkeen, A. 2009. *Teachers in Anglophone Africa. Issues in Teacher Supply, Training and Management. Based on Case Studies in Eritrea, The Gambia, Lesotho, Liberia, Malawi, Uganda, Zambia and Zanzibar*. Washington, DC, World Bank., Africa Region, Human Development.

Mulkeen, A. and Chen, D. (eds). 2008. *Teachers for Rural Schools: Experiences in Lesotho, Malawi, Mozambique, Tanzania, and Uganda*. Washington, DC, World Bank. (Africa Human Development Series.)

Mullis, I., Martin, M. and Foy, P. 2008. *TIMSS 2007 International Mathematics Report: Findings from IEA's Trends in International Mathematics and Science Study at the Fourth and Eighth Grades*. Chestnut Hill, Mass., Boston College, Lynch School of Education, TIMSS & PIRLS International Study Center.

Mundy, K. 2009. Canadian aid for education in conflict-affected states. Background paper for *EFA Global Monitoring Report 2010*.

Munshi, K. and Rosenzweig, M. 2003. *Traditional Institutions Meet the Modern World: Caste, Gender and Schooling Choice in a Globalizing Economy*. Durham, NC, Duke University, Bureau for Research in Economic Analysis of Development. (BREAD Working Paper.)

Nabyonga, J., Desmet, M., Karamagi, H., Kadama, P. Y., Omaswa, F. G. and Walker, O. 2005. Abolition of cost-sharing is pro-poor: evidence from Uganda. *Health Policy and Planning*, Vol. 20, No. 2, pp. 100–8.

Nath, S. R. 2009. Educational marginalization in Bangladesh. Background paper for *EFA Global Monitoring Report 2010*. February.

National Agency to Fight Illiteracy. 2007. *Illiteracy: The Statistics Analysis by the National Agency to Fight Illiteracy of the IVQ Survey Conducted in 2004–2005 by INSEE*. Lyon, France, ANLCI.

National Center for Education Statistics. 2009. *Participation in Education. Preprimary Education*. Washington, DC, US Department of Education, Institute of Education Sciences. http://nces.ed.gov/programs/coe/2009/section1/indicator03.asp (Accessed 31 August 2009.)

National Education Association. 2009. *American Recovery and Reinvestment Act: Frequently Asked Questions. Distribution of Education Funds under American Recovery and Reinvestment Act*. Washington, DC., National Education Association. http://www.nea.org/home/32040.htm (Accessed 2 October 2009.)

National Literacy Trust. 2009. *Adult Literacy Levels*. London, National Literacy Trust. http://www.literacytrust.org.uk/database/stats/adultstats.html#England (Accessed 29 July 2009.)

National Sample Survey Organisation. 2003. *Disabled Persons in India – NSS 58th round*. New Delhi, India Ministry of Statistics and Programme Implementation, National Sample Survey Organisation. (Report No. 485 [58/26/1].)

NCEDR and UNESCO. 2008. *National Report on Mid-term Assessment of Education for All in China*, Beijing, National Center for Education Development Research, Ministry of Education/UNESCO Chinese National Commission.

Nepal Ministry of Education and Sports and UNESCO Kathmandu. 2007. *Education for All Mid-Decade Assessment: National Report.* Kathmandu, Ministry of Education and Sports/UNESCO Office in Kathmandu.

New Zealand Ministry of Education. 2008*a*. *Early Childhood Education Enrolments (Licensed Services): Time-series.* Wellington, New Zealand Ministry of Education. www.educationcounts.govt.nz/__data/assets/excel_doc/0008/34865/ECE_Licensed_Enrolments_2008_tables.xls (Accessed 29 September 2009.)

——. 2008*b*. *MÇori Medium Education July 2008 and MÇori Medium Time-Series Tables.* Wellington, New Zealand Ministry of Education. www.educationcounts.govt.nz/__data/assets/excel_doc/0008/34865/ECE_Licensed_Enrolments_2008_tables.xls (Accessed 29 September 2009.)

——. 2009. *NgÇ Haeata MÇtauranga – The Annual Report on MÇori Education, 2007/08.* Wellington, New Zealand Ministry of Education, Education Information and Analysis Group/Group MÇori.

Nonoyama-Tarumi, Y., Loaizo, E. and Engle, P. 2008. Inequalities in attendance in organised early learning programmes in developing societies: findings from household surveys. *Compare: A Journal of Comparative and International Education*, Vol. 39, No. 3, pp. 385–409.

Nusche, D. 2009. *What Works in Migrant Education? A Review of Evidence and Policy Options.* Paris, Organisation for Economic Co-operation and Development. (OECD Education Working Papers, 22.)

O'Keefe, P. 2007. *People with Disabilities in India: From Commitments to Outcomes.* Washington, DC, World Bank, Human Development Unit, South Asia Region. (Working paper, 41585)

O'Malley, B. 2009. The threat of political and military attacks on schools, students and education staff. Background paper for *EFA Global Monitoring Report 2010.*

Obama, B. 2008. Speech at Plenary Session on Integrated Solutions: Water, Food, and Energy, 2008 Clinton Global Initiative Annual Meeting, New York, 25 September.

Obura, A. and Bird, L. 2009. Education marginalisation in post-conflict settings: a comparison of government and donor responses in Burundi and Rwanda. Background paper for *EFA Global Monitoring Report 2010.*

Ochse, K. 2008. *Fit for Life? Non-formal Post-primary Initiatives in Yemen, Malawi and Namibia.* Eschborn, Germany, Deutsche Gesellschaft für Technische Zusammenarbeit (GTZ).

OECD-DAC. 2007. *Ensuring Fragile States are Not Left Behind.* Paris, Organisation for Economic Co-operation and Development, Development Co-operation Directorate, Development Assistance Committee.

——. 2008*a*. *Aid Effectiveness. A Progress Report on Implementing the Paris Declaration.* Prepared for Third High Level Forum on Aid Effectiveness, Accra, September 2–4. Paris, Organisation for Economic Co-operation and Development, Development Co-operation Directorate, Development Assistance Committee, Working Party on Aid Effectiveness.

——. 2008*b*. *Aid Targets Slipping out of Reach? Final Official Development Assistance (ODA) Data for 2007.* Paris, Organisation for Economic Co-operation and Development, Development Co-operation Directorate, Development Assistance Committee.

——. 2008*c*. *Development Co-operation of the Republic of Korea. DAC Special Review.* Paris, Organisation for Economic Co-operation and Development, Development Co-operation Directorate, Development Assistance Committee.

——. 2009*a*. *2009 DAC Report on Aid Predictability. Survey on Donors' Forward Spending Plans 2009-2011.* Paris, Organisation for Economic Co-operation and Development, Development Co-operation Directorate, Development Assistance Committee.

——. 2009*b*. *Development Aid at Its Highest Level Ever in 2008.* Paris, Organisation for Economic Co-operation and Development, Development Co-operation Directorate, Development Assistance Committee. (Press release.)

——. 2009*c*. *Development Co-operation Report 2009.* Paris, Organisation for Economic Co-operation and Development, Development Co-operation Directorate, Development Assistance Committee. (OECD Journal on Development.)

——. 2009*d*. *International Development Statistics: Online Databases on Aid and Other Resource Flows.* Paris, Organisation for Economic Co-operation and Development, Development Co-operation Directorate, Development Assistance Committee. www.oecd.org/dac/stats/idsonline (Accessed 13 July.)

——. 2009*e*. *Resource Flows to Fragile and Conflict Affected States.* Paris, Organisation for Economic Co-operation and Development, Development Co-operation Directorate, Development Assistance Committee.

OECD. 2004. *Innovation in the Knowledge Economy. Implications for Education and Learning.* Paris, Organisation for Economic Co-operation and Development. (Knowledge Management.)

——. 2006*a*. *Education at a Glance 2006. OECD Indicators.* Paris, Organisation for Economic Co-operation and Development.

——. 2006*b*. *Where Immigrant Children Succeed. A Comparative Review of Performance and Engagement in PISA 2003.* Paris, Organisation for Economic Co-operation and Development, Programme for International Student Assessment.

——. 2006c. *Whole of Government Approaches to Fragile States.* Paris, Organisation for Economic Co-operation and Development.

——. 2007a. *Education at a Glance 2007. OECD Indicators.* Paris, Organisation for Economic Co-operation and Development.

——. 2007b. *PISA 2006: Science Competencies for Tomorrow's World.* Paris, Organisation for Economic Co-operation and Development, Programme for International Student Assessment.

——. 2008a. *2008 Survey on Monitoring the Paris Declaration: Making Aid more Effective by 2010.* Paris, Organisation for Economic Co-operation and Development.

——. 2008b. *Education at a Glance 2008. OECD Indicators.* Paris, Organisation for Economic Co-operation and Development.

——. 2008c. *Jobs for Youth/Des Emplois pour les Jeunes. United Kingdom.* Paris, Organisation for Economic Co-operation and Development.

——. 2009a. *Better Aid. Managing Development Resources. The Use of Country Systems in Public Financial Management.* Paris, Organisation for Economic Co-operation and Development.

——. 2009b. *Jobs for Youth/Des Emplois pour les Jeunes. France.* Paris, Organisation for Economic Co-operation and Development.

——. 2009c. *Jobs for Youth/Des Emplois pour les Jeunes. Japan.* Paris, Organisation for Economic Co-operation and Development.

——. 2009d. *Massive rise in unemployment needs fast, decisive response, says OECD's Gurria.* Paris, Organisation for Economic Co-operation and Development. http://www.oecd.org/document/37/0,3343,en_2649_201185_42459813_1_1_1_1,00.html (Accessed 29 September 2009.)

——. 2009e. *OECD Reviews of Labour Market and Social Policies: Chile 2009.* Paris, Organisation for Economic Co-operation and Development.

——. 2009f. *OECD.Stat, Labour Force Statistics by Sex and Age – Indicators.* Paris, Organisation for Economic Co-operation and Development. http://www.SourceOECD.org/database/OECDStat (Accessed 28 September 2009.)

——. 2009g. *Society at a Glance 2009. OECD Social Indicators.* Paris, Organisation for Economic Co-operation and Development.

Office for the Coordination of Humanitarian Affairs. 2009. *Reliefweb. Financial Tracking Service (FTS).* Geneva, Switzerland, OCHA. http://ocha.unog.ch/fts/pageloader.aspx (Accessed 29 September 2009.)

Oketch, M., Mutisya, M., Ngware, M. and Ezeh, A. C. 2008. *Why are there Proportionately more Poor Pupils Enrolled in Non-State Schools in Urban Kenya in Spite of FPE Policy?* Nairobi, African Population and Health Research Center. (APHRC Working Papers, 40.)

ONE. 2009. *The Data Report 2009.* London, ONE.

Open Society Institute. 2007. *Equal Access to Quality Education for Roma.* Vols. 1 and 2. Budapest, Open Society Institute.

Orfield, G. and Gándara, P. 2009. *CRP Statement on the Flores Decision of the U.S. Supreme Court.* Los Angeles, The Civil Rights Project/Proyecto Derechos Civiles, UCLA. http://www.civilrightsproject.ucla.edu/policy/crp_statement_flores_decision_2009.pdf (Accessed 29 September 2009.)

Orozco, M. 2009. *Understanding the Continuing Effect of the Economic Crisis on Remittances to Latin America and the Caribbean.* Washington, DC, Inter-American Development Bank.

Otaran, N., Sayin, A., Güven, F., Gürkaynak, I. and Atakul, S. 2003. *A Gender Review in Education, Turkey 2003.* Ankara, UNICEF Turkey.

Otieno, W. and K'Oliech, D. 2007. *Factors Affecting Transition to Secondary Education in Africa.* Nairobi, African Population and Health Research Centre (APHRC). (Policy Brief.)

Oxenham, J. 2008. *Effective Literacy Programmes: Options for Policy Makers.* Paris, UNESCO International Institute for Educational Planning. (Fundamentals of Educational Planning, 91.)

Oxford Policy Management and IDL Group. 2008. *Evaluation of the Implementation of the Paris Declaration: Applicability of the Paris Declaration in Fragile and Conflict-Affected Situations. Thematic Study.* Oxford/Bristol, UK, OPM/IDL Group.

Pakistan Ministry of Education. 2003. *National Plan of Action on Education for All (2001-2015).* Islamabad, Ministry of Education.

——. 2008. *Education for All: Mid Decade Assessment. Country Report: Pakistan.* Islamabad, Ministry of Education.

Palmer, R. 2007. Skills for work? From skills development to decent livelihoods in Ghana's rural informal economy. *International Journal of Educational Development,* Vol. 27, No. 4, pp. 397–420.

Pan, E. 2004. *Foreign Aid: Millennium Challenge Account*. New York, Council on Foreign Relations. http://www.cfr.org/publication/7748/#11 (Accessed August 20 2009.)

Panetta, F., Faeh, T., Grande, G., Ho, C., King, M., Levy, A., Signoretti, F. M., Taboga, M. and Zaghini, A. 2009. *An Assessment of Financial Sector Rescue Programmes*. Basel, Switzerland, Bank for International Settlements. (BIS Papers, 48.)

Paxson, C. and Schady, N. 2005*a*. Child health and economic crisis in Peru. *World Bank Economic Review*, Vol. 19, No. 2, pp. 203–23.

——. 2005*b*. *Cognitive Development Among Young Children in Ecuador: The Roles of Wealth, Health and Parenting*. Washington, DC, World Bank. (World Bank Policy Research Working Papers, 3605.)

Payson Center for International Development. 2008. *Second Annual Report. Oversight of Public and Private Initiatives to Eliminate the Worst Forms of Child Labor in the Cocoa Sector in Côte d'Ivoire and Ghana*. New Orleans, La., Tulane University Law School, Payson Center for International Development.

Pearson, M. 2004. *The Case for Abolition of User Fees for Primary Health Services*. London, UK Department for International Development, Health Resource Centre. (Issues Papers.)

PEPFAR. 2009. *1. Overview: the Role of America's Partnerships in the Worldwide Fight against HIV/AIDS*. Washington, DC, the US President's Emergency Plan for AIDS Relief (PEPFAR), US State Department, Office of US Global AIDS Coordinator and the Bureau of Public Affairs. http://www.pepfar.gov/press/fifth_annual_report/113728.htm (Accessed August 2009.)

Peters, S. 2009. Review of marginalisation of people with disabilities in Lebanon, Syria and Jordan. Background paper for *EFA Global Monitoring Report 2010*.

Philippines National Statistical Coordination Board. 2006. *Philippine Poverty Statistics: 2006 Poverty Statistics. Table 1. Annual Per Capita Poverty Thresholds, Poverty Incidence and Magnitude of Poor Families: 2000, 2003 and 2006*. Makati City, Philippines. http://www.nscb.gov.ph/poverty/2006_05mar08/table_1.asp (Accessed October 7 2009.)

Plank, D. 2007. *School Fees and Education for All: Is Abolition the Answer?* Washington, DC, USAID. (EQUIP2 Working Paper.)

Pôle de Dakar. 2002. *Document Statistique MINEDAF VIII*. Dar-es-Salaam, UNESCO-Regional Office for Education in Africa/ World Bank/ISU.

——. 2004. *Education and Sub-regional Approaches in Africa. Basic Education Systems and Policies*. Dakar, UNICEF/UNESCO-Regional Office for Education in Africa/France Ministry of Foreign Affairs/World Bank.

——. 2005. *Dakar + 5. Paving the Way for Action. Education for All in Africa*. Dakar, UNESCO-Regional Office for Education in Africa/France Ministry of Foreign Affairs/World Bank/UNICEF.

——. 2007. *Dakar + 7. EFA -Top Priority for Integrated Sector-wide Policies*. Dakar, UNESCO-Regional Office for Education in Africa/France Ministry of Foreign Affairs/World Bank/UNICEF.

Pôle de Dakar. 2009. *Universal Primary Education in Africa: The Teacher Challenge* Dakar, UNESCO Regional Office for Education in Africa (BREDA), Education Sector Analysis.

Porta Pallais, E. and Laguna, J. R. 2007. *Equidad de la Educación en Guatemala* [Equity in Education in Guatemala]. Ciudad de Guatemala, USAID Guatemala/Academy for Educational Development. (Education Studies Series, vol. 4.) (In Spanish.)

Povey, E. R. 2005. Women and work in Iran (part 1.). *State of Nature*, Vol. 1, Autumn. http://www.stateofnature.org/womenAndWork.html (Accessed 29 September 2009.)

Pratham Resource Centre. 2008. *Annual Status of Education Report (2008)*. Mumbai, India, Pratham Resource Centre.

Pridmore, P. 2008. *Access to Conventional Schooling for Children and Young People Affected by HIV and AIDS in Sub-Saharan Africa: A Cross-national Review of Recent Research Evidence*. London, University of London, Institute of Education, Department of Education and International Development. (SOFIE Opening Up Access Series, 1.)

Qiao, Y. 2007. A system of quality education for adults and youth in China. Singh, M. and Castro Mussot Meyer-Bisch, L. M. (eds), *Literacy, Knowledge and Development: South-South Policy Dialogue on Quality Education for Adults and Young People*. Hamburg, Germany/Mexico City, UNESCO Institute for Lifelong Learning/Mexican National Institute for Adult Education, pp. 197–206.

Quintini, G., Martin, J. P. and Martin, S. 2007. *The Changing Nature of the School to-Work Transition Process in OECD Countries*. Bonn, Germany, Institute for the Study of Labor (IZA). (IZA Discussion Papers, 2582.)

Radelet, S., Clemens, M. and Bhavnani, R. 2005. Aid and growth. *Finance and Development*, Vol. 42, No. 3, pp 16–20.

Radelet, S. and Siddiqi, B. 2007. Global Fund grant programmes: an analysis of evaluation scores. *The Lancet*, Vol. 369, No. 9575, pp. 1807–13.

Raihan, S. 2009. *Impact of Food Price Rise on School Enrolment and Dropout in the Poor and Vulnerable Households in Selected Areas of Bangladesh.* Dhaka, UK Department for International Development. (Report for DFID Bangladesh.)

Ratha, D., Mohapatra, S. and Silwal, A. 2009. *Outlook for Remittance Flows 2009-2011: Remittances Expected to Fall by 7-10 Percent in 2009.* Washington, DC, World Bank, Development Prospects Group, Migration and Remittances Team. (Migration and Development Brief, 10.)

Ravallion, M. 2008. *Bailing out the World's Poorest.* Washington, DC, World Bank. (Policy Research Working Papers, 4763.)

Rawle, G. 2009. *Mid-Term Evaluation of the EFA Fast Track Initiative. Finance and Public Financial Management.* Oxford, UK, Mokoro Ltd/Cambridge Education/Oxford Policy Management. (Draft, Working Paper 2.)

Read, T., Bontoux, V., Buchan, A., Foster, D. and Bapuji, T. 2008. *Secondary Textbook and School Library Provision in Sub-Saharan Africa.* Washington, DC, World Bank. (Africa Human Development Series; Working Papers, 126.)

Reading and Writing Foundation. 2009. *Scope of the Problem.* The Hague, The Netherlands, Stichting Lezen & Schrijven. http://www.lezenenschrijven.nl/en/illiteracy/scope-of-problem/ (Accessed 10 August 2009.)

Research Centre for Educational Innovation and Development. 2003. *Effectiveness of Incentive/Scholarship Programmes for Girls and Disadvantaged Children.* Kathmandu, Tribhuvan University, CERID.

Richmond, M., Robinson, C. and Sachs-Israel, M. 2008. *The Global Literacy Challenge: A Profile of Youth and Adult Literacy at the Mid-Point of the United Nations Literacy Decade 2003–2012.* Paris, UNESCO, Education Sector, Division for the Coordination of United Nations Priorities in Education.

Riddell, A. 2001. *A Review of 13 Evaluations of Reflect.* London, ActionAid UK. (Cirac Paper One.)

___. 2009. *Mid-Term Evaluation of the EFA Fast Track Initiative. Preliminary Paper on Capacity Development.* Cambridge/Oxford, UK, Cambridge Education/Mokoro Ltd/Oxford Policy Management. (Working Paper 4.)

Robinson, C. 2009. *The United Nations Literacy Decade 2003-2012.* Paris, UNESCO.

Roma Education Fund. 2007. *Advancing Education of Roma in Hungary: Country Assessment and the Roma Education Fund's Strategic Directions.* Budapest, Roma Education Fund.

Roodman, D. 2008. *History says financial crisis will suppress aid.* Washington, DC, Center for Global Development. http://blogs.cgdev.org/globaldevelopment/2008/10/history-says-financial-crisis.php (Accessed 31 October 2008.)

Rose, P. 2003. *Out-of-school children in Ethiopia.* Brighton, UK, University of Sussex, Centre for International Education. (Report for DFID Ethiopia Input to the Joint Review Mission of the Education Sector Development Programme II.)

___. 2005. Africa on the Education for All 'Fast Track' to what? Beveridge, M., King, K., Palmer, R. and Ruth Wedgewood (eds), *Reintegrating Education, Skills and Work in Africa: Towards Informal or Knowledge Economies? Towards Autonomy or Dependency in Development?* Edinburgh, UK, Centre for African Studies.

Roy, R., Heuty, A. and Letouzé, E. 2007. *Fiscal Space for What? Analytical Issues from a Human Development Perspective.* Group of Twenty Workshop on Fiscal Policy, Istanbul, UNDP, 30 June–2 July.

RTI International. 2008. *Early Grade Reading Assessment Toolkit.* Washington, DC, Research Triangle Institute International.

Ruel, M. T. 2008. Addressing the underlying determinants of undernutrition: examples of successful integration of nutrition in poverty-reduction and agriculture strategies. *SCN News*, No. 36, pp. 17–21.

Rufa'i, R. A. 2006. The education of the Hausa girl-child in Northern Nigeria. Mutua, K. and Sunal, C. S. (eds), *Research on Education in Africa, the Caribbean, and the Middle East: Crosscurrents and Crosscutting Themes.* Greenwich, Conn., Information Age Publishing, pp. 85–108.

Ruto, S. J., Ongwenyi, Z. N. and Mugo, J. K. 2009. Educational marginalisation in Northern Kenya. Background paper for *EFA Global Monitoring Report 2010.*

Ryan, A., Jennings, J. and White, J. 2007. *BRAC Education Programme. BEP 2004-2009. Mid Term Review Report.* Oslo, Norwegian Agency for Development Cooperation. (NORAD Collected Reviews, 20/2007.)

Ryan, P. 2001. The school-to-work transition: a cross-national perspective. *Journal of Economic Literature*, Vol. 39, No. 1, pp. 34–92.

Ryman, T. K., Dietz, V. and Cairns, K. L. 2008. Too little but not too late: results of a literature review to improve routine immunization programs in developing countries. *BMC Health Services Research*, Vol. 8, No. 134.

Salehi-Isfahani, D. and Dhillon, N. 2008. *Stalled Youth Transitions in the Middle East: A Framework for Policy Reform.* Washington, DC/Dubai, United Arab Emirates, Wolfensohn Center for Development, Brookings Institution/Dubai School of Government. (Middle East Youth Initiative Working Papers, 8.)

Salehi-Isfahani, D. and Egel, D. 2007. *Youth Exclusion in Iran: the State of Education, Employment and Family Formation.* Washington, DC/Dubai, United Arab Emirates, Wolfensohn Center for Development, Brookings Institution/Dubai School of Government. (Middle East Youth Initiative Working Papers, e07-2.)

Sambe, M. and Sprenger-Charolles, L. 2008. *Review of Results from Pilots in French: Senegal.* Paper presented at the Early Grade Reading Assessment (EGRA) Second Workshop, Washington, DC, 12–14 March.

Sanchez, A. 2009. Birth weight, nutrition and the acquisition of cognitive skills: evidence from four developing countries. Initial findings. Background paper for *EFA Global Monitoring Report 2010.*

Sánchez, M. A., Orazem, P. F. and Gunnarson, V. 2009. The Impact of Child Labor Intensity on Mathematics and Language Skills in Latin America. Orazem, P. F., Sedlacek, G. and Tzannatos, Z. (eds), *Child Labor and Education in Latin America: An Economic Perspective.* New York, Palgrave Macmilllan, pp. 117–30.

Sapir, A. 2005. *Globalisation and the Reform of European Social Models.* Brussels, Bruegel. (Bruegel Policy Briefs, 2005/01.)

Save the Children. 2009*a*. *Last in Line, Last in School 2009. Donor Trends in Meeting Education Needs in Countries Affected by Conflict and Emergencies.* London, Save the Children.

——. 2009*b*. Trends in donor policies towards conflict-affected countries. Background paper for *EFA Global Monitoring Report 2010.*

Save the Children UK. 2006. *Children and HIV Prevention, Care and Support in the Tsunami-affected Thailand.* London, Save the Children UK.

Sayed, Y., Subrahmanian, R., Soudien, C. and Carrim, N., with Balgopalan, S., Nekhwevha, F. and Samuel, M. 2007. *Education Exclusion and Inclusion: Policy and Implementation in South Africa and India.* London, UK Department for International Development. (Researching the Issues, 72.)

Sayeh, A. 2009. *Supporting an upswing in Africa through good economic policies.* Washington, DC, International Monetary Fund. http://blog-imfdirect.imf.org/2009/09/09/africa-good-economic-policies/ (Accessed 29 September 2009.)

Scanteam. 2007. *Review of Post-Crisis Multi-Donor Trust Funds. Final Report.* Oslo, Scanteam.

Scheerens, J. 2004. Review of school and instructional effectiveness research. Background paper for *EFA Global Monitoring Report 2005.*

Schnepf, S. V. 2004. *How Different Are Immigrants? A Cross-Country and Cross-Survey Analysis of Educational Achievement.* Bonn, Germany/Southampton, UK, University of Southampton, Southampton Statistical Sciences Research Institute (S3RI)/Institute for the Study of Labor (IZA). (IZA Discussion Papers.)

Schochet, P. Z., McConnell, S. and Burghardt, J. 2003. *National Job Corps Study: Findings Using Administrative Earnings Records Data. Final Report.* Princeton, NJ/Washington, DC, Mathematica Policy Research, Inc./ US Department of Labor. (8140-840.)

Schumacher, R. and Hoffmann, E. 2008. *Family Child Care Ratios and Group Sizes: Charting Progress for Babies in Child Care Research-Based Rationale.* Washington, DC, Center for Law and Social Policy.

Schutz, G., Ursprung, H. W. and Wößmann, L. 2008. Education policy and equality of opportunity. *Kyklos,* Vol. 61, No. 2, pp. 279–308.

Schweinhart, L. J., Montie, J., Xiang, Z., Barnett, W. S., Belfield, C. R. and Nores, M. 2005. *Lifetime Effects: The High/Scope Perry Preschool Study through Age 40.* Ypsilanti, Mich., High/Scope Press.

Sen, A. 2009. *The Idea of Justice.* Cambridge, Mass., Belknap Press of Harvard University Press.

SENAI. 2009. *Portal SENAI.* Brasilia, Serviço Nacional de Aprendizagem Industrial [Brazil National Industrial Training Service]. http://www.senai.br/br/home/index.aspx (Accessed 29 September 2009.)

Shapiro, J. 2006. Guatemala. Hall, G. and Patrinos, H. A. (eds), *Indigenous Peoples, Poverty and Human Development in Latin America.* New York, Palgrave Macmillan, pp. 106–49.

Sharp, K., Brown, T. and Teshome, A. 2006. *Targeting Ethiopia's Productive Safety Net Programme (PSNP).* London, UK Overseas Development Institute/IDL Group Ltd./A-Z Capacity Building Consult.

Shulman, R. 2009. Harlem Program Singled Out as Model Obama Administration to Replicate Plan in Other Cities to Boost Poor Children. *Washington Post,* 2 August.

Sichra Regalsky, I. n.d. *Bolivia. Bilingual Intercultural Education in Bolivia: the Education Reform since 1994.* Cochabamba, Bolivia, Training Program in Bilingual Intercultural Education (PROEIB Andes).

Sidibe, M., Ramiah, I. and Buse, K. 2006. The Global Fund at five: what next for universal access for HIV/AIDS, TB and malaria? *Journal of the Royal Society of Medicine,* Vol. 99, No. 10, pp. 497–500.

Simpson, E. and Tomlinson, B. 2006. *Canada: Is Anyone Listening,* The Reality of Aid/Canadian Council for International Cooperation.

Singal, N. 2009. Education of children with disabilities in India. Background paper for *EFA Global Monitoring Report 2010.*

Singh, A. 2008. *Do School Meals Work? Treatment Evaluation of the Midday Meal Scheme in India.* Oxford, UK, Young Lives. (Young Lives Student Paper, November.)

Slater, R., Ashley, S., Tefera, M., Buta, M. and Esubalew, D. 2006. *PSNP Policy, Programme and Institutional Linkages – Final Report*, UK Overseas Development Institute/IDL Group Ltd./Indak International.

Smits, J. and Gündüz-Hoflgör, A. 2003. Linguistic capital: language as a socio-economic resource among Kurdish and Arabic women in Turkey. *Ethnic and Racial Studies,* Vol. 26, No. 5, pp. 829–53.

Smits, J., Huisman, J. and Kruijff, K. 2008. Home language and education in the developing world. Background paper for *EFA Global Monitoring Report 2009*.

South Africa Department of Education. 2005. *Conceptual and Operational Guidelines for District Based Support Teams*. Pretoria, Department of Education.

Sperling, G. B. 2008. *A Global Education Fund. Toward a True Global Compact on Universal Education*. New York, Center for Universal Education/Council on Foreign Relations. (Working paper.)

Sportcal. 2009. *The Sports Market Insight: 2010 Fifa World Cup in South Africa*. London, Sportscal Global Communications Ltd.

Sridhar, D. 2009. Global Health: Who Can Lead? *The World Today,* Vol. 65, No. 2, pp. 25–26.

Sridhar, D. and Batniji, R. 2008. Misfinancing global health: a case for transparency in disbursements and decision making. *The Lancet,* Vol. 372, No. 9644, pp. 1185–91.

Sridhar, D. and Tamashiro, T. 2009. Vertical funds in health: lessons for education from the Global Fund and GAVI. Background paper for *EFA Global Monitoring Report 2010*.

Sternberg, S. 2008. Study: Nations inflate vaccine numbers to get more aid. *USA Today*, 11 December.

Stirling, M., Rees, H., Kasedde, S. and Hankins, C. 2008. Addressing the vulnerability of young women and girls to stop the HIV epidemic in southern Africa. *AIDS,* Vol. 22, Suppl. 4, pp. S1–3.

Stockholm Challenge. 2008. *Bi-Literacy Project in Productive, Environmental, Gender and Community Health Issues*. Kista, Sweden, Stockholm Challenge. http://www.stockholmchallenge.org/project/data/bi-literacy-project-productive-environmental-gender-and-communitary-health-issues (Accessed 10 February 2009.)

Stofile, S. Y. 2008. Factors affecting implementation of inclusive education policy: a case study in one province in South Africa. PhD dissertation, University of the Western Cape, South Africa.

Sulaiman, M. 2009. Assessing impact of asset transfer on children's education: a case of BRAC's ultra poor programme in Bangladesh. Background paper for *EFA Global Monitoring Report 2010*.

Sweden Ministry of Finance. 2009. *Regeringens Proposition 2008/09:100. 2009 Års Ekonomiska Vårproposition* [Government Bill 2008/09:100. 2009 Economic Bill]. Stockholm, Ministry of Finance.

Sylva, K., Stein, A., Leach, P., Barnes, J. and Malmberg, L.-E. 2007. Family and child factors related to the use of non-maternal infant care: an English study. *Early Childhood Research Quarterly,* Vol. 22, No. 1, pp. 118–36.

Takala, T. 2003. *Analysis of the Education for All Fast-Track Initiative*. Helsinki, Finland Ministry for Foreign Affairs.

Tan, H. 2006. *In-Service Skills Upgrading and Training Policy: Global and Regional Perspectives*. Paper presented at the Regional Conference on Education, Training and the Knowledge Economy in South Asia, New Delhi, 14–15 September. World Bank Institute, Investment Climate Capacity Enhancement Program.

Te Kōhanga Reo National Trust. 2009. *Te Kōhanga Reo*. http://www.kohanga.ac.nz/ (Accessed September 16 2009.)

te Velde, D. W., with Ackah, C., Ajakaiye, O., Aryeetey, E., Bhattacharya, D., Calì, M., Fakiyesi, T., Amoussouga Gero, F., Jalilian, H., Jemio, L. C., Keane, J., Kennan, J., Massa, I., McCord, A., Meyn,, M., Ndulo, M., Rahman, M., Setiati, I., Soesastro, H., Ssewanyana, S., Vandemoortele, M. and others. 2009. *The Global Financial Crisis and Developing Countries: Synthesis of the Findings of 10 Country Case Studies*. London, UK Overseas Development Institute, Investment and Growth Programme. (ODI Working Papers, 306.)

The George Washington University. 2006. *Statistical Data on Brazil: Illiteracy in Brazil as a Percentage of the Population Aged 15 or Older*. Washington, DC, The George Washington University, Institute of Brazilian Business & Public Management Issues. http://www.gwu.edu/~ibi/database/Illiteracy_by_State-Region.pdf (Accessed 8 June 2009.)

Thea, D. and Qazi, S. 2008. Neonatal mortality – 4 million reasons for progress. *The Lancet,* Vol. 371, No. 9628, pp. 1893–5.

Theunynck, S. 2009. *School Construction Strategies for Universal Primary Education in Africa: Should Communities Be Empowered To Build Their Schools?* Washington, DC, World Bank.

Thomas, D., Beegle, K., Frankenberg, E., Sikoki, B., Strauss, J. and Teruel, G. 2004. Education in a crisis. *Journal of Development Economics,* Vol. 74, No. 1, pp. 53–85.

Thomson, A. 2009. Families struggle to survive as flow of dollars dries up. *The Financial Times,* 19 August.

Thomson, A., Woods, E., O'Brien, C. and Onsomu, E. 2009. *Mid-Term Evaluation of the EFA Fast Track Initiative. Country Case Study: Kenya*. Cambridge/Oxford, UK, Cambridge Education/Mokoro Ltd/Oxford Policy Management. (Draft.)

Times of Zambia. 2009. Pande bemoans financial crisis effects on MDGs attainment. *Times of Zambia.* http://www.times.co.zm/news/viewnews.cgi?category=4&id=1237785618 (Accessed 14 October.)

Truong Huyen, C. 2009. Schooling as lived and told: contrasting impacts of education policies for ethnic minority children in Vietnam seen from Young Lives Surveys. Background paper for *EFA Global Monitoring Report 2010.*

Tsujita, Y. 2009. Deprivation of education: a study of slum children in Delhi, India. Background paper for *EFA Global Monitoring Report 2010.*

Tufail, P. 2005. *Situational Analysis of Street Children: Education for All Policy Review and Best Practices Studies on Basic NFE for Children Living and/or Working on the Streets in Pakistan.* Islamabad, AMAL Human Development Network/UNESCO Islamabad.

Tyler, J. H. and Lofstrom, M. 2009. Finishing high school: alternative pathways and dropout recovery. *The Future of Children,* Vol. 19, No. 1, pp. 77–103.

UIL. 2009. *Literate Brazil Programme (Programa Brasil Alfabetizado) – PBA.* Hamburg, Germany, UNESCO Institute for Lifelong Learning. http://www.unesco.org/uil/litbase/?menu=16&country=BR&programme=50 (Accessed 29 September 2009.)

UIS. 2008*a*. *International Literacy Statistics: A Review of Concepts, Methodology and Current Data.* Montreal, Qué., UNESCO Institute for Statistics.

——. 2008*b*. *A View Inside Primary Schools: A World Education Indicators (WEI) Cross National Study.* Montreal, Qué., UNESCO Institute for Statistics.

——. 2009*a*. *Classifying Out-of-school Children.* Montreal, Qué., UNESCO Institute for Statistics.

——. 2009*b*. *Data Center: Custom Tables.* Montreal, Qué., UNESCO Institute for Statistics. http://stats.uis.unesco.org/unesco/TableViewer/document.aspx?ReportId=136&IF_Language=eng&BR_Topic=0 (Accessed 28 July 2009.)

——. 2009*c*. *Literacy Assessment and Monitoring Programme (LAMP): A Brief Introduction and Status.* Montreal, Qué., UNESCO Institute for Statistics.

——. 2009*d*. *The Next Generation of Literacy Statistics: Implementing the Literacy Assessment and Monitoring Programme.* Montreal, Qué., UNESCO Institute for Statistics.

——. 2009*e*. *Projecting Teacher Needs for Universal Primary Education: 2007 to 2015.* Montreal, Qué., UNESCO Institute for Statistics.

UK Department for Children, Schools and Families. 2008. *Deprivation and Education: the evidence on pupils in England. Foundation Stage to Key Stage 4.* London, UK Department for Children, Schools and Families, Schools Analysis and Research Division.

UK Learning and Skills Council. 2007. *Delivering World Class Skills in a Demand-led System.* Coventry, UK/London, UK Learning and Skills Council/UK Department for Education and Skills.

——. 2008. *Government Investment Strategy 2009–10, LSC Grant Letter and LSC Statement of Priorities.* Coventry, UK/London, UK Learning and Skills Council/UK Department for Children, Schools and Families/UK Department for Innovation, Universities and Skills.

UN-HABITAT. 2006. *State of the World's Cities 2006/7.* Nairobi, United Nations Human Settlements Programme.

——. 2008. *State of the World's Cities 2008/2009: Harmonious Cities.* Nairobi, United Nations Human Settlements Programme.

UN Enable. 2009. *Fact Sheet on Persons with Disabilities.* http://www.un.org/disabilities/default.asp?id=18 (Accessed September 16 2009.)

UN General Assembly Security Council. 2009. *Children and Armed Conflict: Report of the Secretary-General.* New York, United Nations.

UN Millennium Project. 2005. *Investing in Development: A Practical Plan to Achieve the Millennium Goals.* New York, United Nations Development Programme, United Nations Millennium Project.

UNAIDS. 2009. *HIV Treatment Data Update – July 2009.* Geneva, Switzerland, Joint United Nations Programme on HIV/AIDS. http://www.unaids.org/en/KnowledgeCentre/Resources/FeatureStories/archive/2009/20090723_AIDS_tratment_Data_UPD_2009.asp (Accessed 24 September 2009.)

UNAIDS, UNICEF, WHO and UNFPA. 2008. *Children and AIDS: Third Stocktaking Report, 2008.* New York, Joint United Nations Programme on HIV/AIDS/UNICEF/World Health Organization/United Nations Population Fund.

Understanding Children's Work. 2009. The twin challenges of eliminating child labour and achieving EFA: evidence and policy options from Mali and Zambia. Background paper for *EFA Global Monitoring Report 2010.*

UNDP. 2007. *Human Development Report 2007/2008. Fighting Climate Change: Human Solidarity in a Divided World.* New York, United Nations Development Programme.

——. 2009. *Arab Human Development Report. Challenges to Human Security in the Arab Countries.* New York, United Nations Development Programme, Regional Bureau for Arab States.

UNESCO-BREDA. 2007. *Dakar +7: EFA Top priority for Integrated Sector-Wide Policies.* Dakar, UNESCO Regional Office for Education in Africa (BREDA).

UNESCO-DME. 2009. *Data Set on Deprivation and Marginalization in Education.* Paris, UNESCO.

UNESCO-IIEP. 2009. Educational marginalization in national education plans. Background paper for *EFA Global Monitoring Report 2010.*

UNESCO-OREALC. 2008. *Los Aprendizajes de los Estudiantes de América Latina y el Caribe: Primer Reporte de los Resultados del Segundo Estudio Regional Comparativo y Explicativo* [Student Achievement in Latin America and the Caribbean: Results of the Second Regional Comparative and Explanatory Study]. Santiago, UNESCO Regional Bureau for Education in Latin America and the Caribbean, Latin American Laboratory for Assessment of the Quality of Education. (In Spanish.)

UNESCO. 1958. *Recommendation Concerning the International Standardization of Educational Statistics.* Adopted by the General Conference. Paris, UNESCO. (10 C/11.)

——. 1960. *Convention against Discrimination in Education.* Adopted by the General Conference at its eleventh session. Paris, UNESCO.

——. 1990. *World Declaration on Education For All.* Adopted by the World Conference on Education for All. Jomtien, Thailand, 5–9 March, UNESCO.

——. 2000. *The Dakar Framework for Action. Education for All: Meeting our Collective Commitments. Including Six Regional Frameworks for Action.* Adopted by the World Education Forum. Dakar, 26–28 April, UNESCO.

——. 2003. *EFA Global Monitoring Report 2003/4.* Paris, UNESCO.

——. 2005. *EFA Global Monitoring Report 2006. Education For All: Literacy for life.* Paris, UNESCO.

——. 2007. *EFA Global Monitoring Report 2008. Education For All by 2015: Will we make it?* Paris, UNESCO.

——. 2008*a*. *EFA Global Monitoring Report 2009. Overcoming Inequality: Why governance matters.* Paris, UNESCO/Oxford University Press.

——. 2008*b*. *United Nations Literacy Decade: Strategic Framework for Action 2008–2012.* Paris, UNESCO.

——. 2009*a*. *Haiti's EFA/FTI Endorsement Process.* Paris, UNESCO. (Unpublished paper.)

——. 2009*b*. *The Impact of the Global Financial and Economic Crisis on the Education Sector. No. 1: the Impact of the Crisis on Public Expenditure on Education: Findings from the UNESCO Quick Survey.* Paris, UNESCO, Education Sector. (ED/EPS/2009/PI/1.)

UNESCO and EduSector AIDS Response Trust. 2008. *Supporting the Educational Needs of HIV-positive Learners: Lessons from Namibia and Tanzania.* Paris, UNESCO.

UNESCO and Spain Ministry of Education and Science. 1994. *The Salamanca Statement and Framework for Action on Special Needs Education.* Paris/Salamanca, Spain UNESCO/Spain Ministry of Education and Science.

UNESCO Bangkok. 2008. *Improving the Quality of Mother Tongue-based Literacy and Learning: Case Studies from Asia, Africa and South America.* Bangkok, UNESCO.

UNESCO Brasilia. 2009. *Youth and Adult Literacy in Brazil: Learning from Practice.* Brasilia, UNESCO.

UNEVOC and UIS. 2006. *Participation in Formal and Vocational Education and Training Programmes Worldwide. An Initial Statistical Study.* Bonn, Germany/Montreal, Qué., UNEVOC International Centre for Technical and Vocational Education and Training/UNESCO Institute for Statistics.

UNHCR. 2007. *UNHCR and Partners to Bring Education to Nine Million Vulnerable Children.* New York, UNHCR. (Press release.) http://www.unhcr.org/46fb5f822.html

——. 2009. *2008 Global Trends: Refugees, Asylum-seekers, Returnees, Internally Displaced and Stateless Persons.* Geneva, Switzerland, UNHCR.

UNICEF. 2007*a*. *Breaking the Cycle of Exclusion. Roma Children in South East Europe.* Belgrade, UNICEF Serbia.

——. 2007*b*. *Progress for Children: A World Fit for Children Statistical Report.* New York, UNICEF.

——. 2007*c*. *The State of the World's Children 2008. Child Survival.* New York, UNICEF.

——. 2007*d*. *Uganda: UNICEF Humanitarian Situation Report.* New York, UNICEF.

——. 2008*a*. *Basic Education for Urban Working Children.* http://www.unicef.org/bangladesh/Education_for_Working_Children_(BEHTRUWC).pdf (Accessed 24 September 2009.)

——. 2008*b*. *The State of the World's Children 2009. Maternal and Newborn Health.* New York, UNICEF.

——. 2009*a*. *Education for All – Fast Track Initiative. Potentials and Challenges for Effective Aid to Basic Education in Sierra Leone*. New York, UNICEF.

——. 2009*b*. *Effective Education Financing in Fragile Contexts. Liberia Education Pooled Fund*. Prepared for INEE Global Consultation: Bridging the Gaps, Istanbul, Turkey, 31 March–2 April.

——. 2009*c*. *Machel Study 10-Year Strategic Review: Children and Conflict in a Changing World*. New York, UNICEF.

UNITAID. 2008. *UNITAID Annual Report 2007*. Geneva, Switzerland, World Health Organization, UNITAID.

United Nations. 1989. *Convention on the Rights of the Child*. New York, United Nations.

——. 2002. *56/116. United Nations Literacy Decade: Education for All*. New York, United Nations. (Resolution adopted by the General Assembly [on the report of the Third Committee (A/56/572)]. Fifty-sixth session. Agenda item 108, A/RES/56/116.)

——. 2007*a*. *Democratic Republic of Congo. Mid-Year Review Humanitarian Action Plan 2007*. New York, United Nations.

——. 2007*b*. *Liberia 2007. Common Humanitarian Action Plan (CHAP)*. New York, United Nations, Office for the Coordination of Humanitarian Affairs.

——. 2008. *Convention on the Rights of Persons with Disabilities*. New York, United Nations.

——. 2009*a*. *Human Rights in Palestine and Other Occupied Arab Territories: Report of the United Nations Fact-Finding Mission on the Gaza Conflict*. New York, United Nations General Assembly. (Human Rights Council, Twelfth session, Agenda item 7.)

——. 2009*b*. *With World at Tipping Point, Inaction Risks Slipping Into Degradation, Despair, Secretary-General Tells Sustainable Development Commission*. New York, United Nations. http://www.un.org/News/Press/docs/2009/sgsm12239.doc.htm (Accessed 5 November 2009.)

United Nations Conference on Trade and Development. 2009. *Trade and Development Report, 2009. Responding to the Global Crisis. Climate Change Mitigation and Development*. Washington, DC, UNCTAD.

United Republic of Tanzania Government. 2008. *General Budget Support Annual Review 2008. Final Report*. Dar es Salaam, Ministry of Finance and Economic Affairs.

——. 2009. *2008 Tanzania Disability Survey*. Dar es Salaam, United Republic of Tanzania National Bureau of Statistics.

Uppsala Conflict Data Program. 2009. *UCDP/PRIO Armed Conflict Dataset v4-2009*. Uppsala, Sweden, Uppsala University, Department of Peace and Conflict Research, Uppsala Conflict Data Program. http://www.pcr.uu.se/research/UCDP/data_and_publications/datasets.htm (Accessed 29 September 2009.)

US Department of Education. 2007. *The Condition of Education in 2007*. Washington, DC, US Department of Education, National Center for Education Statistics. (NCES 2007-064.)

——. 2009. *The American Recovery and Reinvestment Act of 2009: Saving and Creating Jobs and Reforming Education*. Washington, DC, US Department of Education. http://www.ed.gov/policy/gen/leg/recovery/implementation.html (Accessed 23 September 2009.)

US Department of Health and Human Services. 2005. *Head Start Impact Study: First Year Findings*. Washington, DC, US Department of Health and Human Services, Administration for Children and Families.

USAID. 2005. *Fourth Report on the Implementation of USAID Disability Policy*. Washington, DC, USAID.

——. 2007. *President's International Education Initiative Expanded Education for the World's Poorest Children: Liberia Fact Sheet*. Washington, DC, USAID. http://www.usaid.gov/press/factsheets/2007/fs070924_1.html

Van Ravens, J. and Aggio, C. 2005. The costs of achieving Dakar goal 4 in developing and "LIFE" countries. Background paper for *EFA Global Monitoring Report 2006*.

——. 2007. *The Costs and the Funding of Non Formal Literacy Programmes in Brazil, Burkina Faso and Uganda*. Hamburg, Germany, UNESCO Institute for Lifelong Learning.

——. 2008. *Expanding Early Childhood Care and Education: How Much Does It Cost? A Proposal for a Methodology to Estimate the Costs of Early Childhood Care and Education at Macro-level, Applied to the Arab States*. The Hague, Bernard van Leer Foundation. (Working Paper, 46.)

Vegas, E. 2007. Teacher labor markets in developing countries. *Excellence in the Classroom*, Vol. 17, No. 1, pp. 219–32.

Vegas, E. and Petrow, J. 2008. *Raising Student Learning in Latin America. The Challenge for the 21st Century*. Washington, DC, World Bank.

Vegas, E. and Umansky, I. 2005. *Improving Teaching and Learning through Effective Incentives. What can we Learn from Education Reforms in Latin America?* Washington, DC, World Bank.

Victora, C., Hanson, K., Bryce, J. and Vaughan, J. 2004. Achieving universal coverage with health interventions. *The Lancet*, Vol. 364, No. 9444, pp. 1541–48.

Victoria, C. G., Adair, L., Fall, C., Hallal, P. C., Martorell, R. and Richter, L. 2008. Maternal and child undernutrition: consequences for adult health and human capital. *The Lancet,* Vol. 371, No. 9609, pp. 340–57.

Vignoles, A. 2009. Educational marginalization in the UK. Background paper for *EFA Global Monitoring Report 2010.*

Villanger, E. 2008. Cash transfers contributing to social protection: a review of evaluation findings. *Forum for Development Studies,* Vol. 35, No. 2, pp. 221–56.

Visser-Valfrey, M. 2009. *Mid-Term Evaluation of the EFA Fast Track Initiative. Governance.* Cambridge/Oxford, UK, Cambridge Education/Mokoro Ltd/Oxford Policy Management. (Working Paper 5b.)

von Braun, J. 2008. *Food and Financial Crises: Implications for Agriculture and the Poor.* Washington, DC, International Food Policy Research Institute. (Food Policy Report.)

Wachira, N., Root, D., Bowen, P. A. and Olima, W. 2008. *An Investigation into Informal Craft Skilling in the Kenyan and South African Construction Sectors.* Paper presented at the Fifth Post Graduate Conference on Construction Industry Development, 16–18 March, Bloemfontein, South Africa.

Watkins, K. 2000. *The Oxfam Education Report.* Oxford, UK, Oxfam GB.

Weinstein, J. M., Porter, J. E. and Eizenstat, S. E. 2004. *On the Brink: Weak States and US National Security.* Washington, DC, Center for Global Development.

White, H. 2004. *Books, Buildings, and Learning Outcomes: An Impact Evaluation of World Bank Support to Basic Education in Ghana.* Washington, DC, World Bank.

WHO. 2005. *The World Health Report 2005. Make Every Mother and Child Count.* Geneva, Switzerland, World Health Organization

WHO and UNICEF. 2003. *Antenatal Care in Developing Countries: Promises, Achievements and Missed Opportunities. An Analysis of Trends, Levels and Differentials, 1990–2001.* Geneva, Switzerland, World Health Organization/UNICEF.

——. 2008. *World Report on Child Injury Prevention.* Geneva, Switzerland, World Health Organization/UNICEF.

Williamson, T., Agha, Z., Bjornstad, L., Twijukye, G., Mahwago, Y. and Kabelwa, K. 2008. *Building Blocks or Stumbling Blocks? The Effectiveness of New Approaches to Aid Delivery at the Sector Level.* London, UK Overseas Development Institute. (Good Governance, Aid Modalities and Poverty Reduction Working Papers, 8.)

Winthrop, R. 2009*a.* Afghan refugees in Pakistan: certification challenges and solutions. Kirk, J. (ed.), *Certification Counts: Recognizing the Learning Attainments of Displaced and Refugee Students.* Paris, UNESCO International Institute for Educational Planning.

——. 2009*b. Pakistan's Displaced Girls and Women – An Opportunity for Education.* Washington, DC, Brookings. http://www.brookings.edu/opinions/2009/0611_pakistan_education_winthrop.aspx (Accessed 29 September 2009.)

Witter, S., Adjei, S., Armar-Klemesu, M. and Graham, W. 2009. Providing free maternal health care: ten lessons from an evaluation of the national delivery exemption policy in Ghana. *Global Health Action,* Vol. 2. (DOI: 10.3402/gha.v2i0.1881.)

Woldehanna, T. 2009. *Productive Safety Net Programme and Children's Time Use between Work and Schooling in Ethiopia.* Oxford, UK, Young Lives. (Working Paper, 40.)

Woldemikael, T. M. 2003. Language, Education, and Public Policy in Eritrea. *African Studies Review,* Vol. 46, No. 1, pp. 117–36.

Women's Commission for Refugee Women and Children. 2004. *Global Survey on Education in Emergencies.* New York, Women's Commission for Refugee Women and Children.

——. 2005. *Learning in a War Zone.* New York, Women's Commission for Refugee Women and Children.

Woods, E. 2009*a. Mid-Term Evaluation of the EFA Fast Track Initiative. Preliminary Paper on Education Policy and Planning.* Oxford/Cambridge, UK, Mokoro Ltd/Cambridge Education/Oxford Policy Management. (Working Paper 1.)

Woods, N. 2009*b. The International Response to the Global Crisis and the Reform of the International Financial and Aid Architecture.* Strasbourg, France, European Parliament, Directorate-General for External Policies of the Union, Directorate B, Policy Department. (European Parliament Briefing Paper.)

World Bank. 2002*a. World Bank Announces First Group of Countries for 'Education For All' Fast Track.* Washington, DC, World Bank. http://web.worldbank.org/WBSITE/EXTERNAL/NEWS/0,,contentMDK:20049839~menuPK:34463~pagePK:34370~piPK:34424,00.html (Accessed 25 September 2009.)

——. 2002*b. Education for Dynamic Economies: Action Plan to Accelerate Progress towards Education for All (EFA).* Washington, DC, World Bank, Development Committee/International Monetary Fund. (DC2002-0005/Rev1.)

——. 2004. *Vietnam Reading and Mathematics Assessment Study.* Washington, DC, World Bank. (Human Development Sector Reports.)

——. 2005*a*. *Going to School/Going to Work. A Report on Child Labor and EFA in World Bank Projects and Policy Documents*. Washington, DC, World Bank. (Background paper for Third Round Table on the Elimination of Child Labor, Fifth Meeting of the UNESCO High Level Group on Education for All, Beijing, 28–30 November.

——. 2005*b*. *Implementation Completion Report in the Amount of US$50 million to the United Republic of Tanzania for the Primary Education Development Program*. Washington, DC. (IDA-35700 TF-50588.)

——. 2005*c*. *In their own Language*. Washington, DC, World Bank. (Education Notes.)

——. 2005*d*. *Madagascar: Education Sector Development Project – Implementation Completion Report*. Washington, DC, World Bank. (Report N° 33345-MAG.)

——. 2005*e*. *Primary and Secondary Education in Lesotho. A Country Status Report for Education*. Washington, DC, World Bank. (Africa Region Human Development Series. Working Paper, 101.)

——. 2005*f*. *World Development Report 2006: Equity and Development*. Washington, DC, World Bank.

——. 2006*a*. *Cambodia: Halving Poverty by 2015? Poverty Assessment 2006*. Washington, DC, World Bank.

——. 2006*b*. *Indonesia: Making the New Indonesia Work for the Poor*. Washington, DC, World Bank.

——. 2006*c*. *Lao PDR Poverty Assessment Report: From Valleys to Hilltops – 15 Years of Poverty Reduction*. Washington, DC, World Bank.

——. 2006*d*. *Nepal: Resilience Amidst Conflict. An Assessment of Poverty in Nepal, 1995–96 and 2003–04*. Washington, DC, World Bank.

——. 2006*e*. *Project Appraisal Document on a Proposed Loan in the Amount of US$200.00 Million to the Republic of the Philippines for a National Program Support for Basic Education Project*. Washington, DC, World Bank.

——. 2006*f*. *Repositioning Nutrition as Central to Development. A Strategy for Large-scale Action*. Washington, DC, World Bank.

——. 2006*g*. *Skill Development in India. The Vocational Education and Training System*. Washington, DC, World Bank, Human Development Unit, South Asia Region.

——. 2006*h*. *Uganda: Poverty and Vulnerability Assessment*. Washington, DC, World Bank.

——. 2006*i*. *United Republic of Tanzania Public Expenditure and Financial Accountability Review*. Washington, DC, World Bank. (FY05.)

——. 2006*j*. *World Development Report 2007. Development and the Next Generation*. Washington, DC, World Bank.

——. 2007*a*. *Dhaka: Improving Living Conditions for the Urban Poor*. Washington, DC, World Bank. (Bangladesh Development Series, 17.)

——. 2007*b*. *Education in Sierra Leone. Present Challenges, Future Opportunities*. Washington, DC, World Bank. (Africa Human Development Series.)

——. 2007*c*. *Malawi Poverty and Vulnerability Assessment: Investing in Our Future, Synthesis Report: Main Findings and Recommendations)*. Washington, DC, World Bank, Poverty Reduction and Economic Management, Africa Region. (Poverty Assessment, 36546.)

——. 2008*a*. *Double Jeopardy: Responding to Food and Fuel Prices. G8 Hokkaido-Toyako Summit*. Hokkaido, Japan, World Bank, Poverty Reduction and Economic Management Network. (Working Paper, 44951.)

——. 2008*b*. *Meeting Teacher Needs for Education for All Project*. Washington, DC, World Bank.

——. 2008*c*. *Nigeria: A Review of the Costs and Financing of Public Education*. Washington, DC, World Bank, Human Development Unit, Africa Region. (42418-NG.)

——. 2008*d*. *Poverty Assessment for Bangladesh: Creating Opportunities and Bridging the East-West Divide*. Washington, DC, World Bank.

——. 2008*e*. *Rising Food and Fuel Prices: Addressing the Risks to Future Generations*. Washington, DC, World Bank.

——. 2008*f*. *Teacher Employment and Deployment in Indonesia: Opportunities for Equity, Efficiency and Quality Improvement*. Washington, DC, World Bank.

——. 2008*g*. *Thailand Social Monitor on Youth 2008: Development and the Next Generation*. Washington, DC, World Bank.

——. 2009*a*. *EFA Fast Track Initiative (FTI) and the World Bank*. Washington, DC, World Bank. http://go.worldbank.org/8EZE2MXEZ0 (Accessed 1 January 2009.)

——. 2009*b*. *Enhancing Growth and Reducing Poverty in a Volatile World: a Progress Report on the Africa Action Plan*. Washington, DC, World Bank.

——. 2009*c*. *Escaping Stigma and Neglect. People with Disabilities in Sierra Leone*. Washington, DC, World Bank. (Africa Human Development Series.)

——. 2009*d*. *Ethnicity and Development in Vietnam*. Washington, DC, World Bank. (Country Social Analysis.)

——. 2009*e*. *Financial Crisis. What the World Bank Is Doing. (updated September 22)*. Washington, DC, World Bank. http://www.worldbank.org/financialcrisis/bankinitiatives.htm (Accessed 31 September 2009.)

——. 2009*f*. *Kenya: Poverty and Inequality Assessment*. Washington, DC, World Bank.

——. 2009*g*. *Le Système Educatif Béninois. Analyse Sectorielle pour une Politique Educative plus Equilibrée et plus Efficace* [Benin Education System: Sectoral Analysis for a More Balanced and Efficient Education Policy]. Washington, DC, World Bank, Pôle de Dakar. (Africa Human Development Series.)

——. 2009*h*. *Narrative-based Status Report of Countries Receiving Catalytic (CF) Financial Support Under the Provisions of Education for All – Fast Track Initiative (FTI)*. Washington, DC, World Bank. http://go.worldbank.org/QSMZMD2KC0 (Accessed 29 September 2009.)

——. 2009*i*. *Rapid Response Child-focused Social Cash Transfer and Nutrition Security Project, Senegal*. Washington, DC, World Bank. http://web.worldbank.org/external/projects/main?pagePK=64283627&piPK=73230&theSitePK=40941&menuPK=228424&Projectid=P115938 (Accessed 29 September 2009.)

——. 2009*j*. *Six Steps to Abolishing Primary School Fees. Operational Guide*. Washington, DC, World Bank.

——. 2009*k*. *World Development Indicators 2009*. Washington, DC, World Bank.

——. 2009*l*. *Zoellick Calls for 'Vulnerability Fund' Ahead of Davos Forum*. Washington, DC, World Bank. http://go.worldbank.org/76E1GRKBN0 (Accessed 29 September 2009.)

World Bank and Burundi Government. 2008. *Republic of Burundi: Public Expenditure Management and Financial Accountability Review (PEMFAR): Improving Allocative Efficiency and Governance of Public Expenditure and Investing in Public Capital to Accelerate Growth and Reduce Poverty*. Washington, DC, World Bank. (42160-BI.)

World Bank and IMF. 2009. *Global Monitoring Report 2009: A Development Emergency*. Washington, DC, World Bank/International Monetary Fund.

World Bank and UNICEF. 2009. *Abolishing School Fees in Africa: Lessons Learned in Ethiopia, Ghana, Kenya and Mozambique*. Washington, DC/New York, World Bank/UNICEF. (Development Practice in Education.)

World Bank Independent Evaluation Group. 2006. *From Schooling Access to Learning Outcomes: An Unfinished Agenda. An Evaluation of World Bank Support to Primary Education*. Washington, DC, World Bank. (Conference edition.)

World Cocoa Foundation. 2009. *Addressing Child Labor*. http://www.worldcocoafoundation.org/addressing-child-labor/ (Accessed 18 June 2009.)

World Food Programme. 2007. *Global School Feeding Report 2006*. Rome, WFP School Feeding Service.

——. 2009. *WFP in Africa. 2008 Facts, Figures and Partners*. Rome, WFP.

Wrong, M. 2009. *It's our Turn to Eat: the Story of a Kenyan Whistle Blower*. London, Fourth Estate.

Wu, K. B., Goldschmidt, P., Boscardin, C. K. and Azam, M. 2007. Girls in India: poverty, location, and social disparities. Lewis, M. and Lockheed, M. (eds), *Exclusion, Gender and Education: Case Studies from the Developing World*. Washington, DC, Center for Global Development, pp. 119–43.

Wurm, S. 1991. Language death and disappearance: causes and circumstances. *Diogenes*, Issue 39, pp. 1–18.

Yablonski, J. and O'Donnell, M. 2009. *Lasting Benefits – The role of cash transfers in tackling child mortality*. London, Save the Children.

Yates, R. 2009. Universal health care and the removal of user fees. *The Lancet*, Vol. 373, No. 9680, pp. 2078–81.

Yeo, R. and Moore, K. 2003. Including disabled people in poverty reduction work: "Nothing About Us, Without Us". *World Development*, Vol. 31, No. 3, pp. 571–90.

Yoshida, K. 2009. Japan's international cooperation for educational development: review of prospects for scaling up Japan's aid to education. Background paper for *EFA Global Monitoring Report 2010*.

Young, M. 2005. *National Qualifications Framework: Their Feasibility for Effective Implementation in Developing Countries*. Geneva, Switzerland, International Labour Office, Skills and Employability Department, InFocus Programme on Skills, Knowledge and Employability. (Skills Working Papers, 22.)

Zekas, A., Hunter, M., Lombardo, B. and Heyman, C. 2009. *Chad Success Story: Mothers' Associations in Chad Make Headway in Girls' Education: Raising Awareness, Gaining Public Support, and Managing Schools*. Washington, DC, United Nations Girls' Education Initiative.

Zhang, Y., Postlethwaite, T. N. and Grisay, A. 2008. *A View Inside Primary Schools: A World Education Indicators (WEI) Cross-National Study*. Montreal, Qué, UNESCO Institute for Statistics.

Zoellick, R. 2009. Time to herald the Age of Responsibility. *Financial Times*, 25 January.

Abbreviations

AfDF	African Development Fund
AsDF	Asian Development Fund
AIDS	Acquired immune deficiency syndrome
ARRA	American Recovery and Reinvestment Act
BRAC	Formerly Bangladesh Rural Advancement Committee
CIDA	Canadian International Development Agency
CPIA	Country Policy and Institutional Assessment (World Bank)
CONAFE	Consejo Nacional de Fomento Educativo (Mexico)
CONFINTEA	International Conference on Adult Education
DAC	Development Assistance Committee (OECD)
DFID	Department for International Development (United Kingdom)
DHS	Demographic and Health Surveys
DME	Deprivation and Marginalization in Education
EC	European Commission
ECCE	Early childhood care and education
EDI	EFA Development Index
EFA	Education for All
ELA	English Language Arts
EPDF	Education Program Development Fund
ESF	Exogenous Shocks Facility
EU	European Union
EUROSTAT	Statistical Office of the European Communities
FAO	Food and Agricultural Organization of the United Nations
FIFA	International Federation of Association Football
FTI	Fast Track Initiative
FUNDEF	Fundo de Manutenção e Desenvolvimento do Ensino Fundamental e de Valorizaçãodo Magistério (Brazil)
G8	Group of Eight (Canada, France, Germany, Italy, Japan, Russian Federation, United Kingdom and United States, plus EU representatives)
G20	Group of Twenty Finance Ministers and Central Bank Governors
GALP	Global Age-specific Literacy Projections Model
GAVI Alliance	Formerly Global Alliance for Vaccines and Immunisation
GDP	Gross domestic product
GEI	Gender-specific EFA Index
GER	Gross enrolment ratio
GFRP	Global Food Crisis Response Program (World Bank)

GIR	Gross intake rate
GIST	Global Implementation Support Team
GNI	Gross national income
GNP	Gross national product
GPI	Gender parity index
GTZ	Gesellschaft für Technische Zusammenarbeit (German Technical Cooperation)
HCZ	Harlem Children's Zone
HIV	Human immunodeficiency virus
IALS	International Adult Literacy Survey
IBE	International Bureau of Education (UNESCO)
IDB	Inter-American Development Bank
IDS	International Development Statistics
IIEP	International Institute for Educational Planning (UNESCO)
IFFIm	International Finance Facility for Immunisation
ILO	International Labour Organization
IMF	International Monetary Fund
INEE	Inter-Agency Network for Education in Emergencies
INGO	International non-governmental organization
IRC	International Rescue Committee
ISCED	International Standard Classification of Education
LAMP	Literacy Assessment and Monitoring Programme
LDCs	Least developed countries
MDG	Millennium Development Goals
MDTF	Multidonor trust fund
MICS	Multiple Indicator Cluster Surveys (UNICEF)
NCEA	National Certificate of Educational Achievement (New Zealand)
NEPAD	New Partnership for Africa's Development
NER	Net enrolment ratio
NIR	Net intake rate
OA	Official aid
ODA	Official development assistance
OCHA	United Nations Office for the Coordination of Humanitarian Affairs
OECD	Organisation for Economic Co-operation and Development
OHCHR	Office of the High Commissioner for Human Rights (United Nations)
PASEC	Programme d'analyse des systèmes éducatifs de la Conférence des Ministres de l'Éducation des pays ayant le français en partage (CONFEMEN)
PEDP	Primary Education Development Programme
PEPFAR	President's Emergency Plan for AIDS Relief
PIRLS	Progress in Reading Literacy Study

PISA	Programme for International Student Assessment
PRGF	Poverty Reduction and Growth Facility
PPP	Purchasing power parity
PPVT	Peabody Picture Vocabulary Test
PRONADE	Programa Nacional de Autogestión para el Desarrollo Educativo (Guatemala)
PRSP	Poverty Reduction Strategy Paper
PSNP	Productive Safety Net Programme (Ethiopia)
PTA	Parent-teacher association
RSRP	Rapid Social Response Programme (World Bank)
SACMEQ	Southern and Eastern Africa Consortium for Monitoring Educational Quality
SDR	Special drawing rights
SERCE	Segundo Estudio Regional Comparativo y Explicativo
SENAI	Serviço Nacional de Aprendizagem Industrial (Brazil)
Sida	Swedish International Development Cooperation Agency
TIMSS	Trends in International Mathematics and Science Study
UIL	UNESCO Institute for Lifelong Learning
UIS	UNESCO Institute for Statistics
UN	United Nations
UNAIDS	Joint United Nations Programme on HIV/AIDS
UNDP	United Nations Development Programme
UNESCO	United Nations Educational, Scientific and Cultural Organization
UNESCO-BREDA	Regional Bureau for Education in Africa
UNESCO-OREALC	Regional Bureau for Education in Latin America and the Caribbean
UNEVOC	International Centre for Technical and Vocational Training (UNESCO)
UNICEF	United Nations Children's Fund
UNPD	United Nations Population Division
UNRWA	United Nations Relief and Works Agency for Palestine Refugees in the Near East
UPC	Universal primary completion
UPE	Universal primary education
USAID	United States Agency for International Development
WEI	World Education Indicators
WHO	World Health Organization
ZEP	Zone d'Education Prioritaire

Index

This index is in word-by-word order and covers chapters 1 to 5 and the tables on human rights treaties and social protection programmes on pages 291-5. Page numbers in *italics* indicate figures and tables; those in **bold** refer to material in boxes; ***bold italics*** indicates a figure or table in a box. The letter 'n' following a page number indicates information in a note at the side of the page.

The abbreviation ECCE indicates 'early childhood care and education' and the abbreviation TVE indicates 'technical and vocational education'.

Subheadings are filed alphabetically by the significant term, ignoring prepositions and insignificant words (e.g. 'effect on achievement' files as 'achievement').

Definitions of terms can be found in the glossary, and additional information on countries can be found in the statistical annex.

C

F

H

J

K

L

ффективности..

language gap *152*
learning achievement 106, 107, *110*, 154
literacy programmes 103
reading literacy *108*, *109*
relative deprivation *152*, 154
remittances 25, 33
'second chance' programmes 89–90
social protection programmes 48, *295*
micronutrient deficiency 44, 45, 46, 181
Microsoft
 see also Bill and Melinda Gates
 Foundation
 'ninemillion' campaign 232
Mid-Day Meal Scheme (India) 209
Middle East
 see also Arab States; *individual countries*
 economic growth 23, 31
 gender parity/disparity 83
 technical and vocational education 84
 youth unemployment 82, 83, *83*, 86
middle-income countries
 see also countries in transition; *individual*
 countries
 children with disabilities 181
 education aid 228, *229*
 enrolment increase during economic
 downturn 25
 learning achievement *105*, 106, *107*, *109*
 primary education 70
migrants
 effect of ECCE on language development
 50
 effect of economic downturn 25
 and learning achievement 157, *157*
 rights legislation *293*
 slum dwellers 175–6
migration
 effects of 49, 50, **71**
 rural-urban 25, 175–6, **177**
Millennium Challenge Account 238
Millennium Development Goals (MDGs)
 importance of aid 218, 222
 child mortality reduction 46
 malnutrition 43–4
 maternal deaths reduction 46
 need for finance assessment 20
mineral deficiencies 44, 45, 46
Ministry of State for the Development of
 Northern Kenya and other Arid
 Lands **193**
minorities *see* disabilities; disadvantage;
 ethnic minority groups; girls;
 indigenous peoples;
 marginalization; rural areas;
 women
mixed ability teaching 198
mobile schools 193, **193**
Moldova *see* Republic of Moldova
Monaco
 human rights *293*
Mongolia
 ECCE programmes *52*
 education aid
 disbursements 256, *257*
 national systems 236
 education poverty 140, *143*, *162*, *163*
 gender parity/disparity *162*, *163*
 national plan endorsement 253
 out-of-school children *163*
 primary education, enrolment 63
 relative deprivation 151, *151*

rural areas *162*, *163*
school completion *73*
monitoring
 see also data collection systems
 budgets 26–7, 37
 disability 202
 education aid 226
 EFA goals 41, 96, **97**
 role in reducing marginalization 272
Montenegro
 education poverty and gender disparity,
 rural areas *162*, *163*
 out-of-school children *163*
Monterrey conference on financing for
 Millennium Development Goals 249
Morocco
 adult literacy 95, *97*, 99, *100*
 education poverty 139, 141, *141*, 142, *143*,
 162, *163*
 gender parity/disparity 99, *141*, *162*, *163*
 learning achievement 105, *105*, 106, *107*,
 110
 out-of-school children *163*
 primary education, enrolment *63*, *65*
 rural areas *162*, *163*
 school completion 72, *73*
 technical and vocational education 86, **86**
mortality rate, children 25, 42, 43–4, 44, 46,
 47, 179, 184
mothers
 see also women
 access to healthcare 42, 45–7, *47*, **48**, 170
 effect of death on enrolment 185
 educational background, effects 47, *47*,
 52, *52*, 154, 155–6
 effect of health on newborns 45–6
Mozambique
 adult literacy *97*, 101
 basic education *127*, *128*
 child mortality rates 43
 development assistance 218
 disbursements **258**
 education aid
 aid alignment 237
 disbursements 255, *256*
 national systems 219, *236*
 vocational education 230
 education expenditure 26, 34, *126*, *127*, 128
 education poverty *141*, *162*, *163*
 fiscal space *30*, 31
 gender parity/disparity *141*, *162*, *163*
 human rights *292*
 language gap 150, *150*
 national plan endorsement 253
 out-of-school children 56, *60*, 81, *163*
 primary education *126*, 250n
 enrolment **59**, *59*, *63*, *65*
 pupil/teacher ratio 115, *115*
 rural areas *162*, *163*
 school completion 72, *73*
 school grants 189
 stunted children 44
 teacher incentives 198
 teachers *114*, 118
 technical and vocational education 230
 youth unemployment 83
Mubarak-Kohl initiative (Egypt) 86n
multidonor trust funds
 Catalytic Fund *see* Catalytic Fund *main*
 entry

Education Programme Development Fund
 252, **252**
Global Food Crisis Response Programme
 34
multigrade teaching 192–3
multilateral donors
 aid for conflict areas 245, 246, **246**
 education aid 228, 274–5
 health aid *263*
 private-public partnerships 232–3
 trust funds **246**
Musahar community (India) **171**
mute children 182
Myanmar
 basic education *127*, *128*
 education aid, disbursements 242
 education expenditure *127*, 242
 education poverty *141*, *162*, *163*
 gender parity/disparity *141*, *162*, *163*
 out-of-school children *163*
 rural areas *162*, *163*
 stunted children 44

N

Namibia
 education poverty 140, *162*, *163*
 gender parity/disparity *162*, *163*
 HIV and AIDS 185
 learning achievement 106
 out-of-school children *163*
 primary education, enrolment **59**
 rural areas *162*, *163*
 school completion 72
national identity 173
National Industrial Learning Service (Brazil)
 78, **79**
National Literacy Mission (India) 94, 102
national ownership *see* country ownership
national systems (financial management
 systems) 220, 234, 235–7
National Target Programme (Viet Nam) 48
Native Americans, law suit on discrimination
 205
Nauru
 primary education, enrolment *65*
Nazari (Islamic Republic of Iran) **85**
neonatal mortality 25, 46, 47
Nepal
 adult literacy *97*, 98–9, *100*
 aid **48**
 basic education *127*, *128*
 development assistance 218
 education aid 245
 disbursements 234, *242*
 national systems 236
 education expenditure *127*, 242
 education poverty *141*, 153, *162*, *163*
 ethnic minority groups 152–3, *153*
 gender parity/disparity *61*, 98–9, *141*, *162*,
 163
 health costs 48
 language gap *150*, 152
 learning environment 114
 maternal health care 47
 out-of-school children 60, *60*, 61, *163*
 pre-primary education 50
 primary education, enrolment *63*, *65*
 pupil/teacher ratio 114–15
 relative deprivation *152*

O

Q

S

U

V

W

Y

Z